Courts, Judges, & Politics

AN INTRODUCTION TO THE JUDICIAL PROCESS

SIXTH EDITION

Walter F. Murphy

McCormick Professor of Jurisprudence, Emeritus
Princeton University

C. Herman Pritchett

Professor of Political Science, Emeritus (Deceased)
University of California, Santa Barbara

Lee Epstein

Mallinckrodt Distinguished University Professor of Political Science and Professor of Law
Washington University in St. Louis

Jack Knight

Sidney W. Souers Professor of Government
Washington University in St. Louis

Boston   Burr Ridge, IL   Dubuque, IA   Madison, WI   New York
San Francisco   St. Louis   Bangkok   Bogotá   Caracas   Kuala Lumpur
Lisbon   London   Madrid   Mexico City   Milan   Montreal   New Delhi
Santiago   Seoul   Singapore   Sydney   Taipei   Toronto

Mc Graw Hill Higher Education

COURTS, JUDGES, AND POLITICS: AN INTRODUCTION TO THE JUDICIAL PROCESS

Published by McGraw-Hill, a business unit of The McGraw-Hill Companies, Inc. 1221 Avenue of the Americas, New York, NY, 10020. Copyright © 2006, 2002, 1986, 1979, 1974, 1961 by The McGraw-Hill Companies, Inc. All rights reserved. No part of this publication may be reproduced or distributed in any form or by any means, or stored in a database or retrieval system, without the prior written consent of The McGraw-Hill Companies, Inc., including, but not limited to, in any network or other electronic storage or transmission, or broadcast for distance learning.

Some ancillaries, including electronic and print components, may not be available to customers outside the United States.

This book is printed on acid-free paper.

6 7 8 9 10 11 12 DOC/DOC 1 5 4 3 2 1 0

ISBN-13: 978-0-07-297705-9
ISBN-10: 0-07-297705-1

Publisher: *Lyn Uhl*
Senior sponsoring editor: *Monica Eckman*
Development editor: *Margaret Manos*
Marketing manager: *Katherine Bates*
Production editor: *Mel Valentín*
Production supervisor: *Jason Huls*
Design manager: *Kim Menning*
Cover designer: *Kim Menning*
Compositor: *Cenveo (GAC)*
Typeface: *10/12 Palatino*
Printer: *R. R. Donnelley & Sons Company/Crawfordsville, IN*
Cover photo: © *Royalty-Free/Corbis*

Library of Congress Cataloging-in-Publication Data

Courts, judges, & politics : an introduction to the judicial process ; [edited by] Walter F. Murphy, C. Herman Pritchett, Lee Epstein.—6th ed.
     p. cm.
Included bibliographical references and index.
ISBN 0-07-297705-1 (softcover)
  1. Justice, Administration of—United States. 2. Judicial process—United States. 3. Political questions and judicial power—United States. I. Title: Courts, judges, and politics. II. Murphy, Walter F., 1929- III. Pritchett, C. Herman (Charles Herman), 1907- IV. Epstein, Lee, 1958-

KF8700.A7C67 2006
347.73'1—dc22
                                                                              2005041570
http://www.mhhe.com

For Herman and Marguerite Pritchett, in memoriam.

Contents

Part Two

THE AMERICAN LEGAL SYSTEM

Part Three

JUDICIAL POWER

Part Four

JUDICIAL DECISION MAKING

Preface to the Sixth Edition

This book had its origin during the academic year 1956–1957, when I was writing my dissertation at the University of Chicago and serving as C. Herman Pritchett's research assistant. He mentioned in a casual (and, as it turned out, also causal) conversation, probably generated by my having recently read Jack W. Peltason's *The Federal Courts in the Political Process* (New York: Random House, 1955), that he would love to teach a course on the politics of the judicial process, but the materials were too scattered even for a graduate seminar.[1] Because my dissertation was proceeding rapidly, I had begun to think not only of my next project but how my scholarship would develop over the next decades. Thus my application for a fellowship from the Brookings Institution detailed a project for the following year (the uses of stare decisis) and explained how it would fit with plans for a series of books and articles. That scheme closely resembled the table of contents of the first edition of *Courts, Judges, & Politics*.

The year at Brookings provided the opportunity not only to revise my dissertation and get most chapters published in law reviews and journals of political science but also to spend mornings in the Library of Congress or the library of the Supreme Court seeking out materials for a text on the judicial process. (Afternoons were often taken up with attending oral arguments.) By the time I came to Princeton in the late summer of 1958, I had filled in many readings to fit my earlier outline. Then I mustered the courage to invite Herman (who was

---

[1] Henry M. Hart, Jr., and Albert M. Sachs's *The Legal Process* did not come out in its mimeographed form (labeled "tentative edition") until 1958; it did not come out as a book in "normal" form until Foundation Press published a much revised edition in 1994, edited by William N. Eskridge, Jr., and Philip P. Frickey. For an evaluation of the impact of this very important "book," see Anthony J. Sebok, *Legal Positivism in American Jurisprudence* (New York: Cambridge University Press, 1998). Carl A. Auerbach, Lloyd K. Garrison, Willard Hurst, and Samuel Mermin's *The Legal Process: An Introduction to Decision Making by Judicial, Legislative, Executive, and Administrative Agencies* was available only in multilith form, and we were not aware of its existence. It was published in 1961 by Chandler Publishing Co. of San Francisco.

still, in good Chicago style, "Mr. Pritchett"[2]) to join. He readily agreed and provided three necessary gifts: superb judgment about what would and would not be intelligible to students, money to photocopy the materials we agreed on, and a professional reputation for excellence that attracted Random House's editor, Charles Lieber.

During the next two years, we both tried out many of the materials on our students, and by the summer of 1960 we were able to send the manuscript off to the publisher. That edition was more mine than Herman's, though having studied under and worked for him I am certain that he influenced every thing I have written. (Were he alive, he might insist on certain exceptions to that statement.) The second edition represented pretty much equal labor. The third and fourth editions, however, were much more Herman's than mine. My interests had moved to constitutional theory and to comparative politics; in fact, I taught a course on the judicial process only once after the first edition appeared. Although I continued to teach constitutional interpretation, I did so as a form of political jurisprudence rather than as a course in traditional constitutional law. Still, the two of us arrived at a productive arrangement: Herman did the work and I carped.

Alas, Herman died in 1995, as we, under prodding from McGraw-Hill, who had bought Random House's college list, were thinking of how to organize a fifth edition. My own health did not allow me to do the revisions alone. When, in 1958, I initially approached Herman about coauthoring/coediting the first edition, I had read almost every directly relevant article and book published in the preceding three decades. By 1995, the field had burgeoned so that I would have had to spend at least a year, probably two, just to catch up. I decided to wait and hope that McGraw-Hill would forget about the book. Happily, Bert Lummus and his successors, especially Monica Eckman, had long and stubborn memories. The only escape was to undertake the task of revising and to do so in a way that would minimize my burdens. I talked to Sotirios A. Barber of Notre Dame, an old friend with whom I had worked on another project.[3] The two of us sputtered around for almost a year, outdoing each other in producing excuses. Finally, it became clear to both of us that, if the book were going to be reborn, it needed a fresh mind. I then consulted another old friend, Harry P. Stumpf, who had retired from the University of New Mexico in 1995. He knew almost everyone in the field, what each had written, and was willing to share that knowledge as well as his judgments about people and their work. Our discussions convinced both of us that the ideal person was Lee Epstein, the Mallinckrodt Distinguished University Professor of Political Science and Professor of Law at Washington University. Her then-recent publication (with

---

[2]At the University of Chicago of the 1950s, graduate students addressed a member of the faculty as "Mister" not "Professor." (There were then no women teaching the Department of Political Science.) After a few months of collaboration, "Mr. Pritchett" sent me a note saying that "someone named Herman" was answering my mail.

[3]Walter F. Murphy, James E. Fleming, Sotirios A. Barber, and Stephen Macedo, *American Constitutional Interpretation*, 3rd ed. (New York: Foundation Press, 2003).

Jack Knight) of *The Choices Justices Make* (Washington, DC: Congressional Quarterly Press, 1998), with its roots reaching back to my own *Elements of Judicial Strategy* (Chicago: University of Chicago Press, 1964), indicated we shared similar interests, even if her knowledge was far superior to mine. Much to my joy, and that of Monica Eckman at McGraw-Hill, Prof. Epstein accepted the challenge.

The choice turned out to be wonderfully wise, at least for the book and my peace of mind. She played—brilliantly, patiently, and indefatigably—Herman's role for the third and fourth editions, and I resumed mine: She did the work and I carped. I am sure Herman would have been delighted with the final product and both relieved and amused to see someone else subjected to my compulsions about grammar and syntax. That *Courts, Judges, & Politics'* fifth incarnation was principally due to Prof. Epstein's energy, erudition, and patience in dealing with a nearly dead, though still obsessive, white European male.

When McGraw-Hill began to make noises about a sixth edition, Prof. Epstein decided she needed someone to share the burdens of my nit-picking and to help scour professional journals and official reports for readings that would interest as well as educate students. She invited her long-time coauthor and colleague at Washington University, Jack Knight, the Sidney W. Souers Professor of Government. She chose wisely. Changes in this edition are due to their joint endeavors. Again Herman would have been pleased as well as charmed.

Walter F. Murphy

Albuquerque, NM
10 November 2004

Acknowledgments

Prof. Harry P. Stumpf, Emeritus, University of New Mexico, for his willingness to worry about problems of the judicial process and to share his knowledge and judgments; Profs. Judith A. Baer, Gregory A. Caldeira, Micheal Giles, Leslie F. Goldstein, Jeffrey A. Segal, Harold J. Spaeth, and Thomas G. Walker for their individual and collective wisdom of all things judicial and their generosity in imparting it (even at a moment's notice); Ms. Monica Eckman and Ms. Margaret Manos, for their enthusiasm for this project from start to finish; Ms. Stacey Sawyer, for her effort to hone our prose; and the following reviewers:

Frank J. Colucci—*Purdue University, Calumet*

John Kang—*Western Kentucky University*

David N. Atkinson—*University of Missouri, Kansas City*

Peter J. Longo—*University of Nebraska, Kearney*

Mark Landis—*Hofstra University*

Michael C. Gizzi—*Mesa State College*

Larry Bass—*Valparaiso University*

Robert Bradley—*Illinois State University*

PART ONE

The Nature of Judging

CHAPTER 1

Political Jurisprudence

The title of this book might seem irreverent; surveys of public opinion, whether conducted in the United States or abroad, indicate that most people think that a linkage between courts and politics is a bad thing. But we do not use the term *politics* in a pejorative sense to refer to jobbery or partisan manipulations. Quite the contrary. We mean by politics, much as Aristotle did, one of the most important and possibly the most noble of human undertakings: the processes concerned with the authoritative determination of a society's goals and ideals; mobilization of its resources to achieve those goals and ideals; and distribution of rights, duties, costs, benefits, rewards, and punishments among members of that society.

Modern political systems rely on law as one of *the* chief instruments, if not *the* chief instrument, to carry out national objectives and distribute rights and duties. Thus courts and judges, insofar as they help to determine and apply "the law," are inevitably participants in the political processes. But that statement leaves many sets of questions unanswered. First, what is law itself? Second, how and under what conditions do judges become more important participants and under what conditions do they become less important? Third, how do courts and judges operate as they play their various roles? Most of this book directly focuses on the second and third sets of questions, but the first always looms in the background. We directly address it here in the hope that this brief discussion will encourage readers to repeat the question at frequent intervals.

However we define the law, it is not "a brooding omnipresence in the sky" but something that humans have found and made and probably not completely found or made. Thus judges, as well as legislative and executive officials, have to make choices, often hard choices, in determining what the law is. Some clauses of constitutional texts, such as those of the American Fifth and Fourteenth Amendments that forbid the federal and state governments to deprive a person of "life, liberty, or property, without due process of law," cry out for interpretation that goes far beyond parsing sentences or searching for largely lost legislative history to discover specific intentions of particular framers. Statutes are frequently no less general in their commands. The Sherman Antitrust Act, for example, forbids "every contract, combination in the form of trust or otherwise, or conspiracy in restraint of trade." In fact, however, every contract restrains trade to some extent, if only by limiting alternative agreements. Thus it should have come as no surprise that the Supreme Court soon ruled that, for the statute to be enforceable, judges had to read into it a "rule of reason." The Act could prohibit only "unreasonable" restraints of trade; whether restraints were "reasonable" was, of course, a question for judges to decide.

In the context of interpretation and discretion, some authors differentiate between broad or vague clauses, such as those in the Fifth and Fourteenth Amendments, and more specific ones, such as the Third Amendment's prohibition against quartering troops in unwilling civilians' homes during peace. The first kind of clause obviously confers far greater discretion on judges than does the second. As Justice Felix Frankfurter explained this "two clause" theory in *United States v. Lovett* (1946), constitutional issues arising from clauses invoking broad standards of fairness written into the constitutional document permit relatively wide play for individual legal judgments. But specific provisions adopted to prevent the recurrence of historic grievances are defined by history, which channels judicial discretion.

Along with discretion, judges also have power that fits nicely into Harold Lasswell's cynical definition of politics as "who gets what, when, and how." Individual judicial decisions determine a great deal about who gets what from and pays what to the governmental system. Who owes taxes and who is entitled to pensions, unemployment benefits, or welfare are matters that judges frequently decide, just as in civil (noncriminal) disputes between individuals, judges determine who owns a piece of property, what obligations a contract imposes, or how much Citizen A must pay Citizen B for damaging his car.

As later chapters show in some detail, the effects of judicial decisions that apparently concern only two private citizens or a single citizen and a governmental agency may ripple out to include large segments of the population, perhaps even the nation as a whole, as did the U.S. Supreme Court's decision in *Bush v. Gore* (2000), which halted the Florida high court's effort to recount ballots and, in effect, gave George Bush the presidency. Insofar as judicial decisions relate to the legitimate power of governmental officials vis-à-vis one another or private citizens, those rulings may preserve or alter existing structures of authority—the formal and informal means by which a polity is governed. Insofar as judges in justifying their decisions announce fundamental principles, they might affect a nation's ideals and ultimate goals.

CIVIL AND COMMON LAW SYSTEMS

Our emphasis on "might" is deliberate. The ability of judges to affect public policy depends on a number of factors, not least of which is the system under which courts operate. With the exceptions of China and some Islamic countries, most nations are governed by one of two legal systems, the Civil (or Roman) Law or the common law. The name *Civil* was used in the Middle Ages to distinguish this legal mode from canon (ecclesiastical) law, and its use has spread around the European continent, to Latin America through Spanish and Portuguese colonization, through French colonization to the Canadian province of Quebec, Louisiana in the United States, parts of Africa, and through formal adoption to other countries such as Turkey and, strangely enough, Japan. The common law, in contrast, grew up in England and spread to Ireland, the United States, British Canada, Australia, and to those parts of the developing world that came under British domination. At least on the surface, this system provides greater opportunities for judicial discretion and creativity than does the Civil Law.

The Civil Law

The roots of the Civil Law begin in Roman jurisprudence as rediscovered and reinterpreted by legal scholars during the Middle Ages. The model here is a code—a lucid, detailed, and all-encompassing set of interlocking regulations that attempt to lay down in general principle, if not in specific terms, the rules for settling all disputes among human beings. Its first incarnation was in the volumes promulgated by Emperor Justinian in the sixth century; its modern reincarnations came first in the *Code Napoleon* in the early years of the nineteenth century and then in the German codes promulgated ninety years later. Napoleon wanted his Code to be so clear that a peasant in the field could understand it.

The hero of the Civil Law is the scholar, the writer who understands the basic philosophical principles that tie the whole system together into a coherent intellectual whole. His or her nominal superior but actual assistant is the Legislator who adopts the scholar's analysis and gives it binding force within the community. The judge, in contrast, is supposed to be little more than a skilled technician who applies specific sections of the supposedly complete legal corpus. Her or his main task is, to use one of Justice Benjamin N. Cardozo's analogies, like that of a shopper who matches the bright colors of real disputes against the more subtle shades of the Code; in other words, the judge simply discovers the appropriate provisions of the Code and applies them to the case at hand. Such a task requires highly trained understanding but no creativity.

Several very different threads were woven into this normative pattern of a restricted judicial function. The absolutist notion of the law as the will of the sovereign came first. When the emperor—whether he was Roman, French, or German—had spoken, it was the duty of all citizens, including magistrates, to obey, not to add to or subtract from his words as embodied in the law. Later, when democratic ideas were victorious, the same argument was made in relation to the will of the people as expressed through their elected Legislator. (The word *Legislator* is usually singular and often capitalized, implying action by a sovereign, unified will rather than bargaining and compromise among independent interests that typify the American legislative process.) Judges, as appointed officials, have no authority to emend the decisions of the citizens' chosen representatives.

At the heart of the Civil Law is a concept beyond both democratic and authoritarian ideologies: law is a system, closed, self-contained, and self-sustained, a neatly ordered body of principles hierarchically arranged, with the less fundamental principles logically deduced from the more fundamental. Any judicial tampering with this system, even a charitable effort to ease harsh effects of the Code's commands in a particular case, is bound, over the long run, to do more harm than good by destroying the intellectual integrity and conceptual purity of the entire corpus.

As we noted, one of the motives behind the whole movement to codify the law was to curb judicial discretion. It soon became evident, however, that no group of scholars, no matter how learned, could foresee all the forms that human conflict would take. Thus, Civil-Law judges soon began to exercise a great deal of discretion in making law and public policy—and they continue to do so today. The important point here is that, although the official doctrine of the Civil Law prescribes an exceedingly narrow ambit for the exercise of judicial power and discretion, practice is more expansive.

The Common Law

If the hero of the Civil Law has been the scholar, the hero of the common law has been the judge and his or her squire, the practicing attorney. Whereas the Civil Law was formulated in the antiseptic atmosphere of the university and was dependent on abstraction, deep learning, and cool, taut logic, the common law grew out of the muck and mire of courtroom battles. Its rules were efforts to settle immediate human conflicts, with a resultant emphasis on practical results rather than on conceptual purity and logical symmetry. At bottom, common law is judge-made law. Even when enacted into statutes, as much of the common law has been in the United States, the results look more like patchwork quilts than tightly logical syllogisms.

That American judges operate under a common-law tradition is not surprising. The colonists brought with them from England those judge-made rules that had slowly developed over the centuries. Shortly after the Norman Conquest of England, royal officials, who only by rough analogy could be called judges in the modern sense, traveled around the country to settle private disputes and sometimes to punish what we would call—although they did not—public offenses. These officials claimed to apply the common custom of the realm rather than the parochial traditions of a particular shire or village. Which customs were common and which were local depended in large part on the perceptions, experiences, values, and personal judgments of royal officials, for neither sound data nor objective standards were available.

Because one set of judges, operating under the king's central administration, decided the more important cases involving what we would call private litigation, their rulings eventually did become common law if not common custom. During the same period these judges began to follow a doctrine known as *stare decisis*, according to which they applied the rules announced in previous decisions to settle new cases. As we shall see in Chapter 10, deciding precisely what a previous case stands for and how its rule is to be applied to a new situation are hardly simple tasks. Furthermore, even a rigid doctrine of stare decisis allows a judge considerable discretion; still, use of precedents has given the common law a degree of continuity across both space and time.

Judicial discretion takes on added significance when we consider exactly what is meant by the statement that the common law is largely judge-made. It was not until well into the nineteenth century that either the British Parliament or the American Congress began to pass many statutes dealing with the everyday affairs of private citizens. Centuries after it had become an important governmental institution, Parliament met principally to levy taxes, raise armies, fit out navies, declare war, and conclude peace. Occasionally, it would pass a legal monument such as the Bill of Rights of 1689 or the Act of Settlement of 1701, but judges formulated most of the rules, not only in the field of private law, such as property, trespass, wills, contracts, employer-employee relations, but also on issues that in the United States would be regarded as constitutional in character. For example, the basic rights of persons accused of criminal offenses are stated in the so-called Judges' Rules, which originated in a letter written by the Lord Chief Justice in 1906 to the Chief Constable of Birmingham in response to a request for advice.

CONCEPTUALIZATIONS OF LAW: SCHOOLS OF JURISPRUDENCE

So far we have been talking about two specific legal systems, but behind every such system there lurks a network of normative ideas about what should properly be called law. Controversies over the basic question, what is law?, have characterized legal and political discussion since before the time of Plato. The debate basically hinges on a disagreement over whether law is, on the one hand, inherently related to some underlying moral standard or, on the other hand, simply the product of human construction. The two major competitors in this debate in the Western world have historically been natural law and positivism (or legal positivism).

Advocates on both sides of this question believe that the way that we conceptualize law will have an important effect on how we answer a second question: how should judges make decisions? This belief is grounded in the idea that a conception of law has significant implications for what resources a judge can legitimately use to interpret the law and, thus, for how judges should decide cases. The debate over judicial decision making is commonly cast in terms of how much discretion judges have in making their decisions. In the following discussion (and accompanying readings) we will see that these tensions over the appropriate conceptualizations of law and judicial decision making have been a persistent feature of both legal and social-scientific scholarship on the courts.

Natural Law

According to followers of natural law, a putative law's validity depends not merely on lawmakers' having followed correct procedures but also on the inherent justice of that "law." These writers acknowledge that many laws, such as those determining which side of the road cars should drive or whether the nation's currency should be called dollars, pounds, or lire, are inevitably arbitrary and do not raise questions of justice. However, many laws, such as those involving fraud, robbery, rape, and murder, as well as property, taxes, and forms of punishment, involve moral judgments about right and wrong as well as practical judgments about how far society can regulate its citizens' conduct.

The idea around which these writers rally is not that "nature," considered as an abstraction or as a set of immutable laws such as gravity, provides normative standards but rather that, by their human nature, most men and women can reason objectively about what is morally good or bad for themselves and others. These jurists do not deny that specific cultural conditions warp individual judgments, nor do they claim that all humans can or will always reason clearly and impartially, only that under most circumstances most people can see beyond narrow self- or group interest and choose just over unjust actions. Human reason is never perfect, but it is not always warped. Reasons for and against a proposition might even out, sometimes because people are short-sighted or swayed by selfishness and sometimes because several competing ends and means are all moral in themselves, making the question one of prudence. Moreover, moral and legal problems do not necessarily have unique solutions. Because of the human capacity to reason about good and evil, political obedience is not something that reasoning citizens and public officials can blindly give to higher authority, though how and when to resist unjust laws raise additional and very complicated questions of prudence.

Legal Positivism

In contrast, legal positivism contends that a law is a law is a law. Its essence is that it be enacted, through established procedures, by whoever has lawmaking authority in a particular political system. Such laws may be unnecessary, unwise, or even unjust; nevertheless, they remain laws, binding on all citizens within that jurisdiction. For positivists, the core question is whether the law was enacted by the person or the institution on whom the basic rules of the political system confer that authority. Although most of these writers agree that questions of justice are important—indeed, they often urge lawmakers, whoever they might be, to weigh such matters carefully—that lawmakers have made a grossly mistaken or even venal moral judgment remains irrelevant to the notion of law. What citizens must do is obey the law; in a democracy they can vote the rascals out at the next election. What attorneys, scholars, judges, and other public officials must do is to study, explain, and faithfully apply the ramifications of the law.

The Debate

The critical philosophic difference between these two groups is rooted in a dispute about whether moral judgments can have universal validity or whether they are determined, at worst, through idiosyncratic or selfish motives or, at best, according to values relative to time, place, and culture. The twentieth century's leading positivist, Hans Kelsen, himself a Jewish refugee from Nazism, went so far as to argue that the Nazi regime was legitimate and its decrees, like those of any regime that actually controlled its nation's territory, were binding as law as long as they were enacted according to that political system's norms of law-making. Followers of natural law found the entire Nazi regime immoral and its decrees no more than commands from ruthless thugs, deserving of fear but not of respect or freely given obedience.

Emotionally, that particular debate is one positivism cannot win; indeed, it can only lose badly.[1] However, many other issues are not so easily settled as are matters of morality or law—for example, may the law rightly punish a physician who assisted a terminally ill patient to die? Other issues involve complex questions of law, desirable (or even practical) public policy, and morality. For example, should a state enact and enforce a statute that forbids homosexual intercourse between consenting adults?

Further complicating the debate is the fact that since the seventeenth century natural law has been mixed with a close intellectual cousin, natural rights, a doctrine embodied in the Declaration of Independence's claim that all human beings have certain "unalienable rights." Because theories of natural law and natural rights are both based on a belief in the great and innate dignity of every man and woman, the two schools often arrive at the same conclusion about specific problems. Indeed, many proponents of these separate philosophies, especially in the United States, claim dual intellectual citizenship. But this claim of unity is overstated, for the two ask substantially different questions. For natural law, the basic political queries are always these: what is my duty? how must I, acting alone, in combination with others, or through the state, behave toward other beings? For natural rights, the fundamental inquiry is this: what are my rights that other citizens and public officials must respect? A pregnant woman who believed in natural rights might, for instance, assert a right to control her own body, whereas a pregnant woman who believed in natural law might ask: what obligations do I have toward that human life that is developing within me?

Both kinds of issues continually arise in the judicial as well as in the legislative and executive processes. And, following the approach of natural law, many believers in natural rights contend that a law that violates such a right is no law at all. In reply, positivists argue that defining the boundaries of such rights, except as pragmatic judgments for a particular country at a particular time, will produce conflicting markers and lead to anarchy. They hunker down more deeply into their claims that human judgments about morality and justice are relative, and thus whatever the constituted lawmaking authority says is law is law. Nevertheless, often being good democrats and/or constitutionalists, they would establish governmental processes, perhaps including judicial review, to

---

[1] For a more sophisticated version of this debate see: H.L.A. Hart, "Positivism and the Separation of Law and Morals," 71 *Harvard Law Review* 593 (1958); and Lon Fuller, "Positivism and Fidelity to Law—A Reply to Professor Hart," 71 *ibid.* 630 (1958).

make and limit as well as change such choices for society rather than rely on the will of an autocrat.

Civil-Law systems typically follow the positivist school, something of an anomaly considering that most Civil-Law systems operate in Catholic countries, such as France, Spain, Belgium, Austria, and the countries of Latin America, and natural law is the official moral doctrine of the Catholic Church. Under the Civil Law, questions of justice and morality are not for judges but for the Legislator. It should come as no surprise, then, that German and even French judges could unquestioningly apply Nazi decrees. Some common-law systems, such as that still extant in Britain, also instruct judges to follow the tenets of positivism; but others, such as that in the United States, sometimes tell judges to follow positivism, sometimes natural rights, and, far less frequently, natural law. Indeed, one might look at a constitutional text or the ideas embodied in a founding document such as the Declaration of Independence as transforming into positive law some ideals of natural rights. The plain words of the Ninth Amendment offer not merely an invitation but a command for interpreters to attend to such rights: "The enumeration in the Constitution, of certain rights, shall not be construed to deny or disparage others retained by the people."

Even outside the field of constitutional interpretation, natural law and natural rights provoke fascinating questions for common-law judges; for example, to what extent may they use their discretion to shape the law according to norms they deem morally compelling? Two general answers are available. The first, the response of natural law, is that judges must use all discretion reasonably available to arrive at as just a result as the basic principles underlying the legal system allow. If injustice is unavoidable, then the question becomes one of prudence, though not of less importance: Would it do more moral harm, over the long run, to allow the system to function unjustly or to resign in protest? The second, positivist response, says judges should not exercise discretion but merely apply the law as written. If a moral question is present, it is for others to decide, not judges. This sort of answer illustrates what has been called "the declaratory theory" of the judicial function, developed most eloquently by Sir William Blackstone (1723–1780). In one part of his famous *Commentaries on the Laws of England*, he attacked the notion that these wise and virtuous jurists exercised any real degree of discretion. The judge's function, Blackstone explained, was only to declare the law. Judges were the "depositories of the law; the living oracles who are bound by an oath to decide according to the law of the land." Their function was not to decide cases according to private value judgments, to personal preferences over policy matters. Nor were they "delegated to pronounce new law, but to maintain and expound the old one" (Reading 1.1).

Blackstone's influence was great in England and probably greater in America. The *Commentaries* sold more copies in the Colonies than in the mother country. And his prescription for the judicial function was attractive to many people, especially to those who wanted the security—the law and order—that judges would provide against the popular democracy that seemed to be rising in the wake of the American Revolution.

Alas, for the common-law judge's peace of mind, Blackstone was not consistent. Despite his apparent positivism, at times he could sing with the choirs of most theologically oriented natural lawyers. The will of the Maker of mankind, he also said, "is called the law of nature. For as God. . . when he created man, and endued him with freewill to conduct himself in all parts of life, he laid down certain immutable laws of human nature, whereby that freewill is in some degree regulated and restrained, and gave him also the faculty of reason to discover the purport of the whole law." Lest he be misunderstood, Blackstone continued:

> This law of nature, being co-eval with mankind and dictated by God himself, is of course superior in obligation to any other. It is binding over all the globe, in all countries, at all times: no human laws are of any validity if contrary to this; and such of them as are valid derive all their force, and all their authority, mediately or immediately, from this original.[2]

In the early days under the current constitutional text, many American judges apparently believed they had wide discretion to apply what they believed to be natural law and natural rights. By the 1820s, however, most judges retreated, perhaps because slavery, morally wrong under both natural right and natural law, was, nevertheless, constitutionally permissible. Abolitionists invoked both theories—in particular, the latter's having been enshrined in the Declaration of Independence—to brand the constitutional text as "an agreement with Hell, a covenant with death." Faced with threats of tearing the nation apart,[3] judges retreated to positivism, from whence they have later emerged at various times to embrace natural rights and occasionally natural law.

THE INSTITUTIONALIZATION OF DECLARATORY THEORY

In *Federalist* No. 78 Alexander Hamilton made a classic application of Blackstone's declaratory theory to constitutional interpretation. The constitution was a fundamental law, and judges must ascertain its meaning as in the case of all other law. But, as for all other laws, the judges were merely Blackstonian oracles, without discretion. They could "take no active resolution whatever." They had "neither the FORCE nor WILL, but merely judgment" (Reading 1.2).

---

[2] *Commentaries on the Laws of England* (A Facsimile of the First Edition of 1765–1769, with an Introduction by Stanley N. Katz) (Chicago: University of Chicago Press, 1979), I, 2. Like Katz, we believe that Blackstone's endorsement of natural law was merely *pro forma*, but his eloquent, if naive, defense of that theory remained ready at hand for adventurous judges and commentators.

[3] See Robert M. Cover, *Justice Accused: Antislavery and the Judicial Process* (New Haven, CT: Yale University Press, 1975).

Not the least of John Marshall's accomplishments as Chief Justice of the United States (1801–1835) was that, in interpreting the new constitution, he was able to pursue the same freewheeling creativity that common-law judges had historically exercised. He could even occasionally invoke natural law while proclaiming the doctrine that judges had neither force nor will. Marshall successfully asserted in *Marbury v. Madison* (1803) the great power to declare congressional statutes unconstitutional, while making judicial review appear to be nothing more than a simple ministerial act (Reading 2.2). Repugnance between a statute and the constitution, he implied, should be readily apparent to anyone. The difference, as Thomas Reed Powell once put it, was made to seem "equivalent to an objective contradiction in the order of nature and not a mere difference between two difference guessers."[4] And twenty-one years later, in *Osbourn v. Bank of the United States* (1824), by which time Marshall's "active resolution" had done so much to establish the foundations of a strong national government, the Chief was still portraying his Court as the weak tribunal that Hamilton had painted:

> Judicial power, as contradistinguished from the power of laws, has no existence. Courts are the mere instrument of the laws, and can will nothing. When they are said to exercise a discretion, it is a mere legal discretion, a discretion to be exercised in discerning the course prescribed by law. Judicial power is never exercised for the purpose of giving effect to the will of the Judge; always for the purpose of giving effect to the will of the Legislature; or, in other words, to the will of law.

Thomas Jefferson was enraged at Marshall's cleverness. He bitterly attacked the Chief Justice's claims to be simply applying the clear words of the constitutional document. In Marshall's hands, Jefferson complained, the Constitution was "a thing of putty," "nothing more than an ambiguous text, to be explained by his sophistry into any meaning which may subserve his personal malice." What Jefferson perceived was that Marshall was using the power of judicial interpretation to write Federalist principles into the nation's basic law. Jefferson, in fact, was so irate that in 1802 and 1804 he and members of his political party launched several campaigns against the judiciary—first abolishing a whole tier of federal courts, throwing their judges, supposedly protected by tenure during good behavior, out of office and next impeaching a partisan Federalist, Justice Samuel Chase. But Marshall's political jurisprudence, intellectual vigor, and skill in choosing issues raised the Court from third-rate status to a position of near equality in domestic affairs with the president and Congress. In 1835, the year of Marshall's death, Alexis de Tocqueville observed that "the political power which the Americans have entrusted to their courts of justice is immense"(Reading 1.3).

---

[4] Thomas Reed Powell, *Vagaries and Varieties in Constitutional Interpretation* (New York: Columbia University Press, 1956), 14.

EMERGING CHALLENGES: SOCIOLOGICAL JURISPRUDENCE AND LEGAL REALISM

It seemed obvious to Jefferson that judges make law and exercise private judgment in deciding cases, but after the issue of slavery threatened to destroy the Union, positivism, overtly at least, came to dominate U.S. legal education and continued to do so well into the twentieth century. Training for law (Chapter 5 discusses the growth of formal legal education) inculcated in fledgling attorneys a mechanical approach—an approach that borrowed from Blackstone's notion of the duty of judges to declare (and not make) the law. Largely absent was his invocation of natural law. As Yosal Rogat described this positivist mythology: "The judge's techniques were socially neutral, his private views irrelevant: judging was more like finding than making, a matter of necessity rather than choice."[5] Dean (later U.S. Attorney General) Edward Levi was more specific about this orthodox model of legal reasoning, reasoning by example, that this approach enshrines: the judge (1) observes a similarity between cases, (2) announces the rule of law inherent in the first case, and (3) applies that rule to the second case (Reading 10.1).

Just as positivism became the ideal to which judges and lawyers should aspire, new perspectives were starting to emerge from the ranks of the nation's judiciary and, perhaps not so surprisingly, from its law schools. In general, these thinkers denounced pure positivism as overly mechanical and unrealistic,[6] and they urged judges to consider more dynamic factors as bases for decisions. Oliver Wendell Holmes, Jr. (1841–1935) was certainly influential at this time. Although he accepted judicial lawmaking as a fact of life, he did so without Jefferson's partisan rancor. Indeed, Holmes contended that "the Law" had no existence apart from the decisions of courts. In a famous sentence he wrote: "The prophecies of what the courts will do in fact, and nothing more pretentious, are what I mean by the law" (Reading 1.4). Nor did he believe that judges were moved merely by logic. As he explained in what quickly became a widely cited book:

> The life of the law has not been logic; it has been experience. The felt necessities of the time, the prevalent moral and political theories, intuitions of public policy, avowed or unconscious, even the prejudices which judges share with their fellow-men, have had a good deal more to do than the syllogism in determining the rules by which men should be governed.[7]

---

[5] Yosal Rogat, "Legal Realism," in *The Encyclopedia of Philosophy*, ed. Paul Edwards (New York: Macmillan, 1972), 420. Quoted in Jeffrey A. Segal and Harold J. Spaeth, *The Supreme Court and the Attitudinal Model* (New York: Cambridge University Press, 1993), 65.

[6] Roscoe Pound, "The Call for a Realist Jurisprudence," 44 *Harvard Law Review* 697 (1931).

[7] Oliver Wendell Holmes, Jr., *The Common Law* (Boston: Little, Brown, 1881), 1.

Holmes's appointment to the Supreme Court in 1903 gave him the best pulpit in the land for announcing and amplifying his conception of the judicial function and for challenging the declaratory theory. And he seized that opportunity, not only opposing many of his brethren's decisions but also disputing their denials that they were choosing among competing political values and public policies. When, by a five-to-four vote, the Court invalidated a statute from New York that set ten hours as the maximum bakers could work in a day, Holmes charged that the decision was based not on law but upon an economic theory—moreover, "an economic theory which a large part of the country does not entertain." When the Court struck down a state tax in *Baldwin v. Missouri* (1930), he snarled in his final dissent that the Fourteenth Amendment was not "intended to give us carte blanche to embody our economic or moral beliefs in its prohibitions."

As a philosophical pragmatist, Holmes thought that judges should base their decisions primarily on the consequences that follow from a given decision. To adequately assess such consequences, judges should become "the man of statistics and the master of economics"—an ironic claim given that he found both disciplines deadly dull and preferred to spend his hours of leisure reading Proust. Roscoe Pound (1870–1964), who was to become dean of the Harvard Law School and founder of sociological jurisprudence in the United States, believed that the social sciences should shape the development of the law. His principal concern centered on the relationships between the legal system and the society of which it is a part. He saw legal development as the product of adjustments made necessary by the function of law as a controlling and stabilizing force in a constantly changing society. Law, Pound argued, cannot control society if it does not satisfy fundamental public needs for both stability and change. Because understanding the precise nature of those needs depends heavily on sociological knowledge and analysis, lawyers and judges had to broaden their study to include the actual effects of legal rules on society. Indeed, he came to see the study of law as one of the social sciences, living in union with economics, sociology, and political science.

As did Holmes, Pound stressed the critical significance of the judge in providing the really creative element in law. He believed that, historically, legislation had failed to meet the requirements of social change; moreover, the complex conditions of modern life made legislators incapable of drafting statutes that could effectively encompass all eventualities. Judges, deciding on a case-by-case basis, were in a better position than were legislators to achieve the continual adjustment needed for a legal system to harmonize rather than clash with its larger social system. But, Pound emphasized, to play that creative role judges had to abandon the "slot machine theory" of judicial decision making and acquire the learning necessary to become informed "social engineers."

Justice Benjamin N. Cardozo (1870–1938) agreed with Pound about the nature of law and the creative tasks of judges. While he was still a judge on the New York Court of Appeals, he wrote a classic analysis of judicial decision making (Reading 1.5). Again it was Blackstone's concept of judges as mere expounders of known law against which Cardozo contended. Some legal principles—in fact, a great many—he admitted, are well established, and these permit law to exercise a stabilizing influence on society. But when, as often happened, legal principles were not definite, judges must create new rules or refashion old ones. It was in explaining how judges make these creative choices that Cardozo was most effective. And, in so doing, he made no effort to downplay the importance of judges' moral reasoning, of their sense of justice.[8] Although he never specifically invoked natural law, in one of his more famous opinions he did hint that certain natural rights underlay the American constitutional order.[9]

During the 1920s, dissidents calling themselves "legal realists" went even further and mounted a fresh assault on the still highly orthodox declaratory theory. Although realists formed a professionally and intellectually diverse group, which included political scientists, philosophers, economists, and psychologists, most of them were law professors. Taking their cue from Holmes's dictum that law consisted of "prophecies of what the courts will do in fact," they launched a vigorous effort to widen the vista of legal reasoning by using other social sciences, Freudian psychology, and philosophical pragmatism. Legal realism included several varieties of jurisprudence and was more a state of mind than a concerted movement. In general, however, realists argued that judicial decisions and their actual effects on social behavior were the proper foci of legal study. They rejected emphasis on rules as traditionally conceived. Their "science" of law was to be based on observed facts. As Karl Llewellyn, one of the most influential of realists, put it:

> The main thing is what officials [i.e., judges] are going to do . . . is seeing what officials do, do about disputes, or about anything else; and seeing that there is a certain regularity in their doing—a regularity which makes possible prediction of what they and other officials are about to do tomorrow.[10]

Finding out what judges do required improved methods of research and analysis, and the realists were responsible for substantial empirical and quantitative studies of the actual administration of justice. Some of them stressed the importance of trial courts, as opposed to appellate tribunals, which had been at the center of lawyers' interests for several generations. Others wrote about law from the outside, as would social psychologists or cultural anthropologists. In 1930 Jerome Frank (who later became a judge on the United States Court of Appeals for the Second Circuit) produced the clearest statement of a realist position in his seminal work *Law and the Modern Mind*. There he tried to increase understanding of judges and their lawmaking by applying Freudian

---

[8] In addition to Cardozo's *The Nature of the Judicial Process* (New Haven, CT: Yale University Press, 1921), see also Richard Polenberg, *The World of Benjamin Cardozo: Personal Values and the Judicial Process* (Cambridge: Harvard University Press, 1997).

[9] *Palko v. Connecticut*, 302 U.S. 319 (1937).

[10] Karl Llewellyn, *The Bramble Bush* (New York: Oceana Publications, 1951), 13.

psychology and Jean Piaget's theories of child development to empirical data on judicial behavior. In the final book he wrote, he edged close to advocating natural law as a necessary guide to democratic government that was true to its own ideals.[11]

CONTEMPORARY SCHOLARSHIP: THE DEBATES CONTINUE

Karl Llewellyn, Jerome Frank, and other realists such as Edward S. Corwin had a profound effect on the course of legal scholarship, with their general claims providing fodder for law reviews and social science journals. The debates over the appropriate relationship between law and morality and over the appropriate role for judges in the legal process have continued to characterize contemporary scholarship by both legal scholars and social scientists.

Realism's Progeny and Critics

Beginning in the late 1960s a cluster of (then) younger law school professors, calling themselves the Critical Legal Studies movement, renewed and extended the realist critique. Although, like the realists, members of Critical Legal Studies speak with diverse and frequently discordant voices, they agree that legal concepts are inherently indeterminate and so cannot govern decisions in individual cases. The "Crits'" critiques tended to see law as protecting the interests of the dominant classes in society to the serious disadvantage of workers, ethnic minorities, women, and the poor. More recent Critical Legal Studies' writings stress the open-endedness of all legal systems and assert the consequent spuriousness of any claim to a system of "justice" based on neutral applications of coherent principles—the foundation of most conventional legal arguments.

Feminist Jurisprudence and Critical Race Theory run along similar lines, with adherents seeking to demonstrate how the rule of law works against the interests of women and minorities (Reading 1.6). As Gary Minda describes it, "Feminist jurisprudence attempts to tell the woman's story of law—what it feels like to be a woman living in a legal and social world that is defined and manipulated by male attitudes and experiences. The goal is to show how prevailing conceptions of the rule of law fail to respect the experiences and harms of objectifying women under allegedly gender-neutral norms."[12] Richard Delgado provides a glimpse into the establishment and purpose of Critical Race Theory when he writes:

> Critical race scholarship sprang up in the late 1970s with the realization that the civil rights movement of the 1960s had stalled, and many of its gains were being rolled back. It was time to stop perseverating; we no longer could justify

---

[11] Jerome Frank, *Fate and Freedom: A Philosophy for Free Americans* (Boston: Beacon Press, 1953).

[12] Gary Minda, "The Jurisprudential Movements of the 1980s," 50 *Ohio State Law Review* 630 (1989).

depleting our already frustrated energy on what we had been doing all along—filing amicus briefs, coining new litigation strategies, writing another law review article exhorting judges to exercise moral leadership in the search for racial justice—in hope of making things better. We needed new ideas and theories.

Accordingly, we have been borrowing and experimenting with new approaches. We have been showing how areas of law ostensibly designed for our benefit often benefit whites more than blacks.[13]

To make such a demonstration, many critical race scholars have adopted a distinct (and controversial) methodology, the personal narrative. That is, they use "parables, chronicles, stories, and counter stories to show the false necessity and unintentional irony of much current civil rights doctrine and scholarship."[14]

In response to the many variants of legal realism, followers of natural law, such as John Finnis and Robert P. George,[15] began to reformulate and reassert this ancient jurisprudence. Their influence remains centered more in academic than in judicial circles. When he was a judge on the Court of Appeals for the District of Columbia, Clarence Thomas, a former Catholic seminarian, had expressed an interest in exploring how natural law should influence his decision making. When nominated for the Supreme Court in 1991, however, he felt constrained to disavow this line of inquiry lest he irritate positivist senators, worried about how that normative jurisprudence would increase the scope of judicial discretion.

Nevertheless, concerns for a wide and proper role for moral considerations in judging have been flourishing among philosophers, political scientists, and academic lawyers, with natural-law advocates finding ready allies in scholars such as Michael Moore and Sotirios A. Barber, who argue against relativism and positivism, and for "moral realism." They make the case that moral reasoning is not merely a matter of cultural convention. Rather, it is a human capacity, essential to decision making, judicial or otherwise, in a constitutional democracy that takes seriously its commitments to furthering a good life for its citizens.[16] Moreover, some "deep conventionalists" such as Ronald Dworkin[17] have been arguing that even if reason cannot discover universal moral truths, judges and legal scholars alike can and should uncover the norms of their particular societies and apply those norms to problems of law and public policy.

---

[13] Richard Delgado, "Brewer's Plea: Critical Thoughts on Common Cause," 44 *Vanderbilt Law Review* 6–7 (1991).

[14] *Ibid.*

[15] John Finnis, *Natural Law and Natural Rights* (New York: Oxford University Press, 1980); Robert P. George, *In Defense of Natural Law* (Oxford: Clarendon Press, 1999). See also Hadley Arkes, *First Things: An Inquiry into the First Principles of Morals and Justice* (Princeton: Princeton University Press, 1986).

[16] Michael Moore, "A Natural Law Theory of Interpretation," 58 *Southern California Law Review* 277 (1985) and "Moral Reality Revisited," 90 *Michigan Law Review* 2424 (1992); Sotirios A. Barber, *The Constitution of Judicial Power* (Baltimore: Johns Hopkins University Press, 1993).

[17] See especially: "Seven Critics," 11 *Georgia Law Review* 1201 (1977); and *Law's Empire* (Cambridge: Harvard University Press, 1986).

Indeed, concern for moral issues has continuously bubbled beneath the surface of positivism. "Pure positivists" such as Hans Kelsen have been rare outside the Civil Law.

Social Science and the Growth of Political Jurisprudence

As we noted above, strains of legal realism also affected legal scholarship produced by political scientists. Blackstone's declaratory theory had been criticized from the time he formulated it, and few critics were sharper than Edward S. Corwin. The 1920s and 1930s saw a spate of American scholarship in the social sciences that tried to show through quantitative analysis how wrong as descriptions of judicial activities the prescriptions of Blackstone and his followers had been. The landmark work came in 1948 with publication of C. Herman Pritchett's *The Roosevelt Court*. He asked deceptively simple questions: If judges were merely "declaring" the law rather than making it, why did they so often disagree? How, in interpreting the same legal provisions, could they consistently reach different conclusions on important questions of law? When Pritchett concluded that the usual explanations could not provide intellectually acceptable responses, he turned to the answer offered by Jerome Frank and the other legal realists: judges are "motivated by their own preferences." Pritchett, however, did not see "preferences" as mere whims but as opinions, often as deeply thought out as they were felt.

Pritchett's work marked a new beginning, and not an end, to social-scientific inquiry into the legal process. Today, as we shall see throughout this book, political scientists invoke a range of approaches to the study of law—both in the United States and abroad. Some are explicitly normative; others are empirical; and yet a third set, attempts to combine the two. To the basic question of how judges make decisions, political scientists adopt one of three basic approaches. The first, the legal model, is reminiscent of Blackstone's declaratory theory. According to the legal model, judicial decisions "are based on the facts of the case in light of the plain meaning of statutes and the Constitution, the intent of the framers, precedent, and a balancing of societal interests."[18] Thus, the legal model explains a judge's decision by looking at the text of the relevant law and the previous decisions of other judges.

The other two approaches, the attitudinal and strategic models, are direct descendants of the legal realists. According to the attitudinal approach, judicial decisions "are based on the facts of the case in light of the ideological attitudes and values of the justices."[19] Advocates of this approach argue that we can best explain the decisions of judges merely by identifying their personal attitudes about the subject of the relevant case. The strategic approach shares with the attitudinal model the basic idea that judges are goal-oriented actors but offers a

---

[18] Jeffrey A. Segal and Harold J. Spaeth, *The Supreme Court and the Attitudinal Model* (New York: Cambridge University Press, 1993).

[19] *Ibid.*

more nuanced account of how such goals translate into judicial decisions. The advocates of the strategic approach insist that judges cannot achieve their goals without considering the preferences of other relevant actors, the choices they expect those actors to make, and the institutional context.[20] Thus, the strategic model explains judicial decision making by reference to both the goals of the judges and the strategic context in which they exercise their choices. Underlying these last two models is a common understanding: the sociological view of law as a form of social control and its argument that a judge is inevitably a social engineer. Although that picture of the judge might trouble some commentators and members of the public, it deeply perturbs judges. Part of their concern undoubtedly stems from the realists' success in demonstrating not only that judges have a wide range of discretion but also that subconscious forces struggling within judges' own psyches play a major part in molding their decisions.

WHAT IS TO COME

This book is concerned with courts for many of the same reasons that concerned the realists, followers of sociological jurisprudence, critical legal scholars, positive political theorists, and even natural lawyers, moral realists, and "deep conventionalists." Because judges often affect public policy, they are important political actors; because they have discretion, who they are and how they are chosen make a difference to the kinds of public policy the country enjoys or from which it suffers. For the same reasons, we are also interested in how individuals, groups, and public officials can energize and utilize judicial power, as well as in the sorts of instruments judges have at their disposal to shape specific policies and general values. In short, this book examines the judicial process as one of the formal institutions that shape societal change.

By so doing, we hope to encourage students to try to discover a political jurisprudence in judicial decisions and writings—that is, to look for a central set of politically relevant ideas and values that give order and coherence to the work of judges. Most basically, where the substance of judicial decisions is involved, people who want to understand how courts and judges participate in governing society should look for the principal values that decisions are advancing or restricting. For instance: Are judges putting individual liberty ahead of such competing values as equality? Are courts giving priority to the needs of citizens who want stability over the needs of those who want social change? Are judges insisting that freedom of political communication takes precedence over all other values, even the right to privacy? Are judges substituting their own,

---

[20] Lee Epstein and Jack Knight, *The Choices Justices Make* (Washington, DC: CQ Press, 1998). Some years earlier, Walter F. Murphy had suggested similar theories about judicial behavior, but he believes that normative ideas, such as those expressed in natural law, are necessary to choices that are truly rational. See Walter F. Murphy, *Elements of Judicial Strategy* (Chicago: University of Chicago Press, 1964).

perhaps idiosyncratic, values and judgments for those of other, equally responsible and intelligent, officials?

To each of these queries we would append another set of questions: If judges are so acting, should they be? If judges are not so acting, shouldn't they be?

Somewhat less basic are substantive questions about particular public policies and the power of specific governmental officials. To what extent and during what periods of time can a state regulate an individual's decision to take his or her life? What positive action does a school board have to take to overcome racial imbalance in its classrooms? Does putting a duly convicted prisoner to death, even for murder, inflict cruel and unusual punishment? Does denying students in public schools a right, on their own initiative, to engage in public prayers constitute establishment of atheism as the national religion?

By directing attention to these sorts of issues, we also hope to encourage students to ask normative questions: What theories and values should judges advance? What functions are proper to judges in a constitutional democracy, and what functions are improper? By what standards does one draw clear distinctions between the proper and the improper? How (and why) do particular lines of decision support or undermine values and policies central to a viable constitutional democracy?

SELECTED REFERENCES

BAER, JUDITH A. 1999. *Our Lives Before the Law: Constructing a Feminist Jurisprudence.* Princeton, NJ: Princeton University Press.

CARDOZO, BENJAMIN N. 1921. *The Nature of the Judicial Process.* New Haven, CT: Yale University Press.

CLAYTON, CORNELL, AND HOWARD GILLMAN, eds. 1999. *Supreme Court Decision-Making: New Institutionalist Approaches.* Chicago: University of Chicago Press.

DELGADO, RICHARD. 1991. "Brewer's Plea: Critical Thoughts on Common Cause." *Vanderbilt Law Review* 44:6.

DWORKIN, RONALD. 1977. *Taking Rights Seriously.* Cambridge, MA: Harvard University Press.

EPSTEIN, LEE, AND JACK KNIGHT. 1998. *The Choices Justices Make.* Washington, DC: Congressional Quarterly.

FARBER, DANIEL A., AND PHILIP P. FRICKEY. 1991. *Law and Public Choice.* Chicago: University of Chicago Press.

FARBER, DANIEL A., AND SUZANNA SHERRY. 1997. *Beyond All Reason: The Radical Assault on Truth in American Law.* New York: Oxford University Press.

FINNIS, JOHN. 1980. *Natural Law and Natural Rights.* New York: Oxford University Press.

FRANK, JEROME. 1930. *Law and the Modern Mind.* New York: Brentano's.

FRANK, JEROME. 1949. *Courts on Trial.* Princeton, NJ: Princeton University Press.

FRIEDMAN, LAWRENCE M. 1973. *History of American Law.* New York: Simon & Schuster.

FRIEDMAN, LAWRENCE. 2002. *American Law in the Twentieth Century.* New Haven, CT: Yale University Press.

FULLER, LON. 1964. *The Morality of Law.* New Haven, CT: Yale University Press.

GEORGE, ROBERT E. 1999. *In Defense of Natural Law.* Oxford: Clarendon Press.

GUINIER, LANI AND GERALD TORRES. 2002. *The Miner's Canary: Enlisting Race, Resisting Power, Transforming Democracy.* Cambridge, MA: Harvard University Press.

HART, H. L. A. 1961. *The Concept of Law.* Oxford: Oxford University Press.

HUTCHINSON, ALLAN C., AND PATRICK J. MONAHAN. 1984. "Law, Politics, and the Critical Legal Scholars: The Unfolding Drama of American Legal Thought." *Stanford Law Review* 36:199.

KAIRYS, DAVID, ED., 1982. *The Politics of Law.* New York: Pantheon Books.

LLEWELLYN, KARL N. 1951. *The Bramble Bush.* New York: Oceana.

LLEWELLYN, KARL N. 1960. *The Common Law Tradition: Deciding Appeals.* Boston: Little, Brown.

MERRYMAN, JOHN HENRY. 1969. *The Civil Law Tradition.* Stanford, CA: Stanford University Press.

MINDA, GARY. 1989. "The Jurisprudential Movements of the 1980s." *Ohio State Law Review* 50: 630.

MURPHY, WALTER F., AND JOSEPH TANENHAUS. 1972. *The Study of Public Law.* New York: Random House.

MURPHY, WALTER F., AND JOSEPH TANENHAUS. 1977. *Comparative Constitutional Law.* New York: St. Martin's Press.

NEELY, RICHARD. 1981. How Courts Govern America. New Haven, CT: Yale University Press.

NOTE. 1982. "Round and Round the Bramble Bush: From Legal Realism to Critical Legal Scholarship." *Harvard Law Review* 95: 1669.

PINELLO, DANIEL R. 2003. *Gay Rights and American Law.* New York: Cambridge University Press.

POSNER, RICHARD A. 2003. *Law, Pragmatism and Democracy.* Cambridge, MA: Harvard University Press.

POUND, ROSCOE. 1922. *An Introduction to the Philosophy of Law.* New Haven, CT: Yale University Press.

POUND, ROSCOE. 1943. "A Survey of Social Interests." *Harvard Law Review* 57: 1.

PRITCHETT, C. HERMAN. 1948. *The Roosevelt Court.* New York: Macmillan.

PRITCHETT, C. HERMAN. 1968. "Public Law and Judicial Behavior." *Journal of Politics* 30: 480.

RAWLS, JOHN. 1971. A Theory of Justice. Cambridge, MA: Harvard University Press.

RUMBLE, WILFRED E., JR. 1968. *American Legal Realism.* Ithaca, NY: Cornell University Press.

SEBOK, ANTHONY J. 1998. *Legal Positivism in American Jurisprudence.* Cambridge, UK, and New York: Cambridge University Press.

SEGAL, JEFFREY A., AND HAROLD J. SPAETH. 1993. *The Supreme Court and the Attitudinal Model.* New York: Cambridge University Press.

SHAPIRO, MARTIN. 1981. *Courts: A Comparative and Political Analysis.* Chicago: University of Chicago Press.

SMITH, ROGERS M. 1988. "Political Jurisprudence: The New Institutionalism and the Future of Public Law." *American Political Science Review* 82: 89.

SUNSTEIN, CASS R. 2001. *One Case at a Time: Judicial Minimalism on the Supreme Court.* Cambridge, MA: Harvard University Press.

SWEET, ALEC STONE. 2000. *Governing with Judges: Constitutional Politics in Europe.* New York: Oxford University Press.

"[Judges] are the depositaries of the laws; the living oracles . . ."

1.1 COMMENTARIES ON THE LAWS OF ENGLAND

Sir William Blackstone

Sir William Blackstone was an eighteenth-century English jurist. This set of volumes (1765–1768) ranks among the most influential writings in Anglo-American legal theory.

[A] very natural, and very material, question arises: how are these customs and maxims to be known, and by whom is their validity to be determined? The answer is, by the judges in the several courts of justice. They are the depositaries of the laws; the living oracles, who must decide in all cases of doubt, and who are bound by an oath to decide according to the law of the land. Their knowledge of that law is derived from experience and study and from being long personally accustomed to the judicial decisions of their predecessors. And indeed these judicial decisions are the principal and the most authoritative evidence, that can be given, of the existence of such a custom as shall form a part of the common law. The judgment itself, and all the proceedings previous thereto, are carefully registered and preserved, under the name of records, in public repositories set apart for that particular purpose; and to them frequent recourse is had, when any critical question arises, in the determination of which former precedents may give light or assistance. For it is an established rule to abide by former precedents, where the same points come again in litigation: as well to keep the scale of justice even and steady, and not liable to waver with every new judge's opinion; as also because the law in that case being solemnly declared and determined, what before was uncertain, and perhaps indifferent, is now become a permanent rule which it is not in the breast of any subsequent judge to alter or vary from according to his private sentiments: he being sworn to determine, not according to his own private judgment, but according to the known laws and customs of the land; not delegated to pronounce a new law, but to maintain and expound the old one. Yet this rule admits of exception, where the former determination is most evidently contrary to reason; much more if it be clearly contrary to the divine law. But even in such cases the subsequent judges do not pretend to make a new law, but to vindicate the old one from misrepresentation. For if it be found that the former decision is manifestly absurd or unjust, it is declared, not that such a sentence was bad law, but that it was not law; that is, that it is not the established custom of the realm, as has been erroneously determined.

From Sir William Blackstone, *Commentaries on the Laws of England,* American ed. (Chicago: Callaghan & CockCroft, 1871), 1:69–70.

*"[Courts] may truly be said to have neither FORCE nor WILL,
but merely judgment . . ."*

1.2 THE FEDERALIST, NO. 78

Alexander Hamilton

Alexander Hamilton (1755–1804), in collaboration with James Madison and John Jay, wrote a series of essays (now known as *The Federalist Papers*) that were designed to defend the Constitution against attacks mounted by those who opposed ratification. Hamilton also served as first secretary of the treasury.

Whoever attentively considers the different departments of power must perceive that, in a government in which they are separated from each other, the judiciary, from the nature of its functions, will always be the least dangerous to the political rights of the Constitution; because it will be least in capacity to annoy or injure them. The Executive not only dispenses honors, but holds the sword of the community. The legislature not only commands the purse, but prescribes the rules by which the duties and rights of every citizen are to be regulated. The judiciary, on the contrary, has no influence over either the sword or the purse; no direction either of the strength or of the wealth of the society; and can take no active resolution whatever. It may truly be said to have neither FORCE nor WILL, but merely judgment; and must ultimately depend upon the aid of the executive arm for the efficacy of its judgment.

Some perplexity respecting the rights of the courts to pronounce legislative acts void, because contrary to the constitution, has arisen from an imagination that the doctrine would imply a superiority of the judiciary to the legislative power. It is urged that the authority which can declare the acts of another void, must necessarily be superior to the one whose acts may be declared void. As this doctrine is of great importance in all the American constitutions, a brief discussion of the ground on which it rests cannot be unacceptable.

There is no position which depends on clearer principles, than that every act of a delegated authority, contrary to the tenor of the commission under which it is exercised, is unacceptable.

There is no position which depends on clearer principles, than that every act of delegated authority, contrary to the tenor of the commission under which it is exercised, is void. No legislative act, therefore, contrary to the Constitution, can be valid. To deny this, would be to affirm that the deputy is greater than his principal; that the servant is above his master; that the representatives of the people are superior to the people themselves; that men acting by virtue of powers may do not only what their powers do not authorize, but what they forbid.

If it be said that the legislative body are themselves the constitutional judges of their own powers, and that the construction put on them is conclusive upon the other departments, it may be answered, that this cannot be the natural presumption, where it is not to be collected from any particular provisions in the Constitution. It is not otherwise to be supposed, that the Constitution could intend to enable the representatives of the people to substitute their will to that of their constituents. It is far more rational to suppose, that the courts were designed to be an intermediate body between the people and the legislature, in order, among other things, to keep the latter within the limits assigned to their authority. The interpretation of the laws is the proper and peculiar province of the courts. A constitution is, in fact, and must be regarded by the judges, as a fundamental law. It therefore belongs to them to ascertain its meaning, as well as the meaning of any particular act proceeding from the legislative body. If there should happen to be an irreconcilable variance between the two, that which has the superior obligation and validity ought, of course, to be preferred; or, in other words, the Constitution ought to be preferred to the statute, the intention of the people to the intention of their agents.

Nor does this conclusion by any means suppose a superiority of the judicial to the legislative power. It only supposes that the power of the people is superior to both; and that where the will of the legislature, declared in its statutes, stands in opposition to that of the people, declared in the Constitution, the judges ought to be governed by the latter rather than the former. They ought to regulate their decisions by the fundamental laws, rather than by those which are not fundamental.

"He only judges the law because he is obliged to judge a case."

1.3 JUDICIAL POWER IN THE UNITED STATES

Alexis de Tocqueville

I am not aware that any nation of the globe has hitherto organized a judicial power on the principle adopted by the Americans. The judicial organization of the United States is the institution which the stranger has the greatest difficulty in understanding. He hears the authority of the judge invoked in the political occurrences of every day, and he naturally concludes that in the United States judges are important political functionaries; nevertheless, when he examines the nature of the tribunals, they offer nothing which is contrary to the usual habits and privileges of those bodies; and the magistrates seem to him to interfere in public affairs by chance, but by a chance which recurs every day.

From Alexis de Tocqueville, *Democracy in America* (1835), Ch. 6. De Tocqueville was a French political analyst whose observations of nineteenth-century American society have become classic.

The first characteristic of judicial power in all nations is the duty of arbitration. But rights must be contested in order to warrant the interference of a tribunal; and an action must be brought to obtain the decision of a judge. As long, therefore, as a law is uncontested, the judicial authority is not called upon to discuss it. When a judge in a given case attacks a law relating to that case, he extends the circle of his customary duties, without however stepping beyond it; since he is in some measure obliged to decide upon the law, in order to decide the case. But if he pronounces upon a law without resting upon a case, he clearly steps beyond his sphere, and invades that of the legislative authority.

The second characteristic of the judicial power is that it pronounces on special cases.

The third characteristic of the judicial power is its inability to act unless it is appealed to. This characteristic is less general than the other two; but notwithstanding the exceptions, I think it may be regarded as essential. The judicial power is by its nature devoid of action; it must be put in motion in order to produce a result. When it is called upon to repress a crime, it punishes the criminal; when a wrong is to be redressed, it is ready to redress it; when an act requires interpretation, it is prepared to interpret it; but it does not pursue criminals, hunt out wrongs, or examine into evidence of its own accord.

The Americans have retained these three distinguishing characteristics of the judicial power. [A judge's] position is therefore perfectly similar to that of the magistrate of other nations; and he is nevertheless invested with immense political power. The cause of this difference lies in the simple fact that the Americans have acknowledged the right of the judges to found their decisions on the Constitution, rather than on the laws. In other words, they have left judges at liberty not to apply such laws as may appear to them to be unconstitutional.

I am aware that a similar right has been claimed—but claimed in vain—by courts of justice in other countries; but in America it is recognized by all the authorities; and not a party, nor so much as an individual, is found to contest it. This fact can only be explained by the principles of the American constitutions. In the United States, the Constitution governs the legislator as much as the private citizen: as it is the first of laws, it cannot be modified by a law; and it is therefore just that the tribunals should obey the Constitution in preference to any law.

Whenever a law which the judge holds to be unconstitutional is argued in a tribunal of the United States, he may refuse to admit it as a rule; this power is the only one which is peculiar to the American magistrate, but it gives him immense political influence. Few laws can escape his searching analysis; for there are few which are not prejudicial to some private interest or other, and none which may not be brought before a court of justice by the choice of the parties, or by the necessity of the case. But from that time a judge has refused to apply any given law in a case, that law loses a portion of its moral sanction. The persons to whose interests it is prejudicial learn that means exist of evading its authority; and similar suits are multiplied, until it becomes powerless. One of two alternatives must then be resorted to: the people must alter the Constitution, or the legislature must repeal the law.

The political power which the Americans have entrusted to their courts of justice is therefore immense; but the evils of this power are considerably diminished by the obligation which has been imposed of attacking the laws through the courts of justice alone. If the judge had been empowered to contest the laws on the ground of theoretical generalities, if he had been enabled to open an attack or to pass a censure on the legislator, he would have played a prominent part in the political sphere; and as the champion or the antagonist of a party, he would have arrayed the hostile passions of the nation in the conflict. But when a judge contests a law, applied to some particular case in an obscure proceeding, the importance of his attack is concealed from the public gaze; his decision bears upon the interest of an individual, and if the law is slighted it is only collaterally. Moreover, although it be censured, it is not abolished; its moral force may be diminished, but its cogency is by no means suspended; and its final destruction can only be accomplished by the reiterated attacks of judicial functionaries. It will ideally be understood that by connecting the censureship of the laws with the private interests of members of the community, and by intimately uniting the prosecution of the law with the prosecution of an individual, the legislation is protected from wanton assailants and from the daily aggressions of party-spirit. The errors of the legislator are exposed whenever their evil consequences are most felt; and it is always a positive and appreciable fact which serves as the basis of a prosecution.

I am inclined to believe this practice of the American courts to be at once the most favorable to liberty as well as to public order. If the judge could only attack the legislator openly and directly, he would sometimes be afraid to oppose any resistance to his will; and at other moments party-spirit might encourage him to brave it every day. The laws would consequently be attacked when the power from which they emanate is weak, and obeyed when it is strong. That is to say, when it would be useful to respect them, they would be contested; and when it would be easy to convert them into an instrument of oppression, they would be respected. But the American judge is brought into the political arena independently of his own will. He only judges the law because he is obliged to judge a case. The political question which he is called upon to resolve is connected with the interest of the parties, and he cannot refuse to decide it without abdicating the duties of his post. He performs his functions as a citizen by fulfilling the strict duties which belong to his profession as a magistrate. It is true that upon this system the judicial censureship which is exercised by the courts of justice over legislation cannot extend equally to all laws, inasmuch as some of them can never give rise to that precise species of contestation which is termed a lawsuit; and even when such a contestation is possible, it may happen that no one cares to bring it before a court of justice. The Americans have often felt this disadvantage, but they have left the remedy incomplete, lest they should give it efficacy which might in some cases prove dangerous. Within these limits, the power vested in the American courts of justice of pronouncing a statute to be unconstitutional forms one of the most powerful barriers which has ever been devised against the tyranny of political assemblies.

"The prophecies of what the courts will do in fact . . .
are what I mean by the law."

1.4 THE PATH OF THE LAW

Oliver Wendell Holmes, Jr.

Holmes was Justice, Massachusetts Supreme Judicial Court, 1882–1899;
Chief Justice, Massachusetts Supreme Judicial Court, 1899–1902;
and Associate Justice, U.S. Supreme Court, 1902–1932.

When we study law we are not studying a mystery but a well known profession. We are studying what we shall want in order to appear before judges, or to advise people in such a way as to keep them out of court. The reason why it is a profession, why people will pay lawyers to argue for them or to advise them, is that in societies like ours the command of the public force is entrusted to the judges in certain cases, and the whole power of the state will be put forth, if necessary, to carry out their judgments and decrees. People want to know under what circumstances and how far they run the risk of coming against what is so much stronger than themselves, and hence it becomes a business to find out when this danger is to be feared. The object of our study, then, is prediction, the prediction of the incidence of the public force through the instrumentality of the courts.

The means of the study are a body of reports, of treatises, and of statutes, in this country and in England, extending back for six hundred years, and now increasing annually by hundreds. In these sibylline leaves are gathered the scattered prophecies of the past upon the cases in which the axe will fall. These are what properly have been called the oracles of the law. Far the most important and pretty nearly the whole meaning of every new effort of legal thought is to make these prophecies more precise, and to generalize them into a thoroughly connected system. The primary rights and duties with which jurisprudence busies itself again are nothing but prophecies. One of the many evil effects of the confusion between legal and moral ideas, about which I shall have something to say in a moment, is that theory is apt to get the cart before the horse, and to consider the right or the duty as something existing apart from and independent of the consequences of its breach, to which certain sanctions are added afterward. But, as I shall try to show, a legal duty so called is nothing but a prediction that if a man does or omits certain things he will be made to suffer in this or that way by judgment of the court; and so of a legal right.

The first thing for a business-like understanding of the matter is to understand its limits, and therefore I think it desirable at once to point out and dispel

From 10 *Harvard Law Review* 39 (1897). Copyright 1897, Oliver Wendell Holmes, Jr.

a confusion between morality and law, which sometimes rises to the height of conscious theory, and more often and indeed constantly is making trouble in detail without reaching the point of consciousness. You can see very plainly that a bad man has as much reason as a good one for wishing to avoid an encounter with the public force, and therefore you can see the practical importance of the distinction between morality and law. A man who cares nothing for an ethical rule which is believed and practiced by his neighbors is likely nevertheless to care a good deal to avoid being made to pay money, and will want to keep out of jail if he can.

I take it for granted that no hearer of mine will misinterpret what I have to say as the language of cynicism. The law is the witness and external deposit of our moral life. Its history is the history of the moral development of the race. The practice of it, in spite of popular jests, tends to make good citizens and good men. When I emphasize the difference between law and morals I do so with reference to a single end, that of learning and understanding the law. For that purpose you must definitely master its specific marks, and it is for that that I ask you for the moment to imagine yourselves indifferent to other and greater things.

I do not say that there is not a wider point of view from which the distinction between law and morals becomes of secondary or no importance, as all mathematical distinctions vanish in presence of the infinite. But I do say that that distinction is of the first importance for the object which we are here to consider,—a right study and mastery of the law as a business with well understood limits, a body of dogma enclosed within definite lines. I have just shown the practical reason for saying so. If you want to know the law and nothing else, you must look at it as a bad man, who cares only for the material consequences which such knowledge enables him to predict, not as a good one, who finds his reasons for conduct, whether inside the law or outside of it, in the vaguer sanctions of conscience. The prophecies of what the courts will do in fact, and nothing more pretentious, are what I mean by the law.

You may assume, with Hobbes and Bentham and Austin, that all law emanates from the sovereign, even when the first human beings to enunciate it are the judges, or you may think that law is the voice of the Zeitgeist, or what you like. It is all one to my present purpose. . . . In every system there are such explanations and principles to be found. It is with regard to them that a second fallacy comes in, which I think it important to expose.

The fallacy to which I refer is the notion that the only force at work in the development of the law is logic. In the broadest sense, indeed, that notion would be true. The danger of which I speak is not the admission that the principles governing other phenomena also govern the law, but the notion that a given system, ours, for instance, can be worked out like mathematics from some general axioms of conduct. This is the natural error of the schools, but it is not confined to them. I once heard a very eminent judge say that he never let a decision go until he was absolutely sure that it was right.

This mode of thinking is entirely natural. The training of lawyers is a training in logic. The processes of analogy, discrimination, and deduction are those in which they are most at home. The language of judicial decision is mainly the language of logic. And the logical method and form flatter that longing for certainty and for repose which is in every human mind. But certainty generally is illusion, and repose is not the destiny of man. Behind the logical form lies a judgment as to the relative worth and importance of competing legislative grounds, often an inarticulate and unconscious judgment, it is true, and yet the very root and nerve of the whole proceeding. You can give any conclusion a logical form. You always can imply a condition in a contract. But why do you imply it? It is because of some belief as to the practice of the community or of a class, or because of some opinion as to policy, or, in short, because of some attitude of yours upon a matter not capable of exact quantitative measurement, and therefore not capable of founding exact logical conclusions. Such matters really are battle grounds where the means do not exist for determinations that shall be good for all time, and where the decision can do no more than embody the preference of a given body in a given time and place. We do not realize how large a part of our law is open to reconsideration upon a slight change in the habit of the public mind. No concrete proposition is self-evident, no matter how ready we may be to accept it: not even Mr. Herbert Spencer's Everyman has a right to do what he wills, provided he interferes not with a like right on the part of his neighbors.

I think that the judges themselves have failed adequately to recognize their duty of weighing considerations of social advantage. The duty is inevitable, and the result of the often proclaimed judicial aversion to deal with such considerations is simply to leave the very ground and foundation of judgments inarticulate, and often unconscious, as I have said. When socialism first began to be talked about, the comfortable classes of the community were a good deal frightened. I suspect that this fear has influenced judicial action both here and in England, yet it is certain that it is not a conscious factor in the decisions to which I refer. . . . I cannot but believe that if the training of lawyers led them habitually to consider more definitely and explicitly the social advantage on which the rule they lay down must be justified, they sometimes would hesitate where now they are confident, and see that really they were taking sides upon debatable and often burning questions.

So much for the fallacy of logical form. Now let us consider the present condition of the law as a subject for study, and the ideal toward which it tends. The development of our law has gone on for nearly a thousand years, like the development of a plant, each generation taking the inevitable next step, mind, like matter, simply obeying a law of spontaneous growth. It is perfectly natural and right that it should have been so. Limitation is a necessity of human nature. Most of the things we do, we do for no better reason than that our fathers have done them or that our neighbors do them, and the same is true of a larger part than we suspect of what we think. The reason is a good one, because our short life gives us no time for a better, but it is not the best. It does not follow, because we all are compelled to take on faith at second hand most of the rules on which we base our action and our thought, that each of us may not try to set some corner of his world in the order of reason, or that all of us collectively should not aspire to carry reason as far as it will go throughout the whole domain. In regard to the law, it is true, no doubt, that an evolutionist will hesitate to affirm universal validity for his social ideals, or for the principles which he thinks should be embodied in legislation. He is content if he can prove them best for here and now. He may be ready to admit that he knows nothing about an absolute best in the cosmos, and even that he knows next to nothing about a permanent best for men. Still it is true that a body of law is more rational and more civilized when every rule it contains is referred articulately and definitely to an end which it subserves, and when the grounds for desiring that end are stated or are ready to be stated in words.

At present, in very many cases, if we want to know why a rule of law has taken its particular shape, and more or less if we want to know why it exists at all, we go to tradition. We follow it into the Year Books, and perhaps beyond them to the customs of the Salian Franks, and somewhere in the past, in the German forests, in the needs of Norman kings, in the assumptions of a dominant class, in the absence of generalized ideas, we find out the practical motive for what now best is justified by the mere fact of its acceptance and that men are accustomed to it. The rational study of law is still to a large extent the study of history. . . . It is a part of the rational study, because it is the first step toward an enlightened scepticism, that is, toward a deliberate reconsideration of the worth of those rules. When you get the dragon out of his cave on to the plain and in the daylight, you can count his teeth and claws, and see just what is his strength. But to get him out is only the first step. The next is either to kill him, or to tame him and make him a useful animal. For the rational study of the law the black-letter man may be the man of the present, but the man of the future is the man of statistics and the master of economics. It is revolting to have no better reason for a rule of law than that so it was laid down in the time of Henry IV. It is still more revolting if the grounds upon which it was laid down have vanished long since, and the rule simply persists from blind imitation of the past.

"We cannot transcend the limitations of the ego . . ."

1.5 THE NATURE OF THE JUDICIAL PROCESS

Benjamin N. Cardozo

Benjamin N. Cardozo was Judge, New York Court of Appeals, 1918–1926;
Chief Judge, New York Court of Appeals, 1926–1932; and Associate
Justice, U.S. Supreme Court, 1932–1939.

The work of deciding cases goes on every day in hundreds of courts throughout the land. Any judge, one might suppose, would find it easy to describe the process which he had followed a thousand times and more. Nothing could be farther from the truth. Let some intelligent layman ask him to explain: he will not go very far before taking refuge in the excuse that the language of craftsmen is unintelligible to those untutored in the craft. Such an excuse may cover with a semblance of respectability an otherwise ignominious retreat. It will hardly serve to still the pricks of curiosity and conscience. In moments of introspection the troublesome problem will recur, and press for a solution. What is it that I do when I decide a case? To what sources of information do I appeal for guidance? In what proportions do I permit them to contribute to the result? In what proportions ought they to contribute? If a precedent is applicable, when do I refuse to follow it? If no precedent is applicable, how do I reach the rule that will make a precedent for the future? At what point shall the quest be halted by some discrepant custom, by some consideration of the social welfare, by my own or the common standards of justice and morals? Into that strange compound which is brewed daily in the cauldron of the courts, all these ingredients enter in varying proportions. I am not concerned to inquire whether judges ought to be allowed to brew such a compound at all. I take judge-made law as one of the existing realities of life. There before us is the brew. Not a judge on the bench but has had a hand in the making. The elements have not come together by chance. Some principle, however unavowed and inarticulate and subconscious, has regulated the infusion. It may not have been the same principle for all judges at any time, nor the same principle for any judge at all times. But a choice there has been, not a submission to the decrees of Fate; and the considerations and motives determining the choice, even if often obscure, do not utterly resist analysis. [T]here will be need to distinguish between the conscious and the subconscious. More subtle are the forces so far beneath the surface that they cannot reasonably be classified as other than subconscious. It is often through these subconscious forces that judges are kept consistent with themselves, and inconsistent with one another. There is in each of us a stream of tendency, whether you choose to call it philosophy or not, which gives coherence and direction to thought and action. Judges cannot escape that current any more than other mortals. All their lives, forces which they do not recognize and cannot name, have been tugging at their inherited instincts, traditional beliefs, acquired convictions; and the resultant is an outlook on life, a conception of social needs, a sense in James's phrase of "the total push and pressure of the cosmos," which, when reasons are nicely balanced, must determine where choices shall fall. In this mental background every problem finds its setting. We may try to see things as objectively as we please. None the less, we can never see them with any eyes except our own.

We reach the land of mystery when constitution and statute are silent, and the judge must look to the common law for the rule that fits the case. He is the "living oracle of the law" in Blackstone's vivid phrase. Looking at Sir Oracle in action, viewing his work in the dry light of realism, how does he set about his task?

From Benjamin N. Cardozo, *The Nature of the Judicial Process* (New Haven, CT: Yale University Press, 1921), pp. 9–13, 18–21, 43, 66–67, 105–106, 113–114, 141, 161–162. Copyright 1921 by Yale University Press. Reprinted with permission.

The first thing he does is to compare the case before him with the precedents, whether stored in his mind or hidden in books. I do not mean that precedents are ultimate sources of the law, supplying the sole equipment that is needed for the legal armory, the sole tools . . . "in the legal smithy." Back of precedents are basic jural conceptions which are postulates of judicial reasoning, and farther back are the habits of life, the institutions of society, in which those conceptions have had their origin, and which, by a process of interaction, they have modified in turn. None the less, in a system so highly developed as our own, precedents have so covered the ground that they fix the point of departure from which the labor of the judge begins. Almost invariably, his first step is to examine and compare them. If they are plain and to the point, there may be need of nothing more. Stare decisis is at least the everyday working rule of our law. It is a process of search, comparison, and little more. Some judges seldom get beyond that process in any case. Their notion of their duty is to match the colors of the case at hand against the colors of many sample cases spread out upon their desk. The sample nearest in shade supplies the applicable rule. But, of course, no system of living law can be evolved by such a process, and no judge of a high court worthy of his office views the function of his place so narrowly. If that were all there were to our calling, there would be little of intellectual interest about it. The man who had the best card index of the cases would also be the wisest judge. It is when the colors do not match, when the references of the index fail, when there is no decisive precedent, that the serious business of the judge begins. He must then fashion Law for the litigants before him. In fashioning it for them, he will be fashioning it for others. Every judgment has a generative power. It begets its own image.

We go forward with our logic, with our analogies, with our philosophies, till we reach a certain point. At first, we have no trouble with the paths; they follow the same lines. Then they begin to diverge, and we must make a choice between them. History or custom or social utility or some compelling sentiment of justice or sometimes perhaps a semi-intuitive apprehension of the pervading spirit of our law must come to the rescue of the anxious judge, and tell him where to go.

The final cause of law is the welfare of society. The rule that misses its aim cannot permanently justify its existence. "Ethical considerations can no more be excluded from the administration of justice than one can exclude the vital air from his room and live." Logic and history and custom have their place. We will shape the law to conform to them when we may; but only within bounds. The end which the law serves will dominate them all. I do not mean, of course, that judges are commissioned to set aside existing rules at pleasure in favor of any other set of rules which they may hold to be expedient or wise. I mean that when they are called upon to say how far existing rules are to be extended or restricted, they must let the welfare of society fix the path, its direction and distance.

There has been much debate among foreign jurists whether the norms of right and useful conduct, the patterns of social welfare, are to be found by the judge in conformity with an objective or a subjective standard. So far as the distinction has practical significance, the traditions of our jurisprudence commit us to the objective standard. I do not mean, of course, that this ideal of objective vision is ever perfectly attained. We cannot transcend the limitations of the ego and see anything as it really is. None the less, the ideal is one to be striven for within the limits of our capacity. This truth, when clearly perceived, tends to unify the judge's function. His duty to declare the law in accordance with reason and justice is seen to be a phase of his duty to declare it in accordance with custom. It is the customary morality of right-minded men and women which he is to enforce by his decree.

My analysis of the judicial process comes then to this, and little more: logic, and history, and custom, and utility, and the accepted standards of right conduct, are the forces which singly or in combination shape the progress of the law. Which of these forces shall dominate in any case must depend largely upon the comparative importance or value of the social interests that will be thereby promoted or impaired.

If you ask how [the judge] is to know when one interest outweighs another, I can only answer that he must get his knowledge just as the legislator gets it; from experience and study and reflection; in brief, from life itself. Here, indeed, is the point of contact between the legislator's work and his. The choice of methods, the appraisement of values, must in the end be guided by like considerations for the one as for the other. Each indeed is legislating within the limits of his competence. No doubt the limits for the judge are narrower. He legislates only between gaps. He fills the open spaces in the law. How far he may go without traveling beyond the walls of the interstices cannot be staked out for him upon a chart. He must learn it for himself as he gains the sense of fitness and proportion that comes with years of habitude in the practice of an art.

[Yet] the judge, even when he is free, is still not wholly free. He is not to innovate at pleasure. He is not a knight-errant roaming at will in pursuit of his own ideal of beauty or of goodness. He is to draw his inspiration from consecrated principles. He is not to yield to spasmodic sentiment, to vague and unregulated benevolence. He is to exercise a discretion informed by tradition, methodized by analogy, disciplined by system, and subordinated to "the primordial necessity of order in the social life." Wide enough in all conscience is the field of discretion that remains.

Our survey of judicial methods teaches us, I think, the lesson that the whole subject matter of jurisprudence is more plastic, more malleable, the moulds less definitively cast, the bound of right and wrong less preordained and constant, than most of us . . . have been accustomed to believe. So also the duty of a judge becomes itself a question of degree, and he is a useful judge or a poor one as he estimates the measure accurately or loosely. He must balance all his ingredients, his philosophy, his logic, his analogies, his history, his customs, his sense of right, and all the rest, and adding a little here and taking out a little there, must determine, as wisely as he can, which weight shall tip the scales.

"At any given time, the more powerful [of the sexes] will create an ideology suitable to help maintain its position and to make this position acceptable to the weaker one. . . . It is the function of such an ideology to deny or conceal the existence of a struggle. Here is one of the answers to the question . . . as to why we have so little awareness of the fact that there is a struggle between the sexes. It is in the interest of men to obscure this fact; and the emphasis they place on their ideologies has caused women, also, to adopt these theories."

1.6 OBSCURING THE STRUGGLE: SEX DISCRIMINATION, SOCIAL SECURITY, AND STONE, SEIDMAN, SUNSTEIN, AND TUSHNET'S *CONSTITUTIONAL LAW*

Mary E. Becker

Mary E. Becker is Professor of Law at DePaul College of Law.

Both sexes have powerful reasons for obscuring the struggle between them. As [Karen] Horney points out in the preceding passage, it is in men's self interest to protect the status quo by obscuring the divergent interests of the two sexes. In the same essay, Horney also observes that both sexes have reason to ignore the struggle: "we see love between the sexes more distinctly than we see hate—because the union of the sexes offers us the greatest possibilities for happiness." Given this expectation, we "are naturally inclined to overlook . . . the destructive forces that continually work to destroy our chances for happiness."

Women have a number of other reasons for obscuring the struggle besides the hope that they will find happiness in relationships with individual men. Many women are (or want to be) economically dependent on individual men because men tend to have greater economic resources and potential than women [do]. For these women, the best strategy is often to act as though women's and men's interests were the same. Even women who reject economic or emotional dependence on individual men have reasons to obscure the struggle: minimizing the conflict helps them maintain their sanity and their ability to operate effectively within the current system.

One important way in which we obscure struggle between the sexes is by obscuring one reason for struggle: inequality between the sexes. If the sexes are already equal, then there is no need to struggle over the (currently skewed) distribution of financial and physical security, power, status, leisure time, and sexual satisfaction.

From 89 *Columbia Law Review* 264 (1989).

In law, inequality is obscured by accepting as discrimination only that which the law prohibits rather than critically examining the law to judge how well it deals with actual discrimination in the real world. If discrimination is that which the law proscribes, then unremedied discrimination must be past. It follows that women and men are now equal. There is no reason to struggle or need for change. . . .

On one level, this Commentary is a critique of a particular and peculiar notion of sex discrimination: the current constitutional standard, which defines sex discrimination as overtly differential treatment of women and men (unless justified by "real" differences). The current constitutional standard thus requires that similarly situated women and men be treated the same. When the law incorporates male norms (as it often does), the current standard requires only that women who are like men be treated like men. Many feminist scholars have written about the inadequacy of this notion. This Commentary contributes to this ongoing critique by noting its weaknesses in the context of the social security system. Modern equal protection doctrine gives lip service to equality in marginal cases (e.g., social security cases banning express distinctions between women and men) but leaves intact laws favoring breadwinners relative to homemakers (the basic structure of the social security system).

This Commentary is not, however, primarily a critique of equality doctrine. I doubt that any abstract standard of equality would entirely eliminate the bias favoring breadwinners over homemakers in the social security system. But the inevitable shortcomings of a constitutional standard should not blind us to existing inequalities and the need for legislative change.

My ultimate purpose is therefore to begin a discussion of how sex discrimination should be presented in constitutional law casebooks. Currently, casebooks focus on the leading constitutional cases and the doctrines therein propounded, with some fairly abstract criticism of the Court's focus on sexually explicit classifications. Indeed, the authors' casebook [Stone, Seidman, Sunstein, and Tushnet's *Constitutional Law*] is the best of the current texts in terms of offering students some exposure to the problems with this focus. We do expect constitutional law casebooks to present the doctrine developed by the Court, with particular attention to the cases important to doctrinal development. But it is the essence of formalism to confine analysis to legal doctrine. Good pedagogy goes beyond the presentation of doctrine to explore the relationship between doctrine and sound policy.

In a subject as complex as constitutional law, dealing with countless historical, social, intellectual, and ideological forces, one cannot describe everything relevant to every case. One must select. I merely point out that the authors' casebook [Stone, Seidman, Sunstein, and Tushnet's *Constitutional Law*], like the other major constitutional law casebooks, contains a selection of material that tends to obscure, rather than highlight, women's inequality. Given the common human tendency to obscure the struggle between the sexes, it is understandable that authors of constitutional casebooks—who must make difficult selections from a wealth of material—tend not to highlight the reality of women's continuing inequality in concrete terms.

Often, law students are able to understand the real issues behind doctrinal development without explanatory material. There is, however, reason to think that in the context of sex discrimination, students are likely to need particularly pointed guidance, rather than abstract hints. Certainly, students are unlikely to appreciate the real issues in cases dealing with the Byzantine social security system without some information about its structure. Nor is such information of only historical importance since structural inequality remains in the system to the present day.

I believe that the author's casebook would be more effective in presenting the constitutional law of sex discrimination had they attempted to describe the effect of the current standard on the status of women. Such a presentation would include material about the heavy costs associated with the current ineffectiveness in concrete contexts [such as] social security, and its benefits. Until such material is added, it seems quite likely that the struggle will continue to be obscured in the classroom. . . .

Throughout this Commentary, I use "discrimination" broadly to refer to that which enforces and reinforces women's subordinate status relative to men, regardless of whether there is "discrimination" under current legal standards. Subordination refers to the fact that, on a systemic basis, a variety of factors and forces operate in such a way that women, on average, enjoy less leisure time, financial and physical security, status, power, and sexual satisfaction than [do] men. These differential distributions tend to ensure that, on an individual basis, women remain subordinated to men, whether on the job or in the home. As a result, women tend to live lives qualitatively different from the lives of men. Social security contributes to the differential distribution of financial security between women and men by affording much better financial security in old age to those who have successfully fulfilled traditional male breadwinner roles than to those who have fulfilled female roles. It thereby contributes to the subordination of individual women to individual men. . . .

The social security cases approach the social security system as though there were only one possible problem with the system from the perspective of sexual equality: that unusual women who are breadwinners for their families might not be treated like male breadwinners. But the problem with social security—from the perspective of *most* women—has never been the inaccuracy of its stereotyped assumptions, but rather that the system has always afforded shaky security system to women in (stereo)typical roles relative to the stronger security system it affords men in (stereo)typical roles.

In light of this systemic problem, casebooks on constitutional law should be changed. Authors of such books either should replace the social security cases with more important sex-discrimination cases or should present the cases together with information about the structural inequities present in the social security system and the possibility of eliminating these structural inequities. Teachers who assign these cases should use them to illustrate the pervasiveness of sexual inequality under formal equality.

Current constitutional law casebooks—such as Stone, Seidman, Sunstein, and Tushnet's—actually obscure the fact that the sexes have competing interests and must struggle if a more equitable distribution of resources, including financial security in old age, is to be achieved. The accepted approach to presenting the law of sex discrimination in a constitutional law casebook—focusing almost exclusively on the Court's definition of discrimination—conflates actual discrimination with legally proscribed discrimination. This obscures the inadequacy of current remedies and leads to the unquestioning acceptance of a conservative legal standard. In addition, students leave law school unaware of the need for change where the constitutional standard is inadequate. For example, it may be that the Court will, for decades to come, be unwilling to hold that the social security system unconstitutionally discriminates on the basis of sex. Students should, nevertheless, leave a class that addresses sex discrimination in the social security system with some appreciation of the real problems and the need for legislative change, rather than with the misguided impression that all significant discrimination against women has been eliminated from the system. Constitutional law cannot remedy all discrimination. But constitutional law casebooks should not obscure inequality between the sexes.

CHAPTER 2

Courts in Constitutional Democracies

According to Martin Shapiro, the essential characteristics of institutions we call courts are (1) an independent judge applying (2) preexisting norms after (3) adversarial proceedings to achieve (4) a dichotomous decision—that is, one party is held to be right and the other wrong.[1] The almost universal existence of courts (or courtlike structures) as thus described suggests that they fulfill certain basic needs in social organization. It is tempting to go back to primitive societies for clues as to why courts develop and what their roles are.

THE ORIGINS OF COURTS

William Seagle speculates that courts originate when a society's size and complexity loosen its foundational bonds of kinship and friendship.[2] Glendon Schubert thinks that the need for courts is a direct function of the concentration of people and wealth. He regards it as significant that, as a nomadic tribe, the Cheyenne Indians had no need for courts, whereas, as subsistence farmers, the Barotse of Northern Rhodesia (now Zambia) did.[3] "Once people stop wandering around the landscape," says Theodore L. Becker, "up go the courts."[4]

Cultural anthropologists have made intensive inquiries into judicial systems of primitive societies. Max Gluckman studied the judicial process among the Barotse and concluded that it corresponded with judicial processes in Western society more than it differed from them.[5] Paul Bohannon examined justice and judgment among the Tiv in northern Nigeria and concluded that it

---

[1] Martin Shapiro, *Courts: A Comparative and Political Analysis* (Chicago: University of Chicago Press, 1981), 1.

[2] William Seagle, *The Quest for Law* (New York: Knopf, 1941), 92.

[3] Glendon Schubert, *Judicial Policy-Making* (Chicago: Scott, Foresman, 1965), 12.

[4] Theodore L. Becker, *Comparative Judicial Politics* (Chicago: Rand McNally, 1970), 103.

[5] Max Gluckman, *The Judicial Process Among the Barotse of Northern Nigeria* (Glencoe, IL: Free Press, 1955).

would be "sociological over-simplification of the most blatant sort" to identify similarities between Tiv law and Western law.[6] Victor Ayoub reviewed both studies and drew the conclusion that the main function of a court is to conciliate and to reintroduce harmony into the social relations of the contending parties, so that the community will again function smoothly. But analogy between primitive and modern judicial systems, he thought, "seems neither to explain nor confirm. It serves only to suggest."[7]

Universal or not, it is clear that nearly all complex societies entrust agencies commonly called courts with a significant role in resolving conflicts. Their function is to decide disputes among individuals about personal or property rights as well as to assess blame and punishment upon transgressors against the community. Supposedly, these decisions accord with the society's laws, customs, traditions, taboos, or holy books. In sum, courts offer an alternative to force and gain respect when they provide a more predictable, more fair, and less disruptive means of settling disputes than does combat. "The primary social purpose of the judicial process," George Christie writes, "is deciding disputes in a manner that will, upon reflection, permit the loser as well as the winner to feel that he has been fairly treated."[8]

Acceptance of judicial decisions as fair derives, first, from the status and the prestige of the decision maker. In some societies the chief may also act as judge, but it generally becomes necessary to treat the task of judging as a specialized role, allocated on the basis of age, reputation for learning, wisdom, spiritual contacts, confidence of the ruling powers, or the consensus of the community. Whatever the means for selecting them, judges occupy positions of high status, often wear distinctive uniforms, are addressed deferentially, and can exercise punitive powers to enforce respect for their office.

It is not, however, merely because judges are regarded as wise or trained in the law that people come to believe the judicial process yields fair decisions. Judicial rulings are the end product of a distinctive process of varying degrees of complexity that determines facts and shapes issues for the ultimate decision maker. Proceedings before judges are typically adversarial, pitting two parties against each other, each intent on establishing the rightness of her or his contentions. In simpler societies—and occasionally even in the Western world— parties may present their own cases, but generally they are represented by counsel skilled in the substantive rules and procedural technicalities of the law. Witnesses offer evidence as to supposed facts, and experts in the field of controversy provide technical information. Lay participants may perform a valued role, either as jurors who "find" the facts or as auxiliary judges. Only after these procedures, which are ritualistic as well as instrumental, and on the basis of the record that has been made, does a judge announce a decision and give reasons

---

[6] Paul Bohannon, *Justice and Judgment Among the Tiv* (New York: Oxford University Press, 1957).

[7] Victor Ayoub, "The Judicial Process in Two African Tribes," in *Judicial Behavior: A Reader in Theory and Research*, ed. Glendon A. Schubert, Jr. (Chicago: Rand-McNally, 1964), 127.

[8] George Christie, "Objectivity in the Law," 78 *Yale Law Journal* 1311, 1329 (1969).

for it. Even then, in more complex societies, the possibility exists of testing the fairness of a decision by appealing to a higher tribunal.

This account of the judicial process is, of course, idealized. Judges might not be wise or learned. They might be irascible, prejudiced, or open to bribes. They are almost by definition representatives of the Establishment, likely to be unsympathetic to dissenters. In addition, judicial proceedings are typically slow and expensive, and lawyers are perennial targets of scorn because of a popular conception of their craft as devious, pettifogging, and manipulative. In Shakespeare's *Henry VI, Part II,* Dick the Butcher proposes to Jack Cade, "The first thing we do, let's kill all the lawyers." Moreover, legal rules themselves might not be fair or reasonable. Told in Dickens's *Oliver Twist* that the law assumed a man controlled the actions of his wife, Mr. Bumble made a classic response: "If the law says that, sir, then the law is a ass."

There is, then, a darker side to the judicial process, which this book does not try to minimize. Critics have contended that in no other serious field of human endeavor where truth must be established or facts verified do participants use the same methods as do courts. These charges minimize the importance of the reality that the purpose of the judicial process is not solely to establish truth but also to legitimize the compulsory power of the legal system. Because the ritualistic and argumentative procedures of courts have been unfavorably contrasted with the methods of hard sciences such as physics, there is considerable irony in the proposal made by a group of physical scientists that courtlike adversarial proceedings be set up as a method for resolving factual disputes about certain scientific issues so as to provide a sounder basis for public decisions.[9]

Distinctive Characteristics of Judicial Processes

The foregoing discussion suggests that the character of courts is somehow distinct from that of other organizations or institutions. Although there is obvious truth to this perception, perhaps the best way to appreciate the peculiar features of judiciaries is to compare them with one of their counterparts, legislative bodies. Conventional wisdom has it that legislatures make law and courts apply general law to specific circumstances. Yet, because courts participate in making policy, it is more accurate to suggest, as J. Woodford Howard, Jr., does, that the two branches are distinguished more by their procedures.[10] The first and perhaps most important procedural characteristic of courts is that they typically cannot initiate action.[11] Unlike legislators and administrators, judges may not— like legendary knights—ride off in search of a damsel in distress to rescue; they must wait for someone to appear in court and complain.

---

[9] 193 *Science* 653 (1976).

[10] J. Woodford Howard, Jr., "Adjudication Considered as a Process of Conflict Resolution," 18 *Journal of Public Law* 339 (1969).

[11] Exceptions exist to each of the characteristics we discuss; for example, some European constitutional courts can initiate suits on their own. We wish to denote only features of courts that, at the very least, fit those in the United States and most other nations.

In Chapter 6 we discuss in more detail limitations on how and when individuals may bring lawsuits; here we note only that a would-be litigant cannot energize judicial power merely by alleging some general wrong. A person in distress cannot obtain a judicial hearing by protesting, say, a lack of protection against menacing dragons. To have a "case," someone must, first of all, point to a specific and personal legal right that is being violated. For example, some litigants might specify the dragon that is causing trouble and assert as a legally protected right something as concrete as their right to enjoy their own property in peace. As a far less probable alternative, the aggrieved parties might point to the existence of a statute that imposes a nondiscretionary duty on some official to exterminate dragons.

Second, the person in distress must ask for a specific remedy—a cure or a solution—and one that the court can grant. The judge cannot order Ye Blue Knight to go forth and slay, or even arrest, one Oliver Dragon, again except in the unlikely event that a statute clearly imposes a nondiscretionary duty on Blue Knight so to act. If there is a relevant statute but it allows officers of the law some discretion in ridding the world of dragons, then the complainants must go not to judges but to law-enforcement officials and request action. If there is no statute at all, they must ask a local legislator for action. Indeed, even if Blue Knight, acting as both police officer and prosecutor, brings Dragon into court, there is nothing the judge can do unless the knight can offer convincing evidence that Dragon has violated a criminal statute.[12]

Normally, in our hypothetical situation, plaintiffs (those who initiate a civil action) can legitimately request two remedies from a judge. First, they can request that the court require Dragon to pay money to them as compensation for injuries caused to their right to enjoy their property. Second, and either alternatively or additionally, they can petition the court to issue an injunction ordering Dragon to cease and desist from trespassing and causing fright with fiery snorts. (In the latter instance, the "plaintiffs" are called "petitioners.")

A third characteristic of the judicial process concerns the kind of evidence that a court will hear and the procedures by which it will receive and weigh evidence. In most trials in nations that follow the common law, much of the evidence is oral. Were the distressed persons in our example to seek monetary damages against Dragon, they would be required to testify, under oath, in response to questions from their attorney, to having witnessed Dragon, on a certain date at a particular time, in the act of trespassing. On that occasion, the testimony would continue, Dragon threatened bodily harm by hissing and snorting flame and smoke, thus depriving plaintiffs of the peaceful enjoyment of their property.

At the conclusion of the replies to questions of the aggrieved's own attorney, counsel for Dragon could conduct cross-examinations. The purpose could be to expose a contradiction (Were the plaintiffs not at fair on the alleged day?);

---

[12] Historically in Britain and the United States, there were such things as "common-law crimes." In *United States v. Hudson and Goodwin* (1812), the Supreme Court ruled that only acts proscribed by congressional statutes can be prosecuted in federal courts. State judges have tended to follow a similar rule.

to make the person concede the possibility of error in testimony (Was the dragon encountered really Oliver and not his cousin Henry—for after all, do not all dragons look alike?); or to impugn credibility (Were plaintiffs really frightened? Only a fortnight ago, had they not boasted at the local pub of having together slain a score of dragons?).

Furthermore, the other side must have the same full opportunity to present its evidence, subject, again, to cross-examination. Oliver Dragon might claim that for fifteen centuries he and his ancestors had used the stream by plaintiffs' castle to cool their engines and that the smoke and fire claimed to have been seen was only steam from his overheated radiator.

Of course, the dispute might necessarily involve some documentary evidence. Dragon might claim that the Romans had given his ancestors title to the stream on the property and produce a grant dated 25 B.C.E. In rebuttal, plaintiffs' attorney might introduce property tax receipts for a period of three centuries. Whatever the specifics, the basic point is that all the evidence, oral or written, that the court may weigh in its decision is introduced in the presence of both sides, and each litigant has full opportunity to examine and reply to the evidence and the arguments of the other. Although judges may "notice" notorious circumstances such as a war or a depression, they, again unlike administrators or legislators, cannot legitimately consider information denied to one of the parties or base a decision on evidence not submitted in open court.

A fourth distinguishing feature of the judicial process is that the proceedings are adversarial. In common law legal systems, attorneys for the two sides produce the evidence, define the issues, and formulate the arguments. They battle as equals, with the judge acting more as an umpire than as a participant. The adversarial nature of the proceedings is less sharp under Civil Law, as practiced in Europe, Latin America, Quebec, parts of Africa, and to some extent Louisiana (see Chapter 1). In that legal system, the judge plays a far more active role in civil suits, both in introducing evidence and in questioning witnesses. Civil-Law judges are also more active in criminal cases, but the central actor in criminal trials is the procurator, whose tasks are much broader than those of a prosecutor in the United States and include introducing evidence and arguments for as well as against the defendant. To say that the procurator controls the trial is an exaggeration, but under Civil Law the defense attorney does not play an equal part in the drama.

A fifth characteristic that sets the judicial process apart from legislative or administrative processes is that the parties—even governmental officials—may legitimately contact the judge or jury only under tightly structured circumstances. Individuals, pressure groups, or public officials may file lawsuits, urge or help others to do so, or even ask a judge to allow them to intervene in a case already in progress if the ultimate decision in that litigation would directly affect their interests. But lobbying in the sense typically used to describe informal presentations of views to legislators and administrators is taboo in the judicial process. It is a serious crime for a litigant even to try to communicate with the jury or any of its members except in open court under the watchful eyes of the judge and opponent's counsel. A litigant or the litigant's attorney may talk to the judge in the judge's chambers, but normally only in the presence of the attorney for the other side.

A sixth distinguishing feature is more subtle and involves the decision itself. When a legislature attacks the cause of social conflict, it usually issues a sweeping pronouncement in the form of a statute that regulates the future conduct of all persons within its territory. An administrative order, detailing more specific rules to carry out a legislative mandate, may be equally far-reaching. In contrast, a judicial decision typically relates to past conduct (Dragon should not have trespassed on the estate), although it might also forbid future actions similar to the one that triggered the lawsuit (Dragon is permanently enjoined from trespassing on the estate). Moreover, a judicial decision, unlike a statute or an administrative order, does not bind everyone but only the parties to the case, their employees, agents, successors in office, and those who cooperate with any of these people. If it had been Oliver Dragon whom the court forbade to trespass, Henry Dragon—as long as he is not working with or for Oliver—may trespass without violating the judicial order. Aggrieved property owners will have to go to court and begin a new lawsuit to enjoin Henry.

Here one encounters a seventh distinction that further differentiates judicial from legislative ways of coping with conflict, although less so than from administrative means. At the same time, this seventh distinction blurs the significance of the sixth. If a jury decides a dispute, it simply reports its verdict and in civil suits its award—usually no more than a single phrase ("Guilty as charged") or statement ("We find for the plaintiffs and award plaintiffs $10,000 against Oliver Dragon"). The jury gives no explanation of or justification for its collective decision.

When, however, judges instruct juries on legal issues and even more so when judges decide cases without juries, they must provide reasons for their choices. Indeed, federal rules of procedure require judges to write out their findings of fact and their conclusions of law, and usually judges preface these with more detailed explanations of their reasoning, called an opinion. That opinion should be an intellectually coherent and convincing statement. It is not supposed to be a psychological explanation of why the judge decided one way or the other but a justification for that decision, phrased in terms of legal principles. Legislators may produce similar statements, and some of the best of these far surpass most judicial opinions in intellectual quality. But whereas a judge, as a matter of course, is supposed to offer such a principled justification for every decision,[13] a legislator need not do so. Indeed, it is perfectly acceptable for a legislator, if later questioned about a vote, to say only, "It benefited my constituents." That the proposal injured 99 percent of other citizens is unfortunate—not illegal and possibly not unethical, merely unfortunate.

---

[13] There are, of course, exceptions to the rule requiring judges to explain their decisions, the most obvious being the practice of the U.S. Supreme Court in refusing to hear certain cases. Owing to the thousands of cases on their docket, the justices usually offer no explanation when they exercise their discretion not to hear a particular case. (See Reading 7.1 for a notable exception.)

Publication of a judicial opinion blurs the sixth distinction because, in effect, such an opinion announces or clarifies general rules that the judge intends to apply to future cases. In doing so, especially if the tribunal is the highest court of a state or a nation, the effect of an opinion may be similar to that of a statute in the sense of serving as a guide for future conduct of all persons within the court's jurisdiction.

THE ROLES OF COURTS

This last point returns us to a question we raised at the outset—What roles do courts play in their societies?—because it suggests that courts, no less than legislatures, can and do establish policy. But that is not the only function that judges perform. At least two others readily come to mind: resolving disputes and monitoring governmental action.

Resolving Disputes

If our discussion about the origin of courts suggests anything, it is that societies created them, in large measure, to settle disputes peacefully. This is no less true today than it was centuries ago. Indeed, perhaps the primary function of judicial bodies is the resolution of disputes among individuals, as well as those between society and individuals accused of violating its rules, norms, or conventions.

Typically, courts carry out this function in highly prescribed ways, but even the most formal processes have informal aspects. For instance, in civil suits—that is, legal actions in which one party seeks compensation from another party—filing papers in court may be only one step toward an informal settlement, a bargaining ploy by one side. Even criminal cases often become matters of negotiation. In the United States, the majority of convictions (and in some cities as many as nine out of ten) come from pleas of guilty that result from bargaining. The prosecutor reduces the charges against the defendant in return for a plea of guilty to the lesser charge. The defendant may prefer a year in jail to the risk of five years' imprisonment. Letting a criminal off with a light sentence may displease prosecutors, but their offices are likely to be understaffed and overworked. Moreover, the prosecutor also faces a risk: a verdict of not guilty. The trial judge, whose swollen docket could have several hundred cases pending, is typically only too happy to see a bargain struck. Supposedly, the Civil Law forbids "plea bargaining," but there are strong suspicions that such negotiations occur informally.[14]

These things virtually all Americans understand. But two issues relevant to this dispute-resolution process deserve special mention. The first is a fact about judicial institutions: even when courts resolve conflicts among individual

---

[14] There is a heated debate on this question. See, for example, Abraham Goldstein and Martin Marcus, "The Myth of Judicial Supervision in Three 'Inquisitorial' Systems: France, Italy, and Germany," 87 *Yale Law Journal* 240 (1977).

claimants, they often set policy for an entire community. Lynn Mather's essay "The Fired Football Coach" (Reading 2.1) makes this point abundantly clear. The judge resolved the coach's suit against Dartmouth before it went to trial, but his decision nonetheless had implications that went well beyond a dispute about one university's personnel policies. This rippling effect is far from atypical. In their formal as well as informal roles as resolvers of conflict, judges often affect public policy. Indeed, to settle a specific case it might be necessary not merely to interpret and apply general rules but also to construct them. How can judges help but make law when they decide what a vaguely worded statute means in a situation that its drafters never foresaw? As we shall see in Chapters 11 and 12, interpretation of statutes, administrative orders, and constitutional clauses is inherently a creative activity.

The second issue is a fact about nonjudicial institutions: courts are not the only instruments for resolving social conflict; a panoply of alternative modes is readily available. Direct negotiation, bargaining, mediation, arbitration, and even violence still abound in almost every industrial nation. Police, social workers, parole officers, and visiting nurses spend a large share of their time acting as informal mediators among neighbors and relatives, quieting disputes before they produce grist for judicial mills. Modern societies also use elections and referenda to help settle conflicts, not only about who will govern but also about what public policies will prevail.

Making Policy

As in the first chapter, we have wandered again into the province of judicial policy making. And we shall continue to do so for a simple reason: although attempts to cope with social conflict may revolve around a limited number of parties arguing about specific factual questions—to return to our earlier example, Did Dragon hiss and spew smoke and fire at the plaintiffs? Would such hissing and spewing create mortal fear in the average, reasonable person?—larger issues frequently lurk beneath such specific inquiries. What proof is sufficient to establish ownership of property? Does long and unchallenged usage of land or a stream confer legal title? If so, how long is long? Suppose the court found that the land belonged to the plaintiffs but that Oliver Dragon had a prescriptive right (both Civil and common law recognize that a right can be established by long and unchallenged usage) to use the stream to replenish his cooling system. What then if the owners decided to build a mill on the property and dammed the stream so that the flow of water was changed? Could Dragon sue for damages to his radiator? What about the family who owned the next parcel of land downstream and used the water to fill the moat around its castle and irrigate its crops? Could that family sue the people who built the dam?

It is evident that the narrow case of *Property Owners v. Dragon* could ignite a series of questions whose answers might affect all people who own property with a stream running through it, as well as affect technological development in an age whose primary sources of energy for manufacturing were muscle and water power. Deciding these issues, even between two private citizens, means preferring one sort of interest or right or value over another sort. The underlying message is both clear and important: legal rules are never neutral. Every legal rule, or even principle, always prefers one interest, right, value, or group over another. Thus, conflict between two private citizens can rapidly escalate into conflicts between competing groups or even social and economic classes—upstreamers against downstreamers, mill owners against farmers, early mill owners against later mill owners. Thus, in the aggregate and over time, judicial decisions on such issues inevitably affect general public policy as well as economic development.

Monitoring Governmental Action

Lynn Mather's essay underscores this last point. But what happens when a private citizen goes into court and asks the judge to order the government to pay damages or to halt a particular policy? When, for instance, a group of poor people file a civil suit, alleging that a town has drafted its zoning ordinances so that they, and others who are economically underprivileged, cannot live in the town? Or suppose both litigants are governmental officials, as, for example, when a state officer asks a court to forbid the attorney general of the United States to enforce a particular federal statute because, the state officer claims, that statute encroaches on authority reserved to the states. Obviously in these sorts of situations, the potential for judicial policy making is both far more direct and vastly greater than in the average suit between private citizens. Where only individuals are involved, it usually takes a line of decisions handed down over a period of some years to have a significant effect on public policy; but where judges forbid a public official to enforce a statute or order the government to act in a positive fashion, they are immediately and deeply involved in shaping public policy.

Even when judges rule in favor of governmental officials, they could be establishing policy; such certainly would be the case if they upheld a local zoning ordinance that kept poor people out of a town. Either way—upholding or striking down acts—when parties ask courts to resolve these sorts of disputes, they are, in essence, asking judges to monitor or review governmental action. "Judicial review," in turn, has at least three meanings. First, it may refer to review by judges of acts of governmental officials to determine whether the officers are acting under authority of law or exceeding powers granted by a statute (that is, acting *ultra vires*). This type of review is generally available to courts in all systems. Second, there is a kind of judicial review, provided for in federal systems, for policing the distribution of power between the states or provinces and the central government. This sort of adjudication forms an important aspect of the work of supreme courts in such federal polities as Australia, Canada, Germany, India, and the United States. Third, judicial review may mean the power of courts to invalidate or refuse to enforce statutes, treaties, or executive orders on the ground that they violate or are unauthorized by constitutional law of the political system. Because exercise of this authority is to be especially important and controversial, a more extensive discussion is in order. The United States makes a reasonable starting point because, as we shall see, many societies have modeled their forms of judicial monitoring on those established here.

Judicial Review in the United States

At the outset, we must note that although the text of the U.S. Constitution makes no specific provision for this third type of judicial review, it has been exercised almost from the beginning and so has become part of the larger constitutional order. Whether the founders intended federal courts to have this authority has been the subject of long debate, which it would be pointless to repeat here. Suffice it to say that there were some precedents for such exercise of judicial review in the American colonial and early state experience. A form of review of legislation in which judges would participate was proposed, although unsuccessfully, by James Madison at the Constitutional Convention. Still, Charles Beard's review of the Convention's proceedings convinced him that 17 of the 25 most influential Founders declared directly or indirectly for judicial review of legislation.

The famous case of *Marbury v. Madison* (1803) (Reading 2.2) marked the first time the U.S. Supreme Court explicitly explained and justified judicial review. Writing for a unanimous Court, John Marshall, fourth Chief Justice of the United States, used syllogistic reasoning. Major premise: The Constitution is the supreme law of the land, and judges take an oath to support it. Minor premise: It falls within the province of the judiciary to interpret the law. Conclusion: Judges must not enforce a statute that they believe violates the Constitution. This logic is not unassailable. In fact, only two decades later, Justice Gibson of the Pennsylvania Supreme Court expressed a powerful opposing view in *Eakin v. Raub* (1825) (Reading 2.3). Other debates and controversies followed (reviewed below). But *Marbury v. Madison* has been ratified by time and practice and has become a cornerstone of the larger constitutional system.

Marbury, of course, stands only for the proposition that judges can declare acts of Congress invalid. In subsequent cases Marshall asserted that judges could also declare invalid executive orders or actions (*Little v. Barreme*, 1804) and upheld the Judiciary Act of 1789, under which Congress gave the Supreme Court power to review and reverse decisions upholding the constitutionality of state statutes (*Martin v. Hunter's Lessee*, 1816; *Cohens v. Virginia*, 1821). Taken collectively, these cases provide federal judges with impressive tools for monitoring governmental actions, tools that they have not always been hesitant to use. Through the end of the 1990s, the Supreme Court has invalidated nearly 140 federal statutes and some 1,200 local laws. State courts too, with their own power to strike down acts passed within their jurisdiction, are active monitors of their governments. One scholar estimates that state justices invalidate nearly 25 percent of all laws challenged in their court rooms.[15]

But exercise of this power, at the federal or state level, does not necessarily imply that executive and legislative officials always accept judges' constitutional interpretations. On the contrary, disagreements about constitutional meaning have triggered some classic battles in American history. For all its formidable

---

[15] Henry R. Glick, "Policy Making and State Supreme Courts," in *The American Courts: A Critical Assessment*, ed. John B. Gates and Charles A Johnson (Washington, D.C: CQ Press, 1991).

position, the federal judiciary is vulnerable in important respects. When judges die or retire, the president can try to affect constitutional interpretation by nominating to the courts persons having different ideas. If vacancies do not occur, the president can propose that Congress increase the size of the Supreme Court or add other federal judgeships; he can also attempt to organize public opinion against the courts. Article III of the constitutional charter forbids Congress to reduce the salaries of sitting justices; but under Jefferson's leadership, Congress did so in the Judiciary Act of 1802 by abolishing a whole tier of federal courts created by the Federalists just before leaving office. In effect, the Jeffersonians simply turned sixteen incumbent judges out of office and did not appropriate money to continue their salaries. Moreover, Article III of the constitutional text authorizes Congress to control the appellate jurisdiction of the Supreme Court as well as control the trial and appellate jurisdiction of the rest of the federal courts. In 1868 Congress used its authority over the Supreme Court's appellate jurisdiction to prevent the justices from invalidating a controversial federal statute. The Senate can, of course, refuse to confirm judicial nominees; and in considering nominations, it can conduct inquiries into the current state of judicial thinking as well as that of the nominee. Because most state judges must first be elected and then periodically stand for reelection, they are even more vulnerable to political pressures. (See Chapters 4 and 8 for elaboration on these and similar points.)

Judicial Review Abroad

Later in this chapter we consider how these and other threats to judicial independence may affect the ability of judges to perform their various roles. For now, let us return to a point we made earlier: Judicial authority to invalidate acts of coordinate branches is not unique to the United States, although it is fair to say that the prestige of the American Supreme Court has provided a model and incentive for other countries. By the middle of the nineteenth century, the Judicial Committee of the British Privy Council was functioning as a kind of constitutional arbiter for colonial governments within the British Empire—but not, of course, for the United Kingdom itself. Then Canada in the late nineteenth century and Australia in the first years of the twentieth created their own systems of constitutional review, although the Canadians allowed the Judicial Committee to sit as a "supreme" supreme court until 1949.

In the nineteenth century, Argentina also modeled its Corte Suprema on that of the United States and even instructed its judges to pay special attention to precedents of the American tribunal. In this century Austria, Ireland, India, and the Philippines adopted judicial review, and variations of this power can be found in Norway, Switzerland, much of Latin America, and some of Africa. After World War II the three defeated Axis powers—Italy, Japan, and West Germany—all institutionalized judicial review in their new constitutional texts. This development was due in part to a revulsion against recent experiences with unchecked political power and in part to the influence of American occupying authorities. Japan, whose constitutional document was largely drafted by Americans, follows the "decentralized" model of the United States: the power of constitutional review is diffused throughout the entire judicial system.[16] Any court of general jurisdiction can declare a legislative or executive act invalid.

Germany and Italy, and later Belgium, Spain, and Portugal, followed a "centralized" model first adopted in the Austrian constitution of 1920. Each country has a single constitutional court (although some sit in divisions, or "senates") that has a judicial monopoly on interpreting the fundamental law. When, in litigation before the ordinary courts, judges confront a law whose constitutionality they doubt, they are obliged to send the case directly to the constitutional court. This tribunal receives evidence on the constitutional issue, sometimes gathers evidence on its own, hears arguments, perhaps consults sources that counsel overlooked, and hands down a decision. But, unlike in the United States and other common-law nations with judicial review, the constitutional court does not decide the case—because it has not heard a case, only addressed a question of constitutional interpretation. Although the court publishes an opinion justifying its ruling and explaining the controlling principles, the case itself must still be decided by "regular" tribunals. German and Italian public officials may also bring suits in their constitutional court to challenge the legitimacy of legislative, executive, or judicial acts; and under some circumstances private citizens may start similar litigation. Where judicial action is challenged, the constitutional court in effect reviews a decision of another court, but the form of the action is very different from an appeal in the United States.

After the Berlin Wall collapsed in 1989 and the Soviet Union disintegrated soon after, many Eastern European republics looked to judges' interpreting a constitutional text with a bill of rights to protect their newly found liberties. Most opted for centralized systems of constitutional review, establishing ordinary tribunals and a separate constitutional court. They made this choice despite familiarity with Marshall's argument for a decentralized court system in *Marbury*—namely, that all judges may face the problem of a conflict between a statute or an executive order, on the one hand, and the terms of a constitutional document on the other; if judges cannot give preference to the constitutional provision over ordinary legislation or an executive act, they violate their oath to support the constitution.

The countries that have rejected Marshall's rationale tend to use the Civil Law, which takes more seriously the idea of separation of powers and endorses a notion of the supremacy of statutory law over judicial rulings. These countries have accepted the charge that invalidation of a statute on constitutional grounds is an act of high policy, inappropriate for a general court. So most Civil Law nations that have accepted judicial review require all courts except one to apply the law as they find it. The most that ordinary judges can do when a constitutional issue is raised is to refer the problem to the specialized constitutional court.

---

[16] See Walter F. Murphy and Joseph Tanenhaus, eds., *Comparative Constitutional Law* (New York: St. Martin's Press, 1977); C. Neal Tate and Torbjörn Vallinder, eds., *The Global Expansion of Judicial Power: The Judicialization of Politics* (New York: New York University Press, 1995).

The experience of these tribunals has been quite varied. The German Constitutional Court, for example, is largely regarded as a success story. In its first 38 years, that tribunal invalidated 292 Bund (national) and 130 Land (state) laws,[17] provoking frequent complaints that it "judicializes" politics. The Court, however, has survived these attacks and has gone on to create a new and politically significant jurisprudence in the fields of federalism and civil liberties. The Russian Constitutional Court stands (or teeters) in stark contrast. It too began to make extensive use of judicial review to strike down governmental acts but quickly paid a steep price: in 1993, President Boris Yeltsin suspended the Court's operations; it did not resume its activities until nearly two years later.

THE BRITISH ALTERNATIVE. While most industrial and many developing nations have opted for the American or the European model of judicial review, the British have never officially accepted judicial power in quite that naked a form, though in recent years they have backed into a version of judicial review. Judges can interpret acts of Parliament—no small thing, as Chapter 11 shows—but they cannot hold that a legislative act violates the English constitution. Rather, Britain has an alternative to judicial review: parliamentary supremacy in constitutional interpretation. It might be true that the British Parliament tends to be more responsive to citizens' demands than is the American Congress, and the integral relationship between the British executive and the legislature through the device of ministerial responsibility prevents the deadlock and irresponsibility that often characterize American institutional arrangements. But because Parliament can pass any legislation it wishes—and on occasion it has abridged civil liberties—the citizen has no constitutional right enforceable in court against the government acting under statute passed by Parliament. Nevertheless, as we noted earlier, the British may have moved closer to a form of judicial review than they admit, because, in joining the European Union, the United Kingdom accepted the jurisdiction of the European Court of Justice. This tribunal has authority to determine the validity, under the treaties establishing the European Union, of a wide range of domestic policies of each member nation. In fact, the Court of Justice had not, as of early 2000, invalidated a British statute, owing in part to British judges' wonderfully creative talent for interpreting acts of Parliament to conform to the European Community's treaties.[18] Moreover, in 2000, the terms of the European Convention on Human Rights became, by act of Parliament, part of British domestic law. During the early decades of that treaty's life, the European Court of Human Rights at Strasbourg had often found Britain to have violated the agreement, usually for torturing Irish prisoners. It will be interesting to see how courts in the United Kingdom

---

[17] Donald P. Kommers, *The Constitutional Jurisprudence of the Federal Republic of Germany,* 2nd ed. (Durham, NC: Duke University Press, 1997), 52.

[18] See, for example, the matter of equal rights for women, a subject that has not especially bothered Parliament's conscience: Sally J. Kenney, *For Whose Protection? Reproductive Hazards and Exclusionary Policies in the United States and Britain* (Ann Arbor: University of Michigan Press, 1992).

handle such cases, though, again, they can now do so under the guise of statutory, rather than constitutional, interpretation.

To What Extent Does Judicial Review Present a Paradox?

Regardless of the model of judicial review a democratic country adopts, when courts invoke the power to strike down acts of government, something of a paradox seems to emerge. Judges, who are, except in most American states, not directly answerable to the electorate, declare unconstitutional acts passed by officials whom the people have elected—hardly a democratic outcome. In 1825 Justice John Gibson of Pennsylvania's supreme court (Reading 2.3) argued that such a power was not only undemocratic but also unauthorized by the American constitutional document. If Congress passed an unconstitutional statute, the voters could turn the rascals out at the next election, because the people, not Congress or the courts, were the ultimate constitutional interpreters.

Gibson was responding both to Alexander Hamilton's reasoning in *Federalist* No. 78 (Reading 1.2) that judicial review is a democratic, not an undemocratic, power and to John Marshall's reasoning in *Marbury* (Reading 2.2) that the structure of the American constitutional text requires judicial review. Hamilton's argument was the more sophisticated: the terms of the constitutional text express the will of the people; thus, when Congress overreaches its authority and judges prefer the commands of the Constitution over those of the Senate and House, they give effect to the people's will, protecting that will against legislative abuses of power. Gibson's answer to Hamilton is that the people can speak for themselves at elections; to Marshall he replied that the question of constitutionality does not arise before judges, only the question of whether the statute had been enacted into law. Again, the people will judge the constitutionality at the next election.

Implicit in both Hamilton's and Marshall's arguments is a claim for judicial protection of minority rights. By their very nature—the fact that they are elected—legislators and executives are supposed to reflect the interests of the majority. But majorities sometimes wish to deprive minorities of their rights to life, liberty, or property. Therefore, it is necessary for one branch of government that lacks an electoral connection to have the power of constitutional review. This implicit claim has generated an empirically based response: judges seldom invalidate legislative acts in order to protect minorities.

In the United States, Robert A. Dahl (Reading 2.4) has concluded, the Supreme Court tends to reflect the interests of the coalition of groups that support the ruling regime; the justices are members of the dominant national alliance. Vacancies occur on the Court on the average once every twenty-two months, giving the president ample opportunity to restaff and reshape the bench. Exceptional circumstances do occur; but, Dahl claims, judges usually cannot—or will not—run counter to the policies of the ruling coalition. They can only fashion specific policies within the general framework of the dominant coalition's goals or, at considerable risk, make new policy when the alliance has not yet arrived at a consensus.

This account offers many useful insights into the ways in which American government actually functions. But Dahl's analysis has its own problems. Some scholars studying Latin America and Europe suggest that it does not fit courts there.[19] Certainly the record of the German Constitutional Court in invalidating hundreds of parliamentary acts in four decades offers evidence that his thesis does not travel well. Indeed, Jonathan D. Casper argues that Dahl's analysis does not even aptly describe certain eras in American history (Reading 2.5). He also criticizes Dahl for failing to consider instances when the Supreme Court strikes down acts passed by local governments or when the justices engage in statutory interpretation in ways that benefit minority interests. Finally, it is of course true that many presidents themselves would take exception to any suggestion, however implicit, that the appointing process yields a precisely predictable result. The list of judicial "errors" is long. For example: Thomas Jefferson was angry that "his man" William Johnson voted with John Marshall (and told Johnson so); Dwight D. Eisenhower called his nomination of Earl Warren as Chief Justice "the biggest damn fool mistake I ever made"; and Lewis Powell and Harry Blackmun sorely disappointed Richard Nixon. Justice David Souter is merely the last in a long line of political surprises judges have presented to presidents who chose them.

There is yet another and very different response to the question of the alleged paradox of judicial review. Some scholars contend that the conflict between democracy and judicial review is the product of muddled thinking about the nature of most modern political systems.[20] They are not representative democracies in which elected officials rule, subject only to the qualifications that they respect rights of free speech and political participation and also periodically stand for reelection. Rather, the government of the United States, as well as of countries such as Australia, Austria, Canada, Germany, France, Ireland, Italy, and Japan, is made of a mass of checks and counterchecks. The American institutional web is the most complex of all. Federalism limits the power of national majorities by reserving certain powers to the states, allowing the almost 55 million people in California and New York to choose only half the number of senators as do the two-and-a-half million who populate Alaska, the Dakotas, and Vermont; and the president is officially chosen by an electoral college that also gives disproportionate power to states with small populations. Furthermore, only one-third of senators stand for election when a new House of Representatives is chosen, and the Senate has formal power equal, if not superior to, that of the more popularly elected House. Moreover, the existence of a

---

[19] See Gretchen Helmke, "Toward a Formal Theory of an Informal Institution: Insecure Tenure and Judicial Independence in Argentina," paper presented at the 1998 annual meeting of the Conference Group on the Scientific Study of Judicial Politics, East Lansing, MI; Christine Landfried, "Germany," in Tate and Vallinder, eds., *The Global Expansion of Judicial Power.*

[20] See, for example, Walter F. Murphy, James F. Fleming, and Sotirios A. Barber, *American Constitutional Interpretation*, 2nd ed. (Westbury, NY: Foundation Press, 1995); and Murphy, "Constitutions, Constitutionalism, and Democracy," in *Constitutionalism and Democracy: Transitions in the Contemporary World*, ed. Douglas Greenberg et al. (New York: Oxford University Press, 1993).

constitutional text that includes restrictions on government also restrains those who elect public officials. "The very purpose of a Bill of Rights," Justice Robert H. Jackson once wrote for the U.S. Supreme Court, "was to withdraw certain subjects from the vicissitudes of political controversy, to place them beyond the reach of majorities and officials and establish them as legal principles to be applied by the courts."[21]

In addition, lines of authority between Congress and the president are blurred, just as they are between these two institutions and the courts as well as between state and national governments, making these officials compete for power. The system, as James Madison explained in *Federalist* No. 51, pits power against power and ambition against ambition. It does not allow any group, institution, or even a majority to govern without engaging in complex negotiations with other groups and institutions. Thus, constitutional democrats contend, judicial review functions as one of many barriers to free exercise of power, which is not to say that constitutional democrats do not often attack specific judicial decisions as wrong or even wrongheaded. Just as legislatures sometimes enact stupid laws, so judges sometimes make stupid decisions, even when interpreting a constitution.

And, as we have already mentioned, nations with judicial review do not give courts unlimited power. They, too, operate within, and are sometimes ensnared by, webs of checks.

THE EXPANSION OF JUDICIAL POWER?

Even so, C. Neal Tate and his colleagues point to the expansion (and growing influence) of courts throughout the world, calling it one of the "most significant trends in late-twentieth and early-twenty-first-century."[22] James L. Gibson and his team of researchers agree: "Though the United States seems to have led the way in transforming political questions into legal questions, much the same is true in polities as diverse as [those of] Russia, Namibia, the Philippines, Canada, the European Union, and Spain. Nor does this trend toward greater judicialization show signs of abating soon."[23] Undoubtedly, as our discussion suggests, there is much truth in these statements: Courts, throughout the world, are playing important roles in their governments. Donald L. Horowitz provides some explanations as to how this occurred in the United States.[24] "Most obvious," he says, "has been the influence of the school desegregation cases," *Brown v. Board of Education* (1954) and its companion cases:

---

[21] *West Virginia v. Barnette* (1943).

[22] Tate and Vallinder, eds. *The Global Expansion of Judicial Power,* 5.

[23] James L. Gibson, Gregory A. Caldeira, and Vanessa A. Baird, "On the Legitimacy of National High Courts," 92 *American Political Science Review* 343 (1998).

[24] Donald L. Horowitz, *Courts and Social Policy* (Washington, D.C.: Brookings Institution, 1977).

These decisions created a magnetic field around the courts, attracting litigation in areas where judicial intervention had earlier seemed implausible. The more general judicial activism of the Warren Court signaled its willingness to test the conventional boundaries of judicial action. [In this process,] significant social groups [who were] thwarted in achieving their goals in other forums turned to adjudication as a more promising course. Some organizations saw the opportunity to use litigation as a weapon in political struggles carried on elsewhere. The National Welfare Rights Organization, for example, is said to have turned to lawsuits to help create a state and local welfare crisis that might bring about a federal guaranteed income. The image of courts willing to "take the heat" was attractive, too, to legislators who were not. Such social programs as the poverty program had legal assistance components, which Congress obligingly provided, perhaps partly because they placed the onus for resolving social problems on the courts. Soon there were also privately funded lawyers functioning in the environmental, mental health, welfare rights, civil rights, and similar fields. They tended to prefer the judicial road to reform over the legislative. They raised issues never before tested in litigation, and the courts frequently responded by expanding the boundaries of judicial activity.[25]

But Horowitz also highlights, just as we have, that when courts take on these roles—especially when they engage in judicial review—they may place themselves in a vulnerable position vis-à-vis the public and elected actors.

The most extreme contemporary examples come out of the emerging constitutional democracies of Eastern Europe. Judges there have yet to establish their independence and authority, and the new constitutional systems have not firmly established their own and more basic authority. Instructive are the results of a poll conducted in March 1998 by the Public Opinion Foundation in Russia. It revealed that only 18 percent of the respondents believe that their Constitutional Court is truly independent. It will be some time before it is clear whether the majority is right or wrong in this judgment.

What this shaky judicial base means, in practical terms, is, first, that elected officials in democratizing societies have not been hesitant to suspend the operations of their courts, ignore their decisions, threaten impeachment against particular justices, or take other steps designed to punish individual justices or nullify their decisions. Second, when these threats occur, judges are often unable or unwilling to mount defenses, at least in part because they toil in countries where, under previous regimes, "it had been unthinkable that an independent institution should exist which could exert constitutional control over the processes of government and law enforcement."[26] Hence, it is not surprising that, when the Russian Constitutional Court in its first decision struck down a presidential decree as unconstitutional, President Boris Yeltsin did not quite know what to make of the ruling; he complied only after "some coaxing"

---

[25] *Ibid.*, p. 10.

[26] Elspeth Reid, "The Russian Constitutional Court, October 1991–October 1993," 32 *Co-existence* 277 (1995).

by the court's chairman.[27] Nor should it have been surprising that, when members of the Russian Constitutional Court asked their U.S. counterparts about how they ensured compliance with their decisions, the Russians were taken aback by the American justices' surprise. "They simply did not understand us. It simply had not entered their heads that the decisions of the Court would not be implemented."

American judges might have professed amazement at their colleagues' concern, but the fact of the matter is, as we have already seen, that they themselves have not always been immune to threats from elected officials who disagree with judicial rulings. And, in at least some of these instances, American judges have retreated. Indeed, judges have occasionally backed away from constitutional conflicts with Congress.[28] A striking example occurred during the first years of the New Deal (1933–1936), when the justices repeatedly exerted the power of judicial review to strike down economic legislation passed by the "dominant national alliance." President Franklin Roosevelt responded with a plan to reshape the bench by increasing the number of justices from nine to fifteen (Reading 8.6). This particular "Court-packing" plan failed, though an earlier plan under Abraham Lincoln to increase the number of justices from nine to eleven had succeeded. Nevertheless, Roosevelt still won on the substantive constitutional issue of economic regulation. A majority of the "Old Court" and all the younger justices who came to the bench in the years after 1937 reversed course, leaving economic affairs to legislative regulation and turning judicial attention to other issues, in particular the Bill of Rights and the Fourteenth Amendment's guarantee—for decades a hollow guarantee—of equal protection of the laws.

This "switch-in-time that saved nine" is the most dramatic American example of judicial retreat, but it is certainly not the only one. Responding to political pressures and putative threats to their own power, legislative and executive officials have often tried and sometimes have been able to change the direction of judicial policy making. That process continues even today, as the furor over the Massachusetts Supreme Court decision on same-sex marriage makes clear (see Readings 3.9 and 8.7).

And so it goes. Although some people argue that judges lack the institutional capacity to make policy or monitor public officials, the very fact that they are governmental officials means that they cannot avoid being participants in struggles for political power. They might meet that struggle in a nonpartisan way; they might bring to bear all the objectivity, all the learning, all the humility that intelligent people, aware of their own emotional attachments, can muster; they might refuse to lay down more doctrine than necessary to decide a specific question. Yet there are times when a judge cannot escape the duty to judge, to choose between competing societal interests and values. And that choice is what politics is all about.

---

[27] Robert B. Ahdieh, *Russia's Constitutional Revolution: Legal Consciousness and the Transition to Democracy, 1985–1995* (University Park: Pennsylvania State University Press, 1997).

[28] Walter F. Murphy, *Congress and the Court* (Chicago: University of Chicago Press, 1962)

SELECTED REFERENCES

BREWER-CARIAS, ALLAN R. 1989. *Judicial Review in Comparative Perspective*. New York: Cambridge University Press.

CANON, BRADLEY C. 1983. "Defining the Dimensions of Judicial Activism." *Judicature* 66: 237.

CASPER, JONATHAN D. 1976. "The Supreme Court and National Policy Making." *American Political Science Review* 70: 50.

CHAYES, ABRAM. 1976. "The Role of the Judge in Public Law Litigation." *Harvard Law Review* 89: 1281.

CHOPER, JESSE H. 1980. *Judicial Review and the National Political Process*. Chicago: University of Chicago Press.

COVER, ROBERT M. 1982. "The Origins of Judicial Activism in the Protection of Minorities." *Yale Law Journal* 91: 1287.

DAHL, ROBERT A. 1957. "Decision Making in a Democracy: The Supreme Court as a National Policy Maker." *Journal of Public Law* 6: 279.

DAHL, ROBERT A. 2002. *How Democratic Is the American Constitution?* New Haven, CT: Yale University Press.

EISGRUBER, CHRISOPHER. 2001. *Constitutional Self-Government*. Cambridge, MA: Harvard University Press.

ELY, JOHN HART. 1980. *Democracy and Distrust*. Cambridge, MA: Harvard University Press.

FALLON, RICHARD H. 2004. *The Dynamic Constitution*. New York: Cambridge University Press.

FELSTINER, WILLIAM L. F., RICHARD L. ABEL, AND AUSTIN SARAT. 1981. "The Emergence and Transformation of Disputes: Naming, Blaming, and Claiming." *Law and Society Review* 15: 631.

GINSBURG, TOM. 2003. *Judicial Review in New Democracies: Constitutional Courts in Asian Cases*. New York: Cambridge University Press.

GLICK, HENRY R. 1991. "Policy Making and State Supreme Courts." In *The American Courts: A Critical Assessment*, ed. John B. Gates and Charles A. Johnson. Washington, DC: CQ Press.

HALPERN, STEPHEN C., AND CHARLES M. LAMB, EDS. 1982. *Supreme Court Activism and Restraint*. Lexington, MA: Heath.

HOROWITZ, DONALD L. 1977. *The Courts and Social Policy*. Washington, DC: Brookings Institution.

HOROWITZ, MORTON J. 1977. *The Transformation of American Law*. Cambridge, MA: Harvard University Press.

HOWARD, J. WOODFORD, JR. 1969. "Adjudication Considered as a Process of Conflict Resolution." *Journal of Public Law* 18: 339.

JACOB, HERBERT. 1984. *Justice in America*. 4th ed. Boston: Little, Brown.

KOOPMANS, TIM. 2003. *Courts and Political Institutions*. New York: Cambridge University Press.

MATHER, LYNN. 1991. "Policy Making in State Trial Courts." In *American Courts*, ed. John B. Gates and Charles A. Johnson. Washington, DC: CQ Press.

MATHER, LYNN. 1995. "The Fired Football Coach (Or, How Trial Courts Make Policy)." In *Contemplating Courts*, ed. Lee Epstein. Washington, DC: CQ Press.

MILLER, ARTHUR S. 1982. *Toward Increased Judicial Activism: The Political Role of the Supreme Court*. Westport, CT: Greenwood Press.

MURPHY, WALTER F. 1962. *Congress and the Court*. Chicago: University of Chicago Press.

MURPHY, WALTER F., AND JOSEPH TANENHAUS. 1972. *The Study of Public Law*. New York: Random House.

SARAT, AUSTIN, AND JOEL B. GROSSMAN. 1975. "Courts and Conflict Resolution: Problems in the Mobilization of Adjudication." *American Political Science Review* 69: 1200.

STONE, ALEC. 1995. *The Birth of Judicial Politics in France*. New York: Oxford University Press.

TATE, C. NEAL, AND TORBJÖRN VALLINDER, EDS. 1995. *The Global Expansion of Judicial Power: The Judicialization of Politics*. New York: New York University Press.

WALDRON, JEREMY. 2001. *Law and Disagreement*. New York: Oxford University Press.

WOLFE, CHRISTOPHER. 1986. *The Rise of Modern Judicial Review*. New York: Basic Books.

"Just as Congress made policy when it passed the Civil Rights Act to protect minority employees, so do state trial courts make policy when they extend common law and equitable remedies to protect employees from arbitrary dismissals."

2.1 THE FIRED FOOTBALL COACH (OR, HOW TRIAL COURTS MAKE POLICY)

Lynn Mather

Lynn Mather is Professor of Government at Dartmouth College.

On November 29, 1985, after a disappointing football season, the head football coach at Dartmouth College, Joseph Yukica, was fired. Three days later, Yukica filed suit in Grafton County, New Hampshire, Superior Court against Edward Leland, Dartmouth's athletic director, charging a breach of contract and seeking a temporary injunction to halt the termination and to prevent Dartmouth from taking steps to hire a new coach. Judge Walter Murphy granted the temporary injunction, but prior to a full hearing on the merits of Yukica's claim, the parties negotiated a settlement out of court. Although the law had clearly favored Dartmouth, Yukica succeeded in continuing as head coach for one more Dartmouth football season.

On the face of it, there is little to commend this case to the student of public policy making. It was a suit involving private law, filed in a New Hampshire county court, that never even went to trial. Although the judge's order to grant a temporary injunction surprised observers, the order had been carefully tailored to the facts of Yukica's contract, and no new law was made. Yet, because of its arguments and the media coverage given it, the case contributed significantly to the politics and law of employment policy, especially in the sports field.

Yukica became coach at Dartmouth in 1978 with a contract that was renewed every two years. During Yukica's early tenure, the team did extremely well, but then the team fell into a slump, winning only two games each in the 1984 and 1985 seasons. Just before the 1985 season, Leland sent Yukica a contract renewal letter with warm praise for his coaching, but after the last game of the 1985 season, Leland suggested to Yukica that he resign as head coach. Yukica refused to resign and contacted Michael Slive, a good friend and local lawyer who was also a nationally known expert in sports law and former university athletic director. Four days later Yukica received an official letter of termination from Leland, along with an offer of compensation. Slive and Yukica hired David Nixon, an experienced litigator, to be the trial lawyer; Nixon then initiated the lawsuit on Yukica's behalf.

From *Contemplating Courts*, Lee Epstein, ed. (Washington, DC: CQ Press, 1995).

In brief, Yukica claimed that he should be allowed to continue for another year as head coach as outlined in his contract. He also charged procedural irregularities in the way Dartmouth had handled the termination. And he sought a temporary injunction, arguing that, were he to be fired, the damage to his professional reputation and career opportunities would cause him "irreparable harm." These arguments were unusual, seeking to stretch principles of equity in a novel way. In response, Dartmouth College and its athletic director narrowed the case into well-established legal categories with the law weighted on their side. They argued that they had every right to reassign Yukica to other duties within the college as long as they paid his salary and benefits for the remaining eighteen months of the contract. Moreover, Dartmouth argued that the court could not force it to accept Yukica as its football coach; that is, the court could not order the specific performance of Yukica's contract. To do so would contradict the legal precedents on personal services contracts, which have held that compensation ("pay-off"), and not specific performance, is the appropriate legal remedy for a breach of contract.

In firing Yukica while offering monetary compensation, Dartmouth had simply done what colleges around the country had traditionally done when they wanted to change coaches. But Yukica and his lawyers were able to draw support from prominent sports figures who agreed with their view that coaching was in some ways unique, that a broken coaching contract could not be repaired simply through the payment of money. At the preliminary hearing on December 13, Yukica called on numerous witnesses, including Joe Paterno, a coach at Pennsylvania State University; Jack Bicknell, a coach at Boston College; and Bob Blackman, a former Dartmouth football coach. Their testimony furthered the already growing public interest in the case and attracted national media attention. The case was transformed from a fairly routine dismissal into a dispute about the quality of Yukica's twenty-year record of coaching football, the importance of not breaking contracts, and the relative power of institutions and coaches.

A week after the hearing, Judge Murphy granted the temporary restraining order preventing Yukica's dismissal and the college's efforts to replace him. In his order, the judge (himself a former football coach) indicated the likelihood that Yukica would win on the merits of his claim, in part because of procedural irregularities in the dismissal. The procedural question was whether Leland had the sole authority to dismiss Yukica or whether the contract required approval of the dismissal by the sixteen-member athletic council. The judge held that such approval was necessary and offered Dartmouth the chance to obtain it and return to court. That happened in January, as the college brought a motion to dismiss the case on the basis of the minutes of the council meeting in which Yukica's termination was approved. Yukica, however, raised additional procedural issues about the council meeting, and the judge refused to dismiss the case. In addition to the judicial orders, time was clearly on Yukica's side in negotiations, since football recruitment was under way and the college was operating in effect without a head coach. Furthermore, the media coverage of the case put public opinion behind Yukica. As a result, Dartmouth finally settled out of court with an agreement to let Yukica coach for another season.

The temporary injunction by Judge Murphy, although only a pretrial order, played a critical role in the outcome of Yukica's case. The order essentially maintained the status quo and prevented Dartmouth from replacing him. The order also operated to shift power between the two parties, providing Yukica the time and opportunity to argue his case in court and in the press.

Yukica had succeeded in shifting the framework of argument, not just in legal terms but in the wider public debate. National publications reported the case through Yukica's view ("A deal is a deal," "All we're asking is that the college honor a contract") rather than as a dispute about the legal remedy for breach of a personal services contract.

Interestingly, reports on the case seemed to indicate its precedential value despite the limits in the judge's ruling to the particular facts of the contract and despite the fact that it was a negotiated outcome. The president of the American Football Coaches Association, Vince Dooley, was widely quoted as calling *Yukica v. Leland* "a landmark case," and the *Boston Globe* called the judge's initial order a "resounding court victory . . . that could have far-reaching ramifications for the collegiate coaching profession." Some might fault the newspapers for oversimplifying and exaggerating the case's import, yet in another sense the accounts were quite accurate.

Finally, and perhaps of most importance, it affected how coaching contracts were written, as athletic administrators and coaches began to look more closely at the contract language. Yukica himself published a detailed account of his case ("A Deal Is a Deal") in the *1986 Summer Manual of the American Football Coaches Association* and provided a fourteen-point listing of his thoughts on contracts. And administrators made comments such as, "Contracts obviously are going to be more carefully written by the institution" and "I think it [the case] means when you make contracts with a coach, you better know what you've done." It is important to remember that contract law is constituted in part by the way people think about and write their contracts, not just by what happens when a contract is breached. If we think of the contracting process as a sequence of legally significant stages, then it seems clear that change has occurred in the early stages involving assumptions, negotiations, and formulation of coaching contracts—even without definitive change at the stage of legal remedy.

Rather than being a completely isolated or aberrant case, *Yukica v. Leland* is one of many recent lawsuits filed by coaches dismissed by their employers. Instead of filing for specific performance, most of the plaintiffs have sought (and some have won) large financial awards not only for compensatory damages but also for the loss of "collateral opportunities" (the perquisites of being a coach beyond salary and benefits). Indeed, another way to understand the policy importance of *Yukica* is to place it in the larger context of current American employment law. In recent decades the legal rights of employees have been greatly expanded through changes in statutory and case law, but the question of how far to expand those rights is still hotly debated. Cases like this one promote a particular normative interpretation of the problem in ways that distinctly favor employees and encourage legal change.

Lawyers for Yukica were thus attempting to accomplish judicially for coaches what had already been done by statute for other groups of employees.

Just as Congress made policy when it passed the Civil Rights Act to protect minority employees, so do state trial courts make policy when they extend common law and equitable remedies to protect employees from arbitrary dismissals.

*"It is, emphatically, the province and duty of the judicial
department to say what the law is."*

2.2 MARBURY V. MADISON

1 Cranch 137 (1803)

The election of 1800, which capped what is still ranked as one of the nastiest of partisan campaigns in American history, cost the Federalist party both the presidency and control of Congress. The constitutionally mandated peculiarities of governmental succession, however, allowed incumbents to stay in office until March 1801; and they took advantage of this opportunity to maintain control of the judiciary. The lame-duck Congress enacted the Circuit Court Act of 1801, which created six new circuit courts and several district courts to accommodate the new states of Kentucky, Tennessee, and Vermont. These new courts required judges and support staff such as attorneys, marshals, and clerks. As a result, during the last few months of his term in office, Adams made more than two hundred nominations, with sixteen judgeships (the "midnight appointments") approved by the Senate during his last two weeks as president.

An even more important opportunity arose in December 1800, when the third chief justice, Oliver Ellsworth, gave in to pleas from fellow Federalists that he resign so that Adams could name a younger and healthier man as his replacement and so frustrate Jefferson. Initially, Adams offered the post to John Jay, who had served as the first chief justice before leaving to run for the more prestigious office of governor of New York. When Jay refused, Adams turned to his secretary of state, John Marshall. A wounded hero of the Revolutionary War, former congressman from Virginia, one of the American emissaries to France in the ill-fated XYZ Affair, and an ardent Federalist, he was easily confirmed by the Senate in January 1801. Nevertheless, he continued as secretary of state during the remaining months of Adams's presidency.

The Federalist Congress also passed the Organic Act, which authorized Adams to appoint forty-two justices of the peace for the District of Columbia; and this seemingly innocuous law set the stage for the dramatic case of *Marbury v. Madison*. Still acting as secretary of state, Marshall instructed his assistant, his brother James, to deliver the commissions; but in the confusion of Adams's final days in office, James left some of them on his desk. On taking office, Jefferson,

---

Corrected by the Twentieth Amendment (1933), which provided that congressional sessions would begin on January 3 after general elections and the term of the newly elected president on January 20.

who had been angered by Federalist efforts to pack the courts, ordered James Madison, the new secretary of state, not to deliver at least five of these commissions.[1] Some years later, Jefferson explained the situation:

> I found the commissions on the table of the Department of State . . . and I forbade their delivery. Whatever is in the Executive offices is certainly deemed to be in the hands of the President, and in this case, was actually in my hands, because when I countermanded them, there was as yet no Secretary of State.[2]

Later in 1801 William Marbury and three others who had been denied their commissions went directly to the Supreme Court and asked it to issue a writ of mandamus, ordering Madison to deliver the commissions. Marbury claimed he could begin his case there because Section 13 of the 1789 Judiciary Act authorized the Supreme Court to issue writs of mandamus to anyone holding federal office. Whether the murky syntax of Section 13 added to the kinds of cases that could be heard under Court's original jurisdiction or simply authorized the Court to issue such orders in cases properly before it was not obvious, though John Marshall would later treat it as so.

Infuriated by the justices' accepting the case, the Jeffersonians in Congress abolished the 1802 term of the Court, effectively delaying a decision. Moreover, they began openly talking about impeaching Federalist judges—with two justices (Chase and Marshall himself) high on their lists. In this volatile political climate, Marshall found himself in a tenuous position. On the one hand, he considered his cousin Thomas Jefferson to be a dangerous radical and was anxious to curb his power. On the other hand, the chief justice, typically a cautious man, was wary of directly confronting Jefferson, fearing that this strong-willed and popular president, with Congress united behind him, would likely crush a hitherto weak judiciary. And an order from the Court to deliver the commission would tempt Jefferson to defy the Court's authority and begin all-out war.

Marshall, a clever strategist, opted for an indirect course. He opened his opinion with an acerbic 9,000-word indictment of Jefferson's ethics, asserting that Marbury was entitled to his commission. To deny him that right was little short of immoral. Next the chief justice held that the laws of the United States afforded Marbury a remedy. Third was the question whether Marbury had sought the proper remedy. Marshall stated that Section 13 of the Act of 1789 on which Marbury relied enlarged the original jurisdiction of the Supreme Court as defined in Article III of the Constitution. This bald assertion allowed the chief justice to claim that the basic issue in the case was whether judges should follow a statute when it ran counter to their interpretation of the constitutional charter.

Mr. CHIEF JUSTICE MARSHALL delivered the opinion of the Court.

The question whether an act, repugnant to the constitution, can become the law of the land, is a question deeply interesting to the United States; but, happily, not of art intricacy proportioned to its interest. It seems only necessary to recognize certain principles, supposed to have been long and well established, to decide it. That the people have an original right to establish for their future government, such principles as, in their opinion, shall most conduce to their own happiness, is the basis on which the whole American fabric has been erected. The exercise of this original right is a very great exertion; nor can it, nor ought it, to be frequently repeated. The principles, therefore, so established, are deemed fundamental: and as the authority from which they proceed is supreme, and can seldom act, they are designed to be permanent.

This original and supreme will organizes the government, and assigns to different departments their respective powers. It may either stop here, or establish certain limits not to be transcended by those departments. The government of the United States is of the latter description. The powers of the legislature are defined and limited; and that those limits may not be mistaken, or forgotten, the constitution is written, To what purpose are powers limited, and to what purpose is that limitation committed to writing, if these limits may, at any time, be passed by those intended to be restrained? The distinction between a government with limited and unlimited powers is abolished, if those limits do not confine the persons on whom they are imposed, and if acts prohibited and acts allowed, are of equal obligation. It is a proposition too plain to be contested, that the constitution controls any legislative and repugnant to it; or that the legislature may alter the constitution by an ordinary act.

Between these alternatives, there is no middle ground. The constitution is either a superior paramount law, unchangeable by ordinary means, or it is on a level with ordinary legislative acts, and, like other acts, is alterable when the legislature shall please to alter it. If the former part of the alternative be true, then a legislative act, contrary to the constitution, is not law; if the latter part be true, then written constitutions are absurd attempts, on the part of the people, to limit a power, in its own nature, illimitable.

Certainly, all those who have framed written constitutions contemplate them as forming the fundamental and paramount law of the nation, and consequently, the theory of every such government must be, that an act of the legislature repugnant to the constitution is void. This theory is essentially attached to a written constitution, and is, consequently, to be considered, by this court, as one of the fundamental principles of our society. It is not, therefore, to be lost sight of, in the further consideration of this subject.

If an act of the legislature, repugnant to the constitution, is void, does it, notwithstanding its invalidity, bind the courts, and oblige them to give it effect? Or, in other words, though it not be law, does it constitute a rule as operative as if it was a law? This would be to overthrow, in fact, what was established in theory; and would seem, at first view, an absurdity too gross to be insisted on. It shall, however, receive a more attentive consideration.

It is, emphatically, the province and duty of the judicial department, to say what the law is. Those who apply the rule to particular cases, must of necessity expound and interpret that rule. If two laws conflict with each other, the courts must decide on the operation of each. So, if a law be in opposition to the constitution; if both the law and the constitution apply to a particular case, so that the court must either decide that case, conformably to the law, disregarding the constitution; or conformably to the constitution, disregarding the law; the court must determine which of these conflicting rules governs the case: this is of the very essence of judicial duty. If then, the courts are to regard the constitution, and the constitution is superior to any ordinary act of the legislature, the constitution, and not such ordinary act, must govern the case to which they both apply.

Those, then, who controvert the principle, that the constitution is to be considered, in court, as a paramount law, are reduced to the necessity of maintaining that courts must close their eyes on the constitution, and see only the law. This doctrine would subvert the very foundation of all written constitutions. It would declare, that if the legislature shall do that which is expressly forbidden, such act, notwithstanding the express prohibition, is in reality effectual. It would be giving to the legislature a practical and real omnipotence, with the same breath which professes to restrict their powers within narrow limits.

The judicial power of the United States is extended to all cases arising under the constitution. Could it be the intention of those who gave this power, to say, that: in using it, the constitution should not be looked into? That a case arising under the constitution should be decided, without examining the instrument under which it arises? This is too extravagant to be maintained. In some cases, then, the constitution must be looked into by the judges. And if they can open it at all, what part of it are they forbidden to read or to obey?

There are many other parts of the constitution which serve to illustrate this subject. It is declared that "no tax or duty shall be laid on articles exported from any state." Suppose, a duty on the export of cotton, of tobacco, or of Hour; and a suit intended to recover it. Ought judgment to be rendered in such a case? Ought the judges to close their eyes on the constitution, and only see the law?

The constitution declares "that no bill of attainder or ex post facto law shall be passed." If, however, such a bill should be passed, and a person should be prosecuted under it; must the court condemn to death those victims whom the constitution endeavors to preserve?

"No person," says the constitution, "shall be convicted of treason, unless on the testimony of two witnesses to the same overt act, or on confession in open court." Here, the language of the constitution is addressed especially to the courts. It prescribes, directly for them, a rule of evidence not to be departed from. If the legislature should change that rule, and declare one witness, or a confession out of court, sufficient for conviction, must the constitutional principle yield to the legislative act?

From these, and many other selections which might be made, it is apparent that the framers of the constitution contemplated that instrument as a rule for the government of courts, as well as of the legislature. Why otherwise does it direct the judges to take an oath to support it? This oath certainly applies, in an especial manner, to their conduct in their official character. How immoral to impose it on them, if they were to be used as the instruments, and the knowing instruments, for violating what they swear to support! . . . Why does a judge swear to discharge his duties agreeably to the constitution of the United States, if that constitution forms no rule for his government? If it is closed upon him, and cannot be inspected by him? If such be the real state of things, this is worse than solemn mockery. To prescribe, or to take the oath, becomes equally a crime.

It is also not entirely unworthy of observation, that in declaring what shall be the supreme law of the land, the constitution itself is first mentioned; and not the laws of the United States, generally, but those only which shall be made in pursuance of the constitution, have that rank.

Thus, the particular phraseology of the constitution of the United States confirms and strengthens the principle, supposed to be essential to all written constitutions, that a law repugnant to the constitution is void; and that courts, as well as other departments, are bound by that instrument.

The rule must be discharged.

"It is by no means clear, that to declare a law void, which has been enacted according to the forms prescribed in the constitution, is not a usurpation of legislative power."

2.3 EAKIN V. RAUB

12 Sargeant & Rawle 330 (Pa. 1825)

Judge John Gibson was a "creative and distinguished jurist" who served on the Pennsylvania Supreme Court for thirty-seven years and nearly obtained a seat on the U.S. Supreme Court. His dissent in *Eakin v. Raub* is not significant because it came in a case of any great moment—indeed, the facts are not particularly important. But even today scholars maintain that it provides one of the finest rebuttals of Marshall's opinion in *Marbury v. Madison.*

GIBSON, J., dissenting.

I am aware, that a right to declare all unconstitutional acts void, without distinction as to either state or federal constitution, is generally held as a professional dogma; but I apprehend, rather as a matter of faith than of reason. It is not a little remarkable, that although the right in question has all along been claimed by the judiciary, no judge has ventured to discuss it, except Chief Justice Marshall; and if the argument of a jurist so distinguished for the strength of his ratiocinative powers be found inconclusive, it may fairly be set down to the weakness of the position which he attempts to defend.

The constitution is said to be a law of superior obligation; and consequently, that if it were to come into collision with an act of the legislature, the latter would have to give way; this is conceded. But it is a fallacy, to suppose, that they can come into collision before the judiciary.

From *Documents of American Constitutional History*, vol. 1, ed. Melvin I. Urofsky, (New York: Knopf, 1989), 183–185.

The constitution and the right of the legislature to pass the act, may be in collision; but is that a legitimate subject for judicial determination? If it be, the judiciary must be a peculiar organ, to revise the proceedings of the legislature, and to correct its mistakes; and in what part of the constitution are we to look for this proud preeminence? It is by no means clear, that to declare a law void, which has been enacted according to the forms prescribed in the constitution, is not a usurpation of legislative power. It is an act of sovereignty; and sovereignty and legislative power are said by Sir William Blackstone to be convertible terms. It is the business of the judiciary, to interpret the laws, not scan the authority of the lawgiver; and without the latter, it cannot take cognizance of a collision between a law and the constitution. So that, to affirm that the judiciary has a right to judge of the existence of such collision, is to take for granted the very thing to be proved.

But it has been said to be emphatically the business of the judiciary, to ascertain and pronounce what the law is; and that this necessarily involves a consideration of the constitution. It does so: but how far? If the judiciary will inquire into anything beside the form of enactment, where shall it stop? There must be some point of limitation to such an inquiry; for no one will pretend, that a judge would be justifiable in calling for the election returns, or scrutinizing the qualifications of those who composed the legislature.

It will not be pretended, that the legislature has not, at least, an equal right with the judiciary to put a construction on the constitution; nor that either of them is infallible; nor that either ought to be required to surrender its judgment to the other. Suppose, then, they differ in opinion as to the constitutionality of a particular law; if the organ whose business it first is to decide on the subject, is not to have its judgment treated with respect, what shall prevent it from securing the preponderance of its opinion by the strong arm of power? The soundness of any construction which would bring one organ of the government into collision with another, is to be more than suspected; for where collision occurs, it is evident, the machine is working in a way the framers of it did not intend.

But the judges are sworn to support the constitution, and are they not bound by it as the law of the land? The oath to support the constitution is not peculiar to the judges, but is taken indiscriminately by every officer of the government, and is designed rather as a test of the political principles of the man, than to bind the officer in the discharge of his duty: otherwise, it was difficult to determine, what operation it is to have in the case of a recorder of deeds, for instance, who, in the execution of his office, has nothing to do with the constitution. But granting it to relate to the official conduct of the judge, as well as every other officer, and not to his political principles, still, it must be understood in reference to supporting the constitution, only as far as that may be involved in his official duty; and consequently, if his official duty does not comprehend an inquiry into the authority of the legislature, neither does his oath.

But do not the judges do a positive act in violation of the constitution, when they give effect to an unconstitutional law? Not if the law has been passed according to the forms established in the constitution. The fallacy of the question is, in supposing that the judiciary adopts the acts of the legislature as its own; whereas, the enactment of a law and the interpretation of it are not concurrent acts, and as the judiciary is not required to concur in the enactment, neither is it in the breach of the constitution which may be the consequence of the enactment; the fault is imputable to the legislature, and on it the responsibility exclusively rests.

> *"Except for short-lived transitional periods when the old alliance is disintegrating and the new one is struggling to take control of political institutions, the Supreme Court is inevitably a part of the dominant national alliance."*

2.4 DECISION MAKING IN A DEMOCRACY: THE SUPREME COURT AS A NATIONAL POLICY MAKER

Robert A. Dahl

Robert A. Dahl is the Sterling Professor of Political Science Emeritus at Yale University.

One influential view of the Court is that it stands in some special way as a protection of minorities against tyranny by majorities. In the course of its 167 years, in seventy-eight cases, the Court has struck down eighty-six different provisions of federal law as unconstitutional, and by interpretation it has modified a good many more. It might be argued, then, that in all or in a very large number of these cases the Court was, in fact, defending the rights of some minority against a "tyrannical" majority. There are, however, some exceedingly serious difficulties with this interpretation of the Court's activities.

One problem, which is essentially ideological in character, is the difficulty of reconciling such an interpretation with the existence of a democratic polity, for it is not at all difficult to show by appeals to authorities as various and imposing as Aristotle, Locke, Rousseau, Jefferson, and Lincoln that the term democracy means, among other things, that the power to rule resides in popular majorities and their representatives. Moreover, from entirely reasonable and traditional definitions of popular sovereignty and political equality, the principle of majority rule can be shown to follow by logical necessity. Thus to affirm that the Court supports minority preferences against majorities is to deny that popular sovereignty and political equality, at least in the traditional sense, exist in the United States; and to affirm that the Court ought to act in this way is to deny that popular sovereignty and political equality ought to prevail in this country.

From 6 *Journal of Public Law* 279 (1958).

Fortunately, however, we do not need to traverse this well-worn ground; for the view of the Court as a protector of the liberties of minorities against the tyranny of majorities is beset with other difficulties that are not so much ideological as matters of fact and logic. If one wishes to be at all rigorous about the question, it is probably impossible to demonstrate that any particular Court decisions have or have not been at odds with the preferences of a "national majority."

In the absence of relatively direct information, we are thrown back to indirect tests. The eighty-six provisions of federal law that have been declared unconstitutional were, of course, initially passed by majorities of those voting in the Senate and in the House. They also had the president's formal approval. We could, therefore, speak of a majority of those voting in the House and Senate, together with the president, as a "lawmaking majority." It is not easy to determine whether any such constellation of forces within the political elites actually coincides with the preferences of a majority of American adults or even with the preferences of a majority of that half of the adult population which, on the average, votes in congressional elections. Such evidence as we have from opinion polls suggests that Congress is not markedly out of line with public opinion, or at any rate with such public opinion as there is after one discards the answers of people who fall into the category, often large, labeled "no response" or "don't know." If we may, on these somewhat uncertain grounds, take a "lawmaking majority" as equivalent to a "national majority," then it is possible to test the hypothesis that the Supreme Court is shield and buckler for minorities against national majorities.

Under any reasonable assumptions about the nature of the political process, it would appear to be somewhat naive to assume that the Supreme Court either would or could play the role of Galahad. Over the whole history of the Court, on the average one new justice has been appointed every twenty-two months. Thus a president can expect to appoint about two new justices during one term of office; and if this were not enough to tip the balance on a normally divided Court, he is almost certain to succeed in two terms. Presidents are not famous for appointing justices hostile to their own views on public policy nor could they expect to secure confirmation of a man whose stance on key questions was flagrantly at odds with that of the dominant majority in the Senate.

The fact is, then, that the policy views dominant on the Court are never for long out of line with the policy views dominant among the lawmaking majorities of the United States. Consequently it would be most unrealistic to suppose that the Court would, for more than a few years at most, stand against any major alternatives sought by a lawmaking majority. The judicial agonies of the New Deal will, of course, quickly come to mind; but Mr. Roosevelt's difficulties with the Court were truly exceptional. Generalizing over the whole history of the Court, the chances are about one out of five that a president will make one appointment to the Court in less than a year, better than one out of two that he will make one within two years, and three out of four that he will make one within three years. Mr. Roosevelt had unusually bad luck: he had to wait four years for his first appointment; the odds against this long an interval are four to one. With average luck, the battle with the Court would never have occurred;

even as it was, although the "court-packing" proposal did formally fail, by the end of his second term, Mr. Roosevelt had appointed five new justices and by 1941 Mr. Justice Roberts was the only remaining holdover from the Hoover era.

It is to be expected, then, that the Court is least likely to be successful in blocking a determined and persistent lawmaking majority on a major policy and most likely to succeed against a "weak" majority; e.g., a dead one, a transient one, a fragile one, or one weakly united upon a policy of subordinate importance.

An examination of the cases in which the Court has held federal legislation unconstitutional confirms, on the whole, our expectations. Over the whole history of the Court, about half the decisions have been rendered more than four years after the legislation was passed.

Of the twenty-four laws held unconstitutional within two years, eleven were measures enacted in the early years of the New Deal. Indeed, New Deal measures comprise nearly a third of all legislation that has ever been declared unconstitutional within four years after enactment.

It is illuminating to examine the cases where the Court has acted on legislation within four years after enactment where the presumption is, that is to say, that lawmaking majority is not necessarily a dead one.

[These] tend to fall into two rather distinct groups: those involving legislation that could reasonably be regarded as important from the point of view of the lawmaking majority and those involving minor legislation. We would expect that cases involving major legislative policy would be propelled to the Court much more rapidly than cases involving minor policy and this is in fact what happens.

Thus a lawmaking majority with major policy objectives in mind usually has an opportunity to seek for ways of overcoming the Court's veto. It is an interesting and highly significant fact that Congress and the president do generally succeed in overcoming a hostile Court on major policy issues.

* * * * *

The role of the Court as a policy-making institution is not simple; and it is an error to suppose that its functions can be either described or appraised by means of simple concepts drawn from democratic or moral theory. It is possible, nonetheless, to derive a few general conclusions about the Court's role as a policy-making institution.

National politics in the United States, as in other stable democracies, is dominated by relatively cohesive alliances that endure for long periods of time. One recalls the Jeffersonian alliance, the Jacksonian, the extraordinarily long-lived Republican dominance of the post–Civil War years, and the New Deal alliance shaped by Franklin Roosevelt. Each is marked by a break with past policies, a period of intense struggle, followed by consolidation, and finally decay and disintegration of the alliance.

Except for short-lived transitional periods when the old alliance is disintegrating and the new one is struggling to take control of political institutions, the Supreme Court is inevitably a part of the dominant national alliance. As an element in the political leadership of the dominant alliance, the Court of course supports the major policies of the alliance. By itself, the Court is almost power-less to affect the course of national policy. In the absence of substantial agree-ment within the alliance, an attempt by the Court to make national policy is likely to lead to disaster, as the early New Deal cases demonstrate. The Supreme Court is not, however, simply an agent of the alliance. It is an essential part of the political leadership and possesses some bases of power of its own, the most important of which is the unique legitimacy attributed to its interpretations of the Constitution. This legitimacy the Court jeopardizes if it flagrantly opposes the major policies of the dominant alliance; such a course of action, as we have seen, is one in which the Court will not normally be tempted to engage.

> *"The Warren Court, by general reputation at least, was quite different from most of its predecessors. Indeed, one associates with it precisely the characteristics that Dahl found lacking in the Supreme Court's activism and influence in national policy and protection of fundamental rights of minorities against tyrannical or indifferent majorities."*

2.5 THE SUPREME COURT AND NATIONAL POLICY MAKING

Jonathan D. Casper

Jonathan D. Casper was Professor of Political Science at Northwestern University.

Dahl's article was published in 1957, appearing at the end of a decade that had seen one of our periodic episodes of national political repression. Fear of internal subversion by Communists and fellow-travelers had produced not only intense public concern but a variety of federal and state programs aimed at control of the thought, expression and behavior of allegedly subversive elements in our soci-ety. The rulings of the Supreme Court in this period did not mark it as a bastion of individual rights standing against a fearful and repressive national majority. The Court vacillated on the civil liberties issues raised by the loyalty-security programs and generally placed the imprimatur of legitimacy upon a variety of constitutionally questionable governmental activities (e.g., prosecutions under the Smith Act, employee loyalty-security screening programs, legislative investi-gations). In this particularly salient issue area, then, the Supreme Court did fol-low the deferential path suggested by Dahl's analysis.

Since then, we have witnessed the work of the Warren Court and are cur-rently in the midst of the emergence of the Burger court. The Warren Court, by general reputation at least, was quite different from most of its predecessors.

From 70 *American Political Science Review* 50 (1976).

Indeed, one associates with it precisely the characteristics that Dahl found lacking in the Supreme Court's activism and influence in national policy and protection of fundamental rights of minorities against tyrannical or indifferent majorities. The first step, then, in examining Dahl's thesis is to look at what has happened since he wrote. Do events since that date suggest the possibility of a different pattern of Supreme Court participation in policy making?

During this period, the Supreme Court declared thirty-two provisions of federal law unconstitutional in twenty-eight cases. In the entire previous 167 year period, eighty-six provisions had been declared unconstitutional in seventy-eight cases. Putting the two sets together, we note that more than a quarter of all cases involving a declaration of unconstitutionality (28 of 106) have occurred since 1957. In terms of frequency, the Supreme Court proved more active in recent years than it typically had been in the past.

The Evidence Excluded

Dahl limits his consideration to cases in which the Court held federal legislation unconstitutional. Yet cases involving tests of constitutionality of federal legislation compose only one segment of the work of the Court. Two other types of activities also stand out as particular important arenas in which the Court contributes to national policy making. The first deals with statutory construction and the second with federal constitutional issues arising out of state and local legislation or practice.

Statutory Construction

The Court is frequently called upon to interpret the meaning of federal statutes, and in the course of doing so, important policy choices must be made. If we adopt for the moment the notion that influence in policy making is most accurately judged in situations in which various participants conflict with one another, it is clear that the interpretations that are made by the Court—even when they are based on "legislative intent"—are often quite different from those that members of Congress and the President had in mind when the legislation was passed. The Court's doctrine that it will, if at all possible, interpret a statute in such a way as to "save" it from being declared unconstitutional means that the Court will often significantly twist and change the ostensible provisions of a statute. Thus, in interpreting statutes the Court often makes important policy choices, and these choices are at least arguably quite contrary to the preferences of the lawmaking majority that passed the legislation. The more influence the Court exercises by virtue of statutory construction, the less influence it will appear to have in terms of Dahl's coding rules. When the Court "saves" a law by interpreting it rather than declaring it unconstitutional, its contribution to the course of public policy is excluded from consideration under Dahl's rules.

Pennsylvania v. Nelson [1956] illustrates the use of statutory construction technique in rather stark detail. The case involved a prosecution under a "little Smith Act," a state statute modeled after the federal Smith Act that punished those who advocated the violent overthrow of the government of the United

States or of Pennsylvania. The Supreme Court struck down the statute, holding that federal legislation dealing with such subversive activity (particularly the Smith Act of 1940) so occupied the field that Congress had left no room for state activity and that problems of possible conflict between federal and state prosecutions required that the supremacy clause be invoked. Forty-three other states as well as Alaska and Hawaii had similar laws, so that the decision had an impact throughout the country.

The State and Local Cases

The second major area of the Court's work that is excluded from Dahl's analysis involves constitutional issues arising in cases involving state and local statutes or practice. As suggested above, this exclusion is justified on the grounds that we lack evidence about the preferences of the lawmaking majority in such cases and that these cases have not been typically cited by defenders of the Court as the basis of their view that the Court plays a significant role in national policy making. Although there are, to be sure, difficulties in establishing the preferences of the national majority in these cases, a review of them suggests that many do indeed involve the Court in important issues of national policy.

In the religion cases, especially the Engel and Schempp decisions, the Court set forth a policy toward devotional exercises in public schools that affected all schools, not just those in particular localities. Though the decisions were by no means greeted with total compliance, they have not been reversed and still stand as national policy. By the same token, a string of decisions dealing with aid to parochial schools has restricted the nature and types of aid that states and the federal government have been permitted to offer. Though the decisions have not cut off such aid, they have shaped these programs in ways that run contrary to the directions that they would have gone without such intervention.

In the area of race relations, the Supreme Court played a vital role in the development of national policy. Its decisions in the 1950s and 1960s placed a stamp of legitimacy upon claims for equality on the part of black citizens that was crucial to the development of organizations and activities that eventually succeeded not only in the streets but in the Congress as well. Though a solid consensus against de jure segregation did subsequently emerge, the Court played a crucial role in this process rather than merely reflecting developments in other political arenas.

This brief review of some of the Court's work in the area of state and local statutes and practice suggests several issues relevant to Dahl's analysis. First and most important, the policy questions at stake in these cases are not narrow, local or regional issues. In all of these areas the policy promulgated by the Court, although emerging in the context of cases arising out of states or localities, was directly aimed at and had an effect upon governmental activities throughout the nation. Yet the policies that were enunciated had relevance to the whole nation in ways much more manifest than many of the cases involving federal legislation with which Dahl deals.

Did the Court prevail? Was it reversed by a subsequent act of the lawmaking majority? Did the Court itself take back what it had said? In some areas, these questions are difficult to answer at this time, for a few of the decisions are recent.

In terms of one crude indicator, the Court has not been substantially reversed in any of these areas by the passage of legislation or constitutional amendment. In some areas, though, the pattern Dahl suggests does seem apposite: unpopular decisions became part of the country's political agenda, and changes in political regimes affected recruitment to the Court. The replacement of the Warren Court by the Burger Court is to some extent verification of his thesis.

So the thrust of this argument is not that new evidence unambiguously indicates a role for the Court that is radically different from the one that Dahl suggests. The Court is a member of ruling alliances and does respond to others. But examination of the state and local cases does reveal that the arena in which the Court makes policy is substantially broader than the limited area Dahl selects for discussion. Moreover, it suggests that the Court can and does get its way a good deal more frequently than his analysis implies.

In sum, there are difficulties with the evidence that Dahl gathers and the ways in which he utilizes it. He also excludes from consideration a large body of evidence that seems highly relevant to determining the Court's role in national policy making. Consideration of this evidence indicates a substantially more influential role that Dahl's argument admits.

NOTES

1. Historical accounts differ, but it seems that Jefferson decreased the number of Adams's appointments to justice of the peace positions to thirty from forty-two. Twenty-five of the thirty appointees received their commissions, but five—including William Marbury—did not. See Francis N. Stites, John Marshall (Boston: Little, Brown, 1981), 84.
2. Quoted in Charles Warren, *The Supreme Court in United States History*, vol. 1 (Boston: Little, Brown, 1922), 244.

PART TWO

The American Legal System

CHAPTER 3

Judicial Organization

The task of judging in the United States is performed under organizational arrangements more complex and confusing than those encountered in most other countries. There are, first of all, two complete systems of courts—federal and state—with all the attendant problems of defining their respective jurisdictions. Then there are fifty separate state systems, which with few exceptions are based on models and assumptions dating from the eighteenth century or earlier. Each of these systems comprises various levels of tribunals arrayed in hierarchical structures that provide channels of communication among courts and that ensure a measure, but only a measure, of control by higher over lower courts.

ESTABLISHING THE AMERICAN LEGAL SYSTEM

The federal legal system is built on a foundation created by two major statements of the 1780s: Article III of the constitutional document and the Judiciary Act of 1789. Both pertained most directly to the establishment of the federal judiciary, but state courts also felt their effect.

Article III

While the Framers of the Constitution spent a considerable amount of time debating the contents of Article I (dealing with the legislature) and Article II (centering on the executive), they had comparatively little trouble drafting Article III. A primary reason is that both the American states and Great Britain had long-entrenched judicial systems, and the Founders had firsthand knowledge about the workings of these courts—knowledge they lacked about the new kinds of political institutions, Congress and the presidency, that they were creating.

The Framers did not, however, see eye-to-eye on all the specifics. They agreed that there would be at least one federal court, the Supreme Court of the United States, but they disagreed about what kinds, if any, of inferior federal tribunals to establish. The Virginia Plan, which served as the basis for many of the proposals debated at the Convention, suggested that Congress should establish lower federal courts. Delegates who favored a strong national government agreed with this plan, with some wanting to use Article III to create such courts.

On the other hand, delegates who wanted to restrict the new national government vehemently objected to the creation of federal tribunals other than the Supreme Court. As one delegate put it, "The people will not hear of such an innovation. The states will revolt at such encroachments."[1] Instead, these delegates proposed that state courts should, in the first instance, hear cases involving federal law, with appeal allowed to the U.S. Supreme Court. This debate led to a compromise: Article III of the Constitution creates one supreme court, but it does not mention state courts. Nor does it establish lower federal tribunals; rather, it gives Congress the authority to do so. The First Congress (with its Federalist majority) took advantage of Article III by immediately passing the Judiciary Act of 1789, which established lower federal courts. That Congress would take such an action is not surprising: the majority of the Founders anticipated the law because much of Article III—specifically Section 2, the longest part—defines the jurisdiction of these federal courts that might be created. By spelling out this jurisdiction, the Framers provided that Congress could give these courts authority to hear cases according to subject matter: the U.S. Constitution or federal laws or treaties; ambassadors, public ministers (in the eighteenth century, that phrase referred to lesser diplomatic officials), or consuls; and admiralty and maritime law. Article III also specified jurisdiction by party to the litigation:

> Controversies to which the United States shall be a Party;—to Controversies between two or more States;—between a State and Citizens of another State;[2]—between Citizens of different States;—between citizens of the same State claiming Lands under Grants of different States, and between a State, or the Citizens thereof, and foreign States, Citizens, or Subjects.

The Framers also defined the authority of the U.S. Supreme Court, the one judicial body they did create, in terms of original jurisdiction—that is, cases that may begin in the Court and appellate cases, those cases involving other federal issues that begin in another court but may be appealed to the Supreme Court. "In all Cases," Article III says, "affecting Ambassadors, other public Ministers and consult, and those in which a State shall be a party, the supreme Court shall have original Jurisdiction." Article III then adds: "In all the other Cases before mentioned, the supreme Court shall have appellate jurisdiction, both as to Law and Fact, with such Exceptions, and under such Regulations as the Congress shall make."

---

[1] Quoted in Daniel A. Farber and Suzanna Sherry, *A History of the American Constitution*. (St. Paul, MN: West, 1990).

[2] The Eleventh Amendment, ratified in 1795, removed federal jurisdiction over cases in which citizens of one state sued another state. A century later, the Supreme Court ruled in *Hans v. Louisiana* (1890) that the framers and ratifiers of the Eleventh Amendment had been guilty of an error of omission, which the Court would repair. They had also meant to exclude from federal jurisdiction suits brought by citizens of one state against their own state.

A second area of contention at the Convention concerned the manner of choosing federal judges. Again, the Virginia Plan's proposal that Congress select these judges served as the focus of debate. Some delegates wanted the language of Article III to reflect the Virginia Plan, while others wanted appointments left to the Senate. Benjamin Franklin facetiously suggested that lawyers should decide who should sit on the courts: after all, he chuckled, attorneys would select "the ablest of the profession in order to get rid of them, and share their clients among themselves."[3] Finally, the delegates decided that the appointment power should be given to the president, with the "advice and consent" of the Senate. Accordingly, the power to appoint federal judges is located in Article II rather than Article I or III, a placement that has not prevented the Senate from playing a significant role in the process: since 1789, it has read "advice and consent" to mean that it must approve presidential nominees by a majority vote. And it has taken that role quite seriously, voting against 12 of the 148 candidates for the U.S. Supreme Court over the past two centuries—a greater number (proportionately speaking) than against any other federal officers requiring senatorial approval (see Chapter 4).[4]

The Judiciary Act of 1789

Federalism does not require that each of the two levels of government have a complete judicial system. In fact, Australia, Canada, and Germany, all of which are federations, have a complete set of state or provincial courts, topped by a single federal supreme court, sometimes with the addition of one or more specialized federal tribunals. Article III made possible a similar arrangement. Thus, few actions of the First Congress were more portentous for the development of American federalism than its decision in the Judiciary Act of 1789 to set up a complete system of lower federal courts that would interpret and apply many aspects of federal law. That Act is long and complex. At its core were two purposes. First, it sought to structure a federal system of courts by fleshing out the provisions of Article III by establishing a Supreme Court, circuit courts, and district courts. The Supreme Court was to have a chief justice and five associate justices. That the Court initially had only six members illustrates an important point: Congress, not the constitutional document or the Court itself, determines the number of justices. It has been fixed at nine since 1869, though it has varied from six to five (to prevent Thomas Jefferson from filling a vacancy), back to six (to allow him a nomination), to seven and then to nine (to accommodate political interests in the West), to eleven (to allow Abraham Lincoln to put loyal Union men on the bench during the Civil War), and then back to nine again (to prevent Andrew Johnson from making any nominations).

---

[3] Quoted in Farber and Sherry, *A History of the American Constitution*, 55.

[4] Seven others were withdrawn or postponed and never made it on to the Court.

The Act of 1789 also created thirteen district courts. Each of the eleven states that had ratified the Constitution received a court, with separate tribunals created for Maine and Kentucky, which were then parts of Massachusetts and Virginia, respectively. District courts, then as now, were presided over by one judge and were grouped geographically into "circuits," eastern, middle, and southern, staffed by a district judge and two justices of the Supreme Court, who "rode circuit," that is, went around the circuit, usually on horseback or in a buggy, hearing cases.

A second goal of the Judiciary Act was to specify the jurisdictions of the various federal courts. As noted above, Section 2 of Article III speaks broadly about the federal judiciary, authorizing it to hear and decide cases involving particular parties or subjects or, in the case of the Supreme Court, original and appellate jurisdiction. The Judiciary Act provided more specific information, defining the parameters of authority for each of the newly established tribunals and for the U.S. Supreme Court. The district courts were to serve as minor trial courts, hearing cases involving admiralty issues, forfeitures and penalties, petty federal crimes, and minor U.S. civil cases. The circuit courts were also trial courts, with jurisdiction over more important federal civil and criminal matters as well as over cases between citizens of different states. Congress also gave these circuit tribunals limited appellate authority to hear civil and admiralty disputes initially decided by district courts.

What the Act did not do was grant the district and circuit courts the full jurisdiction authorized by Section 2 of Article III of the constitutional text. Congress conferred jurisdiction under three principal heads: admiralty, civil controversies within the "party" categories of Article III, and crimes and offenses against the United States. But jurisdiction of practically all other important "federal" cases (that is, cases in law and equity arising under the Constitution, laws, and treaties of the United States) was left in the first instance to state courts, with the Supreme Court having appellate jurisdiction.

Finally, the Act of 1789 contained several important provisions concerning the jurisdiction of the U.S. Supreme Court. Section 13 said: "The Supreme Court shall also have appellate jurisdiction from the circuit courts and courts of the several states, in the cases herein specifically provided for. . . ." That section also spoke of the Court's authority to issue writs of mandamus, "in cases warranted by the principles and usages of law, to any courts appointed, or persons holding office, under the authority of the United States." (A mandamus is a command to a public official to carry out a particular nondiscretionary act or duty.) This provision might seem trivial, but the Court's interpretation—perhaps misinterpretation of Section 13 as applying to its original, instead of appellate, jurisdiction—formed the centerpiece of *Marbury v. Madison* (Reading 2.2).

Another part of the act, Section 25, expanded the Court's appellate authority under Article III, enabling it, as noted above, to review certain kinds of cases coming out of the states (Reading 3.1). The Supreme Court could hear appeals from the highest state courts if those tribunals upheld a state law against claims that the law violated the Constitution or denied some claim based on the U.S. Constitution, federal laws, or treaties.

Judicial Federalism

At first glance, the components of the Act of 1789—its establishment of a federal judicial system and of rules for that system—appear to favor the Federalists' position. Recall that states rights' delegates at the Constitutional Convention did not want the document to even mention lower federal tribunals, much less give Congress the authority to establish them. In some respects, the Act of 1789 goes beyond the Federalists' arguments at Philadelphia: it authorizes the Supreme Court to review decisions of state supreme courts regarding federal matters. This sort of direct supervisory role over states was among Anti-Federalists' worst nightmares. But it would be a mistake to believe that the Act rejected all the claims of advocates of states' rights. To the contrary, in some important ways it contributed to the development of America's system of judicial federalism: the existence, side by side, of two complete systems of courts. For example, the Act of 1789 used state lines as territorial boundaries for district and circuit courts. That Congress tied the boundaries to the states might have been a concession to the Anti-Federalists who wanted federal judges to have experience in the legal and political culture of a particular state. The practice of choosing district judges from the state, and circuit judges from the region in which they will sit, forms one of the bases of the rule of "senatorial courtesy," which gives a senator of the same political party as the president almost a veto over important appointments in his or her state and further ties district, and even circuit, judges to localities. And senatorial courtesy is itself a by-product of federalism.

Moreover, as we just mentioned, congressional opponents of a separate federal judicial system were successful in limiting the Act's grant of jurisdiction to the tribunals it created. Coupled with the facts that the jurisdiction granted to the federal courts was concurrently exercised by state courts and that federal courts were few in number, this limitation nearly guaranteed continued use of state tribunals even for lawsuits over which federal courts had jurisdiction. The situation did not change until 1875 when Congress conferred on federal courts the full jurisdiction it had withheld in 1789. Then victors in the Civil War no longer trusted state judges, especially in the old Confederacy, to exercise federal powers. Under the Act of 1875 any suit asserting a right under the Constitution, laws, or treaties of the United States could be begun in a federal court, and any such action begun in a state court could be removed to a federal court.

Finally, in spite of Section 25 of the Judiciary Act of 1789, the Supreme Court's review of state judicial decisions met strong opposition until the Civil War. Between 1789 and 1860 the courts of seven states denied the Supreme Court's authority to review decisions of state courts, and the legislatures of eight states adopted resolutions or statutes against this power. Between 1821 and 1882, bills were introduced in ten sessions of Congress to deprive the Court of this jurisdiction. The broadest basis for these attacks was the constitutional theory of the Kentucky Resolutions of 1798, drafted by Jefferson, that each state had authority, equal to that of the federal government, to abide by its own interpretation of the Constitution. (The Virginia Resolutions of the same year, drafted by Madison, made a similar though less bold argument for state authority in constitutional interpretation.) The Supreme Court, however, in two classic cases coming from the highest court of Virginia—*Martin v. Hunter's Lessee* (1816) and *Cohens v. Virginia* (1821)—flatly rejected these contentions.

The Kentucky Resolutions also claimed for each state the authority to nullify any federal act that it believed had encroached on its own authority. Such a claim was implicit in much of the opposition to the Court's reviewing state decisions and in some conflicts was quite explicit. Understandably, the Supreme Court has always given very short constitutional shrift to such arguments. Even Roger Brooke Taney, probably the most ardent states' righter among chief justices before William H. Rehnquist, denounced efforts by state judges in Wisconsin to nullify the Fugitive Slave Act and defy the Supreme Court. For a unanimous Court in *Ableman v. Booth* (1859) Taney wrote: "The sphere of action appropriate to the United States is as far beyond the reach of the judicial process issued by a State judge or a State court, as if the line of division was traced by landmarks and monuments visible to the eye."

A century later, Arkansas tried to nullify the effects of the School Segregation cases. The justices responded in *Cooper v. Aaron* (1958) by publishing an opinion signed by each member of the Court (usually one justice speaks for the Court or for the majority of the justices if they are not unanimous) saying that "the federal judiciary is supreme in the exposition of the law of the Constitution" and that no state official can disobey a federal constitutional ruling "without violating his undertaking to support" that Constitution. (The Court limited its condemnation to state officials who rejected federal judicial rulings, for, as we shall see in Chapter 8, some presidents, including Thomas Jefferson, Andrew Jackson, and Abraham Lincoln, have asserted equal and independent authority in constitutional interpretation (Readings 8.4, 8.5, 8.6, 8.7).

While the Court continues to cling to this basic premise, it has taken a new look at the roles of state judges in American society. This look has led it to chip away at some of the traditional mechanisms for federal supervision of states and their courts, as well as to reinforce the doctrine of comity, a principle associated with federalism. We have much more to say about these important developments later in this chapter, for they have helped revitalize state courts in American society. Although contemporary scholars debate the wisdom of this trend, at least some of the delegates to the Constitutional Convention would have been quite pleased.

TODAY'S SYSTEM OF FEDERAL COURTS

Whichever side won or lost, it is true that passage of the Judiciary Act of 1789 was a defining moment in American legal history. It established the first system of federal courts, one that is not altogether different from that of today. As Figure 3.1 shows, the U.S. Supreme Court still sits at the apex of the system, hearing cases from both federal and state courts. But, via various acts of Congress, the federal ladder has changed: it is now a true three-tiered structure. District courts serve as arenas of first instance for almost all cases, courts of

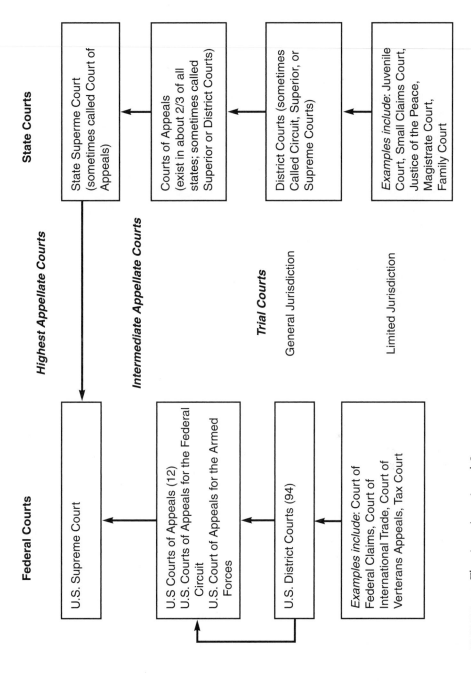

State Courts

Highest Appellate Courts

State Supreme Court (sometimes called Court of Appeals)

Intermediate Appellate Courts

Courts of Appeals (exist in about 2/3 of all states; sometimes called Superior or District Courts)

Trial Courts

General Jurisdiction

District Courts (sometimes Called Circuit, Superior, or Supreme Courts)

Limited Jurisdiction

Examples include: Juvenile Court, Small Claims Court, Justice of the Peace, Magistrate Court, Family Court

Federal Courts

U.S. Supreme Court

U.S Courts of Appeals (12)
U.S. Courts of Appeals for the Federal Circuit
U.S. Court of Appeals for the Armed Forces

U.S. District Courts (94)

Examples include: Court of Federal Claims, Court of International Trade, Court of Verterans Appeals, Tax Court

FIGURE 3.1 The American Legal System

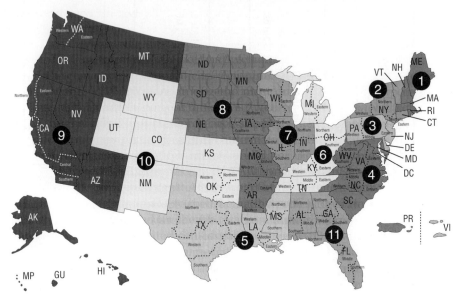

Geographic Boundaries
of United States Courts of Appeals and United States District Courts

FIGURE 3.2 Map of Geographical Boundaries of Federal Circuits and District Courts.

appeals as intermediate appellate bodies—unlike the old circuit courts, these tribunals have their own judges—and with many features typical of bureaucratic organizations (Reading 3.2).

The district courts, one or more of which is located in every state, are the trial courts of the federal system—and its real workhorses (Readings 3.3 and 3.4). These days, the nation's ninety-four district courts process nearly 260,000 civil and 60,000 criminal cases each year.[5] Initially, as we mentioned, there were also federal circuit courts that were trial courts for some classes of cases, but they were finally abolished by statute in 1911. Appeals from the decisions of the district courts go to the courts of appeals, created by Congress in 1891 and known until 1948 as circuit courts of appeals. For judicial purposes the country is divided into eleven numbered circuits; a twelfth court of appeals sits in the District of Columbia (see Figure 3.2). Six to twenty-eight judges staff each circuit. Usually the judges sit in panels of three to hear cases, though for exceptionally important matters they may sit en banc, that is, all together.

Each year litigants file approximately 60,000 cases in the courts of appeals, mostly appeals, asking for review of district courts' decisions. But the character of the judicial business varies from circuit to circuit. The Second Circuit, sitting in New York, is known as the nation's "commercial court" because so much

---

[5] Data on the business of the federal courts are available on the World Wide Web at www.uscourts.gov.

corporate litigation comes to that court for review. For obvious reasons, litigation involving the federal government is heavily concentrated in the Court of Appeals for the District of Columbia Circuit. Until 1981 the Court of Appeals for the Fifth Circuit, based in New Orleans, covered the six states of the Old South and had the most judges and the heaviest caseload of all the circuits. This court along with the Fourth Circuit (Maryland, Virginia, West Virginia, North and South Carolina) had primary responsibility for supervising Southern district judges who were carrying out (or resisting) the Supreme Court's rulings against racial segregation. In 1978, Congress created new judgeships and brought the Fifth Circuit up to twenty-six judges. There had long been pressure, primarily from conservative quarters, to split the Fifth, and it finally succeeded in 1981. Congress redrew the lines of several circuits: Texas, Louisiana, and Mississippi remained in the Fifth, while Georgia, Florida, and Alabama formed a new Eleventh Circuit, headquartered in Atlanta. Discussions of a split of the current Ninth Circuit, covering states in the western part of the country and several territories, are under way. That court, too, is heavily overburdened, with its twenty-eight judges terminating over 11,000 appeals per year or about 2,000 more than the Fifth Circuit, the nation's second busiest.

As J. Woodford Howard, Jr., points out (Reading 3.5), decisions of the courts of appeals make national law in the great majority of cases because less than 1 percent of their decisions are successfully appealed. One factor affecting whether the Supreme Court will grant review is whether two or more courts of appeals have arrived at conflicting interpretations of law. Another factor, of course, is the justices' disagreement with the result reached below. Consequently, it is not surprising that the Supreme Court reverses the courts of appeals in the majority of the cases it accepts and decides.

In certain situations federal statutes have provided for three-judge district courts, typically composed of two circuit judges and one district judge. First authorized in 1903 to try cases arising under the Sherman Antitrust Act, they were subsequently required for other types of proceedings—such as challenges to the constitutionality of state and federal statutes—in which Congress was reluctant to have decisions made by a single judge. There was a right of appeal from a three-judge court directly to the Supreme Court. Staffing these tribunals drained judicial resources, and the right of direct appeal burdened the Supreme Court. As civil rights litigation increased, so did the number of three-judge courts, reaching a peak of 321 in 1973. A sustained effort to reduce this requirement succeeded in 1976, when Congress eliminated the obligation to set up such courts in all cases except those involving reapportionment and a few civil rights claims. Now such courts resolve only about twenty suits per year.

There are also several specialized tribunals in the federal system, including bankruptcy courts, the Court of International Trade, the Court of Military Appeals, the U.S. Court of Veteran Appeals, the Court of Federal Claims, and the Tax Court. The latter four are not actually in the judicial branch but are so-called "Article I" courts created by Congress to help carry out legislative tasks rather than perform the judicial tasks described in Article III of the constitutional text. The Tax Court, for example, hears protests against decisions of the

Internal Revenue Service. Finally there is the Court of Appeals for the Federal Circuit, which hears appeals from district courts in cases involving patents and minor claims against the government, as well as from several specialized federal tribunals, including the Court of Federal Claims and the Court of International Trade. This tribunal, which sits in Washington, D.C., has twelve members who have life terms.

The U.S. Supreme Court

At the apex of the federal hierarchy is the Supreme Court, headed by the Chief Justice of the United States. The office of chief justice, strangely enough, is not mentioned in Article III but is assumed to exist by Article I, Section 3, which provides that the chief justice shall preside over impeachment proceedings in the Senate when the president is on trial.

For a half century the office was designated only as Chief Justice of the Supreme Court, but in the Civil War period Salmon P. Chase successfully claimed the more grandiloquent title of Chief Justice of the United States. The responsibilities of the office are in fact much wider than simply being presiding officer and manager of the Court's affairs. The chief is a ceremonial figure and third-ranking government official after the president and vice president. He or she is concerned with the organization and operation of the entire judicial establishment, which he or she undertakes to represent before Congress, the bar, and the public generally. "I am the head of the judicial branch of government," Chief Justice William Howard Taft claimed in 1922—an exaggeration, surely, but not a far-fetched assertion.

The Supreme Court is primarily an appellate court, but the constitutional text does define two categories of cases that can be heard under the justices' original jurisdiction: those in which a state is a party and those affecting ambassadors, public ministers, and consuls. Generally, however, the Court does not accept a suit invoking its original jurisdiction unless the justices believe there is a compelling reason of public policy. All the remaining business of the Supreme Court comes to it through its appellate jurisdiction, which it exercises, as we have already seen, "with such Exceptions, and under such Regulations as the Congress shall make." In the post–Civil War period, Congress used this authority to prevent the justices from deciding a politically embarrassing case in which the Court had already heard argument. In *Ex parte McCardle* (1869), the Supreme Court agreed that such action was within congressional authority, though *McCardle's* circumstances were so exceptional as to make it hazardous to generalize from this single ruling (Reading 8.8).

To invoke the Court's appellate jurisdiction, litigants can take one of three routes, depending on the nature of their dispute: appeal as a matter of right, certification, or certiorari. Cases falling into the first category (normally called "on appeal") concern issues that Congress has determined are so important that a ruling by the Supreme Court is necessary. Before 1988, these included cases in which a lower court declared a state or a federal law unconstitutional or in which a state court upheld a state statute challenged as being in violation of the U.S. Constitution. Although the justices were supposedly obliged by statute to decide such appeals, they dismissed most of them, particularly those from state courts sustaining the constitutionality of state statutes, offering only the Delphic explanation "Dismissed for want of a substantial federal question." Finally, in 1988, at the Court's urging, Congress virtually eliminated "mandatory" appeals. Today the Court is legally obliged to hear only those few cases (typically involving the Voting Rights Act) appealed from special three-judge district courts. When the Court agrees to hear such cases, it issues an order, noting "probable jurisdiction."

A second, rarely used, route to the Court is certification. Any one of the U.S. courts of appeals can file a writ of certification, asking the justices to respond to questions aimed at clarifying federal law. Because only judges may use this route, very few cases come to the Court this way. Moreover, the justices are not obliged to accept a question certified to them.

The third and most common path of review is a request for a writ of certiorari (from the Latin, "to be made more certain" or "to be informed"). In a petition for a writ of certiorari, the losing litigant in a United States court of appeals, one of the special federal courts, or the highest court of a state (if a question of federal treaty, statutory, or constitutional law is involved) asks the Court to become "informed" about their cases by requesting the lower court to send up the record. If four justices, one less than a majority, vote affirmatively, the Court accepts the case, and it is placed on the calendar for argument.

The Court receives more than 8,000 petitions each year and denies or dismisses about 99 percent of them.[6] Denial of certiorari does not necessarily mean that the Court agrees with the decision below; it simply means that, for whatever reasons, four justices did not find that the case merited the Court's scarcest resource, time. In general, the Court accepts only cases that present substantial issues of law or policy. On some occasions, however, the Court has refused to review decisions raising issues of major importance, usually because the justices felt it would be imprudent for them to become involved at that particular juncture. (Chapters 7 and 13 discuss the Court's decision-making procedures, particularly the handling of certiorari petitions.)

---

[6] To a certain extent the statistics on the Court's burgeoning caseload are misleading, because by far the largest increase is in *in forma pauperis* petitions—those filed without payment of the customary fees. These petitions are typically written by prison inmates seeking review of their convictions. The Court reviews these requests in the same way as it reviews paid petitions. Sometimes they provide the occasion for dramatic decisions. *Gideon v. Wainwright* (1963)—the case that held that all persons accused of felonies have a right to be represented by counsel and that a state must provide free counsel if the defendant cannot hire his own attorney—reached the Supreme Court in the form of a petition printed in pencil by Clarence Gideon while in the Florida penitentiary. Seldom, however, do petitions *in forma pauperis* present valid claims—or at least the justices do not seem to think that they do. In recent years, they have agreed to hear less than a half dozen or so of the nearly 7,000 they received.

Reforming the Federal Courts: The Caseload "Problem"

The Supreme Court's caseload has grown substantially over time. In John Marshall's first term as chief justice, the Court delivered only five opinions; in 1814 that number rose to forty-six, a pitiful handful by today's standards. By 1853, the number of cases docketed had risen to 253, still small compared to the current docket of more than 8,000. So, too, the workloads of lower federal courts have grown.[7] In the 1820s, about 3,500 cases were pending in the nation's circuit and district courts. In 2003 alone, litigants filed more than 328,000 cases in the U.S. district courts and more than 60,000 in the courts of appeals.

This growth, which began in earnest in the 1870s, was the product of many factors, including the expansion of economic life in the aftermath of the Civil War and congressional legislation (particularly the Act of 1875), which, in an effort to protect national power against unrepentant Confederates, extended the jurisdiction of federal tribunals into matters previously left to state courts.[8] That it continued well into the twentieth century is a function both of additional congressional legislation expanding the jurisdiction of federal courts in crime-related areas (especially those involving drugs) and of decisions of the Supreme Court itself—particularly those pertaining to the rights of defendants in criminal cases.

Whatever the causes, the problem of burgeoning dockets has been serious. Federal jurists have frequently expressed concern and even occasionally issued pleas for help. Chief Justice Morrison R. Waite was among the first to call attention to the problem. In a speech delivered in 1887, he sought to convince the public of the need for congressional action to relieve the justices' workload. Virtually all Waite's successors have registered similar complaints—including the current chief justice, William H. Rehnquist. In remarks before the American Law Institute, the chief analyzed, in some detail, the effect that two bills pending in Congress would have on the work of federal judges.

Not all of these cries have fallen on deaf ears. Over the years, Congress has enacted legislation eliminating virtually all the Supreme Court's nondiscretionary jurisdiction. It has also curbed access to federal courts by placing restrictions on the ability of state prisoners to bring appeals of their convictions into federal arenas (see below). Finally, it has created new courts of appeals and new judgeships, though at least the latter may have been aimed more at providing presidents with opportunities to pack the federal bench than at easing caseloads. Scholars and jurists alike disagree about the costs and the benefits of increasing the number of judgeships as a solution to "judicial gridlock" (Reading 3.6).

But Congress has not taken more radical courses of action for which some observers have called. For example, it has not seriously limited Article III's

---

[7] The nineteenth-century data in this paragraph are from Felix Frankfurter and James M. Landis, *The Business of the Supreme Court* (New York: Macmillan, 1928).

[8] Under this act any suit asserting a right under the Constitution, laws, or treaties of the United States can begin in federal courts, and any such action started in state courts can be removed by the defendant to the federal courts for disposition.

allowing of suits between citizens of different states (commonly called "diversity" suits) to be heard in federal courts. The original purpose of opening federal courts to such parties was to provide a neutral forum, because state courts might be biased in favor of their own citizens and against "strangers" from other states. Today there is less likelihood of such bias, and there is considerable opposition to diversity jurisdiction on the ground that it clogs federal courts with a tremendous number of cases growing out of essentially local issues that federal judges must decide according to state law. More than one out of every five private civil cases filed in the federal district courts involve diversity of citizenship. Nor has Congress enacted most of the proposals aimed specifically at reducing the Supreme Court's caseload, such as the creation of a tribunal that would resolve conflicting rulings among the circuits and also screen appeals, passing perhaps four hundred of the most important cases on to the Supreme Court.[9]

With none of these sorts of proposals attracting sufficient support, U.S. judges may have taken matters into their own hands: the nation's circuit courts now publish only about 20 percent of their opinions; the other 80 percent are unpublished decisions, memoranda, or orders that are "erratically distributed and rarely precedential."[10] Why they now so rarely publish their opinions is hardly a mystery. The judges themselves maintain that this approach is necessary if they are able to keep up with their workload.[11]

The justices of the U.S. Supreme Court have taken a different tack. Although the number of cases arriving at the Court has not dropped substantially, the number of those that it is deciding has fallen markedly from 141 in the 1973–1974 term to just 84 three decades later in the 2003–2004 term. Whether this decline reflects the pressures of work or other factors is an interesting question and one about which law professor Arthur D. Hellman speculates.[12] He finds that the decrease has come about because recent appointees to the Court advocate a position different from their predecessors about the roles the Court should play in the American legal system. In Hellman's words, the new justices "are less concerned about rectifying isolated errors in the lower courts, and they believe that a relatively small number of nationally binding precedents is sufficient to provide doctrinal guidance for the resolution of recurring issues."

Is this a positive development? Hellman suggests that many members of the legal community see it that way:

> They share the concern of Justice [Ruth Bader] Ginsburg that centralization of judicial authority tends to carry the "'imperial' judiciary to its logical limits." In

---

[9] See Federal Judicial Center, *Report of the Study Group on the Caseload of the Supreme Court* (Washington, DC: Administrative Office of U.S. Courts, 1972).

[10] Deborah Jones Merritt and James J. Brudney, "Stalking Secret Law: What Predicts Publication in the United States Courts of Appeals," 54 *Vanderbilt Law Review* 71 (2001).

[11] See Judge Boyce F. Martin, Jr., "In Defense of Unpublished Opinions," 60 *Ohio State Law Journal* 177 (1999).

[12] Arthur D. Hellman, "The Shrunken Docket of the Rehnquist Court," *The Supreme Court Review* 403 (1996).

this view, the Court can best serve the needs of the national law by laying down broad principles, leaving their application and elaboration largely to the federal courts of appeals and the state appellate courts. Nor is there any need for the Supreme Court to iron out every wrinkle of statutory interpretation, even some that give rise to apparent intercircuit conflicts.

But, as Hellman points out, there is another, far less "benign" way, of viewing the decline: it "may pose a threat to the effective performance of the Court's functions that is no less serious than that created by an 'imperial judiciary.' At the simplest level, the Court runs the risk that the paucity of decisions will leave wide gaps in the doctrines governing important areas of law."

STATE COURTS

The Framers of the U.S. Constitution probably would be amazed to find a federal judiciary resolving hundreds of thousands of cases, and they most certainly would be astonished at the growth of state courts. At the time of the nation's founding, state courts were simple institutions, lacking not only full-time staffs but also the respect of the public and elected officials. Indeed, because courts were widely viewed as tools of arbitrary colonial governors, state legislatures paid special attention to them, occasionally removing judges or abolishing courts altogether when they disliked their decisions. Over time the situation changed, with judges becoming more professionalized while at the same time bending to local practices and customs. The result was a panoply of legal rulings and judicial structures among the different states.[13]

Many of these early variations persist today. For example, states invoke five different methods of selecting their judges: partisan elections, nonpartisan elections, gubernatorial appointment with state senatorial confirmation, the merit plan, and legislative appointment (see Chapter 4). Their courts also vary in structure, as we describe momentarily. But state legal systems are no longer the simple institutions that they once were; they have evolved into bustling, complex operations that serve as the main source of legal refuge for most Americans (Reading 3.7). Of the nearly 100 million cases filed in the nation's courts each year, more than 97 percent are at the state or local level. To think about it in another way, about one case is filed in the state courts for every third person living in the United States and Puerto Rico.[14] Comparable figures for the federal courts pale in comparison.

---

[13] See Francis R. Aumann, *The Changing American Legal System* (Columbus: Ohio State University Press, 1940); Henry Robert Glick and Kenneth N. Vines, *State Court Systems* (Englewood Cliffs, NJ: Prentice Hall, 1973).

[14] Brian J. Ostrom and Neal B. Krauder, eds., *Examining the Work of State Courts, 2003* (National Center for State Courts, 2003). Available at www.ncsconline.org/index.html. Unless otherwise noted, all data in this section come from this report.

Of course, there is only one federal system of courts but fifty, often quite differently organized state systems, making it difficult to talk about a state judicial system. Even the names states give their courts vary. For example, in some states trial courts are known as circuit courts, superior courts, or even, in New York, supreme courts.

In general, though, most states have developed three-tier systems that parallel those at the federal level: trial courts, intermediate appellate courts, and courts of last resort (see Figure 3.1). At the entry or trial level are typically two kinds of courts: those with limited jurisdiction (such as traffic or juvenile courts) and those with general jurisdiction (usually reserved for more serious criminal or civil offenses). To say that there is one of these courts on every street corner might be to exaggerate but only slightly: there are nearly 16,000 trial courts in the states, staffed by over 29,000 judges. What these figures—as well as the vast jurisdiction of these courts, covering virtually all realms of social life—suggest is that state trial courts are the legal arenas closest to Americans. It is where they are most likely to encounter the "law," be it to appear before a traffic court judge or to watch a trial on Court TV.

This importance commands closer scrutiny of the work of trial judges, and Chapter 9 tries to meet that challenge. For now, however, let us turn to the second tier, the intermediate appellate courts. Here we begin to observe structural variation among the states: eleven states do not have such courts; litigants desiring to appeal their cases must go directly to their state's highest judicial body. In most of the remaining thirty-nine states, they have a right to appeal to an intermediate appellate court, just as they do in the federal ladder—meaning, in turn, that the bulk of intermediate appellate work consists of hearing mandatory appeals from trial courts.[15] Worth noting, though, is that the intermediate appellate courts dispose of most of their cases in short, unsigned opinions (41 percent) or by denying or dismissing them (36 percent). In only 23 percent do they issue published, signed opinions.

Although not all states have intermediate appellate courts, all do have at least one court of last resort, which, depending on the state, is called a supreme court or a court of appeal. These tribunals vary on other dimensions as well. Some have as many as nine judges, others have only five. A handful, including Idaho and Nebraska, receive fewer than 300 cases to review each year; others, such as California, almost as many as the U.S. Supreme Court (more than 7,500 a year). They also exhibit different levels of discretion. Connecticut's Supreme Court grants nearly 20 percent of the petitions it receives; for Kansas's tribunal, that figure is 3 percent. Finally, they invoke different rules and procedures. In Virginia, only one justice need vote to hear a case; in Missouri, four of the seven justices (a majority) must agree to grant review.

---

[15] Depending on the state, some types of trial court cases proceed directly to state courts of last resort; others must go first to intermediate appellate courts. In a handful of states, trial court cases are appealed directly to the state supreme court, which then decides whether the appeal should be heard by an intermediate appellate court.

A NEW JUDICIAL FEDERALISM

Despite these variations, the purpose of state courts of last resort is much the same as their federal counterpart: to serve as the final and ultimate source of judicial authority within their states. And they are performing this role with ever-increasing vigor. In the last few years alone:

- Massachusetts' highest court held that the state could not deny lesbian and gay couples the right to marry.
- California's Supreme Court ruled that a Roman Catholic charity must comply with a state law that requires company health plans cover contraceptives if those plans offer prescription drug benefits—even though the Church considers contraception a sin.
- Wisconsin's Supreme Court upheld a trial court decision ordering a man not to father any more children during his five years of probation "unless he could prove to the court that he could support them all."

What has contributed to this "revitalization" of state supreme courts? Some commentators point the finger directly at the U.S. Supreme Court. They claim that, beginning in the 1970s, the justices took a number of steps to advance a doctrine called "new judicial federalism." In the narrow sense, this doctrine refers to the renewed willingness of state courts to rely solely on state law, especially state constitutional law, when deciding questions of individual rights.[16] In the broader one, it suggests a role of increased importance for state courts in the American governmental system.

Either way, it is clear that the U.S. Supreme Court has encouraged this trend, mainly by chipping away at the various and traditional mechanisms for federal judicial supervision of states and their courts. Specifically, the justices have (1) rearticulated standards for reviewing state decisions, (2) limited the power of federal courts to issue injunctions to prevent state officials from enforcing provisions of state law, (3) restricted the scope of habeas corpus review, and (4) eliminated many exceptions to the Eleventh Amendment.

Reviewing the Decisions of State Supreme Courts

The principles of federalism, says Laurence H. Tribe, require that federal courts further "the twin policies of preserving the integrity of state law and respecting the institutional autonomy of state judicial systems."[17] Potential conflicts between federal and state courts are limited by the principle of comity: The respect that the two systems of courts owe to each other requires federal judges to follow state interpretations of state law and to respect, although not necessarily to defer to, state judges' interpretations of federal statutes and the Constitution.

---

[16] See Shirley S. Abrahamson and Diane S. Gutman, "The New Judicial Federalism: State Constitutions and State Courts," 71 *Judicature* 90 (1987).

[17] Laurence H. Tribe, *American Constitutional Law* (Mineola, NY: Foundation Press, 1988), 196–197.

Following that principle, the Court in *Murdock v. City of Memphis* (1875) said that it would not review state decisions unless the state court's interpretation implicated issues of federal law. This traditional view is called the "adequate and independent state grounds test": so long as a state court's decision rests on adequate and independent state grounds, the Supreme Court will not resolve either the state or the federal issues in the case. Consequently, state courts are entitled to interpret their own statutes and constitutional provisions, and if their reasoning rests on "independent and adequate" state grounds, their decisions are not subject to review by federal courts.

Until the 1970s, the "independent and adequate" doctrine caused little concern among litigants and interest groups seeking expansive interpretations of constitutional rights. For the two previous decades, the U.S. Supreme Court, under the leadership of Earl Warren, had been the most liberal in American history. During the heyday of that era (1962–1968 terms), when the justices were ruling for disadvantaged societal interests in more than 75 percent of their cases, "the notion of a state court['s being] more liberal than the Supreme Court was oxymoronic."[18]

This situation changed dramatically when President Richard Nixon had the opportunity to replace some of the most liberal members of the Warren Court. His choice of Warren Burger for chief justice was particularly telling: whereas Earl Warren supported criminal defendants and other societal "underdogs" in more than 75 percent of the Court's cases, Burger supported these claims in only about 30 percent of cases.

Not surprisingly, commentators perceived that the Burger Court, at least compared with its predecessor, had lessened protection of certain constitutional rights. This perception was shared by holdovers from the Warren Court, particularly Justices William J. Brennan, Jr., and Thurgood Marshall, who were clearly disappointed with the Burger Court's drift. To counter this trend, Brennan began delivering speeches and penning articles that have become something of a bible for those interested in seeking expanded rights and liberties through state courts. He implied that the U.S. Supreme Court, as it was then composed, had halted the expansion of rights, under the federal constitution, ushered in by the Warren Court; and he urged attorneys to consider taking their cases into state courts and state jurists to view their constitutional texts as sources for the expansion of rights rather than to follow blindly the example of the federal bench's interpretations of the national charter (Reading 3.8).

Just as Brennan's arguments were beginning to take hold in the legal community, his (less-rights-oriented) colleagues stepped directly into the debate. Writing for the Court in *Michigan v. Long* (1983), Sandra Day O'Connor—a former state judge—offered a new approach for applying the adequate and independent state grounds standard to ambiguous state court decisions. In her words, the justices would "accept as the most reasonable explanation that the

---

[18] Harold J. Spaeth, "Burger Court Review of State Court Civil Liberties Decisions," 68 *Judicature* 285 (1985).

state court decided the case the way it did because it believed that Federal law required it to do so." To put it another way, as Shirley S. Abrahamson and Diane S. Gutman explain, "the Court set forth a presumption that the state decision rested on federal grounds."[19] Should state judges desire to avoid this presumption, then, O'Connor wrote, they "need only make clear by a plain statement in [their] judgment that the federal cases are being used only for the purpose of guidance, and do not themselves compel the result the court has reached." For, if state judges indicate "clearly and expressly" that their decisions are "based on bona fide separate, adequate, and independent state grounds," then the U.S. Supreme Court will "not undertake to review the decision."

Naturally, the majority of the justices justified this new approach to the adequate and independent state grounds test as a reasonable way to resolve "the vexing issue" of ambiguous state decisions. Even Justice John Paul Stevens, in his dissent, did not take issue with the notion that a clear approach to this area of the law was needed. He simply disliked the one O'Connor fashioned, as did many other commentators, who asserted that the majority's solution was ideologically grounded, designed to provide the conservative justices with a way to counter the liberal state courts' new course. *Long*, itself, shores up this point: by invoking this new approach—the presumption that a state court decision rested on federal grounds—to the independent and adequate state grounds standard, the Court was able to review and overturn a liberal (here, prodefendant) state court decision. Specifically, the Michigan State Supreme Court had ruled that a police search of David Long's car violated both the U.S. Constitution and the state constitution, but the U.S. Supreme Court disagreed. It held that the search was reasonable under its precedents and that the Michigan court's decision did not meet its new approach to the adequate and independent grounds standard, because the state court cited its constitution only twice, relying far more heavily on its understanding of federal case law.

Some scholars have thus suggested that *Long* compromised "the availability of state law as a basis for expanded protection of civil rights and liberties"[20] Support for this claim comes from various studies suggesting that many state jurists do not and, more pointedly, cannot rely exclusively on their own constitutional texts to reach decisions in many areas, including criminal law. The obstacles? Most criminal cases arising under state law deal with issues on which the U.S. Supreme Court has spoken. Moreover, many state criminal constitutional guarantees are worded in much the same language as is the U.S. constitutional document. Therefore, it is possible that state jurists now tend to read state provisions and their federal counterparts in similar ways. From the perspective of those who want state judges to defend minorities and protect the rights of criminally accused, the result has been a resounding defeat. The fear is that state jurists will routinely apply doctrines established by the law-and-order-minded U.S. Supreme Courts of the last few decades.

---

[19] Abrahamson and Gutman, "The New Judicial Federalism," 97.

[20] Spaeth, "Burger Court Review of State Court Civil Liberties Decisions," 286.

Other scholars, however, take a quite different perspective. In their view, *Long* "seeks to protect the integrity of the state. If a state court plainly says that it is relying on state law, the Supreme Court will not review its decision. The Court reaffirms the state court's opportunity to be the final arbiter of its own law and to divest the U.S. Supreme Court of jurisdiction to review."[21] To support this position, analysts point to the willingness of state judges to reconsider their functions and roles, as this telling comment reveals:

> During the years I have been a Montana Supreme Court Justice, I have become more interested in developing the area of law known as "independent state grounds." The new Montana Constitution . . . is a rather unique document and provides a basis for considerable departure from federal precedent. This has been particularly true in the civil rights area where we have developed a new equal protection law relying upon the implication of fundamental rights declared in our State Constitution and requiring a showing of a compelling state interest to justify legislative discrimination.[22]

The Massachusetts Supreme Judicial Court's decision in *Goodridge v. Department of Public Health* (2003) provides a compelling illustration of this general point. In that case the justices held that "barring an individual from the protections, benefits, and obligations of civil marriage solely because that person would marry a person of the same sex violates the Massachusetts Constitution" (Reading 3.9).

At the end of the day, then, the evidence on the extent to which Brennan and Marshall accomplished their particular (ideological) goal is quite mixed. Surely, there does seem to exist a perception among certain segments of the legal community that the Rehnquist Court has encouraged state courts to become more active (if not more liberal) policy makers—with *Goodridge* providing but one example.

Then again we ought consider the Court's decision in *Bush v. Gore* (2000). There, the Court reversed a decision of the Florida Supreme Court, which, among other things, had ordered manual recounts in all counties in the state where "undervotes" had not been recounted by hand. The U.S. Supreme Court's reversal rested largely on equal protection grounds; the majority of the justices believed that the Florida court did not provide the guidance necessary to carry out its command—that manual recounts take into account "the intent of the voter"—and, thus, to ensure the equal application of its order. But the dissenters were quick to take on aspects of the suit implicating federalism. For example, Justice Stevens, in a dissent joined by Justices Ginsburg and Breyer, opened his opinion with the following:

> The Constitution assigns to the States the primary responsibility for determining the manner of selecting the Presidential electors. See Art. I, sec. 1, cl. 2. When questions arise about the meaning of state laws, including election laws,

---

[21] Abrahamson and Gutman, "The New Federalism," 96.

[22] Quoted in Ronald K. L. Collins, Peter J. Galie, and John Kincaid, "State High Courts, State Constitutions, and Individual Rights Litigation Since 1980," 13 *Hastings Constitutional Law Quarterly* 604 (1986).

it is our settled practice to accept the opinions of the highest courts of the States as providing the final answers. On rare occasions, however, either federal statutes or the Federal Constitution may require federal judicial intervention in state elections. This is not such an occasion.

The federal questions that ultimately emerged in this case are not substantial.

He concluded with a paragraph that, at least some suggest, was designed to taunt those justices who agreed with the Court's decision to reverse—Kennedy, O'Connor, Rehnquist, Scalia, and Thomas—the very same justices who have attempted to limit access to the federal courts and enhance the role of state forums:

What must underlie petitioners' entire federal assault on the Florida election procedures is an unstated lack of confidence in the impartiality and capacity of the state judges who would make the critical decisions if the vote count were to proceed. Otherwise, their position is wholly without merit. The endorsement of that position by the majority of this Court can only lend credence to the most cynical appraisal of the work of judges throughout the land. It is confidence in the men and women who administer the judicial system that is the true backbone of the rule of law. Time will one day heal the wound to that confidence that will be inflicted by today's decision. One thing, however, is certain. Although we may never know with complete certainty the identity of the winner of this year's Presidential election, the identity of the loser is perfectly clear. It is the Nation's confidence in the judge as an impartial guardian of the rule of law.

Does *Bush v. Gore* signal a retreat from new judicial federalism? We will not know the answer with certainty until the Court issues new decisions on the subject, but we suspect not; the justices supporting the doctrine have expressed their commitment to it in case after case. Their departure from it—if that is what it was—in *Bush* was, in all likelihood, an anomaly, and not the beginning of the end. Nonetheless, we cannot help but wonder whether it has affected perceptions, especially among state supreme court justices, of the Court's willingness to allow state courts to have the final say on a range of issues—to say nothing of the Court's motives. Indeed, some scholars (and, perhaps, Justice Stevens as well) suggest that *Bush v. Gore* points up the ideological nature of the Court's support for new judicial federalism; that at least five of the justices, the five who supported the disposition in *Bush*, are willing to accept state court decisions only if those decisions comport with their right-of-center values, not if they are "liberal." Inasmuch as *Bush* effectively decided the election in favor of the Republican candidate, commentators may have some justification for this belief.

Issuing Injunctions

A statute of 1793 (28 U.S.C. § 2283) forbade federal courts to issue injunctions staying proceedings in a state court "except as expressly authorized by Act of Congress, or where necessary in aid of its jurisdiction, or to protect or effectuate its judgments." The Supreme Court in *Osbourn v. Bank of the United States* (1824) asserted power to restrain state officials from bringing criminal or civil proceedings in state courts to enforce an invalid state statute, but under that decision an injunction could issue only after a federal court had found the state statute unconstitutional. In 1908 *Ex parte Young* abandoned this requirement. There the Court held that a federal court could enjoin the attorney general of a state from enforcing a state statute in state courts pending a determination of its constitutionality.

Because of exceptions in the anti-injunction act of 1793, federal courts have had considerable leeway in issuing injunctions against state courts but, in pursuance of the principle of comity, had restrained exercise of their authority by the policy of "equitable abstention." This practice is based on the contention that what Justice Hugo L. Black called "Our Federalism" forbids federal courts to interfere with a state's good-faith administration of its criminal laws. Issuance of an injunction by a federal court cuts short the normal adjudication of issues and constitutional defenses in state courts and under traditional equity rules can be justified only if the defendants are threatened with irreparable injury should the state prosecution be allowed to proceed.

Consequently, federal judges seldom enjoined state criminal prosecutions. In *Dombrowski v. Pfister* (1965), however, the Warren Court opened the way for greater federal protection of civil rights by allowing increased federal judicial intervention in state proceedings. But the Burger Court switched course. In *Younger v. Harris* (1971) and in other cases decided the same day, the Court severely limited *Dombrowski* and adopted a stricter view of the obligations comity imposed on federal judges. It ruled that federal courts should not enjoin state officials from enforcing their laws unless continued enforcement would irreparably harm the individual seeking the injunction.

Restricting Habeas Corpus

While *Younger* minimizes the supervision federal courts have over state executive officials, the Supreme Court's rulings on habeas corpus have also lessened federal judges' supervisory role over state courts. Generally speaking, habeas corpus (translated from Latin as "If you have the body") petitions are filed by, or on behalf of, persons held in custody in order to challenge the legality of their detention and to request a court to release them.[23] Until 1867 the writ was not available against any sentence imposed by a court of competent jurisdiction. But in that year Congress, anticipating Southern resistance to new civil rights legislation and constitutional guaranties, conferred on federal courts broad authority to issue writs of habeas corpus for prisoners in custody "in violation of the Constitution or of any treaty or law of the United States." As Justice Brennan commented in *Fay v. Noia* (1963): "A remedy almost in the nature of removal from the state to the federal courts of state prisoners' constitutional contentions seems to have been envisaged."

The result was that defendants convicted in state criminal proceedings had two separate channels for seeking federal judicial redress. First, they could petition for direct review by the U.S. Supreme Court of an adverse decision by the

---

[23] See Victor E. Flango, *Habeas Corpus in State and Federal Courts* (Williamsburg, VA: National Center for State Courts, 1994).

highest state court. If this route failed, prisoners could attack their convictions collaterally by seeking habeas corpus from the federal court for the district in which they were held, with appeal to the court of appeals and finally to the Supreme Court once again. The major accommodation between the two systems required by the Supreme Court in *Fay v. Noia* was that the defendants exhaust their state remedies before seeking habeas corpus in a federal court.

Applications from convicted state prisoners for habeas corpus from federal courts increased rapidly as the Supreme Court became more sensitive to the rights of accused persons. In the 1940s federal judges received about 130 such petitions per year; by the 1990s, that figure exceeded 10,000,[24] with the most common allegation being that evidence used to convict had been secured by unreasonable searches in violation of the Fourth and Fourteenth Amendments.

Scholars, judges, and other public officials differ over the virtue of this upward trend. Those who desire to restrict federal habeas corpus review of convictions in state courts argue that these petitions create tension between state and federal judges because they provide one federal district judge with the opportunity to revisit the judgments of state supreme courts—not to mention all the state tribunals below them. As a result, they dramatically diminish the authority of state judges. Opponents also suggest that petitions for habeas corpus generate long and unnecessary procedural delays, which they say can undermine the deterrent effect of criminal law. Supporters of expansive habeas corpus policies marshal equally impressive arguments. They assert that the procedure is "essential to safeguard Federal constitutional rights in general, ensure national uniformity in the enforcement of rights; overcome the errors of ineffective counsel in state trials; and avoid improper incarceration or, worse, execution of individual defendants."[25] The fact that state courts often wrongly impose death sentences does nothing to weaken claims for postconviction review by federal courts.

Despite these differences, supporters and opponents alike agree that the Rehnquist Court has attempted to reduce the scope of federal habeas corpus and, accordingly, the role of federal courts as a check on state courts. Indeed, with the exception of only one recent case, *Withrow v. Williams* (1993), the justices have time and again restricted the ability of state prisoners to obtain relief in federal courts.

As of 2005, however, these rulings, coupled with congressional legislation limiting the availability of habeas corpus for certain crimes, do not seem to be having much effect on the efforts of state prisoners. While U.S. courts of appeals have recently experienced a decline in the number of habeas corpus petitions, U.S. district courts have seen a rather large increase (over 30 percent). Whether decreases will occur in the future is a matter of speculation. Still, it seems reasonably clear that by placing stricter limits on the ability of losers in state courts to raise claims in federal courts, the justices have advanced the cause of a new

---

[24] *Ibid.,* 14.

[25] Flango, *Habeas Corpus in State and Federal Courts,* 3.

judicial federalism. At the very least, rulings of the Rehnquist Court have increased the probability that decisions of state courts will be the final word in many disputes about criminal justice.

Limiting Exceptions to the Eleventh Amendment

In 1793 the Supreme Court accepted original jurisdiction in *Chisholm v. Georgia,* a suit brought against the state of Georgia by two citizens of South Carolina trying to collect a debt. This action was based on Article III's authorization for federal courts to adjudicate controversies "between a State and citizens of another State." Congress and the states reacted quickly by adopting the Eleventh Amendment giving states immunity from being sued, without their consent, in federal courts by "Citizens of another State, or by Citizens or Subjects of any Foreign State."

Initially, however, the Supreme Court gave the Eleventh Amendment a "stingy" reading. In *Cohens v. Virginia* (1821), Chief Justice Marshall held that the Eleventh Amendment did not preclude the Supreme Court's exercising jurisdiction over a federal question raised on appeal by citizens of their own states (in accord with Section 25 of the 1789 Judiciary Act). This trend continued into the 1980s. In case after case, the Court allowed Congress to make exceptions to the Eleventh Amendment. For example, in *Fitzpatrick v. Bitzer* (1976), the Court held that, because the Fourteenth Amendment expressly authorizes Congress to enforce the Amendment "by appropriate legislation," Congress could, when exercising that authority, abrogate the states' immunity from suit under the Eleventh Amendment. Similarly, in *Pennsylvania v. Union Gas Co.* (1989), a divided Court ruled that the commerce clause of Article II permitted Congress to make an exception to the Eleventh Amendment's grant of immunity, holding that the power to regulate commerce "among the several States" would be "incomplete without the authority to render States liable in damages."

In 1996, however, *Seminole Tribe of Florida v. Florida* overruled *Union Gas.* Writing for the Court, Chief Justice Rehnquist said: "Even when the Constitution vests in Congress complete law-making authority over a particular area, the Eleventh Amendment prevents congressional authorization of suits by private parties against unconsenting States." In other words, the Court asserted that the specific terms of Article I of the constitutional text does not permit Congress to abrogate the states' immunity from suits commenced or prosecuted in the federal courts. Three years later, in *Alden v. Maine* (1999), the justices pushed *Seminole Tribe* even further, ruling that Congress cannot subject nonconsenting states to private suits for damages even in their own courts. And more recently, in *Board of Trustees of the University of Alabama v. Garrett* (2001) they held that state employees cannot sue their employers for violations of the Americans with Disabilities Act of 1990, which prohibits certain employers, including state governments, from "discriminat[ing] against a qualified individual with a disability because of the disability of such individual in regard to job application procedures, the hiring, advancement, or discharge of employees, employee compensation, job training, and other terms, conditions, and privileges of employment."[26]

These decisions may speak more to the current Court's interest in furthering state power than to its interest in pushing new judicial federalism. Nonetheless, to the extent that the two go hand in hand, the justices have done much to invigorate and enhance the roles of state courts in American society.

SELECTED REFERENCES

BANKS, CHRISTOPHER P. 1999. *Judicial Politics in the D.C. Circuit Court.* Baltimore: Johns Hopkins University Press.

BARROW, DEBORAH J., AND THOMAS G. WALKER. 1988. *A Court Divided.* New Haven, CT: Yale University Press.

BARROW, DEBORAH J., GARY ZUK, AND GERALD S. GRYSKI. 1996. *The Federal Judiciary and Institutional Change.* Ann Arbor: University of Michigan Press.

BLACK, CHARLES L., JR. 1974. "The National Court of Appeals: An Unwise Proposal." *Yale Law Journal* 83: 883.

BRENNAN, WILLIAM J. 1977. "State Constitutions and the Protection of Individual Rights." *Harvard Law Review* 90: 502.

BRIGHT, STEPHEN B. 1997. "Is Fairness Irrelevant?: The Evisceration of Federal Habeas Corpus Review and Limits on the Ability of State Courts to Protect Fundamental Rights." *Washington and Lee Law Review* 54: 1.

CASPER, GERHARD, AND RICHARD A. POSNER. 1976. *The Workload of the Supreme Court.* Chicago: American Bar Foundation.

CLARK, DAVID S. 1981. "Adjudication to Administration: A Statistical Analysis of Federal District Courts in the Twentieth Century." *Southern California Law Review* 55: 65.

COHEN, JONATHAN MATTHEW. 2002. *Inside Appellate Courts.* Ann Arbor: University of Michigan Press.

DOUGLAS, WILLIAM O. 1956. *We the Judges.* New York: Doubleday.

DOUGLAS, WILLIAM O. 1960. "The Supreme Court and Its Caseload." *Cornell Law Quarterly* 45: 401.

DUBOIS, PHILIP L., ED. 1982. *The Politics of Judicial Reform.* Lexington, MA: Lexington Books.

FISH, PETER C. 1984. *The Office of Chief Justice of the United States.* Charlottesville: Miller Center, University of Virginia.

---

[26] Worth noting is that the Court bucked this general trend in its most recent statement on the Eleventh Amendment. In *Nevada Department of Human Resources v. Hibbs* (2003), the justices surprised observers when they held that states are not immune from suits brought by their employees under the federal Family and Medical Leave Act (FMLA) of 1993, which provides employees with up to 12 work weeks of unpaid leave annually for the onset of a "serious health condition" in the employee's spouse and for other reasons. One purpose of the act, according to Congress, was "to minimize the potential for employment discrimination on the basis of sex by ensuring generally that leave is available on a gender-neutral basis and to promote the goal of equal employment opportunity for women and men. . . ." Congress believed this was necessary because "due to the nature of the roles of men and women in our society, the primary responsibility for family caretaking often falls on women, and such responsibility affects the working lives of women more than it affects the working lives of men."

FISS, OWEN. 1983. "The Bureaucratization of the Judiciary." *Yale Law Journal* 92: 1442.

FLANGO, VICTOR E. 1994. *Habeas Corpus in State and Federal Courts.* Williamsburg, VA: National Center for State Courts.

FRANKFURTER, FELIX, AND JAMES M. LANDIS. 1928. *The Business of the Supreme Court.* New York: Macmillan.

FRIENDLY, HENRY J. 1973. *Federal Jurisdiction: A General View.* New York: Columbia University Press.

GEORGE, TRACEY E. 1999. "The Dyamics and Determinants of the Decision to Grant En Banc Review." *Washington Law Review* 74: 213.

GILLMAN, HOWARD. 2001. *The Votes That Counted.* Chicago: University of Chicago Press.

GLICK, HENRY ROBERT, AND KENNETH N. VINES. 1973. *State Court Systems.* Englewood Cliffs, NJ: Prentice Hall.

GOLDBERG, ARTHUR J. 1984. "Measuring the Supreme Court's Workload." *Hastings Constitutional Law Quarterly* 11: 353.

HALL, KERMIT, AND ERIC W. RISE. 1991. *From Local Courts to National Tribunals: The Federal Courts of Florida, 1821–1990.* Brooklyn: Carlson.

HART, HENRY M., JR. 1959. "The Time Chart of the Justices." *Harvard Law Review* 73: 84.

HARTMAN, MARSHALL J., AND JEANETTE NYDEN. 1997. "Habeas Corpus and the New Federalism After the Anti-Terrorism and Effective Death Penalty Act of 1996." *John Marshall Law Review* 30: 337.

HELLMAN, ARTHUR D. 1996. "The Shrunken Docket of the Rehnquist Court." *Supreme Court Review* 1996: 403.

HOWARD, J. WOODFORD. 1973. "Litigation Flow in Three U.S. Courts of Appeals." *Law and Society Review* 8: 33.

KAGAN, ROBERT A., BLISS CARTWRIGHT, LAWRENCE M. FRIEDMAN, AND STANTON WHEELER. 1978. "The Evolution of State Supreme Courts." *Michigan Law Review* 76: 961.

LANGER, LAURA. 2002. *Judicial Review in State Supreme Courts: A Comparative Study.* Albany, NY: State University Press of New York.

LYLES, KEVIN. 1997. *The Gatekeepers: Federal District Courts in the Political Process.* Westport, CT: Praeger.

MCGOWAN, CARL. 1967. *The Organization of Judicial Power in the United States.* Evanston, IL: Northwestern University Press.

MERRITT, DEBORAH JONES, AND JAMES J. BRUDNEY. 2001. "Stalking Secret Law: What Predicts Publication in the United States Courts of Appeals." *Vanderbilt Law Review* 54: 71.

"Of High Designs: A Compendium of Proposals to Reduce the Workload of the Supreme Court" [Note]. 1983. *Harvard Law Review* 97: 307.

PORTER, MARY CORNELIA, AND C. ALAN TARR, EDS. 1982. *State Supreme Courts: State Supreme Courts and the Federal System.* Westport, CT: Greenwood Press.

POSNER, RICHARD A. 1985. *The Federal Courts.* Cambridge, MA: Harvard University Press.

Report of the Study Group on the Caseload of the Supreme Court. 1972. Washington, DC: Federal Judicial Center.

ROWLAND, C. K., AND ROBERT CARP. 1996. *Politics and Judgment on the Federal District Courts.* Lawrence: University Press of Kansas.

SCHIAVONI, JOHANNA S. 2002. "Who's Afraid of Precedent?: The Debate over the Precedential Value of Unpublished Opinions." *UCLA Law Review* 49: 1859.

SEGAL, JEFFREY A. AND HAROLD J. SPAETH. 2003. *The Supreme Court and the Attitudinal Model Revisited.* New York: Cambridge University Press.

STAHLKOPF, DEBORAH L. 1998. "A Dark Day for Habeas Corpus: Successive Petitions Under the Antiterrorism and Effective Death Penalty Act of 1996." *Arizona Law Review* 40: 1115.

STUMPF, HARRY P., AND JOHN H. CULVER. 1992. *The Politics of State Courts*. New York: Longman.

TABAK, RONALD J. 1996. "Habeas Corpus as a Crucial Protector of Constitutional Rights: A Tribute Which May Also Be a Eulogy." *Seton Hall Law Review* 26: 1477.

TARR, G. ALAN, ed. 1996. *Constitutional Politics in the States: Contemporary Controversies and Historical Patterns*. Westport, CT: Greenwood Press.

TARR, G. ALAN, AND MARY C. A. PORTER. 1988. *State Supreme Courts in Nation and States*. New Haven, CT: Yale University Press.

UNAH, ISAAC. 1998. *The Courts of International Trade: Judicial Specialization, Expertise and Bureaucratic Policy-Making*. Ann Arbor: University of Michigan Press.

WALTENBURG, ERIC N., AND BILL SWINFORD. 1999. *Litigating Federalism: The States Before the U.S. Supreme Court*. Westport, CT: Greenwood Press, 1999.

YACKLE, LARRY W. 1996. "A Primer on the New Habeas Corpus Statute." *Buffalo Law Review* 44: 381.

3.1 JUDICIARY ACT
OF 1789, SECTION 25

1 U.S. Statutes at Large 85–86

That a final judgment or decree in any suit, in the highest court of law or equity of a State in which a decision in the suit could be had, where is drawn in question the validity of a treaty or statute of or an authority exercised under the United States, and the decision is against their validity; or where is drawn in question the validity of a statute of, or an authority exercised under any State, on the ground of their being repugnant to the constitution, treaties or laws of the United States, and the decision is in favor of their validity, or where is drawn in question the construction of any clause of the constitution, or of a treaty, or statute of, or commission held under the United States, and the decision is against the title, right, privilege or exemption specifically set up or claimed by either party, under such clause of the said constitution, treaty, statute or commission, may be reexamined and reversed or affirmed in the Supreme Court of the United States. . . .[1]

". . . it is not entirely clear that, even to the extent that there has been increasing [judicial] bureaucratization, there has been any change in the quality of the judicial product."

3.2 INSIDE APPELLATE COURTS

Jonathan Matthew Cohen

Jonathan Matthew Cohen is an attorney in Washington, D.C.
He holds a Ph.D. in sociology and a J.D.

The Concept of Judicial Bureaucratization

What do students of judicial administration mean when they speak of the "bureaucratization" of the judiciary? In the past forty years, federal appellate courts

---

[1] *Under Section 25, denial of a federal right by the highest court of a state in the three categories specified was reviewable in the Supreme Court as of right (on writ of error). A 1914 act permitted review by certiorari and also where the state court had upheld the federal right. But an act of 1916 withdrew appeal as of right in cases of the third category, leaving certiorari as the only avenue of review. The Supreme Court Case Selections Act of 1988 eliminated virtually all the Court's nondiscretionary jurisdiction. The Court is no longer obligated to review state court decisions involving federal law. —Eds.*

From Jonathan Matthew Cohen, *Inside Appellate Courts* (Ann Arbor: University of Michigan Press, 2002).

have undergone a "slow, but cumulative, process of change." American courts have witnessed an increasing caseload almost overwhelming in its proportions. The increased demand on federal appellate courts has been accompanied by the addition of many new organizational actors, including increased numbers of law clerks, staff attorneys, and court administrators. Consequently, since at least 1960 there has been an increase in the demands placed on the federal courts, "coupled with a growing reliance on new forms of administration." Critics have termed this increased administrative reliance *bureaucratization*.

Numerous lawyers, judges, and academic commentators have condemned bureaucratization as harmful to the federal appellate judiciary. Judge Patrick E. Higginbotham, for example, has decried bureaucracy as the "carcinoma of the federal judiciary." Judge Robert S. Thompson has called the costs of bureaucratization "unacceptable." Former Solicitor General Wade McCree has asserted that bureaucratization's costs to the quality of justice are "too high."

Nevertheless, even as it is condemned as harmful, the concept of bureaucratization remains elusive. Commentators generally do not mean *bureaucracy* in the technical organizational sense. Rather, *bureaucracy* and *bureaucratization* refer to the lay concept of bureaucracy as demarking an impersonal, inefficient, delay-encumbered organization.

At the core of the concerns about bureaucratization rest certain assumptions about how courts should operate. Those assumptions regard courts as simple triadic structures in which a neutral third party resolves conflicts between antagonistic parties. This triadic structure acts as a "prototype" of the court in which judges have a high degree of independence from external influences. In that prototypical court, each judge makes decisions alone, in isolation from organizational and political influences. Judicial actions "are defined in terms of the actions, judgment, and explanations not of a committee but of an individual. In that idealized court, judges agonize in isolation in an attempt to "find" the right resolution to the conflicts before them—they do not "create" the law. This judicial independence enables judges to maintain the legitimacy necessary for the success of the judicial enterprise.

When a court becomes *bureaucratized*, it moves away from the prototypical court in which decisions stem from the "agony of a lonely isolated judge." Rather, decisions stem from a businesslike mass production. The threat of bureaucratization is that courts will undergo "an equivalent of the industrial revolution" in which they will become the "appellate counterpart of the assembly line." A bureaucratized court no longer functions as a collection of "professionally and collegially controlled, semi feudal domains of judges," but rather acts as a modern administrative agency concerned less with justice and more with speed, efficiency, productivity, simplification, and cost-effectiveness in the delivery of judicial services.

Consequently, a bureaucratized court is depersonalized. Instead of providing the best quality of justice, the bureaucratized court must balance the quality of justice dispensed against the time and cost of each case. As a result, bureaucratization brings about increased hierarchical structure, overspecialization, rigid rules and regulations, impersonality, resistance to change, and delegation of adjudicative duties to judicial staff. In a bureaucratized court, judges' administrative responsibilities overwhelm their adjudicative ones, and the rationality of organizational efficiency overwhelms the goal of reasoned justice.

The Crisis of Volume as the Cause of Bureaucratization

Bureaucratization remains a salient concern because its perceived causes appear to be on the rise. Court observers commonly claim that increases in case volume, case complexity, and the nature of the caseload have forced the courts to become more administrative and more bureaucratic. As these causes continue to increase, judges must rely more heavily on their staff and on the court's bureaucratic safeguards to keep pace. . . . Indeed, many legal scholars have decried the caseload stress as having the potential to damage the court system. . . . Solicitor General McCree called the recent increase in federal litigation "staggering." Judge Richard Posner asserts that the caseload increase constitutes a potentially devastating blow to the appellate judicial process.

The common perception that the caseload has been increasing is far from illusory. Since at least 1960 there has been an "explosion" in the quantity of cases coming to the federal courts. As Judge Posner explained, "The increase in cases filed in the district courts, however dramatic, was dwarfed by the increase in cases filed in the courts of appeals—from 3,765 in 1960 . . . to 29,580 in 1983—an increase of 686 percent. This increase has continued steadily since Judge Posner first published these figures. In 1988 there were 37,524 appeals filed. By 1992, 47,013 appeals were filed, and, by 1993, 50,224 appeals were filed. By 2000, filings in the U.S. Courts of Appeals attained a record high of 54,697 appeals. . . .

The Perceived Consequences of Bureaucratization

Court observers define bureaucratization as harmful to the judicial process, depersonalizing the judiciary, causing judges to spend less time on adjudicative duties and to focus less attention on opinions, and provoking judges to work less collegially. While some judges and commentators claim that these harmful consequences already have come to pass, others warn that continuing bureaucratization potentially will have these effects. Either way, the vast increase in caseload already has produced concern among federal appellate judges. In a 1992 survey of 129 active circuit judges and 59 senior circuit judges conducted by the Federal Judicial Center, 33.5 percent of respondents stated that the volume of civil cases presented a large problem to the judiciary, 37.2 percent of these judges stated that the volume of criminal cases presented a large problem, and 34.6 percent considered the volume of criminal cases to be a grave problem. The study further found that 62.3 percent of the judges considered the increasing complexity of the federal caseload to be problematic. As a result of the caseload, 52.2 percent of the surveyed judges felt that delegation of judges' work to nonjudge personnel had become a problem, 70.8 percent felt that judges have insufficient time for judicial case preparation, and 57.4 percent felt that the impact of the workload on collegiality was problematic. This section considers these perceived consequences of bureaucratization.

The Delegation Dilemma: Increased Reliance on Staff

Bureaucratization commonly is thought to have transformed the judicial process into an administrative process in which judges function as little more than staff managers and opinion editors. The size of the judiciary has increased enormously in the past thirty years. In 1974, there were 97 authorized judgeships. That number jumped to 132 in 1979 and to 156 in 1985. In 1991 the number again increased to 167, where it has remained. Thus, in less than twenty years, the number of judges increased by 72 percent. In 1981 Congress created two new circuits, carving the new Eleventh Circuit out of what had previously been the Fifth Circuit and establishing the Court of Appeals for the Federal Circuit, an appellate court of specialized jurisdiction. Congress currently is considering splitting the Ninth Circuit to create a new Twelfth Circuit. At the same time, the size of judges' personal staffs has increased from one secretary and two clerks to two secretaries and three clerks. Today, federal appellate judges may have as many as four clerks. These trends show no signs of slowing.

As judges use a greater number of staff members—in particular, law clerks—to keep up with the increasing caseload, commentators have expressed concern that the judges must spend more time supervising their clerks and consequently have less time to perform their proper judicial function. The result, some critics assert, is that judges begin to fall into a "judicial torpor" in which they delegate their decision-making power to clerks. These critics aver that when this delegation occurs, judges may become increasingly intellectually lazy, relying on the clerks to rationalize any decisions the judges render. Such commentators argue that when judges rely on clerks for their reasoning, judicial decisions become increasingly arbitrary and opinions become decreasingly imprecise. . . .

Overreliance on law clerks may have a "big impact" on the final judicial opinion. First, . . . this overdelegation enables judges to make decisions without carefully considering the logical or legal reasons for doing so. While judges traditionally have had to agonize over how a decision can be justified, now they merely can decide the case and ask their clerks to agonize over justifications. Second, delegating the initial opinion-drafting responsibility to clerks may seriously and adversely affect the opinions' clarity and style. Judge Posner, for example, perceives clerk-drafted opinions to be stylistically uniform, colorless, and longer, with superfluous arguments, citations, and quotations. As a consequence, Judge Posner worries that clerk-drafted opinions will be less clear and will lack the greatness that marked the opinions of the great jurists of the past. Finally, Judge Posner worries that the perception that clerks draft opinions will threaten the credibility of judicial opinions.

The Collegiality Question: Relationships among Judges

A second concern is that bureaucratization will undermine the collegiality of appellate courts. Unlike trial courts, appellate courts make decisions in panels of three or more judges. Therefore, the ability of appellate judges to work collectively—to share ideas and work together to produce one decision of the court—becomes very important. Accordingly, appellate judges must adjust their behavior to the fact that they can adjudicate cases only collectively. Appellate judges deliberate together, join together in opinions, and make choices as a group.

The term *collegiality* contains two separate but related significances. First, *collegiality* may refer to little more than civility. In that sense, a collegial court is one where its members speak to one another politely and maintain an air of civility in opinions. A second significance of the term *collegiality* is the more technical and more historically accurate sense in which the court acts as a single unit. In that latter sense, the aim of a collegial court is "to produce performances that could in principle represent the unenhanced effort of a single person, but to bring that performance closer to the ideal." A collegial court's trademarks are "collaboration and deliberation" resulting from a "shift in the agency of performance from the individual to the group.

Thus, *collegiality* is not synonymous with multimember decision making. Instead, *collegiality* refers to the continuous, open, and intimate relationship judges share with one another. A collegial court is marked by a lack of competition, pettiness, and enmity and is measured by cohesiveness, friendliness, and mutual respect. Collegiality is important because it promotes judicial efficiency and a better judicial work product. When a judicial opinion represents a unified and collegial court, it produces clearer and weightier precedent. If a court produces fragmented decisions marked by numerous separate opinions, the circuit's precedent becomes murky. . . .

The Organizational Black Box: Organizational Mediation of Judicial Decision Making

Ultimately, the concern over bureaucratization is that its effects will reduce the court's ability to determine the "right" answer and to explain that answer in a relatively clearly reasoned judicial opinion. . . . Commentators generally believe that bureaucratization has caused, or soon will cause, a decline in the quality of the judicial product. Indeed, this conclusion has a certain logical appeal. It seems sensible that increasing the caseload burden while increasing the court's administrative aspects should result in a decrease in the amount of each judge's attention a case receives and ultimately in the quality of that judge's decision.

Nevertheless, it is not entirely clear that, even to the extent that there has been increasing bureaucratization, there has been any change in the quality of the judicial product. Measuring the quality of justice and the judicial product is an extremely difficult endeavor, and there have been almost no systematic empirical studies to establish whether this perceived effect of bureaucratization has come to pass. . . .

Because of the widely held perception of a decline in the quality of the appellate judicial product and regardless of whether such a change actually has taken place, politicians, pundits, and scholars have recommended revolutionary changes to the courts, ranging from dividing courts into smaller subunits to adding a new level to the federal judiciary to creating new courts with limited substantive jurisdiction. These palliatives are sold as being both necessary to avoid a caseload disaster and effective in doing so. Yet these recommendations cannot be evaluated without a firm understanding of how the appellate courts function as organizations.

It is known that the caseload has been increasing and has become more complex. It is known that the courts produce a greater number of decisions in the same amount of time, and some observers believe that this increase has resulted in a decline in the quality of justice. What is not known is precisely what happens between the inputs to the court (a case is filed) and the court's output (the court issues its decision). Without understanding how the court's organizational nature affects the way that judges make their decisions, it is impossible to understand how changes in the court's organizational nature will affect the judicial process and, ultimately, how such changes may affect the quality of justice. Indeed, it is not surprising that, without a more detailed account of how the court functions organizationally, the perception remains widely held that the departure from the ideal type of the solitary judicial sage has caused a decline in the quality of how courts function.

The organizational nature of the court can define an individual judge's ends and shape the means by which judges strive to accomplish those ends. Thus, the organizational nature of the court serves as a significant source of mediation between the increasing caseload and its consequences. This should be no surprise, as it has long been understood that extrinsic factors such as the court's organizational structure act as an important mediator between the law and the way that cases are resolved.

By "organizational nature," I mean both the organization's formal and informal aspects that affect the decision-making process. By "formal aspects" I follow Lauren Edelman in referring to the "configuration of offices and positions and the formal linkages between them (the 'organizational chart') as well as to formal rules, programs, positions, and procedures. "Informal aspects" refer to "the actual communication channels between offices and positions, the actual behavior of individuals who occupy them, and informal norms and practices.

To fully understand the relationship between the inputs, such as the caseload explosion, and the outputs of the court, such as the collegiality or the clarity of the judicial opinion, it is necessary to understand the court's organizational nature and what problems are inherent in its structure. It is necessary to identify how the court's organizational features affect the ways judges do their jobs. Only then is it possible to assess how external pressures and internal changes can affect judicial decision making and to assess proposals to alter the court system to accommodate increasing external pressures. . . .

* * *

The organizational model developed [here] suggests that the federal courts' slow evolution has enabled them to continue to produce a similar quality of justice without sacrificing the ideals that have characterized the appellate process throughout the courts' long history.

This observation comes amid numerous alarmist calls that the judiciary is altering and that revolutionary changes are the only hope for revitalization. For example, Martha Dragich recommends that the court system be overhauled almost entirely by merging the courts of appeals into a single, national appellate court with discretionary jurisdiction and adding an appellate division to the district courts. Most recently, a commission made up largely of federal judges has recommended significant structural changes to the Ninth Circuit, including administering the circuit through regional subdivisions. These and other radical changes could result in unforeseen disaster.

The organizational model suggests pessimism for the efficacy of revolutionary changes. . . .

Because revolutionary changes create the potential consequences, a conservative evolutionary approach is appropriate. Slow evolutionary options constitute relatively small and discrete changes in courts' internal functioning. Evolutionary changes can include such things as changing the way that cases are screened from the oral argument calendar, increasing the use and amount of sanctions and waiver, adopting shared bench memoranda or the min-en banc, and adding small numbers of new judges. The conclusion favoring an evolutionary rather than revolutionary approach is particularly warranted because . . . the courts appear to be functioning reasonably well, even in the face of the severe time constraints resulting from an increased caseload. That is not to say that today's judges are producing the same quality of work as in the past. However, that judges are not functioning at the same level as in the past does not necessarily justify radical changes in the court system. Indeed, the courts I observed . . . have adopted sometimes significant stopgap measures that have enabled them to continue their work unhindered. And aside from general observations about the relative quality of their work, there have been no substantiated empirical claims that even [the courts are] no longer providing just resolutions as frequently as [they] did in the past.

"Trial judges do more than merely enforce norms promulgated by Congress and the appellate courts. Trial courts are also policy-making institutions that allocate social values and privilege."

3.3 POLITICS AND JUDGMENT ON THE FEDERAL DISTRICT COURTS

C. K. Rowland and Robert Carp

C. K. Rowland is Professor of Political Science at the University of Kansas. Robert A. Carp is Professor of Political Science and Associate Dean of the College of Social Sciences at the University of Houston.

From C. K. Rowland and Robert Carp, *Politics and Judgment on the Federal District Courts* (Lawrence: University of Kansas Press, 1996), pp. 2, 3–6.

Importance of District Judge Decision Making

The news media remind us daily that the rulings of our district judges affect all of us in one way or another on a whole panoply of issues: integration of our schools; the availability of abortions; standards for defining obscenity; the quality of the air we breathe and the water we drink; requirements for affirmative action programs; and standards for the maintenance of our prisons, public hospitals, and mental institutions. It is clear that our lives are affected by what federal trial judges say about the U.S. Constitution, federal laws, and the actions of government officials. Judges' decisions affect directly the residents of their own respective districts and, often indirectly, Americans in general insofar as their rulings serve as precedents for jurists in other districts.

Nature of Trial Judge Decision Making

At the most simplistic level, the function of U.S. trial judges is to enforce legal norms by resolving individual disputes. In many cases dispute resolution is largely administrative, as when trial judges facilitate out-of-court settlements. In others it approximates the traditional, mechanical model of judicial norm enforcement—that is, the trial judge "finds" the law, "fits" the law to the facts, and rules in favor of the litigant whose facts fit the law. But trial judges do more than merely enforce norms promulgated by Congress and the appellate courts. Trial courts are also policy-making institutions that allocate social values and privilege. When judges hear cases of first impression, they establish precedent, and in a common-law system this is the essence of policy formation. When opinions are published, they become the rules of the litigation process. When trial judges apply general statutes to individual cases, they implement legislative policies. And when federal trial judges devise and supervise equitable remedies to correct or prevent legal harm, they often impose their own policy judgments on administrators and elected officials.

Judges make policy even when they are acting as "fact finders." When, for example, a district judge supervising mass-tort litigation finds that the "facts" of exposure justify the certification of a plaintiff class, he simultaneously initiates a sequence of value reallocations and establishes evidentiary criteria for analogous future cases. In fact, the policy-making power inherent in fact-finding maximizes district judges' influence over the authoritative allocation of values because it is virtually immune from appellate review. Although litigants may appeal procedural decisions that defined the quantity and quality of the evidence presented, when the evidence convinces our mass-tort judge that the class of people exposed to externalities from a hazardous waste dump extends to a three-mile radius around the dump, that "finding" is virtually immune from appellate oversight.

Thus, judicial policy making in the federal trial courts assumes many overlapping forms. Many traditional distinctions, such as the difference between policy formulation and policy implementation, are obviated when the trial judge formulates specific policies in the process of implementing general legislative, administrative, or constitutional policies. Policy making in the federal trial courts can, however, be divided analytically into two functions—legal interpretation and equitable remediation—that parallel closely the traditional distinction between "law courts" and "equity courts" and require federal trial jurists to involve themselves simultaneously in the formulation and implementation of public policy.

The overlap among factual analysis, legal interpretation, policy formulation, and policy implementation can be illustrated by reference to the model of judicial policy implementation developed by Charles Johnson and Bradley Canon. In the context of this model, federal district judges are part of the "interpreting population," that is, the trial court "responds to the policy decisions of a higher court . . . interprets the meaning of the policy and develops the rules for matters not addressed in the original decision. . . . Interpretations of lower courts are distinguished from the interpretations of [others in the interpreting population] since theirs are viewed as authoritative in a legal sense by others in the political system."

As part of the interpreting population, district judges are key components in the implementation process. However, when judges evaluate evidence and interpret the law, they are also formulating policy. Indeed, absent clear legal guidelines, judges may actually create policy in the process of implementing vague legal guidelines and fitting the interpreted facts of an instant dispute to the interstices of extant law. When, for example, a federal judge rules in a case of first impression that obesity is not a handicap covered by federal antidiscrimination statutes, the jurist is at the same time formulating policy to guide other judges and, more important, potential litigants. Even when a judge is asked to resolve an intensely personal dispute for example, whether an unemancipated minor is mature enough to have an abortion without notifying her parents—his or her judgment becomes part of the common law and defines maturity for potential litigants in that jurisdiction.

Thus, interpretations of facts and law are judicial policy formulations, which are important links in the chain of policy implementation. When trial judges interpret the facts and law to mean that a legal harm has occurred—that is, when they assign legal liability to one or more parties to a dispute—they may be required to devise a legal remedy for that harm. To do so, they must participate in the formulation and implementation of equitable remediation policies designed to correct the causes of that harm and prevent its recurrence. When, for example, a judge finds that a state's prisons are overcrowded and that fact violates prisoners' Eighth and Fourteenth Amendment rights, not only can the judge order state officials to correct the overcrowding, he or she can participate actively in the formulation and administration of policies designed to correct this legal harm and prevent its recurrence.

Because equitable remediation involves district judges in the supervision of elected officials, it involves jurists directly in the highly politicized, authoritative allocation of social values and privilege. When, for example, a judge orders busing to implement school integration, the judge is allocating social values just as surely as if he were a legislator or school board member. Thus, equity judgments have important implications not only for judicial policy making but for the intergovernmental policy process. As such they are important links between the states and the federal government and between the judiciary and other policy-making institutions.

Despite the useful legal distinction between interpretation and remediation, in their eyes and in those of their appellate brethren, it is extremely important to remember that federal district judges are primarily fact finders. Moreover, the fact-finding function transcends remediation and interpretation, often rendering the distinction between the two a distinction without a meaningful difference. The judge's evaluation of the "facts" determines which competing precedent takes priority or which remediation plan will be implemented. Therefore, all forms of judicial policy making give individual judges the discretion and power to exercise judicial judgment—"the act of determining, as in courts, what is comfortable to law and courts." This responsibility is most apparent when judges interpret facts and law; however, it is equally characteristic of the formulation and implementation of remediation policies that require the judge to estimate the scope of legal perceived harm, whether local officials exercise "good faith" in the remediation process, and a host of other determinations about "what is comfortable to law and courts" in the context of the local legal, socioeconomic, and political cultures.

This relationship between judicial discretion, judicial judgment, judicial outcomes, and public policy was encapsulated nicely in district judge C. J. Wyzanski's decision to remain on the trial bench and reject an offer of "promotion" to the appellate bench from Massachusetts Senator Saltonstall in 1959: "The district court gives more scope to a judge's initiative and discretion. The district judge so often has the last word. Even where he does not, heed is given to his estimates of credibility, his determination of the facts, his discretion in framing or denying relief upon the facts he found."

Thus, to the extent facts and laws are ambiguous, federal trial judges' perceptions and interpretations are the product of judicial discretion, even when the judges are "simply" evaluating facts, law, and the fit between the two. This exercise of discretionary judgment is, after all, why we call them "judges" and why these jurists perceive themselves as important policy makers.

While our contention is that significant discretion and policy making are inherent in the work of trial judges, still we readily concede that some judges perceive more room for maneuver in their decision making than others. Role theorists have identified three types of decision makers at the trial court level. First, there are the "lawmakers" who take a broad view of the judicial role. These jurists, often referred to as "activists" or "innovators," contend that they can and must make law in their decisions, because the statutory law and appellate or Supreme Court guidelines are often ambiguous or do not cover all situations and because legislative intent is frequently impossible to determine. In Kitchin's study of federal district judges, only 14 percent were classified in this category.

At the other end of the continuum are the "law interpreters," who take a very narrow, traditional view of the judicial function. Sometimes called "strict constructionists," they don't believe that judges should substitute judicial wisdom for the rightful power of the elected branches of government to make policy. They tend to eschew making innovative decisions that may depart from the literal meaning of controlling precedents. In the Kitchin study, 52 percent of the U.S. trial judges were found to be "law interpreters." Midway between the law interpreters and the lawmakers are judges known as "pragmatists" or "realists," who believe that on occasion they are indeed obliged to make law but that for most cases a decision can be made by consulting the controlling law or appellate court precedents. About a third of federal district judges assume this moderate role. Thus, although ambiguous evidence forces judges to exercise fact finding discretion, judges may have to determine how much discretion they have and how they wish to exercise it. This is obviously a subjective process, and, as has been noted, "activist judges will find more discretion in a given fact situation than will their more restrained colleagues." . . .

"The District Court gives more scope to a judge's initiative and discretion."

3.4 THE IMPORTANCE OF THE TRIAL JUDGE

Charles E. Wyzanski, Jr.

January 12, 1959

Dear Lev:

I am deeply appreciative of your suggestion that my name be presented to the President and the Attorney General for their consideration whether to nominate me as a judge of the United States Court of Appeals for the First Circuit . . . . That you regard me as worthy of that high office is a great compliment. And were I to be appointed to a judgeship in that Court, I should regard it as both an honor and an opportunity for public service.

Yet I am persuaded that it is in both the public interest and my interest for me to decline to allow my name to be considered for the United States Court of Appeals. . . .

The District Court for the District of Massachusetts seems to me to offer at least as wide a field for judicial service as the Court of Appeals for the First Circuit. The District Court gives more scope to a judge's initiative and

---

Letter to Senator Leverett Saltonstall, January 12, 1959. Charles E. Wyzanski, Jr., (died in 1986) was United States District Judge for the District of Massachusetts.

discretion. His width of choice in sentencing defendants is the classic example. But there are many other instances. In civil litigation a District Judge has a chance to help the lawyers frame the issues and develop the facts so that there may be a meaningful and complete record. He may innovate procedures promoting fairness, simplification, economy, and expedition. By instructions to juries and, in appropriate cases, by comments on the evidence he may help the jurors better to understand their high civic function. He is a teacher of parties, witnesses, petitioners for naturalization, and even casual visitors to his court. His conduct of a trial may fashion and sustain the moral principles of the community. More even than the rules of constitutional, statutory, and common law he applies, his character and personal distinction, open to daily inspection in his courtroom, constitute the guarantees of due process.

Admittedly, the Court of Appeals stands higher than the District Courts in the judicial hierarchy, and Congress by attaching a larger compensation to the office of Circuit Judge has expressed its view of the relative importance of the two courts. Yet not all informed persons would concur in that evaluation. My revered former chief, Judge Augustus N. Hand, always spoke of his service in the District Court as being more interesting as well as more revealing of his qualities, and more enjoyable, than his service in the Court of Appeals. . . .

Although less spectacular litigation may ordinarily be carried from the District Court to the Court of Appeals, statistics will show how small a percentage of a reasonably good trial judge's decrees are in fact appealed. The District Judge so often has the last word. Even where he does not, heed is given to his estimates of credibility, his determination of the facts, his discretion in framing or denying relief upon the facts he found. . . .

The District Judge is in more direct relation than is the judge of the Court of Appeals to the bar and its problems. It is within the proper function of a District Court not merely by rules and decisions, but by an informed, intelligent, and energetic handling of his calendar to effectuate prompt as well as unbiased justice. It is the vigor of the District Court more than the action of the Court of Appeals which governs the number of cases which are ripe for appeal, and the time between the beginning of an action and a final judgment in an appellate court. And, paradoxically, it is not infrequently the alertness of the District Judge and his willingness to help counsel develop uncertain points of law (even though the development of such points inevitably increases the risks of error by the trial judge and of reversal by the appellate court) which makes a case significant in the progress of the law when it reaches a court of last resort.

While it may well be true that the highest office for a judge is to sit in judgment on other judges' errors, it is perhaps a more challenging task to seek, from minute to minute, to avoid one's own errors. And the zest of that task is enhanced by the necessity of reacting orally, instead of after the reflection permitted under the appellate judge's uninterrupted schedule of reading and writing.

I realize that the trial judge lacks the opportunity to benefit from the collegiate discussion open to an appellate judge. His ties with his brethren are less intimate. Consequently, he runs the perils of excessive individualism. Few there are who can gently chide him on his foibles, remind him of the grace of manners, or warn against the nigh universal sin of pride.

Yet perhaps the trial judge's relative loneliness brings him closer to the tragic plight of man. Was not Wallace Stevens speaking for the trial judge when he wrote:

"Life consists
   Of propositions about life. The human Reverie is a solitude in which We compose these propositions, torn by dreams"? . . .

Sincerely,
Charles E. Wyzanski, Jr.

> *"[The] federal judicial system . . . is more heterogeneous*
> *than hierarchical in practice."*

3.5 LITIGATION FLOW IN THREE UNITED STATES COURTS OF APPEALS

J. Woodford Howard, Jr.
J. Woodford Howard, Jr., is Thomas P. Stran Professor
Emeritus of Political Science, Johns Hopkins University.

This article reports some findings from an intensive quantitative study of the flow of litigation from federal district courts to three federal courts of appeals (District of Columbia, Second, and Fifth Circuits), and from the three appeals courts to the Supreme Court. The study covered all reported cases decided by the three appeals courts during fiscal years 1965, 1966, and 1967—a total of 4,945. The excerpt reprinted here deals only with the relation of the courts of appeals to the Supreme Court.

The most striking pattern is how little direct supervision the [Supreme Court] Justices exercised over the three courts of appeals. Litigants appealed 1,004 or one-in-five of these circuit decisions [4,945] to the Supreme Court, which granted certiorari in 9.2 percent of those appealed. Discounting eleven dismissals, the Court intervened in ninety-two cases or 1.9 percent of the entire sample . . . affirming 0.5 percent and disturbing 1.4 percent. In effect, the three tribunals became courts of last resort in 98.1 percent of the cases and made decisions that formally prevailed in 98.6 percent. . . .

The upshot is uneven supervision of circuit courts by the Justices. . . . For three years, these courts of appeals were left to their own devices in broad ranges of litigation. The Justices exercised no review at all over their treatment

From 8 *Law and Society Review* 33 (1973). Reprinted with permission.

of insurance and marine contracts, workmen's compensation, fair labor standards, parole, social security, suffrage, and school desegregation. . . . Notwithstanding the high court's propensity to reverse [circuit court decisions], the Justices intervened so rarely and selectively in these federal appeals that controls on the discretion of circuit judges would appear to depend less on fear of formal reversal than on the informal constraints embodied in the notion of "judicial role." . . . Supreme Court review looms as too irregular for rotating circuit judges to worry greatly about reversal or second-guessing Justices. . . .

These frequencies, of course, do not mean that circuit judges were forty-nine times more influential over Federal appeals than the Supreme Court. Just as intermediate appellate courts are highly dependent on litigants and tribunals below, so are they theoretically bound by other Supreme Court decisions in like circumstances and influenced by the decisions of other circuits, too. One Supreme Court decision may control dozens of similar circuit cases, and in a case-law system we cannot assume that a lower court must be reversed in order to follow a higher one. Nor is each appeal in the circuit component of equal significance. . . . Yet these frequencies do help to establish the opportunities of circuit courts to affect national law and further understanding of their appellate roles. . . . The Justices exert direct control over so little federal litigation that those concerned with the distribution of individual justice or the administration of national policy through law should look not only up but down and around. . . .

Circuit judges filter issues on their way to the Supreme Court; they have substantial opportunity to create and to resist judicial policy when the Justices cannot or will not intervene, which is nearly all the time. . . . As courts of last resort in the overwhelming majority of cases, they make national law residually and regionally. Whether courts of appeals are conceived of as political actors with distinct constituencies or as functionaries in a legal bureaucracy, the magnitude of their finality in contexts of regional recruitment and organization produces a federal judicial system that is more heterogeneous than hierarchical in practice. . . .

* * *

[Political scientists Sue Davis and Donald Songer updated Howard's analysis. Their results follow.][1]

Howard found that in the 1960s the Supreme Court exercised very little direct supervision over the courts of appeals. While 20 percent of circuit decisions were appealed, the Supreme Court heard only 9 percent of those requests for review. Thus, in only 1.9 percent of all appeals court cases was the circuit decision reviewed by the Supreme Court; two-thirds of those were reversed.

An examination of the decisions of the courts of appeals for 1986 suggests that review by the Supreme Court of circuit decisions has now become even less frequent. As Table 1 shows, the rate of appeal by the losing party in the courts

---

[1] Reprinted from Sue Davis and Donald Songer, "The Changing Role of the United States Courts of Appeals," *Justice System Journal* 13 (1988–89), 323.

TABLE 1 Supreme Court Review of Three Courts of Appeals (1986)

	Appealed to Supreme Court		Total N	Reviewed by Supreme Court		Affirmed by Supreme Court		Reversed by Supreme Court	
Circuit	%	n		%	n	%	n	%	n
4th	23.1	347	2,032	0.5	11	0.1	3	0.3	7
11th	21.8	294	1,601	0.4	6	0.1	2	0.2	3
D.C.	16.9	59	228	0.9	2	0.4	1	0.4	1
Total	22.0	700	3,861	0.5	19	0.2	6	0.3	11

of appeals has not changed much over the last twenty years. During these two decades, however, the number of cases heard in the courts of appeals has approximately tripled while the number of decisions reviewed by the Supreme Court has remained relatively stable. As a result, the proportion of circuit decisions reviewed by the Supreme Court has dropped dramatically from the already low rates reported in Howard's earlier study and is now less than 1 percent in each of the three circuits. The figures in Table 1 indicate that the Supreme Court still reverses the decision in nearly two-thirds of the cases it accepts for review, but since so few cases are accepted, the result is that in 99.5 percent of all appeals court cases the circuit decision is left undisturbed by the Supreme Court. . . .

"The present number of federal bankruptcy, district, and appellate judges should be increased by at least 50 percent." —VICTOR WILLAMS

"Twenty-one years of service as a federal judge have persuaded me that the most serious threat to the proper functioning of the federal judiciary is the current trend to increase its size beyond tolerable limits." —JON O. NEWMAN

3.6 SOLUTIONS TO FEDERAL JUDICIAL GRIDLOCK VERSUS 1,000 JUDGES— THE LIMIT FOR AN EFFECTIVE FEDERAL JUDICIARY

Victor Williams versus Jon O. Newman

Victor Williams is Assistant Professor of Law, John Jay College of Criminal Justice, City University of New York. Jon O. Newman serves on the U.S. Court of Appeals for the Second Circuit.

From 76 *Judicature* 185 (1993).

Victor Williams

The federal judicial system is in a state of gridlock: Fewer than 850 federal judges are attempting to process the civil actions of a nation of more than 200 million inordinately litigious citizens while adjudicating the criminal trials of a nation at war against drugs and violent crime. Since 1960, federal case filings have increased 900 percent in the courts of appeals and 250 percent in the district courts. This has been exacerbated during the past year by vacancies in up to 135, or one out of six, of all federal judgeships. These vacancies have remained unfilled due to a chronic breakdown in the appointment process. . . .

The dynamic nature of the nation's population and economy guarantee tremendous civil and criminal litigation growth during the next decade. The federal caseload will reach near crisis proportions by the next century without long-term planning and change. The president and Congress, therefore, should develop a long-range plan for the expansion and remodeling of the entire judicial infrastructure, not for the purpose of increasing the power of the judicial bureaucracy, but to ensure that prompt, effective justice is available to all litigants in 2001.

At a minimum, any long-range plan for the renovation of the judicial infrastructure should include the following crucial components. First, the plan should call for the establishment of a United States Court of Bankruptcy Appeals. This Article III appellate court would have twelve circuits, with five to nine judges sitting in each. The court should be vested with exclusive jurisdiction over all appeals from the Article I bankruptcy courts, thus reducing significantly the caseload of district courts and the presently composed court of appeals. Each circuit, in addition, would select one of its own to sit for a limited term on a national intercircuit bankruptcy panel that would settle intercircuit conflicts.

Second, the plan should call for the separation of circuit courts of appeals into civil and criminal divisions. The criminal division of the U.S. Court of Appeals would exercise exclusive jurisdiction over all federal criminal appeals and all collateral civil appeals.

Third, the long-overdue creation of an Intercircuit Court of Appeals should be an integral part of the long term plan. In 1986, then Associate Justice Rehnquist, addressing the American Bar Association, endorsed the establishment of such a court. He advocated the junior supreme court's creation to help alleviate the Supreme Court's overwhelming caseload and to give greater consistency to national law. The idea of constructing an intermediate court having certiorari jurisdiction over select appeals has been considered seriously by Congress, the judiciary, and the bar on numerous occasions since the 1960s.

Fourth, the present number of federal bankruptcy, district, and appellate judges should be increased by at least 50 percent. The call for additional judges represents a substantial departure from existing proposals. Critics of an increased judiciary abound. Consistently, they warn that a federal judiciary of more than 1,000 judges will result in the appointment of unqualified nominees and breed an unmanageable judicial bureaucracy.

Proponents of artificial ceilings on the number of federal judges ignore the trend toward expanding the workload of the federal courts. Propositions to constrain the growth of one of three equal branches of the federal government threaten to sabotage the court system. After considering present and projected gridlock, it is readily apparent that a 1,000-judge ceiling on the federal judiciary is as dangerous as it is arbitrary. Considering the inevitable future growth of the federal caseload, a 50 percent increase in judicial resources is a modest recommendation. . . .

Jon O. Newman

Twenty-one years of service as a federal judge have persuaded me that the most serious threat to the proper functioning of the federal judiciary is the current trend to increase its size beyond tolerable limits.

There are currently 828 authorized federal judgeships. The recent report of the Federal Courts Study Committee and the 1991 year-end report of the Chief Justice of the United States have suggested that 1,000 is the realistic limit for an effective federal judiciary. That limit will inevitably be reached before the end of this decade. The issue to be seriously considered by all who care about the role of the judicial branch in the twenty-first century is whether the number should be held at 1,000 judges or be permitted to go higher.

The line must be held at 1,000 because once that number is exceeded, it will be only a matter of time until the federal judiciary grows to 2,000, 3,000, and then 4,000. Growth of such magnitude will seriously impair the federal judiciary's ability to perform the vital tasks assigned to it under our system of government. . . .

One adverse consequence is the threat to the quality of the federal judiciary. An undue increase in the number of judges will inevitably lead to a reduction in the quality of new appointees. The reason is not that we will be unable to locate 3,000 or 4,000 well-qualified men and women to serve as federal judges. Of course they will be available, indeed eager to serve.

The reason growth impairs quality is that an increase in the number of judicial appointments made every year reduces the visibility of each appointment and permits the political process to select many candidates of mediocre attainments and even a few of marginal competence. . . .

A second adverse consequence of an enlarged federal judiciary is the threat to the proper functioning of each federal court of appeals as its size moves past tolerable limits. I believe a federal court of appeals begins to have its effective functioning impaired as its size moves past nine. The Second Circuit is now at thirteen. We are managing, but as I contemplate our court in the middle of the next century numbering, at current trends, fifty or sixty judges, I despair. It will not be a court; it will be a stable of judges, each one called upon to plough through the unrelenting volume, harnessed on any given day with two other judges who barely know each other.

A third adverse consequence develops as efforts are made to keep the size of each court of appeals within some manageable limits: the circuits are divided and the number of circuits is increased. We have already divided the old Fifth Circuit into the new Fifth and Eleventh Circuits. Many are urging that the mammoth Ninth Circuit, with its current total of twenty-eight appellate judges, be divided into two or three circuits. In a federal judiciary of 3,000 or 4,000, it is inevitable that fragmentation of circuits will occur. The unitary nature of the federal judicial system, with a small number of cohesive circuits, will soon resemble the diverse multi-unit structure of the state systems. They will serve the needs of the fifty states, but their structure is not the model for an effectively functioning national court system.

A fourth adverse consequence of an expanded judiciary is the inevitable decline in the coherence of a body of federal law. With thirteen circuits, most of which number between eleven and fifteen judges, we are quickly approaching a critical point in the history of the federal appellate system. Either we permit each circuit to grow to thirty, forty, or fifty judges, or we maintain the size of each circuit and permit the number of circuits to grow to thirty, forty, or fifty. Either way, the coherence of federal law is bound to decline. As an appellate court of many judges inevitably breeds conflicts among its panels, a nation of many circuits inevitably breeds conflicts among its circuits. It is a threat that the Supreme Court cannot meet. The Court currently reviews less than I percent of the decisions of the federal courts of appeals. It cannot possibly maintain coherence of federal law in a federal judiciary of 2,000, 3,000, or 4,000 judges.

The final and most serious adverse consequence of an enlarged federal judiciary is an impairment in the quality of decision making. This is a somewhat paradoxical phenomenon that requires some explanation. It begins to develop as case volume rises. The initial response is to add more judges. But then an immutable fact of governmental life takes hold: judges are added at a rate that always falls far short of the rate of increase in case volume.

We have seen this occur dramatically in the federal courts of appeals in the past four decades. Their caseload has increased far faster than the increase in judges. In 1947, 387 appeals were filed in the Second Circuit, a court then consisting of six judges. For the court year that ended this past June 30, we received more than 4,000 appeals and our court had increased to thirteen judges. In forty-five years, the case filings increased more than ten times; the number of judges slightly more than doubled. Case filings per judge more than quadrupled.

Once the filings per judge increase at that rate, decline in quality begins to occur because the expanded number of judges is obliged to adopt various expedient measures to handle the growing volume. First, the judges devote less time to each matter, less time to deciding, and less time to crafting opinions. I used to think I was devoting the necessary time to every appeal I heard and every opinion I wrote. As the years go by, I have come to realize, in all candor, that I have been applying a shorter and shorter ruler to measure the time that ought to be devoted to each task. My standards are changing. Heavy volume is taking its toll. . . .

The pressure on the growing judiciary to keep up with a caseload that is growing even faster also impels judges to rely to an increasing extent on supporting staff. The federal judiciary, once renowned for the individualized performances of its judges, tends each year to look and function more like a bureaucracy. When I graduated from law school, each federal circuit judge had one law clerk. Today most have three. In every circuit, staff counsel abound. We have motions clerks, pro se clerks, and other supporting personnel. If growth is not curbed, we can look forward to the day when each federal appellate judge is running a small law office of six law clerks, and each court of appeals has a central staff of 100 lawyers.

In combination, these developments pose a serious threat to the quality of federal court decision making. Thus far, we are coping—just barely. I think the quality of the work being performed by the court on which I serve is quite high, as it is generally throughout the federal judiciary. But I fear for the long-term future. If federal caseloads are permitted to grow at the current pace, we will add judges, always too few to keep up with the increase in volume, and we will see an inevitable decline in the quality of decision making. . . .

"Notwithstanding the distinctive developments in each state, supreme courts in very different states, confronted with rising caseloads, changed in rather similar and predictable ways, although some states were much quicker than others to make those changes."

3.7 THE EVOLUTION OF STATE SUPREME COURTS

Robert A. Kagan, Bliss Cartwright, Lawrence M. Friedman, and Stanton Wheeler

Robert A. Kagan is Professor of Political Science and Law and Director of the Center for the Study of Law and Society, University of California, Berkeley. Lawrence M. Friedman is the Marion Rice Kirkwood Professor of Law at Stanford University. Stanton Wheeler is the Ford Foundation Professor of Law and Social Sciences at Yale Law School.

The population of the sixteen states in our sample increased steadily over time, from fewer than eleven million in 1870 to over seventy-three million in 1970. The sixteen supreme courts issued an average of 131 opinions in 1870, or 170.8 opinions per million persons. From 1870 to 1880, both the average number of supreme court opinions per state and the total opinions per million persons rose with the population. But soon after 1880, these numbers began to diverge. After reaching a peak of 201 in 1880, the number of opinions per million persons per

Reprinted from 76 *Michigan Law Review* 961 (1978).

year has shown a consistent downward trend, averaging a fairly level forty-two since the end of World War II. The average number of opinions per state, however, continued to rise, although at an irregular rate, and reached its high point in 1915, when the sixteen courts issued an average of 291 opinions. It then began a generally downward move, bottoming at 119 opinions per year at the end of World War II. Thereafter, the average number of opinions rose roughly in relation to population growth. In 1970, the sixteen courts wrote an average of 167 opinions per year. . . .

Notwithstanding the distinctive developments in each state, supreme courts in very different states, confronted with rising caseloads, changed in rather similar and predictable ways, although some states were much quicker than others to make those changes. The crucial developments have been in court structure and jurisdiction. Two changes are especially important: grants of power to supreme courts to select their own cases from petitions for review, and the establishment of intermediate appellate courts between the trial courts and supreme courts.

We can distinguish three rough phases in this evolution and three corresponding "types" of state supreme courts. In the first phase, courts had light caseloads and little or no discretion in selecting cases. In the second phase, courts in states with growing populations were burdened by heavy caseloads, but still had little case-selecting discretion. The courts of the third phase had light caseloads (as measured by opinions issued) and great case-selecting discretion; this phase tended to emerge only after extended political struggle. [We] discuss the three phases in turn, pausing to examine the patterns of transition between the second and third phases.

The Low Caseload–Low Discretion State Supreme Court

The United States in 1870 was still predominantly a country of small towns, small farms, and small businesses, run by small government. The national population was about 40,000,000, less than one fifth of what it is today. Illinois, the fourth most populous state (after New York, Pennsylvania, and Ohio) and the largest in our sixteen-state sample, had about 2,500,000 citizens. Oregon's population was 90,000; Nevada's just over 42,000. The absolute volume of litigation was certainly far smaller than it is today, though almost no research exists on this question.

Most states in 1870 had only one level of appeal from their trial courts. Of the sixteen states in our sample, only New Jersey had an appellate court between its trial court of general jurisdiction and its highest court. In none of our sixteen states could the supreme court select cases from those appealed or screen out frivolous or unimportant appeals—the courts were obligated to hear and decide whatever cases litigants chose to appeal. In constructing their dockets of business, supreme courts in the main were *reactive* rather than *proactive*; the volume and content of their caseloads were "litigant-controlled."

This system worked decently enough, especially for states with small populations. Caseloads were not impossibly large; few supreme courts in 1870 decided more than 200 cases with full opinions each year. Seven states in our sample never rose above one million in population in the nineteenth century: Maine, Rhode Island, West Virginia, South Dakota, Idaho, Oregon and Nevada. From 1870 to 1900, their supreme courts averaged fewer than 100 opinions per year. Five of these states remained smaller than one million through 1970: Maine, Rhode Island, South Dakota, Idaho and Nevada. Their annual supreme court caseloads in the twentieth century generally remained below 150 cases, and often below 100.

The High Caseload–Low Discretion State Supreme Court

Other states, however, had larger populations, and some grew quite rapidly. Increases in population generally meant more cases in the trial courts. If the proportion of lower-court litigants who appeal stayed constant (or fell at a rate slower than the rate of increase in the number of lower-court cases), and if appeal remained available as of right, then we would expect population growth to bring more and more appeals. Our data confirm this guess. Supreme court opinions in some of the more populous and faster-growing states reached averages of 400 or 500 a year.

In California and Michigan, population doubled between 1870 and 1895; the number of opinions issued each year jumped from 200 or less in 1870 to over 550 in 1890 and 1895. North Carolina's population took longer to double (its population was 1.1 million in 1870, and 2.2 million in 1910), but its supreme court also doubled its output, from 208 opinions in 1870 to an average of 440 in 1910 and 1915. In Illinois, where the population had reached three million, the supreme court issued 624 opinions in 1875. When population topped one million in Alabama and Minnesota, the supreme court caseloads quickly grew to over 350 per year.

A court whose caseload jumps in a short time to 300, 400, or 500 cases a year cannot be quite the same kind of court as one which decides 50, 75, or 100 cases. Courts, of course, have a certain capacity to accommodate increases in business. Judges can do less research on their own and lean more on the research of lawyers. Judges can spend less time on each case, restrict oral argument, or eliminate it entirely. They can limit the length of briefs and produce shorter or even brief "per curiam" opinions. Still, supreme court judges must read at least some briefs, consider competing arguments, decide cases, and write opinions. If their caseload doubles, the judges are harder pressed to keep up, unless they can devise some drastic shortcuts or divisions of labor.

In any event, judges on busy courts had less time to invest in each case than their predecessors who heard fewer cases. At the least, the flood of cases threatened the quality of decision-making, and some supreme courts clearly saw it that way. Lawyers and legal scholars in the early twentieth century often complained of intolerable delays in the state supreme courts. They also complained that there was not enough time for oral argument or for judges to discuss cases among themselves, and that high courts wasted time on trivial cases. Moreover, some critics contended that the hard-pressed judges relied mechanically on precedent and wrote excessively formalistic opinions which offered only feeble guidance for lower courts and the bar. Of course, our data cannot measure directly the effect of the bursting caseloads on the thoughtfulness and crafts-manship of decisions in the late nineteenth century. But between 1870 and 1900, courts with heavy caseloads did differ from their less burdened counterparts in several distinct ways. . . . [O]n the average, courts with larger caseloads wrote opinions which were shorter, which used fewer citations, and which referred less often to treatises, legal encyclopedias, and law reviews. Although by no means overwhelming, the evidence is fairly consistent.

It would be rash to conclude from these findings that the decisions of heavy-caseload supreme courts were slap-dash or ill-considered; conciseness can be a virtue and long strings of citations can be a vice. These findings are consistent, however, with the idea that courts with massive caseloads were forced to limit the time, effort, and research devoted to each case. This may have increased the risk of routine, poorly crafted opinions.

Patterns of Adaptation to High Caseload

How do organizations in general react to an increasing volume of business? A common way is to hire more staff. More staff means more people to supervise and coordinate, and it leads to functional specialization and more layers of au-thority. The organizations grow and take on the familiar bureaucratic form.

But growth also makes possible economies of scale. The organization works out routines and rules to cover recurring problems. Nonroutine problems are shifted to top officials, who have experts on their staff. A complex organization also tries to stabilize its relationship with the outside world. It attempts to "smooth out" fluctuations in demands that flow in, sometimes by rationing its services. Sometimes it feels it will be better off by taking on some jobs too im-portant to leave to outsiders. A steel mill, for example, might want to control the sources of iron or coal; a police department might patrol aggressively instead of relying entirely on citizens' complaints.

A supreme court faced with growing demands on its time, and worried about the quality of its work, might want to use these classic adaptations. That would mean more staff, new levels of courts, perhaps more specialized appel-late bodies, and more efficient ways to allocate judicial work. Such a court would want to limit the number and kinds of appeals that it received. Ideally, it would enunciate general rules or principles that lower courts could apply routinely and accurately, so that it need hear only the most serious and impor-tant cases.

How could a supreme court ensure that it heard those cases, and only those? It would have to develop a system for identifying significant legal prob-lems and screening out the trivial ones; it would not leave the selection process to the whims and pocketbooks of litigants. A professional staff to help research and write might be more reliable than litigants' lawyers, who differ widely in ability, integrity, and energy. . . . In short, busy state supreme courts would strive to become less reactive, less controlled by litigants, more self-directed and bureaucratically organized. . . .

Reformers pressed for integrated, rational court structures, supported by administrative staffs, to monitor the flow of business and assure that judicial manpower was sensibly allocated. They called in particular for intermediate appellate courts and they felt a supreme court should be able to choose its cases and write its own rules of procedure.

Some of these steps toward reorganization were taken, but some were not. Not until the 1960s did most large and medium-sized states establish intermediate appellate courts and allow supreme courts substantial discretion over caseloads. Through much of the past century, many State supreme courts struggled along year after year, writing 400 or more opinions, using techniques and procedures that had hardly changed in generations. Nonetheless, several different adaptations to the caseload problem can be distinguished.

EARLY INTERMEDIATE APPELLATE COURTS AND DISCRETION Among our sixteen sample states, New Jersey, Tennessee, and West Virginia were unusually successful in controlling the volume of their supreme courts' caseloads, and they began this process remarkably early. New Jersey, [for example], had established an intermediate appellate court for cases "at law" (as opposed to equity) in 1844. This court, called the Supreme Court, was later divided into several three-judge panels, each of which heard appeals from different trial courts. Although New Jersey's highest court, the Court of Errors and Appeals, could not reject appeals from the lower appellate courts, its volume remained extraordinarily small, averaging 145 opinions per year between 1900 and 1935, even though the state's population grew from 1.8 million to 4 million. . . .

FUNCTIONAL EQUIVALENTS FOR INTERMEDIATE APPELLATE COURTS California's experience exemplifies the full battery of methods used to control heavy caseloads. In the late nineteenth century, California responded to rapid growth by increasing the size of its supreme court from three to five judges in the 1860s. In 1879, when the court was hearing over 500 cases a year and writing 350 opinions, the number of justices was increased to seven. The court was also authorized in 1879 to divide into three-judge panels or departments, to hear cases separately. The full court gathered en banc only for extraordinarily important cases. Other states, too, adopted this innovation. The department system was also important because it recognized differences among appeals. Some appeals were more "significant" than others; the less important were treated in one way, more important cases in another. In effect, the division into panels created two intermediate appellate courts—or at least alternative supreme courts—for most appeals.

The California Supreme Court judges issued 402 opinions in 1885, 122 en banc and 280 in departments. At this point, the legislature authorized the court to delegate to three "commissioners" power to bear cases and make preliminary decisions. Commissioners, in effect, were auxiliary judges (or, perhaps, highly trained and experienced staff members). The court could review and modify the commissioners' opinions, but in practice it simply issued them as its own. This innovation, too, gave the Supreme Court some choice of cases it wished to concentrate on. The California Supreme Court continued to produce a prodigious number of opinions (well over 500 in 1995 and 1900), but the judges themselves wrote only 300 per year, 100 en banc, 200 in departments; commissioners handled another 200.

The use of commissioners was discontinued in 1904, when California set up a system of intermediate appellate courts, called courts of appeals. In some types of cases, litigants could appeal only to a court of appeals; in others, they could go directly from the trial court to the supreme court. The California Supreme Court could, however, transfer some of its cases to the court of appeals. It also had discretion to review decisions of the lower appellate courts. Although the supreme court gradually transferred more and more of its cases to the court of appeals, it still averaged over 250 opinions a year from 1910 to 1935, most of them decided en banc.

THE WEAK INTERMEDIATE APPELLATE COURT SYSTEM Illinois wove a different pattern. It created an intermediate appellate court in 1877 (when its supreme court heard over 600 cases) but allowed these courts only a limited role. Appellants could still proceed directly from trial courts to supreme court as of right unless the amount at issue was less than $1,000. Moreover, appeals from the lower appellate court to the supreme court were available as of right.

The Illinois Supreme Court caseload fell to an average of 240 opinions in 1880 and 1885, but by 1900 and 1905, as population and litigation grew, the volume had climbed back to an average of 475 opinions per year. Statutory amendments in 1909 further limited appeals to the supreme court; however, litigants could still appeal directly in felony, tax, real estate, and most constitutional cases. The Supreme Court's caseload remained high. The court seemed reluctant to use its discretionary power to deny appeals from the appellate courts; hence, double appeals were common. As late as 1958, court reformers in Illinois complained that the supreme court was "hamstrung," that it heard "a wide variety of cases with little legal significance."

STATES WITHOUT INTERMEDIATE APPELLATE COURTS Other states dragged their feet even more than Illinois. Minnesota never established an intermediate appellate court, and its supreme court caseload averaged a staggering 425 cases per year from 1890 through 1935. The load declined during the 1940s and 1950s without any notable change in supreme court jurisdiction, but it climbed again in the 1960s, and reached 332 in 1970. Kansas, after brief experiments in the 1890s with commissioners and intermediate appellate courts, abandoned both. Its supreme court averaged 407 opinions a year from 1910 to 1935. Yet here too, without any major structural change, the caseload dropped off; it averaged a high but not unbearable 225 opinions a year from 1950 to 1970. North Carolina had no lower appellate court until the 1960s. Its supreme court had averaged well over 300, and sometimes over 400, opinions per year since the 1890s. . . .

SOME SPECULATIONS ON THE POLITICS OF STATE SUPREME COURT REORGANIZATION We are not sure why supreme court caseloads remained so high so long in so many states, and why structural reform did not come sooner. One crucial factor, it would seem, is that in many states the structure of the judicial system was embedded—one might say frozen—in the state constitution. For many reasons, too, legislators and political leaders were uninterested in reform, or opposed to it outright. Politicians certainly did not see backlogs and overloads in the supreme court as the most pressing problem of the day. Spending money on salaries for new intermediate appellate judges was never politically inviting. The work of some state courts was controversial. Judges were sometimes perceived as reactionaries and as enemies of social legislation; to give such judges more power and discretion would only encourage "government by judiciary." Supreme court reform was often part of a general reform package that included reshaping the lower courts, and thus local magistrates, justices of the peace, court clerks, and others who felt they might suffer in a reorganization outshouted the few reformers. Political and party officials threatened with loss of patronage were also part of the opposition.

Indeed, supreme court judges themselves did not always strongly advocate reorganization. Their self-interest called for caseload control, of course; in modern court systems, more cases do not bring more fees or higher salaries, but simply more work. A court that decides 200 or fewer cases a year and concentrates on difficult and important problems tends to be more prestigious than one struggling through 400 mostly routine cases. But judges also have a tradition of reticence. It is thought unseemly for them to lobby, to seek more power, or to press for reforms that encourage the use of courts. . . .

But ideologies have been shifting over the years. Gradually, judges have espoused a somewhat different view of themselves and their roles. "Sociological jurisprudence" and legal realism have made their mark. At least some state supreme court judges now feel that making policy is an inevitable part of their work, and they wonder whether they should not approach it more systematically. To do so, they must be able to winnow out the trivial cases and concentrate on the important. That cannot be done without structural reform, intermediate appellate courts, control over dockets, and larger staffs.

Meanwhile, reform has become better organized. Since 1917, the American Judicature Society has published a journal which stresses judicial reform. Since the 1920s, state judicial councils, staffed by judges and legislators, have gathered statistics on court business, issued reports and recommendations, and lobbied for reform.

Nevertheless, state supreme courts have not acquired caseload control easily; it has been a long, complicated process, heavily dependent on the political skill of judicial reformers and on the local political climate. Apparent victories have often been subverted. Kansas established an intermediate appellate court in 1895 and abolished it six years later. Illinois set up a lower appellate court, but still allowed direct appeals to the supreme court for cases involving certain politically important interests. Not until the 1960s did the reformers gain real momentum. Only eleven states had intermediate courts in 1948; by 1970, twenty-three did. . . .

The Low Caseload–High Discretion State Supreme Court

By the end of the 1960s, most of the medium-sized and larger states in our sample of sixteen had created intermediate appellate courts and given their supreme courts substantial discretion to select cases from petitions for review. Consequently, supreme court caseloads, as measured by opinions issued, were sharply reduced. . . .

This increasing discretion and diminishing caseload implied corresponding changes in the function of the supreme courts. It suggested an emerging societal consensus that state supreme courts should not be passive, reactive bodies, which simply applied "the law" to correct "errors" or miscarriages of justice in individual cases, but that these courts should be policy-makers and, at least in some cases, legal innovators. After the 1967 reform in North Carolina, the Supreme Court, it was said, could now concentrate on "truly significant questions of law." Even in smaller states, the ideal was a low-volume, well-staffed supreme court which "delegated" routine appeals and supervision of trial courts to lower appellate courts and concentrated on important, far-reaching cases. Rhode Island's supreme court had no case-selecting discretion; one justice complained in 1974 that half of the court's cases "don't belong in the highest court of a state." . . .

A Typology of State Supreme Courts

. . . We grouped the states by the "type" into which they fell during most of the 1870–1970 period. Because of their dramatic shifts, we placed Oregon and California in the type that best characterized them in the last two decades. The three types, which represent different combinations of population, supreme court caseload, and discretion, are as follows:

Type I: Low population states (under one million) with no supreme court case-selecting discretion, no lower appellate court, and relatively light caseloads. Rhode Island, Maine, South Dakota, Idaho, and Nevada were in this category throughout the century. Their supreme courts averaged fewer than 100 opinions per year.

Type II: Medium-sized (over one million) and large states with little or no supreme court case-selecting discretion, and heavy caseloads. Illinois, Michigan, Minnesota, Kansas, North Carolina and Alabama were in this category for most of the century. Oregon joined it in population terms in the 1930s and in caseload terms (over 220 opinions) in the 1915–1930 and 1960–1970 years. These supreme courts averaged well over 200 opinions a year in most time periods, and often 350 or more.

Type III: Medium-sized or large states with substantial controls over supreme court caseloads (lower appellate courts handled most appeals or supreme courts had wide discretion to choose cases) and relatively light caseloads, measured by published opinions. New Jersey, Tennessee and West Virginia were in this category for most of the century. California's Supreme Court joined it about 1940, when it began exercising its discretion to assign most appeals to the court of appeals. These supreme courts averaged under 200 opinions a year, and often fewer than 150. . . .

"Some state courts seem apparently even to be anticipating contrary rulings by the United States Supreme Court and are therefore resting decisions on state law grounds to avoid review."

3.8 GUARDIANS OF OUR LIBERTIES—STATE COURTS NO LESS THAN FEDERAL

William J. Brennan

William J. Brennan served as an Associate Justice of the Supreme Court of the United States from 1957 to 1990.

After his retirement, Chief Justice Earl Warren was asked what he regarded to be the decision during his tenure that would have the greatest consequence for all Americans. His choice was *Baker v. Carr*, because he believed that if each of us has an equal vote, we are equally armed with the indispensable means to make our views felt. I feel at least as good a case can be made that the series of decisions binding the States to almost all of the restraints of the Bill of Rights will be even more significant in preserving and furthering the ideals we have fashioned for our society. Before the Fourteenth Amendment was added to the Constitution, the Supreme Court held that the Bill of Rights did not restrict state, but only federal, action. In the decades between 1868, when the Fourteenth Amendment was adopted, and 1897, the Court decided in case after case that the Fourteenth Amendment did not apply various specific restraints in the Bill of Rights to state action. The breakthrough came in 1897 when prohibition against taking private property for public use without payment of just compensation was held embodied in the Fourteenth Amendment's proscription, "nor shall any state deprive any person of . . . property, without due process of law." But extension of the rest of the specific restraints was slow in coming. It was 1925 before it was suggested that perhaps the restraints of the First Amendment applied to state action. Then in 1949 the Fourth Amendment's prohibition of unreasonable searches and seizures was extended, but the extension was virtually meaningless because the States were left free to decide for themselves whether any effective means of enforcement of the guarantee was to be made available. It was not until 1961 that the Court applied the exclusionary rule to state proceedings.

But the years from 1962 to 1969 witnessed the extension of nine of the specifics of the Bill of Rights, and these decisions have had a profound impact on American life, requiring the deep involvement of state courts in the application of federal law. The Eighth Amendment's prohibition of cruel and unusual

From 15 *Judges Journal* 82 (1976).

punishment was applied to state action in 1962, and is the guarantee under which the death penalty as then administered was struck down in 1971. The provision of the Sixth Amendment that in all prosecutions the accused shall have the assistance of counsel was applied in 1963 and in consequence counsel must be provided in every courtroom of every State of this land to secure the rights of those accused of crime. In 1964, the Fifth Amendment privilege against compulsory self-incrimination was extended. And after decades of police coercion, by means ranging from torture to trickery, the privilege against self-incrimination became the basis of *Miranda v. Arizona*, requiring police to give warnings to a suspect before custodial interrogation. . . .

The thread of this series of holding that the Fourteenth Amendment guarantees citizens the protections of the Bill of Rights in confrontations with state action reflects a conclusion—arrived at only after a long series of decisions grappling with the pros and cons of the question—that there exists in modern America the necessity for protecting all of us from arbitrary action by governments more powerful and pervasive than in our ancestors' time, and that the protections must be construed to preserve their fundamental policies and thereby the maintenance of our constitutional structure of government for a free society.

For the genius of our Constitution resides not in any static meaning that it had in a world that is dead and gone, but in the adaptability of its great principles to cope with the problems of a developing America. A principle to be vital must be of wider application than the mischief that gave it birth. Constitutions are not ephemeral documents, designed to meet passing occasions. The future is their care, and therefore, in their application, our contemplation cannot be only of what has been but of what may be.

Of late, however, more and more state courts are construing state constitutional counterparts of provisions of the Bill of Rights as guaranteeing citizens of their States even more protection than the federal provisions, even those identically phrased. This is surely an important and highly significant development for our constitutional jurisprudence and for our concept of federalism. I suppose it was only natural that when during the 1960s our rights and liberties were in the process of becoming increasingly federalized, state courts saw no reason to consider what protections, if any, were secured by state constitutions. It isn't easy to pinpoint why state courts are beginning to emphasize the protections of their States' own Bill of Rights. It may not be wide of the mark, however, to suppose that these state courts discern in recent opinions of the United States Supreme Court, and disagree with, a pulling back from, or at least, a suspension for the time being of the enforcement of the Boyd principle in respect of application of the federal Bill of Rights and the restraints of the Due Process and Equal Protection Clauses of the Fourteenth Amendment. . . .

In the category of the specific guarantees of the Bill of Rights, the Court has found the First Amendment insufficiently flexible to guarantee access to essential public forums when in our evolving society those traditional forums are under private ownership in the form of suburban shopping centers. It has found that the warrant requirement plainly appearing on the face of the Fourth

Amendment does not require the police to obtain a warrant before arrest, however easy it might have been to get an arrest warrant. It has declined to read the Fourth Amendment to prohibit searches of an individual by police officers following a stop for a traffic violation, although there exists no probable cause to believe the individual has committed any other legal infraction. The Court has found permissible police searches grounded upon consent regardless of whether the consent was a knowing and intelligent one. The Court has found that none of us has a legitimate expectation of privacy in the contents of our bank records, thus permitting governmental seizure of those records without our knowledge or consent.

Moreover, the Court has held . . . that we may not interpose the privilege against self-incrimination to bar Government attempts to obtain our personal papers, no matter how private the nature of their contents. The Court has held that the privilege against self-incrimination is not violated when statements unconstitutionally obtained from an individual are used for purposes of impeaching his testimony, or securing his indictment by a grand jury. . . .

Some state decisions have indeed suggested a connection between these recent decisions of the United States Supreme Court and the state court's reliance on the state's Bill of Rights. For example, the California Supreme Court recently held that statements taken from suspects before first giving them *Miranda* warnings are inadmissible in California courts to impeach an accused who testifies in his own defense; and stated: "We declare that [the decision to the contrary of the U.S. Supreme Court] is not persuasive authority in any state prosecution in California. . . . We pause to reaffirm the independent nature of the California Constitution and our responsibility to separately define and protect the rights of California citizens despite conflicting decisions of the United States Supreme Court interpreting the federal Constitution."

Other examples abound where state courts have independently considered the merits of constitutional arguments and declined to follow opinions of the United States Supreme Court they find unconvincing, even where the state and federal constitutions are similarly or identically phrased. As the Supreme Court of Hawaii has observed, "while this results in a divergence of meaning between words which are the same in both federal and state constitutions, the system of federalism envisaged by the United States Constitution tolerates such divergence where the result is greater protection of individual rights under state law than under federal law. . . ."

And of course state courts that rest their decisions wholly or even partly on state law need not apply federal principles of standing and justiciability that deny litigants access to the courts. Moreover, the state decisions not only cannot be overturned by, they indeed are not even reviewable by, the Supreme Court of the United States. We are utterly without jurisdiction to review such state decisions.

Some state courts seem apparently even to be anticipating contrary rulings by the United States Supreme Court and are therefore resting decisions on state law grounds to avoid review. For example, the California Supreme Court held, as a matter of state constitutional law, that bank depositors have a sufficient expectation of privacy in their bank records to invalidate the voluntary disclosure of such records by a bank to the police without the knowledge or consent of the depositor; thereafter the United States Supreme court ruled that Federal law was to the contrary.

This development puts to rest the notion that state constitutional provisions were adopted to mirror the federal Bill of Rights. The lesson of history is otherwise; indeed, the drafters of the federal Bill of Rights drew upon corresponding provisions in the various state constitutions. Prior to the adoption of the Federal Constitution, each of the rights eventually recognized in the federal Bill of Rights had previously been protected in one or more state constitutions.

The essential point I am making, of course, is not that the United States Supreme Court is necessarily wrong in its interpretation of the Federal Constitution, or that ultimate constitutional truths invariably come prepackaged in the dissents, including my own, from decisions of the Court. It is simply that the decisions of the Court are not dispositive of questions regarding rights guaranteed by counterpart provisions of state law.

"The question before us is whether, consistent with the Massachusetts Constitution, the Commonwealth may deny the protections, benefits, and obligations conferred by civil marriage to two individuals of the same sex who wish to marry. We conclude that it may not."

3.9 GOODRIDGE V. DEPARTMENT OF PUBLIC HEALTH

440 Mass. 309

November 18, 2003

On April 11, 2001, fourteen individuals from five Massachusetts counties filed suit against the state department of public health seeking a judgment that "the exclusion of the [p]laintiff couples and other qualified same-sex couples from access to marriage licenses, and the legal and social status of civil marriage, as well as the protections, benefits and obligations of marriage, violates Massachusetts law." The plaintiffs—all in committed relationships with a partner of the same sex—alleged violation of the laws of the Massachusetts, including but not limited to their rights under numerous provisions of the state Constitution.

The public health department, represented by the state's Attorney General, admitted to a policy and practice of denying marriage licenses to same-sex couples. But it denied that its actions violated any law or that the plaintiffs were entitled to relief.

By a vote of four to three, the highest court in the state ruled in favor of the plaintiffs. As a result, Massachusetts became, on May 17, 2004, the first state in the nation to allow same-sex marriages.

Below we provide an excerpt of the majority opinion, written by Chief Justice Marshall, and one of the dissents.

MARSHALL, C. J.

Marriage is a vital social institution. The exclusive commitment of two individuals to each other nurtures love and mutual support; it brings stability to our society. For those who choose to marry, and for their children, marriage provides an abundance of legal, financial, and social benefits. In return it imposes weighty legal, financial, and social obligations. The question before us is whether, consistent with the Massachusetts Constitution, the Commonwealth may deny the protections, benefits, and obligations conferred by civil marriage to two individuals of the same sex who wish to marry. We conclude that it may not. The Massachusetts Constitution affirms the dignity and equality of all individuals. It forbids the creation of second-class citizens. In reaching our conclusion we have given full deference to the arguments made by the Commonwealth. But it has failed to identify any constitutionally adequate reason for denying civil marriage to same-sex couples.

We are mindful that our decision marks a change in the history of our marriage law. Many people hold deep-seated religious, moral, and ethical convictions that marriage should be limited to the union of one man and one woman, and that homosexual conduct is immoral. Many hold equally strong religious, moral, and ethical convictions that same-sex couples are entitled to be married, and that homosexual persons should be treated no differently than their heterosexual neighbors. Neither view answers the question before us. Our concern is with the Massachusetts Constitution as a charter of governance for every person properly within its reach. "Our obligation is to define the liberty of all, not to mandate our own moral code." *Lawrence v. Texas,* (2003) (Lawrence), quoting *Planned Parenthood of Southeastern Pa. v. Casey* (1992).

Whether the Commonwealth may use its formidable regulatory authority to bar same-sex couples from civil marriage is a question not previously addressed by a Massachusetts appellate court. It is a question the United States Supreme Court left open as a matter of Federal law in *Lawrence,* where it was not an issue. There, the Court affirmed that the core concept of common human dignity protected by the Fourteenth Amendment to the United States Constitution precludes government intrusion into the deeply personal realms of consensual adult expressions of intimacy and one's choice of an intimate partner. The Court also reaffirmed the central role that decisions whether to marry or have children bear in shaping one's identity. The Massachusetts Constitution is, if anything, more protective of individual liberty and equality than the Federal Constitution; it may demand broader protection for fundamental rights; and it is less tolerant of government intrusion into the protected spheres of private life.

Barred access to the protections, benefits, and obligations of civil marriage, a person who enters into an intimate, exclusive union with another of the same sex is arbitrarily deprived of membership in one of our community's most rewarding and cherished institutions. That exclusion is incompatible with the constitutional principles of respect for individual autonomy and equality under law. . . .

For decades, indeed centuries, in much of this country (including Massachusetts) no lawful marriage was possible between white and black Americans. That long history availed not when the Supreme Court of California held in 1948 that a legislative prohibition against interracial marriage violated the due process and equality guarantees of the Fourteenth Amendment, *Perez v. Sharp* (1948), or when, nineteen years later, the United States Supreme Court also held that a statutory bar to interracial marriage violated the Fourteenth Amendment, *Loving v. Virginia* (1967). As both Perez and Loving make clear, the right to marry means little if it does not include the right to marry the person of one's choice, subject to appropriate government restrictions in the interests of public health, safety, and welfare. In this case, as in *Perez and Loving,* a statute deprives individuals of access to an institution of fundamental legal, personal, and social significance—the institution of marriage—because of a single trait: skin color in *Perez and Loving,* sexual orientation here. As it did in *Perez and Loving,* history must yield to a more fully developed understanding of the invidious quality of the discrimination.

The Massachusetts Constitution protects matters of personal liberty against government incursion as zealously, and often more so, than does the Federal Constitution, even where both Constitutions employ essentially the same language. That the Massachusetts Constitution is in some instances more protective of individual liberty interests than is the Federal Constitution is not surprising. Fundamental to the vigor of our Federal system of government is that "state courts are absolutely free to interpret state constitutional provisions to accord greater protection to individual rights than do similar provisions of the United States Constitution."

The individual liberty and equality safeguards of the Massachusetts Constitution protect both "freedom from" unwarranted government intrusion into protected spheres of life and "freedom to" partake in benefits created by the State for the common good. Both freedoms are involved here. Whether and whom to marry, how to express sexual intimacy, and whether and how to establish a family—these are among the most basic of every individual's liberty and due process rights. And central to personal freedom and security is the assurance that the laws will apply equally to persons in similar situations. "Absolute equality before the law is a fundamental principle of our own Constitution." The liberty interest in choosing whether and whom to marry would be hollow if the Commonwealth could, without sufficient justification, foreclose an individual from freely choosing the person with whom to share an exclusive commitment in the unique institution of civil marriage.

The Massachusetts Constitution requires, at a minimum, that the exercise of the State's regulatory authority not be "arbitrary or capricious." Under both the equality and liberty guarantees, regulatory authority must, at very least, serve "a legitimate purpose in a rational way"; a statute must "bear a reasonable relation to a permissible legislative objective." Any law failing to satisfy the basic standards of rationality is void.

The plaintiffs challenge the marriage statute on both equal protection and due process grounds. With respect to each such claim, we must first determine the appropriate standard of review. Where a statute implicates a fundamental right or uses a suspect classification, we employ "strict judicial scrutiny." For all other statutes, we employ the "'rational basis' test." For due process claims, rational basis analysis requires that statutes "bear a real and substantial relation to the public health, safety, morals, or some other phase of the general welfare." For equal protection challenges, the rational basis test requires that "an impartial lawmaker could logically believe that the classification would serve a legitimate public purpose that transcends the harm to the members of the disadvantaged class."

The department argues that no fundamental right or "suspect" class is at issue here, and rational basis is the appropriate standard of review. For the reasons we explain below, we conclude that the marriage ban does not meet the rational basis test for either due process or equal protection. Because the statute does not survive rational basis review, we do not consider the plaintiffs' arguments that this case merits strict judicial scrutiny.

The department posits three legislative rationales for prohibiting same-sex couples from marrying: (1) providing a "favorable setting for procreation"; (2) ensuring the optimal setting for child rearing, which the department defines as "a two-parent family with one parent of each sex"; and (3) preserving scarce State and private financial resources. We consider each in turn.

The judge in the Superior Court endorsed the first rationale, holding that "the state's interest in regulating marriage is based on the traditional concept that marriage's primary purpose is procreation." This is incorrect. Our laws of civil marriage do not privilege procreative heterosexual intercourse between married people above every other form of adult intimacy and every other means of creating a family. General Laws c. 207 contains no requirement that the applicants for a marriage license attest to their ability or intention to conceive children by coitus. Fertility is not a condition of marriage, nor is it grounds for divorce. People who have never consummated their marriage, and never plan to, may be and stay married. While it is certainly true that many, perhaps most, married couples have children together (assisted or unassisted), it is the exclusive and permanent commitment of the marriage partners to one another, not the begetting of children, that is the sine qua non of civil marriage. . . .

The department's first stated rationale, equating marriage with unassisted heterosexual procreation, shades imperceptibly into its second: that confining marriage to opposite-sex couples ensures that children are raised in the "optimal" setting. Protecting the welfare of children is a paramount State policy. Restricting marriage to opposite-sex couples, however, cannot plausibly further this policy. "The demographic changes of the past century make it difficult to speak of an average American family. The composition of families varies greatly from household to household Massachusetts has responded supportively to "the changing realities of the American family," and has moved vigorously to strengthen the modern family in its many variations. . . .

The department has offered no evidence that forbidding marriage to people of the same sex will increase the number of couples choosing to enter into opposite-sex marriages in order to have and raise children. There is thus no rational relationship between the marriage statute and the Commonwealth's proffered goal of protecting the "optimal" child rearing unit. Moreover, the department readily concedes that people in same-sex couples may be "excellent" parents. These couples (including four of the plaintiff couples) have children for the reasons others do—to love them, to care for them, to nurture them. But the task of child rearing for same-sex couples is made infinitely harder by their status as outliers to the marriage laws. While establishing the parentage of children as soon as possible is crucial to the safety and welfare of children, same-sex couples must undergo the sometimes lengthy and intrusive process of second-parent adoption to establish their joint parentage. While the enhanced income provided by marital benefits is an important source of security and stability for married couples and their children, those benefits are denied to families headed by same-sex couples. While the laws of divorce provide clear and reasonably predictable guidelines for child support, child custody, and property division on dissolution of a marriage, same-sex couples who dissolve their relationships find themselves and their children in the highly unpredictable terrain of equity jurisdiction. Given the wide range of public benefits reserved only for married couples, we do not credit the department's contention that the absence of access to civil marriage amounts to little more than an inconvenience to same-sex couples and their children. Excluding same-sex couples from civil marriage will not make children of opposite-sex marriages more secure, but it does prevent children of same-sex couples from enjoying the immeasurable advantages that flow from the assurance of "a stable family structure in which children will be reared, educated, and socialized."

No one disputes that the plaintiff couples are families, that many are parents, and that the children they are raising, like all children, need and should have the fullest opportunity to grow up in a secure, protected family unit. Similarly, no one disputes that, under the rubric of marriage, the State provides a cornucopia of substantial benefits to married parents and their children. The preferential treatment of civil marriage reflects the Legislature's conclusion that marriage "is the foremost setting for the education and socialization of children" precisely because it "encourages parents to remain committed to each other and to their children as they grow."

In this case, we are confronted with an entire, sizeable class of parents raising children who have absolutely no access to civil marriage and its protections because they are forbidden from procuring a marriage license. It cannot be rational under our laws, and indeed it is not permitted, to penalize children by depriving them of State benefits because the State disapproves of their parents' sexual orientation.

The third rationale advanced by the department is that limiting marriage to opposite-sex couples furthers the Legislature's interest in conserving scarce State and private financial resources. The marriage restriction is rational, it argues, because the General Court logically could assume that same-sex couples are more financially independent than married couples and thus less needy of public marital benefits, such as tax advantages, or private marital benefits, such as employer-financed health plans that include spouses in their coverage.

An absolute statutory ban on same-sex marriage bears no rational relationship to the goal of economy. First, the department's conclusory generalization—that same-sex couples are less financially dependent on each other than opposite-sex couples—ignores that many same-sex couples, such as many of the plaintiffs in this case, have children and other dependents (here, aged parents) in their care. The department does not contend, nor could it, that these dependents are less needy or deserving than the dependents of married couples. Second, Massachusetts marriage laws do not condition receipt of public and private financial benefits to married individuals on a demonstration of financial dependence on each other; the benefits are available to married couples regardless of whether they mingle their finances or actually depend on each other for support.

The department suggests additional rationales for prohibiting same-sex couples from marrying, which are developed by some amici. It argues that broadening civil marriage to include same-sex couples will trivialize or destroy the institution of marriage as it has historically been fashioned. Certainly our decision today marks a significant change in the definition of marriage as it has been inherited from the common law, and understood by many societies for centuries. But it does not disturb the fundamental value of marriage in our society.

Here, the plaintiffs seek only to be married, not to undermine the institution of civil marriage. They do not want marriage abolished. They do not attack the binary nature of marriage, the consanguinity provisions, or any of the other gate-keeping provisions of the marriage licensing law. Recognizing the right of an individual to marry a person of the same sex will not diminish the validity or dignity of opposite-sex marriage, any more than recognizing the right of an individual to marry a person of a different race devalues the marriage of a person who marries someone of her own race. If anything, extending civil marriage to same-sex couples reinforces the importance of marriage to individuals and communities. That same-sex couples are willing to embrace marriage's solemn obligations of exclusivity, mutual support, and commitment to one another is a testament to the enduring place of marriage in our laws and in the human spirit.

It has been argued that, due to the State's strong interest in the institution of marriage as a stabilizing social structure, only the Legislature can control and define its boundaries. Accordingly, our elected representatives legitimately may choose to exclude same-sex couples from civil marriage in order to assure all citizens of the Commonwealth that (1) the benefits of our marriage laws are available explicitly to create and support a family setting that is, in the Legislature's view, optimal for child rearing, and (2) the State does not endorse gay and lesbian parenthood as the equivalent of being raised by one's married biological parents. These arguments miss the point. The Massachusetts Constitution requires that legislation meet certain criteria and not extend beyond certain limits. It is the function of courts to determine whether these criteria are met and whether these limits are exceeded. In most instances, these limits are defined by whether a rational basis exists to conclude that legislation will bring about a rational result. The Legislature in the first instance, and the courts in the last instance, must ascertain whether such a rational basis exists. To label the court's role as usurping that of the Legislature, is to misunderstand the nature and purpose of judicial review. We owe great deference to the Legislature to decide social and policy issues, but it is the traditional and settled role of courts to decide constitutional issues. . . .

We also reject the argument suggested by the department, and elaborated by some amici, that expanding the institution of civil marriage in Massachusetts to include same-sex couples will lead to interstate conflict. We would not presume to dictate how another State should respond to today's decision. But neither should considerations of comity prevent us from according Massachusetts residents the full measure of protection available under the Massachusetts Constitution. The genius of our Federal system is that each State's Constitution has vitality specific to its own traditions, and that, subject to the minimum requirements of the Fourteenth Amendment, each State is free to address difficult issues of individual liberty in the manner its own Constitution demands. . . .

The marriage ban works a deep and scarring hardship on a very real segment of the community for no rational reason. The absence of any reasonable relationship between, on the one hand, an absolute disqualification of same-sex couples who wish to enter into civil marriage and, on the other, protection of public health, safety, or general welfare, suggests that the marriage restriction is rooted in persistent prejudices against persons who are (or who are believed to be) homosexual. "The Constitution cannot control such prejudices but neither can it tolerate them. Private biases may be outside the reach of the law, but the law cannot, directly or indirectly, give them effect." Limiting the protections, benefits, and obligations of civil marriage to opposite-sex couples violates the basic premises of individual liberty and equality under law protected by the Massachusetts Constitution.

SPINA, J. (dissenting, with whom SOSMAN and CORDY, JJ., join).

What is at stake in this case is not the unequal treatment of individuals or whether individual rights have been impermissibly burdened, but the power of the Legislature to effectuate social change without interference from the courts, pursuant to art. 30 of the Massachusetts Declaration of Rights. The power to regulate marriage lies with the Legislature, not with the judiciary. Today, the court has transformed its role as protector of individual rights into the role of creator of rights, and I respectfully dissent.

1. *Equal protection.* Although the court did not address the plaintiffs' gender discrimination claim, G.L. c. 207 [the state's policy against same-sex marriages] does not unconstitutionally discriminate on the basis of gender. A claim of gender discrimination will lie where it is shown that differential treatment disadvantages one sex over the other. General Laws c. 207 enumerates certain qualifications for obtaining a marriage license. It creates no distinction between the sexes, but applies to men and women in precisely the same way. It does not create any disadvantage identified with gender as both men and women are similarly limited to marrying a person of the opposite sex.

Similarly, the marriage statutes do not discriminate on the basis of sexual orientation. As the court correctly recognizes, constitutional protections are extended to individuals, not couples. The marriage statutes do not disqualify individuals on the basis of sexual orientation from entering into marriage. All individuals, with certain exceptions not relevant here, are free to marry. Whether an individual chooses not to marry because of sexual orientation or any other reason should be of no concern to the court.

The court concludes, however, that G.L. c. 207 unconstitutionally discriminates against the individual plaintiffs because it denies them the "right to marry the person of one's choice" where that person is of the same sex. To reach this result the court relies on *Loving v. Virginia* (1967), and transforms "choice" into the essential element of the institution of marriage. The *Loving* case did not use the word "choice" in this manner, and it did not point to the result that the court reaches today. In *Loving,* the Supreme Court struck down as unconstitutional a statute that prohibited Caucasians from marrying non-Caucasians. It concluded that the statute was intended to preserve white supremacy and invidiously discriminated against non-Caucasians because of their race. The "choice" to which the Supreme Court referred was the "choice to marry," and it concluded that with respect to the institution of marriage, the State had no compelling interest in limiting the choice to marry along racial lines. The Supreme Court did not imply the existence of a right to marry a person of the same sex. To the same effect is *Perez v. Sharp* (1948), on which the court also relies.

Unlike the *Loving* and *Sharp* cases, the Massachusetts Legislature has erected no barrier to marriage that intentionally discriminates against anyone. Within the institution of marriage, anyone is free to marry, with certain exceptions that are not challenged. In the absence of any discriminatory purpose, the State's marriage statutes do not violate principles of equal protection. This court should not have invoked even the most deferential standard of review within equal protection analysis because no individual was denied access to the institution of marriage.

2. *Due process.* The marriage statutes do not impermissibly burden a right protected by our constitutional guarantee of due process implicit in art. 10 of our Declaration of Rights. There is no restriction on the right of any plaintiff to enter into marriage. Each is free to marry a willing person of the opposite sex.

Substantive due process protects individual rights against unwarranted government intrusion. The court states, as we have said on many occasions, that the Massachusetts Declaration of Rights may protect a right in ways that exceed the protection afforded by the Federal Constitution. However, today the court does not fashion a remedy that affords greater protection of a right. Instead, using the rubric of due process it has redefined marriage.

Although art. 10 may afford greater protection of rights than the due process clause of the Fourteenth Amendment, our treatment of due process challenges adheres to the same standards followed in Federal due process analysis. When analyzing a claim that the State has impermissibly burdened an individual's fundamental or other right or liberty interest, "[w]e begin by sketching the contours of the right asserted. We then inquire whether the challenged restriction burdens that right." Where a right deemed "fundamental" is implicated, the challenged restriction will be upheld only if it is "narrowly tailored to further a legitimate and compelling governmental interest." To qualify as "fundamental" the asserted right must be "objectively, 'deeply rooted in this

Nation's history and tradition,' and 'implicit in the concept of ordered liberty,' such that 'neither liberty nor justice would exist if they were sacrificed.'" Rights that are not considered fundamental merit due process protection if they have been irrationally burdened.

Although this court did not state that same-sex marriage is a fundamental right worthy of strict scrutiny protection, it nonetheless deemed it a constitutionally protected right by applying rational basis review. Before applying any level of constitutional analysis there must be a recognized right at stake. Same-sex marriage, or the "right to marry the person of one's choice" as the court today defines that right, does not fall within the fundamental right to marry. Same-sex marriage is not "deeply rooted in this Nation's history," and the court does not suggest that it is. Except for the occasional isolated decision in recent years, same-sex marriage is not a right, fundamental or otherwise, recognized in this country. Just one example of the Legislature's refusal to recognize same-sex marriage can be found in a section of the legislation amending G.L. c. 151B to prohibit discrimination in the workplace on the basis of sexual orientation, which states: "Nothing in this act shall be construed so as to legitimize or validate a 'homosexual marriage.' . . ." In this Commonwealth and in this country, the roots of the institution of marriage are deeply set in history as a civil union between a single man and a single woman. There is no basis for the court to recognize same-sex marriage as a constitutionally protected right.

CHAPTER 4

Judicial Selection and Retention

When societies design judicial systems, they face many difficult choices, not least being the structure and jurisdiction of the new courts. Among the most controversial problems are those pertaining to judicial selection. How ought a nation select its judges, and for how long should those jurists serve?

Why judicial selection engenders such controversy is an interesting question, with no shortage of answers. But surely a principal one is that political actors and the public alike believe, whether rightly or wrongly, that processes governing judicial selection will affect the types of men and women who will serve and, in turn, the choices they, as judges, will make. Some commentators, for example, assert that providing judges with life tenure leads to a more independent judiciary—one that places itself above the fray of partisan politics. Seen in this way, mechanisms for judicial selection may convey important information about the values societies wish to foster.

And possibilities for choice abound. Some nations, typically those using a Civil-Law system, have chosen to set the ordinary judiciary apart as a distinct profession, one separate even from the practice of law. In Germany, for instance, to become a judge one must be a university graduate with the equivalent of an undergraduate major in law, pass with exceptionally high marks a set of professional examinations, undergo several years of training that combine further study with apprenticeship, and finally sustain another set of rigorous examinations administered by the government. Once in the judicial profession, judges follow careers much like civil servants, moving slowly up the hierarchy from less important to more important courts if they receive good fitness reports from senior jurists. Justices serving on constitutional courts provide a general exception to this rule. Here, Civil-Law societies depart from one another rather dramatically. In Germany, for example, justices are elected by Parliament, although six of the sixteen must be chosen from among professional judges; in Bulgaria and Italy, one-third of the justices are selected by Parliament, one-third by the president, and one-third by judges sitting on other courts. In most Civil-Law countries with judicial review, justices serve for a limited period of time. In Germany, for instance, they serve for a single twelve-year term, in Italy a single nine-year term.

British practice is quite different. For centuries, judges in the United Kingdom held their positions at the pleasure of the king, and their terms of office expired on the death of the sovereign who had appointed them. This dependence on royal favor frequently made for judicial subservience. Their long struggle for free government convinced the English that an independent judiciary was vital to the type of constitutional rule they desired; but not until 1701 did the Act of Settlement provide that judges should serve during good behavior, with removal contingent upon parliamentary approval. And it was not until 1760 that judges' commissions did not expire on the death of the king who had appointed them.[1]

The British belief in the value of an independent judiciary was transplanted to America, and royal abuse of this principle was one of the grievances that gave a moral tinge to the Revolutionary cause. The Declaration of Independence accused George III of having "made Judges dependent on his Will alone, for the Tenure of their Offices, and the Amount and Payment of their Salaries." After the Revolution, American states generally provided that judges should be elected by one or both houses of the legislature or appointed by the governor with the consent of either a special legislative council or the legislature itself. Only one state allowed the governor full appointing power. At the Constitutional Convention in 1787 the Framers were presented with several plans for choosing federal judges. Those delegates, such as George Mason, Elbridge Gerry, and Oliver Ellsworth, who opposed a strong executive, wanted to follow the dominant state practice and vest appointing authority in Congress. Others, such as Alexander Hamilton, James Madison, and Gouverneur Morris, wanted the executive to appoint judges. It was Hamilton who first suggested that the president nominate and the Senate confirm, but the Convention twice rejected this obvious compromise before finally adopting it. Following British practice, the new constitutional charter provided that federal judges should serve during good behavior.

SELECTION OF FEDERAL JUDGES

That the constitutional text specifies one method for selecting federal judges is somewhat deceiving. To be sure, the formal processes are the same regardless if the nominee is to serve on a U.S. district court, a court of appeals, or the Supreme Court: The president nominates and the Senate advises and consents—or not—to the appointment. The informal processes, however, vary from one level to another.[2] When any vacancy on the federal bench arises, the

---

[1] Today in Britain the Lord Chancellor formally appoints judges, though, of course, under the supervision of the Prime Minister. These judges tend to be middle-—and upper-—class males, though more women have joined their ranks in recent years. The more important posts are likely to go to graduates of Oxford and Cambridge; and, although party affiliation no longer seems to be a critical issue, almost all appointees tend to be middle-of-the-road politically.

[2] Sheldon Goldman, *Picking Federal Judges* (New Haven, CT: Yale University Press, 1997), 9–12, describes these processes in some detail.

attorney general's staff begins compiling lists of candidates and putting together files. The names come from many sources, including state and federal officials, interest groups, bar associations, and even the president. Candidates surviving this initial screening receive questionnaires about their personal lives, which they return to the Department of Justice. Traditionally, those surveys also went to American Bar Association's Committee on Federal Judiciary, which the Department of Justice asked to evaluate the candidate "informally." If the ABA Committee's recommendation was favorable, the FBI ran a security check and the ABA Committee was asked to issue a formal report (which includes the votes of its members.) But, in 2001, President George W. Bush ended the Committee's "semi-official" role in conducting prenomination evaluations of judicial candidates. Bush has made a few other changes in the process (see Reading 4.2), but, beyond those, the process continues in much the same way that it did during past administrations. With the FBI report and other political and background information in hand, the president might make the final decision, but usually the attorney general or one of her or his assistants, often the deputy attorney general, makes the selection for vacancies on lower courts. The White House then transmits the nomination to the Senate, which in turn refers the matter to its Committee on the Judiciary. After hearings at which the candidate and other interested parties may testify, the Committee takes a vote; if favorable, it sends the nomination to the full Senate with a formal recommendation to confirm the candidate. Finally, the Senate votes. Nominees receiving the approval of a majority are then sworn in as federal judges.

Lurking beneath this basic process, however, are real differences—both in the process itself and in the expectations of various political actors—depending on the level of the court involved. The president has the widest discretion in filling a vacancy on the Supreme Court in that he can base his decision on any number of factors, including the advancement of his own partisan, political, or personal agenda rather than defer to the preferences of particular members of the Senate. And, yet, because Supreme Court nominations are the most visible to the public, they are likely to be the most controversial. Although the press occasionally covers appointments to the U.S. district courts, front-page stories typically surround Supreme Court nominations. Moreover, proceedings on an appointment to the Supreme Court are often elaborate and explosive. Interest groups can use these hearings as a forum to voice their views on the course of constitutional law, and senators can utilize the publicity of the occasion to express opposition to the candidate, the president, or the Court. This potential for conflict suggests that the president, although free to nominate candidates of his own choosing, still faces real constraints if he wants his candidate confirmed.

Custom imposes much tighter limitations on presidential freedom of choice for judges of district courts. At this level, senators expect to play an important, perhaps the decisive, role. When a vacancy occurs on a district court, a senator from the president's party from that state will normally submit one or more names of candidates to the attorney general's staff for consideration. But the Department of Justice, acting through the deputy attorney general, also conducts its own search for promising talent. If there is a conflict of views between the senator and the administration, the senator can threaten to block confirmation by invoking senatorial courtesy. It is a rule the Senate always follows, except in those instances when it does not. In short, the Senate will not confirm a nominee who would sit in the state of a senator of the same party as the president if the nominee does not meet that senator's approval. On the other hand, although senators—and often even an individual senator—can block an appointment, neither singly nor together can they make a nomination, much less an appointment. Thus a compromise is usually arranged, just as there must be if both senators are from the president's party. Nominees must be satisfactory to both—though perhaps not the first choice of either—or the two have to work out an agreement between them on sharing patronage. Even when both senators are from the opposition party, the president often has to come to terms with them; frequently one side exchanges support for a nomination for backing on a matter the other considers important.

The role that senators play early in the process for nominations to the courts of appeals falls somewhat between those for the Supreme Court and those for district courts. Because each circuit covers more than one state, senators from several states have claims to the appointments. It is generally true, however, that judgeships in each circuit have been allocated by custom among the component states. Consequently, when a vacancy occurs, a senator frequently asserts that the successor should be from the same state as the former incumbent, thus giving the senator from that state a lien on the position.

As a presidential candidate, Jimmy Carter promised to remove federal judges from this system of political patronage. And, after taking office in 1977, he created the U.S. Circuit Nominating Commission, composed of panels in each circuit, appointed by the president and equally divided between lawyers and nonlawyers. These panels were free to search for candidates and to accept applications, not merely to screen persons suggested by senators or the administration. Carter, however, generally found that he had to defer to senatorial prerogative as far as district judges were concerned, though he did urge senators to establish their own merit selection commissions for appointments in their states. Senators in about eighteen states complied, but most ignored the president's suggestion.

In 1981, Ronald Reagan disbanded these commissions; and no chief executive since has seen fit to revive them. Appointments to the courts of appeals now proceed as they did in the pre-Carter years, with senators expecting a good deal of influence at the nominating stage, though, of course, less than for district judgeships. What has changed in recent years: the politics surrounding the appointment of circuit court nominees. Confirmation proceedings have grown increasingly contentious as presidents and senators do battle for political and ideological control of the federal bench. This was as true of the Republicans during the Democratic Clinton administration, as it is in 2005 of the Democrats in the Senate under President George W. Bush (Readings 4.3 and 4.4).

Presidential Considerations

What factors do presidents consider when they make judicial appointments? In a study aimed at answering this question, Sheldon Goldman argues that presidents are usually motivated to advance one or some combination of three agendas: personal, partisan, and policy.[3] Personal agenda refers to using the nominating power to please a friend or associate. Just as senators typically try to build up power bases within their home states by rewarding supporters (sometimes campaign aides or donors) with federal judgeships, so, too, have presidents used their authority to put close friends and supporters on the bench. Lyndon Johnson's nominations of his long-time friend and advisor Abe Fortas, first as an associate justice and then as chief justice, provide the most obvious examples in the twentieth century.

Presidents may also attempt to further a partisan agenda by using nominations as vehicles for shoring up electoral support for their party or for themselves within their party. In 1978, after the Democratically controlled Congress added 117 district and 39 court of appeals judgeships, Carter had the opportunity to accomplish both goals as well as to set a new course for the federal judiciary. Congress had required the president to establish standards for selection of judges on the basis of merit, and to give "due consideration to qualified individuals regardless of race, color, sex, religion, or national origin." Together with the usual number of vacancies, Carter thus had an unprecedented opportunity not only to reshape the federal judiciary but also to satisfy core constituents of the Democratic party: ethnic minorities and women. His nominees to the federal bench included forty women, thirty-seven blacks, and sixteen Hispanics (Reading 4.1). A dozen years later, Bill Clinton continued along the same lines. At least in part to further the agenda (and electoral success) of his party, he was quite attentive to minority groups, with about 20 percent of his 366 nominations going to blacks, Hispanics, and Native Americans and nearly a third to women. During his first two years in office, George W. Bush seemed less concerned than Clinton was about choosing judges from diverse social backgrounds. "When all three court levels are combined," as Sheldon Goldman and his colleagues tell us, "the percentage of [female, black, and Hispanic] judges in active service increased 6.7 percent (as compared to 36.2 percent in Clinton's first two years."[4] Bush, however, has (as of 2004) nominated more blacks to the federal bench than did Ronald Reagan over the course of his eight years in office, and about 20 percent of Bush's appointees are women (Reading 4.1).

In nominating the first woman to the Supreme Court, Sandra Day O'Connor, Reagan tried to woo women away from the Democratic party. Most commentators, however, believe that Reagan was also pursing the third goal that Goldman lists: furthering a policy agenda, that is, enhancing the substantive policy objectives of an administration (Reading 4.2). Indeed, with the possible exception of Richard Nixon, no president has ever been so frank and explicit as Reagan was in publicly announcing what qualifications he would look for in his nominees: He hoped to balance the "activist" Carter-appointed

---

[3] Goldman, *Picking Federal Judges.*

[4] Sheldon Goldman, et al., "W. Bush Remaking the Judiciary: Like Father Like Son?" 86 *Judicature,* 295 (2003).

judges by conservatives who would practice "judicial restraint," a term that translates as "agree with me on social and political issues."[5] Reagan, no doubt, saw himself as doing little more than carrying out the Republican Party Platform of 1980, which had promised selection of judges who "respect and reflect the values of the American people, and whose judicial philosophy is characterized by the highest regard for protecting the rights of law-abiding citizens . . . who respect traditional family values and the sanctity of innocent human life . . . and who share our commitment to judicial restraint." During the campaign, however, reality began to set in, and Reagan said that he would not adopt a single-issue litmus test for judges but would look for nominees whose views were "broadly similar" to his own.

To ensure that nominees would meet these standards, the White House staff took a much more active role in the search for or approval of candidates than had been customary. Creation of a nine-person joint White House–Department of Justice committee, called the President's Committee on Federal Judicial Selection, institutionalized an active White House role in judicial selection. Never before had any administration so systematically taken into account matters of patronage, relations with senators, and influence on public policy.

Reagan's White House rejected candidates supported by Republican senators or governors if those would-be nominees failed the president's ideological tests. Carter's emphasis on selection of women and minorities, while not totally abandoned, became a distinctly minor objective. As one official of the Department of Justice said, "We're not going to sacrifice those things we feel most important simply to adjust the numbers." In general, Reagan's selections were white, male, rich, and almost 93 percent Republican (Reading 4.1).

Professional Qualifications

Above all else, the nomination of federal judges is a partisan process. In the fifteen administrations from Warren Harding to George W. Bush, the percentage of judges appointed from the president's own party ranged from 83 (George W. Bush) to 93 (Ronald Reagan). Given the importance of judges as policy makers, these figures are hardly surprising. At the same time, however, even the Reagan administration could not ignore what is a threshold concern of all participants in the nominating process: professional qualifications. Regardless of their particular objectives, presidents generally select persons of competence and integrity but not necessarily the most able members of the bar. Nominees to the lower federal courts have usually been state judges, prosecuting attorneys, legislators, administrators, or lawyers in private practice who have been politically active.

Opinions differ about the value of prior judicial experience, and throughout its history only about half the members of the Supreme Court had previously been judges. President Eisenhower, after appointing as Chief Justice Earl

---

[5] See Walter F. Murphy, "Reagan's Judicial Strategy," in *Looking Back on the Reagan Presidency*, ed. Larry Berman (Baltimore: Johns Hopkins University Press, 1990).

Warren, who had been California's attorney general and governor but not a judge, made judicial experience a prerequisite for his remaining four nominees. In fact, the policy of Republican presidents has generally been to nominate persons with prior judicial experience, whereas Democratic presidents before Clinton preferred nominees with broad political or administrative backgrounds (Reading 4.1).

Another approach to assessing professional qualifications centers on the reactions of the American Bar Association (ABA). Since 1947, that organization has maintained, as we noted earlier, a Committee on Federal Judiciary, which has sought with varying degrees of success to influence appointments by rating candidates as "extremely well qualified," "well qualified," "qualified," or "not qualified." The committee at first hoped to be permitted to suggest candidates for vacancies, but neither Democratic nor Republican regimes have agreed. The Truman administration, however, did consult with the ABA's committee, and under Eisenhower the committee exercised almost a veto power over nominations. The next three administrations displayed less deference. Kennedy went ahead with eight nominations despite the committee's having rated the candidates as unqualified. Johnson's record was similar. Carter's nominating commissions and their concern for widening the opportunities for judicial selection temporarily cost the ABA committee much of its influence. Three of Carter's nominees rated by the ABA as "unqualified" were confirmed by the Senate. (In one case the ground for the rating was age, a standard the committee subsequently abandoned.) During the Reagan years, the ABA Committee received a good deal of attention when its members split over Judge Robert H. Bork's fitness for the bench, with ten members viewing him as extremely qualified, one voting "not opposed," and four rating him "not qualified."

Confirmation

The ABA's committee's division over Judge Bork, along with some of its other decisions, has led a number of critics to question the propriety of its having such a prominent part in recruiting judges and may have been a factor in the Bush administration's decision to terminate the committee's role in screening candidates. The organization's membership has usually included fewer than half of the nation's practicing attorneys, and it espouses not merely professional "improvements" designed to benefit certain interests within the legal profession but also occasionally controversial, and ideological, political goals. Historically, the ABA was a bedrock of reaction, founded to reverse Supreme Court decisions that legitimized governmental regulation of big business. The Association was, Edward S. Corwin said, "a juristic sewing circle for mutual education in the gospel of laissez faire."[6] As late as World War II, it largely excluded African Americans, Jews, and women from membership. In recent decades, it has become

---

[6] Edward S. Corwin, *Liberty against Government* (Baton Rouge: Louisiana State University Press, 1948), 138.

more liberal, even choosing a Jewish woman as its president in 1995. But, whatever the center of its political gravity, it has for a half century played an important role in judicial selection. Even though, under the Bush administration, it no
longer receives prenomination information about candidates, it continues to
rate them. Of Clinton's first 296 nominees, the ABA rated only three as "not
qualified." Two-thirds were ranked as "well qualified" or "extremely well qualified," the remainder as "qualified." And, interestingly enough, by the ABA's
lights, George W. Bush's are among the most qualified in contemporary U.S.
history—with nearly 70 percent ranked as "well" or "extremely well" qualified.

More generally, systematic research supports the commonsense view that
an important factor for a successful confirmation is the Senate's perception of
the professional qualifications of a candidate.[7] For example, even liberal
Democrats voted for Antonin Scalia and Anthony Kennedy, both nominated by
Reagan for the Supreme Court. At least part of the Senate's near-unanimity on
these two nominees was due to their being, by professional training and moral
character, highly qualified for the job. Scalia, who was and is more conservative
than Bork, also demonstrated considerable intellectual agility in dodging senators' questions, taking great care not to waken the liberal guard dogs who had
chewed up Robert Bork.

But, again, professional qualifications may be only a threshold matter for the
Senate, as they are for the president. By the time nominations reach that body,
many other considerations can come into play, and whether these favor the president or not will determine the success of particular candidates. By virtue of the
fact that the Senate has the final say on nominees, it can impose effective restraints on presidential choices, even if it does not control the selection of candidates. George Washington saw the Senate reject one of his Supreme Court
nominees; and, during the nineteenth century, more than 25 percent of nominations to the Court failed to negotiate the senatorial maze—eight were rejected,
five withdrew because of opposition, and the Senate did not act on another ten.
In contrast, during the first two-thirds of the twentieth century, the Senate rejected only one nominee to the Supreme Court, Judge John J. Parker. He was defeated in 1930, partly because of opposition from labor and black organizations.
In 1916, Louis D. Brandeis had also met strong opposition, as did Charles Evans
Hughes in 1931, but both were confirmed by substantial margins. It was, there-
fore, a stunning reversal of practice when, between 1968 and 1970, President
Johnson and President Nixon each saw the Senate reject two of his nominees.
Reagan, too, failed to obtain confirmation of Bork; and Reagan's successor,
George Bush, almost lost on his nomination of Clarence Thomas. Clinton's two
Supreme Court nominees, however, had an easier time; both Ruth Bader
Ginsburg and Stephen Breyer received near unanimous votes from the Senate.

---

[7] See Charles M. Cameron, Albert D. Cover, and Jeffrey A. Segal, "Senate Voting on Supreme Court
Nominees: A Neo-Institutional Model," 84 *American Political Science Review* 525 (1990); Lee Epstein,
Jeffrey A. Segal, and Nancy Staudt, "The Role of Qualifications in the Confirmation of Nominees to
the Supreme Court," *Florida State University Law Review*, forthcoming (2005).

Still, the Republican-controlled Senate refused to take any action on many of the Democratic president's candidates for lower courts (see Reading 4.3). This refusal to act reflected such blatant partisan maneuvering as to anger even Chief Justice William H. Rehnquist, who had been a Republican stalwart as an aide to Barry Goldwater in the 1964 presidential campaign and as a high official in Richard Nixon's Department of Justice. In a 1997 address, the Chief Justice implored the Republican Senate to act promptly to fill the eighty-two vacancies on the federal bench. "The Senate is surely under no obligation to confirm any particular nominee," Rehnquist said, "but after the necessary time for inquiry, it should vote him up or vote him down." Recently, it has been the Democrats in the Senate who have used a variety of tactics to delay action on Bush's nominees. Fewer than half have been confirmed, with (on average) about 150 days elapsing between nomination and Senate action.[8] The politics surrounding at least some of these nominations has become so contentious that numerous scholars and policy makers have been hard at work at solutions (Reading 4.4).

Why these discrepancies? What can go wrong (or right) for judicial nominees in the Senate?[9] Certainly one factor is the candidate's ideology relative to that of senators or, more precisely, of senators' perceptions of their constituents' political orientations. When a nominee's judicial philosophy is very far to the left or the right of the Senate's, defeat is not unlikely. Knowing how far is "very far" is usually difficult to predict. Another factor centers on the president himself. When his party controls the Senate or he is in his first term, his political resources are usually at their highest. If he decides to use those resources and does so with skill, as Ronald Reagan did, he can even persuade Capitol Hill to overlook its rule of senatorial courtesy.

A final determinant involves the political forces surrounding the nomination, specifically the degree to which organized interest groups mobilize to support or oppose particular nominees. Ideological and partisan considerations have been a part of the process since George Washington imposed the "litmus test" of "deserving Federalist" in choosing the first federal judges, but energetic, public involvement of interest groups is a relatively new phenomenon. Indeed, with scattered exceptions here and there,[10] in most confirmation proceedings during the first half of the twentieth century, both Supreme Court justices and lower court judges were unscathed by the presence of interest groups. The hearings "were predictable and stable affairs, controlled by insiders and cut off from

---

[8] Information on the status of nominations is available at http://judiciary.senate.gov/.

[9] We derive this discussion from Cameron et al., "Senate Voting on Supreme Court Nominees;" Epstein et al., "The Role of Qualifications in the Confirmation of Nominees to the Supreme Court;" and Jeffrey A. Segal, Charles M. Cameron, and Albert D. Cover, "A Spatial Model of Roll Call Voting: Senators, Constituents, Presidents, and Interest Groups in Supreme Court Confirmations," 36 *American Journal of Political Science* 96 (1992).

[10] The confirmation battles over Louis Brandeis and John Parker are two that readily come to mind. Brandeis was confirmed by a vote of 47–22; Parker was rejected by a vote of 39–41. Lee Epstein et al., *The Supreme Court Compendium* (Washington, DC: Congressional Quarterly, 2003) contains votes on all nominees.

public participation"[11] (Reading 4.5). In fact, it was not until 1925 that the Senate Committee on the Judiciary invited a nominee, Harlan Fiske Stone, to testify—and that was at Stone's request. He hoped to defend various decisions made by his law firm and that he himself had made as attorney general. Stone's "the best offense is a good defense" strategy worked: only six senators voted against him.[12] But it did not initiate a new practice. Not until fourteen years later, in 1939, did the Senate call another nominee, Felix Frankfurter, to appear before it. A Harvard Law professor at the time of his nomination, Frankfurter initially declined to testify, claiming that he did not want to miss class. He changed his mind, however, appeared, and was confirmed unanimously. Ten years later, Sherman Minton took a harder stand: He refused to appear on the ground that it would be inappropriate for him to so. The committee withdrew its request.

Since Minton's refusal, the Senate Committee on the Judiciary has requested all nominees to appear, and with one exception they have done so.[13] But the proceedings themselves remained, for the most part, brief, nondivisive events, with few organized interests asking to testify or issuing public statements.

Ronald Reagan's nomination of Robert H. Bork to the Supreme Court brought a halt to this passivity. The reason was, in part, that Bork was a known quantity: He had spent years writing and speaking on his vision of the American constitutional system, a vision that was like Reagan's but much more detailed. For example, he argued that the Supreme Court had been wrong to find a constitutional right to privacy; and women, he contended, could be included under the equal protection clause of the Fourteenth Amendment only if they could show that the framers of that amendment had specifically so intended. Given that we can prove little or nothing about those framers' intentions, many women's groups judged Bork to be a threat to their rights, an opinion shared by other organizations. And leaders of interest groups who did not share his vision had spent nearly as many years plotting and planning what they would do if he were nominated.

When in 1987 that event finally came to pass, those groups were ready. Virtually every segment of the left-of-center interest group community came out against Bork, from environmentalists to consumers to gays and lesbians to unions. They spent millions of dollars on advertising, grassroots campaigns, and polling. And they won—Bork went down in defeat by a vote of 42–58.

Although, as noted previously, interest groups had occasionally publicly opposed other candidates, never had they orchestrated such extraordinary efforts. "Organizational participation in the nomination of Judge Robert Bork," Gregory A. Caldeira and John R. Wright said, "broke all records" (Reading 4.5).

---

[11] Mark Silverstein, *Judicious Choices: The New Politics of Supreme Court Confirmations* (New York: Norton, 1994), 162.

[12] George L. Watson and John A. Stookey, *Shaping America* (New York: HarperCollins, 1995).

[13] The exception was Abe Fortas, when the Senate was considering him for the Chief Justiceship. After he appeared before the Committee, it asked him to return to address ethical questions that had arisen. He refused to do so.

The number of groups testifying against Bork (seventeen) was greater than the number of all groups testifying against all candidates (combined) nominated to the Court in the 1950s. But even these statistics do not relay the massive mobilization of interests: Immediately after Reagan announced the nomination, "more than twenty groups and dozens of individual experts . . . abandoned their families and summer vacations to prepare in-depth analyses and reports that addressed their specific individual or institutional concerns."[14] Their efforts continued unabated until the day of Bork's defeat. The outcome could not have shocked political scientists, who had long suggested that interest groups' participation can taint a candidate, even if senators are ideologically predisposed to vote for him or her. Jeffrey A. Segal and his colleagues make this point with regard to Bork: "A moderate-to-conservative southern senator who might have voted for Bork with a probability of .99 without any interest-group pressure would have a probability of voting for him of .60 after intensive interest-group mobilization."[15]

The judge himself blames his demise on the interest groups' campaign (conducted with the aid of several senators). But other factors were operating, including his own candid ideological reading of the constitutional text and larger constitutional order; even some Republican senators voted against him. The most far ranging effect of Bork's defeat might be that it fundamentally altered the nominating process by putting presidents on notice that candidates, even exceptionally qualified ones, who had spoken out on deeply divisive issues would attract droves of interest groups. Hence, it is hardly surprising that for the most part presidents have since attempted to identify candidates who had not written or said very much on matters that were controversial or even relevant to large segments of the public—Scalia is the notable exception. In other words, presidents have tended to nominate what some have called "stealth" candidates.

This strategy has, for the most part, succeeded. When Bill Clinton nominated Stephen Breyer, only three interest groups testified against him. His nomination won the endorsement of eighty-seven senators, with only nine voting against him.

The Behavior of Judicial Appointees

Research provides less clear answers to the question whether the products of the confirmation process, the judges themselves, vary by presidential and senatorial priorities. Certainly we know that, in the aggregate, presidents have appointed different kinds of people to the bench. If only to further partisan causes, Carter and Clinton placed great emphasis on affirmative action, with the result being nominees of diverse backgrounds. Reagan, in contrast, stressed a commitment to his ideological values, with the result being a more homogeneous group of white, male appointees.

---

[14] Michael Pertschuk and Wendy Schaetzel, *People Rising* (New York: Thunder's Mouth Press, 1989), 68.

[15] Segal et al., "A Spatial Model of Roll Call Voting," 112.

But whether judges, when they reach the bench, reflect the preferences of their appointing presidents is a different matter. On the one hand, Jeffrey A. Segal and his colleagues argue that presidents do occasionally succeed in getting the justices they want; Reagan's appointees, for example, generally have voted in a more conservative fashion than have Johnson's or Clinton's appointees (Reading 4.6). On the other hand, Thomas Walker and Deborah Barrow have disappointing news for those who had hoped to find Carter's "nontraditional" judges on the U.S. Courts of Appeals behaving differently from their white male counterparts: for the most part, they do not (Reading 4.7).

The same mixed results characterize presidential nominations to the Supreme Court. Surely Ronald Reagan must have been pleased with William Rehnquist and Antonin Scalia. Both have consistently taken right-of-center positions on matters of social policy. Sandra Day O'Connor was probably more of an enigma to Reagan, because she steered her own constitutional course. But Richard Nixon, who hoped to appoint law-and-order-minded jurists to the High Court, must have been displeased by Harry A. Blackmun, who, during the latter part of his tenure, consistently ruled in favor of defendants in criminal cases, going so far as to denounce the death penalty as unconstitutional. So, too, George Bush must be puzzled by the way his nominee, David Souter, has often voted with the Court's most liberal justices.

Presidents, of course, try to minimize "surprises." Pondering candidates for the chief justiceship, Lincoln is alleged to have said: "We cannot ask a man what he will do . . . Therefore we must take a man whose views are known."[16] But views held in one phase of life sometimes lose something in the translation to another phase. Lincoln decided on Salmon Portland Chase because he was "right" on emancipation of slaves and "right" on the federal government's authority to issue paper money. Once on the bench, however, Chase voted that the issuance of paper money, a policy he had supported as secretary of the treasury, was unconstitutional. Lincoln's problem indicates that surprises are inevitable, perhaps even to the appointees themselves. Federal judges might not completely ignore the practical political world in which they operate, but the lack of an explicit electoral connection means that neither presidents nor senators, not even the public, can fully control their behavior.

JUDICIAL SELECTION IN THE STATES

Scenarios for recruitment of state judges differ from one another and usually from those for federal jurists. Although, at the time of the nation's founding, the states followed a fairly uniform method of judicial selection—appointment by one or both houses of the legislature—one of the legacies of Jacksonian democracy has been the practice of electing judges. Before 1832 only one state chose all its judges by popular election, but every state admitted to the Union after 1846

---

[16] Quoted in David M. Silver, *Lincoln's Supreme Court* (Urbana: University of Illinois Press, 1956), 208.

provides for the election of all or most of its judges or their reelection after serving minimal terms.

Currently, as Table 4.1 shows, only a few states appoint judges serving on their courts of last resort: the legislatures select the judges in two states; the executive appoints in four states (with the approval of elected bodies in New Jersey and New Hampshire. The others use one of two methods of selection: election and the so-called merit plan.

The merit plan, also known as the Missouri plan, is a compromise between appointing and electing judges. Under this arrangement, a screening committee, typically composed of the state's chief justice, three attorneys elected by the

TABLE 4.1 Initial Selection Methods for Justices Serving on State Courts of Last Resort*

Elected (21)		Appointed (6)	Merit Selection (23)
Partisan Ballot (8)	Nonpartisan Ballot (13)	Gubernatorial (4)	Legislative (2)
Alabama	Arkansas	California	South Carolina
Illinois	Georgia	Maine	Virginia
Louisiana	Idaho	New Hampshire	Colorado
Michigan†	Kentucky	New Jersey	Connecticut
Ohio**	Minnesota		Delaware
Pennsylvania	Mississippi		Florida
Texas	Montana		Hawaii
West Virginia	Nevada		Indiana
	North Carolina		Iowa
	North Dakota		Kansas
	Oregon		Maryland
	Washington		Massachusetts
	Wisconsin		Missouri
			Nebraska
			New Mexico
			New York
			Oklahoma
			Rhode Island
			South Dakota
			Tennessee
			Utah
			Vermont
			Wyoming
			Arizona
			Alaska

*These data are from the American Judicature Society and are available at www.ajs.org/js/materials.htm.

†Candidates appear on the general election ballot without party affiliation but are nominated at political party conventions.

**Candidates appear on the general election ballot without party affiliation but are nominated in partisan primary elections.

state's bar association, and three laypeople appointed by the governor, nominates several candidates for each judicial vacancy. The governor makes the final selection but is usually bound to choose from among the committee's candidates. At the first election after twelve months' service, each new judge is included on the ballot with the question whether she or he should be retained in office. If the voters reject an incumbent, she or he is replaced by another "merit" candidate. If retained, the judge then serves a set term, at the end of which she or he is eligible for reelection. Whether the Missouri plan and its variations really recruit judges on the basis of merit is open to question.[17] What is clear is that selection is no less political, although the political arena tends to be that of bar associations rather than a public forum in which citizens have a vote if not a voice (Reading 4.8).

California has something like the Missouri plan in reverse. The governor has complete discretion in making appointments to the state's appellate courts; but, once named, nominees are subjected to review by a three-person committee composed of the attorney general, the chief justice (or senior supreme court justice if the chief justiceship is being filled), and the presiding justice of the appellate court affected by the nomination (or senior presiding judge when a supreme court nomination is at stake). Rarely has the committee rejected the governor's choice. Once confirmed, appellate court judges must face the voters for retention at the next general election (Reading 4.9).

Debates over State Selection Systems

Given the range of selection systems that states use, it is not surprising that debates have ensued over the "best" method. Some analysts argue that such controversies are pointless because the types of judges yielded by different mechanisms do not vary all that much. After an exhaustive study of the composition of state judiciaries, Henry Glick and Craig Emmert concluded that selection systems do not produce "judges with markedly different or superior judicial credentials or [with different] background characteristics."[18] But, as we saw at the federal level, professional qualifications are a preliminary, not a final, consideration. A critically important question remains: do different methods of selection recruit judges with distinct outlooks toward their roles and/or toward substantive issues of public policy?

We have hints but no definitive answers. Some commentators contend that judges who are elected are not likely to behave any differently from those who are appointed. And it has been strongly argued that accountability to the people, the reason for electing judges, does not occur because voters are usually unaware and uninformed about the activities of judges. So, judges in these

---

[17] There are indeed variations. In New York, for example, the governor makes appointments to the court of appeals (the state's highest court) from a list of names submitted by a nominating commission. But each nominee must be approved by the state senate.

[18] Henry Glick and Craig Emmert, "Selection Systems and Judicial Characteristics," 70 *Judicature* 230 (1987).

electoral states are just as free as their appointed counterparts to ignore the whims of the public and political officials when making their decisions. Other scholars disagree. Melinda Gann Hall shows that judicial elections are as competitive as those for Congress.[19] Given that more than 90 percent of congressional incumbents will win reelection, this figure is not dramatic, but it could mean that elected judges cannot afford to ignore public sentiment when making their decisions. John Wold and John Culver bring some flesh to this argument by detailing the electoral defeat of California Supreme Court justices, which largely came about because they ignored public preferences over the death penalty (Reading 4.9).

The essay by Wold and Culver suggests that judges who face periodic elections must adjust their behavior to fall in line with the public's preference if they wish to keep their jobs, just as legislators must do. This study also points to the growing necessity for judges in electoral systems to engage in active campaigning—and to build up the coffers to do so. Reports out of California, for example, show that the average cost of competing for a judgeship in Los Angeles County grew from $3,000 in the 1970s to $70,000 thirty years later.[20] At the state supreme court level, the stakes are even higher. In 2002, in Ohio alone four candidates raised $6.2 million.[21]

Is such campaigning desirable? Some observers say yes; it offers the public an opportunity to learn about candidates' backgrounds and predict future conduct and, thus, to make more informed electoral decisions. But an increasing number of commentators express grave concerns, particularly about judges' taking campaign money from trial lawyers and organized interests who later litigate cases before them. Critics argue that, in such instances, judges will act no differently from legislators and will make decisions favoring contributors, lest coffers be empty at the next electoral campaign. Because of these concerns, the American Bar Association is considering a proposal that would ask states to limit the amount an individual can contribute to judicial campaigns.

DISCIPLINING JUDGES

When voters do not reelect judges, they are in effect removing them from office. But the reasons for so doing are more likely to center on policy and partisanship than on matters of judicial propriety. Suppose judges engage in unethical or even illegal behavior or are merely habitually rude to litigants and attorneys. What mechanisms exist for punishing or perhaps removing them from the bench?

---

[19] "State Supreme Courts in American Democracy," 95 *American Political Science Review* 315–330 (2001).

[20] "Suit Challenges the Financing of Judge's Campaigns in Los Angeles," *New York Times*, May 19, 1996.

[21] See Brennan Center for Justice et al., *The New Politics of Judicial Elections* (2004), available at www.brennancenter.org. Across the nation, the amount of money raised for candidates seeking to serve on courts of last resort doubled between 1994 and 2000.

Federal Judges

Article III of the constitutional text says that federal judges "shall hold their offices during good Behaviour." That document, however, offers no definition of good behaviour and is silent about who shall define it. In practice, the term has pretty much come to mean life tenure, which many authorities regard as the strongest support for judicial independence. The constitutional text is also silent about what to do about bad judicial behavior. Since Thomas Jefferson's first administration, however, Congress has taken the position that federal judges are subject to impeachment under Article II, which provides: "The President, Vice President, and all civil officers of the United States, shall be removed from office on impeachment for, and conviction of, treason, bribery, or other high crimes and misdemeanors." As with other federal officials, the House votes to impeach (the equivalent of formal accusation or indictment) and the Senate, sitting as a court, tries the case. A two-thirds vote is required for a conviction.

After being defeated in his efforts to impeach and remove Justice Samuel Chase, Jefferson complained that impeachment was a "scarecrow." Certainly as a device for directly removing judges it has been a failure. Since 1789 the House has impeached but thirteen federal judges, and only seven were convicted and removed. These figures, however, do not quite tell the whole story; the House has investigated perhaps as many as fifty judges, some of whom were censured and some of whom resigned during the investigation. Moreover, attempts to impeach became more frequent in the last decades of the twentieth century, with three federal judges removed from office since 1986 and another two nearly impeached. Finally, the Supreme Court has facilitated congressional efforts by giving legislators a reasonably long leash in conducting impeachment proceedings, even permitting the Senate to employ abbreviated processes to speed matters along.[22]

Does this record mean that there is no other method of disciplining and removing federal judges? Some constitutional scholars do, indeed, contend that impeachment is the exclusive remedy. In 1970 Justices William O. Douglas and Hugo L. Black took this position in their dissents in *Chandler v. Judicial Council.* Again, however, the constitutional text merely says that the tenure of federal judges runs "during good behavior," a phrase that, Raoul Berger argued,[23] is not meaningless. He would have followed English precedent by making the writ of scire facias (now quo warranto)[24] available to remove judges guilty of misbehavior. Other scholars have asserted that Congress may by law define good behavior and allow, as a number of states have done, a special court or commission to determine whether a judge's behavior justifies removal.

---

[22] *Nixon v. United States*, 506 U.S. 224 (1993).

[23] Raoul Berger, *Impeachment: The Constitutional Problems* (Cambridge: Harvard University Press, 1973).

[24] *Quo warranto* literally means "by what right?" *Black's Law Dictionary* defines it as being in old English law "a writ against him . . . who claimed or usurped any office, franchise, or liberty, to inquire *by what authority* he supported his claim, in order to determine the right." More recently, Black says, the writ has become "an extraordinary proceeding, prerogative in nature, addressed to preventing a continued exercise of authority unlawfully asserted."

Congress has not gone this far, but in 1980 it adopted legislation providing a means for citizens to file complaints against federal judges. Those complaints are reviewed, in each circuit, by commissions composed of other federal judges who are colleagues and perhaps friends of the accused. A commission can dismiss a complaint—in fact, the typical response—or forward it to other authorities, for example, the chief judge of the circuit who is responsible for assigning cases or, where criminal prosecution seems warranted, to the attorney general. But even before the Act of 1980, judges had taken action, however mild, against some of their own. Several times when justices of the Supreme Court have become senile, the chief justice has refused to assign them opinions and the Court has collectively agreed not to count their votes when they have been in a mere five-judge majority.

The case of United States District Judge Stephen S. Chandler provides an interesting experiment in judicial self-policing at the lower level. Because Judge Chandler had been a defendant in both civil and criminal litigation and had been charged with failing to perform his administrative duties as chief judge in his district, the Judicial Council of the Tenth Circuit forbade him to hear any further cases and reassigned cases pending before him.[25] In effect he remained a judge, but with no functions. Chandler brought suit to recover his authority, but the Supreme Court denied his petition.

Nonetheless, it remains difficult to remove or even discipline federal judges except for conduct that is not merely outrageous, but flagrantly so. These facts have led members of Congress to propose term appointments or even periodic reconfirmation by the Senate, as New Jersey requires for important judgeships. These proposals have all failed, in part because they have often been aimed less at dealing with judicial misconduct in any professional sense than at punishing judges who are ideologically out of step with certain senators and representatives.

A more politically neutral method would be to adopt some variant of a mandatory retirement system. In fact, most other countries require judges to retire at a specified age. Canada, for example, compels its judges to retire at 75, Russia at 70, Germany at 68, and India at 65. But such a practice is hardly a panacea. It reaches only elderly judges, who might or might not be guilty of misbehavior, and leaves untouched younger judges who might need disciplining. There are other significant costs. If the American constitutional text had set compulsory retirement at 70, John Marshall would have served ten less years than he did and Oliver Wendell Holmes twenty-one years less.

State Judges

The historic methods for dealing with judicial misconduct in the states are impeachment, address, and recall. Address is a formal request from the legislature to the governor asking him or her to remove a judge. Recall requires a certain percentage of voters to sign a petition for a special election to vote on whether

---

[25] Each circuit has one judicial council, composed of appeals and trial court judges, over which the chief judge of the circuit presides.

the judge should continue in office. Because these methods are slow and cumbersome, almost every state has adopted some version of a disciplinary committee to police judges. California was the first to establish such a body, which it called the Commission on Judicial Qualifications. Composed of judges, lawyers, and members of the public, the commission can look into complaints brought by citizens or take up cases on its own initiative. Soon the District of Columbia and forty-eight states followed California's lead.

These organizations vary in effectiveness. Where the state supreme court takes a serious interest in judicial discipline and the legislature appropriates enough money for a staff to look into complaints and conduct independent investigations, these commissions can be very useful. Their actions have led to the removal from office of a small but not inconsiderable number of corrupt judges, and even more judges have resigned to avoid investigations.[26]

One must understand that most of the conduct that gets judges into disciplinary trouble does not involve criminal activity but rather insensitivity to real and apparent conflicts of interest, rudeness to lawyers or litigants, or ignorance of the law. In many states, a judge's ignorance of basic legal principles is itself misconduct and can lead to an official reprimand or even removal.

Raw data about how many judges are publicly disciplined and the ratio of complaints to impositions of punishment are misleading in several important respects. First, as with habeas corpus at the federal level, many prisoners file complaints in the false belief that the disciplinary committee sits as an appellate court. "The judge had it in for me" is a typical plea from a prisoner. Many losing civil litigants suffer from a similar misunderstanding. A large percentage of complaints arise from divorce proceedings. There a disappointed litigant often writes: "The judge must have been sleeping with my wife because he awarded her so much alimony."

Second, in addition to providing a means of punishing recalcitrant jurists, these commissions can also help sensitize and educate judges, most of whom, before coming to the bench, had little or no judicial training beyond their own law practices. The commissions' very existence reminds judges of their obligations and the price they will pay for ignoring litigants' and lawyers' legal rights as well as their rights to be treated with dignity and respect. Moreover, it is quite common for disciplinary commissions to call in judges for informal conferences, during which the chair, often a retired justice of the state's highest court, says something to this effect: "Your honor, we've had several complaints about your conduct. None of them is serious enough to warrant formal action against you, but you ought to know that your behavior has worried a lot of people. It worries us, too. Now, I know how quarrelsome attorneys and disrespectful litigants can wear a judge down, but your job is to be patient and treat everyone with courtesy, often with more courtesy than they deserve. So, we

---

[26] In some states, a judge's resigning does not automatically end disciplinary proceedings. In New Jersey, for example, the committee may proceed with its action and recommend to the state supreme court that the offending judge be barred from ever again holding judicial office in that state.

remind you of that duty and tell you of our concern. We hope never to see you in this room again."

Despite much good work, these commissions may not represent the optimal solution to problems of judicial discipline. Basically, they depend on citizens' filing complaints, and most citizens lack the technical and literary skills to write a convincing brief. The people most knowledgeable about judicial conduct, practicing attorneys, are often reluctant to complain or to support their clients when they do so. Lawyers realize that the judge may learn who the accuser is and who supported the charge. If not removed from the bench, the jurist can easily exact revenge against the attorney and his or her future clients. There is also often a tendency among senior judges (just as there is among senators, representatives, administrators, and friends generally) to help hide a colleague's problems with drugs or alcohol by, for example, assigning complicated cases to other judges or suggesting long vacations. The motivation could be charitable, but the long-range effect can harm litigants and bring disrepute on the judiciary.

The state as well as the federal government might look to their counterparts abroad for solutions. In Italy, for example, parties may seek monetary compensation if judges, in the course of performing their duties, commit fraud or act in other harmful ways. France, long concerned with the problem of errant judges, has authorized two bodies, the Conseil Supèrieur de la Magistrature and the Commission de Discipline du Parquet, to undertake disciplinary procedures. Yet, it is worth noting, neither these nor other plans have much of a track record in ridding the bench of bad judges. Mary L. Volcansek tells us that, in the decade between 1986 and 1996, American states formally removed merely 200 jurists. Although this is only a "tiny fraction" of the 30,000 state judges, it exceeds the total number of magistrates (judges and prosecutors) in France and Italy, as well as in U.S. federal courts, plus English judges, removed from office during the twentieth century.[27] It is less likely that these figures reflect judiciaries that are replete with well-behaved men and women than that they indicate a widespread inability to reconcile the need for judicial discipline with the equally important need for judicial independence.

SELECTED REFERENCES

ABRAHAM, HENRY J. 1999. *Justices and Presidents: A Political History of Appointments to the Supreme Court.* New rev. ed. Lanham, MD: Rowman & Littlefield.

ABRAHAM, HENRY J., AND BRUCE A. MURPHY. 1976. "The Influence of Sitting and Retired Justices on Presidential Supreme Court Nominations." *Hastings Constitutional Law Quarterly* 3: 37.

ADAMANY, DAVID, AND PHILIP DUBOIS. 1976. "Electing State Judges." *Wisconsin Law Review* 1976: 731.

---

[27] Mary L. Volcansek et al., *Judicial Misconduct* (Gainesville, FL: University Press of Florida, 1996), 111.

ATKINSON, DAVID N. 1999. *Leaving the Bench: Supreme Court Justices at the End.* Lawrence: University Press of Kansas.

BAUGH, JOYCE A. 2002. *Supreme Court Justice in the Post-Bork Era.* New York: Peter Lang Publishing.

BAUM, LAWRENCE. 1995. "Electing Judges." In *Contemplating Courts*, ed. Lee Epstein. Washington, DC: CQ Press.

BERGER, RAOUL. 1973. *Impeachment: The Constitutional Problems.* Cambridge, MA: Harvard University Press.

BINDER, SARAH A. AND FORREST MALTZMAN. 2002. "Senatorial Delay in Confirming Federal Judges, 1947–98." *American Journal of Political Science* 46 (January): 190.

BRONNER, ETHAN. 1989. *Battle for Justice: How the Bork Nomination Shook America.* New York: W. W. Norton.

BUSHNELL, ELEANORE. 1992. *Crimes, Follies, and Misfortunes: The Federal Impeachment Trials.* Urbana: University of Illinois Press.

CALDEIRA, GREGORY, AND JOHN WRIGHT. 1998. "Lobbying for Justice." *American Journal of Political Science* 42: 499.

CAMERON, CHARLES M., ALBERT D. COVER, AND JEFFREY A. SEGAL. 1990. "Senate Voting on Supreme Court Nominees: A Neo-Institutional Model." *American Political Science Review* 84: 525.

CARTER, STEPHEN L. 1994. *The Confirmation Mess.* New York: Basic Books.

CHAMPAGNE, ANTHONY, AND JUDITH HAYDEL, EDS. 1993. *Judicial Reform in the States.* Lanham, MD: University Press of America.

CHASE, HAROLD W. 1972. *Federal Judges: The Appointing Process.* Minneapolis: University of Minnesota Press.

CHEMERINKSY, ERWIN, 2003. "Ideology and the Selection of Federal Judges." *UC Davis Law Review* 36: 619.

DANELSKI, DAVID J. 1964. *A Supreme Court Justice Is Appointed.* New York: Random House.

DEAN, JOHN W. 2001. *The Rehnquist Choice.* New York: Free Press.

DuBois, PHILIP L. 1980. *From Ballot to Bench.* Austin: University of Texas Press.

EPSTEIN, LEE, JACK KNIGHT, AND ANDREW MARTIN. 2003. The Norm of Prior Judicial Experience and Its Consequences for Diversity on the U.S. Supreme Court. *California Law Review* 91: 903.

EPSTEIN, LEE, JACK KNIGHT, AND OLGA SHVETSOVA. 2001. "Comparing Judicial Selection Systems." *William & Mary Bill of Rights Law Journal.* 107.

GARROW, DAVID J. 2000. Mental Decrepitude on the U.S. Supreme Court: The Historical Case for a 28th Amendment. *University of Chicago Law Review* 67: 995.

GERHARDT, MICHAEL J. 1996. *The Federal Impeachment Process.* Princeton, NJ: Princeton University Press.

GOLDMAN, SHELDON. 1989. "Reagan's Judicial Legacy: Completing the Puzzle and Summing Up." *Judicature* 72: 318.

GOLDMAN, SHELDON. 1997. *Picking Federal Judges.* New Haven, CT: Yale University Press.

GOLDMAN, SHELDON, ET AL. 2003. "W. Bush Remaking the Judiciary: Like Father Like Son?" *Judicature* 86: 282.

GRAHAM, BARBARA LUCK. 1990. "Judicial Recruitment and Racial Diversity on State Courts: An Overview." *Judicature* 74: 28.

GROSSMAN, JOEL B. 1965. *Lawyers and Judges: The ABA and the Politics of Judicial Selection.* New York: Wiley.

HALL, MELINDA GANN. 1987. "Constituent Influence in State Supreme Courts: Conceptual Notes and a Case Study." *Judicature* 63: 78.

MALTESE, JOHN ANTHONY. 1995. *The Selling of Supreme Court Nominees.* Baltimore: John Hopkins University Press.

MORASKI, BRIAN J., AND CHARLES R. SHIPAN. 1999. "The Politics of Supreme Court Nominations: A Theory of Institutional Choice and Constraints." *American Journal of Political Science* 43: 1069.

MURPHY, WALTER F. 1961. "In His Own Image: Mr. Chief Justice Taft and Supreme Court Appointments." In *The Supreme Court Review*, ed. Philip B. Kurland. Chicago: University of Chicago Press.

MURPHY, WALTER F. 1990. "Reagan's Judicial Strategy." In *Looking Back on the Reagan Presidency*, Larry Berman, ed. Baltimore: Johns Hopkins University Press.

PERRY, BARBARA A. 1991. *A "Representative" Supreme Court? The Impact of Race, Religion, and Gender on Appointments.* New York: Greenwood Press.

PINELLO, DANIEL R. 1995. *The Impact of Judicial-Selection Method on State-Supreme-Court Policy: Innovation, Reaction and Atrophy.* Westport, CT: Greenwood Press.

SCHERER, NANCY. 2003. "The Judicial Confirmation Process: Mobilizing Elites, Mobilizing Masses." *Judicature* 86: 240.

SEGAL, JEFFREY A., CHARLES M. CAMERON, AND ALBERT D. COVER. 1992. "A Spatial Model of Roll Call Voting: Senators, Constituents, Presidents, and Interest Groups in Supreme Court Confirmations." *American Journal of Political Science* 36: 96.

SHELDON, CHARLES H., AND NICHOLAS P. LOVRICH, JR. 1991. "State Judicial Recruitment." In *The American Courts: A Critical Assessment*, ed. John B. Gates and Charles A. Johnson. Washington, DC: CQ Press.

SILVERSTEIN, MARK. 1994. *Judicious Choices: The New Politics of Supreme Court Confirmations.* New York: Norton.

SLOTNICK, ELLIOT E. 1983. "The ABA Standing Committee on Federal Judiciary: A Contemporary Assessment." *Judicature* 66: 349.

SONGER, DONALD B. 1982. "The Policy Consequences of Senate Involvement in the Selection of Judges in the U.S. Courts of Appeals." *Western Political Quarterly* 35: 107.

TRIBE, LAURENCE H. 1985. *God Save This Honorable Court: How the Choice of Justices Shapes Our History.* New York: Random House.

VAN TASSEL, EMILY FIELD. 1993. "Resignations and Removals: A History of Federal Judicial Service—and Disservice, 1789–1992." *University of Pennsylvania Law Review* 142: 333.

VAN TASSEL, EMILY FIELD, AND PAUL FINKELMAN. 1999. *Impeachable Offenses: A Documentary History from 1787 to the Present.* Washington, DC: Congressional Quarterly.

VOLCANSEK, MARY L. 1993. *Judicial Impeachment: None Called It Justice.* Urbana: University of Illinois Press.

VOLCANSEK, MARY L., WITH MARIA ELISABETTA DE FRANCISCIS AND JACQUELINE LUCIENNE LAFON. 1996. *Judicial Misconduct: A Cross-National Comparison.* Gainesville: University Press of Florida.

WALKER, THOMAS G., AND DEBORAH J. BARROW. 1985. "The Diversification of the Federal Bench: Policy and Process Ramifications." *Journal of Politics* 47: 596.

WATSON, GEORGE L., AND JOHN A. STOOKEY. 1995. *Shaping America: The Politics of Supreme Court Appointments.* New York: HarperCollins.

YALOF, DAVID ALISTAIR. 1999. *Pursuit of Justices: Presidential Politics and the Selection of Supreme Court Nominees.* Chicago: University of Chicago Press.

4.1 THE COMPOSITION OF THE FEDERAL JUDICIARY

Sheldon Goldman, Elliot Slotnick, Gerard Gryski, Gary Zuk, and Sara Schiavoni.

U.S. district court appointees compared by administration

	W. Bush %	W. Bush (N)	Clinton %	Clinton (N)	Bush %	Bush (N)	Reagan %	Reagan (N)	Carter %	Carter (N)
Occupation										
Politics/government	8.4%	(7)	11.5%	(35)	10.8%	(16)	13.4%	(39)	5.0%	(10)
Judiciary	48.2%	(40)	48.2%	(147)	41.9%	(62)	36.8%	(107)	44.6%	(90)
Large law firm										
100+ members	9.6%	(8)	6.6%	(20)	10.8%	(16)	6.2%	(18)	2.0%	(4)
50-99	6.0%	(5)	5.2%	(16)	7.4%	(11)	4.8%	(14)	6.0%	(12)
25-49	8.4%	(7)	4.3%	(13)	7.4%	(11)	6.9%	(20)	6.0%	(12)
Medium size firm										
10-24 members	4.8%	(4)	7.2%	(22)	8.8%	(13)	10.0%	(29)	9.4%	(19)
5-9	4.8%	(4)	6.2%	(19)	6.1%	(9)	9.0%	(26)	9.9%	(20)
Small firm										
2-4	2.4%	(2)	4.6%	(14)	3.4%	(5)	7.2%	(21)	11.4%	(23)
solo	2.4%	(2)	3.6%	(11)	1.4%	(2)	2.8%	(8)	2.5%	(5)
Professor of law	2.4%	(2)	1.6%	(5)	0.7%	(1)	2.1%	(6)	3.0%	(6)
Other	2.4%	(2)	1.0%	(3)	1.4%	(2)	0.7%	(2)	0.5%	(1)
Experience										
Judicial	53.0%	(44)	52.1%	(159)	46.6%	(69)	46.2%	(134)	54.0%	(109)
Prosecutorial	50.6%	(42)	41.3%	(126)	39.2%	(58)	44.1%	(128)	38.1%	(77)
Neither	22.9%	(19)	28.9%	(86)	31.8%	(47)	28.6%	(83)	31.2%	(63)
Undergraduate education										
Public	42.2%	(35)	44.3%	(135)	46.0%	(68)	37.9%	(110)	55.9%	(113)
Private	51.8%	(43)	42.0%	(128)	39.9%	(59)	48.6%	(141)	34.2%	(69)
Ivy League	6.0%	(5)	13.8%	(42)	14.2%	(21)	13.4%	(39)	9.9%	(20)
Law school education										
Public	53.0%	(44)	39.7%	(121)	52.7%	(78)	44.8%	(130)	52.0%	(105)
Private	39.8%	(33)	40.7%	(124)	33.1%	(49)	43.4%	(126)	31.2%	(63)
Ivy League	7.2%	(6)	19.7%	(60)	14.2%	(21)	11.7%	(34)	16.8%	(34)
Gender										
Male	79.5%	(66)	71.5%	(218)	80.4%	(119)	91.7%	(266)	85.6%	(173)
Female	20.5%	(17)	28.5%	(87)	19.6%	(29)	8.3%	(24)	14.4%	(29)
Ethnicity/race										
White	85.5%	(71)	75.1%	(229)	89.2%	(132)	92.4%	(268)	78.8%	(159)
African American	7.2%	(6)	17.4%	(53)	6.8%	(10)	2.1%	(6)	13.9%	(28)
Hispanic	7.2%	(6)	5.9%	(18)	4.0%	(6)	4.8%	(14)	6.9%	(14)
Asian	—	—	1.3%	(4)	—	—	0.7%	(2)	0.5%	(1)
Native American	—	—	0.3%	(1)	—	—	—	—	—	—
Percentage white male	68.7%	(57)	52.4%	(160)	73.0%	(108)	84.8%	(246)	67.8%	(137)
ABA rating										
EWQ/WQ	69.8%	(58)	59.0%	(180)	57.4%	(85)	53.5%	(155)	51.0%	(103)
Qualified	28.9%	(24)	40.0%	(122)	42.6%	(63)	46.6%	(135)	47.5%	(96)
Not Qualified	1.2%	(1)	1.0%	(3)	—	—	—	—	1.5%	(3)
Political Identification										
Democrat	7.2%	(6)	87.5%	(267)	6.1%	(9)	4.8%	(14)	91.1%	(184)
Republican	83.1%	(69)	6.2%	(19)	88.5%	(131)	91.7%	(266)	4.5%	(9)
Other	—	—	0.3%	(1)	—	—	—	—	—	—
None	9.6%	(8)	5.9%	(18)	5.4%	(8)	3.4%	(10)	4.5%	(9)
Past party activism	56.6%	(47)	50.2%	(153)	64.2%	(95)	60.3%	(175)	61.4%	(124)
Net worth										
Under $200,000	4.8%	(4)	13.4%	(41)	10.1%	(15)	17.9%	(52)	35.8%*	(53)
$200-499,999	21.7%	(18)	21.6%	(66)	31.1%	(46)	37.6%	(109)	41.2%	(61)
$500-999,999	16.9%	(14)	26.9%	(82)	28.4%	(39)	21.7%	(63)	18.9%	(28)
$1+million	56.6%	(47)	38.0%	(116)	32.4%	(48)	22.8%	(66)	4.0%	(6)
Average age at nomination	50.3		49.5		48.2		48.6		49.5	
Total number of appointees	83		305		148		290		202	

* These figures are for appointess confirmed by the 96th Congress for all but six Carter district court appointees (for whom no data were available).

U.S. appeals court appointees compared by administration

	W. Bush %	(N)	Clinton %	(N)	Bush %	(N)	Reagan %	(N)	Carter %	(N)
Occupation										
Politics/government	6.2%	(1)	6.6%	(4)	10.8%	(4)	6.4%	(4)	5.4%	(3)
Judiciary	50.0%	(8)	52.5%	(32)	59.5%	(22)	55.1%	(43)	46.4%	(26)
Large law firm										
100+ members	—	—	11.5%	(7)	8.1%	(3)	5.1%	(4)	1.8%	(1)
50-99	6.2%	(1)	3.3%	(2)	8.1%	(3)	2.6%	(2)	5.4%	(3)
25-49	—	—	3.3%	(2)	—	—	6.4%	(5)	3.6%	(2)
Medium size firm										
10-24 members	12.5%	(2)	9.8%	(6)	8.1%	(3)	3.9%	(3)	14.3%	(8)
5-9	—	—	3.3%	(2)	2.7%	(1)	5.1%	(4)	1.8%	(1)
Small firm										
2-4	—	—	1.6%	(1)	—	—	1.3%	(1)	3.6%	(2)
solo	6.2%	(1)	—	—	—	—	—	—	1.8%	(1)
Professor	12.5%	(2)	8.2%	(5)	2.7%	(1)	12.8%	(10)	14.3%	(8)
Other	6.2%	(1)	—	—	—	—	1.3%	(1)	1.8%	(1)
Experience										
Judicial	68.8%	(11)	59.0%	(36)	62.2%	(23)	60.3%	(47)	53.6%	(30)
Prosecutorial	25.0%	(4)	37.7%	(23)	29.7%	(11)	28.2%	(22)	30.4%	(17)
Neither	25.0%	(4)	29.5%	(18)	32.4%	(12)	34.6%	(27)	39.3%	(22)
Undergraduate education										
Public	43.8%	(7)	44.3%	(27)	29.7%	(11)	24.4%	(19)	30.4%	(17)
Private	37.5%	(6)	34.4%	(21)	59.5%	(22)	51.3%	(40)	51.8%	(29)
Ivy League	18.8%	(3)	21.3%	(13)	10.8%	(4)	24.4%	(19)	17.9%	(10)
Law school education										
Public	50.0%	(8)	39.3%	(24)	32.4%	(12)	41.0%	(32)	39.3%	(22)
Private	25.0%	(4)	31.1%	(19)	37.8%	(14)	35.9%	(28)	19.6%	(11)
Ivy League	25.0%	(4)	29.5%	(18)	29.7%	(11)	23.1%	(18)	41.1%	(23)
Gender										
Male	81.2%	(13)	67.2%	(41)	81.1%	(30)	94.9%	(74)	80.4%	(45)
Female	18.8%	(3)	32.8%	(20)	18.9%	(7)	5.1%	(4)	19.6%	(11)
Ethnicity/race										
White	81.2%	(13)	73.8%	(45)	89.2%	(33)	97.4%	(76)	78.6%	(44)
African American	18.8%	(31)	13.1%	(8)	5.4%	(2)	1.3%	(1)	16.1%	(9)
Hispanic	—	—	11.5%	(7)	5.4%	(2)	1.3%	(1)	3.6%	(2)
Asian	—	—	1.6%	(1)	—	—	—	—	1.8%	(1)
Percentage white male	62.5%	(10)	49.2%	(30)	70.3%	(26)	92.3%	(72)	60.7%	(34)
ABA rating										
EWQ/WQ	68.8%	(11)	78.8%	(48)	64.9%	(24)	59.0%	(46)	75.0%	(42)
Qualified	31.2%	(5)	21.3%	(13)	35.1%	(13)	41.0%	(32)	25.0%	(14)
Political Identification										
Democrat	12.5%	(2)	85.2%	(52)	2.7%	(1)	—	—	82.1%	(46)
Republican	81.2%	(13)	6.6%	(4)	89.2%	(33)	96.2%	(75)	7.1%	(4)
Other	—	—	—	—	—	—	1.3%	(1)	—	—
None	6.2%	(1)	8.2%	(5)	8.1%	(3)	26.2%	(3)	10.7%	(6)
Past party activism	75.0%	(12)	54.1%	(33)	70.3%	(26)	66.7%	(52)	73.2%	(41)
Net worth										
Under $200,000	6.2%	(1)	4.9%	(3)	5.4%	(2)	15.6%*	(12)	33.3%**	(13)
$200-499,999	12.5%	(2)	14.8%	(9)	29.7%	(11)	32.5%	(25)	38.5%	(15)
$500-999,999	18.8%	(3)	29.5%	(18)	21.6%	(8)	35.1%	(27)	17.9%	(7)
$1+million	62.5%	(10)	50.8%	(31)	43.2%	(16)	16.9%	(13)	10.3%	(4)
Total number of appointees	16		61		37		78		56	
Average age at nomination	50.6		51.2		48.7		50.0		51.8	

* Net worth was unavailable for one appointee.

** Net worth only for Carter appointees confirmed by the 96th Congress, with the exception of five appointees for whom net worth was unavailable.

Sheldon Goldman is Professor of Political Science at the University of Massachusetts, Amherst. Elliot Slotnick is Professor of Political Science at The Ohio State University and Associate Dean of the Graduate School. Gerard Gryski and Gary Zuk are Professors of Political Science at Auburn University. Sara Schiavoni is a doctoral candidate in political science at The Ohio State University.

From "W. Bush Remaking the Judiciary: Like Father, Like Son?" *Judicature* 86 (2003), 289–293

*"Judicial selection was a high-stakes activity for
the Reagan administration."*

4.2 PICKING FEDERAL JUDGES (WITH A POSTSCRIPT ON THE GEORGE W. BUSH ADMINISTRATION)

Sheldon Goldman

Sheldon Goldman is Professor of Political Science at the
University of Massachusetts, Amherst.

Ronald Reagan came to the presidency with a political ideology or belief system in place. He was determined to promote his economic and social policy agenda as well as his partisan agenda to establish the Republican Party as the nation's majority party. Reagan and his backers made it no secret that judicial selection would be geared to carrying out these agendas. Indeed, the Republican platform of 1980 included a pledge to direct judicial positions to those sharing conservative values. But how would Ronald Reagan conduct judicial selection and to what extent would he involve himself in the process? . . .

For judicial selection, Ronald Reagan relied primarily on three men: Attorney General William French Smith, who had been Reagan's personal attorney; Edwin Meese III, who in the first term served as a presidential counselor and during the second term replaced Smith as attorney general; and the White House counsel, who until mid-1986 was Fred E. Fielding (later followed by Peter J. Wallison, who served for fifteen months and was then replaced by A. B. Culvahouse, who remained to the end of the Reagan presidency). There is little indication that Reagan took the initiative or was actively involved in the establishment and conduct of the judicial selection process during his presidency. Reagan seems to have routinely approved what a consensus of his advisers recommended. This also appears to have been the case with specific judicial appointments and was consistent with Reagan's presidential management style.

The Reagan administration formalized the judicial selection process by institutionalizing interaction patterns and job tasks that in previous administrations were more informal and fluid. Before Reagan, the center of judicial selection activity had been the deputy attorney general's office, with an assistant to the deputy responsible for the details and, at times negotiations associated with the selection process. In the Carter administration the attorney general and associate attorney general oversaw selection. During the Reagan administration these responsibilities shifted to the newly created Office of Legal Policy.

From Sheldon Goldman, Picking Federal Judges (New Haven, CT: Yale University Press, 1997), pp. 286,291–293, 297, 305-307.

The Justice Department's Office of Legal Policy was headed by an assistant attorney general for legal policy, who reported to the deputy attorney general. The Office of Legal Policy, among its other concerns, became the center of the screening process for judicial selection at the justice Department. The attorney general, the deputy attorney general, the assistant attorney general for legal policy, and the special counsel for judicial selection (another position established by the Reagan administration), along with some of their assistants, met regularly within the Justice Department to make specific recommendations for judgeships to the President's Federal judicial Selection Committee, still another major Reagan administration innovation.

The Federal Judicial Selection Committee or Working Group on Appointments, as it became known (because it also dealt with filling United States attorney and United States marshal positions) institutionalized, and formalized an active White House role in judicial selection. During Reagan's first term, the committee was chaired by White House counsel Fred Fielding and included presidential counselor Edwin Meese III, the White House chief of staff, the assistant to the president for presidential personnel, the assistant to the president for political affairs, and the assistant to the president for legislative affairs. From the Justice Department, members of the committee during the first term included the attorney general, the deputy attorney general, the associate attorney general, the special counsel for judicial selection, and the assistant attorney general for legal policy.

The highest levels of the White House staff thus played an ongoing, active role in the selection of judges. Legislative, patronage, political, and policy considerations were systematically scrutinized for each judicial nomination to an extent never before seen. This assured policy coordination between the White House and the Justice Department, as well as White House staff supervision of judicial appointments. The president was thus presented with a consensus recommendation for judicial nominations.

The committee did not merely react to the Justice Department's recommendations; it was also a source of names of potential candidates and a vehicle for the exchange of relevant information. For example, the assistant to the president for presidential personnel informally checked out each prospective candidate for a judgeship as to political acceptability to party officials in the candidate's home state. This and other background on the candidates informed the discussion. The committee, like the Justice Department, was determined to place on the bench, insofar as it was possible to do so, those compatible with the administration's overall ideological and judicial-philosophical perspective. Thus the formal mechanism of the committee permitted consistent screening of judicial candidates. . . .

Throughout the Reagan presidency the committee held meetings (usually weekly) at the White House. Although this certainly was convenient given the larger number of committee members from the White House, it also symbolized White House primacy in the selection process and the importance the Reagan administration placed on judicial selection and its central role in furthering the president's agenda. . . .

The president's domestic policy agenda, aside from economic and government regulatory concerns, was shaped by opposition to civil libertarian decisions of the Supreme Court. Those decisions included the establishment of the right of a woman to abort a nonviable fetus, the use of remedies such as busing to bring about desegregation of the public schools, the exclusionary rule (barring the use in court of evidence seized in violation of the Fourth Amendment), generous readings of the Bill of Rights to provide for the rights of the accused, prohibitions on prayer rituals in the public schools, and affirmative action in employment and education. In terms of judicial philosophy, the Reagan administration was looking for those who believed in "judicial restraint." Such judges would likely share Reagan's conservative political beliefs and therefore be opposed to these and similar policy positions in court decisions. A political conservative, Reagan no doubt believed, would read the Constitution narrowly. By framing his appointment goals in terms of the judicial philosophy he believed would accomplish his political purposes, Reagan placed a more legitimate public and professional face on his policy agenda for the judiciary. . . .

The Reagan administration did not proceed with a judicial nomination, particularly to the appeals courts, unless it felt assured that the nominee shared the administration's judicial philosophy. When a potential nominee had strong political backing but doubts were raised about the candidate's philosophical reliability, the burden was on the candidate's backers to demonstrate that the doubts were unfounded.

An example of this occurred with the filling of an Illinois seat on the Seventh Circuit. In 1981, Republican senator Charles Percy and Republican governor Jim Thompson, of Illinois, strongly recommended the elevation of Judge Joel M. Flaum. Before Flaum had been appointed to the federal district bench by Gerald Ford, he had been first assistant United States attorney under Thompson, who was then United States attorney. Flaum had the strong support of the organized bar as well. But the vacancy was filled by Professor Richard Posner of the University of Chicago Law School. Senator Percy, by his own account, agreed to support Posner with the understanding that Flaum would be considered for the next vacancy. When Seventh Circuit Judge Robert Sprecher died in May 1982, another Illinois seat on the Seventh came open. Once again Senator Percy and Governor Thompson strongly recommended Flaum.

When it became known that Judge Flaum was being seriously considered, a number of letters from far-right conservatives were sent to administration officials. For example, an Illinois state senator sent a "Dear Ed" letter to then presidential counselor Ed Meese in early July 1982: "Several members of the Chicago Bar have talked to me regarding the Flaum appointment. They express concern with Mr. Flaum's 'bleeding heart' philosophy. I have received similar comments from people more knowledgeable about Mr. Flaum than myself." Even more perilous for the Flaum candidacy was the "Dear Ed" letter from Paul M. Weyrich, the president of the ultra-conservative Coalition for America:

> Our own examination of Flaum's opinions has convinced me that his judicial tendencies are worrisome. Specifically, he seems to have a predilection for

"class action" suits. In addition, at least one of his rulings raises questions as to how he would interpret the recently passed Voting Rights Act Amendments. He has also shown a tendency to intervene in clearly local or state matters, such as the academic decision-making processes. In sum, he is not the sort of judge we would expect from this Administration. We would oppose the elevation of Judge Flaum to the Circuit seat.

The Flaum candidacy seemed to stall, and Senator Percy met with Meese in late September. Realizing that Flaum had been unfairly labeled a judicial activist, Percy asked the dean of the Loyola University School of Law, Charles W. Murdock, who was known as a conservative, to analyze Flaum's decisions and comment on Flaum's judicial philosophy. Percy sent Murdock's eighteen-page analysis to Meese, which concluded that Flaum's decision making "is a model of judicial restraint." Unbeknownst to Percy, the Justice Department in 1981 had undertaken its own review of Flaum's record, which apparently cast doubt on Flaum's commitment to judicial restraint.

To get the Flaum candidacy back on track, Governor Thompson personally met with Justice Department officials to review every published decision of Judge Flaum. As Senator Percy recounted to Reagan, "I am told that at the end of that session there were only two cases that were cited as causing concern, out of his over 250 published opinions." Percy continued in his letter: "Governor Thompson and I would not urge someone on you who we believed would be a discredit to you or your own beliefs. We believe that the record shows that Judge Flaum has exhibited a philosophy of judicial restraint during his eight years on the bench and that he would contribute to your desire to see additional restraint in the decisions being made by our federal courts."

Flaum, unanimously rated "exceptionally well qualified" by the ABA, was nominated on April 14, 1983, and the following May 4 was confirmed. Meese apparently had hoped to fill the position caused by Judge Sprecher's death with the brilliant young conservative professor from the University of Chicago, Frank H. Easterbrook. Easterbrook in fact was named to the next vacancy on the Seventh Circuit.

Judicial selection was a high-stakes activity for the Reagan administration. There was a genuine commitment to reverse the course of judicial policymaking through the appointment of those sharing the president's judicial philosophy. That philosophy was consistent with the conservative policy positions of the social agenda; thus, in effect, philosophical screening was ideological screening. Available evidence in the presidential papers lends support to this view of the Reagan appointment process. Although many of the presidential papers relating to appointments have yet to be processed, from the information that is available it appears that at least 75 percent of appeals court judges were policy-agenda appointments (thirty-eight out of forty-nine for whom a determination could be reasonably made). The balance probably can be considered partisan-agenda appointments. There is no evidence of the personal agenda coming into play. But the administration never had a free ride in its journey to reshape the judiciary. The Senate played an increasingly important role both before and after the election of 1986, in which the Democrats regained control of the Senate. . . .

Editors' note: In a 2003 article, Goldman and his coauthors point out changes that the George W. Bush administration has made to the selection process:

[President George W. Bush has made two changes in the judicial selection process] that warrant additional exploration because they represent potentially significant departures from the status quo characterizing the approach of past administrations. First, at the outset of his administration, President Bush ended the formal role played by the American Bar Association in the rating of candidates before final decisions on the nominations were made. More recently, on October 30, 2002, the President offered a timetable proposal suggesting the parameters for the flow of all phases of the judicial selection process, from notification requirements suggested for sitting judges regarding their plans for stepping down from the bench through the time taken to conduct various facets of the confirmation process.

From the administration's perspective, the swirl of controversy that surrounded the removal of the ABA's formal participation in the presidential stages of judicial selection could be characterized as much ado about very little. [Assistant Attorney General] Viet Dinh noted that the administration recognized that the ABA,

> through the Senate Judiciary Committee and through individual senators, had a role in this process. It was very clear when I took office that Senator Leahy, then Chairman of the Senate Judiciary Committee, would not clear any person for a hearing unless and until that person had received a rating from the ABA. So the ABA was an integral part of the Senate Judiciary Committee's consideration of the candidacy and we did everything in our power to cooperate in that process.

Toward that end, Dinh established a procedure whereby when a nomination was sent to the Senate for confirmation consideration, the name was concurrently sent to the ABA so that it could start its review processes. . . .

Boyden Gray succinctly summarized the view that little has really changed. "The ABA, I think, is just as honored now as it was when I was here. The only thing is that they don't get the upfront knowledge about it, but they're full players. They're getting everything they've always had." A similar assessment was offered by Makan Delrahim from his perspective as Republican Chief Counsel of the Judiciary Committee which, when first chaired by Orrin Hatch during the Clinton years, had ended the ABA Committee's "most favored" status in the process, a change lasting until the Democrats regained control of the Senate chamber and Patrick Leahy assumed the Judiciary Committee chairmanship.

> Senator Hatch looked at it as a matter of equity. Should the Hispanic Bar Association do a vetting before the Committee acts on it or the president sends

Sheldon Goldman, Elliot Slotnick, Gerard Gryski, Gary Zuk, and Sara Schiavoni. From "W. Bush Remaking the Judiciary: Like Father, Like Son?" 86 *Judicature* 289–293 (2003).

it down? What about the Minority Law Students Association? Any association could provide useful advice and they should. And the ABA is just one of them. . . . They've provided their service and it has been valuable.

Since the advent of the 108th Congress, with the ABA removed from the presidential facets of judicial selection, the Republicans back in control of the Senate, and Senator Orrin Hatch again chairing the Judiciary Committee, the question of what status the ABA's post-hoc ratings will play in the confirmation process looms both larger and on somewhat more tenuous footing. Indeed, as Delrahim [Republican Chief Counsel of the Judiciary Committee] underscored,

> The ABA can do its work, but we're not going to allow the ABA to delay our consideration of judicial nominees. I mean there's no constitutional reason . . . to allow any outside group to delay the advice and consent process of the Senate.

Critics of the administration's posture towards the ABA see the implications of its removal from the front end of the selection process in a much more negative light, with unhappy consequences. Nan Aron [of the Alliance for Justice], for example, argues that,

> one difference between now and the years before is the chilling effect that excluding the ABA has had on the desire and ability of lawyers to be upfront, to share their views of the nominees. It's staggering. I remember from the '80s lawyers would call and say, "Just got word from the ABA that so and so had been nominated. You guys ought to take a look."

Now, as Marcia Kuntz added, "there is a lot of pressure on people "not to be candid. Once somebody is nominated, there is an inevitability to confirmation, so why would they stick their necks out and say anything negative?"

In Aron's view, this reality is consistent with a broader administration motivation for altering the ABA's role in the process in the first place:

> I am convinced, I am absolutely convinced, that the reason the administration removed the ABA, I don't care what they say, is not because they are afraid of the rating, because we all know that ratings were uniformly high. It wasn't the ratings that caused them to take them out. It was their desire for total and complete secrecy, and that's another thing that's a huge departure. It's a major change. It's shrouding the entire judicial selection process in secrecy.

The second major departure of the Bush approach to judicial selection, the nascent effort to regulate the time parameters of the process, was not unveiled until October 30, 2002, just one week before the 2002 congressional elections. The President's proposal, stemming, in part, from his view that the Senate had displayed a poor record in confirming his nominees, contained four central recommendations, collectively targeted at filling vacancies expeditiously as seats on the federal bench became open. To succeed, the President's proposal would require behavioral changes not only in the administration's own behavior, in some instances, but in the institutional behavior of the Senate and the judiciary as well:

1. Federal judges should give a year's notice of their intention to take retirement or senior status.
2. The president should nominate a replacement judge within 180 days of receiving such notice.
3. The Senate Judiciary Committee should hold hearings within 90 days of receiving a nomination.
4. The full Senate should hold a floor vote within 180 days of the initial receipt of the nomination.

Adding to its luster was the notion that the proposal was targeted at the process irrespective of the occupant of the White House. Viet Dinh emphasized this point. "I think it's a perfectly sensible plan. It operates irrespective of who is in power, either in the administration or in the Senate." Recognizing that the plan required considerable cooperation from participants in the process outside of White House control, Dinh noted the administration's flexibility in how meeting the guidelines might be accomplished:

> We would support a Senate rule change to codify this, but we would also support anything short of a rule change. A Judiciary Committee rule change, a bipartisan gentlemen's agreement, Judicial Conference resolutions, whatever it is in order to get as close to the ideal that there should be an orderly process of at least giving a person a full day hearing and an up or down vote.

In a similar vein, Associate White House Counsel Brett Kavanaugh noted that "things rarely happen overnight, but he has set out a marker. The President ultimately would like to see the Senate come around to the view that it would make sense to have a standard process that applies to every judicial nominee." In Kavanaugh's view, such a standardized process would enable the judicial selection process to emerge from the tit-for-tat obstructionism that has characterized both the Clinton and Bush administration's selection efforts. Kavanaugh added:

> Have a process where people know the rules in advance, the rules of the road. We're going to have hearings; we're going to have votes. And if you think someone is out of the mainstream, it is incumbent upon you to make that case, whether you are a Republican objecting to a Clinton nominee or a Democrat objecting to a Bush nominee. And, ultimately, you have to convince your colleagues that is the case and not bottle a nominee. That's not fair to the nominee, it's unfair to the president, it hurts the courts, [and] breaks down the whole process. It deters good people from getting involved.

While committed, in the long run, to the necessity of a Senate rule change as an ultimate goal, Kavanaugh admitted,

> That takes time. A lot of times, ideas like this, you keep plugging, you keep plugging and, ultimately, it may come to fruition. And that's what we plan to do with this. The President said the goal is to have a new judge ready to take office the day the old judge retires. That's the seamless transition we're seeking. That's a process. Perfection will probably never be achieved in every case. But improving the process significantly, we think, can be achieved with these kinds of timetables.

In analyzing the President's mandate, it is important to underscore the critical "end game" of the proposed process—floor action on a nomination. According to Viet Dinh,

> This process is not meant as a way to override . . . prerogatives of home state senators. To the extent that we can accommodate those interests and also succeed in expeditious resolution, great! With respect to holds, a hold is nothing but an intention to filibuster. And its only force is the prerogative to filibuster on the floor. We have absolutely no intention of disturbing [the] century old tradition of Senators to filibuster on the floor. . . . [T]he call for a vote on the floor within 180 days is nothing but a statement, "Hey, let's get it out in the open." It's not necessarily a call that you have to have passed cloture within 180 days. If you want to exercise the floor prerogative of denying cloture, fine, just do it. Do it within 180 days, according to normal rules of floor debate, including filibuster, but do it out in the open.

Some skepticism about the President's proposal can be seen, among the administration's supporters. Boyden Gray, for example, noted

> I think they'll try and hold to it. Maybe they'll be able to. But I, myself, am a little bit skeptical of finite timetables that you have to get so and so out. It's just not quite susceptible to such precision.

In addition to such practical concerns about the plan's operation, substantive criticisms of the proposal were also offered, in this instance, from the Democratic side of the Senate aisle. One aide noted that

> the proposal doesn't take into account when a president stacks nominations, numerous nominees at the beginning. There is no regard to how controversial they may be, how time consuming the records may be. They are just supposed to get a hearing pretty quickly.

Another Senate aide offered,

> Portraying it as a situation that has gotten worse is just playing into their argument. Their argument has now gotten to the point where the President is seriously committed to the proposal that he made right before the election. "Okay, let's just take politics out of this; I'll just take all the marbles. Forget about blue slips, forget about hearings, forget about everybody. We'll just have this arbitrary time clock that says within 180 days I get an up or down vote." A Democratic president's moderate nominees were not allowed to go forth, but now we're supposed to flip the switch.

While not opposed, in principle, to a "neutral" proposal instituted under a veil of ignorance at some future time when nobody could know the identity of the president or the partisan balance of the Senate, he continued,

> We should say we will start this with the next president. This is an interesting set of concepts. Let's start it with the next set of guys so that none of us really benefit." Well, I can assure you that will never be offered.

Synthesizing the multiple concerns raised about the President's proposal Elliot Mincberg of People for the American Way asserted that, "aspirational goals may not be a bad idea to suggest in the abstract, but it's important to always consider individual circumstances." Citing complaints that some of the earliest Bush nominees were still waiting to have their hearings, Mincberg continued:

> Well, from the perspective of the administration of the courts, there is a very good reason for that. If you process nominees first in, first out, you're going to have a huge number of vacancies because if the first ones are the most controversial ones, and you take the most time to review, then the result is that the ones who are less controversial don't get reviewed. So I think it's important, frankly, from my perspective, to add some things of a more qualitative nature. I think that the more moderate, less controversial nominees should get priority in processing and they always have, and they should, because it makes perfect sense from the perspective of helping the courts do their job. And that's something that's hard to write in the rules, but is something that has to be considered. And it's a bit counterintuitive to the notion that every nominee should follow a particular schedule. It is certainly true that there is a need to try and make the process work better, but again, I think where that starts, is not with attempted timetables, but with attempts to try and lower the temperature of the process a little.

In the final analysis, Mincberg noted, there was a certain irony in the President's proposal.

> It really isn't appropriate for a president on the one hand to say, at least quietly, I'm going to put a strong ideological stamp on the judiciary but, on the other hand, I want these guys processed in an assembly line process. It doesn't make sense. It's not consistent with the whole division of authority in advice and consent.

"1998: 'GOP, Its Eyes on High Court, Blocks a Judge'; 1998: 'After Delay, Senate Approves Judge for Court in New York'; 2003: 'Stymied by Democrats in Senate, Bush Court Pick Finally Gives Up.'"

READING 4.3. PARTISANSHIP AND THE APPOINTMENT OF FEDERAL JUDGES

Neil A. Lewis

Neil A. Lewis is a graduate of Princeton University, B.A., and Yale Law School, J.D., 1979. He was Assistant District Attorney, New York County District Attorney's Office, 1979–1984; associate and then partner in the New York law firm Pavia & Harcourt, 1984–1992; and, since 1992, United States District Judge, Southern District of New York.

These articles, the first two written on June 13 and October 3, 1998, and the third on September 5, 2003, by Neil Lewis of the *New York Times*, provide some indication of the partisan and ideological nature of the process leading to the confirmation of federal judges. Republicans in the Senate sought to block President Clinton's nominations; Democrats are attempting to do much the same with George W. Bush's choices.

1998: "GOP, Its Eyes on High Court, Blocks a Judge"

Judge Sonia Sotomayor seemed like a trouble free choice when President Clinton nominated her to an appeals court post a year ago. Hers was an appealing story: a child from the Bronx housing projects who went on to graduate summa cum laude from Princeton and become editor of the *Yale Law Journal* and then a Federal prosecutor.

Moreover, she had been a trial judge since 1992, when she was named to the bench by the last Republican president, George [H. W.] Bush.

But Republican senators have been blocking Judge Sotomayor's elevation to the appeals court for a highly unusual reason: to make her less likely to be picked by Mr. Clinton for the Supreme Court, senior Republican Congressional aides said in interviews.

The delay of a confirmation vote on Judge Sotomayor to the United States Court of Appeals for the Second Circuit, based in New York, is an example of the intense and often Byzantine political maneuverings that take place behind the scenes in many judicial nominations. Several elements of the Sotomayor case are odd, White House officials and Democrats in Congress say, but the chief one is the fact that there is no vacancy on the Supreme Court, and no firm indication that there will be one soon. Nor is there any evidence of a campaign to put Judge Sotomayor under consideration for a seat if there were a vacancy.

Judge Sotomayor's nomination was approved overwhelmingly by the Senate Judiciary Committee in March. Of the judicial nominees who have cleared the committee in this Congress, she is among those who have waited the longest for a final vote on the floor.

Senate Republican staff aides said Trent Lott of Mississippi, the majority leader, has agreed to hold up a vote on the nomination as part of an elaborate political calculus; if she were easily confirmed to the appeals court, they said, that would put her in a position to be named to the Supreme Court. And Senate Republicans think that they would then have a difficult time opposing a woman who had just been confirmed by the full Senate.

"Basically, we think that putting her on the appeals court puts her in the batter's box to be nominated to the Supreme Court," said one senior Republican staff aide who spoke on the condition of anonymity. "If Clinton nominated her it would put several of our senators in a real difficult position."

Mr. Lott declined through a spokeswoman to comment.

Judge Sotomayor sits on Federal District Court in Manhattan, and the aides said some senators believe that her record on the bench fits the profile of an "activist judge," a description that has been used by conservatives to question a jurist's ability to construe the law narrowly. It is a description that Judge Sotomayor's supporters, including some conservative New York lawyers, dispute.

Senator Patrick Leahy of Vermont, the senior Democrat on the Judiciary Committee, was blunt in his criticism of the Republicans who are blocking a confirmation vote. "Their reasons are stupid at best and cowardly at worst," he said.

"What they are saying is that they have a brilliant judge who also happens to be a woman and Hispanic, and they haven't the guts to stand up and argue publicly against her on the floor," Senator Leahy said. "They just want to hide in their cloakrooms and do her in quietly."

The models for the strategy of putting candidates on appeals courts to enhance their stature as Supreme Court nominees are Judge Robert H. Bork and Judge Clarence Thomas. Both were placed on the Court of Appeals for the District of Columbia Circuit in part to be poised for nomination to the Supreme Court. Judge Bork was denied confirmation to the Supreme Court in 1987, and Judge Thomas was confirmed in 1991, in both cases after bruising political battles.

The foundation for the Republicans' strategy is based on two highly speculative theories: that Mr. Clinton is eager to name the first Hispanic person to the Supreme Court and that he will have such an opportunity when one of the current justices, perhaps John Paul Stevens, retires at the end of the current Supreme Court term next month.

Warnings about the possibility of Judge Sotomayor's filling Justice Stevens's seat were raised by *The Wall Street Journal*'s editorial pages this month, both in an editorial and in an op-ed column by Paul A. Gigot, who often reflects conservative thinking in the Senate.

Although justices often announce their retirements at the end of a term, Justice Stevens has not given a clue that he will do so. He has, in fact, hired law clerks for next year's term. The *Journal*'s commentary also criticized Judge Sotomayor's record, particularly her March ruling in a case involving a Manhattan business coalition, the Grand Central Partnership. She ruled that in trying to give work experience to the homeless, the coalition had violated Federal law by failing to pay the minimum wage.

Gerald Walpin, a former Federal prosecutor who is widely known in New York legal circles as a staunch conservative, took issue with the *Journal*'s criticism.

"If they had read the case they would see that she said she personally approved of the homeless program but that as a judge she was required to apply the law as it exists," he said. "She wrote that the law does not permit an exception in this case. That's exactly what conservatives want: a nonactivist judge who does not apply her own views but is bound by the law." Mr. Bush nominated Judge Sotomayor in 1992 after a recommendation from Daniel Patrick Moynihan, New York's Democratic Senator.

It also remains unclear how some Senate Republicans came to believe that Judge Sotomayor was being considered as a candidate for the Supreme Court. Hispanic bar groups have for years pressed the Clinton Administration to name the first Hispanic justice, but White House officials said they are not committed to doing so. The Hispanic National Bar Association has submitted a list of six candidates for the Supreme Court to the White House. But Martin R. Castro, a Chicago lawyer and official of the group, said Judge Sotomayor's name is not on the list.

On Sept. 30, the day of her confirmation hearing, Rush Limbaugh, the conservative radio talk show host, warned the Senate that Judge Sotomayor was an ultraliberal who was on a "rocket ship" to the Supreme Court. That day, Judge Sotomayor was questioned closely by Republicans.

In the end, the only Republicans to vote against her were Senator John Kyl of Arizona and Senator John Ashcroft of Missouri. The committee's other conservative members, including Orrin G. Hatch of Utah and Strom Thurmond of South Carolina, voted in her favor. Mr. Kyl and Mr. Ashcroft declined to comment today.

The confirmation delay comes as Ralph K. Winter, chief judge of the Second Circuit, has complained that unfilled vacancies on the court have created its worst backlog in history. In his annual report, Judge Winter, a conservative Republican, lamented that he had to declare judicial emergencies "several times to allow retired judges and trial judges to sit on appeals panels."

Postscript to Sotomayor Nomination: "After Delay Senate Approves Judge for Court in New York"

After a delay of more than a year, the Senate today voted to elevate Judge Sonia Sotomayor of Federal District Court in New York City to the Court of Appeals for the Second Circuit.

Judge Sotomayor's nomination had become embroiled in the sometimes tortured judicial politics of the Senate. Some Republicans did not want to consider the nomination because, they said, putting her on the appeals court would enhance her prospects for elevation to the Supreme Court.

Those lawmakers said they believed President Clinton was eager to place a Hispanic person, [such as] Judge Sotomayor, on the Supreme Court, and they held up consideration of her nomination for months, even though there was no evidence the Clinton Administration had planned to try to put her on the Court when a vacancy arises.

"At long last, this day has finally arrived," said Senator Patrick J. Leahy of Vermont, the ranking Democrat on the Judiciary Committee, just before the Senate voted in Sotomayor's favor, 68 to 28.

All Democrats present voted for Judge Sotomayor, as did several Republicans, including Senator Orrin G. Hatch of Utah, the chairman of the Judiciary Committee. Senator Trent Lott of Mississippi, the majority leader, who had blocked consideration of the nomination by the full Senate, voted against Sotomayor.

Senator Leahy said that the delay in voting on the nomination had been especially troubling because the Second Circuit, which is based in New York, has great backlogs and its chief judge, Ralph K. Winter, had declared a judicial emergency.

The delay in considering the Sotomayor nomination also occasioned heavy lobbying by Hispanic bar groups and the Congressional Hispanic Caucus. After that, the Republican leadership relented and allowed her name to go forward. Ms. Sotomayor will be the second Hispanic Judge on the Second Circuit.

Her confirmation seemed like a trouble-free choice when President Clinton nominated her more than a year ago. She brought the kind of personal story usually greeted warmly by the Senate: a child from the Bronx housing projects who went on to graduate summa cum laude from Princeton and become editor of the *Yale Law Journal* and then a Federal prosecutor.

She has been a trial judge since 1992, when she was named to the bench by President George Bush.

Senator Daniel Patrick Moynihan, Democrat of New York, told the Senate today that in more than five years on the bench, the judge "presided over cases of enormous complexity with skill and confidence."

Her nomination was approved overwhelmingly by the Senate Judiciary Committee more than a year ago. Of the judicial nominees who have cleared the committee in this Congress, she had waited the longest for a final vote.

Her confirmation leaves seventeen judicial nominees still pending in the Senate, a spokeswoman for the Judiciary Committee said today.

"Stymied by Democrats in Senate, Bush Court Pick Finally Gives Up"

Miguel Estrada, whose nomination by President Bush to an important federal appeals court post was blocked by an extraordinary filibuster mounted by Senate Democrats, gave up his two-year struggle today.

"I write to ask you to withdraw my pending nomination," Mr. Estrada said in a letter to the president. "I believe that the time has come to return my full attention to the practice of law and to regain the ability to make long-term plans for my family."

The fight over Mr. Estrada's nomination was the most prominent and most protracted battle in what has become a nasty ideological and political war with no end in sight between the White House and Senate Democrats over who gets to sit on the federal bench.

Republicans moved swiftly to deplore Mr. Estrada's fate and turn his withdrawal into a mobilizing moment among the party faithful akin to the 1987 defeat of Judge Robert Bork's nomination to the Supreme Court. That event was depicted as a great injustice, and it generated long-term political fervor.

"Despite his superb qualifications and the wide bipartisan support for his nomination, these Democrat Senators repeatedly blocked an up-or-down vote that would have led to Mr. Estrada's confirmation," President Bush said in a statement, referring to the Democratic filibuster or threat of extended debate that prevented the nomination from coming to a vote on the Senate floor.

"The treatment of this fine man is an unfortunate chapter in the Senate's history," Mr. Bush said. Other Republicans were far harsher, noting that Mr. Estrada became the first appeals court nominee defeated through a filibuster strategy. While they were reluctant to say so explicitly, some strongly suggested that he was opposed by Democrats because of his Hispanic heritage. Representative Tom Delay of Texas, the House majority leader, said Mr. Estrada was the victim of a "political hate crime."

Although most of Mr. Bush's judicial choices have been confirmed easily, Democrats have blocked several of his nominees to the federal appeals court, asserting that they are part of an effort by the White House to tilt the courts in a more conservative direction.

Republicans have countered that the ideology of the Bush nominees should not matter as they are all highly qualified lawyers who would enforce the law fairly from the bench, leaving their personal views behind.

Mr. Estrada, a forty-one-year-old Washington lawyer who has argued fifteen cases before the Supreme Court, was widely known as an intellectual star in Washington's conservative legal lineup and is a prominent member of the Federalist Society, a conservative legal group.

But he has such a scant written record that Democrats complained he was a "stealth nominee," whose views were hidden from public view but would come out in his rulings from the bench.

Senate Democrats had demanded that the administration provide them with legal memorandums that Mr. Estrada had written while he was an assistant solicitor general in the Justice Department. The White House refused, noting that several Democratic solicitors general had said that was inappropriate.

For Republicans, Mr. Estrada had the strong advantage of an appealing personal story, that of an immigrant from Honduras who went on to graduate with honors both from Columbia University and the Harvard law School. When Mr. Bush nominated him more than two years ago to be the first Hispanic judge on United States Court of Appeals for the District of Columbia Circuit, the White House celebrated the event as a chapter in the American immigrant success story.

In winning the Estrada battle, Democrats were muted in victory today, saying they hoped the administration would now seek to nominate consensus candidates who would win Senate approval.

"This should serve as a wake-up call to the White House that it cannot simply expect the Senate to rubber-stamp judicial nominations," said Senator Edward M. Kennedy, Democrat of Massachusetts.

But Republicans lined up before microphones on Capitol Hill letting loose storms of outrage and repeatedly noting his Hispanic heritage in a clear effort to make Democrats pay a price with a group of swing voters that both parties are avidly courting.

Republicans called the Estrada outcome "shameful," "sad," and "disgraceful." Senator George Allen of Virginia, son of a famous professional football coach, said the Democrats had committed "a personal foul here."

Senator John Cornyn told reporters that Hispanic voters in his state of Texas would certainly question why the first appeals court nominee in history to be blocked from having a direct floor vote on his nomination was of Hispanic heritage.

When he was pressed if he was asserting that Democrats blocked the Estrada nomination in part because of his ethnic heritage, Mr. Cornyn declined to say if that was what he meant to imply.

From *Extensions*, Spring 2004, pp. 13–18.

But Senator Bill Frist of Tennessee, the Republican leader, addressed the issue more directly. "I don't think it is rank bigotry which brought this man down," he said. Rather, he said, Democrats and other Estrada opponents resented how President Bush had demonstrated his commitment to diversity and "stood by the side of Hispanics."

Dr. Frist said that it was no secret that Mr. Bush was eager to promote Hispanic candidates for the bench and was hoping to name the first Hispanic Supreme Court justice.

Senator Charles E. Schumer, a New York Democrat who helped lead the opposition to Mr. Estrada, said: "The implication that anyone has blocked this because of Mr. Estrada's background is cheap and low. The Republicans can't seem to win the argument on the merits, so they resort to below-the-belt tactics."

Mr. Estrada would have been the first Hispanic judge on the United States Court of Appeals for the District of Columbia, widely viewed as the court second in importance only to the Supreme Court.

The announcement of Mr. Estrada's withdrawal came just hours before the Democratic presidential candidates were to appear at a debate in Albuquerque sponsored by the Democratic National Committee and Congressional Hispanic Caucus, aimed at the same kind of audience Republicans were courting with today's complaints.

But it was unclear if the timing was a coincidence, or if the White House was involved. Friends of Mr. Estrada, who was out of town today and did not respond to telephone messages, have said he had been dismayed for weeks about his poor chances of being confirmed.

Dr. Frist offered an analysis that both sides of the debate might agree with when he said that the fight over judicial nominations had soured relations in the Senate. He said he was considering several options to change the system of judicial confirmations in order to prevent Democrats from being able to use a filibuster to block nominees.

Although the Democrats are in the minority, they have been able to fend off confirmation votes by threatening to hold an extended debate or filibuster, which can only be ended by sixty votes. Republicans, with fifty-one votes, were unable to attract the support of the nine Democrats needed to break the filibuster.

Democrats have used a filibuster or threat of one to block at least three other Bush appeals court candidates.

"The ongoing battle of the makeup of the federal judiciary has spilled over into everyday political discourse."

READING 4.4. PARTIES, PRESIDENTS, AND PROCEDURES: THE BATTLE OVER JUDICIAL NOMINATIONS IN THE U.S. SENATE

Jason M. Roberts.

Jason M. Roberts is Assistant Professor of Political
Science at the University of Minnesota.

Article II of the *U.S. Constitution* creates a fundamental tension between the president and the Senate with regards to judicial nominations by vesting the power of nomination in the president, while requiring the Senate's "advice and consent" before a nominee is appointed. History is ripe with examples of conflict between the president and the Senate over individual nominees, such as President Nixon's failure to get Clement Haynesworth and Harrold Carswell confirmed, the filibuster of Abe Fortas's nomination as Chief Justice of the Supreme Court, and more recently the controversies surrounding the nominations of Robert Bork and Clarence Thomas to the Supreme Court. Historically, when controversy has erupted it has centered on the merits of an individual nominee. Haynesworth and Carswell were seen as mediocre jurists, many senators had ethical concerns about Abe Fortas and Clarence Thomas, and Robert Bork's long academic career provided plenty of fodder for those who wished to question his "judicial temperament."

However, this tension between the Senate and the president has reached a new level of intensity in the past decade as interest groups, political parties, senators, and the president have come to view each nomination, not necessarily on its own merits, but rather as a round in an ongoing battle over the ideological makeup of the federal judiciary. As vacancies on the Supreme Court have become rare, the battle has moved down to the level of the U.S. Courts of Appeals and the U.S. district courts. Presidents Bill Clinton and George W. Bush have experienced great difficulty in securing confirmation for their lower court nominees, in most cases because of long delays or outright obstruction in the U.S. Senate.

The ongoing battle over the makeup of the federal judiciary has spilled over into everyday political discourse. Media coverage of the judicial nomination and confirmation process has become more prominent, as the president and Senate parties have sought to mobilize public opinion on their side of the debate with the hopes of forcing action by the other party. One element of the public debate

From *Extensions*, Spring 2004, pp. 13–18.

over judicial nominees has centered on the maze of Senate rules and norms which can be used to stall nominations. As detailed below, there are many procedural hurdles that nominees must clear before securing appointment, and, in the wake of the recent controversy, there have been numerous proposals to alter Senate rules to make the nomination and confirmation process work more efficiently. This essay analyzes some of the more prominent rules change proposals in terms of the likely effect they would have on the nomination and confirmation process as well as the likelihood of them being adopted.

Recent Trends in Delay

For most of U.S. history, presidents have had little trouble getting their nominees to the federal judiciary confirmed by the Senate. As Binder (2001) points out, despite the Senate's reputation as a "black hole" for nominees, most sail through with little difficulty or delay. Over 90 percent of President Carter's nominees to the U.S. Courts of Appeals were confirmed, with an average wait time of less than eighty days from nomination to confirmation.[1] President Reagan was able to secure confirmation for over 80 percent of his U.S. Courts of Appeals nominees, with an average time from nomination to final Senate action similar to that of Carter's nominees, despite Reagan facing a Democratic Senate during the last two years of his administration. The confirmation process began to get bogged down during the administration of George H. W. Bush, but beginning in the administration of President Clinton and continuing now with President George W. Bush, the process has changed dramatically.

The Senate confirmed less than 60 percent of Clinton's nominees to the U.S. Courts of Appeals with an average of 230 days elapsing between nomination and final Senate action, or inaction as was often the case. The dramatic change in this process during the Clinton administration is best exemplified by Richard Paez, who waited over four years—1,506 days—to be confirmed for a seat on the Court of Appeals for the Ninth Circuit. President George W. Bush saw the Senate confirm less than half of his Courts of Appeals nominees during the 107th Congress (2001-2002), with an average of over 150 days from nomination to Senate action. Miguel Estrada, a Bush nominee for the Court of Appeals for the D.C. Circuit, awaited approval by the Senate Judiciary Committee for almost two years, and then encountered more delay after clearing committee. He eventually withdrew his name from consideration after the Senate failed to take an up or down vote on his confirmation—despite his nomination having been pending for more than two and a half years. The lack of prompt Senate action on many of these nominees has drawn the scorn of many observers at least in part because most of the delayed or blocked nominees would have received a positive confirmation vote in the Senate, had such a vote been cast.

Senate Rules, Norms, and Obstruction

While the Constitution clearly grants the "advice and consent" power to the Senate, the parliamentary rules by which nominations and other Senate business are considered was left to the chamber to decide. Over its history, the Senate has developed a labyrinth of rules and norms that make it possible for a determined minority to delay most Senate business—including judicial nominations. For judicial nominees, the highest hurdle to clear is the Senate Judiciary Committee. All judicial nominees submitted by the president are referred to the Judiciary Committee for consideration. The Senate gives the Judiciary Committee great latitude in determining when or if hearings will be held on nominees. The committee chair is in charge of scheduling hearings, and if hearings are not scheduled, nominees do not reach the floor. Almost one-third of President Clinton's Courts of Appeals nominees did not receive a hearing, while more than half of President George W. Bush's Courts of Appeals nominees did not receive a hearing during the 107th Congress (2001–2002).

The Senate has also developed the norm of "senatorial courtesy," which has often manifested itself in the Senate's "blue slip" procedure. Since the 1910s, the Judiciary Committee has sent out blue sheets of paper asking senators from a nominee's home state his or her opinion of the nominee (Binder 2003). Traditionally, if a home state senator objected to a nominee, he or she would write on the blue slip that the nominee was "personally offensive." Throughout history, negative blue slips have often meant that the Judiciary Committee would not act on a nominee. While this is not always the case today, a negative blue slip usually makes confirmation of the nominee much less likely.

In addition to clearing the necessary hurdles to gaining a hearing from the Judiciary Committee, to be reported favorably to the Senate a nominee must gain majority support in the Judiciary Committee. This can be difficult if the president and the Senate majority are of different parties. For example, President George W. Bush's nomination of Charles Pickering for a seat on the Circuit Court of Appeals for the Fifth Circuit was defeated by the Judiciary Committee in early 2002 by a party line vote in committee, which had the effect of keeping the Pickering nomination off the Senate floor.[2]

Senate Rules also present hurdles for nominees who have been reported favorably from committee. Most business is brought up in the Senate under a unanimous consent agreement negotiated between the majority and minority leaders. Thus, for a nominee to get onto the floor agenda, he or she typically must have bipartisan support in the chamber. In the absence of a unanimous consent agreement, the majority leader must gain passage of a motion to proceed to the consideration of a nominee. This motion, like most Senate business, is subject to extended debate, or filibuster, by any senator or group of senators. While there are limited historical examples of a filibuster on the motion to proceed to a nomination—Abe Fortas's nomination to be chief justice is the only known instance—the threat of a filibuster may have played a significant role in keeping many of President Clinton's nominees off the Senate floor.[3] In many instances placing a "hold", or threatening to object to the consideration of a nominee, is enough to keep the majority leader from attempting to bring the nominee to the floor.

The role of extended debate, or filibusters, in judicial nominations has come to the forefront of debate during the 108th Congress. As a legislative minority,

Senate Democrats are unable to block nominations in the Judiciary Committee and have found that the filibuster is the only means they have of blocking judicial nominees that they find objectionable. As of this writing, Senate Democrats have employed the filibuster on five of President George W. Bush's U.S. Courts of Appeals nominees.[4] Rule XXII of the Senate provides that extended debate on legislation or most other Senate business can be ended only by invoking cloture. A senator wishing to invoke cloture must gain sixteen signatures on a petition, then once the petition is filed with the presiding officer, a vote on the motion to invoke cloture occurs two days later. If three-fifths of the Senate, or sixty senators, vote to invoke cloture, then debate is limited to thirty additional hours; however, if cloture is not invoked, debate may continue unabated (Oleszek 2004).

As of this writing the Senate has failed to invoke cloture on any of the five nominees that have been filibustered. Seven cloture votes failed on the nomination of Miguel Estrada prior to his withdrawal from consideration, four cloture votes on Priscilla Owen's nomination have failed, two failed on William Pryor, and one each failed on Janice Brown and Charles Pickering. While these filibusters have prevented confirmation votes on these nominees, Senate business has continued as the Senate has used "tracking" on these nominations. Tracking is a procedure by which the Senate agrees by unanimous consent to move onto other business unaffected by a filibuster, while the filibuster essentially continues in the background (see Binder, Lawrence, and Smith 2002 for more details on tracking). Tracking is a double-edged sword for the majority party in the Senate; on the one hand it prevents a filibuster from delaying other important Senate business, but it also makes filibustering easier by not forcing the filibustering senator to hold the floor continuously—some have labeled it "filibuster light" for this reason.

By allowing Senate business to continue uninterrupted, tracking also keeps a filibuster out of the public eye. This has caused a great deal of frustration for Senate Republicans as they seek to highlight what they view as abuses of Senate rules and traditions. As a result, the Senate staged a forty-hour continuous debate on judicial nominees in November 2003. Labeled a "reverse filibuster" by some, Republicans sought to highlight the unprecedented use of the filibuster on U.S. Courts of Appeals nominees, while Democrats used their time to point out that they had used the filibuster only sparingly to prevent "extremist" judges from gaining a lifetime tenured seat on the federal bench. The "reverse filibuster" provided some interesting political theatre, but likely only served to further escalate the battle over the makeup of the federal judiciary. The battle has continued as President Bush has used his constitutional right to make appointments while the Senate is in recess to seat two of the filibustered nominees—Charles Pickering and William Pryor—on the Court of Appeals for the Fifth Circuit.

Proposed Rules Changes

As the previous section details, the rules and norms of the Senate provide numerous means for delaying and/or defeating judicial nominees, and over the past decade senators of all political stripes have not hesitated to use these tools to delay or block nominees. Unlike legislation, obstruction of a nominee is difficult to overcome; there is no room for compromise; a nominee cannot by amended or modified; the Senate must either accept, reject, or obstruct the nomination. Because of the growing use of obstruction and the difficulty in overcoming it, numerous proposals to alter Senate rules have been proposed in the past few years. President George W. Bush suggested a complete change in the process by proposing a rules change guaranteeing each nominee a hearing and a floor vote after a set amount of time. However, such a fundamental change in the Senate's "advice and consent" role did not receive serious consideration. Two other changes have been widely discussed in the past year: the first, a proposal labeled the "nuclear option," whereby the presiding officer of the Senate would issue a ruling upholding the majority party's position that Rule XXII does not apply to debate on executive nominations; and second, a proposal by Majority Leader Bill Frist to formally change Rule XXII to set up a declining threshold of votes needed to invoke cloture on nominations.

The Nuclear Option

The most drastic proposed change in Senate policy regarding judicial nominations is the one known as the "nuclear option." There are several ways in which this option could potentially play out, but they all share the same "nuclear" feature. The presiding officer, presumably the vice-president, would rule against existing precedents and, likely, the advice of the non-partisan Senate parliamentarian, in favor of the position of the majority party that closing debate on executive business, such as judicial nominations, requires only a majority vote. This move would undoubtedly draw a "point of order," or objection, from a member of the minority party. The presiding officer of the Senate would then rule in favor of the majority party on the point of order. After the ruling by the presiding officer, a member of the minority party would appeal the ruling of the chair, at which time a member of the majority would move to table the appeal. A motion to table an appeal is not debatable and is decided by majority vote. If the vote to table the appeal was successful, the ruling of the presiding officer would stand, reversing or altering existing precedents and, in some way, bringing the Senate to a vote on the nominee. This option is referred to as the "nuclear option" because the fallout from such a strategy would be devastating to the operation of the Senate. Senators who object to this option could stall Senate business for months and the ability of the Senate to transact routine business would be compromised. The Senate often operates via unanimous consent agreements and it is difficult to imagine senators consenting to such agreements in the wake of a forced rule change such as this.

It is also not clear that this proposal would be particularly helpful in dealing with the problem of delay on judicial nominations. Most of the nominees who have encountered significant delay have found the Judiciary Committee, not the Senate floor, to be the major obstacle to confirmation. Rendering Rule XXII invalid for judicial nominations would not help nominees who were stalled in the Judiciary Committee. Given the high costs and low benefits involved in this strategy it seems unlikely that the Senate will pursue this option.

The Frist Proposal

The Frist proposal also seeks to change the floor procedure for judicial nominees but, unlike the "nuclear option," the Frist proposal is grounded in Senate
rules. Frist and eleven cosponsors introduced Senate Resolution 138 in May
2003, and the Senate Rules Committee reported it favorably in June 2003.[5] The
proposal would amend Rule XXII of the Senate to provide that after twelve
hours of floor debate on a nominee,

> . . . the affirmative vote required to bring to a close debate upon that nomina-
> tion shall be reduced by 3 votes on the second such motion, and by 3 additional
> votes on each succeeding motion, until the affirmative vote is reduced to a
> number equal to or less than an affirmative vote of a majority of the Senators
> duly chosen and sworn. The required vote shall then be a simple majority.

This proposal would change current procedure in numerous ways, for example,
the Senate would not be able to attempt to invoke cloture until twelve hours of
debate had passed, and multiple cloture petitions could not be pending at one
time. However, the most important difference would be the declining number
of votes needed to end debate. Under the Frist proposal, the fourth cloture vote
would require only a simple majority to pass, thus clearing the way for an up or
down vote on the nominee in question. This would allow opponents of a nominee to hold up a vote for several days if they so desired, but no longer would a
legislative minority be able to keep a nominee who has reached the Senate floor
from having a confirmation vote.

Much like the nuclear option, the Frist proposal deals only with obstruction
on the floor of the Senate; committee obstruction and delay would be unaffected
by this proposal. As such, his proposal would likely only speed up the process
when the president was facing a Senate controlled by the same party as the
president. Thus the delays encountered during the final six years of Bill
Clinton's presidency and most of the first two years of George W. Bush's presidency would not have been mitigated by the Frist proposal.

Adoption of the Frist proposal would likely not end obstruction on judicial
nominations. A determined minority could object to the tracking procedure
outlined above and prevent the Senate from considering other matters while
a nomination was pending. Given the large number of judicial nominees
put forward each year, and the "waiting period" required before each cloture
vote, a Senate majority could find themselves forced to choose between confirming judicial nominees and transacting other legislative business. Opponents
of the proposal also fear that altering Rule XXII for nominations would eventually lead to a change in debate rules for other legislation, and that setting
specific cloture procedures for nominees might encourage more filibusters
on nominees.

The Frist proposal seems unlikely to secure the necessary two-thirds majority for a change to Rule XXII. The Senate, which carefully guards its norms and
traditions, is generally reluctant to undertake wholesale changes in its rules.
Further, current Senate Democrats are unlikely to support the proposal as they

see themselves as the target of the rule, and many Republicans fear that they may one day find themselves in the minority and unable to block judicial nominees that they find objectionable. Thus while Senator Frist has promised to bring the proposal to the floor at some point during the 108th Congress, the odds of it actually being adopted by the Senate are not high.

Concluding Thoughts

The past decade has seen an unprecedented level of conflict between the president and the Senate over the ideological makeup of the federal judiciary. Actions such as the "reverse filibuster" and President Bush's recent use of recess appointments to overcome Senate obstruction seem to have only further entrenched the partisan divide that is at the heart of the battle over the composition of the federal judiciary. This conflict has produced extraordinarily long delays in the confirmation process, heated partisan rancor both inside and outside of the Senate, and a backlog of cases in the federal courts that continue to find themselves understaffed.

While some of the proposed changes in Senate rules and procedures with regards to nominations could close off some opportunities for delaying action on nominees, none of the proposals are comprehensive enough to fully close off opportunities for delaying Senate action. The provisions in the U.S. Constitution requiring cooperation between the Senate and president in order to staff the judicial branch of government are the direct causes of the current conflict—rules changes in the Senate will not alter this fundamental tension. While members of both parties have sought to put the blame for the increase in delays on the other party, the truth is that both parties have gone to extraordinary lengths to prevent a president of the opposite party from gaining confirmation of judicial nominees. There appears to be no end to this battle in sight. Elections seem to only embolden the "out" party rather than weakening their resistance. Until the level of acrimony between Democrats and Republicans lessens, battles over the makeup of the federal judiciary are likely to continue with or without changes in Senate rules and procedures.

References

Binder, Sarah A. 2001. "The Senate as a Black Hole: Lessons Learned from the Judicial Appointment Experience." *The Brookings Review* 19(2): 37–40.

Binder, Sarah A. 2003. *Blue Slips Sink Ships: Institutionalizing Senatorial Courtesy.* Paper presented at the Annual Meeting of the Midwest Political Science Association.

Binder, Sarah A., Eric D. Lawrence, and Steven S. Smith. 2002. "Tracking the Filibuster, 1917–1996." *American Politics Research* 30(4): 407–423.

Oleszek, Walter J. 2004. *Congressional Procedures and the Policy Process.* 6th ed. Washington DC: CQ Press.

Rutkus, Denis S., and Mitchel A. Sollenberger. 2003. "Judicial Nomination Statistics: U.S. District and Circuit Courts, 1977–2003." *CRS Report for Congress.*

"Senators and presidents came to expect interest groups to stake out positions and work on judicial nominations; organized conflict became part of the political calculus of participants."

4.5 LOBBYING FOR JUSTICE

Gregory A. Caldeira and John R. Wright

Gregory A. Caldeira is Distinguished University Professor of Political Science, and John R. Wright is Professor of Political Science, both at Ohio State University.

Until recently, the active participation of a diverse set of organized interests in the selection of federal judges had not been a regular feature of our politics, or had not been, in the parlance of political science, "institutionalized." This changed during the 1980s. As Republican judges chosen by Ronald Reagan took their seats alongside the liberal appointees of Jimmy Carter, organized interests clashed again and again in the Senate Judiciary Committee and on the floor of the Senate, fighting for control of the federal bench. As a result, the selection of federal judges—once a "cozy triangle" of senators, the executive branch, and the bar—became a major arena for the participation of interest groups. Senators and presidents came to expect interest groups to stake out positions and work on judicial nominations; organized conflict became part of the political calculus of participants. What is more, despite changes in administration, the broad participation of organized interests and the battle lines drawn in the 1980s over the politics of judicial nominations have persisted in the 1990s . . .

Why has organized conflict become a regular part of the game of choosing federal judges? The reasons center on changes occurring within (1) the interest group environment, (2) Congress, (3) the Courts, and (4) the Executive Branch.

The Interest Group Environment

In explaining the rise and institutionalization of organized conflict, surely we should consider how interest group politics have changed during the past few decades. Below we highlight five of those changes and explain how they help us to address our question.

The Mobilization of Interests

The mobilization of organized interests on federal judgeships derives in part from three broader trends in the pressure group environment. The first is the explosion of organizations of every sort during the 1960s and 1970s. Prior to the 1960s, there were simply not that many organized interest groups. And those

From *Contemplating Courts*, Lee Epstein, ed. (Washington DC: CQ Press, 1995), pp. 44, 59–69.

that did exist tended to represent commercial or private interests (such as business, trade, and professional associations). These commercial-type interests used litigation where appropriate, but they did not see the courts as a central forum for the vindication of their interests—largely because New Deal Democrats (that is, economic liberals) dominated the federal judiciary from the onset of the Roosevelt presidency. Accordingly, existing groups had little incentive to involve themselves in judicial confirmations. Beginning in the 1960s and continuing through the 1980s, however, that changed radically. Numerous (liberal) public interest groups formed to represent the interests of disadvantaged segments of society. Since these new organizations often used the courts to achieve their objectives, it is hardly a surprise that they took an interest in judicial nominees.

Second, representation in Washington, D.C., has grown tremendously. Every conceivable organized interest now has some presence there. Those who took part in the nominating fights of the last couple of decades, most of whom maintain an office in the capital, simply reflect the national trend. . . .

Finally, organized interests now have the tools to do the job. They can send flyers to target groups, mobilize constituents important to senators, take out advertisements in newspapers, conduct polls, and so forth. All of these tools facilitate their efforts to influence key decision makers in the executive and legislative branches.

Conservative Counter-Mobilization

Once upon a time, cozy triangles made up of unified groups, members of congressional committees, and bureaucrats made policy with little guidance from Congress or the executive. They were able to do so because they agreed on the direction that policy should take. But the entry of diverse and divisive interests has brought conflict where once harmony reigned. Now, instead of cozy triangles, organized interests come into conflict with one another and complicate the lives of those who make decisions.

The rise of organized conflict came about as two movements sought to counterbalance liberal public interest groups that had arisen during the 1960s and 1970s. The first was the "New Right," which was dissatisfied with a wide range of federal policies, including those on civil rights, law enforcement, welfare, school prayer, abortion, the Equal Rights Amendment, and gay rights. . . .

At the same time as the New Right was attracting supporters, big business began to challenge liberal public interest groups, which had been quite successful in obtaining passage of legislation—at the expense of the business community—that protected consumers and the environment. Beginning in the 1970s, big business attempted to educate the American public about the wonders of free enterprise; corporations advertised in newspapers and magazines. . . .

Organizational Membership and Fundraising

If organized interests took action only to further policy goals in the federal courts, we should anticipate a significant allocation of resources if and only if opposition to a nomination had a reasonable probability of success. Organized interests would not, therefore, take up hopeless causes. Yet organized interests pursue multiple goals. For some of the organizations we have studied, taking a position on a nomination helped them to achieve other goals—maintaining or increasing membership or raising funds. Thus, for example, in 1991, more than thirty women's organizations, along with the ACLU and Planned Parenthood, took out advertisements in the *New York Times* and other places in order to seek support for the close questioning of Judge Souter's views on the right to privacy. The advertisement advised readers to write to and telephone senators and the president and, of course, to write a check to support the coalition. Direct mail, advertisements, and grass-roots organizing against Judge Souter did not go to waste; these efforts contributed to the mobilization of women concerned about abortion rights.

Learning and the Institutionalization of Conflict

Prior to the early 1980s, few organized interests would have contemplated opposition to a nominee for the federal courts. The leadership of many organizations saw the opposing of nominations as a hopeless task; after all, only a handful of nominees had met defeat through the early 1980s. For those active in litigation, the leadership feared reprisals by those against whom it might have taken a position. Furthermore, since only a handful of organizations had taken a position against a judicial nominee, organized interests lacked the cover of a large coalition. By the early 1990s, hundreds of organizations on both sides had adopted positions on and worked for or against nominees to all levels of the federal courts. A position once unthinkable is today within the realm of options for hundreds of organizations at the national level and thousands at the state and local levels. Each time an organization takes a position on a nomination, the next decision is just a little bit easier. . . .

The Rise of the Grand Coalition against Bork

It may have been during confirmation battles of the late 1960s that organized interests began developing their strategies and tactics, but it was during the Bork proceedings that they perfected them—particularly the art of building coalitions. In fact, this single nomination, perhaps more than any other, helps us to understand why conflict is now such a regular part of the confirmation scene.

To be sure, the fight over the Bork nomination has blessed us with a number of lively and well-written books about the formation of the giant coalition against Judge Bork. These books do not, however, give one a proper sense of perspective about how many years the coalition was in the making and the many battles through which the eventual partners had suffered together and oftentimes alone during the early years of the Reagan administration. The coalition against Judge Bork did not come together by accident; it was the product of a series of skirmishes during the 1980s. It represented, in a sense, a great reprisal against the Reagan administration for the blows that the parts of the coalition had taken at its hands during the earlier part of the decade. The uprisings on a smaller scale against a series of nominations before and after Bork brought together parts of this gigantic coalition. . . .

Congress

Pressure group politics is not the only thing that has changed during the past two decades. The congressional political climate has undergone alterations as well. In what follows we consider two aspects of that climate and explain how they helped to contribute to the institutionalization of organized conflict surrounding judicial nominations.

Changes in the Electoral Environment of the Senate

In the 1980s and even in the 1970s, members of the Senate faced an electoral environment markedly different from the politics of the 1950s and 1960s. The extraordinary mobilization of interests has translated into the empowerment of a diverse array of new constituencies in the electoral arena. These "new" constituencies include women, blacks, Hispanics, the mentally ill, the disabled, senior citizens, Christians, and homosexuals. Demonstrated electoral clout provided good reason for members of the Senate to listen carefully to the entreaties of organized interests for or against particular nominees to the federal bench. These newly mobilized interests—together with persistent older ones—are ingredients in the constituencies of many senators; and the new mix has changed the calculus on judicial nominations for many senators, especially in the South but elsewhere as well.

Nominating Politics in an Environment of Scarce Information

Staffing the federal government constitutes one of the most difficult and intractable problems any administration faces. Lack of experienced people, weak or unestablished networks of communication, and rapid turnover of staff plague the executive branch.

Those in the executive and legislative branches who select federal judges confront a similar lack of relevant and reliable information about potential candidates. Only recently has the Senate Judiciary Committee hired a significant number of people to investigate nominees; and, even now, most nominees receive only the most cursory review. In an environment of little information, the ability of organized interests to present sound information about candidates gives them distinctive advantages. Credibility as providers of information about the candidates and preferences of constituencies may permit organized interests to force the hands of those senators who do not wish to cause a disturbance over a nomination.

Divided Government

From 1969 to 1977 and again from 1981 to 1993, divided government presided over national policy making. Until the waning days of the Bush administration, most observers thought divided government a likely feature of national government: Democrats would hold the House and usually the Senate; the Republicans would control the executive branch.

Divided government makes compromise and the building of coalitions more difficult than under government controlled by one party. It dramatically raises the costs of making decisions, in the politics of appointments as elsewhere. The president cannot sit down with the leaders of his party within Congress and come to a meeting of minds; he must consider the preferences of the leaders of the opposition, who control one or more houses. Historically, nominees to the Supreme Court have met with defeat more often under divided government. If, as in much of the Reagan and Bush [and later Clinton] administrations, the opposing party controls one or more houses of the legislature, the chief executive must reckon with the independent power of often-hostile committee chairs. The political conflict inherent in divided government provides a welcome haven for the thrusts of organized interests eager to shape the federal bench.

The Partisan and Ideological Balance in the Federal Courts

The Supreme Court, at the departure of Justice Lewis F. Powell, Jr., in 1987, stood evenly divided on many issues; the courts of appeals, in some circuits, stood in a similar situation at various points during the 1980s. The closer the balance, perceived or actual, the greater the incentive for organized interests to take part in the monitoring of and fights against nominations. In a number of fights during the Reagan era, opponents of a nominee used partisan and ideological balance as an argument against the appointment of a committed conservative; the fight over Judge Bork was only the most salient example. . . .

Increased Importance of the Federal Courts

Conservatives realized much later than did liberals the strategic importance of the federal courts. This changed in the 1970s, as conservatives organized and began to use strategies and tactics in the federal courts on which liberals had relied for decades. The reason why conservatives began to litigate is not difficult to discern: they believed that the Supreme Court of the 1960s, then under the leadership of Earl Warren, had damaged their causes and that liberal interests had engineered some of the more devastating of those rulings (such as *Brown v. Board of Education* and *Miranda v. Arizona*). Conservatives, thus, went into court to counterbalance their ideological opponents, the result being that the federal judiciary took on new importance. It became a battlefield in the ensuing ideological war.

The Executive Branch

No account of the institutionalization of organized conflict, as our historical discussion reveals, would be complete without consideration of the president's role and the changing partisan landscape under which the presidential office has operated. In what follows, we consider three ways in which changes in the executive branch contributed to the conflict that now characterizes judicial nominations.

Success of the Republicans at the Presidential Level

Until the 1968 election, Democrats could hope to make many nominations to the federal courts as the parties naturally alternated in the presidency, for the two major political parties competed on an equal basis for control of the executive. But from 1968 through 1992, the electoral map made a Democratic presidency a long- shot. Reagan's election, in particular, dramatically worsened the fortunes of liberals. Neither Congress nor the executive showed much sympathy to the causes of the liberal interest groups; and the Supreme Court of the late 1970s and early 1980s was no longer the reliable partner of liberal interest groups it had been during the 1960s. By the mid-1980s, many organizations on the left attempted to avoid the Supreme Court whenever possible and, instead, sought to keep their claims in the lower courts. Thus, nominations to the lower federal courts looked very important even as early as 1982. The aggressiveness of early Reagan appointees did nothing to ease the concerns of liberals. . . .

Change in the Presidential Policy Agenda

Unlike Carter and Ford and even Nixon, President Reagan made a serious attempt to push forward an agenda of many controversial social issues. President Reagan's emphasis gave organized interests in opposition strong incentives to worry about the outcome of these issues. The items on President Reagan's legislative agenda—opposition to abortion and busing, support for prayer in school, and so on—called into question many of the decisions closest to the heart of those in organized interests of the liberal stripe. This legislative agenda would have overturned, via statutory or constitutional means, a wide variety of decisions made in the federal courts over a period of three decades. Ultimately, President Reagan failed to gain legislative acceptance for this agenda—some conservatives and liberals would say, for lack of real effort—but, at the outset, no one could predict the outcome with any degree of certainty. President Reagan, after all, dominated Congress during the first part of his first term, and the Republicans did control the Senate. The threat of legislative overruling of judicial decisions and stripping of some areas from the purview of the federal courts made the federal courts even more central to the agenda of liberal organized interests.

The Sophisticated Picking of Judges

President Carter had placed a high priority on affirmative action for women, blacks, and Hispanics in the selection of federal judges, and that infuriated the "New Right" and motivated it to begin the systematic monitoring of nominations to the federal courts. In response, President Reagan, and to a lesser extent President Bush, made the picking of judges a high priority.

The boldness and sophistication of the Reagan judge pickers infuriated organized interests on the liberal side. Officials in the Reagan administration showed little aversion to risk, unlike past and subsequent administrations; tough battles were simply the price one had to pay for "good" judges. Decision makers in the White House and the Department of Justice knew in advance of most of the "problems" that turned up concerning nominees; in some cases what the liberals saw as troubling problems, the conservatives in the administration perceived as attractive qualities. Reaganites, at any rate, pushed forward on controversial nominations despite the threat of a fight from liberal interests. In turn, leaders of liberal interest groups saw the systematic nature of Reagan's judicial strategy as a severe threat to the gains made in the federal courts through the years. It provided a powerful incentive to organize the monitoring of nominations and to engage in direct and grass-roots lobbying in opposition to candidates found unacceptable.

* * *

Does the organizational activity of which we have written really make much of a difference? Some commentators do not think so. The new conventional wisdom—more groups, less clout—does not, however, take into account the more subtle forms of influence. If organized interests face other organizations in the selection of federal judges, we might at first glance decide that there was no net effect. Yet it is quite possible to imagine both organizations influencing the shape of federal judicial selections. That is our reading of President Bush's nomination of David Souter. He could not nominate a moderate, or someone whose views on privacy could be determined, for fear of an uprising among a coalition of conservative organizations. And he could not nominate a known conservative, because of the difficulties President Reagan had encountered from liberal organizations with essentially the same Senate in several fights in the late 1980s. Thus, Bush adopted a strategy of ambiguity. No one on either side of the political spectrum can be sure of Souter's location, even though most have a clear guess. The institutionalization of organized pressures from both the left and the right limited Bush's options. The same sort of pressures might account for President Clinton's nominations of Ruth Bader Ginsburg and Stephen Breyer to the Supreme Court. . . .

"Presidents since Franklin Roosevelt have been fairly successful from a policy standpoint in their Supreme Court appointments."

4.6. BUYER BEWARE? PRESIDENTIAL SUCCESS THROUGH SUPREME COURT APPOINTMENTS

Jeffrey A. Segal, Richard J. Timpone, and Robert M. Howard

Jeffrey A. Segal, Richard J. Timpone, and Robert M. Howard. 2000. "Buyer Beware? Presidential Influence through Supreme Court Appointments." *Political Research Quarterly.* 53(3): 557–573.

Presidents clearly attempt to mold politics through the use of their formal and informal powers. While presidents engage in numerous explicit battles with other branches of government over the direction of policy, as well as the extent of executive power itself, less direct approaches can often have a dramatic effect. The appointment power allows presidents the opportunity to extend their agenda into a variety of areas that they could not control on their own. While such influence is usually limited to the sitting president's term of office, judicial appointments can provide policy-minded presidents with an enduring legacy long after their terms are through. This is clearly the reason that Supreme Court nominations have become major partisan and ideological battles.

Whether or not presidents can extend their policy goals through appointments to the Supreme Court has normative implications for the nature of American institutions as well as practical ones for presidential influence. One area of debate over the Supreme Court is its undemocratic and potentially counter-majoritarian nature. Dahl (1957) has argued that the appointment process is an important constraint on counter-majoritarian impulses of the Court. Thus, appointing presidents and Senates attempting to exert a policy influence in this manner may be considered a beneficial democratic constraint on the Supreme Court.

Given the normative and practical issues involved, we examine the question of just how successful presidents have been in using Supreme Court appointments to extend their policy goals. This requires appointees to follow the path supported by the president. Thus, the critical first question to ask is whether or not their appointees share their views. Concordance, the relative agreement between judicial behavior and presidential policy preferences in this case, is critical for understanding presidential success.

Political Research Quarterly. 53(3): 557–573. (Abridged from 2000).

We explicitly choose "concordance" over the more commonplace "responsiveness." Responsiveness suggests that presidential preferences directly influence justices' decisions. Concordance requires only that the justices act in agreement with the presidential preferences. This could be due to direct influence on the justices' decision-making, but it could also be due to an indirect influence through the appointment of justices with shared values. Given the institutional structure and independence of the Court, the latter approach of choosing like-minded justices is key to any endurance of a president's policy influence in this domain.

Measuring concordance between justices and presidents requires a measure of presidential preferences. In order to create such a measure, we conducted a random mail survey in the Spring of 1995 of political scientists listed in the American Political Science Association *Directory of Membership* (1994) as belonging to the presidency section. We asked respondents to reply to the following statement: "Using whatever criteria you believe appropriate, please evaluate the following presidents on their liberalism in economic policy and social policy (0 = conservative; 100 = extremely liberal)." Sixty-one of the 100 scholars replied, yielding between 57 and 59 sets of usable responses.

Results

We present the results for both economic and social liberalism in Table 1. The table shows a clear split between Democrats and Republicans, with Democratic presidents ranking more liberal on both social and economic scales than their Republican counterparts. Nevertheless, presidents within each party vary considerably. Of the presidents under consideration, Lyndon Johnson ranks the most socially liberal, followed by Truman, then Bill Clinton and Franklin

TABLE 1 Presidential Policy Liberalism

President	Social Liberalism		Economic Liberalism	
	Mean (Rank)	S.E.	Mean (Rank)	S.E.
Johnson	83.5 (1)	1.27	78.2 (2)	1.75
Truman	74.3 (2)	1.69	74.6 (3)	1.67
Clinton	72.0 (3)	1.57	63.1 (5)	1.57
Roosevelt	71.6 (4)	1.97	82.5 (1)	1.45
Carter	67.0 (5)	1.69	60.3 (6)	1.58
Kennedy	66.4 (6)	1.59	65.4 (4)	1.83
Nixon	44.9 (7)	2.07	47.7 (7)	1.64
Ford	39.3 (8)	1.66	38.8 (8)	1.43
Eisenhower	36.9 (9)	1.76	38.8 (8)	1.78
Bush	32.8 (10)	1.79	33.1 (10)	1.67
Reagan	18.0 (11)	1.82	17.6 (11)	1.76

Note: Social and Economic Liberalism ratings are derived by the authors from their presidential experts survey. Scores range from 0 (most conservative) to 100 (most liberal).

Roosevelt. John F. Kennedy ranks the most conservative of the group, with a score just below that of Carter.

The Republican judged the most liberal on social policy in the group is Richard Nixon, although still far below the score of the most conservative ranked Democrat, John Kennedy. Despite his well-known opposition to civil rights and civil liberties, Nixon expanded entitlement programs, established wage and price controls, created the EPA, and proposed major reforms of the welfare system. Five and one-half points below Nixon is Ford, and two and one-half points below Ford is Eisenhower. Not surprising is Reagan's placement, by far, as the most conservative of any American President since the Great Depression.

On the scale of economic liberalism, the Democrats again all rank higher than the Republican presidents. Unlike his placement on social liberalism, Roosevelt scores the highest on economic liberalism, outranking even Johnson. Truman again ranks right below these two, followed by Kennedy, scoring comparatively higher for economic liberalism than for social liberalism. Clinton and Carter round out the Democratic presidents' rankings.

General Concordance

We assess presidential policy success in Supreme Court appointments with the justices' voting in both civil liberties cases and economic cases. We derive both from Harold Spaeth's U.S. Supreme Court Database, which we merged with data from the 1937 through 1945 terms.

Civil liberties data include questions of First Amendment rights, criminal procedure, equal protection, due process, privacy, and attorneys. In all cases except those dealing with the Fifth Amendment's takings clause, a liberal vote upholds individual rights against governmental intrusion. Economics data include all economics and union cases. Liberal votes support governmental regulations in the regular economics cases and unions in the union cases.[1]

We ran a regression analysis to determine how well the voting behavior of Supreme Court nominees could be predicted from the ideology of their appointing president. The analysis (not shown) demonstrates that for each ten points more liberal the presidential scholars rated a president in the domain, an appointed justice is predicted to vote liberally in 4.22 percent more civil liberties cases and 3.41 percent more economics cases. On an aggregate level, we can see that presidents do reasonably well in appointing justices who follow their policy preferences.

The overall success that presidents appear to have in Supreme Court appointments might still mask some significant differences. The first of these is possible differences among presidents. To provide a descriptive baseline, we calculated the predicted civil liberties and economics scores for each president's appointees from the regression equations. We present these results in Table 2. Thus, given his ideology, we predict that Roosevelt's appointees should have voted liberally about 59 percent of the time in civil liberties cases and about 64

---

[1]We provide that raw data at www.sunsb.edu/polsci/jsegal/data.

TABLE 2 Predicted Voting Behavior of Supreme Court Appointees in Civil Liberties and Economics Cases

Appointing President (n)[a]	Civil Liberties			Economics		
	Votes	Predicted AAD[b]	AD[c]	Votes	Predicted AAD[b]	AD[c]
F. Roosevelt (7)	59.28	15.56	4.10	65.47	10.49	3.58
Truman (4)	60.41	22.61	−22.61	62.77	8.49	−5.27
Eisenhower (5)	44.62	15.86	13.56	50.57	15.65	4.41
Kennedy (2)	57.08	23.90	8.62	59.64	1.41	1.41
Johnson (2)	64.30	17.30	17.30	64.00	3.55	3.55
Nixon (4)	48.00	15.80	−13.45	53.60	8.05	−6.65
Ford (1)	45.63	17.17	17.17	50.57	8.13	8.13
Reagan (4)	36.59	5.62	−5.62	43.34	1.65	1.33
Bush(2)	42.88	13.50	−2.38	48.63	8.65	−3.48
Clinton (2)	59.44	2.96	2.96	58.85	8.05	−7.90

[a]Number of justices appointed by president

[b]Average Absolute Deviation

[c]Average Deviation

percent of the time in economic cases. From these predicted scores, we calculate two measures of relative "success": average absolute deviations (AAD) and average deviation (AD). The average absolute deviation states how far the average appointee is from what is predicted from the model given the president's policy liberalism. If one president's appointee is six points more liberal than predicted, given the president's ideology, while another is eight points more conservative, then the AAD equals seven. For the AAD, pluses and minuses do not balance out.

The average absolute deviations are fairly high for civil liberties, except for the Reagan and Clinton appointees. The Reagan appointees' AAD for Civil Liberties issues is 5.62. Clinton's appointees' AAD scores are 2.96 for Civil Liberties. No other president's AAD is less than thirteen. Given that Reagan appointed a relatively high number of appointees, four, his performance may appear to be remarkable. Several possible explanations may explain this: the salience of Court nominees to his agenda; change over career (and the fact that recent presidents' appointees are by definition not very far removed from their appointment temporally); and finally his promotion of William Rehnquist to chief justice, which entailed less uncertainty than other appointments given his track record on the bench as an associate justice.

Regardless of why Clinton and Reagan appear to have done well, this does not mean that the other presidents' appointees, taken as a group, constitute failure from a policy perspective. Franklin Roosevelt's appointees illustrate this perfectly. William O. Douglas voted much more liberally (24.6 points) than we would expect from even a Roosevelt appointee. But Stanley Reed voted much more conservatively than expectations (−18.2). Overall, Roosevelt's justices average deviation (AD), where pluses and minuses can cancel each other out, is just 4.10 points more liberal as a group than we would have expected from our model, given Roosevelt's ideology. On the other hand, each of Truman's appointees voted significantly more conservatively than we would have expected. Not surprisingly, Eisenhower's overall appointments also appear to be a failure from presidential policy perspective. This result is driven by two of his five appointees: Warren and Brennan. Warren was 33.2 points more liberal than expected for an Eisenhower appointee, a mark surpassed in the data set by only Brennan, who was 34.7 points more liberal than expected.

In general, the presidents seem to fare better in economic cases. With the exception of Clinton, each of the president's AAD is lower in economic cases than in civil liberties cases, some dramatically so. So too are most presidents' ADs closer to zero. For instance, Truman's justices appear much closer to his predicted preferences in economics cases than in civil liberties cases. Reagan's appointees are, across the board, exactly where our model would predict, although Clinton's appointees perform only slightly better than the average AAD for presidents in the economic domain.

Further analyses (not shown) demonstrate that the substantive relationship between presidential policy preferences and justice behavior declines over time. In both domains, the early terms of the justices' careers drive concordance, with the substantive impact of presidential ideology declining the longer justices sit on the bench. In the domain of economic policy, justices' votes cannot be statistically distinguished from being unrelated to their appointing presidents' positions after ten terms on the bench. In the less salient domain of civil liberties, presidents fare even worse, with the relationship being statistically insignificant after merely four terms on the bench. Thus, while presidents have been reasonably successful in their Supreme Court appointments, this influence is not as enduring as the aggregate results imply.

Discussion

We conclude, based on the data presented, that presidents since Franklin Roosevelt have been fairly successful from a policy standpoint in their Supreme Court appointments. However, the finer examination shows that this success is somewhat fleeting and that change in judicial behavior diminishes the long-run impact of presidential appointments. This has implications for both normative and practical politics.

Supreme Court justices vote relatively concordantly with their appointing president in the early years of their appointment to the bench. However, this relationship declines over time. If justices shift their views with the rest of society over time, then moving away from appointing presidents may be considered desirable from a democratic theory perspective. However, many studies in this area thus far have not found a clear link between justices' attitude change and shifts in public opinion. Thus, life tenure on the Court may be considered a problem from a counter-majoritarian perspective if the constraining influence of the appointment process is only short-lived.

Some limitations of this study for making normative and practical conclusions deserve attention. For instance, this study focuses on success in terms of the presumed policy goals of the presidents at hand. Some presidents, though, may have had goals other than public policy in mind in nominating Supreme Court justices. Thus it may be unfair to judge presidents on criteria that were not of relevance to them. Eisenhower's two "failures" illustrate the situation well. Though no smoking gun exists, payment of a massive political debt from the 1952 Republican convention may have mattered crucially in the president's selection of Earl Warren. Similarly, the 1956 election featured prominently in the October 1956 recess appointment of Democrat William Brennan. Presumably, Eisenhower could have been more successful from a policy standpoint had judicial policy been more important to him.

The statistical analyses also treat all cases as equivalent, when clearly they are not. Reagan's general success in his appointees must be measured against O'Connor's failure to vote to overrule *Roe v. Wade*.[2] So too, Burger's support for racial busing could hardly have been of comfort to President Nixon.[3] Nevertheless, the general pattern of results is not too different from that which might be obtained by more subjective analyses.

Finally, the data cannot answer the normative question about whether presidents *should* attempt to pack the Court. But examining whether or not presidents *can* pack the Court, and for how long, certainly amplifies the importance of addressing this normative question. Thus, our results help clarify important issues in terms of the democratic nature of the Supreme Court while also raising new questions about the nature and inter-relationships of American governmental institutions. The ephemeral relationship between presidents and appointments returns us to fundamental questions about the nature of American democracy.

"For those who feared either that the affirmative action judges would be inferior to the traditional candidates or that the largely white, male federal court system would not successfully assimilate nontraditional judges, our data offer no support."

4.7 THE DIVERSIFICATION OF THE FEDERAL BENCH: POLICY AND PROCESS RAMIFICATIONS

Thomas G. Walker and Deborah J. Barrow

Thomas G. Walker is Chair of the Political Science Department at Emory University.
Deborah J. Barrow is Associate Professor of Political Science at Auburn University.

Abridged from 47 *Journal of Politics* 596 (1985).

Following his 1976 election to the Presidency, Jimmy Carter carried through on his campaign pledge to diversify the federal bench through an affirmative effort to identify and appoint qualified women, African Americans, and Hispanics. As a result, Carter's female and minority appointments exceeded that of all previous presidents. Of his fifty-six appeals court appointments, 20 percent were women, 16 percent black, and 4 percent Hispanic. At the trial court level, Carter's 206 confirmed judges included 14 percent females, 14 percent blacks, and 7 percent Hispanics.

Undoubtedly, Carter's affirmative action policies opened the process to segments of the population largely shunned by prior chief executives. He improved the representativeness and the perceived legitimacy of the federal courts. Whether Carter's alteration of the judiciary's composition had substantive effects as well is a question of some importance. Consequently, the primary thrust of the research presented here is to discover if Carter's appointment of women and minorities made demonstrable differences in the policies and processes of the judiciary. If such differences did occur, then the impact of Carter's affirmative action initiatives extended far beyond their symbolic and legitimizing contribution.

Research Strategies and Questions

Carter's appointment policies touched off a heated debate over what they might mean for the federal courts. Supporters of increased diversification argued that placing women and minorities in positions of judicial authority would make the courts more receptive to the claims of the disadvantaged, thus resulting in more liberal rulings. Opponents of Carter's policies, while accepting the notion that women and minorities may be prone to more liberal rulings, feared that emphasizing sex and race characteristics at the necessary expense of merit considerations would lead to the appointment of inferior judges, thus lowering the quality of the bench. . . .

Those who believed that women and minorities would have decision-making proclivities different from white male judges based much of their argument on the fact that females and blacks often have taken different routes to the bench than is traditionally the case. For example, Carter's nontraditional nominees were younger, less affluent, and had fewer ties to the local political power structure. White male appointees were more apt to come from private law firms; whereas nontraditional appointees had a higher incidence of governmental service. Women scored higher on measures of academic achievement; white males had higher levels of political activity. . . .

Scientific research on racial and gender differences in attitudes and behavior has led to somewhat mixed conclusions. Public opinion studies have demonstrated that blacks tend to be more liberal than whites over a significant range of domestic and foreign policy issues. Similarly, women, when compared to men, tend to be more dovish on foreign policy issues, more humanitarian on social issues, and more supportive of government intervention in such policy areas as the environment. However, at the elite level these differences become much less pronounced after controlling for political party affiliation. Studies of the judiciary have been limited in number, and have found few clear cut racial or gender differences. Where such differences have been identified, they have been relatively modest in size.

By examining the behavior of judges in areas in which differences have been suggested or might otherwise plausibly be found, we can evaluate the relative merit of the arguments advanced by the proponents and opponents of Carter's selection policies.

The federal district courts provide the best opportunity for the study of female and minority judges because their number is the greatest at this level of the federal judiciary. President Carter appointed twenty-nine women and an equal number of blacks to the district court bench.

Conducting research at the district court level presents some difficult challenges. Cases are almost exclusively heard and decided by a single judge. This makes an evaluation of decision making more difficult than studying collegial courts at the appellate level. In a collegial court, like the United States Supreme Court, multiple judges hear the same case and express their preferences as to how the case should be resolved. When disagreement occurs it is relatively easy to measure the differences among the jurists. Students of trial courts are not afforded this convenience. Each district judge individually hears cases arising out of his or her own judicial district. Obvious problems of valid comparison procedures occur when judges decide independent sets of cases. We simply can never know how the judges would have ruled had they traded dockets.

In order to minimize the difficulties in making meaningful comparisons and to isolate possible differences based on sex and race, a set of cases for study was constructed using the following procedures.

1. We identified the twenty-nine women appointed by Carter to the district court bench.

2. We searched for a male judge to "pair" with each of Carter's female appointees. . . . In order to qualify as a partner in such a pairing, the male judge had to meet three criteria: the potential partner had to be a Carter appointee, sit in the same judicial district, and be of the same race as the female judge. If no such partner could be identified, the female judge was eliminated from further study. If more than one potential partner met these criteria, preference was given first to the potential partner sitting in the same city as the female judge and second to the male judge whose appointment date was closest to the date of the female judge's appointment.

3. The *Federal Supplement* was searched to identify all published decisions handed down by the identified judges from the date of their appointments through 1982. A pair was eliminated from study if either judge was not responsible for at least ten published opinions.

4. Steps 1–3 were repeated beginning with the twenty-nine African American Carter appointees, attempting to pair each with a white judge of the same gender.

This procedure yielded twelve male/female pairs and ten black/white pairs.

All the decisions appearing in the *Federal Supplement* for each of the judges were read and relevant information coded. For our gender comparison sample, this procedure resulted in a total of 743 rulings, of which 340 (45.8 percent) were issued by female judges and 403 (54.2 percent) by male judges. For our racial comparison sample, the final data set included 658 decisions, of which 267 (40.6 percent) were handed down by African American judges and 391 (59.4 percent) by white judges.

Findings

Our exploration for possible behavioral differences between traditional and nontraditional judges focused on two areas of concern. First, we were interested in the policy-making behavior of the judges. Second, we examined certain process characteristics that might provide an indication of the relative quality of the work being produced by the nontraditional judges and how well those judges were being received by other participants in the legal system.

Judicial Policymaking

We examined judicial policymaking in several areas. First, we looked at personal liberties cases (noncriminal constitutional and statutory disputes involving issues such as speech, press, religion, privacy, and discrimination). Second, we examined rulings in cases involving the rights of criminal defendants. Third, we studied decisions dealing with federal economic regulation (antitrust, securities, consumer protection, taxes, labor, banking, etc.). For our gender comparisons we additionally analyzed cases involving issues of particular concern to women (gender discrimination, sexual harassment, reproductive freedom, affirmative actions for women, etc.) as well as issues of interest more generally to minorities (racial and ethnic discrimination, fair housing, welfare rights, poverty rights, etc.). We followed a similar procedure for our racial comparisons, looking at cases involving issues of particular concern to African Americans (racial discrimination, school segregation, employment rights for blacks, etc.) and then at cases presenting questions of concern to women and nonblack minorities. In conducting our analysis, we expected (if the supporters and opponents of Carter's affirmative action policies were correct) that women and blacks would support civil rights claimants, the disadvantaged, and the federal government at higher rates than traditional white, male judges.

Table 1 summarizes our gender comparisons. In two of the five legal areas, significant differences were found, but not in the expected direction. Male judges supported individual claimants in personal liberty and minority policy cases at significantly higher rates than did female judges. In the economic area, however, women, as predicted, supported federal regulation at significantly higher rates than did men. In the areas of criminal rights and women's policy issues, significant male/female differences were not found. Yet in each instance male judges handed down liberal rulings more often than did female judges.

The racial comparisons are illustrated in Table 2. In none of the five areas did significant differences between white and black judges occur.

TABLE 1 Gender and Policymaking

Policy Area	Female Judges	Male Judges
Personal (Noncriminal) Liberties ($N = 198$)		
Supports Liberty Claim	41	47
	(36.6)	(54.7)
Opposes Liberty Claim	71	39
	(63.4)	(45.3)
Criminal Rights ($N = 108$)		
Pro Defendant	17	35
	(43.6)	(50.7)
Pro Prosecution	22	34
	(56.4)	(49.3)
Federal Economic Regulation ($N = 142$)		
Supports Government Policy	48	40
	(72.7)	(52.6)
Opposes Government Policy	18	36
	(27.3)	(47.4)
Women's Policy Issues ($N = 33$)		
Supports Women's Position	8	9
	(47.1)	(56.3)
Opposes Women's Position	9	7
	(52.9)	(43.8)
Minority (Nonfemale) Policy Issues ($N = 73$)		
Supports Minority Position	21	20
	(47.7)	(69.0)
Opposes Minority Position	23	9
	(52.3)	(31.0)

Note: Percentages appear in parentheses.

Judicial Quality

The introduction of nontraditional judges to the federal bench in substantial numbers inevitably led to questions concerning the quality of decision making and how well the newly appointed women and minorities were being accepted by the system. Therefore, we analyzed three factors that allowed us to make some initial judgments in response to these questions.

One measure of both the quality of a judge's decisions and how well he or she is being accepted is the rate at which rulings are challenged. Therefore, we collected data on how often the decisions of the judges in our sample were appealed.

A second indicator of quality is the percentage of appealed cases that are reversed by the higher court. This measure taps a slightly different aspect of the process. Whereas appeal rates are controlled by the attorneys who appear in a judge's court, treatment on appeal reflects the judgment of the appellate judges as to the quality of the trial judge's work. If appeals courts view the rulings of the nontraditional judges as being inferior, then this evaluation would manifest

TABLE 2 Race and Policymaking

Policy Area	Black Judges	White Judges
Personal (Noncriminal) Liberties (*N* = 196)		
Supports Liberty Claim	29	56
	(37.7)	(47.1)
Opposes Liberty Claim	48	63
	(62.3)	(52.9)
Criminal Rights (*N.* = 74)		
Pro Defendant	16	20
	(50.0)	(47.6)
Pro Prosecution	16	22
	(50.0)	(52.4)
Federal Economic Regulation (*N* = 132)		
Supports Government Policy	28	48
	(62.2)	(55.2)
Opposes Government Policy	17	39
	(37.8)	(44.8)
Black Policy Issues (*N* = 40)		
Supports Black Position	10	8
	(47.6)	(42.1)
Opposes Black Position	11	11
	(52.4)	(57.9)
Minority (Nonblack) Policy Issues (*N* = 64)		
Supports Minority Position	13	30
	(68.4)	(66.7)
Opposes Minority Position	6	15
	(31.6)	(33.3)

Note: Percentages appear in parentheses.

itself in higher reversal rates for women and blacks than for their male or white counterparts.

Finally, we examined how the decisions of our judges were used by other courts. By referring to Shepard's Citations, we were able to collect data on the number of times decisions were followed as precedent by other judges as well as the number of times the opinions were questioned or criticized. High-quality opinions have a tendency to be followed as precedent by other judges, whereas inferior rulings are vulnerable to attracting criticism. The ratio of favorable to unfavorable reactions provides some indication of the quality of judicial output.

The results of our comparisons are summarized in Tables 3 and 4. While male and white judges did slightly better on the measures used here than their female or African-American counterparts, none of the differences are great enough to reach levels of statistical significance.

For those who feared either that the affirmative action judges would be inferior to the traditional candidates or that the largely white, male federal court system would not successfully assimilate nontraditional judges, our data offer

TABLE 3 Gender and Process

Process Characteristic	Female Judges	Male Judges
Appeal Rate (*N* = 743)		
Decisions Appealed	48	65
	(14.1)	(16.1)
Decisions Not Appealed	292	338
	(85.9)	(83.9)
Appellate Disposition (*N* = 112)[a]		
Affirmed	22	38
	(45.8)	(59.4)
Reversed	26	26
	(54.2)	(40.6)
Reaction of Other Courts (*N* = 63)		
Followed	19	32
	(76.0)	(84.2)
Criticized	6	6
	(24.0)	(15.8)

Note: Percentages appear in parentheses.

[a]One appealed case was pending at the time the data were collected and, therefore, not included in this analysis.

TABLE 4 Race and Progress

Process Characteristic	Black Judges	White Judges
Appeal Rate (*N* = 658)		
Decisions Appealed	37	58
	(13.9)	(14.8)
Decisions Not Appealed	230	333
	(86.1)	(85.2)
Appellate Disposition (*N* = 94)[a]		
Affirmed	19	32
	(52.8)	(55.2)
Reversed	17	26
	(47.2)	(44.8)
Reaction of Other Courts (*N* = 45)		
Followed	9	28
	(75.0)	(84.8)
Criticized	3	5
	(25.0)	(15.2)

Note: Percentages appear in parentheses.

[a]One appealed case was pending at the time the data were collected and, therefore, not included in this analysis.

no support. Female and black judges seem to have been accepted by the system quite well. Their work appears to be on a par with that of their white and male colleagues and not be the object of discriminatory tendencies by other key participants in the process.

Conclusion

Did it make a difference that President Carter appointed unprecedented numbers of women and minorities to the bench? Undoubtedly, increasing the numbers of female and black judges improved the representative character of the judiciary. However, the data reported here do not indicate that nontraditional judges have assumed a strong advocacy role on behalf of any racial or gender-based interests, nor have they followed a more liberal or activist path than their white, male counterparts. In most respects, decision-making patterns of traditional and nontraditional judges do not differ radically.

Similarly, predictions that the work of female and black judges would be inferior do not stand in light of the data presented here. So, too, falls the assertion that the traditional white, male-dominated judicial system would not fully accept the opinions of female and black jurists. These arguments appear to have been based on either wishful thinking or unjustified fears.

Our data do not allow us to substantiate the reasons why the traditional and nontraditional judges do not radically differ on most counts. Perhaps the common socialization experiences of a legal education have muted the racial or gender differences that might otherwise exist. Similarly, the formal and informal stages of the selection process, which involve participation by local party officials, legislators, interest groups, the Justice Department, and the Senate, screen out potential judges with unconventional views. Women and minorities selected for federal judgeships, therefore, may well be "safe" candidates from the perspective of the political establishment.

The conclusions reached here must be tempered by the acknowledged limitations of this study. Our data are restricted to decisions handed down by Carter appointees in the first few years following the introduction of his affirmative actions selection policies. As a consequence, the number of judges examined and the number of cases they decided are small. This is particularly constricting when analysis beyond very general behavioral propensities is attempted. Similar studies will need to be done as increasing numbers of nontraditional judges are appointed.

"This is not to say that the merit plan is wholly meritless or evil."

4.8 COMMENTS ON THE MISSOURI PLAN

Thurgood Marshall

[In 1977] President Carter issued an executive order creating a new mechanism for selecting federal appellate judges. Under this order, each time a vacancy on a court of appeals occurs, a panel will be activated to report to the President the names of the five persons considered "best qualified" to fill the vacancy. These panels will consist of approximately equal numbers of lawyers and nonlawyers and will be drawn, in part, from the circuit in which the vacancy occurs. Presumably, the President will make every effort to select his nominees from these lists, as he did while Governor of Georgia.

The President's plan, you will note, to a large degree follows the so-called "merit plan" or "Missouri Plan" for selecting judges. This plan, first proposed by Dean Kales of Northwestern Law School in 1914, has spread rapidly in recent years; since 1970 the number of States using it has more than doubled, and almost half the States presently select some or all of their judges under the merit system. My aim, today, is to raise some questions—and express some reservations—about this system.

Of course, no one opposes selecting judges on merit; the alternative, after all, is a meritless selection system, hardly an appealing prospect. Nor can one quarrel with the goal, perhaps first voiced in this country by George Washington, of choosing "the fittest characters to expound the laws and dispense justice": again one need only consider the alternative. The crucial questions are what types of persons make "the fittest" judges, and by what process are they best elevated to the bench.

In theory, at least, the Missouri Plan speaks only to the second question—the question of process. Its answer is that "the fittest"—however defined—are best selected by creating a commission of lawyers and laymen to submit a small list of names to the executive from which he must choose judges. My concern, as I shall explain, is that this process will subtly influence the definition of "fitness," by giving preeminent weight to technical or professional selection criteria.

Insofar as the merit plan is designed simply to put an end to cronyism and patronage in judicial appointments, no one can quarrel with it. I can think of no task that judges are properly called upon to perform that requires prior experience as a friend or backer of the appointing official (or his party). I might add, however, that the one major study that has been done of the first twenty years of the merit plan in Missouri gives substantial reason to question whether the plan can remove friendship with the executive as a criterion for judicial selection.

But questions of effectiveness aside, creating an elaborate set of commissions with broad powers seems unnecessary simply to eliminate cronyism; I cannot help believing that there is an easier way. Perhaps for this reason, proponents of the merit plan never rest their defense on this limited, essentially negative ground. Rather, they contend that it is affirmatively desirable to have a group of lawyers and laypersons assigned the tasks of ferreting out candidates for judgeships, developing information about the candidates, and determining who is best qualified.

Remarks by Mr. Thurgood Marshall at the spring meeting of the American College of Trial Lawyers in Coronado, California, March 14, 1977. Reprinted with permission. Marshall was appointed to the Supreme Court in 1967 by President Johnson.

I see no basis for objecting to commissions which perform the first two tasks. But I know of no one who suggests that the commissions should simply gather names and information for use by the executive. The crux of the merit system, in the eyes of its advocates, is the selection function of the commissions.

It is this crux that I find troubling. That is not just because I come from Washington, where skepticism about committees is almost as prevalent as committees; indeed in Washington it is said that "nothing is impossible—until you assign it to a committee." I am troubled by judicial selection by committee because it seems to me that two biases, or risks of biases, inhere in the process: (1) objective criteria will be given undue weight; and (2) to the extent subjective factors are considered, they will be value-free or technical ones.

The temptation for committees to rely on objective criteria is obvious. Such criteria simplify the task of paring down long lists of names to manageable numbers. Moreover, they can avoid endless debates as to which candidates have demonstrated the best knowledge of the law, for example, by providing seemingly clear measurements.

Perhaps the clearest example of the over-emphasis on objective factors is the weight nominating committees have assigned to prior judicial experience. A national study of members of such commissions found that after mental and physical health, this was the background factor the commissioners considered most important. Similarly, the twenty-year study in Missouri found that 57 percent of the intermediate court judges and 70 percent of the Supreme Court judges appointed under the merit plan had prior judicial experience. Yet I know of no evidence indicating that appellate judges with prior experience make better judges than those lacking such experience; to the contrary, evaluations of Supreme Court Justices demonstrate, as Felix Frankfurter put it, that at least with respect to my court, "the correlation between prior judicial experience and fitness . . . is zero."

Much the same may be true of two other objective criteria on which many place great weight: the requirement that nominees have (1) "at least fifteen years significant legal experience," and, (2) for trial judges, that the nominees have had "substantial experience in the adversary system." The first of these requirements effectively excludes all lawyers under the age of forty and many lawyer-politicians; the second excludes from the trial bench the overwhelming majority of lawyers. It is clear to me, however, that at the very least some of those disqualified for lack of experience—Learned Hand, for one should not be excluded from consideration. Persons like Judge Hand either already have acquired or could readily acquire the knowledge that experience is thought to guarantee. On the other hand, some who are included by virtue of their experience actually should be disqualified on this basis. These persons have spent too many years learning undesirable practices or approaches. In fact, I know of no empirical evidence to justify either experience requirement. The study of Supreme Court Justices to which I earlier referred found that more of those appointed at a younger age (in this context, under fifty-three) went on to greatness—including Justice Joseph Story, appointed at age thirty-two.

But what troubles me most about the merit system is not that it precludes the appointment of some well-qualified persons who don't meet more-or-less arbitrary standards. I am more concerned that the merit plan may compel or induce the appointment of judges simply because they are technically well-qualified, without regard to their basic values, philosophy, or life experience.

It is to be expected that nominating commissions will tend to ignore value-related considerations. We live in an age in which values are viewed as subjective. Unless a nominating committee happens to be homogenous, therefore, it is unlikely to agree on the values that judges should hold. Moreover, even if the committee could agree, it would be improper for it to impose its values on the selection process. These committees typically are neither representative nor accountable bodies. The national study of state nominating committees found, for example, that 98 percent of the committee members are white, 90 percent are male, and that the lay members are largely businessmen and bankers.

Rather than looking to the values of would-be nominees, then, nominating committees may be expected to look exclusively to the nominees' professional abilities: their knowledge of the law, proficiency at writing, and ability to "think like a lawyer." As my late friend and colleague Judge Charles Clark put it with characteristic grace, such committees look to the head exclusively and not to the heart. But as Charlie Clark also insisted, judging is more than just an exercise in technique or craft; it calls for value judgments. This is true of the trial judge required to decide, for example, whether the risk of prejudice outweighs the probative value of a piece of evidence, or whether the risk that an offender will commit more crimes outweighs the offender's interest in retaining his liberty before trial or pending appeal. It is equally true of the appellate judge, required to resolve conflicting claims between liberty and order, equality and efficiency, states' rights and federal power. Indeed studies of judicial behavior have uniformly found clear voting patterns traceable to the attitudes or values of the judges. Thus, as Judge Clark concluded, "it is of truly vital importance that the inner convictions or bias of candidates for judicial appointment be appraised."

Of course, nothing in the merit system necessarily disables the appointing official—who is popularly elected—from considering "inner convictions or bias" in making his selections. But it is at least possible that, by excluding values from their inquiry, nominating committees inadvertently will develop lists of ideologically similar persons. It is also possible that the members of a nominating committee will all agree as to the values that judges should hold, and will make their selections accordingly. In either event, the executive could be precluded from appointing judges who share his—and presumably his constituency's—basic philosophical orientation. And even when nominating committees produce ideologically diverse lists, the thrust of merit selection may persuade some appointing officials that it is somehow illegitimate for them to consider the attitudes or experiences of potential nominees. This, I submit, would be tragic. . . .

This is not to say that the merit plan is wholly meritless or evil. As I said at the outset, I intend only to raise questions and concerns—not to pass definitive judgments. And since I earlier referred to President Carter's executive order, I should note that it may avoid many of the problems I have noted, since it first guarantees women and minority groups representation on the nominating panels; second, requires the panels to recommend only those who have demonstrated "commitment to equal justice under laws"; and third, does not oblige the President to accept every panel's choices. Nevertheless, I am not persuaded that it is either necessary or desirable to give any nominating panel the power to choose the three or five most qualified persons; it seems to me sufficient to allow the panels to search for candidates, generate information, and perhaps make evaluations. But whatever one's ultimate views on the merit system I think it essential that the biases and risks inherent in the process be carefully exposed so that those involved in making selections can be attentive to them. . . .

"Californians opposing Rose Bird's retention obviously rejected the view that citizens should restrict themselves to standards that enhance judicial independence over accountability."

4.9 THE DEFEAT OF THE CALIFORNIA JUSTICES

John T. Wold and John H. Culver

John T. Wold is Professor of Politics at California State University at Stanislaus. John H. Culver is Professor of Political Science at California Polytechnic State University at San Luis Obispo.

For the first time since retention elections were adopted for the [California's] appellate justices in 1934, the public not only rejected a chief justice [Rose Bird], but defeated two other justices, Cruz Reynoso and Joseph Grodin, as well. In renouncing the three jurists, the voters in one stroke removed from the high court three of the four remaining appointees of former Governor Edmund G. (Jerry) Brown, Jr. . . .

Upon what standards did California voters base their ouster of Justices Bird, Reynoso, and Grodin? To attempt to answer this question, we examined relevant data collected by the California (Field) Poll between 1972 and 1986. Our examination led us to conclude that a majority of the California electorate employed an exclusively decisional standard of accountability in 1986. The voters appeared to have been particularly exercised by two lines of decisions handed down by the state court. Of apparent primary concern was the three jurists' perceived opposition to the death penalty; of secondary concern, the justices' perceived leniency toward criminal defendants generally.

From 6 *Judicature* 348–355 (1987)

One month before the election, for example, the reasons most frequently cited by potential voters for opposing Bird were that she "opposes the death penalty" (45 percent of respondents) and that she was "too lenient, soft on criminals/she lets killers go free" (26 percent). Another four percent claimed that the chief justice "ignores the rights of victims." These three sets of responses together constituted 54 percent of all the reasons voiced by Bird's opponents for opposing her retention.

Other comments cited in the same survey may also have reflected voters' concerns about crime and the death penalty. For instance, 15 percent of those interviewed remarked that they did not "like [Bird's] positions, where she stands on the issues." Another 15 percent claimed that Bird had not "held up the will of the people [or] enforce[d] the law." . . .

The data from earlier surveys reinforced the conclusion that voters were almost exclusively concerned with the perceived trend of decisions in the Bird Court. For example, as far back as May 1985 voters emphasized Bird's decisions, her asserted leniency on crime, and her alleged opposition to the death penalty as the primary reasons for opposing her retention.

Voters also had long been overwhelmingly critical of what they viewed as either Bird's or the supreme court's leniency toward "murderers" and criminal defendants generally. For instance, the foremost criticism of the high court voiced in May 1985—an opinion held by 67 percent of respondents—was that the court had "gone too far in protecting the rights of convicted murderers." Seventy-two percent expressed a similar complaint three months later. And in August 1986, interviewees agreed by a margin of 35 percentage points (62 percent to 27 percent) with the statement that Chief Justice Bird had "gone too far in protecting criminal defendants." Likewise, voters agreed by a similar margin (61 percent to 25 percent) with the statement that Bird "allows her own opposition to the death penalty to affect her decisions."

The public also had long held two other related sets of attitudes. One concerned the death penalty itself. Survey data indicated a consistent and increasing level of support for capital punishment over time. By April 1985, retention of the death penalty as a punishment for serious crimes was reportedly favored by 83 percent of California voters, an all-time high.

Another set of attitudes concerned the issue of crime. As early as 1973, and as recently as 1985, a plurality of Californians (35 percent and 24 percent, respectively) had expressed the opinion that crime/law enforcement was the most pressing problem facing the community and the state.

In sum, survey data gathered by the California Poll strongly suggested that voter opposition to Bird, and ultimately to two other liberal members of the California court, was animated by two basic attitudes. One view was that the court had persistently been too lenient toward criminal defendants generally and convicted murderers in particular; the other was that the justices had repeatedly exhibited hostility toward capital punishment. As the Field Institute itself concluded shortly before the election: "The public's strong support for the death penalty and the belief that the Chief Justice is personally opposed to it are directly linked to the desire to have Bird removed from the high court."

Californians opposing Rose Bird's retention obviously rejected the view that citizens should restrict themselves to standards that enhance judicial independence over accountability. For instance, voters clearly rejected the concept that they should retain all justices except those guilty of impeachable offenses, or those who were "behavioral misfits," or those they deemed unqualified in terms of professional ability. In fact, public attitudes were apparently quite favorable toward Bird from a "professional" standpoint. Three months before the election, respondents expressed disagreement by a wide margin (52 percent to 33 percent) with the view that the chief justice was "not qualified to be a justice of the California Supreme Court."

Opponents of Bird, Reynoso, and Grodin nonetheless also appeared to reject extreme concepts of judicial accountability. For example, the survey data indicated that voters did not base their opposition to the three justices upon merely a few unpopular decisions, or only a single decision, that the jurists had handed down. Also, opposition to and support for Bird were apparently not primarily based upon partisan or ideological considerations. Although Democrats and political liberals in fact tended to support her retention, the disposition to vote against the chief justice cut across many demographic, partisan and ideological lines.

Respondents likewise only rarely suggested that it was legitimate to remove judges for merely "personal" or idiosyncratic reasons. For instance, just seven percent of those opposed to Bird did so because of her "personality" or "style." Voters also apparently did not oppose Bird because of her gender. By a margin of 61 percent to 31 percent, respondents to one survey disagreed with the view that the attacks on the chief justice stemmed partly from the fact that she was the first woman on the state high court.

In sum, opposition to Bird, Reynoso, and Grodin appears to have been galvanized by a series of decisions involving the death penalty and other criminal cases. There is little evidence, however, that voters were willing to oust judges for "nonjudicial" factors such as the judge's gender, religious affiliation, racial or ethnic background, or other "personal" characteristics. The California vote suggests that, although a majority of the electorate spurned standards that stress judicial independence, they also were not motivated, at least in the 1986 election, by extreme concepts of judicial accountability or by concepts extraneous to judicial performance. . . .

CHAPTER 5

The Bar

"Law," Jeremy Bentham observed, is made not by judges alone but by "judge and company." Attorneys are by far the most numerous members of this company. Indeed, in the United States the proliferation of lawyers has far outstripped the general population explosion. There are now nearly a million attorneys in the United States, or about one for every 280 citizens.

The law in America used to be something of a stag affair, with men outnumbering women about 36 to 1 in 1970; there was an even greater disparity a decade earlier, before law schools first tried to recruit women. But times have changed. Women now constitute 28.9 percent of the nation's legal profession and 47 percent of law school classes. Current projections show that by 2010 about 40 percent of U.S. lawyers will be women.[1] At the same time—and despite efforts by many law schools to find and admit qualified students from minority racial and ethnic groups—the legal profession remains dominated by whites. Blacks make up only about 3.6 percent of the bar and Hispanics about 4 percent.

As one might expect, the geographic distribution of lawyers is similarly skewed. About 25 percent of all lawyers live in two states, New York and California. More than 40 percent of practicing attorneys are located in nation's most populous cities, with the greatest concentration in Washington, D.C., where there is one lawyer for every fifteen people.

BECOMING AN ATTORNEY

Historically, the common law and Civil Law employed very different methods of training lawyers. Education in Roman law was basically under the control of the universities, and today it is still a subject for undergraduates, not graduate students, at European universities. Admission to the various legal professions is now, however, conditioned on also completing several years of apprenticeship

---

[1] Unless otherwise indicated, we derive data in this chapter from sources on the American Bar Association's Web site (www.abanet.org/media/factbooks/) and the U.S. Department of Labor's Bureau of Labor Statistics (www.bls.gov/).

and passing rigorous examinations. In England the bar has never had close connections with the universities, and lawyers have been trained at Inns of the Court by practitioners.

It was, naturally enough, the British method that carried over to colonial America; and until the early years of the twentieth century, most attorneys received their preparation by apprenticing with a lawyer or by reading law on their own. In the late eighteenth century, however, several professorships of law were established at American colleges, including one at William and Mary held by George Wythe, who had the future Chief Justice John Marshall as a student when he was recovering from wounds before the battle of Yorktown. At about the same time, attorneys set up a number of private law schools. The most influential of these was run by Judge Tapping Reeve at Litchfield, Connecticut, from 1784 to 1833. This school trained more than a thousand young men in the law, including three Supreme Court justices and two vice presidents (Aaron Burr and John C. Calhoun).

The coming of age of the American law school is usually dated from 1870, when Christopher Columbus Langdell became dean of the Harvard Law School and brought about a revolution in the study and teaching of law. Naively but fully convinced that the common law could be reduced to a relatively small number of principles found in opinions of appellate courts, he abandoned lectures in favor of discussing actual cases. In addition, Langdell recruited a full-time faculty and helped make the teaching of law a recognized career within the legal profession.

In one form or another, both of Langdell's innovations spread beyond Harvard to other institutions. His case method became a standard teaching tool in most, if not all, law schools in the United States (Reading 5.1) and remains so today, although contemporary law schools now supplement the case approach with social-scientific and other non-case-based material. Moreover, many medical and business schools have adapted this approach to learning to their own disciplines.

Although by the early 1900s the university-affiliated law school had become the font of legal education, as late as 1953 only 80 percent of practicing lawyers had graduated from law school. This held for even famous "lawyers" of the day, including Franklin D. Roosevelt, who attended but did not graduate from Columbia Law School. It was not until the last decade of the nineteenth century that law schools began to require that their students have some college training, and even today an undergraduate degree is not a formal requirement for admission to most law schools. As a practical matter, however, it is almost impossible for a student to be admitted to a good law school without having graduated in the upper section of his or her college class and without having done very well on the Law School Admission Test (LSAT).

Admission to the Bar

"Membership in the bar," Judge Benjamin N. Cardozo said for the New York Court of Appeals in 1917, "is a privilege burdened with conditions." Each state sets up standards for admission to the bar and for the conduct of practicing attorneys. Although these rules vary greatly from state to state, they all draw essentially on the English statute of 1402: "All attorneys should be examined by the justices, and in their discretion, only those found to be good and virtuous, and of good fame, learned and sworn to do their duty, be allowed to put upon the roll and all others put out." Good moral character and technical competence have remained the two basic requirements for admission. Definitions of these terms, however, vary widely.

Admission to the bar means no more than that the candidate is allowed to practice in the courts of the admitting state. Admission to the courts of another state requires an entirely new procedure, although most states, while demanding that a migrant lawyer become a bona-fide local resident, do not ask an established attorney to take the student bar examination.

Standards for admission to practice before federal courts are even less fixed. Lower federal courts have only minimal consistency in their admission standards. In general, however, if an attorney is a resident of the area covered by the court's jurisdiction, has been admitted to practice before state courts, and is in good standing (that is, is not under suspension or disbarment), she or he will be allowed to appear before federal courts. To join the bar of the U.S. Supreme Court, a lawyer must only (1) have been admitted for three years to practice before the highest court of her or his state; (2) be in good standing before that court; (3) appear to the justices "to be of good moral and professional character"; (4) be sponsored by two members of the Supreme Court bar; and (5) pay a $100 fee. Despite these low barriers, lawyers admitted to practice before the Supreme Court hardly form a representative sample of the American legal profession. On the contrary, as Kevin McGuire reports, these lawyers are an elite within an elite. Fully one-third of the Court's counsel were educated at the nation's most distinguished law schools, and the great majority of them have sought employment in urban law firms, primarily in Washington, New York, and Chicago. Moreover, Supreme Court lawyers are older and have practiced longer than most lawyers in the United States.[2]

The publicly proclaimed standards of professional conduct for practicing lawyers are idealistic. Like a boy scout or a girl scout, the attorney is supposed to be loyal, truthful, trustworthy, courteous, kind, clean, and prompt. On the other hand, lawyers are no less inclined toward sin than are other mortals, and their temptations may be greater. Certainly promptness is not a virtue lawyers practice. The usual formula "in due course" usually means "when I get around to it, which, you should earnestly pray, will be in your lifetime." Policing the bar is a difficult task, and each state has its own method of disciplining attorneys for unethical or illegal conduct. Some states leave the matter largely up to bar associations; others place discipline in the hands of the courts. Increasingly, states are requiring both judges and the organized bar to share this onerous work.

---

[2] Kevin T. McGuire, *The Supreme Court Bar: Legal Elites in the Washington Community* (Charlottesville: University Press of Virginia, 1993).

THE LAWYER'S WORK

In the American political system, lawyers perform three critical functions. First, they translate legal rules for their clients and occasionally for broader segments of the public as well and then try to shape their clients'—or the public's—conduct to conform to those rules. Because clients may include private citizens, leaders of interest groups, universities, foundations, unions, corporations, and public officials, this shaping is no mean function. Second, attorneys often try to persuade lawmakers—who may be judges, jurors, other lawyers, police, legislators, or bureaucrats—to change legal rules to legitimate what their clients want to do. The third function is less explicit, although not less far-reaching, because in a sense it encompasses the other two: At their best, lawyers are problem solvers, as much concerned with accommodation and negotiation as with application of technical rules—and perhaps more so. In short, they seek to arrange a compromise so that their clients and potential opponents can avoid a confrontation in any public forum (Reading 5.2).

Development of the Bar

In England, the legal profession was historically divided into two groups: a small, rather select number of barristers, who alone could argue cases before the higher courts; and solicitors, who met with a client, drew up legal documents, represented him or her in petty cases, and, when a client had to go to a higher court, selected and "briefed" a barrister. Responding to demands of membership in the European Union, which permits lawyers of one member country to bring cases in the courts of other member states, as well as to domestic pressure to permit litigants to hire only one attorney, the United Kingdom has recently set up procedures to allow solicitors to argue cases in all courts.

In Civil-Law systems, there are even greater compartmentalizations. Before they begin their professional career, fledgling lawyers must decide whether they wish to be an attorney in private practice, an administrator in the executive branch of government, a notary,[3] or a judge or a prosecutor. (In some Civil-Law countries, such as Italy, judges and prosecutors form a single corps. And in all Civil-Law systems, prosecutors, or procurators as they are called, have broader functions than their common-law cousins; they must present evidence for as well as against an accused.) For all practical purposes, the young person's initial choice—which is pretty much determined by performance on a series of examinations—is his or her final choice. There is little lateral movement between the branches of the legal profession.

---

[3] Civil-Law notaries should not be confused with the common-law notary public, who is merely a person authorized to administer oaths. In Civil-Law systems, notaries are graduates of law faculties who have also completed several years of apprenticeship. They are officers of the court, who must keep posted office hours in the vicinity of the courthouse; in addition to performing various functions for the court, they draw up such legal documents as wills, contracts, and corporate charters for private clients.

Although the American bar lacks the formal divisions of either England or the Civil-Law countries, the United States has its own specializations, no less real because they are informal. Until the end of the Civil War American attorneys typically had face-to-face relationships with their clients and served as general counselors to their neighbors. The war and the growth of large corporate enterprises did much to change those relationships. The new corporate economic system needed lawyers' skills both to expand its potentialities and to defend it against attacks from labor and farm groups. The attorney became, as Adolph A. Berle said, "an intellectual jobber and contractor in business matters." Lawyers assumed the task of remolding the legal framework of a predominantly agrarian society to fit, as well as to protect and foster, the interests of a burgeoning industrial system.

But the attorney has become more than the servant of the huge corporation. Indeed, lawyers have infiltrated the top levels of business. There is a heavily trod path from the legal staff to boards of directors of banks, airlines, or pharmaceutical companies. Nor is this progression from adviser to director restricted to businesses; much the same phenomenon can be seen in foundations, universities, and labor unions. Handling an organization's myriad legal problems and negotiating with its allies and competitors can give an astute lawyer rare insights into that institution's needs and goals.

The country and small-town lawyer can still enjoy the personal relationships of the early nineteenth century, as can the big-city lawyer who is willing to sacrifice income for variety in work. But to meet the demands of industrialization, the bulk of the legal profession has changed its mode of operation. The large urban law office—which may have more than a thousand attorneys and staff members—is organized much like an efficient factory, divided into departments and, sometimes, subdepartments, each handling only a single type of problem. At the top of the personnel are the partners. Often these are public figures, including former presidents, senators, and judges. Below them are layers of salaried associates, men and women, usually recent graduates of law schools or professionals who have stayed around for five or more years hoping to be chosen as partners. During the summers, young law students, picked because of their promise and in the hope of future recruitment as full-time employees, work with partners or senior associates. A large firm's staff will also include accountants, investigators, librarians, receptionists, and dozens of stenographers as well as several Web masters and specialists in computer hardware and software.

The Contemporary Practice of Law

Although large firms remain important players in the legal world, they hardly dominate the contemporary practice of law. Data show that, upon graduation, many lawyers go to work for universities, businesses, public interest law firms, or various levels of government, including one-year stints as clerks for judges. But most (approximately 75 percent) will work in private practice, a division of labor that continues to hold across all age groups. Currently, 71 percent of women and 75 percent of men are in private practice as solo practitioners or in law firms of varying sizes. Of those in a solo practice, about 24 percent are women.

Some attorneys, of course, choose to pursue careers outside law, working as lobbyists in Washington, D.C., or state capitals, serving as administrators, or even entering electoral politics. In fact, usually more than half of representatives in Congress and about two-thirds of senators are attorneys. The percentage in state legislatures is typically lower; but because of their control of key positions and their ability to devote energy to what are really part-time jobs, lawyers may have even greater influence there than at the federal level.

Accounting for this high degree of political activism has fascinated social scientists and attorneys themselves, and they have offered a number of explanations: Lawyers' schedules allow them to fit politics easily into their lives. Limitations on advertising, though less stringent now than in the past, encourage attorneys to seek other means of bringing their names before the public; and politics is an ideal way. The social prestige of attorneys and their personal financial resources make it relatively easy for them to become elected. Their conditioning as problem solvers skilled in the arts of accommodation and negotiation equips them for democratic politics, and their training in legal technicalities allows them to manipulate formal rules. A final explanation has it that whatever the original reasons, the historic success of lawyers in politics draws to law schools young people with political ambitions, so that the ensuing heavy participation is in large part the result of careful self-selection.

Beyond the source of their employment, attorneys differ in the kinds of law they practice, either criminal or civil. Criminal lawyers, be they public defenders or in private practice, represent clients accused of committing criminal offenses; civil lawyers engage in a wide array of tasks, from helping clients draft wills and contracts to advising corporations on their business practices. Either may litigate, but both (in the main) attempt to avoid trials by settling their cases. (Compare Reading 5.2 and Reading 5.3.) Further, although either may be forced to confront ethical dilemmas, those facing criminal lawyers are often much more painful. Should they defend people they know to be guilty of the crimes of which they are accused? When, if ever, should a defense attorney tell the police about a crime in which their clients may be involved (Reading 5.4)?

Finally, vast distinctions exist in the incomes lawyers can expect to receive. Although the median annual earnings of all lawyers is now about $90,000, those choosing solo practice could have difficulty eking out a living. At the other end of the spectrum are lawyers attached to firms, especially large firms, who can harvest rich returns. By the early 2000s, for example, some Wall Street firms began paying as much as $150,000 to young men and women fresh out of law school, well over twice the median family income in the United States. What senior partners of large law firms take for themselves is in large part a function of the tax laws, with many attorneys preferring to have expense accounts and long consultations with clients in Miami in the winter or Paris in the spring to making additional contributions to the Internal Revenue Service. Chief counsel for large corporations can expect salaries of hundreds of thousand dollars plus fringe benefits such as stock options and pension plans. Despite these sacrifices, senior partners in large firms are likely to take home more than half a million dollars a year in cash, with those in the most prestigious firms reaping twice that much.

Whether in low- or high-paying positions, women continue to lag behind men. A survey of the Massachusetts Bar Association conducted in 1997 showed that half of its male members, but only one-fifth of its female members, made more than $75,999 per year, even though the women billed more hours per week than did the men.[4] National data reveal that the annual median salary of women lawyers is but 73 percent of men's.

CHALLENGES CONFRONTING THE LEGAL PROFESSION

Equalizing salaries of men and women presents an important challenge for the legal profession, but it is surely not the only one. Despite their (on average) relatively high incomes, the trust people place in attorneys, and the frequency with which they are elected to public office, lawyers have an "image problem"[5]—and one that has worsened with time. A survey conducted in 1977 asked respondents to rank the prestige of fifteen occupations; the legal profession ranked fourth. Twenty years later, the profession fell to tenth place, trailing federal legislators.[6]

These ratings may reflect deep ambivalence about attorneys, feelings that are not at all unique to American society. Plato was wary of the divisive force that lawyers exert in a society. The churchmen in the Middle Ages feuded with the "civilians," the Roman lawyers. In the Puritan Revolution, the Levellers—a group far more moderate than their title implied—referred to lawyers as "vermin and caterpillars." The satire of Dean Swift in the next century was devastating. Often frustrated in efforts at legal reform at the turn of the nineteenth century, Jeremy Bentham claimed that attorneys were "obsequious to the whisper of interests and to the beck of power." In 1939 Fred Rodell of the Yale Law School castigated the legal profession as "a high class racket." "In tribal times," he wrote, "there were the medicine men. In the Middle Ages, there were the priests. Today there are the lawyers. For every age, a group of bright boys, learned in their trade and jealous of their learning, who blend technical competence with plain and fancy hocus pocus to make themselves masters of their fellow men."[7]

This ambivalence toward the bar is understandable, because, unlike judges, practicing attorneys have seldom been successful in cloaking their activities in a myth of self-denying impartiality. Lawyers usually possess technical expertise as well as a command of serpentine language that allows them to skate very closely around, when they do not actually fall over, the edges of deception. Those skills are in great demand in a society that regulates itself by complicated legal rules and often depends on cunning half-truths to prosper. Meeting this demand certainly brings money and even power, but any accompanying prestige is often

---

[4] See *Woman and the Law*, 5.

[5] Herbert Kritzer, *The Justice Broker* (New York: Oxford University Press, 1990), 166.

[6] Reported in Amy E. Black and Stanley Rothman, "Shall We Kill All the Lawyers First? Insider and Outsider Views of the Legal Profession," 21 *Harvard Journal of Law and Public Policy* 850 (1998).

[7] Fred Rodell, *Woe Unto You, Lawyers* (New York: Reynal and Hitchcock, 1939), 8.

tinged with a moral suspicion that can breed resentment as well as respect. "Lawyers," Herbert M. Kritzer notes, "are praised when they work for you and damned when they work against you."[8]

But it is not only the public who view the legal profession with some measure of disdain; lawyers also experience moral qualms about many of their fellow practitioners as well as some moral difficulties with their own work. Echoing a speech that Justice Harlan Fiske Stone made in 1934,[9] Justice Sandra Day O'Connor reported that a majority of the practicing bar express dissatisfaction with their profession (Reading 5.5). Reversing these trends is not impossible, she said (again echoing Stone), but it will take much serious effort on the part of the legal community.

SELECTED REFERENCES

ABEL, RICHARD L. 1989. *American Lawyers*. New York: Oxford University Press.

ABEL, RICHARD L., AND PHILIP S. C. LEWIS, EDS. 1995. *Lawyers in Society: An Overview*. Berkeley: University of California Press.

BAKER, NANCY V. 1992. *Conflicting Loyalties: Law and Politics in the Attorney General's Office, 1789–1990*. Lawrence: University Press of Kansas.

BLUMBERG, ABRAHAM S. 1967. "The Practice of Law as a Confidence Game." *Law and Society Review* 1: 15.

BURKE, THOMAS F. 2002. *Lawyers, Lawsuits, and Legal Rights: The Battle over Litigation in American Society*. Berkeley: University of California Press.

CLAYTON, CORNELL W. 1992. *The Politics of Justice: The Attorney General and the Making of Legal Policy*. New York: M. E. Sharpe.

CLAYTON, CORNELL W., ED. 1995. *Government Lawyers: The Federal Legal Bureaucracy and Presidential Politics*. Lawrence: University Press of Kansas.

COFFIN, FRANK M. 1994. *On Appeal: Courts, Lawyering, and Judging*. New York: Norton.

DAVIS, MARTHA F. 1993. *Brutal Need: Lawyers and the Welfare Rights Movement, 1960–1973*. New Haven, CT: Yale University Press.

DERSHOWITZ, ALAN M. 1996. *Reasonable Doubts: The Criminal Justice System and the O. J. Simpson Case*. New York: Simon & Schuster.

DRACHMAN, VIRGINIA G. 1998. *Sisters in Law: Women Lawyers in Modern American History*. Cambridge, MA: Harvard University Press.

FLEMMING, ROY B. 1986. "Client Games: Defense Attorney Perspectives on their Relations with Criminal Clients." *American Bar Foundation Research Journal* 1986: 253.

GALANTER, MARC, AND THOMAS PALAY. 1991. *Tournament of Lawyers: The Transformation of the Big Law Firm*. Chicago: University of Chicago Press.

GOULDEN, JOSEPH C. 1971. *The Superlawyers: The Small and Powerful World of the Great Washington Law Firms*. New York: Weybright & Talley.

HAGAN, JOHN, AND FIONA KAY. 1995. *Gender in Practice: A Study of Lawyers' Lives*. New York: Oxford University Press.

HASKELL, PAUL G. 1998. *Why Lawyers Behave as They Do*. Boulder, CO: Westview Press.

HEINZ, JOHN P., AND EDWARD O. LAUMANN. 1982. *Chicago Lawyers: The Social Structure of the Bar*. New York: Russell Sage.

---

[8] Herbert Kritzer, *The Justice Broker*, 166.

[9] Harlan Fiske Stone, "The Public Influence of the Bar," 48 *Harvard Law Review* 1 (1934).

HEUMANN, MILTON. 1977. *Plea Bargaining: The Experiences of Prosecutors, Judges, and Defense Attorneys*. Chicago: University of Chicago Press.

HURST, WILLARD. 1950. *The Growth of American Law*. Boston: Little, Brown.

IRONS, PETER H. 1982. *New Deal Lawyers*. Princeton, NJ: Princeton University Press.

KAGAN, ROBERT A. 2003. *Adversarial Legalism: The American Way of Law*. Cambridge, MA: Harvard University Press.

KELLY, MICHAEL J. 1994. *Lives of Lawyers: Journeys in the Organizations of Practice*. Ann Arbor: University of Michigan Press.

KRITZER, HERBERT M. 1990. *The Justice Broker: Lawyers and Ordinary Litigation*. New York: Oxford University Press.

KRITZER, HERBERT M. 1991. *Let's Make a Deal: Understanding the Negotiation in Ordinary Litigation*. Madison: University of Wisconsin Press.

KRONMAN, ANTHONY T. 1993. *The Lost Lawyer: Failing Ideals of the Legal Profession*. Cambridge, MA: Belknap.

LAPIANA, WILLIAM P. 1994. *Logic and Experience: The Origins of Modern American Legal Education*. New York: Oxford University Press.

LAUMANN, EDWARD O., AND JACK P. HEINZ, WITH ROBERT L. NELSON AND ROBERT H. SALISBURY. 1985. "Washington Lawyers and Others: The Structure of Washington Representation." *Stanford Law Review* 37: 495.

LAWRENCE, SUSAN E. 1990. *The Poor in Court*. Princeton, NJ: Princeton University Press.

MANN, KENNETH. 1988. *Defending White-Collar Crime: A Portrait of Attorneys at Work*. New Haven, CT: Yale University Press.

MATHER, LYNN, CRAIG A. MCEWEN, AND RICHARD J. MAIMAN. 2001. *Divorce Lawyers at Work*. New York: Oxford University Press.

MCGUIRE, KEVIN T. 1993. *The Supreme Court Bar*. Chapel Hill: University of North Carolina Press.

MESTITZ, ANNA, AND PATRIZIA PEDERZOLI. 1995. "Training the Legal Profession in Italy, France, and Germany." In *The Global Expansion of Judicial Power*, ed. C. Neal Tate and Torbjorn Vallinder. New York: New York University Press.

NARDULLI, PETER F., ROY B. FLEMMING, AND JAMES EISENSTEIN. 1984. "Unraveling the Complexities of Decision Making in Face-to-Face Groups: A Contextual Analysis of Plea-Bargained Sentences." *American Political Science Review* 78: 912.

OLSEN, SUSAN M. 1984. *Clients and Lawyers: Securing the Rights of Disabled Persons*. Westport, CT: Greenwood.

POUND, ROSCOE. 1953. *The Lawyer from Antiquity to Modern Times*. Minneapolis: West.

RODELL, FRED. 1939. *Woe unto You, Lawyers!* New York: Reynal & Hitchcock.

SALOKAR, REBECCA MAE. 1992. *The Solicitor General: The Politics of Law*. Philadelphia: Temple University Press.

SARAT, AUSTIN, AND WILLIAM L. F. FELSTINER. 1995. *Divorce Lawyers and Their Clients: Power and Meaning in the Legal Process*. New York: Oxford University Press.

SERON, CARROLL. 1996. *The Business of Practicing Law: The Work Lives of Solo and Small-Firm Attorneys*. Philadelphia: Temple University Press.

STEVENS, ROBERT. 1971. "Two Cheers for 1870: The American Law School." In *Perspectives on American History: Law in American History*, Vol. 5, ed. Donald Fleming and Bernard Bailyn. Cambridge, MA: Charles Warren Center for Studies in American History, Harvard University.

TWISS, BENJAMIN. 1942. *Lawyers and the Constitution*. Princeton, NJ: Princeton University Press.

WARREN, CHARLES. 1939. *A History of the American Bar*. New York: Howard Fertig.

WICE, PAUL. 1991. *Judges and Lawyers: The Human Side of Justice*. New York: HarperCollins.

"Tried tonight to read a case for the first time. It is harder than hell."

5.1 ONE L: AN INSIDE ACCOUNT OF LIFE IN THE FIRST YEAR AT HARVARD LAW SCHOOL

Scott Turow

Scott Turow is a senior partner in the mammoth law firm of Sonnenschein, Nathan, et al., headquartered in Chicago. He is also the author of several best-selling novels set in the legal profession, including *The Burden of Proof* (1990) and *Personal Injuries* (1999).

9/3/75
(Wednesday)

They called us "One Ls," and there were 550 of us who came on the third of September to begin our careers in the law. For the first three days we would have Harvard Law School to ourselves while we underwent a brief orientation and some preliminary instruction. Then, over the weekend, the upper-year students would arrive, and on Monday all classes would officially commence.

A pamphlet sent in August to all first-year students—the One Ls (1Ls) as they are known at HLS—instructed me to be at the Roscoe Pound Classroom and Administration Building at 10 A.M. to register and to start orientation. I took the bus into Cambridge from Arlington, the nearby town where my wife and I had found an apartment. . . .

At 2 [P.M.] I went to the first meeting of Legal Methods. Rather than a full-blown law school course, Methods was regarded as an introductory supplement to the first-year curriculum. It would run for only ten weeks, a little longer than half of the first term, and the instructor would be a teaching fellow, instead of a member of the faculty. For the next three days, though, Methods would be at the center, concentrated instruction aimed at bringing us to the point where we could start the work of our regular courses, which would begin meeting on Monday.

Normally, Legal Methods would gather in classes of twenty-five, but today for the introductory session three groups had been joined and the small classroom was crowded. There was a lot of commotion as people went about introducing themselves to each other. . . .

At the front of the room the instructor was calling us to order.

"I'm Chris Henley," he said. He was short and had a full beard. He looked to be in his early thirties. "I'd like to welcome you to Harvard Law School.

From Scott Turow, *One L: An Inside Account of Life in the First Year at Harvard Law School* (New York: Penguin Books, 1977), pp. 15, 21–25, 29–31, 35–37, 43–49.

This'll be a brief session. I just want to give you a few ideas about what we'll be doing for the next few days and then in the rest of the course."

Before he went on, Henley told us a little about himself. He had been a lawyer with OEO in Washington for seven years. Now he was here, working on a graduate law degree; next year he would probably move on to another school to become a law professor. Then he introduced the three members of the Board of Student Advisors who would be working with each of the Methods groups. . . . After that, Henley described the course.

"In the Legal Methods program," he said, "you'll be learning skills by practicing them. Each of you will act as attorney on the same case. You'll assume the role of a law firm associate who's been asked to deal with the firing of an employee by a corporation."

It would all be highly fictionalized, but we'd follow the matter through each of its stages, gaining some taste of many aspects of a lawyer's work. Among other things, Henley said we would be involved with a client interview, the filing of suit, preparing and arguing a brief for summary judgment. At the very end we would see how two experienced attorneys would handle the suit in a mock trial. I had only the vaguest idea of what many of the words Henley used meant—*depositions* and *interrogatories* and *summary judgment*—and perhaps for that reason alone, the program sounded exciting.

Henley said our first assignment would be handed out at the end of class. It consisted of a memo from our mythical law-firm boss and a "case" the boss had asked the associate to consult. "Case" here means the published report of a judge's resolution of a dispute which has come before him [or her]. Typically, a case report contains a summary of the facts leading up to the lawsuit, the legal issues raised, and what the judge has to say in resolving the matter. That portion of the case report in which the judge sets forth his views is called an "opinion." Cases and opinions form the very center of a law student's world. Virtually every American law school adheres to the "case-study method," which requires students to learn the law by reading and discussing in class a steady diet of case reports. Most of those are the decisions of appellate courts, designated higher courts to which lawyers carry their objections to some point of law ruled on by a trial judge. Because they deal with closely defined legal questions, appellate opinions are considered especially apt tools for teaching students the kind of precise reasoning considered instrumental to a lawyer's work.

The case Henley assigned us was from the Supreme Court of New Hampshire. He asked us to read it and to be ready to discuss it the next time the Methods group met. That did not sound like much. . . .

In [other] law school classes there would be no "introductory day" like the ones I'd experienced in college and graduate school, none of that business of the professor's displaying himself to prove he does not have to mumble and hoping that students won't drop. "Lectures begin on the opening day of the year," the catalog sternly announced. Assignments would be posted in advance so that we would be fully prepared when we entered class on Monday.

In Criminal Law, Professor Mann had simply assigned the first chapter of the casebook. But Professor Perini's announcement was longer:

For Monday's class, please read pages 1–43 in the casebook, Baldridge and Perini, *Selected Cases in the Law of Contracts*. Also read, at page 46, the case of *Hurley v. Eddingfield* and the case of *Poughkeepsie Buying Service, Inc. v. Poughkeepsie Newspaper* Co. at p. 50.

    Do not forget to bring your casebook and supplement to class.

    Be certain to read all material CAREFULLY.

It was not a good sign. As I copied the announcement, one man beside me said he had looked at the casebook and that the assignment would take hours. And as I finished writing I also noticed that Professor Perini had underlined the last word, *carefully*, twice. . . .

9/3/75

(near midnight)

Tried tonight to read a case for the first time. It is harder than hell.

When I started, I thought the Legal Methods assignment would be easy. The memo from the boss was straightforward. A man named Jack Katz is "our firm's" client. Katz, who had worked for years as the comptroller of a company that makes raincoats, was fired a few months ago by the president of the corporation. His name is Elliot Grueman, and he is the son of the man, now dead, who hired Katz ages ago. Grueman and Katz differed about expansion plans for the company; when Katz carried his objections to a member of the board of directors, Grueman showed Katz the door.

The memo from the boss indicates that Katz probably doesn't have a leg to stand on. It looks like Grueman had every right to fire him, since Katz did not have an employment contract. But still, the boss says, read this New Hampshire case, *Monge v. Beege Rubber Company*, which may indicate some limitations in an employer's right to discharge a worker.

OK. It was nine o'clock when I started reading. The case is four pages long and at 10:35 I finally finished. It was something like stirring concrete with my eyelashes. I had no idea what half the words meant. I must have opened *Black's Law Dictionary* twenty-five times and I still can't understand many of the definitions. There are notations and numbers throughout the case whose purpose baffles me. And even now I'm not crystal-clear on what the court finally decided to do.

Even worse, Henley asked us to try our hand at briefing the case—that is, preparing a short digest of the facts, issues, and reasoning essential to the court in making its decision. Briefing, I'm told, is important. All first-year students do it so they can organize the information in a case, and the various student guide books make it sound easy. But I have no idea of what a good brief looks like or even where to start. What in the hell are "the facts," for instance? The case goes on for a solid page giving all the details about how this woman, Olga Monge, was fired primarily because she would not go out on a date with her foreman. Obviously, I'm not supposed to include all of that, but I'm not sure what to pick, how abstract I'm supposed to be, and whether I should include items like her hourly wage. Is a brief supposed to sound casual or formal? Does it make any difference how a brief sounds? Should I include the reasoning of the judge who dissented, as well? Is this why students hate the case-study method?

Twenty minutes ago, I threw up my hands and quit.

I feel overheated and a little bit nervous. I wouldn't be quite so upset if I weren't going to be reading cases every day and if understanding them weren't so important. Cases are the law, in large part. That fact came as news to me when David explained it this summer. I had always thought that the legislature makes all the rules and that judges merely interpret what has been said. I'm not sure where I got that idea, either in high-school civics or, more likely, from TV.

Anyway, that is not right. When the legislature speaks, the judge obeys. But most of the time, nobody has spoken to the point, and the judge decides the law on his own, looking to what other judges have done in similar circumstances. Following precedent, that's called. Much of what lawyers do in court, apparently, is to try to convince judges that the present situation is more like one precedent than another.

This system of judges making law case by case is called the "common law." I am a little embarrassed that I did not understand what that meant when I applied to law school, particularly since the first page of the HLS catalog says that the law school prepares lawyers to practice "wherever the common law prevails."

Well, tonight the common law has prevailed over me, beaten me back. I suppose it will not be the last time, but I feel frustrated and disturbed.

I am going to sleep.

9/8/75
(Monday)

Today is the start of regular classes. We will now commence "normal" law-school life. The 2Ls and 3Ls will be present, and the section will begin the schedule we'll be on for much of the year. This semester we'll have Contracts, Civil Procedure, Criminal Law, and Torts. The latter two courses last only one term, and they'll be the subjects on which we'll take our first exams in January. Second semester, Contracts and Civil Pro continue, Property will be added, and we'll each be allowed to choose an elective.

We've been warned that today's classes—Criminal and Contracts—will not seem much like Legal Methods. The courses we begin now are considered the traditional stuff of law school, analytical matter, rather than mere how-to. Unlike Methods, these courses will be graded, and they'll be taught by professors, not teaching fellows. The classes will be made up of the whole 140-person section instead of a small group. And, most ominous to me, the instruction will be by the noted "Socratic method."

In a way I'm looking forward to Socratic instruction. I've heard so much about it since I applied to law school it will at least be interesting to see what it's like.

The general run of student reaction is most succinctly expressed in a comment I heard from [a friend] David this summer, the day he showed me around the law school. He was kind of mimicking a tour guide, whining out facts and names as he took me from building to building. When we reached Langdell, he stood on the steps and lifted his hand toward the columns and the famous names of the law cut into the granite border beneath the roof.

"This is Langdell Hall," he said, "the biggest building on the law-school campus. It contains four large classrooms and, on the upper floors, the Harvard Law School library, the largest law-school library in the world.

"The building is named for the late Christopher Columbus Langdell, who was dean of Harvard Law School in the late nineteenth century. Dean Langdell is best known as the inventor of the Socratic method."

David lowered his hand and looked sincerely at the building.

"May he rot in hell," David said.

The Socratic method is without question one of the things which makes legal education—particularly the first year, when Socraticism is most extensively used—distinct from what students are accustomed to elsewhere. While I was teaching, it was always assumed that there was no hope of holding a class discussion with a group larger than thirty. When numbers got that high, the only means of communication was lecture. But Socraticism is, in a way, an attempt to lead a discussion with the entire class of 140.

Generally, Socratic discussion begins when a student—I'll call him Jones—is selected without warning by the professor and asked a question. Traditionally, Jones will be asked to "state the case," that is, to provide an oral rendition of the information normally contained in a case brief. Once Jones has responded, the professor—as Socrates did with his students—will question Jones about what he has said, pressing him to make his answers clearer. If Jones says that the judge found that the contract had been breached, the professor will ask what specific provision of the contract had been violated and in what manner. The discussion will proceed that way, with the issues narrowing. At some point, Jones may be unable to answer. The professor can either select another student at random, or—more commonly—call on those who've raised their hands. The substitutes may continue the discussion of the case with the professor, or simply answer what Jones could not, the professor then resuming his interrogation of Jones. . . .

Despite student pain and protest, most law professors, including those who are liberal—even radical—on other issues in legal education, defend the Socratic method. They feel that Socratic instruction offers the best means of training students to speak in the law's unfamiliar language and also of acquainting them with the layered, inquiring style of analysis which is a prominent part of thinking like a lawyer.

For me, the primary feeling at the start was one of incredible exposure. Whatever its faults or virtues, the Socratic method depends on a tacit license to violate a subtle rule of public behavior. When grounds are too large for any semblance of intimacy, we usually think of them as being divided by role. The speaker speaks and, in the name of order, the audience listens—passive, anonymous, remote. In using the Socratic method, professors are informing students what would normally be a safe personal space is likely at any moment to be invaded.

* * *

In Austin [Hall] the rooms were ancient and enormous. The seats and desks were in rows of yellowed oak, tiered steeply toward the rear. At its highest, the classroom was nearly forty feet, with long, heavy curtains on the windows and dark portraits of English judges, dressed in their wigs and robes, hanging in gilt frames high on the wall. It was an awesome setting, especially when its effect was combined with the stories we had all heard about Perini. There was a tone of tense humor in the conversations around me, most voices somewhat hushed. As I headed for my seat, I overheard a number of people say, "I don't want it to be me," referring to whom Perini would call on.

It was already a few minutes after ten, the hour when we were supposed to start. The class was assembled and almost everyone was in his seat.

Perini moved slowly down the tiers toward the lectern. He held his head up and he was without expression. My first thought was that he looked softer than I'd expected. He was around six feet, but pudgy and a little awkward, Although the day was warm, he wore a black three-piece suit. He held the book and the seating chart under his arm.

The room was totally silent by the time he reached the lectern. He slapped the book down on the desk beneath. He still had not smiled.

"This is Contracts," he said, "Section Two, in case any of you are a little uncertain about where you are." He smiled then, stiffly. "I have a few introductory comments and then we'll be going on to the cases I asked you to look at for today. First, however, I want to lay out the ground rules on which this class will run, so that there will be *no* confusion in the future."

He spoke with elaborate slowness, emphasis on each word. His accent was distinctly southern.

Perini picked up the casebook in one hand.

"The text for this class is *Selected Cases in the Law of Contracts*. The editors are Baldridge and"—Perini lifted a hand to weight the silence—"et cetera." He smiled again, without parting his lips. Around the room a few people snickered. Then he said, "Needless to mention, I hope you bought it new," and got his first outright laugh.

"We will proceed through the book case by case," Perini told us. "Now and then we may skip a case or two. In that event, I'll inform you in advance, or you will find a notice on the bulletin boards. You should stay three cases ahead, each day."

Between the desk on which the lectern sat and the students in the front row, there was a narrow area, a kind of small proscenium. Perini began to pace there slowly, his hands behind his back. I watched him as he came toward our side of the room, staring up harshly at the faces around him. He looked past fifty, coarse-skinned and dark. He was half-bald, but his black hair was styled carefully. There was a grim set to his mouth and eyes.

"This class will deal with the law of obligations, of bargains, commercial dealings, the law of promises," Perini said. "It is the hardest course you will take all year. Contracts has traditionally been the field of law of the most renowned intellectual complexity. Most of the greatest legal commentators of the past century have been Contracts scholars: Williston, Corbin, Fuller, Llewellyn, Baldridge—." He lifted his hand as he had done before. "Et cetera," he said again and smiled broadly for the first time. Most people laughed. One or two applauded. Perini waited before he began pacing again.

"Some of your classmates may find the Property course in the spring the hardest course they take. But you will not feel that way, because you will be taking Contracts with me. I am not"—he looked up—"an easy person.

"I expect you to be here *every* day. And I expect you to sit where the registrar has assigned you. On the so-called back benches, I should see only those persons who are visiting us seeking a momentary glimpse of something morbid." Laughter again from a few places.

"I expect you to be very well prepared, *every* day. I want to be absolutely clear on that. I have *never* heard the word 'pass.' I do not *know* what 'unprepared' means. Now and then, of course, there are personal problems—we all have them at times—which make full preparation impossible. If that is the case, then I want a written note to be handed to my secretary at least two hours before class. You can find her on the second floor of the Faculty Office Building in room two eighty-one."

I wrote it all down in my notebook: "No absence. No pass. No unprepared. Note to sec'ty 2 hrs. b-4 class, FOB 281."

Holy Christ, I thought.

As expected, Perini told us to read nothing aside from class assignments for the first few months—not even "a certain hornbook" we might have heard of. For the present, he assured us, we would have our hands full. Then he described the course in some detail. In that discussion, too, Perini maintained that tone of barely veiled menace. We may have been Phi Beta Kappas and valedictorians, but this was Harvard Law School now—things would not be easy.

There were moments when I was certain that Perini was only half serious. There was such obvious showmanship in all of this, the deliberateness of the gestures, the archness of his smile. It was almost a parody of the legendary tough professor, of the Perini of rumor. But if it was an act, it was one which he was determined would be compelling. He revealed no more than a trace of irony, and there were often moments, as when he had looked up at us, that he seemed full of steel.

As he went on describing the subjects with which we would soon be dealing—offer, acceptance, interpretation; the list was extensive—I began to think that, like Mann, he would let the hour slip away. No one would be called and we'd all be safe for one more day. But at six or seven minutes to twelve he returned to the lectern and looked down at the seating chart.

"Let's see if we can cover a *little* ground today." Perini took a pencil from his pocket and pointed it at the chart. It might as well have been a pistol. Please, no, I thought.

"Mr. Karlin!" Perini cried sharply.

Nearby, I heard a tremendous thud. Five or six seats from me a man was scrambling to grab hold of the books that had been piled before him, two or three of which had now hit the floor. That, I was sure, was Karlin who had jolted when he heard his name called. He was a heavyset man, pale, with black eyeglasses. He was wearing a yarmulke. His eyes, as he struggled with his books, were quick with fright, and at once I felt terribly sorry for him and guilty at my own relief.

"Mr. Karlin," Perini said, ambling toward my side of the room, "why don't you tell us about the case of *Hurley v. Eddingfield*?"

Karlin already had his notebook open. His voice was quavering.

"Plaintiffs intestate," he began. He got no further.

"What does *that* mean?" Perini cried from across the room. He began marching fiercely up the aisle toward Karlin. "In-tes-tate," he said, "'in-*tes*-tate. What is that? Something to do with the *stomach*? Is this an anatomy class, Mr. Karlin?" Perini's voice had become shrill with a note of open mockery and at the last word people burst out laughing. Louder than at anything Perini had said before.

He was only five or six feet from Karlin now. Karlin stared up at him and blinked and finally said, "No."

"No, I didn't think so," Perini said. "What if the word was 'testate'? What would that be? Would we have moved from the stomach"—Perini waved a hand and there was more loud laughter when he leeringly asked his question—"elsewhere?"

"I think," Karlin said weakly, "that if the word was 'testate' it would mean he had a will."

"And 'intestate' that he didn't have a will. I see." Perini wagged his head. "And who is this 'he,' Mr. Karlin?"

Karlin was silent. He shifted in his seat as Perini stared at him. Hands had shot up across the room. Perini called rapidly on two or three people who gave various names—Hurley, Eddingfield, the plaintiff. Finally someone said that the case didn't say.

"The case doesn't *say*!" Perini cried, marching down the aisle. "The case does not say. Read the case. *Read* the case! *Care*fully!" He bent with each word, pointing a finger at the class. He stared fiercely into the crowd of students in the center of the room, then looked back at Karlin. "Do we really care who 'he' is, Mr. Karlin?"

"Care?"

"Does it make any *difference* to the outcome of the case?"

"I don't think so."

"Why not?"

"Because he's dead."

"He's *dead*!" Perini shouted. "Well, that's a load off of our minds. But there's one problem then, Mr. Karlin. If he's dead, how did he file a *law*suit?"

Karlin's face was still tight with fear, but he seemed to be gathering himself.

"I thought it was the administrator who brought the suit."

"Ah!" said Perini, "the ad*mini*strator. And what's an administrator? One of those types over in the Faculty Building?"

It went on that way for a few more minutes, Perini striding through the room, shouting and pointing as he battered Karlin with questions, Karlin doing his best to provide answers. A little after noon Perini suddenly announced that we would continue tomorrow. Then he strode from the classroom with the seating chart beneath his arm. In his wake the class exploded into chatter.

I sat stunned. Men and women crowded around Karlin to congratulate him. He had done well—better, it seemed, than even Perini had expected. At one point the professor had asked where Karlin was getting all the definitions he was methodically reciting. I knew Karlin had done far better than I could have, a realization which upset me, given all the work I had done preparing for the class. I hadn't asked myself who was suing. I knew what "intestate" meant, but not "testate," and was hardly confident I could have made the jump while under that kind of pressure. I didn't even want to think about the time it would be my turn to face Perini.

And as much as all of that, I was bothered by the mood which had taken hold of the room. The exorbitance of Perini's manner had seemed to release a sort of twisted energy. Why had people laughed like that? I wondered. It wasn't all good-natured. It wasn't really laughter with Karlin. I had felt it too, a sort of giddiness, when Perini made his mocking inquiries. And why had people raised their hands so eagerly, stretching out of their seats as they sought to be called on? When Socratic instruction had been described for me, I had been somewhat incredulous that students would dash in so boldly to correct each other's errors. But if I hadn't been quite as scared I might have raised my hand myself. What the hell went on here? I was thoroughly confused, the more so because despite my reservations the truth was that I had been gripped, even thrilled, by the class. Perini, for all the melodrama and intimidation, had been magnificent, electric, in full possession of himself and the students. The points he'd made had had a wonderful clarity and directness. He was, as claimed, an exceptional teacher. . . .

> *"While many clients think of the legal process as an arena*
> *for a full adversarial contest, most divorce disputes*
> *are not resolved in this manner."*

5.2 LAW AND STRATEGY IN THE DIVORCE LAWYER'S OFFICE

Austin Sarat and William L. F. Felstiner

Austin Sarat is William Nelson Cromwell Professor of Jurisprudence and Political Science at Amherst College. William L. F. Felstiner is Professor in the Law and Society Program at the University of California, Santa Barbara, and Distinguished Research Professor of Law at the University of Wales College of Cardiff.

In the research from which this paper is derived, we developed an account of lawyer-client interaction in divorce cases. We chose to examine divorce because it is a serious and growing social problem in which the involvement of lawyers

---

is particularly salient and controversial. Concern among many divorce lawyers about their role suggested that field research on lawyer-client interaction in this area would encounter less resistance than in other areas of legal practice.

We observed cases over a period of thirty-three months in two sites, one in Massachusetts and one in California. This effort consisted in following one side of forty divorce cases, ideally from the first lawyer-client interview until the divorce was final. We followed these cases by observing and tape-recording lawyer-client sessions, attending court and mediation hearings and trials, and interviewing both lawyers and clients about those events. Approximately 115 lawyer-client conferences were tape-recorded. . . .

In this paper we focus on one lawyer-client conference to provide the reader with the maximum opportunity to follow these themes and see them at work "on location." Only through such concentration are we able to convey the level of detail that we believe is necessary to convey the full social significance of the interplay between the lawyer and client. . . .

The lawyer involved in this case graduated from one of the country's top-ranked law schools. He was forty years old at the time of the conference and had practiced for fourteen years. His father was a prominent physician in a neighboring city. The lawyer had spent four years as a public defender after law school and had been in private practice for ten years. He considers himself a trial lawyer and states that he was drawn to divorce work because of the opportunity it provides for trial work. He is married and has never been divorced.

The client and her husband were in their late thirties and had no children. Their marriage had been stormy, involving both substantial separations and infidelity by the husband. Both had graduate degrees and worked full-time; financial support was not an issue. They owned a house, bank stocks, several limited partnerships in real estate, his retirement benefits, and personal property. The house was their major asset. It was an unconventional building to which the husband was especially attached. Housing in the area is very expensive. This divorce was the client's second; there were no children in the first marriage either. She had received extensive psychological counseling prior to and during the case which we observed.

The parties in this divorce initially tried to dissolve their marriage by engaging a mediator and did not at that time individually consult lawyers. The mediator was an established divorce lawyer with substantial experience in divorce mediation. At the first substantive session, the mediator stated that he did not think that further progress could be made if both the spouses continued to live in the house. Although she considered it to be a major sacrifice, the wife said that she had moved out of the house to facilitate mediation after her husband absolutely refused to leave. Thereafter, she visited the house occasionally, primarily to check on plants and pets. The client reported that she was careful to warn her husband when she intended to visit.

Over time, however, this arrangement upset her husband. Rather than raise the problem at a mediation session, he hired a lawyer and secured an *ex parte* order restraining the client from entering the property at any time for any reason. The husband had previously characterized the lawyer that he hired as "the meanest son-of-a-bitch in town." The restraining order ended any prospects for mediation and the client, on the advice of the mediator and another lawyer, hired the lawyer involved in this conference.

Subsequently, a hearing about the propriety of the *ex parte* order was held by a second judge. The issues at this hearing were whether the order should be governed by a general or a divorce-specific injunction statute, what status quo the order was intended to maintain, and whether the husband's attempt to secure the order violated a moral obligation undertaken when the client agreed to move out of the house. The second judge decided against the client on the first two issues, but left consideration of the bad faith question open to further argument. The client's therapist attended the hearing and the lawyer-client conference that immediately followed. At that conference the therapist stressed that contesting the restraining order further might not be in the client's long-term interest even if it corrected the legal wrong.

The conference analyzed in this paper followed the meeting attended by the therapist and was the seventh of twelve that occurred during the course of the case. It took place in the lawyer's office five weeks after the first meeting between lawyer and client. Its two phases, interrupted for several hours at midday, lasted a total of about two hours.

The people referred to in this conference are (fictional names have been assigned to all the participants and places):

Lawyer	Peter Edmunds
Client	Jane Carroll
Spouse	Norb
Spouse's lawyer	Paul Foster
First judge	John Hancock
Second judge	Mike Cohen
Therapist	Irene

* * *

To Fight or To Settle?

[H]ow should divorce disputes be managed? This concern is central in most of the cases that we observed, and it is an issue that may recur as lawyer and client discuss each of the major controversies in a divorce case. Generally the question is whether the client should attempt to negotiate a settlement or insist on resolution before a judge. This question is sometimes posed issue by issue and sometimes across many issues.

While many clients think of the legal process as an arena for a full adversarial contest, most divorce disputes are not resolved in this manner. Although not all lawyers are equally dedicated to reaching negotiated agreements, most of those we observed advised their clients to try to settle the full range of issues in the case. This is not to say that these divorces were free of conflict, for the negotiations themselves were often quite contentious. Although some of our lawyers occasionally advised clients to ask for more than the client had originally

contemplated or to refuse to concede on a major issue when the client was inclined to do so, most seemed to believe that it is generally better to settle than
contest divorce disputes. Thus, we are interested in the ways in which lawyers
get their clients to see settlement as the preferred alternative.

The conference we are examining revolves around two major issues:
(1) whether to ignore or to contest the restraining order; and (2) what position
to take concerning disposition of the family residence. Much of the conference
is devoted to discussing the restraining order—its origins, morality, and legality; the prospects for dissolving it; the lawyer's stake in contesting it; and the
client's emotional reaction to it. Substantively the order is not as important as
the house itself, which received much less attention and generated much less
controversy. Both issues, however, force the lawyer and client to decide whether
they will retain control of the case by engaging in negotiations or cede control
to the court for hearing and decision. The lawyer definitely favors negotiations.

> LAWYER: Okay. What I would like your permission to do then is to meet with
> Foster, see if I can come up with or negotiate a settlement with him that,
> before he leaves . . . I leave his office or he leaves my office, he says, we've
> got something here that I can recommend to my client, and I can say, I've
> got something here that I can recommend to my client. My feeling is, Jane,
> that if we reach that point, both lawyers are prepared to make a recom-
> mendation on settlement to their respective clients, if either of the clients,
> either you or Norb, find something terribly disagreeable with the pro-
> posal that we have, the lawyers have come to between themselves, then
> the case just either can't be settled or it's not ripe for settlement. But we
> would have given it the best shot. But I wouldn't . . . as you know, I'm
> very concerned about wasting a lot of time and energy trying to settle a
> case where two previous attempts have been dismally unsuccessful.

The major ingredient of this settlement system is the primacy of the
lawyers. They produce the deals while the clients are limited to initial instructions and after-the-fact ratification. The phrase "we would have given it the best
shot" is crucial. The "we" seems to refer to the lawyers. Indeed, their efforts
could come to nothing if either client backs out at the last minute. The settlement process as described thus has two dimensions—a lawyer-to-lawyer phase,
in which an arrangement is worked out, and a lawyers-versus-clients phase, in
which the opposing lawyers join together to sell the deal to their clients. If the
clients do not accept the settlement as a package, the only alternative is to go to
trial. Furthermore, if the professionals are content with the agreement they have
devised, dissatisfied clients not only have nothing to contribute but also had
perhaps better seek psychotherapy:

> LAWYER: And if we have to come down a little bit off the 10 percent to
> something that is obviously a real good loan—9 percent—a percentage
> point on a one-year, eighteen-month, $25,000 loan does not make that
> much difference to you. And that's worth settling the case, and I'll say,
> Jane, if we're going to court over what turns out to be one percentage

point, go talk to Irene some more. So that's the kind of a package that I see putting together.

The client in this case is reluctant to begin settlement negotiations until some attention is paid to the restraining order. While she acknowledges that she wants a reasonable property settlement, she reminds her lawyer that that is not her exclusive concern:

> CLIENT: Yes, there's no question in my mind that that [a property settlement] is my first goal. However, that doesn't mean it's my only goal. It's just my first one. And I have done a lot of thinking about this and so it's all this kind of running around in my head at this point. I've been looking very carefully at the parts of me that want to fight and the parts of me that don't want to fight. And I'm not sure that any of that ought to get messed up in the property settlement.

The lawyer responds by acknowledging that he considers the restraining order to be legally wrong and that he believes it could be litigated. Thus, he confirms his client's position and inclination on legal grounds. Yet he dissents from her position and opposes her inclination to fight on other grounds. First, he states that the restraining order, although legally wrong, is "not necessarily. . . completely wrong" because it might prevent violence between spouses. This complicated position is a clear example of a tactic frequently used by lawyers in divorce cases—the rhetorical "yes . . . but." The lawyers we observed often appeared to be endorsing the adversarial pursuit of one of the client's objectives only to remind the client of a variety of negative consequences associated with it. In this way, lawyers present themselves as both an ally and an adviser embracing the wisdom of a long-term perspective.

Second, the lawyer is worried that an effort to fight the restraining order would interfere with the resolution of the case, that is, of the outstanding property issues. Although the lawyer considers the restraining order to be a legal mistake, its effect would end upon final disposition of the house. In the meantime, the client can either live with the order or pay for additional hearings. He believes that it would be unwise for her to fight further not only because the contest would be costly but also because it would postpone or derail entirely negotiations about the house and other tangible assets. Thus when the client asks whether the issue of the restraining order has been raised with her husband's lawyer, her lawyer says:

> LAWYER: Well, we've talked to him. My feelings are still the same. They're very strong feelings that what has been done is illegal, that I want to take it to the Supreme Court. I told Foster off. I basically told him the contents of the letter. I said that I think that Judge Cohen is dead wrong and I would very much like to litigate the thing. On the other hand, I have to be mindful of what Irene said, which is absolutely correct, does that move us toward or away from the ultimate goal, which is the resolution of the case and what you told me when we started off now in very certain terms.

The lawyer's position in this case can be interpreted as a preference for negotiations over litigation based on his determination that this client has more to lose than gain by fighting the restraining order and for the house. In this view the lawyer is neutral about settlement in general and is swayed by the cost-benefit calculation of specific cases. Thus there is a conflict between the client's desire for vindication on what the lawyer perceives to be a peripheral issue and the lawyer's interest in reaching a satisfactory disposition on what for him is a much more important issue. Time and again in our study we observed lawyers attempting to focus their client's attention on the issues the lawyers thought to be major while the clients often concentrated on matters that the lawyers considered secondary. While the disposition of the house in this case will have long-term consequences for the client, the restraining order, as unjust as the lawyer understands it to be, is in his view a temporary nuisance. His sense of justice and of the long-term best interests of his client lead him to try to transform this dispute from a battle over the legality and morality of the restraining order to a negotiation over the more narrow and tangible issue of the ultimate disposition of the house and other assets, which he believes can and should be settled.

In attempting this transformation, the lawyer allies himself with the therapist:

> LAWYER: I agree with Irene that that [fighting the restraining order] is not the best way . . . it's probably the worst way. This [negotiating] hopefully is the best way.

This reliance on the therapist is noteworthy because it is often assumed that a therapeutic orientation is antithetical to the adversarial inclination of law and the legal profession. Yet in this case the lawyer uses the therapist to validate his own position. The legal ideology and the therapeutic ideology seem to him to be compatible; both stress settlement and disvalue legal struggles. . . . However we interpret this observation, it is clear that this lawyer, and most of those we observed, construct an image of the appropriate mode of disposition of a case that is at odds with the conventional view in which lawyers are alleged to induce competition and hostility, transform noncontentious clients into combatants, and promulgate a "fight theory of justice."

The client's own ambivalence toward settlement continues throughout the conference. . . .

> CLIENT: Are you familiar with Chief Joseph?
> LAWYER: No.
> CLIENT: He was a Nez Perce Indian, and he fought the troops of the U.S. government for years and finally he saw that his whole tribe would be killed off and the land devastated so he put down his weapons. And I think the full quote is something like: "From the time the moon sets, I will fight no more forever." I went away that day, that Monday, feeling that this fight had to end, and that's still what I feel. . . .
>
> One of the thoughts I had that afternoon was that probably it came a lot from what Irene had to say—that I've been arguing with this man for

a good many years of my life. You know, first in the living room, then involving family and friends, then involving therapists, and now involving attorneys. How many forums am I going to spend arguing with this person? And I really want the war to end. So that's my basic conflict. I feel I've been treated unjustly. I feel there's a very good case here, but I don't want to fight any more. And that's what this really is about—a continuing war. So a part of me is still very much with Chief Joseph—I don't want to fight any more. There are other and better things to do with this life.

However, as they move further into the discussion of whether to fight or to settle, the client begins to interpret settlement as a capitulation and to reiterate her own ambivalence about how to proceed.

CLIENT: And I think I feel some level of fear about this process of negotiation and how much more I'm going to have to give up. I don't feel tremen—, you know, there's a part of me that does not feel very satisfied with having capitulated repeatedly, and now we're simply doing it with a property settlement.

LAWYER: That's, yeah, that's a . . .

CLIENT: I mean, I don't want to fight and I do want to fight, right? That's exactly what it comes down to.

LAWYER: Yes, you're ambiguous.

CLIENT: Oh, boy, am I ever. And I have to live with it.

She may have to live with her ambivalence, but her lawyer needs a resolution of this issue. The lawyer seeks this resolution by allying himself with the "don't fight" side of the struggle. Her advocate, her "knight," has thus become the enemy of adversariness. Through him the legal system becomes the champion of settlement. Ironically, the client's ambivalence serves to validate the lawyer's earlier suggestion that he might be wasting his time and her money trying to settle this case because she might refuse at the last minute to agree to a deal. The conference reaches closure on the fight/settle issue when the lawyer again asks whether he has her authority to negotiate on the terms they had discussed and repeats his earlier warning that this is their last chance for a settlement:

LAWYER: Well, then I will make a . . . my best effort—we are now coming full circle to where we were this morning, which is fine, which is where we should be. I will make my best effort to effect a settlement with Foster along the lines that you and I have discussed and the specific terms of which I can say to you, Jane, I recommend that you sign this. The decision, of course, is yours. If you don't want to sign it, we're going to go ahead with the litigation on the restraining order and probably a trial. Things can change. We can effect a settlement before the restraining order, which is highly unlikely, or between the time the restraining order issue is resolved and the actual time of trial, maybe there will be another settlement. I'm not going to suggest or advise, after this attempt, that either one of us put any substantial energy in another try at settlement. I just think it's a waste of time and money.

The lawyer's reference to "coming full circle" reflects both the centrality of the dispositional question and the amount of time spent talking about issues the lawyer considers to be peripheral. Having invested that time the lawyer secures what he wanted, both an authorization to negotiate and an agreement on the goals that he will pursue. The client, on the other hand, has aired her ambivalence and resolved to try to end this dispute without a legal contest. Both her ambivalence and her eventual acceptance of settlement are typical of the clients we observed. . . .

"The client . . . is a secondary figure in the court system as in certain other bureaucratic settings."

5.3 THE PRACTICE OF LAW AS A CONFIDENCE GAME

Abraham S. Blumberg

Abraham S. Blumberg was Professor of Sociology and Law at the University of Missouri at Kansas City.

The overwhelming majority of convictions in criminal cases (usually over 90 percent) are not the product of a combative trial by jury process at all but instead merely involve the sentencing of the individual after a negotiated, bargained-for plea of guilty has been entered. Although more recently the overzealous role of police and prosecutors in producing pretrial confessions and admissions has achieved a good deal of notoriety, scant attention has been paid to the organizational structure and personnel of the criminal court itself. Indeed, the extremely high conviction rate produced without the features of an adversary trial in our courts would tend to suggest that the "trial" becomes a perfunctory reiteration and validation of the pretrial interrogation and investigation.

The institutional setting of the court defines a role for the defense counsel in a criminal case radically different from the one traditionally depicted. Sociologists and others have focused their attention on the deprivations and social disabilities of such variables as race, ethnicity, and social class as being the source of an accused person's defeat in a criminal court. Largely overlooked is the variable of the court organization itself, which possesses a thrust, purpose, and direction of its own. It is grounded in pragmatic values, bureaucratic priorities, and administrative instruments. These exalt maximum production and the particularistic career designs of organizational incumbents, whose occupational and career commitments tend to generate a set of priorities. These priorities

From 1 *Law and Society Review* 15 (1967).

exert a higher claim than the stated ideological goals of "due process of law," and are often inconsistent with them.

Organizational goals and discipline impose a set of demands and conditions of practice on the respective professions in the criminal court, to which they respond by abandoning their ideological and professional commitments to the accused client, in the service of these higher claims of the court organization. All court personnel, including the accused's own lawyer, tend to be coopted to become agent-mediators who help the accused redefine his situation and restructure his perceptions concomitant with a plea of guilty.

Of all the occupational roles in the court the only private individual who is officially recognized as having a special status and concomitant obligations is the lawyer. His legal status is that of "an officer of the court," and he is held to a standard of ethical performance and duty to his client as well as to the court. This obligation is thought to be far higher than that expected of ordinary individuals occupying the various occupational statuses in the court community. However, lawyers, whether privately retained or of the legal-aid, public defender variety, have close and continuing relations with the prosecuting office and the court itself through discreet relations with the judges via their law secretaries or "confidential" assistants. Indeed, lines of communication, influence and contact with those offices, as well as with the Office of the Clerk of the court, Probation Division, and with the press, are essential to present and prospective requirements of criminal law practice. Similarly, the subtle involvement of the press and other mass media in the court's organizational network is not readily discernible to the casual observer. Accused persons come and go in the court system schema, but the structure and its occupational incumbents remain to carry on their respective career, occupational and organizational enterprises. The individual stridencies, tensions, and conflicts a given accused person's case may present to all the participants are overcome, because the formal and informal relations of all the groups in the court setting require it. The probability of continued future relations and interaction must be preserved at all costs.

This is particularly true of the "lawyer regulars," i.e., those defense lawyers, who by virtue of their continuous appearances in behalf of defendants, tend to represent the bulk of a criminal court's non-indigent case workload, and those lawyers who are not "regulars," who appear almost casually in behalf of an occasional client. Some of the "lawyer regulars" are highly visible as one moves about the major urban centers of the nation, their offices line the back streets of the courthouses, at times sharing space with bondsmen. Their political "visibility" in terms of local club house ties, reaching into the judge's chambers and prosecutor's office, are also deemed essential to successful practitioners. Previous research has indicated that the "lawyer regulars" make no effort to conceal their dependence upon police, bondsmen, jail personnel. Nor do they conceal the necessity for maintaining intimate relations with all levels of personnel in the court setting as a means of obtaining, maintaining, and building their practice. These informal relations are the sine qua non not only of retaining a practice, but also in the negotiation of pleas and sentences.

The client, then, is a secondary figure in the court system as in certain other bureaucratic settings. He becomes a means to other ends of the organization's incumbents. He may present doubts, contingencies, and pressures which challenge existing informal arrangements or disrupt them; but these tend to be resolved in favor of the continuance of the organization and its relations as before. There is a greater community of interest among all the principal organizational structures and their incumbents than exists elsewhere in other settings. The accused's lawyer has far greater professional, economic, intellectual and other ties to the various elements of the court system than he does to his own client. In short, the court is a closed community.

This is more than just the case of the usual "secrets" of bureaucracy which are fanatically defended from an outside view. Even all elements of the press are zealously determined to report on that which will not offend the board of judges, the prosecutor, probation, legal-aid, or other officials, in return for privileges and courtesies granted in the past and to be granted in the future. Rather than any view of the matter in terms of some variation of a "conspiracy" hypothesis, the simple explanation is one of an ongoing system handling delicate tensions, managing the trauma produced by law enforcement and administration, and requiring almost pathological distrust of "outsiders" bordering on group paranoia.

The hostile attitude toward "outsiders" is in large measure engendered by a defensiveness itself produced by the inherent deficiencies of assembly line justice, so characteristic of our major criminal courts. Intolerably large caseloads of defendants which must be disposed of in an organizational context of limited resources and personnel, potentially subject the participants in the court community to harsh scrutiny from appellate courts, and other public and private sources of condemnation. As a consequence, an almost irreconcilable conflict is posed in terms of intense pressures to process large numbers of cases on the one hand, and the stringent ideological and legal requirements of "due process law," on the other hand. A rather tenuous resolution of the dilemma has emerged in the shape of a large variety of bureaucratically ordained and controlled "work crimes," short cuts, deviations, and outright rule violations adopted as court practice in order to meet production norms. Fearfully anticipating criticism on ethical as well as legal grounds, all the significant participants in the court's social structure are bound into an organized system of complicity. This consists of a work arrangement in which the patterned, covert, informal breaches, and evasions of "due process" are institutionalized, but are, nevertheless, denied to exist.

These institutionalized evasions will be found to occur, to some degree, in all criminal courts. Their nature, scope and complexity are largely determined by the size of the court, and the character of the community in which it is located, e.g., whether it is a large, urban institution, or a relatively small rural county court. In addition, idiosyncratic, local conditions may contribute to a unique flavor in the character and quality of the criminal law's administration in a particular community. However, in most instances a variety of stratagems are employed—some subtle, some crude—in effectively disposing of what are often too large caseloads. A wide variety of coercive devices are employed against an accused-client, couched in a depersonalized, instrumental, bureaucratic version of due process of law, and which are in reality a perfunctory obeisance to the ideology of due process. These include some very explicit pressures which are exerted in some measure by all court personnel, including judges, to plead guilty and avoid trial. In many instances the sanction of a potentially harsh sentence is utilized as the visible alternative to pleading guilty, in the case of recalcitrants. Probation and psychiatric reports are "tailored" to organizational needs, or are at least responsive to the court organization's requirements for the refurbishment of a defendant's social biography, consonant with his new status. A resourceful judge can, through his subtle domination of the proceedings, impose his will on the final outcome of a trial. Stenographers and clerks, in their function as record keepers, are on occasion pressed into service in support of a judicial need to "rewrite" the record of a courtroom event. Bail practices are usually employed for purposes other than simply assuring a defendant's presence on the date of a hearing in connection with his case. Too often, the discretionary power as to bail is part of the arsenal of weapons available to collapse the resistance of an accused person. The foregoing is a most cursory examination of some of the more prominent "short cuts" available to any court organization. There are numerous other procedural strategies constituting due process deviations, which tend to become the work style artifacts of a court's personnel. Thus, only court "regulars" who are "bound in" are really accepted; others are treated routinely and in almost a coldly correct manner.

The defense attorneys, therefore, whether of the legal-aid, public defender variety, or privately retained, although operating in terms of pressures specific to their respective role and organizational obligations, ultimately are concerned with strategies which tend to lead to a plea. It is the rational, impersonal elements involving economies of time, labor, expense and a superior commitment of the defense counsel to these rationalistic values of maximum production of court organization that prevail, in his relationship with a client. The lawyer "regulars" are frequently former staff members of the prosecutor's office and utilize the prestige, know-how and contacts of their former affiliation as part of their stock in trade. Close and continuing relations between the lawyer "regular" and his former colleagues in the prosecutor's office generally overshadow the relationship between the regular and his client. The continuing colleagueship of supposedly adversary counsel rests on real professional and organizational needs of a *quid pro quo*, which goes beyond the limits of an accommodation or *modus vivendi* one might ordinarily expect under the circumstances of an otherwise seemingly adversary relationship. Indeed, the adversary features which are manifest are for the most part muted and exist even in their attenuated form largely for external consumption. The principals, lawyer and assistant district attorney, rely upon one another's cooperation for their continued professional existence, and so the bargaining between them tends usually to be "reasonable" rather than fierce. . . .

"The question that laymen put to me most frequently is
'Would you defend a guilty man?' Or, 'How can
you defend a man you know is guilty?'"

5.4 THE DEFENSE NEVER RESTS

F. Lee Bailey

F. Lee Bailey is a criminal defense attorney whose clients have included
Sam Sheppard, Patty Hearst, and O. J. Simpson.

The rate of acquittal for all the cases I have handled is between sixty and seventy percent. For the forty homicides I have handled, the rate is much higher. One client pleaded guilty in the murder of a teenage girl. Only three of the accused killers I have represented were convicted. I'm not saying I have never gotten a guilty man out of prison on a point of law or that I have not won acquittal for a guilty man. But in none of those three convictions was it proved beyond a reasonable doubt that the defendant had committed murder. When there isn't the slightest doubt that my client committed the crime, he pleads guilty. Otherwise, we fight.

Even if I know a client is guilty, it's not that simple. The question that laymen put to me most frequently is: "Would you defend a guilty man?" Or, "How can you defend a man you know is guilty?"

The questioner is rarely satisfied with my answer. He sees no justification for defending someone who really did it. He can afford to play the moralist; it's not his neck on the guillotine. If lawyers were to shun every case in which they knew the defendant was guilty, there would be no courts. Every person who was arrested and indicted would go right to jail unless his defense counsel judged him innocent.

Guilt, like most things, is scarcely ever black or white. Yes, I have defended a number of men I knew to be guilty. Two were acquitted. One of them was James Martin, and his story is indeed a case in point.

I met Jimmy Martin in the summer of 1961. His cousin, a former classmate of mine, had asked me to take his case. Jimmy could have posed for a Pepsi-Cola ad; he was a good-looking eighteen-year-old with rosy cheeks, clear blue eyes, and curly brown hair. He didn't look as if he were capable of murder, but few people do. And under sufficient pressure, any one of us is capable of killing another human being.

Jimmy was accused of an especially ugly slaying—the murder of an elderly nurse in Roxbury, one of Boston's poorest suburbs. She had been found dead on a church lawn, her uniform ripped open and the back of her skull crushed.

From F. Lee Bailey, *The Defense Never Rests* (New York: Signet, 1971), pp. 57–63.

The night of the incident Jimmy, who had finished a pint of Southern Comfort, was standing drunk on the sidewalk near his home. He spotted the nurse, crossed the street in front of her, stooped as if to tie his shoe, and then suddenly shot up with a haymaker right to her eye as she was about to pass. She fell to the sidewalk, and Jimmy grabbed her pocketbook and ran. There was thirty-eight cents in the purse, but Jimmy had committed an unarmed robbery, an offense punishable in Massachusetts by a maximum sentence of life imprisonment.

As Jimmy fled, the woman got to her feet and continued walking toward the hospital. Meanwhile, Jimmy threw up some of the whiskey and began to feel sorry about the attack. He decided that the only way he could make amends would be to help her. He caught up with her in front of a church whose front lawn was surrounded by a rough stone waft. Still drunk, he tried to tell her that he would help her to a hospital. The woman told him to leave her alone, but Jimmy was adamant about carrying her to the hospital. Although she was small and light, she struggled in his arms as he picked her up, and they fell to the sidewalk. The back of her head struck the stone wall.

Jimmy hauled her onto the church lawn beneath an oak tree. He tried unsuccessfully to have intercourse with her. That was all he could remember.

When the woman's body was discovered, an investigation led police to Jimmy within a few days. Held for several hours without food or a chance to consult with a parent or lawyer, he confessed that he was involved and told his story. When he first talked to me, he said that his mind had been a blank and that he couldn't vouch for the accuracy of what he had told police.

The case was a legal nightmare. If it were found that Jimmy had caused the woman's death—even unintentionally—in the commission of the robbery, then it was felony murder, which carried a penalty of life imprisonment or death. If the victim had died as a result of attempted rape, that too was felony murder—punishable by death only.

I believed that Jimmy Martin was guilty of robbery and attempted rape and that the woman's death was accidental. My belief was based on his own story and on the medical examiner's findings that the crushed skull was the cause of death and that the nature of the injury was consistent with the woman's having fallen against a stone wall. But I knew a jury might be too repelled by the facts of the case to draw such fine distinctions.

I arranged for Jimmy to be examined by psychiatrists, who found that he suffered from epilepsy and that the fits were triggered by alcohol. It was determined that he was not competent to stand trial, and in the fall of 1961 he was confined to the state prison hospital at Bridgewater.

Four years later, hospital authorities reported that he had shown unusual improvement and could be brought to court. The chess game began.

My first move was an attempt to persuade the district attorney to accept a manslaughter plea. I pointed out that changes in the law during the four years Jimmy was hospitalized probably would void his confession. Without the confession, there was little evidence linking him to the nurse's death. Furthermore, we had a strong case for insanity; some of the state's own psychiatrists were convinced that Jimmy had been unable to control his actions at the time of the incident. I didn't want Jimmy convicted of murder, but I didn't want him acquitted by reason of insanity and sent back to Bridgewater, which was more dungeon than hospital. On the other hand, I felt he needed supervision and continued medical help. He had already served four years toward a sentence. If he were allowed to plead guilty to manslaughter, he could be closely supervised during a long probationary period.

The district attorney felt that even without the confession he had enough to force me to defend on insanity grounds. In order to show insanity, I would have to admit Jimmy's complicity. No deal, he said. We would go all the way. I urged the trial judge to accept the manslaughter plea without the district attorney's consent, but he refused.

The trial opened in December, 1965. The judge was Frank J. Murray, an extremely able jurist who would subsequently be named to the U.S. District Court. The prosecutor was assistant district attorney Jack Mulhern, a former Boston College hockey star and a skilled lawyer.

Mulhern presented his case quickly and without fanfare. There was no nonsense; Judge Murray ran a tight court. "Gentlemen," he would say whenever Jack or I seemed puzzled by one of his rulings, "this is a courtroom, not a classroom. Proceed."

As expected, Jimmy's confession was excluded because it had been "extracted" from him under circumstances that showed it to be clearly involuntary. There were no eyewitnesses to the incident. One person had seen Jimmy near the woman, but no one had seen him kill her. When the state rested, it was obvious that its case was weak.

To show insanity, I would have to give the state's case a boost. I had no desire to put Jimmy Martin in the electric chair by proving what the state had been unable to show. On the other hand, the defense could rest without raising the insanity plea, but that might be equally dangerous. In an effort to create a third alternative, I approached Judge Murray in the lobby.

"How about a bifurcated trial in the California manner?" I asked him. "Let the jury decide if he's guilty, and if they convict him, we'll try the issue of sanity."

"I like the idea," the judge said. "And if this case were not capital I might do it. But that's not the law, and it seems to me a question for the Supreme Court, not me."

"We take no position, ladies and gentlemen," I said in my opening statement, "as to whether or not the defendant committed the crime. That's for you to decide. But if you find that he did do it, upon the evidence I am about to present you should also find that he was insane, and therefore not responsible for his act."

The opening left some of the jurors looking puzzled, and I couldn't blame them.

My problems became obvious when I called Dr. Robert Mezer to testify. He had been working with Jimmy since his arrest, and I was counting on him to show that Jimmy was mentally ill. But I had to be very careful. I couldn't ask him a question that would give Jack Mulhern a chance to drag in the confession on cross-examination.

"Doctor," I asked, "do you have an opinion as to whether or not, on June 26, 1961, the defendant was suffering from any disease or defect of the mind?"

Mezer was also taking it slow. "I have an opinion," he said.

"Please let us have it."

"Objection," said Mulhern.

"Sustained," said Judge Murray.

Mulhern and I approached the bench. "I think I'm entitled to that evidence," I said. "If permitted to answer, Dr. Mezer would say that on the day in question, Martin was suffering from schizophrenia and alcoholically triggered epilepsy, each of which is a mental disease and defect."

"No," said the judge. "I won't permit that question. If you wish to show a defense of insanity, you may ask the doctor to assume that Martin committed the crime and then inquire as to what his mental condition was, whether it affected his ability to know right from wrong, and so forth."

"The effect of that ruling is that in order to raise insanity, I have to admit guilt," I said.

"You may view the situation any way you choose," he said. "I have ruled."

I asked for a recess, and explained our dilemma to Jimmy. Which way did he want to go?

"That stuff's all over my head," he said. "Do whatever you think is best."

When court reconvened, I asked to see Judge Murray in his chambers with Mulhern and the stenographer. I had one more idea. "I would like to make a statement for the record, if your honor pleases," I began as we settled into our chairs, "after which the defense will rest."

Judge Murray looked at me sharply, but there was the hint of a smile in his eyes.

"The decision to rest the case at this time," I said, "is mine alone and not that of the defendant. In my judgment, his mental condition, youth, and lack of education are such that he cannot understand the avenues open to him and the attendant risks.

"It is my opinion that the state has failed to make out a case, and on the present state of the record the jury should not be allowed to convict on the principal offense. If I proceed to advance my insanity plea along the lines required by the court, I will in essence be proving the guilt of my client. Because I am an appointed lawyer I do not feel that I have the right to do this. Further, I object to a proceeding where the state can put in half a case, and force the rest of the proof out of a defendant who wishes to avail himself of a collateral defense."

The statement was as important as any I would make in open court, and I pushed a little harder. "In addition," I said, "I do not feel that there is now before this jury any evidence at all of rape-murder. A conviction of that crime would require that the defendant be executed. I will not subject him to that jeopardy. Experience has taught that operating within the archaic rules of our present insanity law, juries are apt to reject the insanity defense even where the medical evidence is overwhelming in support of it, especially where the crime is as grisly as this one. Our Supreme Court has sustained convictions where all the psychiatrists testified that the defendant was insane, and this despite the rule that the burden of proving sanity is on the prosecution, not the defendant. In view of all of these defects in our system, I am forced to rest at this point, I do not waive the defendant's right to his insane defense, and he does not. If he is convicted of murder in any degree, I will take the position that he is entitled to a new trial. As evidence that the defendant is not attempting to unconscionably escape punishment, I will state that our offer to plead guilty to manslaughter is still open."

What happened next was up to Judge Murray. He looked out the window for a few minutes, and then made his decision. "In the circumstances," he said, "I am satisfied that counsel's position is correct. We will split the trial. You gentlemen will give your arguments on the merits, and I will charge. If the defendant is convicted, we will not record the jury's verdict. We will litigate the issue of sanity, and resubmit the case, after further arguments and charge, on the sole issue of guilt or insanity."

My summation was brief. I emphasized the gaps in the state's evidence and the many areas for reasonable doubt. Jack was also brief; without the confession he had little evidence to discuss. The judge's charge was crisp and precise; there was no sense in trying to note errors for future objection.

The jury was ready with its verdict in just a few hours. "Guilty," said the foreman. "Guilty—of assault and battery." There would be no need for an insanity defense. And Jimmy had already served more time in jail than the charge carried.

The following day, I saw the judge at a local restaurant. He would pass sentence the next morning. He mentioned that he had heard very little of the psychiatric evidence. "I'm concerned about releasing this boy if he's still dangerous," he said. "The court will appreciate all the help you can give it in disposing of this case."

I felt the same way about Jimmy's release, and so did Jimmy. At the sentencing, I suggested a solution. "It is apparent," I said, "that the defendant has served more time in jail while awaiting trial, four and one half years, than he can be given for his conviction of assault and battery—three years. However, counsel has no desire to see him released to absolute freedom if he is not ready, or if he will be a threat to the community. The defendant agrees. Therefore, I submit affidavits setting forth what is known of his present mental condition and suggest that he be sent for further evaluation to a state mental hospital." I added that the proposal had Jimmy's consent.

Judge Murray read the affidavits and agreed. He committed Jimmy for thirty-five days' observation. At the end of that time, the hospital reported that his condition was relatively good. Jimmy was released, and has been in no trouble since.

Epilogue

Would I defend a guilty man? In a real sense, Jimmy Martin was guilty—if not of murder, then of something more than a simple assault and battery. In a technical sense, however, he may not have been guilty—there was ample evidence available to show he was not mentally responsible for whatever he did that day.

Was justice done? That question is personal and subjective, and each of you can answer it for yourself. But the question of whether he should have been defended in every possible way is not personal or subjective. It is professional and legal. And any lawyer worth his license would answer it the same way.

> *"I urge you to focus on the broader moral and ethical*
> *implications of your work."*

5.5 PROFESSIONALISM

Sandra Day O'Connor

Sandra Day O'Connor is an Associate Justice on
the Supreme Court of the United States.

It is a great pleasure to be here at Washington University to dedicate this magnificent new home for the law school. . . .

As lovely as it is, what I would like to talk to you about today is not your new building. I would like to discuss my granddaughter. You see, I recently returned from an extended period of grandmother-granddaughter bonding—sort of a cross-generational in-the-family version of Thelma and Louise—and she is often on my mind. At one point during the visit, my granddaughter came to me, disappointed about having to perform some task or another. It was pointless, she said. Well, she didn't actually say "pointless." Pointless, in the vocabulary of a young child, is replaced by two words: "But why?" Her meaning was clear nonetheless. Her second objection was that it was "no fun."

"Pointless and no fun," one of my friends quipped. "If those were legitimate objections, we wouldn't have anyone practicing law." The comment seemed funny at that moment, but in retrospect it seems disconcerting. Is that what the practice of law has become—pointless and no fun? It seems that, in the eyes of many lawyers, it has. More than half of all practitioners report dissatisfaction with the profession. According to one lawyer, the economic pressures of the legal marketplace have escalated workdays to a point where practice is "like drinking water from a fire hose." In this climate, attending to any professional obligations beyond billable hours seems impossible. Nor is dissatisfaction limited to those within the legal community. In society at large—that is among those we would call "non-lawyers"—lawyers are compared frequently, and unfavorably I might add, with skunks, snakes, and sharks. Few Americans recall the trust that our society once placed in its lawyers; it hardly seems possible that Alexis de Tocqueville, were he to come to America today, would conclude that lawyers are our nation's "natural aristocracy."

From 76 *Washington University Law Quarterly* 5 (1998).

Partially responsible for this decline, I suspect, is a decline in professionalism. Dean Roscoe Pound said that a profession is "a group . . . pursuing a learned art as a common calling in the spirit of public service—no less a public service because it may incidentally be a means of livelihood." And, while my granddaughter undoubtedly is a far more interesting subject, what I really want to talk about today—for a few minutes—are the obligations of professionalism: obligations in dealings with other attorneys; obligations toward legal institutions; and obligations to the public whose interests lawyers must serve. Personal relationships lie at the heart of the work that lawyers do. Even in the face of the vast technological advances of the information age, the human dimension remains constant, and these professional obligations will endure.

I

It has been said that a nation and its laws are an expression of the highest ideals of its people. Unfortunately, the conduct of our nation's lawyers has sometimes been an expression of the lowest. Clients increasingly view lawyers as mere vendors of services, and law firms perceive themselves as businesses in a competitive marketplace. As the number of lawyers in this country approaches one million, the legal profession has narrowed its focus to the bottom line, to winning cases at all costs, and to making larger amounts of money. Almost every complaint about the decline of ethics and civility "sounds the dirge of the profession turning into a trade." Practice at the turn of the century, we are told, "promises to be nasty, brutish and, for some, short."

One lawyer who recently stopped practicing law explained his decision to leave the profession in these bleak terms: "I was tired of the deceit. I was tired of the chicanery. But most of all, I was tired of the misery my job caused other people . . . Many attorneys believe that zealously representing their clients means pushing all rules of ethics and decency to the limit." This complaint is not unique. In a *National Law Journal* study, over fifty percent of the attorneys surveyed used the word "obnoxious" to describe their colleagues.

Indeed, sometimes attorney conduct crosses over from rude to downright scandalous. Two lawyers from prominent New York firms recently turned a deposition into an actual brawl. And attorneys have been spotted exchanging invectives and even engaging in shoving matches in front of various court clerks' offices, an image that recalls the description of modern-day litigation as ice hockey in business suits. A sitting federal judge, who may deserve a medal, became so exasperated with a pair of lawyers in a case before him that he wrote an order noting that both counsel had violated the local lawyers' creed of civil conduct. The order stated:

> This is an aspirational creed not subject to enforcement by this court, but violative conduct does call for judicial disapproval at least. If there is a hell to which disputatious, uncivil, vituperative lawyers go, let it be one in which the damned are eternally locked in discovery disputes with lawyers of equally repugnant attributes.

It is no wonder that one magazine has run an article entitled "Lawyers' Lot Not a Happy One."

Most of us probably never encounter such outrageous conduct. I would hope that it is not that often that lawyers encounter even ordinary discourtesy. But a Seventh Circuit study conducted in 1991 revealed that forty-two percent of lawyers, and forty-five percent of the judges, in that circuit think that civility is a profession-side problem. And the problem seems to be growing. In a 1996 survey of the D.C. Bar, sixty-nine percent of the lawyers polled identified civility as a problem. A recent survey of presidents of state and local bar associations produced an even more startling result: ninety percent of the respondents reported both problems with civility and diminished respect among lawyers in their jurisdictions. These statistics mean that lawyers far too often breach their professional obligations to other lawyers—that many lawyers are caught up in a system of behavior that is "structurally, morally, and emotionally exhausted." When the lawyers themselves generate conflict, rather than focusing on the dispute between the parties they represent, it distorts our adversarial system. More civility and greater professionalism can only enhance the pleasure lawyers find in practice, increase the effectiveness of our system of justice, and improve the public's perception of lawyers. We have lost sight of a fundamental attribute of our profession, one that Shakespeare described in *The Taming of the Shrew*. Adversaries in law, he wrote, "[s]trive mightily, but eat and drink as friends." In contemporary practice, however, we speak of our dealings with other lawyers as war—and too often we act accordingly.

But one need not envision litigation as war, argument as battle, or trial as siege. Argument, for example, can be thought of as discourse. I know that when I ask a question at oral argument, it is not meant as an attack; it is an invitation for counsel to address an area of particular concern to me. The most effective advocates respond accordingly, answering honestly and directly. Indeed, one good approach to oral advocacy is to pretend that each judge or justice really wants to vote your way—and will—but *only* if you can set the judge's concerns to rest by answering that question which the judge finds troubling.

Trial similarly can be envisioned as an investigation in which the jury must choose between competing versions of the facts. Ranting and raving in front of the jury probably does little to convince. A more persuasive technique is to present oneself as a reasonable person who wants to see justice done—it just so happens that justice is done by finding for your client, not opposing counsel's. All too often attorneys forget that the whisper can be more dramatic (and more compelling) than the scream. Justice Holmes, no slouch of an advocate, believed that "a lawyer [can] try [a] case like a gentleman"—or gentle woman, I would add—"without giving up any portion of his [or her] energy and force." Hemingway used the vernacular. "Guts," he told us, "is grace under pressure." Grace, however, is not a virtue many of today's lawyers choose to advertise, as underscored by one lawyer's characterization of his "marketing strategy": clients, he explained are "not looking for a guy who coaches Little League. They don't want a wimp. They want a lawyer who means business, an animal who's going to get the job done, whatever it takes." It is appalling that any member of our profession would describe himself in these terms. "Getting the job done" should go hand in hand with courtesy; a lawyer can "mean business" without remaking himself as an "animal."

The common objection to civility is that it will somehow diminish zealous advocacy for the client. I see it differently. In my view, incivility disserves the client because it wastes time and energy—time that is billed to the client at hundreds of dollars an hour, and energy that is better spent working on the case than working over the opponent. According to an English proverb, "[t]he robes of lawyers are lined with the obstinacy of clients." In our experience, the obstinacy of one lawyer lines the pockets of another; and the escalating fees are matched by escalating tensions. I suspect that, if opposing lawyers were to calculate for their clients how much they could save by foregoing what has been called "Rambo-style" litigation (in money and frustration), many clients, although not all, would pass in the pyrotechnics and happily pocket the difference. It is not always the case that the least contentious lawyer loses. It is enough for the ideas and positions of the parties to clash; the lawyers don't have to.

The bench and the bar have begun to address the issue of professionalism in lawyer-lawyer relations. Codes of ethics and professional conduct are good starting points and no doubt necessary. But they focus on what a lawyer should not do rather than teaching lawyers what they affirmatively ought to do. More recently, some jurisdictions have created so-called civility codes—unenforceable guidelines that articulate the basics of common courtesy. Unfortunately, civility is hard to codify or legislate. Discourtesy is notoriously subjective—you know it when you see it—and assessing blame is somewhat akin to asking a pair of fighting fourth-graders "who started it." More important, without a fundamental change in attorney conscience, even the best codification of civility can become, to extend the war metaphor still more, just another battleground. Lawyers simply take up the code of conduct and club each other with that, levying accusations of incivility and bringing motions for sanctions. One court has noted that complaints of this nature are "akin to static in a radio broadcast [that] tends to blot out legitimate argument."

In the end, it is by deed rather than by decree that attorneys teach each other that it is possible to "disagree without being disagreeable." The first place where young lawyers can learn to disagree agreeably is right here—in law school. Although there may be no remedy for the competitive nature of the law school experience, schools can do something about how that experience shapes a young lawyer's approach to practice. Good professors may employ the Socratic method, but not in the interest of disparaging students; rather, they should engage the students in a dialogue which, although sometimes painful, helps students explore the law and develop critical thinking skills. And outside of class, students can learn collegiality from an atmosphere in which each person is treated with respect and understanding. Of course, some schools are more successful in this respect than others [are]: I am sure the Washington University School of Law can stand tall.

Many law schools have moved beyond acculturation and have begun to meet the issue of professional conduct head-on. "Being a lawyer," one professor points out, involves handling the inherent tension among the demands "of a client, fulfilling one's own interests, being an officer of the court, and engaging in fair play towards third parties." Through its first-rate faculty, outstanding lawyering-skills program, and clinical opportunities, Washington University goes a long way toward preparing students for the tensions they will encounter in practice—and training them to respond professionally, but without sacrificing vigor or zeal. It is my hope that the bench and the bar, through example and further training, will reinforce that sense of professionalism, a sense that accrues to the benefit of all.

II

You may have noticed that although I have already spoken for a while, I have not yet met head-on my granddaughter's central question: "But why?" There is a common frustration in the legal community that all our long hours and hard work are not producing anything socially worthwhile. Indeed, there is an old joke to that effect. It involves two men on a balloon expedition who became hopelessly lost in a storm. When the storm cleared, they found themselves floating above a one-lane road, with nothing in sight but wheat fields. There was no one, absolutely no one, around. Finally, they spotted a woman walking down the road.

[Calling down] "Hey!" they called out. "W-h-e-r-e a-r-e w-e?"
To which the woman responded [calling up]:
"You're up in a balloon, about twenty-five feet off the ground."
"She's a lawyer," one man commented to the other.
"How do you know?" [his] companion asked.
"Well," he responded, "her answer was clear, precise, perfectly accurate and totally useless."

I think we can all agree that perfect accuracy in the interest of utter futility is not the highest calling of the profession; nor is it, in my opinion, the answer to why lawyers do what they do. In my view, "[b]oth the special privileges incident to membership in [our] profession and the advantage those privileges give [us] in the necessary task of earning a living are means to a goal that transcends the accumulation of wealth. *That* goal is public service." It is this aspect of professionalism—service to the public—that I want to touch upon last.

Lawyers have in their possession the keys to justice under a rule of law—the keys that open the courtroom door. Those keys are not held for lawyers' own private purposes; they are held in trust for all those who would seek justice, rich and poor alike. We can be proud of the strides the legal community has made toward fulfilling that trust. The bar has never before been involved in greater amounts and more diverse types of *pro bono* work. Never before have law schools contributed so greatly by providing opportunities for their students to represent and advise those who, but for the students, would have no access to legal advice or legal remedies. My law clerks tell me that those who participate remember their experiences long after they leave the law school; that in practice, they feel both an obligation and a desire to donate a portion of their time and learning to public service.

Yet, despite progress and innovations, a great and crying need for legal services for the poor remains. The most recent estimates suggest that as many as eighty-five percent of the poor's legal needs go unmet. And there is evidence—tragic costly evidence—that a substantial number of citizens believe that equality is but an unrealized slogan; that justice is for "just us"—the powerful, the educated, the privileged. If that perception is to be changed and the factors that created it eliminated, the legal community must dedicate an even greater portion of its time and resources to public service. The ever-increasing pressure on the billable hour, combined with the tremendous emphasis on the bottom line, has made fulfilling the obligation to public service quite difficult. But public service marks the difference between a business and a profession. A business can focus only on profits. A profession cannot. It must focus first on the community it is supposed to serve. And that community needs more legal help now than ever before.

The notion that lawyers have a responsibility to their community, and that they are uniquely capable of making a contribution, is nothing new. Lawyers were a critical group in the building of our own Constitution: at the Convention in 1787, thirty-three of the fifty-five participants were lawyers. And when it proved necessary to drastically revise that document after the Civil War, once again lawyers were the dominant force: at least nine of the fifteen drafters of the Fourteenth Amendment were lawyers. It was lawyers who helped express our society's highest ideals in law then. It is lawyers who now must ensure that those ideals are realized and realizable now—not just for the wealthy, but for the poor, for the disenfranchised, and for the disadvantaged.

Conclusion

I wanted to finish where I started—with my granddaughter. However, she has yet to produce a great quote about professionalism appropriate to this occasion. (Give her time—she's still young.) Accordingly, I will close instead with the words of John W. Davis, a former U.S. Solicitor General and (unsuccessful) candidate for president, who reminded the legal community of its sometimes humble but always professional role: "True, we build no bridges," he said. "We raise no towers. We construct no engines. We paint no pictures. There is little of all that we do which the [human] eye . . . can see. But we smooth out difficulties; we relieve stress; we correct mistakes; we take up other men and women's burdens and by our efforts we make possible the peaceful life of men and women in a peaceful state."

At the Court on which I sit, we do not render advisory opinions. But today, I make an exception and offer one specific piece of advice. As you begin to use this splendid new building, I urge you to focus on the broader moral and ethical implications of your work. You should make it the Law School's commitment to teach the importance of doing good while doing well.

PART THREE

Judicial Power

CHAPTER 6

Access to Judicial Power

As heirs to the common-law tradition, American judges cannot exercise their power until someone brings a case before them. Courts, Justice Robert H. Jackson once said, lack a self-starter. Judges can decide issues only when they come to court in accordance with the jurisdictional rules that the constitutional text or the legislature has prescribed. Yet even then, the judicial process does not automatically go into operation. Judges, especially justices of the U.S. Supreme Court, have long believed that overuse can cheapen the value of their decisions, and they refuse to decide a dispute simply because someone has money enough to hire a lawyer. The barriers judges impose on would-be litigants' access to courts are often stated in such technical language as "standing to sue"; and, to understand the judicial process, it is necessary to know something about these rules. One must, however, keep in mind that these technical devices are basically instruments of diplomacy, created by judges to conserve their own time and energy, avoid conflict with other public officials, and protect citizens against the legal system's inability to handle certain kinds of controversies.

Most of the restrictions governing "standing" date from the time when the typical litigants were those who went to court to promote or protect their own personal interests, usually their property. But lawsuits have increasingly been brought by individuals or groups who think of themselves as representing broad social, economic, or ideological interests. These newer litigants have pushed judges to rethink traditional rules of access to judicial power.

FORMAL BARRIERS TO ENTRY IN THE AMERICAN LEGAL SYSTEM

Given the attention that scholars and public officials alike shower on constitutional review (Chapter 2), it is easy to forget that judicial authority has substantial limits. In fact, Article III of the constitutional text—or at least the Supreme Court's interpretation of it—places four major constraints on the authority of federal tribunals to hear and decide questions, restrictions that, by and large, state judges have applied to themselves as well: The court must have authority to hear the case (jurisdiction); there must be a "case or controversy"; the case must be appropriate for judicial resolution (that is, it must be "justiciable'); and the appropriate party must be bringing the case (a potential litigant must have "standing to sue").

Jurisdiction

Jurisdiction refers to the authority of a court to hear and decide a case. In Civil-Law systems, only the legislature or the constitutional document can grant this authority. Under the common law, courts may obtain jurisdiction from a statute, the constitutional text, or from custom. As Chapter 2 explained about the United States, Article III, Section 2, of the constitutional text defines the outer limits of the jurisdiction of federal courts. Congress can authorize lower courts to hear disputes involving particular parties or subject matters. That Article divides the Supreme Court's jurisdiction into original and appellate: the former involves cases that begin in the Court; the latter, authority to review decisions of lower courts.

To what extent does jurisdiction actually constrain the federal courts? The answer, according to Chief Justice Salmon Portland Chase, is clear: "Without jurisdiction the court cannot proceed at all in any cause. Jurisdiction is power to declare the law, and when it ceases to exist, the only function remaining to the court is that of announcing the fact and dismissing the cause."[1] Chase was generally correct, but clever judges can sometimes find room in which to maneuver. *Marbury v. Madison* (Reading 2.2) provides an illustration of power that is constrained but not cabined. William Marbury had asked the Court, under its original jurisdiction, for a writ to compel the secretary of state to issue Marbury's commission as a justice of the peace. Chief Justice Marshall began his opinion with an explanation that Marbury was indeed entitled to receive his commission. By ordering the secretary not to deliver that commission, President Jefferson had violated Marbury's rights—a scathing indictment of the author of the Declaration of Independence. But, after offering this moral critique, Marshall said the Court could not issue the writ because Section 13 of the Judiciary Act of 1787 had expanded the Court's original jurisdiction, a deed that lay beyond Congress's authority. (As we saw in Chapter 3, this reading of Section 13 required considerable creativity.) Thus Marshall was able to blast Jefferson and, having done so, say the Court had no authority to decide what it had just decided. Because the justices had issued no writ and, technically, had ruled in Jefferson's favor, the president could only fume at his public humiliation, while the justices could smirk at their successful assertion of judicial review.

---

[1] *Ex parte McCardle* (1869). (See Reading 8.8.)

Marbury remains authoritative on original jurisdiction: Congress may not expand or contract it. The issue of appellate jurisdiction is more complex. Article III explicitly states that for "Federal questions," as Article III's list of disputes by parties and subject matter is called, over which the Court does not have original jurisdiction, it "shall have appellate Jurisdiction . . . with such Exceptions, and under such Regulations as the Congress shall make." The plain words of this "Exceptions Clause" authorize Congress to alter the Court's appellate jurisdiction.

Martin v. Hunter's Lessee (1816) and *Cohens v. Virginia* (1821) upheld congressional authority to interpret the Supreme Court's appellate jurisdiction to include federal questions that initially arose in state tribunals. And in *Ex parte McCardle* (1869) the justices ruled that the Exceptions Clause authorized Congress to remove the Court's appellate jurisdiction over a particular category of cases (Reading 8.8). Since *McCardle*, however, Congress has only considered, but not enacted, legislation—at least legislation aimed directly at the Supreme Court—to limit the Court's appellate jurisdiction. Many of these proposals have involved controversial issues (e.g., abortion, busing, and prayers in public schools), indicating that many legislators view the Exceptions Clause as a tool to "correct" the Supreme Court's constitutional interpretation. Nevertheless, Congress has not enacted such legislation in the contemporary era.

Despite *McCardle*, there are several reasons to believe that the Court might narrowly interpret the Exceptions Clause. First, *McCardle* was an odd case. The Court probably had no choice but to acquiesce if it wanted to continue to exist as a coequal branch of government. The justices were still living under the stigma of *Dred Scott* (1857) and, in *Ex parte Milligan* (1866), had held that Lincoln had acted unconstitutionally in imposing martial law during the Civil War, a broad and infuriating hint that the justices might well invalidate much of Reconstruction in the South. Thus the Radical Republicans who controlled both houses of Congress and were trying to remove Andrew Johnson from the White House were also angry at the justices. Indeed, one Radical had introduced a bill to abolish the existing Supreme Court and replace it with another institution. Thus some of the justices, most certainly Chief Justice Chase, thought it was necessary for the Court's survival that it placate Congress—a set of circumstances not likely to recur in such an extreme form.

Another reason to doubt the strength of *McCardle* as a precedent is that a few years later, when the constitutional crisis was subsiding, the Court shifted course. In *United States v. Klein* (1872), the justices considered a statute of 1870 that restricted the president's authority to issue amnesties. In particular, the law required those who wished to recover property seized by the Union government during the Civil War to prove their loyalty, even if they had received a presidential pardon. Moreover, the law withdrew the U.S. Supreme Court's (and a lower appellate court's) jurisdiction to hear challenges to the statute's constitutionality. Although the justices acknowledged that the Exceptions Clause authorized Congress to remove their appellate jurisdiction "in a particular class of cases," it could not do so only as "a means to an end." That is, in previous cases the Court had stated that the constitutional text meant what it said: the president had authority to pardon for offenses against the United States. Therefore, Congress was using the Exceptions Clause to limit presidential authority. If the Court allowed such evasion, it would permit Congress to "prescribe rules of decision to the Judicial Department . . . in cases pending before it," in violation of the constitutionally guaranteed integrity of the judiciary.

Still, *Klein* did not settle the issue. Compare, for example, the views of three twentieth-century justices. In 1948 Justice Felix Frankfurter wrote: "Congress need not give this Court any appellate power; it may withdraw appellate jurisdiction once conferred and it may do so even while a case is sub judice,"[2] that is, before a judge. Only a year later, retired Justice Owen J. Roberts supported a constitutional amendment that would have removed congressional authority to tamper with the Court's appellate jurisdiction.[3] But in 1962, Justice William O. Douglas remarked, "There is a serious question whether the McCardle case could command a majority view today."[4]

Whether the Court would bow to Congress's again using the Exceptions Clause will remain an open question until such litigation occurs. Until then, Chief Justice Chase perhaps summed up the situation best when he noted, after *McCardle* had been decided, that use of the Exceptions Clause was "unusual and hardly to be justified except upon some imperious public exigency."[5] Not all nations have been willing to take that chance. Several European constitutional texts written in the twentieth century contain "McCardle Clauses," which forbid the legislature to alter the jurisdiction of the highest court.

Case or Controversy

"The judicial Power," Article III says, shall extend to "Cases" and "Controversies." These are terms of art. A case or controversy exists only where there is a real, live, dispute between two parties, with adverse interests, about the nature and scope of a legally protected right. To put it in the converse, federal judges often say they will not issue advisory opinions or resolve suits that are collusive, unripe, moot, or raise political questions—no matter how important and interesting. (Most state judges follow a similar policy.)

Advisory Opinions

A few states, and some foreign countries (Canada, most notably) require judges of the highest court to advise the executive or legislature, when so requested, as

---

[2] *National Mutual Insurance Co. v. Tidewater Transfer Co.* (1949).

[3] Owen J. Roberts, "Now Is the Time: Fortifying the Supreme Court's Independence," 35 *American Bar Association Journal* 1 (1949). The Senate approved the amendment in 1953, but the House tabled it.

[4] *Glidden Co. v. Zdanok* (1962).

[5] *Ex parte Yerger* (1869).

to their views on the constitutionality of a proposed policy. Since the time of Chief Justice John Jay, however, federal judges have claimed that the absence of a case or a controversy prevents them from performing that service (Reading 6.1). Nevertheless, on occasion judges have found ways of offering advice. For example, they have sometimes offered political leaders informal suggestions in private conversations or correspondence.[6]

Furthermore, justices of the Supreme Court have often given advice in an institutional but indirect manner. The Judiciary Act of 1925, which granted the Court wide discretion in controlling its docket, was largely drafted by Justice Willis van Devanter; and Chief Justice William Howard Taft and several associate justices openly lobbied for its passage, "patrolling the halls of Congress," as Taft put it. In 1937 when the Senate was considering Roosevelt's Court-packing plan, opponents arranged for Chief Justice Charles Evans Hughes to send a letter to Senator Burton K. Wheeler, advising not only that increasing the number of justices would impede rather than facilitate the Court's work but also that the justices' sitting in separate panels to hear cases—a procedure that increasing the number of justices was supposed to allow—would probably violate the constitutional command that there be "one Supreme Court." Like recent chief justices, William H. Rehnquist has sent an annual State of the Judiciary Address, explaining to Congress not only what kind of legislation he deems good for the courts but also the likely effect of proposed legislation on the federal judicial system.

Finally, judges have occasionally used their opinions to provide advice to other decision makers. In *Regents of the University of California v. Bakke* (1978), for instance, the Court held that a state medical school's version of affirmative action had deprived a white applicant of equal protection of the laws by rejecting him in favor of minority applicants whom the school ranked lower on all the relevant academic criteria. But, in a concurring opinion, Justice Lewis Powell volunteered the advice that the kind of affirmative action program Harvard offered would be constitutionally acceptable.

Collusion

Another corollary of the requirement of a case is a refusal to hear collusive disputes, that is, disputes in which the litigants (1) want the same outcome, (2) evince no real adverse interests, or (3) are merely testing a law that does not pose an immediate danger to their legal rights. Indeed, Chief Justice Roger Brooke Taney once said that collusion is "contempt of the court, and highly reprehensible."[7] *Muskrat v. United States* (1911) is the leading case on point. Congress had passed a statute authorizing Cherokee Indians to contest the

---

[6] For early instances, see Stewart Jay, Most *Humble Servants: The Advisory Role of Early Judges* (New Haven, CT: Yale University Press, 1997); for later: William Cibes, "Extra-Judicial Activities of Justices of the United States Supreme Court, 1790–1960," unpublished Ph.D. diss., Princeton University, 1975.

[7] *Lord v. Veazie* (1850).

validity of earlier legislation restricting their rights to certain lands. The Supreme Court, however, ruled that no actual controversy existed; for, although both parties had real interests, there was no live disagreement between them, only an effort by both parties to obtain a judicial ruling on the constitutionality of earlier regulations.

The justices, however, had not and have not always meticulously followed *Muskrat's* dogma. In fact, many important decisions have come about as a result of collusive suits. Consider *Pollock v. Farmers' Loan and Trust Co.* (1895), in which the Court struck down a federal income tax. The litigants, a bank and a stockholder in the bank, both wanted the same outcome—the death of the tax. Or *Carter v. Carter Coal Co.* (1936), in which the Court struck down as unconstitutional a major piece of New Deal legislation. The litigants were a company president and the company, which included the president's father; both parties wanted to eradicate the statute.

Why did the justices resolve these disputes? "The Court's decision to hear or dismiss such a test case," one pair of analysts claim, "usually turns on whether it presents an actual conflict of legal rights susceptible to judicial resolution."[8] In other words, the Court might overlook some element of collusion if the suit itself presents a real controversy or the potential for one. Other scholars are more skeptical. The temptation to set "good" public policy (or strike down "bad" public policy) is sometimes too strong for the justices to follow rules they themselves have made.

Ripeness and Mootness

If a lawsuit challenges governmental action, that action must be sufficiently final to be "ripe" for review by federal courts. This rule forms the basis for the doctrine of "exhaustion of administrative remedies," which requires that persons aggrieved by administrative decisions must have used all the procedures available for correcting the action, as allowed by the agency itself, before they have standing to be heard in court. For instance, if the Department of the Interior increases the fees it charges ranchers to have their cattle graze on national land, the ranchers cannot go to court to contest the increase until they have used whatever methods of appeal the Department itself provides.

The doctrine of "ripeness" also bars access to court until the threat of adverse governmental action is immediate and highly probable, if not absolutely certain, as the experience of civil service workers in *United Public Workers v. Mitchell* (1947) demonstrates. They challenged the Hatch Act, which prohibits some types of federal employees from participating in political campaigns. But only one of the workers had actually violated the Act; the rest had simply expressed an interest in working in campaigns. According to the justices, only the employee who had violated the statute had a ripe claim because "the power of

---

[8] Joan Biskupic and Elder Witt, *Guide to the U.S. Supreme Court*, 3rd ed. (Washington, DC: Congressional Quarterly, 1997), 300.

courts, and ultimately of this Court to pass upon the constitutionality of acts of Congress arises only when the interests of the litigants require the use of this judicial authority for their protection against actual interference. A hypothetical threat is not enough. We can only speculate as to the kinds of political activity the [other] appellants desire to engage in. . . ."

Conversely, events might have proceeded since the filing of the suit to a point where judicial action is no longer needed or cannot provide the relief requested. In these situations the case may be dismissed as "moot." Judges occasionally resort to such holdings to avoid difficult decisions. Thus in *DeFunis v. Odegaard* (1974) a white applicant to a state law school, who had been rejected for admission, showed that less-qualified minority applicants had been accepted under an affirmative action program, and the trial judge ordered his admission. The university appealed. By the time the case reached the Supreme Court, DeFunis was in his third year of law school; and the university had guaranteed his graduation. By a five-to-four vote the justices held the proceeding moot, though recognizing that the same issue would arise in subsequent suits (Reading 6.2) as, in fact, it soon did in *Bakke*.

Of course, given backlogs, strict application of the mootness doctrine would prevent many cases from ever being decided by any federal court. In *Dunn v. Blumstein* (1972), for instance, a new resident of Tennessee challenged the law requiring one year's residence in the state as a qualification for voting. By the time the case reached the Supreme Court, Dunn had lived in the state for two years; but the Court did not regard his suit as moot for that reason. In *Roe v. Wade* (1973), one of the original decisions invalidating state laws regulating abortion, Roe said she was pregnant and wanted an abortion. She argued that she had a constitutional right to an abortion, but Texas law prevented her from exercising that right. The Court decided the case thirty-two months later, a somewhat longer time than most pregnancies last. (Years later she admitted to having had an abortion before filing the suit.) The majority of the justices, however, held that "pregnancy provides a classic justification for a conclusion of nonmootness" (Reading 6.2).

Political Questions and Justiciability

Earlier we said that federal judges insist that they will decide only issues that are "justiciable," that is, appropriate for judicial resolution. At a general level of abstraction, the underlying concept is clear: courts decide certain kinds of questions, Congress and the president decide others. At a more specific level, justiciability becomes a very slippery concept, based on several sets of judgments. First are those about problems of what constitutes a legally protected right, whether that right is personal to an individual litigant or shared by the public generally, whether apparently clashing interests are truly in conflict, and whether a dispute is ripe for judicial action. Second, justiciability also requires a practical judgment about whether the questions litigants present are more properly decided by Congress and/or the president.

To address this second problem of practical judgment, the justices have invented the doctrine of "political questions," essentially the flip side of justiciability. Questions that are justiciable are not political, whereas questions that are not justiciable may be political. One commentator has likened the Court's use of these two terms to an eighteenth-century dictionary's defining a violin as a small cello and a cello as a large violin.[9] And surely the justices can be sharply criticized for their inability to give a crystalline explanation of whatever principle underlies the distinction; but perhaps the basic reason lies in the human difficulties James Madison described in *Federalist* No. 37 as creating imprecision in constitutional language: "indistinctness of the object, imperfections of the organ of conception, inadequateness of the vehicle of ideas. Any one of these must produce a certain degree of obscurity." Still, it is likely that the justices have on occasion used the vagueness of the doctrine of political questions to avoid issues they thought might get them into political trouble.

When the Supreme Court has applied this doctrine, its explanation has typically been that the issue was one whose settlement the Constitution had entrusted to another branch of the government, that the problem lies in a field where judges have no special competence, or that as a practical matter the issue is one with which the judicial process cannot cope. The Court made its first explicit application of political questions in *Luther v. Borden* (1849), a case arising out of efforts in 1841 to reform the government of Rhode Island. At that time, the state had been operating largely under a royal charter of 1663. Led by Thomas Dorr, liberal elements had joined in a rebellion, and for a time two rival state governments coexisted, although not always peacefully. Luther originated as a suit by a private citizen against an official of the charter government for trespassing on his property. In his defense, the official claimed that he was executing a command of the lawful state government.

A judicial decision would have hinged on the question of which government was legitimate; but the Supreme Court refused to stir up the embers of this controversy, which, as a practical matter, had been settled by the time the case reached Washington. Congress had already seated representatives elected under authority of the charter government, and the president had likewise recognized it as the legal government. These decisions, Chief Justice Roger Brooke Taney held, were within the constitutional power of Congress and the president and beyond the competence of judges to review.

For similar reasons the justices have held that the president and Congress have exclusive authority to decide whether a constitutional amendment has been properly ratified or whether the use of the referendum and recall destroyed the republican status of a state government. In *Colegrove v. Green* (1946), a plurality of the Court used the doctrine of political questions to justify a refusal to consider whether gross disparities in population among congressional districts in Illinois violated the Constitution. In *Baker v. Carr* (1962), however, the Court reconsidered *Colegrove*, and in the process Justice William J. Brennan, Jr.,

---

[9] John P. Roche, "Judicial Self-Restraint," 49 *American Political Science Review* 762 (1955).

developed a more restricted definition of political questions. He held for the majority that the doctrine amounted to nothing more than a general self-imposed obligation on the Court to show appropriate deference to the president and Congress[10] (Reading 6.3).

Judicial deference has tended to be the rule in the field of foreign affairs, where judges have generally disclaimed any competence and emphasized that the other branches of government have plenary authority. The Supreme Court has labeled as political rather than justiciable issues those questions involving recognition of foreign governments, the authority of foreign diplomats, the validity of treaties, and the beginning and ending of wars. Likewise, persistent efforts to get the Supreme Court to rule on the constitutionality of American military operations in Vietnam were uniformly unsuccessful.[11] The Court, however, has not been hesitant to enter the fray when war-related litigation implicated judicial power. In *Hamdi v. Rumsfeld* (2004), it ruled that those labeled "enemy combatants" by the Bush administration are entitled to challenge their detention before a federal judge or other "neutral decision maker." "A state of war," the Court wrote, is not a blank check for the president."

Standing

In addition, plaintiffs must show that the interests they are asserting are legally protected. Traditionally, to acquire the status of a legal right, a claim had to be grounded in a specific statutory or a constitutional provision or, more generally, to involve one of those property or "pocketbook" interests that the common law recognized as deserving judicial protection. But even more than a legally protected right must be at stake. To gain "standing," plaintiffs must also establish that the right asserted is personal, not one belonging to other parties or the public at large—with the latter being quite a tricky issue, for, one might cogently argue, all citizens have an interest in government's acting properly. Many state

---

[10] More recently, in 1993 *Nixon v. United States* relied heavily on *Baker* to examine another domestic issue. The House had impeached and the Senate had removed Judge Walter L. Nixon, Jr.; but he went to the Supreme Court, claiming that, by allowing a committee rather than the full Senate to hear the evidence, that body had used unconstitutional procedures. The Court, however, ruled that the procedures used by Congress to handle impeachments are not subject to judicial review. The constitutional text grants the Senate the sole power to try all impeachments, and how the Senate organizes itself to discharge that duty constitutes a political question.

Despite the ruling in *Nixon*, some scholars continue to believe that the Court has weakened the political questions doctrine over the last four decades. By way of proof, they point to *Bush v. Gore* (2000), in which the justices effectively decided the outcome of the presidential election of 2000 and suggest that the Court should have dismissed it as raising a political question. To these observers, *Bush* is merely the last in a line of cases beginning with *Baker* that signaled a "weakening of the traditional 'political questions doctrine' and the expanded application of the equal protection clause to voting rights and democratic process."

[11] See, e.g., *Katz v. Tyler* (1967), *Mora v. McNamara* (1967), and *Massachusetts v. Laird*. The Supreme Court denied certiorari in these and other similar cases, although Justice Douglas (occasionally joined by other colleagues) thought the challenges should be heard.

courts allow an exception to this requirement of a personal injury, in the form of a "taxpayer's suit," a favorite method for initiating litigation to test state or local expenditures, bond issues, or special assessments. As the title implies, the only requirement is that of being a taxpayer in the jurisdiction involved.

Frothingham v. Mellon (1923), however, held that federal courts could not hear such suits. This bar was rigidly maintained until 1968 when *Flast v. Cohen* relaxed the rule by permitting suits to test whether congressional grants benefiting parochial schools amounted to an establishment of religion in violation of the First Amendment. *Flast* symbolized what was at that time a general trend toward lowering barriers to access to federal courts. Twenty-two years earlier, Congress had passed the Administrative Procedure Act of 1946, which, among other things, provided that any person "suffering legal wrong because of agency action, or adversely affected or aggrieved within the meaning of a relevant statute, is entitled to judicial review thereof." Congress had been reacting to pressure from the American Bar Association and business organizations concerned about regulation by federal administrative agencies; but other groups have been able to use this statute. *Association of Data Processing Service Organizations v. Camp* (1970) gave this provision a broad interpretation by specifically rejecting the old standing test of a "recognized legal interest."

But the days of easing standing requirements soon came to an end. During the last three decades, a majority of the justices have been bent on restoring strict standing requirements and, thus, limiting access to federal courts.[12] For example, they have rather narrowly read *Flast*, virtually restricting its reach to precisely the kind of suit at issue there—a challenge to use of federal funds allegedly in violation of the First Amendment's ban against establishment of religion.

Standing and Organized Interests

By the same token, the justices have made it increasingly difficult for interest groups to bring suit. Because we have more to say about organizations later in this chapter, we note here only that the problem of standing is likely to present special problems for groups that wish to use courts to achieve public policies. One reason is that, like individuals, organizations seeking to litigate public issues must demonstrate a legally protected interest and a right not shared with the public generally. This problem has been particularly difficult for conservationists and ecologists fighting environmental damage. Judges had often recognized that organizations such as the Sierra Club had standing to sue; but in one important case, *Sierra Club v. Morton* (1972), the Supreme Court ruled that the Club had failed to allege that its members would be affected by a proposed ski resort in a national forest. Consequently the Club lacked standing to protest the development under the Administrative Procedure Act. Justice William O. Douglas, dissenting, proposed that a river should be given standing as a plaintiff to speak

---

[12] For more on the current Court's inclination to limit access, see our discussion of sovereign immunity in Chapter 4 and of habeas corpus in Chapters 4 and 7.

for "the ecological unit of life that is part of it." More recently, *Lujan v. Defenders of Wildlife* (1992) held that members of an environmental group lacked standing to challenge the Interior Department's reinterpretation of the Endangered Species Act of 1973, under which it would no longer apply the law to federally financed projects overseas. The environmentalists had failed to show, a majority of the justices held, how Interior's new policy threatened them with "imminent" injury.

Although environmentalists, buttressed by strong federal legislation, have been fairly successful in overcoming this barrier and gaining access to the courts, many interest groups have been unable to meet the tightened standing requirements. Ad hoc citizens' organizations protesting alleged governmental abuses have often failed to obtain a judicial hearing because they could not show they suffered more harm or had a greater interest than did the general public. Thus in *Laird v. Tatum* (1972) the Court refused to hear a complaint against military surveillance of private citizens who were opposed to the war in Vietnam; *United States v. Richardson* (1974) denied standing to a group seeking to compel publication of the CIA's budget. To no avail, the group invoked the plain words of Article I, Section 9 of the constitutional text: "No Money shall be drawn from the Treasury, but in Consequence of Appropriations made by Law; and a regular Statement and Account of the Receipts and Expenditures of all public Money shall be published from time to time." *Schlesinger v. Reservists Committee to Stop the War* (1974) rejected a suit asking the courts to declare it unconstitutional for members of Congress to hold commissions in the armed forces's reserves, commissions that usually earned them money and, when on active duty, subjected them to military orders. In vain, plaintiffs cited the plain words of Article I, Section 6: "no Person holding any Office under the United States, shall be a Member of either House during his Continuance in Office."

Warth v. Seldin, decided by the Burger Court in 1975, further narrowed access to federal courts by holding that African Americans, Puerto Ricans, and poor people who were not residents of the town in which they worked lacked standing to challenge that town's zoning laws. Plaintiffs had argued that the zoning regulations effectively excluded them from living in the town because the regulations banned low-cost housing. By a five-to-four vote the Supreme Court denied that plaintiffs had suffered "injury in fact" because they could not point to any particular low-cost housing project that would actually have been built but for the town's ordinances.

Continuing this trend, the Court denied standing in two suits challenging the Internal Revenue Service's practices regarding tax exemptions. In *Simon v. Eastern Kentucky Welfare Rights Organization* (1975) an organization of low-income individuals, too poor to afford hospital services, had challenged tax exemptions granted to certain private hospitals. In *Allen v. Wright* (1984) African American parents of children attending public schools in seven states brought a class-action suit (that is, a suit in which one or a few litigants sue for themselves and "all others similarly situated"), asking for more rigorous enforcement of federal rules denying tax exemption to racially discriminatory private schools. The injury alleged was that black children were unable to attend fully desegregated public schools because large numbers of white children went to private schools that did not admit minority children and could, because of their tax-exempt status, charge lower tuition than would otherwise be possible. In a five-to-three ruling, the Court held this injury only to be "abstract" though "stigmatic"; recognition of standing in such circumstances, Justice Sandra Day O'Connor said, would transform the courts into "no more than a vehicle for the vindication of the value interests of concerned bystanders."

Even when groups advance First Amendment claims of the sort raised in *Flast*, there is no guarantee that the Court will resolve them. *Valley Forge Christian College v. Americans United* (1982) denied standing to a nonprofit organization, dedicated to the maintenance of the separation between church and state, to attack the transfer of an outmoded armed forces hospital to a religious educational institution. Rehnquist rehearsed at length all the virtues of strict adherence to rules regarding cases or controversies and to a showing of an "actual injury" redressable by the courts. William J. Brennan, Jr., dissenting, protested the Court's failure to honor *Flast* and sharply criticized use of "standing to slam the courthouse door against plaintiffs who are entitled to full consideration of their claims on the merits."

Formal Barriers to Access as Gatekeeping Devices

What Justice Brennan's dissent in *Valley Forge* suggested is that standing is a pliable constraint on judicial power. Various opinions filed in *Raines v. Byrd* (1997) make the same point with even greater force. Substantively, Raines involved the Line Item Veto Act of 1996, which gave the president authority to cancel certain tax and spending benefits after signing them into law. As a threshold matter, however, the justices decided that the six members of Congress who brought the suit did not have standing to challenge the law. Writing for the majority, Chief Justice William H. Rehnquist concluded: "these individual members of Congress do not have a sufficient 'personal stake' in this dispute and have not alleged a sufficiently concrete injury to have established Article III standing." In a dissenting opinion, Justice John Paul Stevens disagreed:

> The Line Item Veto Act purports to establish a procedure for the creation of laws that are truncated versions of bills that have been passed by the Congress and presented to the President for signature. If the procedure were valid, it would deny every Senator and every Representative any opportunity to vote for or against the truncated measure that survives the exercise of the President's cancellation authority. Because the opportunity to cast such votes is a right guaranteed by the text of the Constitution, I think it clear that the persons who are deprived of that right by the Act have standing to challenge its constitutionality.

The very fact that different justices could reach such different conclusions serves only to underscore the notion that standing is a much more amorphous concept than judges pretend. Some critics are less kind, asserting that judges approach questions of standing in ways that reflect their ideologies. For example, federal trial judges who seem to be right-of-center on the political spectrum are much less likely to believe that "underdogs"—including labor unions, employees, minority group members—have met the standing requirement than they are to believe that business corporations have.[13]

Allegations of a somewhat different nature have been leveled at judicial interpretations of other barriers to access, such as jurisdiction and justiciability. Donald Horowitz concludes that "the old prohibition on the decision of moot cases is now so riddled with exceptions that it is almost a matter of discretion whether to hear a moot case."[14] *DeFunis* and *Roe v. Wade* neatly illustrate the point (Reading 6.2). Ideology need not have been the determining factor. Having decided *Roe* in 1973 and ignited an explosion of controversy, the justices may have thought it imprudent to immediately wade into another battle.

INFORMAL BARRIERS TO ENTRY

Some scholars suggest that flexible use of barriers to access as discretionary gatekeeping devices reveals certain "passive virtues,"[15] for surely judges cannot function as the nation's omniscient problem solvers, nor, in a constitutional democracy, should they try to do so. Debate over this issue reaches beyond questions about the judiciary's proper roles to the nature of the American political system. One fact, however, remains undisputed: although Article III of the constitutional text places certain limits on the power of the federal judiciary, its language is sufficiently vague to allow judges a good deal of latitude.

However much discretion judges have to shut out (or let in) litigants, it is important to know that the formal barriers they may impose are not the only ones that citizens who wish to access the American legal system might confront. Others are more informal in nature. Money, for example, is often a barrier. Even if a potential litigant believes that she has a legitimate grievance, say, against an employer, a doctor, or a spouse, financial considerations may prevent her from transforming that "grievance" into a lawsuit.[16] Given the costs of hiring an attorney, paying filing fees, taking time off from a job, and so on, she may calculate that accessing the legal system is not financially feasible. These costs partially explain why only one out of thirty people who believe they have been

---

[13] See C. K. Rowland and Bridgett Todd, "Where You Stand Depends on Who Sits: Platform Promises and Judicial Gatekeeping in the Federal District Courts," 53 *Journal of Politics* 175 (1991); see also Nancy Staudt, "Modeling Standing." 79 *New York University Law Review* 612 (2004).

[14] Donald Horowitz, *The Courts and Social Policy* (Washington, DC: Brookings Institution, 1977), 8.

[15] Alexander M. Bickel, *The Least Dangerous Branch of Government* (Indianapolis: Bobbs-Merrill, 1962); see also Bickel's "Forward: The Passive Virtues," 75 *Harvard Law Review* 40 (1961) and the response by Gerald Gunther: "The Subtle Vices of the Passive Virtues—A Comment on Principle and Expediency in Judicial Review," 64 *Columbia Law Review* 1 (1964). For a revisit to the issues here, see Cass R. Sunstein, *One Case at a Time: Judicial Minimalism on the Supreme Court* (Cambridge, MA: Harvard University Press, 1999).

[16] For more on the process through which grievances transform into legal claims, see William L. Felstiner, Richard L. Abel, and Austin Sarat, "The Emergence and Transformation of Disputes: Naming, Blaming, Claiming . . . ," 15 *Law and Society Review* 631–654 (1980–1981).

the victims of discrimination even bother to hire an attorney and only 1 in 100 file a claim in court.[17]

Even if our potential litigant decides to initiate a claim, other obstacles could stand in the way of a trial. Whether to ensure the collection of their fees, to avoid a trial they believe they cannot win, or for any number of other reasons, attorneys might advise their clients to settle out of court (see Reading 5.2). And, even if their lawyers do not provide such advice, litigants might receive it from judges. Indeed, many judges—especially those already overburdened with cases—actively encourage parties to settle their disputes before trial.

Moreover, encouragement to settle need not come directly from inside the legal system. Although it is probably true that most Americans regard courts and judges as the usual instruments for resolving conflicts, a panoply of alternative modes is readily available. Direct negotiation, bargaining, mediation, and even violence still abound in almost every industrial nation. Police, social workers, and parole officers are only three of the many kinds of officials who spend a large share of their time acting as informal mediators among neighbors and relatives, quieting disputes before they produce grist for judicial mills. Modern societies also use elections and referenda to help settle conflict, not only about who will govern but also about what public policies will prevail. Statutes may provide for compulsory arbitration in labor disputes or labor and management may include such provisions in their contract.

With the possible exception of this last form of conflict resolution, mandatory arbitration, these are not necessarily formal barriers to access. But they do serve as alternative mechanisms to litigation and, thus, as ways to reduce the workload of courts. Whether or not they are always preferable to judgment by a court remains an open question, with at least some scholars suggesting—in response to movements aimed at reducing litigation even further by pushing alternative methods of dispute resolution—that out-of-court settlement should not be "institutionalized on a wholesale and indiscriminate basis."[18]

ACCESSING THE LEGAL SYSTEM: WHO USES THE COURTS?

Despite the existence of alternatives to litigation and of various barriers to the courts, each year millions of Americans obtain access to the judiciary, some of them unwillingly and unhappily. People charged with violating criminal laws or sued for allegedly treading on another's rights may have no choice but to appear before a judge. Others go to court to promote their own personal or

---

[17] See Richard E. Miller and Austin Sarat, "Grievances, Claims, and Disputes: Assessing the Adversary Culture," 15 *Law and Society Review* 544 (1980–1981); Herbert M. Kritzer, Neil Vidmar, and W. A. Bogart, "To Confront or Not to Confront: Measuring Claiming Rates in Discrimination Grievances," 25 *Law and Society Review* 883 (1991).

[18] See, e.g., Owen Fiss, "Against Settlement," 93 *Yale Law Journal* 1073 (1984).

proprietary interests. For the most part, they are what Marc Galanter calls "one-shotters," claimants who "have only occasional recourse to the court" and may suffer disadvantages because of their relative inexperience and lack of resources (Reading 6.4).

Finally, the broad scope of judicial power and its potential for affecting public policy have made it inevitable that organized interest groups would seek judicial support for their broader societal or ideological goals by bringing what are really public actions. Lawsuits have been especially attractive instruments for groups whose small size, lack of prestige, and limited cash curtail their influence in electoral processes. Although their supply of the usual political weapons might be short, these groups sometimes have moral, statutory, or constitutional claims that can be persuasive to judges. Racial desegregation, legislative reapportionment, limitations on capital punishment, prison reform, and protection of illegitimate children against legal discrimination stand out among dozens of examples.

Of course, groups of all types, including those representing more "advantaged" elements of society, have used courts for their goals. During the New Deal, the Liberty League and other business organizations supported hundreds of lawsuits against federal regulation of the economy. Other sorts of interest groups, seeking different goals, soon mimicked the Liberty League's strategy. The basic reason is clear: Judges are important policy makers; therefore, groups who wish to shape public policy—or prevent others from shaping policy—find it necessary to influence judges' choices of issues to address as well as solutions they will apply to problems of law and policy. In response, other groups are likely to deem it expedient to defend their interests in court by filing their own suits or participating as amici curiae in ongoing litigation. When the Supreme Court agreed to hear *Lawrence v. Texas* (2003), opposing coveys of interest groups swarmed into the battle. The case posed the constitutional question whether a state could criminalize adult, consensual sex between people of the same gender. Supporters of Lawrence and of the state nearly matched constituency for constituency. The Alliance of Baptists backed Lawrence, and the orthodox Jewish group, Agudath, supported the state; the NOW Legal Defense and Education Fund filed a brief for Lawrence; Concerned Women for America filed for the state; several professors of history wrote in support of Lawrence; and the Center for the Original Intent of the Constitution backed the state.

Groups also go to the Court to publicize themselves and their causes. The NAACP's Legal Defense Fund's (LDF) legendary campaigns to end racial discrimination provide an excellent example.[19] The NAACP's resort to the courts

---

[19] In 1939, the NAACP created the NAACP Legal Defense and Educational Fund to provide a full-time civil rights litigation staff and to enable donors to make tax-deductible contributions. About twenty years later, in 1957, the two formally separated. For more information on the split, see Stephen L. Wasby, *Race Relations Litigation in an Age of Complexity* (Charlottesville: University Press of Virginia, 1995), 61–63.   For the standard study of the LDF's strategy, see Clement E. Vose, *Caucasians Only: The Supreme Court, the NAACP, and the Restrictive Covenant Cases* (Berkeley: University of California Press, 1959).

produced not only favorable policy decisions regarding fair trials for blacks, voting rights, and desegregation in schools, trains, buses, and other public facilities but also established the LDF as the foremost organizational litigant on these issues. Indeed, one southern senator lamented that the LDF's chief, Thurgood Marshall, was mesmerizing the justices of the Supreme Court, an allegation that did nothing to diminish Marshall's reputation or that of the LDF.

The Strategies of Interest Groups

The first questions that leaders of an interest group confront are whether to use the courts at all and, if that answer is affirmative, when, how, and for what purposes. The answers depend on a mélange of factors, including: a group's numerical strength and that of its potential allies, its (and their) financial resources, its ease of access to other governmental agencies, the specific policies it seeks to pursue, what opposing groups are doing, what this group's leaders believe leaders of other groups will do in response to or anticipation of its actions, and, not least of all, the likely attitudes of judges toward the group's arguments and interests.

In the 1950s, for example, it made great sense for the NAACP to try to end segregation through the courts. Southern state legislators were uniformly and vehemently hostile to racial equality. Congress was divided; and, though civil rights legislation might have passed the House, it would have been filibustered to death in the Senate. Moreover, in the Deep South, where the major battles would have to be fought, most African Americans could not vote, so their chances of electing more sympathetic legislators were nonexistent. The justices of the Supreme Court, however, were quite receptive to arguments about the meaning of equal protection of the laws; they would not be looking over their shoulders counting votes at the next election; and the NAACP had in place a staff of superb attorneys.

For their part, white supremacists saw little point in using the courts as instruments to advance their policies, although they could—and did—use state judges to harass the NAACP. The supremacists' best avenues of attack lay through state legislatures and governors. Nevertheless, supremacists had to show up in courtrooms to try to repel the Legal Defense Fund's attacks. Their judicial strategy was to protect the status quo through delaying actions: defend against the NAACP's attacks in court; if defeated, as they usually were, appeal; if they lost again, persuade legislatures to enact new laws; then defend, lose, appeal, lose, and again retreat to state capitols for new legislation. Meanwhile, the supremacists would persuade state legislators to pass laws that aimed at outlawing the NAACP, forcing the organization onto the defensive. The strategy was to wear the NAACP out, to force its attorneys, as one white Southern leader said, "to litigate by day and to litigate by night." The hope was that eventually the NAACP would become physically exhausted and financially bankrupt, and "Nigras" would return to their "proper" places as servants and menial workers.

But the NAACP's attorneys found the strength to continue, the organization did not go bankrupt, and blacks were not about to resubmit to white supremacy. Furthermore, the effects of the NAACP's victories in the courts, especially in *Brown v. Board of Education* (1954), rippled far beyond the judicial arena.[20] Knowledge that segregation was not merely unjust but also unconstitutional spawned new leaders such as Reverend Martin Luther King, Jr., who thought that the time was ripe to exploit electoral as well as judicial processes. Sit-ins, freedom marches, and campaigns to register black voters triggered bitter and often violent resistance. Nightly TV newscasts of state police using attack dogs, fire hoses, and billy clubs against American citizens, both black and white, who dared ask for respect for their constitutional rights generated massive national energy for new legislation. The civil rights hymn "We Shall Overcome" became President Lyndon Johnson's battle cry. Moderate and even conservative Republican lawmakers abandoned their erstwhile Southern Democratic allies and joined with liberal Democrats to push through a bevy of new laws, most especially the Civil Rights Act of 1964, the Voting Rights Act of 1965, and the Civil Rights Act of 1968. What had begun as a series of legal battles in quiet courtrooms had ignited an explosion that changed the American nation.

The drama of such victories should not obscure the fact that interest groups must not attempt to persuade judges the same way they deal with legislators or administrators. It would be grossly improper, indeed typically criminal, for lobbyists to approach judges directly. Instead, groups try to influence judicial decisions by sponsoring a case or submitting a brief amicus curiae ("a friend of the court"; plural amici curiae) (Reading 6.5).

Sponsorship, which entails providing litigants with attorneys and other resources necessary to pursue their cases, takes two basic forms. The first occurs when a group waits for a case to arise within its field of concern and then assumes all or part of the task of representing a litigant in court. The American Civil Liberties Union typically uses this tactic. Parties who believe that their constitutional rights are being violated by prosecution or other governmental coercive action often ask the ACLU to represent them in a legal action. The organization, having limited resources, generally agrees to handle only those cases that it believes present an important constitutional principle.

The other type of sponsorship involves searching for abuses that can be attacked by filing test cases—deliberately bringing a case to secure a judicial ruling on a constitutional issue. The campaign against Connecticut's statute that forbade the use, or aiding or abetting the use, of contraceptives provides an excellent illustration. The law had been passed in the nineteenth century when a majority of the state's citizens were Protestants; when Catholics became a majority, their bishops convinced the legislature that repeal would be unpopular, leaving resort to courts an attractive option for the statute's opponents. In the early 1940s, a physician asked a state court for a declaratory judgment against enforcement of the law because it prevented him from giving advice necessary to his patients' health. Eventually Connecticut's supreme court denied the request, holding the law constitutional. On appeal, the U.S. Supreme Court found the doctor had no standing because, according to his own allegations, he was

---

[20] Not all scholars agree on this point. For a different view, see Reading 14.6 and our discussion in Chapter 14.

not in danger, his patients were.[21] Some years later, another physician and two of his patients brought a similar suit, alleging they would be prosecuted for disobeying the law. In 1961, the U.S. Supreme Court again dismissed the case, saying there was no immediate threat of harm because there was no recorded prosecution under the statute.[22] Finally, the director of the state's Planned Parenthood League and a physician flouted the law by publicly advising married couples about how to use birth-control devices. Arrested and convicted, the defendants appealed to the Supreme Court. This time, in *Griswold v. Connecticut* (1965), the justices reached the merits of the case and held that the law invaded defendants' right to freedom of association and to privacy in their associations, a sweeping though not tightly reasoned opinion.

Historically, bringing test cases raised problems of professional ethics for lawyers: stirring up litigation was a crime under the common law. As we shall see, the Supreme Court has changed those rules; but, even where ethical standards are met, the person in whose name the suit is filed still has to meet all standing and jurisdictional requirements. The surest way to get a judicial hearing on the merits is, as in *Griswold*, by violating a statute. But that tactic is risky. If the courts uphold the constitutionality of the statute, the challenger may go to jail.

A safer tactic involves bringing a civil suit, typically asking for an injunction (an order forbidding the defendant from acting in particular ways) against a public official. Many organizations use this strategy, but it has been most associated with the NAACP, especially in the years immediately before and after *Brown v. Board of Education* (1954), when the Legal Defense Fund's attorneys traveled around the South looking for favorable situations in which to bring desegregation suits and also for plaintiffs who had the courage to lend their names to such suits. Authorities in several Southern states countered the NAACP's efforts by charging that its attorneys were committing the crime of fomenting litigation. In *National Association for the Advancement of Colored People v. Button* (1963), however, the Supreme Court held that these laws could constitutionally forbid stirring up litigation only for private gain; a state's applying them to prevent lawsuits brought to vindicate associational rights would violate the First Amendment. As the Court said, "for such a group [as the NAACP], association for litigation may be the most effective form of political association."

In addition to sponsoring cases, as we noted earlier, an organization or an individual not a party to a lawsuit may participate by securing status as an amicus curiae. Almost all courts regulate the filing of such briefs. These rules vary at the margins, but most allow participation when both parties agree or, if one objects, with the permission of the court. Usually judicial rules allow governmental agencies to file without seeking the parties' consent. Indeed, the U.S. Supreme Court often asks the solicitor general, the official responsible for arguing the federal government's position before the justices, to submit an amicus brief because he or she can present a broader view than counsel for individual

---

[21] *Tileston v. Ullman* (1943).

[22] *Poe v. Ullman* (1961).

litigants. Moreover, when the Supreme Court reviews the constitutionality of an important policy operative in several states, it is customary for state attorneys general to ask their counterparts in other states to support their position by amici briefs. Thus, when the New York public school prayer case came up in *Engel v. Vitale* (1962), twenty-two states submitted a brief asking that New York be permitted to continue the ceremony. In *Lawrence v. Texas* (2003) Alabama, South Carolina, and Utah supported Texas's prohibition against same-sex sodomy. *Brewer v. Williams* (1977), where an admitted murderer's conviction was threatened on the ground of denial of counsel, attorneys general from twenty-one states plus the National District Attorneys Association and a citizens' group called Americans for Effective Law Enforcement filed amici briefs. But in the landmark right-to-counsel case, *Gideon v. Wainwright* (1963), the effort of Florida's attorney general to secure support from other states backfired. Only two states responded favorably, while, largely through the initiative of the attorney general of Minnesota, twenty-three states filed a brief supporting Gideon's constitutional right to counsel.

That interest groups make regular use of amici briefs is an understatement. Today, it is an unusual case before the U.S. Supreme Court that does not attract such submissions. On average, organized interests filed at least one amicus brief in 75.5 percent of all cases decided by full opinion between 1986 and 1996;[23] in fact, during a typical term in the 1990s (the most recent decade for which reliable data exist), 4.5 amici co-signed each brief amicus curiae, for a total of about 1,800 organizational participants. Some cases, particularly those involving such controversial issues as abortion and affirmative action, have attracted even wider participation. In Regents of the University of *California v. Bakke* (1978), involving admission of minority students to medical school, more than a hundred organizations filed fifty-eight amici briefs, of which forty-two backed the university's affirmative action policy and sixteen supported Bakke. Twenty-five years later, when the University of Michigan's affirmative action programs came under fire, once again a wide of array of amici participated—including twenty-one states, numerous business and corporations, and a group of former officers and civilian leaders of the U.S. military, all of which filed in support of the programs, and the governor of Florida (Jeb Bush), the U.S. government, and a dozen or so public policy groups, all of which supported those challenging the plans.[24]

So, too, groups have not ignored state supreme courts, which, since the 1980s, have become increasingly important policy-making bodies (see Chapter 3). Between 1965 and 1975, the average state supreme court received only about four amici briefs per term; between 1980 and 1994, that figure rose to nearly thirteen. But quite clearly some states are more attractive targets for interest groups than others are. In one year in the 1990s, New Jersey's Supreme Court received seventy-four briefs amici curiae; its counterpart in Idaho only seven.

---

[23] Lee Epstein et al., *The Supreme Court Compendium* (Washington, DC: Congressional Quarterly, 2003), Table 7-25.

[24] *Gratz v. Bollinger* (2003); *Grutter v. Bollinger* (2003).

Such discrepancies probably reflect calculations about the relative influence of particular states, as well as about their ability to succeed in seeing judicial decisions reflect their preferences.[25] Then, of course, there is the matter of the relative salience of the case itself. So, for example, in *Goodridge v. Department of Public Health*, in which the Massachusetts high court held that the state could not deny gays and lesbians the right to marry (Reading 3.9), more than twenty-five amici participated.

The Influence of Interest Groups

This explosion of interest group activity raises an interesting question: do groups influence the outcomes of judicial decisions? Any answer to this question must be both complex and tentative. First of all, when interest groups participate on both sides, it is reasonable to speculate that one or more of them did exert some intellectual influence or at least that intervention of groups on the winning side neutralized the arguments of those who lost. To know how much influence any group or private party exerted, an analyst would have to psychoanalyze all the judges who participated in the decision, because a citation to a brief may indicate that a judge is seeking support for a conclusion he or she had already reached.

We can be more certain that many cases would not get into any court, much less the U.S. Supreme Court, without the help of an interest group. Thus, we can say that, because judges have to wait for cases to come before them, groups help set the judicial agenda. It could be that many judges, especially judges on appellate courts, look on interest groups as sources of important information that otherwise would not come to their attention. Gregory A. Caldeira and John R. Wright's research on amici's participation at the agenda-setting stage supports this contention (Reading 6.6), as does the proportion of U.S. Supreme Court opinions that cite amici's arguments. During the Warren Court, the justices cited briefs amici curiae in about 40 percent of their opinions; that figure rose to 66 percent for the Burger Court and to 68 percent for the Rehnquist Court.[26] It thus seems clear that the justices—or their young clerks, who often write first drafts of opinions—are learning enough from amici briefs to cite them in their opinions.

And, once having gained the attention of a court, attorneys for some groups, such as the Women's Rights Project of the American Civil Liberties Union and the NAACP, are often more experienced and their staffs are more adept at research than counsel for "one-shotters." For the NAACP, Thurgood Marshall would orchestrate help from allied groups, allocating to each the task of making specific arguments and enlisting sympathetic social scientists to muster supporting data. Before going to the Supreme Court for oral argument, he would sometimes have a practice session with friendly law professors, each

---

[25] Lee Epstein, "Exploring the Participation of Organized Interests in State Court Litigation," 47 *Political Research Quarterly* 335 (1994).

[26] See Epstein, et al., *The Supreme Court Compendium*, Table 7-27.

one playing the role of a particular justice and trying to pose the sorts of question that the justice would be likely to ask. That sort of preparation can pay off; indeed, Linda Greenhouse, who covers the Supreme Court for the *New York Times* and is one of the Court's most astute students, has argued that good lawyers and amici played crucial roles in the litigation over the Michigan affirmative action plan in *Grutter v. Bollinger* (2003) and same-sex sodomy in *Lawrence v. Texas* (2003).[27] In the former, the justices appeared particularly impressed by the briefs filed by the military officers and corporations in support of affirmative action; in the latter, the Court—which struck down Texas's ban on homosexual sodomy and, in so doing, overruled its decision in *Bowers v. Hardwick* (1986)—wrote:

> The *Bowers* Court said: "Proscriptions against that conduct have ancient roots." In academic writings, and in many of the scholarly amicus briefs filed to assist the Court in this case, there are fundamental criticisms of the historical premises relied upon by the majority and concurring opinions in *Bowers*. Brief for Cato Institute as Amicus Curiae; Brief for American Civil Liberties Union et al. as Amici Curiae; Brief for Professors of History et al. as Amici Curiae. . . . [I]t should be noted that there is no longstanding history in this country of laws directed at homosexual conduct as a distinct matter.

On the other hand, preparation and, more generally, good lawyering need not be decisive. In oral argument, Bakke's attorney showed ignorance of constitutional law and curtly told one justice who tried to help him that he would like to argue the case his own way. Despite this poor performance, Bakke won. There also is some evidence at the trial level suggesting that attorneys working for interest groups are no more successful than private counsel. One study paired similar cases decided by the same district court judge, the same year, with the only major difference being that one case was sponsored by a group, the other brought by attorneys unaffiliated with an organized interest. Despite Galanter's contentions about "one-shotters" (Reading 6.4), the authors found no major differences between the two.[28] Whether these findings hold for other trial judges or for federal and state appellate tribunals remains an interesting and open question.

SELECTED REFERENCES

BARKOW, RACHEL E. 2002. "More Supreme Than Court? The Fall of the Political Question Doctrine and the Rise of Judicial Supremacy." *Columbia Law Review* 102: 237-334.

BERGER, RAOUL. 1969. "Standing to Sue in Public Actions." *Yale Law Journal* 78: 816.

---

[27] Linda Greenhouse, What Got Into the Court? What Happens Next?, *The William Timbers Lecture*, Dartmouth College, November 20, 2003. Available at http://epstein.wustl.edu/courses/supctU/index.html.

[28] Lee Epstein and C. K. Rowland, "Debunking the Myth of Interest Group Invincibility in the Court," 85 American *Political Science Review* 205–217 (1991)

BICKEL, ALEXANDER. 1962. The Least Dangerous Branch of Government. Indianapolis: Bobbs-Merrill.

CALDEIRA, GREGORY A., AND JOHN R. WRIGHT. 1988. "Interest Groups and Agenda Setting in the U.S. Supreme Court." *American Political Science Review* 82: 1109.

EPP, CHARLES. 1998. *The Rights Revolution.* Chicago: University of Chicago Press.

EPSTEIN, LEE. 1993. "Interest Group Litigation During the Rehnquist Court Era." *Journal of Law and Politics* 9: 639.

EPSTEIN, LEE. 1994. "Exploring the Participation of Organized Interests in State Court Litigation." *Political Research Quarterly* 47: 335.

EPSTEIN, LEE, AND JOSEPH F. KOBYLKA. 1995. *The Supreme Court and Legal Change.* Chapel Hill: University of North Carolina Press.

FELSTINER, WILLIAM L., RICHARD L. ABEL, AND AUSTIN SARAT. 1980–81. "The Emergence and Transformation of Disputes: Naming, Blaming, Claiming . . ." *Law and Society Review* 15: 631.

FRANCK, THOMAS M. 1992. *Political Questions/Judicial Answers: Does the Rule of Law Apply to Foreign Affairs?* Princeton, NJ: Princeton University Press.

GALANTER, MARC. 1974. "Why the 'Haves' Come Out Ahead: Speculations on the Limits of Social Change." *Law and Society Review* 9: 95.

GETTIEMAN, MARVIN E. 1973. *The Dorr Rebellion.* New York: Random House.

GREENBERG, JACK. 1994. *Crusaders in Court.* New York: Basic Books.

GROFMAN, BERNARD, ED. 1990. *Political Gerrymandering and the Courts.* New York: Agathon Press.

GUNTHER, GERALD. 1964. "The Subtle Vices of the Passive Virtues—A Comment on Principle and Expediency in Judicial Review." *Columbia Law Review* 64: 1.

HENKIN, LOUIS. 1976. "Is There a 'Political Question' Doctrine?" *Yale Law Journal* 85: 597.

HORN, ROBERT A. 1965. *Groups and the Constitution.* Stanford, CA: Stanford University Press.

KOBYLKA, JOSEPH F. 1991. *The Politics of Obscenity: Group Litigation in a Time of Legal Change.* Westport, CT: Greenwood Press.

KOSHNER, ANDREW JAY. 1998. *Solving the Puzzle of Interest Group Litigation.* Westport, CT: Greenwood Press.

KRISLOV, SAMUEL. 1963. "The Amicus Curiae Brief: From Friendship to Advocacy." *Yale Law Journal* 72: 694.

KRITZER, HERBERT M., NEIL VIDMAR, AND W. A. BOGART. 1991. "To Confront or Not to Confront: Measuring Claiming Rates in Discrimination Grievances." *Law and Society Review* 25: 883.

MILLER, RICHARD E., AND AUSTIN SARAT. 1980–1981. "Grievances, Claims, and Disputes: Assessing the Adversary Culture." *Law and Society Review* 15: 544.

ORREN, KAREN. 1976. "Standing to Sue: Interest Group Conflict in the Federal Courts." *American Political Science Review* 70: 723.

PELTASON, JACK W. 1955. *Federal Courts in the Political Process.* New York: Random House.

RADCLIFFE, JAMES E. 1978. *The Case-or-Controversy Provision.* University Park: Pennsylvania State University Press.

RATHJEN, GREGORY J., AND HAROLD J. SPAETH. 1979. "Access to the Federal Courts: An Analysis of Burger Court Policy Making." *American Journal of Political Science* 23: 360.

ROWLAND, C. K., AND BRIDGETT TODD. 1991. "Where You Stand Depends on Who Sits: Platform Promises and Judicial Gatekeeping in the Federal District Courts." *Journal of Politics* 53: 175.

SCHUCKMAN, JOHN S. 1972. "The Political Background of the Political Question Doctrine: The Judges and the Dorr War." *American Journal of Legal History* 16: 111.

SHEEHAN, REGINALD, WILLIAM MISHLER, AND DONALD R. SONGER. 1992. "Ideology, Status, and the Differential Success of Direct Parties Before the Supreme Court." *American Political Science Review* 86: 464.

SONGER, DONALD R., AND REGINALD S. SHEEHAN. 1992. "Who Wins on Appeal? Upperdogs and Underdogs in the United States Courts of Appeals." *American Journal of Political Science* 36: 235.

SORAUF, FRANK J. 1976 *The Wall of Separation: The Constitutional Politics of Church and State.* Princeton, NJ: Princeton University Press.

STAUDT, NANCY. 2004. "Modeling Standing." 79 *New York University Law Review* 612.

STRASSER, SARAH E. 1995/1996. "Evolution and Effort: Docket Control and Preliminary References in the European Court of Justice." *Columbia Journal of European Law* 2: 49.

STRUM, PHILIPPA. 1974. *The Supreme Court and Political Questions.* Tuscaloosa, AL: University of Alabama Press.

SUNSTEIN, CASS R. 1999. *One Case at a Time: Judicial Minimalism on the Supreme Court.* Cambridge, MA: Harvard University Press.

TRUMAN, DAVID B. 1971. *The Governmental Process*, 2nd ed. New York: Knopf.

VOSE, CLEMENT E. 1959. *Caucasians Only: The Supreme Court, the NAACP and the Restrictive Covenant Cases.* Berkeley: University of California Press.

WASBY, STEPHEN L. 1995. *Race Relations Litigation in an Age of Complexity.* Charlottesville: University of Virginia Press.

ZEMANS, FRANCES KAHN. 1983. "Legal Mobilization: The Neglected Role of the Law in the Political System." *American Political Science Review* 77: 690.

"The President . . . would be much relieved if he found himself free to refer questions of this description to the opinions of the judges of the Supreme Court of the United States."

6.1 THE WASHINGTON ADMINISTRATION'S REQUEST FOR AN ADVISORY OPINION AND THE JUSTICES' RESPONSE

In July 1793, George Washington's secretary of state, Thomas Jefferson, asked the justices if they would be willing to address questions concerning the appropriate role America should play in the ongoing British-French war.

Philadelphia
July 18, 1793

Gentlemen:

The war which has taken place among the powers of Europe produces frequent transactions within our ports and limits, on which questions arise of considerable difficulty, and of greater importance to the peace of the United States. These questions depend for their solution on the construction of our treaties, on the laws of nature and nations, and on the laws of the land, and are often presented under circumstances *which do not give a cognizance of them to the tribunals of the country.* Yet, their decision is so little analogous to the ordinary functions of the executive, as to occasion much embarrassment and difficulty to them. The President therefore would be much relieved if he found himself free to refer questions of this description to the opinions of the judges of the Supreme Court of the United States, whose knowledge of the subject would secure us against errors dangerous to the peace of the United States, and their authority insure the respect of all parties. He has therefore asked the attendance of such of the judges as could be collected in time for the occasion, to know, in the first place, their opinion, whether the public may, with propriety, be availed of their advice on these questions? And if they may, to present, for their advice, the abstract questions which have already occurred, or may soon occur, from which they will themselves strike out such as any circumstances might, in their opinion, forbid them to pronounce on. I have the honor to be with sentiments of the most perfect respect gentlemen,

> Your most obedient and humble servant,
> Thomas Jefferson

From Henry M. Hart, Jr., and Albert M. Sacks, *The Legal Process*, William N. Eskridge, Jr., ed., and Philip P. Frickey (Westbury, NY: Foundation Press, 1994), 630–631, 637.

The following are some of the questions submitted by the president to the Justices.

1. Do the treaties between the United States and France give to France or her citizens, a right, when at war with a power with whom the United States are at peace, to fit out originally in and from the ports of the United States vessels armed for war, with or without commission?

2. If they give such a *right*, does it extend to all manner of armed vessels, or to particular kinds only? If the latter, to what kinds does it extend?

3. Do they give to France or her citizens, in the case supposed, a right to re-fit or arm anew vessels, which, before their coming within any port of the United States, were armed for war, with or without commission?

4. If they give such a right, does it extend to all manner of armed vessels, or to particular kinds only? If the latter, to what kinds does it extend? Does it include an *augmentation* of force, or does it only extend to replace the vessel *in status quo*?

17. Do the laws of neutrality, . . . considered as aforesaid, authorize the United States to permit France, her subjects, or citizens, the sale within their ports of prizes made of the subjects or property of a power at war with France, before they have been carried into some port of France and there condemned, refusing the like privilege to a power at war with France?

18. Do those laws authorize the United States to permit to France the erection of courts within their territory and jurisdiction for the trial and condemnation of prizes, refusing that privilege to a power at war with France?

Less than a month later the justices denied Jefferson's request, with the following reply written directly to the president.

We have considered . . . [the] letter written by your direction to us by the Secretary of State [regarding] the lines of separation drawn by the Constitution between the three departments of government. These being in certain respects checks upon each other, and our being judges of a court in the last resort, are considerations which afford strong arguments against the propriety of our extra-judicially deciding the questions alluded to, especially as the power given by the Constitution to the President, of calling on the heads of departments for opinions, seems to have been purposely as well as expressly united to the executive departments. . . .

> *"Pregnancy provides a classic justification for a conclusion of nonmootness." —ROE V. WADE*

> *"DeFunis will never again be required to run the gantlet of the Law School's admission process." —DEFUNIS V. ODEGAARD*

6.2 ROE V. WADE VERSUS DEFUNIS V. ODEGAARD

Roe v. Wade, 410 U.S. 113 (1973)

A single woman, claiming to be pregnant, challenged the constitutionality of Texas's criminal abortion laws, which proscribed procuring or attempting an abortion except on medical advice for the purpose of saving the mother's life. Among the many questions the justices addressed was whether her case was moot because she was not pregnant at the time her case was presented to them.

Mr. JUSTICE BLACKMUN delivered the opinion of the Court.

The usual rule in federal cases is that an actual controversy must exist at stages of appellate or certiorari review, and not simply at the date the action is initiated.

But when, as here, pregnancy is a significant fact in the litigation, the normal 266-day human gestation period is so short that the pregnancy will come to term before the usual appellate process is complete. If that termination makes a case moot, pregnancy litigation seldom will survive much beyond the trial stage, and appellate review will be effectively denied. Our law should not be that rigid. Pregnancy often comes more than once to the same woman, and in the general population, if man is to survive, it will always be with us. Pregnancy provides a classic justification for a conclusion of nonmootness. It truly could be "capable of repetition, yet evading review."

We therefore agree with the District Court that Jane Roe had standing to undertake this litigation, that she presented a justiciable controversy, and that the termination of her 1970 pregnancy has not rendered her case moot. . . .

DeFunis v. Odegaard, 416 U.S. 312 (1974)

Rejected for admission to the University of Washington Law School, Marco DeFunis, Jr., brought suit against the school, alleging that it had engaged in reverse discrimination—that it had denied him a place but had accepted statistically less qualified minority students. In 1971 a trial court found merit in his claim and ordered that the university admit him. While DeFunis was in his second year of law school, the state's high court reversed the trial judge's ruling. He then appealed to the U.S. Supreme Court. By that time, DeFunis had registered for his final quarter in school. In a per curiam (unsigned) opinion, the Court refused to rule on the merits of DeFunis's claim, asserting that it was moot. Four justices dissented from this disposition.

In response to questions raised from the bench during the oral argument, counsel for the petitioner has informed the Court that DeFunis has now registered "for his final quarter in law school." Counsel for the respondents have made clear that the Law School will not in any way seek to abrogate this registration. In light of DeFunis's recent registration for the last quarter of his final law school year, and the Law School's assurance that his registration is fully effective, the insistent question again arises whether this case is not moot, and to that question we now turn. . . .

The respondents have represented that, without regard to the ultimate resolution of the issues in this case, DeFunis will remain a student in the Law School for the duration of any term in which he has already enrolled. Since he has now registered for his final term, it is evident that he will be given an opportunity to complete all academic and other requirements for graduation, and, if he does so, will receive his diploma regardless of any decision this Court might reach on the merits of this case. In short, all parties agree that DeFunis is now entitled to complete his legal studies at the University of Washington and to receive his degree from that institution. A determination by this Court of the legal issues tendered by the parties is no longer necessary to compel that result, and could not serve to prevent it. DeFunis did not cast his suit as a class action, and the only remedy he requested was an injunction commanding his admission to the Law School. He was not only accorded that remedy, but he now has also been irrevocably admitted to the final term of the final year of the Law School course. The controversy between the parties has thus clearly ceased to be "definite and concrete" and no longer "touch[es] the legal relations of parties having adverse legal interests.". . .

It might . . . be suggested that this case presents a question that is "capable of repetition, yet evading review" *Roe v. Wade* (1973) and is thus amenable to federal adjudication even though it might otherwise be considered moot. But DeFunis will never again be required to run the gantlet of the Law School's admission process, and so the question is certainly not "capable of repetition" so far as he is concerned. Moreover, just because this particular case did not reach the Court until the eve of the petitioner's graduation from law school, it hardly follows that the issue he raises will in the future evade review. If the admissions procedures of the Law School remain unchanged, there is no reason to suppose that a subsequent case attacking those procedures will not come with relative speed to this Court, now that the Supreme Court of Washington has spoken. This case, therefore, in no way presents the exceptional situation in which [we] might permit a departure from "the usual rule in federal cases . . . that an actual controversy must exist at stages of appellate or certiorari review, and not simply at the date the action is initiated" *Roe v. Wade*.

Because the petitioner will complete his law school studies at the end of the term for which he has now registered regardless of any decision this Court might reach on the merits of this litigation, we conclude that the Court cannot, consistently with the limitations of Art. III of the Constitution, consider the substantive constitutional issues tendered by the parties.

Accordingly, the judgment of the Supreme Court of Washington is vacated, and the cause is remanded for such proceedings as by that court may be deemed appropriate.

Mr. JUSTICE BRENNAN, with whom Mr. JUSTICE DOUGLAS, Mr. JUSTICE WHITE, and Mr. JUSTICE MARSHALL concur, dissenting.

I respectfully dissent. Many weeks of the school term remain, and petitioner may not receive his degree despite respondents' assurances that petitioner will be allowed to complete this term's schooling regardless of our decision. Any number of unexpected events—illness, economic necessity, even academic failure—might prevent his graduation at the end of the term. Were that misfortune to befall, and were petitioner required to register for yet another term, the prospect that he would again face the hurdle of the admissions policy is real, not fanciful; for respondents warn that "Mr. DeFunis would have to take some appropriate action to request continued admission for the remainder of his law school education, and some discretionary action by the University on such request would have to be taken." Thus, respondents' assurances have not dissipated the possibility that petitioner might once again have to run the gantlet of the University's allegedly unlawful admissions policy. The Court therefore proceeds on an erroneous premise in resting its mootness holding on a supposed inability to render any judgment that may affect one way or the other petitioner's completion of his law studies. For surely if we were to reverse the Washington Supreme Court, we could insure that, if for some reason petitioner did not graduate this spring, he would be entitled to re-enrollment at a later time on the same basis as others who have not faced the hurdle of the University's allegedly unlawful admissions policy.

In these circumstances, and because the University's position implies no concession that its admissions policy is unlawful, this controversy falls squarely within the Court's long line of decisions holding that the "mere voluntary cessation of allegedly illegal conduct does not moot a case." Since respondents' voluntary representation to this Court is only that they will permit petitioner to complete this term's studies, respondents have not borne the "heavy burden" of demonstrating that there was not even a "mere possibility" that petitioner would once again be subject to the challenged admissions policy. On the contrary, respondents have positioned themselves so as to be "free to return to [their] old ways."

I can thus find no justification for the Court's straining to rid itself of this dispute. . . .

Moreover, in endeavoring to dispose of this case as moot, the Court clearly disserves the public interest. The constitutional issues which are avoided today concern vast numbers of people, organizations, and colleges and universities, as evidenced by the filing of twenty-six amicus curiae briefs. Few constitutional questions in recent history have stirred as much debate, and they will not disappear. They must inevitably return to the federal courts and ultimately again to this Court. Because avoidance of repetitious litigation serves the public interest, that inevitability counsels against mootness determinations, as here, not compelled by the record. Although the Court should, of course, avoid unnecessary decisions of constitutional questions, we should not transform principles of avoidance of constitutional decisions into devices for sidestepping resolution of difficult cases.

On what appears in this case, I would find that there is an extant controversy and decide the merits of the very important constitutional questions presented.

"The nonjusticiability of a political question is primarily
a function of the separation of powers."

6.3 BAKER V. CARR

369 U.S. 186 (1962)

The constitutional text allocates seats in the House of Representatives according to the
population of the state. Once that figure has been established, it is up to the state to de-
termine specific congressional districts. Article I specifies:

> *Representatives . . . shall be apportioned among the several States which may be in-*
> *cluded within this Union, according to their respective Numbers. . . . The actual*
> *Enumeration shall be made within three Years after the first Meeting of the Congress of*
> *the United States, and within every subsequent Term of ten Years, in such Manner as*
> *they shall by Law direct. The Number of Representatives shall not exceed one for every*
> *thirty Thousand, but each State shall have at Least one Representative.*

The document, however, is silent about how states are to set up electoral districts or even
if representatives may be chosen, as are senators, "at large."

As population shifts from rural to urban areas occurred, some states redrew their
congressional district lines. Many, however, did not, leaving huge disparities in popu-
lation between districts. Reform groups representing urban voters began to bring liti-
gation to force legislatures to reapportion. In one of the most important of these efforts,
Colegrove v. Green *(1946), they did so under Article IV of the constitutional charter,*
the Guarantee Clause: "The United States shall guarantee to every State in the Union
a Republican Form of Government, and shall protect each of them against Invasion; and
on Application of the Legislature or of the Executive (when the Legislature cannot be
convened) against Domestic violence." They argued that failure to reapportion legisla-
tive districts deprived some voters of their right to a republican form of government and
demonstrated that, because Illinois had not redistricted since 1901, citizens in some
rural districts had, in effect, nine times the voting power of their cousins in the cities.

The justices could not agree on a majority opinion, but the vote was 4–3 against
Colegrove's *claim. Justice Felix Frankfurter, writing for three of the justices, invoked*
the logic of Luther v. Borden *to argue that the Constitution left open the question of*
legislative reapportionment within states. If the Court intervened in this matter, he as-
serted, it would be acting in a way "hostile to a democratic system." Reapportionment
constituted a "political thicket" into which "courts ought not enter."

As a result of Colegrove, *states that had not reapportioned since the turn of the*
century were under no federal constitutional mandate to do so, and disparities between
the voting power of urban and rural citizens continued to grow. Naturally, many citi-
zens and organizations wanted to force legislatures to reapportion, but under
Colegrove *they could not do so using the guarantee clause. They looked, therefore, to*
another section of the constitutional document, the Fourteenth Amendment's equal pro-
tection clause, which says that no state shall "deny to any person within its jurisdiction
the equal protection of the laws." They argued that the failure to reapportion led to un-
equal treatment of voters.

Although this strategy represented a clever legal attempt to reframe the issue of reapportionment, when attorneys sought to apply it to the Tennessee situation, a federal district court dismissed their suit. Relying on Colegrove *and other cases, that court held reapportionment to pose a political question on which it could not rule. The voters then appealed to the Supreme Court.*

Mr. JUSTICE BRENNAN delivered the opinion of the Court . . .

In holding that the subject matter of this suit was not justiciable, the District Court relied on *Colegrove v. Green* (1946), and subsequent per curiam cases. . . . We understand the District Court to have read the cited cases as compelling the conclusion that since the appellants sought to have a legislative apportionment held unconstitutional, their suit presented a "political question" and was therefore nonjusticiable. We hold that this challenge to an apportionment presents no nonjusticiable "political question. . . ."

Of course the mere fact that the suit seeks protection of a political right does not mean it presents a political question. Such an objection "is little more than a play upon words." *Nixon v. Herndon.* . . . Rather, it is argued that apportionment cases, whatever the actual wording of the complaint, can involve no federal constitutional right except one resting on the guaranty of a republican form of government, and that complaints based on that clause have been held to present political questions which are nonjusticiable.

We hold that the claim pleaded here neither rests upon nor implicates the Guaranty Clause and that its justiciability is therefore not foreclosed by our decisions of cases involving that clause. . . .

Our discussion . . . requires review of a number of political question cases, in order to expose the attributes of the doctrine—attributes which, in various settings, diverge, combine, appear, and disappear in seeming disorderliness. . . . That review reveals that in the Guaranty Clause cases and in the other "political question" cases, it is the relationship between the judiciary and the coordinate branches of the Federal Government, and not the federal judiciary's relationship to the States, which gives rise to the "political question."

We have said that "in determining whether a question falls within [the political question] category, appropriateness under our system of government of attributing finality to the action of the political departments and also the lack of satisfactory criteria for a judicial determination are dominant considerations." *Coleman v. Miller* (1939). The nonjusticiability of a political question is primarily a function of the separation of powers. Much confusion results from the capacity of the "political question" label to obscure the need for case-by-case inquiry. Deciding whether a matter has in any measure been committed by the Constitution to another branch of government, or whether the action of that branch exceeds whatever authority has been committed, is itself a delicate exercise in constitutional interpretation, and is a responsibility of this Court as ultimate interpreter of the Constitution. To demonstrate this requires no less than to analyze representative cases and to infer from them the analytical threads that make up the political question doctrine. We shall then show that none of those threads catches this case.

Foreign relations. There are sweeping statements to the effect that all questions touching foreign relations are political questions. Not only does resolution of such issues frequently turn on standards that defy judicial application, or involve the exercise of a discretion demonstrably committed to the executive or legislature; but many such questions uniquely demand single-voiced statement of the Government's views. Yet it is error to suppose that every case or controversy which touches foreign relations lies beyond judicial cognizance. Our cases in this field seem invariably to show a discriminating analysis of the particular question posed, in terms of the history of its management by the political branches, of its susceptibility to judicial handling in the light of its nature and posture in the specific case, and of the possible consequences of judicial action. . . .

Dates of duration of hostilities. Though it has been stated broadly that "the power which declared the necessity is the power to declare its cessation, and what the cessation requires," here too analysis reveals isolable reasons for the presence of political questions, underlying this Court's refusal to review the political departments' determination of when or whether a war has ended. Dominant is the need for finality in the political determination. . . .

Validity of enactments. In *Coleman v. Miller*, this Court held that the questions of how long a proposed amendment to the Federal Constitution remained open to ratification, and what effect a prior rejection had on a subsequent ratification, were committed to congressional resolution and involved criteria of decision that necessarily escaped the judicial grasp. . . .

The status of Indian tribes. This Court's deference to the political departments in determining whether Indians are recognized as a tribe, while it reflects familiar attributes of political questions . . . also has a unique element in that "the relation of the Indians to the United States is marked by peculiar and cardinal distinctions which exist nowhere else. . . ."

It is apparent that several formulations which vary slightly according to the settings in which the questions arise may describe a political question, although each has one or more elements which identifies it as essentially a function of the separation of powers. Prominent on the surface of any case held to involve a political question is found a textually demonstrable constitutional commitment of the issue to a coordinate political department; or a lack of judicially discoverable and manageable standards for resolving it; or the impossibility of deciding without an initial policy determination of a kind clearly for nonjudicial discretion; or the impossibility of a court's undertaking independent resolution without expressing lack of the respect due coordinate branches of government; or an unusual need for unquestioning adherence to a political decision already made; or the potentiality of embarrassment from multifarious pronouncements by various departments on one question.

Unless one of these formulations is inextricable from the case at bar, there should be no dismissal for nonjusticiability on the ground of a political question's presence. The doctrine of which we treat is one of "political questions," not one of "political cases." The courts cannot reject as "no law suit" a bona fide controversy as to whether some action denominated "political" exceeds constitutional authority. . . .

But it is argued that this case shares the characteristics of decisions that constitute a category not yet considered, cases concerning the Constitution's guaranty, in. Art. IV, ß 4, of a republican form of government. A conclusion as to whether the case at bar does present a political question cannot be confidently reached until we have considered those cases with special care. We shall discover that Guaranty Clause claims involve those elements which define a "political question," and for that reason and no other, they are nonjusticiable. In particular, we shall discover that the nonjusticiability of such claims has nothing to do with their touching upon matters of state governmental organization. . . .

[The opinion then reviewed at length Luther v. Borden *(1849) and other cases involving the "republican form of government" issue.]*

We come, finally, to the ultimate inquiry whether our precedents as to what constitutes a nonjusticiable "political question" bring the case before us under the umbrella of that doctrine. A natural beginning is to note whether any of the common characteristics which we have been able to identify and label descriptively are present. We find none: The question here is the consistency of state action with the Federal Constitution. We have no question decided, or to be decided, by a political branch of government coequal with this Court. Nor do we risk embarrassment of our government abroad, or grave disturbance at home if we take issue with Tennessee as to the constitutionality of her action here challenged. Nor need the appellants, in order to succeed in this action, ask the Court to enter upon policy determinations for which judicially manageable standards are lacking. Judicial standards under the Equal Protection Clause are well developed and familiar, and it has been open to courts since the enactment of the Fourteenth Amendment to determine, if on the particular facts they must, that a discrimination reflects *no* policy, but simply arbitrary and capricious action. . . .
    Reversed and remanded.

Mr. JUSTICE FRANKFURTER, whom Mr. JUSTICE HARLAN joins, dissenting.[27]
    The present case involves all of the elements that have made the Guarantee Clause cases non-justiciable. It is, in effect, a Guaranty Clause claim masquerading under a different label. But it cannot make the case more fit for judicial action that appellants invoke the Fourteenth Amendment rather than Art. IV, § 4, where, in fact, the gist of their complaint is the same—unless it can be found that the Fourteenth Amendment speaks with greater particularity to their situation. We have been admonished to avoid "the tyranny of labels." Art. IV, § 4, is not committed by express constitutional terms to Congress. It is the nature of the controversies arising under it, nothing else, which has made it judicially unenforceable. Of course, if a controversy falls within judicial power, it depends "on how he [the plaintiff] casts his action," whether he brings himself within a jurisdictional statute. But where judicial competence is wanting, it cannot be created by invoking one clause of the Constitution rather than another.

---

[27]For an extended version of this dissent, see Reading 14.3.

"What this analysis does is to define a position of advantage in the configuration of contending parties and indicate how those with other advantages tend to occupy this position of advantage and to have their other advantages reinforced and augmented thereby."

6.4 WHY THE "HAVES" COME OUT AHEAD: SPECULATIONS ON THE LIMITS OF SOCIAL CHANGE

Marc Galanter

Marc Galanter is the John and Rylla Bosshard Professor of Law and Professor of South Asian Studies at the University of Wisconsin, Madison.

I would like to try to put forward some conjectures about the way in which the basic architecture of the legal system creates and limits the possibilities of using the system as a means of redistributive (that is, systemically equalizing) change. Our question, specifically, is, under what conditions can litigation be redistributive, taking litigation in the broadest sense of the presentation of claims to be decided by courts (or court-like agencies) and the whole penumbra of threats, feints, and so forth, surrounding such presentation. . . .

Most analyses of the legal system start at the rules end and work down through institutional facilities to see what effect the rules have on the parties. I would like to reverse that procedure and look through the other end of the telescope. Let's think about the different kinds of parties and the effect these differences might have on the way the system works.

Because of differences in their size, differences in the state of the law, and differences in their resources, some of the actors in the society have many occasions to utilize the courts (in the broad sense) to make (or defend) claims; others do so only rarely. We might divide our actors into those claimants who have only occasional recourse to the courts (one-shotters or OS) and repeat players (RP) who are engaged in many similar litigations over time. The spouse in the divorce case, the auto injury claimant, the criminal accused are OSs; the insurance company, the prosecutor, the finance company are RPs. . . .

We would expect an RP to play the litigation game differently from an OS. Let us consider some of his advantages:

1. RPs, having done it before, have advance intelligence; they are able to structure the next transaction and build a record. . . .
2. RPs develop expertise and have ready access to specialists. They enjoy economies of scale and have low start-up costs for any case.

From 9 *Law and Society Review* 95 (1974).

3. RPs have opportunities to develop facilitative informal relations with institutional incumbents.

4. The RP must establish and maintain credibility as a combatant. His interest in his "bargaining reputation" services as a resource to establish "commitment" to his bargaining positions. . . .

5. RPs can play the odds. The larger the matter at issue looms for OS, the more likely he is to adopt a minimax strategy (minimize the probability of maximum loss). Assuming that the stakes are relatively smaller for RPs, they can adopt strategies calculated to maximize gain over a long series of cases, even where this involves the risk of maximum loss in some cases.

6. RPs can play for rules as well as immediate gains. First, it pays an RP to expend resources in influencing the making of the relevant rules by such methods as lobbying. (And his accumulated expertise enables him to do this persuasively.)

7. RPs can also play for rules in litigation itself, whereas an OS is unlikely to. That is, there is a difference in what they regard as a favorable outcome. Because his stakes in the immediate outcome are high and because by definition OS is unconcerned with the outcome of similar litigation in the future, OS will have little interest in that element of the outcome which might influence the disposition of the decision-maker next time around. For the RP, on the other hand, anything that will favorably influence the outcomes of future cases is a worthwhile result. The larger the stake for any player and the lower the probability of repeat play, the less likely that he will be concerned with the rules which govern future cases of the same kind. Consider two parents contesting the custody of their only child, the prizefighter vs. the IRS for tax arrears, the convict facing the death penalty. On the other hand, the player with small stakes in the present case and the prospect of a series of similar cases (the IRS, the adoption agency, the prosecutor) may be more interested in the state of the law.

   Thus, if we analyze the outcomes of a case into a tangible component and a rule component, we may expect that in case 1, OS will attempt to maximize tangible gain. But if RP is interested in maximizing his tangible gain in a series of cases $1...n$, he may be willing to trade off tangible gain in any one case for rule gain (or to minimize rule loss). We assumed that the institutional facilities for litigation were overloaded and settlements were prevalent. We would then expect RPs to "settle" cases where they expected unfavorable rule outcomes. Since they expect to litigate again, RPs can select to adjudicate (or appeal) those cases which they regard as most likely to produce favorable rules. On the other hand, OSs should be willing to trade off the possibility of making "good law" for tangible gain. Thus, we would expect the body of "precedent" cases—that is, cases capable of influencing the outcome of future cases—to be relatively skewed toward those favorable to RP. . . .

In stipulating that RPs can play for rules, I do not mean to imply that RPs pursue rule-gain as such. If we recall that not all rules penetrate (i.e., become effectively applied at the field level) we come to some additional advantages of RPs.

8. RPs, by virtue of experience and expertise, are more likely to be able to discern which rules are likely to "penetrate" and which are likely to remain merely symbolic commitments. RPs may be able to concentrate their resources on rule-changes that are likely to make a tangible difference. They can trade off symbolic defeats for tangible gains.

9. Since penetration depends in part on the resources of the parties (knowledge, attentiveness, expert services, money), RPs are more likely to be able to invest the matching resources necessary to secure the penetration of rules favorable to them.

It is not suggested that RPs are to be equated with "haves" (in terms of power, wealth, and status) or OSs with "have-nots." In the American setting most RPs are larger, richer, and powerful than are most OSs, so these categories overlap, but there are obvious exceptions. RPs may be "have-nots" (alcoholic derelicts) or may act as champions of "have-nots" (as government does from time to time); OSs such as criminal defendants may be wealthy. What this analysis does is to define a position of advantage in the configuration of contending parties and indicate how those with other advantages tend to occupy this position of advantage and to have their other advantages reinforced and augmented thereby. This position of advantage is one of the ways in which a legal system formally neutral as between "haves" and "have-nots" may perpetuate and augment the advantages of the former.

Editors' Note: Twenty-five years after publication of this seminal work, the Institute of Legal Studies at the University of Wisconsin held a conference on whether "The 'Haves' Still Come Out Ahead." Below we reprint Galanter's comments at that conference, which were later published in the Law & Society Review. *(This is from Marc Galanter, Comment: Farther Along.* 33 Law and Society Review *1113 (1999).*

If I were writing the "Haves" now, I would try to go beyond the configuration of litigants to the organizational characteristics of the legal actors.

More and more of our encounters and relations are with corporate entities rather than natural persons. More and more of our common life is pursued under the auspices of "artificial persons." With them has come a pervasive legalization of life. The sheer amount of law in American society has increased enormously since 1970 and with it the total amount of legal services provided by a much larger and more proficient body of lawyers. To take just a single summary indicator, the portion of the gross domestic product consisting of legal services rose from 0.6 percent in 1967 to 1.6 percent in 1993. As the size of the legal services "pie" has increased, a greater and greater share of that pie has been consumed by business and government organizations and a shrinking share by individuals. In 1967, individuals bought 55 percent of the product of the legal services industry, and businesses bought 39 percent. With each subsequent five-year period, the business portion has increased and the share consumed by individuals has declined. By 1992, the share bought by businesses increased (from 39 percent) to 51 percent, and the share bought by individuals dropped to 40 percent (from 55 percent).

The increasing predominance of organizations as users of law is displayed in Heinz and Laumann's replication of *Chicago Lawyers*. They found law practice in 1975 divided into lawyers who represent large organizations (corporations, labor unions, or government) and those who represent individuals. The two kinds of law practice are two hemispheres of the profession. Most lawyers reside exclusively in one hemisphere or the other and seldom, if ever, cross the equator.

They estimated that in 1975, "more than half (53 percent) of the total effort of Chicago's bar was devoted to the corporate client sector, and a smaller but still substantial proportion (40 percent) is expended on the personal client sector." When the study was replicated 20 years later, the researchers found that there were roughly twice as many lawyers working in Chicago. In 1995, however, about 61 percent of the total effort of all Chicago lawyers was devoted to the corporate client sector and only 29 percent to the personal/small business sector. Because the number of lawyers in Chicago had doubled, the total effort devoted to the personal sector had increased by 45 percent, yet the corporate sector grew by 126 percent. To the extent that lawyers serving the corporate sector were able to command more staff and support services with their effort, these figures understate the gap in services delivered.

The increasing presence of these organizational players—and I include governments and associations as well as corporations—means more occasions to deploy the structural advantages that are discussed in the "Haves" paper. In addition to these structural advantages, artificial persons enjoy "cultural" advantages in the legal forum. U.S. courts have been very receptive to the notion that corporate actors are persons with rights of their own rather than merely instruments of natural persons. Corporations have won, in a string of contemporary Supreme Court opinions, significant Bill of Rights protections involving double jeopardy, search and seizure, and free speech protection on corporate political spending and advertising. One commentator characterized these opinions as symbolic of "the transformation of our constitutional system from one of individual freedoms to one of organizational prerogatives."

Although they enjoy an array of rights, corporations are largely immune from criminal punishment. They cannot be imprisoned, and fines are typically minimal from a corporate vantage, because they are designed with natural persons in mind. On the other hand, corporate actors are frequent and successful users of the criminal justice system to punish offenses against themselves. We tend to be forgiving of corporate folly. Rather than chastening, many of the blunders of corporations are deemed worthy of solace in the form of tax deductions.

Corporations enjoy a relative impunity to moral condemnation for single-minded pursuit of advantage that would be condemned as unworthy if done by natural persons (for example, changing residence or status to secure tax advantages, locating assets to avoid liability). Although individuals who invoke the legal system arouse suspicion and reproach, corporate actors are rarely condemned for aggressively using litigation in pursuit of their interests. Compare the outrage at the McDonald's coffee spill case with the sanguine response to the Texaco-Pennzoil award. A couple of years ago, I found that about 95 percent of a very skeptical class of Wisconsin undergraduates were outraged at the McDonald's coffee spill verdict, but after my persuasive briefing about the facts and the context, this fine dropped to no more than 92 percent. At the same time, they were quite sanguine about the Texaco-Pennzoil award, which they saw as unexceptionable protection of business interests.

A similar cultural slant is found within the legal profession itself. Heinz and Laumann report that the prestige ranking of legal fields mirrors the structural division of the profession, "with fields serving big business clients at the top and those serving individual clients (especially clients from lower socioeconomic groups) at the bottom." In other words, "The higher a specialty stands in its reputation for being motivated by altruistic (as opposed to profitable) considerations, the lower it is likely to be in the prestige order."

The emergence of the notion that legal action is appropriate for corporate bodies but not for individuals is obscure. As many of you know, I have been occupying my time examining lawyer jokes and their history. From this source, I have a sense that several generations back, corporations drew more moral condemnation for their misdeeds. Jokes about lawyers, as about many things, are usually long-lived, but some do drop out of the joke corpus. One cluster of such dropouts is jokes about corporate manipulation of law. These jokes flourished beginning in the 1910s but are pretty much gone by the end of World War II. Here are three examples.

1. The big business magnate entered the famous lawyer's office wearing a worried frown. "That law I spoke to you about is stopping a big deal of mine," he said, "and I'd like to know if you can prove it unconstitutional?" "Very easily," declared the lawyer. "All right; then get busy and familiarize yourself with the law," he was instructed. "No need to," replied the lawyer. "It's that same law you had me prove constitutional a couple of years ago."

2. The eminent trust magnate was going over the books with his new systems expert.

   "Whew!" Whistled the systems expert "Your legal department costs you a heap. Still, I suppose you have to maintain it?"

   "Well, I don't know. Sometimes I think it would be cheaper to obey the law."

3. A New York Lawyer tells of a conversation that occurred in his presence between a bank president and his son who was about the leave for the West, there to engage in business on his own account.

   "Son," said the father, "on this, the threshold of your business life, I desire to impress one thought upon your mind. Honesty, ever and always is the policy that is best."

"Yes, father," said the young man.

"And, by the way," added the gray beard, "I would advise you to read up a little on corporation law. It will amaze you to discover how many things you can do in a business way and still be honest."

These stories express not only a generic suspicion of corporations but distinct notions about law: (1) that despite its air of solidity and majesty, law is malleable; (2) that despite its avowed link to morality, law can be used to circumvent morality; and (3) that despite their pretension to magisterial dignity, lawyers are hired guns who manipulate the law for their clients. Does the demise of these jokes indicate that people no longer believe these things? I think there is solid evidence that they continue to believe these things, perhaps even more intensely than before.

Although wide publics buy into much of the "litigation explosion" lore promulgated by corporate, media, and political elites, there is a widespread and abiding popular perception that the law's departure from justice is not random, but that it systematically favors the rich and powerful. That those with superior fiscal and organizational resources enjoy advantages in litigation has been appreciated by most observers (not just on the left) for a long time. Although survey researchers seem to avoid asking questions about organizational potency, the responses to their questions about treatment of rich and poor reveal a sanguine public estimation that the legal system is biased in favor of the "haves." Twenty years ago, 59 percent of a national sample agreed that "the legal system favors the rich and powerful over everyone else." Ten years ago, when asked whether "the justice system in the United States mainly favors the rich" or "treats all Americans as equally as possible," 57 percent of respondents chose the "favored the rich" response and only 39 percent the "equally" response. In a 1995 survey conducted by U.S. News & World Report, fully three-quarters of the respondents thought that the U.S. legal system affords less access to justice to "average Americans" than [it does] to rich people, and four out of five of these thought "much less." In August 1998, only 33 percent of respondents to a national survey agreed with the statement, "Courts try to treat poor people and wealthy people alike," but 90 percent agreed that "wealthy people or companies often wear down their opponents by dragging out the legal proceedings." Half a year later in another national survey, 80 percent of respondents thought that the "wealthy" receive better treatment from the courts than do other people, and two-thirds agreed with the statement, "When a person sues a corporation, the courts generally favor the corporation over the person."

There seems to be no shortage of cynical knowledge. It is no secret that the "haves" come out ahead. (Were we, scholars of the legal system, the last to know?) How do we square these views with the response to the claims of Stella Liebeck (the McDonald's coffee claimant) and of Pennzoil? Maybe people believe at some level that the "haves" ought to come out ahead. They are supposed to; that is the proper shape of things. Perhaps that is why verdicts for plaintiffs in product liability cases are twelve times more likely to attract newspaper coverage than are verdicts for defendants. David beating Goliath is still a good story, one that is both reassuring and upsetting.

Another possible explanation for the demise of the "haves" jokes is that we are so suffused with cynical knowledge that the notions in the jokes (the malleability of law, its use for immoral purposes, lawyers as whores) are no longer sufficiently surprising (or difficult to acknowledge) to support a punchline. Our doubts about the high expectations of law and lawyers against which the deviance portrayed in the jokes is measured no longer require the indirection of the joke form.

We arrive at a tangle of questions about the relationship between our growing knowledge about the legal world, public perceptions of that world, and the way people act in that world. Does our knowledge affect the working of the legal world? Does the effective functioning of legal institutions require the support of myths about the law's moral grandeur? How much cynical knowledge can the public—or scholars—absorb? How do we manage to have both myths of legality and cynical knowledge? One of the curiosities of our current situation is that the more established and advantaged sections of the population, those who know more about the system and benefit most from its working, tend to be the most disconsolate and angry with it. The "haves" sponsor campaigns against the legal system, trying to persuade the public that it is "demented" and "spun out of control." Some people are never satisfied!

". . . there is no incompatibility between the activity of organizations in litigation and the integrity or independence of the judiciary."

6.5 LITIGATION AS A FORM OF PRESSURE GROUP ACTIVITY

Clement E. Vose

Clement E. Vose was John F. Andrus Professor of Government, Wesleyan University.

Organizations support legal action because individuals lack the necessary time, money, and skill. The form of group participation in court cases is set by such factors as the type of proceeding, standing of the parties, legal or constitutional issues in dispute, the characteristics of the organization, and its interest in the outcome. Perhaps the most direct and open participation has been by organizations which have been obliged to protect their own rights and privileges. The cases have sometimes placed organizations as parties, but more often the organization supports a member or an officer in litigation. One example must suffice.

The constitutional concept of religious freedom has been broadened in recent years by the Supreme Court decisions in cases involving members of the sect known as Jehovah's Witnesses. Most of the cases began when a Jehovah's

From 319 *The Annals of the American Academy of Political and Social Science* 20 (1958). Copyright 1958 the American Academy of Political and Social Science. Reprinted with permission.

Witness violated a local ordinance or state statute. Since 1938, the Witnesses, incorporated as the Watch Tower Bible and Tract Society and represented by its counsel, Hayden Cooper Covington, have won forty-four of fifty-five cases in the United States Supreme Court.

The NAACP

Since 1909 the National Association for the Advancement of Colored People has improved the legal status of Negroes immeasurably by the victories it has won in more than fifty Supreme Court cases. During its early years, the NAACP relied upon prominent volunteer lawyers to represent Negroes in the courts. Limited success coupled with its failure to win gains from Congress led the NAACP in the 1930s to make court litigation fundamental to its program. A separate organization, the NAACP Legal Defense and Educational Fund, was incorporated for this purpose. The goal of the NAACP was to make Negroes "an integral part of the nation, with the same rights and guarantees that are accorded to other citizens, and on the same terms." This ambition meant that beginning in 1938 Thurgood Marshall as special counsel for the NAACP Legal Defense and Educational Fund held what was "probably the most demanding legal post in the country."

In aiming to establish racial equality before the law on a broad basis, the Legal Defense Fund has not functioned as a legal aid society. Limited resources have prevented the Fund from participating in all cases involving the rights of Negroes. As early as 1935 Charles Houston, an imaginative Negro lawyer who preceded Marshall as special counsel, set the tone of NAACP efforts when he declared that the legal campaign against inequality should be carefully planned "to secure decisions, rulings and public opinion on the broad principle instead of being devoted to merely miscellaneous cases."

By presenting test cases to the Supreme Court, the NAACP has won successive gains protecting the right of Negroes in voting, housing, transportation, education, and service on juries. Each effort has followed the development of new theories of legal interpretation and required the preparation of specific actions in the courts to challenge existing precedent. The NAACP Legal Defense Fund has accomplished these two tasks through the cooperation of associated and allied groups. First, as many as fifty Negro lawyers practicing in all parts of the country have been counsel in significant civil rights cases in the lower courts. Many of these men received their legal education at the Howard University Law School in Washington, D.C., and have shared membership in the National Bar Association since its founding in 1925. . . . Second, the NAACP has long benefited from its official advisory group, the National Legal Committee composed of leading Negro and white lawyers. . . . Third, other organizations with no direct connection with the Legal Defense Fund have sponsored a few cases. State and local chapters of the NAACP have often aided Negroes who were parties in cases, especially in the lower courts. The St. Louis Association of Real Estate Brokers was the chief sponsor of the important restrictive covenant case of Shelley v. Kraemer. A Negro national college fraternity, Alpha Phi Alpha, sponsored quite completely the successful attack on discrimination in interstate railway dining cars. . . .

The American Liberty League

The experience of the American Liberty League, organized in 1934 by conservative businessmen to oppose the New Deal, provides another variation on the theme of organizations in litigation. When the League proved unable to prevent enactment of economic regulation by Congress, a National Lawyers' Committee was formed to question the constitutionality of the legislation. In August 1935, the National Lawyers' Committee of fifty-eight members announced plans to prepare a series of reports to the public on whether particular federal laws were "consonant with the American constitutional system and American traditions." These reports "would be of a strictly professional nature and would in no case go into the question of social and economic advisability or the need for constitutional change to meet new conditions." This intention led the Committee during the next two years to conclude that a dozen New Deal statutes were unconstitutional.

The most celebrated Liberty League "brief" prepared by the National Lawyers' Committee questioned the constitutionality of the National Labor Relations Act. That analysis was prepared by a subcommittee of eight attorneys under the chairmanship of Earl F. Reed. It was then submitted to the other members and made public by Raoul E. Desverine, Chairman of the entire group, on Constitution Day, 1935. The reports of the Committee were given wide publicity through press releases, the distribution of pamphlets, and radio talks by leading conservative lawyers like James M. Beck. . . .

Members of the National Lawyers' Committee of the American Liberty League, but not the organization itself, participated in litigation. . . . Although the intention was to offer free legal services to citizens without funds to defend their constitutional rights, members of the National Lawyers' Committee actually represented major corporations which challenged the constitutionality of New Deal legislation in the Supreme Court. Earl F. Reed simply adapted the Liberty League report to apply to the specific facts of the case when he represented the Jones and Laughlin Steel Corporation against the National Labor Relations Board. Another member of the National Lawyers' Committee, John W. Davis, represented the Associated Press in a companion case.

Organizations as "Friends of the Court"

The appearance of organizations as amici curiae has been the most noticed form of group representation in Supreme Court cases. During the last decade amici curiae have submitted an average of sixty-six briefs and seven oral arguments in an average total of forty cases a term.

The frequent entrance of organizations into Supreme Court cases by means of the amicus curiae device has often given litigation the distinct flavor of group combat. This may be illustrated by the group representation in quite different cases. In 1943, when a member of the Jehovah's Witnesses challenged the constitutionality of a compulsory flag salute in the schools, his defense by counsel for the Watchtower Bible and Tract Society was supported by separate amici curiae, the American Civil Liberties Union and the Committee on the Bill of Rights of the American Bar Association. The appellant state board of education was supported by an amicus curiae brief filed by the American Legion. In 1951, in a case testing state resale price maintenance, the United States was an amicus against a Louisiana statute while the Commonwealth of Pennsylvania, the Louisiana State Pharmaceutical Association, American Booksellers, Inc., and the National Association of Retail Druggists entered amici curiae briefs in support of the statute. . . .

Regulation of Organizations in the Courts

Judges, lawyers, legislators, and citizens have reacted to appearances that organizational activity in court cases touches the integrity of the judicial process. A number of limitations have resulted. But in protecting the legal system against these dangers, regulations may be too harsh on organizations and interfere unduly with the freedom of association their functioning represents. Especially is this true when the barriers against group participation in litigation are erected by legislative bodies, but it is not entirely absent when the rules are established by bar associations or by courts themselves. Some practices by organizations require control, but most of the practices of organizations in conducting litigation are perfectly compatible with an independent judiciary. . . .

During the trial of the leaders of the Communist party under the Smith Act in the Federal District Court for the Eastern District of New York located at Foley Square in New York City, picketing and parading outside the court was a daily occurrence. When the Senate Judiciary Committee was considering bills to limit this practice, it received many statements like the following: "Assuming under our form of representative government pressure groups must be tolerated in our legislative and executive branches, I feel there is no good reason why our courts should be subjected to such pressures." In accord with this view, Congress, in 1950, enacted legislation prohibiting any person from parading, picketing, or demonstrating in or near a federal courthouse with the intent of "interfering with, obstructing, or impeding" the administration of justice or of "influencing any judge, juror, witness, or court officer" in the discharge of his duty.

In 1953, the National Committee to Secure Justice in the Rosenberg Case addressed a petition claimed to have the support of 50,000 persons to the Supreme Court. . . . No rule prevents groups from such indecorous action but Justice Hugo Black has expressed the intense disapproval of the Supreme Court. In 1951, when granting a stay of execution to Willie McGhee, a Negro under the death penalty in Mississippi, Justice Black lamented the "growing practice of sending telegrams to judges in order to have cases decided by pressure." Declaring that he would not read them, he said that "the courts of the United States are not the kind of instruments of justice that can be influenced by such pressures." Justice Black gave an implied warning to the bar by noting that "counsel in this case have assured me they were not responsible for these telegrams."

The offer of the National Lawyers' Committee of the American Liberty League to donate its services in test cases led a critic to make a formal complaint to the American Bar Association. The League was charged with unethical conduct for having "organized a vast free lawyers' service for firms and individuals 'bucking' New Deal laws on constitutional grounds." The ABA Committee on Professional Ethics and Grievances ruled, in a formal opinion, that the activities of the Liberty League were perfectly proper, even laudable. The Committee found that neither the substance of the offer, to provide legal defense for "indigent citizens without compensation," nor the "proffer of service," even when broadcast over the radio, was offensive to the ethical code of the American bar. . . .

* * *

. . . Considering the importance of the issues resolved by American courts, the entrance of organizations into cases in these ways seems in order. Indeed the essential right of organizations to pursue litigation would appear to follow from the generous attitude of American society toward the freedom of individuals to form associations for the purpose of achieving a common goal. Of course, traditional judicial procedures should be followed and the attorneys for organizations, as well as for individuals, must address their arguments to reason. If these standards of conduct are followed there is no incompatibility between the activity of organizations in litigation and the integrity or independence of the judiciary.

"We believe . . . that powerful interests will not stand by passively as the Supreme Court legitimizes literally hundreds of decisions in the lower courts each year and calls many others into question."

6.6 ORGANIZED INTERESTS AND AGENDA SETTING IN THE U.S. SUPREME COURT

Gregory A. Caldeira and John R. Wright

Gregory A. Caldeira is Distinguished University Professor of Political Science, and John R. Wright is Professor of Political Science at Ohio State University.

Each year a multitude of interest groups participate in various guises before the Supreme Court. It is clear that in the last couple of decades interest groups have stepped up their activities before the courts, just as they have in other political arenas. Interest groups can of course choose to take part before the Supreme

From 82 *American Political Science Review* 1109 (1988), with adjustments made to facilitate accessibility.

Court in many different roles, and they most often do so as amici curiae. Organized interests have long participated actively as amici curiae for decisions on the merits. But political scientists, with few exceptions, have not measured the impact of these briefs, and no one has done so for decisions on writs of certiorari and appeal.

We contend that not only are amicus curiae briefs important, but that the decision to review a case ranks as important as—if not more important than—the decision on the merits. In setting its agenda, the Supreme Court each year determines new winners and losers in the struggle for economic, political, and social power. We believe, therefore, that powerful interests will not stand by passively as the Supreme Court legitimizes literally hundreds of decisions in the lower courts each year and calls many others into question. And so, as Justice Brandeis once remarked, "the most important thing the Court does is not doing." Thus we ask, to what extent does amicus curiae participation by organized interests influence the Supreme Court's selection of cases for plenary hearing? . . .

* * *

The idea that interest groups have significance in litigation before the Supreme Court goes back at least as far as Bentley's *Process of Government* (1908): "So far from being a sort of legal machine, courts are a functioning part of this government, responsive to the group pressures within it, representatives of all sorts of pressures, and using their representative judgment to bring these pressures to balance, not indeed in just the same way, but on just the same basis that any other agency does." The tactics groups can use to influence legislation are considerable, including "class actions" and test cases; participation as amici curiae; giving of advice and service; expert testimony, and financial assistance; and taking control of the law suit. Vose (1959) blazed a trail with his meticulous and intriguing case study of how the NAACP Legal Defense Fund used a variety of strategies and tactics in its campaign of litigation to end the restrictive covenant in housing. . . .

[S]cholars have demonstrated over and over again the vigorous, extensive, and continuing efforts on the part of interest groups to lobby the courts. At least since the 1960s evidence of the participation of interest groups as amici curiae or sponsors has virtually leaped from the pages of the United States Reports even on the most cursory inspection.

Although the filing of amicus curiae briefs is just one of many tactics available to organized interests, participation as amicus has figured as an indicator of interest group activity in virtually every pertinent study. More important, we have good reason to believe that such filings are consequential. The filing of an amicus brief, apart from the quality or persuasiveness of the arguments presented, provides the justices with an indication of the array of social forces at play in the litigation. In *Bakke v. Regents* of the University of California, for example, the Court had fifty-seven briefs from "friends" and without doubt obtained a vivid picture of whose interests were at risk. The Supreme Court, as Krislov has remarked, sometimes views the amicus as a "potential litigant in future cases, as an ally of one of the parties, or as the representative of an interest not otherwise represented.". . .

So, clearly, interest groups have used the vehicle of amicus briefs often and, in recent years, with increased frequency. There is, in addition, some fragmentary evidence that participation as an amicus curiae constitutes an efficacious route for interest groups to take in their attempt to influence the Court. Puro found that groups on the "liberal" side participated more often as friends of the Court and were more likely than conservatives to triumph on the merits.

We, too, believe that amici curiae make a difference in litigation. And we propose that their impact will be apparent at the agenda-setting phase. The presence of amici during case selection communicates to the Supreme Court information about the constellation of interests involved, and this information, we suggest, is both valued and heeded by the justices and their clerks . . .

Quite simply, our theory assumes that the potential significance of a case is proportional to the demand for adjudication among affected parties and that the amount of amicus curiae participation reflects the demand for adjudication. We propose that amicus curiae participation by organized interests provides information, or signals—otherwise largely unavailable—about the political, social, and economic significance of cases on the Supreme Court's paid docket and that justices make inferences about the potential impact of their decisions by observing the extent of amicus activity. Although potential amici have the option of filing briefs either in support of, or in opposition to, petitions for writs of certiorari, our theory suggests that both types of briefs should have the same effect—that is, increase the likelihood of a grant. The reason is simply that both kinds of briefs draw attention to the potential significance of a case. Consequently, the mere presence or absence of a brief amicus curiae may weigh in more heavily than the substantive arguments presented. . . .

Our primary hypothesis [then] is that the greater number of amicus curiae briefs filed for a given case—either in favor of, or in opposition to, certiorari—the greater the likelihood that the case will be granted a writ of certiorari. We test this hypothesis using data we have collected on all paid cases in which the Supreme Court granted or denied a writ of certiorari or affirmed, dismissed, reversed, or noted probable jurisdiction on a writ of appeal during the 1982 term (N 5 2,061). Of these 2,061 cases, 1,906 involved petitions for writs of certiorari, and the rest were decided on appeal. We confine our analysis to petitions for writs of certiorari, of which 145 (7.6 percent) succeeded. . . .

A simple . . . analysis of decisions on certiorari and filing of amicus briefs indicates considerable preliminary support for our main hypothesis. At least one brief was filed in 148 of the 1,906 petitions (108 cases with briefs in support only, twenty-nine cases with briefs in opposition only, and eleven with briefs both for and against), and the Court granted certiorari in fifty-four, or 36 percent, of these cases. In contrast, when no one filed an amicus brief on a petition, the Court granted only 5 percent of the cases.

Not only does one brief in favor of certiorari significantly improve the chances of a case being accepted, but two, three, and four briefs improve the chances even more. [This finding holds even after we (statistically) take into account other important forces in the certiorari process, such as whether conflict existed in the lower courts.] . . .

Importantly [too] briefs amicus curiae in *opposition* to a petition for certiorari significantly *increase*—rather than decrease—the likelihood that the Supreme Court will grant a review. This result is not nearly so striking as that for briefs in support of certiorari, but [it is statistically significant.] . . . In any event, this result further supports our theory that an amicus brief at the agenda-setting stage is a signal by organized interests to the Supreme Court about the practical importance of a case. The direction of the statistical result suggests that what matters most is the presence or absence of an amicus brief per se, not the direction of the substantive arguments presented. If justices were strongly influenced by the contents of the briefs themselves, it is quite unlikely that briefs in opposition to certiorari would significantly increase the likelihood of certiorari being granted. Briefs amicus curiae in opposition, plainly and simply, pique the Court's interest in a case. . . .

We believe this result is important both for understanding judicial behavior and for understanding the strategies and influence of organized interests in national politics. The U.S. Supreme Court, in our estimation, is quite responsive to the demands and preferences of organized interests when choosing its plenary docket. In this regard, the Supreme Court is very much a representative institution, and we think it both useful and important to analyze the Court from this perspective. We view the Court's openness to outside demands when choosing its plenary docket as not only necessary for a smoothly functioning representative polity but also as a natural consequence of rational political decision making. To be sure, how well or whether judicial responsiveness to the demands of organized interests comports with more traditional theories of decision making is a matter of considerable controversy and is best left for fuller treatment elsewhere.

Organized interests are generally influential during the Court's agenda phase because they solve an informational problem for the justices. Through participation as amici, organized interests effectively communicate to the justices information about the array of forces at play in the litigation, who is at risk, and the number and variety of parties regarding the litigation as significant. Obtained elsewhere, this information would surely be much more costly than as provided through amicus participation, if it could be obtained elsewhere at all. In this regard, organized interests function effectively as interest articulators, a result that generally adds stability to political systems.

CHAPTER 7

Instruments of Judicial Power

The judge's chair is a seat of power. Not only do judges have power to make binding decisions on private citizens, their rulings may also legitimate or negate the use of power by other public officials. Judges are the custodians of authority because their putative expertise in the law, their presumed independence from partisan political control, and their ritualized fact-finding procedures supposedly make their decisions more objective than those of other officials.

The power that judges exercise is not, of course, directly related to the physical force they command. They have only a few officers of the court at their disposal, merely enough to keep order in the courtroom and to move prisoners safely to and from jail. But judicial orders are generally obeyed without overt compulsion. Presumably, even the losers either believe in the fairness of the adjudicative process or recognize that nonacquiescence would be futile because the substantial power of the executive branch usually stands ready to enforce judicial decisions.[1] The constitutional text commands that the president "shall take Care that the Laws be faithfully executed," and specific congressional statutes direct executive assistance in carrying out judicial decisions. Without orders to the contrary, U.S. marshals will enforce decrees of federal courts, and the Department of Justice will cooperate in protecting the integrity of the judicial process. Occasionally, as in 1809, when the governor of Pennsylvania used militia to defy the Supreme Court's judgment in *United States v. Peters,* or when mob violence prevented school desegregation in Little Rock in 1957 and at the University of Mississippi in 1962, additional force might be necessary to secure obedience to a court's order. The marshal can summon a posse, as was done in the *Peters* case, or the president might send in federal troops, as happened in Little Rock and Mississippi. But the fact that force must be used indicates that courts in such cases are approaching the limits of their authority.

---

[1] Judges, of course, have power to command only the parties in the proceeding before them. Whether their decision in a particular case will become effective as a legal standard controlling conduct or be accepted as a precedent in subsequent litigation pose other questions, which we shall examine in Chapters 10 and 14.

WRITS OF CERTIORARI

Before judges resolve disputes in cases before them, they must ascertain whether those suits belong in their courts. Chapter 6 detailed some of the considerations that guide their decisions about who can have access to judicial power and under what circumstances. But, as we saw, simply because a dispute meets these requirements does not mean judges will decide it. The U.S. Supreme Court and many state courts of last resort enjoy wide discretion in shaping their dockets, accepting less than 5 percent of the cases that reach their doorsteps. Writs of certiorari provide the most common method for exercising that discretion.

These writs, as we noted in Chapter 3, are essentially requests by losing litigants to have their records reviewed by a higher court. That court may grant or deny their requests. These writs hark back to a long tradition.[2] Mentions of them in English law come as early as the thirteenth century, and they developed in Britain much as they began—as a "tool to ensure justice by allowing a superior court to remove proceedings from an inferior court."[3] The colonists carried over this process to America, where it was used in much the same way: high courts could issue extraordinary writs—such as certiorari and habeas corpus (discussed later in this chapter)—unless a statute prohibited them from so doing.

This common-law practice, however, is not what the contemporary Supreme Court typically invokes to hear disputes. Rather, the justices rely on "statutory certiorari," that is, on laws passed by Congress that allow them discretion to issue or deny such writs. One such statute, enacted in 1891, allowed the Court some choice in reviewing decisions of circuit courts (now the courts of appeal) via writs of certiorari. Another, enacted in 1914, extended certiorari to certain decisions of state courts. But it was the Judiciary Act of 1925 that established "statutory certiorari" as the principal method for obtaining access to the Court. Under this Act, the justices were obliged to hear only a few categories of cases, such as those in which a federal court had invalidated a state law or a state court had invalidated a federal law. For the rest, the Supreme Court had discretion to grant or deny "cert." In 1988, Congress further extended the justices' freedom to choose among cases. Today the Court is legally obliged to hear only very few controversies (mostly those involving the Voting Rights Act of 1965) appealed from special three-judge district courts.

Over the years, the Court has promulgated rules to explain what makes a case worthy of cert; and scholars have extensively studied the process in order to identify precisely what factors the justices consider and what weight they give to each in deciding to grant or deny cert. The resulting research, which we describe in some detail in Chapter 13 (see also Reading 6.6), is important to

---

[2] This discussion draws on H. W. Perry, *Deciding to Decide* (Cambridge, MA: Harvard University Press, 1991), 295–298, and Felix Frankfurter and James M. Landis, *The Business of the Supreme Court* (New York: Macmillan, 1928).

[3] Perry, *Deciding to Decide*, 296.

scholars, policy makers, and attorneys alike because the justices, although occasionally providing explanations for granting certiorari, typically issue a one-line order: "The petition for a writ of certiorari is denied."

Hopwood v. Texas (1996) is among the exceptions to the justices' general silence. There, the Court declined to hear an affirmative action case in which a lower court had essentially refused to follow the Supreme Court's doctrine laid down in *Bakke*. Perhaps because such action by a lower tribunal is so unusual, two justices felt compelled to explain why they voted to deny cert (Reading 7.1). Intriguingly, the Court waited nearly a decade after *Hopwood* before it jumped back into the fray over affirmative action. In a pair of cases it decided in 2004 (*Grutter v. Bollinger* and *Gratz v. Bollinger*), the Court held that universities may maintain affirmative action programs for the purpose of diversifying their student body so long as those programs are "holistic" and "individualized" in approach, and are not quota systems.

DECISIONS, OPINIONS, AND ORDERS

A judge's authority varies, depending on the particular level of the court and on whether the case is heard with or without a jury. But, even when the final decision is left to a jury, the judge's instructions to the jurors and rulings on what evidence they may or may not consider typically have great influence in determining the outcome of litigation.

The judge's capacity to command is made more palatable by the general assumption that judicial decisions are based on reason and knowledge of the law. Federal rules of procedure require judges of district courts to file findings of fact and conclusions of law to explain their decisions, and judges of appellate courts typically support their rulings with lengthy essays—opinions—justifying those decisions. Jurists have long recognized that carefully drafted explanations of their interpretations and applications of the law not only help demonstrate the correctness of particular decisions but can also increase their impact on public policy. John Marshall fully realized the potential of judicial opinions as instruments to achieve fundamental political goals. His opinions in *Marbury v. Madison* (1803) (first fully asserting judicial review), *McCulloch v. Maryland* (1819), and *Gibbons v. Ogden* (1824) (marking the constitutional expansion of federal power) stand among the most significant of American political writings.

Marshall was the original master of this technique, but many later judges such as Oliver Wendell Holmes, Louis D. Brandeis, Harlan Fiske Stone, and Robert H. Jackson have rivaled his persuasiveness, if not his authoritative voice. Judicial opinions can have a great impact not only on other jurists but also on public officials and even on national public opinion. Phrases like "one person, one vote" may become political slogans around which interest groups and political parties rally. Equally eloquent statements, such as this by Justice Jackson—"If there is any fixed star in our constitutional constellation, it is that no official, high or petty, can prescribe what shall be orthodox in politics, nationalism, religion, or other matters of opinion or force citizens to confess by word or act their faith therein"—can encapsulate an entire political philosophy and set ideals for public policy.

The results of an opinion often come years, even decades, later. Dissenting in *Olmstead v. United States* (1928), Justice Louis D. Brandeis made an impassioned argument for a constitutional right to privacy, but his eloquent reasoning did not bear full fruit for thirty-seven years, when *Griswold v. Connecticut* (1965) so ruled. In the intervening decades, however, his ringing claim for recognition of privacy as "the most comprehensive of rights and the right most valued by civilized men" gnawed at the consciences of the justices and of the nation.

The compelling element in every judicial decision is the order, which terminates the proceeding and appears at the conclusion of the written opinion. Most litigation ends with a simple order that prescribes imprisonment for a period, imposes a fine, commands payment of a sum of money in settlement of a claim, terminates a marriage, or announces who owns a piece of property. On occasion, however, an order can be quite lengthy and complex—for example, a detailed set of instructions as to what specific steps public officials must take to end racial segregation in a school system or to provide proper care and medical treatment for inmates of state mental institutions. At the Supreme Court level, the order typically issued merely affirms or reverses a contested decision of a lower court and remands the case to the lower court for further proceedings in conformity with the Supreme Court's opinion.

THE INJUNCTION

As we suggested above, common-law judges in England invented a number of specialized orders, or writs (including certiorari), that were available to litigants for achieving particular purposes. Most of these writs, however, were adapted only to the settlement of disputes over money, property, or office. In many situations a case concerned not a past wrong that could be compensated for by monetary damages, but a continuing or potential source of injury that a complainant wanted to have stopped or prevented. Because writs at common law looked backward rather than forward, judicial intervention to control future action was not possible.

This gap was filled by courts of equity,[4] which developed a writ called an injunction: a command the court directed to named defendants forbidding them to perform certain specified acts. It may also take the form of a mandatory injunction commanding performance of specific acts. Under traditional rules of

---

[4] Historic English practice created a dichotomy between cases in law and cases in equity. In its early development the common law had gone through periods of extreme rigidity during which courts simply turned away would-be litigants if their suits could not be settled by issuance of certain specific technical writs. These litigants began appealing to the king for his personal justice. By the fourteenth century such petitions for grace were being referred to the king's chancellor for settlement. Out of this practice, courts of chancery, or equity, grew up alongside the courts of law. In the Judiciary Act of 1789, the first Congress made a major, perhaps revolutionary, reform in judicial administration by providing that federal courts would have jurisdiction both in law and equity, a practice now followed in almost all American states and even in England.

equity, to obtain an injunction a litigant must show that she or he has a real right at stake, is suffering or is about to suffer "irreparable injury," no action at law offers an adequate remedy (that is, the injury is of a type that cannot be compensated for by an award of money), and when "the equities are balanced," righting this wrong will outweigh any inconvenience or damage suffered by the defendant or the public at large.

The injunction fulfills a very important function for public policy, because it is the principal instrument available to private parties for testing the constitutionality or legality of official action or restraining other private parties from committing allegedly illegal acts. (Sometimes public officials also use injunctions to compel private citizens to comply with the law.) This writ may take one of three basic forms:

1. *Ex parte restraining orders* are issued at the request of a complainant, without hearing the opposing party; these simply maintain the status quo until the court can hold a full hearing.
2. *Temporary injunctions* are issued after both parties have been heard, but these writs control action only for a specified time, after which the situation will presumably have stabilized or no longer exist. At the end of that period, the court may consider a motion to dissolve the injunction, continue it for another set term, or make it permanent.
3. *Permanent injunctions* control acts into the indefinite future.

Although an injunction addresses named defendants, it binds not only those people but also their servants, agents, attorneys, and employees, as well as all other persons who, knowing the injunction is in effect, conspire with the defendants to violate it. If the defendant is a public official, the injunction runs against the office rather than the incumbent, thus binding his or her successors. The writ differs from a statute in that it does not bind all persons within a particular jurisdiction, only those people described above.

An important feature of an injunction is that the judge can draft a decree with specific provisions aimed to secure the goal that she or he believes equity requires. For example, in 1972 a federal judge in Mississippi issued an injunction aimed at ending discrimination against blacks in the hiring policies of the state highway patrol. The writ ordered the state to stop refusing to give employment applications to blacks, to withdraw a recruiting motion picture portraying an all-white patrol, to advertise vacancies thirty days in advance, and to make recruiting visits to black colleges. In 1974, three years after Judge Frank M. Johnson in Alabama had issued a similar order, that state had a larger percentage of blacks in its state police force than any other state in the nation.

In more recent years, detailed and specific injunctions against people protesting against abortion clinics have generated a good deal of controversy. In an effort to protect their workers and patients from both physical intimidation and moral arguments, operators of those clinics have often asked courts to enjoin pro-life advocates from engaging in certain activities near their facilities. The pro-life demonstrators have countered that such injunctions violate their First Amendment rights to freedom of speech and association. The Supreme Court attempted to resolve the issue in *Madsen v. Women's Health Center, Inc.*

(1994) (Reading 7.2) and *Schenck v. Pro-Choice Network of Western New York* (1997). In both cases, the majority upheld most, but not all, parts of the lower courts' injunctions.[5]

On the use of injunctions to halt efforts to persuade or even physically prevent women from going to abortion clinics, courts have received reinforcement from Congress. The Freedom of Access to Clinic Entrances Act of 1994 specifically authorizes judges to enjoin people threatening or intimidating "persons seeking to obtain or provide reproductive health services." In other instances, however, Congress has attempted to curtail the injunctive power. During the first few decades of the twentieth century, many federal judges were willing, indeed eager, to use injunctions to break strikes or block unions' efforts to organize workers. In response, Congress adopted in 1932 the Norris-LaGuardia Act, which largely withdrew jurisdiction from federal courts to issue injunctions in labor disputes. There was some initial question whether this statute imposed an unconstitutional limit on judicial discretion and perhaps also on the rights of businessmen. *Truax v. Corrigan* (1921) had seemed to say that employers had a constitutionally protected right to seek an injunction in a dispute with their workers, for in that case the Supreme Court invalidated a state statute prohibiting state courts from enjoining certain kinds of actions in labor disputes. But, in *Lauf v. E. G. Shinner and Co.* (1938), the Supreme Court sustained the Norris-LaGuardia Act as an exercise of congressional authority "to define and limit the jurisdiction of the inferior courts of the United States." Nevertheless, the Court has subsequently recaptured for federal judges a substantial measure of power to issue injunctions in labor disputes by narrowly interpreting the prohibitions of the Norris-LaGuardia Act or finding them in conflict with more recent congressional legislation. Moreover, in 1947, Congress enacted the Taft-Hartley Act, which authorized federal courts to issue injunctions against strikes imperiling the national health or safety. Such injunctions, however, cannot be sought by private parties. Only the attorney general of the United States can ask for the writ, and the order is limited to barring strikes during an eighty-day "cooling-off" period so that negotiations to end the dispute can proceed.

Injunctions and Positive Action

As many of these examples indicate, judges traditionally have issued injunctions to bar continuance of particular actions already begun or to prohibit acts not yet begun—forbidding, for instance, people from trying to dissuade or

---

[5] See Reading 7.2 for details on the injunction at issue in *Madsen*. The injunction in *Schenck* created a fixed buffer zone requiring anti-abortion protesters to stay at least fifteen feet away from clinic doors and driveways to ensure access to the building. It also imposed a floating buffer zone, banning protesters from coming within fifteen feet of people and vehicles entering and leaving the clinic. The justices upheld the fixed buffer zone as reasonable, but found that the floating buffer zone violated the First Amendment by burdening speech more than necessary to achieve relevant government interests. As in *Madsen*, Justices Scalia, Kennedy, and Thomas dissented, asserting that the fixed buffer zone as well as the floating zone should have been found to violate the First Amendment rights of the demonstrators.

threatening women seeking to obtain abortions. As prohibitions, injunctions are typically negative orders, with the purpose of maintaining the status quo or returning the parties in the suit to the relation that had existed before one of them had taken the injunction action.

In recent years, negative orders have continued, but many of the sorts of decrees involved in operating schools, jails, and hospitals or in redistricting states have required positive action—and not merely in the sense of demanding that officials undo some particular past wrong. These writs have also ordered officials to pursue indefinitely new and complicated public policies that judges think are necessary to achieve the ends of the constitutional system. *Wyatt v. Stickney* provides an example. In a widely publicized instance of judicial involvement, Federal District Judge Frank M. Johnson issued a precedent-setting order asserting the constitutional rights of patients committed to Alabama state hospitals "to receive such individual treatment as will give each of them a realistic opportunity to be cured or to improve his or her mental condition." His order detailed minimum constitutional standards for treatment and accommodations and required human rights committees to monitor their enforcement. (Reading 7.3)

Such commands relegate vast power to judges and turn high governmental officers into subordinates. The impact of such injunctions on people not directly involved in the litigation also increases markedly. The state legislature, for instance, might be forced to raise taxes to finance the execution of a court's orders or to find the money by reducing the budgets of other agencies or by curtailing certain public services. For example, to comply with *Wyatt,* Alabama increased its spending on mental health from $14 million in 1971 to $58 million in 1973.[6]

One might cogently argue that, in cases that have spawned such sweeping decrees, judges have done no more than mandate policies that elected officials should have been—but were not—carrying out of their own free will. Judge Johnson made precisely that point in defending his orders regarding reform of the "barbaric and shocking" conditions in Alabama's mental hospitals.[7] But many others, including judges and serious scholars, have been troubled by the alleged specter of government by judiciary. As Donald L. Horowitz has put it: "When it comes to framing and modifying programs, administrators are far better situated [than judges] to see things whole, to obtain, process, and interpret complex or specialized data, to secure expert advice, to sense the need to change course, and to monitor performance after decision. Courts can limit the discretion of others, but they find it harder to exercise their own discretion where that involves choosing among multiple, competing alternatives."[8]

---

[6] See Alfred M. Mamlet, "Reconsideration of Separation of Powers and the Bargaining Game: Limiting the Policy Discretion of Judges and Plaintiffs in Institutional Suits," 33 *Emory Law Journal* 685 (1984).

[7] Frank M. Johnson, Jr., "The Role of the Judiciary with Respect to the Other Branches of Government," *John A. Sibley Lecture in Law,* University of Georgia, 1977.

[8] Donald L. Horowitz, "The Hazards of Judicial Guardianship," 37 *Public Administration Review* 148 (1977).

THE CONTEMPT POWER

The contempt power is one of the oldest of judicial weapons. Its purpose is to provide judges with the means to protect the dignity of their courts and to punish disobedience of their orders. There are distinctions between criminal and civil contempt, a distinction that, though often difficult to discern, is nonetheless important. The major difference relates to purpose. The aim of a charge of criminal contempt is to vindicate the dignity of the court, whereas an action for civil contempt tries to protect the rights of one of the litigants. The two types of action also differ as to procedure. In criminal cases, the judge or some other governmental official generally initiates prosecution; the usual presumption of innocence present in a criminal trial applies; and, to convict, the court must find the defendant guilty beyond a reasonable doubt. Civil contempt proceedings are commonly initiated by one of the parties to a suit, and the judge can decide the case on the preponderance of the evidence. Although the president may pardon a person found guilty of criminal contempt of a federal court, it is doubtful that he can pardon for civil contempt, at least when the offended party is a private citizen.

The most tangible difference between the two types of contempt action lies in the punishment meted out. Within limits set by legislatures, judges may impose fines or prison sentences for criminal contempt as in other criminal cases. Judges have the same option in civil cases, again within limits set by legislatures; but here their power is far more extensive. Because the object of a civil contempt action is to secure the rights of one of the parties, the sentence is normally conditional. The judge may, for example, sentence recalcitrants to be imprisoned until they agree to comply with the court's orders, a decision that, of course, could mean life imprisonment, a possibility that judges have recognized. The usual judicial response is that such prisoners carry the keys to their cells in their own pockets; they will be released as soon as they agree to obey the judge. Such an indeterminate sentence is usually more persuasive than a specific fine or short jail term.

The simplest kind of contempt issue is presented when an individual is disrespectful or disorderly in the courtroom. In this situation, the judge has traditionally had the power immediately and summarily, without notice, hearing, or representation by counsel, to charge, try, convict, and sentence the contemnor to jail for a specified term. If it is the defendant who is in contempt, his removal to jail would normally bring the trial to a halt. To prevent aborting the proceedings, judges have in some cases dealt with obstreperous defendants by chaining or gagging them in court and continuing the trial. In *Illinois v. Allen* (1970) the Supreme Court reluctantly approved such a practice. The justices, however, expressed preference for trial judges' using their traditional contempt power to punish disruptions. Furthermore, the Court held that, under extreme provocation, the judge could continue the trial after jailing the defendants without violating their constitutional rights. (Reading 7.4.) On the other hand, some judges have waited until after a trial, then charged, convicted, and sentenced offenders for contempt.

Judges may also hold in civil contempt those who refuse to testify or otherwise obstruct proceedings before a grand jury, if the prosecutor has obtained a judicial order requiring them to give evidence. Although imprisonment is limited to the term of the grand jury, a determined prosecutor can repeat the process before the next grand jury and so keep recalcitrant witnesses in jail for long periods. The two most famous cases in recent memory both involved President William Jefferson Clinton, though only the first resulted in a jailing. Special Prosecutor Kenneth Starr repeatedly tried to get Susan McDougal, an old friend of the Clintons, to answer questions before a grand jury about the First Family's financial dealings in Arkansas. Just as doggedly she refused and spent eighteen months in prison for these refusals. Eventually she was tried and acquitted on charges of criminal contempt and obstruction of justice.

In the other case, the president himself was the contemnor. In August 1999, he gave oral testimony that was televised nationally and video taped for a grand jury. There, under oath, he denied having had sexual relations with a young White House aide, Monica Lewinsky, despite conclusive evidence in the form of semen stains, identified by DNA testing as his. Federal District Judge Susan Weber, one of the president's former students, found his denials to constitute perjury, held him guilty of civil contempt, and fined him. Nothing would have been gained by a jail sentence because the perjury was an accomplished fact. Besides, an order from a federal judge to imprison the president of the United States would have presented constitutional and practical problems as fascinating as they are complex. For instance, who could carry out the order? Federal marshals fall under the command of the executive department.

The contempt power raises similarly serious, if less salacious, problems when used to require journalists, subpoenaed by a grand jury, to give information concerning stories they have written. In *Branzburg v. Hayes* (1972), three reporters, one from Kentucky, one from Massachusetts, and one from New York, refused to testify on the ground that the First Amendment gives them immunity from being forced to reveal the sources of their stories or details of actions they had been allowed to witness under the condition that they would not make public the names of identities of participants. By a five-to-four vote the Supreme Court sustained the convictions. The majority saw no First Amendment problem and declined "to grant newsmen a testimonial privilege that other citizens do not enjoy." The dissenters were distraught: Justice Potter Stewart, who in his youth had worked as a reporter for a Cincinnati newspaper and also edited the *Yale Daily News* while in college, condemned the "Court's crabbed view of the First Amendment."

Predictably, the media reacted even more vehemently, with outpourings of condemnation of *Branzburg* and calls for federal and state statutes that would excuse reporters from revealing their sources or information they had promised not to publish. As a result of this pressure, twenty-six states (but not Congress) enacted "shield laws" allowing journalists to refuse to divulge information about certain news-gathering activities. But because these laws often limit protections to specific circumstances, they are not always particularly effective. Branzburg was from Kentucky, which already had a shield law on the books at the time of his conviction. Unfortunately for him, it covered only sources of information and not personal observation. In many states as well as in the federal system, journalists still face the threat of imprisonment if they refuse to answer questions pertaining to their stories.

THE WRIT OF HABEAS CORPUS

Another major instrument of judicial power is the writ of habeas corpus. Called by Blackstone "the great writ of liberty," it is an order from a judge directing a jailer or other official who has custody of a prisoner to bring that person to court so that the judge can determine the legality of his or her detention. Originally the purpose of habeas corpus was to protect the jurisdiction of the English common-law courts against encroachments by courts of chancery or by the Crown. Gradually, however, the purpose of the writ shifted to become the classic means of protecting individuals against unlawful imprisonment. The Habeas Corpus Act of 1679 established the writ as one of the fundamental rights of Englishmen, and American colonial practice generally accorded habeas corpus the same high standing. Article I of the constitutional text provides that the privilege of the writ may not be suspended "unless when in Cases of Rebellion or Invasion the public Safety may require it."

As we saw in Chapter 3, modern American practice, while retaining habeas corpus as protection against executive authority, has also made it a means of tighter federal judicial control over state courts, usually through state prisoners' seeking another forum in which to challenge their convictions ("collateral review"). During the last few decades, however, the justices, in keeping with their efforts to curb access to federal courts, have limited the ability of state prisoners to use the writ to challenge their convictions.[9] In the Antiterrorism and Effective Death Penalty Act of 1996, Congress tried to further narrow the doors of federal courthouses to these prisoners as well as to immigrants subject to deportation. Somewhat surprisingly, given earlier attitudes, the justices have so far treated this statute rather warily, perhaps looking on it as an unwanted congressional intrusion into judicial business. And, as of late 2000, the total number of filings for habeas corpus in federal district courts had not dropped dramatically.

As a potential judicial weapon against executive power, habeas corpus poses a threat of intragovernmental conflict. On occasion the conflict has become a reality. In 1861, for instance, Chief Justice Roger Brooke Taney, sitting as a circuit court judge as the justices then did, ruled in *Ex parte Merryman* that only Congress, and not the president, could suspend the writ and ordered that a civilian prisoner, John Merryman, who had been arrested by the army, be brought into court. Lincoln met this challenge to his war power by ignoring the Chief Justice's order. Shortly thereafter, the president put a federal judge in the District of Columbia under virtual house arrest to prevent his hearing a different petition for habeas corpus. After the war, the full Supreme Court sustained Taney's doctrine in *Ex parte Milligan* (1866), but this decision could not undo the military rule that Lincoln had for years imposed on the border states. This experience was repeated almost exactly in World War II, when the Court invalidated the executive's suspension of habeas corpus in Hawaii only after the war

---

[9] Laurence H. Tribe summarizes the cases in *American Constitutional Law*, 3rd ed. (New York: Foundation Press, 2000), I, 501–518.

was over. It would thus appear, as Clinton Rossiter put it, that the fate of habeas corpus in times of emergency depends on what executives do and not on what judges say.[10]

SELECTED REFERENCES

BRIGHT, STEPHEN B. 1997. "Is Fairness Irrelevant?: The Evisceration of Federal Habeas Corpus Review and Limits on the Ability of State Courts to Protect Fundamental Rights." *Washington and Lee Law Review* 54: 1.

COVER, ROBERT, AND T. ALEXANDER ALEINIKOFF. 1977. "Dialectical Federalism: Habeas Corpus and the Court." *Yale Law Journal* 86: 1035.

DUKER, WILLIAM F. 1980. *A Constitutional History of Habeas Corpus.* Westport, CT: Greenwood Press.

FISS, OWEN M. 1978. *The Civil Rights Injunction.* Bloomington: Indiana University Press.

FRANKFURTER, FELIX, AND JAMES M. LANDIS. 1928. *The Business of the Supreme Court.* New York: Macmillan.

FREUND, PAUL A. 1952. "The Year of the Steel Case." *Harvard Law Review* 66: 89.

GOLDFARB, RONALD L. 1963. *The Contempt Power.* New York: Columbia University Press.

HARTMAN, MARSHALL J., AND JEANETTE NYDEN. 1997. "Habeas Corpus and the New Federalism After the Anti-Terrorism and Effective Death Penalty Act of 1996." *John Marshall Law Review* 30: 337.

KRAUSE, STEPHEN J. 1996. "Punishing the Press: Using Contempt of Court to Secure the Right to a Fair Trial." *Boston University Law Review* 76: 537.

MADANCY, ROBERT S., JR., SHAWN M. BATES, AND TIMOTHY LAMBERT. 1998. "Habeas Corpus Relief for State Prisoners." *Georgetown Law Review* 86: 1896.

MILLER, AMY E. 1998. "The Collapse and Fall of Floating Buffer Zones: The Court Clarifies Analysis for Reviewing Speech-Restrictive Injunctions in *Schenck v. Pro-Choice*." *University of Richmond Law Review* 32: 275.

NEUBAUER, MARK. 1976. "The Newsmen's Privilege after *Branzburg*." *UCLA Law Review* 24: 160.

PANG, AMBER M. 1998/1999. "Speech, Conduct, and Regulation of Abortion Protest by Court Injunction: From *Madsen v. Women's Health Center* to *Schenck v. Pro-Choice Network*." *Gonzaga Law Review* 34: 201.

PERRY, H. W. 1991. *Deciding to Decide.* Cambridge, MA: Harvard University Press.

SCHUCK, PETER. 1983. *Suing Government: Citizen Remedies for Official Wrongs.* New Haven, CT: Yale University Press.

SMITH, CHRISTOPHER E., AND DARWIN L. BURKE. 1997. "Judges' Views on Habeas Corpus: A Comparison of State and Federal Judges." *Oklahoma City University Law Review* 22: 1125.

STAHLKOPF, DEBORAH L. 1998. "A Dark Day for Habeas Corpus: Successive Petitions Under the Antiterrorism and Effective Death Penalty Act of 1996." *Arizona Law Review* 40: 1115.

---

[10] Clinton Rossiter, *The Supreme Court and the Commander-in-Chief.* Expanded edition, with an introductory note and additional text by Richard P. Longaker (Ithaca, NY: Cornell University Press, 1976), 39.

TABAK, RONALD J. 1996. "Habeas Corpus as a Crucial Protector of Constitutional Rights: A Tribute Which May Also be a Eulogy." *Seton Hall Law Review* 26: 1477.

WERDEGAR, MATTHEW MICKLE. 1999. "Enjoining the Constitution: The Use of Public Nuisance Abatement Injunctions Against Urban Street Gangs." *Stanford Law Review* 51: 409.

YACKLE, LARRY W. 1996. "A Primer on the New Habeas Corpus Statute." *Buffalo Law Review* 44: 381.

"Whether it is constitutional for a public college or graduate school to use race or national origin as a factor in its admissions process is an issue of great national importance."

7.1 TEXAS V. HOPWOOD

518 U.S. 1033 (1996)

In Regents of the University of California v. Bakke, *(1978), the Supreme Court ruled that, under certain circumstances, universities may take race and other factors into account when they make admission decisions. Since that time the justices have never overruled* Bakke.

In 1992, after four white students from the state of Texas were rejected for admission to the University of Texas Law School, they sued the law school alleging that the admission process that took race into account violated their rights under the Equal Protection Clause of the U.S. Constitution. The federal district court held, consistent with Bakke, *that the University of Texas could continue to use racial preferences in its law school admissions process. The white students appealed; and in 1996, a three-judge panel of the U.S. Court of Appeals for the Fifth Circuit reversed that decision, holding "that the University of Texas School of Law may not use race as a factor in deciding which applicants to admit in order to achieve a diverse student body, to combat the perceived effects of a hostile environment at the law school, to alleviate the law school's poor reputation in the minority community, or to eliminate any present effects of past discrimination by actors other than the law school."*

With these words, the panel of the court of appeals took the highly unusual step of refusing to apply a controlling ruling by the U.S. Supreme Court. Then the court of appeals, sitting en banc, refused to grant Texas a rehearing. Seven judges dissented, accusing their colleagues of overturning Bakke:

> *The label "judicial activism" is usually found in the lexicon of those voicing concern about judges whom they perceive to be "liberal," fashioning remedies beyond the scope of what is deemed to be appropriate under the law. Such judicial legislating is generally excoriated as a "bad thing."* Hopwood v. State of Texas *is a textbook example of judicial activism. Here, two members of the three-judge panel determined to bar any consideration of race in the Law School's admission process. This "injunction" is wholly unnecessary to the disposition of the matter appealed and thus is clearly dictum; yet dictum that is a frontal assault on contrary Supreme Court precedent and thus not the kind of dictum we can ignore. By tenuously stringing together pieces and shards of recent Supreme Court opinions that have dealt with race in such diverse settings as minority set asides for government contractors, broadcast licenses, redistricting, and the like, the panel creates a gossamer chain which it proffers as a justification for overruling* Bakke.

Texas then asked the U.S. Supreme Court to grant certiorari, but the justices denied the petition. Justice Ginsburg filed the following opinion.

Opinion of JUSTICE GINSBURG, with whom JUSTICE SOUTER joins, respecting the denial of the petition for a writ of certiorari.

Whether it is constitutional for a public college or graduate school to use race or national origin as a factor in its admissions process is an issue of great national importance. The petition before us, however, does not challenge the lower courts' judgments that the particular admissions procedure used by the University of Texas Law School in 1992 was unconstitutional. Acknowledging that the 1992 admissions program "has long since been discontinued and will not be reinstated," the petitioners do not defend that program in this Court. Instead, petitioners challenge the rationale relied on by the Court of Appeals. "This Court," however, "reviews judgments, not opinions." *Chevron U.S.A. Inc. v. Natural Resources Defense Council, Inc.* (1984). Accordingly, we must await a final judgment on a program genuinely in controversy before addressing the important question raised in this petition.

> *"An injunction, by its very nature, applies only to a particular group (or individuals) and regulates the activities, and perhaps the speech, of that group."*

7.2 MADSEN V. WOMEN'S HEALTH CENTER, INC.

512 U.S. 753 (1994)

The respondents to this suit operated women's clinics, including one in Melbourne, Florida. In 1992 their attorneys asked a state judge to issue an injunction prohibiting the petitioners—Judy Madsen, other individuals, and groups, such as Operation Rescue—from blocking or interfering with public access to the clinic and from physically abusing people entering or leaving the premises. In September 1992 the trial judge granted the injunction.

Six months later the Women's Health Center asked the judge to broaden the injunction, contending that protesters against abortion were continuing to block access to the clinic, approach patients, sing, and use loudspeakers. These acts, the clinic argued, were taking their toll on patients. One doctor told the judge that his patients "manifested a higher level of anxiety and hypertension causing [them] to need a higher level of sedation to undergo the surgical procedures, thereby increasing the risk associated with such procedures." The protesters' noise could be heard throughout the clinic, "causing stress in the patients both during surgical procedures and while recuperating in the recovery rooms." Doctors and clinic workers also were targeted. Protesters picketed in front of their homes, rang neighbors' doorbells, and gave neighbors literature accusing a particular worker of being a "baby killer."

After hearing this testimony and watching a videotape of the protesters, the trial judge concluded that the original injunction was not sufficient "to protect the health, safety and rights of women" and amended the order to prohibit protesters from a range of activities, including:

1. *At all times from entering the property or premises of the clinic.*
2. *At all times from blocking, impeding, or inhibiting people going in or out of the clinic.*
3. *At all times from picketing, demonstrating, or entering within thirty-six feet of the property line of the clinic. An exception to the thirty-six-foot buffer zone is the area immediately to the east of the clinic, where protesters must stay five feet from the clinic property line.*
4. *From 7:30 A.M. through noon, Mondays through Saturdays, during surgical procedures and recovery periods, from singing, chanting, et cetera, or using amplification equipment or other sounds or images that patients inside the clinic can see or hear.*
5. *At all times within three hundred feet of the clinic from physically approaching any person seeking the services of the clinic unless the person indicates a desire to communicate by approaching the protesters.*
6. *At all times from approaching, picketing, demonstrating, or using amplification equipment within three hundred feet of the residence of any clinic employee, and from in any way blocking entrance to the residence of any clinic employee.*
7. *At all times from physically abusing, grabbing, harassing, or touching people entering or leaving the clinic or trying to gain access to the residence of any clinic employee.*
8. *At all times from harassing, intimidating, or physically abusing any health care professional associated with the clinic.*
9. *At all times from encouraging or inciting any other persons to commit any of the acts prohibited by the injunction.*

The protesters challenged this injunction in both state and federal courts as a violation of the First Amendment. Florida's supreme court upheld the injunction, but a federal court of appeals struck it down. The U.S. Supreme Court granted certiorari, according to Chief Justice Rehnquist, "to resolve the conflict between the Florida Supreme Court and the Court of Appeals over the constitutionality of the state court's injunction."

CHIEF JUSTICE REHNQUIST delivered the opinion of the Court.

Petitioners challenge the constitutionality of an injunction entered by a Florida state court which prohibits antiabortion protesters from demonstrating in certain places and in various ways outside of a health clinic that performs abortions. We hold that the establishment of a 36-foot buffer zone on a public street from which demonstrators are excluded passes muster under the First Amendment, but that several other provisions of the injunction do not. . . .

We begin by addressing petitioners' contention that the state court's order, because it is an injunction that restricts only the speech of antiabortion protesters, is necessarily content or viewpoint based. Accordingly, they argue, we should examine the entire injunction under the strictest standard of scrutiny. We disagree. To accept petitioners' claim would be to classify virtually every injunction as content or viewpoint based. An injunction, by its very nature, applies only to a particular group (or individuals) and regulates the activities, and perhaps the speech, of that group. It does so, however, because of the group's past actions in the context of a specific dispute between real parties. The parties seeking the injunction assert a violation of their rights; the court hearing the action is charged with fashioning a remedy for a specific deprivation, not with the drafting of a statute addressed to the general public.

The fact that the injunction in the present case did not prohibit activities of those demonstrating in favor of abortion is justly attributable to the lack of any similar demonstrations by those in favor of abortion, and of any consequent request that their demonstrations be regulated by injunction. There is no suggestion in this record that Florida law would not equally restrain similar conduct directed at a target having nothing to do with abortion; none of the restrictions imposed by the court were directed at the contents of petitioner's message.

Our principal inquiry in determining content neutrality is whether the government has adopted a regulation of speech "without reference to the content of the regulated speech." *Ward v. Rock Against Racism* (1989). We thus look to the government's purpose as the threshold consideration. Here, the state court imposed restrictions on petitioners incidental to their antiabortion message because they repeatedly violated the court's original order. That petitioners all share the same viewpoint regarding abortion does not in itself demonstrate that some invidious content- or viewpoint-based purpose motivated the issuance of the order. It suggests only that those in the group whose conduct violated the court's order happen to share the same opinion regarding abortions being performed at the clinic. In short, the fact that the injunction covered people with a particular viewpoint does not itself render the injunction content or viewpoint based. Accordingly, the injunction issued in this case does not demand the level of heightened scrutiny set forth in *Perry Education Assn.* [*v. Perry Local Educators' Assn.*, 1983]. And we proceed to discuss the standard which does govern.

If this were a content-neutral, generally applicable statute, instead of an injunctive order, its constitutionality would be assessed under the standard set forth in *Ward v. Rock Against Racism* and similar cases. Given that the forum around the clinic is a traditional public forum, we would determine whether the time, place, and manner regulations were "narrowly tailored to serve a significant governmental interest."

There are obvious differences, however, between an injunction and a generally applicable ordinance. Ordinances represent a legislative choice regarding the promotion of particular societal interests. Injunctions, by contrast, are remedies imposed for violations (or threatened violations) of a legislative or judicial decree. Injunctions also carry greater risks of censorship and discriminatory application than do general ordinances. Injunctions, of course, have some advantages over generally applicable statutes in that they can be tailored by a trial judge to afford more precise relief than a statute where a violation of the law has already occurred.

We believe that these differences require a somewhat more stringent application of general First Amendment principles in this context. In past cases evaluating injunctions restricting speech, we have relied upon such general principles while also seeking to ensure that the injunction was no broader than necessary to achieve its desired goals. Our close attention to the fit between the objectives of an injunction and the restrictions it imposes on speech is consistent with the general rule, quite apart from First Amendment considerations, "that injunctive relief should be no more burdensome to the defendants than necessary to provide complete relief to the plaintiffs." Accordingly, when evaluating a content-neutral injunction, we think that our standard time, place, and manner analysis is not sufficiently rigorous. We must ask instead whether the challenged provisions of the injunction burden no more speech than necessary to serve a significant government interest.

[Applying this standard to the injunction at hand, Rehnquist upheld the lower-court injunction to the extent that restricting the rights of the protesters was necessary to ensure access to the clinic and to guarantee that the abortion protesters would not engage in noise or disruption that might compromise the medical procedures being performed. Where he found that the injunction's restrictions went beyond what was necessary to achieve these goals, the chief justice held in favor of the protesters. Consequently, the noise restrictions and the thirty-six-foot buffer zone were upheld. However, the bans on observable images, communicating with clinic clients within three hundred feet of the facility, and entering a three-hundred-foot zone around clinic employee residences were found to be excessive and in violation of the First Amendment.]

JUSTICE SCALIA, with whom JUSTICE KENNEDY and JUSTICE THOMAS join, concurring in the judgment in part and dissenting in part.

The parties to this case invited the Court to employ one or the other of the two well established standards applied to restrictions upon this First Amendment right. Petitioners claimed the benefit of so-called "strict scrutiny," the standard applied to content-based restrictions: the restriction must be "necessary to serve a compelling state interest and . . . narrowly drawn to achieve that end." Respondents, on the other hand, contended for what has come to be known as "intermediate scrutiny" (midway between the "strict scrutiny" demanded for content-based regulation of speech, and the "rational basis" standard that is applied—under the Equal Protection Clause—to government regulation of nonspeech activities). That standard, applicable to so-called "time, place and manner regulations" of speech, provides that the regulations are permissible so long as they "are content-neutral, are narrowly tailored to serve a significant government interest, and leave open ample alternative channels of communication." The Court adopts neither of these, but creates, brand-new for this abortion-related case, an additional standard that is (supposedly) "somewhat more stringent," than intermediate scrutiny, yet not as "rigorous," as strict scrutiny. The Court does not give this new standard a name, but perhaps we could call it intermediate-intermediate scrutiny. The difference between it and intermediate scrutiny (which the Court acknowledges is inappropriate for injunctive restrictions on speech) is frankly too subtle for me to describe, so I must simply recite it: whereas intermediate scrutiny requires that the restriction be "narrowly tailored to serve a significant government interest," the new standard requires that the restriction "burden no more speech than necessary to serve a significant government interest.". . .

The real question in this case is not whether intermediate scrutiny, which the Court assumes to be some kind of default standard, should be supplemented because of the distinctive characteristics of injunctions; but rather whether those distinctive characteristics are not, for reasons of both policy and precedent, fully as good a reason as "content-basis" for demanding strict scrutiny. That possibility is simply not considered. Instead, the Court begins . . . with the following optical illusion: "If this were a content-neutral, generally applicable statute, instead of an injunctive order, its constitutionality would be assessed under the [intermediate scrutiny] standard"—and then proceeds to discuss whether petitioners can sustain the burden of departing from that presumed disposition.

But this is *not* a statute, and it *is* an injunctive order. The Court might just as logically (or illogically) have begun "If this were a content-based injunction, rather than a non-content-based injunction, its constitutionality would be assessed under the strict scrutiny standard"—and have then proceeded to discuss whether *respondents* can sustain the burden of departing from *that* presumed disposition. The question should be approached, it seems to me, without any such artificial loading of the dice. And the central element of the answer is that a restriction upon speech imposed by injunction (whether nominally content-based or nominally content-neutral) is *at least* as deserving of strict scrutiny as a statutory, content-based restriction.

That is so for several reasons: The danger of content-based statutory restrictions upon speech is that they may be designed and used precisely to suppress the ideas in question rather than to achieve any other proper governmental aim. But that same danger exists with injunctions. Although a speech-restricting injunction may not attack content as *content* (in the present case . . . even that is not true), it lends itself just as readily to the targeted suppression of particular ideas. When a judge, on the motion of an employer, enjoins picketing at the site of a labor dispute he enjoins (and he *knows* he is enjoining) the expression of pro-union views. Such targeting of one or the other side of an ideological dispute cannot readily be achieved in speech-restricting general legislation except by making content the basis of the restriction; it is achieved in speech-restricting injunctions almost invariably. The proceedings before us here illustrate well enough what I mean. The injunction was sought against a single-issue advocacy group by persons and organizations with a business or social interest in suppressing that group's point of view.

The second reason speech-restricting injunctions are at least as deserving of strict scrutiny is obvious enough: they are the product of individual judges rather than of legislatures—and often of judges who have been chagrined by prior disobedience of their orders. The right to free speech should not lightly be placed within the control of a single man or woman. And the third reason is that the injunction is a much more powerful weapon than a statute, and so should be subjected to greater safeguards. Normally, when injunctions are enforced through contempt proceedings, only the defense of factual innocence is available. The collateral bar rule of *Walker v. Birmingham* (1967) eliminates the defense that the injunction itself was unconstitutional. Thus, persons subject to a speech-restricting injunction who have not the money or not the time to lodge an immediate appeal face a Hobson's choice: they must remain silent, since if they speak their First Amendment rights are no defense in subsequent contempt proceedings. This is good reason to require the strictest standard for issuance of such orders. . . .

What we have decided seems to be, and will be reported by the media as, an abortion case. But it will go down in the law books, it will be cited, as a free-speech injunction case—and the damage its novel principles produce will be considerable. The proposition that injunctions against speech are subject to a standard indistinguishable from (unless perhaps more lenient in its application than) the "intermediate scrutiny" standard we have used for "time, place, and manner" legislative restrictions; the notion that injunctions against speech need not be closely tied to any violation of law, but may simply implement sound social policy; and the practice of accepting trial-court conclusions permitting injunctions without considering whether those conclusions are supported by any findings of fact—these latest by-products of our abortion jurisprudence ought to give all friends of liberty great concern.

For these reasons, I dissent from that portion of the judgment upholding parts of the injunction.

"There can be no legal (or moral) justification for the State of Alabama's failing to afford treatment ... to the several thousand patients. . . ."

7.3 WYATT V. STICKNEY

325 F. Supp. 781 (1971)

This case began as a labor dispute in 1970 when reductions in revenue from Alabama's tax on cigarettes precipitated a cut in the state's appropriations for mental health. Plans to cope with the problem included dismissal of ninety-nine employees from Bryce Hospital. These employees and a group of patients then filed suit in a U.S. District Court against the governor, the Mental Health Board, and several other state officials. In passing, plaintiffs alleged that reducing the staff would leave patients without adequate care.

At a pretrial conference in his chambers, the presiding judge, Frank M. Johnson, Jr., indicated that he thought that state courts could adequately protect any rights of employees possibly injured by the dismissals; but he also expressed concern about the general level of care at Bryce. Largely in response to these remarks, plaintiffs amended their suit to focus on the claim that patients had a constitutional right to adequate treatment, a right that Alabama was denying them. They asked the court to enjoin the state from sending any more patients to Bryce and to appoint a special master to determine the adequacy of current treatment at the mental hospital and the means the state should use to raise those practices to meet minimal medical and constitutional standards.

JOHNSON, CHIEF JUDGE

Bryce Hospital is located in Tuscaloosa, Alabama, and is a part of the mental health service delivery system for the State. . . . Bryce Hospital has approximately 5,000 patients, the majority of whom are involuntarily committed through civil proceedings by the various probate judges in Alabama. Approximately 1,600 employees were assigned to various duties at the Bryce Hospital facility when this case was heard. . . .

During October 1970, the Alabama Mental Health Board and the administration of the Department of Mental Health terminated ninety-nine of these employees. These terminations were made due to budgetary considerations. . . . The employees who were terminated included forty-one persons who were assigned to duties . . . not involving direct patient care. . . . Twenty-six persons were discharged who were involved in patient activity and recreational programs. . . . The remaining thirty-two employees who were discharged included nine in the department of psychology, eleven in the social service department, . . . three registered nurses, two physicians, one dentist and six dental aides. After the termination of these employees, there remained at Bryce Hospital seventeen physicians, approximately 850 psychiatric aides, twenty-one registered nurses, twelve patient activity workers, and twelve psychologists, . . . together with thirteen social service workers. Of the employees remaining whose duties involved direct patient care in the hospital therapeutic programs, there are only one Ph.D. clinical psychologist, three medical doctors with some psychiatric training (including one board eligible but no board-certified psychiatrist), and two M.S.W. social workers. . . .

Included in the Bryce Hospital patient population are between 1,500 and 1,600 geriatric patients who are provided custodial care but no treatment. The evidence is without dispute that these patients are not properly confined at Bryce Hospital since these geriatric patients cannot benefit from any psychiatric treatment or are not mentally ill. Also included in the Bryce patient population are approximately 1,000 mental retardates, most of whom receive only custodial care without any psychiatric treatment. . . .

The evidence further reflects that Alabama ranks fiftieth among all the states in the Union in per-patient expenditures per day. This Court must, and does, find from the evidence that the programs of treatment in use at Bryce Hospital . . . were scientifically and medically inadequate. These programs of treatment failed to conform to any known minimums established for providing treatment for the mentally ill.

The patients at Bryce Hospital, for the most part, were involuntarily committed through noncriminal procedures and without the constitutional protections that are afforded defendants in criminal proceedings. When patients are so committed for treatment purposes, they unquestionably have a constitutional right to receive such individual treatment as will give each of them a realistic opportunity to be cured or to improve his or her mental condition. *Rouse v. Camerion . . . Covington v. Harris*. . . . Adequate and effective treatment is constitutionally required because, absent treatment, the hospital is transformed "into a penitentiary where one could be held indefinitely for no convicted offense." *Ragsdale v. Overholser*. . . . The purpose of involuntary hospitalization for treatment purposes is treatment and not mere custodial care or punishment. This is the only justification, from a constitutional standpoint, that allows civil commitments to mental institutions. . . . The failure of Bryce Hospital to supply suitable and adequate treatment to the mentally ill cannot be justified by lack of staff or facilities. . . .

There can be no legal (or moral) justification for the State of Alabama's failing to afford treatment—and adequate treatment from a medical standpoint—to the several thousand patients who have been civilly committed to Bryce's for treatment purposes. To deprive any citizen of his or her liberty upon the altruistic theory that the confinement is for humane therapeutic reasons and then fail to provide adequate treatment violates the very fundamentals of due process. . . .

Judge Johnson deferred a decision on plaintiffs' request for a special master. Instead, he ordered the defendants within six months to implement fully their own plans to raise the level of care to minimal standards. The judge also invited the United States, through the Department of Justice and what was then the Department of Health, Education, and Welfare, to assist the court in evaluating defendants' plans and to aid the hospital in qualifying for federal financial aid.

In September 1971 the defendants submitted their final report. Judge Johnson found that they had failed to promulgate and implement a treatment program satisfying minimal medical and constitutional requisites. The court ordered new hearings in which both sides and amici curiae, who now included the National Mental Health Law Project and the American Civil Liberties Union as well as federal officials, presented evidence. When the proceedings were finished, Johnson said that he believed he had heard testimony from the foremost authorities on mental health in the United States. (In the meantime, plaintiffs amended their complaint to include another state institution, Searcy Hospital.)

WYATT V. STICKNEY

344 F. Supp. 373 (1972)

JOHNSON, CHIEF JUDGE . . .

In addition to asking that their proposed standards be effectuated, plaintiffs and amici have requested other relief designed to guarantee the provision of constitutional and humane treatment. Pursuant to one such request for relief, this Court has determined that it is appropriate to order the initiation of human rights committees to function as standing committees of the Bryce and Searcy facilities. The Court will appoint the members of these committees who shall have review of all research proposals and all rehabilitation programs, to ensure that the dignity and the human rights of patients are preserved. The committees also shall advise and assist patients who allege that their legal rights have been infringed or that the Mental Health Board has failed to comply with judicially ordered guidelines. At their discretion, the committees may consult appropriate, independent specialists who shall be compensated by the defendant Board. Seven members shall comprise the human rights committee for each institution, the names and addresses of whom are set forth in Appendix B to this decree. . . .

This Court will reserve ruling upon other forms of relief advocated by plaintiffs and amici, including their prayer for the appointment of a master and a professional advisory committee to oversee the implementation of the court-ordered minimum constitutional standards. Federal courts are reluctant to assume control of any organization, but especially one operated by a state. This reluctance, combined with defendants' expressed intent that this order will be implemented forthwith and in good faith, causes the Court to withhold its decision on these appointments. Nevertheless, defendants, as well as the other parties and amici in this case, are placed on notice that unless defendants do comply satisfactorily with this order, the Court will be obligated to appoint a master.

Because the availability of financing may bear upon the implementation of this order, the Court is constrained to emphasize at this juncture that a failure by defendants to comply with this decree cannot be justified by a lack of operating funds. . . .

Despite the possibility that defendants will encounter financial difficulties in the implementation of this order, this Court has decided to reserve ruling also upon plaintiffs' motion that defendant Mental Health Board be directed to sell or encumber portions of its land holdings in order to raise funds. Similarly, this Court will reserve ruling on plaintiffs' motion seeking an injunction against the treasurer and the comptroller of the State. . . . The Court stresses, however, the extreme importance and the grave immediacy of the need for proper funding of the State's public mental health facilities. The responsibility for appropriate funding ultimately must fall, of course, upon the State Legislature and, to a lesser degree, upon the defendant Mental Health Board of Alabama. For the present time, the Court will defer to those bodies in hopes that they will proceed with the realization and understanding that what is involved in this case is not representative of ordinary governmental functions such as paving roads and maintaining buildings. Rather, what is so inextricably intertwined with how the Legislature and Mental Health Board respond to the revelations of this litigation is the very preservation of human life and dignity. Not only are the lives of the patients currently confined at Bryce and Searcy at stake, but also at issue are the well-being and security of every citizen of Alabama. As is true in the case of any disease, no one is immune from the peril of mental illness. The problem, therefore, cannot be overemphasized and a prompt response from the Legislature, the Mental Health Board and other responsible State officials, is imperative.

In the event, though, that the Legislature fails to satisfy its well-defined constitutional obligation, and the Mental Health Board . . . fails to implement fully the standards herein ordered, it will be necessary for the Court to take affirmative steps, including appointing a master, to ensure that proper funding is realized.[1] . . .

This Court now must consider that aspect of plaintiffs' motion . . . seeking an injunction against further commitments to Bryce and Searcy until such time as adequate treatment is supplied in those hospitals. Indisputably, the evidence in this case reflects that no treatment program at the Bryce-Searcy facilities approaches constitutional standards. Nevertheless, because of the alternatives to commitment . . . the Court is fearful that granting plaintiffs' request at the present time would serve only to punish and further deprive Alabama's mentally ill. . . .

To assist the Court in its determination of how to proceed henceforth, defendants will be directed to prepare and file a report within six months from the date of this decree detailing the implementation of each standard herein ordered. This report shall be comprehensive and shall include a statement of the progress made on each standard not yet completely implemented, specifying the reasons for incomplete performance. The report shall include also a statement of the financing secured since the issuance of this decree and of defendants' plans for procuring whatever additional financing might be required. Upon the basis of this report and other available information, the Court will evaluate defendants' work and, in due course, determine the appropriateness of appointing a master and of granting other requested relief.

Accordingly, it is the order, judgment and decree of this Court:

1. That defendants be and they are hereby enjoined from failing to implement fully and with dispatch each of the standards set forth in Appendix A attached hereto and incorporated as a part of this decree;

2. That human rights committees be and are designated and appointed. . . . These committees shall have the purposes, functions, and spheres of operation previously set forth in this order. . . .

3. That the court costs incurred in this proceeding, including a reasonable attorneys' fee for plaintiffs' lawyers, be and they are hereby taxed against the defendants;

4. That jurisdiction of this cause be and the same is hereby specifically retained. . . .

---

[1] The Court understands and appreciates that the Legislature is not due back in regular session until May, 1973. Nevertheless, special sessions of the Legislature are frequent occurrences in Alabama, and there has never been a time when such a session was more urgently required. If the Legislature does not act promptly to appropriate the necessary funding for mental health, the Court will be compelled to grant plaintiffs' motion to add various State officials and agencies as additional parties to this litigation, and to utilize other avenues of fund raising.

Appendix A: Minimum Constitutional Standards for Adequate Treatment of the Mentally Ill . . .

Humane Psychological and Physical Environment

1. Patients have a right to privacy and dignity.
2. Patients have a right to the least restrictive conditions necessary to achieve the purposes of commitment.
3. No person shall be deemed incompetent to manage his affairs, to contract, to hold professional or occupational or vehicle operator's licenses, to marry and obtain a divorce, to register and vote, or to make a will solely by reason of his admission or commitment to the hospital.
4. Patients shall have the same rights to visitation and telephone communications as patients at other public hospitals, except to the extent that the Qualified Mental Health Professional, responsible for formulation of a particular patient's treatment plan writes an order imposing special restrictions. The written order must be renewed after each periodic review of the treatment plan if any restrictions are to be continued. Patients shall have an unrestricted right to visitation with attorneys and with private physicians and other health professionals.
5. Patients shall have an unrestricted right to send sealed mail. Patients shall have an unrestricted right to receive sealed mail from their attorneys, private physicians, and other mental health professionals, from courts, and government officials. Patients shall have a right to receive sealed mail from others, except to the extent that the Qualified Mental Health Professional responsible for formulation of a particular patient's treatment plan writes an order imposing special restrictions on receipt of sealed mail. The written order must be renewed after each periodic review of the treatment plan if any restrictions are to be continued.
6. Patients have a right to be free from unnecessary or excessive medication. No medication shall be administered unless at the written order of a physician. . . .
7. Patients have a right to be free from physical restraint and isolation. Except for emergency situations, in which it is likely that patients could harm themselves or others and in which less restrictive means of restraint are not feasible, patients may be physically restrained or placed in isolation only on a Qualified Mental Health Professional's written order which explains the rationale for such action. . . .

Physical Facilities

A patient has a right to a humane psychological and physical environment within the hospital facilities. These facilities shall be designed to afford patients with comfort and safety, promote dignity, and ensure privacy, The facilities shall be designed to make a positive contribution to the efficiency attainment of the treatment goals of the hospital.

1. *Resident Unit.* The number of patients in a multi-patient room shall not exceed six persons. There shall be allocated a minimum of eighty square feet of floor space per patient in a multi-patient room. Screens or curtains shall be provided to ensure privacy within the resident unit. Single rooms shall have a minimum of 100 square feet of floor space. Each patient will be furnished with a comfortable bed with adequate changes of linen, a closet or locker for his personal belongings, a chair, and a bedside table.

2. *Toilets and Lavatories.* There will be one toilet provided for each eight patients and one lavatory for each six patients. A lavatory will be provided with each toilet facility. The toilets will be installed in separate stalls to ensure privacy, will be clean and free of odor, and will be equipped with appropriate safety devices for the physically handicapped.

3. *Showers.* There will be one tub or shower for each fifteen patients. If a central bathing area is provided, each shower area will be divided by curtains to ensure privacy. Showers and tubs will be equipped with adequate safety accessories.

4. *Day Room.* The minimum day room area shall be forty square feet per patient. Day rooms will be attractive and adequately furnished with reading lamps, tables, chairs, television and other recreational facilities. They will be conveniently located to patients' bedrooms and shall have outside windows. There shall be at least one day room area on each bedroom floor in a multi-story hospital. Areas used for corridor traffic cannot be counted as day room space; nor can a chapel with fixed pews be counted as a day room area.

5. *Dining Facilities.* The minimum dining room area shall be ten square feet per patient. The dining room shall be separate from the kitchen and will be furnished with comfortable chairs and tables with hard, washable surfaces.

The order went on to list in detail standards for record keeping, linen service, housekeeping, heating, air conditioning, hot water, fire and safety regulation, nutrition, and number and qualifications of staff; it also required that a comprehensive, frequently reviewed plan of treatment be developed for each patient.

Alabama then appealed to the United States Court of Appeals for the Fifth Circuit. That court, in Wyatt v. Aderholt *(1974), unanimously affirmed that "civilly committed mental patients have a constitutional right to such individual treatment as will help each of them to be cured or to improve his or her mental condition." Furthermore, speaking through Judge Minor Wisdom, the court held: "That being the case, the state may not fail to provide treatment for budgetary reasons alone."*

The court of appeals found that the matter of a proper remedy raised "profound Questions" about the role of the federal judiciary in managing state institutions. But because the state had conceded that its treatment fell below minimal constitutional requirements, the circuit judges said: "We need not and do not reach a decision as to whether the standards prescribed by the district court are constitutionally minimum requirements or whether it is within the province of a federal district court to prescribe

standards as distinguished from enjoining the operations of such institutions while constitutional rights are being violated."

According to a close analysis of the first two years of implementation of Wyatt,
Judge Johnson's decree effected substantial improvements in the conditions in the mental hospital, making it safer, more sanitary, and generally more habitable for the residents. But a large disparity still exists between the existing institution and the
standards in the decree.[2] More recent reports suggested that "a miserable situation" at
least regarding medications, persisted for some time after the decision, despite a huge increase in the portion of Alabama's budget devoted to mental institutions (from $14 mil-
lion in 1971 to $58 million in 1973). Nonetheless, Wyatt, which has gone down in the
legal annals as a landmark case, largely because it is seen as creating a right to treatment for mentally ill persons who are involuntarily committed became the prototype for
almost innumerable other lawsuits.[3]

> "The flagrant disregard in the courtroom of elementary standards of
> proper conduct should not and cannot be tolerated."

7.4 ILLINOIS V. ALLEN

397 U.S. 337 (1970)

MR. JUSTICE BLACK delivered the opinion of the Court.

The Confrontation Clause of the Sixth Amendment to the United States
Constitution provides that: "In all criminal prosecutions, the accused shall enjoy the right . . . to be confronted with the witnesses against him. . . ." We have
held that the Fourteenth Amendment makes the guarantees of this clause oblig-
atory upon the States. One of the most basic of the rights guaranteed by the
Confrontation Clause is the accused's right to be present in the courtroom at
every stage of his trial. The question presented in this case is whether an accused can claim the benefit of this constitutional right to remain in the courtroom while at the same time he engages in speech and conduct which is so
noisy, disorderly, and disruptive that it is exceedingly difficult or wholly impossible to carry on the trial.

The issue arose in the following way. The respondent, Allen, was convicted
by an Illinois jury of armed robbery and was sentenced to serve 10 to 30 years

---

[2] Note, "The Wyatt Case: Implementation of a Judicial Decree Ordering Institutional Change," 84
Yale Law Journal 1338 (1975) —Eds.

[3] Sheldon Gelman, "The Law and Psychiatry Wars, 1960–1980," 34 *California Western Law Review* 153
(1997) —Eds.

in the Illinois State Penitentiary. The evidence against him showed that on August 12, 1956, he entered a tavern in Illinois and, after ordering a drink, took $200 from the bartender at gunpoint. The Supreme Court of Illinois affirmed his conviction, and this Court denied certiorari. Later Allen filed a petition for a writ of habeas corpus in federal court alleging that he had been wrongfully deprived by the Illinois trial judge of his constitutional right to remain present throughout his trial. Finding no constitutional violation, the District Court declined to issue the writ. The Court of Appeals reversed.

The facts surrounding Allen's expulsion from the courtroom are set out in the Court of Appeals' opinion sustaining Allen's contention:

> "After his indictment and during the pretrial stage, the petitioner [Allen] refused court-appointed counsel and indicated to the trial court on several occasions that he wished to conduct his own defense. After considerable argument by the petitioner, the trial judge told him, 'I'll let you be your own lawyer, but I'll ask Mr. Kelly [court-appointed counsel] [to] sit in and protect the record for you, insofar as possible.'
>
> "The trial began on September 9, 1957. After the State's Attorney had accepted the first four jurors following their voir dire examination, the petitioner began examining the first juror and continued at great length. Finally, the trial judge interrupted the petitioner, requesting him to confine his questions solely to matters relating to the prospective juror's qualifications. At that point, the petitioner started to argue with the judge in a most abusive and disrespectful manner. At last, and seemingly in desperation, the judge asked appointed counsel to proceed with the examination of the jurors. The petitioner continued to talk, proclaiming that the appointed attorney was not going to act as his lawyer. He terminated his remarks by saying, 'When I go out for lunchtime, you're [the judge] going to be a corpse here.' At that point he tore the file which his attorney had and threw the papers on the floor. The trial judge thereupon stated to the petitioner, 'One more outbreak of that sort and I'll remove you from the courtroom.' This warning had no effect on the petitioner. He continued to talk back to the judge, saying, 'There's not going to be no trial, either. I'm going to sit here and you're going to talk and you can bring your shackles out and straight jacket and put them on me and tape my mouth, but it will do no good because there's not going to be no trial.' After more abusive remarks by the petitioner, the trial judge ordered the trial to proceed in the petitioner's absence. The petitioner was removed from the courtroom. The voir dire examination then continued and the jury was selected in the absence of the petitioner.
>
> "After a noon recess and before the jury was brought into the courtroom, the petitioner, appearing before the judge, complained about the fairness of the trial and his appointed attorney. He also said he wanted to be present in the court during his trial. In reply, the judge said that the petitioner would be permitted to remain in the courtroom if he 'behaved [himself] and [did] not interfere with the introduction of the case.' The jury was brought in and seated. Counsel for the petitioner then moved to exclude the witnesses from the courtroom. The [petitioner] protested this effort on the part of his attorney, saying: 'There is going to be no proceeding. I'm going to start talking and I'm going to keep on talking all through the trial. There's not going to be no trial like this. I want my

sister and my friends here in court to testify for me.' The trial judge thereupon ordered the petitioner removed from the courtroom."

After this second removal, Allen remained out of the courtroom during the presentation of the State's case-in-chief, except that he was brought in on several occasions for purposes of identification. During one of these latter appearances, Allen responded to one of the judge's questions with vile and abusive language. After the prosecution's case had been presented, the trial judge reiterated his promise to Allen that he could return to the courtroom whenever he agreed to conduct himself properly. Allen gave some assurances of proper conduct and was permitted to be present through the remainder of the trial, principally his defense, which was conducted by his appointed counsel. . . .

It is essential to the proper administration of criminal justice that dignity, order, and decorum be the hallmarks of all court proceedings in our country. The flagrant disregard in the courtroom of elementary standards of proper conduct should not and cannot be tolerated. We believe trial judges confronted with disruptive, contumacious, stubbornly defiant defendants must be given sufficient discretion to meet the circumstances of each case. No one formula for maintaining the appropriate courtroom atmosphere will be best in all situations. We think there are at least three constitutionally permissible ways for a trial judge to handle an obstreperous defendant like Allen: (1) bind and gag him, thereby keeping him present; (2) cite him for contempt; (3) take him out of the courtroom until he promises to conduct himself properly.

Trying a defendant for a crime while he sits bound and gagged before the judge and jury would to an extent comply with that part of the Sixth Amendment's purposes that accords the defendant an opportunity to confront the witnesses at the trial. But even to contemplate such a technique, much less see it, arouses a feeling that no person should be tried while shackled and gagged except as a last resort. Not only is it possible that the sight of shackles and gags might have a significant effect on the jury's feelings about the defendant, but the use of this technique is itself something of an affront to the very dignity and decorum of judicial proceedings that the judge is seeking to uphold. Moreover, one of the defendant's primary advantages of being present at the trial, his ability to communicate with his counsel, is greatly reduced when the defendant is in a condition of total physical restraint. It is in part because of these inherent disadvantages and limitations in this method of dealing with disorderly defendants that we decline to hold with the Court of Appeals that a defendant cannot under any possible circumstances be deprived of his right to be present at trial. However, in some situations which we need not attempt to foresee, binding and gagging might possibly be the fairest and most reasonable way to handle a defendant who acts as Allen did here.

In a footnote the Court of Appeals suggested the possible availability of contempt of court as a remedy to make Allen behave in his robbery trial, and it is true that citing or threatening to cite a contumacious defendant for criminal contempt might in itself be sufficient to make a defendant stop interrupting a trial. If so, the problem would be solved easily, and the defendant could remain in the courtroom. Of course, if the defendant is determined to prevent any trial, then a court in attempting to try the defendant for contempt is still confronted with the identical dilemma that the Illinois court faced in this case. And criminal contempt has obvious limitations as a sanction when the defendant is charged with a crime so serious that a very severe sentence such as death or life imprisonment is likely to be imposed. In such a case the defendant might not be affected by a mere contempt sentence when he ultimately faces a far more serious sanction. Nevertheless, the contempt remedy should be borne in mind by a judge in the circumstances of this case.

Another aspect of the contempt remedy is the judge's power, when exercised consistently with state and federal law, to imprison an unruly defendant such as Allen for civil contempt and discontinue the trial until such time as the defendant promises to behave himself. This procedure is consistent with the defendant's right to be present at trial, and yet it avoids the serious shortcomings of the use of shackles and gags. It must be recognized, however, that a defendant might conceivably, as a matter of calculated strategy, elect to spend a prolonged period in confinement for contempt in the hope that adverse witnesses might be unavailable after a lapse of time. A court must guard against allowing a defendant to profit from his own wrong in this way.

The trial court in this case decided under the circumstances to remove the defendant from the courtroom and to continue his trial in his absence until and unless he promised to conduct himself in a manner befitting an American courtroom. As we said earlier, we find nothing unconstitutional about this procedure. Allen's behavior was clearly of such an extreme and aggravated nature as to justify either his removal from the courtroom or his total physical restraint. Prior to his removal he was repeatedly warned by the trial judge that he would be removed from the courtroom if he persisted in his unruly conduct, and, as Judge Hastings observed in his dissenting opinion, the record demonstrates that Allen would not have been at all dissuaded by the trial judge's use of his criminal contempt powers. Allen was constantly informed that he could return to the trial when he would agree to conduct himself in an orderly manner. Under these circumstances we hold that Allen lost his right guaranteed by the Sixth and Fourteenth Amendments to be present throughout his trial.

It is not pleasant to hold that the respondent Allen was properly banished from the court for a part of his own trial. But our courts, palladiums of liberty as they are, cannot be treated disrespectfully with impunity. Nor can the accused be permitted by his disruptive conduct indefinitely to avoid being tried on the charges brought against him. It would degrade our country and our judicial system to permit our courts to be bullied, insulted, and humiliated and their orderly progress thwarted and obstructed by defendants brought before them charged with crimes. As guardians of the public welfare, our state and federal judicial systems strive to administer equal justice to the rich and the poor, the good and the bad, the native and foreign born of every race, nationality, and religion. Being manned by humans, the courts are not perfect and are bound to make some errors. But, if our courts are to remain what the Founders intended, the citadels of justice, their proceedings cannot and must not be infected with the sort of scurrilous, abusive language and conduct paraded before the Illinois trial judge in this case. The record shows that the Illinois judge at all times conducted himself with that dignity, decorum, and patience that befit a judge. Even in holding that the trial judge had erred, the Court of Appeals praised his "commendable patience under severe provocation."

We do not hold that removing this defendant from his own trial was the only way the Illinois judge could have constitutionally solved the problem he had. We do hold, however, that there is nothing whatever in this record to show that the judge did not act completely within his discretion. Deplorable as it is to remove a man from his own trial, even for a short time, we hold that the judge did not commit legal error in doing what he did.

The judgment of the Court of Appeals is reversed.

Reversed.

CHAPTER 8

Limitations on Judicial Power

Dissenting in *United States v. Butler* (1936) against a decision that invalidated one of the more important policies of the New Deal, Harlan F. Stone warned his colleagues: "The only check upon our own exercise of power is our own sense of self-restraint." Within months the Court had surrendered to the New Deal in the famous "switch in time that saved nine," but it had not been Stone's legal learning or his colleagues' sense of self-restraint alone that had persuaded the Court of the error of its ways. Earlier chapters noted some of the political limitations on judicial power, such as those inherent in the appointing process or in limiting access to courts. This chapter seeks to identify more explicitly the limitations imposed on judges by their political and institutional settings.

INTERNAL CHECKS

We should begin by recognizing the relevance of what Stone called "self-restraint" as an operative force in judicial decision making. Robert A. Dahl has stressed the importance of beliefs in democratic processes among political elites in preserving stability in America. These political professionals, Dahl says, accept a certain political culture, including rules of the game that sometimes restrict their own power in the short run, such as respecting the results of elections or allowing opponents to speak.[1] American judges are also products of a democratic culture, though, if sophisticated, they temper that culture with constitutionalism. They rarely believe themselves entitled to impose their personal values and views on the country. Rather, they are aware that they are officials of a constitutional democracy and internalize certain norms to govern their own behavior.

Other chapters reprint essays that are relevant to such a discussion, including material on historical institutionalism, a line of scholarship arguing that judges, deeply concerned with sustaining the legitimacy of their institution,

---

[1] Robert A. Dahl, *Who Governs?* (New Haven: Yale University Press, 1961).

follow a prescribed set of internal norms rather than their own political values.[2] Here we want only to underline the potential importance of such self-limiting concepts. We know, for example, that Stone himself found much of the New Deal politically distasteful; yet, because he could not find any constitutional prohibitions against these policies, he voted to sustain them. In much the same fashion Oliver Wendell Holmes dissented against rulings that read laissez faire into the constitutional system. Still, he distrusted governmental intervention in economic processes—the Sherman Act he characterized as "humbug." But, as he noted in one of his most biting dissents, "The Fourteenth Amendment does not enact Mr. Herbert Spencer's Social Statics." Harry Blackmun's opinion in the capital punishment case of *Furman v. Georgia* (1972)—in which the Court voted that the death penalty, as then applied in the United States, was unconstitutional—runs along the same lines: "Although personally I may rejoice in the Court's result, I find it difficult to accept or to justify as a matter of history, of law, or of constitutional pronouncement. I fear the Court has overstepped. It has sought and has achieved an end." In 1994, Blackmun had a change of heart, claiming that "From this day forward, I no longer shall tinker with the machinery of death."[3] But his vote had been critical in *Gregg v. Georgia*, decided just four years after *Furman*, in which the Court held that the death penalty was not per se unconstitutional.

Blackmun's dissent in *Furman*, though at odds with the Court's decision, was gentle in tone. Not so Justice Antonin Scalia's response to Justice Sandra Day O'Connor in *Webster v. Reproductive Health Services* (1989). (Reading 8.1.) In the name of judicial restraint, O'Connor argued against overturning *Roe v. Wade* (1973). This "assertion," Scalia, sometimes an eloquent apostle of self-restraint, replied, "cannot be taken seriously." This exchange raises one of the more serious problems of self-restraint: Which is more restrained, to overrule a decision or merely cripple it?

We must be careful here, for calls for "judicial self-restraint" are often no more than anguished cries from people (sometimes including judges) disappointed at the course of constitutional interpretation. In fact, there is a faint line between judicial restraint and judicial abdication; and judges, like scholars, often disagree about where to draw that line. It is one thing for a judge to defer to Congress or the president where the constitutional text is ambiguous and the reasons on both sides pretty much equally strong. It is quite another to defer to the judgment of others where "the constitution," whether conceived as merely the document or as the document plus established traditions and/or underlying political theories of democracy and constitutionalism, are quite clear. On such

---

[2] See Ronald Kahn, "Institutional Norms and Supreme Court Decision-Making: The Rehnquist Court on Privacy and Religion," in *Supreme Court Decision-Making,* ed. Cornell W. Clayton and Howard Gillman, (University of Chicago Press, 1999); Howard Gillman and Cornell W. Clayton, eds., *The Supreme Court in American Politics: New Institutionalist Interpretations* (Lawrence: University Press of Kansas, 1999).

[3] *Callins v. Collins* (1994).

occasions, the question becomes should the Court defer to Congress and the president or to the constitution. And that query can be extraordinarily difficult to answer. In 1937, Justice George Sutherland dissented against the Court's validating a New Deal statute that he thought unconstitutional. He conceded that a justice must give "due weight" to the constitutional views of colleagues, Congress, and the president, but:

> in passing upon the validity of a statute, he discharges a duty imposed upon him, which cannot be consummated justly by an automatic acceptance of the views of others which have neither convinced, nor created a reasonable doubt in, his mind. If upon a question so important he thus surrenders his deliberate judgment, he stands forsworn.[4]

As Justice Felix Frankfurter, another self-anointed prophet of self-restraint,[5] once commented: "In the end, judgment cannot be escaped, the judgment of this Court."

INSTITUTIONAL CHECKS

The judicial system imposes certain institutional as well as moral restrictions on judges. Some of these limits are internal to courts. Perhaps most obvious is the judicial practice of writing opinions to justify decisions. This requirement—and it is a requirement for federal trial judges and a hallowed practice on appellate courts—limits the range of judicial choice. These reasons are publicly given and thus can be publicly analyzed, praised, criticized, or even ridiculed. Although legislators can justify their votes by saying a bill will bring money and jobs to their constituents, judges must offer reasons grounded in legal principles. Few jurists have the temerity (or the stupidity) to expose themselves to the scorn of fellow judges, scholars, and journalists by announcing decisions for which they cannot give good, even if controversial, reasons.

Judges of trial courts face other restrictions. In all important criminal cases as well as in many civil suits, litigants have a right to trial by jury. Although a judge may shield the jurors from some untrustworthy evidence and give them detailed explanations of "the law," the final decision is theirs. Moreover, under existing legal rules, a judge is not supposed to overturn a jury's verdict unless it appears that reasonable people could not have reasonably arrived at such a conclusion.

---

[4] *West Coast Hotel v. Parrish*, 300 U.S. 379 (1937).

[5] In many Supreme Court opinions, Frankfurter declared his adherence to the doctrine of judicial restraint. But analyses of his voting behavior, at least according to some scholars, suggest that he was "a staunch economic conservative" who was willing to strike down laws that impinged on his policy preferences. See, e.g., Jeffrey A. Segal and Harold J. Spaeth, *The Supreme Court and the Attitudinal Model Revisited* (New York: Cambridge University Press, 2002), 409-417

Appellate judges also operate within a network of internal restraints. Probably the most effective limitation is that all appellate courts are multijudge tribunals. Judges on lower appellate courts typically sit in panels of three; to give a ruling the weight of precedent, a majority must agree on an opinion as well as a decision. The same holds for courts of last resort. In the U.S. Supreme Court, a justice who wishes to have his or her jurisprudence translated into public law must marshal at least four other colleagues behind his or her reasoning. Because this mustering involves creating consensus, it also thereby often requires crafting opinions that may not exactly reflect the preferences of the writers or of others who join in those opinions. Collective responsibility thus acts as a powerful constraint on appellate judges. (Reading 8.2; see also Chapter 13.)

Other institutional restrictions are functions of the hierarchical structures in which both federal and state judges operate. A potentially serious limit on trial judges, for example, is the right of a losing litigant (except, of course, the prosecution in a criminal case) to appeal a decision. Although appellate judges give a certain presumption to the judgment of a colleague who presided over the actual combat, reversals of lower courts' rulings do occur. By the same token, tribunals of last resort may have the opportunity to review decisions made by intermediate appellate courts; and they, too, have not hesitated to reverse their colleagues on lower courts. William H. Rehnquist once explained why the U.S. Supreme Court had, in the early 1980s, reversed twenty-seven of twenty-eight rulings by the Court of Appeals for the Ninth Circuit: "When all is said and done, some panels of the Ninth Circuit have a hard time saying no to any litigant with a hard luck story."[6] Such extensive monitoring of one particular circuit may be exceptional; but, for the reasons suggested by Jeffrey A. Segal and his colleagues, the mere threat of review by the Supreme Court may restrain judges of intermediate appellate courts. (Reading 8.3.)

In these examples, the hierarchical structure imposes limits on lower courts from tribunals above them. But it can also work the other way: Lower-court judges can hamper the commands of higher courts by avoiding, limiting or even defying them—as many lower courts did with the U.S. Supreme Court's desegregation decisions. Indeed, one Alabama jurist not only declined to follow the Court's decisions in this field but declared the Fourteenth Amendment unconstitutional as well.[7]

That judges of lower courts occasionally frustrate the efforts of judges of higher courts should not be surprising; bureaucratic resistance in administrative hierarchies is a heavily documented fact of life in governmental, ecclesiastical, and commercial organizations. Moreover, the Supreme Court usually does not issue a final order when it decides a case but only remands it—sends it back—to a lower court for "proceedings consistent with this opinion." Not

---

[6] Quoted in *Los Angeles Times*, August 16, 1984.

[7] Bradley C. Canon and Charles A. Johnson, *Judicial Policies: Implementation and Impact* (Washington, DC: CQ Press), 38 (1999); see, more generally, Walter F. Murphy, "Lower Court Checks on Supreme Court Power," 53 *American Political Science Review* 1017 (1959).

infrequently, a party who wins on appeal to the Supreme Court still winds up the loser on remand. Ernesto Miranda—the defendant whose name has since 1966 been attached to the famous warning about rights to silence and to free counsel that the Court has required police to give people whom they arrest—was convicted again when he was retried.[8]

Apart from evasion or even attacks on a higher court, there is ample room for conflict when a trial judge senses a shift in the Supreme Court's policy. "It is a little difficult," Charles Curtis once observed, "for the lower court to have to follow the Supreme Court of the next succeeding year." Two schools of thought tell lower courts how to handle such problems. One, represented by Jerome Frank, thinks that "when a lower court perceives a pronounced new doctrinal trend in Supreme Court decisions, it is its duty, cautiously to be sure, to follow not to resist it." Frank added: "To use mouthfilling words, cautious extrapolation is in order."[9]

But prediction and extrapolation are risky enterprises. Guesses, no matter how well intentioned and well informed, can be wrong. This risk has led other judges to assert that inferior courts should follow doubtful precedents until the higher court specifically overturns them. As Chief Judge Calvert Magruder of the First Circuit said: "We should always express a respectful deference to controlling decisions of the Supreme Court, and do our best to follow them. We should leave it to the Supreme Court to overrule its own cases."[10] When, in *Hopwood v. Texas* (1996) (Reading 7.1), a panel of judges on the U.S. Court of Appeals for the Fifth Circuit refused to apply the U.S. Supreme Court's decision (actually Justice Powell's opinion for a "fractured" court) in *Bakke*, the affirmative action ruling, they seemed to agree with Jerome Frank. As we noted in Chapter 7, the dissenters asserted that *Bakke* was still good law and should have been followed. And, seven years later, in *Grutter v. Bollinger* (2003) the Supreme Court seemed to agree. In upholding the University of Michigan Law School's affirmative action program, the Court wrote: "In the wake of our fractured decision in *Bakke*, courts have struggled to discern whether Justice Powell's diversity rationale, set forth in part of the opinion joined by no other Justice, is nonetheless binding precedent. . . [T]oday we endorse Justice Powell's view that student body diversity is a compelling state interest that can justify the use of race in university admissions."

If confronted with systematic evasion, the Supreme Court can, as a last resort, invoke its inherent power to punish for contempt in order to coerce either state or federal judges. But this power is almost as unlikely to be used as is the impeachment power of Congress. More probably, the Court would do as John

---

[8] Alternatively, when the justices remand cases, losers in the Supreme Court can become winners in lower tribunals. See Richard L. Pacelle and Lawrence Baum, "Supreme Court Authority in the Judiciary: A Study of Remands," 20 *American Politics Quarterly* 169–191 (1992).

[9] *Perkins v. Endicott Johnson Corp.* (1942).

[10] Calvert Magruder, "The Trials and Tribulations of an Intermediate Appellate Court," 44 *Cornell Law Quarterly.* 1, 4 (1958).

Marshall did in *McCulloch v. Maryland* (1819) when faced with militant state resistance: bring the full weight of its statutory and constitutional authority to bear on the substantive issues in dispute and make the final determination of the problems itself. In such a fashion, this aspect of judicial decision making comes full circle. The Supreme Court must take into account the reaction of inferior judges, and lower courts must attempt to divine the counter reaction of the Supreme Court. Meanwhile, both must keep a wary eye on public opinion and maneuverings within the other branches of government to ascertain how these will affect the policy concerned as well as their own authority.

CHECKS IMPOSED BY THE AMERICAN SYSTEM OF SEPARATED INSTITUTIONS

If judges hope to generate enduring policy, they must also be attentive to the preferences of legislative and executive officials.[11] Under the constitutional design of the federal and the state political systems, separate institutions compete for shared powers.[12] "I am a part of the legislative process," President Dwight D. Eisenhower said; and, like every other modern president, he learned that senators and representatives often have more knowledge of and control over executive officials than do presidents. So, too, in choosing judges, establishing rules for judicial procedure, and carrying out (or not carrying out) judicial decisions, both these branches play roles in the operations of the other branch of government. That complex institutional design, along with the informal rules (such as judicial review) that have evolved over time, endows each branch of government with significant authority over the spheres of the other branches as well as over its own. This mingling of powers is coupled with checks on other institutions so that each branch can impose limits on the primary functions of the others. For example, the judiciary may interpret statutes and executive orders; judges can even strike down laws or orders as violating constitutional provisions, but legislatures can pass fresh laws, which the executive may sign or veto; and, if he signs, can then interpret or even refuse to enforce. Moreover, the threat of impeachment, even though it is usually hollow, always stands like a shotgun behind the door.

The checks and balances inherent in systems of shared powers force every political actor to come to grips with the fact that *almost all public policy, whether state or federal, emanates not from the separate actions of the branches of government but from interactions among them.* For any set of actors to make authoritative policy, be they justices, legislators, or executives, they must be sensitive to the desires and likely actions of other relevant actors. Judges may be especially vulnerable here.

---

[11] For a detailed discussion, see Lee Epstein and Jack Knight, *The Choices Justices Make* (Washington, DC: CQ Press, 1998); and Walter F. Murphy, *Elements of Judicial Strategy* (Chicago: University of Chicago Press, 1964).

[12] Charles Jones, The Separated Presidency," in The New American Political System, ed. Anthony King, 2nd ed. (Washington, DC: American Enterprise Institute, 1990), 3.

Controlling neither "the sword or the purse," as Alexander Hamilton put it in *Federalist* No. 78, they directly depend on legislators and executives for the money and means to enforce their decisions. Indirectly, judges also depend on "public confidence" (see later in this chapter) to pressure the other branches of government. To ignore the wishes of legislators and executives and to lose public confidence might spell disaster for judges hoping to see their rulings implemented. On the other hand, to be no more than lackeys of the other branches or automatons reacting to transient public moods would destroy the very purpose of the judiciary, bring judges into disrepute, and end their moral, and probably political, influence.

Political Checks by Executives

In their experiences with presidents who refused to execute judicial decrees, Chief Justices John Marshall and Roger Brooke Taney reacted differently, Marshall with more political adroitness than his successor in office. With good reason, Marshall thought that Thomas Jefferson was ready to defy the expected decision in *Marbury v. Madison* (1803) that Marbury should have his commission. The chief justice shrewdly avoided this clash. (Reading 2.2.) But in 1807 he and Jefferson had a second confrontation when, as part of his circuit-riding duties, Marshall presided over the trial of Aaron Burr for treason. At the request of Burr's counsel, the chief justice ordered Jefferson to produce some highly relevant correspondence between the president and one of the witnesses for the prosecution. Subsequent events are somewhat unclear, and some historians have contended that Jefferson successfully defied the subpoena. Although he did not personally appear, as the subpoena commanded, he did submit some, but not all, of the subpoenaed correspondence—only as a matter of grace, he said, not because he recognized any judicial authority to compel him to do anything whatever. Marshall ignored repeated requests of Burr's counsel to hold Jefferson in contempt, and the jury's return of a verdict of not guilty mooted the issue, much, one would guess, to the chief justice's relief.

Taney had a more direct clash with executive power and handled it more like a bulldog than a fox. After Lincoln had suspended the writ of habeas corpus and substituted military tribunals for civilian courts in Maryland, the army arrested John Merryman, a notorious secessionist, and confined him in Fort McHenry. After Taney's effort to serve a writ of habeas corpus on the commander of the fort had been rebuffed, the chief justice attempted to have the commanding general arrested for contempt; but the marshal was refused admission to the fort. Taney could only lecture the president in a blistering opinion charging him with violating his oath to support the Constitution.

These were, of course, exceptional cases, but the thread connecting judicial decisions with executive enforcement has often been thin. Andrew Jackson refused to carry out one of the decisions of the Marshall Court protecting the treaty rights of Indians against violation by the state of Georgia. Franklin D. Roosevelt had prepared a radio address to explain why he was not going to comply with an expected decision by the Supreme Court declaring unconstitutional the statute taking the United States off the gold standard. Because, by a vote of five to four, the judges refused to rule against the government's action, FDR did not give the speech. In 1957 when Governor Orval Faubus of Arkansas called out the National Guard to prevent execution of a federal court order to integrate the schools, President Eisenhower was more than willing to compromise and for some days took no action to assist the district court. If he had not eventually concluded that Faubus was negotiating in bad faith, *Brown v. Board of Education* (1954) might have become a monument to judicial futility.

Earlier, President Eisenhower had apparently made a clumsy effort to influence the ruling in *Brown*. Shortly before the decision came down, Earl Warren reports in his memoirs, he was invited to a White House dinner. John W. Davis, counsel for the school board in South Carolina, was also present. During the dinner, the president went to great lengths to tell Warren what a "great man" Davis was. He also said that white southerners were not "bad people. All they are concerned about is to see that their sweet little girls are not required to sit in school alongside some big overgrown Negroes." Not long afterward the Court announced the decision in *Brown* and, Warren added, "with it went our cordial relations."[13]

During oral argument before the Supreme Court in *United States v. Nixon* (1974), the president's counsel refused to assure the justices that Nixon would surrender the Watergate tapes if ordered to do so. Had the president in fact not done so, the mood in Congress, the press, and the country ensured that his impeachment would have quickly followed. It is less clear, however, that other popular presidents—John F. Kennedy, Ronald Reagan, or either Roosevelt, for instance—would have paid a high political price for defying the Court. And, of course, both Andrew Jackson and Abraham Lincoln did defy the justices.

Aside from refusing to execute decisions (and, of course, nominating new justices), perhaps the most effective pressure the president can exert on the Court is to throw his prestige onto the policy-making scales and openly attack individual decisions or an entire line of judicial rulings, as did not only Jackson and Lincoln but also both Roosevelts, Reagan, and, most recently, George W. Bush. All six of them tried to reverse judicial policies, whether pronounced by the Supreme Court or other judicial bodies, by arousing public opposition. (Readings 8.4, 8.5, 8.6, 8.7.)

Still, these public attacks in the United States, especially recent ones, are mild compared to many launched by executives elsewhere. In newly developing constitutional democracies in Eastern Europe, presidents have sometimes failed to comply with the decisions of their courts, threatened impeachment, or taken other steps to punish justices or render their decisions ineffective. An extreme example came in 1993 when Russian President Boris Yeltsin, angry at its ability to check his power, suspended his nation's constitutional court. The justices were not able to resume their work until nearly two years later, when Russia adopted a new constitutional text.

---

[13] *The Memoirs of Chief Justice Earl Warren* (New York: Doubleday & Co., 1977), 291–292.

Legislative Restrictions

In the United States, legislative checks on judicial power are potentially far more sweeping than those of the executive acting alone. On the other hand, because a successful attack requires consensus between both houses of Congress and between Congress and the White House, the chances of the two fully cooperating are small. The first legislative control is that over the purse strings. Although the U.S. constitutional text explicitly says that judges' salaries shall not be reduced during their terms of office, under President Jefferson's leadership, Congress in 1802 simply abolished a whole tier of federal courts and refused to appropriate money to pay the (now idle) judges' salaries. In 1937, in an effort to end the war between the Court and the New Deal, Congress employed a reverse tactic, enacting a statute that offered more favorable retirement benefits to encourage older justices, particular Justice Willis Van Devanter, to retire. Individual representatives or senators sometimes try to persuade Congress to refuse to appropriate funds to carry out particular decisions. Congress actually took this tack in 1980, when it attached a rider to an appropriations bill prohibiting the Department of Justice to use money to support school busing. Had it not been for President Jimmy Carter's veto, this bill would have handcuffed implementation of several desegregation rulings.

Additionally, Congress (or a state legislature against its own courts) can invoke its own lawmaking powers to erase judicial interpretations of statutes. And Congress has not been shy about invoking this power. In a comprehensive study, William Eskridge found that Congress overrode or modified the Supreme Court's interpretation of federal statutes 121 times between 1967 and 1990.[14]

Congress can also propose amendments to overturn judicial decisions grounded in constitutional interpretation, either by repudiating the Court's doctrine or striking at judicial power itself. These sorts of efforts have succeeded four times in response to decisions of the U.S. Supreme Court, producing the Eleventh, which removed a portion of federal jurisdiction, and Fourteenth, Sixteenth, and Twenty-fourth Amendments, which proclaimed new constitutional law directly contradicting what the Supreme Court had said. Such amendments are much more frequent at the state level. For example, after an Hawaiian court held that the denial of marriage licenses to same-sex couples constituted gender discrimination under the state's Equal Rights Amendment, various legislators proposed several amendments to the Hawaiian constitutional text to overturn the court's interpretation. One, giving the state legislature the power to define marriage, received support from more than 70 percent of the voters in the state and so became part of Hawaii's constitutional document. The U.S. Congress also reacted to the Hawaiian court's decision by passing the Defense of Marriage Act, which relieved states of any obligation to recognize the validity of same-sex marriages performed in other states. (see also Reading 8.7.)

---

[14] William N. Eskridge, Jr., "Overriding Supreme Court Statutory Interpretation Decisions," 101 *Yale Law Journal* 331 (1991).

The Defense of Marriage Act shores up an important point: Even when courts interpret the constitution, legislatures have occasionally attempted to overturn or undermine their rulings through simple legislation rather than the more cumbersome (and typically unsuccessful) amending route. An example, at the federal level, was the Religious Freedom Restoration Act (RFRA) of 1993. In this statute, Congress attempted to supplant the doctrine the justices had developed in *Employment Division v. Smith* (1990), upholding a state's authority to fire Native American employees who used Peyote in their religious ceremonies. In place of the Court's approval of broad state control over this aspect of the freedom of religion, Congress enacted rules more respectful of the First Amendment's command of "no law" restricting free exercise of religion.

So far, Congress's attack on Smith has failed. In *Boerne v. City of Flores* (1997), not only did the Court strike down the RFRA, but it also took the opportunity to give Congress a self-serving lecture on the justices' version of civics:

> Our national experience teaches that the Constitution is preserved best when each part of the government respects both the Constitution and the proper actions and determinations of the other branches. When the Court has interpreted the Constitution, it has acted within the province of the Judicial Branch, which embraces the duty to say what the law is. *Marbury v. Madison.* When the political branches of the Government act against the background of a judicial interpretation of the Constitution already issued, it must be understood that in later cases and controversies the Court will treat its precedents with the respect due them under settled principles, including stare decisis, and contrary expectations must be disappointed. RFRA was designed to control cases and controversies, such as the one before us; but as the provisions of the federal statute here invoked are beyond congressional authority, it is this Court's precedent, not RFRA, which must control.

The Court reiterated this message in *Dickerson v. United States* (2000), involving provisions of the Crime Control and Safe Streets Act. Passed by Congress in 1968, this law was specifically aimed at undoing the effects of three of the Warren Court's decisions strengthening the procedural rights of criminal defendants. The statute lay moribund for some years because successive presidents, including Richard Nixon, refused to enforce it. Then, unexpectedly, in 1999 a federal appellate court relied on this law to hold admissible a suspect's voluntary statement about a crime made before he was advised of his rights to silence and an attorney. As had Congress, the judges read the Supreme Court's opinion in *Miranda v. Arizona* (1966), to invite Congress to formulate new rules that would protect defendants' rights and held Congress had done so in the Act of 1968.

The Supreme Court disagreed. In an opinion written by Chief Justice Rehnquist, no great fan of *Miranda,* the majority admitted that, although there was some language in the various opinions to support the court of appeals, *Miranda* had announced a "constitutional rule." And, although "Congress retains the ultimate authority to modify or set aside any judicially created rules of evidence and procedure that are not required by the Constitution," it "may not legislatively supersede our decisions interpreting and applying the Constitution. See, e.g., *City of Boerne v. Flores* (1997)."

Despite these words, it seems inevitable that Congress will try again to modify constitutional decisions and, under different circumstances, may succeed. What is important to know for now is that legislative power to change (or attempt to change) judicial interpretations of statutes and constitutional clauses is not the only weak spot in judges' armor. At the federal level, as we noted earlier, Article III of the constitutional text gives Congress control over the appellate jurisdiction of the Supreme Court. As we have seen, in the nineteenth century, Congress exercised that power to punish the Court; and, in the *McCardle* case, the justices meekly accepted the rebuke. (Reading 8.8.) More recently, some senators and representatives have tried to remove the Court's authority to hear many kinds of controversial cases, such as abortion and prayers in public schools.

Those threats, just as have occasional calls for the impeachment of federal judges who disagree with particular legislators on constitutional interpretation, have failed. But congressional power over the number of judgeships and the organization and jurisdiction of the federal courts is a reality. Beginning with the last Federalist Congress in 1801, legislators have regularly attempted to pack the federal courts, especially at times when they and the president have shared the same general political philosophy. Such agreement enables presidents to make many appointments at one time and "relieves Congress of the need to monitor and discipline the judiciary as such judges would be expected to share a common sense of justice with the legislators."[15] On the flip side, Congress has occasionally sought to reduce the number of judges to punish either presidents or judges. To deny Thomas Jefferson a nomination for the Supreme Court, the Judiciary Act of 1801 provided that, when the next vacancy occurred on the Court, the number of justices should be reduced from six to five. When Jefferson's party came to power, Congress enacted the Judiciary Act of 1802, which abolished a tier of federal courts; and in 1869, to deny Andrew Johnson a nomination, Congress eliminated an unfilled seat on the U.S. Supreme Court.

Do these and other attempts at curbing the courts have any effect on the judiciary? Scholars are divided. On one side are those who argue that judges must take into account the preferences of Congress if they hope to see their decisions followed and their institutions remain serious players in the governmental process. In support of this position, some scholars point to specific judicial about-faces, such as the "switch in time that saved nine" in 1937 and the Supreme Court's backing down in the late 1950s after fiery reactions against its rulings on loyalty-security, and the reach of congressional investigations. These scholars also provide data showing that presumably "conservative" courts occasionally reach "liberal" rulings when liberals control the various elected institutions of government.[16]

---

[15] John M. Figuierdo and Emerson H. Tiller, "Congressional Control of the Courts: A Theoretical and Empirical Analysis of Expansion of the Federal Judiciary," 39 *Journal of Law and Economics* 435 (1996).

[16] See, e.g., Pablo T. Spiller and Rafael Gely, "Congressional Control or Judicial Independence: The Determinants of U.S. Supreme Court Labor-Relations Decisions," 23 *RAND Journal of Economics* 463 (1992).

On the other side are two camps, both of which argue that congressional re-straints do not seriously deter judges. These scholars base their claims on dif-ferent assumptions about judicial motivations. Some, the "attitudinalists," suggest that, for federal judges and some of their state counterparts, absence of an electoral connection enables them to act in accord with their own political values: Because legislators do not control their jobs, judges can attempt to max-imize their own policy preferences. This camp has mustered substantial evi-dence in support of its position; Jeffrey A. Segal's work is illustrative. In a series of systematic examinations of the voting patterns of justices of the Supreme Court, he finds that they do not change in response to changes in the partisan political environment. Because "the federal courts were designed to be inde-pendent," Segal concludes, "we should not be surprised that they are capable of actually being independent."[17] Scholars falling into the historical institutional school would not necessarily disagree with Segal's conclusion; they too believe that judges are "autonomous from direct and indirect political pressure." But they would certainly take issue with his assumption that judges seek (or should seek) to etch their own values into law. On their account, as noted earlier, judges attempt to maximize the legitimacy of their institution by adhering to precedent and other norms—a goal they cannot necessarily achieve by following personal policy desires[18]. (see Chapter 10.)

CHECKS FROM THE STATES

Although state executives or legislators have no direct means of limiting federal judicial power, they can utilize their access to Congress or the White House to try to deploy the weapons these institutions have. The Civil War buried nullifi-cation, a venerable means of direct state resistance. This doctrine, which justi-fied a state's "interposing" itself against federal power, dates back to the Kentucky Resolutions of 1798 and 1799, drafted by Thomas Jefferson. Despite James Madison's authorship of the somewhat less assertive Virginia Resolutions of 1798 and his deep respect for Jefferson, he later denounced nul-lification as a "colossal heresy," a "poison," and a "preposterous and anarchical pretension." In 1955 the attorney general of Mississippi commented that his state's effort to nullify the school segregation decisions was based on "legal poppycock"; earlier the governor of Alabama had characterized his legislators who were proposing nullification as "just a bunch of hound dawgs, bayin' at the moon." A more recent Alabama governor, Fob James, apparently did not share this view. Although he did not call for nullification, he did suggest that state officials do not have to follow rulings they consider unconstitutional.

---

[17] Jeffrey A. Segal, "Supreme Court Deference to Congress: An Examination of the Markist Model," in *Supreme Court Decision-Making*, ed. Cornell W. Clayton and Howard Gillman (University of Chicago Press, 1999).

[18] Kahn, "Institutional Norms and Supreme Court Decision-Making."

When a federal district court in 1996 issued a ruling against voluntary public school prayer, James promised to "resist [the] order by every legal and political means, with every ounce of strength I possess." Surely these words were constituted hyperbole, but it is also true that state officials have often attempted, and sometimes successfully so, to check federal judicial power. School prayer, the subject prompting James's remark, provides but one example. After the U.S. Supreme Court, in *School District of Abington Township v. Schempp* (1963), prohibited schools from prescribing readings from the Bible, Tennessee's state commissioner of education said that, despite *Schempp*, local officials could retain Bible readings in their schools if they so desired.[19] Perhaps not so surprisingly, most took up the commissioner's invitation.

State judges, too, as we have suggested, may attempt to thwart implementation of federal rulings and, in so doing, may have tactical advantages over their colleagues in the legislative and executive branches, at least with regard to decisions of the U.S. Supreme Court. Because the Supreme Court will review only those cases from state courts in which the decision was based on a substantial federal question, matters pertaining strictly to state law do not come under federal authority. Thus, state judges can sometimes conceal the real bases of decisions from overworked justices and so avoid review and reversal. And, even when state judges are more candid, they can still prevail, for there are nearly 30,000 of them, a number far beyond the capacity of nine justices on the U.S. Supreme Court to supervise closely. Losing litigants have an incentive to help, but as one man said after losing his case when Utah's supreme court refused to apply the U.S. Supreme Court's interpretations of the Fourteenth Amendment: "The fine will cost me a thousand dollars. It will cost me several hundred thousand dollars to appeal and win. I'd rather lose."

The differences between state and national interests and outlooks and the perennial friction between trial and appellate judges create a substantial reservoir of potential conflict within the judicial system. In 1958, for instance, when attacks on the liberal decisions of the Warren Court had almost produced a constitutional crisis, the Conference of State Chief Justices issued an unprecedented report on federal-state relationships, accusing the Supreme Court of usurping state powers. By the 1970s, in an interesting reversal, the Court had become rather too conservative for tribunals of last resort in such states as California, New Jersey, and Hawaii. Judges in those states declined to follow the Burger (and now Rehnquist) Court's jurisprudence and relied instead on provisions of their own state constitutions to which they are free to give independent meanings. (see Chapter 3, especially Reading 3.9.) For example, the Burger Court ruled in *San Antonio School District v. Rodriguez* (1973) that the Fourteenth Amendment does not require states to ensure that all public school children receive an equally financed education. But two years earlier the California Supreme Court had come to the opposite conclusion in *Serrano v. Priest* (1971)

---

[19] See Robert H. Birkby, "The Supreme Court and the Bible Belt: Tennessee Reaction to the *Schempp* Decision," 10 *Midwest Journal of Political Science* 305–319 (1966).

on the basis of the state constitution. In spite of *Rodriguez*, the state's policy was subsequently confirmed when the Supreme Court refused to review in *Clowes v. Serrano* (1977). Other states followed California's lead in enforcing stricter standards than those approved by *Rodriguez*. New Jersey's supreme court, for example, imposed an equal-financing requirement on that state by interpreting the state constitutional clause mandating "a thorough and efficient system of free public schools" to mean "equally financed" public schools.[20]

CHECKS FROM THE PEOPLE

The public may also play a role in limiting judicial power—one that is most obvious in the many states that elect their judges. Through their votes, citizens can unseat jurists who consistently rule in ways that they dislike. (Reading 4.9.) Even the mere threat of electoral punishment may be sufficient to keep judges in line. Melinda Gann Hall and Paul Brace show that judges who must face the electorate are more likely to uphold sentences of death than are their nonelected counterparts.[21] And work by James Kuklinski and John E. Stanga indicates that even those state judges who rarely face electoral competition bend to public sentiment. (Reading 8.9.)

The role public opinion plays in constraining federal judges is less obvious and, thus, much more subject to dispute. Some commentators argue that because these judges have life tenure there is no reason for them to take account of public opinion when reaching decisions. Others beg to differ, asserting that particular rulings do not deviate significantly from the views of the citizenry. Thomas Marshall claims that "When a clear-cut poll majority or plurality exists, over three-fifths of the [Supreme] Court's decisions reflect the polls. By all arguable evidence the modern Supreme Court appears to reflect public opinion about as accurately as other policy makers."[22] Moreover, some scholars argue that the Court's decisions also may reflect more general societal trends. Two researchers claim a correspondence between decisions and public moods: the justices "are broadly aware of fundamental trends in the ideological tenor of public opinion, and that at least some justices, consciously or not, may adjust their decisions at the margins to accommodate such fundamental trends."[23]

---

[20] *Robinson v. Cahill* (1976).

[21] Melinda Gann Hall and Paul Brace, "The Vicissitudes of Death by Decree: Forces Influencing Capital Punishment in State Supreme Courts," 75 *Social Science Quarterly* 136 (1994). See also Melinda Gann Hall, "Electoral Politics and Strategic Voting in State Supreme Courts," 54 *Journal of Politics* 427 (1992), and Reading 13.3

[22] Thomas Marshall, *Public Opinion and the Supreme Court* (New York: Unwin Hyman, 1989), 97.

[23] William Mishler and Reginald S. Sheehan, "The Supreme Court as a Counter-Majoritarian Institution? The Impact of Public Opinion on Supreme Court Decisions," 87 *American Political Science Review* 89 (1993).

The direction in which influence travels is, however, often unclear. Without doubt, the justices sometimes lag far behind public opinion, as in the battle with the New Deal over governmental regulation of the economy, and have had to beat a hasty retreat back toward public consensus. At other times, the Court has been ahead of public opinion, as it was in its decisions on gerrymandering, racial discrimination, and capital punishment. On the first two issues the Warren Court led the country into a world that was politically, legally, and morally different from that which had existed. On the other hand, the American public continued to support killing convicted murderers, and most state legislatures reenacted laws authorizing the death penalty, albeit with greater procedural protections for the accused. And a majority of the justices who have come to the Court since *Furman* (1972) have shared the public's approval of executions.

Research showing a link between public opinion and judicial decisions, of course, raises many interesting questions: Not least is why would judges who do not depend on voters to retain their jobs would bother to take public opinion into account when they reach their decisions. One response is that courts require legitimacy—in the form of public support for their mission—to ensure the implementation of their decisions and to help them fend off attacks from elected officials.

But public attitudes toward courts and their doctrines are not likely to be static. In a series of studies of national samples conducted in 1964, 1966, and 1967, during the heyday of the Warren Court, Murphy and Tanenhaus found that the most powerful factor explaining support for the Court was political liberalism. In 1975, six years into the more conservative Burger Court, re-interviews of the most knowledgeable third of the sample of 1966 showed that many political liberals and conservatives had switched sides, with the latter now providing the bulk of the Court's support.[24]

Public attitudes are also likely to be complex. Murphy and Tanenhaus's studies demonstrated that, although citizens were more apt to remember specific decisions of the Warren Court of which they disapproved than they approved, they still thought highly of the Court as an institution. Nevertheless, in each of these national surveys a larger proportion of people said they trusted Congress more than the Supreme Court.[25] Two decades later, in 1995, James L. Gibson and his colleagues found that nearly two-thirds of all Americans still trusted the Supreme Court to "reach decisions that are right for country as a whole". (Reading 8.10.) And, interestingly enough, the Court's decision in *Bush v. Gore* (2000), despite scholarly predictions to the contrary, had virtually no affect on public support for the Court. Indeed, if anything, Americans grew even more trusting perhaps because, as Gibson and his colleagues write: "the effect

---

[24] Because of Tanenhaus's sudden death, the only published report of these re-interviews is Joseph Tanenhaus and Walter F. Murphy, "Patterns of Public Support for the Supreme Court: A Panel Study," 43 *Journal of Politics* 24 (1976)

[25] Citations to six of Murphy and Tanenhaus's articles reporting the data and analyses of their studies can be found in their "Publicity, Public Opinion, and the Supreme Court," 84 *Northwestern University Law Review* 985 (1990).

of pre-existing legitimacy on evaluations of the decision was stronger than the effect of evaluations on institutional loyalty, and institutional loyalty predisposed most Americans to view the decision as based on law and therefore legitimate" (see the update to Reading 8.10).

Americans are not alone in trusting courts and judges. Gibson's data suggest that citizens living in constitutional democracies throughout the world tend to support their national courts of last resort. What remains unclear is the extent to which these new citizens would translate their verbal expressions into political action were judicial institutions threatened.

SELECTED REFERENCES

BAKER, LEONARD. 1967. *Back to Rack: The Duel Between FDR and the Supreme Court*. New York: Macmillan.

BERGER, RAOUL. 1969. *Congress v. the Supreme Court*. Cambridge, MA: Harvard University Press.

BERGER, RAOUL. 1974. "The President, Congress, and the Courts." *Yale Law Journal* 83: 1111.

BRENNAN, WILLIAM J., JR. 1977. "State Constitutions and the Protection of Individual Rights." *Harvard Law Review* 90: 489.

CALDEIRA, GREGORY A. 1986. "Neither the Purse Nor the Sword: Dynamics of Public Confidence in the U.S. Supreme Court." *American Political Science Review* 80: 1209.

CALDEIRA, GREGORY A. 1987. "Public Opinion and the U.S. Supreme Court: FDR's Court-Packing Plan." *American Political Science Review* 81: 1139.

CALDEIRA, GREGORY A. 1991. "Courts and Public Opinion." In *The American Courts*, ed. John B. Gates and Charles A. Johnson. Washington, DC: CQ Press.

DE FIGUIERDO, JOHN M., AND EMERSON H. TILLER. 1996. "Congressional Control of the Courts: A Theoretical and Empirical Analysis of Expansion of the Federal Judiciary." *Journal of Law and Economics* 39: 435.

ELLIOTT, SHELDON D. 1958. "Court-Curbing Proposals in Congress." *Notre Dame Lawyer* 33: 597.

EPSTEIN, LEE, AND JACK KNIGHT. 1998. *The Choices Justices Make*. Washington, DC: CQ Press.

EPSTEIN, LEE, JACK KNIGHT, AND ANDREW MARTIN. 2001. "The Supreme Court as a Strategic National Policy Maker." *Emory Law Journal* 50: 583.

ESKRIDGE, WILLIAM N., JR. 1991. "Civil Rights Legislation in the 1990s: Reneging on History?" *California Law Review* 79: 613.

ESKRIDGE, WILLIAM N., JR. 1991. "Overriding Supreme Court Statutory Interpretation Decisions." *Yale Law Journal* 101: 331.

ESKRIDGE, WILLIAM N., JR. 1994. *Dynamic Statutory Interpretation*. Harvard University Press.

FRIEDMAN, BARRY, AND ANNA HARVEY. 2003. "Electing the Supreme Court." *Indiana Law Journal* 78: 123.

GIBSON, JAMES L., GREGORY A. CALDEIRA, AND VANESSA BAIRD. 1998. "On the Legitimacy of National High Courts." *American Political Science Review* 92: 343.

GIBSON, JAMES L., GREGORY A. CALDEIRA, AND LESTER KENYATTA SPENCE. 2004. "The Supreme Court and the U.S. Presidential Election of 2000." *British Journal of Political Science*, forthcoming.

GILLMAN, HOWARD, AND CORNELL W. CLAYTON, eds., 1999. The Supreme Court in American Politics: New Institutionalist Interpretations. Lawrence: University of Kansas Press, 1999.

GUNTHER, GERALD. 1984. "Congressional Power to Curtail Federal Court Jurisdiction." *Stanford Law Review* 36: 895.

HALL, MELINDA GANN. 1992. "Electoral Politics and Strategic Voting in State Supreme Courts." *Journal of Politics* 54: 427.

HALL, MELINDA GANN, AND PAUL BRACE. 1994. "The Vicissitudes of Death by Decree: Forces Influencing Capital Punishment in State Supreme Courts." *Social Science Quarterly* 75: 136.

KAHN, RONALD. 1999. "Institutional Norms and Supreme Court Decision-Making: The Rehnquist Court on Privacy and Religion." In *Supreme Court Decision-Making*, ed. Cornell W. Clayton and Howard Gillman. Chicago: University of Chicago Press.

KATZMANN, ROBERT A. 1997. *Courts and Congress.* Washington, DC: Brookings Institution.

KUKLINSKI, JAMES H., AND JOHN E. STANGA. 1979. "Political Participation and Government Responsiveness: The Behavior of California Superior Courts." *American Political Science Review* 73: 1090.

LEUCHTENBURG, WILLIAM F. 1966. "The Origins of Franklin D. Roosevelt's 'Court-Packing' Plan." In *The Supreme Court Review*, ed. Philip B. Kurland. Chicago: University of Chicago Press.

MALTZMAN, FORREST, JAMES F. SPRINGGS II, AND PAUL J. WAHLBECK. 2000. *Crafting Law on the Supreme Court: The Collegial Game.* Cambridge: Cambridge University Press.

MARSHALL, THOMAS. 1989. *Public Opinion and the Supreme Court.* New York: Unwin Hyman.

MILLER, MARK, AND JEB BARNES, eds. 2005. *Making Policy, Making Law: An Interbranch Perspective.* Georgetown University Press.

MURPHY, WALTER F. 1959. "Lower Court Checks on Supreme Court Power." *American Political Science Review* 53: 1017.

MURPHY, WALTER F. 1962. *Congress and the Court.* Chicago: University of Chicago Press.

MURPHY, WALTER F., AND JOSEPH TANENHAUS. 1990. "Publicity, Public Opinion, and the Supreme Court." *Northwestern University Law Review* 84: 985.

NAGEL, STUART S. 1965. "Court-Curbing Periods in American History." *Vanderbilt Law Review* 18: 925.

NOTE. 1958. "Congressional Reversal of Supreme Court Decisions: 1945–1957." *Harvard Law Review* 71: 1324.

NOTE. 1998. "Congressional Reversal of Supreme Court Decisions: 1945–1957." *Harvard Law Review* 71: 1324.

PRITCHETT, C. HERMAN. 1961. *Congress Versus the Supreme Court 1957–1960.* Minneapolis: University of Minnesota Press.

SCHMIDHAUSER, JOHN B., AND LARRY L. BERG. 1972. *The Supreme Court and Congress: Conflict and Interaction.* New York: Free Press.

SCIGLIANO, ROBERT. 1971. *The Supreme Court and the Presidency.* New York: Free Press.

SEGAL, JEFFREY A. 1997. "Separation-of-Powers Games in the Positive Theory of Law and Courts." *American Political Science Review* 91: 28.

SONGER, DONALD R., JEFFREY A. SEGAL, AND CHARLES M. CAMERON. 1994. "The Hierarchy of Justice: Testing a Principal-Agent Model of Supreme Court-Circuit Court Interactions." *American Journal of Political Science* 38: 673.

TANENHAUS, JOSEPH, AND WALTER F. MURPHY. 1976. "Patterns of Public Support for the Supreme Court: A Panel Study." *Journal of Politics* 43: 24.

ZEPPOS, NICHOLAS S. 1993. "Deference to Political Decisionmakers and the Preferred Scope of Judicial Review." *Northwestern Law Review* 88: 296.

". . . reconsideration of Roe *falls not into any 'good-cause
exception' to [the] 'fundamental rule of judicial restraint . . .'"*
—JUSTICE SANDRA DAY O'CONNOR

*"JUSTICE O'CONNOR'S assertion that a 'fundamental rule
of judicial restraint' requires us to avoid reconsidering* Roe,
cannot be taken seriously." —JUSTICE ANTONIN SCALIA

8.1 WEBSTER V. REPRODUCTIVE HEALTH SERVICES

492 U.S. 490 (1989)

*With legal assistance from Planned Parenthood and the ACLU, Reproductive Health
Services, an abortion counseling facility, challenged numerous provisions of a 1986
Missouri law regulating abortions. After a federal district court struck down most of the
act's provisions as violative of* Roe v. Wade *(1973), which had ruled that the
Constitution guarantees women an unfettered right to terminate their pregnancies during the first trimester with a more restricted right thereafter. The court of appeals affirmed, and the state appealed to the Supreme Court.*

Because the Court's composition had changed since it handed down Roe, *many observers believed that the justices would use* Webster *to overturn that decision.
Although the Court did uphold some of the restrictive provisions of Missouri's law,
Chief Justice Rehnquist, a long-time critic of* Roe, *could not muster a majority of his
colleagues behind an opinion to overrule that case.*

In her concurring opinion, Justice O'Connor, another critic of Roe, *explained why
she was unwilling to reverse the earlier decision. Justice Scalia responded to her rationale with a very sharp concurrence of his own.*

JUSTICE O'CONNOR, concurring in part and concurring in the judgment.
. . . [T]here is no necessity to accept the State's invitation to reexamine the
constitutional validity of *Roe v. Wade* (1973). Where there is no need to decide a
constitutional question, it is a venerable principle of this Court's adjudicatory
processes not to do so, for "[t]he Court will not 'anticipate a question of constitutional law in advance of the necessity of deciding it.'" Neither will it generally
"formulate a rule of constitutional law broader than is required by the precise
facts to which it is to be applied." Quite simply, "[i]t is not the habit of the court
to decide questions of a constitutional nature unless absolutely necessary to a decision of the case." The Court today has accepted the State's every interpretation
of its abortion statute and has upheld, under our existing precedents, every provision of that statute which is properly before us. Precisely for this reason reconsideration of *Roe* falls not into any "good-cause exception" to this "fundamental

rule of judicial restraint. . . ." When the constitutional invalidity of a State's abortion statute actually turns on the constitutional validity of *Roe v. Wade*, there will be time enough to reexamine *Roe*. And to do so carefully.

JUSTICE SCALIA, concurring in part and concurring in the judgment.

I share Justice Blackmun's view that [the opinion of the Court] effectively would overrule *Roe v. Wade* (1973). I think that should be done, but would do it more explicitly. Since today we contrive to avoid doing it, and indeed to avoid almost any decision of national import, I need not set forth my reasons, some of which have been well recited in dissents of my colleagues in other cases. . . .

Justice O'Connor's assertion that a "fundamental rule of judicial restraint" requires us to avoid reconsidering *Roe*, cannot be taken seriously. By finessing *Roe* we do not, as she suggests, adhere to the strict and venerable rule that we should avoid "decid[ing] questions of a constitutional nature." We have not disposed of this case on some statutory or procedural ground, but have decided, and could not avoid deciding, whether the Missouri statute meets the requirements of the United States Constitution. The only choice available is whether, in deciding that constitutional question, we should use *Roe v. Wade* as the benchmark, or something else. What is involved, therefore, is not the rule of avoiding constitutional issues where possible, but the quite separate principle that we will not "formulate a rule of constitutional law broader than is required by the precise facts to which it is to be applied."

The latter is a sound general principle, but one often departed from when good reason exists. Just this Term, for example, in an opinion authored by Justice O'Connor, despite the fact that we had already held a racially based set-aside unconstitutional because unsupported by evidence of identified discrimination, which was all that was needed to decide the case, we went on to outline the criteria for properly tailoring race-based remedies in cases where such evidence is present. *Richmond v. J. A. Croson Co*, (1989). Also this Term, in an opinion joined by Justice O'Connor, we announced the constitutional rule that deprivation of the right to confer with counsel during trial violates the Sixth Amendment even if no prejudice can be shown, despite our finding that there had been no such deprivation on the facts before us—which was all that was needed to decide that case. *Perry v. Leeke* (1989). I have not identified with certainty the first instance of our deciding a case on broader constitutional grounds than absolutely necessary, but it is assuredly no later than *Marbury v. Madison* (1803), where we held that mandamus could constitutionally issue against the Secretary of State, although that was unnecessary given our holding that the law authorizing issuance of the mandamus by this Court was unconstitutional.

The Court has often spoken more broadly than needed in precisely the fashion at issue here, announcing a new rule of constitutional law when it could have reached the identical result by applying the rule thereby displaced. To describe two recent opinions that Justice O'Connor joined: In *Daniels v. Williams* (1986), we overruled our prior holding that a "deprivation" of liberty or property could occur through negligent governmental acts, ignoring the availability of the alternative constitutional ground that, even if a deprivation had occurred, the State's postdeprivation remedies satisfied due process. In *Illinois v. Gates* (1983), we replaced the pre-existing "two-pronged" constitutional test for probable cause with a totality-of-the-circumstances approach, ignoring the concurrence's argument that the same outcome could have been reached under the old test. It is rare, of course, that the Court goes out of its way to acknowledge that its judgment could have been reached under the old constitutional rule, making its adoption of the new one unnecessary to the decision, but even such explicit acknowledgment is not unheard of. . . . It would be wrong, in any decision, to ignore the reality that our policy not to "formulate a rule of constitutional law broader than is required by the precise facts" has a frequently applied good-cause exception. But it seems particularly perverse to convert the policy into an absolute in the present case, in order to place beyond reach the inexpressibly "broader-than-was-required-by-the-precise-facts" structure established by *Roe v. Wade*.

The real question, then, is whether there are valid reasons to go beyond the most stingy possible holding today. It seems to me there are not only valid but compelling ones. Ordinarily, speaking no more broadly than is absolutely required avoids throwing settled law into confusion; doing so today preserves a chaos that is evident to anyone who can read and count. Alone sufficient to justify a broad holding is the fact that our retaining control, through *Roe*, of what I believe to be, and many of our citizens recognize to be, a political issue, continuously distorts the public perception of the role of this Court. We can now look forward to at least another Term with carts full of mail from the public, and streets full of demonstrators, urging us—their unelected and life-tenured judges who have been awarded those extraordinary, undemocratic characteristics precisely in order that we might follow the law despite the popular will—to follow the popular will. Indeed, I expect we can look forward to even more of that than before, given our indecisive decision today. And if these reasons for taking the unexceptional course of reaching a broader holding are not enough, then consider the nature of the constitutional question we avoid: In most cases, we do no harm by not speaking more broadly than the decision requires. Anyone affected by the conduct that the avoided holding would have prohibited will be able to challenge it himself and have his day in court to make the argument. Not so with respect to the harm that many States believed, pre-*Roe*, and many may continue to believe, is caused by largely unrestricted abortion. That will continue to occur if the States have the constitutional power to prohibit it, and would do so, but we skillfully avoid telling them so. Perhaps those abortions cannot constitutionally be proscribed. That is surely an arguable question, the question that reconsideration of *Roe v. Wade* entails. But what is not at all arguable, it seems to me, is that we should decide now and not insist that we be run into a corner before we grudgingly yield up our judgment. The only sound reason for the latter course is to prevent a change in the law—but to think that desirable begs the question to be decided.

It was an arguable question today whether the Missouri law contravened this Court's understanding of *Roe v. Wade*, and I would have examined *Roe* rather than examining the contravention. Given the Court's newly contracted abstemiousness, what will it take, one must wonder, to permit us to reach that fundamental question? The result of our vote today is that we will not reconsider that prior opinion, even if most of the Justices think it is wrong, unless we have before us a statute that in fact contradicts it—and even then (under our newly discovered "no-broader-than-necessary" requirement) only minor problematical aspects of *Roe* will be reconsidered, unless one expects state legislatures to adopt provisions whose compliance with *Roe* cannot even be argued with a straight face. It thus appears that the mansion of constitutionalized abortion law, constructed overnight in *Roe v. Wade*, must be disassembled doorjamb by doorjamb, and never entirely brought down, no matter how wrong it may be.

Of the four courses we might have chosen today—to reaffirm *Roe*, to overrule it explicitly, to overrule it sub silentio, or to avoid the question—the last is the least responsible. On the question of the constitutionality of [the Missouri law], I concur in the judgment of the Court and strongly dissent from the manner in which it has been reached.

> *"Justices are strategic actors who realize that their ability to achieve their goals depends on a consideration of the preferences of other actors, the choices they expect others to make, and the institutional context in which they act."*

8.2 THE CHOICES JUSTICES MAKE

Lee Epstein and Jack Knight

Lee Epstein is the Edward Mallinckrodt Distinguished University Professor of Political Science and Professor of Law at Washington University. Jack Knight is the Sidney W. Souers Professor of Government at Washington University.

Driving while intoxicated (DWI) and driving under the influence (DUI) are now familiar terms to most Americans but that was not true during the 1960s. With the Vietnam War and the Civil Rights movement, drunk driving was not one of the pressing issues of the day.

Even so, various researchers and government agencies began to explore the problem as early as 1968. Although these initial studies differed in design and sampling, they reached the same general conclusion: teens, particularly males, had a greater tendency than the general population to be involved in alcohol-related traffic incidents. . . .

From Lee Epstein and Jack Knight, *The Choices Justices Make* (Washington, DC: CQ Press, 1998), Ch. 1–10, 12–13, with adjustments made by the authors.

Despite this accumulation of statistical evidence, another decade elapsed before most states even considered raising the legal drinking age. Oklahoma was a notable exception. In 1972 it passed a law prohibiting men from purchasing beer until they reached the age of twenty-one, but allowing women to buy low-alcohol-content beer at eighteen.

Regarding the Oklahoma law as a form of sex discrimination, Curtis Craig, a twenty-year-old male who wanted to buy beer, and Carolyn Whitener, a beer vendor who wanted to sell it, brought suit in a federal trial court. Among the arguments they made was that laws discriminating on the basis of gender should be subject, at least according to the U.S. Supreme Court, to a "strict scrutiny" test. Under this standard of review, a court presumes a law to be unconstitutional and, to undermine that assumption, the government must demonstrate that its legislation is the least restrictive means available to achieve a compelling state interest. As one might imagine, laws reviewed under this standard almost never survived tests in court. In Craig and Whitener's opinion, the Oklahoma statute was no exception: no compelling state interest was achieved by establishing different drinking ages for men and women.

In response, the state argued that the U.S. Supreme Court had never explicitly applied the strict scrutiny test to laws discriminating on the basis of sex. Rather, the justices had ruled that such laws ought to be subject to a lower level of review—a test called "rational basis." Under this test the state need demonstrate only that the law is a reasonable measure designed to achieve a legitimate (as opposed to compelling) government purpose. Surely, Oklahoma contended, its law met this standard because statistical studies indicated that men "drive more, drink more, and commit more alcohol-related offenses."

The trial court held for the state. While it acknowledged that existing U.S. Supreme Court decisions were murky, it felt that the weight of the case law supported the state's reliance on the lower-level standard. Moreover, the state had met its obligation of establishing a rational basis for the law: given the statistical evidence, Oklahoma's goal of reducing drunk driving seemed a legitimate one.

Refusing to give up the battle, Craig and Whitener appealed to the U.S. Supreme Court. While they and the state continued to press the same claims that they had at trial, a third party advanced a somewhat different approach. The American Civil Liberties Union entered the case as an amicus curiae, a friend of the court, on behalf of Craig. ACLU attorneys Ruth Bader Ginsburg and Melvin Wulf argued that the Oklahoma law "could not survive review whatever the appropriate test": strict scrutiny or rational basis or "something in between." This argument . . . was interesting in two regards: it suggested that (1) the Court could apply the lower rational basis standard and still hold for Craig, or (2) the Court might consider developing a standard "in between" strict scrutiny and rational basis.

What would the Supreme Court do? That question loomed large during the justices' conference, held a few days after oral arguments. As it is traditional for the chief justice to speak first, Warren Burger led off the discussion. He asserted that Craig was an "isolated case" that the Court should dismiss on procedural grounds. The problem was that, because Curtis Craig had turned twenty-one after the Court agreed to hear the case, his claim was moot. So, to Burger, the dispositive issue was whether Whitener, "the saloon keeper," had standing to bring the suit. Burger thought that she did not. But, if his colleagues disagreed and thought Whitener had standing, Burger said he was willing to find for Craig if the majority opinion was narrowly written. By this, Burger meant that he did not want to apply strict scrutiny to classifications based on sex.

Once Burger had spoken, the other justices presented their views in order of seniority, another of the Court's norms. They were all over the map. (See Table 1.) Lewis Powell and Harry Blackmun agreed with the chief justice: both would dismiss on the standing issue, and both thought they could find for Craig. William Rehnquist also wanted to dismiss on standing but would hold for Oklahoma should the Court resolve the dispute. The remaining five justices would rule in Craig's favor, (See Table 1.) but disagreed on the appropriate standard. Thurgood Marshall favored strict scrutiny, as did William Brennan, but Brennan suggested that a standard in between rational and strict might be viable. Byron White seemed to go along with Brennan. Potter Stewart intimated that the Court need only apply the rational basis test to find in Craig's favor.

TABLE 8.1 Comparison of Justices' Conference and Final Positions in *Craig v. Boren*

	Conference Position			*Final Position*		
Justice	*Standing*	*Standard*	*Disposition*	*Standing*	*Standard*	*Disposition*
Burger	No	Rational?	Dismiss/ Craig	No	Rational	Oklahoma
Brennan	Yes	Strict/In-Between*	Craig	Yes	Heightened	Craig
Stewart	Yes	Rational	Craig	Yes	Unclear	Craig
White	Yes	Strict/In-Between?	Craig	Yes	Heightened	Craig
Marshall	Yes	Strict	Craig	Yes	Heightened	Craig
Blackmun	No	Undeclared	Dismiss/ Craig	Yes	Heightened	Craig
Powell	No	Rational?	Dismiss/ Craig	Yes	Heightened	Craig
Rehnquist	No	Rational	Dismiss/ Oklahoma	No	Rational	Oklahoma
Stevens	Yes	Above rational	Craig	Yes	Heightened	Craig

? = Implicit but not explicit from conference discussion.

*"Strict" represented Brennan's most preferred position, but, at conference, he offered the "in between" standard.

John Paul Stevens argued that some "level of scrutiny above mere rationality has to be applied," but he wasn't clear on what that standard should be.

According to the Court's procedures, if the chief justice is in the majority after the conference vote, he decides who will write the opinion of the Court. If he is not part of the majority, the most senior member of the majority—Brennan, in the *Craig* case—takes on that responsibility. According to Court records, Brennan assigned the *Craig* opinion to himself. When he took on the responsibility, Brennan knew, as do all justices, that he needed to obtain the signatures of at least four others if his opinion was to become the law of the land. If he failed to get a majority to agree to its contents, his opinion would become a judgment of the Court and would lack precedential value.

The majority requirement for precedent is yet another of the Court's many norms, which for Brennan, in *Craig*, must have seemed an imposing one. Only three others—Marshall and possibly White and Stevens—tended to agree with his most preferred positions in the case: (1) Whitener had standing; (2) a strict scrutiny standard should be used; and (3) the Court should rule in Craig's favor. From whom would the fourth vote come? Rehnquist seemed out of the question since his position was diametrically opposed to Brennan's on all the main points; he would surely dissent. Blackmun, Powell, and Burger also favored dismissal but were closer to Brennan on point three.

That left Stewart. He, as do all justices, had several feasible courses of action: join the majority opinion, concur "regularly," concur "specially," or dissent. Based on his conference position—he had voted in favor of standing and Craig but was not keen on the strict scrutiny approach—it was possible that Stewart, as well as Blackmun, Powell, and Burger, might join Brennan's disposition of the case (that Craig should win) but disagree with the strict scrutiny standard the opinion articulated. This situation would not be good news from Brennan's perspective, because such (dis)agreement—called a "special" concurrence—means that Stewart would fail to provide the crucial fifth signature. Stewart might, however, join the majority opinion coalition and write a regular concurrence. A regular concurrence, in contrast to a special concurrence, counts as an opinion "join," Brennan would have his fifth vote.

After several opinion drafts, all revised to accommodate the many suggestions of his colleagues, Brennan succeeded in marshaling a Court. The final version took up the ACLU's invitation, as well as Brennan's own conference alternative, and articulated a test for sex discrimination cases. Called "heightened" (or midlevel) scrutiny, it lies somewhere between strict scrutiny and rational basis. From there, the votes and positions fell out as Table 1 indicates. Note that Powell, Burger, and Blackmun did not join opinions that coincided with their conference positions; that Marshall signed an opinion advocating a standard that was less than ideal from his point of view; and that Brennan's writing advanced a sex discrimination test that fell short of his most preferred standard. Even the votes changed. Powell, Blackmun, and Burger switched their positions, though in different directions.

In the end, thus, *Craig* leaves us with many questions. Why did Powell, Blackmun, and Burger alter their votes? Why did Brennan advance the heightened scrutiny test when he clearly favored strict scrutiny? Why did Marshall join Brennan's opinion, when it adopted a standard he found less than appealing? More generally, why did *Craig* come out the way it did?

These questions take on added importance when we consider that *Craig* is not at all an anomaly. In more than half of all orally argued cases, the justices switch their votes, make changes in their opinions to accommodate the suggestions of colleagues, or join writings that do not necessarily reflect their sincere preferences.

* * *

We believe that a strategic account of judicial decisions helps to answer these questions. On this account, justices are strategic actors who realize that their ability to achieve their goals depends on a consideration of the preferences of other actors, the choices they expect others to make, and the institutional context in which they act. . . . By "strategic," we mean that judicial decision making is interdependent. From *Craig*, we learn that it is not enough to say that Justice Brennan chose heightened scrutiny over rational basis or strict scrutiny because he preferred heightened scrutiny; we know he actually preferred strict scrutiny. Rather, interdependency suggests that Brennan chose heightened scrutiny because he believed that other relevant actors—including his colleagues—would choose rational basis, and, given this choice, heightened scrutiny led to a better outcome for Brennan than the other alternative actions. . . .

Occasionally, strategic calculations will lead justices to make choices that reflect their sincere preferences. Suppose, in *Craig*, that all the justices agreed on all the important issues: Whitener had standing; a strict scrutiny standard should be used; and the Court should rule in Craig's favor. If those conditions held, then Brennan would have been free to write an opinion that reflected his true preferences, because they were the same as the Court's. In other instances, strategic calculations lead justices to act in a sophisticated fashion; that is, they act in a way that does not accurately reflect their true preferences so as to avoid the possibility of seeing their colleagues reject their most preferred policy in favor of their least preferred. Brennan may have followed this thinking in *Craig*. We know that he had to choose among three possible standards but preferred strict scrutiny over heightened scrutiny over rational basis. Yet, he didn't select his most preferred standard, opting instead for his second choice. Why? A possibility is that Brennan thought an opinion advancing strict scrutiny would be completely unacceptable to certain members of the Court, who would push for a rational basis standard, his least preferred standard. He may have chosen heightened scrutiny because, based on his knowledge of the preferences of other justices, it allowed him to avoid his least preferred position, not because it was his first choice. . . .

> "[A] general prediction of many hierarchical models is that decision
> making in the circuit courts depends both on the preferences of the
> nominal superiors, the Supreme Court, and those of the nominal
> subordinates, the circuit court judges."

8.3 DECISION MAKING ON THE U.S. COURTS OF APPEALS

Jeffrey A. Segal, Donald R. Songer, and Charles M. Cameron

Jeffrey A. Segal is Professor of Political Science at SUNY–Stony Brook. Donald R. Songer is Professor of Political Science at the University of South Carolina. Charles M. Cameron is Professor of Political Science at Princeton University.

. . . Since their creation in the 1890s, [the U.S. courts of appeals] have been responsible for ensuring the uniformity of national law in a diverse republic in which sectional pressures constantly seek to undermine that uniformity. More recently, they have become the principal means of supervising the myriad federal regulatory agencies. In both these roles, they are important policy makers: the final authoritative interpreters of federal law and the Constitution in the overwhelming majority of all civil and criminal cases filed in the federal courts.

We consider decision making on the U.S. courts of appeals by examining three different models of behavior—the legal model, the attitudinal model, and the hierarchical model. Briefly, the legal model, as its name suggests, holds that judges make decisions based on legal factors such as the intent of the framers of the Constitution and precedent. Alternatively, the attitudinal model holds that judges make decisions based on their own attitudes and values. Finally, the hierarchical model holds that judges on the courts of appeals have attitudes and values but, as intermediate-level players in a complex judicial hierarchy, are limited in their ability to pursue their values. Hence, the hierarchical model combines elements of the other two and encompasses them as extreme cases. We examine these models using a sample of search and seizure cases decided by the U.S. courts of appeals between 1961 and 1990.

* * *

The Hierarchical Model

Arguably, the pure attitudinal model has particular relevance for decision making on the Supreme Court. The Supreme Court is a court of last resort whose decisions cannot be overturned by other courts. Supreme Court justices

---

From Jeffrey A. Segal, Donald R. Songer, and Charles M. Cameron, "Decision Making on the U.S. Court of Appeals," in *Contemplating Courts,* ed. Lee Epstein (Washington, DC: CQ Press, 1995), 227, 232–233, 235–237, 242–243.

lack electoral or (for the most part) political accountability and have no ambition for higher office. In general, then, they need please no one but themselves. Finally, the Court controls its own jurisdiction and thus can weed out frivolous suits in which text or intent or precedent might be perfectly clear.

These arguments have limited applicability to the judges who sit on the U.S. courts of appeals. First, ambition might be a constraint on the decisions of circuit court judges. Whereas Supreme Court justices have little room to improve their job stature, the same is not true of circuit court judges. We have no accurate count, but it strikes us as reasonable to assume that many of these judges dream of being promoted to the Supreme Court. Thus, the politically acceptable might impinge on the personally preferable. Second, decisions made in circuit courts can be appealed to the Supreme Court. Lower-court judges must then at least consider the preferences of courts above them, although as we shall see, the extent to which they must do so is not always clear. Finally, lack of docket control means that circuit court judges get some cases to decide in which legal discretion is at a minimum, perhaps because of the clarity of a statute or the settling of the issue by the Supreme Court. Although it is impossible to know how often appeals court judges feel that the law or precedents are so clear that any judge would feel constrained to reach the same conclusion, one study estimated that such constraint may exist in as many as 62 percent of their cases (that is, judges may have substantial discretion in only a little over a third of their cases).

How might one construct a model of judicial decision making by judges who are constrained by their location in the judicial hierarchy? A detailed answer is far beyond the scope of this chapter; nevertheless, one way to proceed is to use insights from what social scientists refer to as "principal-agent" theory, a theory of strategic decision making within hierarchical settings. Principal-agent theory focuses on situations in which subordinates have different preferences from their hierarchical superiors and the ability to take hidden actions or exploit hidden information relevant to the decisions. According to the theory, monitoring, auditing, and sanctioning become critical in such situations; the theory provides tools for analyzing these and other features of hierarchies.

Application of principal-agent theory to the federal judiciary suggests a "hierarchical model" of circuit courts. At the level considered here, the hierarchical model is mainly conceptual; exact predictions depend on the detailed procedures followed in the hierarchy. For example, tightening or loosening the certiorari process used by the Supreme Court might well alter the decisions coming from the circuit courts. One very general prediction, however, is common across a wide variety of hierarchical models: superiors rarely find it in their interest to control the behavior of subordinates completely, [as the costs of perfect compliance will outweigh the benefits]. . . . Accordingly, a general prediction of many hierarchical models is that decision making in the circuit courts depends both on the preferences of the nominal superiors, the Supreme Court, and those of the nominal subordinates, the circuit court judges. . . .

TABLE 1. Factors Affecting Circuit Court Decisions: Predictions from Three Models

| | Prediction | | |
| | Supreme Court | Circuit court | |
Model	Case Facts Matter	Doctrine Matters	Preferences Matter
Legal	yes	yes	no
Attitudinal	yes	no	yes
Hierarchical	yes	yes	yes

Hypotheses about Circuit Court Decision Making

The legal, attitudinal, and hierarchical models make different predictions about the factors influencing the decisions of circuit court judges. These differences create the opportunity to test the models. In Table 1 we summarize the different predictions.

The first thing to glean from Table 1 is that case facts are crucial to all three models. The legal model holds that judges consider the facts of the case in light of text, intent, and precedent. The attitudinal model holds that judges consider the facts of the case in light of their own personal policy preferences. The hierarchical model combines both perspectives: judges consider the facts of the case in light of their own personal policy preferences but are likely to be somewhat constrained by text, intent, and precedent, depending on the tools available to higher courts to control lower ones. Because all three models agree about the importance of case facts, fact variables cannot be used to test the models. Instead, fact variables must serve as control variables. That is, the inclusion of facts in our model will allow us to make sure that any results we achieve with regard to legal and attitudinal variables are the result of those factors and not changes in the types of cases heard by the courts of appeals.

The situation differs concerning the influence of Supreme Court doctrine. The legal model and the hierarchical model suggest that the decisions of circuit court judges are affected by Supreme Court doctrine. In contrast, the attitudinal model suggests that Supreme Court doctrine plays little role in the decision making of the circuit court judges. So the importance of Supreme Court doctrine can be used to test the legal and hierarchical model versus the attitudinal model, but not against each other. In other words, if Supreme Court doctrine proves to be important in circuit court decision making, the data reject the attitudinal model as a complete explanation of circuit court decision making.

The attitudinal model and the hierarchical model suggest that circuit court decision making will be affected by the attitudes of the judges on the case, independent of the policy or doctrinal trends on the Supreme Court. The legal model, however, suggests that attitudinal variables play little role in judicial decision making. Therefore, attitudinal variables can distinguish the attitudinal and hierarchical model from the legal model. In other words, if attitudinal variables prove important, the data reject the legal model as a complete explanation of circuit court decision making.

Combining these tests implies the following: if either the attitudinal or the doctrinal variables prove unimportant, the data reject the hierarchical model. If both prove important, both the attitudinal and legal models are dominated by the hierarchical model as an explanation of circuit court decision making.

Results

We test the three models on a random sample of votes by circuit court judges in search and seizure cases between 1961 and 1990. Critical variables are the facts of the case, contemporary Supreme Court doctrine, and the attitudinal predisposition of the particular judge. . . .

[W]e combine our legal and attitudinal variables into a single model to create the hierarchical model. Thus, we can statistically determine whether attitudinal and legal factors exert independent influence on circuit court decisions after each is controlled for the other. Note the following: Between 1969 and 1990, the Supreme Court became increasingly conservative because of the appointments by Richard Nixon, Gerald Ford, Ronald Reagan, and George Bush. So too did the circuit courts become more conservative, for essentially the same reasons. The hierarchical model allows us to determine whether the conservatism of the circuit court judges was due to their own conservatism, the Supreme Court's conservatism, or both.

The results indicate that our legal variable, Supreme Court Change, and our attitudinal variables, measuring region and party, continue to exert a strong influence on the decisions of circuit court judges. . . . [A]ll have the ability to shift dramatically the likelihood that a search will be upheld.

Conclusions

[W]e can now draw some conclusions about the three models. The data reject the legal model as a complete explanation of circuit court decisions because the attitudes of circuit court judges clearly have an effect on their decisions, even when there is a control for the facts in the cases. The data also reject the pure attitudinal model as a complete explanation of their decisions because changes in Supreme Court doctrine affect the decisions of circuit court judges, even when there are controls for facts and attitudes. Instead, the data demonstrate that the hierarchical model, as applied to circuit court decisions, dominates both alternatives: as predicted by that model, both attitudes and Supreme Court doctrine matter. Of course, this does not mean the hierarchical model is "true" in some transcendental sense. But the hierarchical model does provide a simple and useful starting place for understanding the decision making of lower-court judges. Clearly this class of models deserves more attention. . . .

"The Congress, the Executive, and the Court must each . . . be guided
by its own opinion of the Constitution."

8.4 ANDREW JACKSON'S VETO
OF THE BANK BILL

On July 4, 1832, Congress passed an act to continue the Bank of the United States. On July 10, 1832, President Andrew Jackson vetoed the bank bill as unwise, unfair, and unconstitutional. The portion of his veto message dealing with the argument that the constitutionality of the bank had been definitively settled by the decision of the United States Supreme Court in McCulloch v. Maryland *(1819) is reprinted here. This part of the message was largely drafted by Roger Brooke Taney, who was soon to succeed John Marshall as Chief Justice of the United States.*

It is maintained by the advocates of the bank that its constitutionality in all its features ought to be considered as settled by precedent and by the decision of the Supreme Court. To this conclusion I can not assent. Mere precedent is a dangerous source of authority, and should not be regarded as deciding questions of constitutional power except where the acquiescence of the people and the States can be considered as well settled. So far from this being the case on the subject, an argument against the bank might be based on precedent. One Congress, in 1791, decided in favor of a bank; another, in 1811, decided against. One Congress, in 1815, decided against a bank; another, in 1816, decided in its favor. Prior to the present Congress, therefore, the precedents drawn from that source were equal. If we resort to the States, the expressions of legislative, judicial, and executive opinions against the bank have been probably to those in its favor as 4 to 1. There is nothing in precedent, therefore, which, if its authority were admitted, ought to weigh in favor of the act before me.

If the opinion of the Supreme Court covered the whole ground of this act, it ought not to control the coordinate authorities of this Government. The Congress, the Executive, and the Court must each for itself be guided by its own opinion of the Constitution. Each public officer who takes an oath to support the Constitution swears that he will support it as he understands it, and not as it is understood by others. It is as much the duty of the House of Representatives, of the Senate, and of the President to decide upon the constitutionality of any bill or resolution which may be presented to them for passage or approval as it is of the supreme judges when it may be brought before them for judicial decision. The opinion of the judges has no more authority over Congress than the opinion of Congress has over the judges, and on that point the President is independent of both. The authority of the Supreme Court must not, therefore, be permitted to control the Congress or the Executive when act-

From James D. Richardson, ed., *A Compilation of the Messages and Papers of the Presidents* (Washington, DC: Bureau of National Literature and Art, 1908), 2, 581–582.

ing in their legislative capacities, but to have only such influence as the force of their reasoning may deserve.

". . . if the policy . . . is to be irrevocably fixed by decisions of the Supreme Court . . . the people will have ceased to be their own rulers."

8.5 ABRAHAM LINCOLN'S FIRST INAUGURAL ADDRESS, MARCH 4, 1861

. . . A majority, held in restraint by constitutional checks, and limitations, and always changing easily, with deliberate changes of popular opinions and sentiments, is the only true sovereign of a free people. Whoever rejects it, does, of necessity, fly to anarchy or to despotism. Unanimity is impossible; the rule of minority, as a permanent arrangement, is wholly inadmissible; so that rejecting the majority principle, anarchy, or despotism in some form, is all that is left.

I do not forget the position assumed by some, that constitutional questions are to be decided by the Supreme Court; nor do I deny that such decisions must be binding in any case, upon the parties to a suit, as to the object of that suit, while they are also entitled to a very high respect and consideration, in all parallel cases, by all other departments of government. And while it is obviously possible that such decision may be erroneous in any given case, still the evil effect following it, being limited to that particular case, with the chance that it may be overruled, and never become a precedent for other cases, can better be borne than could the evils of a different practice. At the same time the candid citizen must confess that if the policy of the government, upon vital questions, affecting the whole people, is to be irrevocably fixed by decisions of the Supreme Court, the instant they are made, in ordinary litigation between parties, in personal actions, the people will have ceased to be their own rulers, having to that extent, practically resigned their government, into the hands of that eminent tribunal. Nor is there, in this view, any assault upon the court, or the judges. It is a duty, from which they may not shrink, to decide cases properly brought before them; and it is no fault of theirs, if others seek to turn their decisions to political purposes.

*"We must find a way to take an appeal from the Supreme Court
to the Constitution itself."*

8.6 REORGANIZING THE FEDERAL JUDICIARY

Franklin D. Roosevelt

In 1933 you and I knew that we must never let our economic system get completely out of joint again—that we could not afford to take the risk of another great depression.

We also became convinced that the only way to avoid a repetition of those dark days was to have a government with power to prevent and to cure the abuses and the inequalities which had thrown that system out of joint.

We then began a program of remedying those abuses and inequalities—to give balance and stability to our economic system—to make it bombproof against the causes of 1929.

Today we are only part way through that program—and recovery is speeding up to a point where the dangers of 1929 are again becoming possible, not this week or month perhaps, but within a year or two.

National laws are needed to complete that program. Individual or local or State effort alone cannot protect us in 1937 any better than ten years ago. . . . The American people have learned from the depression. For in the last three national elections an overwhelming majority of them voted a mandate that the Congress and the President begin the task of providing that protection—not after long years of debate, but now.

The courts, however, have cast doubts on the ability of the elected Congress to protect us against catastrophe by meeting squarely our modern social and economic conditions.

We are at a crisis in our ability to proceed with that protection. It is a quiet crisis. There are no lines of depositors outside closed banks. But to the far-sighted it is far-reaching in its possibilities of injury to America.

I want to talk with you very simply about the need for present action in this crisis—the need to meet the unanswered challenge of one-third of a nation ill-nourished, ill-clad, ill-housed.

Last Thursday I described the American form of government as a three-horse team provided by the Constitution to the American people so that their field might be plowed. The three horses are, of course, the three branches of government—the Congress, the executive, and the courts. Two of the horses are

From James D. Richardson, ed., *A Compilation of the Messages and Papers of the Presidents* (Washington, DC: Bureau of National Literature and Art, 1908), 6, 9.

Speech presented March 9, 1937. *Senate Report No. 711*, 75th Cong., 1st Sess., pp. 41–44.

pulling in unison today; the third is not. Those who have intimated that the President of the United States is trying to drive that team overlook the simple fact that the President, as Chief Executive, is himself one of the three horses.

It is the American people themselves who are in the driver's seat.

It is the American people themselves who want the furrow plowed.

It is the American people themselves who expect the third horse to pull in unison with the other two.

I hope that you have reread the Constitution of the United States. Like the Bible, it ought to be read again and again.

It is an easy document to understand when you remember that it was called into being because the Articles of Confederation under which the Original Thirteen States tried to operate after the Revolution showed the need of a National Government with power enough to handle national problems. In its preamble the Constitution states that it was intended to form a more perfect Union and promote the general welfare; and the powers given to the Congress to carry out those purposes can be best described by saying that they were all the powers needed to meet each and every problem which then had a national character and which could not be met by merely local action.

But the framers went further. Having in mind that in succeeding generations many other problems then undreamed of would become national problems, they gave to the Congress the ample broad powers "to levy taxes . . . and provide for the common defense and general welfare of the United States."

That, my friends, is what I honestly believe to have been the clear and underlying purpose of the patriots who wrote a Federal Constitution to create a National Government with national power, intended as they said, "to form a more perfect union . . . for ourselves and our posterity." . . .

But since the rise of the modern movement for social and economic progress through legislation, the Court has more and more often and more and more boldly asserted a power to veto laws passed by the Congress and State legislatures in complete disregard of this original limitation.

In the last four years the sound rule of giving statutes the benefit of all reasonable doubt has been cast aside. The Court has been acting not as a judicial body, but as a policy-making body.

When the Congress has sought to stabilize national agriculture, to improve the conditions of labor, to safeguard business against unfair competition, to protect our national resources, and in many other ways to serve our clearly national needs, the majority of the Court has been assuming the power to pass on the wisdom of these acts of the Congress—and to approve or disapprove the public policy written into these laws.

That is not only my accusation. It is the accusation of most distinguished justices of the present Supreme Court. I have not the time to quote to you all the language used by dissenting justices in many of these cases. But in the case holding the Railroad Retirement Act unconstitutional, for instance, Chief Justice Hughes said in a dissenting opinion that the majority opinion was "a departure from sound principles," and placed "an unwarranted limitation upon the commerce clause." And three other justices agreed with him.

In the case holding the A.A.A. unconstitutional, Justice Stone said of the majority opinion that it was a "tortured construction of the Constitution." And two other justices agreed with him.

In the case holding the New York Minimum Wage Law unconstitutional, Justice Stone said that the majority were actually reading into the Constitution their own "personal economic predilections" and that if the legislative power is not left free to choose the methods of solving the problems of poverty, subsistence, and health of large numbers in the community, then "government is to be rendered impotent." And two other justices agreed with him. . . .

In the face of such dissenting opinions, it is perfectly clear that as Chief Justice Hughes has said, "We are under a Constitution, but the Constitution is what the judges say it is."

The Court in addition to the proper use of its judicial functions has improperly set itself up as a third House of the Congress—a super-legislature, as one of the justices has called it—reading into the Constitution words and implications which are not there, and which were never intended to be there.

We have, therefore, reached the point as a Nation where we must take action to save the Constitution from the Court and the Court from itself. We must find a way to take an appeal from the Supreme Court to the Constitution itself. We want a Supreme Court which will do justice under the Constitution—not over it. In our courts we want a government of laws and not of men.

I want—as all Americans want—an independent judiciary as proposed by the Framers of the Constitution. That means a Supreme Court that will enforce the Constitution as written—that will refuse to amend the Constitution by the arbitrary exercise of judicial power—amendment by judicial say-so. It does not mean a judiciary so independent that it can deny the existence of facts universally recognized. . . .

What is my proposal? It is simply this: Whenever a judge or justice of any federal court has reached the age of seventy and does not avail himself of the opportunity to retire on a pension, a new member shall be appointed by the President then in office, with the approval, as required by the Constitution, of the Senate of the United States.

That plan has two chief purposes: By bringing into the judicial system a steady and continuing stream of new and younger blood, I hope, first, to make the administration of all federal justice speedier and therefore less costly; secondly, to bring to the decision of social and economic problems younger men who have had personal experience and contact with modern facts and circumstances under which average men have to live and work. This plan will save our National Constitution from hardening of the judicial arteries. . . .

Those opposing this plan have sought to arouse prejudice and fear by crying that I am seeking to "pack" the Supreme Court and that a baneful precedent will be established.

What do they mean by the words "packing the Court"?

Let me answer this question with a bluntness that will end all honest misunderstanding of my purposes.

If by that phrase "packing the Court" it is charged that I wish to place on the bench spineless puppets who would disregard the law and would decide specific cases as I wished them to be decided, I make this answer: That no President fit for his office would appoint, and no Senate of honorable men fit for their office would confirm, that kind of appointees to the Supreme Court.

But if by that phrase the charge is made that I would appoint and the Senate would confirm justices worthy to sit beside present members of the Court who understand those modern conditions; that I will appoint justices who will not undertake to override the judgment of the Congress on legislative policy; that I will appoint justices who will act as justices and not as legislators—if the appointment of such justices can be called "packing the Courts"—then I say that I, and with me the vast majority of the American people, favor doing just that thing—now. . . . Our difficulty with the Court today rises not from the Court as an institution but from human beings within it. But we cannot yield our constitutional destiny to the personal judgment of a few men who, being fearful of the future, would deny us the necessary means of dealing with the present.

This plan of mine is no attack on the Court; it seeks to restore the Court to its rightful and historic place in our system of constitutional government and to have it resume its high task of building anew on the Constitution "a system of living law." . . .

> *"Activist judges . . . have begun redefining marriage*
> *by court order, without regard for the will of the people*
> *and their elected representatives."*

READING 8.7 GEORGE W. BUSH'S STATEMENT ON SAME-SEX MARRIAGES, 2004

Editors' note: President Bush made this statement in his State of the Union Address, January 20, 2004—shortly after the Massachusetts high court issued its opinion in Goodridge v. Department of Public Health (Reading 3.9.) The President has subsequently expressed his support for a constitutional amendment that would define marriage as a union between a man and a woman.

A strong America must also value the institution of marriage. I believe we should respect individuals as we take a principled stand for one of the most fundamental, enduring institutions of our civilization. Congress has already taken a stand on this issue by passing the Defense of Marriage Act, signed in 1996 by President Clinton. That statute protects marriage under federal law as a union of a man and a woman, and declares that one state may not redefine marriage for other states.

Activist judges, however, have begun redefining marriage by court order, without regard for the will of the people and their elected representatives. On an issue of such great consequence, the people's voice must be heard. If judges insist on forcing their arbitrary will upon the people, the only alternative left to the people would be the constitutional process. Our nation must defend the sanctity of marriage.

The outcome of this debate is important—and so is the way we conduct it. The same moral tradition that defines marriage also teaches that each individual has dignity and value in God's sight.

"Without jurisdiction the court cannot proceed at all in any cause."

8.8 *EX PARTE MCCARDLE*

7 *Wall. 506, 19 L. Ed. 264 (1869)*

In 1866 and 1867, the Supreme Court declared unconstitutional military trials for civilians in areas where regular civil courts were open and also voided a federal statute requiring a "test oath" for admission to certain public professions. These decisions threatened to outlaw the military rule that the Radical Republicans had established in the South. William McCardle, a Mississippi editor, who was being held for trial before a military commission, appealed to the Supreme Court. Ironically, he utilized a statute of 1867 aimed at protecting officials administering the Reconstruction program. To avert a decision that most of the Reconstruction program was unconstitutional, Congress in 1868 repealed—over Johnson's veto—the act of 1867 that gave the Supreme Court appellate jurisdiction in the case. The Court heard the McCardle case in time to decide it prior to repeal of the statute; but over bitter protests from two justices the majority delayed a decision until after the repeal.

Argument of Counsel . . .

Mr. Sharkey, for the appellant:

The prisoner alleged an illegal imprisonment. The imprisonment was justified under certain acts of Congress. The question then presents a case arising under "the laws of the United States"; and by the very words of the Constitution the judicial power of the United States extends to it. By words of the Constitution, equally plain, that judicial power is vested in one Supreme Court. This court, then, has its jurisdiction directly from the Constitution, not from Congress. The jurisdiction being vested by the Constitution alone, Congress cannot abridge or take it away. The argument which would look to Congressional legislation as a necessity to enable this court to exercise "the judicial power" (any and every judicial power) "of the United States," renders a power, expressly given by the Constitution, liable to be made of no effect by the inaction of Congress. Suppose that Congress never made any exceptions or any regulations in the matter. What, under a supposition that Congress must define when, and where, and how, the Supreme Court shall exercise it, becomes of this "judicial power of the United States," so expressly, by the Constitution, given to this court? It would cease to exist. But this court is coexistent and coordinate with Congress and must be able to exercise the whole judicial power of the United States, though Congress passed no act on the subject. . . .

Now, can Congress thus interfere with cases on which this high tribunal has passed, or is passing, judgment? Is not legislation like this an exercise by the Congress of judicial power? . . .

Messrs. L. Trumbull and M. H. Carpenter, contra:

1. The Constitution gives to this court appellate jurisdiction in any case like the present one was, only with such exceptions and under such regulations as Congress makes.
2. It is clear, then, that this court had no jurisdiction of this proceeding—an appeal from the Circuit Court—except under the act of February 5th, 1867. . . .
3. The act conferring the jurisdiction having been repealed, the jurisdiction ceased; and the court had thereafter no authority to pronounce any opinion or render any judgment in this cause. . . .

THE CHIEF JUSTICE [Chase] delivered the opinion of the court.

The first question necessarily is that of jurisdiction; for, if the act of March, 1868, takes away the jurisdiction defined by the act of February, 1867, it is useless, if not improper, to enter into any discussion of other questions.

It is quite true, as was argued by the counsel for the petitioner, that the appellate jurisdiction of this court is not derived from acts of Congress. It is, strictly speaking, conferred by the Constitution. But it is conferred "with such exceptions and under such regulations as Congress shall make." . . .

The source of that jurisdiction, and the limitations of it by the Constitution and by statute, have been on several occasions subjects of consideration here. In the case of *Duroussean v. The United States* [1810], particularly, the whole matter was carefully examined, and the court held, that while "the appellate powers of this court are not given by the judicial act, but are given by the Constitution," they are, nevertheless, "limited and regulated by that act, and by such other acts as have been passed on the subject." The court said, further, that the judicial act was an exercise of the power given by the Constitution to Congress "of making exceptions to the appellate jurisdiction of the Supreme Court." "They have described affirmatively," said the court, "its jurisdiction, and this affirmative description has been understood to imply a negation of the exercise of such appellate power as is not comprehended with it."

The principle that the affirmation of appellate jurisdiction implies the negation of all such jurisdiction not affirmed having been thus established, it was an almost necessary consequence that acts of Congress, providing for the exercise of jurisdiction, should come to be spoken of as acts granting jurisdiction, and not as acts making exceptions to the constitutional grant of it.

The exception to appellate jurisdiction in the case before us, however, is not an inference from the affirmation of other appellate jurisdiction. . . . The provision of the act of 1867, affirming the appellate jurisdiction of this court in cases of habeas corpus is expressly repealed. It is hardly possible to imagine a plainer instance of positive exception.

We are not at liberty to inquire into the motives of the legislature. We can only examine into its power under the Constitution; and the power to make exceptions to the appellate jurisdiction of this court is given by express words.

What, then, is the effect of the repealing act upon the case before us? We cannot doubt as to this. Without jurisdiction the court cannot proceed at all in any cause. Jurisdiction is power to declare the law, and when it ceases to exist, the only function remaining to the court is that of announcing the fact and dismissing the cause. And this is not less clear upon authority than upon principle. . . .

It is quite clear, therefore, that this court cannot proceed to pronounce judgment in this case, for it has no longer jurisdiction of the appeal; and judicial duty is not less fitly performed by declining ungranted jurisdiction than in exercising firmly that which the Constitution and the laws confer.

Counsel seem to have supposed, if effect be given to the repealing act in question, that the whole appellate power of the court, in cases of habeas corpus, is denied. But this is an error. The act of 1868 does not except from that jurisdiction any cases but appeals from Circuit Courts under the act of 1867. It does not affect the jurisdiction which was previously exercised.

The appeal of the petitioner in this case must be *Dismissed for want of jurisdiction.*

> "... the communication to governmental actors of policy preferences
> held by citizens may well be a central component if not the core
> of a responsible system of government."

8.9 POLITICAL PARTICIPATION AND GOVERNMENT RESPONSIVENESS: THE BEHAVIOR OF CALIFORNIA SUPERIOR COURTS

James H. Kuklinski and John E. Stanga

James H. Kuklinski is Professor of Political Science at the University of Illinois.
John E. Stanga is Associate Professor of Political Science at Wichita State University.

. . . [R]esearchers have tended to equate participation with voting. It is natural that scholars should focus their attention on the most common mode of partici-

From James H. Kuklinski and John E. Stanga, "Political Participation and Government Responsiveness: The Behavior of California Superior Courts," 73 *American Political Science Review* 1090 (1979).

pation, but concentration on voting also seems to reflect an underlying assumption that the predominant if not single purpose of participation is to exert pressure on public officials. Mass voting presumably sustains politicians' fear of being tossed out of office, which in turn ensures that government will remain sensitive to the citizens it serves. . . .

[P]articipation can serve a second and distinct purpose: to communicate information about citizen preferences. Here efforts to influence government take the form of increasing officials' awareness of the public's wishes. Whereas electoral coercion involves applying diffuse pressure without specifying how leaders should respond, citizen communication of preferences provides relatively precise guidelines within which officials are to make policy decisions.

As a research matter, considering participation as a communication activity has two positive consequences. First, it underscores the often-overlooked point that responsiveness . . . involves officials and the mass public simultaneously. To conclude that government is unresponsive when the public is apathetic or noncommunicative may be ill-conceived, or at best trivial. Even government leaders dedicated to carrying out the public will would be hard put to do so if that will were unknown. Second, interest is extended to non-elected officials. Study of the participation-responsiveness nexus can include the large proportion of government officials (many bureaucrats and judges, for example) who are isolated from any real electoral sanction but who play important, often decisive, roles in the policy-making process. . . .

. . . [W]e have chosen the California superior court as our unit of analysis. The superior court can be regarded as consisting not only of the judges who sit on the bench, but also of the police, parole officers, prosecutors, and defense attorneys whose interactions shape its final decision. Because these lower courts are legally defined as policy-making bodies having general jurisdiction coterminous with the state's counties, it is possible to ask whether the decisions of the courts are related to variations in public preferences across the counties, and whether this relationship, in turn, is affected by citizen communication of policy preferences.

These questions require data on both the public's preferences and judicial decisions within a specific policy area. We chose as a measure of opinion aggregate voting returns on an initiative ballot proposition proposed during the 1972 general election to remove criminal penalties for the personal use of or preparation for personal use of marijuana. . . . For each county we use the percent support for the marijuana issue. The higher the percentage, the more liberal is a county toward the personal use of marijuana.

In addition to providing a valid measure of public preferences, the initiative vote serves our research objective in two ways. First, it is an initiative. Members of the public both brought the issue and chose to express themselves on it. Over 90 percent of those voting in the general election registered their opinions on the marijuana question. Second, since the vote itself represents a participatory act, we can ask whether participation leads to government response by comparing the levels of policy agreement before and after the communication of preferences.

We therefore computed a measure of judicial policy for each of three years—1971, 1972, and 1973. The policy measure is the mean sentencing severity score of all decisions involving possession of marijuana convictions. It is based on a scale first proposed by the Administrative Office of the United States Courts. . . .

The marijuana decisions, from which the judicial policy measure is constructed, are ideal to study the relationship between political participation and government response. For one thing, the state legislature has given broad sentencing discretion to California superior courts. During the period under examination, judges had authority in marijuana cases to impose prison terms of one to ten years, to order jail sentences, to fine offenders, or to suspend any sentence with or without probation. For another, both the sentencing decisions and public opinion deal specifically and only with the simple possession and use of marijuana. There should be no doubt that we are measuring a direct and well-defined policy linkage between the public and one set of its officials. . . .

Results

The absolute changes in sentencing provide the most compelling...evidence that the proposition vote, as a clear articulation of citizen opinion, drew forth a response from the courts. A schema for analyzing such changes is presented in Table 1. Examining data from the earlier years, 1971 and 1972, one finds that three sentencing situations are possible relative to opinion: courts are oversentencing, undersentencing, or sentencing consistently with opinion. If response did occur, the first group should become more lenient in its sentencing in 1973; undersentencing courts should become more severe, and courts nearest to opinion should display relatively little change.

Table 2 reports the mean change for each of the three categories of courts. The differential movements accord fully with our expectations. Courts originally oversentencing become discernibly more lenient following expression of public preferences on the marijuana issue, while those originally undersentencing increase the severity of their sentences. The only anomalous finding in Table 2 is the 1972–1973 change among courts originally sentencing consistently with opinion. A careful analysis of the individual courts within this category indi-

TABLE 1. A Schema for Measuring Change in Court Sentencing Behavior

Relative Public Support for Legislation of Marijuana	Relative Sentencing Severity in 1971 or 1972		
	Lenient	*Moderate*	*Severe*
High	C	O	O
Medium	U	C	O
Low	U	U	C

Key: O = oversentencing; U = undersentencing: C = sentencing consistently

TABLE 2. Change in Sentencing Policy, by Original Level of Policy Agreement*

Years	Originally Oversentencing	Originally About Correct	Originally Undersentencing
1971–1973	−12.2	−1.1	+11.2
	(N = 15)	(N = 20)	(N = 8)
1972–1973	−16.6	+9.3	+13.4
	(N = 14)	(N = 25)	(N = 5)

*Entries are mean changes in sentencing scores.

cates that this higher-than-expected mean is attributable to the change in sentencing policy of two courts. If these courts are removed from analysis, the mean change drops to +5.6.

The figures in Table 2 take on more meaning when given substantive interpretation. They represent, for example, the difference between a probation of six months and a probation of three years; or the difference between a $50 fine and no fine at all. In short, the changes in sentencing policy had obvious and meaningful impacts on the lives of individuals convicted of possession.

Our initial findings give us reason to believe, then, that the explicit communication of preferences elicited a response from California superior courts. Not only did the cases increase policy agreement in marijuana cases increase significantly after the initiative vote, but also the courts displayed appropriate and differential movement: those courts less in line with opinion in the earlier years showed greater absolute change in sentencing behavior and adjusted their decisions in the predicted direction.

* * *

To consider more fully the implications of the preceding analysis for democratic governance, we now speculate about one final bit of evidence, namely, that the communication of citizen preferences appears to have elicited government response in the absence of any meaningful electoral accountability of public officials. Consider the situation of California superior court judges. These judges have been expressly removed from the vagaries of the electoral process through the institution of staggered six-year terms. Not only are they chosen in technically nonpartisan elections, but also significant numbers in fact obtain their positions through gubernatorial appointment rather than election. . . . Most significant, sitting judges rarely face 'reelection' opposition. In 1972, one of the years included in this study, only 4 of 149 elected judgeships were contested. . . .

If we are correct in suggesting that government response occurred in the absence of meaningful electoral accountability, at least two implications follow. The first is that electoral accountability may not be, as sometimes is supposed, the sine qua non of political responsiveness. Noncoercive or voluntary response may be more common than is generally assumed. Indeed, several other recent research efforts also report findings indicating that public officeholders are inclined to respond even in the absence of electoral coercion. Cook has presented evidence, for example, that federal district court judges responded to their political environments with regard to sentencing in draft cases during the height of the Vietnam War. Such judges are appointed for life terms.

The second implication, closely related to the first, is the one we wish to stress: the communication to governmental actors of policy preferences held by citizens may well be a central component if not the core of a responsible system of government. . . .

> *"The high courts of the Netherlands, Denmark, Germany, Greece,*
> *and even Poland have at least as much institutional legitimacy as*
> *the [U.S.] Supreme Court."*

8.10 ON THE LEGITIMACY OF NATIONAL HIGH COURTS AND THE SUPREME COURT AND THE U.S. PRESIDENTIAL ELECTION OF 2000

James L. Gibson, Gregory A. Caldeira, and Vanessa Baird

James L. Gibson is the Souers Professor of Government at Washington University.
Gregory A. Caldeira is Distinguished University Professor of Political Science
at Ohio State University. Vanessa Baird is Assistant Professor
of Political Science at the University of Colorado.

. . . One of the most significant developments in comparative politics is the growing influence of judicial institutions in national and international politics. . . . Though the United States seems to have led the way in transforming political questions into legal questions, much the same is true in politics as diverse as Russia, Namibia, the Philippines, Canada, the European Union, and Spain. Nor does this trend toward greater judicialization show signs of abating soon.

As courts move more squarely into the political limelight, a host of new questions emerges. Among them is how these institutions relate to their constituents, especially their mass publics. Not even the most powerful courts in the world have the power of the "purse" or "sword"; with limited institutional resources, courts are therefore uncommonly dependent on the goodwill of their

From James L. Gibson, Gregory A. Caldeira, and Vanessa Baird, "On the Legitimacy of National High Courts," 92 *American Political Science Review* 343 (1998).

constituents for both support and compliance. Indeed, since judges often make decisions contrary to the preferences of political majorities, courts, more than other political institutions, require a deep reservoir of goodwill. Without institutional legitimacy, courts find it difficult to serve as effective and consequential partners in governance.

One would find no quarrel from social scientists in the United States with the foregoing sentiments. American political scientists have long evidenced concern about the mass legitimacy of judicial institutions, and a considerable volume of empirical work on mass attitudes toward U.S. courts has been reported. Outside the United States, however, social scientists have devoted little attention to how ordinary people perceive and evaluate courts. Scholars often assume, for instance, that the U.S. Supreme Court is one of the most revered (and unusual) courts in the world, but no rigorous empirical evidence exists to support that claim. Researchers commonly observe in the United States that those who are more knowledgeable about law and courts are more supportive of judicial institutions. But is this a universal relationship; is it invariably the case that to know courts is to love them; or is it simply that American courts are particularly lovable? How would the public have evaluated the Supreme Court during the early years of the Republic, when Jeffersonians battled the institution? Would Germans who knew much about the Nazi courts have loved them as well? And what of Germany today—do knowledgeable Germans love the Bundesverfassungsgericht? We have little idea whether the flock of important hypotheses generated by the American case has any generalizability whatsoever. This is a lacuna of significant proportions for judicial process scholars. . . .

Accordingly, our goal is to broaden the study of the relationships between courts and their publics by examining mass attitudes toward the legitimacy of national high courts, mainly in Europe, East and West. Based on twenty surveys we conducted in eighteen countries in the period 1993 through 1996, we first assess the salience of these institutions to their mass publics. We then investigate the degree of support—diffuse and specific—these courts enjoy. . . .

Awareness of National High Courts

We first asked the respondents about their level of awareness of their national high court. Table 1 reports the results.

Although there is considerable cross-national variability, most high courts are reasonably well known. At one extreme lies West Germany, where nearly half the respondents claimed to be very aware of their constitutional court. Other countries in which awareness is widespread include Great Britain, the United States, Ireland, the former East Germany, Denmark, and perhaps Spain as well. It is interesting to note that awareness of the U.S. Supreme Court is quite high when compared with most other countries, even if awareness is higher (or as high) in a few other countries. In Germany, Great Britain, and the United States, more than four-fifths of the respondents claimed a moderate degree of consciousness of the highest national court. Countries in which the highest court has very little visibility include Russia, Bulgaria, Luxembourg,

TABLE 1. National High Courts

| | Level of Awareness[a] | | | | | | | |
| | Percentage | | | | | | | |
Court	Never Heard of	Don't Know	Not very Aware	Somewhat Aware	Very Aware	Mean	Std. Dev.	N
Russia	50.8	2.2	29.4	17.0	.6	.7	.77	772
Bulgaria	13.4	13.7	47.9	22.7	2.0	1.1	.69	1,183
Luxembourg	25.0	2.5	46.0	17.5	9.0	1.1	.89	200
Belgium	9.2	6.0	56.6	23.3	4.8	1.2	.70	249
France (1993)	7.6	.0	69.4	20.3	2.7	1.2	.60	301
France (1995)	9.2	3.7	64.8	18.1	4.2	1.2	.65	759
Portugal	17.7	4.0	45.0	30.3	3.0	1.2	.76	300
Italy	9.0	.7	54.3	31.0	5.0	1.3	.71	300
Poland	11.7	3.0	50.8	27.9	6.6	1.3	.77	821
Greece	6.1	3.5	51.1	32.5	6.8	1.4	.72	311
Hungary	9.0	1.4	48.3	37.7	3.6	1.4	.70	785
Spain (1995)	10.7	3.8	35.8	43.2	6.5	1.4	.79	773
The Netherlands	6.0	.0	55.3	36.0	2.7	1.4	.64	300
Spain (1993)	10.3	3.7	27.3	35.7	23.0	1.7	.95	300
Denmark	1.3	.3	26.7	62.0	9.7	1.8	.62	300
Germany (East)	1.0	1.3	27.5	52.8	17.5	1.9	.71	309
Ireland	1.6	7.8	22.1	44.5	24.0	1.9	.83	321
Great Britain	1.7	.0	11.3	55.3	31.7	2.2	.69	300
United States	.6	.1	16.8	49.8	32.7	2.2	.71	810
Germany (West)	1.5	.5	12.1	38.4	47.5	2.3	.76	198

Note: Countries rank in order on the mean level of awareness. In the first five columns, each row totals to 100%, except for rounding errors. The range of the variable "awareness" is from 0 to 3.

[a]The question read: "And what about the [HIGHESTCOURTOFTHECOUNTRY], that is, one of the [NATIONALITY] courts? Would you say that you are very aware, somewhat aware, not very aware, or have never heard of the [HIGHESTCOURTOFTHECOUNTRY]?"

Portugal, and perhaps France as well. We should reiterate, however, that substantial cross-national differences exist in the visibility of the national high court. Strikingly, when we combine the two highest levels of awareness, the percentage fairly aware of the national high court ranges from a low of 17.6 in Russia to a high of 85.9 in West Germany.

Even a cursory examination of Table 1 reveals that awareness is not necessarily related to the age of the institution [see Table 2]. With the exception of Russia, awareness of the high court in some of the new democracies is not particularly low. In Hungary, for instance, awareness is about the same as in the Netherlands and Greece; Poland is comparable to Italy; and Bulgaria is similar to Luxembourg. . . . It is clear that there is not necessarily a strong relationship between the age of the institution and its salience within the mass public.

Awareness of the national high courts may indicate something of their politicization. After all, these courts become known primarily when they make decisions that attract mass media attention. Rulings on arcane legal issues are

TABLE 2. National High Courts

Country	National High Court	Year of Creation
Belgium	Hof van Cassatie (Cour de Cassation)	1831
Bulgaria	Kohctutyzuoheh Cad	1991
Denmark	Højesteret	1753
France	Cour de Cassation	1790
Germany (East)	Bundesverfassungsgericht	1990
Germany (West)	Bundesverfassungsgericht	1949
Greece	Anótato Eidikó Dikastério	1975
Hungary	Alkotmánybíróság	1990
Ireland	Supreme Court of Ireland (Chúirt Uachtarach)	1924
Italy	Corte Constituzionale	1956
Luxembourg	Cour Supérieure de Justice	1868
The Netherlands	De Hoge Raad der Nederlanden	1838
Poland	Sad Najwy'zszy	1984
Portugal	Tribunal Constitucional	1982
Russia	Verkhovniy Sud	1993
Spain	Tribunal Constitucional	1979
United Kingdom	Court of Appeal	1876
United States	Supreme Court	1790

unlikely to interest many; decisions on issues of public law—Sunday closing, abortion, gender equality—are much more likely to penetrate the public consciousness. To the extent that a court is salient, it probably has made decisions of interest and concern to ordinary people.

Support

[Respondents were asked three questions pertaining to their degree of support of their high courts:]

- Court jurisdiction: "The Right of the [highest court of the country] to decide certain types of controversial issues would be reduced." [Disagreement with this statement indicates support of the court.]
- Institutional Commitment: "If the [highest court of the country] started to make a lot of decisions that most people disagreed with, it might be best to do away with the [highest court of the country] altogether."[Disagreement with this statement indicates support of the court.]
- Trust: "The [highest court of the country] can usually be trusted to make decisions that are right for the country as a whole." [Agreement with this statement indicates support of the court.]

There is a great deal of variability across countries in their support of the national high courts. Consider institutional commitment, which, among the attentive publics, ranges from a low of 18.6 % in Bulgaria to a high of 76 % in the United States. In less than half the countries, a majority of respondents support

TABLE 3. Average Diffuse Support for National High Court among Attentive Publics

	Mean Support
Spain (1993)	46.3
Bulgaria	48.8
Germany (East)	49.4
Belgium	52.2
Spain (1995)	53.9
Ireland	54.5
France (1995)	55.0
France (1993)	55.2
Russia	56.6
Hungary	57.1
Italy	57.8
Great Britain	58.0
Luxembourg	58.8
Portugal	61.6
United States	62.2
Poland	62.5
Greece	65.0
Germany (West)	65.4
Denmark	66.6
The Netherlands	69.9

Note: The countries are rank ordered on the degree of support for the national high court (lowest to highest).

their national high court. . . . Yet, trust in the national high court is quite wide-spread in most countries, with, for instance, an astounding 89 % of the Dutch expressing some trust in the De Hoge Raad. Apparently, people trust their national high court even if they support reigning it in or even abolishing it should it fail to perform satisfactorily over a lone period of time.

To simplify comparisons across countries, we have created [an index of support based on responses to the three statements above]. Table 3 reports the means . . . for each country. According to this index, the Dutch are the most supportive of their national court; the Spanish are least supportive; and the Italians and Hungarians score at the middle of the twenty countries.

The data in Table 3 provide an enlightening perspective on the U.S. Supreme Court. It is certainly a widely supported institution in the United States, but, in comparative perspective, it is not inordinately well supported. The high courts of the Netherlands, Denmark, Germany, . . . Greece, and even Poland have at least as much institutional legitimacy as the Supreme Court. . . . [T]he U.S. Supreme Court does not have an exceptionally deep reservoir of goodwill among its mass public.

Connecting Awareness and Support

To what degree does increased awareness of the national high court contribute to increased support for the institution? Research from the United States strongly suggests that greater awareness of the Supreme Court directly translates into greater support for it.

Our data show widely varying relationships between awareness of the national high court and support for it. The connection is strongest in Belgium. The relationship is also quite strong in the Netherlands and France. But awareness and support are completely unrelated in Russia. To know a court is not necessarily to love it but there is a fairly strong tendency in most countries for the more aware to be more supportive of their national high court.

Editors' Note. In the wake of the Court's controversial decision in Bush v. Gore *(2001), Gibson, Caldeira, and Lester Spence conducted a follow-up survey in the United States to determine whether Americans' support for the Court had declined. In what follows we reprint their primary findings.*

The U.S. presidential election of 2000 reminds us once again of the importance of the legitimacy of political institutions. Consider this highly simplified view of the election.

A bitter political controversy arises. The dispute bounces around various institutions, with no definitive resolution. Finally, the US Supreme Court intervenes and makes a decision. Some grumble about the ruling, but political elites call for it to be "respected," much if not most of the mass public seems to accept the decision, and the brouhaha ends. The country gets on with its business. Scholars then talk of the Court expending its "political capital," and wonder about the efficacy of the Court in future clashes, but the Court seems to have enough legitimacy to "get away with" its ruling and make it "stick."

The circumstances surrounding *Bush v. Gore* may well enter our textbooks one day as a stellar example of the power and efficacy of institutional legitimacy.

The Supreme Court decision settling the outcome of the U.S. presidential election unleashed a torrent of criticism. Not only was the logic of the opinion assailed, but many also judged the Court's opinion, and even the Court itself, as illegitimate. For instance, 585 law professors placed an advertisement in the *New York Times* on 13 January 2001, condemning the Court's decision as illegitimate. Perhaps for the first time, public opinion pollsters queried the American people using words like "legitimate" and "legitimacy." Scholars complained about a "self-inflicted wound" on the Court, as many questioned whether *Bush v. Gore* undermined the ability of the Court to rule on controversial issues in the future. In short, in the eyes of many, *Bush v. Gore* subtracted mightily from the institutional legitimacy enjoyed by the U.S. Supreme Court.

A great deal of hyperbole surrounded the U.S. election, and politicians, professors, and pundits made many outlandish empirical claims at the time. Terms [such as] "legitimacy" were nearly always used loosely, without rigorous definition. Unfortunately, because serious scholarly inquiry into the Court's legitimacy has been limited, we have little systematic knowledge about how the election may actually have influenced the legitimacy of the Court.

The theoretical issues raised by this dispute are not, however, unfamiliar to scholars. Researchers have long been interested in the question of how an institution's performance affects its legitimacy, and in particular how the Supreme Court's decisions shape people's views of it. Still, the relationship between judgments of particular decisions and more general attitudes toward political institutions like the Supreme Court is under-analyzed and poorly understood within political science.

How legitimate is the U.S. Supreme Court today, and how did the 2000 election affect the legitimacy of the institution? Though the question of change in support is difficult to answer, we adduce some new evidence on the Court's legitimacy in the period shortly after the conclusion of the presidential election. One purpose of this article is thus to provide empirical results on how Americans viewed the Court in the aftermath of the 2000 presidential election, based on a nationally representative sample interviewed at the beginning of 2001. . . .

Table 1 reports the responses from the six statements we use to measure loyalty toward the U.S. Supreme Court. The first three columns of figures represent the frequencies after collapsing "strong" and not so strong responses, and the column labeled "Supportive of the Court" reports the percentage of respondents giving answers indicating loyalty to the institution, regardless of whether loyalty requires an agree or disagree reply. The means and standard deviations are based on the uncollapsed data, and in every instance higher scores indicate more loyalty toward the Supreme Court.

These data indicate at least a moderate level of loyalty toward the Supreme Court among most Americans. On average, 3.8 of the statements elicit support for the Court, and 77.7 percent of the respondents endorse at least three of the six statements (data not shown). Except for the two items on partisanship, strong majorities express support for the Court on four of the six statements. On the clearest measure of institutional loyalty, the first (but also easiest) item, support is extremely widespread: Over four of five Americans assert that it would *not* be better to do away with the Court, even if there were fairly widespread displeasure with its decisions. Although a significant minority worries about politics and partisanship on the Court, over three-fourths of the sample asserts that the Court—not the leaders of the Court—can generally be trusted. These data indicate that the Supreme Court enjoys a reasonably solid reservoir of good will, even in the aftermath of the tumultuous presidential election of 2000. Placing these findings in the context of cross-national research, the U.S. Supreme Court is a fairly legitimate institution.

Change in Loyalty toward the Court

It is impossible in a cross-sectional survey to analyze individual-level change in opinions. [But] we can compare the 2001 data to a similar survey conducted in 1995. Table 2 reports these results. The 2001 figures we report in Table 2 are identical to those reported in Table 1, above.

Consider the mean scores. In every instance, the mean is higher (more support) in 2001 than it was in 1995. The differences are not enormous, but they are in every instance statistically significant. From these data it is *impossible to conclude that loyalty toward the Supreme Court plummeted after the presidential election of 2000*. Indeed, the percentage of Americans saying the Court can be trusted is 12.5 percentage points higher in 2001 than it was in 1995. Americans were somewhat more likely to have an opinion toward the Supreme Court in 2001, and their opinions were more likely to be positive than in 1995.

TABLE 1. Indicators of Loyalty Toward the US Supreme Court, 2001

	Percentages (Totalling to 100%)					
	Not Supportive of the Court	Uncertain	Supportive of the Court	Mean	Std. Dev.	N
Do away with the Court	12.9	4.4	82.7	4.23	1.16	1418
Limit the Court's jurisdiction	28.3	11	60.7	3.55	1.34	1418
Court can be trusted	17	5.1	77.8	3.89	1.17	1418
Court favors some groups	43.7	14.4	41.9	3.02	1.37	1409
Court gets too mixed up in politics	40.8	15.9	43.3	3.05	1.36	1418
Court should interpret the Constitution	22.7	8.1	69.2	3.73	1.31	1418

Note: The percentage are calculated on the basis of collapsing the five-point Likert response set (e.g., "agree strongly" and "agree" responses are combined). The mean and standard deviations are calculated on the uncollapsed distributions. Higher mean scores indicate more institutional loyalty.

The propositions are:

If the US Supreme Court started making a lot of decisions that most people disagree with, it might be better to do away with the Supreme Court altogether.

The right of the Supreme Court to decide certain types of controversial issues should be reduced.

The Supreme Court can usually be trusted to make decisions that are right for the country as a whole.

The decisions of the US Supreme Court favor some groups more that others.

The US Supreme Court gets too mixed up in politics.

The US Supreme Court should have the right to say what the Constitution means, even when the majority of the people disagree with the Court's decision.

TABLE 2. Loyalty Toward the Supreme Court, 1995–2001

Item Year	Level of Diffuse Support for the Supreme Court					
	Percentage					
	Not Supportive	Undecided	Supportive	Mean	Std. Dev.	N
Limit the Court's Jurisdiction						
1995	35.5	11.7	52.8	3.2	1.1	803
2001	28.3	11	60.7	3.6	1.3	1418
Do Away with the Court						
1995	16.8	7.2	76	3.8	1.0	803
2001	12.9	4.4	82.7	4.2	1.2	1418
Court Can be Trusted						
1995	25.1	9.6	65.3	3.4	1.0	804
2001	17	5.1	77.8	3.9	1.2	1418

Limit the Court's Jurisdiction:

  1995: The right of the Supreme Court to decide certain types of controversial issues should be reduced.

  2001: The right of the Supreme Court to decide certain types of controversial issues should be reduced.

Do Away with the Court:

  1995: If the US Supreme Court started making a lot of decisions that most people disagreed with, it might be better to do away with the Supreme Court altogether.

  2001: If the US Supreme Court started making a lot of decisions that most people disagreed with, it might be better to do away with the Supreme Court altogether.

Court Can be Trusted:

  1995: The Supreme Court can usually be trusted to make decisions that are right for the country as a whole.

  2001: The Supreme Court can usually be trusted to make decisions that are right for the country as a whole.

Summary

This analysis yields several conclusions. First, the U.S. Supreme Court enjoys at least a moderate degree of loyalty from the American people –its "reservoir of good will" is certainly not shallow. [Second,] support for the Court does not seem to have been depressed by the justices' involvement in the presidential election: It would be difficult indeed to conclude from these cross-sectional data that the basic legitimacy of the Court was threatened by the justices' involvement in the 2000 election imbroglio.

PART FOUR

Judicial Decision Making

CHAPTER 9

Fact Finding in the Courts

A judicial decision involves two formal processes: determining the facts and then choosing—often crafting, sometimes even creating—the appropriate rules of law to apply to these facts. This double process, we add, in no way excludes the possibility that the perceptions and judgments of those who find "the facts," apply "the law," or both are affected by emotional as well as intellectual considerations.

Some lawsuits, of course, do not involve disputes about the relevant facts. In a criminal case, for example, the defendant may plead guilty and thus relieve the prosecutor of the burden of establishing that the accused has violated the law. In a civil proceeding, both parties may agree about the facts and disagree only about the legal rules applicable to the situation. Still, trial courts must be prepared to discover the facts in any controversy brought before them, and much of the peculiar character of judicial proceedings is attributable to their fact-finding methods.

Television has probably sensitized much of the American population to the importance of judicial fact finding and in this respect, if no other, has performed a public service. Nevertheless, scholars still tend to concentrate on the work of appellate tribunals. The "upper-court myth," as Judge Jerome Frank called it, holds that legal rules announced by appellate courts control decisions of trial courts and that trial judges' mistakes can be remedied on appeal. In reality, however, American appellate judges receive a case in the form of a record shaped by the procedural rulings and findings of fact in the trial court. The litigation, like rough dough, has already been mixed and partly molded. When the record consists largely of documents, as, for instance, in an antitrust suit, appellate judges may feel at least as competent as the trial judge to weigh the evidence. But when the evidence consists mostly of oral testimony and the witnesses have contradicted one another (as they often do), appellate judges, because they themselves neither saw nor heard those witnesses, are loath to overturn a trial judge's findings. Indeed, the U.S. Supreme Court regularly, albeit not always, adheres to the "two-court rule"; that is, the justices will not question facts established by a trial court and accepted by an appellate court in the same case. The "two-court" practice is merely a logical extension of the

Federal Rules of Civil Procedure, which shield from appellate review a district judge's finding of fact unless that finding is "clearly erroneous." By contrast, an appeal in Civil-Law systems typically means that the higher court conducts a complete retrial of alleged facts as well as a review of the applicability of particular legal rules.

THE ADVERSARIAL PROCESS

When the common law was in its infancy, the judicial process leaned heavily on the Deity to determine the critical facts in dispute. One method, trial by combat, allowed the litigants to do physical battle with each other. Supposedly, God dropped all other pressing matters in the universe and intervened to bestow victory on the just man. But because at least one of the litigants was unjust and because the Almighty was known to be quite busy and to think in long-range rather than short-range terms, there were risks as well as inconveniences in such trials. To ease these problems, a group of professional champions made themselves available to do combat, albeit for a fee that only the more affluent could afford.[1]

During the Middle Ages, lesser folk in England frequently tried to gain the Deity's attention by resorting to various trials by ordeal, the hot iron being the most common form: during Mass a litigant would grasp a white-hot iron. His smoldering hand was then bandaged and examined three days later. If it was free of infection, God had spared him because he had told the truth; if it was infected, he had lied. Most Catholic theologians had frowned on such practices, and in 1215 the Fourth Lateran Council forbade clergy to participate in them. This ban threw the British law of evidence into chaos, and only after fifty years of experimentation did the jury—in a form familiar to us—come into existence as a substitute for divine fact finding. The Church had long provided an alternative—if, to English tastes, peculiar—model, which had to some extent been followed in lay tribunals on the continent. In ecclesiastical tribunals, a judge heard and questioned witnesses, examined documents, and then decided the issues in dispute. He might have prayed for wisdom, but he neither expected, nor apparently habitually received, explicit directions from heaven.

The trial procedures that eventually developed in the common law form an adversarial system. The trial judge, even when sitting without a jury, properly acts more like a referee than a player in this contest. Opposing counsel carry the burden of uncovering the facts by waging all-out intellectual warfare in order to reveal their versions of the truth. Each side calls its own witnesses and questions them about their knowledge of the dispute; then the attorney for the other side has an opportunity to cross-examine those witnesses, to try to discredit

---

[1] In 1985 two Scottish brothers accused of armed robbery unsuccessfully sought the option of trial by combat with the royal champion. This type of trial was last recorded in 1603, but the honorary office of royal champion still exists.

damaging testimony by showing that the witnesses are mendacious, mistaken, or biased or that the evidence offered is irrelevant to the issues at trial. At the conclusion of these sometimes dramatic confrontations, the judge or the jury is supposed to sort out truth from falsehood and decide what the "real" facts are (Reading 9.1).

JURIES

The Sixth and Seventh Amendments to the U.S. Constitution recognize a right to a trial by jury in all federal cases. The Seventh Amendment, however, excepts civil disputes in which the amount in controversy is twenty dollars or less, and the Supreme Court has upheld legislation that exempts criminal prosecutions for "petty offenses," a vague term that usually refers to crimes for which the penalty does not exceed six months' imprisonment. On the other hand, the Court has ruled that trial by jury is so fundamental a constitutional right that the Fourteenth Amendment's due process clause imposes on states the duty to accord defendants this right in serious criminal cases, although again not for petty offenses.[2]

The justification for the fundamental nature of the protection of a trial by jury does not lie in a belief that untrained people, selected pretty much at random from the community, are especially adept at finding facts. (Nevertheless, if judges are skilled at discovering the truth, it must follow that most juries are also reasonably capable in that work. A thorough empirical study—some of whose results are reprinted in Reading 9.2—reported that judges and juries agreed on the verdict in more than three-quarters of the cases studied.)[3] Rather, the basic argument for the jury, as eloquently stated by Justice Byron R. White in *Duncan v. Louisiana*, is a political one: "jury trial is granted to criminal defendants in order to prevent oppression by the Government . . . an inestimable safeguard against the corrupt or overzealous prosecutor and against the compliant, biased, or eccentric judge." Another important justification has been that jurors, drawn as they are from the community at large rather than from among lawyers and public officials, may temper enforcement of unpopular, outdated, or harsh laws.

Even so, defendants in criminal cases may make a "knowing" waiver of the right to jury trial. Moreover, as many as nine out of ten criminal prosecutions are settled by plea bargaining—negotiations between the prosecutor and defense counsel in which the defendant agrees to plead guilty in exchange for the prosecutor's lessening the charge, agreeing to ask the judge for leniency, or

---

[2] *Duncan v. Louisiana* (1968); *Baldwin v. New York* (1970).

[3] Harry Kalven and Hans Zeisel, *The American Jury* (Boston: Little, Brown, 1966). More recent studies confirm a high level of agreement between judges and juries on verdicts. See, e.g., R. Perry Sentell, Jr., "The Georgia Jury and Negligence: The View from the Bench," 26 *Georgia Law Review* 85 (1991). We also should note that judges do have ways to override jury decisions. Upon the request of a losing party, judges can set aside jury verdicts or enter judgments notwithstanding the verdicts; but only if they find the jury's decisions to have been unreasonable.

both. On the civil side, too, the vast majority of cases filed in court are settled by negotiation; and a judge sitting alone decides a large portion of the remainder.

Jury Trials

When litigants opt for a jury, they are, as we noted above, taking advantage of their Sixth or Seventh Amendment right to a trial by "jury." But what does the term jury mean now, and what did it mean to the drafters and ratifiers of those amendments? We can speculate about what those people thought but cannot definitively ascertain their understanding. Most probably, they thought that the system they had inherited from the British required that a jury be composed of the defendant's peers, that it consist of twelve persons, and that it reach unanimous verdicts. Today, none of these three features is fully operative.

Composition of Juries

Presumably, in England being tried by a jury of one's peers meant that one would face members of one's social class. In other words, a commoner would be tried by a jury of commoners and a nobleman by a jury of noblemen. Because the United States does not recognize such class distinctions, a jury of one's peers means a jury that represents a cross section of the community. To put together representative panels, most jurisdictions follow a procedure that works this way:

1. Individuals living within a specified geographical area are called for jury duty. Most localities use voter registration lists, property tax records, or driver's license rosters from which to select names at random.
2. Those selected form the jury pool, or venire, the group from which attorneys choose the jury.
3. The judge may conduct initial interviews excusing certain classes of people (felons, illiterates, the mentally ill) and certain occupational groups, as allowed under the laws of the particular jurisdiction.
4. The remaining individuals are available to be chosen to serve on a trial jury.

In the final phase of selection, the so-called voir dire occurs (Reading 9.3). This is a pretrial proceeding in which opposing counsel, either directly or through the judge, may question prospective jurors about their backgrounds and opinions. If a juror indicates bias in the case, counsel may challenge her or him "for cause"; if the judge believes the lawyer is correct, the challenged person will be dismissed from the panel of potential jurors. The law provides additional protection by allowing each side a certain number of "peremptory" challenges, which require no justification. (The number of challenges "for cause" is unlimited.) In extreme cases in which most community members have apparently formed an opinion (perhaps because of extensive pretrial publicity), the defense may ask for a change of venue, that is, that the trial be held in another locality.

The objective of this long-standing procedure is to form a trial, or "petit," jury representing a cross section of the community. (*Petit* is French for "small"; the petit jury is distinguished from the grand jury, which has twenty-three members.) Does the procedure work effectively? This question has been the center of numerous scholarly analyses and is still being debated. One common complaint is that the process of selecting jurors is too time consuming, sometimes taking longer than the trial itself. The principal reason for slowness is that in most states competing attorneys control the voir dire, and they may ask long strings of petty questions about each potential juror's occupation, neighborhood, reading habits, hobbies, and acquaintances—all in the hope of gaining some insight into how he or she would vote if empaneled. In federal courts, such delays are less likely because the judge controls the voir dire, asking questions submitted by counsel.

Another criticism is that the processes of selection produce unacceptable biases. Here critics point to a variety of supposed flaws. One stems from the fact that most states allow numerous exemptions from jury service. Often professionals such as lawyers, doctors, teachers, professors, architects, social workers, and public officials are automatically excused; and many other intelligent, educated people who do not wish to spend a week or more in court for two or three dollars a day may know enough to make counsel for one side or the other sufficiently nervous to challenge them. The all-too-frequent result is a jury composed mostly of people who are unemployed or elderly and looking for something to do, or too poor and uneducated to give answers that set off lawyers' alarms. (The criticism that juries are staffed by the old and the poor was also lodged in ancient Athens, where jurors were paid an average day's wage for their work.[4]) Quite different, but still related to bias, is the criticism that juries underrepresent the poor. Many localities draw their jury pools from voter registration lists, which means that jury pools are likely to reflect the average voter—white, middle-aged, and middle-class. The composition of the entire pool, of course, could well differ from that of any actual jury.

One additional source of bias may come from the way attorneys, specifically prosecutors, use their peremptory challenges systematically to excuse members of some groups, such as African Americans. This particular choice has typically been based on a belief that black jurors are reluctant to convict black defendants; and, in many jurisdictions, defendants in criminal cases include a disproportionately large number of blacks. Although trial judges long recognized that prosecutors engaged in this practice, they could do little about it because peremptory challenges do not require their approval. Indeed, in *Swain v. Alabama* (1965), the Supreme Court rejected an argument that prosecutors should be prohibited from using peremptory challenges to remove prospective jurors

---

[4] See Mogens Herman Hansen, *The Athenian Democracy in the Age of Demosthenes.* Norman, OK: University of Oklahoma Press, 1999, J. A. Crook, trans.

for reasons of race. In *Batson v. Kentucky* (1986), however, the Court reexamined *Swain* and startled the legal community by holding that even peremptory challenges are subject to judicial scrutiny. The justices went on to sketch a framework within which defendants could challenge prosecutors who appeared to be using their peremptory challenges in a racially discriminatory way.

Batson, however, was just the beginning of the Court's reevaluation of peremptory challenges. *Powers v. Ohio* (1991) ruled that criminal defendants may object to race-based exclusion of jurors through peremptory challenges whether or not the defendant and the excluded jurors are of the same race. In the same term, *Edmonson v. Leesville Concrete Co.* extended Batson's reasoning to civil cases, holding that private litigants may not use their peremptory challenges in a racially biased manner. Finally, in *J. E. B. v. Alabama ex rel. T. B.* (1994), lawyers convinced the justices to apply *Batson* to intentional sex discrimination in selecting jurors.

Yet an additional criticism comes from the practice of "jury stacking." Counsel have always tried to use their challenges to eliminate jurors likely to be unsympathetic to their side, but they have generally proceeded only on the basis of their personal experience, professional judgment, and idiosyncratic hunches (Reading 9.4). More recently—and more expensively—lawyers have engaged firms that sample public opinion in a community to map the backgrounds of ideal jurors and have hired social psychologists to sit in the courtroom during the voir dire and observe potential jurors in order more accurately to predict jurors' attitudes (Readings 9.5 and 9.6). These experts have a right to be in the courtroom, for in *Press-Enterprise Co. v. Superior Court of California* (1984) the Supreme Court held that trial judges must ordinarily permit the press and public to attend the proceedings in which jurors are chosen.

Number of Jurors

Another long-standing tradition Americans adopted from the British relates to the size of the jury. Since the fourteenth century, all English juries had twelve people, a number of disputed origin. Some suggest that it represents the twelve apostles; others claim it emanates from the twelve tribes of Israel. The point on which all scholars agree is that in early America twelve was considered the proper number of jurors.

Beginning in the mid 1960s, however, many states began to experiment, substituting six-person juries in noncapital cases. These states reasoned that smaller juries would be more economical, faster, and more likely to reach a verdict than to end up hopelessly divided. Was the use of less than twelve people consistent with the demands of the Sixth Amendment? In 1970 *Williams v. Florida* answered this question. The Supreme Court reviewed a state conviction for robbery after a trial before a jury of six people. For the majority, Justice White explained that the number twelve had no special constitutional significance; rather, it was the result of historical accident. All the constitutional text requires, according to the Court, is a jury sufficiently large to allow actual deliberation and to represent a cross section of the community. The six-person jury used to convict Williams met these standards.[5]

In the wake of Williams, many states followed Florida's lead and now use juries of less than twelve members for some offences. Nonetheless, White's reasoning has been closely scrutinized by legal scholars, and numerous empirical investigations have tried to determine whether six-person juries reach conclusions significantly different from their twelve-person counterparts.[6] Although the scholarly verdict is far from unanimous, many now agree that "research on the effects of panel size on jury performance indicates that the use of six-member juries does not result in significant differences in either trial outcome or quality of deliberation."[7] On the other hand, there seems to be consensus over the obvious: the fewer the jurors, the less time it takes to reach a verdict.

Jury Verdicts

For several centuries American practice followed the English tradition of requiring a unanimous verdict to convict or to acquit in criminal cases. In the event the jury was deadlocked, judges would declare the jury "hung." The prosecutor could then either schedule a retrial or drop the charges. Allegedly to make the administration of justice more efficient, some states have altered the unanimity rule for twelve-person juries, requiring instead the agreement of nine or ten of the twelve in noncapital criminal prosecutions.

Two cases, *Johnson v. Louisiana* and *Apodaca v. Oregon*, decided together in 1972, tested the constitutionality of convictions reached by juries that were not unanimous. Louisiana and Oregon claimed that requiring unanimity was obsolete in modern society and, because this requirement made hung juries more likely, often led to miscarriages of justice. In contrast, Johnson and Apodaca asserted that the very essence of a jury's decision making is the presence or absence of doubt. If no reasonable doubt exists about a person's guilt, the jury is supposed to reach a guilty verdict; if doubt is present, the jury should come to the opposite conclusion. And the very fact that jurors are divided indicates the

---

[5] Neither Congress nor the Court has authorized such ultra-petite juries in federal criminal cases, but *Colgrove v. Battin* (1973) approved civil juries of only six people in federal civil trials; and such small panels now sit in most United States district courts. In *Ballew v. Georgia* (1978), however, the Court refused to allow five-person juries in state criminal cases.

[6] This has come about at least in part because many scholars agree with Bernard Grofman: the Court's use of empirical evidence [in the jury size cases] is uniformly dreadful. See his "The Slippery Slope: Jury Size and Jury Verdict Requirements: Legal and Social Science Approaches," 2 *Law and Policy Quarterly* 285 (1980).

[7] Reid Hastie, Steven D. Penrod, and Nancy Pennington, *Inside the Jury* (Cambridge: Harvard University Press, 1983), 38. Bernard Grofman, "The Slippery Slope," concludes that the difference between the conviction rates of six- and twelve-person juries will be small: perhaps as low as 3 percent and less than 14 percent. Other scholars have found differences between large and small juries but agree that "regardless of which jury type is chosen some desirable features of the unchosen type are lost" [Michael J. Saks, *Jury Verdicts* (Lexington, MA: Lexington Books, 1977), 107.]

existence of reasonable doubt. But according to Justice White, who again wrote for the Court, lack of unanimity is not the equivalent of doubt. Thus, a state's relaxing the traditional requirement does not violate the Sixth and Fourteenth Amendments., White did insist, however, that juries in federal criminal cases had to arrive at unanimous verdicts. Because this latter issue was not before the Court, White's views on federal juries were merely obiter dicta (words spoken in passing), not only presenting a question about the logical consistency of the Sixth Amendment's terms but also raising doubts about how seriously the justices took their own oft-repeated rule of not reaching constitutional questions unless raised by a litigant who met all the qualifications of standing to sue (discussed in Chapter 6).

The Critics and the Defenders of Juries

As the foregoing discussion implies, juries remain a controversial part of the American legal system. The "scientific" selection of jurors, not to mention the use of peremptory challenges to eliminate particular types of jurors, raises questions about the degree to which juries conform to the Sixth Amendment's mandate that they be "impartial." But that concern is not the only one that academics and jurists alike have expressed. Despite Justice White's panegyric in *Duncan* to the sacredness of the right, many judges, prosecutors, and scholars have severely criticized the jury for both its expense and its slowness in administering justice. Perhaps it was in response to such criticisms that the Supreme Court permitted experimentation with two historic features of juries under the common law—twelve persons and a unanimous verdict.

Although these decisions may have helped quicken the pace of justice and lowered the costs of judicial administration, they have not mitigated other criticisms of the American jury system. Many of these concerns, including the process of selecting jurors—be they centered on biases within the process or the plight of prospective jurors who often spend days sitting around dingy anterooms waiting to be called—continue to provide fodder for intense debates.[8] At the same time, others, especially criticisms concerning "jury nullification"—when jurors refuse to convict because they dislike a law or dislike the way the government is attempting to apply a law in a particular context—have emerged as particularly pressing issues within the American system of criminal justice (Readings 9.3, 9.7).

And yet, despite the plethora of concerns, there are few scholars, lawyers, or judges who argue for the total elimination of the jury. To the contrary: Most seem to agree with Tracy Weiss: "Although the jury system is far from being perfect, it acts as a great democratizing principle which brings the people of our country directly into the government system" (Reading 9.8). Indeed, variations on the jury, often in the form of "lay judges" who sit and vote with professional jurists, have become common in Civil-Law systems.

---

[8] See, e.g., Richard K. Willard, "What Is Wrong with American Juries and How to Fix It," 20 *Harvard Journal of Law and Public Policy* 483 (1996).

Standards for Fact Finding

To make decisions, judges and juries require varying standards of proof depending on the seriousness of the proceeding. To obtain an indictment (an accusation) from a grand jury, a prosecutor need show only that the facts make a prima facie case, that is, on their face point toward, without necessarily conclusively proving, the guilt of the accused. This standard is so easily met that a standing joke among prosecutors is the claim: "I can persuade a grand jury to indict a ham sandwich." That defense counsel might be able to rebut the evidence the grand jury heard, prove it is incomplete and biased, or demonstrate more plausible interpretations of the alleged facts does not invalidate an indictment. Similarly, a court applies the standard of a prima facie case when it grants a temporary injunction in an ex parte proceeding, that is, a proceeding in which only the person seeking the injunction comes into court. To secure a conviction on a criminal charge or to obtain a permanent injunction, the standard of proof is, of course, much higher.

In civil suits a plaintiff need show only that "the preponderance of the evidence" supports his or her contentions. As its name indicates, this rule requires that the fact finder(s) conclude(s) that more evidence supports than contradicts the plaintiff's allegations of "facts." Much more stringent is the standard required for a conviction in a criminal case: "beyond a reasonable doubt." Here before returning a verdict of guilty, the trial court—either jury or judge—must be convinced that the "facts" presented by the prosecution so overwhelm the "facts" offered by the defense and any alternative explanations of the prosecution's evidence that no reasonable doubt of guilt remains in the fact finders' minds. Reasonable is a slippery word that defies precise definition, but trial judges typically instruct juries that it means a doubt of real weight. As one federal judge explained to a jury, a reasonable doubt "is just such a doubt as the term implies; a doubt for which you can give a reason. It must not arise from a merciful disposition or kindly, sympathetic feeling or desiring to avoid a possibly disagreeable duty. . . . It is a doubt which is created by the want of evidence, or maybe by the evidence itself; not speculative, imaginary, or conjectural."[9]

Since the early days of the Republic, courts have routinely insisted that prosecutors meet the standard of "beyond a reasonable doubt"; but neither the constitutional text of 1787 nor any subsequent amendment contains a word about such a requirement. It was not until 1970 that *In re Winship* explicitly ruled that the standard was imbedded in the larger constitution. There the Supreme Court said that this strict criterion was inherent in the concept of due process of law expressed in both the Fifth and Fourteenth Amendments and applied to proceedings against juveniles as well as against adults. Nevertheless, the defendant may have to carry the burden of proof under some circumstances. Where, for example, a person offers as a defense that he or she acted

---

[9] *United States v. Olmstead* (1928); quoted in Walter F. Murphy, *Wiretapping on Trial* (New York: Random House, 1965), 42–43.

under the pressure of an "extreme emotional disturbance" that might explain or excuse the crime, it is constitutional for the trial court to require an accused prove this claim by a preponderance of the evidence.[10]

Adjudicative Facts

Some analysts distinguish between adjudicative and legislative facts.[11] Adjudicative facts are of the kind that courts have traditionally had to discover to resolve disputes involving a limited number of persons and fairly specific incidents. Controversies over such matters as whether Sam struck his wife, whether his wife aimed a weapon at Sam, or whether IBM and Microsoft made a contract, are adjudicative facts that can usually be established by ordering persons who were at the scene to testify about what, to their direct knowledge, actually occurred. These are the facts that normally go to a jury. They relate to the parties, their activities, their properties, or their businesses. Findings of adjudicative facts must be supported by evidence and, depending on the sort of case, meet the test of either "preponderance of the evidence" or "beyond a reasonable doubt."

Under the strictures of the rule against hearsay, witnesses may testify only about what they themselves have seen or heard. But duly qualified "expert" witnesses, such as people skilled in ballistics, may offer their professional opinions. Efforts to supplement witnesses' testimony by more precise or scientific fact-finding methods have not been fully successful. On the one hand, courts routinely accept data regarding fingerprints as well as blood and breath tests for drunkenness; on the other hand, judges remain skeptical about lie detectors, voice prints, and narcoanalysis. Interestingly, some judges have permitted or requested experts on morals or ethics—clergy, philosophers, professors of religion—to testify on such subjects as conscientious objection to military service, the right to die, religious rights of prisoners, and blood transfusions or other medical treatments resisted on moral grounds.

Legislative Facts and Public Issues

Contrasting with litigation involving disputes about individual actions are cases in which the controversy concerns application or validity of social or economic legislation aimed at establishing governmental control over conduct. In those disputes, the actual, if not formal, litigants are large groups or classes of people, typically including public officials. In such cases the "facts" often concern attitudes or opinions or social practices or economic conditions. These are

---

[10] *Patterson v. New York* (1977).

[11] Donald L. Horowitz prefers the terms *historical facts* and *social facts*. He explains: "Historical facts are the events that have transpired between the parties to a lawsuit. Social facts are the recurrent patterns of behavior on which policy must be based. Historical facts, as I use the term, have occasionally been called *adjudicative facts* by lawyers, and social facts have also been called *legislative facts*. I avoid these terms because of the preconceptions they carry and the division of labor they imply" [*The Courts and Social Policy* (Washington, DC: Brookings Institution, 1977), 45.]

sometimes called legislative facts—facts that help the tribunal exercise its judgment or discretion in determining what course of action to take. Legislative facts are ordinarily general and do not concern merely the immediate parties. When courts must find facts of such breadth, the usual practice of relying on testimony by eyewitnesses or participants becomes both inadequate and inappropriate. As Kenneth C. Davis says, "legislative facts need not be, frequently are not, and sometimes cannot be supported by evidence."[12]

And, as Justice Felix Frankfurter once complained, "the types of cases now calling for decision to a considerable extent require investigation of voluminous literature far beyond the law reports and other legal writings."[13] One needs little imagination to grasp the difficulties of using traditional judicial procedures to obtain information about such broad and complex issues as the potential effect on young children's minds of having a teacher who has had surgery to change his or her sex; whether a war really began at the firing of the first shots, the formal declaration by one of the belligerents, or some time in between; or the injury—which will show up, if ever, only many years later—to nearby residents by an accident at a nuclear power plant or a laboratory engaged in recombinant DNA research.

One means judges have used to take broad societal conditions into account is called "judicial notice." The judge merely "notices" certain more or less obvious situations. Such noticing is a long-established judicial tradition, but it has characteristically operated within fairly narrow limits. In *Ohio Bell Telephone Co. v. Public Utilities Commission* (1937), for example, the Supreme Court said it would take notice of the fact that there had been an economic depression and that market values decline during a depression. But litigants would have to prove, by evidence, the precise extent of that decline. Beyond judicial notice a judge may determine social or economic facts by independent research, just as in dealing with legal points at issue in a trial. Justice Frankfurter made a significant comment from the bench to counsel during the first reargument of the School Segregation Cases:

> Can we not take judicial notice of writing by people who competently deal with these problems? Can I not take judicial notice of [Gunnar] Myrdal's book [*An American Dilemma*] without having him called as a witness? . . . How to inform the judicial mind, as you know, is one of the most complicated problems. It is better to have witnesses, but I did not know that we could not read the works of competent writers.

Social and Economic Data

Judicial notice is limited in scope, and a busy judge cannot do a great deal of original research. Thus, even together, these two sources of information cannot entirely fulfill a judge's need for information. There are other ways of satisfying

---

[12] *Administrative Law and Government* (St. Paul: West Publishing Co., 1960), 284.

[13] *Ferguson v. Moore-McCormack Lines* (1957).

this need, of course. One is for counsel to gather relevant data and summarize and analyze them in briefs. Each side can then present and defend its interpretations and attack those of the opposition.

The most celebrated breakthrough involving use of this approach was the brief prepared by Louis D. Brandeis, then a practicing attorney in Boston, and presented to the Supreme Court in *Muller v. Oregon* (1908), in which he was defending the constitutionality of a state law setting ten hours as the maximum working day for women. This brief, the usefulness of which the Court specifically acknowledged in its opinion, gathered an enormous amount of information on foreign and American laws limiting hours for women and utilized governmental reports that stressed the dangers to women's health and morals posed by long hours of labor. Such laws and opinions "may not be, technically speaking, authorities," the Supreme Court said, but "they are significant of a widespread belief that woman's physical structure, and the functions she performs in consequence thereof, justify special legislation restricting or qualifying the conditions under which she should be permitted to toil." This technique of presenting social data to a court has become known as a "Brandeis brief."

Brandeis's triumph was, however, an island of victory in a sea of defeat. When Congress and the states began enacting minimum-wage laws and setting maximum hours of work for men as well as women, judges grew quite hostile. Indeed, Brandeis had used his factual brief because a few years earlier the Supreme Court had, in *Lochner v. New York* (1905), invalidated a statute setting maximum hours for bakers. And in 1923, defending a challenge to the validity of an act of Congress regulating hours of work for women and children in the District of Columbia, Felix Frankfurter, a protegé of Brandeis, who was then on the Court, filed a Brandeis brief. By a vote of five to three, however, the Court invalidated the law. For the majority Justice George Sutherland noted that counsel had included a large number of materials supporting minimum wages and that the Court's own research had revealed additional writings on the other side. He concluded:

> These are all proper enough for the consideration of lawmaking bodies, since their tendency is to establish the desirability or undesirability of the legislation; but they reflect no legitimate light upon the question of its validity, and that is what we are called upon to decide. (*Adkins v. Children's Hospital.*)

Not unexpectedly, then, the Court was antagonistic to the New Deal's efforts to regulate the national economy. A majority of the justices considered it their prerogative either to examine economic conditions and arrive at their own conclusions about the necessity of governmental regulation, or, alternatively, to refuse to look at economic conditions at all and merely rely on the dogma that laissez faire had been constitutionally mandated, even though that economic theory could not be found in the constitutional text. After Justice Owen Roberts and to a lesser extent Chief Justice Charles Evans Hughes changed their minds and pulled off "the switch in time that saved nine," the justices had to rethink their role vis-à-vis Congress and the states on economic regulation. The eventual decision was to presume such statutes constitutional, especially when they were supported by information obtained through legislative hearings. As Harlan Stone wrote for the Court in 1938: "regulatory legislation affecting ordinary commercial transactions is not to be pronounced unconstitutional unless in the light of the facts made known or generally assumed it is of such a character as to preclude the assumption that it rests upon some rational basis within the knowledge and experience of the legislators."[14]

The rule now is that, if there is a rational relation between economic legislation and a valid governmental purpose (and the justices have sometimes shown considerable creativity in imagining such a relation), courts will presume the regulation to be constitutional. Citing legislative hearings or reports by administrative agencies reinforces this presumption, but no longer is it necessary for counsel defending the constitutionality of economic legislation to use a Brandeis brief.

Another method of presenting social science data to a court continues to rely on the Brandeis brief but goes beyond that technique. At the trial of the original School Segregation Cases, for example, the NAACP not only included in its briefs studies of the effects of segregation on black children but also called social scientists to the stand to testify as expert witnesses, much as a prosecutor might call a ballistics technician to testify whether a bullet was fired from a certain gun or as a defense attorney might summon a psychiatrist to testify about a client's mental health. The social sciences, however, are still considered "soft" compared to "hard" sciences such as chemistry and physics; and in a society in which most educated citizens fancy themselves experts on politics, economics, and sociology, establishing expertise is not always easy.[15] The following colloquy during the trial in the case from South Carolina illustrates some of the difficulties:

> JUDGE [JOHN J.] PARKER: It seems to me that any lawyer or any man who has any experience in government would be just as well qualified as he [Kenneth Clark, a social psychologist] would to express an opinion on that [the effects of segregation] on Black school children. He is not a scientist in the field of education. . . . Do you seriously contend he is qualified to testify as an educational expert? What do you say about that, Mr. Marshall?
>
> MR. [THURGOOD] MARSHALL: . . . we have been trying to . . . present as many experts in the field with as many different reasons why we consider that segregation in and of itself is injurious.
>
> JUDGE PARKER: Are you going to offer any more witnesses along this line?
>
> MR. MARSHALL: No sir. The other witnesses are real scientists.
>
> JUDGE PARKER: Well, I'll take it for what it's worth. Go ahead.

---

[14] *United States v. Carolene Products* (1938).

[15] See Wallace D. Loh, ed., *Social Research and the Judicial Process* (New York: Russell Sage Foundation, 1984).

In the subsequent oral argument before the Supreme Court, Justice Frankfurter expressed what must be a common judicial concern over the weight to be given to social science evidence: "I do not mean that I disrespect it. I simply know its character. It can be a very different thing from, as I say, things that are weighed and measured and are fungible. We are dealing here with very subtle things, very subtle testimony."

When the Supreme Court decided the School Segregation Cases, usually cited under the title of *Brown v. Board of Education*, Chief Justice Earl Warren, in what became a famous (or infamous) footnote, referred to several sociological studies as supporting the Court's conclusion that racial segregation injured the segregated. Opponents of integration utilized these references to charge that the justices were preaching sociology rather than interpreting the Constitution—and bad sociology at that, for the tests these "experts" used were crude at best, misleading at worst.

Contemporary Use of Social Science Evidence: The Death Penalty Cases

Despite Warren's opinion in *Brown* and despite the growing sophistication of social-scientific analyses, judges continue to express skepticism about the use of such evidence. Perhaps no area better exemplifies this fact of legal life than capital punishment. For decades lawyers opposed to the death penalty have invoked studies by social scientists to question—with only limited success—various aspects of this most severe form of punishment.

Of paramount interest to many of these attorneys were data purporting to show that states applied the death penalty in a racially discriminatory fashion (See Reading 9.10). Indeed, the evidence was so powerful that many defense counsel believed they could use it to convince judges to find the death penalty unconstitutional on the ground that states could never apply it in a fair manner. In *Furman v. Georgia* (1972), five members of the U.S. Supreme Court seemed sympathetic to this claim, or at least sufficiently sympathetic to write opinions indicating that all existing state laws imposing the death penalty were unconstitutional. To be sure, the views presented in the opinions of these five justices varied considerably—three justices (Byron White, Potter Stewart, and William O. Douglas) thought capital punishment, as currently imposed, was unconstitutional; and two (William J. Brennan, Jr., and Thurgood Marshall) said it was unconstitutional in all circumstances. But, beyond these splits, the five agreed that those states using capital punishment were doing so in an arbitrary manner, at least with regard to race.

Attorneys in favor of abolishing the death penalty, especially those working for the NAACP Legal Defense Fund (LDF), were ecstatic. One called it "the biggest step forward criminal justice has taken in 1,000 years."[16] But, as it turned out, the abolitionists celebrated a bit too soon, for neither the states nor

---

[16] Quoted in Frederick Mann, "Anthony Amsterdam," 3 *Juris Doctor* 31–32 (1973).

the justices were finished with the death penalty. Barely three years after *Furman*, the Court agreed to hear *Gregg v. Georgia* (1976) to consider the constitutionality of a new breed of death penalty laws written to overcome the defects of the old laws. And, in *Gregg*, a majority of the justices found that these new laws, in fact, reduced the chance for "wanton and freakish" punishment of the sort the Court found so distasteful in *Furman*.

After *Gregg*, opponents of capital punishment began considering new ways of challenging the laws. One of their hopes was that courts would pay attention to a study published in 1986 that demonstrated purposeful race discrimination in the imposition of the death penalty—specifically that African Americans convicted of murdering whites received death sentences at disproportionately high rates.

Initially, it seems difficult to understand why attorneys would pin their hopes to such a study; after all, they had gone down this path before. But the new research was different from its predecessors; it was far more grandiose in design and sophisticated in analysis. Named for one of the investigators, Professor David Baldus (the others were George Woodworth and Charles Pulaski), the study examined 2,484 murder cases prosecuted in Georgia from 1973 to 1979, coded for some 230 variables. To analyze this mammoth amount of data, Baldus used multivariate analysis, which allows researchers to demonstrate the individual effects of possible explanatory variables (such as the race of the defendant or the victim) on outcomes (such as the decision to sentence to death).[17]

Baldus's conclusions were dramatic. Among the most noteworthy were the following:

- The chances of receiving a death sentence were 4.3 times greater for defendants whose victims were white than for defendants whose victims were black.
- Of the 128 cases in which death was imposed, 108, or 87 percent, involved white victims.
- Prosecutors sought the death penalty in 70 percent of cases involving black defendants and white victims, but in only 32 percent in which both the defendant and the victim were white.
- Black defendants were 1.1 times more likely than other defendants to receive death sentences.

Armed with this study, the LDF tried to convince the justices, in the case of *McCleskey v. Kemp* (1987), that the disparate application of death penalty laws led to unacceptable violations of the Equal Protection and Due Process clauses of the U.S. constitutional text. But the Court would not take the bait (Reading 9.9). Although *McCleskey* caused great division among the justices, the majority of the Court—in an opinion written by Justice Lewis Powell—upheld the

---

[17] For more on this study, see David Baldus, George Woodruff, and Charles Pulaski, *Equal Justice and the Death Penalty* (Boston: Northeastern University Press, 1990).

constitutionality of the death penalty. To Powell, *McCleskey* had offered "no evidence specific to his own case that would support an inference that racial considerations played a part in his sentence. Instead, he relies solely on the Baldus study."

As if this loss was not bitter enough for the LDF and Baldus's team (Reading 9.10), imagine their frustration when they learned, along with the rest of the legal community, that Lewis Powell had, some years later, expressed regret over supporting Georgia's claims in the 1987 case (Reading 9.11). Had he adopted the LDF's position, the case would have been decided by a five-to-four vote in McCleskey's favor.

SELECTED REFERENCES

ABRAMSON, JEFFREY. 1994. *We, the Jury: The Jury System and the Ideal of Democracy.* New York: Basic Books.

ADLER, STEPHAN J. 1994. *The Jury: Trial and Error in the American Courtroom.* New York: Times Books.

ALSCHULER, ANDREW W., AND ALBERT G. DEISS. 1994. "A Brief History of the Criminal Jury in the United States." *University of Chicago Law Review* 61: 867–875.

BALDUS, DAVID C., GEORGE G. WOODWORTH, AND CHARLES A. PULASKI, JR. 1990. *Equal Justice and the Death Penalty.* Boston Northeastern University Press.

BURNETT, D. GRAHAM. 2002. *A Trial by Jury.* New York: Vintage.

DANIELS, STEPHEN, AND JOANNE MARTIN. 1995. *Civil Juries and the Politics of Reform.* Evanston, IL: Northwestern University Press and American Bar Foundation.

DIAMOND, SHARI SEIDMAN. 1990. "Scientific Jury Selection: What Social Scientists Know and Do Not Know." *Judicature* 73: 178.

DIAMOND, SHARI SEIDMAN, AND JESSICAN BINA. 2004. "Puzzles about Supply-Side Explanation for Vanishing Trials: A Look at New Fundamentals. *Journal of Empirical Legal Studies* 1: 637.

FRANKEL, MARVIN E. 1976. "The Adversary Judge: The Experience of the Trial Judge." *Texas Law Review* 54: 465.

GROFMAN, BERNARD. 1980. "The Slippery Slope: Jury Size and Jury Verdict Requirements: Legal and Social Science Approaches." *Law and Policy Quarterly* 2: 285.

HAINES, HERBERT H. 1996. *Against Capital Punishment: The Anti-Death Penalty Movement in America, 1972–1994.* New York: Oxford University Press.

HASTIE, REID, AND NANCY PENNINGTON. 1996. "Perceptions and Decision Making: The Jury's View." *University of Colorado Law Review* 67: 957.

HASTIE, REID, STEVEN D. PENROD, AND NANCY PENNINGTON. 1983. *Inside the Jury.* Cambridge, MA: Harvard University Press.

HANS, VALERIE. 2000. *Business on Trial: The Civil Jury and Corporate Responsibility.* New Haven, CT: Yale University Press.

HOROWITZ, DONALD L. 1977. *The Courts and Social Policy.* Washington, DC: Brookings Institution.

JONAKAIT, RANDOLPH. 2003. *The American Jury System.* New Haven: Yale University Press.

KAGAN, ROBERT A. 2001. *Adversarial Legalism: The American Way of Life.* Cambridge, MA: Harvard University Press.

KALVEN, HARRY, AND HANS ZEISEL. 1966. *The American Jury.* Boston: Little, Brown.

KARST, KENNETH L. 1960. "Legislative Facts in Constitutional Litigation." *Supreme Court Review* 1960: 75.

KLUGER, RICHARD. 1976. *Simple Justice*. New York; Knopf.

LEVIN, BETSY, AND WILLIS D. HAWLEY, eds. 1977. *The Courts, Social Science, and School Desegregation*. New York: Transaction Books.

LEVINE, JAMES P. 1992. *Juries and Politics*. Pacific Grove, CA: Brooks/Cole.

LOH, WALLACE D., ed. 1984. *Social Research in the Judicial Process*. New York: Russell Sage Foundation.

MacRAE, DUNCAN. 1976. *The Social Function of Social Science*. New Haven, CT: Yale University Press.

MILLER, ROBERT H. 1998. "Six of One Is Not a Dozen of the Other." *University of Pennsylvania Law Review* 146: 621.

NOTE. 1980. "Peremptory Challenges and the Meaning of Jury Representation." *Yale Law Journal* 89: 1177.

NOTE. 1983. "Public Disclosures of Jury Deliberations." *Harvard Law Review* 96: 886.

ROSEN, PAUL L. 1972. *The Supreme Court and Social Science*. Urbana: University of Illinois Press.

RUSSELL, GREGORY D. *The Death Penalty and Racial Bias: Overturning Supreme Court Assumptions*. Westport, CT: Greenwood Press.

SAKS, MICHAEL. 1976. "The Limits of Scientific Jury Selection." *Jurimetrics Journal* 17:3.

SPERLICH, PETER W. 1980. "Social Science Evidence in the Courts." *Judicature* 63: 280.

THALER, PAUL. 1994. *The Watchful Eye: American Justice in the Age of the Television Trial*. Westport, CT: Praeger.

VIDMAR, NEIL. 1998. "The Performance of the American Civil Jury: An Empirical Perspective." *Arizona Law Review* 40: 849.

WEISS, TRACEY GILSTRAP. 1997. "The Great Democratizing Principle: The Effect on South Africa of Planning a Democracy with a Jury System." *Temple International and Comparative Law Journal* 11: 107.

"How does it all look and feel to the impartial judge, regulating the contest, waiting to see whether the jury arrives at findings he knows to be correct or is successfully kept from doing so?"

9.1 THE ADVERSARY JUDGE: THE EXPERIENCE OF THE TRIAL JUDGE

Marvin E. Frankel

Marvin E. Frankel was U.S. District Court Judge, Southern District of New York.

Much of the time, the script, cues, and setting of the courtroom drama support the judge in performing his role as impartial arbiter between the parties and faithful guide of the jury toward the truth. The prescribed role has been learned by the judge during a (usually) long course of training and observation in the lists. The professed expectations of all the other participants, which are basic determinants of the role to begin with, support the prescription. The standard doctrine, respected for its own sake and as a weapon in the hands of higher courts, is a potent force. The ceremonial business is also a congruent pressure. The two sides, in the well, are physically equal. The judge sits between them, usually on a raised bench, and is called upon to reaffirm more than once the equality of the contestants before the law. The jurors are enjoined, over and over again, to be impartial, and the judge is both their mentor and their colleague in this effort. The usual pressures to conform encourage and drive the judge to be neutral.

But there are contradictions, powerful pressures in a different direction, that constitute the focus of this essay. The pressures may be of several kinds. I mean to consider only those that may be called systematic, inherent in the trial process as we conduct it. This excludes, among other things, an array of possible obstacles to impartiality that vary with cases, litigants, and judges—matters like legal or ideological preconceptions, biases touching people or groups, and things still more sinister and, it is hoped, more rare. The exclusions leave enough, I think, to warrant our concern.

The very nature of our accepted trial procedures generates forces that work against the judge's efforts to be neutral and detached. All of the several conditions and circumstances I plan to identify under this heading have in common a tendency to embroil the judge in the battle, to enlist him [or her] as an ally or to identify him as an enemy. Upon some reflection, however, I find these factors subdividing into two categories: those that cause the judge to take on combat-

---

From Marvin E. Frankel, "The Adversary Judge: The Experience of the Trial Judge," 54 *Texas Law Review* 465 (1976).

ive qualities and those that serve to frustrate or impede or visibly depreciate his duty of leadership toward truth. It seems convenient at any rate to divide the topic in this way.

The Judge Embattled

The supreme concern of the parties on trial, and therefore of counsel, is to win. Of course, the battle should be fought by the rules, but the goal is victory—not the triumph of "Justice" viewed in detachment, but triumph. The high objective of the defense lawyer on trial is acquittal—not an acquittal because the client is innocent, just an acquittal. To be reminded of the clichè about criminal defense lawyers who say they could not bear the responsibility of representing an innocent man is amusing, not startling. We know that the great (and desired, and expensive) defense lawyers are those believed to be most likely to achieve vindication for clients who are not innocent. . . .

The preeminence of the concern for victory is less total for the prosecutor, but it is not a subordinate matter either. Prosecutors seek convictions. Under the rules, which seem increasingly to be obeyed, they have other, broader obligations. But their goal on trial is a guilty verdict, and their behavior in court is oriented accordingly.

With partisan counsel fighting to win, and with the judge as umpire to enforce the rules of the fight, there might seem a priori no reason in the nature of the contest why the judge should himself be, or seem to be, or perceive himself as being drawn into the fray. The trial judge, likely to have moved to the bench from the ranks of advocates, may not start out wholly indisposed or unused to combat, but that progression is not unusual; all kinds of umpires are former contestants. The adversary trial, however, happens to be a game in which the role of umpire includes unorthodox features. Although it has no instant replays of particular events, its participants have a large stake in increasing the probability that the whole game be replayed, This possibility depends largely, of course, on whether the judicial umpire himself commits fouls—"errors," as we say—in the regulating of the contest. And this element is liable to cause the detachment of the trial judge to be tested, threatened, and sometimes impaired, if not entirely lost.

The "big cases," heavily populated with lawyers, heighten the tension. When the crucial question has been asked, or almost asked, the courtroom explodes as people spring up at the several tables shouting objections, usually loudly because they are in some haste and heat to cut off forbidden answers. All perhaps look somehow menacing from combined effects of tension, hostility to the questioner, and anticipated conflict. Viewed from the bench, the rising warriors sometimes have an assaultive look, which is surely a fantasy, but a palpable one to be not, I think, experienced exclusively by judicial paranoids. Whatever the individual emotional impact, the occasion is a testing time for the judge. It may be an easy chance or a hard one. If the latter, the sense of being challenged and opposed by the demand for a ruling is a recurrent experience.

Nobody doubts the range of adversary implications in our description of the judge as being "on trial." Among the more explicit references to trying the judge are the usually proper things lawyers must do or say "for the record." But propriety or no, the statement may have a cutting edge. When the lawyer says, "Just for the record, judge," depending upon the degree of the judge's self-confidence, the phrase may seem to mean simply "to preserve our rights." Or, perhaps it means "This is too much for you, judge, but it is to be your undoing above." And the lawyer may in fact intend that it be heard either way. Judge-baiting, if not one of the approved techniques, is, after all, not an utter rarity, although perhaps less common than some judges perceive it to be.

In viewing the judge as a probable adversary, the defendant manifests an attitude, and continues a tradition, that is ancient and far from dishonorable with us. Along with the prestige often attached to the office, along with the rituals of deference, we view trial judges with a deep strain of mistrust and hostility. We remember more trial judges in history as notorious than as notable. The hardy survival of the jury with us, as distinguished from its tendency to atrophy elsewhere, reflects a fundamental skepticism about judges. The Constitution itself teaches the lesson, commanding in effect that the fact findings of a jury be less vulnerable than a judge's. The low pay of judges, in a society prone to estimate people in dollars, is part of the same story.

The Judge Discomforted

Apart from the threats to his detachment and neutrality, the adversary battle before the jury is frequently conducted under conditions that entail a potential sense of frustration, even stultification, for the presiding judge. Each of the contestants seeks to win. For either or both, in part or in whole, the goal of victory may be inconsistent with the quest for truth, which represents the public goal the judge is commissioned to pursue. "The very premise of our adversary system of criminal justice is that partisan advocacy on both sides of a case will best promote the ultimate objective that the guilty be convicted and the innocent go free." If premises could be vindicated by reiteration, that one would by now have overwhelmed the skepticism it tends on its face to inspire. Whatever the case, the trial judge spends a good deal of his time solemnly watching clear, deliberate, entirely proper efforts by skilled professionals to block the attainment of "the ultimate objective."

When I say efforts are "clear" and "deliberate," I mean nothing less. This is not a jaundiced hunch; it is an open and shared professional understanding, concealed only from the jury. Often, the judge has been made explicitly aware before trial that the prosecution's assertions, though they will be contested at every step, are true. Less often, but often enough, the concession is made after trial, at sentencing or some other point when confession seems prudent or advantageous.

A whole class of examples arises in courts where plea bargaining is practiced. The bargaining, in which the judge frequently participates, starts from an understanding that the defendant has done approximately the wrong with which he is charged. In many cases, however, no deal is made. The defendant goes to trial. In the trial, the defense, by cross-examination and otherwise, fights to prevent demonstration of facts that were conceded before trial and are thus, in a sufficient and meaningful sense, known by the judge and counsel to be true.

Every trial judge could add illustrations from his own experience. I tender one here, perhaps more dramatic than routine, but apposite, I think, for our theme. A trial about two years ago involved a group of defendants charged with major dealings (multikilogram, hundreds of thousands of dollars) in heroin and cocaine. Important for both conspiracy and substantive counts was a suitcase that had been opened in a Toledo railroad baggage room and found to contain over five kilograms of heroin and a kilogram of cocaine. . . .

The motion was eventually denied, both because the quaint claim of retained title proved defective and because the Toledo search was held in any event to have been reasonable. But the points of particular interest here came later.

After other evidentiary hearings on pretrial motions adding to a total of eleven court days, we proceeded to a nineteen-day trial. While defendants did not take the stand, the considerable talents of numerous defense counsel were bent for four weeks on destroying any suggestion by any witness that would place their clients within miles at any time of any narcotics, including, of course, the Toledo shipment. Counsel for one of the erstwhile movants opened with the observation to the jury that there would "not be a shred of credible evidence," but only incredible assertions from "Individuals who are the scum of the earth." A chemist who offered the opinion, novel only to the jury, that the substances in the Toledo suitcase were heroin and cocaine was raked by cross-examination for some three hours, his experience tested, his veracity and motives questioned, the modesty of his academic rank (and the fact that he was a mere Ph.D., not an M.D.) being duly brought to his attention when it became apparent he had a tendency to irascibility.

Altogether, a total of forty-nine witnesses appeared. The jury heard over six hours of summation and a charge requiring (or at least lasting) nearly two hours. In deliberations extending over three days, including two nights of sequestration in a hotel, the jury called for testimony and exhibits reflecting questions, inter alia, that the movant-defendants had answered adversely to themselves, under oath, many weeks before. In the end, the defendants were convicted.

The purposes of and justifications for that four-week trial are familiar and (mostly) precious. The prosecution bears the burden of proof. Only lawful evidence is allowed. Defendants are presumed to be innocent, jurors are to search out the truth, but doubts are to be resolved in favor of the defense. Granted all that and more, our immediate subject is role strain. How does it all look and feel to the impartial judge, regulating the contest, waiting to see whether the jury arrives at findings he knows to be correct or is successfully kept from doing so? Judges vary, of course, so there is no single answer, not even for any single judge. . . .

"The jury is . . . an exciting experiment."

9.2 THE AMERICAN EXPERIMENT

Hans Zeisel and Harry Kalven, Jr.
Hans Zeisel is and Harry Kalven, Jr., was a professor
at the Law School, University of Chicago.

The Anglo-American jury is a remarkable political institution. It recruits a group of twelve [laypeople], chosen at random from the widest population; it convenes them for the purpose of the particular trial; it entrusts them with great official powers of decision; it permits them to carry on deliberations in secret and to report out their final judgment without giving reasons for it; and, after their momentary service has been completed, the state orders them to disband and return to private life.

The jury thus represents a deep commitment to the use of [laypeople] in the administration of justice, a commitment that finds its analogue in the widespread use of lay judges in the criminal courts of other countries. It opposes the cadre of professional, experienced judges with this transient, ever-changing, ever-inexperienced group of amateurs.

The jury is thus almost by definition an exciting experiment in the conduct of serious human affairs, and it is not surprising that, virtually from its inception, it has been the subject of deep controversy, attracting at once the most extravagant praise and the most harsh criticism.

As a matter of both theoretical interest and methodological convenience, we have studied the performance of the jury measured against the performance of the judge as a baseline. Our material is a massive sample of actual criminal jury trials conducted in the United States in recent years. For each of these trials we have the actual decision of the jury and a communication from the trial judge, telling how he [or she] would have disposed of that case had it been tried before him without a jury.

For one reason or another the jury feels, at times, that the defendant at the time of the trial has already been sufficiently punished so that the addition of any further punishment would be excessive. The readiest occasion is where the defendant himself is hurt as a consequence of the crime. In one case the defendant fires a shot into the family home of his estranged wife. The judge finds him guilty of shooting with intent to kill; the jury convicts only of the lesser charge

From Hans Zeisel and Harry Kalven, Jr., "The American Experiment," *Chicago Today*, 3 (Winter 1966), 3–35. Reprinted by permission of the University of Chicago.

of pointing and discharging a firearm. The decisive circumstance appears to be that the defendant's shot did not injure anyone, but when the brother-in-law shot back in self-defense, he seriously injured the defendant. The punished-enough theme comes through in the comment of the judge: "Defendant had long experience of marital strife with his wife. Jury felt since the only person hurt was defendant himself they could not punish him further. . . ."

Sometimes, in the jury's eyes, the defendant has been sufficiently punished by the death of a loved one. In a prosecution for negligent auto homicide, the victim is the intended bride of the defendant, a 21-year-old member of the Air Force. It is clear from the judge's description of the case that not only the jury but the parents of the girl feel the defendant has been punished enough by the event: "Her mother and father were character witnesses for the defendant, and he makes his home with them when not on duty. Defendant had never been in trouble and it was obvious that the family of the girl did not want him convicted . . . ."

Indeed the jury may respond to this sentiment even where the victim in the case is a stranger to the defendant. Thus, the jury acquits a young boy, a high school senior, who kills a ten-year-old boy while negligently using a rifle. The judge, after describing the boy defendant as of "high moral character, religious, clean-cut appearing," offers as explanation of the disagreement: "The jury felt that having the charge and killing on his conscience was sufficient punishment."

We get just a glimpse here of the profound but disturbing idea that at times the crime may be its own punishment.

The pattern of these cases indicates that the jury is again engaging in a delicate calculus. It is not simplistically treating every injury to every defendant in the course of a crime as punishment. It appears to weigh this factor only where the crime has been a crime of negligence, or where the crime has been limited to an attempt.

The punished-enough theme is found in a second group of cases where there has been long imprisonment while defendant awaited trial. It is customary for the judge in sentencing to give the defendant credit for the time he has already spent in jail; the jury, however, would at times not only give him credit but would set him free. The point is most obvious if the offense itself is considered trivial as in the case where the defendant was charged with stealing two pieces of lumber. He had already spent two months in jail and—"The jury felt sorry for the defendant because he had been in jail for over two months and the lumber allegedly stolen was worth $2.40."

The harm may, however, be quite serious. In a domestic quarrel, the defendant shoots and wounds his common-law wife so seriously that she is in the hospital for almost a year. The trial is not held until she is discharged, with the result that the defendant spends the interval in jail awaiting the trial. This circumstance seems to be a major factor in moving the jury to acquit.

In one set of circumstances the jury carries out the punished-enough theme a wild dimension further. The defendant is charged with rape of his ten-year-old daughter and at the first trial of the case is found guilty and sentenced to life imprisonment. On appeal, a new trial is granted with a change of venue. At the second trial, the jury hangs. The case is tried a third time, and it is for this third trial that we have the actual jury report. At this trial it is disclosed that the defendant has by now been in jail for 13 months. The extraordinary reaction of his third and last jury which acquits is set forth by the judge as follows: "They were out just 30 minutes. The jury took up a collection of $68 and gave it to the defendant after the case was over."

A final variation on the punished-enough theme arises when the defendant has been plagued by such misfortunes, dating from the time of the crime, that the jury feels life or Providence has already punished him sufficiently. This equity is illustrated in a case of income tax evasion, which brings to mind the story of Job. During the period for which the defendant, originally well-to-do, is charged with failing to file tax returns, he is subject to misfortunes [that] the judge inventories as follows:

> Defendant did not testify but the evidence shows that during the years in question his home burned, he was seriously injured, and his son was killed. Later he lost his leg, his wife became seriously ill, and several major operations were necessary. About three years before the trial, his wife gave birth to a premature child [who] was both blind and spastic. These, however, are only a portion of the calamities the defendant has suffered during the years he failed to file his income tax return. . . .

It is a commonplace that the American society is to an unusual degree not a single homogeneous culture; in a favorite word of social science, the society is pluralistic. Conceivably, the law might recognize cultural differences and apply different norms to subcultures within the society, as indeed British colonialism appears to have done on occasion. But only in rare instances has American law encountered this issue. The examples that come to mind are of religious sects such as the Mormons and the Quakers. In the case of the Mormons the law has forced them to accept the general standard of monogamy, while in the case of the Quakers, when the law recognized their distinctive claim, it did this in the form of a general exemption for conscientious objectors.

In a handful of disagreements the judges' explanations do seem to open suggestively onto this large theme of subculture. But while the judge's comments are insistent, there is a good deal of doubt that this time they succeed in isolating a special jury sentiment.

Not unexpectedly, the cases have a racial cast. In crimes of violence committed by Negroes against Negroes, or Indians against Indians, the jury is, as the judge sees it, moved at times to leniency because it views the defendant as not fully acculturated and, therefore, incapable of white standards of self-control. It scarcely needs mentioning that this explanation, uncongenial as it is to contemporary mood, tends to speak more in the language of contempt than that of tolerance.

In the end, the theme remains evanescent. The materials are sketchy and crossed with other interpretations. Thus, we do little more here than the reporting out of these cases.

In a case from the south where a Negro woman shoots and kills her husband, the judge would have given the death penalty on a finding of first-degree murder, the jury reduces the charge to first-degree manslaughter and the judge comments: "Negroes are not held to the same moral responsibility as white people. . . . Negroes kill each other without reason other than the immediate urge at the time. . . . Community regards the law as too severe for some Negro cases because of lack of moral sense."

In another case from the south where a Negro man and woman living in the same house get into a quarrel and the man kills her with a shotgun, the judge explains the disagreement in much the same way: "This verdict in my opinion is due somewhat to the fact that juries give much more latitude to colored folks than to white. They know how liable colored folks are to act on impulse by shooting and cutting. . . ."

The point may not be confined to Negroes. There is more than a suggestion of it in a homicide case where the judge, after giving other reasons for the disagreement, states: "None, except the complaining parties are Indians, and the jury cannot be excited about the fact one Indian kills another."

Despite the emphasis with which the judge's comments have been made there are substantial difficulties with accepting his subculture explanation. To begin with, there are not enough cases to persuade. The explanation is couched in simple general terms and requires only Negro parties to a crime of violence; yet we have many disagreement cases in intraracial crimes of violence [that] the judge explains on other grounds while keeping silent about the subculture theme. More troublesome, the few cases we do have here are largely instances of domestic violence between Negroes. We have already seen that the jury is sensitive to domestic tensions and is ready to treat its eruption into violence on generous analogy to self-defense. . . .

As a sort of postscript of dissatisfaction with this line of explanation, we may have one case too many: The defendant, a Negro, shoots the mother of his child. The jury finds murder in the first degree, and the judge comments that the verdict "was fully supported by the proof." But he would have found only second-degree murder, because the defendant was a Negro and the real reason was "just anger and resentment." He then goes on to say: "The ancestors of this defendant came from the jungle of Africa only a few generations ago. Society expected too much from him. He killed the woman because he had insufficient intelligence to solve his problem any other way." The power with which the judge puts this to explain his own verdict rounds out the doubt that we have located a distinctive jury sentiment.

This is perhaps the appropriate place to note that we originally expected the study to yield considerable evidence on whether or not the jury is color-blind. Actually it has been possible to collect only a few scattered findings. The Negro appears as defendant more frequently than the Negro share of the population would predict, although he elects jury trial proportionately. He is at some disadvantage in the quality of counsel, even when we take economic factors into account.

The Negro defendant, furthermore, is less likely to be seen as sympathetic, a factor established as a major influence on jury leniency. The data offer the suggestion that this is aggravated in interracial crimes. Finally, there is the possible offset, examined here, that in intraracial crimes the Negro may occasionally be the beneficiary of an unfriendly sentiment.

"I could have brought a book. A Russian novel."

9.3 JUROR FUROR

Geoffrey Norman

Geoffrey Norman is editor at large for *Forbes FYI*.

When you are called to jury duty, you are inclined to feel a little surge of self-importance along with a sense of pride that goes along with doing your duty. But it passes quickly. When called to participate in my first jury pool (a few months before listening to Cochran), I was warned to be at the courthouse promptly at 9 a.m. I live in the country (Vermont), and it is a forty-five minute drive from my home to the courthouse. I gave it an hour and a half just to be sure and bought the morning paper in case I was early and had some time to kill. I could have brought a book. A Russian novel.

I found a place to park—there were no designated spots for jurors as there were for all the judges and other members of the courthouse crowd. Jurors may be the anchor of all our liberties but that doesn't mean they rate parking privileges.

I located the clerk's office and announced myself. Once my name had been found on the list and a check mark entered next to it, I was asked if my employer was compensating me for my time spent doing jury duty. I said I was self-employed.

Well, the clerk asked, did I want to be compensated? The implication was, plainly, that a "yes" answer would put me in the company of welfare cheats and doctors who scam Medicare for millions.

I took the money anyway. I have no shame. It came to $30 a day, for sitting around and mainly doing nothing. Much less than the government pays its full-time employees for doing the same thing.

I was directed to a courtroom and told to wait there for instructions.

By nine o'clock, there were about thirty of us waiting in the courtroom. Some of these people became instant acquaintances and talked. Some, like me, read. A few women (old hands, I figured) did needlepoint.

From Geoffrey Norman, "Juror Furor," *The American Spectator,* March 1998.

Nine o'clock passed. Then nine-thirty. I finished my paper. At ten, nobody had bothered even to stick his head in the room and tell us that things were running late—which was self-evident—and apologize for the delay. The reason for this, it became clear, was that nobody was a damned bit sorry for making us wait or keeping us uninformed. We were jurors. It was our job to be treated with high-handed contempt, and we were being paid for it. Thirty bucks a day.

I went to the door and was stopped by a man who wore a uniform and carried a sidearm. He was so fat that the exertion of pulling the gun would have probably given him a coronary. His presence did not make me feel all that secure but, of course, he wasn't there to protect us; he was our jailer.

"Sorry," he said, "but you can't leave the room. We got lawyers and defendants out in the halls."

I said—politely, I thought—that I didn't quite understand. Defendants—people who were charged with crimes—were free to roam the halls. Jurors—those of us doing our civic duty for a cool thirty bucks a day—had to be confined to a room with an armed guard at the door.

The fat man with the Glock gave me a look that pretty much summed up what the courthouse gang thought of jurors.

"Well," I said, "when are we going to get started?"

"When the judge gets ready."

It was then that I began to understand that the judicial system runs at its own, leisurely pace; one that is not inconvenienced, like the rest of the world, by deadlines. Lawyers and judges take as much time as they feel they need. They will not be hurried. Which explains, no doubt, why it takes a decade or more to execute a convicted murderer.

Jurors' time might be wasted but—to use the punch line of an old joke—what is time to a pig?

I went back to my uncomfortable seat and my newspaper. I had been reduced to reading the bridge column.

Still, nobody came to tell us anything.

At 10:40, the courtroom was opened. Bailiffs entered and a couple of men in dark suits took places at tables in the front of the courtroom. The prosecutor and the lawyer for the defendant. We all knew that from watching the television.

The defendant also took his place. He was a surly looking young man who had dressed in his newest jeans and cleanest sweatshirt for the occasion.

The bailiff instructed us to rise. The judge entered and told us to be seated. More and more, I felt like I was back in kindergarten.

Over the next half hour or so, the judge and the lawyers went through the motions of a plea and sentencing for the man in the stylish sweatshirt who had been accused of beating up his girlfriend. While those of us in the jury pool had been confined to our room, his lawyers and the judge had worked out a guilty plea and a suspended sentence. This, I was told by a man who'd done several tours of jury duty, is pretty much routine. Defendants wait until the last possible moment to deal. Which often means jurors are not needed.

The deal was done. The defendant and his lawyer left the courtroom. The bailiff called the next case. Another scruffy defendant walked up to the front table, accompanied by his lawyer, who then asked the judge to continue the case. The judge didn't have a problem with this. What's a couple of months, after all, against the imperatives of justice?

The case was rescheduled.

By now it was 11:45, and since court normally recessed for lunch at 12:00, the judge decided there was no point in working for a mere fifteen minutes. He called recess.

I ate chicken and dumplings at the local diner and was back in my assigned seat at one o'clock sharp. No sign of the judge.

He finally showed at about 2:40, and, once again, we all stood up when he entered the room, as though we were honored.

But this time it looked like we might get a case. We had a defendant who wasn't going to cop a plea. A stocky, middle-aged man with the look of someone who had done hard jobs for small pay, he was seated at his table, alone, since he had decided to act as his own lawyer. As our names were read off, we took our places in the jury box. Then the prosecutor and the judge asked us the predictable questions. Did any of us know the defendant? Did any of us have relatives on the police force? Had any of us been the victims of a crime? The defendant asked if any of us thought that kids should not be held accountable for their actions. It was the one question that contained any hint of what the trial would be about or any element of originality.

We made it through the questions in a little less than an hour. Then before the trial could actually begin, the judge called another recess.

"The guy must have a prostate problem," one of my fellow jurors said.

Twenty minutes later, the first witness was called.

It was now after three. Like the rest of the jurors, I was eager and impatient to do some justice. What we got was a case involving some stolen bottles.

The essentials of the case were as follows: A couple of kids—young teenage boys—were on their way to school one morning and saw some returnable bottles stacked outside a neighbor's trailer. Needing some cash so they could play the video games, they decided to "take" the bottles and cash them in for the deposit. The man who owned the trailer—and the bottles—and was now sitting in front of us as a criminal defendant, happened to look out of his window and see the theft in progress. He went out and gave chase. The boys dropped the bottles and split up. The man chased one of them through the neighborhood and across a city street. The kid went into an apartment building to hide, but the man followed, cornered him, and gave the kid the business.

As jurors, our job was to consider the case against the man whose bottles the kids had tried to steal. He was charged with recklessly endangering the kid when he chased him across the street and with menacing him when he caught up with him in the apartment building and got in his face.

The prosecutor seemed to read my mind.

"The state," he intoned in his opening remarks, "does not condone the theft of private property. But that is not what this case is about. This case is about a defendant who took the law into his own hands. . . ."

The judicial system, when it is not on break, takes a very dim view of anyone who does this. It reacts pretty much the same way any monopoly does when faced with competition. It sets out to annihilate its rival.

The defendant said that he would attempt to prove to the jury that he had not threatened anyone, that he had done what anyone in his shoes would have done, and that his conduct had actually been fairly restrained.

After these opening arguments, we heard from the cop who had arrested the defendant, a couple of women who had called to complain about the disturbance, and the boy whom the defendant had chased. The prosecutor made his case smoothly. The defendant, who had the impertinence to act as his own lawyer, was repeatedly interrupted by the judge and told to frame his questions properly.

"The bottles were clearly mine, right, anybody would know that?"

"Objection."

"Sir, I must remind you again that your questions must be framed in such a way that the witness can respond as to matters of fact."

"Sorry, Your Honor. I'll try again. Is it true that the bottles were found on the ground, approximately 200 yards from my trailer?"

"Yes."

And on it went.

The star witness, of course, was the kid. The prosecutor stressed the chase. The defendant, when his time came, got the kid to admit that, yeah, he and his buddy knew those bottles didn't belong to them, but they had decided to take them anyway. And, yeah, he'd heard somebody yelling at him to stop, but he kept running anyway. And, no, he hadn't been hit when he was cornered in the building. Just yelled at and cuffed a little, maybe.

"Do you recognize the man who yelled at you?"

"Yeah. It was you."

I had my mind made up even before the judge spent thirty minutes or so telling us what our duties were and how we had a solemn duty to find according to the law and blah, blah, blah. He spoke very slowly, as though we might not understand the epistemological subtlety of "reasonable doubt."

Who does? According to polls, two-thirds of the people on any jury believe in alien abductions. So what is reasonable? For that matter, what is doubt?

I had no doubt when I walked into the jury room.

Neither did two other jurors. Both men. We all believed that the defendant ought to get a medal. He had probably done the kid a favor by throwing a scare into him. If the defendant had called the police to report the theft and the police had been able to find the boy and charge him, he would have been delivered into the hands of the juvenile justice system where he would have learned that nothing much happens to you if you steal someone's property. You will be counseled.

The three of us made our argument. The other jurors—all but one, women—wanted to convict the defendant. "Because he did break the law," one of them said.

We argued, back and forth. And slowly, our side wore their side down. Our most persuasive argument was experience. We all knew about boys who did worse than the kid who stole the bottles and never suffered. But more than that, we all had our own immediate experience with the judicial system—our day of jury duty. If this was the way they ran things, my side argued, then we needed more vigilantes.

After an hour or so, we prevailed in a clear cut case of jury nullification. According to the judge's instructions, we should have found the defendant guilty. We went with justice instead of the law.

The judge thanked us, with some distaste. And then he spoke to us from the heart. If we felt inconvenienced by the delays and the inefficiencies of the system, he said, there was an easy remedy. Tell your legislator to vote for more money for the courts. The problem was overwork.

He said it with a straight face. And then adjourned the court. We had actually worked about four hours of a nine-hour day. Like the O. J. jury we had returned a flawed verdict, based largely on our resentments.

We were, I fear, increasingly typical.

"You are not interested in the morals of the juror. If a man is instinctively kind and sympathetic, take him."

9.4 HOW TO PICK A JURY

Clarence Darrow

Clarence Darrow (1857–1938) served as defense attorney in the Leopold and Loeb trial (1924) and the Scopes "Monkey" trial (1925), among many others.

In spite of the power that the courts exercise over the verdict of the jury, still the finding of the twelve men is very important, sometimes conclusive. It goes without saying that lawyers always do their utmost to get men on the jury who are apt to decide in favor of their clients. It is not the experience of jurors, neither is it their brain power that is the potent influence in their decisions. A skillful lawyer does not tire himself hunting for learning or intelligence in the box; if he knows much about man and his making, he knows that all beings act from emotions and instincts, and that reason is not a motive factor. If deliberation counts for anything, it is to retard decision. The nature of the man himself is the element that determines the juror's bias for or against his fellow-man. Assuming that a juror is not a half-wit, his intellect can always furnish fairly good reasons for following his instincts and emotions. Many irrelevant issues in

From Clarence Darrow, "How to Pick a Jury," *Esquire* (May 1936). Available on the World Wide Web at.

choosing jurors are not so silly as they seem. Matters that apparently have nothing to do with the discussion of a case often are of the greatest significance.

In the last analysis, most jury trials are contests between the rich and poor. If the case concerns money, it is apt to be a case of damages for injuries of some sort claimed to have been inflicted by someone. These cases are usually defended by insurance companies, railroads, or factories. If a criminal case, it is practically always the poor who are on trial. The most important point to learn is whether the prospective juror is humane. This must be discovered in more or less devious ways. As soon as "the court" sees what you want, he almost always blocks the game. Next to this, in having more or less bearing on the question, is the nationality, politics, and religion of the person examined for the jury. If you do not discover this, all your plans may go awry. Whether you are handling a damage suit, or your client is charged with the violation of law, his attorney will try to get the same sort of juror. . . .

[L]et us assume that we represent one of "the underdogs" because of injuries received, or because of an indictment brought by what the prosecutors name themselves, "the state." Then what sort of men will we seek? An Irishman is called into the box for examination. There is no reason for asking about his religion; he is Irish; that is enough. We may not agree with his religion, but it matters not, his feelings go deeper than any religion. You should be aware that he is emotional, kindly and sympathetic. If he is chosen as a juror, his imagination will place him in the dock; really, he is trying himself. You would be guilty of malpractice if you got rid of him, except for the strongest reasons.

An Englishman is not so good as an Irishman, but still, he has come through a long tradition of individual rights, and is not afraid to stand alone; in fact, he is never sure that he is right unless the great majority is against him. The German is not so keen about individual rights except where they concern his own way of life; liberty is not a theory, it is a way of living. Still, he wants to do what is right, and he is not afraid. He has not been among us long, his ways are fixed by his race, his habits are still in the making. We need inquire no further. If he is a Catholic, then he loves music and art; he must be emotional, and will want to help you; give him a chance.

If a Presbyterian enters the jury box and carefully rolls up his umbrella, and calmly and critically sits down, let him go. He is cold as the grave; he knows right from wrong, although he seldom finds anything right. He believes in John Calvin and eternal punishment. Get rid of him with the fewest possible words before he contaminates the others; unless you and your clients are Presbyterians you probably are a bad lot, and even though you may be a Presbyterian, your client most likely is guilty.

If possible, the Baptists are more hopeless than the Presbyterians [are]. They, too, are apt to think that the real home of all outsiders is Sheol, and you do not want them on the jury, and the sooner they leave the better. The Methodists are worth considering; they are nearer the soil. Their religious emotions can be transmuted into love and charity. They are not half bad; even though they will not take a drink, they really do not need it so much as some of their competitors for the seat next to the throne. If chance sets you down between a Methodist and a Baptist, you will move toward the Methodist to keep warm.

Beware of the Lutherans, especially the Scandinavians; they are almost always sure to convict. Either a Lutheran or Scandinavian is unsafe, but if both in one, plead your client guilty and go down the docket. He learns about sinning and punishing from the preacher, and dares not doubt. A person who disobeys must be sent to hell; he has God's word for that.

As to Unitarians, Universalists, Congregationalists, Jews, and other agnostics, don't ask them too many questions; keep them anyhow, especially Jews and agnostics. It is best to inspect a Unitarian, or a Universalist, or a Congregationalist with some care, for they may be prohibitionists; but never the Jews and the real agnostics! And do not, please, accept a prohibitionist; he is too solemn and holy and dyspeptic. He knows your client would not have been indicted unless he were a drinking man, and anyone who drinks is guilty of something, probably much worse than he is charged with, although it is not set out in the indictment. Neither would he have employed you as his lawyer had he not been guilty.

I have never experimented with Christian Scientists; they are much too serious for me. Somehow, solemn people seem to think that pleasure is wicked. Only the gloomy and dyspeptic can be trusted to convict. Shakespeare knew: "Yon Cassius has a lean and hungry look; he thinks too much; such men are dangerous." You may defy all the rest of the rules if you can get a man who laughs. Few things in this world are of enough importance to warrant considering them seriously. So, by all means, choose a man who laughs. A juror who laughs hates to find anyone guilty. Never take a wealthy man on a jury. He will convict, unless the defendant is accused of violating the anti-trust law, selling worthless stocks or bonds, or something of that kind. Next to the Board of Trade, for him, the penitentiary is the most important of all public buildings. These imposing structures stand for capitalism. Civilization could not possibly exist without them. Don't take a man because he is a "good" man; this means nothing. You should find out what he is good for. Neither should a man be accepted because he is a bad sort. There are too many ways of being good or bad. If you are defending, you want imaginative individuals. You are not interested in the morals of the juror. If a man is instinctively kind and sympathetic, take him.

". . . the technique raises serious doubts about the very integrity of the jury system."

9.5 SCIENCE: THREATENING THE JURY TRIAL

Amitai Etzioni

Amitai Etzioni is Director of the Center for Policy Research, Washington, D.C.

Man has taken a new bite from the apple of knowledge, and it is doubtful whether we will all be better for it. This time it is not religion or the family that [is] being disturbed by the new knowledge but that venerable institution of being judged by a jury of one's peers. The jury's impartiality is threatened because defense attorneys have discovered that by using social science techniques, they can manipulate the composition of juries to significantly increase the likelihood that their clients will be acquitted.

The problem is not that one may disagree with a particular jury verdict that has resulted in such cases; enough different defendants have been freed with the help of social science jury-stacking to disturb observers on all sides. The trouble is that the technique raises serious doubts about the very integrity of the jury system, that it increases the advantage of rich and prominent defendants over poor and obscure ones and, most ominously, that it may prompt the state to start hiring social scientists of its own. It would seem only a matter of time before prosecutors, with all the resources at their disposal, get fed up with losing cases partly because the defense has scientifically loaded panels with sympathetic jurors.

Prosecutors have already had to swallow a number of such defeats. A team headed by sociologist Jay Schulman and psychologist Richard Christie, for example, took an active role in selecting juries [that] discharged radical defendants in the Harrisburg Seven case, the Camden Twenty-Eight trial over a draft-office raid, and the Gainesville Eight case involving Vietnam Veterans Against the War; Schulman is now working in Buffalo, N.Y., for the Attica defendants. A team of black psychologists, moreover, helped choose the jury that acquitted Angela Davis, and nothing of late has done more to publicize scientific intervention in jury selection than the Mitchell-Stans trial in New York.[1]

In that case, helping to choose the jury was Marty Herbst, a "communication" specialist versed in social science techniques. He advised the defense to seek a jury of working-class persons, of Catholic background, neither poor nor rich ("average income of $8,000 to $10,000"), and readers of New York's *Daily News*. To be avoided were the college-educated, Jews, and readers of the *New York Post* and the *New York Times*. These sociological characteristics are widely associated with conservative politics, respect for authority, and suspicion of the media.

In the original jury, the defense succeeded in getting eleven out of twelve jurors who matched the specifications. By a fluke, the twelfth juror became ill and was replaced by another who, though college educated, was a conservative banker, thus completing the set.

Amitai Etzioni, "Science: Threatening the Jury Trial," *Washington Post*, May 20, 1974. Reprinted with permission. © The Washington Post.

[1] *The trial of former Attorney General John Mitchell and Maurice Stans, one of Richard Nixon's chief fundraisers, for offenses growing out of the Watergate scandals. The jury acquitted both men, although Mitchell was later convicted after another trial on different charges. —Eds.*

Interviewing Acquaintances

The more elaborate ways in which social science can help select acquittal-prone juries are illustrated by the Schulman-Christie team's work in the trial of Indian militants at Wounded Knee.

As described in a May, 1973 report, the team first assembled a sociological profile of the community through interviews with 576 persons chosen at random from voter registration lists. The interviews allowed the research team to cross-tabulate such characteristics as occupation and education with attitudes favorable toward the defense—especially toward Indians—and to select out the best "predictor variables." Such analysis was needed because people of the same social background hold different attitudes in different parts of the country; hence a generalized sociological model would not suffice. (In Harrisburg, where the Berrigan trial was held, for example, women proved more friendly toward the defense than men, but the reverse was true in Gainesville.)

Next, observers were placed in the courtroom to "psych out" prospective jurors, using anything from the extent to which they talked with other prospective jurors to their mode of dress. (In the Angela Davis case, handwriting experts analyzed the signatures of prospective jurors.)

Information gained in this way was compared to what the computer predicted about the same "type" of person, based on the interview data [that] had been fed into it. This double reading was further checked, especially when the two sources of information did not concur, by field investigators who interviewed acquaintances of the prospective jurors.

How Many Challenges?

Such information becomes more potent in the hands of defense lawyers the more challenges there are and the more unevenly the challenges are distributed. The number is important because the more persons one can challenge, the more one can select a jury to one's liking. The unevenness is important to prevent the other side from applying the same procedures and nullifying one's work.

The number of challenges varies with the seriousness of the offense and from state to state. A common pattern is that if the prospective penalty is death, each side receives thirty challenges, plus three for each of four alternate jurors. If ten years' imprisonment is at stake, the respective numbers are twenty and two, and so on down the scale. The original intention was to allow the fairest selections in the weightiest cases. But with the introduction of social science into jury picking, the unwitting result is that the more serious the trial, the more jury-stacking is allowed.

Similarly, uneven challenges are introduced, at the judge's discretion, to make up for other imbalances. While a judge can severely limit the challenges on both sides to avoid a long jury selection process, this significantly increases the chances of having any convictions that might be overturned by a higher court on the ground of a biased jury—and reversals are considered a blot on a judge's record. In the Mitchell-Stans case, the judge allowed the defense twenty peremptory challenges, the prosecution eight, to make up for adverse publicity preceding the trial. This obviously helped the defense lawyers secure the kind of jury they favored.

Social scientists, of course, did not invent the idea of using challenges to help get a favorable jury. But until recently lawyers commonly could not use much more than rules of thumb, hunches, or experience to guide their challenges. As Justice John M. Murtagh put it: "One human being cannot read the mind of another." The lawyers on both sides, moreover, were more or less equal in their ability to exercise this kind of homespun social psychology.

The new methods are quite a bit more accurate, though fortunately they are far from foolproof. People do not always act out their predispositions. Social science data is statistical, not absolute. At best survey techniques, even when supplemented with psychological analysis, can produce only "probabilistic" profiles, not guaranteed results. At the Berrigan trial, two of the defense attorneys' careful selections—one a woman with four conscientious objector sons—held out for a guilty verdict on the conspiracy charge, causing a hung jury.

Nevertheless, the recent spate of acquittals demonstrates that the impact can be considerable and that, on the average, the method will work well. Hence we are surely in for more frequent use of the technique.

It Takes Money

It might be said that soon both sides to all trials will be equipped with the same capability, and that so long as the granting of an uneven number of challenges is curbed, giving both sides similar selection power, the edge of the social science helpers will be dulled. But the extent to which this takes place will be limited by the costliness of the technique.

Radical defendants have benefited from the free labor of scores of volunteers and the time donations of high-powered consultants, though even they needed expensive computers. As Howard Moore, Jr., Angela Davis's chief counsel, put it: "We can send men to the moon, but not everyone can afford to go. Every unpopular person who becomes a defendant will not have the resources we used in the Davis case." The Mitchell and Stans bills for their social science helpers may run to a five-digit figure.

Clearly, the average defendant cannot avail himself of such aid. Therefore, the net effect of the new technique, as is so often the case with new technology, will be to give a leg up to the wealthy or those who command a dedicated following. This is hardly what the founders of the American judicial system had in mind.

It might also be argued that juries are, on the average, far from representative anyhow; studies do show that too many higher income, higher-educated people do not serve, that juries end up disproportionately filled with "housewives, clerical workers, craftsmen, and retired persons." Furthermore, the legal defense of those who can pay or otherwise attract top talent has always been much better than that of the average defendant. But a society moving toward greater justice would seek to correct these flaws, not to accentuate them.

Also, it should be noted that up to now the procedure has been used, as far as we know, solely by defense attorneys. The state has not provided any district attorneys with social science teams and computers. However, what would happen if the state did resort to systematic reliance on such techniques? Could any but the wealthiest defendants then compete with the state?

No Good Remedies

Unfortunately, one cannot unbite the apple of knowledge. Even sadder is that we see here, as we have seen so often before, that attempting to contain the side-effects of the application of science is costly, at best partially effective, and far from uncontroversial itself. To put it more succinctly, there seem to be no half-good, let alone good, remedies.

Probably the best place to start is with prospective jurors. If fewer persons were excused from jury duty, the universe from which jurors are drawn would be more representative of the community and, to a degree, less easy to manipulate. Next, serious consideration could be given to reducing challenges, especially peremptory ones. This approach, though, constitutes not only a wide departure from tradition but limits the possibility of uncovering prejudicial attitudes in would-be jurors.

More powerful but even more problematic is to extend the ban on tampering with the jury to all out-of-court investigations of prospective jurors. It could be defined as a serious violation of law to collect data about prospective jurors, to investigate their handwriting, to interview their neighbors and the like, and any discovery of such data-gathering could be grounds for a mistrial. This would not eliminate the lawyers' courtroom use of sociology and psychology or the usefulness of community profiles based on studies of citizens at large. But it could curb the more sophisticated application of those techniques which require homing in on the characteristics of particular jurors.

Another potent but controversial answer is for the judge alone to be allowed to question and remove prospective jurors. In this way the judge could seek both an open-minded jury and one which represents a cross section of the community, not sociologically loaded dice. To the extent that judges themselves are free of social bias, this would probably work quite well. However, since jury selection has some effect on the outcome of each case, such a relatively active role by the judge flies in the face of the prevalent Anglo-Saxon tradition, according to which the judge is a neutral referee between the sides, not a third party. The challenges, though, could become the task of a specialist attached to the courts.

The most radical remedy would be to follow Britain's lead and restrict the conditions under which citizens are entitled to a jury trial. (In Britain only 2 to 3 percent of the cases still go to a jury.) Moreover, the jury is considered by many to be a major cause of rising court costs and delays in cases coming to trial. Nor is there any compelling evidence that trial by jury is fairer than trial by judges. These are hardly the days, though, in which reforms entailing less participation by the people and greater concentration of power in the hands of the elected or appointed officials are likely to be either very popular or wise.

But until one remedy or another is applied, the state will almost surely have to do its own research, if only to even the odds. District attorneys or U.S. attorneys cannot be expected to stand by doing nothing while defendants in the most serious cases buy themselves a significant edge in trial after trial. The champions of the technique will have to realize that the days when it could be reserved for their favorite defendants will soon be over.

"It is safe to say that scientific jury selection works; juror characteristics do influence the decisions they make."

9.6 THE LIMITS OF SCIENTIFIC JURY SELECTION

Michael Saks

Michael Saks is Professor of Law and Psychology at the University of Iowa.

[T]he defense of the scientific jury selection might begin by pointing out that it is thoroughly legal. Prospective jurors are not themselves approached or tampered with. They are merely compared to statistical profiles of the population from which they are drawn. They are questioned only during voir dire, and only to the extent permitted by the trial judge, as has been the way for generations. All that has changed is that lawyers can now know the hidden meaning of the answers and of jurors' background characteristics.

The practice of voir dire and of challenging jurors was not invented by [scholars]. [I]t has been part of the jury system for centuries. And for those centuries lawyers have sought to impanel the most favorable possible juries for their clients. This has always been widely regarded as a proper goal for the lawyer. Why should the fact that he has finally been given the means to achieve that goal be so objectionable? If the goal was good, why has the ability to actually achieve it become bad? . . .

[T]he goal of jury selection is not, I think, an unwise one. The intent is to impanel an impartial jury, that is, a jury whose members do not have biases that would make them unable to fairly weigh the evidence. Jurors are supposed to reach a verdict shaped by the weight of the evidence and not by the decision-makers' biases. The strategy for achieving that goal—allowing both advocates some opportunity to exclude from the jury persons thought to be biased against their side—also seems to me a wise and workable one. Scientific jury selection can add substantially to the achievement of that goal. Instead of guessing at who will be biased and will therefore not respond impartially to the evidence, lawyers can make informed judgments. If both sides have social science help, each will more effectively exclude jurors favorable to the other side, and the

Michael Saks, "The Limits of Scientific Jury Selection," 17 *Jurimetrics Journal* 3 (1976).

final panel will consist of the neutral jurors, the very ones who will be most able to do what a jury is intended to do. Thus, juror attitudes and personality would play a minimal role in determining the outcome of the trial. Evidence would be permitted to play the greatest possible role, which is how it was always supposed to be. Thus, scientific jury selection would make the goal of impartial jury decisions more attainable than has ever before been possible. . . .

I have saved for last what is perhaps the most interesting reason for not worrying excessively about scientific jury selection: the empirical reason. No evidence exists to support the apparently widely held belief that scientific jury selection is a powerful tool. What has most people upset about the technique is the fact that no one who has used it has lost a case. By the usual standards for evaluating empirical evidence, the same standards used by the social and behavioral scientists who developed the basic principles for the technique, this seemingly impressive evidence is really no evidence at all. The venerated scientific method usually calls for a control group, that is, a comparison group to tell you what an observation really means. To elucidate, suppose there were a control group. Suppose each of the cases had been tried before two juries—one selected the scientific way and one selected the old way. We could then compare the verdicts delivered by the scientific juries with those delivered by the conventional juries (the control juries.) We know that all of the scientifically selected juries refused to convict. What would the conventionally selected juries have done? The answer to this question is absolutely essential to an assessment of how effective scientific jury selection is or even whether it works at all. Without such comparisons it simply is impossible to know. If a significant number of control juries convicted we would know that the use of scientific jury selection techniques helped the defense effort.

If all of the conventional juries also refused to convict, we would know that scientific jury selection offered no help to the defense in those cases. . . .

[A] balanced assessment of the effectiveness of scientific jury selection, based on what is generally known about human decision making and on the data offered by the studies that have been done is, I believe, the following. It is safe to say that scientific jury selection "works"; juror characteristics do influence the decisions they make. But it is evidence that that determines the outcome of trials, rather than the characteristics of the jurors. If the evidence against a defendant is very strong or very weak, it isn't going to matter who is on the jury. If the evidence is close, then the jury selection could make the difference. One wouldn't be wasting money or time if he employed scientific jury selection, but if he did so at the expense of building a strong case out of evidence, he would be making a mistake. In cases where the evidence is close or ambiguous, scientific jury selection would be especially helpful.

*"There is an increasing perception that some African-American jurors
vote to acquit black defendants for racial reasons, sometimes explained as
the juror's desire not to send another black man to jail. There is
considerable disagreement over whether it is appropriate
for a black juror to do so."*

9.7 BLACK JURORS: RIGHT TO ACQUIT?

Paul Butler

Paul Butler is Associate Professor of Law
at the George Washington University Law School.

In 1990 I was a Special Assistant United States Attorney in the District of
Columbia. I prosecuted people accused of misdemeanor crimes, mainly the
drug and gun cases that overwhelm the local courts of most American cities. As
a Federal prosecutor, I represented the United States of America and used that
power to put people, mainly African-American men, in prison. I am also an
African-American man. During that time, I made two discoveries that profoundly changed the way I viewed my work as a prosecutor and my responsibilities as a black person.

The first discovery occurred during a training session for new assistants
conducted by experienced prosecutors. We rookies were informed that we
would lose many of our cases, despite having persuaded a jury beyond a reasonable doubt that the defendant was guilty. We would lose because some black
jurors would refuse to convict black defendants who they knew were guilty.

The second discovery was related to the first but was even more unsettling.
It occurred during the trial of Marion Barry, then the second-term mayor of the
District of Columbia. Barry was being prosecuted by my office for drug possession and perjury. I learned, to my surprise, that some of my fellow African-
American prosecutors hoped that the mayor would be acquitted, despite the
fact that he was obviously guilty of at least one of the charges—an FBI videotape plainly showed him smoking crack cocaine. These black prosecutors
wanted their office to lose its case because they believed that the prosecution of
Barry was racist.

There is an increasing perception that some African-American jurors vote to
acquit black defendants for racial reasons, sometimes explained as the juror's
desire not to send another black man to jail. There is considerable disagreement
over whether it is appropriate for a black juror to do so. I now believe that, for
pragmatic and political reasons, the black community is better off when some

Paul Butler, "Black Jurors: Right to Acquit?" *Harper's Magazine* (December 1995). Adapted from the
Yale Law Journal (December 1995).

nonviolent lawbreakers remain in the community rather than go to prison. The decision as to what kind of conduct by African Americans ought to be punished is better made by African Americans, based on their understanding of the costs and benefits to their community, than by the traditional criminal justice process, which is controlled by white lawmakers and white law enforcers. Legally, African-American jurors who sit in judgment of African-American accused persons have the power to make that decision. Considering the costs of law enforcement to the black community, and the failure of white lawmakers to come up with any solutions to black antisocial conduct other than incarceration, it is, in fact, the moral responsibility of black jurors to emancipate some guilty black outlaws.

Why would a black juror vote to let a guilty person go free? Assuming the juror is a rational, self-interested actor, she must believe that she is better off with the defendant out of prison than in prison. But how could any rational person believe that about a criminal?

Imagine a country in which a third of the young male citizens are under the supervision of the criminal justice system—either awaiting trial, in prison, or on probation or parole. Imagine a country in which two-thirds of the men can anticipate being arrested before they reach age thirty. Imagine a country in which there are more young men in prison than in college.

The country imagined above is a police state. When we think of a police state, we think of a society whose fundamental problem lies not with the citizens of the state but rather with the form of government, and with the powerful elites in whose interest the state exists. Similarly, racial critics of American criminal justice locate the problem not with the black prisoners but with the state and its actors and beneficiaries.

The black community also bears very real costs by having so many African Americans, particularly males, incarcerated or otherwise involved in the criminal justice system. These costs are both social and economic, and they include the large percentage of black children who live in female-headed, single-parent households; a perceived dearth of men "eligible" for marriage; the lack of male role models for black children, especially boys; the absence of wealth in the black community; and the large unemployment rate among black men.

According to a recent *USA Today*/CNN/Gallup poll, 66 percent of blacks believe that the criminal justice system is racist, and only 32 percent believe it is not racist. Interestingly, other polls suggest that blacks also tend to be more worried about crime than whites; this seems logical when one considers that blacks are more likely to be victims of crime. This enhanced concern, however, does not appear to translate to black support for tougher enforcement of criminal law. For example, substantially fewer blacks than whites support the death penalty, and many more blacks than whites were concerned with the potential racial consequences of the strict provisions of last year's crime bill. Along with significant evidence from popular culture, these polls suggest that a substantial portion of the African-American community sympathizes with racial critiques of the criminal justice system.

African-American jurors who endorse these critiques are in a unique position to act on their beliefs when they sit in judgment of a black defendant. As jurors, they have the power to convict the accused person or to set him free. May the responsible exercise of that power include voting to free a black defendant who the juror believes is guilty? The answer is "yes" based on the legal doctrine known as jury nullification.

Jury nullification occurs when a jury acquits a defendant who it believes is guilty of the crime with which he is charged. In finding the defendant not guilty, the jury ignores the facts of the case and/or the judge's instructions regarding the law. Instead, the jury votes its conscience.

The prerogative of juries to nullify has been part of English and American law for centuries. There are well-known cases from the Revolutionary War era when American patriots were charged with political crimes by the British crown and acquitted by American juries. Black slaves who escaped to the North and were prosecuted for violation of the Fugitive Slave Law were freed by Northern juries with abolitionist sentiments. Some Southern juries refused to punish white violence against African Americans, especially black men accused of crimes against white women.

The Supreme Court has officially disapproved of jury nullification but has conceded that it has no power to prohibit jurors from engaging in it; the Bill of Rights does not allow verdicts of acquittal to be reversed, regardless of the reason for the acquittal. Criticism of nullification has centered on its potential for abuse. The criticism suggests that when twelve members of a jury vote their conscience instead of the law, they corrupt the rule of law and undermine the democratic principles that made the law.

There is no question that jury nullification is subversive of the rule of law. Nonetheless, most legal historians agree that it was morally appropriate in the cases of the white American revolutionaries and the runaway slaves. The issue, then, is whether African Americans today have the moral right to engage in this same subversion.

Most moral justifications of the obligation to obey the law are based on theories of "fair play." Citizens benefit from the rule of law; that is why it is just that they are burdened with the requirement to follow it. Yet most blacks are aware of countless historical examples in which African Americans were not afforded the benefit of the rule of law: think, for example, of the existence of slavery in a republic purportedly dedicated to the proposition that all men are created equal, or the law's support of state-sponsored segregation even after the Fourteenth Amendment guaranteed blacks equal protection. That the rule of law ultimately corrected some of the large holes in the American fabric is evidence more of its malleability than its goodness; the rule of law previously had justified the holes.

If the rule of law is a myth, or at least not valid for African Americans, the argument that jury nullification undermines it loses force. The black juror is simply another actor in the system, using her power to fashion a particular outcome. The juror's act of nullification—like the act of the citizen who dials 911 to report Ricky but not Bob, or the police officer who arrests Lisa but not Mary, or the prosecutor who charges Kwame but not Brad, or the judge who finds that Nancy was illegally entrapped but Verna was not—exposes the indeterminacy of law but does not in itself create it.

A similar argument can be made regarding the criticism that jury nullification is antidemocratic. This is precisely why many African Americans endorse it; it is perhaps the only legal power black people have to escape the tyranny of the majority. Black people have had to beg white decision makers for most of the rights they have: the right not to be slaves, the right to vote, the right to attend an integrated school. Now black people are begging white people to preserve programs that help black children to eat and black businesses to survive. Jury nullification affords African Americans the power to determine justice for themselves, in individual cases, regardless of whether white people agree or even understand. At this point, African-Americans should ask themselves whether the operation of the criminal law system in the United States advances the interests of black people. If it does not, the doctrine of jury nullification affords African-American jurors the opportunity to exercise the authority of the law over some African-American criminal defendants. In essence, black people can "opt out" of American criminal law.

How far should they go—completely to anarchy, or is there someplace between here and there that is safer than both? I propose the following: African-American jurors should approach their work cognizant of its political nature and of their prerogative to exercise their power in the best interests of the black community. In every case, the juror should be guided by her view of what is "just." (I have more faith, I should add, in the average black juror's idea of justice than I do in the idea that is embodied in the "rule of law.")

In cases involving violent malum in se (inherently bad) crimes, such as murder, rape, and assault, jurors should consider the case strictly on the evidence presented, and if they believe the accused person is guilty, they should so vote. In cases involving nonviolent, malum prohibitum (legally proscribed) offenses, including "victimless" crimes such as narcotics possession, there should be a presumption in favor of nullification. Finally, for nonviolent, malum in se crimes, such as theft or perjury, there need be no presumption in favor of nullification, but it ought to be an option the juror considers. A juror might vote for acquittal, for example, when a poor woman steals from Tiffany's but not when the same woman steals from her next-door neighbor.

How would a juror decide individual cases under my proposal? Easy cases would include a defendant who has possessed crack cocaine and an abusive husband who kills his wife. The former should be acquitted and the latter should go to prison.

Difficult scenarios would include the drug dealer who operates in the ghetto and the thief who burglarizes the home of a rich white family. Under my proposal, nullification is presumed in the first case because drug distribution is a nonviolent malum prohibitum offense. Is nullification morally justifiable here? It depends. There is no question that encouraging people to engage in self-destructive behavior is evil; the question the juror should ask herself is whether the remedy is less evil. (The juror should also remember that the criminal law does not punish those ghetto drug dealers who cause the most injury: liquor store owners.)

As for the burglar who steals from the rich white family, the case is troubling, first of all, because the conduct is so clearly "wrong." Since it is a nonviolent malum in se crime, there is no presumption in favor of nullification, but it is an option for consideration. Here again, the facts of the case are relevant. For example, if the offense was committed to support a drug habit, I think there is a moral case to be made for nullification, at least until such time as access to drug-rehabilitation services are available to all.

Why would a juror be inclined to follow my proposal? There is no guarantee that she would. But when we perceive that black jurors are already nullifying on the basis of racial critiques (i.e., refusing to send another black man to jail), we recognize that these jurors are willing to use their power in a politically conscious manner. Further, it appears that some black jurors now excuse some conduct—like murder—that they should not excuse. My proposal provides a principled structure for the exercise of the black juror's vote. I am not encouraging anarchy; rather I am reminding black jurors of their privilege to serve a calling higher than law: justice.

I concede that the justice my proposal achieves is rough. It is as susceptible to human foibles as the jury system. But I am sufficiently optimistic that my proposal will be only an intermediate plan, a stopping point between the status quo and real justice. To get to that better, middle ground, I hope that this essay will encourage African Americans to use responsibly the power they already have.

Support for the jury system in South Africa among scholars and even among the major political parties was almost non-existent."

9.8 THE GREAT DEMOCRATIZING PRINCIPLE: THE EFFECT ON SOUTH AFRICA OF PLANNING A DEMOCRACY WITHOUT A JURY SYSTEM

Tracey Gilstrap Weiss

On December 10, 1996, South Africa embarked on the voyage to creating a new democracy when President Mandela signed the South African Constitution into law. . . . The framers of the South African constitution had many different considerations in creating this democracy. They were attempting to determine what

From Tracey Gilstrap Weiss, "The Great Democratizing Principle: The Effect on South Africa of Planning a Democracy Without a Jury System," 11 *Temple International and Comparative Law Journal* 107 (1997).

form the government would take; whether a bill of rights would be necessary, and what should be included therein; how to ensure the people are involved in the government sufficiently; and other such considerations. While the serious-ness of these discussions concerning the overall structure of the government can, and indeed should, overshadow the specific details, the framers should have considered all viable options in creating the constitution. One option which was absent from the constitutional discussions was the possibility of im-plementing a jury system in the new democracy. . . .

On the other hand, critics of the jury system point out that the United States is the only country which presently uses a full jury system. Critics also pose se-rious questions concerning the effectiveness of the jury system in serving its democratic purpose. There are questions concerning the ability of the jury to understand cases, especially those involving complex business issues or thorny legal matters; there are questions about jury bias; and other similar complaints which question the effect on justice of these problems. Further, there has been much controversy in the United States surrounding the jury's ability to effec-tively fill this role particularly when race becomes an issue in the case, which will be apropos in a discussion of South Africa.

South Africa's racial composition provides a fertile basis on which to begin evaluating the effectiveness of its jury system. South Africa has unsuccessfully implemented the jury system in the past. Therefore, it came as no surprise to the politicos in South Africa that the "democratic" constitution did not include a guar-antee of a right to trial by jury. Support for the jury system in South Africa among scholars and even among the major political parties was almost non-existent. The irony in this is that the new democratic South Africa could fail if it realizes belat-edly that one of the most important challenges to the creation of a democracy is to bestow power to the people. Yet even if the new South African system does not fail, a failure to fully incorporate the people within a government that is "by the people" will create serious repercussions to future generations. . . .

Arguments in Favor of the Jury System

The United States; History/Success with the Jury System

. . . After much, and at times heated, debate, the United States Constitution in-cluded the right to trial by jury in Article III for criminal proceedings and in Amendment Seven of the Bill of Rights for civil proceedings.

Since this decision, the jury system has been the subject of much criticism in the United States. The following reasons are often cited by critics for concern over the effectiveness of the system: jurors' lack of understanding in complex cases; jury responsibility regarding their decision making; racism by the jury and in jury selection (i.e., use of preemptory challenges to take certain races off of the jury); big awards against corporations; and the administrative costs of im-plementing the jury system—both in dollars and in time. As these are serious concerns regarding the jury system, research has been done and is ongoing to correct these problems. Indeed, "no one would suggest, of course, that the jury is an ideal institution; its critics raise many important concerns."

Despite these serious concerns about the jury system, most scholars, judges, and citizens are not willing to abandon it. The first use of empirical data to support the continued use of the jury system in the United States came from Harry Kalven, Jr., and Hans Zeisel in their book, *The American Jury*. Their analysis led them to conclude that "the civil jury was a superior institution of adjudicating disputes involving complex societal values, that the jury served as an important instrument of popular control over law enforcement, and that the jury brought a superior sense of social equity to the decision making process."

In the late twentieth century, there has been another crisis of faith in the jury system in the United States. Those who fear the competency of the current jury system base their fear on a few specific jury decisions. The fear that juries may have gone awry comes from several key areas, the first in the area of business or complex litigation.

There have been numerous calls for tort reform leveled against the jury for lack of knowledge in deciding complex tort cases. There have been cases *like Liggett & Myers v. Brown & Williamson*, involving complex securities and antitrust laws. During post trial interviews, the jury in *Liggett* admitted to knowing nothing about the technicalities of the case, yet awarded millions of dollars. That case was ultimately reversed by the Supreme Court which stated, "a reasonable jury is presumed to know and understand the law, the facts of the cases and the realities of the market." The Supreme Court found that the jury [that] decided that case did not know the law. . . .

The second area where there have been cries for reform in the U.S. jury system is in cases involving race. The Rodney King trial is one such example. In that case, the jury had to decide if four white police officers used excessive force in beating a black motorist, Rodney King, where a videotape showed the officer's violently beating King. The government requested a change of venue to a predominantly white locale with all white jurors. The jury found that the officers had not used excessive force. This decision sparked race rioting in Los Angeles of unprecedented proportion. The officers were re-tried later by a more racially mixed jury and found guilty. The criticism is that the race of the jury affected the outcome of the case.

Yet critics point out that . . . even the Rodney King verdict does not seem to have greatly affected public devotion to the jury.

One reason for strong support for the jury system, despite its obvious difficulties and inherent problems, is that the alternatives do not satisfy the democratic needs of the country. One alternative is for judges alone or a panel of judges to decide cases. Several problems exist when the judge, without the assistance of the jury, decides cases. The first is that it is through the jury system, "where ordinary people come together to exercise extraordinary power," that we "come the closest" to being a democracy. "It is the jury rather than judges that serve the interests of democracy and inject the values of the 'many' into judicial proceedings."

There exists an additional risk that judges or a panel of judges will be too prejudiced. It is more likely that the jurors who only serve for one particular case will be more impartial. Since the judges will have previously analyzed similar cases, the judges may be improperly swayed. Furthermore, if they have heard an excuse before that was found untrue, they may unjustifiably believe it to be untrue again. If we allow judges, who are appointed to the Federal bench, as well as to many state and local benches, to decide all cases alone, there is the risk that "in spite of their own natural integrity [they] will have an involuntary bias towards those of their own rank and dignity. . . ."

Conversely, the jury reflects the community's values, and allowing the community's values to be heard through the jury's voice legitimatizes the court system in the eyes of the rest of the community. To endorse the use of the jury system, Judge John A. Gibbons stated that "in the process of gaining public acceptance for the imposition of sanctions, the role of the jury is highly significant."

Although the United States' jury system is far from being perfect, it acts as a great democratizing principle [that] brings the people of our country directly into the government system. The jury system has been evolving since the country began and must continue to evolve to meet the changing needs of the judicial system. Although "the civil jury is not invincible [as] demonstrated by its disappearance in England . . . ," we seem committed to working to save it. Indeed, "if we fail . . . we will lose the most potent and ingenious vehicle for self-rule ever invented."

Reasons Why the Jury System Is Compatible with South Africa's New Democratic Principles

An important part of the constitutional discussions in South Africa was the need for an independent judiciary. The current judicial structure in South Africa is having a legitimacy crisis. Some recognized problems with the current judiciary are that it is an all white preserve, the appointments are made giving greater priority to political factors than merit, and the judiciary has been used to legitimize the domination by the majority over the minority. The current South African judiciary is composed of judges who are appointed by the "state president in consultation with the minister of justice but may be dismissed only by Parliament." In South Africa's history, there has been only one black man and one white woman on the court; the rest are upper- or middle-class white males.

However, the old judiciary can not immediately be replaced with native Africans, for, at present, there are very few native Africans among those qualified to be judges. Since it will take time to educate native Africans in enough numbers to even out the judiciary, the jury system could fill this role. Although the judges would still predominantly be white middle class males, the jurors themselves could even out the representation.

Another problem with the South African judiciary is that the judicial appointments have been based on political affiliations rather than merit. The party in power has used the judiciary as a way to "uphold the laws of apartheid." The judiciary complied by "refusing to confront [apartheid] and, on occasions, expanding its severity." However, as South African constitutional scholar John Dugard points out, even if the judges were appointed based on merit, it is difficult for human nature to ignore subconscious stimuli. The subconscious stimuli referred to is the constant barrage in South Africa by the "media, schools and society at large" that whites are superior. There have even been cases where the judiciary has refused to rule for native Africans when the law could easily have been interpreted in the native African's favor, simply to maintain the status quo, at the jeopardy of the individual's rights.

Due to the inadequacy of the minority judges to mete out justice for the majority and the inherent, even subconscious, racism, the judges often make inequitable decisions not founded on fact. There are instances where judges have taken judicial notice of extremely ridiculous and racist things.

The jury would help solve these problems because it allows for flexibility in the legal decision. When the community members interpret the laws, they will be infusing the community's values, not the values of one judge who is appointed by the political power. That the community members themselves will be making the decisions will help abate the legitimacy crisis currently surrounding the judiciary in South Africa.

"Statistics at most may show only a likelihood that a particular factor entered into some decisions."

9.9 MCCLESKEY V. KEMP

481 U.S. 279 (1987)

On May 13, 1978, Warren McCleskey, a black man, and three accomplices attempted to rob a furniture store in Atlanta, Georgia. One of the employees hit a silent alarm button, which was answered by a white, thirty-one-year-old police officer. As the officer entered the store, he was shot and killed. Several weeks later, when police arrested McClesky on another charge, he confessed to the robbery. At his trial, McCleskey was identified by one of the accomplices as the individual who killed the officer. The prosecution also entered evidence indicating that McCleskey had bragged about the shooting.

Three months after the robbery, a jury of eleven whites and one black convicted McCleskey and sentenced him to death. At that point, the NAACP's Legal Defense Fund (LDF) took over his defense and based his appeal in the federal courts on Baldus's study showing that blacks convicted of murdering whites received death sentences at disproportionately high rates (see the text of this chapter and Reading 9.10 for details about the study). Armed with this study the LDF tried to convince the justices that the disparate application of death penalty laws led to unacceptable violations of the Equal Protection and Due Process Clauses, as well as the Eighth Amendment's prohibition against Cruel and Unusual Punishments.

JUSTICE POWELL delivered the opinion of the Court.

This case presents the question whether a complex statistical study that indicates a risk that racial considerations enter into capital sentencing determinations proves that petitioner McCleskey's capital sentence is unconstitutional under the Eighth or Fourteenth Amendment.

Our analysis begins with the basic principle that a defendant who alleges an equal protection violation has the burden of proving "the existence of purposeful discrimination." A corollary to this principle is that a criminal defendant must prove that the purposeful discrimination "had a discriminatory effect" on him. Thus, to prevail under the Equal Protection Clause, McCleskey must prove that the decision makers in his case acted with discriminatory purpose. He offers no evidence specific to his own case that would support an inference that racial considerations played a part in his sentence. Instead, he relies solely on the Baldus study. McCleskey argues that the Baldus study compels an inference that his sentence rests on purposeful discrimination. McCleskey's claim that these statistics are sufficient proof of discrimination, without regard to the facts of a particular case, would extend to all capital cases in Georgia, at least where the victim was white and the defendant is black.

The Court has accepted statistics as proof of intent to discriminate in certain limited contexts. First, this Court has accepted statistical disparities as proof of an equal protection violation in the selection of the jury venire in a particular district. Although statistical proof normally must present a "stark" pattern to be accepted as the sole proof of discriminatory intent under the Constitution, "[b]ecause of the nature of the jury-selection task, . . . we have permitted a finding of constitutional violation even when the statistical pattern does not approach [such] extremes." Second, this Court has accepted statistics to prove statutory violations under Title VII [of the Civil Rights Act of 1964, which generally prohibits employment discrimination based on race, color, religion, sex, or national origin].

But the nature of the capital sentencing decision, and the relationship of the statistics to that decision, are fundamentally different from the corresponding elements in the venire-selection or Title VII cases. Most importantly, each particular decision to impose the death penalty is made by a petit jury selected from a properly constituted venire. Each jury is unique in its composition, and the Constitution requires that its decision rest on consideration of innumerable factors that vary according to the characteristics of the individual defendant and the facts of the particular capital offense. Thus, the application of an inference drawn from the general statistics to a specific decision in a trial and sentencing simply is not comparable to the application of an inference drawn from general statistics to a specific venire-selection or Title VII case. In those cases, the statistics relate to fewer entities, and fewer variables are relevant to the challenged decisions.

Another important difference between the cases in which we have accepted statistics as proof of discriminatory intent and this case is that, in the venire selection and Title VII contexts, the decision maker has an opportunity to explain the statistical disparity. Here, the State has no practical opportunity to rebut the Baldus study.

Finally, McCleskey's statistical proffer must be viewed in the context of his challenge. McCleskey challenges decisions at the heart of the State's criminal justice system. "[O]ne of society's most basic tasks is that of protecting the lives of its citizens and one of the most basic ways in which it achieves the task is through criminal laws against murder." Implementation of these laws necessarily requires discretionary judgments. Because discretion is essential to the criminal justice process, we would demand exceptionally clear proof before we would infer that the discretion has been abused. The unique nature of the decisions at issue in this case also counsel against adopting such an inference from the disparities indicated by the Baldus study. Accordingly, we hold that the Baldus study is clearly insufficient to support an inference that any of the decision makers in McCleskey's case acted with discriminatory purpose. . . .

McCleskey also argues that the Baldus study demonstrates that the Georgia capital sentencing system violates the Eighth Amendment. . . .

Two principal decisions guide our resolution of McCleskey's Eighth Amendment claim. In *Furman v. Georgia* (1972), the Court concluded that the death penalty was so irrationally imposed that any particular death sentence could be presumed excessive.

In *Gregg [v. Georgia* (1976)], the Court specifically addressed the question left open in Furman—whether the punishment of death for murder is "under all circumstances, 'cruel and unusual' in violation of the Eighth and Fourteenth Amendments of the Constitution." . . . We noted that any punishment might be unconstitutionally severe if inflicted without penological justification, but concluded that the infliction of death as a punishment for murder is not without justification and thus is not unconstitutionally severe. . . .

[McCleskey] contends that the Georgia capital punishment system is arbitrary and capricious in application, and therefore his sentence is excessive, because racial considerations may influence capital sentencing decisions in Georgia. We now address this claim.

To evaluate McCleskey's challenge, we must examine exactly what the Baldus study may show. Even Professor Baldus does not contend that his statistics prove that race enters into any capital sentencing decisions or that race was a factor in McCleskey's particular case. Statistics at most may show only a likelihood that a particular factor entered into some decisions. There is, of course, some risk of racial prejudice influencing a jury's decision in a criminal case. There are similar risks that other kinds of prejudice will influence other criminal trials. The question "is at what point that risk becomes constitutionally unacceptable." McCleskey asks us to accept the likelihood allegedly shown by the Baldus study as the constitutional measure of an unacceptable risk of racial prejudice influencing capital sentencing decisions. This we decline to do.

Because of the risk that the factor of race may enter the criminal justice process, we have engaged in "unceasing efforts" to eradicate racial prejudice from our criminal justice system. Our efforts have been guided by our recognition that "the inestimable privilege of trial by jury . . . is a vital principle, underlying the whole administration of criminal justice." Specifically, a capital sentencing jury representative of a criminal defendant's community assures a "'diffused impartiality'" in the jury's task of "express[ing] the conscience of the community on the ultimate question of life or death."

Individual jurors bring to their deliberations "qualities of human nature and varieties of human experience, the range of which is unknown and perhaps unknowable." The capital sentencing decision requires the individual jurors to focus their collective judgment on the unique characteristics of a particular criminal defendant. It is not surprising that such collective judgments often are difficult to explain. But the inherent lack of predictability of jury decisions does not justify their condemnation.

McCleskey's argument that the Constitution condemns the discretion allowed decision makers in the Georgia capital sentencing system is antithetical to the fundamental role of discretion in our criminal justice system. Discretion in the criminal justice system offers substantial benefits to the criminal defendant. Not only can a jury decline to impose the death sentence, it can decline to convict, or choose to convict of a lesser offense. Whereas decisions against a defendant's interest may be reversed by the trial judge or on appeal, these discretionary exercises of leniency are final and unreviewable. Similarly, the capacity of prosecutorial discretion to provide individualized justice is "firmly entrenched in American law." As we have noted, a prosecutor can decline to charge, offer a plea bargain, or decline to seek a death sentence in any particular case. Of course, "the power to be lenient [also] is the power to discriminate," but a capital-punishment system that did not allow for discretionary acts of leniency "would be totally alien to our notions of criminal justice."

At most, the Baldus study indicates a discrepancy that appears to correlate with race. Apparent disparities in sentencing are an inevitable part of our criminal justice system. Despite these imperfections, our consistent rule has been that constitutional guarantees are met when "the mode [for determining guilt or punishment] itself has been surrounded with safeguards to make it as fair as possible." Where the discretion that is fundamental to our criminal process is involved, we decline to assume that what is unexplained is invidious. In light of the safeguards designed to minimize racial bias in the process, the fundamental value of jury trial in our criminal justice system, and the benefits that discretion provides to criminal defendants, we hold that the Baldus study does not demonstrate a constitutionally significant risk of racial bias affecting the Georgia capital-sentencing process.

Two additional concerns inform our decision in this case. First, McCleskey's claim, taken to its logical conclusion, throws into serious question the principles that underlie our entire criminal justice system. The Eighth Amendment is not limited in application to capital punishment, but applies to all penalties. Thus, if we accepted McCleskey's claim that racial bias has impermissibly tainted the capital sentencing decision, we could soon be faced with similar claims as to other types of penalty. Moreover, the claim that his sentence rests on the irrelevant factor of race easily could be extended to apply to claims based on unexplained discrepancies that correlate to membership in other minority groups, and even to gender. Similarly, since McCleskey's claim relates to the race of his victim, other claims could apply with equally logical force to statistical disparities that correlate with the race or sex of other actors in the criminal justice system, such as defense attorneys, or judges. Also, there is no logical reason that such a claim need be limited to racial or sexual bias. If arbitrary and capricious punishment is the touchstone under the Eighth Amendment, such a claim could—at least in theory—be based upon any arbitrary variable, such as the defendant's facial characteristics, or the physical attractiveness of the defendant or the victim, that some statistical study indicates may be influential in jury decision making. As these examples illustrate, there is no limiting principle to the type of challenge brought by McCleskey. The Constitution does not require that a State eliminate any demonstrable disparity that correlates with a potentially irrelevant factor in order to operate a criminal justice system that includes capital punishment. As we have stated specifically in the context of capital punishment, the Constitution does not "plac[e] totally unrealistic conditions on its use." Second, McCleskey's arguments are best presented to the legislative bodies. It is not the responsibility—or indeed even the right—of this Court to determine the appropriate punishment for particular crimes. Legislatures also are better qualified to weigh and "evaluate the results of statistical studies in terms of their own local conditions and with a flexibility of approach that is not available to the courts." Capital punishment is now the law in more than two thirds of our States. It is the ultimate duty of courts to determine on a case-by-case basis whether these laws are applied consistently with the Constitution. Despite McCleskey's wide ranging arguments that basically challenge the validity of capital punishment in our multiracial society, the only question before us is whether in his case the law of Georgia was properly applied. We agree with the District Court and the Court of Appeals for the Eleventh Circuit that this was carefully and correctly done in this case. Accordingly, we affirm the judgment of the Court of Appeals for the Eleventh Circuit.

It is so ordered.

JUSTICE BRENNAN, with whom JUSTICE MARSHALL, JUSTICE BLACKMUN, and JUSTICE STEVENS join, dissenting.

At some point in this case, Warren McCleskey doubtless asked his lawyer whether a jury was likely to sentence him to die. A candid reply to this question would have been disturbing. First, counsel would have to tell McCleskey that few of the details of the crime or of McCleskey's past criminal conduct were more important than the fact that his victim was white. Furthermore, counsel would feel bound to tell McCleskey that defendants charged with killing white victims in Georgia are 4.3 times as likely to be sentenced to death as defendants charged with killing blacks. In addition, frankness would compel the disclosure that it was more likely than not that the race of McCleskey's victim would determine whether he received a death sentence: six of every eleven defendants convicted of killing a white person would not have received the death penalty if their victims had been black, while, among defendants with aggravating and mitigating factors comparable to McCleskey's, twenty of every thirty-four would not have been sentenced to die if their victims had been black. Finally, the assessment would not be complete without the information that cases involving black defendants and white victims are more likely to result in a death sentence than cases featuring any other racial combination of defendant and victim. The story could be told in a variety of ways, but McCleskey could not fail to grasp its essential narrative line: there was a significant chance that race would play a prominent role in determining if he lived or died.

The Court today holds that Warren McCleskey's sentence was constitutionally imposed. It finds no fault in a system in which lawyers must tell their clients that race casts a large shadow on the capital sentencing process. . . .

The Court's decision today will not change what attorneys in Georgia tell other Warren McCleskeys about their chances of execution. Nothing will soften the harsh message they must convey, nor alter the prospect that race undoubtedly will continue to be a topic of discussion. McCleskey's evidence will not have obtained judicial acceptance, but that will not affect what is said on death row. However many criticisms of today's decision may be rendered, these painful conversations will serve as the most eloquent dissents of all.

JUSTICE BLACKMUN, with whom JUSTICE MARSHALL, JUSTICE STEVENS, and JUSTICE BRENNAN join, dissenting.

The Court today sanctions the execution of a man despite his presentation of evidence that establishes a constitutionally intolerable level of racially based discrimination leading to the imposition of his death sentence. I am disappointed with the Court's action not only because of its denial of constitutional guarantees to petitioner McCleskey individually, but also because of its departure from what seems to me to be well-developed constitutional jurisprudence.

Justice Brennan has thoroughly demonstrated that, if one assumes that the statistical evidence presented by petitioner McCleskey is valid, as we must in light of the Court of Appeals' assumption, there exists in the Georgia capital sentencing scheme a risk of racially based discrimination that is so acute that it violates the Eighth Amendment. His analysis of McCleskey's case in terms of the Eighth Amendment is consistent with this Court's recognition that, because capital cases involve the State's imposition of a punishment that is unique both in kind and degree, the decision in such cases must reflect a heightened degree of reliability under the Amendment's prohibition of the infliction of cruel and unusual punishments. . . .

Yet McCleskey's case raises concerns that are central not only to the principles underlying the Eighth Amendment, but also to the principles underlying the Fourteenth Amendment. Analysis of his case in terms of the Fourteenth Amendment is consistent with this Court's recognition that racial discrimination is fundamentally at odds with our constitutional guarantee of equal protection. The protections afforded by the Fourteenth Amendment are not left at the courtroom door. Nor is equal protection denied to persons convicted of crimes. The Court in the past has found that racial discrimination within the criminal justice system is particularly abhorrent: "Discrimination on the basis of race, odious in all aspects, is especially pernicious in the administration of justice." *Rose v. Mitchell* (1979). Disparate enforcement of criminal sanctions "destroys the appearance of justice, and thereby casts doubt on the integrity of the judicial process."

JUSTICE STEVENS, with whom JUSTICE BLACKMUN joins, dissenting.

The Court's decision appears to be based on a fear that the acceptance of McCleskey's claim would sound the death knell for capital punishment in Georgia. If society were indeed forced to choose between a racially discriminatory death penalty (one that provides heightened protection against murder "for whites only") and no death penalty at all, the choice mandated by the Constitution would be plain. But the Court's fear is unfounded. One of the lessons of the Baldus study is that there exist certain categories of extremely serious crimes for which prosecutors consistently seek, and juries consistently impose, the death penalty without regard to the race of the victim or the race of the offender. If Georgia were to narrow the class of death-eligible defendants to those categories, the danger of arbitrary and discriminatory imposition of the death penalty would be significantly decreased, if not eradicated. . . . [S]uch a restructuring of the sentencing scheme is surely not too high a price to pay. . . .

> *"During the period since McCleskey, no one has repudiated or invalidated any of the findings in this research."*

9.10 THE DEATH PENALTY DIALOGUE BETWEEN LAW AND SOCIAL SCIENCE

David C. Baldus

David C. Baldus is Joseph B. Tye Professor of Law at the
University of Iowa College of Law.

. . . There has been a long dialogue in the courts on the issue of race and the death penalty. It started in 1966 when Marvin Wolfgang presented compelling evidence of race-of-defendant discrimination in the imposition of the death penalty for rape in Arkansas. His data were presented in *Maxwell v. Bishop*, an Arkansas decision challenging an individual death sentence. Then-Judge Harry Blackmun, sitting on the Eighth Circuit Court of Appeals, denied relief to the black defendant on a methodological ground. The results showing a pattern of purposeful discrimination throughout the state against black defendants were based on a sample of cases that had been randomly drawn. The fatal flaw was that the sample did not include the claimant's case or any other cases from his county; therefore, no relief was available.

From David C. Baldus, "The Death Penalty Dialogue Between Law and Social Science," 70 *Indiana Law Journal* 1033 (1995).

In the study of homicide cases, where we have seen the most extensive analyses of race discrimination, the pioneer was Bill Bowers. In some very creative work in the 1970s, he sensitized the courts and the entire research community to the nature and implications of race-of-victim discrimination. Although Bowers's early work was persuasive, it was limited by small numbers of control variables in the FBI data set with which he was working. This gave the Fifth Circuit a methodological justification, when he presented his data in cases there in the 1970s and 1980s, to say that race-of-victim discrimination had not been proven.

This early research, including work in progress by Barry Nakell, provided the foundation for the work that I did in Georgia with two colleagues, George Woodworth and Charles Pulaski. We also studied carefully the methodological critiques in Maxwell and in the Fifth Circuit cases that rejected Bowers's work. We were determined to do our best to overcome the omitted-variable problems that had weakened the persuasiveness of his work.

In the end, with the help of grants from the Justice Department and the Edna McConnell Clark Foundation, we developed empirical evidence suggesting that, on average, Georgia prosecutors were more likely to seek a death sentence and Georgia juries were more likely to impose a death sentence in white-victim cases. We also found that these effects were particularly concentrated in what we characterized as the "mid-range" of cases—those cases where there truly was a close choice as to the life or death decision. It turned out that Warren McCleskey's was located in this category of cases.

McCleskey's lawyers argued that the statistical evidence we presented supported a presumption that race had influenced decisions in his case, and that the State had failed to rebut that presumption. As a consequence, McCleskey argued, his proof established a violation of the Eighth and Fourteenth Amendments.

The Court's dilemma here was real. Race discrimination is an important constitutional matter. In other contexts, under both the Constitution and the civil rights laws, the Court has generally upheld similar claims of racial discrimination. A grant of relief for McCleskey, however, could threaten the legitimacy of death sentencing in Georgia and possibly beyond. At the very least, such a ruling would complicate its administration.

In *McCleskey v. Kemp*, five Justices voted to reject Warren McCleskey's claim. They could have done so on the methodological grounds suggested by the trial court, but that approach could have been construed as an invitation to the social science community to cure the defects and return to court another day. Instead, the Court, in an opinion written by Justice Powell, rejected the claim by establishing burdens of proof for the use of statistical evidence to establish discrimination in death penalty cases that were impossible to meet.

The Court's justification, based on federalism concerns, had some plausibility. But the methodological arguments about the impossibility of proving discrimination in a death-sentencing system were quite unpersuasive.

So also were the suggestions that these disparities are inevitable in the system, and that abolition is the only real cure for the problem. On these points, an internal memorandum by Justice Scalia is particularly relevant. His memo surfaced recently in Justice Marshall's papers when they were opened at the Library of Congress. It was a short note to all the Justices, written three months before the *McCleskey* decision. In it, Justice Scalia rejects Justice Powell's methodological arguments but goes on to state that race discrimination in the death penalty is "'real, acknowledged in the decisions of this Court, and ineradicable.'"

Where did the *McCleskey* data figure into all this, particularly for Justice Powell, the key swing vote and author of the majority opinion? Even though the Court accepted the validity of our research, the trial court's very strong criticism of the methodology left lingering doubts, which were carried over into Justice Powell's footnotes. Also, the research was complex and difficult to understand. Further, it has been reported to me that Justice Powell was uncomfortable basing any decision on statistical evidence.

But perhaps most important, in my estimation, is that race-of-victim discrimination does not raise the same sort of moral concerns as race-of-defendant discrimination—even though, from a constitutional standpoint, discrimination on the basis of any racial aspect of the case is illegitimate. Justice Powell may well have voted differently if the evidence had shown race-of-defendant discrimination rather than race-of-victim discrimination. After all, it is the defendants who pick their victims.

In addition, the core race-of-victim findings do not conform to ordinary knowledge about race discrimination. In this regard, it is worth noting that most lay and many professional people who know anything about the case think that what we actually established was race-of-defendant discrimination, not race-of-victim discrimination.

After *McCleskey*, the dialogue on race and the death penalty shifted to Congress. In 1991 and again last year, the House of Representatives approved what is known as the Racial Justice Act, which would have bypassed *McCleskey* and permitted condemned prisoners to raise statistical challenges to their death sentences on the ground of race. Those challenges would have been evaluated under standards and presumptions similar to those used in Title VII employment discrimination cases and jury discrimination cases under the Fourteenth Amendment. In both those years, however, the measure was killed in a conference committee.

Supporters of the Racial Justice Act gathered some strength for their position from a General Accounting Office study which reviewed all of the literature on race-of-victim discrimination and put its imprimatur on it—the whole corpus of twenty-eight studies—suggesting that it showed real effects. Also, during the period since *McCleskey*, no one has repudiated or invalidated any of the findings in this research.

Nevertheless, most opposition to the new legislation was based on three key *McCleskey*-like themes. First, existing race-of-victim discrimination research is unreliable and does not establish the reality of race-of-victim discrimination. Second, for methodological reasons, race discrimination simply cannot be proven. And third, even if you could prove it, racial discrimination cannot be corrected, without either de facto abolition of the death penalty, or a requirement that prosecutors use "quotas" to guide their charging decisions.

My research colleagues and I think that these are specious claims.

In closing, the recent statements of Justice Powell and Justice Blackmun provide additional evidence of the long-term percolating effects of social science research on elite and public opinion. Both Powell and Blackmun now believe that the death penalty experience of the last twenty years was a failure, and that the system should be declared unconstitutional. Justice Blackmun was clearly influenced by the cumulative evidence of the arbitrariness, discrimination, and miscarriages of justice documented since 1973. In contrast, Justice Powell seems much more concerned that the death penalty system cannot be made to work properly, and that the public attributes this failure to the Court, which has the effect of undercutting the legitimacy of the institution he loves so dearly.

*"I have come to think that capital punishment
should be abolished."—JUSTICE POWELL*

9.11 LEWIS F. POWELL, JR.

John C. Jeffries, Jr.

John C. Jeffries, Jr., clerked for Justice Powell and is now the Emerson
Spies Professor and the Horace Goldsmith Research Professor
at the University of Virginia School of Law.

Powell stated his position most succinctly in an early memorandum, urging his colleagues not to hear McCleskey's case. First, it was hard to know what to make of statistics. "Sentencing judges and juries are constitutionally required to consider a host of individual-specific circumstances in deciding whether to impose capital punishment. No study can take all of these individual circumstances into account, precisely because they are fact-specific as to each defendant." Of course, taking all factors into account was precisely what Baldus and his colleagues had tried to do, but Powell was uneasy with this kind of evidence. As he said elsewhere, "My understanding of statistical analysis . . . ranges from limited to zero."

He also did not know what constitutional weight to give to the statistical effect of the victim's race. "One would expect that if there were race-based sentencing, the Baldus study would show a bias based on the defendant's race," but the "study suggests no such effect. . . ." Differential treatment of defendants based on the race of their victims was hard to understand as racial bias against defendants.

From John C. Jeffries, Jr., Lewis F. Powell, Jr. (New York: Charles Scribner's, 1994).

Finally, Powell thought the overall picture revealed by the figures was decidedly positive. The "study tends to show that the system operates rationally as a general matter: The death penalty was most likely in those cases with the most severe aggravating factors and the least mitigating factors, and least likely in the opposite cases. The pattern suggests precisely the kind of careful balancing of individual factors that the Court required in Gregg." . . .

[P]owell did not see the case as condoning racism but simply as recognizing the inevitable variations in any nonmandatory death penalty. . . .

[I]n conversation with the author in the summer of 1991, Powell was asked whether he would change his vote in any case:

"Yes, *McCleskey v. Kemp.*"

"Do you mean you would now accept the argument from statistics?"

"No, I would vote the other way in any capital case."

"In any capital case?"

"Yes."

"Even in *Furman v. Georgia?*"

"Yes. I have come to think that capital punishment should be abolished."

CHAPTER 10

Precedents and Legal Reasoning

Not only must a court determine the facts of a case, it must also decide what rules of law control the kind of dispute before it and how to apply those rules. A trial judge may share with a jury responsibility for finding facts, but the judge alone is supposed to determine "the law." On occasion, of course, a group of jurors might choose to ignore what the judge tells them, but formal responsibility for selecting appropriate legal rules, interpreting those rules, and even sometimes creating them rests on the judge alone, a burden made abundantly clear by the fact that appellate courts do not use juries at all.

It is customary to say that there are three sources for the law applied by American judges: constitutional texts (federal and state), statutes (federal and state), and common law. (In fact, of course, judges often look to their own beliefs about good public policy and, especially in constitutional interpretation, to political theories of democracy and constitutionalism.) In the sense used here, common law refers to that part of the law of England, the United States, and other English-speaking countries that is found in judicial decisions and in textbooks discussing these decisions, as distinguished from the law enacted by legislatures, constitutional conventions, or public referenda.

This chapter is not concerned with the substantive rules of the common law, but rather with the techniques by which judges develop and apply that body of law. The common law's model of decision making is inductive, a process by which judges draw general principles from decisions in particular controversies. Once stated, these principles become imbedded as precedents and part of the "law" that judges apply in future controversies raising the same sorts of questions. But applying precedents—following stare decisis—is neither a simple nor an automatic process. It involves both skill and art. Each new controversy requires a reexamination of precedents in light of the immediate case as well as any new social conditions. In courts where the common law tradition prevails, judges have a unique responsibility for providing elements of both stability and change in the law. By force of their commissions rather than by reason of their competence, as Robert H. Jackson once noted, they operate as social engineers.

In contrast to the common law, the Civil Law is supposedly based on an all-encompassing code enacted by the legislature and expounded by scholars more than by judges. Indeed, it has sometimes been unlawful for judges to cite previous cases in their opinions. Nevertheless, judges in Civil–Law systems are often very aware of what other, especially higher, courts have done. Indeed, for more than a quarter century, most Italian courts have had in place computer programs that can call up from an immense database judicial interpretations of every article of the civil, commercial, and criminal codes. Moreover, some tribunals, most especially the Constitutional Court of Germany, now freely cite, discuss, and claim to rely on as well as to differ from earlier rulings.

REASONING BY EXAMPLE

The basic technique employed by common-law judges to determine the law is reasoning by example (Readings 10.1 and 10.2). The source of the law applied in a particular case matters very much; consequently, the two following chapters are devoted to special problems of statutory construction and constitutional interpretation. But, whatever the source of the law, the fundamental character of the judicial task includes a comparison of facts and decisions in related controversies.

Let us take a situation that presents the common law's techniques of legal reasoning in clearest form. A controversy comes before a judge in which facts A, B, C, and D are present. Aided by briefs of counsel (and now by huge databases that can be retrieved by programs such as Lexis and WestLaw), the judge searches earlier cases for similar situations. If she or he finds another case in which facts A, B, C, and D were present, then that case is a precedent, and the judge will feel a strong—though not necessarily an absolutely binding—obligation to decide the present case the same way. When a substantial number of cases involving similar facts have been decided the same way, judges will say that a rule of law exists: A general rule has emerged from a series of particular instances. Over a period of decades or centuries, rules of law covering a wide variety of factual situations develop in this fashion. Periodically, legislatures may enact or revise some of these rules of law by adopting them in statutes, and occasionally they will nullify a rule of common law by enacting a contrary statute. And, as we shall see, judges also periodically reexamine and modify or even replace these rules.

Meanwhile, new controversies constantly challenge existing rules. Moreover, the facts in a current case never exactly duplicate those of an earlier case. Thus there is constant opportunity for counsel to contend that a rule previously applied to an apparently similar case is not really applicable to a current dispute. An attorney may argue, for example, that the facts in the earlier case were A, B, C, and D, whereas here they are A, B, C, and E. The judge must then decide whether the similarities are so close that he or she should apply the same rule. If so, the judge must reformulate the rule to cover situations where the facts are A-B-C-E as well as A-B-C-D. Alternatively, he or she may decide that replacement of D by E so changes the situation that the court must apply a different rule; in that event, he or she may merely modify the older rule or create a new one.

Justice Benjamin N. Cardozo ridiculed the notion that adherence to precedent is simply a matter of a judge's "match[ing] the colors of the case at hand against the colors of many sample cases spread out upon the desk." If matching were all there were to judging, he said, then the judge with the best card index of cases would be the wisest jurist. (Today we would say that the wisest judge would be the one whose computer had access to the largest database.) "It is when the colors do not match," Cardozo continued, "when the references in the index fail, when there is no decisive precedent, that the serious business of the judge begins. He must then fashion law for the litigants before him. In fashioning it for them, he will be fashioning it for others" (Reading 1.5)

In such cases counsel for opposing litigants urge on the judges precedents that, they insist, fit the present controversy. Lawyers try to explain away as inapplicable precedents that apparently conflict with the result they are being paid to secure. Attorneys as well as judges must thus engage in a complicated process of comparing decisions in a search for similarities that are significant enough to guide judicial wisdom (Readings 10. 3 and 10.4).

What transpires in a court of common law, then, is not only a controversy about facts. The court is also a forum in which attorneys argue the relevance of previous decisions to current questions and the applicability of rules of law embodied in those earlier decisions. But because rules of law are basically ways of explaining and justifying decisions, the emphasis is typically less on concepts and more on demonstrating how the facts of the present case are similar to or different from those of previous controversies.

RATIO DECIDENDI VERSUS DICTA

Judges and commentators often say that, to decide whether a previous decision qualifies as a precedent, one must strip away the nonessentials of a case and expose the basic reasons for the court's decision. This process is generally referred to as "establishing the principle," or the "ratio decidendi," of the case. Many jurists have tried to explain how this task can be accurately performed, but no set of rules is entirely satisfactory. Judges are often imprecise in their language; furthermore, as they learn from experience, they or their successors may change their minds about what an earlier case stands for. With the understanding that judicial principles are elusive targets, we can look at the five rules suggested by Arthur L. Goodhart, which are as useful as any.[1] His first two rules explain how the principle of the case is not to be found:

---

[1] Arthur L. Goodhart, "Determining the Ratio Decidendi of a Case," 40 *Yale Law Journal* 161 (1930).

1. The principle of a case is not found in the reasons given in the opinion.
2. The principle is not found in the rule of law set forth in the opinion.

These first two rules suggest that it is not enough to know what the judge said. What is missing in these first two situations is any relationship between the facts of the case and the decision. The principle of a case cannot be established without knowing the facts of that case.

But Goodhart's third rule indicates that there is even more to the problem:

3. The principle is not necessarily found by a consideration of all the ascertainable facts of the case and the judge's decision.

This rule emphasizes that not all the facts of a case were relevant to establishing the principle of the decision. One must have a standard to determine which facts were relevant.

So, Goodhart's fourth rule provides:

4. The principle of the case is found by taking account (a) of the facts treated by the judge as material and (b) his or her decision as based on them.

Here we finally have a rule on what to look for in the search for the ratio decidendi.

But Goodhart gives one final guide to relevance.

5. In finding the principle it is also necessary to establish what facts were held to be immaterial by the judge, because the principle may depend as much on exclusion as it does on inclusion.

Dicta

Rule 4, the basic positive guide, deserves further elaboration. In stressing the relationship between the judge's decision and the facts that she or he treated as material, Goodhart merely reformulated what is generally referred to as the rule of dicta in judicial opinions. A dictum (or obiter dictum; plural: obiter dicta) is any expression in an opinion that is unnecessary to the decision reached in the case or that relates to a factual situation other than the one actually before the court. The task of the judge is to decide the immediate case. Any comments not essential to the reasoning necessary to decide that case are, consequently, surplus verbiage and, although sometimes useful, are not authoritative in discovering the principle underpinning the earlier case. A judicial opinion supposedly has value as a precedent only insofar as it is squarely based on the facts of the controversy being adjudicated. As Chief Justice John Marshall explained in *Cohens v. Virginia* (1821):

> It is a maxim not to be disregarded that general expressions in every opinion are to be taken in connection with the case in which those expressions are used. If they go beyond the case, they may be respected but ought not to control the judgment in a subsequent suit. . . . The reason of this maxim is obvious. The

question actually before the Court is investigated with care and considered in its lull extent. Other principles which may serve to illustrate it are considered in their relation to the case decided, but their possible bearing on all other cases is seldom completely investigated.

Chief Justice William Howard Taft's opinion in *Myers v. United States* (1926) provides a classic example of a dictum. There the Court was dealing with a statute that forbade the president to remove a postmaster from office without the consent of the Senate. For the Court, Taft held that this legislation unconstitutionally restricted the president's authority to direct the executive branch of government. But the chief justice did not confine his opinion to the office of postmaster. Instead, he declared that the constitutional principles behind the Court's decision applied to all presidential appointees, including heads of federal regulatory commissions.

In 1935, *Humphrey's Executor v. United States* presented the Supreme Court with a controversy involving presidential removal of precisely such an official, a member of the Federal Trade Commission. Explaining why Taft's broad statement did not fit the case of an officer with quasi-legislative and quasi-judicial functions, Justice George Sutherland wrote:

> The office of a postmaster is so essentially unlike the office now involved that the decision in the Myers case cannot be accepted as controlling our decision here. A postmaster is an executive officer restricted to the performance of executive functions. He is charged with no duty at all related to either the legislative or judicial power. The actual decision in the Myers case finds support in the theory that such an officer is merely one of the units in the executive department and hence inherently subject to the exclusive and illimitable power of removal by the chief executive, whose subordinate and aide he is. Putting aside dicta, which may be followed if sufficiently persuasive but which are not controlling, the necessary reach of the decision goes far enough to include all purely executive officers. It goes no further.

Often, however, the matter of dicta is not so simply settled. First of all, as no reader of judicial opinions need be reminded, judges are seldom skilled in clear writing. What was dogma and what was dictum in an opinion are frequently a mystery. Second, as we have noted, judges may change their minds or wish to change the rules contained in earlier decisions. When they carry out these wishes, they may find justification for their new directions in the dicta of previous opinions. In time, frequent reliance on logically extraneous words changes the meaning of an earlier case from what its author intended to what its users prefer.

Two shockingly illiberal decisions from World War II provide a pair of illustrations. In *Hirabayashi v. United States* (1943) and *Korematsu v. United States* (1944) the Court sustained, first, the constitutionality of a curfew directed at all persons of Japanese descent, most of whom were native-born American citizens, living on the West Coast, then upheld a program that forcibly herded all such people into concentration camps. In justifying the first decision, Chief Justice Harlan Fiske Stone conceded that "distinctions between citizens solely because of their ancestry are by their very nature odious to a free people whose institutions are founded upon the doctrine of equality." But, Stone added, "Because racial discriminations are in most circumstances irrelevant and therefore prohibited, it by no means follows that, in dealing with the perils of war, Congress and the Executive are wholly precluded from taking into account those facts." Thus the Court found it reasonable for the government in fighting a war against Japan to restrict the movement of people whose ancestors had been born in Japan.

Writing for the Court in *Korematsu*, Justice Hugo Black threw a similar sop to the Bill of Rights, noting that "all legal restrictions which curtail the civil rights of a single racial group are immediately suspect." Then Black, as had Stone, went on to find that the "pressing public necessity" of war could justify imprisonment of citizens of a particular race, even though they had been neither accused nor convicted of any crime.

Because no case has again arisen involving such hysteria, the Court has never had a full opportunity to repent its sins. But the justices soon found an indirect way. They ripped out of context Stone's and Black's dicta about racial equality and cited these sentences as authorities for invalidating a state statute restricting the right of Japanese aliens to own land, for sustaining a state statute forbidding segregated seating in public or private transportation, for forbidding a state court from enforcing an agreement between private citizens not to sell property to blacks, for striking down state efforts to keep ethnic minorities off juries, and for outlawing segregation in public schools.[2] In 1943 or 1944, no one in his or her right mind, least of all a judge, would have dreamed that *Hirabayashi* and *Korematsu* stood for libertarian principles.

Further complicating analysis, judges might deliberately plant dicta in their opinions, hoping that they themselves or those who come after them will cite these words as authority for changing the law. Although he di⸱⸱⸱ ⸱⸱⸱intend in *Hirabayashi*, Stone was a master of this technique. To gain a ⸱⸱⸱ would often write an opinion with a very narrow holding, ⸱⸱⸱ footnotes to that opinion he would strew an occasional s⸱⸱⸱ later pluck out as evidence that the Court had really inte⸱⸱⸱ ruling. As a former law clerk reported, Stone was "like a ⸱⸱⸱ be pulled out at some later time. And there was mischie⸱⸱⸱ his delight when his ruse was undetected and the chestn⸱⸱⸱

TREATMENT OF PRECEDENT

Declaring parts of an opinion to be dicta is not the only method judges and lawyers invoke to avoid applying earlier rulings. Other means include distinguishing, limiting, ignoring, or even overruling precedents.

---

[2] See Walter F. Murphy, "Civil Liberties and the Japanese American Cases: A Study in the Uses of Stare Decisis," 11 *Western Political Quarterly* 3 (1958).

[3] Memorandum by Herbert Wechsler, Law Clerk File, *The Stone Papers*, the Library of Congress.

Distinguishing a Precedent

Distinguishing a precedent involves a demonstration that the principle of the earlier case is, when "properly" understood, inapplicable to the present problem. Because the facts of two cases are never identical, it is always possible to find grounds for refusing to follow the earlier decision, although sometimes the reasons offered strain credulity.

Examples are numerous. In *Oyama v. California* (1948) the Supreme Court "assumed" the constitutionality of a California statute forbidding aliens (that is, Japanese) ineligible for American citizenship to acquire agricultural land, though it managed to render the act unenforceable on other grounds. Five months later in *Takahashi v. Commission* the Court considered the constitutionality of a similar California law banning alien Japanese from commercial fishing. Justice Stanley Reed thought that "the right to fish is analogous to the right to own land"; but, speaking for the majority, Justice Black managed to distinguish the two statutes. *Oyama* and the cases on which it relied "could not in any event be controlling here. They rested solely upon the power of states to control the devolution and ownership of land within their borders, a power long exercised and supported on reasons peculiar to real property." In other words, earth is different from water.

In 1937 Chief Justice Charles Evans Hughes treated a pair of precedents even more curtly when, in *National Labor Relations Board v. Jones & Laughlin Steel Corp.* (1937), the Court allowed Congress, under the commerce clause of the constitutional text, to regulate labor relations. Standing directly in the way were two recent rulings, *Schechter Poultry Corp. v. United States* (1935) and *Carter v. Carter Coal Co.* (1936), both of which had emphatically denied that the federal government had authority to regulate labor relations. The Chief Justice merely wrote: "These cases are not controlling here."

Limiting a Precedent

Distinguishing a precedent presumably leaves it with full validity for the circumstances to which it originally applied; a judge simply finds it inapplicable to the current controversy. But occasionally reconsideration of a precedent will convince a court that the doctrine of the earlier opinion should be restated in a more limited way to conform to current understandings. *Carter v. Carter Coal Co.* suffered such a fate. As just noted, Chief Justice Hughes merely distinguished it in 1937, and yet it was obvious that much of *Jones & Laughlin* directly contradicted *Carter*. In 1941, in *United States v. Darby Lumber Co.*, the Supreme Court upheld another congressional statute regulating labor relations on grounds that once more contradicted *Carter*. This time the Court thought it prudent to recognize that something had happened to the vitality of the earlier case and stated that *Carter* was "limited in principle." Although the Court did not explain how the principle was limited, the justices in subsequent cases continued to ignore *Carter's* restrictive interpretation of congressional power. That is, they did so until 1995 when, for the first time since the battles over the New Deal, the justices struck down a federal statute because it allegedly fell outside the authority the commerce clause granted to Congress.[4] The majority opinion cited *Carter Coal* only once, and in passing at that; but Justice Clarence Thomas, in a concurring opinion, invoked it with approval.

Running along somewhat different lines is the way that three members of the Court, Justices Sandra Day O'Connor, Anthony Kennedy, and David Souter, treated *Roe v. Wade* (1973) in *Planned Parenthood of Southeastern Pennsylvania v. Casey* (1992) (Reading 10.5; see also Reading 10.8). On the one hand, the trio did not vote to overrule *Roe*; to the contrary, they reaffirmed its "central holding" that a woman should have "some" freedom to terminate a pregnancy. On the other, the "joint opinion" severely limited (some might even say "gutted") the core of *Roe*. In his separate opinion, Justice Antonin Scalia made this point with some force (Reading 8.1).

Ignoring a Precedent

An embarrassing precedent can be handled by simply not mentioning it at all. This technique may seem rather untidy, even cowardly, because it impairs the validity of the ignored precedent and leaves what Justice William O. Douglas used to call "a derelict on the stream of the law." In *Lochner v. New York* (1905), for example, the Supreme Court held unconstitutional a state ten-hour law for bakers. Then in *Bunting v. Oregon* (1917) a somewhat differently constituted Court upheld Oregon's ten-hour law for factory workers in an opinion that never mentioned *Lochner*. The result of this silence was that when a still different majority of the justices decided in *Adkins v. Children's Hospital* (1923) to invalidate a minimum-wage law for women, they were able to cite *Lochner* as a precedent, contending that "the principles therein stated have never been disapproved." Chief Justice William Howard Taft found all this very confusing, for, as he noted in his dissenting opinion in *Adkins*, he had always supposed that Bunting had overruled *Lochner* "sub silentio."

Again, in *United States v. Classic* (1941) Justice Stone held for the Court that federal primary elections were subject to congressional regulation, without mentioning *Grovey v. Townsend* (1935), which had asserted that party primaries were outside the scope of constitutional protection. Stone had deliberately omitted any such reference because he needed the vote of Justice Owen J. Roberts, who had written the Court's opinion in *Grovey*. Later, in *Smith v. Allwright* (1944), when Roberts's vote was no longer necessary, the Court held that in fact *Grovey* had been dead ever since *Classic*. Realizing that he had been tricked, Roberts protested angrily:

> It is suggested that *Grovey v. Townsend* was overruled sub silentio in *United States v. Classic*. If this Court's opinion in the *Classic* case discloses its method of overruling earlier decisions, I can only protest that, in fairness, it should rather

---

[4] *United States v. Lopez* (1995).

have adopted the open and frank way of saying what it was doing than, after the event, characterize its past action as overruling *Grovey v. Townsend*, though those less sapient never realized the fact.

Overruling a Precedent

Lest it be thought that old precedents never die but just fade away, it should be noted that occasionally a court does specifically overrule a case. Overturning is more likely to occur when a precedent has become a notorious political as well as a legal liability. In the decade from 1937 to 1947, as a new Supreme Court liquidated many of the constitutional doctrines of the old Court, the justices overruled at least thirty-two previous decisions, thirty of which turned on issues of constitutional interpretation. One of the most famous victims of this judicial reorientation was *Hammer v. Dagenhart* (1918), in which the Court had by a five-to-four vote declared unconstitutional the Federal Child Labor Act of 1916. This ruling was based on such a tortured construction of the Court's previous decisions that its authority had always been slight, and in *United States v. Darby Lumber Co.* (1941) the justices welcomed the opportunity to bury it. For a unanimous Court, Justice Stone said:

> The conclusion is inescapable that *Hammer v. Dagenhart* was a departure from the principles which have prevailed in the interpretation of the commerce clause both before and since the decision and that such vitality, as a precedent, as it then had has long since been exhausted. It should be and now is overruled.

In the more contemporary era, justices have advocated overruling decisions in a wide array of legal areas, from federalism to defendants' rights. Indicative of this trend are Justice Scalia's separate opinions in *Webster v. Reproductive Health Services* (Reading 8.1) and *Planned Parenthood* (Reading 10.5).

Because overruling (or even attempting to do so) often attracts much publicity, such events may seem to occur far more frequently than they in fact do. The Supreme Court has many times repeated that it is always ready to reconsider its interpretations of the Constitution, but even there a clean reversal of precedent is unusual. Moreover, where issues essentially involve only private individuals and where many people have in good faith built thick layers of relations around the framework of an earlier rule, judges are reluctant to scrap that rule, even when they think that the rule is ill-advised and inconsistent with other decisions. Judges have the obvious—and realistic—fear that a sudden switch to a different rule will create chaos. One means of avoiding such horrendous results and still formulating new, more preferred rules is the practice of "prospective overruling," a declaration by a court that it will decide cases arising in the future by a new principle but will neither upset old decisions nor apply that new principle to disputes that began in the past, when the older rule was in effect. In addition, as a general policy, the Supreme Court will not overturn its earlier interpretations of a congressional statute, even when the justices now disagree with the earlier interpretation. Congress, the justices usually say, can undo the Court's error, if error there be, by passing a new statute.

Deeper reasons of policy may also lie behind the Court's refusal to overturn a previous decision in any field of the law. For instance, in *Runyon v. McCrary* (1977) Justice John Paul Stevens offered a candid explanation for joining a majority of the Court in a holding that a congressional statute enacted during Reconstruction forbade private citizens to decline to sign a contract with other citizens because of their race. The majority based Runyon on *Jones v. Mayer* (1968), but later research convinced Stevens that *Jones* had misstated the intentions of Congress. Furthermore, Jones had involved a different statute, although Congress had later codified the two as successive sections in the same chapter and title of the United States Code. Despite his view of *Jones* and his misgivings about the differences between the two statutes, Stevens joined the majority, explaining that "even if Jones did not accurately reflect the sentiments of the Reconstruction Congress, it surely accords with the prevailing sense of justice today." He continued:

> The policy of the Nation as formulated by the Congress in recent years has moved constantly in the direction of eliminating racial segregation in all sectors of society. This Court has given a liberal and sympathetic construction to such legislation. For the Court now to overrule Jones would be a significant step backwards, with effects that would not have arisen from a correct decision in the first instance. Such a step would be so clearly contrary to my understanding of the mores of today that I think the Court is entirely correct in adhering to Jones.

Nonetheless, overrulings do occur—one study found that the U.S. Supreme Court had, as of 1995, overturned 154 of its own decisions.[5] Moreover, and despite this relatively low number (after all, the Court has issued thousands of opinions), scholars have sought to identify the features of cases that make them ripe for reversal. One, to which we have already alluded, centers on whether the precedent has become a liability. James Spriggs and Thomas Hansford find that the more often the Court has distinguished or limited a precedent, the more likely the justices will overrule it.[6] Spriggs and Hansford also discover that courts they classify as liberal are more willing to override precedents established by "conservative" courts, and vice versa. Such would not have come as a surprise to Justice Thurgood Marshall. In response to the Court's decision in *Payne v. Tennessee* (1991), which overruled *Booth v. Maryland* (1987) and *South Carolina v. Gathers* (1989), Marshall quipped: "It takes little real detective work to discern just what has changed since this Court decided *Booth* and *Gathers*: this Court's own personnel."

Extending a Precedent

So far we have been talking mostly about restricting precedents, but just as the importance of some decisions diminish or die, the reach of others expands. In

---

[5] Saul Brenner and Harold J. Spaeth, *Stare Indecisis* (New York: Cambridge University Press, 1995).

[6] J. Spriggs and T. Hansford, "Explaining the Overruling of U.S. Supreme Court Precedent." Paper presented at the 1998 annual meeting of the Midwest Political Science Association, Chicago.

fact, Justice Cardozo stressed the "tendency of a principle to expand itself to the limit of its logic," and his opinion in *MacPherson v. Buick Motor Co.* (Reading 10.3) beautifully illustrates the point. *Hirabayashi* and *Korematsu* supply another excellent case study. In the first decision, sustaining the curfew, Justice Stone carefully explained that the Court was restricting itself to deciding that single issue: "It is unnecessary," he wrote, "to consider whether or to what extent such findings [of military danger] would support orders differing from the curfew order." But the following year Justice Black in *Korematsu* squarely based his reasoning on "the principles we announced in the *Hirabayashi* Case." In vain, Justice Robert H. Jackson dissented: "The Court is now saying that in *Hirabayashi* we did decide the very things we there said that we were not deciding. . . . How far the principle of this case would be extended before plausible reasons would play out, I do not know."

A decade later *Brown v. Board of Education* (1954) spoke of the fundamental importance of the public school system to American life and of the deleterious effects of compelling children to attend racially segregated schools. With no further elaboration about the evil effects of segregation either in general or in some noneducational settings, the Court cited *Brown* to justify, in terse opinions, invalidating laws requiring racial separation in public parks, golf courses, swimming pools, and transportation.

PRECEDENTS AND DECISION MAKING

In sum, when a court makes a decision, it brings into being a force that is itself potentially creative. Like parents with their children, no judge can foretell how an intellectual offspring will develop. At the hands of other jurists principles may wither, remain healthy, or grow into giants. Indeed, these principles might go through several cycles of expansion and contraction as circumstances—and judges—change. Thus, the accordion-like qualities of stare decisis allow judges to adapt the law incrementally, step-by-step, usually preserving some of the old rules while fashioning new ones. The whole process is much more disorderly and unpredictable than judges sometimes like to admit. "I was much troubled in spirit, in my first years on the bench," Justice Cardozo wrote, "to find how trackless was the ocean on which I had embarked. I sought for certainty. . . . [But] I have grown to see that the process in its highest reaches is not discovery, but creation."[7]

Cardozo's claim (or at least the implications of it) finds support within the scholarly literature. Recall Chapter 1's discussion of the Legal Realists, many of whom regarded citing precedents as mere "smokescreens" used by judges to mask their own values and attitudes. At least some contemporary analysts

---

[7] Benjamin N. Cardozo, *The Nature of the Judicial Process* (New Haven, CT: Yale University Press, 1921), 166.

agree. Jeffrey A. Segal and Harold J. Spaeth, for example, cast doubt on the degree to which precedents affect the decisions reached by U.S. Supreme Court justices (Reading 10.6). And research by Frank B. Cross and Emerson H. Tiller suggests that judges of U.S. Court of Appeals are less-than-faithful followers of precedents they do not like. When there is a "whistleblower" on the court—that is, a judge "whose policy preferences differ from the majority's" and who will expose the majority's failure to apply relevant precedents—the majority will follow stare decisis. But when a whistleblower is not present, according to Cross and Tiller, the court will attempt to manipulate precedents to conform to its political values (Reading 13.3).

In contrast comes the voice of Justice Lewis F. Powell, who said that he "cannot agree" with those who assert that the Court ignores stare decisis (Reading 10.7). Powell too could have laid claim to scholarly support for his position. Some comes from historical institutionalists, who argue that precedent informs judicial decision making in "important ways." Ronald Kahn's essay (Reading 10.8) exemplifies this school of thought. Variants of rational choice scholarship, with Jack Knight and Lee Epstein's response to Segal and Spaeth's work being illustrative, would agree with Kahn's bottom line but take a different route to arrive there (Reading 10.6). While Kahn argues that justices follow precedent at least in part because of their "conceptions of their professional obligations," Knight and Epstein suggest that the justices—even those who do not share the view that the Court should be tightly constrained by past decisions—will take precedent into account because they are concerned with protecting the integrity of their institution and with establishing rules that will engender public compliance.

SELECTED REFERENCES

ACKERMAN, BRUCE. 1991. *We the People.* Cambridge, MA: Harvard University Press.

BENESH, SARA C. AND MALIA REDDICK, 2001. "Overruled: An Event History Analysis of Lower Court Reaction to Supreme Court Alteration of Precedent." *Journal of Politics* 63: 534.

BRENNER, SAUL, AND HAROLD J. SPAETH. 1995. *Stare Indecisis.* Cambridge, MA: Cambridge University Press.

BRIGHAM, JOHN. 1978. *Constitutional Language: An Interpretation of Judicial Decision.* Westport, CT: Greenwood Press.

BUENO DE MESQUITA, ETHAN AND MATTHEW STEPHENSON. 2002. "Informative Precedent and Intrajudicial Communication," *American Political Science Review* 96:755.

CARDOZO, BENJAMIN N. 1921. *The Nature of the Judicial Process.* New Haven, CT: Yale University Press.

CARTER, LIEF H., AND THOMAS BURKE. 2001. *Reason in Law.* New York: Longman.

CROSS, FRANK B., AND EMERSON H. TILLER. 1998. "Judicial Partisanship and Obedience to Legal Doctrine: Whistleblowing on the Federal Court of Appeals." *Yale Law Journal* 107: 2155.

DOUGLAS, WILLIAM O. 1949. "Stare Decisis." *The Record of the Association of the Bar of the City of New York* 4: 152.

DWORKIN, RONALD. 1977. *Taking Rights Seriously*. Cambridge, MA: Harvard University Press.

FRIEDMAN, LAWRENCE. 1968. "On Legalistic Reasoning." *Wisconsin Law Review* 1968: 148.

FULLER, LON L. 1946. "Reason and Fiat in Case Law." *Harvard Law Review* 59: 376.

GELY, RAFAEL. 1998. "Of Sinking and Escalating: A (Somewhat) New Look at Stare Decisis." *University of Pittsburgh Law Review* 60: 89.

GILLMAN, HOWARD. 1993. *The Constitution Besieged: The Rise and Demise of Lochner Era Police Powers Jurisprudence*. Durham, NC: Duke University Press.

GOODHART, ARTHUR L. 1930. "Determining the Ratio Decidendi of a Case." *Yale Law Journal* 40: 161.

KAHN, PAUL M. 1999. *The Cultural Study of Law: Reconstructing Legal Scholarship*. Chicago: University Of Chicago Press.

KAHN, RONALD. 1999. "Institutional Norms and Supreme Court Decision Making: The Rehnquist Court on Privacy and Religion Supreme Court Decision Making." In *Supreme Court Decision Making*. Chicago: University of Chicago Press.

LEE, THOMAS R. 1999. "Stare Decisis in Historical Perspective: From the Founding Era to the Rehnquist Court." *Vanderbilt Law Review* 52: 647.

LEVI, EDWARD H. 1948. *An Introduction to Legal Reasoning*. Chicago: University of Chicago Press.

LLEWELLYN, KARL N. 1960. *The Common Law Tradition: Deciding Appeals*. Boston: Little, Brown.

MERRYMAN, JOHN HENRY. 1971. *The Civil Law Tradition: An Introduction to the Legal Systems of Western Europe and Latin America*. Stanford, CA: Stanford University Press.

MURPHY, WALTER F. 1958. "Civil Liberties and the Japanese American Cases: A Study in the Uses of Stare Decisis." *Western Political Quarterly* 11: 3.

POUND, ROSCOE. 1923. "The Theory of Judicial Decision." *Harvard Law Review* 36: 641.

SHAPIRO, MARTIN. 1965. "Stability and Change in Judicial Decision-Making: Incrementalism or Stare Decisis?" *Law in Transition Quarterly* 2: 134.

SHAPIRO, MARTIN. 1972. "Toward a Theory of Stare Decisis." *Journal of Legal Studies* 1972: 125.

SPAETH, HAROLD J., AND JEFFREY A. SEGAL. 1999. *Majority Rule or Minority Will?* Cambridge: Cambridge University Press.

SPRIGGS, JAMES F., AND THOMAS C. HANSFORD. 2001. "Explaining the Overruling of U.S. Supreme Court Precedent." *Journal of Politics* 63: 1091.

SUNSTEIN, CASS. 2001. *Designing Democracy: What Constitutions Do*. Oxford: Oxford University Press.

"The basic pattern of legal reasoning is reasoning by example."

10.1 AN INTRODUCTION TO LEGAL REASONING

Edward H. Levi

Edward Levi is Glen A. Lloyd Distinguished Service Professor, Emeritus, and President, Emeritus, of the University of Chicago.

. . . [I]t is important that the mechanism of legal reasoning should not be concealed by its pretense. The pretense is that the law is a system of known rules applied by a judge. . . . In an important sense legal rules are never clear, and, if a rule had to be clear before it could be imposed, society would be impossible. The mechanism accepts the differences of view and ambiguities of words. It provides for the participation of the community in resolving the ambiguity by providing a forum for the discussion of policy in the gap of ambiguity. On serious controversial questions, it makes it possible to take the first step in the direction of what otherwise would be forbidden ends. The mechanism is indispensable to peace in a community.

The basic pattern of legal reasoning is reasoning by example. It is reasoning from case to case. It is a three-step process described by the doctrine of precedent in which a proposition descriptive of the first case is made into a rule of law and then applied to a next similar situation. The steps are these: similarity is seen between cases; next the rule of law inherent in the first case is announced; then the rule of law is made applicable to the second case. This is a method of reasoning necessary for the law, but it has characteristics which under other circumstances might be considered imperfections. . . .

The determination of similarity or difference is the function of each judge. Where case law is considered and there is no statute, he [or she] is not bound by the statement of the rule of law made by the prior judge even in the controlling case. The statement is mere dictum, and this means that the judge in the present case may find irrelevant the existence or absence of facts which prior judges thought important. It is not what the prior judge intended that is of any importance; rather it is what the present judge, attempting to see the law as a fairly consistent whole, thinks should be the determining classification. In arriving at his result he will ignore what the past thought important; he will emphasize facts which prior judges would have thought made no difference. It is not alone that he could not see the law through the eyes of another, for he could at least try to do so. It is rather that the doctrine of dictum forces him to make his own decision.

Reprinted from *An Introduction to Legal Reasoning* by Edward H. Levi, by permission of The University of Chicago Press. Copyright University of Chicago Press, 1948. Pp. 1–7.

Thus it cannot be said that the legal process is the application of known rules to diverse facts. Yet it is a system of rules; the rules are discovered in the process of determining similarity or difference. But if attention is directed toward the finding of similarity or difference, other peculiarities appear. The problem for the law is: When will it be just to treat different cases as though they were the same? A working legal system must therefore be willing to pick out key similarities and to reason from them to the justice of applying a common classification. The existence of some facts in common brings into play the general rule. If this is really reasoning, then by common standards, thought of in terms of closed systems, it is imperfect unless some overall rule has announced that this common and ascertainable similarity is to be decisive. But no such fixed prior rule exists. It could be suggested that reasoning is not involved at all; that is, that no new insight is arrived at through a comparison of cases. But reasoning appears to be involved; the conclusion is arrived at through a process and was not immediately apparent. It seems better to say there is reasoning, but it is imperfect.

Therefore it appears that the kind of reasoning involved in the legal process is one in which the classification changes as the classification is made. The rules change as the rules are applied. More important, the rules arise out of a process which, while comparing fact situations, creates the rules and then applies them. . . . In a sense all reasoning is of this type, but there is an additional requirement which compels the legal process to be this way. Not only do new situations arise, but in addition people's wants change. The categories used in the legal process must be left ambiguous in order to permit the infusion of new ideas. And this is true even where legislation or a constitution is involved. The words used by the legislature or the constitutional convention must come to have new meanings. Furthermore, agreement on any other basis would be impossible. In this manner the laws come to express the ideas of the community and even when written in general terms, in statute or constitution, are molded for the specific case.

But attention must be paid to the process. A controversy as to whether the law is certain, unchanging, and expressed in rules, or uncertain, changing, and only a technique for deciding specific cases misses the point. It is both. . . .

Reasoning by example in the law is a key to many things. It indicates in part the hold which the Law process has over the litigants. They have participated in the law making. They are bound by something they helped to make. Moreover, the examples or analogies urged by the parties bring into the law the common ideas of the society. The ideas have their day in court, and they will have their day again. This is what makes the hearing fair, rather than any idea that the judge is completely impartial, for of course he cannot be completely so. Moreover, the hearing in a sense compels at least vicarious participation by all the citizens, for the rule which is made, even though ambiguous, will be law as to them.

Reasoning by example shows the decisive role which the common ideas of the society and the distinctions made by experts can have in shaping the law. The movement of common or expert concepts into the law may be followed. . . .

The idea achieves standing in the society. It is suggested again to a court. The court this time reinterprets the prior case and in doing so adopts the rejected idea. In subsequent cases, the idea is given further definition and is tied to other ideas which have been accepted by courts. It is now no longer the idea which was commonly held in the society. It becomes modified in subsequent cases. Ideas first rejected but which gradually have won acceptance now push what has become a legal category out of the system or convert it into something which may be its opposite. The process is one in which the ideas of the community and of the social sciences, whether correct or not, as they win acceptance in the community, control legal decisions. Erroneous ideas, of course, have played an enormous part in shaping the law. An idea, adopted by a court, is in a superior position to influence conduct and opinion in the community; judges, after all, are rulers. And the adoption of an idea by a court reflects the power structure in the community. But reasoning by example will operate to change the idea after it has been adopted.

Moreover, reasoning by example brings into focus important similarity and difference in the interpretation of case law, statutes, and the constitution of a nation. There is a striking similarity. It is only folklore which holds that a statute if clearly written can be completely unambiguous and applied as intended to a specific case. . . . Hence reasoning by example operates with all three. But there are important differences. What a court says is dictum, but what a legislature says is a statute. The reference of the reasoning changes. Interpretation of intention when dealing with a statute is the way of describing the attempt to compare cases on the basis of the standard thought to be common at the time the legislation was passed. While this is the attempt, it may not initially accomplish any different result than if the standards of the judge had been explicitly used. Nevertheless, the remarks of the judge are directed toward describing a category set up by the legislature. These remarks are different from ordinary dicta. They set the course of the statute, and later reasoning in subsequent cases is tied to them. As a consequence, courts are less free in applying a statute than in dealing with ease law. The current rationale for this is the notion that the legislature has acquiesced by legislative silence in the prior, even though erroneous, interpretation of the court. . . .

Under the United States experience, contrary to what has sometimes been believed when a written constitution of a nation is involved, the court has greater freedom than it has with the application of a statute or case law. . . . The constitution sets up the conflicting ideals of the community in certain ambiguous categories. . . . The constitution, in other words, permits the court to be inconsistent. The freedom is concealed either as a search for the intention of the framers or as a proper understanding of a living instrument, and sometimes as both. But this does not mean that reasoning by example has any less validity in this field.

It may be objected that this analysis of legal reasoning places too much emphasis on the comparison of cases and too little on the legal concepts which are created. It is true that similarity is seen in terms of a word, and inability to find a ready word to express similarity or difference may prevent change in the law.

The words which have been found in the past are much spoken of, have acquired a dignity of their own, and to a considerable measure control results. . . . Thus the connotation of the [phrase] *For a time* has a limiting influence—so much so that the reasoning may even appear to be simply deductive.

But it is not simply deductive. In the long run a circular motion can be seen. The first stage is the creation of the legal concept which is built up as cases are compared. The period is one in which the court fumbles for a phrase. Several phrases may be tried out; the misuse or misunderstanding of words itself may have an effect. The concept sounds like another, and the jump to the second is made. The second stage is the period when the concept is more or less fixed, although reasoning by example continues to classify items inside and out of the concept. The third stage is the breakdown of the concept, as reasoning by example has moved so far ahead as to make it clear that the suggestive influence of the word is no longer desired.

The process is likely to make judges and lawyers uncomfortable. It runs contrary to the pretense of the system. It seems inevitable, therefore, that as matters of kind vanish into matters of degree and then entirely new meanings turn up, there will be the attempt to escape to some overall rule which can be said to have always operated and which will make the reasoning look deductive. The rule will be useless. It will have to operate on a level where it has no meaning. . . . It is window dressing. Yet it can be very misleading. Particularly when a concept has broken down and reasoning by example is about to build another, textbook writers, well aware of the unreal aspect of old rules, will announce new ones, equally ambiguous and meaningless, forgetting that the legal process does not work with the rule but on a much lower level. . . .

"Legal rules change every time they are applied because no two
cases ever have exactly the same facts."

10.2 REASON IN LAW

Lief H. Carter

Lief Carter is McHugh Distinguished Professor of American
Institutions and Leadership at Colorado College.

. . . Precedents help narrow the range of legal choices judges face when they resolve a cas[e], . . . but they never provide complete certainty. Reasoning by example also perpetuates a degree of unpredictability in law. To see why, we proceed through six analytical stages.

From Lief H. Carter, *Reason in Law* 4th ed. (New York: HarperCollins, 1988).

Stage One: Reasoning by Example in General

Reasoning by example, in its simplest form, means accepting one choice and rejecting another because the past provides an example that the accepted choice somehow "worked." Robert, for example, wants to climb a tree but wonders if its branches will hold. He chooses to attempt the climb because his older sister has just climbed the tree without mishap. Robert reasons by example. His reasoning hardly guarantees success: His older sister may still be skinnier and lighter. Robert may regret a choice based on a bad example, but he still reasons that way. If he falls and survives, he will possess a much better example from which to reason in the future.

The most important characteristic of reasoning by example in any area of life is that no rules tell the decider *how* to select the facts that are similar or different. Let us therefore see how this indeterminacy occurs in legal reasoning.

Stage Two: Examples in Law

In law, decisions in prior cases provide the examples for legal reasoning. For starters, a precedent contains the analysis and the conclusion reached in an earlier case in which the facts and the legal question(s) resemble the current conflict a judge has to resolve. Even when a statute or a constitutional rule is involved, a judge will look at what other judges have said about the meaning of that rule when they applied it to similar facts and answer similar legal questions. . . .

To understand more fully how precedents create examples we must return to the distinction between law and history. How does a judge know whether facts of a prior case really do resemble those in the case now before him [or her]?

Trials themselves do *not*, as a rule, produce precedents. As we have seen, trials seek primarily to find the immediate facts of the dispute, to discover who is lying, whose memory has failed, and who can reliably speak to the truth of the matter. When a jury hears the case, the judge acts as an umpire, making sure the lawyers present the evidence properly to the jury so that it decides the "right" question. Often judges do the jury's job altogether. The law does not allow jury trials in some kinds of cases. When the law does allow jury trials, the parties may elect to go before a judge anyway, perhaps because they feel the issues are too complex for laypeople or perhaps because "bench trials" take less time.

Of course, a trial judge must decide the issues of law that the lawyers raise. The conscientious trial judge will explain to the parties orally for the record why and how he resolves the key legal issues in their case. In some instances he will give them a written opinion explaining his legal choices, and some of these find their way into the reported opinions. But since at trial the judge pays most attention to the historical part of the case, deciding what happened, he usually keeps his explanations at the relatively informal oral level. As a result other judges will not find these opinions reported anywhere; they cannot discover them even if they try. Hence few trial judges create precedents even though they resolve legal issues.

Thus the masses of legal precedents that fill the shelves of law libraries mostly emerge from the appellate process. You should not, however, lose sight of the fact that lawyers use many of the same legal reasoning techniques when they base their recommendations to their clients on appellate precedents to avoid trials as well as when they manipulate precedents to their advantage in litigation.

Stage Three: The Three-Step Process of Reasoning by Example

Legal reasoning often involves reasoning from the examples of precedents. Powerful legal traditions impel judges to solve problems by using solutions to similar problems reached by judges in the past. Thus a judge seeks to resolve conflicts by discovering a statement about the law in a prior case—his example—and then applying this statement or conclusion to the case before him. Lawyers who seek to anticipate problems and prevent conflicts follow much the same procedure. Professor Levi calls this a three-step process in which the judge sees a factual similarity between the current case and one or more prior cases, announces the rule of law, on which the earlier case or cases rested, and applies the rule to the case before him.

Stage Four: How Reasoning by Example Perpetuates Unpredictability in Law

To understand this stage we must return to the first step in the three-step description of the legal reasoning process, the step in which the judge decides which precedent governs. The judge must choose the facts in the case before him that resemble or differ from the facts in the case, or line of cases, in which prior judicial decisions first announced the rule. The judge no doubt accepts his obligation, made powerful by legal tradition, to "follow precedent," but he is under no obligation to follow any particular precedent. He completes step one by *deciding for himself* which of the many precedents are similar to the facts of the case before him and by *deciding for himself* what they mean.

No judicial opinion in a prior case can require that a judge sift the facts of his present case one way or another. He is always free to do this himself. A judge writing his opinion can influence a future user of the precedent he creates by refusing to report or consider some potentially important facts revealed in the trial transcript. But once he reports them, precedent users can use the facts in their own way. They can call a fact critical that a prior judge reported but deemed irrelevant; they can make a legal molehill out of what a prior judge called a mountain. Thus the present judge, the precedent user, retains the freedom to choose the example from which the legal conclusion follows.

I call this judicial freedom to choose the governing precedent by selectively sifting the facts "fact freedom." Our inability to predict with total accuracy how a judge will use his fact freedom is the major source of uncertainty in law. Thus we cannot say that "the law" applies known or given rules to diverse factual situations, because we don't know the applicable rules until after the judge uses his fact freedom to choose the precedent.

Stage Five: An illustration of Unpredictability in Law

Consider the following example from the rather notorious history of enforcing the Mann Act. The Mann Act, passed by Congress in 1910, provides in part that "Any person who shall knowingly transport or cause to be transported . . . in interstate or foreign commerce . . . any woman or girl for the purpose of prostitution or debauchery, or for any other immoral purpose . . . shall be deemed guilty of a felony." Think about these words for a minute. Do they say that if I take my wife to Tennessee for the purpose of drinking illegal moonshine whiskey with her I shall be deemed guilty of a felony? What if I take her to Tennessee to rob a bank? Certainly robbing a bank is an "immoral purpose." Is it "interstate commerce"? [(No need to answer the question now.)] . . . For the moment, you should see only that the Congress has chosen some rather ambiguous words and then move to the main problem: choosing the "right" example to decide the following case.

Mr. and Mrs. Mortensen, owners and operators of a house of prostitution in Grand Island, Nebraska, decided to take some of the employees for a well-earned vacation at Yellowstone and Salt Lake City. The girls did lay off their occupation completely during the entire duration of the trip. Upon their return they resumed their calling. Over a year later federal agents arrested the Mortensens and, on the basis of the vacation trip, charged them with violation of the Mann Act. The jury convicted the Mortensens. Their lawyer appealed to an appellate court judge.

Unpredictability in law arises when the judge cannot automatically say that a given precedent is or isn't factually similar. To simplify matters here, let us now assume that he examines only one precedent, the decision of the U.S. Supreme Court in *Caminetti v. United States*, announced in 1917. He must choose whether this example does or does not determine the result in Mortensen. Assume that in *Caminetti* a man from Wichita met but did not linger with a woman during a brief visit to Oklahoma City. After his return home, he sent this "mistress" a train ticket, which she used to travel to Wichita. There she did spend several nights with her friend, but not as a commercial prostitute. Assume that on these facts the Supreme Court in *Caminetti* upheld the conviction under the Mann Act. Does this case determine the Mortensens' fate? Does this precedent bind the court in Mortensen? To answer these questions the judge must decide whether this case is factually similar to Mortensen. Is it?

In one sense, of course it is. In each case the defendants transported women across state lines, after which sex out of wedlock occurred. In another sense it isn't. Without her ticket and transportation the Oklahoma woman could not have slept with the defendant. But if the Mortensens had not sponsored the vacation, the women would have continued their work. The Mortensens' transportation *reduced* the frequency of prostitution. The rancher maintained or increased "illicit sex." Should this difference matter? The judge is free to select one interpretation of the facts or the other in order to answer this question. Either decision will create a new legal precedent. It is precisely this freedom to decide either way that increases unpredictability in law.

Stage Six: Reasoning by Example Facilitates Legal Change

Why does judicial fact freedom make law change constantly? Legal rules change every time they are applied because no two cases ever have exactly the same facts. Although judges treat cases as if they were legally the same whenever they apply the rule of one case to another, deciding the new case in terms of the rule adds to the list of cases a new and unique factual situation. To rule in the Mortensens' favor, as the Supreme Court did in 1944, gave judges new ways of looking at the Mann Act. With those facts, judges after 1944 could, if they wished, read the Mann Act more narrowly than *Caminetti* did. Mortensen thus potentially changed the meaning of the Mann Act, thereby changing the law.

But as the situation turned out, the change did not endure. In 1946 the Court upheld the conviction, under the Mann Act, of certain Mormons, members of a branch known as Fundamentalists, who took "secondary" wives across state lines. No prostitution at all was involved here, but the evidence did suggest that some of the women did not travel voluntarily. Fact freedom worked its way again. The Court extended *Caminetti* and by implication isolated Mortensen. The content of the Mann Act, then, has changed with each new decision and each new set of facts.

Is law always as confusing and unclear as these examples make it seem? In one sense certainly not. To the practicing lawyer, most legal questions the client asks possess clear and predictable answers. But in such cases . . . the problems probably do not get to court at all. Uncertainty helps convert a human problem into a legal conflict. We focus on uncertainty in law because that is where reason in law takes over.

In another sense, however, law never entirely frees itself from uncertainty. Lawyers always cope with uncertainties about what happened, uncertainties that arise in the historical part of law. If they go to trial on the facts, even if they think the law is clear, the introduction of new evidence or the unexpected testimony of a witness may raise new and uncertain legal issues the lawyers didn't consider before the trial. Lawyers know they can never fully predict the outcome of a client's case, even though much of the law is clear to them most of the time.

The Other Side of the Coin: Stare Decisis as a Stabilizing and Clarifying Element in Law

I hope that this discussion of unpredictability in law has not left the impression that law is never clear at all. If rules of law amounted to nonsense—lacked any meaning—government by law could not function. If society is to work, most law must be clear much of the time. We must be able to make wills and contracts, to insure ourselves against disasters, and to plan hundreds of other decisions with the confidence that courts will back our decisions if the people we trust with our freedom and our property fail us.

There is indeed a force pushing toward stability within reasoning by example itself: Once judges determine that a given precedent is factually similar enough to determine the outcome in the case before them, then in normal circumstances they follow the precedent. We call this the doctrine of stare decisis, "we let the prior decision stand." . . .

. . . [I]n fact, most law is clear enough to prevent litigation most of the time. Lawyers can advise us on how to make valid wills and binding contracts. . . . Without a system of precedents it would be harder for us to predict judicial decisions and therefore more difficult for us to plan to avoid legal conflicts.

There is a paradox here. Because courts do exist to apply law to solve legal problems, and because we trust them in fact to do so, courts, particularly the appellate courts that concern us here, don't actually have to do this in the majority of disputes. In anticipation, private citizens who know what the law means in their case will, if for no other reason than to save money, usually resolve their problem without asking a court to review the law. They don't need to ask the meaning of the law; they know its meaning.

Perhaps in our legal system both clarity and unpredictability, and stability and change, can benefit us, depending on the type of problem the law tries to address in a given case. . . .

> "*. . . whatever the rule in* Thomas v. Winchester *may once have been, it has no longer that restricted meaning.*"

10.3 MACPHERSON V. BUICK MOTOR CO.

217 N.Y. 382, 111 N.E. 1060 (1916) (Court of Appeals of New York)

CARDOZO, J. The defendant is a manufacturer of automobiles. It sold an automobile to a retail dealer. The retailer dealer resold to the plaintiff. While the plaintiff was in the car, it suddenly collapsed. He was thrown out and injured. One of the wheels was made of defective wood, and its spokes crumbled into fragments. The wheel was not made by the defendant; it was bought from another manufacturer. There is evidence, however, that its defects could have been discovered by reasonable inspection, and that inspection was omitted. There is no claim that the defendant knew of the defect and willfully concealed it. . . . The question to be determined is whether the defendant owed a duty of care and vigilance to anyone but the immediate purchaser.

The foundations of this branch of the law, at least in this state, were laid in *Thomas v. Winchester*. A poison was falsely labeled. The sale was made to a druggist, who in turn sold to a customer. The customer recovered damages from the seller who affixed the label. "The defendant's negligence," it was said, "put human life in imminent danger." A poison falsely labeled is likely to injure any one who gets it. Because the danger is to be foreseen, there is a duty to avoid injury. Cases were cited by way of illustration in which manufacturers were not subject to any duty irrespective of contract. The distinction was said to be that their conduct, though negligent, was not likely to result in injury to any one except the purchaser. We are not required to say whether the chance of injury was always as remote as the distinction assumes. Some of the illustrations might be rejected today. The *principle* of the distinction is for present purposes the important thing.

Thomas v. Winchester became quickly a landmark of the law. In the application of its principle there may at times have been uncertainty or even error. There has never in this state been doubt or disavowal of the principle itself. The chief cases are well known. *Loop v. Litchfield* was the case of a defect in a small balance wheel used on a circular saw. The manufacturer pointed out the defect to the buyer, who wished a cheap article and was ready to assume the risk. The risk can hardly have been an imminent one, for the wheel lasted five years before it broke. In the meanwhile the buyer had made a lease of the machinery. It was held that the manufacturer was not answerable to the lessee. . . . *Losee v. Clute,* the case of the explosion of a steam boiler, must be confined to its special facts. It was put upon the ground that the risk of injury was too remote. The buyer in that case had not only accepted the boiler but had tested it. The manufacturer knew that his own test was not the final one. The finality of the test has a bearing on the measure of diligence owing to persons other than the purchaser. . . .

These early cases suggest a narrow construction of the rule. Later cases, however, evince a more liberal spirit. First in importance is *Devlin v. Smith.* The defendant, a contractor, built a scaffold for a painter. The painter's servants were injured. The contractor was held liable. He knew that the scaffold, if improperly constructed, was a most dangerous trap. He knew that it was to be used by the workmen. He was building it for that very purpose. Building it for their use, he owed them a duty, irrespective of his contract with their master, to build it with care.

. . . [T]he latest case in this court in which *Thomas v. Winchester* was followed . . . is *Statler v. Ray Mfg. Co.* The defendant manufactured a large coffee urn. It was installed in a restaurant. When heated, the urn exploded and injured the plaintiff. We held that the manufacturer was liable. We said that the urn "was of such a character inherently that, when applied to the purposes for which it was designed, it was liable to become a source of great danger to many people if not carefully and properly constructed."

It may be that *Devlin v. Smith* and *Statler* have extended the rule of *Thomas v. Winchester.* If so, this court is committed to the extension. The defendant argues that things imminently dangerous to life are poisons, explosives, deadly weapons—things whose normal function it is to injure or destroy. But whatever the rule in *Thomas v. Winchester* may once have been, it has no longer that restricted meaning. A scaffold . . . is not inherently a destructive instrument. It becomes destructive only if imperfectly constructed. A large coffee urn . . . may have within itself, if negligently made, the potency of danger, yet no one thinks of it as an implement whose normal function is destruction. . . . We have mentioned only cases in this court. But the rule has received a like extension in our courts of intermediate appeal.

We hold, then, that the principle of *Thomas v. Winchester* is not limited to poisons, explosives, and things of like nature, to things which in their normal operation are implements of destruction. If the nature of a thing is such that it is reasonably certain to place life and limb in peril when negligently made, it is then a thing of danger. Its nature gives warning of the consequences to be expected. If to the element of danger there is added knowledge that the thing will be used by persons other than the purchaser, and used without new tests, then, irrespective of contract, the manufacturer of this thing of danger is under duty to make it carefully. That is as far as we are required to go for the decision of this case. There must be knowledge of a danger, not merely possible, but probable. . . . There must also be knowledge that in the usual course of events the danger will be shared by others than the buyer. Such knowledge may often be inferred from the nature of the transaction. But it is possible that even knowledge of the danger and of the use will not always be enough. The proximity or remoteness of the relation is a factor to be considered. . . . We are not required at this time to say that it is legitimate to go back to the manufacturer of the finished product and hold the manufacturers of the component parts [liable]. . . . We leave that question open. We shall have to deal with it when it arises. . . .

From this survey of the decisions, there thus emerges a definition of the duty of a manufacturer which enables us to measure this defendant's liability. Beyond all question, the nature of an automobile gives warning of probable danger if its construction is defective. This automobile was designed to go fifty miles an hour. Unless its wheels were sound and strong, injury was almost certain. It was as much a thing of danger as a defective engine for a railroad. The defendant knew the danger. It knew also that the car would be used by persons other than the buyer. This was apparent from its size; there were seats for three persons. It was apparent also from the fact that the buyer was a dealer in cars, who bought to resell. The maker of this car supplied it for the use of purchasers from the dealer just as plainly as the contractor in *Devlin v. Smith* supplied the scaffold for use by the servants of the owner. The dealer was indeed the one person of whom it might be said with some approach to certainty that by him the car would not be used. Yet the defendant would have us say that he was the one person whom it was under a legal duty to protect. The law does not lead us to so inconsequent a conclusion. Precedents drawn from the days of travel by stage coach do not fit the conditions of travel to-day. The principle that the danger must be imminent does not change, but the things subject to the principle do change. They are whatever the needs of life in a developing civilization require them to be.

In reaching this conclusion, we do not ignore the decisions to the contrary in other jurisdictions. . . . Some of them, at first sight inconsistent with our conclusion, may be reconciled upon the ground that the negligence was too remote, and that another cause had intervened. But even when they cannot be reconciled, the difference is rather in the application of the principle than in the principle itself. . . .

. . . The English courts . . . agree with ours in holding that one who invites another to make use of an appliance is bound to the exercise of reasonable care.

... That at bottom is the underlying principle of *Devlin v. Smith*. The contractor who builds the scaffold invites the owner's workmen to use it. The manufacturer who sells the automobile to the retail dealer invites the dealer's customers to use it. . . .

... We may find an analogy in the law which measures the liability of landlords. If A leases to B a tumbledown house he [A] is not liable, in the absence of fraud, to B's guests who enter it and are injured. This is because B is then under duty to repair it. . . . But if A leases a building to be used by the lessee at once as a place of public entertainment, the rule is different. There injury to persons other than the lessee is foreseen, and the foresight of the consequences involves the creation of a duty (*Junkermann v. Tilyou R. Co.* and cases there cited).

In this view of the defendant's liability there is nothing inconsistent with the theory of liability on which the case was tried. . . .

The judgment should be affirmed with costs.

> "In holding that Congress' power under Article I, Section 5 allowed it 'to judge only the qualifications expressly set forth in the Constitution,' Powell established that the only qualifications and disqualifications for membership in Congress are to be found in the Constitution, and that even a constitutional grant of authority to judge qualifications did not include the power to add any." —BRIEF FOR THE RESPONDENT

> "The Arkansas pluality cited Powell v. McCormack (1969); but there this Court expressly declined to consider state power, and held only that when a single House sits as 'Judge,' then the term 'Qualifications' as used in Article I, § 5, refers only to those set forth in the Constitution." —BRIEF FOR THE PETITIONERS

10.4 BRIEFS FILED IN U.S. TERM LIMITS V. THORNTON

514 U.S. 779 (1995)

Article I of the U.S. Constitution contains the requirements that must be met by all prospective members of Congress:

- *A senator must be at least thirty years old and have been a citizen of the United States not less than nine years (Section 3, Clause 3).*

- *A representative must be at least twenty-five years old and have been a citizen not less than seven years (Section 2, Clause 2).*

- *Every member of Congress must be, when elected, an inhabitant of the state that he or she is to represent (Section 2, Clause 2, and Section 3, Clause 3).*

- *No one may be a member of Congress who holds any other "Office under the United States" (Section 6, Clause 2).*

Finally, Section 3 of the Fourteenth Amendment states that no person may be a senator or a representative who, having previously taken an oath as a member of Congress to support the Constitution, has engaged in rebellion against the United States or given aid or comfort to its enemies, unless Congress has removed such disability by a two-thirds vote of both houses.

With only a few exceptions, these standards qua standards have not caused much controversy or litigation. Some legal questions, however, have arisen with respect to their relationship to Article I, Section 5, which reads: "Each House shall be the Judge of the Elections, Returns and Qualifications of its own Members." Several interpretations are possible. One is that this clause ought to be read in conjunction with Article I requirements for membership. That is, Congress cannot deny a duly elected person a seat in the institution unless that person fails to meet the specified criteria. Another interpretation is that Congress is free to develop additional qualifications, independent of those specified in the constitutional text.

It was not until Powell v. McCormack in 1969 that the Supreme Court sought to resolve this matter. There the Court held that the House of Representatives could not refuse to seat a duly elected individual who met the constitutional standards for membership. As Chief Justice Warren emphatically noted, "Congress is limited to the standing qualifications prescribed in the Constitution."

The Court's decision in Powell became highly relevant to debates in the 1990s over term limits and, in particular, to U.S. Term Limits v. Thornton (1995), the first challenge to reach the Court. Did Powell prevent states from limiting the terms of office of members of the U.S. Congress? Attorneys for the respondents (who wanted the Court to strike down Amendment 73 to the Arkansas state constitution, which prohibited from the ballot anyone seeking reelection who previously had served two terms in the U.S. Senate or three terms in the U.S. House of Representatives) and for the petitioners (who wanted the Court to uphold the Amendment) provided the Court with very distinct responses and, as such, nicely illustrate the malleability of precedent.

Brief for Respondent Congressman Ray Thornton

Question Presented

Whether a State may unilaterally impose qualifications upon candidates for the United States Congress by restricting access to the ballot for certain candidates, even though Article I of the United States Constitution sets forth the qualifications for members of Congress as part of a comprehensive scheme for the election of national legislators.

This Court's Precedents Confirm That the Qualifications Prescribed by the Constitution Are Exclusive

. . . [T]his Court's precedents confirm what the language, structure and history of Article I make clear. In *Powell*, this Court addressed whether courts could review a House determination that an individual was "unqualified" to sit as a member because he had been accused of misappropriating public funds and abusing the process of the New York courts. The issue of justiciability in *Powell* thus turned on whether the Constitution's specified qualifications for members are exclusive, or whether they constitute a mere baseline to which other qualifications may be added. In holding that Congress's power under Article I, Section 5 allowed it "to judge only the qualifications expressly set forth in the Constitution," *Powell* established that the only qualifications and disqualifications for membership in Congress are to be found in the Constitution and that even a constitutional grant of authority to judge qualifications did not include the power to add any.

The Court recently affirmed this reading of *Powell* in *Nixon v. United States*. Distinguishing the justiciability of congressional action under the impeachment clause from congressional action under Section 5, the Court explained that "[o]ur conclusion in *Powell* was based on the fixed meaning of 'qualifications' set forth in Article I, Section 2. The claim [of] . . . textual commitment of unreviewable authority was defeated by the existence of this separate provision specifying the only qualifications which might be imposed for House membership."

Petitioners attempt to dismiss *Powell* on the ground that it did not explicitly address whether qualifications can be added either through legislation or by the States. These distinctions are unavailing. First, petitioners fail to recognize that Congress's authority under Section 5 is, if anything, broader than any "reserved" or implied power it or the States could possibly have over the composition of the national legislature. Section 5 is the only provision in the Constitution that delegates any authority at all to any entity concerning the qualifications of federal legislators. If the express grant of authority to judge the qualifications of Members of Congress does not include authority to prescribe qualifications, the States (and Congress) cannot derive greater authority from constitutional silence.

Second, Article I, Section 4 makes clear that Congress can enjoy no less authority than the States in this area. Under this provision, Congress is effectively empowered to sit as the legislature of individual States for the purpose of making or altering state election laws. Again, if, as petitioners acknowledge, Congress has no power to add qualifications through its own legislation, the States cannot possess such authority either. To hold otherwise would be to conclude that the Framers conferred through a veto right over state elections laws a power to add qualifications that they did not confer through an express constitutional grant of authority to judge qualifications. In sum, the reasoning in Nixon and the holding in Powell directly support the Arkansas Supreme Court's determination that Amendment 73 is unconstitutional.

Brief for Petitioners U.S. Term Limits, Inc., et al.

Question

Does Article I of the Constitution forbid a state to decline to print on its election ballots the names of multi-term incumbents in the House of Representatives and Senate?

Arguments

1. Amendment 73 does not set a qualification for office. Certainly it was advocated by supporters of turnover in elective offices, and is designed to lessen the overwhelming election advantages, many of them governmentally conferred, that are enjoyed by multi-term incumbents. But it does so only by not continuing to print such incumbents' names on ballots. It does not disqualify them from running, being elected, or serving in office.

This Court has never held that Article I bars a state ballot restriction. That claim once was urged against a California law that restricted access to the ballot based on prior political affiliation and activity. *Storer v. Brown* (1974). The argument that the ballot law was a qualification and violated Article I was dismissed by this Court with incredulity, as "wholly without merit." Practically all state election laws, and ballot regulations in particular, influence election outcomes— none more so than the ballot restrictions accompanying primary-election laws, which States have enacted for nearly a century now, and whose usual beneficiaries are incumbents. Until this year the courts have consistently held that Article I simply is not implicated by state laws that deny benefits or make election more difficult, but do not prohibit election and service. . . .

. . . To depart from *Storer v. Brown* and the many decisions like it, and now equate a state ballot regulation with a disqualification for office, would open to Article I challenge the state primary laws and hundreds of other provisions by which fifty states tightly regulate congressional elections. For the courts to try to decide which of these state election laws should now be recharacterized as qualifications would be particularly unnecessary when the institution affected—the Congress—is specifically assigned full authority in Article I, § 4, to override Arkansas Amendment 73, or any other state law on congressional elections that it deems unwise.

2. Even if the Arkansas Supreme Court were correct in its assertion that Amendment 73 added qualifications for holding congressional office,[1] still Article I would not be violated. Article I, in both § 2 and § 4, explicitly assigns the States broad power over congressional elections. It restricts such state regulations only by establishing Congress' power to annul them, which later was supplemented by the Fourteenth Amendment. Its disqualification provisions, in Article I, §§ 2 and 3, set minimums but contain no restrictions on state laws.

The Arkansas court believed that Article I by implication takes away state power without saying so. But from the time of Chief Justice Marshall, this Court has repeatedly declined to imply prohibitions of state power from the Constitution's silence. The Tenth Amendment further confirms that constitutional limitations on state power are normally express, e.g., Article I, § 10, and only rarely to be implied. . . .

---

[1]The Arkansas courts uniformly ruled against Amendment 73. The lower court struck it down as a violation of Article I of the U.S. Constitution, and, in 1994, the Arkansas Supreme Court affirmed. According to the justices, "The qualifications clauses fix the sole requirement for congressional service. This is not a power left to the states." —Eds.

The Arkansas plurality cited *Powell v. McCormack* (1969); but there this Court expressly declined to consider state power, and held only that when a single House sits as "Judge," then the term "Qualifications" as used in Article I, § 5, refers only to those set forth in the Constitution. See *Nixon v. United States* (1993). The Arkansas opinion postulated a need for "uniformity" in qualifications for Congress. But state congressional-election laws have never been uniform. And no State whose people limit how long their representatives will stay in a House of Congress casts any burden on other States, any more than if its people voted unwisely against a particular candidate. In fact, the States' central role in selecting their national representatives is an important protection in maintaining the balance of the federal system.

It would be late in the day, given the volume of contemporaneous state, and even federal, disqualification legislation, and the ballot-restriction and disqualification laws in dozens of jurisdictions, now to hold that it all was and is unconstitutional, under an unstated implication from the Constitution's silence. Nor is it necessary in any sense to do so. No federal function is threatened. No majority is seeking to suppress ideas or to impose its will on a powerless minority or protected class. The voters of Arkansas were not altering the structure of the federal government. They were simply trying, in choosing their representation, to open the political process and to remove one of the many election advantages that long-term incumbents enjoy. The usual state power to regulate congressional elections should not be eliminated by an unstated negative implication when (1) the Constitution is silent; (2) two centuries of lawmaking are to the contrary; and (3) Congress, although specifically empowered by the Constitution to do so, has not seen fit to interfere.

In a 5–4 decision, the Supreme Court ruled for the respondents. In so doing, the majority reaffirmed Powell v. McCormack: *The Constitution's age, residency, and citizenship requirements are a complete statement of congressional eligibility standards. Neither Congress nor the states may add to or delete from those requirements. Term limits, however, remains a hot political topic. The public continues to support them, and many Republican members of Congress remain committed to keeping the issue on the political agenda. The Court's ruling, however, makes it probable that term limits could be imposed only by constitutional amendment—or a change in the Court's membership.*

"Within the bounds of normal stare decisis analysis . . . and subject to the considerations on which it customarily turns, the stronger argument is for affirming Roe's *central holding, with whatever degree of personal reluctance any of us may have, not for overruling it."*

10.5 PLANNED PARENTHOOD OF SOUTHEASTERN PENNSYLVANIA V. CASEY

505 U.S. 833 (1992)

At issue in Planned Parenthood of Southeastern Pennsylvania v. Casey *was a Pennsylvania law containing the following provisions:*

Informed consent/twenty-four-hour waiting period. *At least twenty-four hours before a physician performs an abortion, a physician must inform the woman of "the nature of the procedure, the health risks of the abortion and of childbirth, and the 'probable gestational age of the unborn child.'" The physician also must provide women with a list of adoption agencies. Abortions may not be performed unless the woman "certifies in writing" that she has given her informed consent. Twenty-four hours must elapse between the time women give their consent and the abortion procedure is performed (§ 3205).*

Spousal notice. *Before performing an abortion on a married woman, a physician must receive a statement from her stating that she has notified her spouse that she "is about to undergo an abortion." Alternatively, the woman may "provide a statement certifying that her husband is not the man who impregnated her; that her husband could not be located; that the pregnancy is the result of spousal sexual assault which she has reported; or that the woman believes that notifying her husband will cause him or someone else to inflict bodily injury upon her" (§ 3209).*

Parental consent. *Unless she exercises a judicial bypass option, a woman under the age of eighteen must obtain the informed consent of one parent prior to obtaining an abortion (§ 3206).*

Reporting and record keeping. *All facilities performing abortions must file reports containing information about the procedure, including: the physician, the woman's age, the number of prior pregnancies or abortions she has had, "preexisting medical conditions that would complicate the pregnancy," the weight and age of the aborted fetus, whether or not the woman was married, and, if relevant, the reason(s) the woman has failed to notify her spouse. If the abortion is performed in a facility funded by the state, the information becomes public (§ 3207).*

Before these provisions went into effect, five women's clinics challenged their constitutionality. A federal district court generally agreed with the clinics, but the Court of Appeals for the Third Circuit reversed. In a move designed to intensify the debate over abortion before the 1992 elections, Planned Parenthood asked the Supreme Court to issue a nonambiguous decision: either affirm or overturn Roe v. Wade. *The state, joined by President George Bush's solicitor general, Kenneth Starr, also asked the Court "to end the current uncertainty" surrounding the abortion issue. Their position was clear: "*Roe v. Wade *was wrongly decided and should be overruled." Given changes in the Court's membership—two of Bush's nominees, David Souter and Clarence Thomas, had replaced William Brennan and Thurgood Marshall, who had voted with the majority in* Roe—*many observers predicted the Court would do precisely that (see Reading 10.8).*

JUSTICE O'CONNOR, JUSTICE KENNEDY, and JUSTICE SOUTER announced the judgment of the Court and delivered the opinion of the Court with respect to Parts I, II, III, V-A, V-C, and VI, an opinion with respect to Part V-E, in which JUSTICE STEVENS joins, and an opinion with respect to Parts IV, V-B, and V-D.

I

Liberty finds no refuge in a jurisprudence of doubt. Yet nineteen years after our holding that the Constitution protects a woman's right to terminate her pregnancy in its early stages, *Roe v. Wade* (1973), that definition of liberty is still questioned. Joining the respondents as amicus curiae, the United States, as it has done in five other cases in the last decade, again asks us to overrule *Roe.*

And at oral argument in this Court, the attorney for the parties challenging the statute took the position that none of the enactments can be upheld without overruling *Roe v. Wade.* We disagree with that analysis; but we acknowledge that our decisions after *Roe* cast doubt upon the meaning and reach of its holding. Further, the chief justice admits that he would overrule the central holding of *Roe* and adopt the rational relationship test as the sole criterion of constitutionality. State and federal courts as well as legislatures throughout the Union must have guidance as they seek to address this subject in conformance with the Constitution. Given these premises, we find it imperative to review once more the principles that define the rights of the woman and the legitimate authority of the State respecting the termination of pregnancies by abortion procedures.

After considering the fundamental constitutional questions resolved by *Roe,* principles of institutional integrity, and the rule of stare decisis, we are led to conclude this: the essential holding of *Roe v. Wade* should be retained and once again reaffirmed.

While we appreciate the weight of the arguments made on behalf of the State in the case before us, arguments which in their ultimate formulation conclude that *Roe* should be overruled, the reservations any of us may have in reaffirming the central holding of *Roe* are outweighed by the explication of individual liberty we have given combined with the force of stare decisis. We turn now to that doctrine. . . .

III

The sum of precedential inquiry shows Roe's underpinnings unweakened in any way affecting its central holding. While it has engendered disapproval, it has not been unworkable. An entire generation has come of age free to assume *Roe*'s concept of liberty in defining the capacity of women to act in society, and to make reproductive decisions; no erosion of principle going to liberty or personal autonomy has left *Roe*'s central holding a doctrinal remnant; *Roe* portends no developments at odds with other precedent for the analysis of personal liberty; and no changes of fact have rendered viability more or less appropriate as the point at which the balance of interests tips. Within the bounds of normal stare decisis analysis, then, and subject to the considerations on which it customarily turns, the stronger argument is for affirming *Roe*'s central holding, with whatever degree of personal reluctance any of us may have, not for overruling it.

In a less significant case, stare decisis analysis could, and would, stop at the point we have reached.

Our analysis would not be complete, however, without explaining why overruling *Roe*'s central holding would not only reach an unjustifiable result under principles of stare decisis but would seriously weaken the Court's capacity to exercise the judicial power and to function as the Supreme Court of a Nation dedicated to the rule of law. To understand why this would be so it is necessary to understand the source of this Court's authority, the conditions necessary for its preservation, and its relationship to the country's understanding of itself as a constitutional Republic.

The root of American governmental power is revealed most clearly in the instance of the power conferred by the Constitution upon the Judiciary of the United States and specifically upon this Court. As Americans of each succeeding generation are rightly told, the Court cannot buy support for its decisions by spending money, and, except to a minor degree, it cannot independently coerce obedience to its decrees. The Court's power lies, rather, in its legitimacy, a product of substance and perception that shows itself in the people's acceptance of the Judiciary as to determine what the Nation's law means and to declare what it demands.

The underlying substance of this legitimacy is of course the warrant for the Court's decisions in the Constitution and the lesser sources of legal principle on which the Court draws. That substance is expressed in the Court's opinions, and our contemporary understanding is such that a decision without principled justification would be no judicial act at all. But even when justification is furnished by apposite legal principle, something more is required. Because not every conscientious claim of principled justification will be accepted as such, the justification claimed must be beyond dispute. The Court must take care to speak and act in ways that allow people to accept its decisions on the terms the Court claims for them, as grounded truly in principle, not as compromises with social and political pressures having, as such, no bearing on the principled choices that the Court is obliged to make. Thus, the Court's legitimacy depends on making legally principled decisions under circumstances in which their principled character is sufficiently plausible to be accepted by the Nation.

The need for principled action to be perceived as such is implicated to some degree whenever this, or any other appellate court, overrules a prior case. This is not to say, of course, that this Court cannot give a perfectly satisfactory explanation in most cases. People understand that some of the Constitution's language is hard to fathom and that the Court's Justices are sometimes able to perceive significant facts or to understand principles of law that eluded their predecessors and that justify departures from existing decisions. However upsetting it may be to those most directly affected when one judicially derived rule replaces another, the country can accept some correction of error without necessarily questioning the legitimacy of the Court.

In two circumstances, however, the Court would almost certainly fail to receive the benefit of the doubt in overruling prior cases. There is, first, a point beyond which frequent overruling would overtax the country's belief in the Court's good faith. Despite the variety of reasons that may inform and justify a decision to overrule, we cannot forget that such a decision is usually perceived (and perceived correctly) as, at the least, a statement that a prior decision was wrong. There is a limit to the amount of error that can plausibly be imputed to prior courts. If that limit should be exceeded, disturbance of prior rulings would be taken as evidence that justifiable reexamination of principle had given way to drives for particular results in the short term. The legitimacy of the Court would fade with the frequency of its vacillation.

That first circumstance can be described as hypothetical; the second is to the point here and now. Where, in the performance of its judicial duties, the Court decides a case in such a way as to resolve the sort of intensely divisive controversy reflected in *Roe* and those rare, comparable cases, its decision has a dimension that the resolution of the normal case does not carry. It is the dimension present whenever the Court's interpretation of the Constitution calls the contending sides of a national controversy to end their national division by accepting a common mandate rooted in the Constitution.

The Court is not asked to do this very often, having thus addressed the Nation only twice in our lifetime, in the decisions of *Brown* [*v. Board of Education*] and *Roe*. But when the Court does act in this way, its decision requires an equally rare precedential force to counter the inevitable efforts to overturn it and to thwart its implementation. Some of those efforts may be mere unprincipled emotional reactions; others may proceed from principles worthy of profound respect. But whatever the premises of opposition may be, only the most convincing justification under accepted standards of precedent could suffice to demonstrate that a later decision overruling the first was anything but a surrender to political pressure, and an unjustified repudiation of the principle on which the Court staked its authority in the first instance. So to overrule under fire in the absence of the most compelling reason to reexamine a watershed decision would subvert the Court's legitimacy beyond any serious question. . . .

The Court's duty in the present case is clear. In 1973, it confronted the already-divisive issue of governmental power to limit personal choice to undergo abortion, for which it provided a new resolution based on the due process guaranteed by the Fourteenth Amendment. Whether or not a new social consensus is developing on that issue, its divisiveness is no less today than in 1973, and pressure to overrule the decision, like pressure to retain it, has grown only more intense. A decision to overrule *Roe*'s essential holding under the existing circumstances would address error, if error there was, at the cost of both profound and unnecessary damage to the Court's legitimacy, and to the Nation's commitment to the rule of law. It is therefore imperative to adhere to the essence of *Roe*'s original decision, and we do so today.

IV

The woman's right to terminate her pregnancy before viability is the most central principle of *Roe v. Wade*. It is a rule of law and a component of liberty we cannot renounce.

Yet it must be remembered that *Roe v. Wade* speaks with clarity in establishing not only the woman's liberty but also the State's "important and legitimate interest in potential life." That portion of the decision in *Roe* has been given too little acknowledgment and implementation by the Court in its subsequent cases. Those cases decided that any regulation touching upon the abortion decision must survive strict scrutiny, to be sustained only if drawn in narrow terms to further a compelling state interest. Not all of the cases decided under that formulation can be reconciled with the holding in *Roe* itself that the State has legitimate interests in the health of the woman and in protecting the potential life within her. In resolving this tension, we choose to rely upon *Roe*, as against the later cases.

Roe established a trimester framework to govern abortion regulations. Under this elaborate but rigid construct, almost no regulation at all is permitted during the first trimester of pregnancy; regulations designed to protect the woman's health, but not to further the State's interest in potential life, are permitted during the second trimester; and during the third trimester, when the fetus is viable, prohibitions are permitted provided the life or health of the mother is not at stake. Most of our cases since *Roe* have involved the application of rules derived from the trimester framework.

We reject the trimester framework, which we do not consider to be part of the essential holding of *Roe*. Measures aimed at ensuring that a woman's choice contemplates the consequences for the fetus do not necessarily interfere with the right recognized in *Roe*, although those measures have been found to be inconsistent with the rigid trimester framework announced in that case. A logical reading of the central holding in *Roe* itself, and a necessary reconciliation of the liberty of the woman and the interest of the State in promoting prenatal life, require, in our view, that we abandon the trimester framework as a rigid prohibition on all previability regulation aimed at the protection of fetal life. The trimester framework suffers from these basic flaws: in its formulation it misconceives the nature of the pregnant woman's interest; and in practice it undervalues the State's interest in potential life, as recognized in *Roe*.

As our jurisprudence relating to all liberties save perhaps abortion has recognized, not every law which makes a right more difficult to exercise is, ipso facto, an infringement of that right. An example clarifies the point. We have held that not every ballot access limitation amounts to an infringement of the right to vote. Rather, the States are granted substantial flexibility in establishing the framework within which voters choose the candidates for whom they wish to vote.

The abortion right is similar. Numerous forms of state regulation might have the incidental effect of increasing the cost or decreasing the availability of medical care, whether for abortion or any other medical procedure. The fact that a law which serves a valid purpose, one not designed to strike at the right itself, has the incidental effect of making it more difficult or more expensive to procure an abortion cannot be enough to invalidate it. Only where state regulation imposes an undue burden on a woman's ability to make this decision does the power of the State reach into the heart of the liberty protected by the Due Process Clause.

The concept of an undue burden has been utilized by the Court as well as individual members of the Court, including two of us, in ways that could be considered inconsistent. Because we set forth a standard of general application to which we intend to adhere, it is important to clarify what is meant by an undue burden.

A finding of an undue burden is a shorthand for the conclusion that a state regulation has the purpose or effect of placing a substantial obstacle in the path of a woman seeking an abortion of a nonviable fetus. A statute with this purpose is invalid because the means chosen by the State to further the interest in potential life must be calculated to inform the woman's free choice, not hinder it. And a statute which, while furthering the interest in potential life or some other valid state interest, has the effect of placing a substantial obstacle in the path of a woman's choice cannot be considered a permissible means of serving its legitimate ends. To the extent that the opinions of the Court or of individual Justices use the undue burden standard in a manner that is inconsistent with this analysis, we set out what in our view should be the controlling standard. Understood another way, we answer the question, left open in previous opinions discussing the undue burden formulation, whether a law designed to further the State's interest in fetal life which imposes an undue burden on the woman's decision before fetal viability could be constitutional. See, e.g., *Akron I* (O'CONNOR, J., dissenting). The answer is no.

Some guiding principles should emerge. What is at stake is the woman's right to make the ultimate decision, not a right to be insulated from all others in doing so. Regulations which do no more than create a structural mechanism by which the State, or the parent or guardian of a minor, may express profound respect for the life of the unborn are permitted, if they are not a substantial obstacle to the woman's exercise of the right to choose. Unless it has that effect on her right of choice, a state measure designed to persuade her to choose childbirth over abortion will be upheld if reasonably related to that goal. Regulations designed to foster the health of a woman seeking an abortion are valid if they do not constitute an undue burden.

Even when jurists reason from shared premises, some disagreement is inevitable. That is to be expected in the application of any legal standard which must accommodate life's complexity. We do not expect it to be otherwise with respect to the undue burden standard. We give this summary:

(a) To protect the central right recognized by *Roe v. Wade* while at the same time accommodating the State's profound interest in potential life, we will employ the undue burden analysis as explained in this opinion. An undue burden exists, and therefore a provision of law is invalid, if its purpose or effect is to place a substantial obstacle in the path of a woman seeking an abortion before the fetus attains viability.

(b) We reject the rigid trimester framework of *Roe v. Wade*. To promote the State's profound interest in potential life, throughout pregnancy the State may take measures to ensure that the woman's choice is informed, and measures designed to advance this interest will not be invalidated as long as their purpose is to persuade the woman to choose childbirth over abortion. These measures must not be an undue burden on the right.

(c) As with any medical procedure, the State may enact regulations to further the health or safety of a woman seeking an abortion. Unnecessary health regulations that have the purpose or effect of presenting a substantial obstacle to a woman seeking an abortion impose an undue burden on the right.

(d) Our adoption of the undue burden analysis does not disturb the central holding of *Roe v. Wade*, and we reaffirm that holding. Regardless of whether exceptions are made for particular circumstances, a State may not prohibit any woman from making the ultimate decision to terminate her pregnancy before viability.

(e) We also reaffirm *Roe*'s holding that "subsequent to viability, the State in promoting its interest in the potentiality of human life may, if it chooses, regulate, and even proscribe, abortion except where it is necessary, in appropriate medical judgment, for the preservation of the life or health of the mother." *Roe v. Wade*.

The Court went on to uphold the informed consent/twenty-four-hour waiting period and parental consent provisions of the law and strike down the spousal notice and reporting sections.

JUSTICE SCALIA, with whom THE CHIEF JUSTICE, JUSTICE WHITE, and JUSTICE THOMAS join, concurring in the judgment in part and dissenting in part.

My views on this matter are unchanged from those I set forth in my separate opinion . . . in *Webster v. Reproductive Health Services* (1989) (SCALIA, J., concurring in part and concurring in judgment).[2] The States may, if they wish, permit abortion-on-demand, but the Constitution does not require them to do so. The permissibility of abortion, and the limitations upon it, are to be resolved like most important questions in our democracy: by citizens trying to persuade one another and then voting.

Beyond that brief summary of the essence of my position, I will not swell the United States Reports with repetition of what I have said before; and applying the rational basis test, I would uphold the Pennsylvania statute in its entirety. I must, however, respond to a few of the more outrageous arguments

---

[2]See Reading 8.1 .—Eds.

in today's opinion, which it is beyond human nature to leave unanswered. I shall discuss each of them under a quotation from the Court's opinion to which they pertain.

"Liberty finds no refuge in a jurisprudence of doubt."

One might have feared to encounter this august and sonorous phrase in an opinion defending the real *Roe v. Wade*, rather than the revised version fabricated today by the authors of the joint opinion. The shortcomings of *Roe* did not include lack of clarity: Virtually all regulation of abortion before the third trimester was invalid. But to come across this phrase in the joint opinion—which calls upon federal district judges to apply an "undue burden" standard as doubtful in application as it is unprincipled in origin—is really more than one should have to bear.

The joint opinion frankly concedes that the amorphous concept of "undue burden" has been inconsistently applied by the Members of this Court in the few brief years since that "test" was first explicitly propounded by Justice O'Connor in her dissent in *Akron I*. Because the three Justices now wish to "set forth a standard of general application," the joint opinion announces that "it is important to clarify what is meant by an undue burden." I certainly agree with that, but I do not agree that the joint opinion succeeds in the announced endeavor. To the contrary, its efforts at clarification make clear only that the standard is inherently manipulable and will prove hopelessly unworkable in practice.

The joint opinion explains that a state regulation imposes an "undue burden" if it "has the purpose or effect of placing a substantial obstacle in the path of a woman seeking an abortion of a nonviable fetus." An obstacle is "substantial," we are told, if it is "calculated [not] to inform the woman's free choice [but to] hinder it." This latter statement cannot possibly mean what it says. Any regulation of abortion that is intended to advance what the joint opinion concedes is the State's "substantial" interest in protecting unborn life will be "calculated [to] hinder" a decision to have an abortion. It thus seems more accurate to say that the joint opinion would uphold abortion regulations only if they do not *unduly* hinder the woman's decision. That, of course, brings us right back to square one: defining an "undue burden" as an "undue hindrance" (or a "substantial obstacle") hardly "clarifies" the test. Consciously or not, the joint opinion's verbal shell game will conceal raw judicial policy choices concerning what is "appropriate" abortion legislation.

> "While we appreciate the weight of the arguments . . . that Roe should be overruled, the reservations any of us may have in reaffirming the central holding of Roe are outweighed by the explication of individual liberty we have given combined with the force of stare decisis."

The Court's reliance upon stare decisis can best be described as contrived. It insists upon the necessity of adhering not to all of *Roe*, but only to what it calls the "central holding." . . .

I am certainly not in a good position to dispute that the Court has saved the "central holding" of *Roe*, since to do that effectively I would have to know what the Court has saved, which in turn would require me to understand (as I do not) what the "undue burden" test means. I must confess, however, that I have always thought, and I think a lot of other people have always thought, that the arbitrary trimester framework, which the Court today discards, was quite as central to *Roe* as the arbitrary viability test, which the Court today retains. It seems particularly ungrateful to carve the trimester framework out of the core of *Roe*, since its very rigidity (in sharp contrast to the utter indeterminability of the "undue burden" test) is probably the only reason the Court is able to say, in urging stare decisis, that *Roe* "has in no sense proven 'unworkable.'" I suppose the Court is entitled to call a "central holding" whatever it wants to call a "central holding"—which is, come to think of it, perhaps one of the difficulties with this modified version of stare decisis. I thought I might note, however, that the following portions of *Roe* have not been saved:

- Under *Roe*, requiring that a woman seeking an abortion be provided truthful information about abortion before giving informed written consent is unconstitutional, if the information is designed to influence her choice, *Thornburgh; Akron I*. Under the joint opinion's "undue burden" regime (as applied today, at least) such a requirement is constitutional.
- Under *Roe*, requiring that information be provided by a doctor, rather than by nonphysician counselors, is unconstitutional, *Akron I*. Under the "undue burden" regime (as applied today, at least) it is not.
- Under *Roe*, requiring a 24-hour waiting period between the time the woman gives her informed consent and the time of the abortion is unconstitutional, *Akron I*. Under the "undue burden" regime (as applied today, at least) it is not.
- Under *Roe*, requiring detailed reports that include demographic data about each woman who seeks an abortion and various information about each abortion is unconstitutional, *Thornburgh*. Under the "undue burden" regime (as applied today, at least) it generally is not. . . .

The Imperial Judiciary lives.

We should get out of this area, where we have no right to be, and where we do neither ourselves nor the country any good by remaining.

*"While we have no argument with claims that stare decisis should be
the rule and not the exception . . . Potter Stewart and Lewis Powell are
the sole exceptions among modern Supreme Court justices who
virtually never subjugate their preferences to the norms of stare decisis."*
—SEGAL AND SPAETH

*"The justices' behavior is consistent with a belief that a norm
favoring precedent is a fundamental feature of the general
conception of the function of the Supreme Court in
society at large."* —EPSTEIN AND KNIGHT

10.6 THE INFLUENCE OF STARE DECISIS ON THE VOTES OF UNITED STATES SUPREME COURT JUSTICES

Jeffrey A. Segal and Harold J. Spaeth

Jeffrey A. Segal is Professor of Political Science at SUNY–Stony Brook.
Harold J. Spaeth is Professor of Political Science at Michigan State University.

To determine whether justices are influenced by precedent, we focus on the voting patterns of dissenting justices in landmark cases. We examine dissenting justices because we know that their revealed preferences differ from the established precedent, and thus we can distinguish whether or not these justices arguably were influenced by the established precedent in future cases. We choose landmark cases because they are more likely to establish precedential guidelines for future cases and because landmark cases are more likely to actually generate progeny that we can analyze. . . . For each dissenting justice we will determine whether that justice accepts the relevant landmark decision in subsequent cases dealing with the same issue. Thus, if we were to examine *Roe v. Wade* (1973) and its progeny, we would ask whether Roe dissenters Rehnquist or White subsequently: (1) adopted the position that abortion statutes are subject to a compelling interest standard and (2) agreed that the Constitution accepts the fundamental right to abortion until the fetus is viable.

This is not an unobtainable standard. Examples of justices changing their votes in response to established precedents clearly exist. In *Griswold v. Connecticut* (1965), Stewart rejected the creation of a right to privacy and its application to married individuals. Yet in *Eisenstadt v. Baird* (1972) he accepted

Jeffrey A. Segal and Harold J. Spaeth, "The Influence of Stare Decisis on the Votes of United States Supreme Court Justices," 40 *American Journal of Political Science* 971 (1996). See also Harold J. Spaeth and Jeffrey A. Segal, *Majority Rule or Minority Will* (Cambridge: Cambridge University Press, 1999).

Griswold's right to privacy and was even willing to apply it to unmarried persons. . . . The question, then, is not whether precedent influences any of the justices' decisions, for surely it does. The question is whether such behavior exists at systematic and substantively meaningful levels.

We believe that our operational definition is both reasonable and, unlike other definitions, falsifiable. Compare our definition to one that counts a justice as following precedent as long as he or she cites some case or cases that are consistent with that Justice's vote. Since there are always some cases supporting both sides in virtually every conflict decided by the Court, such a definition turns stare decisis into a trivial concept, at least for explanatory purposes. Moreover, a justice-centered view of precedent makes precedent a personal decision, not the institutional decision that it so clearly is supposed to be. . . .

Results

We list the effect of precedent on the votes of justices who dissented in our landmark cases in Appendix 11 [excluded but available in the article]. These are arrayed in chronological order. . . .

Space does not allow a full discussion of our evaluation of the 346 votes in question. [But], in summary, 90.8 percent of the votes conform to the justices' revealed preferences. That is, only 9.2 percent of the time did a justice switch to the position established in the landmark precedent.

. . . Only Stewart and Powell remotely display adherence to precedent, with the others overwhelmingly supportive of their preferences at a minimum rate of at least 80 percent. No justice cast more than six precedential votes (Stewart), followed by Powell with five. Half of Stewart's, however, result from *Benton v. Maryland* (1969), while all of Powell's conform to *Furman v. Georgia* (1972). Indeed, the eleven Furman progeny account for ten of the thirty-two precedential votes, with the three Benton progeny producing five others. Accordingly, two of our fifty-four landmark decisions (3.7 percent) spawn 45.7 percent of the precedential votes.

Court watchers might notice that our two most precedential justices [Stewart and Powell] are also justices who have situated themselves at or about the median position on the Court. Perhaps precedent plays a substantial role in Supreme Court decision making due to the behavior of one or two highly influential justices. Unfortunately, the results do not bear out the hypothesis. Of the 146 progeny, the results in only five can arguably be tied to the influence of precedent: four death penalty cases, where Powell, Powell and Blackmun, and O'Connor were instrumental in forging a liberal majority; and one campaign finance case, where Brennan and Marshall were instrumental in striking expenditure prohibitions by nonprofit advocacy groups. . . .

The evidence is rather convincing. While we have no argument with claims that stare decisis should be the rule and not the exception, the empirical results are to the contrary. Potter Stewart and Lewis Powell are the sole exceptions among modern Supreme Court justices who virtually never subjugate their preferences to the norms of stare decisis.

THE NORM OF STARE DECISIS

Jack Knight and Lee Epstein

Jack Knight is the Sidney W. Souers Professor of Government,
and Lee Epstein is the Edward Mallinckrodt Distinguished
University of Political Science at Washington University.

The Mechanisms of Precedential Effect

Precedent might affect Supreme Court decision making in a number of ways. For this discussion we concentrate on two possible mechanisms of precedential effect. . . .

Precedent as the Primary Reason for Justices' Decisions

The first mechanism is that precedent provides the primary reason why justices make the decisions that they do. On this account justices use the rules that are established by previous court cases as the basis for their subsequent judicial decisions. . . .

Segal and Spaeth's analysis can be understood as testing this mechanism of precedential effect. Yet, it is worth noting at the onset that Segal and Spaeth (as they acknowledge) do not seek to test the effect of precedent on justices whose preferences match precedent [justices in the majority of the precedent-setting opinion]. . . .

What they do test is the effect of precedent on justices whose preferences in the original cases do not match the precedent established in those cases. And this is an important area of analysis: if precedent matters, then it ought to affect the subsequent decisions of members of the Court. The problem is that Segal and Spaeth propose an unduly narrow test of these effects. They focus on the influence of precedent on the disposition of cases (on the votes to affirm or re-verse the decisions of lower courts)—a focus that will always reject the effect of precedent on judicial choice whenever the subsequent votes of dissenters in precedent-setting cases do not exactly match the majority vote in the original case—while we suggest elsewhere that such focus is not the most appropriate way of assessing judicial decision making. More specifically, we argue that analyses of courts ought to center on the law that is established by judicial decisions. By law we refer to the substantive rules of behavior that are created by courts through their holdings and justificatory arguments. If legal rules become the primary focus for analyzing the effect of precedent on judicial decision making, then the possibilities for such effects expand beyond the determination of judicial preferences. And such effects cannot be adequately tested through a narrow focus on the disposition of cases.

From Jack Knight and Lee Epstein. "The Norm of Stare Decisis" *American Journal of Political Science* 40:1018–1035.

Precedent as a Constraint on Justices

With this focus on the substantive content of judicial decisions in mind, we suggest a second mechanism of precedential effect: precedent can serve as a constraint on justices acting on their personal preferences. On this account, justices have a preferred rule that they would like to establish in the case before them, but they strategically modify their position to take account of a normative constraint in order to produce a decision as close as is possible to their preferred outcome. A norm favoring respect for precedent can serve as such a constraint.

To see this, consider the task facing Justices: they seek to establish a rule as close as possible to their most preferred policy position but, to accomplish this, they must take account of the strategic nature of their choice. On the one hand, they must be attentive to the strategic dimensions of the decision making process within the Court itself: only those rules to which at least five members of the Court subscribe will be established. Thus, they may have to modify their most preferred policy choice in order to accommodate the preferences of the other members of the Court. On the other hand, they must be attentive to the strategic dimensions of Judicial decision making outside of the Court: if justices want to establish a legal rule of behavior that will govern the future activity of the members of the society in which their Court exists, they will be constrained to choose from among the set of rules that the members of that society will recognize and accept. If the Court seeks to establish rules that the people will not respect and with which they will not comply, the fundamental efficacy of the Court is undermined.

For at least two reasons, it is on this external strategic dimension that a norm favoring respect for precedent can significantly affect decision making by constraining judicial choice. First, there are prudential reasons to suggest that Justices might follow precedent rather than their own policy preferences. Stare decisis is one way in which courts respect the established expectations of a community. To the extent that the members of a community base their future expectations on the belief that others in that community will follow existing laws, the Court has an interest in minimizing the disruptive effects of overturning existing rules of behavior. If the Court seeks to radically change existing rules, then the changes may be more than that to which the members of the community can adapt, resulting in a decision that does not produce a rule that will be efficacious.

Second, there are normative reasons why justices may follow precedent as opposed to their own preferences. If a community has a fundamental belief that the "rule of law" requires the Court to be constrained by precedent, then justices can be constrained by precedent even if they personally do not accept that fundamental belief. The constraint follows from the effect of the community's belief on its willingness to accept and comply with the decisions of the Court. If the members of the community believe that the legitimate judicial function involves the following of precedent, then they will reject as normatively illegitimate the decisions of any court that regularly and systematically violate precedent. To the extent that justices are concerned with establishing rules that will engender the compliance of the community, they will take account of the fact that they must establish rules that are legitimate in the eyes of that community. In this way a norm of stare decisis can constrain the actions of even those Court members who do not share the view that justices should be constrained by past decisions.

But the task of empirically testing the effect of this norm is a complicated one. Just as the norm of consensus made its presence known in ways other than the ideological content of the vote, the norm of stare decisis manifests itself in ways other than the vote to continue to dissent from precedent-setting cases. The question, thus, becomes: if a norm of respecting precedent exists on the Court, in what ways would it manifest itself?

The problem in answering this, not unlike the obstacle posed by empirically assessing the norm of consensus, is that the norm of respecting precedent is quite general, and individual cases are quite specific. Individual violations of the norm will not result in a general rejection of the Court by the society as a whole; only regular and systematic deviations from the norm will undermine the Court's legitimacy. Accordingly, evidence of individual instances of deviation will not demonstrate that the norm has no effect. As long as justices generally comply with the norm, they will be free to deviate from precedent in those cases in which their personal preferences so differ from the precedent that they feel compelled to change the existing law. Thus, the best we can do in this brief essay is to offer widespread evidence of the existence of behavior that is consistent with the existence of a norm and that is inconsistent with the lack of such a norm. It is through this indirect evidence that we can make the case for the existence of a norm of stare decisis.

A Conceptual and Empirical Look at Behaviors Consistent with a Norm of Stare Decisis

To determine whether such evidence exists, we begin by conceptualizing Court decision making as occurring in the three stages: pre-vote, conference, and opinion circulation and publication. Our argument, elaborated below, is that each presents opportunities for a norm about the respect of precedent to structure judicial choices.

Pre-Vote Stage: Attention to Precedent

As many scholars of the judicial process recognize, the foundations of Court decisions are laid after the Court "decides to decide" a case—when attorneys present written and oral arguments to the justices. And, while analysts dispute the extent to which these arguments influence the votes of the justices, none would seriously claim that attorneys do not attempt to exert such influence.

Scholars also agree that the primary way in which attorneys seek to influence judicial decision making is by persuading the justices to adopt legal rules that will produce outcomes favorable to the interests of their clients. To accomplish this, they offer arguments that identify various legal sources, which they claim reflect the law most appropriate to govern the facts of the extant case. It seems reasonable to infer from these attorneys' arguments those legal sources—

be they citations to precedent or other authorities—that they believe will most likely affect Court decisions.

Our examination of one of Segal/Spaeth's precedent creation-progeny series, *Edelman v. Jordan* (1974), suggests that attorneys believe in the power of precedent. We gathered the lists of authorities in briefs filed in *Edelman* and its twelve successors and counted the number of citations to cases and to all other authorities. The results are clear: in all but six of the twenty-six briefs did citations to precedent exceed those to all other sources, including scholarly works, state and federal constitutional provisions, statutes, and regulations.

Of course, this evidence merely suggests that attorneys believe that precedent is an important influence on Court decision making; it does not demonstrate that precedent actually has the anticipated effect. Yet, it is behavior consistent with the existence of a norm favoring respect for precedent. For if attorneys truly believed that precedent was not an effective way for them to influence the Court, there would be no reason for them to give precedent such emphasis in their briefs. . . .

Conference Discussion: Appeals to Precedent

After a case is briefed and argued, the Court holds a private conference to discuss it. During conference, the justices state their views on the case (beginning with the Chief Justice and moving in order of seniority) and, frequently, how they would dispose of it (e.g., reverse, remand, affirm). Clearly, as many scholars have demonstrated, justices engage in various forms of strategic behavior during conference. For example, Murphy [in *Elements of Judicial Strategy*] suggests that justices view their conference statements as tools of persuasion; indeed, in preparing them, Court members and their clerks are often mindful of the preferences of other justices and the positions they are likely to take. So one justice may try to demonstrate to others how a particular legal rule will lead them to a result more in line with their goals than other courses of action. When justices take this tack, they offer various arguments in support of the superiority of their proposed rule.

One important source of evidence in support of the existence of a norm of stare decisis, we believe, is the extent to which justices invoke precedent in their arguments during these private conferences. There are two reasons why this is important. First, it is evidence of the existence of the norm among the justices themselves. The very fact that precedent would be employed as a source of persuasion in their private communications suggests that the justices believe that it can have an effect on the choices of their colleagues. It is one thing for the justices to ground their public proclamations in the rhetoric of precedent; it is quite another for them to use it in their private deliberations. Second, the invocation of precedent in conference discussions lends support to the claim that a general norm favoring precedent exists in society at large. For justices who seek to establish legal rules that will engender compliance in the community as a whole, priority will be given to those rules that are consistent with a norm favoring respect for precedent if they believe that such a norm exists. Thus, one reason why justices might be persuaded to adjust their position on the holding in a case in the direction of precedent is that such an adjustment will enhance the probability that the resulting decision will be considered legitimate by society.

To determine whether such evidence exists, we examined Justice Brennan's notes of conference discussions over *Edelman* and its progeny; more specifically, we coded whether or not justices invoked precedent in their remarks.

[The results indicate that] in all but [one case] did at least one justice mention a previously-decided case. And, in many of those instances, a particular precedent formed the centerpiece of their conference statements—as in *Atascadero State Hospital v. Scanlon* (1985), when O'Connor simply said, "Pennhurst [*State Hospital v. Halderman*, 1984] decided this case and I'd reverse," or in *Green v. Mansour* (1985), when Blackmun noted that he would "reverse on *Atascadero*." . . .

Clearly, these kinds of statements—not to mention the overall results—provide documentation of the use of precedent in the private deliberations of the Court. Of course, we recognize that this is not definitive evidence of a precedential effect on decision making; yet, at the same time, it is clearly evidence of behavior consistent with the existence of a norm favoring respect for precedent. And it is important to note that it is behavior that makes little sense if the justices know that precedent has no impact on their ultimate decisions. . . .

Opinion Circulation and Publication: Claims About and Treatment of Precedent

After the Court discusses a case, the Chief Justice (or the most senior member of the majority, if the Chief Justice is not in the majority) assigns the opinion to himself/herself or to another member of the Court. The next step, typically, is for the writers to circulate drafts of their opinions.

Although there are many ways that the norm favoring precedent could manifest itself during this process, we have chosen to focus on the products of that process: the final, published versions of the opinion. And we draw attention to two aspects of these products—the claims writers make in their opinions and the way they treat precedent within them.

CLAIMS ABOUT PRECEDENT   Court members invoke numerous justifications for their opinions, from the intent of the framers to the plain meaning of the words of statutes. Yet, as even Segal and Spaeth acknowledge, "appeal to precedent is the primary justification justices provide for the decisions they reach." . . . [Indeed,] very few Supreme Court opinions—majority, dissenting, or concurring—do not cite previously decided cases. A perusal of any volume of the *U.S. Reports* supports this, as does our analysis of a sample of Segal and Spaeth's cases. In particular, we counted the number of citations to cases and to all other authorities in the majority and dissenting opinions cast in Edelman and its progeny. In all but three of the twenty-eight opinions, citations to precedent exceeded those to all other sources combined. What is more, the average opinion cited 2.01 previously decided cases per *U.S. Reports* page; that figure was .93 for all other authorities. . . .

Of course, the data reported here are limited to a few cases, but we doubt that any scholar of the judicial process would take issue with our conclusion that precedent is a prominent feature of most opinions. What they may suggest, though, is that the data actually support Segal and Spaeth's argument. The invocation of the precedent justification by both dissenting and majority opinions renders it meaningless. But this position begs the question of why: Why would justices (for whom precedent was unimportant, as Segal and Spaeth maintain) feel compelled to invoke it, and not just occasionally but regularly—especially since so many other justifications exist?

The answer is clear. The justices' behavior is consistent with a belief that a norm favoring precedent is a fundamental feature of the general conception of the function of the Supreme Court in society at large. To the extent that compliance with this norm is necessary to maintain the fundamental legitimacy of the Supreme Court, such a belief will constrain the justices from deviating from precedent in a regular and systematic way.

TREATMENT OF PRECEDENT Perhaps the most important evidence of a norm of stare decisis comes in the way the Court treats existing precedent. If the justices consistently and often overturned principles established in past cases, then we could hardly label stare decisis a "norm"—in the sense that norms establish expectations about future behavior.

But this is not the case. No matter how one counts the number of alterations of precedent, the numbers border on the trivial. . . .

To be sure, we recognize that the explicit abandonment of precedent is the most extreme method of disposing of prior decisions the justices no longer find useful; certainly, they maintain rulings on the books that they have effectively gutted. But, the key point, as Baum highlights, is this:

> The Court adheres to precedents far more often than it overturns them, either explicitly or implicitly. . . . Certainly most justices accept the principle that "any departure from the doctrine of stare decisis demands special justification." Like the law in general, the rule of adhering to precedent hardly controls the Court's decisions, but it does structure and influence them.

[T]he relevant data support Baum's sentiment, and they are consistent with the claim that a norm of stare decisis exists in the Supreme Court.

". . . elimination of constitutional stare decisis would represent explicit endorsement of the idea that the Constitution is nothing more than what five Justices say it is."

10.7 STARE DECISIS AND JUDICIAL RESTRAINT

Lewis F. Powell, Jr.

Leslie H. Arps Lecture, The Association of the Bar of the City of New York, October 17, 1989.
Lewis F. Powell, Jr., served on the U.S. Supreme Court from 1971 to 1987.

Current Health of Stare Decisis

. . . [I]t may be of interest to consider broadly the current health of the principle of stare decisis. Some lawyers and academics have suggested that the principle is now ignored, or is at least in serious decline. I cannot agree. I am reminded of Mark Twain's often quoted cable from Europe to the Associated Press: "The reports of my death are greatly exaggerated." In my view, Justice Stevens's 1983 assessment in his New York University Law Review article remains correct today. Overrulings occur with some frequency, but when considered in light of the business of the Court as a whole they are rare. As Justice Stevens pointed out, "Two or three overrulings each Term are, indeed, significant." But the Court, in the exercise of certiorari jurisdiction, considers thousands of cases a year. The vast majority involve nothing more than application of previously decided cases. This is stare decisis.

A review of the Burger and Warren Courts illustrates my view of stare decisis, as a rule of stability, but not inflexibility. The Burger and Warren Courts spanned a roughly equal number of years: Chief Justice Warren presided for the sixteen-year period between 1953 and 1969; Chief Justice Burger for seventeen years between 1969 and 1986. Counting the overruled decisions of each era reveals that during Warren's tenure the Court overruled sixty-three cases. The Burger Court, of which I was a member, overruled some sixty-one cases. Of course, the precise numbers can vary depending on the method of counting. I have chosen to rely primarily on explicit overrulings. The point in any event is plain. On a rough average the Court has overruled less than four cases per term. Thus it has overruled a significant and fairly constant number of prior decisions over time. But when the totality of cases is considered, the general rule of stare decisis remains a fundamental component of our judicial system.

Of course, the importance of cases overruled is also relevant. It can be said fairly that the overruling of major decisions was infrequent under both Chief Justices. I mention briefly some of the more celebrated overrulings of the Warren and Burger Courts.

By far the most important of the Warren Court cases is *Brown v. Board of Education*. It explicitly overruled the 1899 case of *Cumming v. Board of Education*, the 1927 case *Gong Lum v. Rice*, and of course rejected *Plessy v. Ferguson*. The Warren Court overruled a number of criminal procedure decisions in a series of cases that "incorporated" the Bill of Rights through the Fourteenth Amendment. In its overall effect on the structure of constitutional judicial review, the incorporation cases are perhaps of unique significance. In other areas, *Baker v. Carr* overruled *Colegrove v. Green* and brought legislative apportionment controversies under judicial review.

The Burger Court also had its share of important overrulings. In *Miller v. California* the Court overruled the *Memoirs* case and established a new standard for obscenity. In *Gregg v. Georgia*, the Court overruled *McGautha v. California* and began the present course of Eighth Amendment scrutiny of capital punishment. Several cases broke new ground in expanding the rights of women. For example, *Taylor v. Louisiana* invalidated restrictions on jury service by women, overruling a case decided only four Terms earlier. And in *Batson v. Kentucky*, an opinion I wrote in 1986, the Court overruled *Swain v. Alabama*, easing the evidentiary burden of defendants who claim racial discrimination in jury selection.

Proper Role of Stare Decisis

The records of the Burger and Warren Courts are consistent with the traditional role of stare decisis that I have described. For example, the Burger Court demonstrated a greater sensitivity to the public interest in law enforcement than that reflected in some of the decisions of the Warren Court. Yet it did not overrule those Warren Court decisions, such as *Mapp v. Ohio, Massiah v. United States*, and *Miranda v. Arizona*, that announced broad principles protecting the rights of criminal defendants. Rather, the Burger Court, with due regard for stare decisis, set about the difficult task of clarifying the scope of these sweeping decisions.

Fortunately, there is no absolute rule against overruling prior decisions. *Brown* itself stands as a testament to the fact that we have a living Constitution. And where it becomes clear that a wrongly decided case does damage to the coherence of the law, overruling is proper. But I repeat that the general rule of adherence to prior decisions is a proper one. This is true both for statutory and constitutional cases. Justice Frankfurter aptly noted the critical importance of stare decisis when he described it as the principle "by whose circumspect observance the wisdom of this Court as an institution transcending the moment can alone be brought to bear on the problems that confront us." The specific merits of stare decisis are familiar; I comment on them briefly.

(i) The first is one of special interest to judges: it makes our work easier. As Justice Cardozo put it: "The labor of judges would be increased almost to the breaking point if every past decision could be reopened in every case, and one could not lay one's own course of bricks on the secure foundation of the courses laid by others who had gone before him." Few cases that reach the Supreme Court are easy. Most involve hours of study and reflection; the conscientious judge must make many close calls. It cannot seriously be suggested that every case brought to the Court should require reexamination on the merits of every relevant precedent that has gone before.

(ii) Stare decisis also enhances stability in the law. This is especially important in cases involving property rights and commercial transactions. Even in the area of personal rights it also is necessary to have a predictable set of rules on which citizens may rely in shaping their behavior.

(iii) Perhaps the most important and familiar argument for stare decisis is one of public legitimacy. The respect given the Court by the public, and by the other branches of government, rests in large part on the knowledge that the Court is not composed of unelected judges free to write their policy views into law. Rather, the Court is a body vested with the duty to exercise the Judicial Power prescribed by the Constitution. An important aspect of this is the respect the Court shows for its own previous opinions.

Recent Threats to Traditional Stare Decisis

Though the doctrine of stare decisis as I have described it remains strong, challenges to the traditional conception of stare decisis have appeared recently in two areas.

The first of these concerns stare decisis in statutory cases. The idea has long been advanced that stare decisis should operate with special vigor in statutory cases. This is because Congress has the power to pass new legislation correcting any statutory decision by the Court that Congress deems erroneous. Thus, if Congress fails to respond to a statutory decision, the courts can assume that Congress believes the statutory interpretation was correct.

I am in general agreement with this view. But it can be taken to extremes. Three Justices last Term joined with Justice Stevens in suggesting that where a significant time has passed without action by Congress, the Supreme Court's prior statutory decisions become as binding on the Supreme Court itself as on lower courts.

In my view the Court should hesitate to adopt such a categorical rule. It reflects an unrealistic view of the political process and Congress's ability to fine-tune statutes. Correction of erroneous statutory interpretations may in some cases be vital to the effective administration of justice and the coherence of the law. But correction may have little political constituency in Congress. The Court therefore has a responsibility both to ensure that its statutory interpretations follow the intent of the drafting Congress, and to ensure that erroneous interpretations do not damage the fabric of the law. Some statutes are a mishmash of ambiguities. Indeed, some "statutory" law consists of an open-ended statute that has been left almost entirely to "common law" development in the courts. Federal antitrust law is an example.

A second recent challenge to traditional stare decisis is the renewal of calls for a relaxation, or even outright elimination, of stare decisis in constitutional cases. Some Court opinions hint at this. And the argument has been made directly by a former Assistant Attorney General in the *Cornell Law Review*. This view of stare decisis also has little to commend it.

Those who would eliminate stare decisis in constitutional cases argue that the doctrine is simply one of convenience. They say it is useful only to judges who would defend their own erroneous decisions against shifting majorities on the Court. It is true that stare decisis, as applied, can be based on subjective standards that are unprincipled. True also that it is cited far more often by dissenters when a case has been overruled than by a Justice who relies on stare decisis to uphold a case he or she thinks wrongly decided. But elimination of constitutional stare decisis would represent explicit endorsement of the idea that the Constitution is nothing more than what five Justices say it is. This would undermine the rule of law. . . .

*"[I]nstitutional norms, including the following of precedent,
or stare decisis; respect for the difference between law and politics;
and concerns for institutional legitimacy inform Court
decision making in important ways."*

10.8 INSTITUTIONAL NORMS AND SUPREME COURT DECISION MAKING: THE REHNQUIST COURT ON PRIVACY AND RELIGION

Ronald Kahn

Ronald Kahn is the James Monroe Professor of Politics and Law at Oberlin College.

Supreme Court decision making can be viewed as instrumental or constitutive. While drawing on quite disparate explanations, all instrumental approaches reject constitutional principles, institutional norms, and legal concepts, such as the rule of law, as significant to Supreme Court decision making. They are united in a central premise, really a heuristic device, that justices draw upon institutional norms, precedent constitutional principles, and theories of interpretation only to justify preconceived policy preferences. Two prominent instrumental approaches center on the individual justice. One, the attitudinal approach, argues that justices decide cases on the basis of their personal policy preferences; the other, the strategic approach, argues that justices are rational actors whose decisions reflect a desire to promote policy preferences, in a way that

In *Supreme Court Decision Making*, ed. Cornell W. Clayton and Howard Gillman (Chicago: University of Chicago Press, 1999).

is attentive to the competitive preferences of their colleagues and other policy makers. A second major set of instrumental approaches centers on external influences on the Court—proceeding on such assumptions as that the Court follows election returns, responds to interest group pressures, or responds to other political events.

By contrast, the constitutive approach to Supreme Court decision making is based on the premise that justices' decisions are "constituted" of a distinctive set of institutional norms and customs, including legal principles and theories. It assumes that members of the Supreme Court believe that they are required to act in accordance with particular institutional and legal expectations and responsibilities. Thus, the constitutive approach is consistent with the assumptions about institutional behavior held by the new wave of "historical institutional" scholars who seek to meld the study of politics and history. They argue that institutions both structure one's ability to act on a set of beliefs that are external to the institution and are a source of distinctive political purposes, goals, and preferences. Therefore, the constitutive approach assumes that justices make decisions in the institutional context which informs the choices they make. It assumes that the Court's institutional norms and commitments are important for the maintenance of constitutional principles and Court decision making. Moreover, justices must be principled in their decision-making process if they are to have the continued respect of their colleagues, the wider interpretive community, citizens, and leaders. Justices must convince us [not only] that a specific case decision is wise but also that the principles upon which they base their decision, and upon which future cases are based, are appropriate. . . .

I will analyze landmark privacy cases from the 1990s to ask whether the Rehnquist Court (1986–present) continues to be constitutive in its decision making. As with the Warren Court (1953–1969) and Burger Court (1969–1986) before it, Rehnquist Court justices do not follow election returns, the policies of the presidents who appointed them, or even personal policy wants, as my evidence will show. I find that institutional norms, including the following of precedent, or stare decisis; respect for the difference between law and politics; and concerns for institutional legitimacy inform Court decision making in important ways. . . .

Rights of Privacy and Abortion Choice

The key Rehnquist Court right of abortion choice case, *Planned Parenthood of S.E. Pennsylvania v. Casey*, was not decided until 1992. By 1991, there were six Reagan-Bush appointees on the Supreme Court: Sandra Day O'Connor (1981); William H. Rehnquist as Chief Justice (1986); Antonin Scalia (1986); Anthony Kennedy (1988); David Souter (1990); and Clarence Thomas (1991). Before the 1991–1992 term, it was not clear what direction the Rehnquist Court would take in crucial areas such as the right of privacy and abortion choice and freedom of religion. Would the Rehnquist Court, like the Warren and Burger Court eras before it, be constitutive in its decision making; or would it change the pattern, by following election returns; disregarding important legal norms, such as stare decisis; and failing to protect the institutional needs of the Court? . . .

The Supreme Court, Presidents, and Election Returns

If justices on the Rehnquist Court are simply instrumental in their decision making, what might we expect from this Court? Pushed by the religious right, the Reagan-Bush Administration sought to end the right of abortion choice, except where the life of the mother is threatened. They also opposed the expansion of various rights of sexual intimacy. Nevertheless, in the face of such pressure, the Rehnquist Court refused to reject the basic holdings of *Roe*, that a woman has a right to abortion choice prior to viability. Rehnquist Court justices refused to vote their personal policy preferences on abortion, or those of the Presidents who appointed them, even in the face of the Reagan-Bush Administrations' long-term, spirited attack on the right of abortion choice, as evidenced by their five attempts, over a decade to overturn *Roe*. Justices O'Connor, Souter, and Kennedy—three Reagan-Bush appointees—refused to overturn *Roe*. . . .

Principles, Not Personal Policy Preferences, Followed

As justices do not follow elections returns, they do not simply follow personal policy preferences. In the joint opinion in *Casey*, O'Connor, Kennedy, and Souter wrote, "Some of us as individuals find abortion offensive to our most basic principles of morality but that cannot control our decision. Our obligation is to define the liberty of all, not to mandate our own moral code." . . .

. . . One cannot say that personal preferences never enter the calculations; the evidence of attitudinalists makes clear that judicial votes can be quite consistent with what we would expect if we assumed that judges voted on the basis of their political ideologies. However, a new institutional gloss helps us understand some of the circumstances under which judges might subordinate their preferences in order to serve institutional goals and purposes.

The Importance of Precedents

. . . [What] the joint opinion in *Casey* [does] emphasize is that a continuing commitment to stare decisis requires a reaffirmation of *Roe*. It states, "The obligation to follow precedent begins with necessity, and a contrary necessity marks its outer limit." Justices O'Connor, Souter, and Kennedy crafted an important new test in *Casey* to determine when the Court should overturn past decisions. The joint opinion states that decisions will be overruled only if they (1) prove unworkable in practice, (2) cause inequities in effect, (3) damage social stability, and (4) are abandoned by society, or (5) rely on key fact assumptions that have changed. Applying this test to *Roe v. Wade*, the plurality finds that it meets none of the conditions.

In a constitutive decision-making process, the Supreme Court applies polity and rights principles and precedent in light of the nation's reliance that a rule of law will prevail. For example, the *Casey* Court, in deciding whether to overturn *Roe*, considers the reliance people have placed in the rule of law in *Roe* and whether overturning the rule of law in *Roe* would create special hardships. . . .

The Court also considers new doctrine. It finds that the continuation of *Roe*'s essential holdings is supported "not only as an exemplar of *Griswold* liberty but as a rule (whether or not mistaken) of personal autonomy and bodily integrity, with doctrinal affinity to cases recognizing limits on governmental power to mandate medical treatment or to bar its rejection." In stating this the Court refers to *Cruzan v. Director, Missouri Dept. of Health*, a 1990, right-to-die case. Moreover, the Court views prior abortion rights cases, including *Akron v. Akron Center for Reproductive Health* (1983), *Thornburgh v. American College of Obstetricians and Gynecologists* (1986), and *Webster v. Reproductive Health Services* (1989), as either reaffirming *Roe* or as declining "to address the constitutional validity of the central holding of *Roe*." Because the relationship of the right of abortion choice to society's reliance on the basic values of liberty and privacy has grown stronger and has been reinforced by events in the lives of women since the establishment of the right of abortion with *Roe* in 1973, the Court finds that the essential holdings of *Roe* must be retained. To do otherwise in 1992 would seriously undermine the legitimacy of the Supreme Court and the rule of law itself, they asserted.

Institutional Legitimacy

The joint opinion makes frequent mention of the danger to the Court's legitimacy that would come from overturning *Roe*: "To overrule under fire in the absence of the most compelling reason to reexamine a watershed decision would subvert the Court's legitimacy beyond any serious question." Finally, Blackmun's concurring opinion seems to offer a clear rebuke to the Reagan-Bush Administrations and to the instrumental election returns theories. Blackmun writes, "The Court's reaffirmation of *Roe*'s central holding is also based on the force of stare decisis. . . . What has happened today should serve as a model for future Justices and a warning to all who have tried to turn this Court into yet another political branch."

One cannot claim that precedent always controls in a straightforward way; there is extensive evidence that judges do not always mindlessly follow a clear precedent even in those rare circumstances when cases are covered by precedent (Segal and Spaeth 1996).[3] However, Casey demonstrates that there are times, for reasons having to do with the Court's institutional position in the political system and the justices' conceptions of their professional obligations, when a commitment to precedent takes priority over a more instrumental approach to the law, and the new institutionalist perspective helps draw attention to these circumstances. . . .

---

[3]See Reading 10.6. —Eds.

CHAPTER 11

Statutory Interpretation

The great bulk of law interpreted and applied by courts in the United States today is either statutory law or regulations issued by administrative agencies to implement statutes. Congress, the fifty state legislatures, and thousands of city and county councils annually enact huge masses of statutes; and administrative agencies daily multiply this brood in reams of supposedly explanatory regulations. This predominance of law based on statutes is characteristic of only the past century. Earlier, judge-made principles of the common law had controlled most social and economic relationships; but democratization, industrialization, and urbanization have pushed legislators and administrators to become much more active in formulating social and economic policy.

This shift can be seen in startling clarity in the statistics of the Supreme Court's business. According to the calculations of Felix Frankfurter and James M. Landis,[1] as late as 1875 more than 40 percent of the controversies coming to the Court involved common-law litigation; by 1925 only 5 percent of the cases fell into this category. Today the justices would rarely, if ever, accept a case unless it raised an important question of federal constitutional, statutory, or administrative law.

PLAIN MEANING AND THE PROBLEM OF AMBIGUITY

The task of interpreting statutes might seem, on first consideration, to pose fewer problems than does the task of reasoning from case law. There is no need to navigate a sea of precedents for the principle governing the case. There is no need to discern dicta to be excluded from consideration. The court starts with a text—the legislature's effort to state a rule of law in language that will make its meaning clear and plain (Reading 11.1).

---

[1] Felix Frankfurter and James M. Landis, *The Business of the Supreme Court* (New York: Macmillan, 1927), 306.

But complications quickly arise. For one, lawmakers often find it difficult to convey their exact purpose in clear and plain language. It is easy to blame careless drafting; strange and awkward language abounds in statutes. Yet some problems are much too technical and complex to be encompassed in words that are intelligible to the nonspecialist. A statute such as the Securities and Exchange Act, which regulates advertising, buying, and selling stocks and bonds, must use a great deal of esoteric terminology that has meaning only to experts in the field.

There is the additional problem of language itself. Even rules stated in ordinary words often contain ambiguities. A classic example is the city ordinance that reads: "No vehicle shall enter a public park." Does that ordinance exclude baby buggies? tricycles? bicycles? self-propelled wheelchairs? mopeds? skateboards? an ambulance coming to bring an injured person to a hospital? a police car protecting the people enjoying the park? Words, as Judge Jerome Frank explained, "serve as symbols. As such they are necessarily somewhat compressed, condensed. . . . The judges must determine the proper limits of expansion of condensed symbols."[2] Coping with that sort of compressed ambiguity is hardly an easy task, as nicely illustrated by the Supreme Court's struggle in *Smith v. United States* (1993) (Reading 11.2) to explain the meaning of the word *use*. Such linguistic gymnastics make more understandable President William Jefferson Clinton's famous insistence, in giving a deposition regarding his sexual harassment of Paula Jones and his affair with Monica Lewinsky, that the special prosecutor define the word *is*.

A third set of complications arises when legislators are deliberately ambiguous. Sometimes lawmakers who cannot agree among themselves on how to attack a problem compromise by choosing obscure language and thus tossing the basic difficulty to administrators or judges. In other instances legislators believe that certain problems are too complex and varied in form to be successfully met by clear, precise language. In such situations, legislators frequently resort to sweeping phrases, empowering other governmental agencies "to regulate in the public interest," to set "reasonable rates," or to provide "family-planning services." During the debate on what became the Sherman Act of 1890, another senator asked John Sherman what he meant by "monopoly." Sherman candidly responded that he had no exact definition:

> It is difficult to define in legal language the precise line between lawful and unlawful combinations. This must be left for the courts to determine in each particular case. All that we, as lawmakers, can do is to declare general principles, and we can be assured that the courts will apply them so as to carry out the meaning of the law.[3]

If Congress had no exact meaning, then judges faced an enormous difficulty in carrying out "the meaning of the law." It is little wonder that the Supreme Court

---

[2] Jerome Frank, *Courts on Trial* (Princeton, NJ: Princeton University Press, 1950), 294.

[3] 21 *Congressional Record* 2460.

quickly became and has remained, as one standard text says, "the ultimate maker of antitrust policy."[4]

At still other times, legislators hastily enact statutes as a means of easing pressure from interest groups and constituents, employing muddy language so as to allow themselves a ready claim of misinterpretation if the legislation proves unwise. As one English judge complained about such a statute, it was "an ill-penned enactment, like too many others, putting Judges in the embarrassing situation of being bound to make sense out of nonsense, and to reconcile what is irreconcilable."[5]

As an example of intentional ambiguity consider the congressional efforts to enact a standard for exempting conscientious objectors to military service. On the one hand, the older practice of requiring all healthy males to serve required the government to violate the consciences of many loyal citizens. On the other hand, excusing members of pacifist religious sects might have violated the establishment clause of the First Amendment. So in 1948 Congress made exemption depend on an individual's relation to a "Supreme Being," leaving it to administrators and judges to interpret this ethereal language.

DEALING WITH AMBIGUITY: THEORIES OF STATUTORY INTERPRETATION

When, as is so often the case, the words of the text are sufficiently murky that they fail to provide clear, determinative answers, judges must move beyond the words and look to other "contexts" of the law. And, yet, both scholars and judges fervently disagree over which contexts should be relevant.

In the sections to follow we consider four such contexts or approaches—intentionalism, purposivism, new textualism, and dynamic statutory interpretation—all of which have their share of supporters and detractors. Here we want to emphasize only that debates over these various approaches are of relatively recent vintage. As William N. Eskridge, Jr. notes: "Statutory interpretation is the Cinderella of legal scholarship. Once scorned and neglected, confined to the kitchen, it now dances in the ballroom. Although the interpretation of statutes has been an ongoing topic of interest since the colonial period, only since the early 1980s have American legal academics become intensely excited about statutory interpretation."[6]

---

[4] Merle Fainsod, Lincoln Gordon, and Joseph C. Palamountain, Jr., *Government and the American Economy*, 3rd ed. (New York: Norton, 1959), 603.

[5] Quoted in C. K. Allen, *Law in the Making*, 6th ed. (London: Oxford University Press), 468.

[6] William N. Eskridge, *Dynamic Statutory Interpretation* (Cambridge, MA: Harvard University Press, 1994), 1. This intense interest has produced an explosion of scholarship, with three works of particular importance and of immense use to us as we crafted this chapter: Eskridge's *Dynamic Statutory Interpretation*; his casebook (coauthored with Philip P. Frickey), *Cases and Materials on Legislation*, 2nd ed. (St. Paul, MN: West, 1995); and his monograph (coauthored with Frickey and Elizabeth Garrett), *Legislation and Statutory Interpretation* (New York: Foundation Press, 1999). Also useful is Kent Greenawalt, *Statutory Interpretation: 20 Questions* (New York: Foundation Press, 1999).

Why statutory interpretation has only recently sparked the imagination of the legal and social-scientific communities could have a good deal to do with the ultimate interpreter of federal legislation in the United States, the Supreme Court—specifically, with its decision in *United Steelworkers v. Weber* (1979) (Reading 11.3). Part of *Weber's* importance is that it involved an issue of intense societal and political concern—affirmative action. But more relevant here is that it provided an opportunity for the justices to trot out their favored theories of statutory interpretation, from the purposivism in Justice William J. Brennan's majority opinion to the dynamic approach taken by Harry Blackmun in his concurrence to the intentionalism evident in William H. Rehnquist's dissent.

Legislative Intent

What did the legislature intend when it enacted the statute? Many scholars have argued that the answer to this question—that is, the intent of the enacting body—ought to serve as the "cornerstone" of statutory interpretation. And at least some judges have taken this advice, with Rehnquist's dissenting opinion in *Weber* providing but one example. That legislative intent holds such sway with the legal community should not come as a surprise. As Eskridge explains: "Intentionalism is in some respects a natural way to view statutory interpretation in a representative democracy. If the legislature is the primary lawmaker and interpreters are its agents, then requiring interpreters to follow the legislature's intentions constrains their choices and advances democracy by carrying out the will of the elected legislators."[7]

Nonetheless, intentionalism has its share of serious problems. It is, of course, possible that any given legislator did not have an "intention" beyond appearing to please constituents in general, particular interest groups, party leaders, or other legislators. The last may show their gratitude by voting for another bill that the indifferent legislator does badly want enacted. Further, even if a legislator did have an intent in mind, it is usually difficult to glean it from the record surrounding the law: Most members of Congress do not speak on most bills, and when they do they are often less than candid. Finally, because "Congress Is a 'They,' Not an 'It'," as Kenneth A. Shepsle titled a paper, the notion of a single legislative intent may be something of an oxymoron. Given that there are 435 members of the House of Representatives and 100 senators, it would not be surprising to find that a dozen different "intentions" were operating, none of which commanded majority agreement.

Many of the readings in this chapter explore the various shortcomings of intentionalism, and we have more to say about it in the next chapter, where we consider its application to constitutional interpretation. So suffice it to note here that those judges who favor the approach are not unmindful of these and other obstacles confronting any search for original intent. In fact, in light of them, Judge Richard A. Posner proposes a modified version of intentionalism—imaginative

---

[7] Eskridge, *Dynamic Statutory Interpretation*, 14.

reconstruction. Using this approach, judges would assume the position of enacting legislators (usually ones who were pivotal to the passage of the law) and ask themselves how those key legislators would have answered the question at hand (Reading 11.4). To some scholars, Rehnquist's dissent in *Weber* provides a better example of this approach than of traditional intentionalism. To the extent that he attempted to determine whether pivotal members of the enacting Congress would have supported affirmative action, these scholars could be right.[8]

Legislative Purpose

In *Weber*, Justice Brennan, who delivered the opinion of the Court, rejected Rehnquist's exercise in "imaginative reconstruction"; indeed, one of the swipes he took at Rehnquist was that the Court would have reached a decision "completely at variance with the purpose of the statute" had it followed an intentional tack. Instead, Brennan undertook a search for the law's purpose and made an explicit distinction between *intent* and *purpose*—one that all too often gets blurred in judicial opinions and scholarly writings. Perhaps the causes of this failing lie in the huge expense of a good dictionary (as much as $25) and the difficulties of using such a highly technical tool (its entries are arranged alphabetically). In any event, "to have in mind" is a common definition. Thus it usually refers to a psychological state, what writers of a statute, an administrative regulation, or a judicial opinion had in mind. *Purpose* refers to "an object to be attained," an "end" to be accomplished. This word also has psychological implications, but it is easier to express and to discern than is *intent*. At least an avowed purpose is easier to discern than is intent, because a statute or a constitutional text spells out very early in its wording what its purposes are.[9]

In undertaking a search for the statute's purpose in *Weber*, Brennan was not out of step with mainstream views of statutory interpretation, for judges normally presume, not always correctly, that a statute has a purpose, that it is a legislative effort to solve a problem in public policy. Thus it is a widely accepted rule that judges should try to discover that purpose so as to interpret specific phrases in light of that overarching objective. "A formally enacted statement or purpose in a statute," as the legal scholars most closely associated with this approach, Henry M. Hart and Albert M. Sachs, put it, "should be accepted by the Court if it appears to have been designed to serve as a guide to interpretation, is consistent with the words and context of the statute, and is relevant to the question of meaning at issue" (Reading 11.5). This prescription recognizes that judges have a subordinate role to play in applying statutory law; their obligation is to

---

[8] Of course, part of the problem here lies in determining which legislators were pivotal. Scholars who focus on the legislative process differ sharply among themselves on how to discover such persons. And when they do appear, it could turn out that they, too, voted for a bill only as part of a bargain that another proponent would vote favorably on a different measure.

[9] It goes without saying that, as in all of human life, what is said is not always what is meant. And there lie many of the difficulties of interpretation, as we shall see momentarily.

help the legislature achieve its goals. But what are courts to do when the law's purpose is not so clear? Hart and Sachs continue: "In all other situations, the purpose of the statute has in some degree to be inferred."

Unfortunately, this task is no simple matter. A court might employ a wide range of sources and practices in a quest for legislative purpose, and an equally wide range of differences of opinion as to the merits of these sources and practices. In England the usual rule is that courts must examine nothing but the words of the statute itself. They can take no note of any discussions in Parliament during the passage of the act, nor of any statements of members of the Government in presenting the bill, nor of any committee deliberations on the bill. For generations practice in the United States tended to follow the English example. As late as 1921, a majority of the Supreme Court could claim that it was "well established that the debates in Congress expressive of the views and motives of individual members are not a safe guide in ascertaining the meaning and purpose of the law-making body."[10]

But even then judges in the United States were not universally denying themselves information about a statute's genesis and development, and within little more than a decade courts were routinely looking at legislative reports and debates in an effort to discern what purposes underlay social and economic regulations. Today it is accepted practice for judges to place considerable stress on the legislative history of an act in determining its meaning—as the majority did in *Weber* (1979). It is no wonder, therefore, that members of Congress, recognizing the important role of legislative history, regularly take great pains to get statements into the *Congressional Record* that will support their interpretation of the legislative language being adopted. Often those statements are not merely efforts to "create a record" that will help administrators and judges understand the law but also efforts by a bill's opponents to create a record that will mislead interpreters and so minimize the damage that opponents fear a particular piece of legislation will inflict on the interests they are trying to protect.

These problems indicate that most judges in the United States agree on the wisdom of using legislative history to guide statutory interpretation. Justice Antonin Scalia, who is deeply skeptical of approaches that rely on legislative purpose or intent—believing that "it is law that governs, not the intent of the lawgiver"[11]—has lashed out at the use of legislative history to divine purpose especially when an examination of that history supplants the plain meaning of the statute. His concurring opinion in *Conroy v. Aniskoff* (1993) provides a clear example of his reasoning (Reading 11.6).

The New Textualism

Others, most notably Judges Frank H. Easterbrook and Richard A. Posner, also take issue with Hart and Sachs's claim that interpreters should look to a

---

[10] *Duplex Printing Press Co. v Deering* (1921).

[11] Antonin Scalia, *A Matter of Interpretation* (Princeton, NJ: Princeton University Press, 1997). We have more to say about Scalia's approach in Chapter 12.

statute's formal statement of purpose, and they do so for a reason different from that of Scalia: They believe such approaches are inattentive to the realities of the legislative process. Taking their cues from public-choice scholarship, these judges have made the breathtaking discovery, which any journalist or college freshman who had taken a course in American government would have long known, that most legislation is, in part, the product of intensely negotiated bargains struck among interest groups and legislators. Hence, a single legislative intent or purpose seldom exists because most legislation is a child of many compromises, often incoherent, with the final language simply reflecting the "deal" that attracted the support of a majority of legislators.[12]

Although Judges Posner and Easterbrook agree about the nature of legislation, they strongly disagree about what public choice implies for statutory interpretation. Posner, as we noted, contends that courts ought to defer to legislative deals by engaging in a process of "imaginative reconstruction." Dismissing this task as beyond the ability of most judges, Easterbrook (along with Scalia) advocates "new" textualism: "My suggestion is that unless the statute plainly hands courts the power to create and revise a form of common law, the domain of the statute should be restricted to cases anticipated by its framers and expressly resolved in the legislative process." Whether this theory shares the problems of its close relative, the plain-meaning approach, is a question Easterbrook addresses in Reading 11.7.

Dynamic Statutory Interpretation

Despite their differences, all the approaches to statutory interpretation we have considered—textualism, intentionalism, purposivism, and their variants—share a common feature: They place emphasis on laws at the time legislature wrote them, requiring judges to undertake "archeological" digs to interpret them.[13] They are static accounts to the extent that they would have judges, regardless of who they are and when they are interpreting the extant statute, reach the same conclusions about its meaning.

Proponents of another approach, called dynamic statutory interpretation, take issue with this feature of traditional accounts. "Just as modern literary theory has taught that the meaning of literary texts changes from reader to reader and over time," so too, Eskridge and Frickey argue, "the meaning of statutory texts changes over time." Hence, "statutory texts, like literary texts, are transformed every time they are interpreted."[14] According to their argument, dynamic statutory interpretation is an evolving process in which judges take into account changes in the "societal, legal, and constitutional" context of the statute. As changes in this context occur, changes in interpretation follow (Reading 11.8). To ignore this dynamic aspect of statutory interpretation would be to

---

[12] This is but one feature of public choice scholarship invoked by Posner and Easterbrook. See Reading 11.7 for others.

[13] See Alexander Aleinikoff, "Updating Statutory Interpretation," 87 *Michigan Law Review* 20 (1988).

[14] Eskridge and Frickey, *Legislation*, 572.

ignore the realities of Supreme Court practice—at least so this argument goes, an argument, by the way, which is accepted by some of the justices of the Supreme Court (see, e.g., Blackmun's concurring opinion in Reading 11.3).

The changes of which Eskridge and Frickey speak are, of course, broad enough to encompass alterations in the political environment. As Eskridge himself demonstrates, the Supreme Court occasionally reads statutes in a strategic fashion—one that takes into account the preferences of the contemporary Congress rather than the one that enacted the law. This approach could explain why "conservative" courts sometimes interpret statutes in a "liberal" fashion and vice versa,[15] with *Weber* providing an interesting example.

Although many scholars agree that judges do, in fact, read statutes dynamically, debate has ensued over whether they should do so. Even leading proponents of this account, Eskridge and Frickey, acknowledge some of the problems that emerge when judges ignore the purpose of or the intent behind a law and, instead, read it in light of the climate of the times (See Reading 11.8). But other problems—such as a lack of stability and predictability in law that occur when judges pay more heed to the current legislature than the enacting one—are equally apparent.

PRACTICAL MATTERS IN STATUTORY INTERPRETATION

Theoretical approaches aside, judges have developed a number of "maxims," "canons," and "principles"—rules of thumb, really—to aid in the interpretation of statutes when their meanings are not entirely transparent (Readings 11.1 and 11.4). Some are extrinsic to the law under examination. Its legislative history provides one example, but there are others, including legislative inaction. After a statute has been judicially interpreted, courts might study congressional reaction for clues about the correctness of the decision. If disappointed legislators fail to amend the statute, judges often take such inaction as indicating that the original judicial interpretation was correct, or at least within limits that Congress considers acceptable. So too, judges habitually turn to explanatory rules promulgated by the administrative agency to whom the legislature has assigned the task of enforcing the particular statute. Agencies such as the Internal Revenue Service and the National Labor Relations Board issue massive codes of regulations that supposedly carry out the will of Congress—a will that is often expressed in sweeping generalities to meet complex technological, social, and

---

[15] For a strategic account in which the Court pays heed to the preferences of the Congress that enacted the legislation, see John Ferejohn and Barry Weingast, "A Positive Theory of Statutory Interpretation," 12 *International Review of Law and Economics* 263–279 (1992). Also see Jeffrey A. Segal's study, "Separation-of-Powers Games in the Positive Theory of Congress and Courts," 91 *American Political Science Review* 28–44 (1997), which argues that justices rarely operate in the way claimed by Eskridge and Frickey.

economic problems. Although courts retain full authority to modify or reject administrative interpretations of statutes and sometimes exercise that authority, they usually invoke those interpretations to aid their own statutory interpretation, a process captured by the old saw, "the blind leading the blind."

As controversial as extrinsic aids may be (Reading 11.6), intrinsic aids—particularly those beckoning judges to read statutes in light of the so-called canons of construction—are more so (Readings 11.1 and 11.4). At least some of the controversy surrounding these canons stems from their sheer number: Just as there is sufficient precedent for judges to find at least one that supports their position, "there are," as Karl Llewellyn noted, "two opposing canons on almost every point."[16] He went on to provide numerous examples of the "thrust" and "parry" nature of the canons, including: (1) "A statute cannot go beyond its text" (thrust), but "To effect its purpose a statute may be implemented beyond its text" (parry); (2) "If language is plain and unambiguous it must be given effect (thrust), but "Not when literal interpretation would lead to absurd or mischievous consequences or thwart manifested purpose" (parry).

A final set of principles, and ones no less fluid, focuses on presumptions that judges ought to make when interpreting statutes. Along these lines a rule of interpretation frequently utilized by judges and highly recommended by the Supreme Court requires that, whenever possible, legislation be interpreted in such a way as to avoid constitutional questions. Involved here is a recognition of the need to use very cautiously judicial power to declare legislative acts unconstitutional, particularly acts of Congress. Concurring in *Ashwander v. Tennessee Valley Authority* (1936), Justice Louis D. Brandeis listed for the Court's benefit a "series of rules under which it has avoided passing upon a large part of all the constitutional questions pressed upon it for decision." The seventh rule read:

> When the validity of an act of the Congress is drawn in question and even if a serious doubt of constitutionality is raised, it is a cardinal principle that this Court will first ascertain whether a construction of the statute is fairly possible by which the question may be avoided.

Often, of course, judges disagree on how far they may legitimately go in interpreting a statute so as to make it constitutional. Conclusions from the principle of judicial self-restraint usually give conflicting advice. The rule that a judge should not declare a statute invalid if she or he can avoid doing so conflicts with the rule that a judge should not redraft what Congress has enacted. For a court to rewrite a statute to make it constitutional may be a less-warranted exercise of judicial power than to take the legislation at its face value and declare it invalid.

One of the many notable instances of judicial difference on this issue occurred in *Scales v. United States* (1961). The Supreme Court was reviewing the conviction of a communist under the provision of the Smith Act making it a

---

[16] Karl Llewellyn, "Remarks on the Theory of Appellate Decision and the Rules or Canons about How Statutes Are to Be Construed," 3 *Vanderbilt Law Review* 395 (1950).

crime for anyone, "knowing the purposes thereof," to become a member of or affiliate with "any society, group, or assembly of persons" advocating, abetting, advising, or teaching "the duty, necessity, desirability, or propriety" of violent overthrow of the government of the United States or of any state or territory in the United States. Speaking for the majority, Justice John M. Harlan, II, tried to skirt the First Amendment's protection of freedom of association by interpreting the statute as affecting only "active" members who had the "specific intent" of carrying out the proscribed activities, not just nominal members who knew of a group's illegal aims. In dissent Justice Black protested that

> the Court has practically rewritten the statute . . . by treating the requirements of "activity" and "specific intent" as implicit in words that plainly do not include them. . . . It seems clear to me that neither petitioner nor anyone else could ever have guessed that this law would be held to mean what this Court now holds it does mean. For that reason, it appears that petitioner has been convicted under a law that is, at best, unconstitutionally vague and, at worst, ex post facto.

STATUTORY LAW AND JUDICIAL LAW MAKING

This discussion should have made it obvious that, despite the number of theories and rules of thumb, judges may have at least as much leeway in interpreting statutes as in working within the interstices of their own previous decisions. And it should not be forgotten that in interpreting statutes judges look to previous judicial decisions, following a form of stare decisis almost identical to that used in common-law cases. Attorneys worth their fee would never advise clients about the meaning of a statute without first poring over the ways in which courts have construed the legislature's words.

More generally, parsing plain words, seeking legislative intent or purpose, whether static or dynamic, or following any set of clear rules often sends judges on a bootless hunt. As Monroe Smith observed several generations ago:

> the possibilities of lawfinding under cover of interpretation are very great. A distinguished German jurist, Windscheid, has remarked that in interpreting legislation modern courts may and habitually do "think over again the thought which the legislator was trying to express," but that the Roman jurist went further and "thought out the thought which the legislator was trying to think."[17]

Such problems have moved some American jurists to refer to the process of statutory interpretation as an "art." Judge Jerome Frank took this analogy and Windscheid's observation to heart. Only half-smiling, Frank suggested that judges should read a statute as a musician reads a score, as something to be interpreted rather than mechanically applied. "The conscientious, intelligent judge," he continued,

---

[17] Quoted by Thomas Reed Powell, "The Logic and Rhetoric of Constitutional Law," 15 *Journal of Philosophy, Psychology, and Scientific Method* 654 (1918).

will consider government a sort of orchestra, in which, in symphonies authorized by the people, the courts and the legislature each play their parts. The playing may sometimes be bad. There may, occasionally, be some disharmonies. But, after all, modern music has taught us that a moderate amount of cacophony need not be altogether unpleasant.[18]

Whether or not Frank's analogy pleases judges, it is apparent that their roles will, of necessity, be creative when reading many statutes—and "many" will probably include those most important to a particular generation. A court can make as much law by reading a statute too strictly as it can by reading it too loosely, and "too" in each instance defies objective definition. As a result, the "disharmonies" that result as judges rule for or against particular interests are far more frequent—and painful—than Frank cared to admit.

SELECTED REFERENCES

ALEINIKOFF, ALEXANDER. 1988. "Updating Statutory Interpretation." *Michigan Law Review* 87: 20.

BEANEY, WILLIAM M. 1959. "Civil Liberties and Statutory Construction." *Journal of Public Law* 8: 66.

BICKEL, ALEXANDER M., AND HARRY H. WELLINGTON. 1957. "Legislative Purpose and the Judicial Process: The Lincoln Mills Case." *Harvard Law Review* 71: 1.

CALABRESI, GUIDO. 1982. *A Common Law for the Age of Statutes*. Cambridge, MA.: Harvard University Press.

DWORKIN, RONALD. 1982. "Law as Interpretation." *Texas Law Review* 60: 527.

EASTERBROOK, FRANK. 1983. "Statutes' Domains." *University of Chicago Law Review* 50: 533.

ELY, JOHN HART. 1970. "Legislative and Administrative Motivation in Constitutional Law." *Yale Law Journal* 79: 1207.

ESKRIDGE, WILLIAM N., JR. 1990. "The New Textualism." *U.C.L.A. Law Review* 37: 621.

ESKRIDGE, WILLIAM N., JR. 1994. *Dynamic Statutory Interpretation*. Cambridge, MA: Harvard University Press.

ESKRIDGE, WILLIAM N., JR., PHILIP P. FRICKEY, AND ELIZABETH GARRETT. 1999. *Legislation and Statutory Interpretation*. New York: West.

FARBER, DANIEL A. 1989. "Statutory Interpretation and Legislative Supremacy." *Georgetown Law Journal* 78: 281.

FARBER, DANIEL A. 2000. "Do Theories of Statutory Interpretation Matter? A Case Study." *Northwestern University Law Review* 94: 1409

FEREJOHN, JOHN A., AND BARRY R. WEINGAST. 1992. "Limitations of Statutes: Strategic Statutory Interpretation." *Georgetown Law Journal* 565.

FEREJOHN, JOHN A., AND BARRY R. WEINGAST. 1992. "A Positive Theory of Statutory Interpretation." *International Review of Law and Economics* 12: 263.

FRANK, JEROME. 1930. *Law and the Modern Mind*. New York: Brentano's.

FRANK, JEROME. 1947. "Words and Music: Some Remarks on Statutory Interpretation." *Columbia Law Review* 47: 1259.

FRANKFURTER, FELIX. 1947. "Some Reflections on Reading Statutes." *Record of the Association of the Bar of the City of New York* 2: 213.

---

[18] Jerome Frank, *Courts on Trial*, 207–208.

GREENAWALT, KENNETH. 1999. *Legislation: Statutory Interpretation (20 Questions)*. New York: Foundation Press.

HART, HENRY M., JR., AND ALBERT M. SACHS. 1994. *The Legal Process*. William N. Eskridge, Jr., and Philip P. Frickey, eds. Westbury, NY: Foundation Press.

HURST, J. WILLARD HURST. 1982. *Dealing with Statutes*. New York: Columbia University Press.

LLEWELYN, KARL. 1950. "Remarks on the Theory of Appellate Decision and the Rules or Canons About How Statutes Are to Be Construed." *Vanderbilt Law Review* 3: 395.

MACEY, JONATHAN R. 1986. "Promoting Public-Regarding Legislation through Statutory Interpretation: An Interest Group Model." *Columbia Law Review* 86: 223.

MANTEL, HOWARD N. 1959. "The Congressional Record: Fact or Fiction of the Legislative Process." *Western Political Quarterly* 12: 981.

MASHAW, JERRY L. 1997. *Greed, Chaos, and Governance*. New Haven, CT: Yale University Press.

MENDELSON, WALLACE. 1955. "Mr. Justice Frankfurter on the Construction of Statutes." *California Law Review* 43: 652.

MILLER, ARTHUR S. 1956. "Statutory Language and the Purposive Use of Ambiguity." *Virginia Law Review* 42: 23.

POPKIN, WILLIAM D. 1999. *Statutes in Court: The History and Theory of Statutory Interpretation*. Durham, NC: Duke University Press.

POSNER, RICHARD A. 1982. "Economics, Politics, and the Reading of Statutes and the Constitution." *University of Chicago Law Review* 49: 263.

POSNER, RICHARD A. 1985. *The Federal Courts*. Cambridge, MA: Harvard University Press.

POUND, ROSCOE. 1908. "Common Law and Legislation." *Harvard Law Review* 21: 383.

RODRIGUEZ, DANIEL B. 1992. "Statutory Interpretation and Political Advantages." *International Review of Law and Economics* 12: 217.

SCALIA, ANTONIN. 1997. *A Matter of Interpretation*. Princeton, NJ: Princeton University Press.

SEGAL, JEFFREY A. 1997. "Separation-of-Powers Games in the Positive Theory of Congress and Courts." *American Political Science Review* 91: 28.

SHEPSLE, KENNETH A. 1992. "Congress Is a 'They,' Not an 'It': Legislative Intent as an Oxymoron." *International Review of Law and Economics* 12: 239.

STRAUSS, PETER L. 1998. "The Courts and Congress: Should Judges Disdain Political History?" *Columbia Law Review* 98: 242

SUNSTEIN, CASS R. 1989. "Interpreting Statutes in the Regulatory State." *Harvard Law Review* 103: 405.

VERMEULE, ADRIAN. 2001. "The Cycle of Statutory Interpretation." *University of Chicago Law Review* 68: 149.

WALD, PATRICIA M. 1983. "Some Observations on the Use of Legislative History in the 1981 Supreme Court Term." *Iowa Law Review* 68: 195.

"... [J]udges are not unlettered glossators."

11.1 SOME REFLECTIONS ON THE READING OF STATUTES

Felix Frankfurter

Felix Frankfurter served as Associate Justice of
the U.S. Supreme Court between 1939 and 1962.

... Anything that is written may present a problem of meaning, and that is the
essence of the business of judges in construing legislation. The problem derives
from the very nature of words. They are symbols of meaning. But unlike mathematical symbols, the phrasing of a document, especially a complicated enactment, seldom attains more than approximate precision. If individual words are
inexact symbols, with shifting variables, their configuration can hardly achieve
invariant meaning or assured definiteness. Apart from the ambiguity inherent
in its symbols, a statute suffers from dubieties. It is not an equation or a formula
representing a clearly marked process, nor is it an expression of individual
thought to which is imparted the definiteness a single authorship can give. A
statute is an instrument of government partaking of its practical purposes but
also of its infirmities and limitations, of its awkward and groping efforts. . . .
The imagination which can draw an income tax statute to cover the myriad
transactions of a society [such as] ours, capable of producing the necessary revenue without producing a flood of litigation, has not yet revealed itself.
Moreover, government sometimes solves problems by shelving them temporarily. The legislative process reflects that attitude. Statutes as well as constitutional
provisions at times embody purposeful ambiguity or are expressed with a generality for future unfolding. . . .

The intrinsic difficulties of language and the emergence after enactment of
situations not anticipated by the most gifted legislative imagination reveal
doubts and ambiguities in statutes that compel judicial construction. The
process of construction, therefore, is not an exercise in logic or dialectic: The
aids of formal reasoning are not irrelevant; they may simply be inadequate.
The purpose of construction being the ascertainment of meaning, every consideration brought to bear for the solution of that problem must be devoted to that
end alone. To speak of it as a practical problem is not to indulge a fashion in
words. It must be that, not something else. Not, for instance, an opportunity for
a judge to use words as "empty vessels into which he can pour anything he

will"—his caprices, fixed notions, even statesmanlike beliefs in a particular policy. Nor, on the other hand, is the process a ritual to be observed by unimaginative adherence to well-worn professional phrases. . . .

. . . The area of free judicial movement is considerable. . . . The difficulty is that the legislative ideas which laws embody are both explicit and immanent. And so the bottom problem is: What is below the surface of the words and yet fairly a part of them? Words in statutes are not unlike words in a foreign language in that they too have "associations, echoes, and overtones." Judges must retain the associations, hear the echoes, and capture the overtones. . . .

Even within their area of choice the courts are not at large. They are confined by the nature and scope of the judicial function in its particular exercise in the field of interpretation. They are under the constraints imposed by the judicial function in our democratic society. As a matter of verbal recognition certainly, no one will gainsay that the function in construing a statute is to ascertain the meaning of words used by the legislature. To go beyond it is to usurp a power which our democracy has lodged in its elected legislature. . . . A judge must not rewrite a statute, neither to enlarge nor to contract it. . . .

This duty of restraint, this humility of function as merely the translator of another's command, is a constant theme of our Justices. . . . In short, judges are not unfettered glossators. They are under a special duty not to over-emphasize the episodic aspects of life and not to undervalue its organic processes—its continuities and relationships. For judges at least it is important to remember that continuity with the past is not only a necessity but even a duty.

Let me descend to some particulars.

The Text. Though we may not end with the words in construing a disputed statute, one certainly begins there. . . . The Court no doubt must listen to the voice of Congress. But often Congress cannot be heard clearly because its speech is muffled. Even when it has spoken, it is as true of Congress as of others that what is said is what the listener hears. Like others, judges too listen with what psychologists used to call the apperception mass, which I take it means in plain English that one listens with what is already in one's head. One more caution is relevant when one is admonished to listen attentively to what a statute says. One must also listen attentively to what it does not say.

We must, no doubt, accord the words the sense in which Congress used them . . . we assume that Congress uses common words in their popular meaning, as used in the common speech of men, The cases speak of the "meaning of common understanding," "the normal and spontaneous meaning of language," "the common and appropriate use, "the natural straightforward and literal sense," and similar variants. . . .

Sometimes Congress supplies its own dictionary. It did so in 1871 in a statute defining a limited number of words for use as to all future enactments. . . . Or there may be indications from the statute that words in it are the considered language of legislation. "If Congress has been accustomed to use a certain phrase with a more limited meaning than might be attributed to it by common practice, it would be arbitrary to refuse to consider that fact when we come to interpret a statute." . . . Or words may acquire scope and function from the history of events which they summarize or from the purpose which they serve. . . . Words of art bring their art with them. They bear the meaning of their habitat whether it be a phrase of technical significance in the scientific or business world, or whether it be loaded with the recondite connotations of feudalism. . . . The peculiar idiom of business or of administrative practice often modifies the meaning that ordinary speech assigns to language. And if a word is obviously transplanted from another legal source, whether the common law or other legislation, it brings the old soil with it.

The Context. Legislation is a form of literary composition. But construction is not an abstract process equally valid for every composition, not even for every composition whose meaning must be judicially ascertained. The nature of the composition demands awareness of certain presuppositions. . . . And so, the significance of an enactment, its antecedents as well as its later history, its relation to other enactments, all may be relevant to the construction of words for one purpose and in one setting but not for another. Some words are confined to their history; some are starting points for history. Words are intellectual and moral currency. They come from the legislative mint with some intrinsic meaning. Sometimes it remains unchanged. Like currency, words sometimes appreciate or depreciate in value.

Frequently the sense of a word cannot be got except by fashioning a mosaic of significance out of the innuendoes of disjointed bits of statute. Cardozo phrased this familiar phenomenon by stating that "the meaning of a statute is to be looked for, not in any single section, but in all the parts together and in their relation to the end in view." . . .

You may have observed that I have not yet used the word "intention." All these years I have avoided speaking of the "legislative intent," and I shall continue to be on my guard against using it. The objection to "intention" was indicated in a letter by Mr. Justice Holmes which the recipient kindly put at my disposal:

> Only a day or two ago—when counsel talked of the intention of a legislature, I was indiscreet enough to say I don't care what their intention was. I only want to know what the words mean.

Legislation has an aim; it seeks to obviate some mischief, to supply an inadequacy, to effect a change of policy, to formulate a plan of government. That aim, that policy is not drawn, like nitrogen, out of the air; it is evinced in the language of the statute, as read in the light of other external manifestations of purpose. That is what the judge must seek and effectuate. . . .

The difficulty in many instances where a problem of meaning arises is that the enactment was not directed towards the troubling question. The problem might then be stated, as once it was by Mr. Justice Cardozo, "which choice is it the more likely that Congress would have made?" . . . But the purpose which a court must effectuate is not that which Congress should have enacted, or would have. It is that which it did enact, however ineptly, because it may fairly be said to be imbedded in the statute, even if a specific manifestation was not thought of, as is often the very reason for casting a statute in very general terms.

Often the purpose or policy that controls is not directly displayed in the particular enactment. Statutes cannot be read intelligently if the eye is closed to considerations evidenced in affiliated statutes, or in the known temper of legislative opinion. Thus, for example, it is not lightly to be presumed that Congress sought to infringe on "very sacred rights." This improbability will be a factor in determining whether language, though it should be so read if standing alone, was used to effect such a drastic change. . . .

Nor can canons of construction save us from the anguish of judgment. Such canons give an air of abstract intellectual compulsion to what is in fact a delicate judgment, concluding a complicated process of balancing subtle and elusive elements. . . . Insofar as canons of construction are generalizations of experience, they all have worth. In the abstract, they rarely arouse controversy. Difficulties emerge when canons compete in soliciting judgment, because they conflict rather than converge. For the demands of judgment underlying the art of interpretation, there is no vade mecum. . . .

The quality of legislative organization and procedure is inevitably reflected in the quality of legislative draftsmanship. Representative Monroney told the House last July [1947] that "95 percent of all the legislation that becomes law passes the Congress in the shape that it came from our committees. Therefore if our committee work is sloppy, if it is bad, if it is inadequate, our legislation in 95 percent of the cases will be bad and inadequate as well." . . . But what courts do with legislation may in turn deeply affect what Congress will do in the future. Emerson says somewhere that mankind is as lazy as it dares to be. Loose judicial reading makes for loose legislative writing. It encourages the practice illustrated in a recent cartoon in which a senator tells his colleagues "I admit this new bill is too complicated to understand. We'll just have to pass it to find out what it means." . . .

But there are more fundamental objections to loose judicial reading. In a democracy the legislative impulse and its expression should come from those popularly chosen to legislate, and equipped to devise policy, as courts are not. The pressure on legislatures to discharge their responsibility with care, understanding and imagination should be stiffened, not relaxed. Above all, they must not be encouraged in irresponsible or undisciplined use of language. In the keeping of legislatures perhaps more than any other group is the well-being of their fellow-men. Their responsibility is discharged ultimately by words. . . .

*"When someone asks, 'Do you use a cane?' he is not inquiring
whether you have your grandfather's silver-handled walking stick
on display in the hall; he wants to know whether you walk
with a cane." —JUSTICE ANTONIN SCALIA*

*"[I]t does not follow that the only 'use' to which a cane might be put is
assisting one's grandfather in walking. Quite the opposite: The most
infamous use of a cane in American history had nothing to do with
walking at all." —JUSTICE SANDRA DAY O'CONNOR*

11.2 SMITH V. UNITED STATES

508 U.S. 223 (1993)

*Under federal law [18 U.S.C. @ 924(c)(1)], anyone who uses a machine gun, in con-
nection with a drug offense, shall receive a prison sentence of 30 years. In this case, however, the defendant, John Angus Smith, did not use the gun as a weapon; he used it as a
medium for barter: one MAC-10 machine gun for several ounces of cocaine. After he received the mandatory sentence of 30 years, Smith appealed, arguing that §924(c)(1)'s
penalty for using a firearm during and in relation to a drug trafficking offense covers
only situations in which the firearm is used as a weapon and not to defendants who use
a firearm solely as an object for barter.*

*Addressing Smith's contention required the Court to decide whether the exchange
of a gun for narcotics constitutes "use" of a firearm within the meaning of 18 U.S.C.
§924(c)(1). The majority agreed that it did but its interpretation of the word "use" was
the subject of an interesting debate between Justices O'Connor and Scalia.*

JUSTICE O'CONNOR delivered the opinion of the Court.
... [W]e confine our discussion to what the parties view as the dispositive issue
in this case: whether trading a firearm for drugs can constitute "use" of the
firearm within the meaning of §924(c)(1).

When a word is not defined by statute, we normally construe it in accord
with its ordinary or natural meaning. Surely petitioner's treatment of his MAC-
10 can be described as "use" within the everyday meaning of that term.
Petitioner "used" his MAC-10 in an attempt to obtain drugs by offering to trade
it for cocaine. *Webster's* defines "to use" as "to convert to one's service" or "to
employ." *Black's Law Dictionary* contains a similar definition: "to make use of; to
convert to one's service; to employ; to avail oneself of; to utilize; to carry out a
purpose or action by means of." Indeed, over 100 years ago we gave the word
"use" the same gloss, indicating that it means "to employ" or "to derive service
from." Petitioner's handling of the MAC-10 in this case falls squarely within
those definitions. By attempting to trade his MAC-10 for the drugs, he "used"
or "employed" it as an item of barter to obtain cocaine; he "derived service"
from it because it was going to bring him the very drugs he sought.

In petitioner's view, §924(c)(1) should require proof not only that the defendant used the firearm but also that he used it as a weapon. But the words "as a weapon" appear nowhere in the statute. Rather, §924(c)(1)'s language sweeps broadly, punishing any "use" of a firearm, so long as the use is "during and in relation to" a drug trafficking offense. Had Congress intended the narrow construction petitioner urges, it could have so indicated. It did not, and we decline to introduce that additional requirement on our own.

Language, of course, cannot be interpreted apart from context. The meaning of a word that appears ambiguous if viewed in isolation may become clear when the word is analyzed in light of the terms that surround it. Recognizing this, petitioner and the dissent argue that the word "uses" has a somewhat reduced scope in §924(c)(1) because it appears alongside the word "firearm." Specifically, they contend that the average person on the street would not think immediately of a guns-for-drugs trade as an example of "us[ing] a firearm." Rather, that phrase normally evokes an image of the most familiar use to which a firearm is put—use as a weapon. Petitioner and the dissent therefore argue that the statute excludes uses where the weapon is not fired or otherwise employed for its destructive capacity. Indeed, relying on that argument—and without citation to authority—the dissent announces its own, restrictive definition of "use." "To use an instrumentality," the dissent argues, "ordinarily means to use it for its intended purpose."

There is a significant flaw to this argument. It is one thing to say that the ordinary meaning of "uses a firearm" includes using a firearm as a weapon, since that is the intended purpose of a firearm and the example of "use" that most immediately comes to mind. But it is quite another to conclude that, as a result, the phrase also excludes any other use. Certainly that conclusion does not follow from the phrase "uses . . . a firearm" itself. As the dictionary definitions and experience make clear, one can use a firearm in a number of ways. That one example of "use" is the first to come to mind when the phrase "uses . . . a firearm" is uttered does not preclude us from recognizing that there are other "uses" that qualify as well. In this case, it is both reasonable and normal to say that petitioner "used" his MAC-10 in his drug trafficking offense by trading it for cocaine; the dissent does not contend otherwise.

The dissent's example of how one might "use" a cane suffers from a similar flaw. To be sure, "use" as an adornment in a hallway is not the first "use" of a cane that comes to mind. But certainly it does not follow that the only "use" to which a cane might be put is assisting one's grandfather in walking. Quite the opposite: The most infamous use of a cane in American history had nothing to do with walking at all [it was the caning of Senator Charles Sumner on the Senate floor in 1856]; and the use of a cane as an instrument of punishment was once so common that "to cane" has become a verb meaning "to beat with a cane." In any event, the only question in this case is whether the phrase "uses . . . a firearm" in §924(c)(1) is most reasonably read as excluding the use of a firearm in a gun-for-drugs trade. The fact that the phrase clearly includes using a firearm to shoot someone, as the dissent contends, does not answer it. . . .

The dissent suggests that our interpretation produces a "strange dichotomy" between "using" a firearm and "carrying" one. We do not see why that is so. Just as a defendant may "use" a firearm within the meaning of §924(c)(1) by trading it for drugs or using it to shoot someone, so too would a defendant "carry" the firearm by keeping it on his person whether he intends to exchange it for cocaine or fire it in self-defense. The dichotomy arises, if at all, only when one tries to extend the phrase "uses . . . a firearm" to any use "for any purpose whatever."

JUSTICE SCALIA, with whom JUSTICE STEVENS and JUSTICE SOUTER join, dissenting. Section 924(c)(1) mandates a sentence enhancement for any defendant who "during and in relation to any crime of violence or drug trafficking crime . . . uses . . . a firearm." 18 U.S.C. §924(c)(1). The Court begins its analysis by focusing upon the word "use" in this passage and explaining that the dictionary definitions of that word are very broad. It is, however, a "fundamental principle of statutory construction (and, indeed, of language itself) that the meaning of a word cannot be determined in isolation but must be drawn from the context in which it is used." That is particularly true of a word as elastic as "use," whose meanings range all the way from "to partake of" (as in "he uses tobacco") to "to be wont or accustomed" (as in "he used to smoke tobacco"). See *Webster's New International Dictionary*.

In the search for statutory meaning, we give nontechnical words and phrases their ordinary meaning. To use an instrumentality ordinarily means to use it for its intended purpose. When someone asks, "Do you use a cane?" he is not inquiring whether you have your grandfather's silver-handled walking stick on display in the hall; he wants to know whether you walk with a cane. Similarly, to speak of "using a firearm" is to speak of using it for its distinctive purpose, i.e., as a weapon. To be sure, "one can use a firearm in a number of ways," including as an article of exchange, just as one can "use" a cane as a hall decoration—but that is not the ordinary meaning of "using" the one or the other. The Court does not appear to grasp the distinction between how a word can be used and how it ordinarily is used. It would, indeed, be "both reasonable and normal to say that petitioner 'used' his MAC-10 in his drug trafficking offense by trading it for cocaine." It would also be reasonable and normal to say that he "used" it to scratch his head. When one wishes to describe the action of employing the instrument of a firearm for such unusual purposes, "use" is assuredly a verb one could select. But that says nothing about whether the ordinary meaning of the phrase "uses a firearm" embraces such extraordinary employments. It is unquestionably not reasonable and normal, I think, to say simply "do not use firearms" when one means to prohibit selling or scratching with them.

The normal usage is reflected, for example, in the United States Sentencing Guidelines, which provide for enhanced sentences when firearms are "discharged," "brandished, displayed, or possessed," or "otherwise used." As to the latter term, the Guidelines say: "'Otherwise used' with reference to a dangerous weapon (including a firearm) means that the conduct did not amount to the discharge of a firearm but was more than brandishing, displaying, or possessing a firearm or other dangerous weapon." "Otherwise used" in this provision obviously means "otherwise used as a weapon."

Given our rule that ordinary meaning governs, and given the ordinary meaning of "uses a firearm," it seems to me inconsequential that "the words 'as a weapon' appear nowhere in the statute"; they are reasonably implicit. Petitioner is not, I think, seeking to introduce an "additional requirement" into the text but is simply construing the text according to its normal import. . . .

Another consideration leads to the same conclusion: §924(c)(1) provides increased penalties not only for one who "uses" a firearm during and in relation to any crime of violence or drug trafficking crime but also for one who "carries" a firearm in those circumstances. The interpretation I would give the language produces an eminently reasonable dichotomy between "using a firearm" (as a weapon) and "carrying a firearm" (which in the context "uses or carries a firearm" means carrying it in such manner as to be ready for use as a weapon). The Court's interpretation, by contrast, produces a strange dichotomy between "using a firearm for any purpose whatever, including barter," and "carrying a firearm."

> *"Examination of [the background of the legislative history of Title VII and the historical context from which the Act arose] makes clear that an interpretation of the sections that forbade all race-conscious affirmative action would bring about an end completely at variance with the purpose of the statute and must be rejected." —JUSTICE WILLIAM J. BRENNAN, JR.*

> *"[W]ith virtual clairvoyance, the Senate's leading supporters of Title VII anticipated precisely the circumstances of this case and advised their colleagues that the type of minority preference employed by Kaiser would violate Title VII's ban on racial discrimination." —JUSTICE WILLIAM H. REHNQUIST*

11.3 UNITED STEELWORKERS V. WEBER

443 U.S. 193 (1979)

The Kaiser Aluminum Co. reserved for minorities half of all positions in its nationwide training program for skilled craft jobs. The company passed over Brian F. Weber, a white employee, for one of these slots, even though he had more seniority than several of the African-American employees who were chosen for the program. As a private employer, Kaiser was not bound by the Equal Protection Clause of the Fourteenth Amendment.

Title VII of the Civil Rights Act of 1964, however, bars racial discrimination in private employment; and Weber invoked this provision to sue the company. Eventually the case reached the Supreme Court.

MR. JUSTICE BRENNAN delivered the opinion of the Court. . . .

We emphasize at the outset the narrowness of our inquiry. Since the Kaiser-USWA plan does not involve state action, this case does not present an alleged violation of the Equal Protection Clause of the Constitution. Further, since the Kaiser-USWA plan was adopted voluntarily, we are not concerned with what Title VII requires or with what a court might order to remedy a past proven violation of the Act. The only question before us is the narrow statutory issue of whether Title VII forbids private employers and unions from voluntarily agreeing upon bona fide affirmative action plans that accord racial preferences in the manner and for the purpose provided in the Kaiser-USWA plan. That question was expressly left open in *McDonald v. Santa Fe Trail Transp. Co.* (1976), which held, in a case not involving affirmative action, that Title VII protects whites as well as blacks from certain forms of racial discrimination.

Respondent argues that Congress intended in Title VII to prohibit all race-conscious affirmative action plans. Respondent's argument rests upon a literal interpretation of §§703(a) and (d) of the Act. Those sections make it unlawful to "discriminate . . . because of . . . race" in hiring and in the selection of apprentices for training programs. Since, the argument runs, *McDonald v. Santa Fe Trail Transp. Co.* settled that Title VII forbids discrimination against whites as well as blacks, and since the Kaiser-USWA affirmative action plan operates to discriminate against white employees solely because they are white, it follows that the Kaiser-USWA plan violates Title VII.

Respondent's argument is not without force. But it overlooks the significance of the fact that the Kaiser-USWA plan is an affirmative action plan voluntarily adopted by private parties to eliminate traditional patterns of racial segregation. In this context respondent's reliance upon a literal construction of Sec. 703(a) and (d) and upon *McDonald* is misplaced. It is a "familiar rule that a thing may be within the letter of the statute and yet not within the statute, because not within its spirit nor within the intention of its makers." *Holy Trinity Church v. United States* (1892). The prohibition against racial discrimination in §§703(a) and (d) of Title VII must therefore be read against the background of the legislative history of Title VII and the historical context from which the Act arose. Examination of those sources makes clear that an interpretation of the sections that forbade all race-conscious affirmative action would "bring about an end completely at variance with the purpose of the statute" and must be rejected.

Congress' primary concern in enacting the prohibition against racial discrimination in Title VII of the Civil Rights Act of 1964 was with "the plight of the Negro in our economy." (Remarks of Sen. Humphrey.) Before 1964, blacks were largely relegated to "unskilled and semi-skilled jobs." (Remarks of Sens. Humphrey, Clark, [and] Kennedy.) Because of automation the number of such jobs was rapidly decreasing. (See Remarks of Sens. Humphrey [and] Clark.) As a consequence "the relative position of the Negro worker [was] steadily worsening. In 1947 the nonwhite unemployment rate was only 64 percent higher than the white rate; in 1962 it was 124 percent higher." *Id*. (Remarks of Sen. Humphrey.) (See also remarks of Sen. Clark.) Congress considered this a serious social problem. As Senator Clark told the Senate:

> The rate of Negro unemployment has gone up consistently as compared with white unemployment for the past 15 years. This is a social malaise and a social situation which we should not tolerate. That is one of the principal reasons why this bill should pass.

Congress feared that the goals of the Civil Rights Act—the integration of blacks into the mainstream of American society—could not be achieved unless this trend were reversed. And Congress recognized that that would not be possible unless blacks were able to secure jobs "which have a future." (Remarks of Sen. Clark.) (See also remarks of Sen. Kennedy.) As Senator Humphrey explained to the Senate:

> What good does it do a Negro to be able to eat in a fine restaurant if he cannot afford to pay the bill? What good does it do him to be accepted in a hotel that is too expensive for his modest income? How can a Negro child be motivated to take full advantage of integrated educational facilities if he has no hope of getting a job where he can use that education?
>
> Without a job, one cannot afford public convenience and accommodations. Income from employment may be necessary to further a man's education, or that of his children. If his children have no hope of getting a good job, what will motivate them to take advantage of educational opportunities?

These remarks echoed President Kennedy's original message to Congress upon the introduction of the Civil Rights Act in 1963.

> There is little value in a Negro's obtaining the right to be admitted to hotels and restaurants if he has no cash in his pocket and no job.

Accordingly, it was clear to Congress that "the crux of the problem [was] to open employment opportunities for Negroes in occupations which have been traditionally closed to them," . . . (remarks of Sen. Humphrey), and it was to this problem that Title VII's prohibition against racial discrimination in employment was primarily addressed.

It plainly appears from the House Report accompanying the Civil Rights Act that Congress did not intend wholly to prohibit private and voluntary affirmative action efforts as one method of solving this problem. The Report provides:

> No bill can or should lay claim to eliminating all of the causes and consequences of racial and other types of discrimination against minorities. There is reason to believe, however, that national leadership provided by the enactment of Federal legislation dealing with the most troublesome problems will create an atmosphere conducive to voluntary or local resolution of other forms of discrimination.

Given this legislative history, we cannot agree with respondent that Congress intended to prohibit the private sector from taking effective steps to accomplish the goal that Congress designed Title VII to achieve. The very statutory words intended as a spur or catalyst to cause "employers and unions to self-examine and to self-evaluate their employment practices and to endeavor to eliminate, so far as possible, the last vestiges of an unfortunate and ignominious page in this country's history." *Albemarle v. Moody* (1975) cannot be interpreted as an absolute prohibition against all private, voluntary, race-conscious affirmative action efforts to hasten the elimination of such vestiges. It would be ironic indeed if a law triggered by a Nation's concern over centuries of racial injustice and intended to improve the lot of those who had "been excluded from the American dream for so long" (remarks of Sen. Humphrey) constituted the first legislative prohibition of all voluntary, private, race-conscious efforts to abolish traditional patterns of racial segregation and hierarchy.

Our conclusion is further reinforced by examination of the language and legislative history of §703(j) of Title VII. Opponents of Title VII raised two related arguments against the bill. First, they argued that the Act would be interpreted to require employers with racially imbalanced work forces to grant preferential treatment to racial minorities in order to integrate. Second, they argued that employers with racially imbalanced work forces would grant preferential treatment to racial minorities, even if not required to do so by the Act. (See remarks of Sen. Sparkman.) Had Congress meant to prohibit all race-conscious affirmative action, as respondent urges, it easily could have answered both objections by providing that Title VII would not require or permit racially preferential integration efforts. But Congress did not choose such a course. Rather Congress added §703(j), which addresses only the first objection. The section provides that nothing contained in Title VII "shall be interpreted to require any employer . . . to grant preferential treatment . . . to any group because of the race . . . of such . . . group on account of "a de facto racial imbalance in the employer's work force. The section does *not* state that "nothing in Title VII shall be interpreted to *permit*" voluntary affirmative efforts to correct racial imbalances. The natural inference is that Congress chose not to forbid all voluntary race-conscious affirmative action.

The reasons for this choice are evident from the legislative record. Title VII could not have been enacted into law without substantial support from legislators in both Houses who traditionally resisted federal regulation of private business. Those legislators demanded as a price for their support that "management prerogatives and union freedoms . . . be left undisturbed to the greatest extent possible." Section 703(j) was proposed by Senator Dirksen to allay any fears that the Act might be interpreted in such a way as to upset this compromise. The section was designed to prevent §703 of Title VII from being interpreted in such a way as to lead to undue "Federal Government interference with private businesses because of some Federal employee's ideas about racial balance or imbalance." Clearly, a prohibition against all voluntary, race-conscious, affirmative action efforts would disserve these ends. Such a prohibition would augment the powers of the Federal Government and diminish traditional management prerogatives while at the same time impeding attainment of the ultimate statutory goals. In view of this legislative history and in view of Congress' desire to avoid undue federal regulation of private businesses, use of the word "require" rather than the phrase "require or permit" in §703(j) fortifies the conclusion that Congress did not intend to limit traditional business freedom to such a degree as to prohibit all voluntary, race-conscious affirmative action.

We therefore hold that Title VII's prohibition in §§703(a) and (d) against racial discrimination does not condemn all private, voluntary, race-conscious affirmative action plans. . .

III

We need not today define in detail the line of demarcation between permissible and impermissible affirmative action plans. It suffices to hold that the challenged Kaiser-USWA affirmative action plan falls on the permissible side of the line. The purposes of the plan mirror those of the statute. Both were designed to break down old patterns of racial segregation and hierarchy. Both were structured to "open employment opportunities for Negroes in occupations which have been traditionally closed to them."

At the same time the plan does not unnecessarily trammel the interests of the white employees. The plan does not require the discharge of white workers and their replacement with new black hires. Cf. *McDonald v. Santa Fe Trail Transp. Co.* Nor does the plan create an absolute bar to the advancement of white employees; half of those trained in the program will be white. Moreover, the plan is a temporary measure; it is not intended to maintain racial balance but simply to eliminate a manifest racial imbalance. Preferential selection of craft trainees at the Gramercy plant will end as soon as the percentage of black skilled craft workers in the Gramercy plant approximates the percentage of blacks in the local labor force.

We conclude, therefore, that the adoption of the Kaiser-USWA plan for the Gramercy plant falls within the area of discretion left by Title VII to the private sector voluntarily to adopt affirmative action plans designed to eliminate conspicuous racial imbalance in traditionally segregated job categories. Accordingly, the judgment of the Court of Appeals for the Fifth Circuit is
   Reversed.

MR. JUSTICE POWELL and MR. JUSTICE STEVENS took no part in the consideration or decision of this case.

MR. JUSTICE BLACKMUN, concurring.

While I share some of the misgivings expressed in Mr. Justice Rehnquist's dissent, concerning the extent to which the legislative history of Title VII clearly supports the result the Court reaches today, I believe that additional considerations, practical and equitable, only partially perceived, if perceived at all, by the 88th Congress, support the conclusion reached by the Court today, and I therefore join its opinion as well as its judgment.

In his dissent from the decision of the United States Court of Appeals for the Fifth Circuit, Judge Wisdom pointed out that this litigation arises from a practical problem in the administration of Title VII. The broad prohibition against discrimination places the employer and the union on what he accurately described as a "high tightrope without a net beneath them." If Title VII is read literally, on the one hand they face liability for past discrimination against blacks, and on the other they face liability to whites for any voluntary preferences adopted to mitigate the effects of prior discrimination against blacks.

In this litigation, Kaiser denies prior discrimination but concedes that its past hiring practices may be subject to question. Although the labor force in the Gramercy area was approximately 39 percent black, Kaiser's workforce was less than 15 percent black, and its craft workforce was less than 2 percent black. Kaiser had made some effort to recruit black painters, carpenters, insulators, and other craftsmen, but it continued to insist that those hired have five years' prior industrial experience, a requirement that arguably was not sufficiently job-related to justify under Title VII any discriminatory impact it may have had. The parties dispute the extent to which black craftsmen were available in the local labor market. They agree, however, that after critical reviews from the Office of Federal Contract Compliance, Kaiser and the Steelworkers established the training program in question here and modeled it along the lines of a Title VII consent decree later entered for the steel industry. Yet when they did this, respondent Weber sued, alleging that Title VII prohibited the program because it discriminated against him as a white person and it was not supported by a prior judicial finding of discrimination against blacks.

Respondent Weber's reading of Title VII, endorsed by the Court of Appeals, places voluntary compliance with Title VII in profound jeopardy. The only way for the employer and the union to keep their footing on the "tightrope" it creates would be to eschew all forms of voluntary affirmative action. Even a whisper of emphasis on minority recruiting would be forbidden. Because Congress intended to encourage private efforts to come into compliance with Title VII, Judge Wisdom concluded that employers and unions who had committed "arguable violations" of Title VII should be free to make reasonable responses without fear of liability to whites. Preferential hiring along the lines of the Kaiser program is a reasonable response for the employer, whether or not a court, on these facts, could order the same step as a remedy. The company is able to avoid identifying victims of past discrimination and so avoids claims for back pay that would inevitably follow a response limited to such victims. If past victims should be benefited by the program, however, the company mitigates its liability to those persons. Also, to the extent that Title VII liability is predicated on the "disparate effect" of an employer's past hiring practices, the program makes it less likely that such an effect could be demonstrated. Cf. *County of Los Angeles v. Davis* (1979) (hiring could moot a past Title VII claim). And the Court has recently held that work-force statistics resulting from private affirmative action were probative of benign intent in a "disparate treatment" case.

The "arguable violation" theory has a number of advantages. It responds to a practical problem in the administration of Title VII not anticipated by Congress. It draws predictability from the outline of present law and closely effectuates the purpose of the Act. Both Kaiser and the United States urge its adoption here. Because I agree that it is the soundest way to approach this case, my preference would be to resolve this litigation by applying it and holding that Kaiser's craft training program meets the requirement that voluntary affirmative action be a reasonable response to an "arguable violation" of Title VII.

MR. JUSTICE REHNQUIST, with whom CHIEF JUSTICE [BURGER] joins, dissenting.

In a very real sense, the Court's opinion is ahead of its time: it could more appropriately have been handed down five years from now, in 1984, a year coinciding with the title of a book from which the Court's opinion borrows, perhaps subconsciously, at least one idea. Orwell describes in his book a governmental official of Oceania, one of the three great world powers, denouncing the current enemy, Eurasia, to an assembled crowd:

> It was almost impossible to listen to him without being first convinced and then maddened. . . . The speech had been proceeding for perhaps twenty minutes when a messenger hurried onto the platform and a scrap of paper was slipped into the speaker's hand. He unrolled and read it without pausing in his speech. Nothing altered in his voice or manner, or in the content of what he was saying, but suddenly the names were different. Without words said, a wave of understanding rippled through the crowd. Oceania was at war with Eastasia! . . . The banners and posters with which the square was decorated were all wrong! . . .
>
>   [T]he speaker had switched front one line to the other actually in mid-sentence, not only without a pause, but without even breaking the syntax" (G. Orwell, 1949, *Nineteen Eighty-Four*, 182–183).

Today's decision represents an equally dramatic and equally unremarked switch in this Court's interpretation of Title VII.

The operative sections of Title VII prohibit racial discrimination in employment simpliciter. Taken in its normal meaning and as understood by all Members of Congress who spoke to the issue during the legislative debates, this language prohibits a covered employer from considering race when making an employment decision, whether the race be black or white. Several years ago, however, a United States District Court held that "the dismissal of white employees charged with misappropriating company property while not dismissing a similarly charged Negro employee does not raise a claim upon which Title VII relief may be granted." *McDonald v. Santa Fe Trail Transp. Co.* (1976). This Court unanimously reversed, concluding from the "uncontradicted legislative history" that "[T]itle VII prohibits racial discrimination against the white petitioners in this case upon the same standards as would be applicable were they Negroes. . . ."

We have never wavered in our understanding that Title VII "prohibits all racial discrimination in employment, without exception for any particular employees." In *Griggs v. Duke Power Co.* (1971), our first occasion to interpret Title VII, a unanimous court observed that "[d]iscriminatory preference, for any group, minority or majority, is precisely and only what Congress has proscribed." And in our most recent discussion of the issue, we uttered words seemingly dispositive of this case: "It is clear beyond cavil that the obligation imposed by Title VII is to provide an equal opportunity for each applicant regardless of race, without regard to whether members of the applicant's race are already proportionately represented in the work force." *Furuco Construction Corp. v. Waters* (1978)

Today, however, the Court behaves much like the Orwellian speaker earlier described, as if it had been handed a note indicating that Title VII would lead to a result unacceptable to the Court if interpreted here as it was in our prior decisions. Accordingly, without even a break in syntax, the Court rejects "a literal construction of §703(a)" in favor of newly discovered "legislative history," which leads it to a conclusion directly contrary to that compelled by the "uncontradicted legislative history" unearthed in *McDonald* and our other prior decisions. Now we are told that the legislative history of Title VII shows that employers are free to discriminate on the basis of race: an employer may, in the Court's words, "trammel the interests of white employees" in favor of black employees in order to eliminate "racial imbalance." Our earlier interpretations of Title VII, like the banners and posters decorating the square in Oceania, were all wrong.

As if this were not enough to make a reasonable observer question this Court's adherence to the oft-stated principle that our duty is to construe rather than rewrite legislation, *United States v. Rutherford* (1979), the Court also seizes upon §703(j) of Title VII as an independent, or at least partially independent, basis for its holding. Totally ignoring the wording of that section, which is obviously addressed to those charged with the responsibility of interpreting the law rather than those who are subject to its proscriptions, and totally ignoring the months of legislative debates preceding the section's introduction and passage, which demonstrate clearly that it was enacted to prevent precisely what occurred in this case, the Court infers from §703(j) that "Congress chose not to forbid all voluntary race-conscious affirmative action."

Thus, by a tour de force reminiscent not of jurists such as Hale, Holmes, and Hughes but of escape artists such as Houdini, the Court eludes clear statutory language, "uncontradicted" legislative history, and uniform precedent in concluding that employers are, after all, permitted to consider race in making employment decisions. It may be that one or more of the principal sponsors of Title VII would have preferred to see a provision allowing preferential treatment of minorities written into the bill. Such a provision, however, would have to have been expressly or impliedly excepted from Title VII's explicit prohibition on all racial discrimination in employment. There is no such exception in the Act. And a reading of the legislative debates concerning Title VII, in which proponents and opponents alike uniformly denounced discrimination in favor of, as well as discrimination against, Negroes, demonstrates clearly that any legislator harboring an unspoken desire for such a provision could not possibly have succeeded in enacting it into law.

Were Congress to act today specifically to prohibit the type of racial discrimination suffered by Weber, it would be hard pressed to draft language better tailored to the task than that found in §703(d) of Title VII:

> It shall be an unlawful employment practice for any employer, labor organization, or joint labor-management committee controlling apprenticeship or other training or retraining, including on-the-job training programs to discriminate against any individual because of his race, color, religion, sex, or national origin in admission to, or employment in, any program established to provide apprenticeship or other training.

Equally suited to the task would be §703(a)(2), which makes it unlawful for an employer to classify his employees

> In any way which would deprive or tend to deprive any individual of employment opportunities or otherwise adversely affect his status as an employee, because of such individual's race, color, religion, sex, or national origin.

Entirely consistent with these two express prohibitions is the language of §703(j) of Title VII, which provides that the Act is not to be interpreted "to require any employer . . . to grant preferential treatment to any individual or to any group because of the race . . . of such individual or group to correct a racial imbalance in the employer's workforce." Seizing on the word "require," the Court infers that Congress must have intended to "permit" this type of racial discrimination. Not only is this reading of §703(j) outlandish in the light of the flat prohibitions of §§703(a) and (d), but, as explained in Part III, it is also totally belied by the Act's legislative history.

Quite simply, Kaiser's racially discriminatory admission quota is flatly prohibited by the plain language of Title VII. This normally dispositive fact, however, gives the Court only momentary pause. An "interpretation" of the statute upholding Weber's claim would, according to the Court, "'bring about an end completely at variance with the purpose of the statute.'" To support this conclusion, the Court calls upon the "spirit" of the Act, which it divines from passages in Title VII's legislative history indicating that enactment of the statute was prompted by Congress's desire "to open employment opportunities for Negroes in occupations which [had] been traditionally closed to them." Quoting 110 Cong. Rec. 6548 (1964) (remarks of Sen. Humphrey). But the legislative history invoked by the Court to avoid the plain language of §§703(a) and (d) simply misses the point. To be sure, the reality of employment discrimination against Negroes provided the primary impetus for passage of Title VII. But this fact by no means supports the proposition that Congress intended to leave employers free to discriminate against white persons. In most cases, "[l]egislative history . . . is more vague than [is] the statute we are called upon to interpret." Here, however, the legislative history of Title VII is as clear as the language of §§703(a) and (d), and it irrefutably demonstrates that Congress meant precisely what it said in §§703(a) and (d)—that no racial discrimination in employment is permissible under Title VII, not even preferential treatment of minorities to correct racial imbalance.

In undertaking to review the legislative history of Title VII, I am mindful that the topic hardly makes for light reading, but I am also fearful that nothing short of a thorough examination of the congressional debates will fully expose the magnitude of the Court's misinterpretation of Congress' intent.

Introduced on the floor of the House of Representatives on June 20, 1963, the bill—H.R. 7152—that ultimately became the Civil Rights Act of 1964 contained no compulsory provisions directed at private discrimination in employment. The bill was promptly referred to the Committee on the Judiciary, where it was amended to include Title VII. With two exceptions, the bill reported by the House Judiciary Committee contained §703(a) and (d) as they were ultimately enacted.

Amendments subsequently adopted on the House floor added 703's prohibition against sex discrimination and §703(d)'s coverage of "on-the-job training."

After noting that "[t]he purpose of [Title VII] is to eliminate . . . discrimination in employment based on race, color, religion, or national origin," the Judiciary Committee's Report simply paraphrased the provisions of Title VII without elaboration. H.R.Rep. pt. 1, p. 26. In a separate Minority Report, however, opponents of the measure on the Committee advanced a line of attack which was reiterated throughout the debates in both the House and Senate and which ultimately led to passage of §703(j). Noting that the word "discrimination" was nowhere defined in H.R. 7152, the Minority Report charged that the absence from Title VII of any reference to "racial imbalance" was a "public relations" ruse, and that "the administration intends to rely upon its own construction of 'discrimination' as including the lack of racial balance. . . ." H.R.Rep. pt. 1, pp. 67–68. To demonstrate how the bill would operate in practice, the Minority Report posited a number of hypothetical employment situations, concluding in each example that the employer may be forced to hire according to race, to "racially balance" those who work for him in every job classification or be in violation of Federal law.

When H.R. 7152 reached the House floor, the opening speech in support of its passage was delivered by Representative Celler, Chairman of the House Judiciary Committee and the Congressman responsible for introducing the legislation. A portion of that speech responded to criticism "seriously misrepresent[ing] [p*233] what the bill would do and grossly distort[ing] its effects:"

> [T]he charge has been made that the Equal Employment Opportunity Commission to be established by title VII of the bill would have the power to prevent a business from employing and promoting the people it wished, and that a "Federal inspector" could then order the hiring and promotion only of employees of certain races or religious groups. This description of the bill is entirely wrong. . . .
>
> Even [a] court could not order that any preference be given to any particular race, religion or other group, but would be limited to ordering an end of discrimination. The statement that a Federal inspector could order the employment and promotion only of members of a specific racial or religious group is therefore patently erroneous.
>
> The Bill would do no more than prevent . . . employers from discriminating against or in favor of workers because of their race, religion, or national origin.
>
> It is likewise not true that the Equal Employment Opportunity Commission would have power to rectify existing "racial or religious imbalance" in employment by requiring the hiring of certain people without regard to their qualifications simply because they are of a given race or religion. Only actual discrimination could be stopped. 110 *Cong. Rec.* 1518 (1964)

Representative Celler's construction of Title VII was repeated by several other supporters during the House debate.

Thus, the battle lines were drawn early in the legislative struggle over Title VII, with opponents of the measure charging that agencies of the Federal Government such as the Equal Employment Opportunity Commission (EEOC), by interpreting the word "discrimination" to mean the existence of "racial imbalance," would "require" employers to grant preferential treatment to minorities, and supporters responding that the EEOC would be granted no such power and that, indeed, Title VII prohibits discrimination "in favor of workers because of their race." Supporters of H.R. 7152 in the House ultimately prevailed by a vote of 290 to 130, and the measure was sent to the Senate to begin what became the longest debate in that body's history.

The Senate debate was broken into three phases: the debate on sending the bill to Committee, the general debate on the bill prior to invocation of cloture, and the debate following cloture. . . .

Formal debate on the merits of H.R. 7152 began on March 30, 1964. Supporters of the bill in the Senate had made elaborate preparations for this second round. Senator Humphrey, the majority whip, and Senator Kuchel, the minority whip, were selected as the bipartisan floor managers on the entire civil rights bill. Responsibility for explaining and defending each important title of the bill was placed on bipartisan "captains." Senators Clark and Case were selected as the bipartisan captains responsible for Title VII.

In the opening speech of the formal Senate debate on the bill, Senator Humphrey addressed the main concern of Title VII's opponents, advising that not only does Title VII not require use of racial quotas, it does not permit their use. "The truth," stated the floor leader of the bill, "is that this title forbids discriminating against anyone on account of race. This is the simple and complete truth about title VII." 110 *Cong. Rec.* 6549 (1964). Senator Humphrey continued:

> Contrary to the allegations of some opponents of this title, there is nothing in it that will give any power to the Commission or to any court to require hiring, firing, or promotion of employees in order to meet a racial "quota" or to achieve a certain racial balance.
>
> That bugaboo has been brought up a dozen times; but it is nonexistent. In fact, the very opposite is true. Title VII prohibits discrimination. In effect, it says that race, religion and national origin are not to be used as the basis for hiring and firing. Title VII is designed to encourage hiring on the basis of ability and qualifications, not race or religion.

At the close of his speech, Senator Humphrey returned briefly to the subject of employment quotas:

> It is claimed that the bill would require racial quotas for all hiring, when in fact it provides that race shall not be a basis for making personnel decisions.

* * *

A few days later, the Senate's attention focused exclusively on Title VII, as Senators Clark and Case rose to discuss the title of H.R. 7152 on which they shared floor "captain" responsibilities. In an interpretative memorandum submitted jointly to the Senate, Senators Clark and Case took pains to refute the opposition's charge that Title VII would result in preferential treatment of minorities. Their words were clear and unequivocal:

There is no requirement in title VII that an employer maintain a racial balance in his workforce. On the contrary, any deliberate attempt to maintain a racial balance, whatever such a balance may be, would involve a violation of title VII because maintaining such a balance would require an employer to hire or to refuse to hire on the basis of race. It must be emphasized that discrimination is prohibited as to any individual.

Of particular relevance to the instant litigation were their observations regarding seniority rights. As if directing their comments at Brian Weber, the Senators said:

Title VII would have no effect on established seniority rights. Its effect is prospective and not retrospective. Thus, for example, if a business has been discriminating in the past and, as a result, has an all-white working force, when the title comes into effect, the employer's obligation would be simply to fill future vacancies on a nondiscriminatory basis. He would not be obliged—or indeed permitted—to fire whites in order to hire Negroes or to prefer Negroes for future vacancies or, once Negroes are hired, to give them special seniority rights at the expense of the white workers hired earlier.

Thus, with virtual clairvoyance, the Senate's leading supporters of Title VII anticipated precisely the circumstances of this case and advised their colleagues that the type of minority preference employed by Kaiser would violate Title VII's ban on racial discrimination. To further accentuate the point, Senator Clark introduced another memorandum dealing with common criticisms of the bill, including the charge that racial quotas would be imposed under Title VII. The answer was simple and to the point: "Quotas are themselves discriminatory."

Despite these clear statements from the bill's leading and most knowledgeable proponents, the fears of the opponents were not put to rest. Senator Robertson reiterated the view that "discrimination" could be interpreted by a federal "bureaucrat" to require hiring quotas. Senators Smathers and Sparkman, while conceding that Title VII does not, in so many words, require the use of hiring quotas, repeated the opposition's view that employers would be coerced to grant preferential hiring treatment to minorities by agencies of the Federal Government. Senator Williams was quick to respond:

Those opposed to H.R. 7152 should realize that to hire a Negro solely because he is a Negro is racial discrimination, just as much as a "white only" employment policy. Both forms of discrimination are prohibited by title VII of this bill. The language of that title simply states that race is not a qualification for employment. . . . Some people charge that H.R. 7152 favors the Negro at the expense of the white majority. But how can the language of equality favor one race or one religion over another? Equality can have only one meaning, and that meaning is self-evident to reasonable men. Those who say that equality means favoritism do violence to common sense.

* * *

While the debate in the Senate raged, a bipartisan coalition under the leadership of Senators Dirksen, Mansfield, Humphrey, and Kuchel was working with House leaders and representatives of the Johnson administration on a number of amendments to H.R. 7152 designed to enhance its prospects of passage. The so-called "Dirksen-Mansfield" amendment was introduced on May 26 by Senator Dirksen as a substitute for the entire House-passed bill. The substitute bill, which ultimately became law, left unchanged the basic prohibitory language of §§703(a) and (d), as well as the remedial provisions in §706(g). It added, however, several provisions defining and clarifying the scope of Title VII's substantive prohibitions. One of those clarifying amendments, §703(j), was specifically directed at the opposition's concerns regarding racial balancing and preferential treatment of minorities, providing in pertinent part:

> Nothing contained in [Title VII] shall be interpreted to require any employer . . . to grant preferential treatment to any individual or to any group because of the race . . . of such individual or group on account of a racial imbalance in the employer's workforce.

* * *

Contrary to the Court's analysis, the language of §703(j) is precisely tailored to the objection voiced time and again by Title VII's opponents. Not once during the eighty-three days of debate in the Senate did a speaker, proponent or opponent, suggest that the bill would allow employers *voluntarily* to prefer racial minorities over white persons. In light of Title VII's flat prohibition on discrimination "against any individual . . . because of such individual's race," 703(a), 42 U.S.C. §2000e-2(a), such a contention would have been, in any event, too preposterous to warrant response. Indeed, speakers on both sides of the issue, as the legislative history makes clear, recognized that Title VII would tolerate no voluntary racial preference, whether in favor of blacks or whites. The complaint consistently voiced by the opponents was that Title VII, particularly the word "discrimination," would be interpreted by federal agencies such as the EEOC to require the correction of racial imbalance through the granting of preferential treatment to minorities. Verbal assurances that Title VII would not require—indeed, would not permit—preferential treatment of blacks having failed, supporters of H.R. 7152 responded by proposing an amendment carefully worded to meet, and put to rest, the opposition's charge. Indeed, unlike §§703(a) and (d), which are, by their terms, directed at entities—e.g., employers, labor unions—whose actions are restricted by Title VII's prohibitions, the language of §703(j) is specifically directed at entities—federal agencies and courts—charged with the responsibility of interpreting Title VII's provisions.

In light of the background and purpose of §703(j), the irony of invoking the section to justify the result in this case is obvious. The Court's frequent references to the "voluntary" nature of Kaiser's racially discriminatory admission quota bear no relationship to the facts of this case. Kaiser and the Steelworkers acted under pressure from an agency of the Federal Government, the Office of Federal Contract Compliance, which found that minorities were being "underutilized" at Kaiser's plants. That is, Kaiser's workforce was racially imbalanced. Bowing to that pressure, Kaiser instituted an admissions quota preferring blacks over whites, thus confirming that the fears of Title VII's opponents were well founded. Today, §703(j), adopted to allay those fears, is invoked by the Court to uphold imposition of a racial quota under the very circumstances that the section was intended to prevent. . . .

Our task in this case, like any other case involving the construction of a statute, is to give effect to the intent of Congress. To divine that intent, we traditionally look first to the words of the statute and, if they are unclear, then to the statute's legislative history. Finding the desired result hopelessly foreclosed by these conventional sources, the Court turns to a third source—the "spirit" of the Act. But close examination of what the Court proffers as the spirit of the Act reveals it as the spirit animating the present majority, not the 88th Congress. For if the spirit of the Act eludes the cold words of the statute itself, it rings out with unmistakable clarity in the words of the elected representatives who made the Act law. It is equality. Senator Dirksen, I think, captured that spirit in a speech delivered on the floor of the Senate just moments before the bill was passed:

> [T]oday we come to grips finally with a bill that advances the enjoyment of living; but, more than that, it advances the equality of opportunity.
>
> I do not emphasize the word "equality" standing by itself. It means equality of opportunity in the field of education. It means equality of opportunity in the field of employment. It means equality of opportunity in the field of participation in the affairs of government. . . .
>
> That is it.
>
> Equality of opportunity, if we are going to talk about conscience, is the mass conscience of mankind that speaks in every generation, and it will continue to speak long after we are dead and gone. 110 *Cong. Rec.* 14510 (1964).

There is perhaps no device more destructive to the notion of equality than the numerus clausus—the quota. Whether described as "benign discrimination" or "affirmative action," the racial quota is nonetheless a creator of castes, a two-edged sword that must demean one in order to prefer another. In passing Title VII, Congress outlawed *all* racial discrimination, recognizing that no discrimination based on race is benign, that no action disadvantaging a person because of his color is affirmative. With today's holding, the Court introduces into Title VII a tolerance for the very evil that the law was intended to eradicate, without offering even a clue as to what the limits on that tolerance may be. We are told simply that Kaiser's racially discriminatory admission quota "falls on the permissible side of the line." By going not merely *beyond* but directly *against* Title VII's language and legislative history, the Court has sown the wind. Later courts will face the impossible task of reaping the whirlwind.

"[T]he judge should try to put himself in the shoes of the enacting legislators and figure out how they would have wanted the statute applied to the case before him."

11.4 THE FEDERAL COURTS

Richard A. Posner

Richard A. Posner is Chief Judge of the U.S. Court
of Appeals for the Seventh Circuit.

The Canons of Construction

A realistic understanding of legislation is devastating to the canons of construction, a list of ancient interpretive maxims catalogued in such works as
Sutherland on Statutory Construction and invoked with great frequency by federal as by state judges in dealing with questions of statutory interpretation.
Among the principal canons are the following: one starts with the language of
the statute; if the language is plain, construction is unnecessary; repeals by implication are disfavored; penal statutes are to be construed narrowly but remedial statutes broadly; *expressio unius est exclusio alterius* [the expression of one
thing is the exclusion of another].

A frequent criticism of the canons, made forcefully by Professor Llewellyn
many years ago, is that for every canon one might bring to bear on a point there
is an equal and opposite canon. This is an exaggeration; but what is true is that
there is a canon to support every possible result. If a judge wants to interpret a
statute broadly, he does not mention the plain-meaning rule; he intones the rule
that remedial statutes are to be construed broadly, or some other canon that
leans toward the broad rather than the narrow. If he wants to interpret the
statute narrowly, he will invoke some other canon. This point answers the suggestion (for which, incidentally, there is no supporting evidence) that whether
good or bad as an original matter, the canons constitute a code that Congress expects the courts to use in interpreting statutes. That might make some sense if
most questions of statutory interpretation fell within only one canon's domain.
For example, suppose Congress decided that if the meaning of a statute as applied to some problem was plain as a linguistic matter, the statute should be interpreted in accordance with that meaning even if it was contrary to Congress's
actual purpose in enacting the statute. So if Congress grants a tax exemption to
"minister[s] of the gospel," rabbis should not be held eligible, and if this makes
the exemption unconstitutional under the First Amendment because it discriminates against a religion, too bad. The problem with this and virtually any other
example one could give is that the plain-meaning canon is not the only canon;

From Richard A. Posner, *The Federal Courts* (Cambridge, MA: Harvard University Press, 1985), 276, 286–289, 290.

and in the example just given, it runs up against the canon that statutes should be construed if possible to avoid being held unconstitutional. Thus the court has to choose between canons, and there is no canon for ranking or choosing between canons; the code lacks a key.

* * *

An Alternative Approach

As an alternative to viewing statutory interpretation as the application of the canons of construction, I suggest a two-part approach. First, the judge should try to put himself in the shoes of the enacting legislators and figure out how they would have wanted the statute applied to the case before him. This is the method of imaginative reconstruction. If it fails, as occasionally it will, either because the necessary information is lacking or because the legislators had failed to agree on essential premises, then the judge must decide what attribution of meaning to the statute will yield the most reasonable result in the case at hand—always bearing in mind that what seems reasonable to the judge may not have seemed reasonable to the legislators, and that it is their conception of reasonableness, to the extent known, rather than the judge's, that should guide decision.

The limitations of this approach, especially the first part, should be plain from my earlier discussion of the difficulties of reconstructing history. And it invites the criticism that judges do not have the requisite imagination and that what they will do in practice is to assume that the legislators were people just like themselves, with the result that statutory construction will consist of the judge's voting his own preferences and ascribing them to legislators. But the irresponsible judge will twist any approach to yield the outcomes that he desires, and the stupid judge will do the same thing unconsciously.

The judge who follows the suggested approach will not only consider the language, structure, and history of the statute but also study the values and attitudes, as far as they can be known today, of the period when the legislation was enacted. It would be a mistake to ascribe to legislators of the 1930s or the 1960s and early 1970s the skepticism regarding the size of government and the efficiency of regulation that is widespread today, or to impute to the Congress of the 1920s current ideas of conflict of interest. The judge's job is not to keep a statute up to date in the sense of making it reflect contemporary values but to imagine as best he can how the legislators who enacted the statute would have wanted it applied to situations they did not foresee.

The judge will be particularly alert to any sign of legislative intent regarding the freedom with which he should exercise his interpretive function. Sometimes a statute will state whether it is to be broadly or narrowly construed; more often the structure and language of the statute will supply a clue. If the legislature enacts into statute law a common law concept, as Congress did when in the Sherman Act it forbade agreements in restraint of trade, this is a clue that the courts are to interpret the statute with the freedom with which they would construe and apply a common law principle—in which event the legislators' values may not be controlling after all.

The opposite extreme is a statute that sets out its requirements with some specificity, especially against a background of dissatisfaction with judicial handling of the same subject under a previous statute or the common law (much federal labor and regulatory legislation is of this character). Probably the legislature does not want the courts to paint with a broad brush in adapting such a statute to the unforeseeable future. The Constitution contains several such provisions—for example, the provision that the President must be at least 35 years old. This provision does not invite interpretation; it does not invite a court to recast the provision so that it reads "'the President must be mature.'" There is nothing the court could point to in or behind the Constitution that would justify such an interpretation. It is not that the words are plain, but rather that read in context, as words must always be read in order to yield meaning, they do not authorize any interpretation except the obvious one.

Although the approach I have sketched has obvious affinities with the "attribution of purpose" approach of Professors Hart and Sacks, I want to stress one difference. They say that in construing a statute a court "should assume, unless the contrary unmistakably appears, that the legislature was made up of reasonable persons pursuing reasonable purposes reasonably." Coupled with an earlier statement that in trying to divine the legislative will the court should ignore "short-run currents of political expedience," Hart and Sacks appear to be suggesting that the judge should ignore interest groups, popular ignorance and prejudice, and anything else that deflects legislators from the single-minded pursuit of the public interest as the judge would conceive it. But this approach risks attributing to legislation not the purposes reasonably inferable from the legislation itself but the judge's own conception of the public interest. When Hart and Sacks were writing—in the wake of the New Deal—the legislative process was widely regarded as progressive and public-spirited. Today there is less agreement that the motives behind most legislation are benign, and this should make the judge wary about too readily assuming a congruence between his conception of the public interest and the latent purposes of the statutes he is called on to interpret. . . .

I want to end by comparing my suggested approach to [another] position in the current literature on interpretation. Although it would oversimplify Easterbrook's position to describe it as "strict constructionism," it does resemble strict constructionism, a concept that I have already noted is unfriendly to legislation though sometimes promoted as the only philosophy that ensures fidelity to legislative intent. The concept is the lineal descendant of the canon that statutes in derogation of the common law are to be strictly construed, and like that canon it was used in nineteenth-century England to emasculate social welfare legislation. To construe a statute strictly is to limit its scope and its life span—to make Congress work twice as hard to produce the same effect. An anecdote told by Holmes is pertinent here: "There is a story of a Vermont justice of the peace before whom a suit was brought by one farmer against another for breaking a churn. The justice took time to consider, and then said that he had looked through the statutes and could find nothing about churns, and gave judgment to the defendant."

It is not an accident that most "no constructionists" are political liberals and most "strict constructionists" are political conservatives. The former think that modern legislation does not go far enough and want the courts to pick up the ball that the legislators have dropped; the latter think it goes too far and want the courts to rein the legislators in. Each school has developed interpretive techniques appropriate to its political ends.

"A formally enacted statement of purpose in a statute should be accepted by the court if it appears to have been designed to serve as a guide to interpretation, is consistent with the words and context of the statute, and is relevant to the question of meaning at issue. In all other situations, the purpose of a statute has in some degree to be inferred."

11.5 THE LEGAL PROCESS

Henry M. Hart, Jr., and Albert M. Sachs

Henry M. Hart, Jr. was a professor at Harvard Law School,
where Albert M. Sachs served as Dean.

Points A–F have been omitted.

G. The Attribution of Purpose
    1. Enacted statements of purpose

        A formally enacted statement of purpose in a statute should be accepted by the court if it appears to have been designed to serve as a guide to interpretation, is consistent with the words and context of the statute, and is relevant to the question of meaning at issue.

        In all other situations, the purpose of a statute has in some degree to be inferred.

    2. Inferring purpose: the nature of the problem

        In drawing such inferences the court needs to be aware that the concept of purpose is not simple.

        (a) Purposes may be shaped with differing degrees of definiteness.

            The definiteness may be such that resolution of a doubt about purpose resolves, without more, a question of specific application.

            Or a purpose may be deliberately formulated with great generality, openly contemplating the exercise of further judgment by the interpreter even after he [or she] has fully grasped the legislature's

From Henry M. Hart, Jr., and Albert M. Sachs, *The Legal Process* (Westbury, NY: Foundation Press, 1994), 1377–1380. William N. Eskridge, Jr., and Philip P. Frickey prepared this volume for publication from the 1958 Tentative Edition.

thought. E.g., the direction to the Federal Trade Commission to prevent, in certain ways, "unfair methods of competition in commerce."

(b) Purposes, moreover, may exist in hierarchies or constellations. E.g. (to give a very simple illustration), to do *this* only so far as possible without doing *that*.

(c) One form of such a constellation or relationship is invariable in the law and of immense importance. The purpose of a statute must always be treated as including not only an immediate purpose or group of related purposes but a larger and subtler purpose as to how the particular statute is to be fitted into the legal system as a whole.

An isolated enactment, not part of a comprehensive code, always raises the question: What purpose is to be attributed to the statute with respect to the treatment of related matters falling outside the four corners of its immediate application? As contemplating judicial solution of such problems without any reference to the statute whatever? As precluding judicial change in previously announced law relating to them? Or as encouraging or directing judicial change in accordance with the underlying policy or principle of the statute?

A provision in a comprehensive code presents always a distinctive question of interpretive method. In interpreting such a provision, the court must necessarily be aware that the sole agency of growth of the law thereafter will have to be the legislature, if the provision is read as precluding exercise of creative activity on its part. It has to attribute a purpose to the statute in this regard.

3. Inferring purpose: the technique

In determining the more immediate purpose which ought to be attributed to a statute, and to any subordinate provision of it which may be involved, a court should try to put itself in imagination in the position of the legislature which enacted the measure.

The court, however, should not do this in the mood of a cynical political observer, taking account of all the short-run currents of political expedience that swirl around any legislative session.

It should assume, unless the contrary unmistakably appears, that the legislature was made up of reasonable persons pursuing reasonable purposes reasonably.

It should presume conclusively that these persons, whether or not entertaining concepts of reasonableness shared by the court, were trying responsibly and in good faith to discharge their constitutional powers and duties.

The court should then proceed to do, in substance, just what Lord Coke said it should do in Heydon's Case. The gist of this approach is to infer purpose by comparing the new law with the old. Why would reasonable men, confronted with the law as it was, have enacted this new law to replace it? Answering this question, as Lord Coke said, calls for a close look at the "mischief" thought to inhere in the old law and at "the true reason of the remedy" provided by the statute for it.

The most reliable guides to an answer will be found in the instances of unquestioned application of the statute. Even in the case of a new statute there almost invariably are such instances, in which, because of the perfect fit of words and context, the meaning seems unmistakable.

Once these points of reference are established, they throw a double light. The purposes necessarily implied in them illuminate facets of the general purpose. At the same time they provide a basis for reasoning by analogy to the disputed application in hand. E.g., why would the legislature distinguish, for purposes of punishment, between an escaper serving only a single sentence and one serving the first of several?

What is crucial here is the realization that law is being made, and that law is not supposed to be irrational.

4. Inferring purpose: aids from the context

The whole context of a statute may be examined in aid of its interpretation, and should be whenever substantial doubt about its meaning exists in the interpreter's mind, or is suggested by him.

Not only the state of the law immediately before enactment but the course of its prior development is relevant.

The court may draw on general public knowledge of what was considered to be the mischief that needed remedying.

Formal public announcements of those concerned with the preparation or advocacy of the measure may be freely consulted. E.g., messages of the chief executive, reports of commissions, and the like.

The internal legislative history of the measure (that is, its history from the filing of the bill to enactment) may be examined, if this was reduced to writing officially and contemporaneously. But in the use which is made of this material two closely related limitations should be scrupulously observed.

First. The history should be examined for the light it throws on general purpose. Evidence of specific intention with respect to particular applications is competent only to the extent that the particular applications illuminate the general purpose and are consistent with other evidence of it.

Second. Effect should not be given to evidence from the internal legislative history if the result would be to contradict a purpose otherwise indicated and to yield an interpretation disadvantageous to private persons who had no reasonable means of access to the history.

5. Inferring purpose: post-enactment aids

The judicial, administrative, and popular construction of a statute, subsequent to its enactment, are all relevant in attributing a purpose to it.

The court's own prior interpretations of a statute in related applications should be accepted, on the principle of stare decisis, unless they are manifestly out of accord with other indications of purpose. Once these applications are treated as fixed, they serve as points of reference for juristic thinking in the same fashion as verbally clear applications in the case of a new statute.

An administrative or popular construction is relevant for different reasons. Such a construction affords weighty evidence that the words may bear the meaning involved. In the absence of reasons of self interest or the like for discounting the construction, it is persuasive evidence that the meaning is a natural one. Considerations of the stability of transactions and of existing understandings counsel in favor of its acceptance, if possible. In cases where the construction has been widely accepted and consistently adhered, it may be said to fix the meaning-to be the meaning which experience has demonstrated the words to bear.

6. Inferring purpose: presumptions

The court's last resort, when doubt about the immediate purpose of a statute remains, is resort to an appropriate presumption drawn from some general policy of the law.

This is likely to be its only resort when the question concerns more nearly ultimate policy, or the mode of fitting the statute into the general fabric of the law.

Reflection about these presumptions is the most important task in the development of a workable and working theory of statutory interpretation. . . .

"The greatest defect of legislative history is its illegitimacy."

11.6 CONROY V. ANISKOFF

507 U.S. 511 (1993)

Section 525 of the Soldiers' and Sailors' Civil Relief Act of 1940 provides that the "period of military service" shall not "be included in computing any period . . . provided by any law for the redemption of real property sold or forfeited to enforce any obligation, tax, or assessment." According to Conroy, a U.S. Army officer, this provision prevented a town from acquiring and selling his property for failure to pay real estate taxes while he was in military service.

The U.S. Supreme Court agreed. While Justice Scalia concurred with the majority's holding, he took issue with its approach to interpreting §525.

JUSTICE SCALIA, concurring in the judgment.

The Court begins its analysis with the observation: "The statutory command in §525 of the Soldiers' and Sailors' Civil Relief Act of 1940 is unambiguous, unequivocal, and unlimited." In my view, discussion of that point is where the remainder of the analysis should have ended. Instead, however, the Court feels compelled to demonstrate that its holding is consonant with legislative history, including some dating back to 1917—a full quarter century before the provision at issue was enacted. That is not merely a waste of research time and ink; it is a false and disruptive lesson in the law. It says to the bar that even an "unambiguous [and] unequivocal" statute can never be dispositive; that, presumably under penalty of malpractice liability, the oracles of legislative history, far into the dim past, must always be consulted. This undermines the clarity of law and condemns litigants (who, unlike us, must pay for it out of their own pockets) to subsidizing historical research by lawyers.

The greatest defect of legislative history is its illegitimacy. We are governed by laws, not by the intentions of legislators. As the Court said in 1844: "The law as it passed is the will of the majority of both houses, and the only mode in which that will is spoken is in the act itself. . . ." *Aldridge v. Williams.* But not the least of the defects of legislative history is its indeterminacy. If one were to search for an interpretive technique that, on the whole, was more likely to confuse than to clarify, one could hardly find a more promising candidate than legislative history. And the present case nicely proves that point.

Judge Harold Leventhal used to describe the use of legislative history as the equivalent of entering a crowded cocktail party and looking over the heads of the guests for one's friends. If I may pursue that metaphor: The legislative history of §205 of the Soldiers' and Sailors' Civil Relief Act contains a variety of diverse personages, a selected few of whom—its "friends"—the Court has introduced to us in support of its result. But there are many other faces in the crowd, most of which, I think, are set against today's result. . . .

> *"[U]nless the statute plainly hands courts the power to create and revise a form of common law, the domain of the statute should be restricted to cases anticipated by its framers and expressly resolved in the legislative process."*

11.7 STATUTES' DOMAINS

Frank H. Easterbrook

Frank H. Easterbrook is a judge on the U.S. Court
of Appeals for the Seventh Circuit.

My suggestion is that unless the statute plainly hands courts the power to create and revise a form of common law, the domain of the statute should be restricted to cases anticipated by its framers and expressly resolved in the

From Frank H. Easterbrook, "Statutes' Domains," 50 *University of Chicago Law Review* 533 (1983), 544–551.

legislative process. Unless the party relying on the statute could establish either express resolution or creation of the common law power of revision, the court would hold the matter in question outside the statute's domain. The statute would become irrelevant, the parties (and court) remitted to whatever other sources of law might be applicable.

This approach overlaps the "clear statement" principle of construction that is often, but erratically, invoked by courts that deny the power to resolve the issue put to them. The court will say something like: "The legislature may well have supported the party relying on the statute, had it thought about this problem, but if the legislature expects us to reach such a result in so sensitive an area, it must state its conclusion clearly." The court then explains why it thinks the subject matter of the legislation counsels hesitation. Perhaps it affects state-federal relations, perhaps it creates startling remedies, perhaps it raises serious constitutional questions, perhaps it departs from the common law (and so from the judges' conception of the good).

As others have pointed out, the "clear statement" principle usually fails as a useful tool of construction because it cannot demonstrate why the legislature would have wanted the court to hesitate just because the subject matter of the law is "sensitive." Likely it thinks that making hard decisions in sensitive areas is what courts are for. The "clear statement" principle can be used by courts seeking to decide by indirection (the very thing they ask the legislature *not* to do) and to elide responsibilities given by statutes. Invocation of the "clear statement" rule thus has been taken by some as a sign of willful *mis*construction of the statute.

The "clear statement" approach nonetheless reflects the truth that some statutes support judicial gap filling more than others do. The problem in the "clear statement" approach lies not in the declaration that courts sometimes will demand explicit legislative resolution and will refuse to fill statutory gaps but rather in the conditions giving rise to that demand. The rule I have suggested above is a "clear statement" approach revised to turn on the method the legislature has adopted. If it enacts some sort of code of rules, the code will be taken as complete (until amended); gaps will go unfilled. If instead it charges the court with a common law function, the court will solve new problems as they arise, but using today's wisdom rather than conjuring up the solutions of a legislature long prorogued.

This is just a slightly different way of making the point that judicial pursuit of the "values" or aims of legislation is a sure way of defeating the original legislative plan. A legislature that seeks to achieve Goal X can do so in one of two ways. First, it can identify the goal and instruct courts or agencies to design rules to achieve the goal. In that event, the subsequent selection of rules implements the actual legislative decision, even if the rules are not what the legislature would have selected itself. The second approach is for the legislature to pick the rules. It pursues Goal X by Rule Y. The selection of Y is a measure of what Goal X was worth to the legislature, of how best to achieve X, and of where to stop in pursuit of X. Like any other rule, Y is bound to be imprecise, to be over- and under-inclusive. This is not a good reason for a court, observing the inevitable imprecision, to add to or subtract from Rule Y on the argument that, by doing so, it can get more of Goal X. The judicial selection of means to pursue X displaces and directly overrides the legislative selection of ways to obtain X. It denies to legislatures the choice of creating or withholding gap-filling authority. The way to preserve the initial choice is for judges to put the statute down once it becomes clear that the legislature has selected rules as well as identified goals.

This approach is faithful to the nature of compromise in private interest legislation. The approach also is supported by a number of other considerations. First, it recognizes that courts cannot reconstruct an original meaning because there is none to find. Second, it prevents legislatures from extending their lives beyond the terms of their members. Third, it takes a liberal view of the relation between the public and private spheres. Fourth, it takes a realistic view of judges' powers. I elaborate on these below.

1. Original Meaning. Because legislatures comprise many members, they do not have "intents" or "designs," hidden yet discoverable. Each member may or may not have a design. The body as a whole, however, has only outcomes. It is not only impossible to reason from one statute to another but also impossible to reason from one or more sections of a statute to a problem not resolved.

This follows from the discoveries of public choice theory. Although legislators have individual lists of desires, priorities, and preferences, it turns out to be difficult, sometimes impossible, to aggregate these lists into a coherent collective choice. Every system of voting has flaws. The one used by legislatures is particularly dependent on the order in which decisions are made. Legislatures customarily consider proposals one at a time and then vote them up or down. This method disregards third or fourth options and the intensity with which legislators prefer one option" over another. Additional options can be considered only in sequence, and this makes the order of decision vital. It is fairly easy to show that someone with control of the agenda can manipulate the choice so that the legislature adopts proposals that only a minority support. The existence of agenda control makes it impossible for a court—even one that knows each legislator's complete table of preferences—to say what the whole body would have done with a proposal it did not consider in fact. . . .

2. Legislatures Expire. Judicial interpolation of legislative gaps would be questionable even if judges could ascertain with certainty how the legislature would have acted. Every legislative body's power is limited by a number of checks, from the demands of its internal procedures to bicameralism to the need to obtain the executive's assent. The foremost of these checks is time. Each session of Congress, for example, lasts but two years, after which the whole House and one-third of the Senate stand for reelection. What each Congress does binds the future until another Congress acts, but what a Congress might have done, had it the time, is simply left unresolved. The unaddressed problem is handled by a new legislature with new instructions from the voters.

If time is classified with the veto as a limit on the power of legislatures, then one customary argument for judicial gap filling—that legislatures lack the time and foresight to resolve every problem—is a reason why judges should not attempt to fill statutory gaps. The shortness of time and the want of foresight and the fear of offending constituents, like the fear of the veto, raise the costs of legislation. The cost of addressing one problem includes the inability, for want of time, to address others. If courts routinely construe statutory gaps as authorizing "more in the same vein," they reduce this cost.

In a sense, gap-filling construction has the same effects of extending the term of the legislature and allowing that legislature to avoid submitting its plan to the executive for veto. Obviously no court would do this directly. If the members of the Ninety-Third Congress reassembled next month and declared their legislative meaning, the declaration would have absolutely no force. This rump body would get no greater power by claiming that its new "laws" were intimately related to, and just filled gaps in, its old ones. Is there a better reason why the members of the Ninety-Third Congress, the Eighty-Third, and the Seventy-Third "sitting" in the minds of judges should continue to be able to resolve new problems "presented" to them? The rule I have suggested reduces the number of times judges must summon up the ghouls of legislatures past. In order to authorize judges to fill statutory gaps, the legislature must deny itself life after death and permit judges or agencies to supply their own conceptions of the public interest.

3. Liberal Principles. A principle that statutes are inapplicable unless they either plainly supply a rule of decision or delegate the power to create such a rule is consistent with the liberal principles underlying our political order. Those who wrote and approved the Constitution thought that most social relations would be governed by private agreements, customs, and understandings, not resolved in the halls of government. There is still at least a presumption that people's arrangements prevail unless expressly displaced by legal doctrine. All things are permitted unless there is some contrary rule. . . . A rule declaring statutes inapplicable unless they plainly delegate the solution of the matter respects this position. . . .

4. Judicial Abilities. Statutory construction is an art. Good statutory construction requires the rarest of skills. The judge must find, clues in the structure of the statute, hints in the legislative history, and combine these with mastery of history, command of psychology, and sensitivity to nuance to divine how deceased legislators would have answered unasked questions.

It is all very well to say that a judge able to understand the temper of 1871 (and 1921), and able to learn the extent of a compromise in 1936, may do well when construing statutes. How many judges meet this description? How many know what clauses and provisos, capable of being enacted in 1923, would have been unthinkable in 1927 because of subtle changes in the composition in the dominant coalitions in Congress? It is hard enough to know this for the immediate past, yet who could deny that legislation that could have been passed in 1982 not only would fail but also could be repealed in 1983? The number of judges living at any time who can, with plausible claim to accuracy, "think [themselves] . . . into the minds of the enacting legislators and imagine how they would have wanted the statute applied to the case at bar," may be counted on one hand.

* * *

This is most certainly not to say that statutory construction is bad, or even that it is a necessary evil. Most statutes contain a substantial core of understandable commands. Most exercises of construction are ordinary attempts to supply a meaning where legislators plainly intended the statute to apply but did not say what the application entailed. It is clear they did something, and the question is what, particularly, with respect to some unanticipated set of events. Finding out what the statute means, even if this calls for creation as well as re-creation, is an essential part of government, lest statutes become brittle and fail of their essential purposes. I have been addressing the problems that arise when legislators did nothing about some sizable class of cases, when the community of readers does not agree on meaning, and agencies or judges must determine whether to take the legislators at their (non)word, and declare the legislation inapplicable, or leap into the gap with an exercise of construction, as if the legislators had spoken.

Declaring legislation inapplicable unless it either expressly addresses the matter or commits the matter to the common law (or administrative) process would not produce unalloyed benefits. It is easy enough to imagine some horror in which nonapplication perpetrates gross injustice. The price principals pay for reducing the discretion of their agents includes the lost opportunities to carry out the principals' goals in ways the principals could not have anticipated when they issued their commands. Yet it is well understood that a decision to grant or withhold discretion from agents requires a careful balancing of costs. A reduction in discretion may mean lost opportunities, but an increase in discretion may mean that agents distort or deviate from the principals' plans. . . .

"There is nothing revolutionary about understanding statutes
in dynamic rather than static terms."

11.8 DYNAMIC STATUTORY INTERPRETATION

William N. Eskridge, Jr.

William N. Eskridge, Jr., is John A. Garver Professor
of Jurisprudence at Yale Law School.

. . . [A]rchaeological theories do not and cannot satisfactorily describe what courts do in statutory interpretation. Problems identified with originalist theory can help us understand the dynamism of statutory interpretation. Originalists theories cannot limit statutory interpretation to a single factor or exclude

From William N. Eskridge, Jr., *Dynamic Statutory Interpretation*, (Cambridge, MA: Harvard University Press, 1994), 48–49.

postenactment considerations, do not yield objective and determinate answers in the hard cases, and cannot convincingly tie results in statutory cases to the expectations of original legislative majorities. Statutory interpretation is multi-faceted and evolutive rather than single-faceted and static, involves policy choices and discretion by the interpreter over time as she applies the statute to specific problems, and is responsive to the current as well as the historical political culture.

There is nothing revolutionary about understanding statutes in dynamic rather than static terms. American scholars have long recognized that the Constitution and the common law are interpreted dynamically and early in this century applied this insight to statutory interpretation as well. Scholars in other industrial countries have long recognized that statutory interpretation is evolutive. The standard reasons given for evolutive interpretation by scholars in other countries are equally applicable to statutory interpretation in the United States.

Because they are aimed at big problems and must last a long time, statutory enactments are often general, abstract, and theoretical. Interpretation of a statute usually occurs in connection with a fact-specific problem (a case or an administrative record) which renders it relatively particular, concrete, and practical. As an exercise in practical rather than theoretical reasoning, statutory interpretation will be dynamic. It is a truism that interpretation depends heavily on context, but the elasticity of context is less well recognized. The expanded context of cases and problems engenders dynamic interpretations. Because statutes have an indefinite life, they apply to fact situations well into the future. When successive applications of the statute occur in contexts not anticipated by its authors, the statute's meaning evolves beyond original expectations. Indeed, sometimes subsequent applications reveal that factual or legal assumptions of the original statute have become (or were originally) erroneous; then the statute's meaning often evolves against its original expectations.

Under a system of separated powers, the statutory interpreter (an administrator or judge) is a different person from the people enacting the statute (legislators). The interpreter's perspective makes a difference in statutory interpretation: two different people acting in good faith often interpret the same text in different ways. Because of differences in perspective, dynamic interpretation can occur early in the statute's evolution, especially if the statute submerges or falls to resolve controversial issues. As time passes, the interpreter's perspective is likely to diverge in an increasing number of ways from the perspective of the statute's authors, and changing societal and legal contexts afford her more discretion to interpret the statute in ways not anticipated by its authors. To the extent that people rely on official interpretations to structure their conduct and expectations, their reliance may be a practical or equitable barrier to efforts by subsequent interpreters to reestablish the statute's original meaning.

Statutory interpretation is hierarchical and sequential. Interpretations by private parties can be corrected by administrators, who can be reversed by judges, who can be overridden by the legislature. Even if agencies and courts seriously sought to enforce original intent, text, or purpose, they would not do so because of a hydraulic process of feedback and anticipation which occurs as the system works out statutory meaning for issues that arise. Thus it is that agencies and courts are constantly pressed from below—by private communities of interpretation, by interest groups, by ground-level implementers of the statute—to interpret the statute in ways that are responsive to new facts, new needs, new ideas. They are also pressed from above—by congressional committees, by the threat of legislative override, by the president—to interpret the statute in ways that are responsive to current rather than historical political preferences.

As Francis Bennion of the United Kingdom put it in 1984, a statutory act "takes on a life of its own . . . [T]he ongoing Act resembles a vessel launched on some one-way voyage from the old world to the new. The vessel is not going to return; nor are its passengers. Having only what they set out with, they cope as best they can. On arrival in the present, they deploy their native endowments under conditions originally unguessed at." I think Bennion's description holds for statutory interpretation in the United States as well.

* * *

In 1992, five years after Eskridge and Frickey published a book advocating the dynamic approach to statutory interpretation described above, they took the opportunity to comment on work that had built on theirs:[1]

Since our casebook went to press in 1987, there have been a number of articles advocating theories of dynamic statutory interpretation. We should like to make three points about the trend in these articles.

First, there seems to be a provisional academic consensus that the Supreme Court's actual practice in statutory interpretation is incomprehensible if one tries to view it as re-creating original legislative intent, or any kind of answer that ignores the evolution of the statute and current policy. In short, as a descriptive matter, the Court—and any likely collection of intelligent human beings—interprets statutes dynamically and not "archaeologically" over time.

Second, the commentators are working through the reasons why statutory interpretation will be dynamic over time. The main reasons are practical: The enacting legislature cannot anticipate all the applications of statutes it passes, or even the ways in which the statute will change the world or be undone by the future. To make a statutory scheme work, it must be interpreted dynamically to adapt the statute to changed, and usually unanticipated, circumstances. The pragmatics of applying statutes to new circumstances augur against inflexible, foundational approaches to statutory interpretation.

Commentators have also emphasized institutional reasons for dynamic statutory interpretation. Edward Rubin has reminded us that most official statutory interpretation is done not by courts but by agencies—which are by their

---

[1]William N. Eskridge, Jr., and Philip P. Frickey 1992. *Supplement to Cases and Materials on Legislation* (St. Paul, MN: West, 1992), 125–127. —Eds.

political nature going to be more responsive to the political preferences of the current Congress and President than they are to the preferences of the enacting Congress. One of us has argued that the Supreme Court is often more responsive to current legislative preferences than to historic ones.

Third, even though recent scholarship suggests that the Court interprets statutes dynamically and sometimes should do so, some scholars have normative qualms about certain aspects of it. For example, it may seem illegitimate if an interpretation goes against both the text and legislative history of the statute to promote current values, for in that instance the court might be seen as violating a clear legislative command. Moreover, even if a court may sometimes do that, are we confident that the current values reflected in the Supreme Court's opinions are defensible ones? Might dynamic statutory interpretation become just another way the "Haves" in our polity advance their interests, at the expense of the "Have Nots"?

The most interesting recent development promoting dynamism in statutory interpretation is the Rehnquist Court's development of its own canons-based approach to dynamic statutory interpretation (that is, the Court is developing or revising canons based upon its own constitutional values). Stephen Ross argues that the Republican Rehnquist Court is reading its own conservative values into statutes enacted by more liberal Democratic Congresses. Even if one rejects the direct partisan explanation, it still may be that the Rehnquist Court, thus far so restrained in constitutional interpretation (few federal statutes have been invalidated), will be activist in statutory interpretation (clipping back on liberal policies and pushing Congress to spend increasing amounts of its time on override efforts).

CHAPTER 12

Constitutional Interpretation

One way most constitutional democracies limit political power is by allowing judges to share in interpreting the constitution and to declare invalid any legislative or executive action that, in their judgment, violates that constitution. Fulfilling this function is certainly the most visible role that judges play; it is also among the most important. Deciding what the constitution permits or forbids can affect not only immediate public policy but also the future shape of the political system and affect possibly its very survival.

CONSTITUTIONAL TEXTS, CONSTITUTIONS, AND CONSTITUTIONALISM

At the outset, we should distinguish among three distinct concepts that bear semantically similar titles: a "constitutional text," a "constitution," and "constitutionalism."[1] A constitutional text is a document that, at very least, purports to map the nation's fundamental political arrangements, what Americans, following the Framers in Philadelphia, call the Constitution of the United States. That document may also proclaim certain moral values, perhaps even aspirations, to which the people claim to dedicate themselves. Those values and aspirations may be openly expressed in a statement of purposes, such as to "establish justice" and "secure the blessings of Liberty," and more subtly in institutional arrangements and procedures.

It is, of course, not necessary that a nation have a constitutional text. New Zealand and the United Kingdom have long survived without one. Israel has only a partial constitutional document that was formally declared to be

---

[1] For a more detailed discussion, see Walter F. Murphy, "Constitutions, Constitutionalism, and Democracy," in Douglas Greenberg, Stanley N. Katz, Melanie Beth Oliviero, and Stephen C. Wheatley, eds., *Constitutionalism and Democracy*, (New York: Oxford University Press, 1993).

supreme law not by a convention or an assembly chosen to write such a script but by the Supreme Court.[2] Even when a nation has a constitutional document, its authority—that is, the extent to which it is a sham or to which its descriptions of political processes are accurate and its commands and prohibitions obeyed—is a question for empirical research. Some such texts are mere fig leaves, as were Josef Stalin's for the Soviet Union and Mao Zedong's for the People's Republic of China; others, such as those of the United States, Canada, and the Federal Republic of Germany, come close to speaking political truth, though even these do not perfectly mirror reality.

The authority a text carries is partly a function of its relation to the second concept, the larger "constitution," or, as the German Constitutional Court calls it, "the constitutional order." It includes those sets of principles, practices, understandings, traditions, and interpretations that the country actually follows or believes it follows. The more of the constitutional text "the constitution" includes—that is, the more public officials and private citizens shape their behavior and values to conform to the text's provisions—the more authoritative that text is. It may have generated some of the constitutional order's principles, practices, and traditions. Others may have become embedded in the text's margins, or may, perhaps, have come to substitute, in part or in whole, for its terms. The relationships here are complex. Just as a constitutional text can shape the values and the behavior of both public officials and private citizens, so, too, the values and the behavior of these people can change what the terms of the constitutional text come to signify.

The third concept, "constitutionalism," refers to a normative political theory, contending that all political power, even of democratically chosen and responsible officials, should be limited. Like democratic theory, constitutionalism holds human dignity and liberty as its central value; but, unlike democratic theory, constitutionalism would put substantive as well as procedural restrictions on what "the people" and their elected representatives can do.

Judges, legislators, executives, private citizens, and even learned scholars often confuse these three concepts, muddling the already complicated business of constitutional interpretation. Justices of the United States Supreme Court, for example, typically speak of what "the Constitution" means as if they were merely parsing the document of 1787 and its relevant amendments. But that text does not speak of such matters as:

- "Judicial review," the authority of judges to invalidate acts of coordinate branches of government, which John Marshall defended in *Marbury v. Madison* (1803) (Reading 2.2)
- "Executive privilege," the authority of the president to withhold information from other branches of government, the point of the dispute in *United States v. Nixon* (1974) (Reading 12.1)

---

[2] *United Mizrahi Bank plc v. Migdal Cooperative Village* (1995) 49 (iv) P. D. 221, translated and excerpted in 31 *Israel Law Review* 764–802 (1997).

- "Senatorial courtesy," which Chapter 4 addressed in describing the recruitment of judges
- The "right to privacy," first clearly enunciated in *Griswold v. Connecticut* (1965), and the long and boisterous debate over abortion, reflected in this volume only in *Webster v. Reproductive Health Services* (1989) (Reading 8.1) and *Planned Parenthood v. Casey* (1992) (Reading 10.6)

WHAT IS TO BE INTERPRETED?

The differences between "the constitution" and "the constitutional text" suggest that when we begin to engage in "constitutional interpretation," the first question we confront is, What is it we should be interpreting? Is it only the text? Or is it the larger "constitution"?

Making the text the sole target might appear to provide the simplest answer; but that appearance is deceptive, because a document seldom makes much sense when read out of intellectual and practical context. Even were interpreters to agree that it is the larger constitutional order they must confront, they would face problems of exquisite difficulty. What does that "constitution" include? Does it reflect some concepts, such as a presumption of innocence for those accused of crime, that were so obvious to the founding generation as not to have required mention in the text? If so, what are they? How do we find them? How do we justify the validity of our "discovery"? Further, have some usages—again, senatorial courtesy, for example—become such integral parts of the political tradition as to acquire constitutional status? Have some documents, such as the second paragraph of the Declaration of Independence, played such a formative role that they, too, have entered the constitutional canon? Which documents, and how can we justify our choices? We must repeat the same queries for earlier interpretations, political theories, and traditions.

Another set of questions concerns the stability of constitutional provisions. To what extent does "the constitution," whether text or more than text, always mean the same thing? Can "the constitution" change only through the process of formal amendment that Article V spells out? Can it also change through usage and interpretation? Was it legitimate in 1954 for the Supreme Court in *Brown v. Board of Education* to declare that the Fourteenth Amendment forbade racial segregation in public schools more than eighty years after the Congress that proposed the Fourteenth Amendment had established racially segregated schools in the District of Columbia and fifty-eight years after the Court itself had upheld segregation? Brown profoundly changed the nature not only of the American "constitution" but also of American society.[3] If that sort of sweeping reform through constitutional (re)interpretation is legitimate, what limits are left on change through interpretation?

---

[3] But see Gerald N. Rosenberg, *The Hollow Hope* (Chicago: University of Chicago Press, 1991) (Reading 14.6). We discuss this work in Chapter 14.

The challenges that these questions pose make it easier to understand why so many constitutional interpreters, on and off the bench, prefer to believe that they are working only with a text augmented, perhaps, with earlier constructions of those words.

WHO SHALL INTERPRET?

If interpreters could solve the questions about what exactly it is that they interpret, they would then have to look at their own duty and authority to engage in that task. To some extent, all public officials and citizens in the United States share an obligation to interpret their constitution. Legislators who take their oaths of office seriously must decide whether any bill meets constitutional standards. A conscientious administrator has to make a similar judgment when carrying out a statutory command or an executive order. Indeed, one can cogently argue not only that all public officials should interpret the constitution but also that they inevitably do so, because even a decision that interpreting the constitution is someone else's responsibility is itself an interpretation of the constitution. When citizens vote, give money to help finance electoral campaigns, write their representatives, or contact executive officials, they, too, have both an opportunity and a duty to remember that their primary allegiance is not to a candidate, a party, or an interest but to "the constitution."

We spoke, however, not only of duty but also of authority, a different notion that implies an obligation of others. Thus authority to interpret means that others, whether public officials or private citizens, have an obligation to treat that interpretation with respect, perhaps even to accept it as binding. Congress, the president, and the Supreme Court each demonstrate great deference to the others' constitutional interpretation. Indeed, the Supreme Court often asserts that, except where a "fundamental right" or a "suspect classification" is at issue, it will presume that an act of Congress is constitutional. An individual citizen's constitutional interpretation seldom gains much respect, unless he or she is a noted scholar; and even then few people, except perhaps when writing final examinations, feel an obligation to follow it.

On the other hand, when the "people" speak en masse, most public officials, including judges, usually listen intently. In 1935–1936, for example, the Supreme Court invalidated much of Franklin D. Roosevelt's New Deal. At the election of 1936, which many interpreted as a kind of constitutional referendum, FDR swept forty-six of the then forty-eight states. Very quickly, the Court began what has been called "the switch in time that saved nine and revised its former constitutional jurisprudence. "Looking back," Justice Owen Roberts, who had been one of the justices who changed his mind, later said, "it is difficult to see how the Court could have resisted the popular urge for uniform standards throughout the country—for what in effect was a unified economy."[4]

---

[4] Owen J. Roberts, *The Supreme Court and the Constitution* (Cambridge, MA: Harvard University Press, 1951), 61.

Democratic theory, of course, demands great deference to the "people's" interpretations and to those of its elected representatives. Interpretations by appointed judges do not carry the same democratic weight. Constitutionalism, however, is very comfortable with judicial review. Indeed, judicial review and a bill of rights have become the two primary institutions of constitutionalism. And not only the United States but also Canada, India, Ireland, Japan, Korea, some countries in Latin America, and almost all the nations on the European continent, east, west, and central, have modified their operative versions of democracy with both of these institutions.

During the past two centuries, judges in the United States provided one important model of judicial control over basic constitutional issues by asserting a broad measure of authority to invalidate acts of coordinate branches of government. Furthermore, although specific decisions have often met fierce resistance and sometimes that resistance has brought about a new and quite different interpretation, as after 1936, Congress, the president, and the electorate have, by and large, accepted the legitimacy of judicial authority. The Supreme Court's role as a principal, though not certainly not always the final, constitutional interpreter is so firmly established that it can precipitate the resignation of a president, as it did in *United States v. Nixon* (1974) (Reading 12.1); or the election of a president, as it did in *Bush v. Gore* (2000). At one swoop it can declare more than 200 federal statutory provisions unconstitutional, as it did in *Immigration and Naturalization Service (INS) v. Chadha* (1983); or invalidate almost every law in the country regulating abortion, as it did in *Roe v. Wade* (1973).

Nevertheless, American judges have never pretended to have a monopoly on constitutional interpretation; and very seldom have they been so bold as to assert they were the "ultimate" interpreters within the federal government. *United States v. Nixon* (1974) (Reading 12.1) offers one of those rare instances in which the Court has made such a claim. More recently, *City of Boerne v. Flores* (1997), striking down a portion of the Religious Freedom and Restoration Act of 1993, and *Dickerson v. United States* (2000), asserting that *Miranda v. Arizona* (1966) announced constitutional rules binding on Congress, both contain language that strongly asserts judicial supremacy in constitutional interpretation. Ironically, *Boerne* and *Dickerson*, just as *Bush v. Gore*, were decided by the Rehnquist Court, a majority of whose justices frequently preach the necessity of judicial self-restraint, and the opinion of the Court in *Nixon* was written by Chief Justice Warren Earl Burger, who was chosen, so President Richard Nixon said, because he believed in and would practice judicial self-restraint. Despite these claims, as Chapter 8 showed, presidents of such stature as Thomas Jefferson, Andrew Jackson, and Abraham Lincoln were not willing to concede that they or Congress were obliged to accept the Supreme Court's constitutional interpretations as legally binding (Readings 8.4–8.7).

Moreover, as Chapters 6 and 11 indicated, judges in the United States often sidestep constitutional questions. Among the formal doctrines the Supreme Court has created to avoid constitutional issues are standing to sue and political questions. The Court's control over its own docket increases the justices' ability to evade whatever disputes they do not wish to hear (see Chapter 13).

The reasons for avoidance vary from respect for democratic processes to misgivings about the limited reach of judges' interpretive authority, to concern that courts are not competent to handle particular problems, to strategic considerations of timing, to worry about legislative or executive retaliation or sabotage, and to fear that judges will not be able to enforce an unpopular decision.

HOW SHOULD JUDGES INTERPRET THE CONSTITUTION? INTERPRETIVE STYLE IN THE UNITED STATES

Among the first things a European scholar would notice about constitutional interpretation by judges in the United States is that the work is done in the fashion of the common law, that is, in the context of deciding concrete cases. In contrast, many constitutional democracies (Austria, Belgium, Chile, the Federal Republic of Germany, Italy, Spain, and Portugal, for example) restrict judicial authority to interpret the constitution to a single tribunal, standing outside the regular judicial hierarchy. This "constitutional court" usually answers questions rather than make decisions for one litigant or the other.

In the American judicial system, disputes about facts, statutory law, and constitutional meaning are typically jumbled together. Constitutional interpretation in the United States means "constitutional adjudication,"[5] not analyzing a question in the abstract. Two forces tug at judges' robes: One is the revered practice of common-law judges to decide the case at hand on principles no broader than necessary for that task; the other is the equally revered practice of common-law judges to offer guidance to other public officials, lawyers, and potential litigants by identifying and clarifying the general principles the court is following. The first tug is generally the stronger. The *U.S. Reports*, which reprints the opinions of the Supreme Court, nowhere contains a full, systematic, coherent statement of a theory of what "the constitution" is, who are its ultimate interpreters, and how it should be interpreted.

A European scholar would also notice that, when engaging in constitutional interpretation, U.S. jurists behave like common-law judges in yet another respect: Much of the supposed "constitutional" analysis is actually analysis of what earlier judges have said about the particular issue. Almost immediately, constitutional interpretation leaves the confines of the text to explore the more spacious realm of previous judicial opinions. In this sense, at least, constitutional interpretation by American judges rapidly moves from "the constitutional text" to "the constitution."

---

[5] See Harry H. Wellington, *Interpreting the Constitution: The Supreme Court and the Process of Adjudication* (New Haven, CT: Yale University Press, 1990).

MODES OF INTERPRETATION

U.S. judges interpret both the "constitutional text" and "the constitution" in a wide variety of ways. Moreover, these jurists often use several different interpretive modes, just as they do in statutory interpretation, when addressing the same issue; and, over a period of a few years, the same judge may, without much self-consciousness, use several mutually inconsistent approaches. It is worth trying to abstract out of formal opinions some of those modes that judges frequently employ. In what follows, we consider eight: the text, stare decisis, original intent or understanding, structural analysis, purposive analysis, polls of other jurisdictions, balancing of interests, and cost-benefit analysis.

The Text

The most obvious way to engage in constitutional interpretation is to look at the words of the document itself. Those words, just as the words of statutes (see Chapter 11), do solve many problems. No one, for example, expects a president to stand for reelection every year. The constitutional text specifies four years as the term, and that issue is closed. So, too, military officers are not likely to try to billet their troops in civilian homes in peacetime. The Third Amendment's prohibition is crystal clear on that point: "No soldier shall, in time of peace, be quartered in any house, without the consent of the owner. . . ."

Alas for judges' peace of mind, where the document's meaning is straightforward, they are not likely to be asked to interpret it. It is where the words are unplain or plain words are arranged in unplain clauses that disputes arise. A document plus a dictionary cannot tell us much about what phrases such as "due process of law," commerce "among the several states," or "cruel and unusual punishment" mean. The text itself may even command interpreters to go beyond its four corners. The Ninth Amendment does so: "The enumeration in the Constitution of certain rights shall not be construed to deny or disparage others retained by the people." "Shall not," of course, is imperative in mood; it does not advise, it commands. If interpreters must move beyond the text and a dictionary, to where do they go?

Stare Decisis and Doctrinal Analysis

As we noted in Chapter 10, American judges, being children of the common law, are quick to look to precedents for guidance. This practice can provide helpful guidance to lower-court judges, when other courts have written on the same or very similar issues as those currently being litigated. Stare decisis can also be of some aid to justices of the Supreme Court in laying out reasoning for and against a particular interpretation. Guidance, however, differs from control. The current case may present new issues on which previous opinions cast little light. And, even if the Court did once decide the precise question, the U.S. doctrine of stare decisis does not automatically trigger reaffirmation. Indeed, the justices often repeat that, when constitutional issues are involved, stare decisis is even less rigid a rule than it normally is.[6]

In *Planned Parenthood v. Casey* (1992) (Reading 10.6), Justices Sandra Day O'Connor, Anthony M. Kennedy, and David H. Souter took a quite different tack. They argued that the Court should keep *Roe v. Wade* (1973) alive, lest the justices seem to be backing down under fire. But even as the three wrote this warning, they modified Roe's doctrine about the status of abortion as a fundamental right.

Stare decisis, however, operates subtly and pervasively in constitutional interpretation. As our European commentator would note, one of the hallmarks of constitutional interpretation in the United States, at least by judges, is to weave webs of doctrine around the text. When dealing with racial discrimination in the 1890s, for example, the justices developed the doctrine of "separate but equal" and tested the validity of racially restrictive regulations within that framework rather than the constitutional charter's "equal protection of the laws." Later, as the Court retreated from "separate but equal," the justices slowly developed a new doctrinal test called "strict scrutiny," a phrase that is also remote from the Fourteenth Amendment's "equal protection of the laws." To withstand judicial scrutiny now, legislation based on race or other "suspect" classifications must be necessary to effect a "compelling governmental interest" that is not attainable without the law's utilizing these "suspect" criteria. And, as anyone familiar with the common law would have guessed, the exact terms of this newer doctrine and what other classifications are "suspect" continue to change. We look in vain to the words of the document for enlightenment and so must rely on case-by-case development.

One could multiply examples from a dozen other areas of constitutional disputes, such as federal and state regulation of business or the establishment of religion. Judges create doctrines and use them as frameworks for constitutional analysis. For example, the justices use the phrase "liberty interest" as term of art to denote a right or an interest not specifically listed in the constitutional text but somehow included in the "liberty" that the Fifth Amendment protects against the federal government or the Fourteenth protects against the states. This sort of development dates back to the days of Chief Justice John Marshall when the Court invented the "original package" doctrine: A state could not tax or regulate commerce from abroad or another state as long as the goods remained in their "original package."

Judges have become even more doctrinally fertile. More than a half century ago, Thomas Reed Powell, who taught constitutional law at the Harvard Law School, would warn his students not to read the constitutional text. "It will only confuse you," he would say. What students had to understand were the doctrines the Court had constructed around the document. These, not the words of

---

[6] Such flexibility is prudent; the constitutional text is difficult to amend and judges make mistakes—or come to see problems quite differently as their perspectives change.

the text, determined whether a presidential power was constitutional, a statute was valid, or a right existed.

The problems this sort of constitutional interpretation creates are obvious. But some such development is inevitable in a common-law system. There is no way of escaping accretion that builds on a broader "constitution" around a constitutional text.

Original Intent or Understanding

When interpreters find insufficient nourishment in "plain words," earlier rulings, or broader doctrines, they sometimes try to discover the "intent" of the framers of either the text of 1787 or an amendment to it, or search for something close to intent but yet different, the "original understanding" of the founding generation, again of the text of 1787 or the relevant amendment. But those two usually contain even more wiggly worms than the quest for legislative intent behind a statute. Such searches make several assumptions. The first is that the founders' intentions or understandings—rather than the words they actually adopted—should bind future generations. This assumption is one that Justice Antonin Scalia questions when interpreting statutes. As Chapter 11 pointed out, Scalia ridicules those who, on a fairly full if not always completely accurate record, would try to discern "legislative intent." Instead, he asks what the words of the statute would ordinarily mean. That usual meaning would govern interpretation unless there were strong indications that, in the particular context of the statute, the words had an unusual meaning.

In constitutional interpretation, Scalia embraces the difficulties he rejects when interpreting a statute and seeks to use history not to find "original intent" "original understanding" of the text's meaning (Reading 12.2). This search is almost impossible for a court to undertake. Not only is the concept of "original understanding" as elusive as "intent" but the documentary evidence for both is missing. Both depend heavily on the meaning of words and language is in a constant state of change. Samuel Johnson, the great British lexicographer of the 18th century, admitted that his dictionary did not work for the colonies; and the first dictionary of American English, that by Noah Webster, was not published until 1828, forty years after ratification. At least most statutes judges must interpret are recent so that they can be more aware of linguistic changes.

The second assumption is that the founders had a single intention or understanding—as opposed to many different and perhaps irreconcilable intentions and understandings. This assumption is as tenuous in constitutional interpretation as it is in statutory analysis. "Every man," William Anderson noted, "being a different individual, unavoidably has intentions that are somewhat different from those of someone else. Such a thing as a solid, unified intention of all the members in any group would be hard if not impossible to find."[7] A unified understanding is equally unlikely to have existed.

---

[7] William Anderson, "The Intention of the Framers: A Note on Constitutional Interpretation," 49 *American Political Science Review* 340, 343 (1955).

There is a third and even more attenuated assumption: We can reconstruct the intentions or understandings of those who adopted the constitutional text of 1787 or its amendments. In fact, for 1787 the historical record is incomplete.[8] Moreover, some of what passes for "records" of the Philadelphia convention are jumbled, even forged. During the debates, the secretary became confused and thoroughly botched the minutes; and James Madison, who took the most complete and most reliable notes on what was said, edited them after the convention adjourned. The accounts of debates in the state ratifying conventions are often in worse shape: few secretaries knew anything like modern shorthand and were often partisans of one side or the other, determined to "prove" their spokesmen made the better case. It is no wonder that some participants claimed that what they were reported as saying badly mangled what they actually did say.

Those who would rely on "original understanding" might claim that the condition of the historic record is less of a barrier to their approach. The popular debate on ratification was full; millions of pamphlets (heavily outnumbering the entire population) argued for and against the new political system. This mass of literature, however, demonstrates not one but dozens of understandings of what the new constitution would constitute.

The interpretive utility of the "history" of amendments vary. In general one can say that the more recent the amendment, the more reliable the record. For the Bill of Rights, we know almost nothing of what was said in the Senate and precious little about ratification in the states. It is thus no wonder that contemporary scholars engage in heated debates over such things as whether the Framers intended the Second Amendment's guarantee of the "right to keep and bear arms" to serve as a barrier to gun control. The congressional record for the Fourteenth Amendment is probably complete though not always helpful; the issues senators and representatives were most interested in were not those that have plagued future generations. At the state level, it is difficult to piece together much beyond the final votes in the ratifying legislatures.

There are other problems with using original intent or understanding, based on democratic theory and on prudence. Whatever the Framers had in their minds, the democratic argument runs, the people of the times accepted only what the Framers wrote, not what they meant to write or some people understood them to write. Later generations have not known, much less endorsed, what earlier generations intended or understood.

The prudential argument was best stated by Justice Benjamin N. Cardozo in an opinion he decided not to publish. At issue had been the validity of a Minnesota statute, enacted to combat the Great Depression, providing for a moratorium on foreclosures on farms whose owners were unable to pay their mortgages. The statute ran afoul not only of the plain words of Article I, §10 of the Constitution, "No State shall . . . Pass any law impairing the obligation of

---

[8] See James H. Hutson, "The Creation of the Constitution: The Integrity of the Documentary Record," 65 *Texas Law Review* 1 (1986).

contracts," but also of some evidence of the "intent" of the Framers. Nevertheless, the Supreme Court by a five-to-four vote sustained the statute. Chief Justice Charles Evans Hughes's opinion for the Court was a mishmash of reasoning, partly based on a distinction between the obligation of a contract and the remedy for enforcing a contract and also partly on the notion that the constitution's meaning changes over time. Cardozo had wanted to put the issue more bluntly:

> To hold this [statute constitutional] may be inconsistent with things that men said in 1787 when expounding to compatriots the newly written constitution. They did not see the changes in the relation between states and nation or in the play of social forces that lay hidden in the womb of time. It may be inconsistent with things that they believed or took for granted. Their beliefs to be significant must be adjusted to the world they knew.[9]

Despite all these difficulties, many judges and scholars still look on the "intent of the Framers" or original understanding as magical charms for constitutional interpretation.[10] Former court of appeals judge and (failed) Supreme Court nominee Robert H. Bork is perhaps most associated with this approach (Reading 12.3), but he is joined by a few current justices. In *Minneapolis Star & Tribune v. Minnesota Commissioner of Revenue* (1983), where the state had levied a special sales tax on paper and ink used by newspapers, Justice O'Connor said in her opinion for the Court striking down the tax: "There is substantial evidence that differential taxation of the press would have troubled the Framers of the First Amendment." To that statement she appended a footnote about constitutional interpretation generally:

> It is true that our opinions rarely speculate on precisely how the Framers would have analyzed a given regulation of expression. In general . . . we have only limited evidence of exactly how the Framers intended the First Amendment to apply. There are no recorded debates in the Senate or in the States, and the discussion in the House of Representatives was couched in general terms, perhaps in response to Madison's suggestion that the representatives not stray from simple acknowledged principles. Consequently, we ordinarily simply apply those general principles. . . . But when we do have evidence that a particular law would have offended the Framers, we have not hesitated to invalidate it on that ground alone.

Justice Clarence Thomas has been less equivocal. Since his ascension to the bench, he has invoked originalism to offer answers to a wide range of questions, from caps on campaign spending to the appropriate balance of power between the states and the federal government. Such a jurisprudential tack would have

---

[9] Unpublished opinion in *Home Owners Loan Association v. Blaisdell* (1934). Most of Cardozo's opinion is printed in Walter F. Murphy, James E. Fleming, Sotirios A. Barber, and Stephen Macedo, *American Constitutional Interpretation*, 3rd ed. (New York: Foundation Press, 2003).

[10] For an intelligent defense of originalism, see Keith E. Whittington, *Constitutional Interpretation: Textual Meaning, Original Intent, and Judicial Review* (Lawrence: University Press of Kansas, 1999).

angered his predecessor, Thurgood Marshall (Reading 12.4) and Thomas's self-assured judgments on heatedly contested historical issues bemuse scholars.

Structural Analysis

Individual clauses of any constitutional text often make little sense on their own, and they may even conflict with one another. The First Amendment, for instance, forbids Congress both "to establish" a religion and to prohibit "the free exercise thereof." The two clauses "are cast in absolute terms, and either of which, if expanded to a logical extreme, would tend to clash with the other."[11] Suppose Congress did not exempt Quakers from compulsory military service. Might not such action violate their free exercise of religion? Suppose Congress did exempt Quakers from compulsory military service. Might not that action give them preferred status because of their religious beliefs and so constitute indirect establishment of a religion?

Theologians and literary critics, who have long faced similar interpretive problems of opacity and conflict, have recognized a "hermeneutic dilemma": One cannot understand the whole—of a document, a story, or a political system—without understanding the parts; but neither can one understand the parts without understanding the whole. Constitutional commentators label as "clause-bound" interpretation that looks at a particular clause of the text as an isolated unit and ignores connections with the larger entity. In contrast, structuralism breaks into the circle at the macrolevel. As James Madison put it in *Federalist* No. 40:

> There are two rules of construction, dictated by plain reason, as well as founded on legal axioms. The one is that every part of the expression ought, if possible, be made to conspire to some common end. The other is that where the several parts cannot be made to coincide, the less important should give way to the more important part; the means should be sacrificed to the end, rather than the end to the means.

Poe v. Ullman (1961) and *Griswold v. Connecticut* (1965) exemplify structuralist interpretation. Both cases involved challenges to the validity of a state's forbidding advising people about contraception. Dissenting in *Poe*, William O. Douglas wrote that the "notion of privacy is not drawn from the blue. It emanates from the totality of the constitutional scheme under which we live." John Marshall Harlan's dissent made a similar argument. The "liberty" protected by the due process clauses

> is not a series of isolated points pricked out in terms of the taking of property; the freedom of speech, press, and religion, the right to keep and bear arms; the freedom from unreasonable searches and seizures; and so on. It is a rational continuum which, broadly speaking, includes a freedom from all substantial arbitrary imposition and purposeless restraints.

---

[11] *Walz v. Tax Commission* (1970).

In *Griswold*, Douglas and Harlan mustered a majority. Writing for the Court, Douglas began by looking at the document, but he did not restrict analysis to any one clause. Instead, he examined the interplay among the values he thought underlay the First, Third, Fourth, Fifth, and Ninth Amendments. These clauses provided textual roots for partial rights to privacy in specific areas. Next he spoke of these individual provisions as having "penumbras formed by emanations from those guarantees that give them life and substance." Douglas then began to construct a general theory of privacy, and his structural analysis, echoing his reference in *Poe* to "the totality of the constitutional scheme," transcended the text and sought meaning from a theory of constitutionalism.

Of necessity, deciding distributions of powers among the branches of the federal government and between federal and state government all partake of structural analysis. In problems involving federalism, it is almost impossible for interpreters to restrict themselves to the text because the document's words on the issue are so few and so cryptic. It is only somewhat easier to do so in disputes between branches of the national government; even when addressing relations among Congress, the president, and the judiciary, the text allocates powers less by specific verbal directions than by intricately woven patterns of sharing and dividing.

Among the greatest attractions of structural analysis is that it makes intuitive sense to deal with a whole rather than with individual pieces. It posits a coherence to constitutional interpretation. Its drawbacks stem from the fact that it is the interpreter who must articulate the structure on which "the constitution," whatever it includes, hangs. And different interpreters are apt to perceive different structures.

Purposive Analysis

Purposive analysis, sometimes called "teleological jurisprudence," asks what are the general aims of the constitutional text or the larger "constitution," then uses answers to organize interpretation. We shall discuss two examples of this sort of interpretation, reinforcing representative democracy and giving effect to fundamental rights. Both have peculiar relevance to U.S. constitutional interpretation, for that constitutional text opens by specifying the purposes of "the new order for the ages."

Interpreters who see the basic purpose of a constitution as creating and maintaining a representative democratic system argue that the main judicial function in constitutional interpretation is to keep the political processes open by protecting all citizens' rights to speak, assemble, organize, and vote. Judges, so the reasoning continues, also should protect members of various minorities from any indirect as well as direct discriminatory governmental action that would reduce the minorities' ability to compete politically. Responsibility for most constitutional interpretation, these democratic theorists contend, rests with Congress, the president, and state officials chosen through processes that are truly free and open.

In its early incarnation, this method of constitutional interpretation was called the "doctrine of preferred freedoms" and had its modern origin in Justice Harlan Stone's Footnote 4 in an otherwise trivial case, *United States v. Carolene Products* (1938). There Stone appended the second two paragraphs of the note to a statement that in general the Court would presume that statutes were constitutional (see Chapter 9), then added the first paragraph in response to criticism from Chief Justice Charles Evans Hughes:

> There may be narrower scope for operation of the presumption of constitutionality when legislation appears on its face to be within a specific prohibition of the Constitution, such as those of the first ten amendments, which are deemed equally specific when held to be embraced within the Fourteenth.
>
> It is unnecessary to consider now whether legislation which restricts those political processes which can ordinarily be expected to bring about a repeal of undesirable legislation is to be subjected to more exacting judicial scrutiny under the general prohibitions of the Fourteenth Amendment than are most other types of legislation. . . .
>
> Nor need we inquire whether similar considerations enter into the review of statutes directed at particular religious, or national, or racial minorities; whether prejudice against discrete and insular minorities may be a special condition, which tends seriously to curtail the operation of those political processes ordinarily to be relied upon to protect minorities, and which may call for a correspondingly more searching judicial inquiry.

This statement was modest and tentative, but other justices were soon applying Stone's ideas as if they were settled and expansive constitutional doctrine; and several scholars, including Alpheus Thomas Mason,[12] John Hart Ely,[13] and Louis Lusky[14] (Stone's clerk, who helped write the footnote) further developed Stone's ideas into several related but distinct constitutional theories.

Other judges and commentators agree, as did Stone himself,[15] that interpreters should look to constitutional purpose but see constitutionalism as at least equal if not superior in rank to democracy. They view the system as designed not merely to protect citizens' rights to participate freely and equally in the political processes but also to defend *substantive*, fundamental rights against governmental interference. These "constitutionalists" contend that judges should protect not only participatory rights but also other basic rights such as to privacy. "Constitutionalists" argue that the first paragraph of Footnote 4 shows that "democrats" read too narrowly the jurisprudence immanent in *Carolene Products*. Once again we are in the realm of precedents and even that spacious terrain, jurisprudence, rather than in the narrow domain of a text.

---

[12] Alpheus Thomas Mason, *Security through Freedom* (Ithaca, NY: Cornell University Press, 1955); *Harlan Fiske Stone* (New York: Viking, 1956); and *The Supreme Court from Taft to Burger* (Baton Rouge: Louisiana State University Press, 1979).

[13] John Hart Ely, *Democracy and Distrust: A Theory of Judicial Review* (Cambridge, MA: Harvard University Press, 1980).

[14] Louis Lusky, *By What Right?* (Charlottesville, VA: Michie, 1975).

[15] See his dissenting opinion in *Minersville School District v. Gobitis* (1940).

It was the supposed centrality of rights of property and "liberty of contract" to individual autonomy that had propelled the Court to curb governmental regulation of the economy during the period 1890–1937. In *Meyer v. Nebraska* (1923), Justice James C. McReynolds, a crusty advocate of laissez faire, put the notion of fundamental rights in terms the Court still quotes. His textual anchor was the word *liberty* in the Fifth and Fourteenth Amendments. That concept, he wrote,

> denotes not merely freedom from bodily restraint but also the right of any individual to contract, to engage in any of the common occupations of life, to acquire useful knowledge, to marry, establish a home and bring up children, to worship God according to the dictates of his own conscience, and generally to enjoy those privileges long recognized at common law as essential to the orderly pursuit of happiness by free man.

Fourteen years later, Justice Cardozo, a foe of laissez faire, also endorsed the notion of fundamental rights. In *Palko v. Connecticut* (1937), he explained that some rights imbedded in the Bill of Rights were "so rooted in the traditions and conscience of our people as to be ranked as fundamental." The Fourteenth Amendment's due process clause "incorporated" those rights that were "of the very essence of a scheme of ordered liberty," and so protected them against state as well as federal infringement.

For much of the rest of the twentieth century, the justices, like elected public officials and scholars, argued about which rights, listed in or read into the text, are fundamental and how to justify that doubly distinctive status. (Without doubt, this debate will continue as long as constitutional interpretation does.) The Court has included freedom to marry, worship or not worship, have or not have children, travel, retain one's citizenship, and perhaps receive minimal education. Disputes over governmental regulation of such practices as abortion (*Planned Parenthood v. Casey* [1992]) and sodomy (*Lawrence v. Texas* [2003]) have centered not only on which rights are included in the constitutional document but also which of those rights is "fundamental," and so deserving of special judicial protection.

Even these brief descriptions of two similar but not always mutually compatible versions of purposive interpretation show that it provides no magic key to unlock constitutional meaning. Apart from their conflicts with each other, both versions have internal difficulties. Advocates of "reinforcing democracy" have to acknowledge that the text provides a weak basis for their jurisprudence. Thus, to limit judicial discretion to move beyond the text, they want judges to move beyond that text. Furthermore, critics claim, participatory rights are merely one species of fundamental rights, thus "the democrats" make arbitrary choices among rights.[16]

And the problems with "fundamental rights" are huge. No advocate has yet produced a calculus to demonstrate which listed rights are more or less

---

[16] See, for example, Laurence H. Tribe, "The Puzzling Persistence of Process-Based Constitutional Theories,"89 *Yale Law Journal* 1063 (1980); reprinted as Chapter 2 of his *Constitutional Choices* (Cambridge, MA: Harvard University Press, 1985).

important and which unlisted rights are so basic as to be accorded constitutional status. Justice Harlan's efforts in *Poe v. Ullman* (1961) were heroic, but his message that U.S. constitutional democracy was a synthesis of "liberty of the individual" and "the demands of organized society," based on "what history teaches are the traditions from which it developed as well as the traditions from which it broke," was no more precise than his call for "judgment and restraint" in discovering that synthesis and the rights it safeguarded.[17]

Polls of Other Jurisdictions

As a variant on the historical approach, a judge might probe English traditions or early colonial or state practices to determine how public officials of the times—or later—interpreted similar words or phrases. The Supreme Court has frequently used such evidence. For instance, when *Wolf v. Colorado* (1949) presented the Court with the question whether the Fourth Amendment, as applied to the states by the due process clause of the Fourteenth Amendment, barred use in state courts of evidence obtained through an unconstitutional search, Justice Felix Frankfurter surveyed the law in all the states and in ten jurisdictions within the British Commonwealth. He used this poll to bolster a conclusion that, while "the Constitution" forbade unreasonable searches and seizures, it did not prohibit state officials from using such ill-gotten evidence against a defendant.

In 1952, however, when *Rochin v. California* confronted the justices with the question whether a state could use evidence it had obtained from a defendant by pumping out his stomach—evidence admissible in the overwhelming majority of states at that time—Frankfurter declined to call the roll. Instead he declared that gathering evidence by a stomach pump was "conduct that shocks the conscience" and so its fruits could not be used in courts, state or federal. When in 1961 *Mapp v. Ohio* overruled *Wolf* and held that state courts must exclude all unconstitutionally obtained evidence, the justices again surveyed the field. For the Court, Justice Tom C. Clark said: "While in 1949 almost two-thirds of the States were opposed to the exclusionary rule, now, despite the *Wolf* Case, more than half of those since passing upon it, by their own legislative or judicial decision, have wholly or partly adopted or adhered to the [rule]."

The point of this set of examples is not that Frankfurter or the Court was inconsistent, but that the method itself, while it offers insights, is far from foolproof. First of all, the constitutional text of 1787 as it initially stood and has been since amended rejects many English and some colonial and state practices. Second, even a steady stream of precedents from the states may mean no more than that judges, too busy to give the issue much thought, imitated one another

---

[17] For a fascinating debate about what makes a particular right fundamental, see Carlos Nino, *The Ethics of Human Rights* (Oxford: Oxford University Press, 1991) and the essays, which Nino provoked, by Thomas Nagel, Bernard Williams, Martin D. Farrell, and Elaine Scarry, in Harold Hongju Koh and Ronald C. Slye, eds., *Deliberative Democracy and Human Rights*, (New Haven, CT: Yale University Press, 1999).

under the rubric of stare decisis. Third, if one is seeking for original intent or understanding, it is difficult to imagine the relevance of state practices in the twentieth and twenty-first centuries to what was in the minds of people in the eighteenth century. If one wants to know what other judges, now and in the recent past, have thought about the constitution, writ large or small, polls are useful. Nevertheless, they say nothing about the correctness of those thoughts—and the correctness of a lower court's interpretation may be precisely the issue before the Supreme Court.

Polls of Courts Abroad

While the Supreme Court continues to take into account the practices of other U.S. jurisdictions—particularly in the area of criminal procedure—foreign courts occasionally look to their counterparts in other countries for guidance. The South African ruling in *The State v. Makwanyane* (1995) provides a vivid example. To determine whether the death penalty violated its nation's constitution, the Republic's Constitutional Court surveyed practices elsewhere, including those in the United States. At the end of the day, the justices decided not to "follow the path" taken by the U.S. Supreme Court, ruling instead that their constitution prohibited the state from imposing capital punishment. (Reading 12.5). Rejection of American practice was made all the more interesting (ironic?) in light of a speech delivered by Justice Harry Blackmun, just a year before *Makwanyane*.[18] In that address, Blackmun chastised his colleagues for failing to take into account a decision of the South African high court dismissing a prosecution against a person kidnapped from a neighboring country. This ruling, Blackmun argued, was far more faithful to international conventions than the one his Court reached in *United States v. Alvarez-Machain* (1992), which permitted U.S. agents to abduct a Mexican national.

Alvarez-Machain aside, there does seem to be an increasing tendency for U.S. American judges to consider the rulings of courts abroad and practices elsewhere as they go about the task of interpreting the constitution. This trend is particularly evident in opinions regarding capital punishment, wherein justices opposed to this form of punishment often point to the nearly one hundred countries that have abolished the death penalty.

Whether this practice will become more widespread or filter into other legal areas is an interesting question, and one likely to cause debate among the justices. Although some support efforts to expand their horizons beyond U.S. borders, others apparently agree with Justice Scalia, who has argued that "the views of other nations, however enlightened the Justices of this court may think them to be, cannot be imposed upon Americans through the Constitution."[19]

---

[18] "Justice Blackmun Addresses the ASIL Annual Dinner," *American Society of International Law Newsletter*, March 1994.

[19] *Thompson v. Oklahoma* (1987). See also Robert H. Bork, *Coercing Virtue: The Worldwide Rule of Judges* (Washington, DC: American Enterprise Institute Press, 2003).

Balancing of Interests

Where the constitutional text voices apparently contradictory commands, as with the two prohibitions of the First Amendment's clause relating to religion, some interpreters have claimed to "balance" the conflicting rights and powers. Seldom, however, do "balancers" explain the nature of the scale on which they weigh competing values or, more important, the weights they attach to various values.

John Marshall Harlan's opinion for the Court in *Barenblatt v. United States* (1959) provides a typical example. A witness compelled to testify before a congressional committee had invoked the First Amendment to justify refusing to answer question about his alleged membership in the Communist party. Convicted for contempt of Congress and having lost on appeal, Barenblatt obtained certiorari from the Supreme Court. For the majority, Harlan spoke both of the protection that the First Amendment gave to freedom of association as well as the threat that the Communist party posed to national security and the authority of Congress to meet that threat by obtaining information. "In the last analysis," he wrote, "this power rests on the right of self-preservation, 'the ultimate value of any society.'" After laying out these competing values, Harlan cryptically explained: "We conclude that the balance between the individual and the governmental interests here at stake must be struck in favor of the latter, and that therefore the provisions of the First Amendment have not been violated."

But "the balance" is often hidden within a black box. If no one knows how the scale is calibrated or has any precise notion of even the relative weights of the values involved until after a decision is announced, it is difficult to escape the conclusion that the judge has by fiat decided that one value is more important than another. The particular decision may be wise and even in keeping with some general jurisprudence, but "balancers" usually ask readers to accept their conclusions on faith rather than reason.[20] Perhaps balancers are groping toward the notion that certain values are more important than the others and that extracting them from the tangled web of litigation makes their relative importance clearer. Some justices have openly said that they find in the larger constitution and the constitutional text such a hierarchy and have tried to identify at least some of the "fundamental" values and rights. And here we return to the problems our discussion of purposive interpretation raised.

Cost-Benefit Analysis

Balancing might also tie in with cost-benefit analysis. As Chapter 14 points out, judges often appraise alternative rulings by forecasting their consequences. These estimates can, of course, influence choices among plausible constitutional interpretations. And here we might have, if not balancing, an effort to maximize benefits and minimize costs.

---

[20] Justice Antonin Scalia is among the most severe critics of balancing. See Antonin Scalia, "The Rule of Law as a Law of Rules," 56 *University of Chicago Law Review* 1175 (1989).

One of the recurrent issues the Supreme Court confronted during much of the twentieth century concerned application of the exclusionary rule, which forbids use in criminal proceedings of evidence secured in violation of the Fourth Amendment. Claims that the rule hampers the conviction of criminals have affected judicial attitudes, as Justice Byron White frankly admitted in *United States v. Leon* (1984): "The substantial social costs exacted by the exclusionary rule for the vindication of Fourth Amendment rights have long been a source of concern." In *Leon* a majority of the Court applied a "cost-benefit" calculus to justify a "good faith" seizure by police on an invalid search warrant. (Readings 12.6 and 12.7). An observer might ask a general question about this sort of analysis: By what account of values should judges weigh costs and benefits, and how do they take into account the different people whom a decision may simultaneously punish and reward?

CONSTITUTIONAL INTERPRETATION AS A FORM OF STATECRAFT

We could make a much longer list of modes—and criticisms of those modes—of constitutional interpretation. But no method or rule of interpretation, either singly or in combination with others, offers much hope of attaining final constitutional truth. Acceptance of this fact has caused judges and scholars to react in ways that can be arranged along a broad spectrum. At one end is endorsement of a judicial role of breathing life into the vague terms of the constitutional text so that it is "relevant to solutions of current problems"—in sum, a judicial license to make that document a "living" reality. The other extreme posits for elected officials and the amending process the task of modernizing the text or the larger constitution and leaves to judges the ostensibly simple function of "saying what the law is" (Readings 12.8, 12.9).

Part of the difficulty lies in the nature of language, part in the nature of what cries out for interpretation—not only a text but practices, traditions, previous interpretations, and perhaps political theories. In a critical sense, constitutional interpretation also partakes of statecraft, because deciding what "the constitution" means—what it allows as well as what it forbids—can have immense long-range as well as immediate effects both on public policy and the institutions and processes of government. At very least, as U.S. American judges have been fond of repeating, the constitution is not a suicide pact. At very best, it is a charter for a people as well as for their government.

The difficulties here are as huge as they are obvious. Untangling webs of political theory is work that we associate more with professional philosophers than practical politicians or lawyers. Untangling webs of history is work we associate more with professional historians than judges. Furthermore, we look in vain for clear standards to tell us when an interpretation or practice has entered the constitutional canon. And constitutional texts themselves are often little more clear than the practices, interpretations, traditions, and political theories that surround them. These documents are, after all, drafted by human beings who, living at given moments in history, try to cope with concrete problems as well as formulate general principles. It is no easy task for judges, legislators, executive officials, scholars, or private citizens, to transfer meaning to later—and unforeseen—problems that occur in vastly different political, social, economic, technological, and intellectual contexts.

SELECTED REFERENCES

ACKERMAN, BRUCE A. 1984. "Discovering the Constitution?" *Yale Law Journal* 93: 1013.

ACKERMAN, BRUCE A. 1989. "Constitutional Politics/Constitutional Law." *Yale Law Journal* 99: 453.

ACKERMAN, BRUCE A.1991. *We the People: The Foundations*. Cambridge, MA: Harvard University Press.

AGRESTO, JOHN. 1984. *The Supreme Court and Constitutional Democracy*. Ithaca, NY: Cornell University Press.

ALEXANDER, LARRY, ED. 1998. *Constitutionalism: Philosophical Foundations*. Cambridge: Cambridge University Press.

AMAR, AKHIL REED. 1988. "Philadelphia Revisited: Amending the Constitution Outside Article V." *University of Chicago Law Review* 55: 1043.

AMAR, AKHIL REED. 1998. *The Bill of Rights: Creation and Reconstruction*. New Haven, CT: Yale University Press.

ANDERSON, WILLIAM. 1955. "The Intention of the Framers: A Note on Constitutional Interpretation." *American Political Science Review* 49: 340.

ARKES, HADLEY. 1990. *Beyond the Constitution*. Princeton, NJ: Princeton University Press.

BARBER, SOTIRIOS A. 1984. *On What the Constitution Means*. Baltimore: John Hopkins University Press.

BARBER, SOTIRIOS A. 1993. *The Constitution of Judicial Power*. Baltimore: Johns Hopkins University Press.

BERNS, WALTER. 1987. *Taking the Constitution Seriously*. New York: Simon & Schuster.

BICKEL, ALEXANDER M. 1962. *The Least Dangerous Branch*. Indianapolis: Bobbs-Merrill.

BICKEL, ALEXANDER M. 1970. *The Supreme Court and the Idea of Progress*. New York: Harper & Row.

BOBBITT, PHILIP. 1991. *Constitutional Interpretation*. Cambridge, MA: Basil Blackwell.

BORK, ROBERT H. 1971. "Neutral Principles and Some First Amendment Problems." *Indiana Law Journal* 47: 1.

BORK, ROBERT H. 1990. *The Tempting of America: The Political Seduction of the Law*. New York: Free Press.

BORK, ROBERT H. 2003. *Coercing Virtue: The Worldwide Rule of Judges*. Washington, D.C.: AEI Press.

BURT, ROBERT A. 1992. *The Constitution in Conflict*. Cambridge, MA: Belknap Press.

CARTER, LIEF H. 1985. *Contemporary Constitutional Lawmaking*. New York: Pergamon Press.

CARTER, LIEF H. 1991. *An Introduction to Constitutional Interpretation: Cases in Law and Religion*. New York: Longman.

CHERMERINSKY, ERWIN. 1987. *Interpreting the Constitution*. New York: Praeger.

CHOPER, JESSE H. 1980. *Judicial Review and the National Political Process*. Chicago: University of Chicago Press.

CORTNER, RICHARD C. 1981. *The Supreme Court and the Second Bill of Rights*. Madison: University of Wisconsin Press.

CROSSKEY, W. W., AND WILLIAM JEFFREY, JR. 1980. *Politics and the Constitution in the History of the United States.* 3 vols. Chicago: University of Chicago Press.

DUXBURY, NEIL. 1995. *Patterns of American Jurisprudence.* Oxford: Clarendon Press, 1995.

DWORKIN, RONALD. 1977. *Taking Rights Seriously.* Cambridge, MA: Harvard University Press.

ELY, JOHN HART. 1980. *Democracy and Distrust: A Theory of Judicial Review.* Cambridge, MA: Harvard University Press.

EPSTEIN, LEE, AND THOMAS G. WALKER. 2000. *Constitutional Law for a Changing America.* 4th ed. Washington, DC: CQ Press.

FINN, JOHN E. 1991. *Constitutions in Crisis: Political Violence and the Rule of Law.* New York: Oxford University Press.

GILLMAN, HOWARD. 1993. *The Constitution Besieged: The Rise and Demise of Lochner Era Police Powers Jurisprudence.* Durham, NC: Duke University Press.

GOLDSTEIN, LESLIE FRIEDMAN. 1991. *In Defense of the Text.* Savage, MD: Rowman & Littlefield.

HARRIS, WILLIAM F., II. 1993. *The Interpretable Constitution.* Baltimore: Johns Hopkins University Press.

HIRSCH, HARRY N. 1992. *A Theory of Liberty: The Constitution and Minorities.* New York: Routledge.

HUTSON, JAMES H. 1986. "The Creation of the Constitution: The Integrity of the Documentary Record." *Texas Law Review* 65: 1.

JACOBSOHN, GARY J. 1986. *The Supreme Court and the Decline of Constitutional Aspiration.* Totowa, NJ: Rowman & Littlefield.

KAHN, RONALD. 1994. *The Supreme Court and Constitutional Theory.* Lawrence: University of Kansas Press.

KRAMER, LARRY D. 2004. The People Themselves: Popular Constitutionalism and Judicial Review. Oxford: Oxford University Press.

LEVINSON, SANFORD V. 1988. *Constitutional Faith.* Princeton, NJ: Princeton University Press.

LUSKY, LOUIS. 1975. *By What Right? A Commentary on the Supreme Court's Power to Revise the Constitution.* Charlottesville, VA: Michie Co.

LYNCH, JOSEPH M. 1999. *Negotiating the Constitution: The Earliest Debates over Original Intent.* Ithaca, NY: Cornell University Press.

MARSHALL, THURGOOD. 1987. "Reflections on the Bicentennial of the United States Constitution." *Harvard Law Review* 101: 1

MASON, ALPHEUS T. 1979. *The Supreme Court from Taft to Burger.* Baton Rouge: Louisiana State University Press.

MCCLOSKEY, ROBERT G. 1960. *The American Supreme Court.* Chicago: University of Chicago Press.

MILLER, CHARLES A. 1969. *The Supreme Court and the Uses of History.* Cambridge, MA: Harvard University Press.

MONAGHAN, HENRY P. 1975. "Foreword: Constitutional Common Law." *Harvard Law Review* 89: 1.

MOORE, WAYNE D. 1996. *Constitutional Rights and Powers of the People.* Princeton, NJ: Princeton University Press.

MURPHY, WALTER F. 1980. "An Ordering of Constitutional Values." *Southern California Law Review* 53: 703.

MURPHY, WALTER F. 1990. "The Right to Privacy and Legitimate Constitutional Change." In *The Constitutional Bases of Political and Social Change in the United States,* Shlomo Slonim, ed. New York: Praeger.

MURPHY, WALTER F. 1992. "Staggering Toward the New Jurisprudence of Constitutional Theory." *American Journal of Jurisprudence* 37: 337.

MURPHY, WALTER F. 1993. "Constitutions, Constitutionalism, and Democracy." In *Constitutionalism and Democracy*, Douglas Greenberg, Stanley N. Katz, Melanie Beth Oliviero, and Steven C. Wheatley, eds. New York: Oxford University Press.

MURPHY, WALTER F., JAMES E. FLEMING, AND SOTIRIOS A. BARBER. 1995. *American Constitutional Interpretation*. 2nd ed. Westbury, NY: Foundation Press.

MURPHY, WALTER F., AND JOSEPH TANENHAUS, EDS. 1977. *Comparative Constitutional Law: Cases and Commentaries*. New York: St. Martin's Press.

NELSON, WILLIAM E. 1986. "History and Neutrality in Constitutional Adjudication." *Virginia Law Review* 72: 1237.

PERRY, MICHAEL J. 1988. *Morality, Politics, and Law*. New York: Oxford University Press.

PORTO, BRIAN L. 1998. *The Craft of Legal Reasoning*. Fort Worth: Harcourt Brace.

POSNER, RICHARD. 1990. *The Problems of Jurisprudence*. Cambridge, MA: Harvard University Press.

POSNER, RICHARD. 2003. Law, Pragmatism, and Democracy. Cambridge, MA: Harvard University Press.

POWELL, JEFFERSON H. 1985. "The Original Understanding of Original Intent." *Harvard Law Review* 98: 885.

REHNQUIST, WILLIAM. 1976. "The Notion of a Living Constitution." *Texas Law Review* 54: 693.

SAGER, LAWRENCE G. 2004. Justice in Plainclothes. New Haven, CT: Yale University Press.

SCHAUER, FREDERICK. 1982. "An Essay on Constitutional Language." *UCLA Law Review* 29: 797.

SCHROCK, THOMAS S., AND ROBERT C. WELSH. 1978. "Reconsidering the Constitutional Common Law." *Harvard Law Review* 91: 1117.

THAYER, JAMES BRADLEY. 1893. "The Origin and Scope of the American Doctrine of Constitutional Law." *Harvard Law Review* 7: 129.

TRIBE, LAURENCE H. 1985. *Constitutional Choices*. Cambridge, MA: Harvard University Press.

TRIBE, LAURENCE H., AND MICHAEL C. DORF. 1991. *On Reading the Constitution*. Cambridge, MA: Harvard University Press.

TUSHNET, MARK. 2003. The New Constitutional Order. Princeton, NJ: Princeton University Press.

WECHSLER, HERBERT. 1959. "Toward Neutral Principles of Constitutional Law." *Harvard Law Review* 43: 1.

WELLINGTON, HARRY H. 1990. *Interpreting the Constitution: The Supreme Court and the Process of Adjudication*. New Haven, CT: Yale University Press.

WHITTINGTON, KEITH E. 1999. *Constitutional Interpretation: Textual Meaning, Original Intent, and Judicial Review*. Lawrence: University Press of Kansas.

*". . . this presumptive must be considered in light of our historic
commitment to the rule of law."*

12.1 UNITED STATES V. NIXON

418 U.S. 683 (1974)

*This case was one of many judicial actions the Watergate scandal spawned. The contro-
versy began on June 17, 1972, when seven men broke into the Democratic National
Committee headquarters located in the Watergate complex in Washington, D.C. The
seven were apprehended and charged with criminal offenses. All had ties either to the
White House or to the Committee to Re-elect the President. Five of the seven pleaded
guilty, and the other two were convicted. At the end of the trial, one of the defendants,
James McCord, Jr., claimed that he had been pressured to plead guilty and that there
were others involved in the break-in who had not been prosecuted. It was clear to many
observers that the break-in was only the tip of a very large iceberg of shady dealings and
cover-ups engaged in by influential persons closely tied to the Nixon administration.*

*In response to these events, the Senate began an investigation. The star witness was
John Dean III, Special Counsel to the President, who testified under a grant of immunity.
He implicated high officials in the president's office and claimed that even Nixon had
known about the burglary and subsequent cover-ups. As surprising as this testimony
was, Alexander Butterfield, another of Nixon's aides, made the most shocking revelation:
the president had installed a secret taping system that automatically recorded all conversations in the Oval Office. Obviously, these tapes held information that would settle the
dispute between witnesses claiming the White House was deeply involved in the
Watergate affair and those officials who were denying the administration's involvement.*

*In addition to the Senate's investigation, a special prosecutor was appointed to look
into the Watergate affair. The first person to hold this position, Archibald Cox, asked
Nixon to turn over the tapes. When he refused, Cox went to court to get an order compelling the president to deliver the materials. The district court as well as the Court of
Appeals for the District of Columbia ruled in favor of the prosecutor. Nixon then offered
to release summaries of the recordings, but that did not satisfy Cox, who continued to
demand the complete tapes. In response, Nixon ordered Cox fired. When the two highest officials in the Department of Justice resigned rather than comply with the order,
Solicitor General (later Judge) Robert H. Bork became the acting attorney general and
dismissed Cox. (Bork had planned to resign as well, but the other two officials persuaded
him to stay on so that someone with professional integrity would be running the
Department.) The firing of the prosecutor and the resignation of the other officials, popularly known as the "Saturday Night Massacre," enraged public officials from both parties as well as many journalists and a large segment of the American people. Calls for
impeachment echoed around Washington and the rest of the country.*

*A new special prosecutor, Leon Jaworski, was appointed. He pursued the tapes with
the same zeal as had Cox. Finally, Nixon relented and agreed to produce some of the materials. But when he did so, the prosecutor found that the tapes had been heavily edited.*

One contained eighteen and one-half minutes of mysterious buzzing at a crucial point, indicating that conversation had been erased.

Jaworski obtained criminal indictments against several of Nixon's aides. Although no criminal charges were brought against the president, a grand jury named him an "unindicted co-conspirator." At about the same time, the House Committee on the Judiciary began its own investigation into whether the president should be impeached. And both that committee and Jaworski sought more of the tapes to review. Nixon steadfastly refused to comply, claiming that executive privilege allowed him and him alone to decide what would be released and what would remain secret. The district court issued a final subpoena duces tecum, an order to produce the tapes and other documents. Both the United States and Nixon requested that the Supreme Court review the case, and the justices accepted the case on an expedited basis, bypassing the court of appeals.

CHIEF JUSTICE BURGER delivered the opinion of the Court. . . .

IV

A

. . . [W]e turn to the claim that the subpoena should be quashed because it demands "confidential conversations between a President and his close advisors that it would be inconsistent with the public interest to produce." The first contention is a broad claim that the separation of powers doctrine precludes judicial review of a President's claim of privilege. The second contention is that if he does not prevail on the claim of absolute privilege, the court should hold as a matter of constitutional law that the privilege prevails over the subpoena duces tecum.

In the performance of assigned constitutional duties each branch of the Government must initially interpret the Constitution, and the interpretation of its powers by any branch is due great respect from the others. The President's counsel, as we have noted, reads the Constitution as providing an absolute privilege of confidentiality for all presidential communications. Many decisions of this Court, however, have unequivocally reaffirmed the holding of *Marbury v. Madison* (1803) that "it is emphatically the province and duty of the judicial department to say what the law is."

No holding of the Court has defined the scope of judicial power specifically relating to the enforcement of a subpoena for confidential presidential communications for use in a criminal prosecution, but other exercises of powers by the Executive Branch and the Legislative Branch have been found invalid as in conflict with the Constitution. *Powell v. McCormack* (1969); *Youngstown Sheet & Tube Co. v. Sawyer* (1952). In a series of cases, the Court interpreted the explicit immunity conferred by express provisions of the Constitution on Members of the House and Senate by the Speech or Debate Clause, U.S. Const. Art. I, § 6. . . . Since this Court has consistently exercised the power to construe and delineate claims arising under express powers, it must follow that the Court has authority to interpret claims with respect to powers alleged to derive from enumerated powers.

Our system of government "requires that federal courts on occasion interpret the Constitution in a manner at variance with the construction given the document by another branch." *Powell v. McCormack*. And in *Baker v. Carr* the Court stated: "Deciding whether a matter has in any measure been committed by the Constitution to another branch of government, or whether the action of that branch exceeds whatever authority has been committed, is itself a delicate exercise in constitutional interpretation, and is a responsibility of this Court as ultimate interpreter of the Constitution."

Notwithstanding the deference each branch must accord the others, the "judicial power of the United States" vested in the federal courts by Art. III, § 1 of the Constitution can no more be shared with the Executive Branch than the Chief Executive, for example, can share with the Judiciary the veto power, or the Congress share with the Judiciary the power to override a presidential veto. Any other conclusion would be contrary to the basic concept of separation of powers and the checks and balances that flow from the scheme of a tripartite government. *The Federalist*, No.47. We therefore reaffirm that it is "emphatically the province and the duty" of this Court "to say what the law is" with respect to the claim of *Marbury v. Madison*.

B

In support of his claim of absolute privilege, the president's counsel urges two grounds, one of which is common to all governments and one of which is peculiar to our system of separation of powers. The first ground is the valid need for protection of communications between high government officials and those who advise and assist them in the performance of their manifold duties; the importance of this confidentiality is too plain to require further discussion. Human experience teaches that those who expect public dissemination of their remarks may well temper candor with a concern for appearances and for their own interests to the detriment of the decision-making process. Whatever [is] the nature of the privilege of confidentiality of presidential communications in the exercise of Art. II powers, the privilege can be said to derive from the supremacy of each branch within its own assigned area of constitutional duties. Certain powers and privileges flow from the nature of enumerated powers; the protection of the confidentiality of presidential communications has similar constitutional underpinnings.

The second ground asserted by the President's counsel in support of the claim of absolute privilege rests on the doctrine of separation of powers. Here it is argued that the independence of the Executive Branch within its own sphere . . . insulates a president from a judicial subpoena in an ongoing criminal prosecution, and thereby protects confidential presidential communications.

However, neither the doctrine of separation of powers nor the need for confidentiality of high-level communications, without more, can sustain an absolute, unqualified presidential privilege of immunity from judicial process under all circumstances. The President's need for complete candor and objectivity from advisers calls for great deference from the courts. However, when the privilege depends solely on the broad, undifferentiated claim of public interest in the confidentiality of such conversations, a confrontation with other values arises. Absent a claim of need to protect military, diplomatic or sensitive national security secrets, we find it difficult to accept the argument that even the very important interest in confidentiality of presidential communications is significantly diminished by production of such material for in-camera inspection with all the protection that a district court will be obliged to provide.

The impediment that an absolute, unqualified privilege would place in the way of the primary constitutional duty of the Judicial Branch to do justice in criminal prosecutions would plainly conflict with the function of the courts under Art. III. In designing the structure of our Government and dividing and allocating the sovereign power among three coequal branches, the Framers of the Constitution sought to provide a comprehensive system, but the separate powers were not intended to operate with absolute independence. . . . To read the Art. II powers of the President as providing an absolute privilege as against a subpoena essential to enforcement of criminal statutes on no more than a generalized claim of the public interest in confidentiality of nonmilitary and nondiplomatic discussions would upset the constitutional balance of "a workable government" and gravely impair the role of the courts under Art. III.

C

Since we conclude that the legitimate needs of the judicial process may outweigh presidential privilege, it is necessary to resolve those competing interests in a manner that preserves the essential functions of each branch. The right and indeed the duty to resolve that question does not free the judiciary from according high respect to the representations made on behalf of the President. *United States v. Burr* (1807).

The expectation of a President to the confidentiality of his conversations and correspondence, like the claim of confidentiality of judicial deliberations, for example, has all the values to which we accord deference for the privacy of all citizens and added to those values the necessity for protection of the public interest in candid, objective, and even blunt or harsh opinions in presidential decision making. A President and those who assist him must be free to explore alternatives in the process of shaping policies and making decisions and to do so in a way many would be unwilling to express except privately. These are the considerations justifying a presumptive privilege for presidential communications. The privilege is fundamental to the operation of government and inextricably rooted in the separation of powers under the Constitution. In *Nixon v. Sirica* (1973), the Court of Appeals held that such presidential communications are "presumptively privileged," and this position is accepted by both parties in the present litigation. We agree with Mr. Chief Justice Marshall's observation, therefore, that: "in no case of this kind would a court be required to proceed against the President as against an ordinary individual." *United States v. Burr.*

But this presumptive privilege must be considered in light of our historic commitment to the rule of law. This is nowhere more profoundly manifest than in our view that "the twofold aim [of criminal justice] is that guilt shall not escape or innocence suffer." *Berger v. United States* (1935). We have elected to employ an adversary system of criminal justice in which the parties contest all issues before a court of law. The need to develop all relevant facts in the adversary system is both fundamental and comprehensive. The ends of criminal justice would be defeated if judgments were to be founded on a partial or speculative presentation of the facts. The very integrity of the judicial system and public confidence in the system depend on full disclosure of all the facts, within the framework of the rules of evidence. To insure that justice is done, it is imperative to the function of courts that compulsory process be available for the production of evidence needed either by the prosecution or by the defense.

Only recently the Court restated the ancient proposition of law, albeit in the context of a grand jury inquiry rather than a trial,

> "that the public . . . has a right to every man's evidence" except for those persons protected by a constitutional, common law, or statutory privilege. *United States v. Bryan (1950).*

The privileges referred to by the Court are designed to protect weighty and legitimate competing interests. Thus, the Fifth Amendment to the Constitution provides that no man "shall be compelled in any criminal case to be a witness against himself." And, generally, an attorney or a priest may not be required to disclose what has been revealed in professional confidence. These and other interests are recognized in law by privileges against forced disclosure, established in the Constitution, by statute, or at common law. Whatever their origins, these exceptions to the demand for every man's evidence are [neither] lightly created nor expansively construed, for they are in derogation of the search for truth.

In this case the President challenges a subpoena served on him as a third party requiring the production of materials for use in a criminal prosecution on the claim that he has a privilege against disclosure of confidential communications. He does not place his claim of privilege on the ground they are military or diplomatic secrets. As to these areas of Art. II duties the courts have traditionally shown the utmost deference to presidential responsibilities. . . . No case of the Court, however, has extended this high degree of deference to a President's generalized interest in confidentiality. Nowhere in the Constitution, as we have noted earlier, is there any explicit reference to a privilege of confidentiality, yet to the extent this interest relates to the effective discharge of a President's powers, it is constitutionally based.

The right to the production of all evidence at a criminal trial similarly has constitutional dimensions. The Sixth Amendment explicitly confers upon every defendant in a criminal trial the right "to be confronted with the witnesses against him" and "to have compulsory process for obtaining witnesses in his favor." Moreover, the Fifth Amendment also guarantees that no person shall be deprived of liberty without due process of law. It is the manifest duty of the courts to vindicate those guarantees and to accomplish that it is essential that all relevant and admissible evidence be produced.

In this case we must weigh the importance of the general privilege of confidentiality of presidential communications in performance of his responsibilities against the inroads of such a privilege on the fair administration of criminal justice. The interest in preserving confidentiality is weighty indeed and entitled to great respect. However we cannot conclude that advisers will be moved to temper the candor of their remarks by the infrequent occasions of disclosure because of the possibility that such conversations will be called for in the context of a criminal prosecution.

On the other hand, the allowance of the privilege to withhold evidence that is demonstrably relevant in a criminal trial would cut deeply into the guarantee of due process of law and gravely impair the basic function of the courts. A President's acknowledged need for confidentiality in the communications of his office is general in nature, whereas the constitutional need for production of relevant evidence in a criminal proceeding is specific and central to the fair adjudication of a particular criminal case in the administration of justice. Without access to specific facts a criminal prosecution may be totally frustrated. The President's broad interest in confidentiality of communications will not be vitiated by disclosure of a limited number of conversations preliminarily shown to have some bearing on the pending criminal cases.

We conclude that when the ground for asserting privilege as to subpoenaed materials sought for use in a criminal trial is based only on the generalized interest in confidentiality, it cannot prevail over the fundamental demands of due process of law in the fair administration of criminal justice. The generalized assertion of privilege must yield to the demonstrated, specific need for evidence in a pending criminal trial. . . .

E

. . . Since this matter came before the Court during the pendency of a criminal prosecution, and on representations that time is of the essence, the mandate shall issue forthwith.

Affirmed.

MR. JUSTICE REHNQUIST took no part in the consideration or decision of these cases.

> *"If the Constitution were . . . a novel invitation to apply current societal values, what reason would there be to believe that the invitation was addressed to the courts rather that to the legislature?"*

12.2 ORIGINALISM: THE LESSER EVIL

Antonin Scalia

Antonin Scalia has been an Associate Justice on the U.S. Supreme Court since 1986.

From Antonin Scalia's "Originalism:The Lesser Evil" 57 *University of Cincinnati Law Review* 849, in Walter F. Murphy, et al. 2003. *American Constitutional Interpretation.* 3rd ed. New York: Foundation Press, p. 243–248.

. . . It may surprise the layman . . . to learn that originalism is not, and had perhaps never been, the sole method of constitutional exegesis. It would be hard to count on the finders of both hands and the toes of both feet, yes, even on the hairs of one's youthful head, the opinions that have in fact been rendered not on the basis of what the Constitution originally meant, but on the basis of what the judges currently thought it desirable for it to mean. . . . But in the past, nonoriginalist opinions have almost always had the decency to lie, or at least to dissemble, about what they were doing—either ignoring strong evidence of an original intent congenial to the court's desires, or else not discussing original intent at all, speaking in terms of broad constitutional generalities with no pretense of historical support. . . . It is only in relatively recent years . . . that nonoriginalist exegesis has . . . come out of the closet, and put itself forward overtly as an intellectually legitimate device. To be sure, in support of its venerability as a legitimate interpretive theory there is often trotted out John Marshall's statement in *McCulloch v. Maryland* [1819] that "we must never forget it is a constitution we are expounding "—as though the implication of that statement was that our interpretation must change from age to age. But that is a canard. The real implication was quite the opposite: Marshall was saying that the Constitution had to be interpreted generously because the powers conferred upon Congress under it had to be broad enough to serve not only the needs of the federal government originally discerned but also the needs that might arise in the future. If constitutional interpretation could be adjusted as changing circumstances required, a broad initial interpretation would have been unnecessary. . . .

The principal theoretical defect of nonoriginalism . . . is its incompatibility with the very principal that legitimizes judicial review of constitutionality. Nothing in the text of the Constitution confers upon the courts the power to inquire into, rather than passively assume, the constitutionality of federal statutes. That power is, however, reasonably implicit because, as Marshall said in *Marbury v. Madison*, (1) "[i]t is emphatically the province and duty of the judicial department to say what the law is," (2) "[i]f two laws conflict with each other, the courts must decide on the operation of each," and (3) "the constitution is to be considered, in court, as a paramount law." Central to that analysis, it seems to me, is the perception that the Constitution, though it has an effect superior to other laws, is in its nature the sort of "law" that is the business of the courts—an enactment that has a fixed meaning ascertainable through the usual devices familiar to those learned in the law.

If the Constitution were not that sort of a "law," but a novel invitation to apply current societal values, what reason would there be to believe that the invitation was addressed to the courts rather that to the legislature? One simply cannot say, regarding that sort of novel enactment, that "[i]t is emphatically the province and duty of the judicial department" to determine its content. Quite to the contrary, the legislature would seem a much more appropriate expositor of social values, and its determination that a statute is compatible with the Constitution should, and in England, prevail.

Apart from the frailty of its theoretical underpinning, nonoriginalism confronts a practical difficulty reminiscent of the truism of elective politics that "You can't beat somebody with nobody." It is not enough to demonstrate that the other fellow's candidate (originalism) is no good: one must also agree upon another candidate to replace him. . . . If the law is to make any attempt at consistency and predictability, surely there must be general agreement not only that judges reject one exegetical approach (originalism) but that they adopt another. And it is hard to discern any emerging consensus among the nonoriginalists as to what this might be. Are the "fundamental values " that replace original meaning to be derived from the philosophy of Plato, or of Locke, or [John Stuart] Mill, of [John] Rawls , or perhaps from the latest Gallup poll? This is not to say that originalists are in entire agreement as to what the nature of their methodology is. . . . but as its name suggests, it by and large represents a coherent approach, or at least an agreed-upon point of departure. As the name "nonoriginalism" suggests (and I know no other, more precise term by which this school of exegesis can be described), it represents agreement on nothing except what is the wrong approach.

Finally, I want to mention what is not a defect of nonoriginalism but one of its supposed benefits that seems to me illusory. . . . [O]ne of the most prominent nonoriginalists, Professor [Lawrence] Tribe . . . [wrote] that the Constitution "incites us, and our judges, to expand on the . . . freedoms that are uniquely our heritage." I think it fair to say that that is a common theme of nonoriginalists in general. Bur why, one may reasonably ask—once the original import of the Constitution is cast aside to be replaced by the "fundamental values" of the current society—why are we invited only to "expand on" freedoms, and not to contract them as well? . . . Nonoriginalism, in other words is a two-way street that handles traffic both to and from individual rights.

Let me turn next to originalism, which is also not without its wars. Its greatest defect, in my view, is the difficulty of applying it correctly. Not that I agree with, or even take very seriously, the intricately elaborated scholarly criticisms to the effect that (believe it or not) words have no meaning. They have meaning enough, as the scholarly critics themselves must surely believe when they choose to express their views in text rather than music. But what is true is that it is often exceedingly difficult to plumb the original understanding of an ancient text. Properly done, the task requires the consideration of an enormous mass of material—in the case of the Constitution and its Amendments, for example . . . the records of the ratifying debates in all the states. Even beyond that, it requires an evaluation of the reliability of that material—many of the reports of the ratifying debates, for example, are thought to be quite unreliable. And further still, it requires immersing oneself in the political and intellectual atmosphere of the time—somehow placing out of mind knowledge that we have which an earlier age did not, and putting on beliefs, attitudes, philosophies, prejudices and loyalties that are not those of our day. It is, in short, a task sometimes better suited to the historian that the lawyer. . . .

[T]he second most serious objection to originalism: In its undiluted form, at least, it is medicine that seems too strong to swallow. Thus, almost every originalist would adulterate it with the doctrine of stare decisis—so that *Marbury v. Madison* would stand even if Professor Raoul Berger should demonstrate unassailably that it got their meaning of the Constitution wrong. (Of course recognizing stare decisis is seemingly even more incompatible with nonoriginalist theory: if the most solemnly and democratically adopted text of the Constitution and its Amendments can be ignored on the basis of current values, what possible basis could there be of enforced adherence to a legal decision of the Supreme Court?) But stare decisis alone is not enough to prevent originalism from being what many would consider too bitter a pill. What if some state should enact a new law providing public lashing, or branding of the right hand, as punishment for certain criminal offenses? Even if it could be demonstrated unequivocally that these were not cruel and unusual measures in 1791, and even though no prior Supreme Court decision has specifically disapproved them, I doubt whether any federal judge—even among the many who consider themselves originalists—would sustain them against an eighth amendment challenge. . . . [A]ny espousal of originalism as a practical theory of exegesis must somehow come to terms with that reality.

One way of doing so, of course, would be to say that it was originally intended that the cruel and unusual punishment clause would have an evolving content—that "cruel and unusual" originally meant "cruel and unusual for the age in question" and not "cruel and unusual in 1791." But to be faithful to originalist philosophy, one must not only say this but demonstrate it to be so on the basis of some textual or historical evidence. Perhaps the mere words "cruel and unusual" suggest an evolutionary intent more than other provisions of the Constitution, but that is far from clear; and I know of no historical evidence for that meaning. And if the faint-hearted originalist is willing simply to posit such an intent for the "cruel and unusual punishment" clause, the privileges and immunity clause, etc.? When one goes down, there is really no difference between the faint-hearted originalist and the moderate nonoriginalist, except that the former finds it comforting to make up (out of whole cloth) an original evolutionary intent, and the latter thinks that superfluous. It is, I think, the fact that most originalists are faint-hearted and most nonoriginalists are moderate (that is, would not ascribe evolving content to such clear provisions as the requirement that the President be no less than thirty-five years of age) which accounts for the fact that the sharp divergence between the two philosophies does not produce an equivalently sharp divergence in judicial opinions.

Having described what I consider the principal difficulties with the originalist and nonoriginalist approaches . . . I owe it to the listener to say which of the two evils I prefer. It is originalism. I take the need for theoretical legitimacy seriously, and even if one assumes (as many nonoriginalists do not even bother to do) that the Constitution was originally meant to expound evolving rather that permanent values[,] . . . I see no basis for believing that supervision of the evolution would have been committed to the courts. At an even more general theoretical level originalism seems to me more compatible with the nature and purpose of a Constitution in a democratic system. A democratic society does not, by and large, need constitutional guarantees—and in particular those constitutional guarantees of individual rights . . .—is precisely to prevent the law from reflecting certain changes in original values that the society adopting the Constitution thins fundamentally undesirable. Or, more precisely, to require the society to devote to the subject the long and hard consideration required for a constitutional amendment before those particular values can be cast aside.

I also think that the central practical defect of nonoriginalism is fundamental and irreparable: the impossibility of achieving any consensus on what, precisely is to replace original meaning, once that is abandoned. The practical defects of originalism, on the other hand, while genuine enough, seem to me less severe. While it may indeed be unrealistic to have substantial confidence that judges and lawyers will find the correct historical answer to such refined questions of original intent as the precise content of "the executive Power" for the cast majority of questions the answer is clear. The death penalty, for example, was not cruel and unusual punishment because it is referred to in the Constitution itself; and the right of confrontation by its plain language meant, at least, being face-to-face with the person testifying against one at trial. For the nonoriginalist, even these are open questions.

As for the fact that originalism is strong medicine, and that one cannot realistically expect judges (probably myself included) to apply it without a trace of constitutional perfectionism," I suppose I must respond that this is a world in which nothing is flawless and fall back upon G. K. Chesterton's observation that a thing worth doing is worth doing badly. It seems to me, moreover, that the practical defects of originalism are defects more appropriate for the task at hand—that is, less likely to aggravate the most significant weakness of the system of judicial review and more likely to produce results acceptable to all. . . .

Now the main dander in judicial interpretation to the Constitution—or, for that matter, in judicial interpretation of any law—is that the judges will mistake their own predilections for the law. Avoiding this error is the hardest part of being a conscientious judge: perhaps no conscientious judge ever succeeds entirely. Nonoriginalism, which under one or another formulation invokes "fundamental values" as the touchstone of constitutionality, plays precisely to this weakness. It is very difficult for a person to discern a difference between those political values that he personally thinks most important and those political values that are "fundamental to our society." Thus, by the adoption of such a criterion judicial personalization of the law is enormously facilitated. (One might reduce this danger by insisting that the new "fundamental values" invoked to replace original meaning be clearly and objectively manifested in the laws of the society. But among all the varying tests suggested by nonoriginalist theoreticians, I am unaware that that one ever appears. Most if not all nonoriginalists, for example, would strike down the death penalty, though it continues to be widely adopted in both state and federal legislation.)

Originalism does not aggravate the principal weakness of the system, for it establishes a historical criterion that is conceptually quite separate form the preferences of the judge himself. And the principal defect of that approach—that historical research is always difficult and sometimes inconclusive—will, unlike nonoriginalism, lead to a more moderate rather than a more extreme result. The inevitable tendency of judges to think that the law is what they would like it to be will, I have no doubt, cause most errors in judicial historiography to be made in the direction of projecting upon the age of 1789 current, modern values—so that as applies, even as applies in the best of faith, originalism will (as the historical record shows) end up as something of a compromise. Perhaps not a bad characteristic for a constitutional theory. . . .

Having made that endorsement, I hasten to confess that in a crunch I may prove a faint-hearted originalist. I cannot imagine myself, any more than any other federal judge, upholding a statute that imposes the punishment of flogging. But then I cannot imagine such a case's arising either. In any event, in deciding the cases before me I expect I will rarely be confronted with making the stark choice between giving evolutionary content (not yet required by stare decisis) and not giving evolutionary content to particular constitutional provisions. The vast majority of my dissents from nonoriginalist thinking (and I hope at least some of those dissents will be majorities) will, I am sure, be able to be framed in the terms that, even if the provision in question has an evolutionary content, there is inadequate indication that any evolution in social attitudes has occurred. That . . . is the real dispute that appears in the case: not between nonoriginalists on the one hand and pure originalists on the other, concerning the validity of looking at all to current values but rather between, on the one hand, nonoriginalists, faint-hearted originalists, and pure-originalists-accepting-for-the-sake-of-argument-evolutionary-content and, on the other hand, other adherents of the same three approaches, concerning the nature and degree of evidence necessary to demonstrate that constitutional evolution has occurred.

I am left with a sense of dissatisfaction, as I am sure you are, that a discourse concerning what one would suppose to be a rather fundamental—indeed, the most fundamental—aspect of constitutional theory and practice should end so inconclusively. But it should come as no surprise. We do not yet have an agreed-upon theory for interpreting statutes, either. I find it perhaps too laudatory to say that this is the genius of the common law system; but it is at least its nature.

"If the Constitution is law, then presumably its meaning, like that of all other law, is the meaning the lawmakers were understood to have intended."

12.3 THE TEMPTING OF AMERICA

Robert H. Bork

Robert H. Bork, formerly a judge on the U.S. Court of Appeals for the District of Columbia and defeated nominee for the Supreme Court, is John M. Olin Scholar in Legal Studies at the American Enterprise Institute.

What was once the dominant view of constitutional law—that a judge is to apply the Constitution according to the principles intended by those who ratified the document—is now very much out of favor among the theorists of the field.

From Robert H. Bork, *The Tempting of America* (New York: Free Press, 1990), pp. 143–153.

In the legal academies in particular, the philosophy of original understanding is usually viewed as thoroughly passè, probably reactionary, and certainly—the most dreaded indictment of all—"outside the mainstream." That fact says more about the lamentable state of the intellectual life of the law, however, than it does about the merits of the theory.

In truth, only the approach of original understanding meets the criteria that any theory of constitutional adjudication must meet in order to possess democratic legitimacy. Only that approach is consonant with the design of the American Republic.

The Constitution as Law: Neutral Principles

When we speak of "law," we ordinarily refer to a rule that we have no right to change except through prescribed procedures. That statement assumes that the rule has a meaning independent of our own desires. Otherwise there would be no need to agree on procedures for changing the rule. Statutes, we agree, may be changed by amendment or repeal. The Constitution may be changed by amendment pursuant to the procedures set out in Article V. It is a necessary implication of the prescribed procedures that neither statute nor Constitution should be changed by judges. Though that has been done often enough, it is in no sense proper.

What is the meaning of a rule that judges should not change? It is the meaning understood at the time of the law's enactment. Though I have written of the understanding of the ratifiers of the Constitution, since they enacted it and made it law, that is actually a shorthand formulation, because what the ratifiers understood themselves to be enacting must be taken to be what the public of that time would have understood the words to mean. It is important to be clear about this. The search is not for a subjective intention. If someone found a letter from George Washington to Martha telling her that what he meant by the power to lay taxes was not what other people meant, that would not change our reading of the Constitution in the slightest. Nor would the subjective intentions of all the members of a ratifying convention alter anything. When lawmakers use words, the law that results is what those words ordinarily mean. If Congress enacted a statute outlawing the sale of automatic rifles and did so in the Senate by a vote of 51 to 49, no court would overturn a conviction because two senators in the majority testified that they really had intended only to prohibit the use of such rifles. They said "sale," and "sale" it is. Thus, the common objection to the philosophy of original understanding—that Madison kept his notes of the convention at Philadelphia secret for many years—is off the mark. He knew that what mattered was public understanding, not subjective intentions. Madison himself said that what mattered was the intention of the ratifying conventions. His notes of the discussions at Philadelphia are merely evidence of what informed public men of the time thought the words of the Constitution meant. Since many of them were also delegates to the various state ratifying conventions, their understanding informed the debates in those conventions. As Professor Henry Monaghan of Columbia has said, what counts is what the public understood. Law is a public act. Secret reservations or intentions count for nothing. All that counts is how the words used in the Constitution would have been understood at the time. The original understanding is thus manifested in the words used and in secondary materials, such as debates at the conventions, public discussion, newspaper articles, dictionaries in use at the time, and the like. Almost no one would deny this; in fact almost everyone would find it obvious to the point of thinking it fatuous to state the matter—except in the case of the Constitution. Why our legal theorists make an exception for the Constitution is worth exploring.

The search for the intent of the lawmaker is the everyday procedure of lawyers and judges when they must apply a statute, a contract, a will, or the opinion of a court. To be sure, there are differences in the way we deal with different legal materials, which was the point of John Marshall's observation in *McCulloch v. Maryland* that "we must never forget, that it is a constitution we are expounding." By that he meant that narrow, legalistic reasoning was not to be applied to the document's broad provisions, a document that could not, by its nature and uses, "partake of the prolixity of a legal code." But he also wrote there that it was intended that a provision receive a "fair and just interpretation," which means that the judge is to interpret what is in the text and not something else. And, it will be recalled, in *Marbury v. Madison* Marshall placed the judge's power to invalidate a legislative act upon the fact that the judge was applying the words of a written document. Thus, questions of breadth of approach or of room for play in the joints aside, lawyers and judges should seek in the Constitution what they seek in other legal texts: the original meaning of the words.

We would at once criticize a judge who undertook to rewrite a statute or the opinion of a superior court, and yet such judicial rewriting is often correctable by the legislature or the superior court, as the Supreme Court's rewriting of the Constitution is not. At first glance, it seems distinctly peculiar that there should be a great many academic theorists who explicitly defend departures from the understanding of those who ratified the Constitution while agreeing, at least in principle, that there should be no departure from the understanding of those who enacted a statute or joined a majority opinion. A moment's reflection suggests, however, that Supreme Court departures from the original meaning of the Constitution are advocated precisely because those departures are not correctable democratically. The point of the academic exercise is to be free of democracy in order to impose the values of an elite upon the rest of us.

If the Constitution is law, then presumably its meaning, like that of all other law, is the meaning the lawmakers were understood to have intended. If the Constitution is law, then presumably, like all other law, the meaning the lawmakers intended is as binding upon judges as it is upon legislatures and executives. There is no other sense in which the Constitution can be what article VI proclaims it to be: "Law." It is here that the concept of neutral principles, which [Herbert] Wechsler said were essential if the Supreme Court was not to be a naked power organ, comes into play. Wechsler . . . , in expressing his difficulties with the decision in *Brown v. Board of Education*, said that courts must choose principles which they are willing to apply neutrally, apply, that is, to all cases that may fairly be said to fall within them. This is a safeguard against political judging. No judge will say openly that any particular group or political position is always entitled to win. He will announce a principle that decides the case at hand, and Wechsler had no difficulty with that if the judge is willing to apply the same principle in the next case, even if it means that a group favored by the first decision is disfavored by the second. . . .

The Court cannot, however, avoid being a naked power organ merely by practicing the neutral application of legal principle. The Court can act as a legal rather than a political institution only if it is neutral as well in the way it derives and defines the principles it applies. If the Court is free to choose any principle that it will subsequently apply neutrally, it is free to legislate just as a political body would. Similarly, if the Court is free to define the scope of the principle as it sees fit, it may, by manipulating the principle's breadth, make things come out the way it wishes on grounds that are not contained in the principle it purports to apply . . . but only according to the personal preferences of the Justices. The philosophy of original understanding is capable of supplying neutrality in all three respects—in deriving, defining, and applying principle.

Neutrality in the Derivation of Principle

When a judge finds his principle in the Constitution as originally understood, the problem of the neutral derivation of principle is solved. The judge accepts the ratifiers' definition of the appropriate ranges of majority and minority freedom. . . . He need not, and must not, make unguided value judgments of his own.

This means, of course, that a judge, no matter on what court he sits, may never create new constitutional rights or destroy old ones. Any time he does so, he violates not only the limits to his own authority but, and for that reason, also violates the rights of the legislature and the people. To put the matter another way, suppose that the United States, like the United Kingdom, had no written constitution and, therefore, no law to apply to strike down acts of the legislature. The U.S. judge, like the U.K. judge, could never properly invalidate a statute or an official action as unconstitutional. The very concept of unconstitutionality would be meaningless. The absence of a constitutional provision means the absence of a power of judicial review. But when a U.S. judge is given a set of constitutional provisions, then, as to anything not covered by those provisions, he is in the same position as the U.K. judge. He has no law to apply and is, quite properly, powerless. In the absence of law, a judge is a functionary without a function.

This is not to say, of course, that majorities may not add to minority freedoms by statute, and indeed a great deal of the legislation that comes out of Congress and the state legislatures does just that. The only thing majorities may not do is invade the liberties the Constitution specifies. In this sense, the concept of original understanding builds in a bias toward individual freedom. Thus, the Supreme Court properly decided in *Brown* that the equal protection clause of the Fourteenth Amendment forbids racial segregation or discrimination by any arm of government, but, because the Constitution addresses only governmental action, the Court could not address the question of private discrimination. Congress did address it in the Civil Rights Act of 1964 and in subsequent legislation, enlarging minority freedoms beyond those mandated by the Constitution.

Neutrality in the Definition of Principle

The neutral definition of the principle derived from the historic Constitution is also crucial. The Constitution states its principles in majestic generalities that, we know cannot be taken as sweepingly as the words alone might suggest. The first amendment states that "Congress shall make no law . . . abridging the freedom of speech," but no one has ever supposed that Congress could not make some speech unlawful or that it could not make all speech illegal in certain places, at certain times, and under certain circumstances. . . .

But the question of neutral definition remains and is obviously closely related to neutral application. Neutral application can be gained by defining a principle so narrowly that it will fit only a few cases. Thus, [in] Griswold,[1] we can make neutral application possible by stating the principle to be that government may not prohibit the use of contraceptives by married couples. But that tactic raises doubts as to the definition of the principle. Why does it extend only to married couples? Why, out of all forms of sexual behavior, only to the use of contraceptives? Why, out of all forms of behavior in the home, only to sex? There may be answers, but if there are, they must be given.

Thus, once a principle is derived from the Constitution, its breadth or the level of generality at which it is stated becomes of crucial importance. The judge must not state the principle with so much generality that he transforms it. The difficulty in finding the proper level of generality has led some critics to claim that the application of the original understanding is actually impossible. That sounds fairly abstract, but an example will make clear both the point and the answer to it.

In speaking of my view that the fourteenth amendment's equal protection clause requires black equality, Dean Paul Brest said:

> The very adoption of such a principle, however, demands an arbitrary choice, among levels of abstraction. Just what is "the general principle of equality that applies to all cases"? Is it the "core idea of black equality" that Bork finds in the original understanding (in which case Alan Bakke [a white who sued because a state medical school gave preference in admissions to other races] did not state a constitutionally cognizable claim), or a broader principle of "racial equality" (so that, depending on the precise content of the principle, Bakke might have a case after all), or is it a still broader principle of equality that encompasses discrimination on the basis of gender (or sexual orientation) as well? . . .
>
> . . . The fact is that all adjudication requires making choices among the levels of generality on which to articulate principles, and all such choices are inherently nonneutral. No form of constitutional decision making can be salvaged if its legitimacy depends on satisfying Bork's requirements that principles be "neutrally derived, defined, and applied."

---

[1]*See the text for a description of Griswold. —Eds.*

If Brest's point about the impossibility of choosing the level of generality upon neutral criteria is correct, we must either resign ourselves to a Court that is a "naked power organ" or require the Court to stop making "constitutional" decisions. But Brest's argument seems to me wrong, and I think a judge committed to original understanding can do what Brest says he cannot. We may use Brest's example to demonstrate the point.

The role of a judge committed to the philosophy of original understanding is not to "choose a level of abstraction." Rather, it is to find the meaning of a text—a process which includes finding its degree of generality, which is part of its meaning—and to apply that text to a particular situation, which may be difficult if its meaning is unclear. With many if not most textual provisions, the level of generality which is part of their meaning is readily apparent. The problem is most difficult when dealing with the broadly stated provisions of the Bill of Rights. . . . In dealing with such provisions, a judge should state the principle at the level of generality that the text and historical evidence warrant. The equal protection clause was adopted in order to protect the freed slaves, but its language, being general, applies to all persons. As we might expect, and as Justice Miller found in the *SlaughterHouse* Cases, the evidence of what the drafters, the Congress that proposed the clause, and the ratifiers understood themselves to be requiring is clearest in the case of race relations. It is there that we may begin in looking for evidence of the level of generality intended. Without meaning to suggest what the historical evidence in fact shows, let us assume we find that the ratifiers intended to guarantee that blacks should be treated by law no worse than whites, but that it is unclear whether whites were intended to be protected from discrimination in favor of blacks. On such evidence, the judge should protect only blacks from discrimination, and Alan Bakke would not have had a case. The reason is that the next higher level of generality above black equality, which is racial equality, is not shown to be a constitutional principle, and therefore there is nothing to be set against a current legislative majority's decision to favor blacks. Democratic choice must be accepted by the judge where the Constitution is silent. The test is the reasonableness of the distinction, and the level of generality chosen by the ratifiers determines that. If the evidence shows the ratifiers understood racial equality to have been the principle they were enacting, Bakke would have a case. In cases concerning gender and sexual orientation, however, interpretation is not additionally assisted by the presence of known intentions. The general language of the clause, however, continues to subject such cases to the test of whether statutory distinctions are reasonable. Sexual differences obviously make some distinctions reasonable while others have no apparent basis. That has, in fact, been the rationale on which the law has developed. Society's treatment of sexual orientation is based upon moral perceptions, so that it would be difficult to say that the various moral balances struck are unreasonable.

Original understanding avoids the problem of the level of generality in equal protection analysis by finding the level of generality that interpretation of the words, structure, and history of the Constitution fairly supports. This is a solution generally applicable to all constitutional provisions as to which historical evidence exists. There is, therefore, a form of constitutional decision making that satisfies the requirement that principles be neutrally defined. . . .

Neutrality in the Application of Principle

The neutral or nonpolitical application of principle has been discussed in connection with Wechsler's discussion of the *Brown* decision. It is a requirement, like the others, addressed to the judge's integrity. Having derived and defined the principle to be applied, he must apply it consistently and without regard to his sympathy or lack of sympathy with the parties before him. This does not mean that the judge will never change the principle he has derived and defined. Anybody who has dealt extensively with law knows that a new case may seem to fall within a principle as stated and yet not fall within the rationale underlying it. As new cases present new patterns, the principle will often be restated and redefined. There is nothing wrong with that; it is, in fact, highly desirable. But the judge must be clarifying his own reasoning and verbal formulations and not trimming to arrive at results desired on grounds extraneous to the Constitution. This requires a fair degree of sophistication and self-consciousness on the part of the judge. The only external discipline to which the judge is subject is the scrutiny of professional observers who will be able to tell over a period of time whether he is displaying intellectual integrity.

An example of the nonneutral application of principle in the service of a good cause is provided by *Shelley v. Kraemer*, a 1948 decision of the Supreme Court striking down racially restrictive covenants. Property owners had signed agreements limiting occupancy to white persons. Despite the covenants, some whites sold to blacks, owners of other properties sued to enforce the covenants, and the state courts, applying common law rules, enjoined the blacks from taking possession.

The problem for the Supreme Court was that the Constitution restricts only action by the state, not actions by private individuals. There was no doubt that the racial restrictions would have violated the equal protection clause of the Fourteenth Amendment had they been enacted by the state legislature. But here state courts were not the source of the racial discrimination, they merely enforced private agreements according to the terms of those agreements. The Supreme Court nonetheless held that "there has been state action in these cases in the full and complete sense of the phrase."

In a 1971 article in the *Indiana Law Journal*, I pointed out the difficulty with *Shelley*, for which I was severely taken to task in my Senate hearings and elsewhere. That criticism consisted entirely of the observation that I had disapproved of a case that favored blacks and was therefore hostile to civil rights. Both the fact that many commentators had criticized *Shelley* and my approval of other cases that favored blacks were ignored. The implicit position taken by some senators and activist groups was that a judge must always rule for racial minorities. That is a position I reject, because it requires political judging. Members of racial minorities should win when the law, honestly applied, supports their claim and not when it does not. *Shelley v. Kraemer* rested upon a theory that cannot be honestly applied and, in the event, has not been applied at all.

The Supreme Court in *Shelley* said that the decision of a state court under common law rules constitutes the action of the state and therefore is to be tested by the requirements of the Constitution. The racial discrimination involved was not the policy of the state courts but the desire of private individuals, which the courts enforced pursuant to normal, and neutral, rules of enforcing private agreements. The impossibility of applying the state action ruling of *Shelley* in a neutral fashion may easily be seen. Suppose that a guest in a house becomes abusive about political matters and is ejected by his host. The guest sues the host and the state courts hold that the property owner has a right to remove people from his home. The guest then appeals to the Supreme Court, pointing out that the state, through its courts, has upheld an abridgment of his right of free speech guaranteed by the First Amendment and made applicable to the states by the Fourteenth. The guest cites *Shelley* to show that this is state action and therefore the case is constitutional. There is no way of escaping that conclusion except by importing into the rule of *Shelley* qualifications and limits that . . . have no foundation in the Constitution or the case. Whichever way it decided, the Supreme Court would have to treat the case as one under the First Amendment and place state law with constitutional law.

It is necessary to remember that absolutely anything, from the significant to the frivolous, can be made the subject of a complaint filed in a state court. Whether the state court dismisses the suit out of hand or proceeds to the merits of the issue does not matter; any decision is, according to *Shelley*, state action and hence subject to constitutional scrutiny. That means that all private conduct may be made state conduct with the result that the Supreme Court will make the rules for all allowable or forbidden behavior by private individuals. That is not only a complete perversion of the Constitution of the United States, it makes the Supreme Court the supreme legislature. The result of the neutral application of the principle of *Shelley v. Kraemer* would be both revolutionary and preposterous. Clearly, it would not be applied neutrally, and it has not been, which means that it fails Wechsler's test.

Shelley was a political decision. As such, it should have been made by a legislature. It is clear that Congress had the power to outlaw racially restrictive covenants. Subsequently, in fact, in a case in which as Solicitor General I filed a brief supporting the result reached, the Supreme Court held that one of the post–Civil War civil rights acts did outlaw racial discrimination in private contracts. That fact does not, however, make *Shelley* a proper constitutional decision, however much its result may be admired on moral grounds.

Judicial adherence to neutral principles, in the three senses just described, is a crucial element of the American doctrine of the separation of powers. Since the Court's invocation of the Constitution is final, the judiciary is the only branch of the government not subject to the ordinary checks and balances that pit the powers of the other branches against each other. If it is to be faithful to the constitutional design, therefore, the Court must check itself. . . .

"I cannot accept this invitation [to celebrate the 200th anniversary
of the Constitution], for I do not believe that the meaning of the
Constitution was forever "fixed" at the Philadelphia Convention.
Nor do I find the wisdom, foresight, and sense of justice exhibited
by the Framers particularly profound."

12.4 REFLECTIONS ON THE BICENTENNIAL OF THE UNITED STATES CONSTITUTION

Thurgood Marshall

Thurgood Marshall served as Associate Justice of
the U.S. Supreme Court from 1967 to 1991.

The year 1987 marks the 200th anniversary of the United States Constitution. A Commission has been established to coordinate the celebration. The official meetings, essay contests, and festivities have begun.

The planned commemoration will span three years, and I am told 1987 is "dedicated to the memory of the Founders and the document they drafted in Philadelphia." We are to "recall the achievements of our Founders and the knowledge and experience that umpired them, the nature of the government they established, its origins, its character, and its ends, and the rights and privileges of citizenship, as well as its attendant responsibilities."

Like many anniversary celebrations, the plan for 1987 takes particular events and holds them up as the source of all the very best that has followed. Patriotic feelings will surely swell, prompting proud, proclamations of the wisdom, foresight, and sense of justice shared by the Framers and reflected in a written document now yellowed with age. This is unfortunate—not the patriotism itself but the tendency for the celebration to oversimplify, and overlook, the many other events that have been instrumental to our achievements as a nation. The focus of this celebration invites a complacent belief that the vision of those who debated and compromised in Philadelphia yielded the "more perfect Union" it is said we now enjoy.

I cannot accept this invitation, for I do not believe that the Constitution was forever "fixed" at the Philadelphia Convention. Nor do I find the wisdom, foresight, and sense of justice exhibited by the Framers particularly profound. To the contrary, the government they devised was defective from the start, requiring several amendments, a civil war, and momentous social transformation to attain

Thurgood Marshall, "Reflections on the Bicentennial of the United States Constitution," 101 *Harvard Law Review* 1 (1987).

the system of constitutional government, and its respect for the individual free-doms and human rights, that we hold as fundamental today. When contemporary Americans cite "The Constitution," they invoke a concept that is vastly different from what the Framers barely began to construct two centuries ago.

For a sense of the evolving nature of the Constitution we need look no further than the first three words of the document's preamble: "We the People." When the Founding Fathers used this phrase in 1787, they did not have in mind the majority of America's citizens. "We the People" included, in the words of the Framers, "the whole Number of free Persons." On a matter so basic as the right to vote, for example, Negro slaves were excluded, although they were counted for representational purposes—at three-fifths each. Women did not gain the right to vote for over a hundred and thirty years.

These omissions were intentional. The record of the framers' debates on the slave question is especially clear: the Southern states acceded to the demands of the New England states for giving Congress broad power to regulate commerce, in exchange for the right to continue the slave trade. The economic interests of the regions coalesced: New Englanders engaged in the "carrying trade" would profit from transporting slaves from Africa as well as goods produced in America by slave labor. The perpetuation of slavery ensured the primary source of wealth in the Southern states.

Despite this clear understanding of the role slavery would play in the new republic, use of the words "slaves" and "slavery" was carefully avoided in the original document. Political representation in the lower House of Congress was to be based on the population of "free Persons" in each state, plus three-fifths of all "other Persons." Moral principles against slavery, for those who had them, were compromised, with no explanation of the conflicting principles for which the American Revolutionary War had ostensibly been fought: the self-evident truths "that all men are created equal, that they are endowed by their Creator with certain unalienable Rights, that among these are Life, Liberty, and the pursuit of Happiness."

It was not the first such compromise. Even these ringing phrases from the Declaration of Independence are filled with irony, for an early draft of what became that declaration assailed the King of England for suppressing legislative attempts to end the slave trade and for encouraging slave rebellions. The final draft adopted in 1776 did not contain this criticism. And so again at the Constitutional Convention eloquent objections to the institution of slavery went unheeded, and its opponents eventually consented to a document which laid a foundation for the tragic events that were to follow.

Pennsylvania's Gouverneur Morris provides an example. He opposed slavery and the counting of slaves in determining the basis for in Congress. At the Convention he objected that

> the inhabitant of Georgia [or] South Carolina who goes to the coast of Africa, and in defiance of the most sacred laws of humanity tears away his fellow creatures from their dearest connections and damns them to the most cruel bondages, shall have more votes in a Government for protection of the rights of mankind than the Citizen of Pennsylvania or New Jersey who views with a laudable horror, so nefarious a practice.

And yet Gouverneur Morris eventually accepted the three-fifths accommodation. In fact, he wrote the final draft of the Constitution, the very document the bicentennial will commemorate.

As a result of compromise, the right of the Southern states to continue importing slaves was extended, officially, at least until 1808. We know that it actually lasted a good deal longer, as the Framers possessed no monopoly on the ability to trade moral principles for self-interest. But they nevertheless set an unfortunate example. Slaves could be imported, if the commercial interests of the North were protected. To make the compromise even more palatable customs duties would be imposed at up to ten dollars per slave as a means of raising public revenues!

No doubt it will be said, when the unpleasant truth of the history of slavery in America is mentioned during this bicentennial year, that the Constitution was a product of its times, and embodied a compromise which, under other circumstances, would not have been made. But the effects of the Framers' compromise have remained for generations. They arose from the contradiction between guaranteeing liberty and justice to all and denying both to Negroes.

The original intent of the phrase, "We the People," was far too clear for any ameliorating construction. Writing for the Court in 1857, Chief Justice Taney penned the following in the *Dred Scott* case, on the issue of whether, in the eyes of the Framers, slaves were "constituent members of the sovereignty" and were to be included among "We the People": "We think they are not, and that they are not included, and were not intended to be included. . . ."

* * *

And so, nearly seven decades after the Constitutional Convention, the Supreme Court reaffirmed the prevailing opinion of the Framers regarding the rights of Negroes in America. It took a bloody civil war before the Thirteenth Amendment could be adopted to abolish slavery, though not the consequences slavery would have for future Americans.

While the Union survived the civil war, the Constitution did not. In its place arose a new, more promising basis for justice and equality, the Fourteenth Amendment, ensuring protection of the life, liberty, and property for all persons against deprivations without due process, and guaranteeing equal protection of the laws. And yet almost another century would pass before any significant recognition was obtained of the rights of black Americans to share equally even in such basic opportunities as education, housing, and employment and to have their votes counted, and counted equally. In the meantime, blacks joined America's military to fights its wars and invested untold hours working in its factories and on its farms, contributing to the development of this country's magnificent wealth and waiting to share in its prosperity.

What is striking is the role legal principles have played throughout America's history in determining the condition of Negroes. They were enslaved by law, emancipated by law, disenfranchised and segregated by law; and, finally, they have begun to win equality by law. Along the way, new constitutional principles have emerged to meet the challenges of a changing society. The progress has been dramatic, and it will continue.

The men who gathered in Philadelphia in 1787 could not have envisioned these changes. They could not have imagined, nor would have accepted, that the document they were drafting would one day be construed by a Supreme Court to which had been appointed a woman and the descendant of an African slave. "We the People" no longer enslave, but the credit does not belong to the Framers. It belongs to those who refused to acquiesce in outdated notions of "liberty," "justice," and "equality" and who strived to better them.

And so we must be careful, when focusing on the events which took place in Philadelphia two centuries ago, that we not overlook the momentous events which followed and thereby lose our proper sense of perspective. Otherwise, the odds are that for many Americans the bicentennial celebration will be little more than a blind pilgrimage to the shrine of the original document now stored in a vault in the National Archives. If we seek, instead, a sensitive understanding of the Constitution's inherent defects, and its promising evolution through 200 years of history, the celebration of the "Miracle at Philadelphia" will, in my view, be a far more meaningful and humbling experience. We will see that the true miracle was not the birth of the Constitution, but its life, a life nurtured through two turbulent centuries of our own making, and a life embodying much good fortune that was not.

Thus, in this bicentennial year, we may not all participate in the festivities with flag-waving fervor. Some may more quietly commemorate the suffering, struggle, and sacrifice that have triumphed over much of what was wrong with the original document and observe the anniversary with hopes not realized and promises not fulfilled. I plan to celebrate the bicentennial of the Constitution as a living document, including the Bill of Rights and the other amendments protecting individual freedoms and human rights.

> "The acceptance by a majority of the United States Supreme Court of the proposition that capital punishment is not per se unconstitutional, but that in certain circumstances it may be arbitrary, and thus unconstitutional, has led to endless litigation, [c]onsiderable expense and interminable delays. . . . The difficulties that have been experienced in following this path persuade me that we should not follow this route."

12.5 THE STATE V. MAKWANYANE

(Constitutional Court of the Republic of South Africa)
1995 (3) SA 391 (CC)

At issue in this case was whether a South African law, adopted in 1977, permitting "the imposition of the death penalty in murder cases, conflicted with a provision of the country's 1993 constitutional text prohibiting "cruel, inhuman, or degrading treatment or punishment." To make its determination, the Court conducted an extensive survey of precedent and practices elsewhere. We reprint but a small sampling of its results.

Arbitrariness and Inequality

In holding that the imposition and the carrying out of the death penalty in the cases then under consideration constituted cruel and unusual punishment in the United States, Justice Douglas, concurring in *Furman v. Georgia*, said that "[a]ny law which is nondiscriminatory on its face may be applied in such a way as to violate the Equal Protection Clause of the Fourteenth Amendment." Discretionary statutes are

> ... pregnant with discrimination, and discrimination is an ingredient not compatible with the idea of equal protection of the laws that is implicit in the ban on "cruel and unusual" punishments.

It was contended that we should follow this approach and hold that the factors to which I have referred, make the application of [the 1977 law], in practice, arbitrary and capricious, and, for that reason, any resulting death sentence is cruel, inhuman, and degrading punishment.

The differences that exist between rich and poor, between good and bad prosecutions, between good and bad defence, between severe and lenient judges, between judges who favour capital punishment and those who do not, and the subjective attitudes that might be brought into play by factors such as race and class, may in similar ways affect any case that comes before the courts and is almost certainly present to some degree in all court systems. Such factors can be mitigated, but not totally avoided, by allowing convicted persons to appeal to a higher court. Appeals are decided on the record of the case and on findings made by the trial court. If the evidence on record and the findings made have been influenced by these factors, there may be nothing that can be done about that on appeal. Imperfection inherent in criminal trials means that error cannot be excluded; it also means that persons similarly placed may not necessarily receive similar punishment. This needs to be acknowledged. What also needs to be acknowledged is that the possibility of error will be present in any system of justice and that there cannot be perfect equality as between accused persons in the conduct and outcome of criminal trials. We have to accept these differences in the ordinary criminal cases that come before the courts, even to the extent that some may go to [jail] when others similarly placed may be acquitted or receive noncustodial sentences. But death is different, and the question is, whether this is acceptable when the difference is between life and death. Unjust imprisonment is a great wrong, but if it is discovered, the prisoner can be released and compensated; but the killing of an innocent person is irremediable.

In the United States, the Supreme Court has addressed itself primarily to the requirement of due process. Statutes have to be clear and discretion curtailed without ignoring the peculiar circumstances of each accused person. Verdicts are set aside if the defense has not been adequate, and persons sentenced to death are allowed wide rights of appeal and review. This attempt to ensure the utmost procedural fairness has itself led to problems. The most notorious is the "death row phenomenon" in which prisoners cling to life, exhausting every possible avenue of redress, and using every device to put off the date of execution, in the natural and understandable hope that there will be a reprieve from the Courts or the executive. It is common for prisoners in the United States to remain on death row for many years, and this dragging out of the process has been characterized as being cruel and degrading. The difficulty of implementing a system of capital punishment which on the one hand avoids arbitrariness by insisting on a high standard of procedural fairness and on the other hand avoids delays that in themselves are the cause of impermissible cruelty and inhumanity is apparent. Justice Blackmun, who sided with the majority in *Gregg*'s case, ultimately came to the conclusion that it is not possible to design a system that avoids arbitrariness. To design a system that avoids arbitrariness and delays in carrying out the sentence is even more difficult.

The United States jurisprudence has not resolved the dilemma arising from the fact that the Constitution prohibits cruel and unusual punishments but also permits, and contemplates that there will be, capital punishment. The acceptance by a majority of the United States Supreme Court of the proposition that capital punishment is not per se unconstitutional, but that in certain circumstances it may be arbitrary, and thus unconstitutional, has led to endless litigation. Considerable expense and interminable delays result from the exceptionally high standard of procedural fairness set by the United States courts in attempting to avoid arbitrary decisions. The difficulties that have been experienced in following this path, to which Justice Blackmun and Justice Scalia have both referred,[2] but from which they have drawn different conclusions, persuade me that we should not follow this route. . . .

Cruel, Inhuman and Degrading Punishment

The United Nations Committee on Human Rights has held that the death sentence by definition is cruel and degrading punishment. So has the Hungarian Constitutional Court and three judges of the Canadian Supreme Court. The death sentence has also been held to be cruel or unusual punishment and thus unconstitutional under the state constitutions of Massachusetts and California.

The California decision is *People v. Anderson.* Capital punishment was held by six of the seven judges of the Californian Supreme Court to be "impermissibly cruel" under the California Constitution, which prohibited cruel or unusual punishment. Also,

> It degrades and dehumanizes all who participate in its processes. It is unnecessary to any legitimate goal of the state and is incompatible with the dignity of man and the judicial process.

In the Massachusetts decision in District Attorney for the *Suffolk District v. Watson*, where the Constitution of the State of Massachusetts prohibited cruel or unusual punishment, the death sentence was also held, by six of the seven judges, to be impermissibly cruel.

In both cases the disjunctive effect of "or" was referred to as enabling the Courts to declare capital punishment unconstitutional even if it was not "unusual." Under our Constitution it will not [be permitted] if it is cruel, or inhuman, or degrading.

Proportionality is an ingredient to be taken into account in deciding whether a penalty is cruel, inhuman, or degrading. No Court would today uphold the constitutionality of a statute that makes the death sentence a competent sentence for the cutting down of trees or the killing of deer, which were capital offences in England in the eighteenth century. But murder is not to be equated with such "offences." The willful taking of an innocent life calls for a severe penalty, and there are many countries which still retain the death penalty as a sentencing option for such cases. Disparity between the crime and the penalty is not the only ingredient of proportionality; factors such as the enormity and irredeemable character of the death sentence in circumstances where neither error nor arbitrariness can be excluded, the expense and difficulty of addressing the disparities which exist in practice between accused persons facing similar charges, and which are due to factors such as race, poverty, and ignorance, and the other subjective factors which have been mentioned, are also factors that can and should be taken into account in dealing with this issue. It may possibly be that none alone would be sufficient under our Constitution to justify a finding that the death sentence is cruel, inhuman, or degrading. But these factors are not to be evaluated in isolation. They must be taken together, and they must be evaluated with other relevant factors, including the two fundamental rights on which the accused rely, the right to dignity and the right to life.

The carrying out of the death sentence destroys life, which is protected without reservation [in] our Constitution, it annihilates human dignity which is protected under [our Constitution], elements of arbitrariness are present in its enforcement, and it is irremediable. Taking these [and other] factors into account . . . I am satisfied that in the context of our Constitution the death penalty is indeed a cruel, inhuman and degrading punishment. . . .

"The substantial social costs exacted by the exclusionary rule
for the vindication of Fourth Amendment rights
have long been a source of concern."

12.6 UNITED STATES V. LEON

468 U.S. 897 (1984)

Weeks v. United States *(1914) excluded from use in federal trials evidence obtained by unlawful searches and seizures.* Mapp v. Ohio *(1961) extended this exclusionary rule to state trials and provoked bitter and long-lasting opposition by police, prosecutors, and many other public officials, including state and federal judges. In this case, law enforcement officers had obtained a search warrant to seize evidence linking Alberto Leon to large-scale drug dealing. Partially on the basis of this evidence, a federal grand jury indicted him for conspiracy to possess and distribute cocaine. At a pretrial hearing, however, the district judge found that, although the officers had acted in good faith, the affidavit on which the warrant was based had been inefficient to establish "probable*

cause," as required by the Fourth Amendment. Thus the judge ruled that the seized ev-
idence must be excluded from the trial. The Department of Justice appealed to the Court
of Appeals for the Ninth Circuit and, after that tribunal affirmed, sought and obtained
certiorari from the United States Supreme Court.

JUSTICE WHITE delivered the opinion of the Court. . . .

Language in opinions of this Court and of individual Justices has sometimes implied that the exclusionary rule is a necessary corollary of the Fourth
Amendment, *Mapp v. Ohio* (1961); *Olmstead v. United States* (1928), or that the
rule is required by the conjunction of the Fourth and Fifth Amendments. These
implications need not detain us long. The Fifth Amendment theory has not
withstood critical analysis or the test of time, see *Andersen v. Maryland* (1976),
and the Fourth Amendment "has never been interpreted to proscribe the introduction of illegally seized evidence in all proceedings or against all persons."
Stone v. Powell (1976).

The Fourth Amendment contains no provision expressly precluding the use
of evidence obtained in violation of its commands, and an examination of its
origin and purposes makes clear that the use of fruits of a past unlawful search
or seizure "work[s] no new Fourth Amendment wrong." *United States v.*
Calandra (1974). The wrong condemned by the Amendment is "fully accomplished" by the unlawful search or seizure itself, *ibid.*, and the exclusionary rule
is neither intended nor able to "cure the invasion of the defendant's rights
which he has already suffered." *Stone v. Powell* (WHITE, J., dissenting). The rule
thus operates as "a judicially created remedy designed to safeguard Fourth
Amendment rights generally through its deterrent effect, rather than a personal
constitutional right of the person aggrieved." *United States v. Calandra.*

Whether the exclusionary sanction is appropriately imposed in a particular
case, our decisions make clear, is "an issue separate from the question whether
the Fourth Amendment rights of the party seeking to invoke the rule were violated by police conduct." *Illinois v. Gates* (1983). Only the former question is currently before us, and it must be resolved by weighing the costs and benefits of
preventing the use in the prosecution's case-in-chief of inherently trustworthy
tangible evidence obtained in reliance on a search warrant issued by a detached
and neutral magistrate that ultimately is found to be defective.

The substantial social costs exacted by the exclusionary rule for the vindication of Fourth Amendment rights have long been a source of concern. "Our
cases have consistently recognized that unbending application of the exclusionary sanction to enforce ideals of governmental rectitude would impede unac-
ceptably the truth-finding functions of judge and jury." *United States v. Payner*
(1980). An objectionable collateral consequence of this interference with the
criminal justice system's truth-finding function is that some guilty defendants
may go free or receive reduced sentences as a result of favorable plea bargains.
Particularly when law enforcement officers have acted in objective good faith or
their transgressions have been minor, the magnitude of the benefit conferred on
such guilty defendants offends basic concepts of the criminal justice system.
Stone v. Powell. Indiscriminate application of the exclusionary rule, therefore,

may well "generat[e] disrespect for the law and the administration of justice." Accordingly, "[a]s with any remedial device, the application of the rule has been restricted to those areas where its remedial objectives are thought most efficaciously served." *United States v. Calandra.* . . .

Close attention to those remedial objectives has characterized our recent decisions concerning the scope of the Fourth Amendment exclusionary rule. The Court has, to be sure, not seriously questioned, "in the absence of a more efficacious sanction, the continued application of the rule to suppress evidence from the [prosecution's] case where a Fourth Amendment violation has been substantial and deliberate. . . ." *Franks v. Delaware* (1978), *Stone v. Powell.* Nevertheless, the balancing approach that has evolved in various contexts—including criminal trials—"forcefully suggest[s] that the exclusionary rule be more generally modified to permit the introduction of evidence obtained in the reasonable good-faith belief that a search or seizure was in accord with the Fourth Amendment." *Illinois v. Gates.* (WHITE, J., concurring in the judgment).

JUSTICE BRENNAN, with whom JUSTICE MARSHALL joins, dissenting.

Ten years ago in *United States v. Calandra* (1974), I expressed the fear that the Court's decision "may signal that a majority of my colleagues have positioned themselves to reopen the door [to evidence secured by official lawlessness] still further and abandon altogether the exclusionary rule in search-and-seizure cases." Since then, in case after case, I have witnessed the Court's gradual but determined strangulation of the rule. It now appears that the Court's victory over the Fourth Amendment is complete. That today's decision represents the *piece de resistance* of the Court's past efforts cannot be doubted, for today the Court sanctions the use in the prosecution's case-in-chief of illegally obtained evidence against the individual whose rights have been violated—a result that had previously been thought to be foreclosed.

The Court seeks to justify this result on the ground that the "costs" of adhering to the exclusionary rule in cases like those before us exceed the "benefits." But the language of deterrence and of cost/benefit analysis, if used indiscriminately, can have a narcotic effect. It creates an illusion of technical precision and ineluctability. It suggests that not only constitutional principle but also empirical data support the majority's result. When the Court's analysis is examined carefully, however, it is clear that we have not been treated to an honest assessment of the merits of the exclusionary rule but have instead been drawn into a curious world where the "costs" of excluding illegally obtained evidence loom to exaggerated heights and where the "benefits" of such exclusion are made to disappear with a mere wave of the hand.

The majority ignores the fundamental constitutional importance of what is at stake here. While the machinery of law enforcement and indeed the nature of crime itself have changed dramatically since the Fourth Amendment became part of the Nation's fundamental law in 1791, what the Framers understood then remains true today—that the task of combating crime and convicting the guilty will in every era seem of such critical and pressing concern that we may be lured by the temptations of expediency into forsaking our commitment to protecting individual liberty and privacy. It was for that very reason that the Framers of the Bill of Rights insisted that law enforcement efforts be permanently and unambiguously restricted in order to preserve personal freedoms. In the constitutional scheme they ordained, the sometimes unpopular task of ensuring that the government's enforcement efforts remain within the strict boundaries fixed by the Fourth Amendment was entrusted to the courts. . . .

JUSTICE STEVENS [concurring in *Leon* and dissenting in a similar case decided the same day]. . . .

It is appropriate to begin with the plain language of the Fourth Amendment:

> The right of the people to be secure in their persons, houses, papers, and effects, against unreasonable searches and seizures, shall not be violated; and no Warrants shall issue but upon probable cause, supported by Oath or affirmation, and particularly describing the place to be searched, and the persons or things to be seized.

The Court assumes that the searches in these cases violated the Fourth Amendment yet refuses to apply the exclusionary rule because the Court concludes that it was "reasonable" for the police to conduct them. In my opinion an official search and seizure cannot be both "unreasonable" and "reasonable" at the same time. The doctrinal vice in the Court's holding is its failure to consider the separate purposes of the two prohibitory clauses in the Fourth Amendment.

The first clause prohibits unreasonable searches and seizures, and the second prohibits the issuance of warrants that are not supported by probable cause or that do not particularly describe the place to be searched and the persons or things to be seized. We have, of course, repeatedly held that warrantless searches are presumptively unreasonable and that there are only a few carefully delineated exceptions to that basic presumption. But when such an exception has been recognized, analytically we have necessarily concluded that the warrantless activity was not "unreasonable" within the meaning of the first clause. Thus, any Fourth Amendment case may present two separate questions: whether the search was conducted pursuant to a warrant issued in accordance with the second clause, and, if not, whether it was nevertheless "reasonable" within the meaning of the first. On these questions, the constitutional text requires that we speak with one voice. We cannot intelligibly assume arguendo that a search was constitutionally unreasonable but that the seized evidence is admissible because the same search was reasonable.

I. . . .

In *Leon*, there is also a substantial question whether the warrant complied with the Fourth Amendment. There was a strong dissent on the probable cause issue when *Leon* was before the Court of Appeals, and that dissent has been given added force by this Court's intervening decision in *Illinois v. Gates* (1983), which constituted a significant development in the law. It is probable, though admittedly not certain, that the Court of Appeals would now conclude that the warrant in *Leon* satisfied the Fourth Amendment if it were given the opportunity to reconsider the issue in the light of Gates. Adherence to our normal practice following the announcement of a new rule would therefore postpone, and probably obviate, the need for the promulgation of the broad new rule the Court announces today. . . .

Judges, more than most, should understand the value of adherence to settled procedures. By adopting a set of fair procedures, and then adhering to them, courts of law ensure that justice is administered with an even hand. "These are subtle matters, for they concern the ingredients of what constitutes justice. Therefore, justice must satisfy the appearance of justice." *Offutt v. United States* (1954). Of course, this Court has a duty to face questions of constitutional law when necessary to the disposition of an actual case or controversy. *Marbury v. Madison* (1803). But when the Court goes beyond what is necessary to decide the case before it, it can only encourage the perception that it is pursuing its own notions of wise social policy, rather than adhering to its judicial role. I do not believe the Court should reach out to decide what is undoubtedly a profound question concerning the administration of criminal justice before assuring itself that this question is actually and of necessity presented by the concrete facts before the Court. Although it may appear that the Court's broad holding will serve the public interest in enforcing obedience to the rule of law, for my part, I remain firmly convinced that "the preservation of order in our communities will be best insured by adherence to established and respected procedures." *Groppi v. Leslie* (CA7 1971) (en banc) (STEVENS, J., dissenting), rev'd (1972). . . .

IV. . . .

The exclusionary rule is designed to prevent violations of the Fourth Amendment. "Its purpose is to deter-to compel respect for the constitutional guaranty in the only effectively available way, by removing the incentive to disregard it." *Elkins v. United States* (1960). If the police cannot use evidence obtained through warrants issued on less than probable cause, they have less incentive to seek those warrants, and magistrates have less incentive to issue them.

Today's decisions do grave damage to that deterrent function. Under the majority's new rule, even when the police know their warrant application is probably insufficient, they retain an incentive to submit it to a magistrate, on the chance that he may take the bait. No longer must they hesitate and seek additional evidence in doubtful cases. . . .

The Court is of course correct that the exclusionary rule cannot deter when the authorities have no reason to know that their conduct is unconstitutional. But when probable cause is lacking, then by definition a reasonable person under the circumstances would not believe there is a fair likelihood that a search will produce evidence of a crime. Under such circumstances well-trained professionals must know that they are violating the Constitution. The Court's approach—which, in effect, encourages the police to seek a warrant even if they know the existence of probable cause is doubtful—can only lead to an increased number of constitutional violations.

Thus, the Court's creation of a double standard of reasonableness inevitably must erode the deterrence rationale that still supports the exclusionary rule. But we should not ignore the way it tarnishes the role of the judiciary in enforcing the Constitution. For the original rationale for the exclusionary rule retains its force as well as its relevance:

> The tendency of those who execute the criminal laws of the country to obtain conviction by means of unlawful seizures . . . should find no sanction in the judgments of the courts which are charged at all times with the support of the Constitution and to which people of all conditions have a right to appeal for the maintenance of such fundamental rights. *Weeks v. United States* (1914).

Thus, "Courts which sit under our Constitution cannot and will not be made party to lawless invasions of the constitutional rights of citizens by permitting unhindered governmental use of the fruits of such invasions. . . ." *Terry v. Ohio* (1968). . . . Today, for the first time, this Court holds that although the Constitution has been violated, no court should do anything about it at any time and in any proceeding. In my judgment, the Constitution requires more. Courts simply cannot escape their responsibility for redressing constitutional violations if they admit evidence obtained through unreasonable searches and seizures, since the entire point of police conduct that violates the Fourth Amendment is to obtain evidence for use at trial. If such evidence is admitted, then the courts become not merely the final and necessary link in an unconstitutional chain of events but its actual motivating force. "If the existing code does not permit district attorneys to have a hand in such dirty business it does not permit the judge to allow such iniquities to succeed." *Olmstead v. United States* (1928) (HOLMES, J., dissenting). Nor should we so easily concede the existence of a constitutional violation for which there is no remedy. To do so is to convert a Bill of Rights into an unenforced honor code that the police may follow in their discretion. The Constitution requires more; it requires a remedy. If the Court's new rule is to be followed, the Bill of Rights should be renamed.

It is of course true that the exclusionary rule exerts a high price—the loss of probative evidence of guilt. But that price is one courts have often been required to pay to serve important social goals. That price is also one the Fourth Amendment requires us to pay, assuming as we must that the Framers intended that its strictures "shall not be violated." For in all such cases, as Justice Stewart has observed, "the same extremely relevant evidence would not have been obtained had the police officer complied with the commands of the fourth amendment in the first place."

> [T]he forefathers thought this was not too great a price to pay for that decent privacy of home, papers, and effects which is indispensable to individual dignity and self-respect. They may have overvalued privacy, but I am not disposed to set their command at naught. *Harris v. United States* (1947) (JACKSON, J., dissenting).

We could, of course, facilitate the process of administering justice to those who violate the criminal laws by ignoring the commands of the Fourth Amendment—indeed, by ignoring the entire Bill of Rights—but it is the very purpose of a Bill of Rights to identify values that may not be sacrificed to expediency. In a just society those who govern, as well as those who are governed, must obey the law. . . .

> "... the technocratic approach of the policy analyst is ill-suited to the judicial task of construing law—especially the law of the Constitution."
> —LAURENCE H. TRIBE

> "All goods are scarce. . . . Judges must respond to scarcity." —FRANK H. EASTERBROOK

12.7 ECONOMIC REASONING AND CONSTITUTIONAL INTERPRETATION

In the November 1984 issue of the Harvard Law Review, *Frank H. Easterbrook published an article entitled "Foreword: The Court and the Economic System." In it he argued that economic principles of reasoning permeated the Supreme Court's work and defended this approach to legal problems. Soon thereafter, Laurence H. Tribe wrote a rebuttal and Easterbrook a reply.*

Constitutional Calculus: Equal Justice or Economic Efficiency?

Laurence H. Tribe

Laurence H. Tribe is Tyler Professor of Constitutional Law, Harvard Law School.

The Constitution cannot be cabined in any calculus of costs and benefits. Yet Professor Frank Easterbrook, an exponent of an increasingly influential school of thought regarding the relationship of law to economics, comes to the defense of a recent Supreme Court trend toward discharging the federal judicial mission in the manner of an economic manager armed with the hard-edged tools of cost-benefit analysis. Whether the Court actually uses those tools as aids to decision making, or merely employs them to legitimate decisions arrived at in other ways, the thrust of my critique is that the substantive values implicit in the Court's emerging approach are deeply at odds with the constitutional enterprise. Professor Easterbrook's spirited defense of the Supreme Court's increasingly apparent affinity for a technocratic perspective is welcome because it renders transparent what might otherwise have been obscure. And because it comes from an unabashed advocate rather than a critic of the new approach, the Easterbrook analysis helps to rebut any suggestion that the managerial mode neither motivates the Court's actions nor provides a mask for the Court's decisions, but is only a mirage conjured by observers unsympathetic with the substantive results of a series of recent decisions.

Like Professor Easterbrook, I will be concerned here less with the outcomes of selected Supreme Court cases than with the Court's methods and the premises on which those methods necessarily rest. Specifically, I will focus on what sorts of questions the Court asks or fails to ask both itself and us about power and powerlessness, about public purposes and private interests, about the nature of laws and constitutions, and about the mission of courts in our political system.

In Professor Easterbrook's world, the Supreme Court is little more than a "regulator": a "governor of the government." Its Justices, like all judges, are pulled in opposite directions by their work. From one side, the nature of litigation invites judges to apply an ex post approach to dispute resolution, an approach that requires a court to take the positions of the parties as given and to apportion losses and profits fairly among them. From the other side, sophisticated judges who "appreciate" the economic system are pulled toward an ex ante approach, in which a court is interested less in doing justice in the case at hand than in creating sound rules to govern the behavior of the world at large. In the Easterbrook vision, rule creation is thus forward-looking, and, in his felicitous phrase, the rule "knows not its subjects."

One salient feature of Professor Easterbrook's distinction is that concern for fairness surfaces principally in the ex post, not the ex ante, approach. That is, if courts seek to do justice among the parties actually before them by merely slicing up the pie fairly, they must forfeit the opportunity to expand the pie as a whole by formulating an appropriate forward-looking and general legal rule. For, in Professor Easterbrook's opinion, a focus on the equities in the individual case almost invariably leads to the promulgation of rules that tend to impoverish people generally, by snatching from them the opportunity to order their activities more efficiently in the future. According to Professor Easterbrook, the lawyer's concept of fairness is a "suitcase full of bottled ethics from which one freely chooses to blend his own type of justice"; only those unable to appreciate the importance of increasing overall productivity will engage in such childish pursuits. It is instrumental rather than moral values that truly matter.

Given this perspective on the role of the judiciary in general, it is unsurprising that Professor Easterbrook concentrates primarily on nonconstitutional adjudication. The Supreme Court's constitutional rules, as he sees them, are addressed solely to the lower courts and only remotely and indirectly influence anyone's behavior or shape any aspect of the public's general attitudes. But regardless of whom constitutional decisions are thought to address, and regardless of whether Professor Easterbrook believes that his instrumental lens is primarily suited to the analysis of statutory decisions, he apparently considers utilitarian policy analysis to be appropriate in constitutional cases as well. According to Professor Easterbrook, it is not for the judiciary to concern itself with criticizing or changing the distribution of wealth and power, or to decide what is to count as a cost or a benefit; those matters are solely the province of the political branches, whose legislative deals the judiciary must faithfully enforce whatever the subject matter of a rule, be it securities regulation or freedom of expression, Professor Easterbrook endorses a nearly exclusive focus on each rule's marginal impact—its probable incremental effect on a suitably weighted sum of the variables made relevant by the political compromises the judiciary is charged to effectuate.

But to treat the underlying choice of variables, and the social reality they represent, as beyond the judiciary's proper concern is to render the answer derived by a court both trivial and at best half-right. Professor Easterbrook tells us that what we need to ask is what effect the alternative rules will have on the future behavior of individuals; but he does not bother to inquire how those same alternatives will affect the future distribution of power and wealth among those individuals, nor does he care to know how the parties actually before the court initially arrived at their unequal positions. This disregard of the *distributional* dimension of any given problem is characteristic of the entire law-and-economics school of thought, which assumes a world in which no one is economically coerced and in which individuals who do not "buy" things are said to be "unwilling," rather than unable, to do so.

Treating a constitutional court's task as merely one of toting up marginal costs and benefits also ignores the crucial questions of what *counts* as a cost or a benefit—and who gets to decide that issue. The approach applauded by Professor Easterbrook thus fails to recognize the *constitutive* dimension of constitutional decisions: the fact that constitutional choices affect, and hence require consideration of, the way in which a polity wishes to *constitute* itself. In making such choices, we reaffirm and create, select and shape, the values and truths we hold sacred. Such decisions determine much about how we define our society and specify much about what we stand for and what sort of country we wish to become. Contrary to Professor Easterbrook's assumption, the constitutional decisions of courts—and, to a lesser but still significant degree, all legal decisions—serve not merely to implement "given" systems of acknowledged values but also to define and reshape the values—indeed, the very identity—of the nation. A court not only chooses *how* to achieve preexisting ends but also affects *what* those ends are to be and *who* we are to become.

It is for this reason above all others that the technocratic approach of the policy analyst is ill-suited to the judicial task of construing law—especially the law of the Constitution. The instrumental methods of which Professor Easterbrook is so fond are incapable of grasping and addressing that dimension of human choice that permits the simultaneous transformation of the system of ends and values that characterizes the chooser; such methods cannot address the question of what the chooser's system of ends *should be*. Yet the core of the

Supreme Court's function, in any but the most shallow conception, must rotate precisely about these questions of value, not merely about questions of relative efficiency.

The appeal of utilitarian policy analysis, as well as its power, lies in its ability to reduce the various dimensions of a problem to a common denominator. The inevitable result is not only that "soft" variables—such as the value of vindicating a fundamental right or preserving human dignity—tend to be ignored or understated but also that entire problems are reduced to terms that misstate their structure and that ignore the nuances that give these problems their full character. Thus, for example, the law-and-economics school of thought typically argues that rights should be awarded on grounds of efficiency to reflect the discontinuous preferences of those who would refuse any inducement to cede those "rights." Even if this analytic approach occasionally generates a result with which most of us would agree, by assigning a right in accord with the individual feelings and collective traditions that underlie those discontinuous preferences, the method nonetheless remains defective and distorting. Being "assigned" a right on efficiency grounds, after an appraisal of the relevant cost curves, hardly satisfies the particular human need that can be met only by a shared social and legal understanding that the right belongs to the individual because the capacity and opportunity it embodies are organically and historically a part of the person that she is, and not for any purely contingent and essentially managerial reason. As Justice Stewart concisely put the matter for the Court in *Faretta v. California*, "Personal liberties are not rooted in the law of averages."

One final flaw in the utilitarian approach championed by Professor Easterbrook is its embrace of one of the most persistent myths of policy analysis: that the analytical techniques *in themselves* lack significant substantive bias or controversial content—that the techniques are neutral in regard to matters of value precisely because such matters may simply be inserted in the analysis. But the disregard of those techniques for distributive and other constitutive concerns cannot be corrected merely by punching in one or more dummy variables labeled "values." The cost-benefit comparisons and marginal analyses are already engineered, whether intentionally or not, to serve a specific agenda. The intellectual and social heritage of these ideas, as well as their natural tendency, lies in the classical eighteenth and nineteenth century economics of unfettered contract, consumer sovereignty, social Darwinism, and perfect markets—the classical economies that the Supreme Court in fact exalted as federal constitutional law from the 1890s to 1937. This brings those ideas within a paradigm of actions guided by a preexisting set of personal preferences—a paradigm inclined toward the exaltation of possessive individualism, "efficient" resource allocation, and maximum productivity, as against respect for distributive justice, procedural fairness, and the irreducible and sometime inalienable values associated with personal rights and public goods. It is thus little wonder that Professor Easterbrook's courts, cut adrift from the Constitution's emphasis on fundamental rights as well as its structural concern for a democratic separation of powers, are but passive and empty vessels.

In this respect, the myth that judges are but "honest agents," "faithfully executing decisions made by others," is a cornerstone both of Professor Easterbrook's argument and of the judicial approach that arguments [such as] his are calculated to encourage and to legitimate. But surely courts cannot enhance the quality of constitutional adjudication by abdicating responsibility for the difficult choices such adjudication inevitably entails. We must thus examine with the deepest skepticism any claim that there exists some neutral technique that, if followed with care and competence, can serve to make our judges mere agents of political bargains struck on our behalf by others.

The not-so-hidden premise of the methods that Professor Easterbrook endorses must therefore be that process, structure, distribution, and constitutive notions of what count as costs or benefits are somehow "given" in advance and therefore need not actively concern those who are charged with construing and enforcing laws and constitutions. But, as will by now be apparent, I believe that precisely those dimensions of constitutional—and general judicial—decision making should be of paramount concern. Relegating them to an unexamined background entails self-deception, ensures the triumph of extant distributions of wealth and power, and abdicates responsibility for the choices that courts and others necessarily make in accepting or rejecting competing claims to legal protection. Indeed, in a political era increasingly dominated by narcissistic inattention to the public realm, and marked particularly by a lack of concern for the least powerful within society, the Supreme Court's failure to address the plight of those most in need reinforces what I see as a dismal moral vacuum.

A final point deserves reiteration. Nothing in my critique makes it necessary to prove that the Supreme Court's increasingly frequent invocation of cost-benefit modes of analysis and argument actually mirrors the thought processes that motivate the Court's decisions. The vital fact is that the Court's actions, like the steely cost-benefit analyses with which they comport so well, are sadly insensitive to constitutional concerns bearing on the distribution of wealth and power and to the broader constitutive dimensions of all legal decisions. Because it is those concerns and dimensions that should be most prominent on the agenda of a court dealing with constitutional issues, the Supreme Court's failure to take such concerns seriously is no less troubling if the cost-benefit patina is but a mask for substantive judgments arrived at through other means, than it is if the cost-benefit imagery genuinely mirrors what the Court understands itself to be doing. . . .

Method, Result, and Authority: A Reply

Frank H. Easterbrook

Frank H. Easterbrook is a judge on the U.S. Court of Appeals for the Seventh Circuit.

Frank H. Easterbrook, "Method, Result, and Authority: A Reply," 98 *Harvard Law Review* 622 (1985).

I.

All good things are scarce. Self-interested conduct is the handmaiden of scarcity. These are facts of life. Given scarcity, judicial decisions inevitably create, transfer, or destroy valuable things and affect people's decisions. Even justice is scarce. Disputes about attorneys' fees stem from the high costs of litigation, and rules about harmless error grow out of the costs of retrials (including the delay other litigants encounter when one case receives extra process).

Judges must respond to scarcity. The effects of a court's decision on who gets how much of what good things may or may not be what the judges anticipated. Private and public responses to the decision may or may not undercut what the judges sought to achieve.

The foundation of my Foreword is the belief that knowledge of potential effects and responses is preferable to ignorance. The Foreword contains three principal normative propositions:

(1) judges should be aware that their decisions create incentives influencing conduct ex ante and that attempts to divide the stakes fairly ex post will alter or reverse the signals that are desirable from an ex ante perspective;

(2) judges should be aware that marginal effects, and not average effects, influence the responses to their decisions and that responses are pervasive; and

(3) judges should be aware of the interest-group nature of much legislation, for this influences its meaning.

Appreciation of each of these propositions is an essential ingredient in any intelligent response to the problem of scarcity.

The Foreword also offers two descriptive propositions:

(1) the Justices are better aware of these three principles and act on them more intelligently than they used to do; and

(2) their recognition and action cuts across many parts of the law. Both of these propositions seem to me reasons to applaud the Justices.

A number of propositions do not appear in the Foreword. The following are among the missing:

(a) all human concerns can be monetized in practice and deployed by courts in a grand cost-benefit analysis;

(b) an application of the three normative principles leads to a determinate outcome in all (or even most) cases; and

(c) utilitarian principles should govern all kinds of disputes.

Professor Tribe's Article largely agrees with the Foreword's descriptive propositions. He does not question my analysis of how the Court's thinking has changed, though he obviously would prefer that the Court follow a noninstrumental path. He also does not question much of the normative analysis, though his preference for noninstrumental values leads him to think that the analysis turns judges' heads in the wrong direction.

Most of the bite in Professor Tribe's Comment comes from his vigorous denial of propositions (a), (b), and (c). He believes, for example, that many human concerns cannot be (or ought not to be) monetized, that cost-benefit calculations may be indeterminate, and that the Constitution often instructs judges to disregard utilitarian calculations in favor of recognizing personal rights and reshaping preferences.

I am delighted to agree. My Foreword does not mention "cost-benefit analysis," for example; judges have neither the information nor the incentive to do such analysis well, and even a dispassionate analysis done by a team of superb economists is apt to be incomplete and misleading. . . .

. . . I think Professor Tribe's comment is based on the belief that those interested in the economics of legal institutions *must* believe propositions (a), (b), and (c), even if they deny them. Why be interested in economic analysis if it does not give universal answers? Professor Tribe's reaction is common among those who see red whenever someone mentions economics. I therefore think it helpful briefly to explore why people ask economic questions even if they do not think the inquiry will yield dispositive answers to all legal disputes.

II.

Law is not a closed logical system. Every legal dispute worth having involves some propositions about the state of the world. These disputes have answers, though they may be very hard to find. Professor Tribe tells us, for example, that if people can sleep in the parks near the White House, the homeless will become better off because they likely will get some income transfers in their favor. This may or may not be true—whether it is true depends on the reactions of other, competing lobbyists, on the substitution among programs of income redistribution, and so forth. The effects of an increase in one group's public exposure are hard to calculate. We need some way to evaluate Professor Tribe's assertion, as we need a way to evaluate the other predictions that are the stuff of litigation.

No litigant argues before the Supreme Court without making predictions about how the decision will affect society. Few opinions omit predictions about effects. Litigants and judges alike believe that these effects are important in determining the outcome of the case. These predictions usually rest on a tacit economic analysis. Better to make the analysis express, to give more knowledge of these consequences.

It really does not matter that the ex ante perspective, attention to marginal effects, and recognition of the interest-group character of legislation are not dispositive in this search. No one insists that any single method or piece of evidence be dispositive. In litigation we call evidence "relevant" if it makes the truth of a pertinent fact more or less likely; we do not demand that each piece of evidence be dispositive. In the design of aircraft, the principles of aerodynamics and fluid motion are important but not dispositive, because no computer is powerful enough to model all aspects of the flow of air over an airfoil. Some designs therefore lead to crashes. Yet only a fool would argue that because aerodynamics is not dispositive, it should be discounted as a useful source of knowledge in the design of aircraft.

It is the same with economic analysis. The consideration of marginal effects in deciding cases is not apt to be dispositive, but it is informative and in many instances will tip the balance. Because more knowledge is better than less, economic analysis is valuable. The alternative ways of predicting effects of decisions—often unfounded guesses, counterfactual beliefs, and superstition—do not become more attractive just because economic analysis is incomplete.

Professor Tribe appears to believe, however, that economic inquiry contains misinformation that imposes unwarranted costs on the legal process. . . . He thinks that economic analysis directs attention toward what is monetizable and away from personal rights and the goal of changing values. Perhaps it does for some; any tool can be misused. Knives can kill people as well as cut the food at dinner. But economics need not mislead. Economics is about maximization subject to constraints. Economics is applied rationality. Someone can name the maximand (say, freedom of speech and the value proposing new political arrangements) or the constraint (usually scarcity of some valuable thing) without affecting the nature of the analysis. True, there are formal models that have no room for personal relationships, but there is also an economics of the family in which altruism, concern for future generations, and the development of more fulfilling lives play the central role. Economists have no difficulty understanding education, although the role of education in changing the values of those being educated is an essential part of the venture. People often want to change their own preferences, and anything they want to do—even if they do not know where they will end up—can be evaluated. Nothing in the approach requires the exclusion of other values. . . .

III.

Finally, we are entitled to ask why courts are authorized to pursue the path marked for them by Professor Tribe—marching off toward reconstituting society. Why is this a part of the judicial mission? Legislatures "reconstitute society" daily; they are the mechanism for aggregating preferences, setting change in motion, and expressing aspirations. The Civil Rights Act of 1964 is a profound and increasingly successful effort to overcome and reshape preferences. Judges have a different role. The argument for judicial review in The Federalist and in *Marbury v. Madison* is that judges serve as a brake on the other branches by insisting that they pursue their goals in ways that respect both the structure of government and the rights won in the Revolution and Civil War. The idea that judges should spur the other branches on to ever greater reconstitutions of society is alien to the original design.

It is here that Professor Tribe and I conclusively part company. The difference between us is not so much about the role of economics in judging as it is about the role of judges in society. Our differences could not be deeper if neither of us had heard of Adam Smith. . . .

Judges have no authority to reconstitute the values of the people or to exalt redistribution at the expense of competing objectives selected by the political branches. Our Constitution is based on the ideas of Locke and Montesquieu, not the view of Rousseau that the state should imbue its citizens with the "true" values they "ought" to hold. The Framers were skeptical about both the existence of such values and the wisdom of trusting the government to choose among them. They rejected the arguments of the anti-Federalists, which were very similar to those of Rousseau and Professor Tribe. The choice made in 1787 was to separate powers, not to give judges the functions of both making and executing decisions about the fundamental values of society. As Hamilton quoted Montesquieu in *The Federalist* No. 78, "[T]here is no liberty, if the power of judging be not separated from the legislative and executive powers." The choice was to recognize and rely on the self-interest of factions—public and private—rather than to scorn faction and seek the instruction of Platonic guardians.

The Constitution demands that all power be authorized. It is not enough to say that judicial decisions are about "how we define our society and specify much about what we stand for and what sort of country we wish to become." "We the People" speak through the Constitution itself, through representatives in the legislature, through the amending process. Judges are granted tenure to *insulate* them from the wishes of today's majorities, not to enable them to claim inspiration about the "true will" of the people. The passage of time cannot make Rousseau the courts' guiding star—not, at least, without another revolution. The Court's drift from economic substantive due process to other forms of substantive intervention did not occur because of a new grant of legitimate authority. Judges applying the Constitution we have, rather than the one Professor Tribe wishes we had, must take their guidance and authority from decisions made elsewhere. Otherwise they speak with the same authority they and Professor Tribe and I possess when we fill the law reviews with our speculations and desires: none. And the other branches owe no obedience to those who speak without authority.

This is not to say that the judicial process is mechanical. Far from it. The process involves the most delicate assessment of meaning. Knowledge is ephemeral, and doubts about both the meaning of words and the effects of rules tax the greatest interpreters. But none of this changes the source of the power to decide. Judges can legitimately demand to be obeyed only when their decisions stem from fair interpretations of commands laid down in the texts. This principle—the real source of the disagreement between Professor Tribe and me, and between Tribe and the Court—has nothing to do with economics. Professor Tribe would be dismayed no matter why judges took a restricted view of the considerations they deemed to be appropriate in deciding cases. Professor Tribe would not be happy with a Court staffed by Justices with Felix Frankfurter's view of the role of judges, even though Justice Frankfurter thought ill of economics. An understanding of economics does not cause people to invent limits on the role of judges. Causation runs the other way. Those who believe that judges have but a limited role to play in government are also more likely to be comfortable using the liberal, individualist premises that Professor Tribe rightly sees as important parts of economic thought.

IV.

Determining how "we reaffirm and create, select and shape, the values and truths we hold sacred" is the most pressing task for the political society. But the execution of this task falls on the people and their representatives. The delicacy and indeterminacy of the task is no reason for judges to pretend that there is no scarcity.

Once they must deal with scarcity, they must deal with economics. They may discharge this obligation expressly or by implication, well or poorly, but deal with it they will. Utopian visions yield political aspiration, but aspiration and adjudication must be separated. Hopes for a better society do not justify unreflective treatment of the tradeoffs we must make in a world of scarcity.

"Surely there is no justification for a third legislative branch in the federal government."

12.8 THE NOTION OF A LIVING CONSTITUTION

William H. Rehnquist

William H. Rehnquist is Chief Justice of the United States.

At least one of the more than half-dozen persons nominated during the past decade to be an Associate Justice of the Supreme Court of the United States has been asked by the Senate Judiciary Committee at his confirmation hearings whether he believed in a living Constitution. It is not an easy question to answer; the phrase "living Constitution" has about it a teasing imprecision that makes it a coat of many colors. . . .

. . . The phrase is really a shorthand expression that is susceptible of at least two quite different meanings.

The first meaning was expressed . . . by Mr. Justice Holmes in *Missouri v. Holland* (1920).

> . . . When we are dealing with words that also are a constituent act, like the Constitution of the United States, we must realize that they have called into life a being the development of which could not have been foreseen completely by

From William H. Rehnquist, "The Notion of a Living Constitution," 54 *Texas Law Review* 693 (1976). Quoted with the permission of the copyright owner, *Texas Law Review*, The University of Texas School of Law, 2500 Red River, Austin, Texas 78705.

the most gifted of its begetters. It was enough for them to realize or to hope that they had created an organism; it has taken a century and has cost their successors much sweat and blood to prove that they created a nation.

. . . The framers of the Constitution wisely spoke in general language and left to succeeding generations the task of applying that language to the unceasingly changing environment in which they would live. . . . Merely because a particular activity may not have existed when the Constitution was adopted, or because the framers could not have conceived of a particular method of transacting affairs, cannot mean that general language in the Constitution may not be applied to such a course of conduct. Where the framers of the Constitution have used general language, they have given latitude . . . to make that language applicable to cases that the framers might not have foreseen.

. . . I have sensed a second connotation of the phrase "living Constitution." . . . Embodied in its most naked form, it recently came to my attention in some language from a brief that had been filed in a United States District Court on behalf of state prisoners asserting that the conditions of their confinement offended the United States Constitution . . . :

> We are asking a great deal of the Court because other branches of government have abdicated their responsibility. . . . Prisoners are like other "discrete and insular" minorities for whom the Court must spread its protective umbrella because no other branch of government will do so. . . . This Court, as the voice and conscience of contemporary society, as the measure of the modern conception of human dignity, must declare that the [named prison] and all it represents offends the Constitution of the United States and will not be tolerated.

Here we have a living Constitution with a vengeance. Although the substitution of some other set of values for those which may be derived from the language and intent of the framers is not urged in so many words, that is surely the thrust of the message. Under this brief writer's version of the living Constitution, nonelected members of the federal judiciary may address themselves to a social problem simply because other branches of government have failed or refused to do so. These same judges, responsible to no constituency whatever, are nonetheless acclaimed as "the voice and conscience of contemporary society."

. . . [T]hose who have pondered the matter have always recognized that the ideal of judicial review has basically antidemocratic and antimajoritarian facets that require some justification in this Nation, which prides itself on being a self-governing representative democracy. . . .

All who have studied law, and many who have not, are familiar with John Marshall's classic defense of judicial review in his opinion for the Court in *Marbury v. Madison*. . . . [W]hile it supports the Holmes version of the phrase "living Constitution," it also suggests some outer limits for the brief writer's version.

The ultimate source of authority in this Nation, Marshall said, is not Congress, not the states, not for that matter the Supreme Court. . . . The people are the ultimate source of authority; they have parceled out the authority that originally resided entirely with them by adopting the original Constitution and by later amending it. . . .

In addition, Marshall said that if the popular branches of government . . . are operating within the authority granted to them by the Constitution, their judgment and not that of the Court must obviously prevail. When these branches overstep the authority given them by the Constitution . . . or invade protected individual rights, and a constitutional challenge to their action is raised in a lawsuit brought in federal court, the Court must prefer the Constitution to the government acts.

John Marshall's justification for judicial review makes the provision for an independent federal judiciary not only understandable but also thoroughly desirable. Since the judges will be merely interpreting an instrument framed by the people, they should be detached and objective. A mere change in public opinion since the adoption of the Constitution, unaccompanied by a constitutional amendment, should not change the meaning of the Constitution. . . .

Clearly Marshall's explanation contains certain elements of either ingenuousness or ingeniousness. . . . The Constitution is in many of its parts obviously not a specifically worded document but one couched in general phraseology. There is obviously wide room for honest difference of opinion over the meaning of general phrases in the Constitution; any particular Justice's decision when a question arises under one of these general phrases will depend to some extent on his own philosophy of constitutional law. One may nevertheless concede all of these problems . . . yet feel that [Marshall's] justification for nonelected judges exercising the power of judicial review is the only one consistent with democratic philosophy of representative government. . . .

One senses no . . . connection with a popularly adopted constituent act in . . . the brief writer's version of the living Constitution. The brief writer's version seems instead to be based upon the proposition that federal judges, perhaps judges as a whole, have a role . . . , quite independent of popular will, to play in solving society's problems. Once we have abandoned the idea that the authority of the courts to declare laws unconstitutional is somehow tied to the language of the Constitution that the people adopted, a judiciary exercising the power of judicial review appears in a quite different light. Judges then are no longer the keepers of the covenant; instead they are a small group of fortunately situated people with a roving commission to second-guess Congress, state legislatures, and state and federal administrative officers concerning what is best for the country. Surely there is no justification for a third legislative branch in the federal government, and there is even less justification for a federal legislative branch's reviewing on a policy basis the laws enacted by the legislatures of the fifty states. . . . If there is going to be a council of revision, it ought to have at least some connection with popular feeling. Its members either ought to stand for reelection on occasion, or their terms should expire and they should be allowed to continue serving only if reappointed by a popularly elected Chief Executive and confirmed by a popularly elected Senate.

The brief writer's version of the living Constitution is seldom presented in its most naked form but is instead usually dressed in more attractive garb. The argument in favor of this approach generally begins with a sophisticated wink—why pretend that there is any ascertainable content to the general phrases of the Constitution as they are written since, after all, judges constantly disagree about their meaning? . . . We all know the basis of Marshall's justification for judicial review, the argument runs, but it is necessary only to keep the window dressing in place. Any sophisticated student of the subject knows that judges need not limit themselves to the intent of the Framers, which is very difficult to determine in any event. Because of the general language used in the Constitution, judges should not hesitate to use their authority to make the Constitution relevant and useful in solving the problems of modern society. . . .

At least three serious difficulties flaw the brief writer's version of the living Constitution. First, it misconceives the nature of the Constitution, which was designed to enable the popularly elected branches of government, not the judicial branch, to keep the country abreast of the times. Second, the brief writer's version ignores the Supreme Court's disastrous experiences when in the past it embraced contemporary, fashionable notions of what a living Constitution should contain. Third, however socially desirable the goals sought to be advanced by the brief writer's version, advancing them through a freewheeling, nonelected judiciary is quite unacceptable in a democratic society.

It seems to me that it is almost impossible, after reading the record of the Founding Fathers' debates in Philadelphia, to conclude that they intended the Constitution itself to suggest answers to the manifold problems that they knew would confront succeeding generations. The Constitution that they drafted was indeed intended to endure indefinitely, but the reason for this very well-founded hope was the general language by which national authority was granted to Congress and the Presidency. These two branches were to furnish the motive power within the federal system, which was in turn to coexist with the state governments. . . . Limitations were indeed placed upon both federal and state governments. . . . These limitations, however, were not themselves designed to solve the problems of the future, but were instead designed to make certain that the constituent branches, when they attempted to solve those problems, should not transgress these fundamental limitations.

Although the Civil War Amendments [XIII–XV] were designed more as broad limitations on the authority of state governments, they too were enacted in response to practices that the lately seceded states engaged in to discriminate against and mistreat the newly emancipated freed men. To the extent that the language of these amendments is general, the courts are of course warranted in giving them an application coextensive with their language. Nevertheless, I greatly doubt that even men like Thad Stevens and John Bingham, leaders of the radical Republicans in Congress, would have thought any portion of the Civil War Amendments, except section five of the Fourteenth Amendment, was designed to solve problems that society might confront a century later. I think they would have said that those amendments were designed to prevent from ever recurring abuses in which the states had engaged prior to that time.

The brief writer's version of the living Constitution, however, suggests that if the states' legislatures and governors, or Congress and the President, have not solved a particular social problem, then the federal court may act. I do not believe that this argument will withstand rational analysis. Even in the face of a conceded social evil, a reasonably competent and reasonably representative legislature may decide to do nothing. It may decide that the evil is not of sufficient magnitude to warrant any governmental intervention. It may decide that the financial cost of eliminating the evil is not worth the benefit which would result from its elimination. It may decide that the evils which might ensue from the proposed solution are worse than the evils which the solution would eliminate.

Surely the Constitution does not put either the legislative branch or the executive branch in the position of a television quiz show contestant so that when a given period of time has elapsed and a problem remains unsolved by them, the federal judiciary may press a buzzer and take its turn at fashioning a solution.

The second difficulty with the brief writer's version of the living Constitution lies in its inattention to or rejection of the Supreme Court's historical experience gleaned from similar forays into problem solving. . . .

The third difficulty with the brief writer's notion of the living Constitution is that it seems to ignore totally the nature of political value judgments in a democratic society. If such a society adopts a constitution and incorporates in that constitution safeguards for individual liberty, these safeguards indeed do take on a generalized moral rightness or goodness. They assume a general social acceptance neither because of any intrinsic worth nor because of any unique origins in someone's idea of natural justice but instead simply because they have been incorporated in a constitution by the people. Within the limits of our Constitution, the representatives of the people in the executive branches of the state and national governments enact laws. The laws that emerge after a typical political struggle in which various individual value judgments are debated likewise take on a form of moral goodness. . . . It is the fact of their enactment that gives them whatever moral claim they have upon us as a society, however, and not any independent virtue they may have in any particular citizen's own scale of values.

Beyond the Constitution and the laws in our society, there simply is no basis other than the individual conscience of the citizen that may serve as a platform for the launching of moral judgments. There is no conceivable way in which I can logically demonstrate to you that the judgments of my conscience are superior to the judgments of your conscience, and vice versa. Many of us necessarily feel strongly and deeply about our own moral judgments, but they remain only personal moral judgments until in some way given the sanction of law. . . .

. . . Representative government is predicated upon the idea that one who feels deeply upon a question as a matter of conscience will seek out others of like view or will attempt to persuade others who do not initially share that view. When adherents to the belief become sufficiently numerous, he will have the necessary armaments required in a democratic society to press his views upon the elected representatives of the people, and to have them embodied into positive law.

Should a person fail to persuade the legislature, or should he feel that a legislative victory would be insufficient because of its potential for future reversal, he may seek to run the more difficult gauntlet of amending the Constitution. . . .

I know of no other method compatible with political theory basic to democratic society by which one's own conscientious belief may be translated into positive law and thereby obtain the only general moral imprimatur permissible in a pluralistic, democratic society. It is always time consuming, frequently difficult, and not infrequently impossible to run successfully the legislative gauntlet. . . . It is even more difficult for either a single individual or indeed for a large group of individuals to succeed in having such a value judgment embodied in the Constitution. All of these burdens and difficulties are entirely consistent with the notion of a democratic society. It should not be easy for any one individual or group of individuals to impose by law their value judgments upon fellow citizens who may disagree with those judgments. Indeed, it should not be easier just because the individual in question is a judge. . . .

The brief writer's version of the living Constitution, in the last analysis, is a formula for an end run around popular government. To the extent that it makes possible an individual's persuading one or more appointed federal judges to impose on other individuals a rule of conduct that the popularly elected branches of government would not have enacted and the voters have not and would not have embodied in the Constitution, the brief writer's version of the living Constitution is genuinely corrosive of the fundamental values of our democratic society.

"Those who ignore the distinction between concepts and conceptions . . .
are forced to argue in a vulnerable way."

12.9 TAKING RIGHTS SERIOUSLY

Ronald Dworkin

Ronald Dworkin, is Quayne Professor of Jurisprudence at University College, London and Professor of Law and Philosophy at New York University.

[I]n what follows I shall use the name "Nixon" to refer not to Nixon but to any politician holding the set of attitudes about the Supreme Court that he made explicit in his political campaigns. There was, fortunately, only one real Nixon, but there are, in the special sense in which I use the name, many Nixons.

What can be the basis of this composite Nixon's opposition to the controversial decisions of the Warren Court? He cannot object to these decisions simply because they went beyond prior law, or say that the Supreme Court must never change its mind. Indeed the Burger Court itself seems intent on limiting the liberal decisions of the Warren Court. . . . The Constitution's guarantee of 'equal protection of the laws,' it is true, does not in plain words determine that "separate but equal" school facilities are unconstitutional, or that segregation was so unjust that heroic measures are required to undo its effects. But neither does it provide that as a matter of constitutional law the Court would be wrong to reach these conclusions. It leaves these issues to the Court's judgment, and the Court would have made law just as much if it had, for example, refused to hold [segregation] unconstitutional. . . .

So we must search further to find a theoretical basis for Nixon's position. . . .

2

The constitutional theory on which our government rests is not a simple majoritarian theory. The Constitution, and particularly the Bill of Rights, is designed to protect individual citizens and groups against certain decisions that a majority of citizens might want to make, even when that majority acts in what it takes to be the general or common interest. Some of these constitutional restraints take the form of fairly precise rules. . . . But other constraints take the form of what are often called "vague" standards, for example, the provision that the government shall not deny men due process of law, or equal protection of the laws.

This interference with democratic practice requires a justification. The draftsmen of the Constitution assumed that these restraints could be justified by appeal to moral rights which individuals possess against the majority and which the constitutional provisions, both "vague" and precise, might be said to recognize and protect.

The "vague" standards were chosen deliberately . . . in place of the more specific and limited rules that they might have enacted. But their decision . . . has caused a great deal of legal and political controversy, because even reasonable men of good will differ when they try to elaborate, for example, the moral rights that the due process clause or the equal protection clause brings into the law. They also differ when they try to apply these rights, however defined, to complex matters of political administration. . . .

The practice has developed of referring to a "strict" and a "liberal" side to these controversies, so that the Supreme Court might be said to have taken the "liberal" side in the segregation cases and its critics the "strict" side. Nixon has this distinction in mind when he calls himself a "strict constructionist." But the distinction is in fact confusing because it runs together two different issues that must be separated. Any case that arises under the "vague" constitutional guarantees can be seen as posing two questions: (1) Which decision is required by strict, that is to say faithful, adherence to the text of the Constitution or to the intention of those who adopted that text? (2) Which decision is required by a political philosophy that takes a strict, that is to say narrow, view of the moral rights that individuals have against society? Once these questions are distinguished, it is plain that they may have different answers. The text of the First Amendment, for example, says that Congress shall make no law abridging the freedom of speech, but a narrow view of individual rights would permit many such laws. . . .

In the case of the "vague" provisions, however, like the due process and equal protection clauses, lawyers have run the two questions together because they have relied, largely without recognizing it, on a theory of meaning that might be put this way: If the Framers of the Constitution use vague language . . . then what they "said" or "meant" is limited to the instances of official action that they had in mind as violations, or, at least, to those instances that they would have thought were violations if they had had them in mind. . . .

This theory makes a strict interpretation of the text yield a narrow view of constitutional rights, because it limits such rights to those recognized by a limited group of people at a fixed date of history. . . .

But the theory of meaning on which this argument depends is far too crude; it ignores a distinction that philosophers have made but lawyers have not yet appreciated. Suppose I tell my children simply that I expect them not to treat others unfairly. I no doubt have in mind examples of the conduct I mean to discourage, but I would not accept that my "meaning" was limited to these examples, for two reasons. First I would expect my children to apply my instructions to situations I had not and could not have thought about. Second, I stand ready to admit that some particular act I had thought was fair when I spoke was in fact unfair, or vice versa, if one of my children is able to convince me of that later; in that case I should want to say that my instructions covered the case he cited, not that I had changed my instructions. I might say that I meant the family to be guided by the concept of fairness, not by any specific conception of fairness I might have had in mind.

This is a crucial distinction. . . . Suppose a group believes in common that acts may suffer from a special moral defect which they call unfairness and which consists in a wrongful division of benefits and burdens, or a wrongful attribution of praise or blame. Suppose also that they agree on a great number of standard cases of unfairness and use these as benchmarks against which to test other, more controversial cases. In that case, the group has a concept of unfairness, and its members may appeal to that concept in moral instruction or argument. But members of that group may nevertheless differ over a large number of these controversial cases, in a way that suggests that each either has or acts on a different theory of why the standard cases are acts of unfairness. They may differ, that is, on which more fundamental principles must be relied upon to show that a particular division or attribution is unfair. In that case, the members have different conceptions of fairness.

If so, then members of this community who give instructions or set standards in the name of fairness may be doing two different things. First they may be appealing to the concept of fairness, simply by instructing others to act fairly; in this case they charge those whom they instruct with the responsibility of developing and applying their own conception of fairness as controversial cases arise. That is not the same thing, of course, as granting them a discretion to act as they like; it sets a standard which they must try—and may fail—to meet. . . . The man who appeals to the concept in this way may have his own conception . . . but he holds this conception only as his own theory of how the standard he set must be met, so that when he changes his theory he has not changed that standard.

On the other hand, the members may be laying down a particular conception of fairness; I would have done this, for example, if I had listed my wishes with respect to controversial examples or if, even less likely, I had specified some controversial and explicit theory of fairness. . . . The difference is a difference not just in the detail of the instructions given but in the kind of instructions given. When I appeal to the concept of fairness I appeal to what fairness means, and I give my views on that issue no special standing. When I lay down a conception of fairness, I lay down what I mean by fairness, and my view is therefore the heart of the matter. . . .

Once this distinction is made it seems obvious that we must take what I have been calling 'vague' constitutional clauses as representing appeals to the concepts they employ, like legality, equality, and cruelty. . . .

Those who ignore the distinction between concepts and conceptions. . . are forced to argue in a vulnerable way. If those who enacted the broad clauses had meant to lay down particular conceptions, they would have found the sort of language conventionally used to do this, that is, they would have offered particular theories of the concepts in question.

Indeed the very practice of calling these clauses "vague" . . . can now be seen to involve a mistake. The clauses are vague only if we take them to be botched or incomplete or schematic attempts to lay down particular conceptions. If we take them as appeals to moral concepts they could not be made more precise by being more detailed.

The confusion I mentioned between the two senses of "strict" construction is therefore very misleading indeed. If courts try to be faithful to the text of the Constitution, they will for that very reason be forced to decide between competing conceptions of political morality. So it is wrong to attack the Warren Court, for example, on the ground that it failed to treat the Constitution as a binding text. On the contrary, if we wish to treat fidelity to that text as an overriding requirement of constitutional interpretation, then it is the conservative critics of the Warren Court who are at fault, because their philosophy ignores the direction to face issues of moral principle that the logic of the text demands.

I put the matter in a guarded way because we may not want to accept fidelity to the spirit of the text as an overriding principle of constitutional adjudication. It may be more important for courts to decide constitutional cases in a manner that respects the judgments of other institutions of government, for example. Or it may be more important for courts to protect established legal doctrines, so that citizens and the government can have confidence that the courts will hold to what they have said before. But it is crucial to recognize that these other policies compete with the principle that the Constitution is the fundamental and imperative source of constitutional law. They are not, as the "strict constructionists" suppose, simply consequences of that principle.

3

Once the matter is put in this light . . . we are able to assess these competing claims of policy, free from the confusion imposed by the popular notion of "strict construction." For this purpose I want now to compare and contrast two very general philosophies of how the courts should decide difficult or controversial constitutional issues. I shall call these two philosophies by the names they are given in the legal literature—the programs of "judicial activism" and "judicial restraint"—though it will be plain that these names are in certain ways misleading.

The program of judicial activism holds that courts should accept the directions of the so-called vague constitutional provisions in the spirit I described. . . . They should work out principles of legality, equality, and the rest, revise these principles from time to time in the light of what seems to the Court fresh moral insight, and judge the acts of Congress, the states, and the President accordingly. . . .

The program of judicial restraint, on the contrary, argues that courts should allow the decisions of other branches of government to stand, even when they offend the judges' own sense of the principles required by the broad constitutional doctrines, except when these decisions are so offensive to political morality that they would violate the provisions on any plausible interpretation, or, perhaps, when a contrary decision is required by clear precedent. . . .

The Supreme Court followed the policy of activism rather than restraint in cases like the segregation cases because the words of the equal protection clause left it open whether the various educational practices of the states concerned should be taken to violate the Constitution, no clear precedent held that they did, and reasonable men might differ on the moral issues involved. . . . But the program of restraint would not always act to provide decisions that would please political conservatives, In the early days of the New Deal . . . it was the liberals who objected to Court decisions that struck down acts of Congress in the name of the due process clause.

It may seem, therefore, that if Nixon has a legal theory it depends crucially on some theory of judicial restraint. We must now, however, notice a distinction between two forms of judicial restraint, for there are two different, and indeed incompatible, grounds on which that policy might be based.

The first is a theory of political skepticism that might be described in this way. The policy of judicial activism presupposes a certain objectivity of moral principle; in particular it presupposes that citizens do have certain moral rights against the state, like a moral right to equality of public education or to fair treatment by the police. Only if such moral rights exist in some sense can activism be justified as a program based on something beyond the judge's personal preferences. The skeptical theory attacks activism at its roots; it argues that in fact individuals have no such moral rights against the state. They have only such legal rights as the Constitution grants them, and these are limited to the plain and uncontroversial violations of public morality that the framers must have had actually in mind, or that have since been established in a line of precedent.

The alternative ground of a program of restraint is a theory of judicial deference. Contrary to the skeptical theory, this assumes that citizens do have moral rights against the state beyond what the law expressly grants them, but it points out that the character and strength of these rights are debatable and argues that political institutions other than courts are responsible for deciding which rights are to be recognized.

This is an important distinction, even though the literature of constitutional law does not draw it with any clarity. The skeptical theory and the theory of deference differ dramatically in the kind of justification they assume, and in their implications for the more general moral theories of the men who profess to hold them. These theories are so different that most American politicians can consistently accept the second, but not the first.

A skeptic takes the view . . . that men have no moral rights against the state and only such legal rights as the law expressly provides. But what does this mean, and what sort of argument might the skeptic make for his view? . . . I shall rely, in trying to answer these questions, on a low-keyed theory of moral rights against the state. . . . Under that theory, a man has a moral right against the state if for some reason the state would do wrong to treat him in a certain way, even though it would be in the general interest to do so. . . .

I want to say a word about the virtues of this way of looking at moral rights against the state. . . . [I]t simply shows a claim of right to be a special, in the sense of a restricted, sort of judgment about what is right or wrong for governments to do.

Moreover, this way of looking at rights avoids some of the notorious puzzles associated with the concept. It allows us to say, with no sense of strangeness, that rights may vary in strength and character from case to case, and from point to point in history. If we think of rights as things, these metamorphoses seem strange, but we are used to the idea that moral judgments about what it is right or wrong to do are complex and are affected by considerations that are relative and that change.

The skeptic who wants to argue against the very possibility of rights against the state of this sort has a difficult brief. He must rely, I think, on one of three general positions: (a) He might display a more pervasive moral skepticism, which holds that even to speak of an act being morally right or wrong makes no sense. . . . (b) He might hold a stark form of utilitarianism, which assumes that the only reason we ever have for regarding an act as right or wrong is its impact on the general interest. Under that theory, to say that busing may be morally required even though it does not benefit the community generally would be inconsistent. Or He might accept some form of totalitarian theory, which merges the interest of the individual in the good of the general community, and so denies that the two can conflict.

Very few American politicians would be able to accept any of these three grounds. . . .

I do not want to suggest, however, that no one would in fact argue for judicial restraint on grounds of skepticism; on the contrary, some of the best-known advocates of restraint have pitched their arguments entirely on skeptical grounds. In 1957, for example, the great judge Learned Hand . . . argued for judicial restraint and said that the Supreme Court had done wrong to declare school segregation illegal. . . . It is wrong to suppose, he said, that claims about moral rights express anything more than the speakers' preferences. If the Supreme Court justifies its decisions by making such claims, rather than by relying on positive law, it is usurping the place of the legislature, for the job of the legislature, representing the majority, is to decide whose preferences shall govern.

This simple appeal to democracy is successful if one accepts the skeptical premise. . . . But a very different, and much more vulnerable, argument from democracy is needed to support judicial restraint if it is based not on skepticism but on deference, as I shall try to show.

4

. . . [A] theory of restraint based . . . on deference [holds] that courts ought not to decide controversial issues of political morality because they ought to leave such decisions to other departments of government. . . .

There is one very popular argument in favor of the policy of deference, which might be called the argument from democracy. It is at least debatable, according to this argument, whether a sound conception of equality forbids segregated education or requires measures like busing to break it down. Who ought to decide these debatable issues of moral and political theory? Should it be a majority of a court in Washington, whose members are appointed for life and are not politically responsible to the public whose lives will be affected by the decision? Or should it be the elected and responsible state or national legislators? A democrat, so this argument supposes, can accept only the second answer.

But the argument from democracy is weaker than it might first appear. The argument assumes, for one thing, that state legislatures are in fact responsible to the people in the way that democratic theory assumes. But in all the states, though in different degrees and for different reasons, that is not the case. . . . I want to pass that point, however, because it does not so much undermine the argument from democracy as call for more democracy. . . . I want to fix attention on the issue of whether the appeal to democracy in this respect is even right in principle.

The argument assumes that in a democracy all unsettled issues, including issues of moral and political principle, must be resolved only by institutions that are politically responsible in the way that courts are not. Why should we accept that view of democracy? To say that that is what democracy means does no good, because it is wrong to suppose that the word, as a word, has anything like so precise a meaning. Even if it did, we should then have to rephrase our question to ask why we should have democracy, if we assume that is what it means. Nor is it better to say that that view of democracy is established in the American Constitution, or so entrenched in our political tradition that we are committed to it. We cannot argue that the Constitution, which provides no rule limiting judicial review to clear cases, establishes a theory of democracy that excludes wider review, nor can we say that our courts have in fact consistently accepted such a restriction. . . .

So the argument from democracy is not an argument to which we are committed either by our words or our past. We must accept it, if at all, on the strength of its own logic. In order to examine the arguments more closely, however, we must make a further distinction. The argument . . . might be continued in two different ways: one might argue that judicial deference is required because democratic institutions, like legislatures, are in fact likely to make sounder decisions than courts . . . about the nature of an individual's moral right against the state.

Or one might argue that it is for some reason fairer that a democratic institution rather than a court should decide such issues. . . . The distinction between these two arguments would make no sense to a skeptic, who would not admit that someone could do a better or worse job at identifying moral rights against the state, any more than someone could do a better or worse job of identifying ghosts. But a lawyer who believes in judicial deference rather than skepticism must acknowledge the distinction. . . .

I shall start with the second argument, that legislatures and other democratic institutions have some special title to make constitutional decisions. . . . One might say that the nature of this title is obvious, because it is always fairer to allow a majority to decide any issue than a minority. But that . . . ignores the fact that decisions about rights against the majority are not issues that in fairness ought to be left to the majority. Constitutionalism—the theory that the majority must be restrained to protect individual right—may be a good or bad political theory, but the United States has adopted that theory, and to make the majority judge in its own cause seems inconsistent and unjust. So principles of fairness seem to speak against, not for, the argument from democracy.

Chief Justice Marshall recognized this . . . in *Marbury v. Madison*. . . . He argued that since the Constitution provides that the Constitution shall be the supreme law of the land, the courts . . . must have power to declare statutes void that offend that Constitution. Many legal scholars regard his argument as a non sequitur; because, they say, although constitutional constraints are part of the law, the courts, rather than the legislature itself, have not necessarily been given authority to decide whether in particular cases that law has been violated. But the argument is not a non sequitur if we take the principle that no man should be judge in his own cause to be so fundamental a part of the idea of legality that Marshall would have been entitled to disregard it only if the Constitution had expressly denied judicial review.

Some might object that it is simple-minded to say that a policy of deference leaves the majority to judge its own cause. Political decisions are made, in the United States, not by one stable majority but by many different political institutions each representing a different constituency which itself changes its composition over time. The decision of one branch of government may well be reviewed by another branch that is also politically responsible, but to a larger or different constituency. . . .

But this objection is itself too glib, because it ignores the special character of disputes about individual moral rights as distinct from other kinds of political disputes. Different institutions do have different constituencies when, for example, labor or trade or welfare issues are involved. . . . But this is not generally the case when individual constitutional rights, like the rights of accused criminals, are at issue. It has been typical of these disputes that the interests of those in political control of the various institutions of the government have been both homogeneous and hostile. Indeed that is why political theorists have conceived of constitutional rights as rights against the "state" or the "majority" as such, rather than against any particular body or branch of government. . . .

It does seem fair to say, therefore, that the argument from democracy asks that those in political power be invited to be the sole judge of their own decisions. . . . That is not a final proof that a policy of judicial activism is superior to a program of deference. . . . But the point does undermine the argument that the majority, in fairness, must be allowed to decide the limits of its own power.

We must therefore turn to the other continuation of the argument from democracy, which holds that democratic institutions, like legislatures, are likely to reach sounder results about the moral rights of individuals than would courts. In 1969 the late Professor Alexander Bickel . . . argued for the program of judicial restraint in a novel and ingenious way. He allowed himself to suppose, for purposes of argument, that the Warren Court's program of activism could be justified if in fact it produced desirable results. He appeared, therefore, to be testing the policy of activism on its own grounds, because he took activism to be precisely the claim that the courts have the moral right to improve the future, whatever legal theory may say. . . . Bickel accepted it, at least provisionally, but he argued that activism fails its own test.

The future that the Warren Court sought has already begun not to work, Bickel said. The philosophy of racial integration it adopted was too crude, for example, and has already been rejected by the more imaginative leaders of the black community. Its thesis of simple and radical equality has proved unworkable in many other ways as well; its simple formula for one-man- one-vote for passing on the fairness of election districting, for instance, has produced neither sense nor fairness.

Why should a radical Court that aims at improving society fail even on its own terms? Bickel has this answer: courts, including the Supreme Court, must decide blocks of cases on principle, rather than responding in a piecemeal way to a shifting set of political pressures. They must do so not simply because their institutional morality requires it but because their institutional structure provides no means by which they might gauge political forces even if they wanted to. But government by principle is an inefficient and in the long run fatal form of government, no matter how able and honest the statesmen who try to administer it. For there is a limit to the complexity that any principle can contain and remain a recognizable principle, and this limit falls short of the complexity of social organization.

The Supreme Court's reapportionment decisions, in Bickel's view, were not mistaken just because the Court chose the wrong principle. One-man-one-vote is too simple, but the Court could not have found a better, more sophisticated principle that would have served as a successful test for election districting across the country, or across the years, because successful districting depends upon accommodation with thousands of facts of political life and can be reached, if at all, only by the chaotic and unprincipled development of history. Judicial activism cannot work as well as government by the more-or-less democratic institutions, not because democracy is required by principle but, on the contrary, because democracy works without principle, forming institutions and compromises as a river forms a bed on its way to the sea.

What are we to make of Bickel's argument? His account of recent history can be, and has been, challenged. It is by no means plain, certainly not yet, that racial integration will fail as a long-term strategy; and he is wrong if he thinks that black Americans, of whom more still belong to the NAACP than to more militant organizations, have rejected it. No doubt the nation's sense of how to deal with the curse of racism swings back and forth as the complexity and size of the problem become more apparent, but Bickel may have written at a high point of one arc of the pendulum.

He is also wrong to judge the Supreme Court's effect on history as if the Court were the only institution at work, or to suppose that if the Court's goal has not been achieved the country is worse off than if it had not tried. . . . Nor do we have much basis for supposing that the racial situation in America would now be more satisfactory, on balance, if the Court had not intervened, in 1954, and later, in the way that it did.

But there is a very different, and for my purpose much more important, objection to take to Bickel's theory. His theory is novel because it appears to concede an issue of principle to judicial activism, namely that the Court is entitled to intervene if its intervention produces socially desirable results. But the concession is an illusion, because his sense of what is socially desirable is inconsistent with the presupposition of activism that individuals have moral rights against the state. In fact, Bickel's argument cannot succeed, even if we grant his facts and his view of history, except on a basis of a skepticism about rights as profound as Learned Hand's.

I presented Bickel's theory as an example of one form of the argument from democracy, the argument that since men disagree about rights, it is safer to leave the final decision about rights to the political process, safer in the sense that the results are likely to be sounder. Bickel suggests a reason why the political process is safer. He argues that the endurance of a political settlement about rights is some evidence of the political morality of that settlement. He argues that this evidence is better than the sorts of argument from principle that judges might deploy if the decision were left to them. . . .

. . . [Bickel] argues that the organic political process will secure the genuine rights of men more certainly if it is not hindered by the artificial and rationalistic intrusion of the courts. In this view, the rights of blacks, suspects, and atheists will emerge through the process of political institutions responding to political pressures in the normal way. If a claim of right cannot succeed in this way, then for that reason it is, or in any event it is likely to be, an improper claim or right. But this bizarre proposition is only a disguised form of the skeptical point that there are in fact no rights against the state.

Perhaps, as Burke and his modern followers argue, a society will produce the institutions that best suit it only by evolution and never by radical reform. But rights against the state are claims that, if accepted, require society to settle for institutions that may not suit it so comfortably. The nerve of a claim of right . . . is that an individual is entitled to protection against the majority even at the cost of the general interest. Of course the comfort of the majority will require some accommodation for minorities but only to the extent necessary to preserve order; and that is usually an accommodation that falls short of recognizing their rights.

Indeed the suggestion that rights can be demonstrated by a process of history rather than by an appeal to principle shows either a confusion or no real concern about what rights are. A claim of right presupposes a moral argument and can be established in no other way. Bickel paints the judicial activists . . . as eighteenth-century philosophers who appeal to principle because they hold the optimistic view that a blueprint may be cut for progress. But this picture confuses two grounds for the appeal to principle and reform, and two senses of progress.

It is one thing to appeal to moral principle in the silly faith that ethics as well as economics moves by an invisible hand, so that individual rights and the general good will coalesce, and law based on principle will move the nation to a frictionless utopia. . . . But it is quite another matter to appeal to principle as principle, to show, for example, that it is unjust to force black children to take their public education in black schools, even if a great many people will be worse off if the state adopt the measures needed to prevent this.

This is a different version of progress. It is moral progress, and though history may show how difficult it is to decide where moral progress lies, and how difficult to persuade others once one has decided, it cannot follow from this that those who govern us have no responsibility to face that decision or to attempt that persuasion.

5

This has been a complex argument, and I want to summarize it. Our constitutional system rests on a particular moral theory, namely, that men have moral rights against the state. The difficult clauses or the Bill of Rights, like the due process and equal protection clauses, must be understood as appealing to moral concepts rather than laying down particular conceptions; therefore a court that undertakes the burden of applying these clauses fully as law must be an activist court, in the sense that it must be prepared to frame and answer questions of political morality.

It may be necessary to compromise that activist posture to some extent, either for practical reasons or for compelling reasons of principle. But Nixon's public statements about the Supreme Court suggest that the activist policy must be abandoned altogether, and not merely compromised, for powerful reasons of principle. If we try to state these reasons of principle, we find that they are inconsistent with the assumption of a constitutional system, either because they leave the majority to judge its own cause, or because they rest on a skepticism about moral rights that neither Nixon nor most American politicians can consistently embrace.

So Nixon's jurisprudence is a pretense and no genuine theory at all. . . . Constitutional law can make no genuine advance until it isolates the problem of rights against the state and makes that problem part of its own agenda. That argues for a fusion of constitutional law and moral theory, a connection that, incredibly, has yet to take place. . . .

CHAPTER 13

The Processes of Judicial Decision Making

As previous chapters have shown, judicial decision making is far from being a mechanical act. Fact-finding in the courts differs from the search for truth in a laboratory or a library; judicial reasoning is not like the formal logic of the philosopher; and trial and appellate procedures differ in structure from those of legislatures and administrative agencies. Together these processes and structures narrow the alternatives that judges are likely to perceive and from among which they will choose; but singly or together these peculiar processes channel, rather than determine, judicial behavior. They leave room for the play of personal values, including moral judgments, philosophies of law, conceptions of proper judicial functions, weighings of probable effects of a decision, and perceptions of the political environment and likely reactions of other actors.

TRIAL COURTS

Lawsuits confront trial judges with a long and, occasionally, difficult series of questions (Reading 13.1; see also Chapters 3 and 9). Before criminal trials begin, judges rule on various motions raised by counsel and make determinations of the utmost concern to defendants, including whether to set bail and, if so, how high to set it; judges also accept any pleas negotiated between prosecuting attorneys and defense attorneys. Civil cases, too, often require judges to consider motions of opposing counsel as well as, in many instances, to encourage and accept settlement agreements. At trial, a judge must rule on motions almost as a reflex action. A lawyer may object to an opponent's questioning and ask the judge to resolve the issue. Especially when a jury is present, judges do not like to suspend proceedings while they research and meditate, although they sometimes must because of the complexity of the issue.

In contrast to the necessity for quick decisions while a trial is in progress, the judge has some opportunity to reflect on the instructions to be given to the jurors at the close of the trial. He or she usually asks the lawyers on each side to assist by drafting proposed instructions. Because the final decision in the case is the jury's, these instructions are usually not published, although they are kept with the records of the trial so that they can be reviewed in the event of an appeal. The sole record of the jury's deliberative process is the verdict itself.

Because proceedings before a judge sitting without a jury are much less formal than those with a jury present, the trial judge has to make relatively fewer rulings on procedural technicalities. After hearing the evidence and arguments and reading any briefs submitted, the judge decides the case either immediately or after deliberation that often lasts as long as several weeks and occasionally several months. That decision is accompanied by a written opinion that consists of at least two parts, findings of fact and conclusions of law; it might also include a statement explaining the reasoning by which the court arrived at these results.[1]

How judges of trial courts reach decisions is an interesting question with no shortage of answers. Some scholars argue that judges are primarily motivated to etch their policy preferences or values into law. This penchant could explain why judges affiliating with the Democratic party or appointed by Democratic presidents vote in a more liberal fashion than do their Republican colleagues (see Reading 4.6); generally Democrats are more liberal in their political orientations than are Republicans. Others have suggested that values tell only part of the story. In a comprehensive study of state judges in Iowa, James L. Gibson found that their political attitudes (which he derived from personal interviews) did not provide a very good predictor of their sentencing decisions. Only when Gibson considered the role orientations of these judges—that is, "their beliefs about the kind of behavior proper for a judge"—did political attitudes exert any influence.[2] Judges who believe that their own values and attitudes are legitimate criteria for decision making are in fact strongly influenced by those values and attitudes and reach sentencing outcomes accordingly; judges who believe that it is improper to consider their own preferences fail to take them into account when making their decisions. This finding led Gibson to conclude that role orientations may not predict judicial behavior but do "predict the criteria" of decisions.

Yet others have pointed to the influence of localism.[3] All state judges will be longtime residents of that state, and trial judges almost always longtime residents of the city, town, or county in which they sit. At the federal level, the

---

[1] It is up to trial court judges, at least U.S. District Court judges, to determine whether their opinions ought be published. The criterion they are supposed to use is whether the opinion "is of general precedential value." Apparently, they do not believe that most of their opinions meet this standard, given that as many as 90 percent go unpublished. See Donald R. Songer, "Nonpublication in the United States District Courts: Official Criteria versus Inferences from Appellate Review," 50 *Journal of Politics* 206 (1988).

[2] James L. Gibson, "Judges' Role Orientations, Attitudes, and Decisions: An Interactive Model," 72 *American Political Science Review* 918 (1978).

[3] We hasten to note that, although localism may have its greatest impact on trial courts, is not always absent at the federal appellate levels. Judges on each of the courts of appeals, except for that for the District of Columbia Circuit, will always be from that area, with every state in the circuit having a claim to one or more seats on that bench. Considerations of federalism operate even in selecting members of the Supreme Court. No longer can the justices "represent," in the sense of being "chosen from," each of the circuits; but geography is a nontrivial consideration for the precise reason that senators and other political leaders want people on the bench who understand their peculiar

situation is somewhat, but only somewhat, different for trial judges. As Chapter 4 pointed out, senatorial courtesy means that district judges are usually acceptable to their states' senators, which, in turn, means that they are apt to be not merely prominent lawyers but prominent local lawyers, men and women who have lived much of their lives in the communities in which they will serve. That connection often causes them to share many of the values that dominate the local community, assuming such exist. For instance, it was federal district judges who had the hard and sometimes dangerous task of overseeing racial integration in the South. Initially many, probably most, of these jurists (all of the fifty-eight were white males) shared the predominant southern white opposition to "racial mixing." The majority of these men were able to overcome, though not without difficulty, their prejudices; but others were determined to comply, if at all, only with the barest letter of the law.[4] As George Bell Timmerman, Sr., the Judge for the Eastern District of South Carolina and father of the governor, said in rebuffing the NAACP's efforts to desegregate public buses: "One's personality is not formed on a bus."

There is yet another form of localism, and it too can influence judicial decisions. For trial court judges to process cases efficiently and effectively, they must interact frequently with other (typically) local participants in the process, such as, in criminal cases, defense and prosecuting attorneys. Because these other actors and judges come to rely on one another to perform various tasks, they often develop (especially in small towns and cities) close personal and working relationships—or what some have called a courtroom "work group" or "community."[5] Those groups or communities, especially if they are stable, can affect the behavior of all their members, along with the outcomes of cases (Reading 13.2).

On a related note, scholars posit that trial judges are especially concerned with the efficient operation of their courtrooms, ruling in ways to maximize its effective operation and minimize work load demands.[6] Finally, some specialists argue that lower court judges are forward-looking actors, who make decisions that they believe higher courts will respect. We have more to say about this momentarily.

---

problems. In 1930, for instance, President Herbert Hoover hesitated to nominate Benjamin N. Cardozo because he was from New York and Chief Justice Charles Evans Hughes was also a New Yorker and Justice Harlan Fiske Stone, though born in New Hampshire, had lived much of his adult life in New York City. (Stone, a close personal friend of Hoover, pressured the president by offering to resign to overcome the geographical objection.) The way was eased when a western senator announced that Cardozo did not belong to New York but to the United States.

[4] See the superb study by Jack W. Peltason: *Fifty-Eight Lonely Men: Southern Federal Judges and School Desegregation* (New York: Harcourt, Brace & World, 1961).

[5] See, e.g., James Eisenstein and Herbert Jacob, *Felony Justice* (Boston: Little, Brown, 1977); Peter F. Nardulli, James Eisenstein, and Roy B. Flemming, *The Tenor of Justice* (Urbana: University of Illinois Press, 1988); James Eisenstein, Roy B. Flemming, and Peter Nardulli, *The Contours of Justice* (Boston: Little, Brown, 1988).

[6] See, for example, Malcolm M. Feeley, *The Process Is Punishment: Handling Cases in a Lower Court* (New York: Russell Sage, 1979).

INTERMEDIATE APPELLATE COURTS

On appellate courts the decision-making process takes place under the much more complex conditions of group life. Whether sitting on an intermediate appellate court, or a supreme court, the appellate judge does not make decisions alone; rather, he or she casts but one vote on a bench that may include as few as three judges, as is typical on intermediate appellate courts, or as many as nine (or more), as is the case for some state supreme courts and, of course, the U.S. Supreme Court. Moreover, the task confronting appellate judges differs considerably from that of trial judges. In appellate proceedings, there are no juries or witnesses; there is simply a written record of the events at the trial and the briefs and oral arguments of attorneys. It is up to the judges alone to determine which side has made the better case.

In so doing, judges may take into account the factors or invoke the theories that we considered in previous chapters, including precedents, the putative intent of the Framers regarding a particular law or constitutional provision, and the purpose legislators may have had in mind when they enacted the legislation—along with judges' own political values. Indeed, just as research indicates that the decisions of judges of trial courts often reflect their political preferences, scholars suggest that judges of appellate courts are no less interested in etching their values into law.[7] In attempting to read the law in accord with their own values, however, intermediate appellate (and trial) judges face a substantial constraint—the possibility of sanctioning from a higher court. To the extent that supreme courts cannot hire, fire, promote, demote, financially reward, or penalize members of trial or intermediate courts, that sanction can take only one form: reversal. But reversal can itself take many shapes, from publication of an opinion sympathizing with the difficulties facing the lower court and the intelligent, if less than perfect, way in which that judge coped with the problem, to a scathing rebuke that casts doubt on the judges' learning, intelligence, or even integrity. In and of itself, reversal is unpleasant; coupled with a searing critique, it can produce public humiliation. And most judges are famous for having egos that are both large and tender (see Chapter 8 and Reading 8.3).

We do not mean, however, that judges of lower courts never defy supreme courts.[8] As we mentioned in Chapter 8, in *Hopwood v. Texas* (1996) a panel on the Fifth Circuit, at least according to their dissenting colleagues, took the dramatic step of defying a precedent established by the Supreme Court of the United

---

7 Support for this proposition comes from a multitude of studies. See Jeffrey A. Segal and Harold J. Spaeth, *The Supreme Court and the Attitudinal Model Revisited* (New York: Cambridge University Press, 2002) for an analysis of the U.S. Supreme Court. For a recent study of the U.S. Court of Appeals, see Cass Sunstein, David Schkade, and Lisa Michelle Ellman, *Ideological Voting on Federal Courts of Appeals: A Preliminary Investigation*. Virginia Law Review 90 (2004): 301. See also Reading 13.2.

8 We draw this and the following paragraph from Charles Cameron, Lee Epstein, and Jeffrey A. Segal's ongoing research on lower-court responses to the U.S. Supreme Court.

States. More than fifty years earlier, a special three-judge district court had refused to apply the doctrine of the First Flag Salute Case. Two of the judges said they sensed a change of heart on the Supreme Court, and the subsequent appeal, in *West Virginia v. Barnette* (1943), vindicated that judgment. These decisions are merely the most striking instances of a more general phenomenon, lower-court deviation from precedents set by a higher court—a phenomenon that can take the subtler forms we discussed in Chapter 10, such as distinguishing, limiting, or avoiding precedents. As one observer noted in 1941: "[Many] precedents have been rejected through the stratagem of distinguishment; others have been the subject of conscious judicial oversight. As a consequence, judicial discretion among 'inferior' judges is not so confined and limited as legal theorists would have it."[9]

This observation raises a question that, depending on one's perspective, can be posed two different ways: Why do lower courts defy higher courts? Or, given the small percentage of intermediate appellate court cases that higher courts hear and reverse: why do lower courts comply with higher courts? Attempts to address these queries take several forms. One is a line of inquiry aimed at identifying the circumstances that lead to deviations, subtle or overt. Lawrence Baum, for example, suggests that lower courts will be less responsive to the U.S. Supreme Court in controversial civil liberties cases and that the clarity of the precedent, the legitimacy other judges accord to the Court's ruling, and estimates of the chances of the justices reviewing their rulings also affect the likelihood of compliance.[10] Another set of investigations has focused on role orientations as the critical causal mechanism. For example, Robert Cover's noted study of abolitionist judges' enforcement of the Fugitive Slave Act emphasizes the moral quandary created by these judges' twin commitments to abolition and the rule of law.[11]

More recently, scholarly efforts, conducted both by social scientists and legal scholars, have shifted focus from individual socialization to structural incentives created by the ways in which judicial hierarchies are designed and operated. The resulting studies have taken several different forms. Segal, Cameron, and Songer (Reading 8.3), for example, focus on the relationship we have emphasized here—between lower and higher courts. Cross and Tiller (Reading 13.3) too are concerned with the extent to which a lower court follows (or defies) a higher court, but their emphasis is how internal dynamics within a panel of judges affect that relationship.

---

[9] Comment, "The Attitude of Lower Courts to Changing Precedents," 50 *Yale Law Journal* 1448-1449 (1941).

[10] Lawrence Baum, "Lower Court Response to Supreme Court Decisions: Reconsidering a Negative Picture." 3 *Justice System Journal* 208 (1978).

[11] Robert Cover, *Justice Accused* (New Haven, CT: Yale University Press, 1975). See also J. Woodford Howard, "Role Perceptions and Behavior in Three U.S. Courts of Appeals," 39 *Journal of Politics* 916 (1977).

STATE SUPREME COURTS

When it comes to decision making, the nation's fifty highest courts follow roughly the same procedures: After deciding which petitions merit their full consideration, they receive written briefs, hear oral arguments, discuss the case among themselves, and, then, issue opinions. But the detailed plans these tribunals follow differ. Chapter 4 discussed the various selection procedures that states invoke to choose their justices and how those mechanisms affect judicial decisions. Melinda Gann Hall's research on the Louisiana Supreme Court examined how the justices' perceptions of the electorate's potential responses affect their decision making. Based on personal interviews and voting data, she found that the justices occasionally suppress dissents if they believe those minority views do not accord with those of their constituents (Reading 13.4).

Chapter 4 also noted differences in the way courts select cases to review. Some state supreme courts choose to hear as many as 80 percent of the cases appealed to them and others less than 5 percent. Moreover, even after state justices decide which disputes they will resolve, they use different procedures to reach decisions.[12] They invoke five basic methods to determine which justice will write the opinion of the Court: (1) a random draw or rotation that occurs prior to oral arguments, before the justices discuss the case; (2) a random draw or rotation that occurs after oral arguments or the court's discussion of the case; (3) a completely discretionary decision made by the Chief Justice; (4) a completely discretionary decision made by the Chief Justice if he or she is in the majority or by the most senior member of the majority when the Chief is in the minority; or (5) a consensus of the justices following their consideration of the case. By the same token, after hearing oral arguments, the courts use different procedures to reach decisions on the merits. On some courts, the most junior members speak and vote first; on others, the Chief Justice casts the first vote; and on still others, no sequence of discussion exists—any justice wishing to speak may do so once the colleague preceding her or him has relinquished the floor.

These and other procedural or institutional variations raise the question: do they affect decision making? Although evidence pertaining to the range of judicial behavior is far from conclusive, Melinda Hall and Paul Brace present strong support for the proposition that institutional arrangements influence judges' decisions to dissent. Because there are "opportunities for sanctions and rewards" on courts "where opinions are assigned at the discretion of the Chief Justice, where conference discussion occurs in order of seniority, and where voting takes place in order of reverse seniority," low dissent rates should result.[13] Conversely, because

> randomization of the opinion-writing process removes opportunities to reward the loyal and punish the recalcitrant . . . [J]oining a winning coalition on one de-

---

[12] We derive this discussion from Melinda Gann Hall, "Opinion Assignment and Conference Practices in State Supreme Courts," 73 Judicature (1987) 209-214. See also Stanford McConkie, "Decision Making in State Supreme Courts," 59 Judicature 337 (1976).

[13] Paul Brace and Melinda Gann Hall, "Neo-Institutionalism and Dissent in State Supreme Courts," 52 Journal of Politics 58-59 (1990).

cision will not result in any tangible reward on later decisions, such as being assigned an opinion in one's area of substantive expertise or on a significant issue. As a result, the incentives for consensus are reduced.

Supreme courts that use a random opinion assignment procedure can expect 14 percent more cases with dissent than do states that use discretionary procedures.

But, of course, these sorts of procedures are not the only factors that affect the choices that state high court justices make. In a recent study of sex discrimination, Epstein and her colleagues show that the justices are far more likely to rule in favor of the party alleging discrimination if their state's constitution contains an equal rights amendment and if they are left-leaning in their politics. In other words, both law and ideology affect their decisions—hardly an unsurprising finding but interesting nonetheless, especially in light of debates over same-sex marriage.[14]

THE U.S. SUPREME COURT

We come finally to the apex of the American legal system, the Supreme Court of the United States. Unlike the highest state tribunals, there is, of course, but one U.S. Supreme Court. And, over time, that Court has developed a multitude of procedures to structure its decision making. Some—those listed in the Rules of the Supreme Court of the United States[15]—are formal. For the most part, however, unwritten norms and conventions shape the way the justices reach their decisions. Such is in direct contradistinction to many of the world's constitutional courts, which operate under a closely prescribed set of procedures. Consider, for example, the Armenian Constitutional Court's rules "Concerning the Chairman" [Chief Justice]:

The Chairman of the Constitutional Court shall:

I. Prepare sessions of the Constitutional Court;
II. Charge any member of the Constitutional Court with preparation of the cases to be heard at the session;
III. Call and chair the sessions of the Constitutional Court;
IV. Present the cases on the agenda to the members of the Constitutional Court;
V. Follow the procedures of case hearing, and shall issue orders to the litigants and invited persons, which shall have binding force;
VI. Represent the Constitutional Court in its relations with other agencies and organizations;
VII. Supervise the staff of the Constitutional Court, nominate and dismiss the chief of staff of the Constitutional Court, approve the inner regulations and the nomination of staff members;

---

[14] This study is available at: http://epstein.wustl.edu/research/ERA.html.

[15] These are available at www.supremecourtus.gov/ctrules/ctrules.html.

VIII.   Supervise the funds of the Constitutional Court, and be responsible for functioning of the Constitutional Court;

IX.   Exercise other duties as provided by this law.

Although the Chief Justice of the United States, as we describe momentarily (see also Reading 13.6), has many special responsibilities, they are not set out in this level of detail anywhere in the Court's rules. One rule that the Court has formalized concerns the start of its business year (called a "term"). Under Rule 4, the term always begins on the first Monday in October; the rule is silent on when terms conclude, but they usually run until sometime in June or July. Normally, the Court sits for two-week periods to hear arguments and announce decisions and then adjourns for two weeks to allow the justices to research, think, and write their opinions. During the weeks the Court is sitting, the justices meet a few minutes before ten in the robing room behind the courtroom. Precisely at ten the maroon velvet curtains part, and the justices take their places behind the bench as the crier gavels the courtroom to attention and chants:

> The Honorable, the Chief Justice and Associate Justices of the Supreme Court of the United States! Oyez, Oyez, Oyez! All persons having business before the Honorable, the Supreme Court of the United States are admonished to draw near and give their attention, for the Court is now sitting. God save the United States and this Honorable Court.

The Court receives more than 8,000 appeals and petitions for certiorari each term (see Chapter 3). In the 2001 term for example it acted on 7,936 cases. But it decided only eighty-eight petitions on the merits—far fewer than it decided just ten years previous (see Chapter 3). Many of these petitions (6,127 of 7,936) were in forma pauperis (filed without payment), originated mostly by convicts in state and federal prisons, and often handwritten. Most of these cases present no substantial grounds for review, but occasionally one will raise a significant issue, as in *Gideon v. Wainwright* (1963) wherein the Court held that defendants in all serious criminal prosecutions had a right to counsel, appointed and paid for by the government if defendants were too poor to afford their own attorneys.

Case Selection

Most of the justices have found it possible to handle this huge workload only by giving major responsibilities to their law clerks. The first clerk was hired by Justice Horace Gray in 1882 at his own expense. But within a few decades it became an established practice for each justice to have one clerk, with two for the Chief Justice. The number has now been increased to four (five for the Chief Justice), with each generally serving for one term. The method of selection is entirely a personal matter for the justices, who often have had a preference for graduates of particular law schools (usually highly ranked ones) or residents of certain states or areas. At the start of its 1998 term, however, the justices experienced heavy pressure to hire minority clerks.[16] In light of their then-existing

---

[16] "Protest Outside High Court," *New York Times*, October 6, 1998, p. A19.

record—of the 428 clerks hired over time, less than 5 percent had been Asian American, 2 percent African American, and 1 percent Hispanic—NAACP President Kweisi Mfume told the justices that they "ought to be ashamed of [themselves]." Perhaps they received the message: Among the 1999–2000 class of clerks were two African Americans and three Asian Americans.

Justices typically delegate responsibility for initial review of all appeals and petitions to their clerks, who prepare for each case a summary of the facts, questions presented, and a recommended course of action. In 1972, as the workload mounted, a majority of the justices had their clerks join a "cert pool." Filings were divided among the clerks in the pool, and a single clerk's memo would then be circulated to all the participating justices. Now, in 2005, eight of the nine justices (all but John Paul Stevens) participate in this pool.

During the selecting process, the Chief Justice plays a special role. Before the full Court meets to decide which cases to take, he circulates a "discuss list" containing those cases he feels worthy of consideration by the entire court; any justice (in order of seniority) may add to (but not subtract from) this list. Less than 15 percent of the cases that come to the Court make it onto the list and are actually discussed by the justices in conference.[17] The rest are automatically denied review, and the lower court decision stands.

This much we know. Because the Court's conferences are attended only by the justices, we cannot say precisely what transpires; but we can offer a relatively clear picture based on notes and papers of the Court's members. These sources tell us that the discussion of each petition takes place at a meeting called a conference. The conference room itself is austerely furnished with a long table and nine chairs, law books, a portrait of John Marshall, a marble fireplace, a desk for the Chief Justice in one corner, and a window with an undiverting view of Second Street, N.E. When the justices meet there, they lock themselves in. The junior justice answers all knocks at the door, and no one is allowed in except a waiter who brings in desperately needed coffee. Even he or she is quickly relieved of the burden by one of the justices.[18]

---

[17] Ruth Bader Ginsburg, "Remarks for the American Law Institute Annual Dinner," 38 *St. Louis University Law Journal* 881 (1994). For more general information on the discuss list, see Gregory A. Caldeira and John R. Wright, "The Discuss List: Agenda Building in the Supreme Court," 24 *Law and Society Review* 807-836 (1990).

[18] In these days of "government in the sunshine," judges stand pretty much alone in insisting that decisions take place in secret. Congress has agreed to this arrangement by exempting the federal courts from legislation regarding open government and freedom of information. There are two basic reasons. First, all federal judges and especially those of the Supreme Court are supposed to base their decisions on factors other than public opinion. After all, they are not elected officials. Opening up their deliberations to scrutiny by the press, for example, might encourage judges to take notice of popular sentiment. Or so the argument goes. Although they often do have an electoral connection, state judges usually also operate in secret once briefs are filed arguments are heard. That exemption is usually justified, as is the one for federal judges, on grounds that judicial decisions can have major effects on financial dealings and political negotiations. It is easy to imagine, for example, the advantages a shareholder might have if he or she knew the Supreme Court was going to order the break up of a large corporation because of its violations of the antitrust laws. It is worth noting that the secrecy of judicial proceedings is not universally approved of. Judges of the Swiss Constitutional Court meet on the stage of a small theater to discuss and vote on cases. The number of spectators is usually small.

UNITED STATES, Petitioner

vs.

ANTHONY SALERNO AND VINCENT CAFARO

07/21/86 – cert

11/3/86 — cert. granted

HOLD FOR	CERT.			JURISDICTIONAL STATEMENT				MERITS		MOTIONS			
	G	D	G&D	N	FOBT	DIS	AFT	REV	AFT	G	D		
Rehnquist, Ch. J. ... *assigned*	✓							✓					
Brennan, J.	✓								✓				
White, J.	✓							✓					
Marshall, J.		✓							✓				
Blackman, J.	✓							✓					
Powell, J.	✓							✓					
Stevens, J.	✓								✓				
O'Connor, J.	✓							✓					
Scalia, J.	✓							✓					

FIGURE 13.1 A Page from the Docket Book of Justice Thurgood Marshall

Note: In this case, eight of the nine justices voted to grant certiorari (only Justice Marshall voted to deny). But they were not so united on the decisions on the merits. Six justices voted to reverse the lower court's decision, which had struck down a congressional law allowing Federal courts to deny bail to defendants who present a risk to society or to other persons; three (Brennan, Marshall, and Stevens) voted to affirm. Because Rehnquist was in the majority, he had the authority to select the opinion writer and he assigned that task to himself.

The conference begins with the Chief Justice presenting a short summary of the facts and, typically, stating his vote (see Reading 8.2). The associate justices, who sit at the table in order of seniority, then comment on each petition, with the most senior justice speaking first and the newest member last. The justices record their own and their colleagues' votes on certiorari (and later on the merits) in their docket books (see Figure 13.1). But, given the large number of petitions, they apparently discuss few cases in detail.

By tradition, the Court adheres to the so-called Rule of Four: it grants certiorari to those cases receiving the affirmative vote of at least four justices.[19] This

---

[19] The Court is required by statute to accept appeals, but, as noted in Chapter 3, these now constitute a trivial portion of the justices' workload.

rule has no statutory basis.[20] It rests simply on practice and assurances given by Chief Justice William Howard Taft and other members of the Court to Congress in 1925, when access to the Court was made largely discretionary, that the Court would not abuse its new freedom.

But allowing a minority of the Court to determine what cases it will consider does create some problems. As Justice Stevens has said: "The Rule of Four must inevitably enlarge the size of the Court's argument docket and cause it to hear a substantial number of cases that a majority of the Court deems unworthy of review." It occasionally happens that a case placed on the docket by a vote of four justices will be dismissed by vote of the other five justices as "improvidently granted."[21] It appears, however, that more than 90 percent of all the Court's decisions on certiorari are unanimous and that only 22 percent are accepted by less than a majority.[22]

Refusal to grant certiorari does not necessarily mean that the justices have approved the decision below. As Justice Felix Frankfurter said in *State v. Baltimore Radio Show* (1950), it means only that four justices did not deem the case important enough, for whatever reason, to justify the Court's attention. Nevertheless, it cannot be denied that refusal to grant certiorari does lend some credence to the lower court's ruling.

Factors Affecting Selection of Cases

Before turning to the path of the cases the Court agrees to decide, let us consider an equally intriguing issue—what factors influence the Court's decision to

---

[20] To the extent that Congress has not passed a law requiring the Court to follow the Rule of Four, this is true. Nonetheless, Justice Thurgood Marshall-in response to a proposal offered by Justice John Paul Stevens to change the Rule of Four to a majority rule-thought that Congress needed to approve any modification: "While there is nothing in the Court's jurisdictional grant prohibiting such a substitution, I have serious reservations whether the Court could properly abandon the Rule of Four [on its own]. Members of the Court have represented to Congress that the Rule of Four is the policy of the Court, and Congress has relied on those representations. While we do not generally hold private industry to every assurance its lobbyists make before a congressional committee, I believe that when our representative appear before a co-equal branch of the federal government, we should hold ourselves to a higher standard." Thurgood Marshall, "Memorandum to the Conference," September 21, 1983, 4-5. *The Papers of Thurgood Marshall*, The Library of Congress.

[21] See, e.g., New York v. Uplinger, 467 U.S. 246 (1984). In *United States v. Shannon* (1952), Justice William O. Douglas protested that such action would impair the "integrity of the four-vote rule."

[22] These data, based on the 1990 term, are from David M. O'Brien, *Storm Center*, 5th ed. (New York: Norton, 2000), 211, 214. If a justice disagrees with the Court's decision to deny certiorari, he or she can file a dissenting opinion. Some dissents to denial of certiorari are nothing more than boilerplates, such as some of the ones Brennan and Marshall filed when the Court denied certiorari in death sentence cases: "Adhering to our views that the death penalty is in all circumstances cruel and unusual punishment prohibited by the Eighth and Fourteenth Amendments, we would grant certiorari and vacate the death sentence in this case." Others read more like full-fledged opinions, with the author sometimes stating how she or he would vote on the merits of the case.

review? Scholars have offered two: legal (or principled) considerations and political considerations.[23]

The first suggests that justices seek to reach "principled" decisions at the case-selection stage—those based largely on the dictates of Rule 10. This rule, which the Court created to govern the cert process, specifies that the justices will accept cases decided differently between state and federal courts or against the Supreme Court's own precedents. When justices follow this rule, they are engaging in "principled" agenda setting, some scholars argue, because the rule itself is impartial as to the type of possible result over a particular petition. If justices looked only at whether conflict existed, their agenda-setting decisions would not reflect their own policy preferences over the substantive consequences of a case but, rather, those of the dictates of the rule itself. By its own terms, however, Rule 10 expresses policy preferences: uniformity of decisions within the federal judicial system and the superiority of the national over state courts. That most of us agree with those policies does not make them less policies.

There is some support for believing that the Court takes Rule 10 seriously. Based on interviews with justices and their clerks, H. W. Perry concluded that conflict in the circuits is "without a doubt, one of the most important things to all the justices. All of them are disposed to resolve conflicts when they exist and want to know if a particular case poses a conflict" (Reading 13.5). And a 1988 study of the Court's records support Perry's findings: If actual conflict is present in a case, a 33 percent chance exists that the Court will grant review—compared with the then 5 percent certiorari rate.[24] On the other hand, as Gregory A. Caldeira and John R. Wright explain, Rule 10 is not especially helpful in understanding "how the Court makes gatekeeping decisions."[25] The justices may use the existence of actual conflict as a threshold (cases that do not present conflict may be rejected), but they do not accept all cases with conflict because there are too many. In fact, during any given term, the Court rejects hundreds of cases in which real conflicts exist.[26]

The considerations listed in Rule 10 thus may act as constraints on the justices' behavior, but they do not necessarily further our understanding of what occurs in cases meeting the criteria. Scholars have, therefore, looked to other factors that may influence the Court's selection of cases; and three are particularly important. The first is the U.S. solicitor general (SG), the attorney who repre-

---

[23] Some scholars have noted a third set: procedural considerations. These emanate from Article III, which—under the Court's interpretation-places constraints on the ability of federal tribunals to hear and decide cases. These constraints are reviewed in Chapter 6. Here we note the two that are particularly important for the review decision: the case must be appropriate for judicial resolution in that it presents a real "case" and "controversy" (justiciability), and the appropriate person must bring the case (standing). Unless these procedural criteria are met, the Court-at least supposedly-will deny review. It is worth noting, however, that because most petitions meet these criteria, they are not especially useful in helping the justices make decisions select cases to hear on the merits.

[24] See Gregory A. Caldeira and John R. Wright, "Organized Interests and Agenda Setting in the U.S. Supreme Court," 82 *American Political Science Review* 1109-27 (1988) (Reading 6.6).

[25] Caldeira and Wright, "Organized Interests and Agenda Setting in the U.S. Supreme Court," 1115

[26] See Lawrence Baum, *The Supreme Court*, 7th ed. (Washington, DC: CQ Press, 2001), 111.

sents the U.S. government before the Supreme Court. Simply stated, when the SG files a petition, the Court far more often than not grants certiorari (70 to 80 percent of the government's cases). These numbers could reflect the SG's expertise. Because he and the members of his staff are involved in so much litigation before the Supreme Court, they acquire a great deal of knowledge that other litigants do not have and so are able to structure their petitions to attract the attention and interest of the justices. Even more to the point, the justices have come rely on the solicitor general to act as a filter; that is, they expect the SG to examine carefully the cases to which the government is a party and bring only the most important to their attention. The SG's success could also reflect the justices' awareness of his special role. A presidential appointee whose decisions often mirror the administration's philosophy, the SG is also supposed to represent the interests of the United States. As members of the nation's highest court, the justices may believe that they cannot ignore these interests.

The second political factor is the amicus curiae (friend of the court) brief. Recall our discussion from Chapter 6: the presence of amicus briefs significantly enhances a case's chance to be heard, and multiple briefs have a greater effect (see Reading 6.6). Even when groups file in opposition to granting certiorari, they increase—rather than decrease—the probability that the Court will hear the case. In other words, although the justices may not be strongly influenced by the arguments contained in these briefs (if they were, why would briefs in opposition to certiorari not have the opposite effect?), they seem to use them as cues: If interest groups are sufficiently interested in an appeal to file briefs in support of (or against) the Court's reviewing a decision, the petition for certiorari is probably worth serious consideration. After all, in deciding which cases to decide, the Court is expressing its view about which issues are of national importance.

Finally, we have good reasons to suspect that justices' ideology affects actions on certiorari petitions. Researchers tell us that the justices of the liberal Warren Court were more likely to grant review to cases in which the lower court reached a conservative decision so that they could reverse, whereas the more conservative Burger Court accepted liberal decisions to reverse. At this point, we lack sufficient data on the Rehnquist Court to reach any firm conclusions, but it would be hard to believe that the current justices would be any less likely than their predecessors to vote on the basis of their ideology.

Scholarly studies also suggest that justices engage in strategic voting behavior at the certiorari stage. It would be amazing if, as intelligent men and women, they were not forward-thinking and did not consider the implications of their cert vote for decisions on merits, asking themselves: if I vote to grant a particular petition, what are the odds of my position winning down the road? As one justice explained his calculations, "I might think the Nebraska Supreme Court made a horrible decision, but I wouldn't want to take the case, for if we take the case and affirm it, then it would become precedent."[27] Scholars, along with various justices and their clerks, label this action as "defensive denial."

---

[27] Quoted in H. W. Perry, *Deciding to Decide* (Cambridge, MA: Harvard University Press, 1991), 200.

Oral Argument

If the justices grant certiorari, the Clerk of the Court (an administrative officer, not one of the justices' young aides) puts the case on the docket and schedules oral argument. Well before that date, each side submits written briefs detailing its contentions and reprinting relevant portions of the record from lower courts. Once again, it is not always possible for the justices to read all the material. They examine the briefs with care; but, because it is not unusual for a trial record in a complicated case to run to several thousand pages, the justices have to learn which parts can be skipped or perused and which need close study. (Having once been college students undoubtedly helps them.) The Supreme Court's Rules require that briefs contain specific page citations to those parts of the record being discussed, but there are limits to specificity. *Sacher v. United States* (1952), for example, involved review of several lawyers' convictions for contempt of court for their general conduct during a trial whose record took up 13,000 pages.

The justices hear oral argument from 10:00 A.M. until Noon on Mondays, Tuesdays, and Wednesdays, then recess for an hour for lunch and return for two more hours of argument at 1:00 P.M. Although the Court will grant exceptions in very important cases, counsel for each side usually have only thirty minutes. Thus the Court can hear an average of twelve cases each week it sits.

The attorney stands at a lectern facing the justices in their high-backed leather chairs. A white light flashes when counsel has five minutes left, and when time is up, a red light goes on. Although lavishly generous with its time during its initial decades, in the twentieth century the Court became miserly. The story is told that Chief Justice Charles Evans Hughes once cut a prominent lawyer off in the middle of the word *if*.

Oral argument can be an arduous experience for counsel. Especially if an attorney merely repeats what is already written in the brief, the justices sometimes stare impassively at the draperies, chat among themselves, write notes, read, send pages for law reports, or even occasionally nap, apparently bored by what is being said to them. On the other hand, they may suddenly turn a turgid presentation into an exciting debate by posing a rapid series of piercing questions and counterquestions, as the following exchange between Justice Byron White and Sarah Weddington, the attorney representing Jane Roe in *Roe v. Wade* (1973), indicates. White got the ball rolling when he asked Weddington to respond to an issue her brief had not addressed: whether abortions should be performed during all stages of pregnancy or should somehow be limited. The following discussion ensued:

> WHITE: And the statute doesn't make any distinction based upon at what period of pregnancy the abortion is performed?
>
> WEDDINGTON: No, Your Honor. There is no time limit or indication of time, whatsoever. So I think—
>
> WHITE: What is your constitutional position there?
>
> WEDDINGTON: As to a time limit—
>
> WHITE: What about whatever clause of the Constitution you rest on—Ninth Amendment, due process . . . —that take you right up to the time of birth?

WEDDINGTON: It is our position that the freedom involved is that of a woman to determine whether or not to continue a pregnancy. Obviously I have a much more difficult time saying that the State has no interest in late pregnancy.

WHITE: Why? Why is that?

WEDDINGTON: I think that's more the emotional response to a late pregnancy, rather than it is any constitutional—

WHITE: Emotional response by whom?

WEDDINGTON: I guess by persons considering the issue outside the legal context, I think, as far as the State—

WHITE: Well, do you or don't you say that the constitutional—

WEDDINGTON: I would say constitutional—

WHITE: —right you insist on reaches up to the time of birth, or—

WEDDINGTON: The Constitution, as I read it . . . attaches protection to the person at the time of birth.

This exchange involved only one justice, but others got into the act as well. And trying to race along with nine different minds going off in several directions can provide strenuous mental exercise. When he was solicitor general, before his own appointment to the Court, Stanley Reed once fainted dead away while arguing a case, and many other lawyers have suffered obvious intellectual blackouts.

It is no wonder that contemporary attorneys prepare for weeks, even months, before they appear before the High Court. But to what end? In the Court's early years, there was little doubt about the importance of oral arguments. Because attorneys did not always submit written briefs, the justices relied on orals to provide them with information about the cases and to help them formulate their opinions. Moreover, orals were considered important public events, with the most prominent attorneys of the day participating. Arguments often went on for days: *Gibbons v. Ogden* (1824), the landmark commerce clause case, was argued for five days, and *McCulloch v. Maryland* (1819), the litigation challenging the constitutionality of the national bank, took nine days to argue.

Now, however, scholars, lawyers, and judges debate the effectiveness of oral argument and its role in decision making. Chief Justice Earl Warren maintained that they made little difference to the outcome. Once the justices have read the briefs and studied related rulings, most have relatively firm views on how the case should be decided, and orals change few minds. Justice William J. Brennan, Jr., however, claimed that they were extremely important because they helped justices clarify core arguments. The questions justices ask during oral argument may not be good predictors of the Court's final vote, but they provide some indication of what individual justices believe to be the central issues of the case. In addition, we should not forget the symbolic importance of oral argument: it is the only part of the Court's decision-making process that occurs in public.[28]

---

[28] Professor Jerry Goldman has made the oral arguments of many cases available on the World Wide Web at www.oyez.org/oyez/frontpage.

The Judicial Conference

For a short time on Wednesday afternoons after oral argument and all day on Fridays when the Court is sitting, the justices meet in conference to decide the cases just argued. By custom, only occasionally not followed, any justice who is not present for oral argument does not participate in deciding the case, making a tie vote possible. That result would automatically affirm the judgment of the lower court, create no precedent, and would bind only on the parties to the actual dispute. In such cases, the justices do not reveal how they voted. The Court, of course, can reschedule the case for re-argument, if it wishes.

Justices may recuse (disqualify) themselves if they have had some previous relation with the controversy or with parties or counsel in the case. But, unlike in other countries, the decision to recuse is an individual one each justice makes for him or herself. In *Laird v. Tatum* (1972), which involved military surveillance of private citizens and public officials within the United States, (then Associate) Justice William H. Rehnquist filed a memorandum explaining why he declined to disqualify himself even though, prior to joining the Court, he, as an official of the Department of Justice, had general knowledge of these practices and had defended them before a congressional committee.

Such decisions are highly personal and concern not merely conflicts that a judge may feel but also those that outside observers may reasonably perceive. Justice Brennan would not sit in *Princeton University v. Schmid* (1982) because his son's law firm handled some of the university's legal affairs. However, Chief Justice William Howard Taft did not deem it necessary to recuse himself when his half-brother argued before the Court. Similarly, Felix Frankfurter thought it proper to sit in cases argued by his dear friend Dean Acheson. Far more controversial because of the enormous political stakes were the decisions of Justices Scalia and Thomas not to recuse themselves in *Bush v. Gore* (2000), which stopped the recount of ballots in Florida and gave the presidential election to George W. Bush. Scalia's son worked for the law firm arguing Bush's case before the Court and Thomas's wife was helping review candidates for executive positions if Bush were to become president. But perhaps even more controversial was Justice Scalia's decision against recusing himself from a case involving his "friend" Vice President Dick Cheney.[29] When the media reported that Scalia had gone duck hunting with Cheney just three weeks after the Supreme Court agreed to decide, one of the parties filed a motion for Scalia to recuse himself. In response, Scalia filed a rather extraordinary memorandum, detailing why "established principles and practices do not require (and thus do not permit) recusal." In the course of the twenty-one-page memo, Scalia noted, and accurately we might add, that "a rule that required Members of this Court to remove themselves from cases in which the official actions of friends were at issue would be utterly disabling. Many Justices have reached this Court precisely because they

---

[29] *Cheney v. U.S. District Court* (2004). In his memorandum, Scalia wrote of Cheney: "I am a friend of his."

were friends of the incumbent President or other senior officials—and from the earliest days down to modern times Justices have had close personal relationships with the President and other officers of the Executive."[30]

Justices who are participating in a case—that is, most justices in most cases—participate in conference discussion. Before that discussion begins, each justice shakes hands with every other, a reminder that they remain colleagues even though they may soon be bitterly arguing. The Chief Justice presides and has the difficult and delicate duty of allowing adequate discussion of each case while moving the Court efficiently through its docket (Reading 13.6). To accomplish this task, he must have the skill both to encourage meaningful intellectual debate and to prevent discussion from degenerating into invective or filibustering. The Chief Justice gives his views first, and then the other justices speak in order of seniority of service on the Court. Traditionally, when the Chief called discussion to a close, the justices voted in reverse order of seniority, with the newest justice going first and the Chief last. This procedure conferred on the Chief the advantage of being able to vote with the majority and so assign (or keep to himself) authority to write the opinion of the Court. During his last years on the bench, however, Chief Justice Earl Warren persuaded his brethren to vote in the same order in which they had spoken, a procedure continued under Burger and, now, Rehnquist.

If he votes with the majority, the Chief assigns the task of writing the opinion of the Court. If the Chief Justice is in the minority, the senior associate justice makes the assignment. Before John Marshall, the Court had generally followed the British practice, whereby the judges wrote seriatim, that is, each judge who had the time or inclination wrote his own opinion. There was seldom an institutional opinion of the Court. Believing that the appearance of monolithic unity of reasoning as well as of result would give greater weight to judicial decisions, Marshall made it standard practice to designate one judge, usually himself, to act as speaker for the whole Court.

As we describe below, the Court has retained this practice; whenever possible, the justices attempt to forge one opinion representing the view of the majority. But it no longer habitually, or even usually, follows the "norm of consensus," which Marshall effectuated out of a belief that unanimous rulings would "greatly strengthen the authority" of the Court.[31] Although Marshall's successors through the 1930s attempted to perpetuate the norm, it fell apart under Harlan Fiske Stone's tenure as Chief Justice (1941–1946) and has never

---

[30] Scalia offered some examples: "John Quincy Adams hosted dinner parties featuring such luminaries as Chief Justice Marshall, Justices Johnson, Story, and Todd, Attorney General Wirt, and Daniel Webster. Justice Harlan and his wife often 'stopped in' at the White House to see the Hayes family and pass a Sunday evening in a small group, visiting and singing hymns. Justice Stone tossed around a medicine ball with members of the Hoover administration mornings outside the White House. Justice Douglas was a regular at President Franklin Roosevelt's poker parties; Chief Justice Vinson played poker with President Truman."

[31] William H. Rehnquist, "The Supreme Court: The First Hundred Years Were the Hardest," 42 *University of Miami Law Review* 581 (1996).

resurfaced. Today only about a third of the Court's decisions are the products of a unanimous vote, suggesting that dissensus, not consensus, is the norm.

Writing Opinions

The power to choose the opinion writer provides a source of real power for the Chief Justice, because he can designate that member of the majority, including himself, who, he believes, will write the opinion that best fits the situation. Chief justices have adopted various strategies in assigning opinions (see Reading 13.6). He will usually attempt to deliver the opinion in the major cases, as Warren did in the School Segregation Cases and Burger did in *United States v. Nixon* (Reading 12.1). When the Court is badly divided and it is uncertain whether a narrow majority can be held together, Chief Justices have usually thought it desirable to have one of the Court's more diplomatic justices write the opinion.[32]

Justice Lewis F. Powell described the justices and their law clerks as "nine small, independent law firms."[33] This description is accurate to the extent that each justice and his or her own staff tend to run separate operations, with little direct face-to-face interaction. All the justices rely heavily on their own clerks to research, edit, and even prepare drafts of the opinions they have been assigned to write, though actual practices vary widely. But once the opinion writer has a draft ready and circulates it to all the justices (no matter how they voted), substantial interaction among the chambers ensues. Each justice can make comments and suggestions for change. Any justice who believes that the opinion writer is taking an undesirable path is free to write a separate opinion, concurring or dissenting, or join with another justice in so doing. If enough justices behave in that fashion, the original opinion writer could wind up alone, perhaps even in dissent, with someone else writing for the Court.

The very existence of the possibility of a concurring or a dissenting opinion—not considered proper in such Civil-Law countries as France or Italy and allowed only since the 1970s on a single tribunal in West Germany, the Constitutional Court—is an important facet of legal systems based on the common law. When judges publicly disagree about the meaning of law and perhaps also of the Constitution, "the Law" loses the appearance of majestic certainty. Jurists disagree among themselves as to whether such a loss is desirable, but there can be no doubt that dissenting opinions sometimes provide powerful forces for legal, social, and political change. Actually a dissenter has an easier task than does the justice who speaks for the Court or even one who writes a concurring opinion, for a dissenter speaks without the authority, and therefore

---

[32] For more on the factors affecting opinion assignments, see Forest Maltzman and Paul J. Wahlbeck, "May It Please the Chief? Opinion Assignments in the Rehnquist Court," 40 *American Journal of Political Science* 421 (1996), and Elliot F. Slotnick, "Who Speaks for the Court? Majority Opinion Assignment from Taft to Burger," 23 *American Journal of Political Science* 60 (1979).

[33] "What the Justices Are Saying," 62 *American Bar Association Journal* 1454 (1976).

without the responsibility, of representing a coordinate branch of the federal government. As Justice Benjamin N. Cardozo once said,

> The spokesman of the Court is cautious, timid, fearful of the vivid word, the heightened phrase. He dreams of an unworthy brood of scions, the spawn of careless dicta, disowned by the ratio decidendi. . . . The result is to cramp and paralyze. One fears to say anything when the peril of misunderstanding puts a warning finger to the lips. Not so, however, the dissenter. . . . Deep conviction and warm feeling are saying their last say with knowledge that the cause is lost. . . . The dissenter speaks to the future, and his voice is pitched to a key that will carry through the years.[34]

Whether because of the eloquence of dissenters, the complexity of the issues, or the stubbornness of individual justices, it sometimes happens that they cannot agree on an opinion that at least five of them can sign. In that situation, the Court announces its decision, perhaps through a brief per curiam (unsigned) order that merely states the result. Alternatively, the justice in the majority whose opinion attracted the most votes (called the plurality opinion) announces the Judgment of the Court (usually simply "Affirmed" or "Reversed"). Under such circumstances, especially if each justice writes an opinion or clusters of several justices join together, the result can be a confusing hodgepodge, as indicated by the beginning of *McConnell v. Federal Election Commission* (2003), in which the Court considered the constitutionality of the Bipartisan Campaign Reform Act (BCRA) of 2002:

> Stevens and O'Connor, JJ., delivered the opinion of the Court with respect to BCRA Titles I and II, in which Souter, Ginsburg, and Breyer, JJ., joined. Rehnquist, C. J., delivered the opinion of the Court with respect to BCRA Titles III and IV, in which O'Connor, Scalia, Kennedy, and Souter, JJ., joined, in which Stevens, Ginsburg, and Breyer, JJ., joined except with respect to BCRA §305, and in which Thomas, J., joined with respect to BCRA §§304, 305, 307, 316, 319, and 403(b). Breyer, J., delivered the opinion of the Court with respect to BCRA Title V, in which Stevens, O'Connor, Souter, and Ginsburg, JJ., joined. Scalia, J., filed an opinion concurring with respect to BCRA Titles III and IV, dissenting with respect to BCRA Titles I and V, and concurring in the judgment in part and dissenting in part with respect to BCRA Title II. Thomas, J., filed an opinion concurring with respect to BCRA Titles III and IV, except for BCRA §§311 and 318, concurring in the result with respect to BCRA §318, concurring in the judgment in part and dissenting in part with respect to BCRA Title II, and dissenting with respect to BCRA Titles I, V, and §311, in which opinion Scalia, J., joined as to Parts I, II—A, and II—B. Kennedy, J., filed an opinion concurring in the judgment in part and dissenting in part with respect to BCRA Titles I and II, in which Rehnquist, C. J., joined, in which Scalia, J., joined except to the extent the opinion upholds new FECA §323(e) and BCRA §202, and in which Thomas, J., joined with respect to BCRA §213. Rehnquist, C. J., filed an opinion dissenting with respect to BCRA Titles I and V, in which Scalia and Kennedy, JJ., joined.

---

[34] Benjamin N. Cardozo, "Law and Literature," 14 Yale Review 699, 715-716 (1925).

Stevens, J., filed an opinion dissenting with respect to BCRA §305, in which Ginsburg and Breyer, JJ., joined.

But, however garbled the message, one point remains clear: any opinion that does not command the assent of a majority of the justices who participate in a decision—and at least six justices are necessary for a quorum—does not speak for the Supreme Court of the United States. Such an opinion—plurality, concurring, dissenting, whether in part or in whole—is merely an expression of the views of one or more members of the Court and is entitled to respect. But its reasoning need not be accepted as controlling by other judges, public officials, or private citizens.

Dissenting and concurring opinions, if there are any, are also circulated among all the justices, and authors may make changes to meet points raised by other opinions. When he feels that the justices are satisfied that they can fruitfully say no more to one another, the Chief Justice brings the case up again at conference. If he hears no request for additional time, he puts the case on the list of those whose decision will be announced during the next week the Court is in session.

Negotiating and Bargaining

The preceding discussion fails to convey a realistic sense of the interplay among the justices as they work their way toward a consensus, if that is possible, or toward an effective statement of and support for conflicting views. Few justices have been so insensitive to their responsibilities as simply to plow their own furrows, write their own opinions, and ignore the accommodation of views essential on a collegial tribunal. Rather, justices generally seek to persuade their colleagues of the rightness—even righteousness—of their views. Where possible, they use reason, where necessary they use emotional appeals, bargaining, or all three.[35]

Negotiation and compromise are facts of life on appellate courts. To bargain effectively, one must have something to trade as well as a sanction to apply if the offer is rejected. The most significant items with which judges can negotiate are their votes and concurrences in opinions. Conversely, threats to change votes or write separate opinions, dissenting or concurring, are the sanctions most generally available to judges. The effectiveness of each depends in part on the division within the Court and the skills of the particular jurist. When, for instance, the Supreme Court is divided five to four, any justice in the majority can exercise great influence by dropping hints of a switch in vote. When the vote is nine to zero or eight to one, an individual justice has little clout. Similarly, a threat from a judge whose writing style is dull and whose reasoning is not noted for awesome power is not likely to carry much weight unless the vote is very close. On the other hand, a dissent—even the possibility of a lone dissent—from

---

[35] Walter F. Murphy, *Elements of Judicial Strategy* (Chicago: University of Chicago Press, 1964); Lee Epstein and Jack Knight, *The Choices Justices Make* (Washington, DC: CQ Press, 1998).

a judge with the skill of a Holmes, a Brandeis, a Black, a Jackson, a Frankfurter, a Harlan, or a Brennan is likely to give the majority pause.

Negotiation can be explicit or tacit. One of the most common opportunities for compromise occurs when judges circulate drafts of opinions to colleagues for comments (Reading 13.7). The other judges may then suggest changes, with everyone understanding that the opinion writer ignores these suggestions at the risk of losing support for the opinion. The threat to pull out normally need not be expressed, though some judges prefer to be very explicit. Stone, for example, once wrote Frankfurter: "If you wish to write, placing the case on the ground which I think tenable and desirable, I shall cheerfully join you. If not, I will add a few observations for myself." Only slightly less direct was the note attached to a draft of a concurring opinion that Brennan sent White:

> I've mentioned to you that I favor your approach to this case and want if possible to join your opinion. If you find the following suggestions . . . acceptable, I can, as I stated in the enclosed concurrence, join you. I'm not generally circulating the concurrence until you let me have your reaction.

Although it is probably true that accommodation often prevents a majority from splintering into concurring factions, compromise can also serve to mute dissent. In either circumstance, the threat of a separate opinion may create a bargaining situation in which both gain something. Fearing that publication of a dissent or a concurrence would cause the author of the prevailing opinion to make her or his pronouncements more rigid or perhaps draw attention to and emphasize an "erroneous" ruling, a judge in the minority may reason that it would be more prudent to suppress disagreement if concessions can be won from the majority. As Justice William Johnson, a contemporary of John Marshall, explained his vote in *Sturges v. Crowninshield* (1819): "The Court was, in that case, greatly divided in their views of the doctrine, and the judgment partakes as much of a compromise as of a legal adjudication. The minority thought it better to yield something than risk the whole."[36]

As an integral part of this process, publication of a dissent and circulation within a court of a separate opinion serve two different functions. The latter is essentially an effort to resolve conflict within the family by, in one fashion or another, persuading other judges. The former is basically an attempt to shift the arena of combat. Having lost within the Court, a published dissenting opinion is, as Justice Cardozo said, an appeal to history, particularly to future judges. But a dissent can be more. Whether or not the author intends it, a dissent can become an appeal to contemporaries—to members of Congress, to the president and executive officials, to lower-court judges, to the bar or other interest groups, or to the public at large—to change the decision of the majority. As Frankfurter explained to Murphy in discussing a dissent in *Harris v. United States:*

> This is a protest opinion—a protest at the Bar of the future—but also an effort to make the brethren realize what is at stake. Moreover, a powerful dissent in a

---

[36] It was in *Ogden v. Saunders* (1827) that Johnson explained his earlier vote in Sturges.

case like that is bound to have an effect on the lower courts as well as on the officers of the law, just as a failure to speak out vigorously against what the Court is doing will only lead to further abuse. And so in order to impress our own brethren, the lower courts and enforcement officers, it seems to me vital to make the dissent an impressive document.

Although dissent is a cherished part of the common-law tradition, a judge who persistently refuses collegial accommodation may soon be regarded as an obstructionist. Similarly, colleagues may regard as disloyal to the bench a judge whose dissents frequently become levers for legislative or administrative action reversing judicial policies. It is likely that either appraisal would curtail the influence of a justice. Even in his despair over the course of constitutional adjudication after John Marshall's death, Justice Joseph Story thought this consideration limited the frequency with which he could dissent. He told James Kent that he would stay on the bench and continue to express his—and Marshall's—opinions, "But I shall naturally be silent on many occasions from an anxious desire not to appear contentious, or dissatisfied, or desirous of weakening the [word unclear] influence of the court."

Another factor that might prod a minority judge into accepting compromise is psychological. Most people suffer anxiety when they find themselves in severe disagreement with a group with whom they are intimately associated. Appellate judges tend to be highly independent and individualistic people, but few of them are completely immune to dislike of isolation. Their professional socialization and role orientations—especially their legal training and the accepted norms of judicial behavior—to some extent encourage judges to express their own views, but only to some extent. This socialization also encourages judges to strive for harmony and teamwork with colleagues.

Other factors also push the majority, especially the opinion writer, to accept compromise. As already noted, an eloquent, tightly reasoned dissent can be an upsetting force. Writing without institutional authority—and responsibility—a clever dissenter can sometimes wreak intellectual mayhem on the essay that an opinion writer for the Court has had to patch together out of the not always compatible views of the other justices. The majority can therefore find it profitable to mute criticism from within the Court by giving in to the minority on some issues.

The justice who has the task of writing the opinion of the Court often assumes the role of a broker adjusting the interests of the group. The problems, of course, are dynamic rather than static. Making a change to accommodate one colleague can cost the opinion writer the vote of a different colleague. Moreover, compromising and incorporating several different lines of reasoning in the opinion may encourage an even more damaging dissent or ridicule from journalists, academics, or other public officials, many of whom delight in highlighting what they perceive as judicial lapses in logic.

Most important, a judge will want to avoid watering down an opinion to the point where it ceases to be an operational doctrine—though dilution may be the only alternative to outright rejection. The opinion writer can supply a sort of marginal analysis to the alternatives confronted. The minimum need—the essential need—is to have enough votes to win a majority so that the result and opinion carry the institutional authority of the Court. Thus, given the high value of these votes, the opinion writer should be willing to pay a relatively high price in accommodation to secure them. Once, however, a majority acquiesces, the marginal value of any additional vote declines, as does the price that an opinion writer should be willing to pay. The marginal value of another vote, however, is never zero, although the price may exceed its real value.

Voting on the Merits

Eventually, after what could be considerable negotiation, the final version of the opinion is reached, and each justice expresses a position by writing or signing an opinion of another justice. When all the justices have declared themselves, the only remaining step is for the Court to announce its decision and vote to the public.

Why do justices reach particular decisions? What forces play a role in determining their choices? Previous chapters provide a variety of answers—for example, Chapters 1 ("Political Jurisprudence"), 10 ("Precedents and Legal Reasoning"), 11 ("Statutory Interpretation"), and 12 ("Constitutional Interpretation") considered some of the formal legal components as well as less formal, though usually quite important, political and personal factors. Emphasis on what some scholars call "legally relevant" elements emanates from expectations of how many (perhaps most) Americans, including a large share of members of the legal community, expect judges to behave, particularly what they should and should not consider to reach decisions. Jurists are supposed to shed all their personal biases, preferences, and partisan attachments when they take their seats on the bench, because that sort of baggage, it is argued, should have no bearing on a court's decisions. Rather, judges ought to reach decisions in accord with factors that are grounded in "the law," such as precedents, or "neutral principles." Whether justices behave, or should behave, in accord with these standards is the object of considerable debate, as so many of the readings in this book demonstrate (e.g., compare Readings 10.7 and 10.9).

Stress on philosophical, political, and personal factors in decision making offers a quite different vision of the Supreme Court's decision making—indeed, of all judicial decision making. Although scholars who restrict themselves to formal legal elements contend that judges should divorce themselves from their personal and political biases when they settle disputes, scholars who also utilize extralegal approaches argue that it is unrealistic to expect judges to shed all their preferences and values (many of which are stored in the subconscious) and to ignore public opinion when they go to the bench. Rather, under the black robes there is a person like all of us whose convictions (perhaps biases) and attachments are strong and pervasive. It is one thing to ask judges to abandon partisan preferences for the Democratic or the Republican party or to sever ties to a particular president, senator, or governor. Almost all justices have managed to do so, with *Bush v. Gore* (2000) being one of the most consequential exceptions. It is quite a different thing to ask judges to abandon their moral anchorings. We cannot expect them to become what Chief Justice Earl Warren once called intellectual eunuchs.

Furthermore, there is no such animal as a "neutral principle"; by definition, principles are general propositions that supposedly govern decisions about how to act.[37] The principles of constitutional democracy, for instance, unfold a panoply of personal and public values that are vastly different from the principles of fascism or Stalinism. What we can hope for—indeed, can demand—from judges is "neutral application" of the principles of constitutional democracy. Thus, these scholars—and we count ourselves in these ranks although we are often out of step with many of our colleagues—argue, a judge can and should be impartial between litigants but cannot and should not be impartial between competing political philosophies or moral systems. No political system or its legal subsystem is or can be "value free," for, at root, politics is about values.

Judges usually do not admit that they are swayed by public opinion or that they vote according to their conceptions of what is best for the nation; but battalions of scholars claim that substantial evidence suggests that these factors do affect judges. (Note that we say judges are "swayed" by such factors, not "impelled," and these factors "affect" judges, not "control" them.) Readings in Chapter 8, for example, point to the influence that both elected officials—executives and members of the legislature—and the public can have on judicial decisions.

But perhaps even more prevalent in the literature of social science are explanations of justices' patterns of voting that turn on the (imputed) political perceptions, preferences, attitudes, or values of the justices. Using these attitudinal approaches, analysts draw attention—just as they do for trial and appellate court judges—to the degree to which a justice is conservative or liberal—as in: "Justice X holds conservative views on issues of criminal law" or "Justice Y holds liberal views on free speech." This school of thought holds that when a case comes before the Court, each justice perceives the facts of the dispute through the screen of his or her values and tends to arrive at a decision consistent with his or her personal political philosophy.

As Chapter 1 pointed out, the Legal Realists, who began their work at about the time of World War I, stressed the importance of judges' personal values in the ways in which they perceive and weigh alternative resolutions to legal disputes. A few social scientists took up the challenge and began systematic analyses of judges' votes. Among the first was Charles Grove Haines, who studied the outcomes in New York City's courts of 17,000 prosecutions for the offense of public intoxication.[38] Forty-one magistrates heard these cases, and the results varied dramatically from judge to judge. One magistrate dismissed the charges against only 1 of 566 defendants he tried; another dismissed 54 percent of the charges.

---

[37] See especially Arthur S. Miller and Ronald F. Howell, "The Myth of Neutrality in Constitutional Adjudication," 27 *University of Chicago Law Review* 661 (1960).

[38] Charles Grove Haines, "General Observations on the Effects of Personal, Political, and Economic Influences in the Decisions of Judges," 17 *Illinois Law Review* 96 (1922).

Alas, only a few social scientists tried to carry on Haines's work until C. Herman Pritchett picked up the banner after the end of the Supreme Court's war against the New Deal. Examining the way the justices voted from 1937 to 1953, he observed that dissent had become an institutionalized feature of judicial decisions.[39] If only precedents and other legal factors drove the Court's rulings, why did various justices interpreting the exact same legal materials not merely reach different results but do so consistently over the years? He concluded that the justices were not merely following precedents but were motivated in part by their own values. Pritchett's findings touched off an explosion of research on the influence of attitudes on the Supreme Court's decision making.[40] Much of this scholarship describes how liberal or conservative the various justices were and attempts to predict their voting behavior based on their attitudinal preferences.

How valuable are these efforts in helping us to understand judicial decision making? On the one hand, knowledge of justices' voting records can lead to fairly accurate predictions about their voting behavior in future cases. Suppose, for example, that the current Court hears a case dealing with the death penalty. The members of the Court who most strongly support government's constitutional authority to execute prisoners are Antonin Scalia and Clarence Thomas. Thus we can confidently predict that, if the justices disagree about the outcome, Scalia and Thomas would vote to sustain the death penalty. At the other end of the spectrum, John Paul Stevens is now the most consistent opponent of the death penalty, and we can also confidently predict his votes.[41]

On the other hand, attitudinal approaches are not without their share of problems. First is the matter of labels. Analysts tend to rank justices as more or less "liberal" or more or less "conservative," with "liberal" referring to support for civil liberties and support for governmental regulation of the economy and "conservative" referring to absence of such support. But, even if one accepts these tags as valid, they are relative to other justices on the Court. A "conservative" justice may support civil liberties more strongly than do most state or federal judges, legislators, or executive officials. Furthermore, this characterization is itself arbitrary, for it is doubtful how many true conservatives oppose civil liberties, though they may well oppose the judiciary's defining the content of civil

---

[39] See, especially, C. Herman Pritchett: "Divisions of Opinion among Justices of the U.S. Supreme Court, 1939-1941," 35 *American Political Science Review* (1941): 890; *The Roosevelt Court* (New York: Macmillan, 1948); and *Civil Liberties and the Vinson Court* (Chicago: University of Chicago Press, 1954).

[40] The classic works that followed Pritchett are Glendon A. Schubert, Jr., "The Study of Judicial Decision Making as an Aspect of Political Behavior," 52 *American Political Science Review* 1007 (1958); Schubert, *The Judicial Mind* (Evanston, IL: Northwestern University Press, 1965); and David W. Rohde and Harold J. Spaeth, *Supreme Court Decision Making* (San Francisco: Freeman, 1976). For a lucid, modern-day treatment, see Jeffrey A. Segal and Spaeth, *The Supreme Court and the Attitudinal Model Revisited* (New York: Cambridge University Press, 2002).

[41] We adopt this example from Jeffrey A. Segal and Harold J. Spaeth, *The Supreme Court and the Attitudinal Model,* (New York: Cambridge University Press, 1993), 223.

liberty. And, of course, at times liberals have also opposed not only specific judicial definitions but the very authority of judges to bind the country by those definitions. The *Dred Scott* Case (1857) provides the classic instance, but one can also cite reactions to various rulings from 1890 until 1937 enlarging and protecting the constitutional rights of owners of corporations to be free from governmental regulation.

And it is not always clear how to classify decisions. For people who believe that a woman has an unfettered right to control her body, *Roe v. Wade* (1973) is a landmark ruling in favor of civil rights; for people who believe that a human fetus has a right to life that takes priority over all but the mother's life, *Roe* is profoundly anti–civil rights. *Wisconsin v. Mitchell* (1993) presents similar classificatory difficulties. There the Court upheld a state law that increased the sentence for crimes if the defendant "intentionally selects the person against whom the crime is committed" on the basis of race, religion, national origin, sexual orientation, and other similar criteria. If we view the law as penalizing racial or ethnic hatred, we would count it as defending civil rights; if, however, we see the law as penalizing a person because of what he or she believes or says, we would deem the ruling anti–civil rights. The hard truth is, as Justice Felix Frankfurter once lamented, that great cases often present a clash of rights, not of wrongs.

Moreover, many cases also raise an additional dimension of equally perplexing questions: given the nature of the American political system (and that nature is contestable and contested), which governmental institution should decide these issues? Would a judicial ruling that sets policy for the nation deprive, in effect, the people of their right to elect representatives who will set public policy? Alternatively, would judicial deference to the legislature damage the constitutionalist basis of the political system, which is supposed to protect minorities against majorities?

Second, how do we know if a particular justice, say, Justice Scalia, is liberal or conservative? The answer typically is that we know he is conservative because he casts votes analysts consider conservative. This is circular reasoning indeed, for as we have just seen "liberal" and "conservative" are slippery terms.

Third, we must understand that ideological labels are often time-dependent, bound to a particular historical era. For example, *Muller v. Oregon* (1908) upheld a state law that set a maximum number on the hours women (but not men) could work. How would we twenty-first-century Americans classify this decision? Those of us who believe conservatives have difficulty with the notion of equality between the sexes (and not all people who call themselves conservatives do, any more than all self-proclaimed liberals practice as well as preach equality) would regard it as conservative because it seems to patronize and protect women.[42] In the early 1900s, however, most students of the Court considered

---

[42] Some contemporary observers would find the labels "liberal" and "conservative" to be equally misleading. Because the Nineteenth Amendment would not come into force until 1920, women in 1905 did not yet have a constitutionally recognized right to vote and so could not protect their own interests in the ways they thought proper through the political processes open to men

Muller a liberal ruling because it allowed the government to regulate business. To make things curiouser and curiouser, liberals had historically opposed governmental regulation of economic affairs; thus if *Muller* had been decided some decades earlier, it would have angered liberals.

Even if we acknowledge that many scholars have often attached simplistic labels to judges and their work, we still cannot easily dismiss the importance of attitudinal approaches: As scholar after scholar has pointed out, knowing a justice's ideology enables us, in many instances, to understand why he or she consistently votes on important issues of law and public policy. Nor should we dismiss the importance of the other extralegal factors, be they public opinion, strategy, or pressures imposed by elected actors. The Realists and the social scientists, such as Haines, Pritchett, and those who have come since, have time and again demonstrated that factors such as formal legal rules and precedents simply cannot account for the way in which judges behave.

The picture of justices trying to etch their preferences into law, negotiating with their colleagues, or looking over their shoulders at Congress, the president, or judges of lower courts conflicts with the image of a Supreme Court composed of austere and aloof demigods standing above the dark earth of politics.[43] Although almost all informed students of the judicial process concede (sometimes grudgingly) the accuracy of such a description of what actually goes on in collegial tribunals, many of those scholars—and judges themselves—perceive serious moral and ethical problems. Inevitably the question arises: how far can judges compromise without betraying their oaths to support the Constitution? This very serious question might be turned around: Would judges who had no ideas of their own about what "the constitution," as text or larger political system, meant, who only followed what their predecessors said it meant (if they could figure out what that was), who merely looked up "the law" without concern for doing the best they could to ensure not only that the constitution was interpreted so as to fulfill the lofty purposes the text itself lists, who simply voted and went home without worry about what other people thought or did or what would happen to the country—would such men and women be betraying their oaths of office?

---

[43] Since the 1970s, several books purported to reveal the inside story of various Courts' decisional histories: Bob Woodward and Scott Armstrong, *The Brethren: Inside the Supreme Court* (New York: Simon & Schuster, 1979); Phillip J. Cooper, *Battles on the Bench: Conflict Inside the Supreme Court* (Lawrence: University Press of Kansas, 1995); and Edward Lazarus, *Closed Chambers: The First Eyewitness Account of the Epic Struggles Inside the Supreme Court* (New York: Random House, 1998). The Brethren-an account of seven terms of the Burger Court-remains the most famous (or infamous). One of its authors, Bob Woodward, had earned his reputation as an ace investigative reporter in the Watergate affair. The book, according to the dust jacket, was "the first detailed behind-the-scenes account of the Supreme Court in action." The authors, their advertising claimed, had "pierced the secrecy to give us an unprecedented view of the Chief and Associate Justice-maneuvering, arguing, politicking, compromising, and making the decisions that affect every major area of American life." The writer of this hyperbole was probably unaware that many scholars had already pierced that "veil" and reported with far fewer errors about how the justices made their decisions.

No reader, having come this far in *Courts, Judges, and Politics,* would be shocked by the notion that judges argue and compromise and that constitutional principles are subject to continual reexamination as they challenge and are challenged by a disordered world. Indeed, such a description is likely to seem as exceptional as the notion that professional football is a physical sport.

SELECTED REFERENCES

ARMSTRONG, VIRGINIA, AND CHARLES A. JOHNSON. 1982. "Certiorari Decisions by the Warren and Burger Courts: Is Cue Theory Time Bound?" *Polity* 15: 141.

ATKINS, BURTON M. 1973. "Judicial Behavior and Tendencies toward Conformity in a Three-Member Small Group: A Case Study of Dissent Behavior on the United States Court of Appeals." *Social Science Quarterly* 54: 41.

BAUM, LAWRENCE. 1994. "What Judges Want: Judges' Goals and Judicial Behavior." *Political Research Quarterly* 47: 749.

BAUM, LAWRENCE. 1997. *The Puzzle of Judicial Behavior.* Ann Arbor: University of Michigan Press.

BECKER, THEODORE R. 1966. "A Survey Study of Hawaiian Judges: The Effect of Decisions on Judicial Role Variations." *American Political Science Review* 60: 677.

BOUCHER, ROBERT L., JR., AND JEFFREY A. SEGAL. 1995. "Supreme Court Justices as Strategic Decision Makers: Aggressive Grants and Defensive Denials on the Vinson Court." *Journal of Politics* 57: 812.

BRENNER, SAUL. 1979. "The New Certiorari Game." *Journal of Politics* 41: 649.

BRENNER, SAUL. 1980. "Fluidity on the United States Supreme Court: A Reexamination." *American Journal of Political Science* 24: 526.

BRENNER, SAUL, AND JOHN F. KROL. 1989. "Strategies in Certiorari Voting on the United States Supreme Court." *Journal of Politics* 51: 828.

CALDEIRA, GREGORY A., AND JOHN R. WRIGHT. 1988. "Organized Interests and Agenda-Setting in the U.S. Supreme Court." *American Political Science Review* 82: 1109.

CALDEIRA, GREGORY A., JOHN R. WRIGHT, AND CHRISTOPHER J. W. ZORN. 1999. "Sophisticated Voting and Gate-Keeping in the Supreme Court." *Journal of Law, Economics, and Organization* 15: 549.

CARP, ROBERT, AND RUSSELL WHEELER. 1972. "Sink or Swim: The Socialization of a Federal District Court Judge." *Journal of Public Law* 21: 359.

CROSS, FRANK B., AND EMERSON H. TILLER. 1998. "Judicial Partisanship and Obedience to Legal Doctrine: Whistleblowing on the Federal Courts of Appeals." *Yale Law Journal* 107: 2155.

DAVIS, SUE. 1990. "Power on the Court: Chief Justice Rehnquist's Opinion Assignments." *Judicature* 74: 66.

EISENSTEIN, JAMES, ROY B. FLEMMING, AND PETER F. NARDULLI, 1988. *The Contours of Justice.* Boston: Little, Brown.

EISENSTEIN, JAMES, AND HERBERT JACOB. 1977. *Felony Justice.* Boston: Little, Brown.

EPSTEIN, LEE, AND JACK KNIGHT. 1998. *The Choices Justices Make.* Washington, DC: CQ Press.

EPSTEIN, LEE, AND JOSEPH F. KOBYLKA. 1992. *The Supreme Court and Legal Change.* Chapel Hill: University of North Carolina Press.

FEELEY, MALCOLM M. 1976. *The Process Is Punishment: Handling Cases in a Lower Court.* New York: Russell Sage.

FRANK, JEROME. 1930. *Law and the Modern Mind.* New York: Brentano's.

GEORGE, TRACEY E. 1998. "Developing a Positive Theory of Decision Making on U.S. Courts of Appeals." *Ohio State University Law Review* 58: 1635.

GEORGE, TRACEY E., AND LEE EPSTEIN. 1992. "On the Nature of Supreme Court Decision Making." *American Political Science Review* 86: 323.

GIBSON, JAMES L. 1978. "Judges' Role Orientations, Attitudes, and Decisions: An Interactive Model." *American Political Science Review* 72: 911.

GILLMAN, HOWARD. 2001. *The Votes That Counted.* Chicago: University of Chicago Press.

GLICK, HENRY ROBERT. 1971. *Supreme Courts in State Politics.* New York: Basic Books.

GLICK, HENRY ROBERT, AND KENNETH N. VINES. 1973. *State Court Systems.* Englewood Cliffs, NJ: Prentice Hall.

GOLDMAN, SHELDON. 1966. "Voting Behavior on the United States Courts of Appeals, 1961–1964." *American Political Science Review* 60: 378.

GOLDMAN, SHELDON. 1973. "Conflict on the U.S. Courts of Appeals, 1965–1971: A Quantitative Analysis." *University of Cincinnati Law Review* 42: 635–658.

GROSSMAN, JOEL B., AND JOSEPH TANENHAUS, EDS. 1969. *Frontiers of Judicial Research.* New York: Wiley.

HALL, MELINDA GANN. 1987. "Constituent Influence in State Supreme Court: Conceptual Notes and a Case Study." *Journal of Politics* 49: 1117.

HALL, MELINDA GANN. 1992. "Electoral Politics and Strategic Voting in State Supreme Court." *Journal of Politics* 54: 427.

HALL, MELINDA GANN, AND PAUL BRACE. 1989. "Order in the Court: A Neo-Institutional Approach to Judicial Consensus." *Western Political Quarterly* 42: 391.

HALL, MELINDA GANN, AND PAUL BRACE. 1992. "Toward and Integrated Model of Judicial Voting Behavior." *American Politics Quarterly* 20: 147.

HETTINGER, VIRGINIA, STEFANIE LINDQUIST, AND WENDY L. MARTINEK. 2004. "Comparing Attitudinal and Strategic Accounts of Dissenting Behavior on the U.S. Courts of Appeals." *American Journal of Political Science* 48: 123.

HOWARD, J. WOODFORD. 1968. "On the Fluidity of Judicial Choice." *American Political Science Review* 62: 43.

HOWARD, J. WOODFORD. 1977. "Role Perceptions and Behavior in Three U.S. Courts of Appeals." *Journal of Politics* 39: 916.

JOHNSON, TIMOTHY R. 2004. *Oral Arguments and the United States Supreme Court.* Albany, NY: State University of New York Press.

KROL, JOHN F., AND SAUL BRENNER. 1990. "Strategies in Certiorari Voting on the United States Supreme Court." *Western Political Quarterly* 43: 342.

MALTZMAN, FORREST, JAMES F. SPRIGGS II, AND PAUL J. WAHLBECK. 2000. *Crafting Law on the Supreme Court: The Collegial Game.* Cambridge, UK: Cambridge University Press.

MALTZMAN, FORREST, AND PAUL J. WAHLBECK. 1996. "May It Please the Chief? Opinion Assignments in the Rehnquist Court." *American Journal of Political Science* 40: 421.

MALTZMAN, FORREST, AND PAUL J. WAHLBECK. 1996. "Strategic Policy Considerations and Voting Fluidity on the Burger Court." *American Political Science Review* 90: 581.

MASON, ALPHEUS T. 1956. *Harlan Fiske Stone: Pillar of the Law.* New York: Viking.

MASON, ALPHEUS T. 1968. "The Chief Justice of the United States: Primus Inter Pares." *Journal of Public Law* 20: 17.

MURPHY, WALTER F. 1964. *Elements of Judicial Strategy.* Chicago: University of Chicago Press.

MURPHY, WALTER F., AND JOSEPH TANENHAUS. 1972. *The Study of Public Law.* New York: Random House.

NAGEL, STUART S. 1961. "Political Party Affiliations and Judges' Decisions." *American Political Science Review* 55: 843.

NARDULLI, PETER F., JAMES EISENSTEIN, AND ROY B. FLEMMING. 1988. *The Tenor of Justice.* Urbana: University of Illinois Press.

OAKLEY, JOHN B., AND ROBERT S. THOMPSON. 1981. *Law Clerks and the Judicial Process.* Berkeley: University of California Press.

PELTASON, JACK W. 1961. *Fifty-Eight Lonely Men: Southern Federal Judges and School Desegregation.* New York: Harcourt, Brace & World.

PERRY, H. W., JR. 1991. *Deciding to Decide: Agenda-Setting in the United States Supreme Court.* Cambridge, MA: Harvard University Press.

POWELL, LEWIS F., JR. 1980. "What Really Goes on at the Supreme Court." *American Bar Association Journal* 66: 721.

PRITCHETT, C. HERMAN. 1948. *The Roosevelt Court.* New York: Macmillan.

PRITCHETT, C. HERMAN. 1953. *Civil Liberties and the Vinson Court.* Chicago: University of Chicago Press.

PRITCHETT, C. HERMAN. 1968. "Public Law and Judicial Behavior." In *Political Science: Advance of the Discipline,* Marian D. Irish, ed. Englewood Cliffs, NJ: Prentice Hall.

PROVINE, DORIS MARIE. 1980. *Case Selection in the United States Supreme Court.* Chicago: University of Chicago Press.

ROHDE, DAVID W. 1972. "Policy Goals and Opinion Coalitions in the Supreme Court." *Midwest Journal of Political Science* 16: 208.

ROHDE, DAVID W. 1972. "Policy Goals, Strategic Choice and Majority Opinion Assignments in the U.S. Supreme Court." *American Journal of Political Science* 16: 652.

ROHDE, DAVID W., AND HAROLD J. SPAETH. 1976. *Supreme Court Decision Making.* San Francisco: Freeman.

ROWLAND, C. K., AND ROBERT A. CARP. 1996. *Politics and Judgment in Federal District Courts.* Lawrence: University Press of Kansas.

SCHUBERT, GLENDON. 1958. "The Study of Judicial Decision-Making as an Aspect of Political Behavior." *American Political Science Review* 52: 1007.

SCHUBERT, GLENDON. 1962. "The 1960 Term of the Supreme Court: A Psychological Analysis." *American Political Science Review* 56: 90.

SCHUBERT, GLENDON. 1965. *The Judicial Mind.* Evanston, IL: Northwestern University Press.

SEGAL, JEFFREY A., AND HAROLD J. SPAETH. 2003. *The Supreme Court and the Attitudinal Model Revisited.* New York: Cambridge University Press.

SLOTNICK, ELLIOT F. 1979. "Who Speaks for the Court? Majority Opinion Assignment from Taft to Burger." *American Journal of Political Science* 23: 60.

SMITH, ROGERS M. 1988. "Political Jurisprudence, the 'New Institutionalism,' and the Future of Public Law." *American Political Science Review* 82: 89.

SONGER, DONALD R. 1982. "Consensual and Nonconsensual Decisions in Unanimous Opinions of the United States Courts of Appeals." *American Journal of Political Science* 26: 225.

SONGER, DONALD R., AND SUSAN HAIRE. 1992. "Integrating Alternative Approaches to the Study of Judicial Voting: Obscenity Cases in the U.S. Courts of Appeals." *American Journal of Political Science* 36: 963.

SONGER, DONALD R., JEFFREY A. SEGAL, AND CHARLES M. CAMERON. 1994. "The Hierarchy of Justice: Testing a Principal-Agent Model of Supreme Court-Circuit Court Interactions." *American Journal of Political Science* 38: 673–696.

STEARNS, MAXWELL L. 2000. *Constitutional Process: A Social Choice Analysis of Supreme Court Decision Making.* Ann Arbor: University of Michigan Press.

STUMPF, HARRY, AND JOHN H. CULVER. 1992. *The Politics of State Courts.* New York: Longmans.

TANENHAUS, JOSEPH, JOSEPH SCHICK, MATTHEW MURASKIN, AND DANIEL ROSEN. 1963. "The Supreme Court's Certiorari Jurisdiction: Cue Theory." In *Judicial Decision Making*, Glendon Schubert, ed. New York: Free Press.

TARR, G. ALAN, AND MARY CORNELIA PORTER. 1988. *State Supreme Court in State and Nation*. New Haven, CT: Yale University Press.

ULMER, S. SIDNEY. 1984. "The Supreme Court's Certiorari Decisions: Conflict as a Predictive Variable." *American Political Science Review* 78: 901.

VINES, KENNETH N. 1964. "Federal District Court Judges and Race Relations Cases in the South." *Journal of Politics* 26: 338.

WAHLBECK, PAUL J., JAMES F. SPRIGGS, II, AND FORREST MALTZMAN. 1998. "Marshalling the Court: Bargaining and Accommodation on the U.S. Supreme Court." *American Journal of Political Science* 42: 294.

WALKER, THOMAS G., LEE EPSTEIN, AND THOMAS G. WALKER. 1988. "On the Mysterious Demise of Consensual Norms in the United States Supreme Court." *Journal of Politics* 50: 361.

WILKINSON, J. HARVIE, III. 1974. *Serving Justice: A Supreme Court Clerk's View*. New York: Charterhouse.

"It's a heinous crime that he's charged with, but the fact of the matter is that there is a presumption of innocence and that's what the court is required to act on."

13.1 CRITICAL ISSUES IN THE COURTROOM: EXPLORING A HYPOTHETICAL CASE

Charles Nesson and Associates

At a conference on criminal courts, Charles Nesson of Harvard Law School led a panel of judges, attorneys, and other court personnel in an exchange about a hypothetical case. Among the issues they covered were bail, plea bargaining, and sentencing.

PROFESSOR CHARLES NESSON: You know Vernon Jones to be the reverend of Zion Baptist Church for 15 or 20 years, and he is being arraigned in front of you and when the charges are read, they're very serious. It's rape, attempted rape, and assault. Judge Daffron, you are going to have to set bail. That's the first order of business. Tell me how you are going to proceed.

JUDGE JOHN DAFFRON [a state circuit court judge]: The consideration would be the danger to the community, the likelihood that the accused would appear for future proceedings, and if he, in fact, is an established member of the community. On the point of his likelihood to appear, it seems he would be very likely to have bail set and be able to post bond in spite of the fact that the offenses are very serious.

PROFESSOR NESSON: Do you want to know any details about the offenses?

JUDGE DAFFRON: I would ask the prosecutor or the police officer the facts of the offenses and try to make some determination of the strength of the case, the potential danger to the community, and the effect on the victim.

PROFESSOR NESSON: Here is apparently what happened. Mr. Jones has been molesting young women right in his office at the Zion Baptist Church. He apparently has been making a practice of picking out young, impressionable women who were deeply religious, having sex with them in his office and then following it up with the strictest, scariest direction to them not to disclose to anyone or God will punish them and their mothers. By the way, there are people taking notes out there like mad. Suddenly you see a scurry in the back of the courtroom with people running out and court reporters starting to filter in.

JUDGE DAFFRON: If there is a probability that other charges may be placed or that other people were at risk, then it seems to me that it swings toward pretrial confinement.

72 *Judicature* 12 (1988).

PROFESSOR NESSON: What do you mean it swings towards pretrial confinement? What are you actually going to do now?

JUDGE DAFFRON: If these are all the facts, I'm going to lock him up.

PROFESSOR NESSON: You're going to lock him up period? No bail, no bond, no nothing?

JUDGE DAFFRON: Place him in confinement. I would set a bail. It would be commensurate with what I think the risk is and so far, from what I've heard, there is a significant risk to others.

PROFESSOR NESSON: Judge O'Toole, are you right along with him here?

JUDGE THOMAS O'TOOLE [state superior court judge]: I just want to make sure that if he is going to be released, the community is assured he is going to abide by the conditions of the release, and I would make my decision according to those factors.

PROFESSOR NESSON: You don't have any problems at all using the dangerousness of this fellow as the criterion on which you are making the judgment?

JUDGE DAFFRON: If there is not a significant risk to the community or individual people, then there should be a moderate amount applied that would be designed to assure his appearances at the proceeding. When you add in the factor of potential risk as it has been presented so far, it comes as a matter that requires pretrial detention.

PROFESSOR NESSON: How are those reporters in the back of the room affecting you?

JUDGE DAFFRON: It sounds pompous, but I don't really think I'd be particularly concerned with the fact that it's going to be a news item.

* * *

PROFESSOR NESSON: And it's sounding wiser and wiser to you, at least for the moment, to lock this guy up?

JUDGE DAFFRON: From what I've heard so far, yes. My leaning is to confinement.

PROFESSOR NESSON: Mr. Peruto, you represent this fellow. Now what do you think you could do for him?

CHARLES PERUTO [an attorney]: Well, in the first place, I need a couple of facts that would make me think he's a hell of a man.

PROFESSOR NESSON: We should let our audience know that you have in front of you a little sheet that gives some minor details on this fellow. It's got his name and his date of birth (he's 52 years old), his address (Rocky Peak), and telephone number. He was divorced seven years ago and he's employed. It also includes the date of the offense, the charges, possible penalties, and his employment history. His employment history is basically fairly impressive; it amounts to that he's been a minister here for 20 years.

ATTORNEY PEURTO: In the first place, I'd argue that he's been removed from his position where this was alleged to have occurred, and therefore the likelihood of recurrence is remote. I would point out that he has a splendid record. I'm going to say to the judge that here are alternatives. I have to recognize that rape is a very frightening thing in the community, at least to half of the community, and that the judge is in a ticklish position. I also have to recognize that I'm not going to get very far persuading the judge to release this man on a bail that he can make because I've got to understand that he's going to be incurring the wrath of the press. So I think I would start thinking about alternatives, such as daily calling-in, but confined to his own home. In other words, present a program for a man who otherwise had had a splendid record and obviously has been disturbed in some fashion and promise to present him for psychiatric examination; present a program of reporting to the court with regard to any evidence of propensities along the lines of the charges that he faces and suggest alternatives to prison.

PROFESSOR NESSON: Ms. Washington, should this fellow be locked up right now or not?

FRANCES WASHINGTON [probation officer]: Yes, he should. He's one of the most trusted members of the community. He molested children, little girls who are probably taught to trust him, and he violated that trust. He inflicted physical and long-lasting psychological damage to these children. He should go to jail. I would not release him back to the community, not to call in. He could be molesting more children while he's calling in. Calling in doesn't have anything to do with this.

PROFESSOR NESSON: Judge Murphy, do you have any problem with this reaction? We've got a guy whose got roots in the community that are solid as a rock. He's going to show up on the day of trial and yet the reaction from all of these folks is, "Hey, that's not what counts. What counts, 'Is he dangerous?'" Is that what counts?

CHIEF JUSTICE ROBERT MURPHY: I think the fear of those who are opposed to pretrial detention to some extent may be justified by what we're hearing here. I share defense counsel's view on this entirely. He starts with the presumption of innocence. He's probably going to say, "I was in Chicago when all this happened." But this man, based on what I have before me, does not seem to be a candidate for pretrial detention. I don't know how much space you have in the Rocky Peak jail detention center, but I'd save it for someone who's got a track record of dangerousness.

PROBATION OFFICER WASHINGTON: If this man was a drifter, a drunk, a drug addict, or a burglar who had a history of appearing in court for every hearing, he would still be held with or without bond. I believe that the minister's about to get away with rape because he is "somebody" in the community. Granted, we don't know that he's guilty and I've already found him guilty, but you have to look out for your children and you have an obligation to look out for other people's children.

PROFESSOR NESSON: What does the presumption of innocence mean to you?

PROBATION OFFICER WASHINGTON: That you're innocent until found guilty. But mind you, I work with juveniles, and 90 percent of the juveniles who are caught did what they were accused of doing and that is just the way it is.

JUDGE MERCEDES DEIZ [state circuit court judge]: What we are hearing from the probation officer is clearly what we are all concerned about at this conference. The arraigning judge must make a decision as to whether the individual should be released, recognizing the tremendously terrible crime that he is charged with. I have to somehow push that out of my mind and get input from defense counsel and the attorney who is representing this minister. We're lucky enough in my area to have a closed-street supervision outfit, and so if the closed-street supervision people will take this man under their regular supervision pending the time of trial then, based upon everything I'm hearing from defense counsel and the district attorney, I think I would release him.

PROFESSOR NESSON: Respond to Ms. Washington. She says, "Listen, the presumption of innocence is a very important part of our trial procedure, but let's not set it up as something totally realistic. I've worked day to day for years in the system, and I know that 90 percent of the people that come into the system as arrestees are guilty. If I have to presume that they are innocent, you're asking me to take a totally unrealistic view of the world. And certainly a view of the world that the constituency out there and the reporters scribbling on their pads aren't going to take." What do you say to her?

JUDGE DEIZ: Thank God for the jury system because they listen. The jurors listen to that instruction and literally apply it and recognize that the defendant has to be proven guilty beyond a reasonable doubt on every material aspect of the case. Too often, the DAs goof and forget some material aspect of the case and some guy gets off who is just as guilty and horrible a human being as Ms. Washington is concerned about. But the guy gets off because we have a system that says the person has to be proven guilty.

JUDGE RICARDO URBINA [District of Columbia superior court judge]: You haven't given us the law of the jurisdiction, but I think the judge has to bite the bullet on a case like this. The information you've given us makes it rather clear that there are alternatives to locking this person up before trial. He is presumed innocent, and there's any number of reasons that explains the allegations that have been made. It's a heinous crime that he's charged with, but the fact of the matter is that there is a presumption of innocence, and that's what the court is required to act on. If there is some danger to the community, there's a number of things the court can do to try to insulate the community from being harmed. The first factor in my mind is going to be whether or not he's going to return to court. The second would be trying to set up some system to assure me, as the judge, the court, or the system in the community that they can rest at ease, even based on these allegations about him.

PROFESSOR NESSON: Ms. Washington's got a system. Her system to put the people in that church at ease is to lock him up, and that is very reassuring. And in fact all the rest of this stuff, about keeping him at home and checking in with the probation officer once a week, is not very reassuring.

JUDGE URBINA: I think it's the judge's job to identify the issue and to deal with it directly. It's not the judge's job to make the community feel comfortable with that decision. The judge has got the law to rely on, and often that's what the judge has to do—make a decision that's going to make the community uncomfortable.

LUCY FRIEDMAN [executive director, Victim Services Agency]: I think that in this case the judge's job is not to make the community feel comfortable in general terms but to deal with the specifics of this case. From the victim's perspective, this is a troubling case because although we want to presume innocence, we clearly don't want to have this man take advantage and continue doing what he's been doing. I hope the reporters are out there because the more publicity about this case, the better. If he were then released with some kind of supervision, the community would be protected because people would be aware of what he has been accused of doing.

PROFESSOR NESSON: Judge Daffron, after considering this very difficult problem, winds up making the judgment that he's going to set fairly high bond of $150,000. After bond is set, there is quite a bit of action out there in the community. There's a lot of people raising money in support of this fellow to pay off his bond. And you, Mr. Peruto, kind of like the political support that he's getting. You figure you'll have him out in awhile and I want you to think about talking to Mr. Goldsmith about pleading this one out. Mr. Goldsmith, you're willing to talk with him?

STEPHEN GOLDSMITH [prosecutor]: Yes, I think so.

ATTORNEY PERUTO: I would talk about plea bargaining in the sense of assault and point out that there was no serious injury because I haven't heard anything like that and that this man obviously has mental difficulty, which I can assure him will be taken care of. Now I would have had him thoroughly examined by people whom I hired that knew how to examine people. You'll always find psychiatrists who you can interest in the efficacy of the problem.

PROFESSOR NESSON: You're gonna hire these psychiatrists and you're then going to write the script for them?

ATTORNEY PERUTO: Absolutely, with all due honesty.

PROFESSOR NESSON: Let's assume I'm your psychiatrist. What are your interests in this examination, Mr. Peruto?

ATTORNEY PERUTO: I want you to examine my client because obviously he has some aberration of mind, which has caused this. He's been divorced seven years. He's been very, very morose, and he's been very, very depressed. I think it's worked on him to such a point where it's caused him to be a little bit, well, a little careless. He's misinterpreted the smiles of these young ladies. I think that once you've examined him, you'll agree that this man is not dangerous but really in dire need of medical attention.

PROFESSOR NESSON: Mr. Goldsmith, is this somebody you're gonna press hard with?

PROSECUTING ATTORNEY GOLDSMITH: This is a difficult case for the prosecutor, in fact, an unusual case, because the dynamics are against the prosecution.

The church has rallied, and they're convinced of the man's innocence. It's not a case the prosecutor particularly wishes to test. At the same time, we know there are multiple counts, whether you call them child molesting or rapes. We've gotten your psychiatric report saying he's not a pedophile; he's really a sick person.

The issue is whether this is an aberrational event and he can be treated. We ought to take into consideration whether he is in fact a pedophile who will continue to molest children if he's out. I would say to his attorney, we will not bring the other sixteen counts if you will pick one of these counts for which we want a guilty plea. Leave sentencing open to the judge.

PROFESSOR NESSON: And what's that going to mean if you take the plea to one count?

PROSECUTING ATTORNEY GOLDSMITH: We would require some sort of prison term to be determined by the court.

PROFESSOR NESSON: It's going to be up to the judge to sentence?

PROSECUTING ATTORNEY GOLDSMITH: I'm assuming that either there's a mandatory imprisonment period or the prosecution requires some imprisonment to be determined by the court.

PROFESSOR NESSON: All right, so let me see if I've got this straight. It depends a little bit for you on what the law is in the jurisdiction.

PROSECUTING ATTORNEY GOLDSMITH: What the judge's discretion is under the law.

PROFESSOR NESSON: If the judge has no discretion, then you are in a total position of power, aren't you? You are going to decide whether this guy does time or not? On the other hand, if the judge has discretion, you have a good deal less power? And you'd respond to that by saying I'm gonna be much less willing to bargain away charges?

PROSECUTING ATTORNEY GOLDSMITH: We're trying to get him to plead to something, and what I'm giving up is my requirement he goes for a fixed period of time. We're going to kind of roll the dice. He's gonna put his psychiatrist on before the judge; I get a guilty plea out of it. So long as the guy goes to prison, that's good for the state.

PROFESSOR NESSON: All right; now here's the situation in the jurisdiction. The judge has discretion. He could put this fellow on probation. That's possible. And the law in your jurisdiction is that you can't sentence-bargain. You can charge-bargain; you can't sentence-bargain. You go in front of the judge; he pleads guilty; it's up to the judge to sentence. Now, where does that leave you?

PROSECUTING ATTORNEY GOLDSMITH: The reason we have a lot less with which to deal is because the sentence ranges from the three counts that have been provided to us are twenty to forty years for rape, fifteen to thirty-five for attempted rape and eight to twenty for aggravated assault. If there's no realistic chance the man's ever going to get more than eight years, there's not much advantage for the state to go to trial at all on the top two charges because we know the judges are way to the left of prosecutors and it's going to come down to the minimum sentence. So we say plead guilty to one of the counts, eight to twenty years, and we'll forgive the other two counts.

   If the judge has a full range of discretion on sentencing, which essentially in this case is zero to forty years, we want a guilty plea which will allow the court—after it hears from you and the probation department, thank goodness, and the other psychiatrist—to come in with a range of penalty that's appropriate. Or we way, "Plead guilty to the eight to twenty, that's the lowest one, you reduce your risk of going to prison for forty years, and then let the judge decide."

PROFESSOR NESSON: Mr. Goldsmith, is this the discussion between you and Mr. Peruto that's taking place down in your office?

PROSECUTING ATTORNEY GOLDSMITH: Right.

PROFESSOR NESSON: What happens if Mrs. Robinson wants to present? She's Darlene's mother. Darlene was the victim of charge number one. Ms. Washington, would you be Mrs. Robinson for me? Talk to Ms. Washington here and discourage her.

PROSECUTING ATTORNEY GOLDSMITH: We think, Mrs. Robinson, that if this man is found guilty, the sentence is going to be six or eight years, and there is a chance it could go higher. We could go to trial with your twelve-year-old daughter and the chances of an increased sentence are a little bit greater. We can try to get a guilty plea and not put her through it. I'd like your permission to offer a guilty as charged to the count of eight to twenty years.

PROBATION OFFICER WASHINGTON: I don't want my twelve-year-old to be subjected to a trial after what she has been subjected to by this man. I want him to serve sixteen years, not eight, because when he is released, I want my child to be grown, through college, maybe even out of the area and hopefully over this.

PROSECUTING ATTORNEY GOLDSMITH: Well, I'm going to have a settlement discussion with his attorney. I'll offer him fifteen to thirty-five years. I think it would be easier if you weren't there. If he rejects it, then I'll come back to you and talk to you about whether your daughter wants to go through it. But one thing I want you to understand is even if we do go through this trial, the judge could still give the range of sentence that could go all the way down to zero. We can't guarantee a sentence to you, but I'll take your proposal to the defense attorney.

PROFESSOR NESSON: You're letting her run your office?

PROSECUTING ATTORNEY GOLDSMITH: In this case, the mom has a major say in whether to put her daughter, the victim, through the trial for what could come out of it, much more so than in a robbery or other case that doesn't put her child victim on the stand.

PROFESSOR NESSON: Mr. Peruto, what are you going to do about this?

ATTORNEY PERUTO: Well, I would point out to the district attorney that even with eight years, the man will be sixty, so I don't know where she's coming off with the protection of her own child. I would talk to Mr. Goldsmith about things such as considerations of track record. For example, if he has tried cases against me before that he thought were winners and wound up losers, I would say that one of the bits of input has to do with the possibility of success at the trial. I would point out to him that although he gets great sympathetic appeal from the fact that the child is twelve, he also has a child that is not going to be able to understand the kind of cross-examination that I would put the child through. I would suggest that he speak again to Mrs. Robinson and let her know these things and that it might result in serious damage to the child, far greater than the risk she would fear after his release in eight years. It might cause irreparable harm to her. I would throw in all of these things, and I would suggest to him that if he wants a plea from me to the extent he wants a plea on the higher charge of rape and leave it to the judge, I could not accept that because he's only passing the buck. I am all too familiar with judges saying, "Well, he's already gotten his break on the reduction of the number of counts," and the judge is on the hot seat because now it's not a question of presumption of innocence. You have a guilty person before you, and he's gonna face the press, and we all know the way the press came down on that one judge who made that unfortunate comment, "She'll get over it." No judge is going to give him eight years or less than eight years on a plea to the rape charge. It must be the kind of bargain where we have a cap on the sentence; otherwise, I would have to tell my client, "You're a fool—you may as well face a thousand charges than one which exposes you to ninety-five years total because you can't trust the judge." You gotta put yourself in that judge' position. We just cannot deal under those circumstances on anything higher than the assault charge.

PROFESSOR NESSON: What I hear you saying to me, Mr. Peruto, is if you can't make a firm deal that at least caps the sentence, you don't want any deal at all.

ATTORNEY PERUTO: That's right. I would point out to the DA that I've got my doctors who are going to testify, I've got the great number of parishioners that are going to come in for him; it's going to be a real donnybrook. I'm just going to have to tell my own client you're shooting crap if you come in on a rape plea because then you're defenseless, and you're putting the judge in the position that I've previously described, and I would advise him to go for broke.

PROFESSOR NESSON: Judge O'Toole, should the law permit the prosecutor and defense to make a firm deal on the amount of the sentence? Must it be the law that the prosecution and the defense can make a firm deal on the amount of the sentence?

JUDGE O'TOOLE: The answer to that is no, because the judge has to impose sentence, and if he has no discretion in accepting or rejecting the deal, they're passing the buck to him whether it's a bad deal. The judge gets the buck from the community so to speak, and they don't suffer from it.

PROFESSOR NESSON: Judge Urbina? Do you understand the problem? How should it be?

JUDGE URBINA: I don't like the idea of having the defense and prosecution dictate what the sentence should be in the case. The judge, as more or less of a neutral person in the situation, has oversight of what's going on and has insight into what should ultimately be appropriate as a sentence. Both the prosecution and defense are coming at the problem with a particular point of view in mind, and they've reached a point where they've compromised. I don't think that compromise should really involve the judge.

PROFESSOR NESSON: Judge Murphy, how should it be?

MURPHY: To a large extent, judges know their prosecutors and their defense counsels and, to some extent, will pay deference to their judgment. They certainly don't have all of the facts before them, but by no means or measure can a trial judge be bound by a bad deal on his judgment. As a practical matter on the plea-bargaining process, the bargainers know their judge, and I think they ride on the philosophy that what they agree to will in fact be accepted, but they can never be totally assured.

PROFESSOR NESSON: What would happen in this case if we were to live in a world with no plea bargaining, no sentence bargaining, and no charge bargaining?

MURPHY: It's a cruel, cruel world and a very unrealistic one. Obviously, the court system would probably break itself very, very shortly if you didn't have the plea-bargaining process.

PROSECUTING ATTORNEY GOLDSMITH: It's an unrealistic world that doesn't allow those people closest to the case to negotiate an outcome based on the dynamics of the evidence, the dynamics of the community, and the importance of the charge.

PROFESSOR NESSON: So as far as you're concerned, it's part of the prosecutor's job to negotiate outcomes?

PROSECUTING ATTORNEY GOLDSMITH: Absolutely.

PROFESSOR NESSON: And God help the defense—if they didn't have that to do, what else would they offer their clients?

PROSECUTING ATTORNEY GOLDSMITH: Well, I think we arrive together at a decision that more than anything takes the evidence and predicts the judge.

PROFESSOR NESSON: All right. Let's predict the judge here. Judge O'Toole, just looking for a reaction. What are you going to sentence this man to?

JUDGE O'TOOLE: Well, he's gonna to go prison, it's just a question of how long. It's a very serious crime, and apparently we have mitigating factors and aggravating factors.

PROFESSOR NESSON: He's a distinguished member of the civil liberties movement, civil rights movement, and a pillar in the Baptist Church. Tremendous support from his congregation.

JUDGE O'TOOLE: That isn't at the top of my list of priorities for determining sentence.

PROFESSOR NESSON: And he's sick.

JUDGE O'TOOLE: Is that a factor to consider? That also works the other way because if he's sick, who's to know whether he's going to recover? I would perhaps have a psychiatric examination conducted by a court-appointed expert, and you also have the expert input from the probation department. Included in the expert input would be statements of the victims and interested parties. All these players come in line on a sentence.

Mrs. Robinson rings a loud bell when she talks about the concerns of her daughter. I would want to know the impact on the victim. I'd also want to be satisfied as to the length of incarceration that this man would serve under the particular sentence. I'd want to know the guidelines for release and what type of parole supervision he's going to have. The man's fifty-two years old, perhaps it's somewhat pragmatic, but I'd want to see him incarcerated until he's sixty and put parole on him. I'd propose a sentence that considers not only punishment and deterrence but community safety and also the interests of the defendant. This is a very serious ongoing pattern of conduct, evident not only by this particular charge, but if I understand the facts, this has been occurring with other young females in the parish.

PROFESSOR NESSON : You're going to find out about that during sentencing?

JUDGE O'TOOLE : I would think so.

PROFESSOR NESSON: Commissioner Coughlin, can you use this man? You've got him now, and you've got him for a minimum of eight years. What are you going to do with him?

THOMAS COUGHLIN [commissioner, state correctional services]: Put him to work. I would probably use whatever skills I could get out of him. Not in terms of ministerial skills, but I'd imagine he could read and write pretty good, and we'd probably put him in some setting within the prison system where we could use those skills. . . .

"Negotiation and mutual accommodation dominated workgroup interactions and facilitated guilty pleas."

13.2 FELONY JUSTICE

James Eisenstein and Herbert Jacob

James Eisenstein is Professor of Political Science at Pennsylvania State University; Herbert Jacob was Professor of Political Science at Northwestern University.

Courtroom Workgroups in Chicago

Two sets of courtroom workgroups [preliminary workgroups and trial court workgroups] determined the fate of defendants in Chicago.

From James Eisenstein and Herbert Jacob, *Felony Justice* (Boston: Little, Brown, 1977), pp. 106–109.

Preliminary hearing workgroups in Chicago disposed of almost all defendants charged with felonies. The principal members of [these] workgroups spent considerable [time in] these courtrooms. The associate circuit judges assigned to them remained for a year or two. The two or three assistant prosecutors in each courtroom typically stayed at least six months. The two public defenders stationed there remained about as long. A single more experienced assistant prosecutor alternated between the north side and south side courtrooms to negotiate pleas. The volume of work and physical proximity of Chicago's preliminary hearing courtrooms permitted a few private attorneys to make a living by confining their practice to quick disposition cases there. Finally, bailiffs and clerks staffing these courtrooms often had many years of service in them.

These characteristics produced stable workgroups whose members became quite familiar with each other. Several consequences flowed from this familiarity. Workgroup members depended on one another. Chicago's judges lacked the power to refuse to hold a preliminary hearing. As a result, judges shared control over decisions more with assistant prosecutors, public defenders, and private regulars. The pressure generated by the very heavy case load reinforced tendencies toward cooperation and mutual dependence. Courtroom goals also reflected the effects of case pressure. The goals of disposing of cases and maintaining cohesion were compelling. Everyone realized that the entire felony disposition process depended on these courtrooms to screen out most defendants before they reached the trial court level. Pressures applied to workgroup members by sponsoring organizations gave special importance to the goal of disposing of cases. The preliminary hearing workgroups' physical location in the same building that housed fifteen of the twenty trial courtrooms facilitated the communication of such pressure. Their low visibility to the general public (the media rarely reported their decisions) reduced the urgency of doing justice as a crucial goal.

Workgroup members exhibited considerable cooperation and mutual accommodation. Postponements were easily negotiated, particularly when they facilitated a disposition. When preliminary hearings ultimately were held, they reflected little of the conflict that adversarial proceedings are supposed to show. Rather, they were often informal.

These characteristics did not eliminate all conflict, of course. Nor did they reduce judges to mere equals of the attorneys. The formal authority of judges kept them in the position of greatest influence. Judges' unflattering opinions of some workgroup members' competence, particularly the private regulars and the young assistant state's attorneys, also limited the extent to which judges deferred to others.

Cases that survived the rigorous screening at the preliminary hearing went to trial court workgroups for disposition. These workgroups were even more stable than those at the preliminary hearing stage. Judges had no set term of service in the criminal division, but most spent at least a year there, and some served more than two. The state's attorney's office assigned two assistants to most judges' courtrooms. These assignments were semipermanent, although some assistants shifted periodically. Nevertheless, many remained with a judge at least a year, and most tried cases in other courtrooms only occasionally during that period. The public defender's office assigned an assistant public defender to each courtroom. Most stayed as long as assistant prosecutors did. Finally, some retained regular defense attorneys managed to concentrate many of their cases in a few courtrooms, and assumed the status of a regular workgroup member. The long courthouse experience of some of these attorneys made them familiar to judges and prosecutors even though they did not appear as often as the public defender. Once assigned to a courtroom, defendants' cases almost always remained in that courtroom. Hence, almost no last-minute shifting of courtrooms occurred.

The stability of courtroom workgroups and their members' familiarity with each other produced the expected results. Mutual dependence was very high, nearly equalizing the influence of judge, prosecutor, and defense counsel, except when the defense counsel was an occasional or a maverick. Negotiation and mutual accommodation dominated workgroup interactions and facilitated guilty pleas. Stability produced standard operating procedures that simplified the work of all. Many court days began with an informal conference in the judge's chambers, which the prosecutor, public defender, and regulars attended. The participants briefed the judge on the day's docket, the likely outcome of the cases (which ones were ready for plea negotiations, which needed continuances, the likelihood of a bench or jury trial), and other matters. They often interspersed discussion of such business with social pleasantries and banter about the city's sports teams. The goals of reducing uncertainty and maintaining cohesion assumed considerable importance. When pleas could not be negotiated, workgroup members preferred the reduced uncertainty bench trials provided.

In most courtrooms, informal norms developed. Judges accommodated the work schedules of prosecutors and defense counsel. For instance, attorneys trying cases in a courtroom automatically obtained a continuance in other courtrooms where they had a matter scheduled. Both judges and prosecutors often tried to help retained regulars collect their fees. Prosecutors took care to keep judges informed about what cases were likely to trial and sought to build and preserve a reputation for reliability and reasonableness. Defense attorneys had perhaps the most developed set of courtroom norms, which included the following strictures:

1. Never make the state's attorney answer unnecessary motions.
2. Don't mess up someone else's schedule, especially by leading him to think you are ready to proceed when you are not.
3. Disclose the nature of your case informally in chambers or hallways.
4. Accommodate the prosecution wherever possible, especially with respect to scheduling.
5. Avoid trials for cases that cannot be won. [Trying cases when there is a chance of winning was not considered a violation of the norm.]

Although one or another of these norms could occasionally be violated with impunity, consistent violation met with sanctions from the courtroom workgroup. Violators found themselves waiting half a day for a continuance, while other attorneys were taken care of immediately. The opportunity to show off for a client would be denied, or the attorney would be scolded from the bench for petty matters that ordinarily were overlooked. [T]hese norms bound many defense counsel closely to the courtroom organization.

> *"We suggest that the prospect of a 'whistleblower' on the court—that is, the presence of a judge whose policy preferences differ from the majority's and who will expose the majority's manipulation or disregard of the applicable legal doctrine— is a significant determinant of whether judges will perform their designated role as principled legal decision makers."*

13.3 JUDICIAL PARTISANSHIP AND OBEDIENCE TO LEGAL DOCTRINE: WHISTLEBLOWING ON THE FEDERAL COURTS OF APPEALS

Frank B. Cross and Emerson H. Tiller

Frank B. Cross is the Herbert D. Kelleher Centennial Professor of Business Law at the University of Texas at Austin; Emerson H. Tiller is Professor of Business, Politics and the Law, University of Texas at Austin.

. . . [We] ask the following question: if judges have personal or partisan policy preferences, why would they follow established legal doctrine when it conflicts with those preferences? While there is undoubtedly more than one valid explanation for principled adherence to legal doctrine, we suggest that the prospect of a "whistleblower" on the court—that is, the presence of a judge whose policy preferences differ from the majority's and who will expose the majority's manipulation or disregard of the applicable legal doctrine (if such manipulation or disregard were needed to reach the majority's preferred outcome)—is a significant determinant of whether judges will perform their designated role as principled legal decision makers. We do more than merely propose this theory; we test it empirically and find substantial support for our claim. . . .

Frank B. Cross and Emerson H. Tiller, "Judicial Partisanship and Obedience to Legal Doctrine: Whistleblowing on the Federal Courts of Appeals," 107 *Yale Law Journal* 2155 (1998).

A Theory of Compliance with Doctrine

Once the Supreme Court sets forth doctrines, lower courts may comply or disobey. If lower courts comply, they may do so for a number of reasons: (1) compliance with doctrine enables the lower courts to effect their political preferences; (2) the lower courts are dutifully performing their roles as sincere jurists, applying the principles in an ideologically (or politically) neutral manner; or (3) the lower courts fear exposure of any noncompliance and consequent reversal. Lower courts may disobey because (4) they wish to effect their political preferences; or (5) they mean to apply doctrine dutifully but are influenced to apply the rules in a way that achieves their political preferences. Each of these five modes may operate at different times and under different circumstances.

Our first theoretical proposition is simple: judges are more likely to obey legal doctrine when such doctrine supports the partisan or ideological policy preferences of the court majority. In those cases in which doctrine does not support the partisan or ideological policy preferences of the court majority, we expect somewhat more disobedience. Our second theoretical proposition is that courts are more likely to comply with doctrine (rather than to decide based solely on their political preferences) when the judicial panel is politically or ideologically divided. This results from the presence of a minority position on the panel that creates an opportunity for whistleblowing—a minority member with doctrine on her side and the ability, through a dissent, to expose disobedient decisionmaking by the majority. The minority member may threaten to highlight the disobedience externally to a higher court or to Congress, producing exposure and possible reversal. Alternatively, the minority may expose the subconscious disobedience internally, causing the majority to acknowledge its disregard or unintentional manipulation of doctrine. Consequently, in the presence of such a whistleblower, the majority must sometimes capitulate and keep its decision within the confines of doctrine.

We apply our analysis to the federal courts of appeals. These courts are organized such that three-judge panels are randomly selected to hear appeals from lower federal district courts or federal regulatory agencies. After these panels make their decisions, the outcome may be appealed to the full circuit sitting en banc or to the Supreme Court. . . .

Judicial Obedience to the *Chevron Doctrine*: Applying the Theory to Administrative Law

The Supreme Court in *Chevron U.S.A. Inc. v. Natural Resources Defense Council, Inc.* seemingly commanded lower courts to grant considerable deference to federal administrative agency interpretations of statutes. The decision was of great import for administrative law and also offers an ideal test case for determining whether Supreme Court doctrine has a material effect in restraining the decisions of lower courts. One can examine lower-court decision making in the wake of *Chevron* and observe whether the lower court is granting deference neutrally, as per doctrine, or is manipulating the deference doctrine to achieve politically desirable outcomes. We employ *Chevron* cases to test our theories of judicial decision making. . . .

An Empirical Examination

We reviewed all opinions from the D.C. Circuit Court of Appeals between 1991 and 1995 that cited *Chevron*—according to Shepard's Citations, over two hundred in all. Cases that cited *Chevron* for something other than the deference principle were excluded. Each case was then coded for, among other things, (1) whether the court gave deference to the agency statutory interpretation; (2) whether the court upheld or reversed the agency policy; (3) the direction of the policy outcome (liberal vs. conservative) from the agency; and (4) the partisan makeup of the court panel (Democrats vs. Republicans).

With respect to policy direction, our coding tracked practices relatively common in the political science literature. If an industry group was challenging a federal regulation, then the agency position was coded as liberal. If nongovernmental public interest organizations or individual plaintiffs challenged the agency position, we coded the agency position as conservative, unless the organization or individual was clearly conservative in orientation, in which case we coded the agency position as liberal. Cases without any clear political content were winnowed from the database, leaving about 170 decisions coded. If the court reversed the agency in favor of a liberal challenger, we coded the case outcome as liberal; if the court reversed the agency in favor of a conservative challenger, we coded the outcome as conservative.

With respect to coding the preferences of the reviewing court panel, each judge was assigned a political party affiliation according to the President who appointed the judge. We assumed that, in general, Democratic appointees are more liberal and Republicans more conservative in policy orientation. During the time period under consideration, the D.C. Circuit was dominated by Republican appointees, although a significant number of Democratic appointees were present. Each panel therefore had a majority 2–1 or 3–0) of either Republican or Democratic judges. This coding enabled us to test whether the partisanship of the judicial panel influenced the political outcomes of litigation and the degree to which *Chevron* deference affected this association.

A simple comparison of judicial party affiliation and political decisions reveals a fairly profound partisan effect. . . . [A] panel consisting of a majority of Republicans rendered a conservative decision 54 percent of the time (62 of 114), while a panel consisting of a majority of Democrats rendered a liberal decision 68 percent of the time (28 of 41). The presence of some "liberal" decisions by conservative courts and "conservative" decisions by liberal courts may be a function of a combination of factors. It may be a misspecification problem—politics lie upon a continuum, and some policies may be too conservative for a given "conservative" court or too liberal for a "liberal" court. Or, our coding of agency decisions by nature of the litigant challenging the agency may misidentify some litigants' political affiliations. Alternatively, the mismatch may indicate that doctrine is having a significant effect in constraining all-out partisan decision making. Nonetheless, these simple results suggest that there is a significant political determinant to judicial decision making, at least in *Chevron* review.

Our theory suggests that whether deference is granted (that is, whether the *Chevron* doctrine is being adhered to) is dependent upon the convergence between the partisan policy preferences of the panel's majority and the outcome resulting from the application of *Chevron*. Put differently, the court panel is more likely to follow *Chevron* when the agency has issued a policy consistent with the panel's assumed policy preferences (liberal for Democrats and conservative for Republicans) than when there is no such alignment between the court's policy preferences and the agency policy. To bear out this relationship and to sort out the effects of several other variables that may affect the likelihood that a court will defer to an agency, we ran a statistical test. . . .

[In that test] POLICY CONVERGENCE is both the political variable and the main variable of interest. It indicates whether there is alignment between the assumed preferences of the panel's majority (as measured by the political party affiliation of the majority of members on the panel) and the policy outcome of the agency (as measured by the litigants challenging the agency). We postulate that deference is more likely when the assumed partisan preferences of the panel's majority favor the agency outcome (Republicans favoring conservative agency outcomes and Democrats favoring liberal agency outcomes).

We also include a variable to indicate whether the reviewing panel members were from the same political party (UNIFIED PANEL). Our theory suggests that a politically unified panel, that is 3–0 Republican or 3–0 Democrat, is more likely to disregard the constraints of doctrines that do not support the court's policy preferences when there is no policy convergence. When there is no whistleblower on a panel, that is the panel is politically unified, judges will see doctrine as less of an obstacle to political decision making.

Next, we include a variable for the political party of the majority of the members on the panel (MAJORITY PARTY). It is possible that judges of one party (for a variety of reasons, both political and sincere) are more true to legal doctrine than the judges of the other. Finally, we include the variable YEAR, which represents the actual year in which a particular case was decided, the first year being set at zero. This is intended to capture the possibility that the *Chevron* doctrine has grown weaker over time.

As predicted, the effect of POLICY CONVERGENCE is . . . highly significant. The results indicate that when the agency's policy outcome is consistent with the policy preferences of the panel's majority, the court is more likely to defer than if there is no such convergence. We calculate the impact of this variable to be 31 percent—that is, the panel is 31 percent more likely to defer (that is, follow doctrine) when its policy preferences are consistent with the agency's policies than when they are not. The results also indicate that whether the panel was politically divided (2–1) or united (3–0) had an effect on whether the panel deferred to the agency, although the significance of these results is somewhat less. We calculated the impact of this variable to be 17 percent—that is, it is 17 percent less likely that the court will defer when it is unified than when it is split 2–1. Neither the political party of the panel majority (MAJORITY PARTY) nor the year in which the decision was made (YEAR) proved significant. In other words, neither Democrats nor Republicans appeared any more or less committed to doctrine than judges of the other party. Likewise, the passing of time did not appear to diminish or strengthen the effects of *Chevron*.

While the above results suggest that a division among panel members does affect whether doctrine will be followed (as indicated by the marginal significance of the UNIFIED PANEL variable), they do not necessarily establish that the presence of a whistleblower is the mechanism. It is possible that 2–1 majorities whose policy preferences are consistent with those of the agencies nonetheless decide, with some regularity, to capitulate to the minority member. Recall that our whistleblower theory postulates that there should be an effect when a 2–1 majority is in conflict (in terms of its partisan policy preferences) with the agency over policy outcomes, rather than when the 2–1 majority is in agreement with the agency's policy choice.

To examine the whistleblower hypothesis further, we segregated the data by whether there was a politically unified panel (3–0 Republican and 3–0 Democratic majorities) or politically divided panel (2–1 Republican-to-Democrat majorities and vice versa). We then separated the data with respect to deference (our measure for judicial obedience) and whether there was policy convergence between the deciding court panel and the agency.

Consider first the politically unified panels. In the 21 cases where it appeared to be to the unified panels' policy advantage to disobey *Chevron*, the panels did so two-thirds of the time. In other words, unified panels deferred to the agency only 33 percent (7 of 21) of the time when the policy outcomes that would have resulted from adhering to doctrine appeared inconsistent with the panel's political preferences. In the 14 cases in which it appeared to be to the advantage of the unified panels to obey *Chevron*, the panels did so 71 percent (10 of 14) of the time.

Now consider the divided panels. Of the cases in which it was to the panels' advantage to obey *Chevron*, they did so 84 percent (37 of 44) of the time. This is not surprising, as doctrine in such cases poses no conflict for the majority. Now consider the 76 cases involving the whistleblower scenario, in which it appeared to be to the advantage of the majority not to defer. These panels continued to obey the doctrine 62 percent (47 of 76) of the time. Compare this rate of obedience to that of unified panels whose policy preferences seemed inconsistent with the application of the *Chevron* doctrine (33 percent). In short, the presence of a whistleblower makes it almost twice as likely that doctrine will be followed when doctrine works against the partisan policy preferences of the court majority.

* * *

Partisanship clearly affects how appellate courts review agency discretion. In our study of administrative law decisions by the D.C. Circuit, we have found that panels controlled by Republicans were more likely to defer to conservative agency decisions (that is, to follow the *Chevron* doctrine) than were the panels controlled by Democrats. Similarly, Democrat-controlled panels were more likely to defer to liberal agency decisions than were those controlled by Republicans. Nonetheless, legal doctrine appears to play an important role in the partisan struggle over policy. Minority judges can use doctrine to corral the partisan ambitions of a court majority whose policy preferences would best be accomplished by neglecting the dictates of doctrine. The minority member acts as a whistleblower, ready to expose any cheating by the majority. In our study, we found that the presence of a whistleblower—that is, a minority member with *Chevron* deference favoring the minority member's political preference— significantly increases the chances that the court majority will follow doctrine. While a partisan split panel does not negate all partisan influences on *Chevron* review, it clearly moderates such influences and makes doctrine more likely to be followed.

> *"[J]ustices who strongly desire reelection and fear the possibility of electoral sanction will not distinguish themselves from the rest of the court by dissenting on highly salient political questions."*

13.4 CONSTITUENT INFLUENCE IN STATE SUPREME COURTS

Melinda Gann Hall

Melinda Gann Hall is Professor of Political Science
at Michigan State University.

This paper examines the propensity to dissent in a setting other than the United States Supreme Court—the Louisiana Supreme Court—and argues that, indeed, certain institutional arrangements and strategic calculations seem to affect justices' voting behavior. To wit, the process of facing an electorate may have a subtle but significant impact on the way certain types of justices, who have a strong desire to retain the office and who anticipate possible electoral opposition, vote on highly salient political issues. More generally, the tendency toward unanimity or near unanimity in the decisions of many state courts of last resort may be explained, in part, by constituent influence and strategic voting.

To anticipate some degree of constituent influence in most state supreme courts seems very reasonable. The justices of a majority of these courts are elected for specific terms, either by partisan or nonpartisan election mechanisms, and even justices of the courts chosen by "merit" are forced to face retention elections. Since most state supreme court justices are elected and are

Melinda Gann Hall, "Constituent Influence in State Supreme Courts," 49 *Journal of Politics* 1117–1123 (1987).

forced to appear at given intervals before the voters after having cast large numbers of votes on divisive public policy issues, it is plausible that justices may pursue voting strategies in order to maximize their chances of re-election.

However, judges, unlike other political actors, are generally perceived to make decisions on the basis of such legal constraints as laws, precedents, and constitutions, without the interplay of politics or political preferences. Therefore, even though the most casual observers of courts recognize that judges often have extraordinary discretion in rendering decisions, judges can claim protection of the "purple curtain" and defend their choices with the shield of the law.

For judges, controversial decisions become more difficult to justify on the basis of law when they depart from the majority's decisions and vote in the minority. It can be argued that though voters may accept a legal explanation for a unanimous court's unpopular decision, the mechanism of judicial accountability is more rigidly adhered to on issues where voters have information and strong preferences and where judges have singled themselves out for criticism.

Therefore, it can be hypothesized that justices who strongly desire reelection and fear the possibility of electoral sanction will not distinguish themselves from the rest of the court by dissenting on highly salient political questions. Instead, a justice will either vote with the majority or will mask his or her disagreement in a concurrence rather than a dissent. In other words, we should see a higher level of unanimous voting relative to an overall pattern on controversial, very visible issues for certain types of justices. A limited case study of the Louisiana Supreme Court is utilized to explore this proposition.

The Louisiana Supreme Court is a seven-member state supreme court whose members are elected on partisan ballots (party label on the ballot) after open primaries for ten-year terms. Justices are chosen from specific geographic districts within the state, with two justices representing the district which includes New Orleans, the largest population center within the state. Therefore, each justice is chosen from a limited constituency and is connected to the constituency by a residency requirement. Terms on the court are staggered so that the entire court is never up for re-election at the same time. Interim vacancies are filled through appointments made by the court until elections can be scheduled within the following six months.

In-depth personal interviews were conducted in 1983 with each of the members of the Louisiana Supreme Court, with each interview lasting anywhere from several hours to all day. In order to solicit frank and candid remarks, each justice was guaranteed absolute confidentiality. As a result, the individual justices will not be associated with their specific comments or votes.

A rather wide variety of subjects was covered with each justice, but each was asked to assess the impact of facing reelection on his decision-making propensities. Of particular interest were the responses of the justices who perceived themselves to be much more liberal than their constituencies. It is, after all, in the conflict between decision makers' personal values and their constituents' preferences that the effects of elections can best be examined and understood.

During the interviews, three of the justices who identified themselves as liberals voiced very different reactions to the prospects of facing voters. Justice "A" described rather comprehensively how the process of seeking re-election affects his votes on one subset of criminal cases, the death penalty suits. This justice expressed, in general, a very strong concern for the protection of individual rights and freedoms and the necessity of courts to guard against "tyrannical majorities." In particular, he professed a personal abhorrence of executions and the death penalty, and he was also very critical of the United States Supreme Court's interpretation of the Eighth Amendment. What this particular justice indicated was a strong personal preference against the use of the death penalty.

Yet, at the same time, Justice "A" acknowledged that his perception of his constituents was that they clearly preferred the death penalty as a punishment for murder and that they would retaliate against him at election time if the justice did not reflect constituent preferences in this set of judicial decisions. Justice "A" felt that, of all the cases decided by the court, the decisions involving the death penalty were most likely to be reported by newspapers and most likely to be focused upon by opponents in campaigns. Louisiana is, of course, a state which has always provided for the death penalty and has actually executed several convicted murderers in the past few years. Since a liberal voting pattern in this highly visible and emotional set of decisions would place the justice at odds with his more conservatively oriented constituency, Justice "A" stated that he does not dissent in death penalty cases against an opinion of the court to affirm a defendant's conviction and sentence, expressly because of a perceived voter sanction, in spite of his deeply felt personal preferences to the contrary. He further acknowledged that in decisions prior to 1983, a period when the end of his term was rather distant, he had frequently dissented against the majority's upholding sentences in death cases, and he felt the public reaction was quite negative.

Justice "A" also expressed a great deal of anxiety over potentially losing his position, for which he would be running again in the upcoming few years. This justice, who seemed particularly satisfied with his office, apparently did not have the necessary years of service to draw a pension if defeated.

What Justice "A" described is the use of an uncomplicated, yet interesting and potentially effective strategy to pursue reelection. In order to minimize electoral opposition and maximize his public position, this minority justice professed to pursue a strategy of voting with the majority on issues of high public salience (e.g., the death penalty cases) and not voicing any dissent. Quite simply, although Justice "A" feels relatively free to decide most cases in line with his preferences about civil rights and liberties and other matters of public policy, this member of the Louisiana Supreme Court avoids giving ammunition to potential opponents in campaigns by not singling himself out for attention in highly visible decisions.

The other liberal justices, Justice "B" and Justice "C," when asked about voters, argued that they were relatively unconcerned with winning or losing their next elections. Although both expressed plans to run again for office and certainly claimed the desire to win, they seemed very casual about the prospect of losing. These justices have a great deal of service to the court, seemed somewhat bored with the job, and if defeated would qualify for lifetime pensions from the state. Like Justice "A," Justice "B" and Justice "C" also seemed concerned about defendants' rights but did not voice the same level of abhorrence or philosophical objections to the death penalty as Justice "A."

Both Justice "B" and Justice "C" expressed a lack of concern with constituent reaction and argued that it was their perceptions of justice which prevailed in decisions, even on high-salience issues presented to the court where their personal views were clearly in conflict with those of the voters.

In order to investigate whether the patterns each justice described are reflected in actual votes, data on all criminal decisions of the Louisiana Supreme Court with written opinion for the 1980–1981 term and data on all cases in which the death penalty was given as a sentence from 1981 through June 1986 were collected from the Southern Reporter [containing the decisions of southern state supreme courts]. A vote cast in favor of overturning a defendant's conviction or sentence was classified as a liberal vote, while a vote cast supporting a defendant's conviction or sentence was designated a conservative vote. Table 13.1 ranks the justices of the Louisiana Supreme Court according to their liberal voting tendencies in nonunanimous criminal decisions for 1980–1981, the first term of the most recent complete natural court. As the data demonstrate, Justices "A," "B," and "C" do seem to be the most liberal justices of the Louisiana Supreme Court on criminal cases during this period. To anticipate electoral incompatibility on death penalty cases seems imminently reasonable for these justices.

If Justice "A" is pursuing a process of strategic voting according to the above prescriptions (i.e., not casting liberal dissents on highly visible decisions before a perceived conservative constituency), then for Justice "A" there should be significant differences in dissent rates between criminal cases in general and death penalty cases. Conversely, for Justice "B" and Justice "C," who did not feel pressures from their constituencies, we should see very similar levels of

TABLE 13.1 Liberal Voting Tendencies of the Justices of the Louisiana Supreme Court: 1980–1981

	Criminal Cases Decided with Dissent	
Justice	*N of Votes Cast in Favor of Defendants' Claims*	*% of Votes Cast in Favor of Defendants' Claims*
A	70/102	68.6%
B	59/102	57.8%
C	56/102	54.9%
D	38/101	37.6%
E	35/102	34.3%
F	31/102	30.4%
G	19/102	18.6%

dissent between criminal cases overall and the death penalty cases. Table 13.2 presents this information.

As can be seen from Table 13.2, the expectations about Justice "A"'s behavior are borne out by the data. For the death penalty cases, Justice "A" has a pronounced tendency to dissent less from conservative decisions of the court, to vote with the majority more often, and to cast fewer liberal votes than he does on criminal cases overall. In fact, the only liberal dissent Justice "A" cast in death penalty cases during the period 1981 through 1986 was cast in early 1982, and for four years Justice "A" has not expressed public disagreement with any death case decisions of the court.

As Table 13.2 also indicates, the expectations about Justice "B" and Justice "C" are confirmed by the data. Unlike Justice "A," Justice "B" and Justice "C" do not exhibit differential voting patterns for death cases, and there is no clear evidence in the data that Justice "B" or Justice "C" responds to constituent pressures, even in such controversial cases as death penalty suits.

This look at the Louisiana Supreme Court presents some evidence that suggests that certain types of justices may, indeed, be affected by the pressures of re-election. Justices who find themselves in the court minority, who perceive themselves to have views inconsistent with those of their constituents, and who have very strong ambitions to retain their positions and fear electoral challenge may be extremely hesitant to voice disagreement with the court's decisions on highly controversial issues of public policy. To avoid singling themselves out for criticism during the re-election process, these types of justices may suppress the expression of dissent. Whether voters and opponents are cognizant of the justices' behavior or not, certain justices seem to fear the prospect of electoral sanction and consequently alter their behavior.

TABLE 13.2 Voting Propensities of Justices A, B, and C

	Justice A		Justice B		Justice C	
	All Criminal Cases	Death Penalty Cases	All Criminal Cases	All Death Cases	All Criminal Cases	All Death Cases
Number of Liberal Dissents from Conservative Decisions	33/127 (28%)	1/30 (3.3%)	16/127 (12.6%)	4/30 (13.3%)	17/127 (13.4%)	4/30 (13.3%)
Number of Votes with the Court Majority	165/202 (81.7%)	44/45 (97.8%)	186/202 (92.1%)	41/45 (91.1%)	184/202 (91.1%)	41/45 (91.1%)
Overall Number of Liberal Votes	05/202 (52.0%)	16/45 (35.6%)	91/202 (45%)	19/45 (42.2%)	90/202 (44.6%)	19/45 (42.2%)

> *"If there's a genuine conflict, that's the single most important factor,*
> *though alone it's not enough."*

13.5 DECIDING TO DECIDE

H. W. Perry

H.W. Perry is Professor of Political Science at the University of Texas–Austin.

H. W. Perry's study of the certiorari process relies heavily on interviews with the justices and their clerks. The following reports the results of his investigation into what makes a petition "certworthy"—that is, worthy of review by the Supreme Court.

Criteria for Cert.

It takes a combination of things to make a case certworthy. . . . It is not precisely correct to discuss this process in terms of necessary and sufficient conditions, but it is helpful to think of it that way. Several things are necessary to make a case certworthy, none of which alone is sufficient. . . .

Circuit Conflict

Comments from two justices:

> JUSTICE: A conflict among federal courts is important, particularly. Every now and then we will take a case that is a conflict among states. Many times it is not about state law but about federal law. State law doesn't make much difference up here.
> PERRY: Could you tell me what would make a case an obvious grant?
> JUSTICE: Conflict among the circuits might.

"Might." Few things are said without qualification when it comes to certworthiness, but I shall do so now. Without a doubt, the single most important generalizable factor in assessing certworthiness is the existence of a conflict or "split" in the circuits. The overwhelming majority of my informants, indeed almost all, listed this as the first and most important thing that they looked for in a petition.

When asked what they looked for in a cert. petition, the following clerks gave responses similar to almost all of my informants':

> First, a conflict. Then you had to see if there really was a conflict. . . . I really do believe that a conflict is the reason that most cases are taken. In some ways it is the driving force.

From H. W. Perry, *Deciding to Decide* (Cambridge, MA: Harvard University Press, 1991), pp. 245–249, 251–254; 265–270.

If there's a genuine conflict, that's the single most important factor, though alone it's not enough.

First, is there a conflict. Those really dominated and were clearly the most important reason for taking cert.

A justice said the following:

Some cases obviously should be granted cert. For example, if there is a clear conflict between circuits in interpreting the internal revenue code so that the tax code is being administered differently in different parts of the country—that is simply intolerable. The Supreme Court must grant cert. so that the tax law is administered uniformly over the United States. You could make this decision without even going into the merits of the case. I don't think that anybody would disagree that to hear this case is a proper function of the Supreme Court.

But witness what one of his brethren said:

Naturally, I would took for conflicts, although I don't see if there is a conflict involving some obscure provision of the Internal Revenue Code that means the nation is going to go to hell. I am really looking for more important issues.

The two justices' comments are not necessarily contradictory. All justices believe that a conflict must involve an important issue. But the justices vary somewhat on their willingness to tolerate a conflict. As one justice told me:

One thing I hear around the conference table more and more is that "something is a 'tolerable' conflict," or "there is a conflict out there but . . ." Justice A will say let's consider this but [several years later], although the date is getting pushed back a bit. Justice B and I are both concerned about this. He more than I. We see it as a job of the Court to resolve federal conflicts. It is intolerable to have a certain law for the people in the Second Circuit and something else for people in the Eighth. Sometimes I join Justice B's dissents. I don't always join because I think his notion of conflict is rather strained. But I don't believe that we should have the First Circuit saying something and another interpretation in the Ninth Circuit. But sometimes there are just so many hours in a day.

Justice B is at one extreme believing virtually every conflict should be taken as long as the issue is not completely trivial. The justice just quoted is fairly close to Justice B's position. The following justice, however, is probably at the opposite extreme:

Now as for what I look for, that is really my appraisal of importance. I would say that a conflict is neither necessary nor sufficient to get a case granted. For example, you have case like *Bakke* where the importance just cries out. But also there are cases where the conflict is clear, but I don't think it is important enough for us to deal with it. Justice B is strong on conflicts. He not only believes that we should resolve federal conflicts, but he believes it extends to state courts. . . .

I don't know if you are familiar with a motion for a judgment notwithstanding a verdict. It means the judge can set aside the verdict or the judgment regardless of the verdict of the jury. In one circuit they reversed a district court's refusal to set aside—I don't remember the exact situation—because there they looked at the defendant's testimony as well as the plaintiff's. Whereas in other circuits they look at only the plaintiff's testimony, and in another circuit it is even something else, so there are different standards. But if we ever get a conflict on this, unless there is something more important raised, there is nothing inherently unfair in any of these methods. There are no significant differences. It is not that much different from what different state courts might have. We certainly don't feel the need to go in and make them uniform in this big country. So I don't think the difference is significant, and what is happening in all circuits is basically fair. Now Justice B would certainly take a different view on something like that.

And of course lots of times that a conflict is alleged, there is not really even a conflict. So I look for conflicts, but it is certainly not controlling. I look more for the character of the issue and the need for resolution. Whether or not an issue is ripe.

These statements highlight the differences among the justices with regard to conflicts, but the remarks of the last justice must be put in context. He, too, sees conflicts as very important, and his comments were a reaction to the extreme position of Justice B. In fact, determining whether or not there is a split is one of his clerk's primary responsibilities as it is for all clerks. Justice B is known by all clerks to want to resolve virtually all legitimate conflicts. Since Justice B is a member of the cert. pool, much of the pool memo is involved in analyzing whether or not there is, in fact, a real conflict. Though Justice B is at the extreme, all justices are interested in circuit splits and think they are one of the most important things to establish certworthiness.

The importance of a conflict should be no surprise. It is one of the only explicit criteria for certworthiness given in the Rules of the Court. . . .

[But a] circuit split is not simply a formal criterion for cert.; it is probably the single most important criterion, and those who wish to comprehend the cert. process must realize this. A circuit split is neither necessary nor sufficient, but it is almost both.

Though many cases do not involve a conflict, it is, nevertheless, the first thing looked for. The underlying assumption is that most issues, if important, will arise in the various circuits. If there is no split, then usually there is no need for Supreme Court action. . . .

Importance

When asked what they looked for to determine if a case were certworthy, informants almost invariably would say that first they looked to see if there were a circuit conflict, and then they looked to see if the conflict involved an important issue. Sometimes a case is so important that it must be granted whether or not there is a conflict, but important issues usually generate a conflict. Conflicts, however, do not always involve important issues. Like certworthiness, importance is ultimately subjective. Nevertheless, informants were asked how they determined importance.

Important cases are of several types. Some are important in and of themselves; that is, it is the resolution of the particular case, not necessarily the legal issue, that is important. Such cases usually are, as lawyers say, sui generis, or the only one of their kind, and they are cases that most anybody would recognize as important. A case such as *U.S. v. Nixon* comes to mind. In such a case, there has usually been little or no percolation of the legal issue, but there is a perception that the case is of sufficient importance that it deserves resolution by the U.S. Supreme Court. Flaws such as inadequate percolation and bad facts must be ignored.

A second category of cases are those that present issues that are important to the polity. The Supreme Court is sometimes called upon to decide issues that are of huge political and societal importance. Such issues are ones that most anyone would consider important. The issues presented in *Brown v. Board of Education*, *Roe v. Wade*, and *Bakke* are possible examples. They resolve or address important issues of law, but their importance clearly emanates from their impact on society. . . .

A third category consists of cases that are important to the law. I refer to these cases as ones of legal importance. Clarification of a rule of evidence or some administrative procedure may be crucial to the functioning of the criminal justice system, or some federal agency, but the importance stems from confusion in the legal system. The confusion has usually been generated by conflicting or improper interpretations by courts. Such cases also present important issues and constitute the bulk of the Court's workload.

Obviously, the categories are not neatly separable. Some cases belong in all categories, and many belong jointly in the last two. Cases of public importance often present issues for which resolution is needed for the proper functioning of the legal system; and resolution of the law is, of course, ultimately important to the polity. But for heuristic purposes, types of "important" cases can be thought about separately. What constitutes an "important issue" in the Supreme Court may be a highly technical issue of law, or it might be an issue of profound societal importance. Incidentally, the distinction is not constitutional versus statutory. Resolution of what constitutes double jeopardy may be of great legal importance, and a statutory interpretation of the Civil Rights Act may generate profound societal impact and interest.

There is little to say about "importance" in the first two categories. Aside from issues of obvious societal importance, trying to determine what constitutes importance in the Supreme Court is quite difficult. I received many answers, but two common ones emerged. Importance is often determined by the breadth of effect rather than the depth. In other words, if a ruling below has a potential impact on large numbers of people, that helps establish importance. If it has a large impact on one corporation or individual, that alone does not make it important. A second though related criterion is the effect something has on the federal government. When the solicitor general claims that a ruling or policy has a large effect on the government, and he urges review, such a case is almost always believed to be important whether or not the justices immediately see the importance. Beyond these criteria, however, importance is in the nose of the beholder. . . .

Egregiousness

Try as they might, justices cannot always resist acting as a court of last resort. Sometimes they will take a case that is a flagrant abuse of justice even though it presents no particularly interesting question of law. The term that was invariably used to describe such cases was "egregious." Everyone acknowledged that an egregious result below sometimes prompted review for an otherwise uncertworthy case, but no explanation emerged that one could use systematically to distinguish between those cases that the justices could hold their noses and ignore from those they could not. However, cases that are considered to be egregious come from two categories: those where a severe injustice occurred and those where there has been a flagrant disregard for announced doctrine.

With regard to the first category—blatant injustice—one clerk's imprecise explanation was typical and is probably about the best one can give:

> They all kind of have these tug-at-the-heartstring cases. . . . I mean the justices are human, and when they see something like that [a terrible injustice he had described], sometimes it strikes them.

The justices admitted their behavior without any better explanation.

> JUSTICE: This is not a court to simply assure that justice is done. We cannot right all wrongs.
>
> PERRY: Although [justices] always claim that, there always seem to be a few cases that the Court picks that, to an outsider, the only justification for taking the case seems to be that you felt the result was so egregious.
>
> JUSTICE: That's true. That happens. But not all that often. Basically we see it not as a court of justice.

I was unable to determine what might commonly strike justices as egregious. One justice said:

> I really think it is almost random. We are all influenced to a different degree about different things and when we happen to come together, it is almost random. There are times when I think the Court is simply correcting an error. . . .

The second category of egregious cases has to do with flagrant disregard for precedent. Interestingly, this was described to me only by the clerks—perhaps because this is an artifact of the interview, that is, the context in which the subject arose, or perhaps because justices were unwilling to acknowledge their reactions to opinions below. The clerks frequently talked about the need to "slap the wrist" of a judge below, the following remark typifies the comments from many clerks.

> Yes, that is absolutely the case. It is a relatively small percentage of cases, but when they have a sense of outrage at a misapplication of the law, they will take the case when it doesn't seem to be certworthy for other reasons. They will particularly do this when there is a cavalier disregard for a precedent by a lower court judge. Mostly these are handled by summary reversal.

Another clerk painted the picture more dramatically:

Sometimes they take cases which may seem frivolous. For example, you know there are many more lower courts and lower judges, and there is fear on the Supreme Court, and I think real fear, that these courts seem to think that they can just ignore the Supreme Court because they know that the Court simply can't take but a few cases.

Many Court observers have suggested that judges on Courts of Appeals often play a bit fast and loose with precedent, knowing that the Supreme Court cannot possibly review all decisions. This charge was leveled particularly at the Ninth Circuit prior to the Reagan appointments. Whether willful disregard is a common practice by judges, and whether there is "real fear" by the justices causing them to take cases periodically to stop such behavior, one cannot be sure. If a wrist slap occurs, however, it is usually done by summary disposition.

By way of concluding this section on egregiousness, I quote one justice's response when I asked him why he thought an increase in summary dispositions was occurring:

> JUSTICE: The volume is so enormous. I think part of the reason the volume is so enormous is that we are not a court to correct errors, and a lot of these summary judgments are just correcting errors. My belief is if a guy got a fair shake, even if I believe it was wrong, we can't go around correcting all errors, and I think it's wrong to review these cases.
> PERRY: I know that you justices often say that this isn't a court to correct errors, but sometimes it seems that if there is something egregious . . .
> JUSTICE: [interrupting]: Yes I'm just as guilty as some of the others about doing that, but I'm certainly trying to restrain myself.

"Lead us not into temptation."

13.6 THE INFLUENCE OF THE CHIEF JUSTICE IN THE DECISIONAL PROCESS

David J. Danelski

David J. Danelski was Dean of the Faculty and vice President for Academic Affairs at Occidental College.

The Chief Justice of the United States has a unique opportunity for leadership in the Supreme Court. He presides in open court and over the secret conferences

---

This is an abridged version of a paper delivered in New York City at the 1960 annual meeting of the American Political Science Association.

where he usually presents each case to his associates, giving his opinion first and voting last. He assigns the Court's opinion in virtually all cases when he votes with the majority; and when the Court is divided, he is in a favorable position to seek unity. But his office does not guarantee leadership. His actual influence depends upon his esteem, ability, and personality and how he performs his various roles.

In Conference

The conference is the matrix of leadership in the Court.[1] The Court member who is able to present his views with force and clarity and defend them successfully is highly esteemed by his associates. When perplexing questions arise, they turn to him for guidance. He usually makes more suggestions than his colleagues, gives more opinions, and orients the discussion more frequently, emerging as the Court's task leader. In terms of personality, he is apt to be somewhat reserved; and, in concentrating on the decision of the Court, his response to the emotional needs of his associates is apt to be secondary.

Court members frequently disagree in conference and argue their positions with enthusiasm, seeking to persuade their opponents and the undecided brethren. And always, when the discussion ends, the vote declares the victor. All of this gives rise to antagonism and tension, which, if allowed to get out of hand, would make intelligent, orderly decision of cases virtually impossible. However, the negative aspects of conference interaction are more or less counterbalanced by activity which relieves tension, shows solidarity, and makes for agreement. One Court member usually performs more such activity than the others. He invites opinions and suggestions. He attends to the emotional needs of his associates by affirming their value as individuals and as Court members, especially when their views are rejected by the majority. Ordinarily he is the best-liked member of the Court and emerges as its social leader. While the task leader concentrates on the Court's decision, the social leader concentrates on keeping the Court socially cohesive. In terms of personality, he is apt to be warm, receptive, and responsive. Being liked by his associates is ordinarily quite important to him; he is also apt to dislike conflict.

As presiding officer of the conference, the Chief Justice is in a favorable position to assert task and social leadership. His presentation of cases is an important task function. His control of the conference's process makes it easy for him to invite suggestions and opinions, seek compromises, and cut off debate which appears to be getting out of hand, all important social functions.

It is thus possible for the Chief Justice to emerge as both task and social leader of the conference. This, however, requires the possession of a rare combination of qualities plus adroit use of them. Normally, one would expect the functions of task and social leadership to be performed by at least two Court

---

[1]This study is based largely on private papers of members of the Supreme Court from 1921 to 1946. The theory of conference leadership is derived primarily from the work of Robert F. Bales. See his "Task Roles and Social Roles in Problem-Solving Groups," in Maccoby et al., *Readings in Social Psychology* (New York: Holt, Rinehart & Winston, 1958), pp. 437–447.

members, one of whom might or might not be the Chief Justice. As far as the Chief Justice is concerned, the following leadership situations are possible:

Task Leadership	Social Leadership
I	1	1
II	2	1
III	1	2
IV	2	2

In situation I, the Chief Justice is a "great man" leader, performing both leadership functions. The consequences of such leadership, stated as hypotheses, are (1) conflict tends to be minimal; (2) social cohesion tends to increase; (3) satisfaction with the conference tends to increase; (4) production, in terms of number of decisions for the time spent, tends to increase. The consequences in situations II and III are the same as in I, particularly if the Chief Justice works in coalition with the associate justice performing complementary leadership functions. However, in situation IV, unless the task and social functions are adequately performed by associate justices, consequences opposite to those in situations I, II, and III tend to occur.

Situation II prevailed in the Taft Court (1921–1930): Chief Justice Taft was social leader, and his good friend and appointee, Justice Van Devanter, was task leader. Evidence of Van Devanter's esteem and task leadership is abundant. Taft, for example, frequently asserted that Van Devanter was the ablest member of the Court. If the Court were to vote, he said, that would be its judgment too. The Chief Justice admitted that he did not know how he could get along without Van Devanter in conference, for Van Devanter kept the Court consistent with itself, and "his power of statement and his immense memory make him an antagonist in conference who generally wins against all opposition." At times, Van Devanter's ability actually embarrassed the Chief Justice, and he wondered if it might not be better to have Van Devanter run the conference himself. "Still," said Taft, "I must worry along until the end of my ten years, content to aid in the deliberation when there is a difference of opinion." In other words, Taft was content to perform the social functions of leadership. And he did this well. His humor soothed over the rough spots in conference. "We are very happy with the present Chief," said Holmes in 1922. "He is good-humored, laughs readily, not quite rapid enough, but keeps things moving pleasant,"

Situation I prevailed in the Hughes Court (1930–1941): task and social leadership were combined in Chief Justice Hughes. He was the most esteemed member of his Court. This was due primarily to his performance in conference. Blessed with a photographic memory, he would summarize comprehensively and accurately the facts and issues in each case he presented. When he finished, he would look up and say with a smile: "Now I will state where I come out." Then he would outline his views as to how the case should be decided. Sometimes that is all the discussion a case received, and the justices proceeded to vote for the disposition suggested by the Chief. Where there was discussion, the other Court members gave their views in order of seniority without interruption, stating why they concurred or dissented from the views of the Chief Justice. After they had their say, Hughes would review the discussion, pointing out his agreement and disagreement with the views expressed. Then he would call for a vote.

As to the social side of Hughes' leadership, there is the testimony of Justice Roberts: Never in the eleven years Roberts sat with Hughes in conference did he see him lose his temper. Never did he hear him pass a personal remark or even raise his voice. Never did he witness him interrupting or engaging in controversy with an associate. Despite Hughes' popular image of austerity, several of his associates have said that he had a keen sense of humor which aided in keeping differences in conference from becoming discord. Moreover, when discussion showed signs of deteriorating into wrangling, Hughes would cut it off. On the whole, he was well liked. Justice Roberts said: "Men whose views were as sharply opposed as those of Van Devanter and Brandeis, or those of Sutherland and Cardozo, were at one in their admiration and affectionate regard for their presiding officer." Roberts could have well added justices Holmes, Black, Reed, Frankfurter, Douglas, McReynolds, and perhaps others.

Situation IV prevailed during most of Stone's Chief Justiceship (1941–1946). When Stone was promoted to the center chair, Augustus Hand indicated in a letter to Hughes that Stone did not seem a sure bet as task leader because of "a certain inability to express himself orally and maintain a position in a discussion." Hand proved to be correct. Stone departed from the conference role cut out by Hughes. When he presented cases, he lacked the apparent certitude of his predecessor; and, at times, his statement indicated that he was still groping for a solution. In that posture, cases were passed on to his associates for discussion. Court members spoke out of turn, and Stone did little to control their debate. Instead, according to Justice Reed, he would join in the debate with alacrity, "delighted to take on all comers around the conference table." "Jackson," he would say, "that's damned nonsense." "Douglas, you know better than that."

In other words, Stone was still acting like an associate justice. Since he did not assume the Chief Justice's conference role as performed by Hughes, task leadership began to slip from his grasp. Eventually, Justice Black emerged as the leading contender for task leadership. Stone esteemed Black but distrusted his unorthodox approach; thus no coalition occurred as in the Taft Court. Justices Douglas, Murphy, Rutledge, and, to a lesser degree, Reed acknowledged Black's leadership which he was able to reinforce by generally speaking before them in conference. Justices Roberts, Frankfurter, and Jackson, however, either looked to Stone for leadership or competed for it themselves.

The constant vying for task leadership in the Stone conference led to serious conflict, ruffled tempers, severe tension, and antagonism. A social leader was badly needed. Stone was well liked by his associates and could have performed this function well, but he did not. He did not use his control over the conference process to cut off debates leading to irreconcilable conflict. He did not remain neutral when controversies arose so that he could later mediate them. As his biographer, Alpheus T. Mason, wrote: "He was totally unprepared to cope with the petty bickering and personal conflict in which his Court became engulfed." At times, when conference discussion became extremely heated, Justice

Murphy suggested that further consideration of certain cases be postponed, but in this regard, Stone was a failure.

A consideration of the personalities of the task and social leaders on the Court from 1921 to 1946 is revealing. Of his friend, task leader Van Devanter, William D. Mitchell said: "Many thought him unusually austere, but he was not so with his friends. He was dignified and reserved." Of task leader Black, his former law clerk, John P. Frank, wrote: "Black has firm personal dignity and reserve. . . . [He] is a very, very tough man. When he is convinced, he is cool hard steel. . . . His temper is usually in close control, but he fights, and his words may occasionally have a terrible edge. He can be a rough man in an argument." On the other hand, social leader Taft was a warm, genial, responsive person who disliked conflict of any kind. Stone had a similar personality. He, too, according to Justice Jackson, "dreaded conflict." Hughes' personality contained elements conducive to both task and social leadership. He was "an intense man," said Justice Roberts; when he was engrossed in the work of the Court, "he had not time for lightness and pleasantry." Nonetheless, added Roberts, Hughes' relations with "his brethren were genial and cordial. He was considerate, sympathetic, and responsive."

The consequences of the various Court leadership configurations from 1921 to 1946 may be summarized as follows:

	Taft (II)	*Hughes (I)*	*Stone (IV)*
Conflict	Present but friendly.	Present but bridled by C. J.	Considerable; unbridled and unfriendly.
Cohesion	Good; teamwork and compromise.	Fair; surface personal cordiality; less teamwork than in Taft Court.	Poor; least cohesion in 25-year period; personal feuds in the Court.
Satisfaction	Considerable.	Mixed; Stone dissatisfied prior to 1938; Frankfurter, Roberts, and others highly satisfied.	Least in 25-year period; unrelieved tension and antagonism.
Production	Fair; usually one four- to five-hour conference a week week with some items carried over.	Good; usually one conference a week.	Poor; frequently more than one conference a week; sometimes three and even four.

Except in production, the Taft Court fared better than the Courts under his two successors. The consequences of leadership in the Stone Court were predictable from the hypotheses, but Hughes' "great man" leadership should have produced consequences more closely approximating those in the Taft Court. The difference in conflict, cohesion, and satisfaction in the two courts can be perhaps attributed to the fact that Taft was a better social leader than Hughes.

Opinion Assignment

The Chief Justice's power to assign opinions is significant because his designation of the Court's spokesman may be instrumental in:

1. Determining the value of a decision as a precedent, for the grounds of a decision frequently depend upon the justice assigned the opinion.
2. Making a decision as acceptable as possible to the public.
3. Holding the Chief Justice's majority together when the conference vote is close.
4. Persuading dissenting associates to join in the Court's opinion.

The Chief Justice has maximal control over an opinion when he assigns it to himself; undoubtedly Chief Justices have retained many important cases for that reason. The Chief Justice's retention of "big cases" is generally accepted by his associates. In fact, they expect him to speak for the Court in those cases so that he may lend the prestige of his office to the Court's pronouncement.

When the Chief Justice does not speak for the Court, his influence lies primarily in his assignment of important cases to associates who generally agree with him. From 1925 to 1930, Taft designated his fellow conservatives, Sutherland and Butler, to speak for the Court in about half of the important constitutional cases[2] assigned to associate justices. From 1932 to 1937, Hughes, who agreed more with Roberts, Van Devanter, and Sutherland than the rest of his associates during this period, assigned 44 percent of the important constitutional cases to Roberts and Sutherland. From 1943 to 1945, Stone assigned 55.5 percent of those cases to Douglas and Frankfurter. During that period, only Reed agreed more with Stone than Frankfurter, but Douglas agreed with Stone less than any other justice except Black. Stone had high regard for Douglas' ability, and this may have been the Chief Justice's overriding consideration in making these assignments.

It is possible that the Chief Justice might seek to influence dissenting justices to join in the Court's opinion by adhering to one or both of the following assignment rules:

Rule 1: Assign the case to the justice whose views are the closest to the dissenters on the ground that his opinion would take a middle approach upon which both majority and minority could agree.

Rule 2: Where there are blocs on the Court and a bloc splits, assign the opinion to a majority member of the dissenters' block on the grounds that (a) he would take a middle approach upon which both majority and minority could agree and (b) the minority justices would be more likely to agree with him because of general mutuality of agreement.

---

[2]"Important constitutional cases" were determined by examination of four recent leading works on the Constitution. If a case was discussed in any two of the works, it was considered an "important constitutional case."

There is some evidence that early in Taft's Chief Justiceship he followed Rule 1 occasionally and assigned himself cases in an effort to win over dissenters. An analysis of his assignments from 1925 to 1930, however, indicates that he apparently did not adhere to either of the rules with any consistency. The same is true for Stone's assignments from 1943 to 1945. In other words, Taft and Stone did not generally use their assignment power to influence their associates to unanimity. However, an analysis of Hughes' assignments from 1932 to 1937 indicates that he probably did. He appears to have followed Rule 1 when either the liberal or conservative blocs dissented intact. When the liberal bloc dissented, Roberts, who was then a center judge, was assigned 46 percent of the opinions. The remaining 54 percent were divided among the conservatives, apparently according to their degree of conservatism: Sutherland, 25 percent; Butler, 18 percent; McReynolds, 11 percent. When the conservative bloc dissented, Hughes divided 63 percent of those cases between himself and Roberts.

Hughes probably also followed Rule 2. When the left bloc split, Brandeis was assigned 22 percent of the cases he could have received compared with his 10 percent average for unanimous cases. When the right bloc split, Sutherland was assigned 16 percent of the decisions he could have received compared with his 11 percent average for unanimous cases. He received five of the six cases assigned the conservatives when their bloc split.

Of course, there are other considerations underlying opinion assignment by the Chief Justice, such as equality of distribution, ability, and expertise. It should be noted that opinion assignment may also be a function of social leadership.

Uniting the Court

One of the Chief Justice's most important roles is that of Court unifier. Seldom has a Chief Justice had a more definite conception of that role than Taft. His aim was unanimity, but he was willing to admit that at times dissents were justifiable and perhaps even a duty. Dissents were proper, he thought, in cases where a Court member strongly believed the majority erred in a matter involving important principle or where a dissent might serve some useful purpose, such as convincing Congress to pass certain legislation. But, in other cases, he believed a justice should be a good member of the team, silently acquiesce in the views of the majority, and not try to make a record for himself by dissenting.

Since Taft's conception of the function of the dissent was shared by most of his associates, his efforts toward unity were well received. Justices joining the Taft Court were indoctrinated in the "no dissent unless absolutely necessary" tradition, most of them learning it well. Justice Butler gave it classic expression on the back of one colleague's opinions in 1928:

> I voted to reverse. While this sustains your conclusion to affirm, I still think reversal would be better. But I shall in silence acquiesce. Dissents seldom aid in the right development or statement of the law. They often do harm. For myself I say: "lead us not into temptation."

Hughes easily assumed the role of Court unifier which Taft cut out for him, for his views as to unanimity and dissent were essentially the same as Taft's. Believing that some cases were not worthy of dissent, he would join in the majority's disposition of them, though he initially voted the other way. For example, in a 1939 case involving statutory construction, he wrote to an associate: "I choke a little at swallowing your analysis, still I do not think it would serve any useful purpose to expose my views."

Like Taft, Hughes mediated differences of opinion between contending factions, and in order to get a unanimous decision, he would try to find common ground upon which all could stand. He was willing to modify his own opinions to hold or increase his majority; and if this meant he had to put in some disconnected thoughts or sentences, in they went. In cases assigned to others, he would readily suggest the addition or subtraction of a paragraph in order to save a dissent or a concurring opinion.

When Stone was an associate justice, he prized the right to dissent and occasionally rankled under the "no dissent unless absolutely necessary" tradition of the Taft and Hughes Courts. As Chief Justice, he did not believe it appropriate for him to dissuade Court members from dissenting in individual cases by persuasion or otherwise. A Chief Justice, he thought, might admonish his associates generally to exercise restraint in the matter of dissents and seek to find common ground for decision, but beyond that he should not go. And Stone usually went no further. His activity or lack of it in this regard gave rise to new expectations on the part of his associates as to their role and the role of the Chief Justice regarding unanimity and dissent. In the early 1940s, a new tradition of freedom of individual expression displaced the tradition of the Taft and Hughes Courts. This explains in part the unprecedented number of dissents and separate opinions during Stone's Chief Justiceship.

Nonetheless, Stone recognized that unanimity was desirable in certain cases. He patiently negotiated a unanimous decision in the Nazi Saboteurs case.[3] It should be pointed out, however, that this case was decided early in his Chief Justiceship before the new tradition was firmly established. By 1946, when he sought unanimity in the case of General Yamashita,[4] the new tradition of freedom was so well established that Stone not only failed to unite his Court, but his dissenters, Murphy and Rutledge, apparently resented his attempt to do so.

The unprecedented number of dissents and concurrences during Stone's Chief Justiceship can be only partly attributed to the displacing of the old tradition of loyalty to the Court's opinion. A major source of difficulty appears to have been the free-and-easy expression of views in conference. Whether the justices were sure of their grounds or not, they spoke up and many times took positions from which they could not easily retreat; given the heated debate which sometimes occurred in the Stone conference, the commitment was not simply

---

[3] *Ex parte Quirin* (1942).
[4] *In re Yamashita* (1946).

intellectual, What began in conference frequently ended with elaborate justification as concurring or dissenting opinions in the United States Reports. This, plus Stone's passiveness in seeking to attain unanimity, is probably the best explanation for what Pritchett characterized as "the multiplication of division" in the Stone Court.

Conclusion

Interpersonal influence in the Supreme Court is an important aspect of the judicial process which has been given little attention. Of course, the "why" of the Court's decisions cannot be explained solely or even predominantly in those terms. Yet interpersonal influence is a variable worthy of consideration. Take, for example, the Court's about-face in the flag salute cases. With task leader Hughes presiding in 1940, not a single justice indicated in conference that he would dissent in the *Gobitis*[5] case. Subsequently, Stone registered a solo dissent, but such militant civil libertarians as Black, Douglas, and Murphy remained with Hughes. Only three years later, the Court reversed itself in the *Barnette*[6] case with Black, Douglas, and Murphy voting with Stone. One might seriously ask whether the presence of Hughes in the first case and not in the second had something to do with the switch. Much more work has to be done in this area, but it appears that in future analyses of the Court's work, task and social leadership will be useful concepts.

The importance of the Chief Justice's power to assign opinions is obvious. Equally if not more important is his role in unifying the Court. Taft's success in this regard greatly contributed to the Court's prestige, for unanimity reinforces the myth that the law is certain. In speaking of the Court in 1927, Hughes said that "no institution of our government stands higher in public confidence." As Court unifier, he sought to maintain that confidence after his appointment in 1930. That the Court's prestige is correlated with unanimity was demonstrated in Stone's Chief Justiceship: as dissent rose, the Court's prestige declined.

Thus the activity of the Chief Justice can be very significant in the judicial process. If he is the Court's task leader, he has great influence in the allocation of political values which are inevitably involved in many of the Court's decisions. More than any of his associates, his activity is apt to affect the Court's prestige; this is important, for ultimately the basis of the Court's power is its prestige.

---

[5]*Minersville School District v. Gobitis* (1940).

[6]*West Virginia v. Barnette* (1943).

"The willingness of a majority opinion author to accommodate his or her colleagues appears to be conditioned by the extent to which the author needs the continued support of justices who were part of his or her conference coalition."

13.7 MARSHALLING THE COURT: BARGAINING AND ACCOMMODATION ON THE UNITED STATES SUPREME COURT

Paul J. Wahlbeck, James F. Spriggs, and Forrest Maltzman

Paul J. Wahlbeck and Forrest Maltzman are associate professors of Political Science at George Washington University. James F. Spriggs is Associate Professor of Political Science at the University of California, Davis.

One of the most important and enduring actions a justice can undertake is to write a majority opinion. Opinions contain legal rules that establish referents for future behavior and thus have an impact beyond the parties in the litigation. For this reason, justices relish the opportunity to be assigned a majority opinion and attempt to frame legal rules that most closely match their policy preferences. In other words, justices care not just about the direction of the outcome, but also about the content of the opinions that accompany the Court's rulings.

Although opinion authors clearly have a disproportionate influence over the final opinion, they cannot act unilaterally. The author's choices regarding the opinion's legal reasoning are, in part, structured by the choices of other justices. After circulating an opinion draft, the author commonly receives comments and suggestions. Chief Justice William Rehnquist explains, "If a justice agrees with the general import of the draft, but wishes changes to be made in it before joining, a letter to that effect will be sent. . . ."

The papers of retired justices provide numerous examples of instances in which justices have requested that majority opinion authors make changes to their draft opinions. These requests often state conditions that must be met before a justice will join an opinion. As Justice Potter Stewart once told Justice Hugo Black, "I would be willing to join your opinion, if you would be receptive to two additions. . . ." Similarly, Justice Byron White wrote Justice William Brennan, "if you would consider a minor change or two, I shall join you." Justice Brennan likewise wrote Chief Justice Rehnquist "I am in almost complete agreement with your draft opinion. Before joining, however, I would ask that you make two small changes."

42 *American Journal of Political Science* (1998), 294–315.

A strategic justice who has been assigned the majority opinion will recognize that it is sometimes rational to yield on some issues in order to maintain control of the opinion. Indeed, a justice informed [H. W. Perry] that:

> We don't negotiate, we accommodate. And this is a perfectly appropriate and good procedure because this is a court of nine people and it is our responsibility to have an opinion of the Court—a unanimous opinion if possible when the Court can come up with one. And so it is good to have this accommodation, and attempts to accommodate.

A memo from Justice Brennan to Justice Thurgood Marshall explaining a majority opinion draft that Brennan wrote in *Pennsylvania v. Muniz* (1990) highlights the type of tradeoff that a strategic justice must make:

> Had my draft opinion suggested that no such exception [to the rule established in Miranda v. Arizona] existed, at least five if not more would have written separately to disagree, and I would have had no control over the breadth of the exception they would create. I made the strategic judgment, therefore, to concede the existence of an exception but to use my control over the opinion to define the exception as narrowly as possible. . . . As you will recall, Sandra forced my hand. . . .

Justice Potter Stewart also penned the following to the conference: "I have restructured this opinion somewhat, in an effort to meet the difficulties expressed respectively by John Harlan and Bill Brennan." The changes reflected in subsequent drafts often have the desired effect of enticing a justice to join the opinion. This phenomenon is illustrated by a letter from Justice Brennan to Justice Sandra Day O'Connor: "Thank you very much for the changes in the above. Please join me."

Our principal argument is that the choices majority opinion authors make are, at least in part, a function of the choices made by other justices. Justices pursue their own policy objectives, but they are also constrained by their colleagues. Of course, certain nonstrategic factors may also affect the circulation of majority opinion drafts. In the analyses reported below, we control for a variety of these nonstrategic factors in order to determine the relative influence of bargaining on the circulation of majority opinion drafts.

Strategic Determinants of Accommodation

Decision making on the Court is a collective enterprise among the justices and, as a result, justices' choices are interdependent. The actions and decisions of one justice are, in other words, affected by the positions adopted by his or her colleagues. Opinion authors' decisions about the content of majority opinions are therefore in part a function of the choices made by other justices on the Court. We examine the influence of several strategic considerations on the likelihood of an opinion author accommodating his or her colleagues.

The first calculation a strategic justice makes stems from the author's need to hold together a majority of the Court, that is, the conference decision coalition. An author with a fragile decision coalition should be more amenable to suggestions from colleagues. Indeed, it is precisely this phenomenon that apparently motivated Brennan to accommodate O'Connor in *Pennsylvania v. Muniz* (1990) and led Chief Justice Rehnquist to exclaim, "The willingness to accommodate on the part of the author of the opinion is directly proportional to the number of votes supporting the majority result at conference . . . if the result at conference was reached by a unanimous or a lopsided vote, a critic who wishes substantial changes in the opinion has less leverage." Rehnquist's comment suggests:

> *Hypothesis 1: The likelihood of the majority opinion author accommodating colleagues is inversely related to the size of the majority conference coalition.*

The need for the majority opinion author to moderate his or her views depends upon the acceptability of those views to the majority coalition. When the author's views are acceptable to the coalition, there is little need for accommodation. In contrast, when the author's preferred outcome is more distant from that favored by the majority coalition, the author must make a greater effort to accommodate other coalition members. Therefore:

> *Hypothesis 2: Opinion authors who are ideologically distant from the majority coalition on whose behalf they are writing will make a greater effort to accommodate their colleagues.*

The ideological composition of the supporting coalition also affects the willingness of opinion authors to adjust their opinions. If the majority is particularly heterogeneous, then the opinion author will probably have greater difficulty persuading the coalition members to adopt his or her legal reasoning. Thus:

> *Hypothesis 3: The more ideologically heterogeneous the conference majority coalition, the more likely the author will accommodate other justices.*

We also expect the magnitude of bargaining in the majority coalition to affect the scope of accommodation. As [several justices indicate, they] see a causal relationship between suggestions and changes in the draft opinion. As justices make suggestions about the majority opinion, more accommodation is likely to occur. Still, all suggestions are not equal. For instance, the bargaining strength of the suggesting justice may influence the likelihood that accommodations will follow. If a justice makes it clear that he or she will join the majority only if certain suggestions are incorporated in the draft, such suggestions should carry extra weight and, thus, provoke a greater effort at accommodation. Two hypotheses follow:

> *Hypothesis 4: The larger the number of letters from justices in the conference majority coalition that make suggestions or voice concerns about an opinion, the greater the accommodation.*
>
> *Hypothesis 5: The larger the number of letters from conference majority coalition members making threats (explicit statements that joining an opinion is contingent upon changes), the greater the accommodation.*

After an opinion is circulated, justices do not have to "join" the opinion or make suggestions. One tactic that justices regularly use is to inform the justice who drafted the opinion that they are unwilling to join the opinion until subsequent majority opinion drafts or nonmajority opinions are circulated. Normally, justices who voted with the majority at conference will, [according to Rehnquist], "join [the majority opinion] without waiting for circulation of the dissent." Thus, an opinion author may interpret such a "wait" statement as a strategic move to entice more concessions. It follows that:

> *Hypothesis 6: The effort to accommodate will increase as the number of letters from majority coalition members stating that they are going "to wait" before deciding to join the opinion rises.*

Nevertheless, the majority opinion author should not be expected to respond to every suggestion. Although Brennan, in *Pennsylvania v. Muniz* (1990), clearly made the strategic calculation to accommodate changes O'Connor insisted upon, opinion authors also refuse to accommodate their colleagues. For example, in one case Justice Marshall, who was authoring the majority opinion, decided that, "Since seven of us agree, my current plan is not to make the change suggested in the Chief's ultimatum." A suggestion or statement from a justice who voted with the minority at conference, and is thus likely to dissent, is likely to be discounted by the majority opinion author. Consistent with this idea is Brennan's observation that after circulating a draft majority opinion, the author's particular concern is "whether those who voted with him are still of his view and what they have to say about his proposed opinion." According to Brennan, opinion authors are more concerned about accommodating the views of a majority coalition member than those of a dissenter. Thus:

> *Hypothesis 7: A larger volume of suggestions from justices in the minority conference coalition is unlikely to lead to greater efforts at accommodation.*

> *Hypothesis 8: The effort to accommodate is not related to the number of letters from minority conference coalition members informing the majority opinion author that they will wait before making a final choice.*

Nonstrategic Influences on Accommodation

Nonstrategic factors that stem from characteristics of either the case or opinion author can also account for the variation in the amount of accommodation that occurs. Circulating a new draft in order to accommodate one's colleagues requires an investment of time and energy on the part of the majority opinion author. Because all justices [according to Justice Ginsburg] "operate under one intensely practical constraint—time," the willingness of an opinion author to accommodate colleagues is in part a function of the amount of work that the justice has pending and the time available to complete that work. When a justice has many majority opinions waiting to be written or as the Court approaches the end of its term, we expect greater reluctance to write another draft.

Hypothesis 9: The willingness of a justice to accommodate his peers with a new draft is inversely proportional to the justice's outstanding workload.

Hypothesis 10: In cases argued towards the end of the Court's term, justices are less likely to respond to the concerns of colleagues.

An author's need to engage in accommodation may also depend upon the nature of the case. Because the likelihood that the majority opinion author has dealt successfully with all pertinent concerns in the initial draft is diminished if a case is particularly complex, we expect:

Hypothesis 11: Complex cases will require additional efforts at accommodation.

Likewise, we expect authors to make a greater effort to accommodate their colleagues' concerns in cases that are particularly important. Due to their possible impact, important cases are likely to promote more give-and-take among the justices.

Hypothesis 12: More important cases will require additional efforts at accommodation.

Data and Methods

. . . [J]ustices and scholars alike see the number of drafts as a reasonable, albeit imperfect, measure of the extent to which the majority author accommodates his or her colleagues. Thus, we use the number of draft majority opinions circulated for each of the 2,295 cases where a majority opinion assignment was made or a signed opinion was released during the Burger Court (1969–1985 terms) as our dependent variable. To obtain the data, we relied upon the circulation records maintained by Justice William Brennan and available in his papers at the Library of Congress. For every case, these records provide a listing of all majority opinion drafts, nonmajority opinion drafts, and letters and memoranda written by every member of the Court and circulated to the conference. . . .

Findings

Table 13.3 provides an overview of the circulation of majority drafts. During the Burger Court, the average majority opinion author circulated 2.8 drafts prior to publication. Although multiple circulations were common, there was considerable variability. Of the 2,295 cases, 255 (11.1 percent) had only one draft circulated, 779 (33.9 percent) had two drafts circulated, and 1,259 (54.9 percent) had three or more drafts circulated. . . .

The expectation that the circulation of new draft opinions reflects strategic calculations about the need to accommodate fellow justices is strongly supported. Indeed, the findings are consistent with all eight strategic accommodation hypotheses. Consistent with hypothesis 1, . . . opinion authors are expected to write 20.0 percent more drafts if they are writing on behalf of a minimum winning coalition than if they are writing on behalf of a unanimous bench. Such a finding highlights the strategic nature of the opinion-circulation process. The willingness of a majority opinion author to accommodate his or her colleagues

TABLE 13.3 Circulation of Majority Opinion Drafts

Number of Drafts	Frequency	Percent
0	2	0.1
1	255	11.1
2	779	33.9
3	687	29.9
4	336	14.6
5	146	6.4
6	57	2.5
7	22	1.0
8	10	0.4
14	1	0.0
Total	2,295	100.0

appears to be conditioned by the extent to which the author needs the continued support of justices who were part of his or her conference coalition.

[The analysis also supports hypothesis 2]: . . . [T]he more ideologically distant an author is from the majority coalition, the greater the number of draft opinions he or she is likely to circulate. If an author is ideologically at the mean of the majority coalition, 2.7 drafts are circulated, but if an author is ideologically distant from the core of the majority coalition, 3.1 drafts are required. This represents a 14.8 percent increase in the expected number of drafts. Supportive of hypothesis 3, [the data reveal] that majority opinion authors are more accommodating when the conference coalition is less cohesive. Compared to when the Court is cohesive, majority opinion authors are likely to circulate 15.4 percent more drafts when the conference coalition is heterogeneous.

According to hypotheses 4, 5, and 6, the author's decision to circulate drafts is shaped by the actions of other members of the original coalition. The results of our [investigation] bear out hypothesis 4, which ties the number of drafts to the number of changes requested by members of the majority coalition. In the absence of letters from other members of the majority coalition, 2.7 majority draft opinions are likely to be circulated; in contrast, if three letters with suggestions are received by the opinion author, 3.3 draft opinions are written, and if six letters with suggestions are received, 4.0 draft opinions result. According to hypothesis 5, opinion authors are particularly responsive to suggestions accompanied by an explicit threat, and . . . [in fact] the inclusion of threats enhances a justice's leverage with the majority opinion author. If three explicit threats are sent to the author, we expect 15.2 percent more drafts than if three nonthreatening suggestions are sent instead. In the interest of retaining the original coalition, justices apparently respond to colleagues' threats not to join the opinion unless their suggestions are incorporated in a new draft. Similarly, consistent with hypothesis 6, opinion authors are more likely to revise their opinions when members of the majority coalition inform them that they are going to await further developments.... [W]hereas an opinion with three wait statement results in 3.2 drafts, no wait statements yields 2.7 drafts.

Although majority opinion authors clearly respond to implicit and explicit suggestions and threats from members of the majority coalition, hypotheses 7 and 8 predicted that they would not necessarily respond to suggestions, threats, and wait statements from those justices who had previously announced their intention to dissent.... [The data] are consistent with both of these hypotheses. There is little evidence that majority opinion authors systematically take into account the views of members of the minority conference coalition in deciding whether to circulate a new draft opinion.

While our central concern rests with the strategic interdependencies between majority opinion authors and their colleagues on the Court, we also recognize that nonstrategic factors may affect the circulation of draft opinions. In fact, we find that case characteristics affect the number of revisions that a majority author circulates. Consistent with hypothesis 9, the ... [analysis shows] that the heavier an opinion author's workload, the less likely he or she is to circulate a new draft opinion. When a justice is working on seven majority opinions, compared to an empty workload, the expected number of drafts decreases by 11.5 percent. The eleventh hypothesis—that more drafts would be circulated in complex cases than in relatively straightforward ones—is supported, but [hypotheses 10 and 12 are not. It is particular interesting that] more important cases do not seem to provoke extra efforts at accommodation.

Discussion

Few activities of the members of the United States Supreme Court are more important than the crafting of a majority opinion. It is the legal rule articulated in the majority opinion, not just the disposition of a particular case, that serves as guide for other branches of government, the lower courts, and even the general public. Although relatively little systematic work has been done on how opinions are constructed, it seems reasonable to assert that the process is interdependent. The justices themselves and scholars who have studied the opinion-formation process argue that opinion authors are constrained by their colleagues.... Our analysis makes clear that opinion authors are not unconstrained actors who are free to act on their own policy preferences. Opinion authors' actions are shaped by the interplay of their own policy preferences and the actions of their colleagues....

CHAPTER 14

The Impact of Judicial Decisions

Traditionally, students of law lost interest in a case after the final decision was handed down. But for scholars concerned with relations among law, politics, and society, the most interesting aspect of the judicial process may only be beginning when a court issues its mandate. For there remains the problem of securing compliance with the ruling; and when judges take a position on an important policy issue, their decision inevitably becomes a political event that can set off a chain reaction. If a court miscalculates its capacity to alter political behavior, it will stimulate opposition to its policies and perhaps to the judiciary itself. Justice Felix Frankfurter had these possibilities in mind when he urged the Supreme Court in *Colegrove v. Green* and *Baker v. Carr* (Readings 6.3 and 14.3) not to enter the "political thicket" of legislative reapportionment. As Chapters 8 and 13 pointed out, the opportunities for resistance to the Supreme Court's decisions, both in the lower courts and the political arena, abound.

One of the most effective of recent approaches to understanding the policy-making roles of the courts has been research into the effects of judicial decisions. Impact, according to Bradley C. Canon and Charles A. Johnson, refers to the general reactions and responses following a judicial decision:

> Judicial decisions are not self-implementing; courts must frequently rely on other courts or on nonjudicial actors in the political system to turn law into action. Moreover, the implementation of judicial decisions is a political process; the actors upon whom courts must rely [to translate law into action] are usually political actors and are subject to political pressures as they allocate resources to implement a judicial decision (Reading 14.1).

COMPLIANCE AND IMPACT

In the usual kind of civil litigation, compliance with a decision is routine, at least after all appeals have been exhausted. If the court's verdict in a criminal case is not guilty, police release the defendant immediately. When the verdict is guilty, and there is no reversal on appeal, judicial personnel, police, and prison officials act together or separately to collect the fine or incarcerate the defendant (see Reading 13.2). When a judge determines ownership of property, settles a tax claim, awards compensation, or forbids construction of a dam, the loser typically, if reluctantly, obeys without the court's having to use its coercive power to punish for contempt.

Examining the outcomes in these sorts of routine disputes is an important task because they occupy a substantial portion of the time of most courts, and they are the kind in which most citizens are likely to find themselves involved. So it should come as no surprise that scholars have devoted energy to asking questions such as these: who wins (or comes out ahead), and who loses (or comes out behind), and why? (See Reading 6.4.)[1] Under what circumstances will individuals obey (or disobey) judicial decisions?[2]

Even so, when a controversy concerns broad public policy, when interest groups or governmental officials are the litigants, and when a court's final decree and opinion relate directly to future conduct of persons not actually parties to the litigation, the matter of compliance typically becomes extremely complex. In studying such situations, most analysts prefer to use the word *impact* instead of compliance because the importance of what happens after a court's decision often involves a galaxy of private citizens and public officials—including presidents, governors, state and federal legislators, prosecutors, other judges, and leaders of interest groups—who, technically, are not bound by the court's decision.

The immediate effect of a judicial order, of course, is limited; it binds only the parties to that proceeding, their employees, agents, and people who, knowing the order is in force, cooperate with the defendants to violate it. When the Supreme Court entered its final decree in *Brown v. Board of Education* in 1955, it directed only four school boards "to admit to public schools on a racially nondiscriminatory basis with all deliberate speed the parties to these cases." (A fifth case, *Bolling v. Sharpe*, produced a similar order to schools in the District of Columbia.) But, as Chapter 10 explained, the opinion of any court has status as a precedent under the principles of stare decisis; and, because the Supreme Court is the nation's highest tribunal, its decisions on federal matters should be followed by all other courts. Nevertheless, it is always an open question whether, and to what extent, a ruling of the Supreme Court (or any other court) will be effective outside the confines of the particular piece of litigation. The answer depends on a large variety of factors.

Roberts v. United States Jaycees (1984) provides a textbook example of the Supreme Court's effectiveness. Here the Court upheld the constitutionality of Minnesota's Human Rights Act, which outlawed of the Junior Chamber of

---

[1] See also Stanton Wheeler et al., "Do the Haves Come Out Ahead?" 21 *Law and Society Review* 403 (1987); Peter Van Koppen and Marijbe Malsch, "Defendants and One-Shotters Win After All," 25 *Law and Society Review* 803 (1991); Herbert M. Kritzer and Susan Silbey, eds. *In Litigation, Do the Haves Still Come Out Ahead?* (Palo Alto, CA: Stanford University Press, 2003).

[2] A good deal of this literature is broader in focus, asking why people obey not only courts but also other legal authorities and the law itself. See, e.g., Tom Tyler, *Why People Obey Law* (New Haven, CT: Yale University Press, 1990); Stewart Macaulay, "Images of Law in Everyday Life: The Lessons of School, Entertainment, and Spectator Sports," 21 *Law and Society Review* 185 (1987).

Commerce's practice of limiting membership to young males. Although that organization had, as a general policy, long forbade admission of women and the Court's ruling technically applied only to Minnesota, within one month the national society voted to admit women in all chapters throughout the country. Only a few, scattered, local groups resisted.

To comply with a ruling of the Supreme Court (or any other tribunal), officials and interest groups must know that the order has been issued and be able to understand it. Alas, the justices have not been particularly helpful in making opinions intelligible to the public. Until recently the Court handed down opinions only on Mondays, and this bunching made it difficult for the media to report the decisions adequately, particularly toward the end of the term when the bulk of the most important decisions were announced. Moreover, only a few newspapers, notably *The New York Times* and *The Washington Post*, had reporters competent to handle the legalese in which opinions are usually written, leading to charges that the press tended to concentrate on controversial items or quotable phrases rather than give a clear presentation of all the issues. It is no wonder that Max Friedman declared in 1968 that "the Supreme Court is the worst-reported and worst-judged institution in the American system of government."[3]

Some observers, including Tim O'Brien, ABC News's correspondent for the Court, assert that times have changed: "Max Friedman's observations about the news media and the Court years ago are simply no longer valid; television has changed most dramatically since those days. . . . *The New York Times* and *The Washington Post* both have veterans at the Court. The [news service] wires are similarly staffed with Supreme Court veterans who provide papers around the country with competent coverage." But the wire services' providing factually accurate stories to newspapers in no way ensures that local editors will not butcher those accounts and garble their messages. More generally, Elliot E. Slotnick and Jennifer A. Segal's comprehensive analysis of television news coverage of the Court provides only limited support for O'Brien's observation. They found that the networks were continuing to cover only "leading" cases and were not even giving those the substantive coverage they deserved:

> The news stories infrequently include important . . . substantive information about the Court's docket activities; while many stories . . . included references to case facts, the litigants, and interested individuals and groups, most stories lacked references to the justices, the case vote, the ideological division in a case, the case history, and the amicus briefs filed.[4]

Even more serious, journalists' coverage of certain types of cases—particularly denials of certiorari—can be misleading or downright wrong. It is not unusual to read (or watch) a story that asserts that the Court has upheld a policy, program, or decision when, in fact, it has merely refused to hear a case (Reading 14.2).

---

[3] Quoted in Elliot E. Slotnick and Jennifer A. Segal, Television News and the Supreme Court (New York: Cambridge University Press, 1998), 10.

[4] Ibid., 187.

ANTICIPATED CONSEQUENCES

Concern over the impact of a judicial decision does not begin with the issuance of the final decree. Speculation about possible consequences of a ruling is an inevitable part of the decision-making process not only in legislative and administrative bodies and among the leaders of interest groups but also within judicial chambers. There might be some judges who give no thought to the practical problems a decision would create, who act on the basis of the Latin motto *Fiat justitia, ruat coelum,* "Let Justice Be Done, Though the Heavens Fall." Most judges, however, would be reluctant to announce a judgment that they thought might yield catastrophic results.

Consequently, weighing of possible or likely outcomes of alternative rulings is a normal part of the decision-making calculus. In the Supreme Court one can see concern with consequences at every stage of decision making. Occasionally, as in the *School Segregation* Cases, the justices formally order counsel to focus their arguments on the most efficacious remedy for a past wrong. A much more typical scene at oral argument shows the justices pressing counsel— often unsuccessfully—to discuss what the practical results would be of the desired ruling. Timothy R. Johnson's extensive analysis of the kinds of questions justices asked in civil liberties cases decided between 1972 and 1986 shores up this point. Of the 2,592 questions involving new issues—that is, those the parties did not raise in their written briefs—nearly half attempted to elicit information about the various implications of a decision, including likely effects on congressional, presidential, and state policies.[5]

At conference, the justices also debate likely effects, speculating about probable governmental responses to possible decisions. When, for instance, the Court was considering *Hirabayashi v. United States* (1943), Hugo L. Black advised his brethren that, if he were the general in charge of the program to place American citizens of Japanese ancestry in concentration camps and a court were to order those people released, he would disobey.[6]

Black's reaction probably is indicative of a larger phenomenon. If justices want to generate enduring policy, they must be attentive to the preferences of the other institutions and anticipate reactions of those other officials are likely to take. Our own research leads us to estimate that, in approximately 60 percent

---

[5] Timothy R. Johnson, "Information, Oral Arguments, and Supreme Court Decision Making," 29 *American Politics Research* 331 (2001). See also his *Oral Arguments and the Supreme Court of the United States* (Albany, NY: State University of New York Press, 2004).

[6] Alpheus Thomas Mason, *Harlan Fiske Stone* (New York: Viking, 1956), 674, reported the remark but did not identify the justice. In 1962, Justice William O. Douglas told Walter F. Murphy that Black had made the comment and expressed full confidence in the fairness of his old friend from Alabama, General J. L. DeWitt, who was commanding the programs that would ultimately intern more than a 100,000 Americans of Japanese descent. This friendship between Black and DeWitt, who was in a sense the defendant in the case, raises the interesting question of whether Black should have recused himself. Antonin Scalia probably would not have thought this step necessary. Recall that he refused to recuse himself in litigation involving his friend, Vice President Cheney.

of cases discussed in conference, at least one justice mentions likely reactions of political actors outside the Court.[7]

Occasionally, one can see similar though somewhat less candid debates in published opinions. In denying Mississippi's request in 1867 that the Court enjoin President Andrew Johnson from enforcing the Reconstruction Acts, Chief Justice Salmon P. Chase speculated about the likely effects of issuing the injunction:

> If the President refuses obedience, it is needless to observe that the Court is without power to enforce its process. If, on the other hand, the President complies with the order of the Court and refuses to execute the acts of Congress, is it not clear that a collision may occur between the executive and legislative departments of the government? May not the House of Representatives impeach the President for such refusal? And in that case could this Court interfere, in behalf of the President, thus endangered by compliance with its mandate, and restrain by injunction the Senate . . . from sitting as a court of impeachment? Would the strange spectacle be offered to the public wonder of an attempt by this Court to arrest proceedings in that Court?[8]

Justice Frankfurter's dissent in *Baker v. Carr* (Reading 14.3) voiced a similar warning that courts lacked the means to carry out reapportionment and that even the attempt to do so would lessen judicial prestige by embroiling judges in partisan political debates. Justice John Marshall Harlan's dissent in *Miranda v. Arizona* (1966) argued that the Court's new rules enlarging the rights of suspected criminals would encourage police to lie about having informed such people of their rights and, even if successful in ensuring that suspects understood their rights, would exact a fearsome price in unsolved crimes. In *Webster v. Reproductive Health Services* (1989) (Reading 8.1), Justice Antonin Scalia speculated about the reactions of the public to the Court's modification of, but failure to overturn, *Roe v. Wade* (1973):

> We can now look forward to at least another Term with carts full of mail from the public, and streets full of demonstrators, urging us—their unelected and life-tenured judges who have been awarded those extraordinary, undemocratic characteristics precisely in order that we might follow the law despite the popular will—to follow the popular will. Indeed, I expect we can look forward to even more of that than before, given our indecisive decision today.

And more recently Justice O'Connor took aim at the majority's decision in *Blakely v. Washington* (2004), which held that judges alone cannot impose sentences greater than the range provided under state guidelines. "The practical consequences for trial courts," O'Connor wrote, "will be . . . unsettling: How are courts to mete out guidelines sentences? Do courts apply the guidelines as to mitigating factors, but not as to aggravating factors? Do they jettison the guidelines altogether? The Court ignores the havoc it is about to wreak on trial courts across the country."

---

[7] We base this estimate on an examination of private papers of the justices, realizing that not all such papers are available or that all the notes individual justices take while they themselves are debating are absolutely accurate. Certainly these notes are likely to be incomplete.

[8] *Mississippi v. Johnson* (1867).

ACTUAL CONSEQUENCES

When we speak of the impact of judicial decisions, however, we usually mean actual rather than anticipated consequences. In *Webster* and in *Blakely*, justices speculated about the effect of the Court's decision, but what in fact did happen after the decision was handed down? How and in what way did the court's ruling in these and its many other decisions change behavior and affect—or even effect—public policy? Did problems of enforcement arise? If so, what form did resistance take: foot dragging, new lawsuits, efforts to reverse the decision by legislation or constitutional amendment, threats against the tenure of the judges, attempts to eliminate some categories of jurisdiction?

The first thing one notices about the actual consequences of judicial decisions in the United States, even of the Supreme Court, is how varied they have been. The dramatic ruling in the *Steel Seizure* case during the middle of the Korean War moved President Truman to return quickly, though grudgingly, the steel mills to their regular managers, and, as everyone had expected, a long and costly strike soon occurred. In 1974 the Court's equally dramatic ruling that Richard Nixon should turn over several tapes of conversations in the White House to the special Watergate prosecutor was followed by Nixon's surrender—made far more grudgingly than Truman's (Reading 12.1). Revelations of the tapes' contents led to nearly unanimous support within the House of Representatives for impeachment, and Nixon resigned in disgrace. Less dramatically, Michael McCann documents how various groups and attorneys used litigation to extract from reticent employers compliance with statutes and appellate decisions promoting the cause of equal pay for women.[9]

Other rulings have produced mixed results. Some communities blithely ignored the Supreme Court's decisions that the First and Fourteenth Amendments forbid religious instruction, prayer, and Bible reading in public schools. Elsewhere, communities slightly modified their practice; and still others changed their policies to conform to the Court's views. School segregation, of course, presents the richest pattern of diversity (see Reading 14.5). Initially, the Court's edict in *Brown v. Board* did vastly more to get black children into the courts as litigants than into formerly all-white schools as students. But, after a series of bitter political and legal battles that lasted for more than a decade, and especially after passage of the Civil Rights Act of 1964, staunch southern resistance began to collapse. Ironically, integrated schools became more of a reality in the South than in many eastern, midwestern, and western urban centers, where patterns of housing segregation and later the Court's hostility toward busing helped continue racially segregated education.[10]

---

[9] Michael McCann, *Rights at Work* (Chicago, IL: University of Chicago Press, 1994). McCann describes the results of his study in Reading 14.6.

[10] See, e.g., *Keyes v. Denver* (1973); *Milliken v. Bradley* (1974); *Board of Education of Oklahoma City Public Schools v. Dowell* (1991); and *Freeman v. Pitts* (1992). Nonetheless, in *United States v. Fordice* (1992), the Rehnquist Court made it clear that it was not totally removing itself from controversies about segregation.

The Court's decisions invalidating state statutes restricting abortion had an impact matched in scale only by *Brown v. Board*. Reacting against *Roe v. Wade* (1973), various interest groups opposed to abortion at first attempted to secure a constitutional amendment overturning *Roe* and authorizing states to continue to regulate abortions. When these efforts failed—only about a third of Americans supported a constitutional ban on abortions, perhaps explaining why Congress, ever cognizant of the polls, did not propose any of the "human life" amendments it considered in the 1970s—groups begin lobbying legislators for new statutes. They had considerable success in convincing states to limit rights to abortion by restricting funding and imposing such requirements as parental or spousal consent, a waiting period, abortions only in hospitals, obligations on physicians to explain possible consequences of the procedure, or to obtain the consent of a second physician. The Court invalidated some of these restrictions, most notably those requiring spousal notification; but the justices have allowed others, including limited forms of parental consent. So, too, the Court upheld, in *Harris v. McCrae* (1980), limitations on the use of federal funds to reimburse cost of abortions under state Medicaid programs.

The consequences of all this legislative and judicial activity have been the fodder of lively debates. In the "five years after *Roe*," Susan Hansen claims, "changes in access to abortion have been apparent throughout the U.S. The trend over time has been toward greater equalization of access with the largest increases in abortion rates in the most restrictive states."[11] But Gerald N. Rosenberg, writing two decades after *Roe*, shows that the number of doctors ready to perform abortions declined precipitously between 1982 and 1995.[12] The actual number of abortions has also decreased markedly. Whether these changes are due to harassment of abortion clinics, moral concern among doctors about a process that destroys human fetuses, or some combination of these and other factors is unclear. What is evident, is that lack of providers makes it difficult for women in many states, even populous ones, to exercise what the Supreme Court has said is their constitutional right.

Immigration and Naturalization Service (INS) v. Chadha (1983) produced different but equally hostile and ultimately more successful reactions. There the Court invalidated a very common congressional device, the "legislative veto." In scores of statutes since 1931, Congress had authorized the executive to exercise certain powers; at the same time, however, it had asserted the authority of one or both houses to veto actions taken under those grants. The purpose of this arrangement was to avoid resort to ordinary legislation, which, under the constitutional document, risks a presidential veto. In *Chadha* the attorney general had, under

---

[11] Susan Hansen, "State Implementation of Supreme Court Decisions: Abortion Since *Roe v. Wade*," 42 *Journal of Politics* 372 (1980).

[12] Gerald N. Rosenberg, "The Real World of Constitutional Rights: The Supreme Court and the Implementation of the Abortion Decisions," in *Contemplating Courts*, Lee Epstein, ed. (Washington, DC: CQ Press, 1995). More generally, Rosenberg argues that judges cannot evoke significant societal alterations without the support of the public and other key actors in the system (see Reading 14.5). We return to his argument at the end of the chapter.

statutory authority, suspended the deportation of an alien, but the House had subsequently adopted a resolution vetoing the suspension, as also authorized by statute. The Supreme Court literally applied the textual requirement that all proposed legislation must be presented to the president for his signature or disapproval and found this effort to bypass the president unconstitutional.

Justice Byron R. White dissented. Noting that some 200 statutes provided for a legislative veto, he contended that this device had become a central means by which Congress secures the accountability of executive and independent agencies. Without the legislative veto, Congress faces a Hobson's choice: Refrain from delegating authority, leaving itself with a hopeless task of writing laws with the requisite specificity to cover endless special circumstances across the entire landscape of public policy; or abdicate its lawmaking function to the executive branch and independent agencies. To choose the former would leave major national problems unresolved; to opt for the latter would risk unaccountable policymaking by those not elected to fill that role. In fact, after *Chadha*, Congress avoided both alternatives. Legislative committees found various formal and informal ways (including exchanges of promises not to cut budgets in return for promises to consult about policies) to continue their supervision of administrative action (Reading 14.4).

Even more strikingly negative were the reactions of the states to *Furman v. Georgia* (1972). There, five members of the Court had ruled that capital punishment, as it was then imposed, violated the Constitution. In his dissenting opinion, Chief Justice Warren Earl Burger noted that only two (William J. Brennan, Jr. and Thurgood Marshall) of the five had claimed that capital punishment was unconstitutional under all circumstances, thus making it possible for states to rewrite their laws to meet their objections. "It is clear," Burger asserted, "that if state legislatures and the Congress wish to maintain the availability of capital punishment, significant statutory changes will have to be made. . . . [L]egislative bodies may seek to bring their laws into compliance with the Court's ruling by providing standards for juries and judges to follow . . . or by more narrowly defining crimes for which the penalty is imposed." Privately, however, Burger described his suggestion futile, lamenting: "There will never be another execution in this country."[13] As it turned out, he was dead wrong: Within three years after Furman, two-thirds of the states had rewritten their death penalty laws to overcome the defects of the old ones. In *Gregg v. Georgia* (1976) and its companion cases, the Court upheld, at least in principle, most of the new statutes.

However pessimistic Burger was, he, of course, had hoped that his dissent would lead states to revise their laws. In other instances, judicial decisions—like all decisions—can have important but unintended effects, as *Dred Scott v. Sandford* (1857) so well illustrates. Writing for the majority, Chief Justice Roger Brooke Taney, who had freed his own slaves because he thought slavery was morally wrong, wrote the opinion of the Court. On an historical record that was, at best, dubious, he found, first, that the Framers of the constitutional text had

---

[13] Bob Woodward and Scott Armstrong, *The Brethren* (New York: Simon & Schuster, 1979), 219.

not considered black people, whether slave or free, as citizens. Second, it followed that a black man could not invoke the jurisdiction of federal courts to hear disputes between citizens of different states. Third, Congress could not prohibit slavery in the territories because such a ban would take away the slave owner's "property" without due process of law. Thus Scott had remained a slave even when his master took him into a "free territory."

Taney and the other justices in the majority thought that they were solidifying the Union by putting an end to the bitter debate about how (or even whether) Congress could regulate slavery in the territories. The result was dramatically and catastrophically different. Not only was the actual holding that Scott was still a slave meaningless (his new owner soon freed him), but the Court's opinion on the broader issues only deepened divisions between North and South and helped make bloody civil war more probable. Later, the opening sentence of the Fourteenth Amendment specifically repudiated Scott's pronouncement that African Americans could not be citizens: "All persons born or naturalized in the United States and subject to the jurisdiction thereof, are citizens of the United States and of the State wherein they reside."

The Fourteenth Amendment did not mark the first or the last time Congress has used constitutional amendments to reverse the Court's constitutional doctrine. The initial instance involved the Eleventh Amendment, adopted in 1795 to override the Court's interpretation in *Chisholm v. Georgia* (1793) that a citizen of one state could use a federal court to sue another state for monetary damages. *Pollock v. Farmers' Loan & Trust Co.* (1895) provided a third occasion. A five-to-four majority, with a senile justice casting the decisive vote, ruled that the constitutional text forbade the federal government to levy a tax on personal incomes; but the Sixteenth Amendment, ratified in 1913, explicitly authorized such a tax. The Twenty-Sixth Amendment (1971) reversed the doctrine of *Oregon v. Mitchell* (1970) that Congress could not fix the voting age at eighteen for state and local elections. Moreover, as Chapter 11 noted, congressional staff, as well as the staff of interest groups, continually monitor judicial decisions construing federal statutes; Congress itself frequently passes new legislation to expand, limit, reinterpret, or reverse those interpretations. Between 1967 and 1990 alone, Congress enacted legislation to "correct" more than 340 pieces of statutory interpretation by federal courts.[14]

EXPLAINING AND ASSESSING EFFECTS

It is obvious that the Supreme Court's decisions have had widely varying results, many of which the justices did not anticipate. The real problem lies in explaining why some decisions have been more effective than others in carrying out the policies immanent in the Court's opinions. Philip B. Kurland, a former

---

[14] See William N. Eskridge, Jr., "Overriding Supreme Court Statutory Interpretation Decisions," 101 *Yale Law Journal* 331-417 (1991).

clerk to Justice Felix Frankfurter and a noted professor of law at the University of Chicago, offered a set of tests for the effectiveness of a controversial Supreme Court ruling:

> The first requirement is that the constitutional standard be a simple one. The second is that the judiciary have adequate control over the means of effectuating enforcement. The third is that the public acquiesce—there is no need for agreement, simply the absence of opposition—in the principle and its application.[15]

Bush v. Gore (2000), which effectively settled the presidential election of 2000, came close to meeting all three of Kurland's criteria. First, although the opinion of the Supreme Court was intellectually muddled, it justified a clear and simple decision: Florida could not re-examine disputed ballots to determine for which candidate they had been cast. Second, the order was immediately directed to the state supreme court, but the officials who ultimately had to carry it out were the governor (George Bush's brother), the person who certified electors (one of George Bush's campaign managers), and the state legislature, which was controlled by Republicans. None of these people was averse to stopping the recount before it could be determined if Bush had really won. Third, the country had gone more than a month without knowing who the next president would be, and public opinion polls showed that a majority of people had tired of the whole controversy. (See Reading 8.11 for the public's reaction to the decision.)

Earlier, several scholars had used a larger sample of cases to test the utility of Kurland's standards as well as a few of their own devising. For example, in attempting to explain circumstances that lead federal agencies to comply (or not) with judicial decisions, James F. Spriggs II homed in on a version of Kurland's second factor, the specificity of the Court's opinion, and found that item was, indeed, a significant determinant of an agency's compliance. But also important were the agency's preferences and the degree to which it had the support of interest groups.[16]

Studies examining the reactions of other actors, including judges of lower courts, Congress, the president, and the states show that if (1) the Court's prestige is high, (2) the case concerns a matter over which the Court's jurisdiction is clear, (3) the Court issues a direct order (or commands a lower court to do so) to a named official, (4) to perform or not perform a specified act, (5) that is within the official's power to perform or not to perform, and (6) the Court's decision does not run against the grain of the opinion dominant in the official's constituency, then there is a very high probability that the decision will be carried out. One can place a negative in front of all six circumstances and predict with a high degree of accuracy that the decision will not be carried out. As soon as one of these six circumstances changes, the accuracy of prediction plummets (see Reading 14.1).

---

[15] Philip B. Kurland, "Equal Educational Opportunity: The Limits of Constitutional Jurisprudence Undefined," 35 *University of Chicago Law Review* 583 (1968).

[16] James F. Spriggs II, "The Supreme Court and Federal Administrative Agencies: A Resource-Based Theory of and Analysis of Judicial Impact," 40 *American Journal of Political Science* 1122 (1996).

Scholars have also been concerned with broader questions associated with the consequences of judicial decisions: to what extent can courts, acting alone, generate meaningful social and political change? Long ago, students of the presidency concluded that the White House can seldom bring about lasting changes in public policy. Success typically requires not only strong presidential action but also new legislation—including, very importantly, appropriations—from Congress, enthusiastic enforcement from administrative agencies, sympathetic treatment from courts, and, not least, the active support of politically skilled interest groups. Public policy is almost always the product of a process, a series of actions and reactions, not of a single decision by a legislative, executive, or judicial institution. And this interactive process starts—or sometimes even stops—with the action of an interest group or one of the formal political institutions. Thus it was hardly surprising when Gerald N. Rosenberg.[17] (Reading 14.5) found that *Brown v. Board* (1954) produced little integration in public schools in the South until Congress, at the insistent urging of President Lyndon B. Johnson, the Department of Justice, the U.S. Commission on Civil Rights, and the broader Civil Rights Movement, had enacted the Civil Rights Act of 1964. This statute put the federal spending power and criminal laws behind desegregation. Then the Voting Rights Act of 1965 utilized federal authority to allow blacks to use their right to vote to retire state and federal officials who wished to continue governmentally imposed racial discrimination.

Rosenberg's specific finding is correct: Before 1964, there was little desegregation in southern public schools. His broader claim, however, that *Brown* "contributed little" to furthering the cause of civil rights, is somewhat like an assertion that *Marbury v. Madison* (1803) (Reading 2.2) was unimportant because William Marbury never got his commission. Civil rights bills had been introduced in almost every Congress since the end of Reconstruction; not one of them became law, even those that President Truman had fiercely supported. Southern political influence in Congress was great but so was the segregationists' basic constitutional argument: In a series of decisions beginning with *Plessy v. Ferguson* in 1896, the Supreme Court of the United States had held that it was legitimate for states to treat blacks and whites differently.

Then, on May 17, 1954, Chief Justice Earl Warren said for a unanimous Supreme Court that, like the Declaration of Independence, the American constitutional order forbade a caste society. Many of us living in the twenty-first century find it hard to grasp what a radical statement this was. The Court shook the roots of a way of life, not only of the South but of the entire nation. White clergy, in the South as well as the North, were quicker than public officials to understand the moral revolution that had begun. Within weeks of *Brown*, many

---

[17] Gerald N. Rosenberg, *The Hollow Hope: Can Courts Bring About Social Change?* (Chicago, IL: University of Chicago Press, 1991). For more recent critiques of *Brown*, see Michael J. Klarman, *From Jim Crow to Civil Rights: The Supreme Court and the Struggle for Racial Equality* (New York: Oxford University Press, 2004); Charles J. Ogletree, *All Deliberate Speed: Reflections on the First Half Century of* Brown v. Board of Education (New York: Norton, 2004); Derrick Bell, *Silent Covenants:* Brown v. Board of Education *and the Unfulfilled Hopes for Racial Reform* (New York: Oxford University Press, 2004).

ministers, priests, and rabbis were preaching that their colorblind God had always endorsed the gospel of Earl Warren and Thomas Jefferson: "All men are created equal." And African Americans understood the moral and constitutional messages. They tired of the long, slow fight the NAACP had waged in the courts and, led by people like the Rev. Martin Luther King, Jr., and joined by white sympathizers, marched in the highways, sat in at restaurants, and defied the police who assaulted them with clubs, water hoses, and attack dogs. These men and women demanded—they did not request—the rights the Supreme Court had said the American constitutional system provided. Their struggle was difficult, at times bloody, and has not yet ended; but their hymn "We Shall Overcome" has come much closer to reality. Before *Brown,* white supremacists could claim that they were the party of the "Constitution." But *Brown* fundamentally changed that situation. Now segregation was a constitutional outlaw. As Eldridge Cleaver, one of the leaders of the Black Panthers, wrote:

> Prior to 1954, we lived in an atmosphere of Novocain. Negroes found it necessary, in order to maintain what sanity they could, to remain somewhat aloof and detached from "the problem." We accepted indignities and the mechanics of the apparatus of oppression without reacting by sitting-in or holding mass demonstrations. Nurtured by the fires of the controversy over segregation, I was soon aflame with indignation over my newly discovered social status.[18]

Cleaver and his Panthers preached and practiced violence against whites. The Rev. Martin Luther King, Jr., was more effective in preaching and practicing passive resistance as a means of persuading whites (and blacks) that racial discrimination was morally as well as constitutionally wrong. Rather than stressing litigation, he relied on demonstrations and marches as well as on speeches; but he, too, fully understood how the Justices had made straight the path toward his dream of racial equality. Linking divine and human law, he said: "If we are wrong, the Supreme Court of this nation is wrong. If we are wrong, God Almighty is wrong."[19] In his hands, both forms of law were powerful instruments.

In sum, no *Brown,* no Civil Rights Movement, no Civil Rights Act of 1964, and no Voting Rights Act of 1965, at least within the lifetime of anyone reading this book. More generally, we can say that, although judicial decisions alone are usually insufficient to generate change, those rulings, especially when explained by eloquent opinions, can energize interest groups, sway public opinion, and even convince elected officials, if not of the rightness of the Court's decision, at least of the prudence of worrying about reelection. In these ways, direct and indirect, judges can help reset the agendas of legislative and executive officials, just as a president or a group of senators can help set the agendas of their own and other branches of government. Like the president from his "bully pulpit," the Supreme Court, when it enjoys high public respect, can play

---

[18] Eldridge Cleaver, *Soul on Ice* (New York: McGraw-Hill, 1968), 3-4.

[19] Quoted by Thomas R. Rochon, *Culture Moves: Ideas, Activism, and Changing Values* (Princeton, NJ: Princeton University Press, 1998), 56.

the role of "republican schoolmaster," providing the public with an "example of the way good republicans should behave" (see Reading 14.7).

Why scholars vehemently disagree over whether judicial fora can or do generate real social or political change or both is itself an interesting question. At least part of the answer, as we have indicated, lies in the constantly reacting nature of the American political system. A judicial ruling, like a presidential decision or an act of Congress, is only one element in a complex battle that often begins in the private sphere, is waged in various political arenas, and will return to those arenas—if, indeed, it ever completely leaves them—after judges have had their say. Furthermore, it is likely that most important issues will also reappear in the courts for fresh decisions and will do so not once but several times before they are finally settled, forgotten, or, what is most likely, superseded by new problems of public policy.[20] "The Supreme Court," James Levine has said, "is better understood as a catalyst of change rather than as a singular effector of change."[21]

The real question, the most difficult question, is not whether courts can bring about important changes in public policies and public attitudes but to what extent and under what circumstances can they do so. Unlike physical scientists, scholars who study political behavior can seldom isolate a single phenomenon and hold all other factors constant. Rather, we typically look at a tangled—and moving—web of events; pulling the judicial thread out is usually impossible. So far scholars have identified rather than solved such problems, but they continue to try to untwist the knotted threads of public policy making.

SELECTED REFERENCES

BAAS, LARRY R., AND DAN THOMAS. 1984. "The Supreme Court and Policy Legitimation: Experimental Tests." *American Politics Quarterly* 12: 335.

BAKER, LIVA. 1983. *Miranda: Crime, Law, and Politics.* New York: Atheneum.

BASS, JACK. 1981. *Unlikely Heroes: The Dramatic Story of the Southern Judges of the Fifth Circuit Who Transformed the Supreme Court's* Brown *Decision into a Revolution for Equality.* New York: Simon & Schuster.

BAUM, LAWRENCE. 1976. "Implementation of Judicial Decisions: An Organizational Analysis." *American Politics Quarterly* 4: 86.

BAUM, LAWRENCE. 1978. "Lower Court Response to Supreme Court Decisions: Reconsidering a Negative Picture." *Justice System Journal* 3: 208.

BECKER, THEODORE L., AND MALCOLM M. FEELEY, EDS. 1973. *The Impact of Supreme Court Decisions,* 2nd ed. New York: Oxford University Press.

BEISER, EDWARD N. 1968. "A Comparative Analysis of State and Federal Judicial Behavior: The Reapportionment Cases." *American Political Science Review* 62: 788.

---

[20] For an early but still valuable study of courts' interrelations with other processes of governance, see Jack W. Peltason, *Federal Courts in the Political Process* (New York: Random House, 1955).

[21] James Levine, "Methodological Considerations in Studying Supreme Court Efficacy," 4 *Law and Society Review* 583 (1970).

BERKSON, LARRY C. 1978. *The Supreme Court and Its Publics: The Communication of Policy Decisions.* Lexington, MA: Lexington.

BOND, JON R., AND CHARLES A. JOHNSON. 1982. "Implementing a Permissive Policy: Hospital Abortion Services after *Roe v. Wade." American Journal of Political Science* 26: 1.

BOWEN, LAUREN. 1995. "Do Court Decisions Matter?" In *Contemplating Courts*, Lee Epstein, ed. Washington, DC: CQ Press.

CALDEIRA, GREGORY A. 1991. Courts and Public Opinion. In *The American Courts: A Critical Assessment*, John B. Gates and Charles A. Johnson, eds. Washington, DC: CQ Press.

CANON, BRADLEY C. 1973. "Reactions of State Supreme Courts to a U.S. Supreme Court Civil Liberty Decision." *Law and Society Review* 8: 109.

CANON, BRADLEY C., AND CHARLES A. JOHNSON. 1999. *Judicial Policies: Impact and Implementation.* 2nd ed. Washington, DC: CQ Press.

CANON, BRADLEY C., AND K. KOLSON. 1971. "Compliance with *Gault* in Rural America: The Case of Kentucky." Journal of Family Law 10: 300.

DOLBEARE, KENNETH M., AND PHILLIP F. HAMMOND. 1971. *The School Prayer Decisions: From Court Policy to Local Practices.* Chicago: University of Chicago Press.

FAHLUND, G. GREGORY. 1973. "Retroactivity and the Warren Court." *Journal of Politics* 35: 570.

FLEMMING, ROY B., JOHN BOHTE, AND B. DAN WOOD. 1997. "One Voice Among Many: The Supreme Court's Influence on Attentiveness to Issues in the United States." *American Journal of Political Science* 41: 1224.

FRANKLIN, CHARLES H., AND LIANE C. KOSAKI. 1989. "Republican Schoolmaster: The U.S. Supreme Court, Public Opinion, and Abortion." *American Political Science Review* 83: 751.

GRUHL, JOHN. 1980. "The Supreme Court's Impact on the Law of Libel." *Western Political Quarterly* 33: 518.

HANSEN, SUSAN. 1980. "State Implementation of Supreme Court Decisions: Abortion Since *Roe v. Wade." Journal of Politics* 42: 372.

HOEKSTRA, VALERIE J. 2004. *From the Marble Temple to Main Street: The Effect of Court Decisions on Local Public Opinion.* New York: Cambridge University Press.

HOEKSTRA, VALERIE J., AND JEFFREY A. SEGAL. 1996. "The Shepherding of Local Public Opinion: The Supreme Court and Lamb's Chapel." *Journal of Politics* 58: 1079.

JOHNSON, CHARLES A. 1979. "Lower Court Reactions to Supreme Court Decisions: A Quantitative Examination." *American Journal of Political Science* 4: 792.

JOHNSON, CHARLES A. 1987. "Law, Politics, and Judicial Decision Making: Lower Federal Court Uses of Supreme Court Decisions." *Law and Society Review* 21: 325.

JOHNSON, TIMOTHY R. 2004. *Oral Arguments and the Supreme Court of the United States.* Albany, NY: State University of New York Press.

KAPLAN, DIANE S., AND RICHARD ZUCKERMAN. 1975. "The Wyatt Case: Implementation of a Judicial Decree Ordering Institutional Change." *Yale Law Journal* 84: 1338.

KRISLOV, SAMUEL, ET AL., EDS. 1971. *Compliance and the Law.* Beverly Hills, CA: Sage.

LEVINE, JAMES P. 1970. "Methodological Considerations in Studying Supreme Court Efficacy." *Law and Society Review* 4: 583.

MANWARING, DAVID. 1968. "The Impact of *Mapp v. Ohio.*" In *The Supreme Court as a Policy Maker*, David Everson, ed. Carbondale, IL: Southern Illinois University, Public Affairs Bureau.

MCCANN, MICHAEL. 1994. *Rights at Work: Pay Equity Reform and the Politics of Legal Mobilization.* Chicago: University of Chicago Press.

MEDALIE, RICHARD J., LEONARD ZEITZ, AND PAUL ALEXANDER. 1968. "Custodial Interrogation in Our Nation's Capital: The Attempt to Implement Miranda." *Michigan Law Review* 66: 1347.

Mondak, Jeffrey J. 1990. "Perceived Legitimacy of Supreme Court Decisions: Three Functions of Source Credibility." *Political Behavior* 12: 363.

Muir, William K. 1967. *Law and Attitude Change.* Chicago: University of Chicago Press.

Murphy, Walter F. 1962. *Congress and the Court: A Case Study in the American Political Process.* Chicago: University of Chicago Press.

Murphy, Walter F., and Joseph Tanenhaus. 1972. *The Study of Public Law.* New York: Random House.

Ogletree, Charles. 2004. *All Deliberate Speed: Reflections on the First Half-Century of* Brown v. Board of Education. New York: W. W. Norton.

Peltason, Jack W. 1961. *Fifty-Eight Lonely Men: Southern Federal Judges and School Desegregation.* New York: Harcourt, Brace & World.

Pritchett, C. Herman. 1961. *Congress versus the Supreme Court, 1957–1960.* Minneapolis: University of Minnesota Press.

Reid, Traciel V. 1988. "Judicial Policy-Making and Implementation: An Empirical Investigation." *Western Political Quarterly* 41: 509.

Rodgers, Harrell R., Jr., and Charles S. Bullock III. 1972. *Law and Social Change.* New York: McGraw Hill.

Romans, Neil T. 1974. "The Role of State Supreme Courts in Judicial Policy Making: *Escobedo, Miranda,* and the Use of Judicial Impact Analysis." *Western Political Quarterly* 27: 38.

Rosenberg, Gerald N. 1991. The *Hollow Hope: Can Courts Bring about Social Change?* Chicago: University of Chicago Press.

Scheingold, Stuart. 1974. *The Politics of Rights.* New Haven, CT: Yale University Press.

Slotnick, Elliot E., and Jennifer A. Segal. 1998. *Television News and the Supreme Court.* New York: Cambridge University Press.

Songer, Donald R., and Reginald S. Sheehan. 1990. "Supreme Court Impact on Compliance and Outcomes: *Miranda* and *New York Times* in the United States Courts of Appeals." *Western Political Quarterly,* 43: 297.

Tanenhaus, Joseph, and Walter Murphy. 1982. "Patterns of Public Support for the Supreme Court: A Panel Study." *Journal of Politics* 43: 24.

Tarr, G. Alan. 1977. *Judicial Impact and State Supreme Courts.* Lexington, MA: Lexington Books.

Tyler, Tom. 1990. *Why People Obey Law.* New Haven, CT: Yale University Press.

Wald, Michael, et al. 1967. "Interrogations in New Haven: The Impact of *Miranda.*" *Yale Law Journal* 76: 1550.

Wasby, Stephen L. 1970. *The Impact of the United States Supreme Court: Some Perspectives.* Homewood, IL: Dorsey Press.

"[W]e hope to move away from idiosyncratic, case-by-case or policy-by-policy analyses toward a general theoretical understanding of the events that may follow a judicial decision."

14.1 JUDICIAL POLICIES: IMPLEMENTATION AND IMPACT

Bradley C. Canon and Charles A. Johnson

Bradley C. Canon is Professor of Political Science at the University of Kentucky.
Charles A. Johnson is Professor and Chair of the Department
of Political Science at Texas A&M University.

In this excerpt the authors introduce the notions that judicial decisions are not self-implementing and that courts must frequently rely on other courts or on nonjudicial actors in the political system to turn law into action. Moreover, the implementation of judicial decisions is a political process; the actors on whom the courts must rely to translate law into action are usually political actors and are subject to political pressures as they allocate resources to implement a judicial decision.

[O]ur aim is not to study the aftermath of every judicial decision; instead, we want to make general statements about what has happened or may happen after any judicial decision.[1] That is, we hope to move away from idiosyncratic, case-by-case or policy-by-policy analyses and toward a general theoretical understanding of the events that may follow a judicial decision. . . .

The first step in understanding any political process is to develop a conceptual foundation upon which explanations may be built. We will organize our presentation of what happens after a court decision around two major elements: the actors who may respond to the decision and the responses that these actors may make. Focusing on these two elements enables us to define more precisely who is reacting and how. In studying the responses to judicial policies, we describe and attempt to explain the behavior following a court decision—specifically, what the behavior is, its antecedents, and its consequences. Hence, when we discuss impact, we are describing . . . general reactions [following] a judicial decision. When we discuss implementation, we are describing the behavior of lower courts, government agencies, or other affected parties as it relates to enforcing a judicial decision. When we discuss what many would call compliance/noncompliance or evasion, we are describing behavior that is in some

---

From Bradley C. Canon and Charles A. Johnson, *Judicial Policies: Implementation and Impact* (Washington, DC: CQ Press, 1999), pp. 16–26.

[1] The material reprinted here follows the authors' extensive review of reactions to *Roe v. Wade* (1973), holding that a woman has a constitutional right to an abortion at least during the first trimester of her pregnancy (see Reading 6.2). —Eds.

706

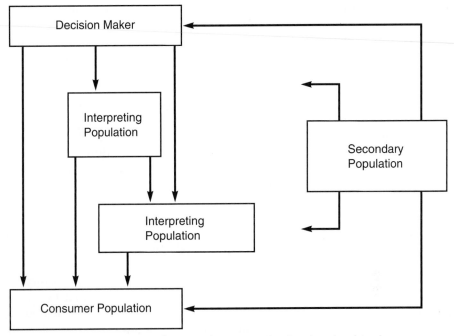

FIGURE 14.1 Populations and Lines of Communication Involved in the Implementation of Judicial Decisions

way consistent or inconsistent with the behavioral requirements of the judicial decision.

Figure 14.1 presents a schematic diagram of the different sets of actors, referred to as populations, that may respond to a judicial policy. The organization of these populations is essentially a functional one, in which their roles in shaping the impact of judicial decisions and their influence on the ultimate impact of judicial policy differ.

The Interpreting Population

For any appellate court decision, the actor most often charged with responding to a decision is a particular lower court, often a trial court. Moreover, in our common law system many appellate court decisions become policies used in deciding future cases. In a general sense, therefore, a higher court's policy affects all lower courts within its jurisdiction. This set of courts is known as the interpreting population. (This population may include state attorneys-general or other nonjudges who have an official role in interpreting the law.) The interpreting population, as the name implies, responds to the policy decisions of a higher court by refining the policy it has announced. Such refinements could have the effect of enlarging or [of] limiting the original policy. This population, in other words, interprets the meaning of the policy and develops the rules for matters not addressed in the original decision. Of course, all populations must "interpret" the decision in order to react to it. Interpretations by lower courts, however, are distinguished from other interpretations since theirs are viewed as authoritative in a legal sense by others in the political system. Hence, this population provides "official" interpretations of a court policy applicable to the other populations under their jurisdiction.

The Supreme Court's *Roe* decision launched the judiciary into a new area of the law, which required considerable refining before complete implementation. Shortly after the decision was announced, lower state and federal courts began hearing cases presenting issues that had not been directly addressed in *Roe*. In Florida, for example, the issue of a father's rights were raised by a father who brought legal action to restrain the mother of his unborn child from obtaining an abortion. The lower court denied relief and the Florida Supreme Court affirmed that decision, arguing that the U.S. Supreme Court's abortion decision was based on the mother's "right of privacy" (*Jones v. Smith*, 1973). The decision to terminate a pregnancy was, therefore, purely the right of the mother and could not be subject to interference by the state or private individuals.

Meanwhile, in Arizona, another matter was before the courts. Arizona law prohibited the advertisement of any medicine or procedures that facilitated abortions. New Times, Inc., a local publisher, was convicted under this statute and appealed to the state supreme court. The conviction was reversed, since the Arizona abortion statutes were found to be similar to the Texas statute struck down in *Roe v. Wade*, even though the issue before the court was different from that decided in the original abortion cases (*State v. New Times, Inc.*, 1973).

In each of these instances, . . . the issue before the court had not been addressed directly in the original decision. Consistent with the common law tradition, the lower courts had the responsibility of making authoritative interpretations of policy in light of the original Supreme Court decision. In their interpretations these courts could limit the application of the original policy, as did the Arizona trial court in convicting the publisher, or could facilitate its implementation, as did the Florida courts. . . .

The Implementing Population

The lower courts apply a higher court's policy only in cases that come before them. Higher court policies, however, usually affect a wider set of actors than those involved in lawsuits. We refer to this set of actors as the implementing population. In most instances, this population is made up of authorities whose behavior may be reinforced or sanctioned by the interpreting population. The implementing population usually performs a policing or servicing function in the political system—that is, implementors apply the system's rules to persons subject to their authority. Prominent examples of this population are police officers, prosecutors, university and public school officials, and welfare and social security workers. In many instances, the original policy and subsequent interpretations by lower courts are intended to impose requirements or set limits on the behavior of the implementing population. A clear example of this activity involves decisions concerning police behavior with regard to the rights of criminal suspects.

When the services or practices of private concerns are subject to a judicial policy, the implementing population is composed of private individuals or institutions. For example, court decisions may require or strongly suggest that corporations implement policies against racial or gender discrimination or harassment. . . . [H]owever, when a private organization has a choice (is not obligated to follow a policy), it is part of the consumer population.

The implementing population may vary from decision to decision. For criminal justice decisions, prosecutors, police officers, and defense attorneys are the primary implementors. For environmental protection decisions, the implementors are most often federal and state environment protection agencies. Reapportionment decisions usually involve legislators as the implementing population. When judicial decisions require no action by government agencies, nongovernmental service agencies may be the implementors. Sometimes, there is no implementing population at all. For example, no one is charged with implementing a case such as *New York Times Co. v. Sullivan* (1964), which significantly decreased the applicability of libel law to public officials. The decision held that when public officials initiated libel suits against the media, they had to show a much greater degree of fault than did private persons who filed libel suits. Sullivan is implemented solely through court rulings made in the course of litigation.

The degree to which a court decision actually benefits those it was intended to benefit depends on the implementing actors and institutions whose activities are affected by the decision. Implementors' reactions may range from full compliance to doing nothing. . . .

The Consumer Population

Those for whom the policies are set forth by the court are identified as the consumer population. This population is the set of individuals (usually not affiliated with the government) who would or should receive benefits or suffer disabilities as a result of a judicial decision; that is, they gain or lose desired rights or resources. Criminal suspects, for example, benefit from judicial policies announced by the Supreme Court in the 1960s. African-American students presumably benefited from school desegregation decisions following *Brown v. Board of Education* (1954). But they were disadvantaged by more recent judicial decisions limiting affirmative action programs in many public universities. Thus, some consumer populations may not benefit from a judicial policy. For example, juvenile court defendants suffer because they do not have the right of trial by jury; stockholders can suffer when their corporation is split up as a result of an antitrust ruling. And there are decisions under which members of the consumer population may either benefit or suffer, depending on their attitudes toward the policy. When led prayer was banned in the public schools (*Abington School District v. Schempp*, 1963), children who wanted to pray became disadvantaged and those who did not want to pray became advantaged.

The consumer population, depending on the policy involved, may include the entire population of the political system, as with judicial decisions concerning general tax legislation. For some decisions, however, a very limited population may be directly involved, such as criminal suspects under arrest. When the policy affects a specific sector but supposedly is for the public good (for example, antitrust decisions), a distinction between direct and indirect consumption must sometimes be made. Also, for some decisions there are two levels of consumer population, those who have to decide whether to offers some previously prohibited service and those who decide whether to use the service. For example, after *Roe* women could still not obtain legal abortions unless hospitals, clinics, and physicians were willing to perform them. . . . [Most] medical facilities and doctors choose not to offer abortion services.

Specifying the consumer population exactly may be troublesome in some cases. For example, while few would dispute that women with unwanted pregnancies are the consumers for the Supreme Court's abortion decision, opponents would likely argue that unborn children are also consumers and receive catastrophic negative benefits from the abortion decision. Others might argue that fathers of unborn children or parents of underage, pregnant girls are part of *Roe's* consumer population. . . .

The Secondary Population

The populations we have discussed so far are those directly (at least potentially) affected by a judicial policy or its implementation. The secondary population is a residual one. It consists of everyone who is not in the interpreting, implementing, or consumer population for any given decision. Members of the secondary population are not directly affected by a judicial policy: however, some members may react to a policy or its implementation. This reaction usually takes the form of some type of feedback directed toward the original policy maker, another policy maker, the implementing population, or the consumer population.

The secondary population may be divided into four subpopulations: government officials, interest groups, the media, and the public at large. First, there are government officials. This subpopulation includes legislators and executive officers who are not immediately affected by the decision. Though usually unaffected directly, these individuals are often in a position to support or hinder the implementation of the original policy. This subpopulation is distinguished from other secondary subpopulations in that its members have direct, legitimate authority in the political system, and they are often the recipients of political pressure from the public. Clearly, for example, Congress and the state legislatures substantially affected implementation of *Roe v. Wade* with the passage of laws restricting the funding of abortions.

The second subpopulation is interest groups, which are often activated by court policies even when they are not directly affected by them. Subsequent actions by these groups may facilitate or block effective implementation of the judicial policy. National, state, and local pro-life organizations have worked diligently to discourage providers from offering abortion services and women from obtaining abortions. These groups have also maintained considerable pressure on public officials and the courts to limit the implementation of pro-choice policies.

The third subpopulation is the media, which communicate the substance of judicial policies to potentially affected populations. Included here are general and specialized media, which may affect implementation or consumption by editorial stance or simply by the way they report (or do not report) judicial policies. Media attention to a policy, descriptions of reactions to it, and support or criticism often can play a large role in determining the amount and direction of feedback courts and implementors get. Media reports of activities by pro-choice and pro-life groups have helped keep the abortion issue at the forefront of American politics.

The fourth subpopulation consists of members of the public at large, insofar as they do not fall within the consumer population. The most important segment of this subpopulation is attentive citizens—those who are most aware of a judicial policy. This segment includes individuals who may be related to the consumer population (e.g., parents of teenage girls seeking an abortion), politically active individuals (e.g., political party workers), or just people who follow the news pretty regularly. . . .

Fluidity and Linkage among Populations

The basis for the foregoing classification of populations is primarily functional. We may, therefore, on some occasions find that particular individuals are members of different populations in different circumstances. For example, it is entirely possible for an attorney general to be an interpreter for one judicial policy and an implementor for another. In the former instance, the attorney general would be issuing an authoritative, legally binding statement interpreting a judicial decision; in the latter instance, the attorney general would be charged with the responsibility of applying a judicial policy to some consumer population or of carrying out some order of the court. School boards may be implementors of a schoolhouse religion decision and consumers of a court decision changing the way the state finances the schools. Media outlets are consumers of a libel decision like Sullivan, but more often they are in the secondary population. Obviously, private citizens are in both the consumer and secondary populations, depending on the nature of the judicial policy.

Attorneys constitute a special set of participants whose function may vary from one setting to another. They assist the interpreting population when they argue for a particular interpretation of a higher court's decision in briefs or oral arguments before lower court judges. They have a role in implementation when they insist that agencies follow the policies promulgated by a higher court. When they advise clients to take advantage (or not to do so) of a judicial policy, attorneys are playing a role as quasi-members of the consumer population.

Perhaps even more often, attorneys are called upon to give their interpretations of judicial policies for potential consumers, implementing groups, and, occasionally, secondary groups such as interested citizens or legislative bodies. Such interpretations are not official like those of the interpreting population. Often, however, their interpretations can be final, since paying clients usually act on lawyers' advice; so it is reasonable to assume that such interpretations play an important role in accounting for the reactions of others to judicial policies. . . .

In a broad sense, as they perform these functions, attorneys serve as linkages between various populations. They provide a means for the communication of decisions downward from higher courts to relevant actors, as well as being unofficial interpreters of these decisions. Their linkage activities may also prompt new litigation or feedback to the courts or other agencies, which, in turn, may affect the implementation of a decision.

Acceptance Decisions and Behavioral Responses

. . . We may observe a large variety of responses to judicial decisions, so precise distinctions are difficult to make. Nonetheless, we believe two general categories of responses are captured in the concepts of acceptance decisions and behavioral responses. The acceptance decision involves psychological reactions to a judicial policy, which may be generalized in terms of accepting or rejecting the policy. An individual's acceptance decision is shaped by several psychological dimensions: intensity of attitude, regard for the policy-making court, perceptions of the consequences of the decision, and the respondent's own role in society.

The intensity of a person's attitude toward the policy prior to the court's decision can be important. Most white southerners, for example, were extremely hostile toward policies of racial integration before *Brown*; thus their unwillingness to accept the decision was not surprising. Many people had similarly intense attitudes about . . . prayers in the public schools. Many minority groups felt strongly about affirmative actions. For most policies, though, feelings are not so intense. Few people feel strongly about such issues as the size and composition of juries or the application of the First Amendment guarantees to commercial advertising. In such instances the acceptance decision is less likely to be governed by prior attitudes.

Another dimension . . . [involves] . . . regard for the court making the decision. People who view the U.S. Supreme Court favorably may be more inclined to accept a decision as legitimate and proper. Those who generally view the Court negatively or who believe it has [usurped] too much authority may transfer these views to particular decisions of the Court.

A third dimension relates to a person's perception of the consequences of a decision. Those who may not quarrel with a decision in the abstract but believe it will have a serious and detrimental effect on society may be reluctant to accept it. In the 1950s, for example, many citizens feared that communism would expand in the United States as a result of the Supreme Court's decisions granting due process to persons suspected of engaging in subversive activities. In the late 1990s many people worry that court decisions voiding affirmative action programs will make it more difficult for minority applicants to obtain jobs.

Finally, acceptance decisions are shaped by a person's own rote in society. An ambitious judge, a school superintendent, or police chief may be reluctant to accept (publicly, at least) an unpopular judicial policy for fear that it will harm his or her career. Corporate officers or citizens may be unwilling to accept a decision if they think it will reduce their profits or cause them great inconvenience. Conversely, people may accept quite willingly decisions that are popular with the public or that bring them financial or other benefits.

Behavioral responses involve reactions that may be seen or recorded and that may determine the extent to which a court policy is actually realized. These responses are often closely linked to acceptance decisions. Persons who do not accept a judicial policy are likely to engage in behavior designed to defeat the policy or minimize its impact. They will interpret it narrowly, try to avoid implementing it, and refuse or evade its consumption. Those who accept a policy are likely to be more faithful or even enthusiastic in interpreting, implementing, and consuming it. Of course, nonacceptors may not always be in a position to ignore a decision or to refuse completely to comply with it. Malapportioned state legislatures, for instance, had little choice but to reapportion themselves after the Supreme Court established a "one person, one vote" criterion for legislative representation in the 1960s. People may adjust some of their behavioral responses to meet the decision's requirements while they have other, less visible, behavioral responses that may more truly reflect their unwillingness to accept the decision. Conversely, acceptors may for reasons of inertia never fully adjust their behavioral responses to a new judicial policy.

Changes in policy often entail changes in rules or formal directives within an organization. But at the day-to-day level, norms, informal understandings, or even behavioral habits within an organization may set the tone. Public and private employers may, for example, adopt formal policies prohibiting sexual harassment, but many informally tolerate violations of those policies. Policy changes may also include changes in organizational structure or function. . . . [The] delivery of [health care services related to abortion] changed after *Roe v. Wade* to the extent that currently most [abortion services] are provided by clinics, not hospitals.

Another type of behavioral response is the actions or inactions of those who consume the policy. Consumption decisions can be affected by the way the interpreting an implementing populations act. Consumers may respond to a court decision by using, ignoring, or avoiding it. For example, many lawyers do not advertise, even though the Supreme Court has ruled that they can do so (*Bates v. Arizona*, 1978). We must examine actual behavior, in addition to policy changes of corporations and agencies, if we are to better understand the consumption of judicial policies.

Feedback is another behavioral response to judicial policies. It is directed toward the originator of the policy or some other policy-making agency. The purpose of feedback behavior is usually to provide support for or make demands upon other political actors (including judges) regarding the judicial policy. Feedback is often communicated through interest groups or the media. Almost immediately after the Supreme Court announced its abortion decision, feedback in the form of letters to the justices began. Also, some members of Congress let the Court know of their displeasure with the abortion decision by introducing . . . [amendments to the Constitution] to overturn *Roe*. Manifestations of displeasure or support by various interest groups have been directed at the Court and other political institutions, such as Congress and state legislatures. In varying degrees, [these attempts at] feedback have led to modifications of the policy—as we can see in the Court's *Webster* and *Casey* decisions . . . allowing states greater leeway in regulating abortion.[2] . . .

> "[T]he largest proportion of stories about the Court's denials of certiorari could not be deemed ambiguous at all. Rather, they were clearly wrong."

14.2 TELEVISION NEWS AND THE SUPREME COURT: ALL THE NEWS THAT'S FIT TO AIR?

Elliot E. Slotnick and Jennifer A. Segal

Elliot E. Slotnick is Associate Dean of the Graduate School and Professor of Political Science at Ohio State University. Jennifer A. Segal is Assistant Professor of Political Science at the University of Kentucky.

If there is one area where the propensity for misreporting the Court's actions is most pronounced, that area would almost certainly be the media's relatively infrequent forays into reporting on the Court's docketing decisions and, in particular, its decision to not hear a case, the denial of certiorari. Indeed, when asked what television news did least well in its coverage of the Court, Supreme Court Public Information Officer Toni House bemoaned, "The cavalier attitude that they have about when we deny cert . . . which misleads people into thinking that we are ruling on things . . . I mean every time Dan Rather says, 'The Supreme Court today upheld . . .' I want to smack him. I pleaded with [CBS correspondents] Fred Graham and Rita Braver to stop him. He has got to know better. He's been around too long." . . .

The pronounced tendency of the media to misreport certiorari decisions has not gone unnoticed by the justices themselves. Indeed, Justice Ginsburg, for one, has written:

From Elliot E. Slotnick and Jennifer A. Segal, *Television News and the Supreme Court* (New York: Cambridge University Press, 1998), pp. 190–191; 193, 198–208.

[2] See Readings 8.1 (Webster) and 10.6 (Casey). —Eds.

Still too often, in my view, the press overstates the significance of an order denying review. Headlines, particularly, may be as misleading as they are eye-catching. For example, when we declined to review a decision of the Illinois Supreme Court in what has come to be known as the "Baby Richard" case, one headline read: "Controversial Illinois Adoption Rule Upheld: Without Comment, Supreme Court Affirms Biological Father's Right to 'Baby Richard.'" And when we declined to hear a constitutional challenge to a curfew for minors in Dallas, Texas, a headline reported: "High Court Appears to Uphold Curfews."

* * *

On the Meaning of Certiorari Denials

Developing examples of mischaracterizations of Court actions such as certiorari decisions would not be significant if the media were not the major source of public information about the Court or if, indeed, decisions on certiorari were generally tantamount to definitive decisions on the merits with widespread precedential value. The dominance of the media, however, particularly television, in informing people of the Court's work has been well documented. Katsh has noted that most people claim to receive all of their information from television, while Iyengar and Kinder have argued, "As television has moved to the center of American life, TV news has become Americans' single most important source of information about political affairs." Clearly, . . . "Public awareness of Supreme Court decisions depends heavily on the quality of coverage provided by the mass media."

Answering the question of whether the Court's decision to not hear a case has substantive meaning is somewhat more difficult, and, indeed, persuasive arguments have been made on both sides of the question. In a technical and legal sense, of course, all that a certiorari denial means is that the Supreme Court, utilizing its appellate discretion, has refused to hear a case, thereby leaving a lower court decision and its immediate holding undisturbed. This formal view of certiorari denial suggests that the Court, in not hearing the case, has not given any indication whatsoever of where it stands on the merits of the lower court judgment or on the issues involved. Consequently, the lower court decision carries no broad legal precedential or policy significance.

Many justices and commentators have consistently and aggressively insisted that this minimalist perspective on the meaning of decisions not to decide is, indeed, an accurate one. Felix Frankfurter argued the position most frequently and in greatest detail. At the most general level, Frankfurter noted that "a denial no wise implies agreement" with a lower court decision. Rather, "it simply means that fewer than four members of the Court deemed it desirable to review a decision of the lower court as a matter 'of sound judicial discretion.'" . . . [3]

Nevertheless, many analysts and jurists continue to dispute this minimalist interpretation of certiorari denials, often taking as their starting point additional words in Justice Jackson's *Brown v. Allen* (1953) concurrence: "Some say denial

---

[3] We discuss the certiorari process in Chapter 13. —Eds.

means nothing; others say it means nothing much. Realistically, the first position is untenable and the second is unintelligible. . . . The fatal sentence that in real life writes finis to many causes cannot in legal theory be a complete blank.". . .

Television Coverage of Certiorari Decisions in the 1989–1990 Term

. . . We have isolated for analysis all network newscast stories from the Court's October 1989 term that were, in fact, focused on docketing decisions, whether or not they were characterized in that fashion by the newscast. In the analysis that follows we will assess both the nature and the magnitude of television's propensity to misreport the Court's certiorari decisions.

. . . [T]he stories were coded according to the Court's actual action in the case at hand (whether it granted or denied certiorari); how the network portrayed the Court's action (whether certiorari was granted or denied or whether the case was treated as a decision on the merits); whether the network projected any policy motivation, direction, or implications from the Court's action; and how definitive the Court's action actually was. This information was crucial in assessing the nature of the networks' coverage of the Court's docketing decisions during the term examined here. Our analysis demonstrated that while the networks' reporting of grants of certiorari was, for the most part, accurate, reporting of the Court's denials of certiorari was considerably more problematic.

Of the forty-two stories on docketing decisions broadcast by the three networks on their evening news programs, thirteen (31.0 percent) covered the Court's granting of certiorari (see Table 14.1). Nine of these stories (69.2 percent) reported on three different cases involving important, controversial issues. These cases centered on flag burning, discrimination against women of childbearing age in work involving hazardous chemicals, and abortion counseling. Each of these certiorari grants was reported by each of the networks, with only [the flag-burning case] actually decided on the merits in the October 1989 term.

TABLE 14.1 Network Newscast Presentation of Docketing Decisions, 1989 Term (Percentages in Parentheses)

| | Supreme Court Docketing Decision | |
	Certiorari grant	Certiorari denial
Number of stories	13	29
Number of cases	7	18
Presented as cert grant	13 (100)	0
Presented as cert denial	0	7 (24.1)
Presented ambiguously	0	8 (27.6)
Presented as merits decision	0	14 (48.3)
Presented "accurately"	13 (100)	7 (24.1)

The remaining four stories focused on four other grants, each reported by only one of the three networks. They involved issues of mandatory life sentencing without the possibility of parole for those in possession of specified amounts of cocaine, a search-and-seizure case involving the establishment of road blocks to catch drunk drivers, a federalism question centering on state control of the deployment of national guard troops, and a trial procedure question of whether an alleged child abuser has the right to face his or her accuser.

Obviously, these cases represent only a small proportion of those that were actually granted certiorari during the 1989–1990 term. Such sparse coverage is not at all surprising, however, as stories on the Court's docketing decisions, particularly the granting of certiorari as distinct from a controversial denial, will generally be less newsworthy and television friendly than a report on a dramatic (and predictably scheduled) oral argument or an emotionally laden and divisive Supreme Court ruling. Television reporters covering the Court today do not have the Court as their sole assignment and, consequently, do not have sufficient time to invest in studying the Court's docketing decisions, which would be necessary to flesh out more than the occasional and seemingly compelling certiorari story, particularly in a setting where such a story would face substantial barriers to getting on the air. As noted by NBC's Pete Williams, "it just depends on how big the case is. I mean the term limits case we covered every step of the way. We covered it when they granted cert, we covered it when it was argued, we covered it when it was decided." Generally, however, the television Court reporter lacks the luxury of paying much attention to the Court's docketing choices. . . .

As one would expect, the stories that did address certiorari grants received very little airtime or prominence in the network newscasts. Ten of the stories were thirty seconds or less, and twelve were presented after the newscast's first commercial break. Only two stories, both about the abortion counseling case, included considerable substantive information such as the identification of the litigants or interested groups, the case facts, and the case history. Nearly half of the stories (six) offered absolutely no such substantive information, with the remainder including bits and pieces of information. Thus, despite the importance of many of the issues that were the subject of these cases, stories covering their certiorari grants were not very substantial.

Nevertheless, and of primary importance to this analysis, all thirteen of these certiorari grant stories reported accurately the Court's decision to review the case at issue. Language such as the Court agreed to "decide," "take up," "take on," make "a quick ruling," "review," "hear arguments," and "consider" made the action in the Court's decision to grant certiorari quite clear. The same, however, is far from true for the stories covering the Court's denials of certiorari, the focus of the remainder of this analysis.

Twenty-nine of the forty-two stories (69.0 percent) focusing on the Court's docketing decisions concerned the decision to deny certiorari. . . . The certiorari denial stories fell broadly into four issue areas: equal protection, privacy, abortion, and the First Amendment. The greatest number of stories (10, 34.5 percent) was about abortion-related cases, despite the fact that these cases constituted only four of the eighteen. These four cases concerned Operation Rescue blockades and demonstrations in Atlanta and New York, the use of racketeering laws to sue antichoice groups, and the legitimacy of tax exemptions for the Roman Catholic Church when it has engaged in antichoice lobbying.

Cases involving the issue of equal protection, including gender discrimination in a Maryland country club, the rights of homosexuals in the armed services, school programs for handicapped children, and an affirmative action suit by Gulf Oil employees were the focus of six stories. Five stories centered on privacy concerns, including three cases about random drug testing, one about seat belt laws, and another about cordless phones. The First Amendment was the focus of two cases that were covered in three stories, two about school dances in a public high school and the other about the sinking of the Greenpeace ship, Rainbow Warrior. Finally, three other cases were the focus of five stories, three about a case that proposed the reevaluation of the trust fund established for the victims of the Dalkon Shield, a faulty birth control device, one about a case involving disputed water rights in Wyoming, and one about a case questioning the immunity from liability for caseworkers involved in the placement of children in foster-care homes.

Thus, the eighteen certiorari denials reported on involved some of the most contentious political issues of the day, particularly as they related to the abortion, equal protection, and privacy domains. This is not surprising since such issues allowed for interesting television stories and were likely to be attractive to the most television viewers. Nevertheless, it must be underscored that these eighteen certiorari denials constituted a minute proportion (substantially less than 1 percent) of the total number of denials made by the Court during its 1989–1990 term ($n = 4,705$) and, by no means, could they be considered broadly representative of all matters the Court chose not to hear. Thus, not surprisingly, viewers were exposed to very select types of cases that were denied certiorari, and they were exposed to only a very few of them.

As was the case in the stories covering the granting of certiorari, almost all of the certiorari denial stories were quite short and not prominently placed in the broadcast. . . . [Moreover,] none of the networks did a very thorough or accurate job in presenting a picture of what the Court had actually done.

Indeed, inaccuracy in the newscasts' characterization of the Court's action is clearly the most important deficiency of these stories. In contrast to the stories about grants of certiorari, most of the stories about certiorari denials (22, 75.9 percent) were coded as fundamentally inaccurate or, at best, misleading or ambiguous in reporting what the Court had done. In nearly half of the certiorari denial stories (14, 48.3 percent), the Court's actions were blatantly misreported as decisions on the merits rather than as denials of certiorari. In eight additional stories (27.6 percent), the terminology used was sufficiently ambiguous to cause the viewer considerable difficulty in determining whether a merits decision had been made or cert had been denied. (In our own coding of these instances, it was only after extensive investigation that we could determine that the cases that were the subject of these "ambiguous" reports were, indeed, denials of certiorari.) Only seven of the twenty-nine stories about denials of certiorari

(24.1 percent) were reported clearly and accurately as Supreme Court decisions not to hear a case! . . .

Ambiguous Language

Ambiguous language such as "refused to overturn" was used in a number of stories including one about the ban on homosexuals in the military. As ABC's [Peter] Jennings stated, "in Washington, the Supreme Court has refused to overturn the regulation that forbid acknowledged homosexuals from being members of the armed forces," language suggesting that the case had been heard by the Court and that an existing policy had been left in place (2/26/90). [Tom] Brokaw used similar terminology in NBC's story on the same case (2/26/90).

In a story about the Dalkon Shield settlement, CBS's Dan Rather reported that "the U.S. Supreme Court turned down the last major challenge and cleared the way today for a $2.5 billion dollar settlement for women injured by the Dalkon Shield birth control device" (11/6/89). The Court's action in a random drug-testing case was also misreported when Rather stated:

> The U.S. Supreme Court today gave qualified approval for random drug testing among government workers in sensitive jobs. The Supreme Court turned down appeals from Justice Department employees and civilian army counselors (1/22/90).

In this instance, imprecise characterization of the Court's action is linked with the assertion of a substantive direction in the Court's holding, thereby compounding the problem.

In reporting this same case quite similarly, NBC's Brokaw stated that, "mandatory drug laws got another vote of confidence today from the Supreme Court. Without comment, the Court rejected challenges to two testing programs for justice Department employees with top security clearance and for the Army's civilian drug counselors" (1/22/90). Finally, when reporting on a petition by a pro-choice group to take away the tax-exempt status of the Roman Catholic Church, Rather stated, "Justices, without comment, killed a lawsuit by an abortion rights group" (4/30/90).

These examples illustrate some of the language that we conservatively (and, we feel, generously) characterized as ambiguous or misleading for this analysis, that was used in many of the stories about the Court's decisions to deny certiorari. While phrases such as "turned down," "refused to overturn," "rejected challenges," and "killed a lawsuit" may have appeared to professionally trained ears as indirect or imprecise ways of describing certiorari denials, such a characterization would not likely be drawn by an average television newscast consumer. It is much more likely that the typical viewer of the evening's news would interpret this language to mean that the Court had heard a case and rendered a substantive judgment. (Even we, as noted previously, had difficulty determining from such news stories what type of action the Court had taken and several errors were made in our initial coding.) In the most positive light, then, the networks failed to portray clearly and accurately the Court's action in these stories.

Blatant Error

Most important, the largest proportion of stories about the Court's denials of certiorari could not be deemed ambiguous at all. Rather, they were clearly wrong. The most frequently used word to characterize the Court's action in such stories was upheld. In reporting on the Court's decision to deny certiorari to the petition challenging a ban on dances in public schools, Brokaw reported that "the Court upheld a ban on dances in the public schools of Purdy, Missouri, where many people are Southern Baptists who believe that dancing is sinful and satanic" (4/16/90). On April 30, Brokaw stated in a story about one of the cases of random drug testing that "the Court upheld random drug testing of thousands of air traffic controllers and other Transportation Department employees in safety-related jobs." The clear implication of these and other stories was that the Court had made a decision on the merits of the cases rather than denying them certiorari.

Other reports included the equally misleading and erroneous words ruled or ruling, stating clearly that a decision had been made. Bob Schieffer of CBS News, when reporting on a case regarding special education programs in public schools for handicapped children, stated that "in effect, today's ruling means that these schools must keep trying to find programs that will help these children" (11/27/89). Similarly, when explaining the Court's action in the aforementioned case involving dances in public schools, Brokaw reported, "the U.S. Supreme Court ruled today on an issue that most youngsters in this country say is a fundamental right: the school dance" (4/16/90).

Somewhat different, yet similarly misguided, language was used in other stories. When reporting on the case of the sinking of Greenpeace's Rainbow Warrior, Rather stated, "the Supreme Court today refused to force the U.S. Central Intelligence Agency to release documents on the 1985 sinking of the Rainbow Warrior" (2/26/90). Jennings, in ABC's coverage of the public school dances case, reported that "the Supreme Court has left in place a law that bans a high school in . . . Missouri from holding school dances" (4/16/90). And in the case involving the attempt to revoke the Roman Catholic Church's tax-exempt status, Jennings reported, "the Court . . . rejected an effort to strip the Catholic Church of its tax-exempt status" (4/30/90).

Another variant of the misreporting of a certiorari denial came in a setting where the Court's inaction was linked to its definitive ruling in a prominent case (*Baltimore City Department of Social Services v. Bouknight*) that was part of our leading case sample for 1989–1990. The Bouknight case was covered at all three decision stages by CBS News. When the merits ruling in Bouknight was reported in a lengthy (about two and a half minutes) piece on decision day, Dan Rather described another "related" Supreme Court action (*Babcock, By and Through Babcock v. Tyler*) at the end of the piece: "In another child abuse case today, the Supreme Court let stand a ruling that public social workers may not be sued when children suffer abuse in court-approved foster homes" (2/20/90). Babcock was, however, simply a certiorari denial, and, we should add, the *Bouknight* case itself was a Fifth Amendment self-incrimination ruling where the legal issue did not deal with the issue of child abuse per se.

Each of these examples illustrates the extent to which network newscasts can be misleading in their reporting of the Court's actions. Television viewers were very likely to believe that the Court had made decisions on the merits in each case when, in fact, the justices had actually denied certiorari in each of these cases except, of course, *Bouknight.*

Perhaps the most blatant misreporting of certiorari denials during the 1989–1990 term occurred in the stories about the demonstrations and protest activities of the antiabortion group Operation Rescue. On May 14, 1990, both ABC and CBS reported on the Court's refusal to hear the group's assertion that blocking access to abortion clinics in Atlanta, Georgia, was protected by the First Amendment's guarantee of free speech. Ted Koppel of ABC introduced the story by reporting that "before the Supreme Court a defeat today for the antiabortion group Operation Rescue. The Court said that a claim of free speech does not give them the right to block access to abortion clinics in Atlanta, Georgia.". . .

CBS's coverage of this case was, perhaps, even more misleading. Schieffer reported:

> The Supreme Court split five to four today and upheld a ban on antiabortion demonstrators who tried to block entrances to Atlanta abortion clinics. The Court rejected the demonstrators' arguments that they were just exercising free speech.

Beyond using the words *upheld* and *rejected* . . . arguments, all of which imply that the Court made a substantive decision, Schieffer's report included the outcome of a vote taken by the justices. By reporting the vote, it appeared (even to us) that the justices had made a decision on the merits. After extensive but unsuccessful searching for such a decision, we found evidence indicating that the vote was actually taken to determine whether an application by Operation Rescue for a stay should be granted. By a vote of five to four, the application was denied.

If this was not confusing enough, a week later (5/21/90) each of the three networks aired stories about Operation Rescue's activities in New York. In this instance the presentation of the litigation setting, which was, indeed, a certiorari denial, was quite problematic. Further, the stories included erroneous references to the earlier Atlanta case, treating it as if a merits decision had been made. For instance, Jennings reported:

> There has been a second legal defeat at the Supreme Court for the antiabortion group Operation Rescue. The justices today agreed with lower courts, which ruled the Operation Rescue pickets may not block access to abortion clinics in New York. Last week the Court made a similar ruling for clinics in Atlanta.

CBS's explanation of the Court's action went even farther down an erroneous road. The opening visual headline for the evening's newscast was, "The Supreme Court Bans Abortion Clinic Blockades"—not the best of beginnings! Dan Rather introduced the story by reporting:

> The U.S. Supreme Court approved new limits today on protests by antiabortion groups. The justices upheld a permanent ban on demonstrators who physically

try to block entrances to abortion clinics. Today's ruling was on a case from New York.

In an expansive follow-up report, [CBS's] Rita Braver repeated the problematic reference to the Atlanta case stating that "last week the Court voted five to four to allow a temporary ban against Operation Rescue to stand in Atlanta. But today's action is considered even more significant because it involves a permanent ban and can have an impact on similar cases now under way in other states."

Elaborating on the seeming implications of the "case," Braver opined, "the Supreme Court action is bad news for Operation Rescue. . . . Abortion rights activists call it a victory for them." Confirmatory interviews were then conducted with spokespersons for the Legal Defense Fund of NOW and the Feminist Women's Health Centers.

For NBC, Tom Brokaw reported that "today, the U.S. Supreme Court upheld the ban on [blocking entrances to abortion clinics] by Operation Rescue in the New York City area. Last week, the Court let stand a similar ban against the group in Atlanta."

These five stories about two abortion-related cases sharply illustrate the extent to which the network news programs may misreport the activities of the Court. Both cases were, at some level, denied review by the Supreme Court, yet the stories that aired about them gave the distinct impression that the Court had made a decision on the merits in each case. This impression was further substantiated for the Atlanta case by subsequent references in the stories about the New York case. Moreover, in addition to mischaracterizing certiorari denials as merits decisions, these examples also demonstrate that network newscasts may unjustifiably draw broad policy implications from the Court's certiorari action. Anyone viewing these stories (as well as the other seventeen that we have characterized as reported ambiguously, at best, or as merits decisions at worst), regardless of which channel they were watching and how knowledgeable they were about the Court, would have likely misperceived the nature of the action the Court had taken and its public policy implications. . . .

". . . to promulgate jurisdiction in the abstract is meaningless."

14.3 BAKER V. CARR

369 U.S. 186 (1962)

Justice Felix Frankfurter's plurality opinion in Colegrove v. Green *(1946) warned that courts would enter a "political thicket" if they tried to settle disputes over legislative districting. Sixteen years later, when* Baker v. Carr *(Reading 6.3) held that legislative apportionment presented questions appropriate for judicial determination, Frankfurter again predicted dire consequences.*

MR. JUSTICE FRANKFURTER, whom MR. JUSTICE HARLAN joins, dissenting.

The Court today reverses a uniform course of decision established by a dozen cases, including one by which the very claim now sustained was unanimously rejected only five years ago. The impressive body of rulings thus cast aside reflected the equally uniform course of our political history regarding the relationship between population and legislative representation—a wholly different matter from denial of the franchise to individuals because of race, color, religion or sex. Such a massive repudiation of the experience of our whole past in asserting destructively novel judicial power demands a detailed analysis of the role of this Court in our constitutional scheme. Disregard of inherent limits in the effective exercise of the Court's "judicial Power" not only presages the futility of judicial intervention in the essentially political conflict of forces by which the relation between population and representation has time out of mind been and now is determined. It may well impair the Court's position as the ultimate organ of "the supreme Law of the Land" in that vast range of legal problems, often strongly entangled in popular feeling, on which this Court must pronounce. The Court's authority—possessed neither of the purse nor the sword—ultimately rests on sustained public confidence in its moral sanction. Such feeling must be nourished by the Court's complete detachment, in fact and in appearance, from political entanglements and by abstention from injecting itself into the clash of political forces in political settlements.

A hypothetical claim resting on abstract assumptions is now for the first time made the basis for affording illusory relief for a particular evil even though it foreshadows deeper and more pervasive difficulties in consequence. The claim is hypothetical and the assumptions are abstract because the Court does not vouchsafe the lower courts—state and federal—guidelines for formulating specific, definite, wholly unprecedented remedies for the inevitable litigations that today's umbrageous disposition is bound to stimulate in connection with politically motivated reapportionments in so many States. In such a setting, to promulgate jurisdiction in the abstract is meaningless. It is devoid of reality as "a brooding omnipresence in the sky" for it conveys no intimation what relief, if any, a District Court is capable of affording that would not invite legislatures to play ducks and drakes with the judiciary. For this Court to direct the District Court to enforce a claim to which the Court has over the years consistently found itself required to deny legal enforcement and at the same time to find it necessary to withhold any guidance to the lower court how to enforce this turnabout, new legal claim, manifests an odd—indeed an esoteric—conception of judicial propriety. One of the Court's supporting opinions, as elucidated by commentary, unwittingly affords a disheartening preview of the mathematical quagmire (apart from divers judicially inappropriate and elusive determinants), into which this Court today catapults the lower courts of the country without so much as adumbrating the basis for a legal calculus as a means of extrication. Even assuming the indispensable intellectual disinterestedness on the part of judges in such matters, they do not have accepted legal standards or criteria or even reliable analogies to draw upon for making judicial judgments. To charge courts with the task of accommodating the incommensurable factors of policy that underlie these mathematical puzzles is to attribute, however flatteringly, omnicompetence to judges. The Framers of the

Constitution persistently rejected a proposal that embodied this assumption and Thomas Jefferson never entertained it.

Recent legislation, creating a district appropriately described as an atrocity of ingenuity," is not unique. Considering the gross inequality among legislative electoral units within almost every State, the Court naturally shrinks from asserting that in districting at least substantial equality is a constitutional requirement enforceable by courts. Room continues to be allowed for weighting. This of course implies that geography, economics, urban-rural conflict, and all the other nonlegal factors which have throughout our history entered into political districting are to some extent not to be ruled out in the undefined vista now opened up by review in the federal courts of state reapportionments. To some extent—aye, there's the rub. In effect, today's decision empowers the courts of the country to devise what should constitute the proper composition of the legislatures of the fifty states. If state courts should for one reason or another find themselves unable to discharge this task, the duty of doing so is put on the federal courts or on this Court, if state views do not satisfy this Court's notion of what is proper districting.

We were soothingly told at the bar of this Court that we need not worry about the kind of remedy a court could effectively fashion once the abstract constitutional right to have courts pass on a state-wide system of electoral districting is recognized as a matter of judicial rhetoric, because legislatures would heed the Court's admonition. This is not only an euphoric hope. It implies a sorry confession of judicial impotence in place of a frank acknowledgment that there is not under our Constitution a judicial remedy for every political mischief, for every undesirable exercise of legislative power. The Framers carefully and with deliberate forethought refused so to enthrone the judiciary. In this situation, as in others of like nature, appeal for relief does not belong here. Appeal must be to an informed, civically militant electorate. In a democratic society like ours, relief must come through an aroused popular conscience that sears the conscience of the people's representatives. In any event there is nothing judicially more unseemly nor more self-defeating than for this Court to make in terrorem pronouncements, to indulge in merely empty rhetoric, sounding a word of promise to the ear, sure to be disappointing to the hope.

"Government requires comity and cooperation among the branches."

14.4 LEGISLATIVE VETOES, PHOENIX STYLE

Louis Fisher

Louis Fisher is a specialist in American national government in the
Congressional Research Service of the Library of Congress

[In] June [1983] the U.S. Supreme Court supposedly sounded the death knell for
the legislative veto, a key tool used by Congress for decades to control the executive branch. The broadness of *INS v. Chadha* seemed to strip Congress of every
variety of legislative veto: two- house, one-house, and committee.

Legislators must now search for substitutes to satisfy the court's belief that
the Framers intended a "finely wrought and exhaustively considered" process
for making law. Instead of using "shortcuts" like the legislative veto, Congress
is supposed to act with full deliberation, including action by both houses and
presentation of a bill or joint resolution to the president for his signature or veto.

Developments since *Chadha* suggest a different conclusion. Congress will
continue to exercise close control over the agencies, but these controls are unlikely to run the gauntlet of the full legislative process. Informal and nonstatutory ways of doing business, perfected over the years by committees and
agencies, will persist and probably flourish.

Is this defiance of the Supreme Court? In a way. But a better explanation is
that the court reached too far and did not take into account accommodations
that have been mutually beneficial to legislators and executive officials. It is unrealistic to think that a single decision, even by the Supreme Court, will eliminate executive-legislative agreements established over the years.

Part of Congress' response to *Chadha* has been to review statutes that contain legislative vetoes and make them conform to the Court's ruling. One-house
and two-house legislative vetoes are being deleted and replaced by joint resolutions. This has been the approach with the Foreign Assistance Act, the Export
Administration Act, the D.C. Home Rule Bill, Amtrak legislation, the Consumer
Product Safety Commission, and the War Powers Resolution.

Joint resolutions are a tempting substitute, a quick way to "doctor" statutes
tainted by the legislative veto. However, a joint resolution of disapproval weak-
ens congressional control over the power it delegates. Congress cannot be expected to pass joint resolutions to stop every agency action it dislikes. The
workload is too great, and if the president vetoed the joint resolution, members

Reprinted with permission from *Extensions*, a publication of the Carl Albert Congressional Research
and Studies Center, Spring 1984. All rights reserved.

would have to forge a two-thirds majority irk each house to override him. Why should Congress produce an extraordinary majority to recapture authority it delegated by majority vote?

On the other hand, a joint resolution of approval shifts the advantage to Congress. The president would have to secure congressional approval within a specific number of days. The results may be ironic. Prior to *Chadha*, it took a two-house legislative veto to disapprove a major arms sale. If Congress now insists on a joint resolution of approval for major sales, they would be "vetoed" if either house refused its support. The administration would face not a two-house but a one-house veto.

Congress has many informal ways of controlling executive agencies. With or without the blessing of the Supreme Court, congressional committees and subcommittees will exercise a veto power over agency actions. And agencies will acquiesce because in return for this level of congressional scrutiny they receive important grants of discretionary power and program flexibility.

It may come as a surprise to some observers in town that Congress has continued to enact legislative vetoes after the *Chadha* decision. Are they constitutional? Not by the court's definition. Will that fact change the behavior between committees and agencies? Probably not. An agency might advise the committee: "As you know, the requirement in this statute for committee prior-approval is unconstitutional under the Court's test." Perhaps agency and committee staff will nod their heads in agreement. After which the agency will seek the prior approval of the committee.

Statutes in the future may rely more heavily on "notification" to committees before an agency acts. Notification does not raise a constitutional issue since it falls within the report-and-wait category already sanctioned by prior Court rulings. But notification can become a code word for committee prior-approval. Only in highly unusual situations will an agency defy a committee or subcommittee.

Agencies know that harsh penalties await them if they ignore review committees. Certainly we see this pattern over the last three to four decades with regard to reprogramming. As an informal accommodation between the branches, agencies are allowed to shift funds within an appropriation account provided they obtain committee approval for major changes. *Chadha* does not affect these nonstatutory legislative vetoes. They existed in the past and will persist in the future, perhaps in even greater number because of the court's decision. They are not legal in effect. They are, however, in effect legal.

Internal congressional rules are another substitute for the legislative veto. In the 1950s, President Eisenhower objected to statutory provisions that required agencies to "come into agreement" with committees before implementing an administrative action. Congress changed the procedure so that funds could be appropriated for a project only after authorizing committees passed a resolution of approval. The Justice Department accepted the committee resolution as a valid form of action because it was directed at Congress (the Appropriations Committees) rather than the executive branch.

The House of Representatives may also want to rewrite its rule governing limitations (riders) on appropriations bills, making it easier to add them during floor action. Riders allow Congress to veto agency actions simply by denying funds. Since a president would seldom veto an appropriations bill because of an offensive rider, the practical effect is at least a two-house veto. Because of House/Senate accommodations, the result in many cases is a one-house veto.

The Court treated a complex issue in simple terms. The unfortunate effect is to convey to the country an impression of government that does not, and cannot, exist in practice. We should not be too surprised or disconcerted if, after the Court closed the door to the legislative veto, we heard a number of windows being raised and perhaps new doors constructed, making the executive-legislative structure as accommodating as before for shared power. It may not be a house of aesthetic quality and certainly does not resemble the neat model envisioned by the Supreme Court, but it will go a long way in meeting the basic needs of executive agencies and congressional committees. Government requires comity and cooperation among the branches. Part of this will depend on legislative vetoes in one form or another.[4]

"Brown and its progeny stand for the proposition that courts are impotent to further the interests of the relatively disadvantaged."

14.5 THE HOLLOW HOPE: CAN COURTS GENERATE SOCIAL CHANGE?

Gerald N. Rosenberg

Gerald N. Rosenberg is Associate Professor of Political Science at the University of Chicago.

... [According to] legal historian Michael Klarman, "constitutional lawyers and historians generally deem *Brown v. Board of Education* to be the most important U.S. Supreme Court decision of the twentieth century, and possibly of all time."' The question I address is whether the decision in *Brown* made the contribution to American society that this comment suggests. In asking this question, I mean

---

From Gerald N. Rosenberg, "African-American Rights after *Brown*," 24 *Journal of Supreme Court History* (1999): 201, which provides a summary of his argument in *The Hollow Hope*, along with some new thoughts.

[4] By March, 1985, Fisher reported, "In the sixteen months between Chadha and the end of the 98th Congress, fifty-three legislative vetoes (generally the committee-veto variety) have been enacted into law in eighteen different statutes." Fisher believes that "the Court's prestige has been damaged by a decision that was broader than necessary and unpersuasive in reasoning." By the end of 1998, "the list of new legislative vetoes," according to Fisher, "had increased to more than four hundred." —Eds.

to disparage no one. Civil rights lawyers [such as] Thurgood Marshall, Jack Greenberg, and countless others dedicated their careers, and sometimes their lives, to a principled belief in justice for all. My question does not challenge their commitment [or] their principles. It does ask whether litigation was the right strategic choice to further their goals, whether their understanding of the strengths and weaknesses of courts as agents of social change was subtle enough to guide them to the best strategy for change.

Underlying this question about *Brown* is a broader question about the role of the Supreme Court in the larger society. Since the mid-twentieth century, there has been a belief that courts can act to further the interests of the relatively disadvantaged. Starting with civil rights and spreading to issues raised by women's groups, environmental groups, political reformers, and others, American courts seemingly have become important producers of political and social change. Cases such as *Brown* and *Roe v. Wade* are heralded as having produced major change. Further, such litigation has often occurred, and appears to have been most successful, when the other branches of government have failed to act. Indeed, for many, part of what makes American democracy exceptional is that it includes the world's most powerful court system, protecting minorities and defending liberty in the face of opposition from the democratically elected branches. Americans look to activist courts, then, as fulfilling an important role in the American scheme.

Courts, many also believe, can bring heightened legitimacy to an issue. Courts deal with rights. Judges, at their best, are not politically beholden nor partisan. Rather, they are independent and principled, deciding not what policy they want but rather what the Constitution requires. This gives judicial decisions a moral legitimacy that is missing from the actions of the other branches. Court decisions can remind Americans of our highest aspirations and chide us for our failings. Courts, [Alexander] Bickel suggests, have the "capacity to appeal to men's better natures, to call forth their aspirations, which may have been forgotten in the moment's hue and cry." For Eugene Rostow, the "Supreme Court is, among other things, an educational body, and the Justices are inevitably teachers in a vital national seminar." Bickel agrees, viewing courts as "a great and highly effective educational institution." Courts, one commentator put it, can provide "a cheap method of pricking powerful consciences.". . .

Reasons for Caution

Before uncritically accepting this view of the Court as correct, there are at least three reasons to be skeptical. First, it is almost entirely lawyers who make this argument. Although lawyers may be no less self-critical than other professionals, they may be no more self-critical either. That is, they may have deep-seated psychological reasons for believing in the importance of the institutions in which they work. This may lead to overvaluing the contribution of the courts to furthering the interests of the relatively disadvantaged.

Second, there is an older view of the role of courts which sees them as much more constrained. Under this view, courts are the least able of any of the branches of government to produce change because they lack all of the necessary tools to do so. They are the "least dangerous branch" because they lack budgetary or coercive power. That courts are uniquely dependent on the executive branch is a view that was most forcefully argued over two hundred years ago by Alexander Hamilton in *Federalist* 78. Hamilton wrote: the judiciary "has no influence over either the sword or the purse; no direction either of the strength or of the wealth of the society, and can take no active resolution whatever. It may truly be said to have neither FORCE nor WILL but merely judgment of and must ultimately depend upon the aid of the executive arm even for the efficacy of its judgments." As President Jackson reportedly commented in response to *Worcester v. Georgia*, a decision with which he disagreed, "[Chief Justice] John Marshall has made his decision, now let him enforce it." This view suggests that Court decisions furthering the interests of the relatively disadvantaged will only be implemented when the other branches are willing to do so.

The third reason for skepticism about the role of courts as producers of progressive change comes from several decades of public opinion research. If courts are dependent on public and elite support for their decisions to be implemented, as Hamilton suggests, this requires both public knowledge of Court decisions and a public willingness to act based on them. Proponents of an activist, progressive Court assume this. According to one defender of the claim, "without the dramatic intervention of so dignified an institution as a court, which puts its own prestige and authority on the line, most middle-class Americans would not be informed about such grievances." However, decades of public opinion research paint a mixed picture, at best. In general, only about 40 percent of the American public report having read or heard something contemporary about the Court. . . . In 1973, 20 percent of respondents to a Harris poll identified the Court as a branch of Congress, as did 12 percent of respondents with college degrees. In a culture in which personality is important, the public, too, is quite ignorant of the Justices' identity. In a 1989 *Washington Post* poll, for example, 71 percent of 1,005 respondents could not name any Justice while only 2 percent could correctly name all nine. Somewhat humorously, while 9 percent named the distinguished Chief Justice of the United States (Rehnquist), a whopping 54 percent, six times as many respondents, correctly identified the somewhat less distinguished "judge of the television show 'The People's Court'" (Judge Wapner). The Supreme Court is not in the forefront of the consciousness of most Americans. . . .

The point of this discussion is that there are good reasons to be wary of claims that the Court can further the interests of the relatively disadvantaged. Lacking the power to implement their decisions, courts are dependent on other elite institutions and the public at large. And given the findings of the survey literature, this is not a comforting thought for those who believe in the efficacy of the courts to further the interests of the relatively disadvantaged. With this background in mind, I return to *Brown*.

Examining the effects of *Brown* raises questions of how to deal with complicated issues of causation. Because it is difficult to isolate the effects of court decisions from other events in furthering the interests of the relatively disadvantaged, special care is needed in specifying how courts can be effective. On a general level, one can distinguish two types of influence courts can exercise.

Court decisions may produce significant social reform through a judicial path that relies on the authority of the court. Alternatively, court influence can follow an extra-judicial path that invokes court powers of persuasion, legitimacy, and the ability to give salience to issues. Each of these possible paths of influence is different and requires separate analysis,

The judicial path of causal influence is straightforward. It focuses on the direct outcome of judicial decisions and examines whether the change required by the courts was made. In civil rights, for example, if a Supreme Court decision ordering an end to public segregation was the cause of segregation ending, then one would see lower courts ordering local officials to end segregation, those officials acting to end it, the community at large supporting it, and, most important, segregation actually ending,

Separate and distinct from judicial effects is the more subtle and complex causal claim of extra-judicial effects. Under this conception of causation, courts do more than simply change behavior in the short run. Court decisions may produce significant social reform by inspiring individuals to act or persuading them to examine and change their opinions. Court decisions, particularly Supreme Court decisions, may be powerful symbols, resources for change. They may affect the intellectual climate, the kinds of ideas that are discussed. The mere bringing of legal claims and the hearing of cases may influence ideas. Courts may produce significant social reform by giving salience to issues, in effect placing them on the political agenda. Courts may bring issues to light and keep them in the public eye when other political institutions wish to bury them. Thus, courts may make it difficult for legislators to avoid deciding controversial issues.

In 1954, in *Brown v. Board Education*, the U.S. Supreme Court found that state laws requiring race-based segregation in public elementary and secondary schools violated the Equal Protection Clause of the Fourteenth Amendment. Overturning nearly sixty years of Court-sanctioned racial segregation, *Brown* is heralded as one of the U.S. Supreme Court's greatest decisions. In particular, *Brown* is the paradigm of the Court's ability to protect rights and bring justice to minorities. To the human rights activist Aryeh Neier, *Brown* is the great "symbol" of courts' ability to protect rights and produce significant social reform." For Jack Greenberg, long-time civil rights litigator, *Brown* is the "principal inspiration to others" who seek change and the protection of rights through litigation."

Given the praise accorded to the *Brown* decision, examining its actual effects produces quite a surprise. The surprise is that a decade after *Brown* virtually nothing had changed for African-American students living in the eleven states of the former Confederacy that required race-based school segregation by law. For example, in the 1963–1964 school year, barely one in one hundred (1.2 percent) of these African-American children was in a nonsegregated school. That means that for nearly ninety-nine of every one hundred African-American children in the South a decade after *Brown*, the finding of a constitutional right changed nothing. A unanimous landmark Supreme Court decision had no effect on their lives. This raises the question of why there was no change.

The answer, in a nutshell, is that there was no political pressure to implement the decision and a great deal of pressure to resist it. On the executive level, there was little support for desegregation until the Johnson presidency. President Eisenhower steadfastly refused to commit his immense popularity or prestige in support of desegregation in general or *Brown* in particular. As Roy Wilkins, executive secretary of the National Association for the Advancement of Colored People (NAACP), put it, "if he had fought World War II the way he fought for civil rights, we would all be speaking German today." . . . Although President Kennedy was openly and generally supportive of civil rights, he took little concrete initiative in school desegregation and other civil rights matters until pressured by events to do so. He did not rank civil rights as a top priority and, like Eisenhower before him, was "unwilling to draw on the moral credit of his office to advance civil rights."

Civil rights were not supported by other national leaders until late in the Kennedy administration. In March 1956, Southern members of Congress, virtually without exception, signed a document entitled a "Declaration of Constitutional Principles," also known as the Southern Manifesto. Its 101 signers attacked the *Brown* decision as an exercise of "naked power" with "no legal basis." They pledged themselves to "use all lawful means to bring about a reversal of this decision which is contrary to the Constitution and to prevent the use of force in its implementation." This unprecedented attack on the Court demonstrated to all that pressure from Washington to implement the Court's decisions in civil rights would not be forthcoming.

If national political leaders set the stage for ignoring the courts, local politicians acted their part perfectly. A study of the 250 gubernatorial candidates in the Southern states from 1950 to 1973 revealed that after *Brown* "ambitious politicians, to put it mildly, perceived few incentives to advocate compliance." This perception was reinforced by Arkansas Governor Orval Faubus's landslide reelection in 1958, after he repeatedly defied court orders to prevent the desegregation of Central High School in Little Rock, demonstrating the "political rewards of conspicuously defying national authority." Throughout the South, governors and gubernatorial candidates called for defiance of court orders. Any individual or institution wishing to end segregation pursuant to court order, that is, to obey the law as mandated by the Supreme Court, would incur the wrath of state political leaders and quite possibly national ones. The best they could hope for was a lack of outright condemnation. Political support for desegregation was virtually nonexistent.

At the prodding of state leaders, state legislatures throughout the South passed a variety of prosegregation laws. By 1957, only three years after *Brown*, at least 136 new laws and state constitutional amendments designed to preserve segregation had been enacted. These ranged from depriving policemen of their retirement and disability if they failed to enforce the state's segregation laws (Georgia), to denying promotion or graduation to any student of a desegregated school (Louisiana), to simply making it illegal to attend a desegregated school (Mississippi) to Virginia's massive resistance including closing public schools, operating a tuition grant scheme, suspending compulsory attendance laws, and building private segregated schools. . . . As the Southern saying went, "as long we can legislate, we can segregate."

Along with opposition to desegregation from political leaders at all levels of government, there was hostility from many white Americans. Law and legal decisions operate in a given cultural environment, and the norms of that environment influence the decisions that are made and the impact they have. In the case of civil rights, decisions were announced in a culture in which slavery had existed and apartheid did exist. Institutions and social structures throughout America reflected a history of, if not a present commitment to, racial discrimination. Cultural barriers to civil rights had to be overcome before change could occur. And courts do not have the tools to do so. This is well illustrated in the decade after *Brown*.

One of the important cultural barriers to civil rights was the existence of private groups supportive of segregation. One type, represented by the Ku Klux Klan, White Citizens' Councils, and the like, existed principally to fight civil rights. Either through their own acts, or the atmosphere these groups helped create, violence against blacks and civil rights workers was commonplace throughout the South. . . . [C]ountless bombings and numerous murders occurred throughout the South. During the summer of 1964 in Mississippi alone there were thirty-five shootings, sixty-five bombings (including thirty-five churches), eighty beatings, and six murders. It was a brave soul indeed who worked to end segregation or implement court decisions. . . .

The cultural biases against civil rights that pervaded private groups also pervaded local governments. Court-ordered action may be fought or ignored on a local level, especially if there is no pressure from higher political leadership to follow the law and pressure from private groups not to. It was common to find, for example, that where bus companies followed the law and removed segregation signs in terminals, state and local officials put them back up. In the five Deep South states, as a matter of principle no school-board member or superintendent openly advocated compliance with the Supreme Court decision. And despite *Cooper v. Aaron*,[5] and the sending of troops to Little Rock in 1957, as of June 1963, only sixty-nine out of 7,700 students at the supposedly desegregated, "formerly" white, junior and senior high schools of Little Rock were black. Public resistance, supported by local political action, can almost always effectively defeat court-ordered civil rights.

In sum, in civil rights, court-ordered change confronted a culture opposed to that change. That being the case, the American judicial system, constrained by the need for both elite and popular support, constrained change.

---

[5] In light of *Brown*, Little Rock, Arkansas developed a plan for desegregating Central High School. A day before the plan was to go into effect, Arkansas Governor Orval Faubus ordered the state's national guard to prevent black students from entering the school. After a federal district court ruled against him, Faubus removed the guards but, because a threatening crowd had gathered around the school, the students still could not enter the building. This led President Eisenhower to send out federal troops to enforce the district court's order.

But this was not the end of the matter. After the district court granted a request made by city officials to delay desegregation for a 2 1/2 year period, the NAACP took the case, *Cooper v. Aaron*, to the U.S. Supreme Court. In an opinion signed by all nine members, the Court refused to allow delay.

The analysis above, however, omits one key institution and one key group: the judiciary, lawyers and their academic counterparts. The South, like the rest of the country, has both state and federal courts as well as lawyers. And the courts have a natural constituency in the American legal profession. Indeed, Justice Frankfurter believed that lawyers' support of the Court's decision in *Brown* would be decisive. As he put it in a letter to a friend, "it is the legal profession of the South on which our greatest reliance must be placed . . . because the lawyers of the South will gradually realize that there is a transcending issue, namely respect for law as determined so impressively by a unanimous court [in *Brown*]." But Justice Frankfurter was to be doubly disappointed; both Southern lawyers and elite lawyers and legal academics throughout the country condemned the case or offered only the most tepid support.

Lawyers and the Legal Profession

While there were undoubtedly some white Southern lawyers who supported the Court, they were few and far between. Opponents, in contrast, were everywhere. And surprisingly, opposition was voiced not merely by white Southerners but also by elite, Northern lawyers as well. A notable example was the American Bar Association (ABA), which is the nation's major professional legal organization. Politically neutral, it claims the legitimacy of professional expertise. However, in the wake of *Brown*, it lent the pages of its journal, the *ABA Journal*, to condemnation of *Brown*, from the vicious to the technical. It published only the most tepid, rule-of-law, defenses of the decision. Not once, in either editorials or articles, was there an argument that *Brown* was morally, constitutionally, or substantively correct. . . .

Elite legal academics also joined the fray. "[S]peaking the rhetoric of institutional legitimacy, a significant number of northeastern, white, liberal lawyers joined with white, southern, never-say-die segregationists in questioning the Court's authority and legitimacy in *Brown*." Although there was some support for the decision in law reviews immediately following *Brown*, it was found mostly in short pieces. In contrast, elite law reviews repeatedly blasted the Court. For example, the Harvard Law Review poured out a torrent of criticism, especially in its annual Forewords. *Brown* was criticized as poorly thought out, insufficient to support other cases, and unprincipled. The most important article was undoubtedly written by Herbert Wechsler, a law professor at Columbia University in New York City. Giving the Holmes Lecture at Harvard, and appearing as the Foreword to the 1959 *Harvard Law Review*, . . . [he criticized] *Brown* as unprincipled. *Brown* lacked a neutral principle, Wechsler argued, because separate but equal, if truly equal, was itself a neutral principle and there was no neutral way of deciding between it and equality. Wechsler's piece is the second most cited law review article in the period 1957 through March 1985! The popularity of his critique of *Brown* as unprincipled is a powerful indicator of the lack of support elite academic lawyers gave to *Brown*.

Local Courts

Judges seldom stepped in where politicians, lawyers, and the public at large were unwilling to go. The "fifty-eight lonely men" who served the federal judiciary in the South were being asked to dismantle a social system they had grown up with and of which they were a part. Even a judge as pro–civil-rights as John Minor Wisdom was sympathetic, finding it "not surprising that in a conservative community a federal judge may feel that he cannot jeopardize the respect due the court in all of his cases by vigorously supporting civil rights." Although there were some outstanding Southern federal judges such as J. Skelly Wright, John Minor Wisdom, Bryan Simpson, and Frank Johnson, there were also some who were not. For example, Judge Elliott (M. Dist. GA) stated that be did not want "pinks, radicals and black voters to outvote those who are trying to preserve our segregation laws." Judge Cox (S. Dist. Miss.), speaking from the Bench in March 1964, referred repeatedly to black voter-registration applicants in derogatory language (as "a bunch of niggers") who were "acting like a bunch of chimpanzees." It is important to note that both Judges Elliott and Cox were Kennedy appointees. . . .

On the state levels judges were even more biased. Chief Justice J. Edwin Livingston of the Alabama Supreme Court, speaking in 1959 to several hundred students and business leaders, announced: "I'm for segregation in every phase of life and I don't care who knows it. . . . I would close every school from the highest to the lowest before I would go to school with colored people." Alabama circuit judge Walter B. Jones wrote a column in the Montgomery Advertiser that he devoted to the "defense of white supremacy." In June 1958 he told readers that in the case against the NAACP, over which be was presiding, he intended to deal the NAACP a "mortal blow" from which it "shall never re-cover." It is no wonder, then, that despite clear Supreme Court rulings, Alabama was able to keep the NAACP in litigation for eight years and effectively inca-pacitated in the State. As Leon Friedman, who talked with scores of civil rights lawyers in the South, concluded, "the states' legal institutions were and are the principal enemy."

The use of the courts in the civil rights movement is considered the para-digm of a successful strategy for social change. Yet, a closer examination reveals that courts had virtually no direct effect on ending discrimination in education, Courageous and praiseworthy decisions were rendered, and nothing changed. *Brown* and its progeny stand for the proposition that courts are impotent to fur-ther the interests of the relatively disadvantaged. *Brown* is a paradigm, but for precisely the opposite view.

This, however, is not the end of the story. By the 1972–1973 school year, more than 91 percent of African-American children in the eleven states of the former Confederacy were in a nonsegregated school. Eighteen years after *Brown,* Southern school systems were desegregated. How did this occur?

Change came to Southern school systems in the wake of congressional and executive branch action. Title VI of the 1964 Civil Rights Act permitted the cut-off of federal funds to programs receiving federal monies where racial discrimi-nation was practiced, and the 1965 Elementary & Secondary Education Act provided a great deal of federal money to generally poor Southern school districts. By the 1971–1972 school year, for example, federal funds [constituted] from between 12 percent and 27.8 percent of Southern state school budgets, up from between 4.6 percent and 11.1 percent in the 1963–1964 school year. This combination of federal funding and Title VI gave the executive branch a tool to induce desegregation when it chose to do so. When the U.S. Department of Health, Education, and Welfare began to threaten fund cut-offs to school districts that refused to desegregate, dramatic change occurred. By the 1972–1973 school year, more than 91 percent of African-American school children in the eleven Southern states were in integrated schools, up from 1.2 percent in the 1963–1964 school year. With only the constitutional right in force in the 1963–1964 school year, no more that 5.5% percent of African-American children in any Southern state were in school with whites. By the 1972–1973 school year, when economic incentives were offered for desegregation, and costs imposed for failure to desegregate, in no Southern state were fewer than 80 percent of African-American children in integrated schools. School desegregation occurred in the years 1968–1972, then, because a set of conditions provided incentives for it and imposed costs for failing to desegregate. When those conditions were lacking, as in the first decade after *Brown*, constitutional rights were flouted. What a Court decision was unable to accomplish, federal dollars were able to achieve. The Supreme Court, acting alone, lacked the power to produce change.

Indirect Effects

The judicial path of influence is not the only way an institution can contribute to civil rights. By bringing an issue to light courts may put pressure on others to act, sparking change. Thus *Brown* and its progeny may have been the inspiration that eventually led to congressional and executive branch action and some success in civil rights. According to one commentator, "*Brown* set the stage for the ensuing rise in black political activism, for legal challenges to racial discrimination in voting, employment, and education, as well as for the creation of a favorable climate for the passage of the subsequent civil rights legislation and the initiation of the War on Poverty." Indeed, most commentators (and I assume most readers) believe this is the case and hold their belief with little doubt. As C. Herman Pritchett put it, "if the Court had not taken that first giant step in 1954, does anyone think there would now be a Civil Rights Act of 1964?"

In the next few pages I examine these claims. What evidence exists to substantiate them? How important was *Brown* to the civil rights struggle? In examining these questions, it must be noted that social scientists do not understand well enough the dynamics of influence and causation to state with certainty that the claims of Court influence (or any other causal claims) are right or wrong. Similarly, social scientists do not understand fully the myriad of factors that are involved in an individual's reaching a political decision. Ideas seem to have feet of their own, and tracking their footsteps is an imperfect science. Thus, even if I find little or no evidence of extra-judicial influence, it is simply impossible to state with certainty that the Court did not contribute in a significant way to civil rights. On the other hand, claims about the real world require evidence. Otherwise, they are merely statements of faith.

Turning to the specifics, I have tried to delineate the links that are necessary for the Court to have influenced civil rights by the extra-judicial path. The bottom line, the last link, is that the action of the President and Congress resulted in change. That is, the passage of the 1964 Civil Rights Act brought about change. . . . The key question, then, is the extent to which congressional and presidential action was a product of Court action.

One hypothesized link postulates that Court action gave civil rights prominence, putting it on the political agenda. Media coverage of civil rights over time could provide good evidence to assess this link. A second link, put quite simply, is that Court action influenced both the President and Congress to act. The Court, in other words, was able to pressure the other branches into dealing with civil rights. A third hypothesized link proposes that the Court favorably influenced white Americans in general about civil rights and they in turn pressured politicians. By bringing the treatment of black Americans to nationwide attention, the Court may have fomented change. A final hypothesized link suggests that the Court influenced black Americans to act in favor of civil rights and that this in turn influenced white political elites either directly or indirectly through influencing whites in general.

Salience

When the Supreme Court unanimously condemned segregation in 1954, it marked the first time since 1875 that one of the three branches of the federal government spoke strongly in favor of civil rights on a fundamental issue. The Court, it is claimed, put civil rights on the political agenda. "*Brown*," Neier writes, "launched the public debate over racial equality." One important way in which the political agenda is created is through the press. Thus, one way in which the Court may have given salience to civil rights is through inducing increased press coverage of it and balanced treatment of blacks. . . .

The most powerful way to determine if there was a sustained increase in press coverage of civil rights in response to *Brown* is to actually count press stories over time. The evidence shows that while press coverage of civil rights, as measured by the number of stories dealing with the issue in the *Readers' Guide to Periodical Literature*, increased moderately in 1954 over the previous year's total, by 1958 and 1959 coverage actually dropped below the level found in several of the years of the late 1940s and early 1950s! In addition, if one examines the magazines in America in the 1950s and early 1960s with the largest circulations, *Reader's Digest*, *Ladies Home Journal*, *Life*, and the *Saturday Evening Post*, the same general pattern again repeats. And it was not until 1962 that *TV Guide* ran a story having to do with civil rights. Thus, press coverage provides no evidence that the Court's decision gave civil rights salience for most Americans. . . .

There was one media outlet that gave enormous coverage to *Brown*: Voice of America! The decision was immediately translated into thirty-four languages and broadcast around the world. In poignant contrast, Universal Newsreels, the company that made news reports for movie theaters in the United States, never mentioned *Brown*.

In sum, press coverage of civil rights provides no evidence for the claim that the Court has important extra-judicial-effects claim. This finding is striking since *Brown* is virtually universally credited with having brought civil rights to national attention.

Elites

The extra-judicial-effects argument claims that the actions of the Supreme Court influenced members of Congress, the President, and the executive branch. The argument might be that because of the "deference paid by the other branches of government and by the American public" to the Supreme Court, its decisions prodded the other branches of the federal government into action. Further, the argument might run that the Court's actions sensitized elites to the legitimate claims of blacks. As Wilkinson puts it, "*Brown* was the catalyst that shook up Congress.

A sensible place to look for evidence of indirect effects is in the legislative history and debates over the 1957, 1960, and 1964 civil rights acts, and in presidential pronouncements on civil rights legislation. If Court action was crucial to congressional and presidential action, one might reasonably expect to find members of Congress and the President mentioning it as a reason for introducing and supporting civil rights legislation. While it is true that lack of attribution may only mean that the Court's influence was subtle, it would cast doubt on the force, if not the existence, of this extra-judicial effect.

At the outset, the case for influence is supported by the fact that civil rights bills were introduced and, for the first time since 1875, enacted in the years following *Brown*. While this makes it seem likely that *Brown* played an important role, closer examination of the impetus behind the civil rights acts of 1957, 1960, and 1964 does not support this seemingly reasonable inference. The 1957 and 1960 bills were almost entirely driven by electoral concerns. Republicans attempted to court Northern urban black voters and, at the same time, embarrass the Democrats by exposing the major rift between that party's Northern and Southern wings. The press and political opponents understood the bills as a response to electoral pressures, not to constitutional mandates.

The story of the 1964 act is similar in that there is no evidence of Court influence and a great deal of evidence for other factors, in this case the activities of the civil rights movement. The Kennedy administration offered no civil rights bill until February 1963 and the bill it offered then was "a collection of minor changes far more modest than the 1956 Eisenhower program." When a House subcommittee modified and strengthened the bill, Attorney General Robert Kennedy met with the members of the full Judiciary Committee in executive session and "criticized the subcommittee draft in almost every detail." It was not until the events of the spring of 1963 that the administration changed its thinking.

In Congress, there is little evidence that *Brown* played any appreciable role. The seemingly endless congressional debates, with some four million words uttered in the Senate alone, hardly touched on the case. References to *Brown* can be found on only a few dozen out of many thousands of pages of Senate debate. While much of the focus of the debate was on the constitutionality of the proposed legislation, and on the Fourteenth Amendment, the concern was not with how *Brown* mandated legislative action, or even how *Brown* made such a bill possible. Even in the debates over the fund cut-off provisions, *Brown* was seldom mentioned. . . . Thus, there does not appear to be evidence for the influence of *Brown* on legislative action.

Reviewing the public pronouncements of Presidents Eisenhower, Kennedy, and Johnson on civil rights legislation, I do not find the Court mentioned as a reason to act. Neither Eisenhower nor Kennedy committed the moral weight of their office to civil rights. When they did act, it was in response to violence or upcoming elections, not in response to Court decisions. While President Johnson spoke movingly and eloquently about civil rights, he did not mention Court decisions as an important reason for civil rights action. In his moving speeches to Congress and the nation in support of the 1964 Civil Rights Act and the 1965 Voting Rights Act he dwelt on the violence that peaceful black protesters were subjected to, the unfairness of racial discrimination, and the desire to honor the memory of President Kennedy. It was these factors that Johnson highlighted as reasons for supporting civil rights, not Court decisions.

In sum, I have not found the evidence necessary to make a case of clear attribution for the Court's effects on Congress or the President. Students of the Civil Rights Acts of 1957, 1960, and 1964 credit their introduction and passage to electoral concerns, or impending violence, not Court decisions. The extra-judicial-effects claim is not supported with Congress or the President.

Whites

The extra-judicial-effects thesis views courts as playing an important role in alerting Americans to social and political grievances. The view here is that the Supreme Court "pricked the conscience" of white America by pointing out both its constitutional duty and its shortcomings. "Except for *Brown*," Aryeh Neier contends, white Americans "would not have known about the plight of blacks under segregation." For this claim to hold, in order for courts to affect behavior, directly or indirectly, people must be aware of what the courts do. While this does not seem an onerous responsibility, I have shown earlier that most Americans have little knowledge about U.S. courts and pay little attention to them. The specific question this leaves unanswered is whether this holds true for a case such as *Brown*.

Surprisingly, and unfortunately, there appear to be no polls addressing awareness of *Brown*. There are, however, polls charting the reaction to *Brown* by Southerners over time. They show both very little support for desegregation and lessening support throughout the 1950s. By 1959, for example, support for desegregation actually dropped, with only 8 percent of white Southerners responding that they would not object, down from 15 percent in 1954.

If there is little evidence that *Brown* changed opinions about school desegregation in the South, perhaps it helped change white opinions more generally. It is clear that throughout the period from the beginning of the Second World War to the passage of the 1964 Act, whites became increasingly supportive of civil rights. Is there evidence that this change was the effect of Court action? The answer appears to be no. Writing in 1956, Hyman and Sheatsley found that the changes in attitude were "solidly based" and "not easily accelerated nor easily reversed." Further, they found that the changes were not due to any specific event, such as Kennedy's assassination, or a Supreme Court decision. They found that changes in national opinion "represent long-term trends that are not easily modified by specific—even by highly dramatic—events."

Another way of examining the indirect-effects claim on white Americans is to look at how the sensitivity of Americans to civil rights changed generally. According to one proponent of judicial influence, the "*Brown* decision was central to eliciting the moral outrage that both blacks and whites were to feel and express about segregation." If the Court served this role, it would necessarily have increased awareness of the plight of blacks. The evidence, however, shows no sign of such an increase. Survey questions as to whether most blacks were being treated fairly resulted in affirmative responses of 66 percent in 1944, 66 percent in 1946, and 69 percent in 1956. The variation of 3 percent is virtually meaningless. By 1963, when Gallup asked if any group in America was being treated unfairly, 80 percent said no. Only 5 percent of the sample named "the Negroes" as being unfairly treated while 4 percent named "the whites.". . . As Burke Marshall, head of the Justice Department's Civil Rights Division put it, "the Negro and his problems were still pretty much invisible to the country . . . until mass demonstrations of the Birmingham type." These results, and the change over time, hardly show an America whose conscience is aroused. If the Court pricked the conscience of white Americans, the sensitivity disappeared quickly.

In sum, in several areas where the Supreme Court would be expected to influence white Americans, evidence of the effect has not been found. Most Americans neither follow Supreme Court decisions nor understand the Court's constitutional role. It is not surprising, then, that change in public opinion appears to be oblivious to the Court. Again, the extra-judicial-effects thesis lacks evidence.

Blacks

The indirect-effects thesis makes claims about the effect of the Supreme Court on black Americans. Here, a plausible claim is that *Brown* was the spark that ignited the black revolution. By recognizing and legitimizing black grievances, the public pronouncement by the Court provided blacks with a new image and encouraged them to act. This assumption is virtually universal among lawyers and legal scholars, and representative quotations can be found throughout this chapter. *Brown* "begot," one legal scholar tells us, "a union of the mightiest and lowliest in America, a mystical, passionate union bound by the pained depths of the black man's cry for justice and the moral authority, unique to the Court, to see that justice realized." Thus, *Brown* may have fundamentally reoriented the views of black Americans by providing hope that the federal government, if made aware of their plight, would help. Black action, in turn, could have changed white opinions and led to elite action and civil rights. If this is the case, then there are a number of places where evidence should be found.

One area where this effect should be seen is in civil rights demonstrations. The evidence plainly indicates that civil rights marches and demonstrations affected both white Americans and elites and provided a major impetus for civil rights legislation. As Wilkinson puts it, "the Court sired the movement, succored it through the early years, [and] encouraged its first taking wing." If this were the case, if, in the words of civil rights litigator Jack Greenberg, the direct-action campaign would not have developed "without the legal victories that we'd won earlier," then one would expect to see an increase in the number of demonstrations shortly after the decision. However, there is almost no difference in the number of civil rights demonstrations in the years 1953, 1954, and 1955. There was a large jump in 1956.[6] But then the numbers drop. For example, 1959 saw fewer civil rights demonstrations than in four of the years of the 1940s! And the number of demonstrations skyrocketed in the 1960s, six or more years after *Brown*. This pattern does not suggest that the Court played a major role. The time period is too long and the 1960s increases too startling to credit the Court with a meaningful effect. . . .

DR. MARTIN LUTHER KING, JR.   One possible way in which *Brown* might have ignited the civil rights movement is by inspiring Dr. King. His ringing denouncements of segregation, his towering oratory, and his ability to inspire and move both blacks and whites appear to have played an indispensable role in creating pressure for government action. Was King motivated to act by the Court? From an examination of King's thinking, the answer appears to be no. King rooted his beliefs in Christian theology and Gandhian nonviolence, not constitutional doctrine. His attitude to the Court, far from a source of inspiration, was one of strategic disfavor. "Whenever it is possible," he told reporters in early 1957, "we want to avoid court cases in this integration struggle." He rejected litigation as a major tool of struggle for a number of reasons. He wrote of blacks' lack of faith in it, of its "unsuitability" to the civil rights struggle, and of its "hampering progress to this day." Further, he complained that to "accumulate resources for legal actions imposes intolerable hardships on the already overburdened." In addition to its expense, King saw the legal process as slow. Blacks, he warned, "must not get involved in legalism [and] needless fights in lower courts" because that is "exactly what the white man wants the Negro to do. Then he can draw out the fight." Perhaps most important, King believed that litigation was an elite strategy for change that did not involve ordinary people. He believed that when the NAACP was the principal civil rights organization, and court cases were relied on, "the ordinary Negro was involved [only] as a passive spectator" and "his energies were unemployed." As he told the NAACP Convention on July 5, 1962, "only when the people themselves begin to act are rights on paper given life blood." King's writings and actions do not provide evidence for the Dynamic Court view that he was inspired by the Court.

---

[6] Rosenberg attributes this jump to the Montgomery bus boycott, sparked by the arrest of Rosa Parks, a black women, who refused to give up her seat to a white and move to the back of a segregated city bus. —Eds.

BLACK GROUPS The founding of the Student Non-Violent Coordinating Committee (SNCC), the Congress of Racial Equality (CORE), and the Southern Christian Leadership Conference (SCLC), the organizations that provided the leadership and the shock troops of the movement, could quite plausibly have been inspired by the Court. Although SNCC was not founded until six years after Brown, and CORE was not revitalized until 1961, it may have taken that long for the effect to be felt.

However, it is quite clear that the Court played no role in inspiring these key groups of the civil rights movement to form. To the contrary, they were formed as an explicit rejection of litigation as a method of social change. . . . The founding of SNCC in 1960 [for example] . . . was aimed at helping students engaged in sit-ins to create at least some communication and organization network."' And CORE was founded in 1942 as a Gandhian-type movement of mass nonviolent direct action. As its Executive Director James Farmer told Roy Wilkins of the NAACP in response to Wilkins's opposition to the Freedom Ride, and preference for litigation, "we've had test cases and we've won them all and the status remains quo." The point is that Brown is simply not mentioned as a source of inspiration. . . .

In sum, the claim that a major contribution of the courts in civil rights was to give the issue salience, press political elites to act, prick the consciences of whites, legitimate the grievances of blacks, and fire blacks up to act is not substantiated. In all the places examined, where evidence supportive of the claim should exist, it does not. The concerns of clear attribution, time, and increased press coverage all cut against the thesis. Public-opinion evidence does not support it and, at times, clearly contradicts it. The emergence of the sit-ins, demonstrations, and marches does not support it. While it must be the case that Court action influenced some people, I have found no evidence that this influence was widespread or of much importance to the battle for civil rights. The evidence suggests that Brown's major positive impact was limited to reinforcing the belief in a legal strategy for change of those already committed to it. The burden of showing that Brown accomplished more now rests squarely on those who for years have written and spoken of its immeasurable importance.

Conclusion: The Fly-Paper Court

[I have] examined whether the Supreme Court's decision in Brown v. Board of Education was able to desegregate schools. Surprisingly, the analysis showed the Court's decision, praiseworthy as it was, did not make much of a contribution. This is the case because, on the most fundamental level, courts depend on political support to produce such reform. Thus, political hostility doomed the Court's contributions.

Courts will also be ineffective in producing change, given any serious resistance because of their lack of implementation powers. The structural constraints built into the American judicial system, make courts virtually powerless to produce change. They must depend on the actions of others for their decisions to be implemented. With civil fights, little changed until the federal government became involved. Where there is local hostility to change, court orders will be ignored. Community pressure, violence or threats of violence, and lack of market response all serve to curtail actions to implement court decisions. When Justice Jackson commented during oral argument in *Brown*, "I suppose that realistically this case is here for the reason that action couldn't be obtained from Congress," he identified a fundamental reason why the Court's action in the case would have little effect.

In general, then, not only does litigation steer activists to an institution that is constrained from helping them, but also it siphons off crucial resources and talent, and runs the risk of weakening political efforts. In terms of financial resources, social reform groups do not have a lot of money. Funding a litigation campaign means that other strategic options are starved of funds. . . . Further, the legal strategy drained off the talents of such as Thurgood Marshall and Jack Greenberg. As Martin Luther King, Jr., complained: "to accumulate resources for legal actions imposes intolerable hardships on the already overburdened."

It is important to note here that there were options other than litigation. Massive voter registration drives could have been started in the urban North and in some major Southern cities. Marches, demonstrations, and sit-ins could have been organized and funded years before they broke out, based on the example of labor unions and the readiness of groups like the CORE. Money could have been invested in public relations. Amazingly, in 1957 the NAACP spent just $7,814 for its Washington Bureau operations. Its entire "public relations and informational activities" spending for 1957 was $17,216. NAACP lobbyists did not even try to cultivate the black press or the black church, let alone their white counterparts. And even in 1959 the public relations budget was only $10,135. When activists succumbed to the "lawyers' vision of change without pain," a "massive social revolution" was side-tracked into "legal channels." Because the NAACP failed to understand the limits on U.S. courts, its strategy was bound to fail.

If this is the case, then there is another important way in which courts effect social change. It is, to put it simply, that courts act as "fly-paper" for social reformers who succumb to the "lure of litigation." Courts, I have argued, can seldom produce significant social reform. Yet if groups advocating such reform continue to look to the courts for aid, and spend precious resources in litigation, then the courts also limit change by deflecting claims from substantive political battles, where success is possible, to harmless legal ones where it is not. Even when major cases are won, the achievement is often more symbolic that real. Thus, courts may serve an ideological function of luring movements for social reform to an institution that is structurally constrained from serving their needs, providing only an illusion of change. . . .

*"My study suggests that Rosenberg's narrow claims discount the wide
range of ways in which legal action has proved . . . consequential."*

14.6 REFORM LITIGATION ON TRIAL: REVIEW OF *THE HOLLOW HOPE*

Michael McCann

Michael McCann is Professor of Political Science at the University of Washington.

The Book's Virtues

The Hollow Hope is a bold, compelling, and important book. Rosenberg offers a most impressive contribution to the tradition of social-scientific studies on judicial impact. That the book has attracted much attention is hardly surprising; it will be required reading in university classes for some years to come. Several strengths of the book in particular deserve mention.

Rosenberg's general message urging skepticism about the transformative impacts of court decisions and effectiveness of legal tactics surely is sound. His admonitions recall, explicitly and implicitly, argument[s] regarding the powerful "myth of rights" in American culture. Several decades of (at least moderately) liberal court action provide clear evidence that judicial proclamations of just sentiments do not automatically translate into just social practices; the courts alone rarely can do much to advance progressive social agendas. Moreover, Rosenberg's contention that reformers sometimes overvalue legal tactics as resources for reform no doubt is correct. His arguments about the "flypaper" attraction of litigation offer new grounds for support of similar skeptical arguments by other respected analysts.

Rosenberg's work also is very impressive in its commitment to high scholarly standards. He is exceptionally erudite, and cites a wide range of secondary literature—by historians, sociologists, economists, and social movement analysts as well as legal scholars—to support his investigation of various policy histories. Equally important is his commitment to extensive empirical study itself. The book offers a vast treasure of data that, while mostly derived from secondary sources, is interesting on its own terms as well as supportive of the author's claims. I was "surprised" by more than a few of Rosenberg's findings, as the book's introduction predicted. In terms of data collection, the work reflects a level of commitment and rigor from the author that is exemplary in the field. Rosenberg thus is on firm ground in challenging fellow students of the courts—critics and supporters alike—to match his data with new empirical studies that can enrich the debate over how and when legal action matters.

From Michael McCann, "Reform Litigation on Trial: Review of *The Hollow Hope*," 17 *Law and Social Inquiry* 715 (1992).

Finally, it is worth noting that *The Hollow Hope* is a good read in many ways. The argument is well organized, and the analytical framework is consistently developed from start to end. Rosenberg also writes well. The book is highly accessible and full of pithy, eloquent lines. This quality both makes the data-laden pages easier to digest and accelerates its sense of dramatic tension. One of the keys to this drama is that, somewhat ironically, the book's form and style resemble to some degree a trial. . . . [Through] repeated cross-examinations, to closing statement, the liberal optimist position is subjected to a trial seeking to verify beyond reasonable doubt Rosenberg's critical allegations. . . . This no doubt will irritate [some] scholars. But the author's dazzling and unremitting critical barrage keeps the book interesting, from first read through continued reflection.

Does, however, this intellectual inquisition generate compelling insights regarding the effectiveness of reform litigation? I will scrutinize the implications of this type of analysis first on its own terms and then by way of contrast with a quite different approach that Rosenberg does not consider.

Evaluating the Arguments: An Internal Critique

Close scrutiny suggests that Rosenberg's analysis, however bold and impressive, is less convincing on various counts than he assumes. Even on its own terms, there is considerable analytical slippage and inconsistency that calls into question both his specific historical assessments and sweeping conclusions. I review here a few of my reservations regarding the internal cogency of his analysis.

Source Selections

As noted above, one undeniable strength of *The Hollow Hope* is Rosenberg's extensive review of secondary source material. That much data is marshaled, however, does not mean that the author's use of that material is always convincing. I will mention three types of evidentiary problems, illustrated by brief examples, that sometimes left me unsatisfied.

First, I was bothered by the palpable absence of certain relevant data that might contradict or qualify the author's assessments. . . . Rosenberg uses only selective quotations by activists and observers that support his points about the lack of indirect effects from litigation while ignoring abundant others. For example, my own reading of writings by, and interviews with, civil rights activists and leaders has revealed many attributions contradicting Rosenberg's view that judicial rulings were irrelevant. . . . Martin Luther King, Jr., . . . was rather more complex and affirmative about the importance of *Brown* than Rosenberg suggests. While King wisely warned against leaving the fight to lawyers, he repeatedly recognized the importance of support from the courts. It is worth recalling, after all, that a large part of King's "Letter from a Birmingham jail" offered a profound reflection about the relationship between justice and law. "Any law that uplifts human personality is just," he wrote. "Thus it is that I can urge men to obey the 1954 decision of the Supreme Court, for it is morally right; and I can urge them to disobey segregation ordinances, for they are morally wrong." Extensive documentation of other such examples is impossible here, but many readers no doubt will wonder why such widely available data were not considered important in this analysis of litigation's significance to primary movement activists.

A second cause for skepticism is that Rosenberg's statistical data at times provide at best shaky support for his conclusions. . . . [H]is own data belies his claim that civil rights organizations did not enjoy significant gains in membership and money following the *Brown* decision. His Table 4.3 reveals that NAACP income climbed from $391,000 in 1953 to over $1,000,000 by 1960, with the biggest jump in 1954–1957. The total for all civil rights groups, moreover, increased almost fivefold from 1948 to 1958 and doubled between 1954 and 1957. One need not cite *Brown* as a sole cause . . . to find plausible evidence of some causal linkages at stake. Rosenberg himself attributes the NAACP rise to an intensive membership campaign, as if that could be separated from the legal campaign and achievement. . . .

Finally, it is relevant to note that many of the historians and social scientists Rosenberg invokes to support specific parts of his argument do not support his overall interpretation about judicial impotence. For example, Doug McAdam and Aldon Morris, two well-known authorities often cited by Rosenberg to interpret the civil rights legacy, provide a rather different account than his. Indeed, both sociologists accord the NAACP legal effort and *Brown* victory much greater—partial and contingent, to be sure, but nonetheless much greater—significance than does Rosenberg. On the combined impact of Supreme Court decisions and federal executive policy from the 1930s to 1950s, for example, McAdam summarizes that "the symbolic importance of the shift would be hard to overstate. It was responsible for nothing less than a cognitive revolution within the black population regarding the prospects for change in this country's racial status quo." And this is one of Rosenberg's primary sources of data and alternative interpretation! . . .

What are we to make of this? Specific examples of unconvincing data can be found in any study, of course. Nor is it improper for an author to use evidence provided by other scholars who interpret its significance differently. Nevertheless, Rosenberg's argument largely hinges on evidence regarding scores of discrete causal connections. If a fair number of these are less convincing than he insists, so might his larger position be for some readers. . . .

Comparative Institutional Analysis

That Rosenberg puts so much weight on the comparative institutional weakness of courts to formulate and implement bold reform policies deserves some further comment. What is striking is that his argument hinges on assumptions about comparative institutional capacity that are not well demonstrated. It certainly is true that courts are limited in their capacities to deal with complex social problems. But what institution is not highly limited, at least in domestic policy? My reading of scholarly literature, and the newspapers for that matter, suggests an overwhelming consensus that executive and legislative institutions at all levels have trouble translating their will into effective social change. Rosenberg himself admits early on that all bureaucratic institutions have limited capacities to implement policy reforms. But that insight is lost in the rest of his analysis. Instead, the other government branches often are romanticized as the heroic saviors of great causes apparently botched by the feckless, hamstrung courts. In sum, to demonstrate only that courts encounter "particular difficulties," in the absence of detailed direct comparative institutional analysis, does not establish their inferiority to other government actors, much less their nearly absolute powerlessness.

More important, this type of zero-sum comparative analysis itself obscures the fact that discrete institutions are almost never solitary organs of change in our political system. Our system of mixed and shared powers usually requires cooperation, or at least consent, from all branches for policy changes (at least major domestic policies) to even receive authorization, much less generate significant social impacts. After all, presidents, bureaucrats, and legislators require deference from judges to be effective in most cases . . . as much as judges need the others to advance change. By ignoring cases where courts withheld support—whether by inaction or opposition—for policy actions of other branches, Rosenberg thus demonstrates little about such dynamics of institutional interaction and interdependence. The result is a tendency to treat courts and other institutions according to different standards: That judicial impact is contingent on support from other branches is invoked to demonstrate the weakness and dependence of courts, while the dependence of those other branches on the courts is mostly ignored. In sum, the book's focus on courts as independent agents of change involves an unrealistic test that every branch would fail.

Policy Impacts versus Political Action

Finally, and perhaps most important, Rosenberg's confident concluding argument that limited judicial impacts confirm the poverty of legal tactics is not demonstrated by his empirical study. The reason is that, even if one accepts—as, literally understood, I do—his argument that courts by themselves rarely "produce significant social change," this is not very revealing about either how or why people litigate and deploy legal tactics. His study does not focus on either the actual practices of legal advocacy or the intentions, understandings, and tactical designs of those who engage in such practices. His aggregate data about national policy effects may be revealing about some types of impacts, but it pretty much leaves legal actors—especially nonjudicial actors—and reform movements themselves unexamined. Rosenberg offers little assessment of competing options available to movement tacticians, potentially empowering effects beyond policy changes, or variations of impact in different venues that may qualify aggregate mass statistics. Nor does he consider the many studies that find compelling defenses of legal action beyond those specified in his inquiry. . . .

Comparing Approaches: Top-Down versus Bottom-Up Studies

So far, my analysis has attempted to unpack Rosenberg's study and evaluate it on its own terms. My reservations have primarily concerned some of his specific conceptual categories, empirical assessments, and overall conclusions rather than the utility of his general analytical approach to analyzing the effectiveness of legal tactics. I now will direct my sights to this latter aspect of the book's contribution. My contention will be that Rosenberg's conceptual framework is generally defensible and useful for evaluating whether "courts can produce significant social change." However, I argue that this narrow formulation itself is less illuminating and important than Rosenberg suggests. . . .

Court-Centered versus Decentered Models of Legal Practice

Among the most interesting and prominent approaches to the study of law that have developed in the last two decades are what might be called "dispute-centered" (or decentered) perspectives. Although such studies have been identified by various labels—including studies of dispute resolution, legal mobilization, legal ideology, and law in society—and diverge in some respects, they share some basic conceptual understandings." Like Rosenberg, they urge a generally skeptical, contingent, empirically grounded, context-specific approach to legal analysis. Yet they build on basic premises and insights that Rosenberg almost completely overlooks.

We can begin to examine these differences by reviewing the essential elements of Rosenberg's analytical scheme. Most important is that Rosenberg places courts at the center of his analysis: "This is not a book about what caused or causes liberal change. . . . It is about whether the courts can or did produce such change." If judges are the legal agents and aspiring producers of change to be scrutinized, the reactions of target citizens (masses and official elites) are the primary measures of how effective such actions are. Causality is presumed to initiate at the top in a discrete judicial source, and trickles down unidirectionally on society, if at all. This impact, we have seen, can be either direct (coercion) or indirect (moral persuasion). In both forms of impact, however, the primary standard of effective change is compliance with, or affirmative action (inspired) toward, the goals of the court by target populations. Judicial rulings thus provide their own determinate, knowable criteria of evaluation. Finally, Rosenberg rejects categorical views of likely judicial impact, arguing instead that we must examine a variety of contingent factors—mostly involving actions by other state elites—to understand whether those judicial actions generated positive change.

The dispute-centered tradition of legal analysis takes a quite different view on every point. For one thing, most such studies begin with, and place primary emphasis on, nonjudicial (both elite and ordinary citizen) actors locked into ongoing but typically conflictual social relations. Social struggles themselves thus define the center of analysis, and nonjudicial actors are viewed as practical legal agents rather than as simply reactors to judicial command. Moreover, legal action begins with the framing of legal demands in such ongoing relations rather than with official court decisions. In fact, courts are viewed as relatively peripheral to most forms of legal action; actual resort to judicial intervention is the exception rather than the rule. Rosenberg's boldly framed conclusion that the courts have little direct impact on—and that they almost never unilaterally "cause"—most aspects of citizen behavior thus is a routine assumption in this alternative framework.

That courts only rarely become directly involved in most disputes hardly means that they are inconsequential, however. If direct effects matter far less than Rosenberg's [work] suggests, then indirect effects matter rather more in the decentered framework. And the latter are more significant because they entail a wide range of manifestations slighted by Rosenberg's focus on compliance and moral inspiration. As John Brigham concludes on the former point, simple "compliance is a very small part of the policy consequences of the Supreme Court's decisions." One reason is that judicial decisions express a whole range of norms, logics, and signals that cannot be reduced to clear commands or rules, which Rosenberg emphasizes. Scholars in the bottom-up tradition instead emphasize that court decisions "work through the transmission and reception of information rather than by concrete imposition of controls." Such judicially generated information and knowledge, moreover, are understood to have far more relevance for tactical judgments about practical action by citizens and officials than for their abstract moral opinions and philosophical convictions. In other words, judicial proclamations are likely to have less impact in altering the substantive values of most citizens (moral persuasion) than in reshaping perceptions of when and how particular values are realistically actionable as claims of legal right. . . .

The bottom-up, dispute-centered approach likewise emphasizes that practical legal knowledge does not simply trickle down on citizens and state officials in unidirectional, determinate fashion. An emphasis on legal knowledge and signals over legal commands and exhortations suggests as well that the effects of judicial opinions instead are inherently indeterminate, variable, dynamic, and interactive. "The messages disseminated by courts do not . . . produce effects except as they are received, interpreted, and used by [potential] actors," observes Galanter. Indeed, differently situated social actors are likely to respond quite differently to judicially authorized norms as they negotiate relations in various venues throughout society. This includes, on the one hand, the fact that many citizens routinely reconstruct legal norms into resources for purposes quite unintended by judicial officials. . . . On the other hand, judicial opinions can reshape the strategic landscape in ways that encourage other citizens and officials to circumvent, defy, and even initiate counter-reform efforts to alter court rulings. In sum, the decentered view emphasizes that judicially articulated legal norms take a life of their own as they are deployed in practical social action. This points to what many analysts refer to as the constitutive capacity of law: Legal knowledge prefigures in part the symbolic terms of material relations and becomes a potential resource in ongoing struggles to refigure those relations. . . .

Applications to Reform Movement Struggles

Most scholarly studies in the bottom-up, dispute-centered tradition have focused on legal tactics and constraints in small-scale civil conflicts among individuals and small groups. Some studies have applied the approach to larger-scale public conflicts and reform campaigns, however. These studies typically focus less on whether courts "produce" intended changes than on the various ways that reform activists deploy legal resources to wage their campaigns in multiple venues outside of courts. The result in most cases is a more complex look at the implications of legal action for issue agenda setting, movement building, negotiating and lobbying efforts, remedial program development, and even personal transformation than suggested by Rosenberg. Two brief examples will illustrate the divergent implications for understanding the role of litigation in actual reform politics.

First, I return to the legacy of *Brown*. Rosenberg's judgment of small indirect effects hinges on the decision's: low salience, measured by media coverage of the opinion itself; failure to coerce or inspire federal elite support; negligible impacts on public opinion among blacks and whites; and small impact on civil rights advocacy groups beyond the elite, legalistic NAACP. From the dispute-centered view, much of the data is of marginal relevance. The initial focus of judicial impact should be specifically on the primary parties in the initial conflict—that is, on organized whites and blacks in the South. Leading social movement scholars on the subject (many cited by Rosenberg) tell a story that not only differs a bit from Rosenberg's but parallels that offered by dispute-oriented legal analysts. . . . In particular, these social movement analysts document at length the significant impact of *Brown* on the NAACP and middle-class southern blacks, emphasizing especially the former's crucial leadership role in mobilizing the latter for action. Sociologist Aldon Morris demonstrates in his outstanding book, for example, that NAACP local activists "were the leaders who spearheaded the resistance of the black community." *Brown* was crucial to this evolving leadership role and radicalism in two ways. First, it raised southern blacks' hopes less by moral inspiration than by "demonstrating that the Southern white power structure was vulnerable at some points" and providing scarce practical resources for defiant action. "The winning of the 1954 decision was the kind of victory the organization needed to rally the black masses behind its program; by appealing to blacks' widespread desire to enroll their children in the better-equipped white schools it reached into black homes and had meaning for people's personal lives."

Second, the increasing "pressure on the Southern white power structure to abolish racial domination" led to a massive, highly visible attack—including legal assaults as well as violent intimidation—on the NAACP itself. These reactions in turn forced a split between local, church-affiliated NAACP leaders urging more radical forms of protest action and the bureaucratic, legally oriented national organization. The result was a marked increased in both the momentum of the grass-roots protest campaign among southern blacks generally and frustration about the effectiveness of legal tactics alone. "The two approaches—legal action and mass protest—entered into a turbulent but workable marriage.". . .

I offer as a second example my own forthcoming study on legal mobilization tactics in the campaign for gender-based pay equity (or comparable worth) reform.[7] Grounded in an intensive study of a dozen pay-equity campaigns and more than 150 in-depth interviews with activists around the nation, my dispute-centered analysis reaches conclusions startlingly different from Rosenberg's.

---

[7] McCann's study, *Rights at Work,* was published by the University of Chicago Press two years after this review appeared. Supporters of "comparable worth" argue that employers should provide equal pay for jobs involving comparable skill, effort, conditions of work, and responsibility. —Eds.

The Hollow Hope does not provide a comparably exhaustive study of this specific legacy, it is true.[8] Rosenberg does, however, invoke secondary sources to register some fairly strong judgments. His analysis begins typically with the courts, noting that in 1981 "the Supreme Court gave the green light to comparable-worth litigation" that challenges widespread patterns of gender-based job segregation and wage discrimination. He then argues that court actions were ineffective in two ways. First, "despite litigation, where comparable worth policies have been instituted, they have been the result of collective bargaining and government action, not litigation." Moreover, despite judicial victories on wage discrimination, the overall patterns of differential earnings between men and women have changed little during the last 30 years. Hence his conclusion: "Litigation has failed to end discrimination. . . . Cases were argued and won but, litigants aside, little was accomplished.". . .

. . . [M]y study suggests that Rosenberg's narrow claims discount the wide range of ways in which legal action has proved most consequential for the pay equity movement. Despite only episodic and limited success in the courts, movement actors have mobilized legal resources in highly effective ways. . . . Legal tactics proved . . . important in battles to win employer concessions on reform demands. Rosenberg again is misleading when he argues that reforms were the product of collective bargaining and legislation rather than litigation. Both my case studies and interviews clearly demonstrated that legal leveraging tactics were a crucial component of effective negotiating activity. "We would never have gotten the plan in bargaining without those pending charges," one local female union organizer summarized in terms repeated to me endlessly. Again, activists at all levels ranked legal action as one of the two most effective tactics for negotiating policy change. What is striking is that the overwhelming percentage of legal leveraging actions never reached the trial stage. In most cases, simply filing formal charges achieved the desired result; in a few cases, mere verbal threats of a lawsuit broke negotiating deadlocks. Even more surprising is that such tactics were effective for a decade in the absence of clear, consistent judicial support for the claims themselves!

The legacy of litigation proved crucial in yet other ways. For one thing, movement activists successfully constructed and justified the basic template for pay equity reform implementation on the basis of judicially approved remedies in other areas of antidiscrimination law, even though the courts themselves rarely authorized such remedies for comparable worth claims. Finally, interviews with rank-and-file activists offered striking evidence about the transformative power of "rights consciousness"—at once committed to radical legal principles and deeply critical of official lawmakers—that evolved through political struggle in which legal tactics loomed large. In sum, activist actions and testimony alike confirmed an empowering "politics of rights" virtually uncompromised by a "myth of rights." The point again thus is not that Rosenberg's specific claim is wrong; courts themselves did not unilaterally produce social change. But his top-down,

---

[8] Though *Brown v. Board of Education* forms the centerpiece of his study, Rosenberg also considers the impact of cases involving women's rights, the environment, reapportionment, and criminal law. —Eds.

court-centered framework overdetermines the inherent tensions between legal tactics and the grass-roots politics that he celebrates. Even if Rosenberg accorded more attention to the pay equity legacy, much of the complementary relationship I found would remain invisible to his analytical scheme. . . .

Conclusion

Much of the preceding discussion has documented the limitations of *The Hollow Hope*. This form of critical evaluation admittedly borders on rebuking the author for not formulating the type of analysis I would prefer. But that has not been my intent. First, my assessment has tried to distinguish the many strengths of the book from its weaknesses. The strengths include an elegant analytical model, a wealth of useful data, and some sound general claims about the limited utility of litigation for advancing justice. The weaknesses include considerable overstatement regarding both the inherent ineffectiveness of legal tactics and the significance of insights regarding judicial effects provided by his top-down, court-centered analytical framework. Second, my discussion has outlined the contours of a potentially important debate among rival analytical approaches that Rosenberg largely skirts. My view is that this debate is valuable in itself as well as supportive of my arguments about the book's limitations. . . .

> *"The Court cannot buy support for its decisions by spending money and, except to a minor degree, it cannot independently coerce obedience to its decrees. The Court's power lies, rather, in its legitimacy, a product of substance and perception that shows itself in the people's acceptance of the Judiciary as fit to determine what the Nation's law means and to declare what it demands." —JUSTICE SANDRA DAY O'CONNOR[9]*

14.7 PUBLIC REACTION TO SUPREME COURT DECISIONS[10]

Valerie J. Hoekstra

Valerie Hoekstra is Assistant Professor of Political Science at Arizona State University.

Introduction

Every few decades, the Supreme Court hands down a monumental decision that grasps both public and elite attention. It is difficult to think about the Court without these decisions coming to mind. Examples of such notable decisions in-

---

[9] *Planned Parenthood of Southeastern Pennsylvania v. Casey* (1992).

[10] Adapted from Valerie J. Hoekstra, *Public Reaction to Supreme Court Decisions* (New York: Cambridge University Press, 2003.)

From Valerie J. Hoekstra, *From the Marble Temple to Main Street: The Effect of Court Decisions on Local Public Opinion.* (New York: Cambridge University Press, 2004.)

clude *Brown v. Board of Education* (1954), *Roe v. Wade* (1973), and most recently, *Bush v. Gore* (2000). Each of these decisions was followed by heated debate about the issues in the cases as well as discussions about the very legitimacy of the Court itself. But what about the ordinary decisions that make up the Court's docket each year? Is there public interest and attention to these other, more ordinary cases? Do these decisions have any effect on public opinion?

In recent years, the Court hears approximately eighty cases, each of which will affect some segment of our population and will attract some media attention. The question is whether these ordinary decisions, representing the vast majority of the Court's work have any effect on public opinion. National attention is rarely focused on such cases. However, these cases often attract more intense and sustained local media interest providing the opportunity to learn how these cases affect members of these local communities. If the effect of decisions is more localized, looking for uniform national level effects would produce misleading results. Moreover, many of the Court's decisions require active implementation, oftentimes by local officials. If the Court can change public opinion on the issues, or at least cast legitimacy on the policy under review, then the probability of successful implementation is greatly enhanced. For these reasons, looking to the local communities that gave rise to the controversies is a better place to investigate the Court's impact on public opinion.

Case Selection and Research Design

In the following pages I present the results from four, two-wave panel studies of the residents in and around the local communities where a Supreme Court case began. In each study, two samples were generated. The first is a random sample of residents from the immediate town. The second is made up of those who reside in the surrounding towns. The surrounding area sample tends to reflect the coverage of the dominant local newspaper. The respondents were randomly selected and were first contacted before the Court's decision and were contacted for the second wave within two weeks of the announcement of the Court's decision.

There were two civil liberties and two economic cases. The first case, the *Center Moriches* case included a mix of First Amendment issues (free speech, free exercise of religion, and religious establishment) (*Lamb's Chapel v. Center Moriches Union Free High School District* [1993]). The controversy in this case began when the Center Moriches high school district refused to allow Lamb's Chapel, a local nondenominational church, to use school facilities, after school hours, to show a film on parenting and family values. The district did so despite the fact that they maintained a policy of allowing other community groups to use school facilities. The Court decided that the school district violated the church's free speech guarantees by prohibiting them from showing the film. They found no religious establishment violation since the topic of the film-parenting and family values-was a secular one.

The *Monroe* case dealt exclusively with a religious establishment controversy (*Board of Education of Kiryas Joel v. Grumet* [1994]). In this case, the court was asked to determine whether New York state's creation of a special school district exclusively for the local Hasidic community violated the establishment clause of the First Amendment. The Court decided that the district did indeed violate the First Amendment.

The *Oklahoma* Case involved state authority to tax the gasoline sold by members of a Native American Indian tribe (*Oklahoma Tax Commission v. Chickasaw Nation* [1995]). The state of Oklahoma imposed a gasoline tax and attempted to collect the tax from Indian-owned gasoline stations. Members of the Chickasaw tribe refused to pay. The Supreme Court ruled in favor of the Chickasaw Nation.

Finally, the *Oregon* Case involved a controversy over the federal government's application of the 1973 Endangered Species Act (*Babbitt, Secretary of the Interior et al. v. Sweet Home Chapter of Communities for a Greater Oregon* [1995]). In this case, private property owners and businesses in Sweet Home, Oregon challenged Babbitt 's interpretation of the word "harm" found in the Endangered Species Act. Babbit interpreted it to prohibit any habitat modification which might affect a threatened or endangered species. This had huge implications for the lumber industry in the Pacific Northwest because the spotted owl tends to nest in old-growth trees. The property owners and businesses argued that Congress intended to protect [only] individual animals not their habitats when it wrote the Endangered Species Act. The Court ruled in favor of Babbitt's broader interpretation.

Media Coverage and Public Knowledge

Except for the occasional and exceptional case, most cases may not resonate on the national agenda. In fact, research using national public opinion polls typically reveals scant knowledge about the Court and its activities. However, most Americans read their local paper, not *The New York Times*. If a story does not appear in the media to which most people are attuned, they simply will not have the opportunity to encounter any information about the Court. Instead, we need to look to those places where access to information is sufficient to produce informed citizens, and we should survey respondents with the Court's calendar in mind.

Thus, one obvious place to look is in the local communities where the controversies began. In those communities, the local media should be more likely to report on a local case that makes it to the Supreme Court than on a similar case that originates in some other part of the country. If the media do report on these cases, then we should also expect local levels of awareness to be high. While research suggests that the media may not be able to change how people think about issues, it can certainly tell them which issues are important to think about. Thus, I expect the local media will cover local cases more extensively than the national media and media from other parts of the nation.

The results for media coverage are presented in Table 14.2. As expected, the local media covered the cases more extensively than did the national media or media from other parts of the nation. The results are most dramatic for the *Monroe* case. There, the local newspaper, *The Times Herald-Record*, published

TABLE 14.2 Local and National Newspaper Coverage of the Cases

	Center Moriches	Monroe	Oklahoma	Oregon
Local newspaper	6 *Newsday*	25 *Times Herald- Record*	3 *Daily Oklahoman* 9 *Ada Evening News*	6 *Oregonian* 2 *Albany Democratic Herald*
The New York Times	2	7	0	4
The St. Louis Post Dispatch	3	5	0	4
The Wall Street Journal	1	3	0	1
The Washington Post	1	4	0	2
The Los Angeles Times	3	3	0	2

Cell entries are the number of stories.

twenty-five stories about the Court's decision about the Hasidic school district, whereas *The New York Times* published only seven. In the other cases, coverage by the local papers produced about twice as many stories about the case, and often more, than did any of the other papers.

Did this extensive media coverage lead to high levels of awareness of the cases? When compared with the results typically reported from national surveys, awareness is very high. In Center Moriches, approximately 82 percent of the respondents had heard about and could correctly describe how the Court had decided the case involving the local church, Lamb's Chapel, and the local high school. Results in Monroe were nearly as high: 71 percent knew about the Court's decision on the Hasidic school district. In the two economic cases, awareness was somewhat lower. In the Oklahoma case about 21 percent knew about the gasoline tax decision and in Oregon about 40 percent knew about the spotted owl case. In each of the four surveys, the residents of the immediate communities were more likely to report knowing about the decision than were those from the surrounding communities. The differences ranged from about 10 to 20 percent. The results for local awareness, even for the economic cases, are dramatic. Beyond extensive media coverage and awareness, can we discern any other effects on public opinion? This is the question I turn to in the following section.

Can Court Decisions Shape Public Opinion?

Many scholars believe that the Court can sway the public in the direction of its decisions. Scholars have attempted to empirically test this question with mixed success. Most of the research relying on aggregate data finds very little evidence of aggregate opinion shifts in the direction of the decisions. Research looking at highly volatile issues such as abortion and capital punishment shows that people may become polarized in their opinions. Other research looking at less controversial issues, like the ones studied here, shows that persuasion is can occur.

TABLE 14.3 Support for the Supreme Court's Decision in the Four Panel Studios among Those Who Knew about the Decision

	Center Moriches	Monroe	Oklahoma	Oregon
First wave	5.12	4.69	3.50	3.15
Second wave	5.42	5.33	3.46	3.15
0	.06	.001	.89	1.00
N	93	88	24	59

Note: Cell entries are average levels of support for the issues. Opinions were measured along a seven-point Likert-type scale where higher values indicate greater agreement with how the Court decided the issue.

Given these previous findings, what kind of effect of Court decisions on public opinion might we expect? Three possibilities emerge from the earlier discussion: Persuasion, no effect, or polarization. Polarization was found following highly salient and controversial decisions dealing with abortion and capital punishment, and is less likely to occur following the more routine kinds of cases the Court hears each term. The null findings are based largely on aggregate data which can obscure individual level effects. With individual level data, more subtle patterns might emerge. Therefore, even though the results from past research appear somewhat contradictory, if we were to examine individual-level opinion, following more routine cases, where media, and hence public attention is high, persuasion effects are quite possible.

Table 14.3 presents the aggregate levels of support for the position the Court takes in the cases both before and after the Court announced its decisions. Responses were measured along seven-point scales where 1 indicates "very strongly disagree (with the position the Court ultimately announces)" and 7 indicates "very strongly agree (with the position the Court ultimately announces)." Thus, higher values at the second wave would suggest the possibility that the Court exerted a persuasive influence on attitudes of members of the local communities. In two of the studies, Center Moriches and Monroe, there is some evidence of an overall shift in favor of the Court's decision. In the first wave of the study, the mean response was 5.12 on the seven-point scale. After the Court's decision, the mean level of support rose to 5.42 on the seven-point scale. This means that following the Court's decision, more of the local residents supported the Church's right to use the school facility than did before the decision. The difference is marginally statistically significant ($p = .07$). There was an even greater shift in the Monroe case. Before the Court announced its decision, average support was 4.69 on the seven-point scale. After the decision, support increased to 5.33. This means that after the decision, more of the local residents viewed New York's creation of the school district as a violation of the separation of church and state than did before the Court handed down it decision. This difference was statistically significant ($p = .001$). This provides some, albeit modest, support for the Court as a persuasive influence on public opinion among those who hear about its decisions. However, it was found only in two of the four studies. Views about the gasoline tax and the endangered species act in Oklahoma and Oregon respectively were unchanged.

Since those in the immediate community should perceive the issue as more important than [do] those in the surrounding communities, their opinions should be more difficult to change. I expect that they will seek out and critically think about the different information, weighing all sides of the issue, making them less susceptible to persuasion Those from the surrounding communities, however, might become more supportive of the Court's decision since they are expected to care less about this issue than their counterparts in the immediate community, and thus spend less time thinking about the different dimensions to the issue. Table 14.4 reports differences in support for the decision among the residents of the different communities.

Table 14.4 shows some support for this expectation. Among the residents of the surrounding communities, there is a statistically significant increase in support for the Court's decision in the Center Moriches and Monroe studies. In fact, virtually all of the increase in support for the Court's decision in the Center Moriches and Monroe studies reported earlier in Table 14.4 is the result of increase in support among those from the surrounding communities. There is no evidence that the opinions of those from the immediate communities changed. Again, however, the results are limited to just two of the four studies. The results provide some support for the expectation that persuasion is most likely to occur among those from the surrounding communities.

Conclusion

Media coverage and local levels of awareness of the four cases were very high. Previous research focusing on national media attention and national awareness tend to paint a discouraging portrait. The four relatively routine cases

TABLE 14.4 Support for the Supreme Court's Decision in the Panel Studies by Geographic Proximity

	Center Moriches	Monroe	Oklahoma	Oregon
Immediate community				
First wave	5.32	4.60	3.31	2.00
Second wave	5.42	4.93	3.50	2.03
$P =$	.50	.16	.65	.87
N	57	40	16	35
Surrounding communities				
First wave	4.81	4.77	3.88	4.83
Second wave	5.42	5.67	3.38	4.79
$P =$	.07	.00	.23	.90
N	63	48	8	24

Note: Cell entries are average levels of support for the issues. Opinions were measured along a seven-point Likert-type scale where higher values indicate greater agreement with hoe the Court decided the issue.

generated intense local media coverage. This local media coverage created a well informed local populace. As expected, those from the immediate community were even more likely to have heard about the Court's decision than were those from the surrounding communities. In both communities, awareness was higher than is typically found in national samples. All the ingredients for the Court to influence public opinion were in place. While I examined local geographic communities, similar effects might occur among other kinds of communities. For example, members of occupational or religious communities might have similar opportunities to become aware of relevant Supreme Court decisions, especially if there is some form of media (e.g., a professional newsletter, Internet Web site, or journal) or some other source of communication.

Did the Court shape public opinion in these local communities? This reading began with the words of Justice Sandra Day O'Connor from her opinion in *Planned Parenthood of Southeastern Pennsylvania v. Casey* (1992). She referred to the Court's legitimacy as the power to command acceptance of its decisions. Is she right? Can the Court expend its legitimacy in order to help mold and shape public reactions? The evidence presented above is mixed. The Court does have a great deal of support among members of the mass public; however, this cache of legitimacy does not automatically translate into greater acceptance of its decisions. At the same time, there was also evidence (see Hoekstra 2003) that agreement or disagreement with the decision affected support for the Court, especially among those from the immediate community. This presents the Court with a difficult dilemma. While its political capital may have some, albeit small, power to shape reactions to its decisions, it risks that capital when its decisions run counter to prevailing public opinion.

Case Index

Subject Index